2000 ★ PEOPLE ENTERTAINMENT ALMANAC

★ 2000 ★
PEOPLE
ENTERTAINMENT
ALMANAC

CREATED AND PRODUCED BY
CADER BOOKS • NEW YORK

YEAR-IN-REVIEW

ROYALS

SCREEN

TUBE

SONG

PAGES

STAGE

20th-CENTURY TIMELINE

PEOPLE EXTRAS

CELEB REGISTER

Cader Books
38 E. 29 Street
New York, NY 10016
www.caderbooks.com
For news and updates, send your e-mail and street address to
people@caderbooks.com

First Edition

1 3 5 7 9 10 8 6 4 2

Printed in the United States of America

CONTENTS

TUBE   155

SONG   215

PAGES 295

STAGE 353

TIMELINE 383

PEOPLE EXTRAS 415

THE PEOPLE REGISTER 439

PHOTO CREDITS

COVER

Front cover (clockwise from top): Robert Deutsch/© 1999 USA TODAY (John Kennedy Jr.); Dan Chung/Reuters (Lady Wessex, Sophie Rhys-Jones); New Line (Mike Myers); Frank Veronsky (Camryn Manheim); Larry Busacca/Jive Records (Britney Spears); Peter Kramer/Galella Ltd. (Peter Jennings); Peter Kramer/Galella Ltd. (Nicole Kidman); Corbis/Bettman-UPI (Joe DiMaggio); Ron Wolfson/London Features International Ltd. (Michelle Pfeiffer); Brendan Beirne/Sygma (Gwyneth Paltrow); Steve Granitz/Retna Ltd., USA (Ricky Martin). *Spine:* Walter McBride/Retna Ltd., USA (Susan Lucci). *Back cover:* Reuters/Jeff Christensen/Archive Photos (Julia Roberts and Benjamin Bratt).

YEAR IN REVIEW

p. 15: Theodore Wood/Camerapress/Retna; p. 16: © Nigel Norrington/Camera Press/Retna, Ltd.; p. 18: Reuters/HO/Archive; p. 20: Reuters/Mike Segar/Archive; p. 21: © Stewart Mark/Camera Press/Retna, Ltd.; p. 23: AP; p. 25: © Ellis O'Brien/All Action/Retna; p. 27: Reuters/Mike Blake/Archive.

ROYALS

p. 59: Reuters/Ian Waldie/Archive; p. 61: AP; p. 65: Christopher Simon Sykes/Camerapress/Retna; p. 68: Reuters/Russell Boyce/Archive; p. 69: Reuters/Ian Waldie/Archive; p. 71: Reuters/Dan Chung/Archive.

SONG

p. 216: Epic; p. 217: Margaritaville/Island; p. 218: Sire; Righteous Babe; p. 219: Atlantic; p. 221: Heartbeat; C2/Colombia; p. 222: Warner Bros.; p. 224: Jive; p. 224: Lava/Atlantic; p. 226: Reprise.

PAGES

p. 297: William Morrow; p. 298: Harcourt Brace; p. 300: Simon & Schuster; p. 301 Scribner; p. 302: Random House; Putnam; p. 303: Random House; p. 304: Rob Weisbach/William Morrow; p. 305: O'Reilly; p. 307: St. Martin's Press; p. 308: William Morrow; p. 309: Little, Brown.

TIMELINE

pp. 384, 385 (2), 386: Hulton Deutsch Collection; p. 387: Archive Photos; pp. 388 (2), 389 (2), 390, 391, 394, 395 (2), 396, 398 (2), 399, 401, 402, 403: Hulton Deutsch Collection; p. 404: Holland/Retna Ltd.; p. 405: Archive Photos; p. 406: Hulton Deutsch Collection; p. 407: AP/Wide World; p. 410: Sarasota County Sheriff's Department/Meg Handler collection; p. 412: Reuters/Sam Mircovich/Archive.

THE PEOPLE REGISTER

p. 450: Reuters/Sam Mircovich/Archive; p. 452: © Bill Davila/Retna; p. 458: © John Spellman/Retna; p. 474: © Armando Gallo/Retna; p. 478: © Joseph Marzullo/Retna; p. 485: © Armando Gallo/Retna; p. 486: © Steve Granitz/Retna; p. 487: Reuters/Fred Prouser/Archive; p. 488: © Walter McBride/Retna; p. 497: © Joseph Marzullo/Retna; p. 502: © Joseph Marzullo/Retna; p. 504: Deidre Davidson/Saga/Archive; p. 505: © Steve Granitz/Retna; p. 509: © Steve Granitz/Retna; p. 517: Reuters/Fred Prouser/Archive; p. 526: © Steve Granitz/Retna; p. 531: © Walter McBride/Retna; p. 532: © Armando Gallo/Retna; p. 536: © Steve Granitz/Retna; p. 554: Reuters/Fred Prouser/Archive; p. 556: AP.

STAFF

Editor in Chief
Michael Cader

Senior Editor
John Jusino

Design
Charles Kreloff, Stephen Hughes

Research
Thomas Hill, Lauren Rubenzahl, Amy Woodbury

Photo Research
Joan Meisel

Consulting Editors
Seth Godin, Steve Baumgartner

PEOPLE WEEKLY
Carol Wallace, Managing Editor
Nora P. McAniff, President
Robert D. Jurgrau, Group Business Manager
Eric Levin, Supervising Editor

PEOPLE Contributors
Jane Bealer, Robert Britton, Richard Burgheim, Betsy Castillo, Steven
Dougherty, Nancy Eils, Carol A. Franklin, Tom Gliatto, Susanne Golden,
Larry Hackett, Jeremy Helligar, Terry Kelleher, Betsey Kittenplan,
James M. Lello, Michael A. Lipton, Denise Lynch, Samantha Miller,
Florence Nishida, James Oberman, Vincent R. Peterson, Leah Rozen,
Lisa Russell, Randy Vest, Paul Zelinski

ACKNOWLEDGMENTS

Many people and organizations have generously lent their time, resources, and expertise to help make this project possible. Special thanks go to: Academy of Recording Arts and Sciences; Bill Adams, Walden Book Company, Inc.; Frank Alkyer, *Down Beat;* Jennifer Allen, PMK; Simon Applebaum, Cablevision; Bridget Aschenberg, ICM; Alan Axelrod; Robert Azcuy, Itsy Bitsy Productions; Michael Barson, Putnam; Anita Bedra, Reprise Records; Michelle Bega, Rogers & Cowan, Inc.; Jennifer Belodeau, Barnes & Noble; Andi Berger, PMK; Cindi Berger; Marion Billings, M/S Billings Publicity, Ltd.; Helen Blake, National Infomercial Marketing Association; Jeff Blitz, Writers Guild of America, west; Judy Boals, Berman, Boals & Flynn; Matthew Bradley, Viking; Sandy Bresler, Bresler, Kelly, and Associates; Gerry Byrne, *Variety;* Brad Cafarelli, Bragman, Nyman, Cafarelli; Fr. John Catoir, Christophers; Center for the Book, Library of Congress; Center for Media and Public Affairs; Vicki Charles, Loud Records; Jennifer Chen, PBS; Marylou Chlipala, Carnegie Mellon School of Drama; Bob Christie, National Academy of Television Arts and Sciences; Robert C. Christopher, The Pulitzer Prizes; Steve Clar; Rosie Cobbe, Fraser & Dunlop; Camille Cline; Dan Cohen, Caroline Records; Sam Cohn; Ace Collins; Sarah Cooper, O. W. Toad Ltd.; Dan Corathers, *Dramatics* magazine; Angela Corio, Recording Industry Association of America; Marie Costanza, NYU/Tisch Musical Theater Dept.; Kendal Culp, Random House; Louise Danton, National Academy of Television Arts and Sciences; Leslie Dart, PMK; Gary N. DaSilva; Jennifer DeGuzman, MTV; Paul Dergarabedian, Exhibitor Relations; Steve Devick, Platinum Records; Mark Dillion, Capitol Records; Joan Dim, NYU, Tisch School of the Arts; Heather Dinwiddie, American Symphony Orchestra League; Dramatists Guild; Steve Dworman, *Infomercial Marketing Report;* Marilyn Egol, RCA Victor; Allen Eichhorn; Ed Enright, *Down Beat;* Rebecca Erbstein, *Jeopardy!;* Kenneth Ewing; Charmaine Ferenczi, The Tantleff Office; Ophir Finkelthal, Virgin Records; Karen Forester, Country Music Association; Diane Fortiay, Island Records; Susan Geller, Susan Geller & Associates; Heather Gifford, National Academy of Recording Artists; Debbie Gilwood; Michelle Gluckman, American Society of Magazine Editors; Bob Gregg, Paramount; Amanda Grossman, Capitol Records; Ned Hammad, *Pulse!;* Mary Lou Henner, Knopf; Heidi, Def Jam Records; Tom Hill, Nick at Nite; Patricia Hodges, Time Warner; Hollywood Chamber of Commerce; Hollywood Foreign Press Association; Dave Howard, Hofflund/Pollone Agency; Jane Huebsch, American Symphony Orchestra League; Patrick Ingram, Bantam; Gary Ink, *Publishers Weekly;* M. Jackson, AUDELCO; A. J. Jacobs; Sarah Jagenow, WaldenBooks; Elizabeth Jarret; Kristin Joerg, Bantam Books; Steve Jukes, Judy Daish Associates; Susan S. Kaplan, *Billboard;* Joyce Ketay, Joyce Ketay Agency; Amanda Kimmel, Dell; John Kings, Texas Center for Writers; Pat Kingsley; Leonard Klady, *Variety;* Judy Krug, American Library Association; Stacy Laufer, Crown; Amy Leavell, Capricorn Records; Marleah Leslie; Ruth Levine, Penguin; Stacey Levitt, Rachel McCallister & Associates; Ed Limato, ICM; Heather Malcolm, *Jeopardy!;* Elizabeth Maas, The League of American Theatres and Producers; Tracy Mann, Righteous Babe Recordings; Joe Marich; Howard Marcantel, National Academy of Cable Programming; Nicole Marti, Viking Books; Angela Medina, Juilliard School of Drama; Gilbert Medina, William Morris Agency; Lisa Meredith, National Cable Forum; Suzanne Mikesell, *Pulse!;* Jason Mitchell, Chronicle; T. J. Mitchell, Hofflund/Pollone Agency; Jessica Morell; Jamie Morris, *Soap Opera Digest;* Nara Nahm, Pantheon; Vincent Nasso, Nielsen Media Research; The National Book Foundation; Karen Kriendler Nelson, Richard Tucker Foundation; Patricia Nicolescu, Quigley Publishing Co., Inc.; Shannon O'Boyle, *Advertising Age;* David O'Connor; Catherine Olim, PMK; Lisa Olsen, O'Reilly & Associates; Bob Palmer; Charlotte Parker, Parker Public Relations; Gilbert Parker, William Morris; Karen Pascho; Whitney Peelin, Houghton Mifflin; Nanette Perez, American Library Association; Liz Perl, Berkley; Craig Phillips, 20th Century Fox International; Eileen Potrock, Itsy Bitsy Productions; Ronnie Pugh, Country Music Hall of Fame; Myra Quinn, Peter Brown Agency; Joe Regal, Irene Reichbach, Harcourt Brace; Russell & Volkening; Tom Reidy, Tuneful Productions; Jonathan S. Renes, DMB&B; Sandy Rice, PMK; Rock and Roll Hall of Fame; Sandee Richardson, *Steve Dworman's Infomercial Marketing Report;* Richard Rodzinski, Van Cliburn Competition; Bradley Roberts, *Pollstar;* Cynthia Robinson, American Library Association's Office for Intellectual Freedom; Bradley J. Rogers, *Pollstar;* Ami Roosevelt; Rachel Rosenberg, Northwestern University School of Speech; Howard Rosenstone, Rosenstone/ Wender; Sheryl Rothmuller, NBC Entertainment Press and Publicity; Lucy Sabini, RCA; Heidi Schaeffer, ICM; Bill Schelble; Melanie Schmidt, American Library Association; Ken Schneider, Knopf; Mitch Schneider, Warner Brothers Records; Rachel Schnoll, Viking; Elaine Schock, RCA Records; Nancy Seltzer, Nancy Seltzer & Associates, Inc.; Greg Sharko, ATP Media Relations; John Sheehan, Center for Media and Public Affairs; Paul Shefrin, The Shefrin Company; Barry Sherman, University of Georgia; Jane Sindell, CAA; Smithsonian Institution, Division of Community Life; Robert Stein, United Talent Agency; Carol Stone, PMK; Laine Sutton, *Jeopardy!;* Jack Tantleff, The Tantleff Office; Jonathan Taylor, *Variety;* Prof. Mark Tucker, Columbia University; Terry Tuma, Yale School of Drama; Georgina Warwick, *Jeopardy!;* Rebecca Watson, Broadway Books; Kate Weaver, Avon Books; Sarah Webster, O. W. Toad Ltd.; Murray Weissman, Weissman Angellotti; Windi Wentworth, PBS; Moira Whalon; *Whitaker's Almanac;* Heather Willis, *Pulse!;* Patricia Willis, Beinecke Library, Yale University; Staci Wolfe; Lea Yardum, Weissman/Delson Communications.

11

THE YEAR IN REVIEW

JANUARY

The Culkin family: Fatal fire, angry questions

People weekly

Julia & Her Law Man

After a string of fizzled romances, the *Stepmom* star gets serious with *Law & Order* heartthrob Benjamin Bratt

Buckingham Palace announces that **Prince Edward**, 35, has proposed marriage to **Sophie Rhys-Jones** and she has accepted (reportedly her precise reply was, "Yes, yes please."). Her engagement ring boasts a two-carat diamond flanked by two smaller heart-shaped ones. Edward and Rhys-Jones have been dating for five years. The wedding is celebrated at St. George's Chapel in Windsor Castle in June (see page 71).

The Baseball Hall of Fame hits a rare triple—**Nolan Ryan**, **George Brett**, and **Robin Yount** are all headed to Cooperstown. For the first time since Babe Ruth was chosen, three first-time candidates are elected to the Hall: Ryan, the greatest power pitcher ever; Brett, the big-game player who almost hit .400; and Yount, the clutch hitter who was Most Valuable Player at shortstop and center field.

Diane Sawyer and **Charles Gibson** step in as co-anchors of ABC's *Good Morning America* for "a few months," says Sawyer, but by May the pair extend their temporary duties for at least another year. They replace Lisa McRee and Kevin Newman. Despite less-than-enthusiastic reviews, especially for their less-than-lifelike banter, the new anchor team boosts the program's ratings significantly (though it still lags far behind NBC's *Today*).

Emulating that success, another former morning show star, **Bryant Gumbel**, announces plans to return to his old time slot—but Gumbel will make his a.m. home at his new network, CBS, on *This Morning*. To skeptics judging the move a demotion, he comments, "I'm not necessarily sure I'd ever look at hosting two hours of live television as a comedown."

The **National Basketball Association**, which came close to becoming the only major professional sports league to lose an entire season because of a labor dispute, dramatically bounces back with a landmark settlement with its players, allowing for a shortened 52-game season beginning February.

The excitement is diminished days later, when the game's premier player, Chicago Bull **Michael Jordan**, 35, announces his retirement. Though Jordan—who led the Bulls to their sixth NBA title last season—

had said he would not return to the team if coach Phil Jackson left, which he did, fans held out hope that he would change his mind.

Debbie Reynolds joins the crusade to keep the landmark **H-O-L-L-Y-W-O-O-D** sign looming above the nation's entertainment capital. "It's just a lot of wood and tin. You have to look after these things," the movie star says, as the Hollywood Historic Trust announces that the famous 50-foot letters were available for corporate adoption at $100,000 a year. Corporate sponsors won't be able to affix logos to the sign but can use it in advertisements.

Home-run king **Mark McGwire**'s record-setting seventieth home-run ball fetches a record-setting $2.7 million at a sports memorabilia auction. The staggering sum eclipses the presale estimate of $1 million as well as the previous high paid for a baseball—$126,500, for the first home-run ball Babe Ruth swatted in Yankee Stadium, sold only last November. McGwire gave the bat he used to belt No. 70 to the Baseball Hall of Fame in Cooperstown, N.Y.

Elvis Presley may not be alive, but a fan receives a letter from him—39 years after asking for his autograph for her eleventh birthday in 1960. Presley had replied to 11-year-old Karen Golz, who was living in what was then West Germany (where Presley served in the American military), but the letter was mislaid by his landlady. He signed the missive "Your friend Elvis" and added a handwritten note: "Dear Karen, May you have a very happy birthday—and lots of Teddy Bears," a reference to one of his hits. The letter is reported to be one of only five such personal ones by the King still in existence.

Barbie, the world's most popular doll, marks her 40th birthday with a huge Milan fashion show, kicking off worldwide celebrations by manufacturer Mattel. "We call it a celebration of Barbie's fortieth anniversary, not her birthday...because ladies don't talk about their age," says a spokesperson. Despite the fanfare, Barbie encounters rocky times in the fast-changing toy marketplace.

After years of artfully dodging the lenses of the world's media, **Prince Charles** and his longtime love, **Camilla Parker Bowles**, finally emerge together for the first of many public appearances. As the couple leave London's Ritz Hotel by a side entrance, approximately 150 photographers crowd into the narrow street and gorge themselves on what until now had been the most elusive royal photograph of all. As the two stood together on the sidewalk, Charles turns and puts an arm around Camilla before helping her into the car. The couple had been attending a fiftieth birthday party for Camilla's sister, Annabel Elliot.

Prince Charles and Camilla Parker Bowles speed away from their first photo op.

Chicago Bears' Hall of Famer **Walter Payton**, gaunt and tearful, announces that he has a rare disease, primary sclerosing cholangitis, and needs a liver transplant to live. The cause of the affliction, which blocks the bile ducts, is unknown, but it isn't related to alcohol, steroids, hepatitis, or immune deficiency, he says. The player known as "Sweetness," Payton, 44, still holds NFL career records for yards gained (16,726) and number of carries (3,838).

The Eagles: Their Greatest Hits, 1971–1975 crosses the 25-million-copy sales mark, equaling Michael Jackson's *Thriller* as one of the bestselling albums of all time.

The Heisman Trophy that was awarded to **O. J. Simpson** in 1968 brings $230,000 in an auction in Los Angeles. The sale was ordered to help settle part of the $33.5 million civil judgment against him for the stabbing and slashing deaths of his ex-wife and her friend. Simpson was acquitted of criminal charges in the killings. The Heisman Trophy is the first ever to go on the auction block, and its plaque contains the misspelling of the word *athletic,* which is missing the letter *h.*

A disgusted **Oprah Winfrey** is calling it a day—in two years, when her current contract runs out. The talk show queen tells the *Sunday Times* of London that she is sick-ened by the sort of TV sleaze made popular by **Jerry Springer**. "I am in disbelief about things that are happening on television talk shows," she says. "How low can it get? Can public taste keep on sinking? Yes, it can. I have to get out." A diplomatic Springer responds, "I hope she doesn't quit. She's great…the best talent there is on television."

But later in the year controversy engulfs Springer and his show again. First corporate bosses at Studios USA, the show's producer, replace new broadcasts with calmer, vintage *Springer* episodes during the end of May sweeps while announcing their intention to once again reduce violence on the show.

Then Springer is called to Chicago's City Hall to defend his show against charges that its fights are faked. (If the fights are real, city officials ask why the off-duty policemen who serve as *Jerry Springer Show* bodyguards have not made any arrests.) Springer ardently maintains the program ridicules violence and the guests who fight one another. "If I thought for one second that my show would be hurtful to society," said Springer, "I wouldn't do it."

An article in the *National Liberty Journal,* edited and published by the Reverend Jerry Falwell, warns parents that **Tinky Winky**, the purple character who sports a triangular antenna on his head on TV's popular *Teletubbies* children's show, may be a gay role model. To support its claim, the publication says Tinky Winky has the voice of a boy but carries a purse. "He is purple—the gay pride color; and his antenna is shaped like a triangle—the gay pride symbol." A spokesman for Itsy Bitsy Entertainment, which licenses the Teletubbies in the United States, said the purse is actually Tinky Winky's magic bag. "It's a children's show, folks," said Steve Rice. To think we would be putting sexual

Nicole Kidman bares her soul—and more, for at least 14 seconds— on Broadway in The Blue Room.

innuendo in a children's show is kind of outlandish."

British supermodel **Kate Moss** reveals that she is a recovering alcoholic who, for 10 years, did not walk down a catwalk sober. Moss, 25, tells British magazine *The Face* about a hedonistic jet-set life of champagne, vodka, and marijuana in her decade as a top international model. She said she started smoking pot and drinking at age 12. Now that she has sobered up (in November she checked into London's posh clinic the Priory) and attends Alcoholics Anonymous meetings, Moss says, "I don't want to go back to how I was." Shortly after her announcement, the model's professional relationship with designer Calvin Klein is reportedly ended.

In the season's most dramatic exit, **George Clooney** appears in his final episode of *ER*—at least as a regular cast member. His character, Dr. Doug Ross, leaves girlfriend Carol Hathaway (Julianna Margulies) to resettle in the Pacific Northwest. But Hathaway becomes pregnant later in the season, and reportedly Clooney will be brought back the next season for guest appearances.

Lauryn Hill, the 23-year-old soul diva who won the hearts of consumers and critics with her debut solo album, grabs five Grammy awards, including the prizes for Album of the Year and Best New Artist. Hill's trophy haul breaks Carole King's 1971 record for most awards nabbed by a female artist in a single night. (King won four awards for her *Tapestry* album.)

It is also a good night for veterans: **Madonna**, who had been largely ignored by Grammy voters during her 15-year career, wins three awards, including Best Pop Album for *Ray of Light*. Other first-time winners include **Jimmy Page** and **Robert Plant**, who were never honored for their work in Led Zeppelin, in the Hard Rock category, and **Elvis Costello**, who shared his only trophy thus far with veteran songwriter **Burt Bacharach**, in the Pop Collaboration with Vocals category.

MARCH

Nicole Kidman's sensational, limited-run, sold-out Broadway show, *The Blue Room*, closes one week early due to the star's persistent

bronchial infection. British playwright David Hare's highly hyped (but very antiseptic) adaptation of the Arthur Schnitzler play *La Ronde* became the hottest drama ticket of the season, thanks largely to Kidman's brief nude scenes—14 seconds' worth, by one count.

Bob Hope, who has received numerous accolades for entertaining U.S. troops, is getting another honor: a G.I. doll created in his likeness. "Hollywood Hero" has been designed to pay homage to the 95-year-old comedian, who spent a half century entertaining U.S. troops around the world. "Hope Enterprises was involved in all of it, right down to the scoop on the nose," noted Jon Fitch, associate marketing manager of Hasbro. "They even asked us to make it more prominent than we originally had it."

Barbara Walters airs two hours of a "very full and frank" discussion with **Monica Lewinsky** to an estimated audience of 70 million people, drawing ratings just below those for Oprah Winfrey's prime-time interview of Michael Jackson in 1993. What will Lewinsky tell her children, Walters asks: "Mommy made big mistake." Sporting an elegant new hairstyle by Richard Keogh (who said he was inspired by Elizabeth Taylor and Snow White) and a dramatic shade of lipstick, the former White House intern makes a strong

Monica Lewinsky and Barbara Walters sit for the interview of the year.

impression with her style, from bookstores to beauty counters. When reporters reveal the "secret" of her lips is Club Monaco's Glaze, stores quickly sell out nationwide. Her book, originally bought by an English publisher and sublicensed to U.S. publisher St. Martin's Press, debuts as a No. 1 bestseller. (Within three months, however, *Monica's Story* joins the ranks of "remaindered" books offered at a big discount, though the publisher happily claims sales of over 500,000 copies.)

Quickly displacing Lewinsky atop the lists is once-trusted Clinton adviser **George Stephanopoulos**'s memoir, *All Too Human*. Stephanopoulos recalls that as soon as he heard the president's denials of an affair with

Monica Lewinsky, "I knew in my gut that Clinton was lying." Stephanopoulos, 38, who now lives in New York, received a $2.85 million advance for his book and is now a commentator on ABC.

American hero **Joe DiMaggio**, baseball's legendary "Yankee Clipper," dies at his home in Harbour Island, Fla., at age 84, after a six-month battle with lung cancer. Perhaps best known for his remarkable 56-game hitting streak in 1941, Joltin' Joe was a private man in life and in death. Only about 30 of his relatives and close friends are allowed to attend the funeral in San Francisco, held in the same church in which he married his first wife, Dorothy Arnold, in 1939.

Iconoclastic director **Stanley Kubrick** dies of a heart attack at his home north of London. He was 70.

His latest film—the psychosexual thriller *Eyes Wide Shut,* starring Tom Cruise and Nicole Kidman—was shown to Warner Bros. top brass only a week before his death. The film holds the record for the longest shooting schedule of any Hollywood movie, surpassing the two-years-plus David Lean spent on *Lawrence of Arabia*.

Three singers who dominated radio in the 1970s—**Bruce Springsteen**, **Paul McCartney**, and **Billy Joel**—join the Rock and Roll Hall of Fame, along with **Dusty Springfield**, who died two weeks prior to the induction. The ceremony features the first live reunion of Springsteen and his E Street Band in a decade (in April the Boss and the band tour the U.S. for the first time in 11 years), even though E Street itself wasn't being inducted. McCartney, who didn't attend when the Beatles were inducted in 1988, makes his first major public appearance since the death of his wife, Linda, last spring. He is accompanied by his daughter Stella, who wears a T-shirt that reads "ABOUT #&@%$! TIME!"

Oscar makes love, not war, as the Elizabethan romantic fantasy *Shakespeare in Love* scores a major upset over Steven Spielberg's WWII drama *Saving Private Ryan*, which had been the favored winner. *Shakespeare* takes home seven gold statuettes—including those for Best Picture, Actress (Gwyneth Paltrow), and Supporting Actress (Dame Judi Dench)—and *Ryan*, five, including one for Best Director to Steven Spielberg. The ceremony itself, the first ever on a Sunday, is the longest on record, running four hours and two minutes.

Actor **David Strickland**, 28, who played the rock critic on the NBC sitcom *Suddenly Susan*, is found dead in a Las Vegas adult motel, having apparently hanged himself with a bedsheet. Strickland, who had been arrested for cocaine possession the previous October and put on 36-month probation, was supposed to be in a Los Angeles court for a progress report the day his body was found. Friend and *Suddenly Susan* star Brooke Shields says in a statement, "I am devastated by the loss of my best friend, whose talent and humor graced all who knew him."

APRIL

Children of war: Aiding Kosovo's littlest victims

People weekly

Suddenly Split

Game, set, mismatch: Wed just two years, BROOKE SHIELDS and ANDRE AGASSI call it quits

Eccentric basketball star **Dennis Rodman** and his actress-wife, **Carmen Electra**, file for divorce to end their six-month marriage, according to their publicist, who says the split is amicable. Rodman, 37, and Electra, 26, were married in Las Vegas on November 14, 1998, after what was reported to be an all-night bender. Less than two weeks later, Rodman filed for an annulment, saying he was of unsound mind when he recited his vows. The two reconciled, and Electra was with Rodman when he announced in February that he would be joining the Los Angeles Lakers. During that news conference, Rodman said he and his wife were happily married but living in separate homes.

The British Academy of Film and Television Arts awards a fellowship—and the evening's only standing ovation—to **Elizabeth Taylor**. "I don't think of myself as an actress,

and I didn't think any of you did—quite rightly too," she told the audience. "But it makes me want to act again."

The Broadway season's most eagerly anticipated drama—a revival of Eugene O'Neill's 1946 classic *The Iceman Cometh*, starring Kevin Spacey—opens to critical raves. The four-hour production carries a top ticket price of $100 a seat. But the show is bested at the Tony Awards later in the year by the Brian Dennehy-led revival of *Death of a Salesman*.

Brooke Shields and tennis star **Andre Agassi** announce that they are divorcing after almost two years of marriage. Shields's publicist issues a statement on behalf of the couple, saying: "We have the utmost love and respect for each other and will remain the best of friends." Only hours after the announcement, Agassi plays in the Hong Kong Open, beating Germany's Hendrik Dreekman (6-3, 6-0) in the semifinals and setting the tone for a furious comeback. Over the summer, Agassi comes roaring out of a two-year slump that had dropped his ranking to No. 141 in the world, culminating in dramatic come-from-behind victories at both the French Open and the U.S. Open. With the victory in France, Agassi becomes only the fifth player to win all four Grand Slam events—the U.S., French, and Australian Opens and Wimbledon.

Magician David Blaine emerges from his underground home after spending seven days buried alive.

Magician **David Blaine** steps out smiling from an underground coffin that he says was his home for seven days. Buried six feet under, the Plexiglas coffin was pumped with air, but Blaine said he had had no food and received only three to four tablespoons of water a day through an intravenous tube. A plastic container and tube handled toilet necessities.

Pamela Anderson Lee reveals that she has had her breast implants removed. Marleah Leslie, a spokeswoman for the actress, reports that the former *Baywatch* beauty and producer-star of *VIP* "just wanted her body to go back to its natural state." Anderson Lee has also requested that a restraining order against her husband, Tommy Lee, be removed so he can spend more time with their two children.

Wayne Gretzky, 38, ends his National Hockey League career to rousing cheers and endless chants from an overflow crowd at Madison Square Garden. Gretzky finishes his career with an assist (his 1,963rd, to go along with his 894 goals), as his New York Rangers lose to Pittsburgh 2-1 in overtime. Smiling through his tears, he notes, "I'm devastated I will no longer be a hockey player. I will miss every part of the game, because I loved every part of the game. But I've made the right decision."

Hip-hop mogul **Sean "Puffy" Combs** is charged with second-degree assault in New York City in connection with an alleged attack on Interscope Records executive Steve Stoute. The dispute was reportedly over a music video. (Stoute manages rapper Nas, whose video *Hate Me Now* apparently has a scene that features Nas and Puffy each nailed to a cross.) Combs, 29, surrenders to police voluntarily and is released from Manhattan Criminal Court after posting $15,000 in bail. In June he announces that he has "talked everything out" with Stoute. Combs comments, "I was embarrassed. That's not a normal action for me. I thought, 'How could you be so stupid? This is not like you.' " Stoute's civil suit is being negotiated out of court, and in September Combs is allowed to plead guilty to a reduced charge of harassment and is sentenced to one day of "anger management."

An aspiring artist from the Sunbelt beats out 6,000 other wannabe video jockeys for an instant taste of fame. **Thalia D. DaCosta**, 21, of Sunrise, Fla., wins MTV's nationwide VJ search. Five finalists from around the country were tested on their music knowledge, poise, and stamina, live on MTV, as viewers voted for the winner. DaCosta also wins a $25,000 prize and a new car.

Divas **Cher**, **Whitney Houston**, **LeAnn Rimes**, **Tina Turner**, **Faith Hill**, **Mary J. Blige**, **Chaka Khan**, and **Brandy**, plus divo **Elton John**, all play Manhattan's Beacon Theater in a broadcast of VH1's *Divas Live '99* concert. VH1 was reportedly turned down by Diana Ross and Lauryn Hill.

Eric Harris, who just turned 18, and **Dylan Klebold**, 17, bring terror and tragedy upon **Columbine High School** in Littleton, Colo. The two teenage gunmen kill 13 people and injure dozens of others in a shooting spree at their school before killing themselves.

It stands grimly as the worst act of violence ever at an American school. Columbine teachers are hailed as heroes for their roles in calming and protecting students and possibly saving many lives.

A note left by Harris indicates the two teenagers acted alone, and with clear forethought: "Do not blame others for our actions," local police paraphrased from the note; "This is the way we wanted to go out."

An estimated 70,000 people attend a memorial service addressed by Vice

Julia Roberts causes a stir with her underarm debut at the premiere of Notting Hill.

President Al Gore, who tells the crowd, "All of us must change our lives to honor these children…More than ever, I realize every one of us is responsible for all of the children."

Ripples of change do indeed appear in short order, as leaders from Hollywood to Washington assess what they can do to stem the tide of teen violence. Immediate actions include the postponing of the season finale of teen favorite *Buffy the Vampire Slayer* due to its violent content; a delay in shock rocker Marilyn Manson's concert tour; new Federal legislative initiatives on gun control; and restricting the access of minors to violent entertainment.

Barbra Streisand will reportedly receive more than $13 million for her Y2K gig at the MGM Grand in Las Vegas. Tickets for the 15,000 Grand seats sell for $2,500, but $1 million buys the deluxe package: a pair of front-row seats, a room at an MGM mansion, pampering sessions at a spa, and a gourmet meal for two.

Julia Roberts turns heads at the London premiere of her latest movie, *Notting Hill*, but this time for a new reason: hairy armpits. "Like two clumps of seaweed," declares a writer for Britain's *Mirror*. "I have to admit, I looked twice over at Julia's hairy armpits," Kate Winslet told the paper. Roberts's rep had no comment.

MAY

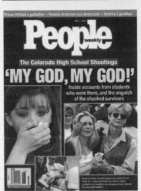

After deliberating for less than seven hours, a jury in Michigan finds **The Jenny Jones Show** negligent in the slaying of gay guest Scott Amedure, who admitted to having a crush on another man, Jonathan Schmitz, now 32, in an episode of the show taped (but never aired) in 1995. The show's producers are ordered to pay more than $25 million in damages.

Schmitz was found guilty of murder in 1996, but his conviction was thrown out on appeal. In August he is found guilty again of second degree murder, and sentenced to 25 to 50 years.

Despite the large verdict, Jones maintains that her program is not to blame: "Of course I did soul searching. Of course, after this happened we went back…We then and now still feel we did nothing wrong…I think it's not fair to blame the show for the actions of someone. That happened three days after they left the show."

After dazzling fans and confounding defenses for 16 years, **John Elway** makes his retirement official (having delayed the announcement because of the school killings in Littleton). As he says the words, the tears flow, too: "I couldn't do it anymore," said Elway, 38. "I can't compete at the level I want to compete at. That's what it came down to."

Actress **Dana Plato**, who, like her fellow *Diff'rent Strokes* child costars, had seen legal troubles in the years since the show was canceled, dies of a drug overdose. Plato, 34, apparently took the painkiller Loritab along with Valium while visiting the home of her fiancé's parents in Oklahoma. Only the week before her death, Plato told Howard Stern on his radio show that she had been drug-free for "over a decade."

Costar **Gary Coleman**, who played the lovable Arnold on the show, pleaded no contest in February to disturbing the peace for punching a female bus driver who heckled him about his career failures. He was arrested later in the year after failing to pay the $400 fine and faces a civil suit over the incident. In a trouble-filled year, he subsequently filed for bankruptcy protection.

Amy Fisher, 24, leaves prison after serving nearly seven years for shooting her lover's wife in the head in a case that once dominated tabloid headlines. Fisher's mother and her attorney, Bruce Barket, noted, "She's obviously extremely happy and thankful to the people who brought this about," including shooting victim Mary Jo Buttafuoco, who helped win an early release for Fisher.

After endless pre-opening hype, including a hit trailer, midnight raids on toy stores, multiple-week lines for opening-day tickets, and fears of opening-day havoc in workplaces around the country, *Star Wars: Episode I—The Phantom Menace* finally debuts, smashing its way to new box office records. But given the enormous anticipation, some claim the film falls short of expectations for the eagerly awaited space adventure. It earns the highest single-day and opening-day grosses ($28.5 million on a Wednesday) and reaches the $100 million, $200 million, and $350 million box office marks faster than any other movie in history (besting *The Lost World: Jurassic Park*, *Independence Day*, and *Titanic* respectively). But its opening weekend gross of $61.8 million is short of the record $72.1 million debut of *The Lost World*.

Daredevil motorcyclist **Robbie Knievel** succeeds in a feat his father, the legendary Evel Knievel, was never allowed to attempt—he jumps over the Grand Canyon at its narrowest point, clearing a gap more than 200 feet wide and more than 1,200 feet deep at a speed of more than 90 mph—as he faces winds of more than 15 mph. Paramedics help Knievel away from the landing site after he injures his leg touching down.

Brazilian model **Luciana Gimenes Morad** gives birth to a baby boy named Lucas and claims the father is **Mick Jagger**. Mick, 55, denies the child is his, but DNA tests confirm that he is the dad. Later in the year, Jagger's estranged wife Jerry Hall agrees to an annulment and a reported settlement of $15 million plus ownership of their $8 million, 26-room London mansion.

Rosie O'Donnell turns an appearance on her talk show by actor **Tom Selleck** into a heated debate on gun control. Selleck, 54, had filmed a commercial for the National Rifle Association; O'Donnell had frequently criticized the NRA since the Columbine-massacre. Addressed by his host as "Mr. NRA," Selleck finally declares: "I didn't come on your show to have a debate," he said. "I came on your show to plug a movie [*The Love Letter*]. That's what I'm doing here."

Conceding the confrontation hadn't gone well, O'Donnell stated, "I strongly do apologize to him personally, but I do not apologize for my feelings about this issue…The people who feel strongly against what the NRA stands for in their lobbying effort need to be heard as well."

Nineteen is the magic number for **Susan Lucci**, who finally wins the Best Actress trophy for her role as the villainous Erica Kane on ABC's *All My Children* after her nineteenth Daytime Emmy Award nomination. Experts had considered this year to be one of Lucci's best shots at winning due to her portrayal of Erica holding a hospital vigil over her anorexic daughter.

As an arena filled with 14,000 spectators looks on in horror, 33-year-old professional wrestler **Owen Hart** falls to his death when the harness that was lowering him to the ring snaps, dropping him 50 feet to the mat. Hart, who wrestled under the name "The Blue Blazer," is believed to have died instantly after the fall at Kemper Arena in Kansas City, Mo. Some 1,300 mourners pack his memorial service, among them pro wrestlers Hulk Hogan, Road Dogg, Gorilla Monsoon, Paul Bearer, Sgt. Slaughter, and "Stone Cold" Steve Austin.

A beaming **Mike Tyson** walks out of a Rockville, Md., jail after serving only three and a half months of his one-year sentence for assaulting two motorists. Tyson will be subject to urine testing at least twice a week and to unannounced home visits by state authorities, said an official. The former boxing champ must also receive permission before leaving Maryland, complete a psychiatric evaluation, and undergo anger management treatment.

It's TV finale time, led by the last episode of ABC's *Home Improvement*, which draws an estimated 35 million viewers, making it the fourth most-viewed series finale of the 1990s. Announcing his retirement after eight seasons earlier in the year, star Tim Allen told reporters, "I don't know how many different ways I can say it, but when it's just about the money and it's just about the ratings, then it's just about over." Allen ranked as TV's highest-paid star, making $1.5 million per episode.

Other notable sign-offs include NBC's *Mad About You* and Fox's *Melrose Place*.

Gregory Omdahl, the executor of **Phil Hartman**'s estate (and his brother-in-law) sues Pfizer Inc., which makes the antidepressant Zoloft. Hartman, 49, star of the TV sitcom *NewsRadio*, was shot to death in 1998 by his wife in the couple's Encino, Calif., home. **Brynn Hartman**, 40, then killed herself. Los Angeles psychiatrist Arthur

Susan Lucci claims her long-sought Emmy Award.

Sorosky, who treated Mrs. Hartman prior to the shootings, was also named in the suit, which claims she wasn't properly diagnosed and that she suffered side effects from the drug that caused her explosion of violence. Tests conducted after Mrs. Hartman's death showed she had Zoloft, alcohol, and cocaine in her system at the time of the shootings.

JUNE

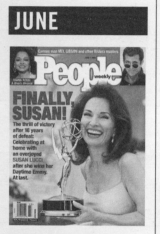

Bob Dylan and **Paul Simon** kick off a 30-city summer tour in Colorado Springs, Colo., performing hits from their respective repertoires as well as a few duets. The two musical legends are touring together for the first time. Simon hasn't toured since 1992, having spent much of his time in recent years on the Broadway flop *The Capeman*.

Readers champ at the bit to get their hands on the latest tale of **Dr. Hannibal "The Cannibal" Lecter**. *Hannibal*,

the new novel by **Thomas Harris**, marks the return of the murderous doctor and FBI agent Clarice Starling—the principal characters from Harris's 1988 novel (and 1991 Oscar-winning movie) *The Silence of the Lambs*.

Adding the Tony Award for Leading Actress in a Drama for her role in David Hare's *Amy's View* to her Best Supporting Actress Oscar for her work in *Shakespeare in Love*, **Judi Dench** joins Audrey Hepburn and a select few others in her rare double victory.
    Rosie O'Donnell, scheduled to present an award, is a no-show. Later reports indicate that a kidnap threat voiced on the *Howard Stern Show* kept Rosie at the side of her son, Parker, 3, and daughter, Chelsea Belle, 18 months.

Rena Mero, known to wrestling fans as **Sable**, files a $110 million lawsuit against Titan Sports Inc., better known as the **World Wrestling Federation**, alleging that the WWF sought to intimidate her into performing obscene and dangerous acts. The suit claims the WWF forced Mero to give up her championship belt after she repeatedly refused to have her gown torn off and her breasts exposed. A confidential settlement is reached later in the year, and the company obtains a temporary restraining order against *Playboy* over a planned nude photo feature of the wrestler.

Michael Jackson pays $1,542,500 at auction for producer David O. Selznick's 1939 Best Picture Oscar for *Gone With the Wind*. The price shattered the previous mark of $607,500 (set in 1996) for the Oscar won by Clark Gable as Best Actor for the 1934 film *It Happened One Night*.

Austin Powers: The Spy Who Shagged Me opens with a groovy $54.7 million in ticket sales, collecting more in its first three days than the original made in its entire theatrical run. Other summer box-office surprises include *The Blair Witch Project,* shot for under $100,000 and grossing well in excess of $100 million, and the blockbuster fright flick *The Sixth Sense,* which becomes the season's No. 2 film.

After nearly a year of negotiations between the filmmaker and the government, **George Lucas's Lucasfilm Ltd.** is granted the right to develop 23 acres of coveted San Francisco land at the former Presidio Army Base. The site will be known as the Letterman Digital Arts Center and will house part of Lucas's film and technology empire, including Industrial Light & Magic, LucasArts Entertainment Company, and the THX Group.

Humphrey Bogart and his *African Queen* co-star, **Katharine Hepburn**, lead the **American Film Insti-**

24

tute's list of the 50 greatest screen legends. (The legends had to begin their careers before 1950.) Cary Grant is No. 2 on the list of greatest male actors, followed in the Top Ten by James Stewart, Marlon Brando, Fred Astaire, Henry Fonda, Clark Gable, James Cagney, Spencer Tracy, and Charlie Chaplin. Following the Great Kate among the female legends are, in order: Bette Davis, Audrey Hepburn, Ingrid Bergman, Greta Garbo, Marilyn Monroe, Elizabeth Taylor, Judy Garland, Marlene Dietrich, and Joan Crawford.

Horror novelist **Stephen King**, 51, is struck by an out-of-control minivan while walking along a road in North Lovell, Maine, where he owns a home. After five operations to stabilize a collapsed lung and multiple fractures to his right leg and hip, King begins a slow recovery. Doctors estimate he will need at least nine months of physical therapy to heal fully. To help heal his soul, King buys the offending vehicle and announces that, "I'm going to take a sledgehammer and beat the hell out of [it]!"

Mattel's **Tarzan** the ape-man action figure is accused of being a little too primitive. Raising the right arm of the 12-inch-high "Rad Repeatin' Tarzan" switches on a recording of his jungle yell. The problem is that the spring-loaded arm must be pumped rapidly up and down from

Eric Clapton holds a favored guitar one more time, before auctioning off 100 instruments to benefit charity.

Tarzan's chest to below his loin cloth, a motion that some call suggestive. The toymaker announces it will change the packaging of the figure.

Fourteen letters written by **J. D. Salinger** (author of *The Catcher in the Rye*) to a young **Joyce Maynard**, with whom he had a May-to-December romance, are sold at auction to software company founder Peter Norton for $156,500. Norton announces, "I plan to return the letters to Mr. Salinger or do whatever else Mr. Salinger lets me know he wants done with them." But the famously reclusive 80-year-old author will still have to face the forthcoming memoir of his daughter Peggy Salinger, 43, which her publisher announces for publication next year.

NBC's soap *Another World* airs its last episode after 35 years. Over the years *World* launched the careers of **Anne Heche, Morgan Freeman, Ray Liotta, Kyra Sedgwick**, and **Eric Roberts**, among others.

Eric Clapton parts with 100 guitars, including a beloved 1956 sunburst Fender he called "Brownie," which sells for $497,500 at a charity auction (beating the previous auction record of $320,000 for a guitar owned by Jimi Hendrix). In all, the sale generates $5 million for a Caribbean drug and alcohol clinic the rocker founded in 1997.

Disgraced broadcaster **Marv Albert** signs a three-year deal with NBC to do the play-by-play for National Basketball Association games and for some Olympic events. The contract represents an almost total reclamation of Albert's reputation, which became tarnished in the fall of 1997 when NBC fired him after he pleaded guilty to sexually abusing a woman in a Virginia hotel room. Since the incident, Albert has undergone therapy and has remarried.

JULY

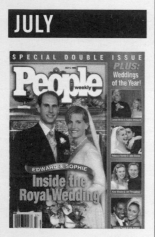

Not with a bang but with a squeak not even worthy of Mickey Mouse, the **Walt Disney Co.** and **Jeffrey Katzenberg** settle their bitter and long-running dispute over profits Katzenberg says he was owed for projects he worked on before he quit the studio in 1994. (Katzenberg had departed because Disney chairman Michael Eisner had refused to make him heir apparent.) Neither side comments on the details, but the *New York Times* estimates the settlement to be

a total of $200 million, $83 million more than the amount Disney had already paid Katzenberg. In his lawsuit, the former studio boss claimed he was owed a bonus of $580 million as a going-away perk when he left Disney to co-found Dream-Works. Disney put the figure as low as $119 million.

Oprah Winfrey is joining the fold—the magazine fold, that is. The talk show host, who is used to gracing magazine covers, announces she is starting one of her own, to debut next spring, in partnership with the Hearst Corp. The new magazine will offer articles on community, family, relationships, health and fitness, fashion and beauty, and books. Says Oprah: "This magazine provides a different way for people to be informed and inspired."

Later in the month, reigning Magazine Queen **Martha Stewart** announces plans to take her empire, Martha Stewart Living Omnimedia, public.

In a thrilling conclusion, the U.S. women's soccer team prevails over China in the **Women's World Cup** finals by the slimmest of margins—a single goal, drilled by Brandi Chastain, to cap a postovertime shootout. More than 90,000 fans cheer the heroics, the largest audience ever for a women's sporting event. Subsequent honors include placing players Michelle Akers, Chastain, Mia Hamm, Kris-

tine Lilly, and goalie Briana Scurry on Wheaties boxes, the first such recognition for soccer players.

In a family tragedy shared by a shocked and grieving nation, **John F. Kennedy Jr.**, 38, plunges to his death in the Atlantic Ocean just miles off of Martha's Vineyard while piloting his private plane. Kennedy's wife, **Carolyn**, 33, and her sister **Lauren Bessette**, 34, also perish. Kennedy and his wife were headed to his cousin Rory's wedding on Cape Cod, and they planned to stop on Martha's Vineyard to drop off Lauren before continuing on to the Cape.

After days of first frantic and then gloomily resigned searching, the bodies are located strapped into the fuselage of the plane on the ocean floor.

In a small family ceremony held aboard the Navy destroyer USS *Briscoe*, the ashes of the victims are scattered at sea. A private Mass for 350 relatives and close friends is held in New York City. Senator Edward Kennedy delivers a stirring eulogy: "He was lost on that troubled night—but we will always wake for him, so that his time, which was not doubled, but cut in half, will live forever in our memory, and in our beguiled and broken hearts."

Cancer survivor **Lance Armstrong**, 37, claims an inspiring victory in the Tour de

France, cycling's equivalent of the Super Bowl. Only the second American to win the famed yellow jersey, he finishes the grueling trek more than seven minutes ahead of his nearest competitor.

Three days of "peace, love, and music" end with rioting crowds and arson at **Woodstock 99**, held in Rome, N.Y. Though most of the 225,000 fans are well behaved and enjoy performances by top acts as varied as Korn, Limp Bizkit, Rage Against the Machine, Jewel, Alanis Morissette, Wyclef Jean, and Elvis Costello, the mayhem at the end (and subsequent allegations of multiple rapes) tarnishes the entire event. The organizers report 3,000 people received medical attention during the festival, and 44 were arrested.

Brandi Chastain celebrates the U.S. women's soccer team overtime victory in the World Cup.

AUGUST

X-Files star **David Duchovny** files suit against 20th Century Fox Film Corp., alleging that the studio has cheated him out of millions of dollars in profits. The lawsuit claims that Fox sold various rights to the hit show to its own or affiliated companies at below-market prices and engaged in other actions that reduced the apparent profits generated by the series.

Duchovny further alleges that series creator and executive producer Chris Carter con-spired with Fox to cover up the self-dealing and was paid hush money amounting to millions of dollars for his compliance. Carter, however, is not named as a defendant in the lawsuit.

In September, TV producer Steven Bochco files his own $61.6 million suit against Fox, similarly claiming the studio cheated him out of profits from his popular *NYPD Blue* show by licensing it at below market value to f/X, a Fox cable network.

Tennis star **Steffi Graf**, 30, announces that she is retiring. Arguably the game's greatest female player, Graf, who won 107 titles, including 22 Grand Slam crowns, is the only player to have won each of the four Grand Slam titles at least four times. Shortly after the announcement, Graf is linked romantically to the newly-single Andre Agassi.

Warren Beatty, 62, indicates elliptically that he is considering a run on the White House. The politically liberal actor is said to be displeased with the current crop of Democratic candidates. Alec Baldwin summed up the feelings of many, commenting, "Why would you give up being Warren Beatty to go to Washington and be president?... Every president wants to be Warren Beatty." But shortly thereafter, **Donald Trump** and **Cybill Shepherd** both express similar thoughts of vying for the Oval Office.

The **Planet Hollywood** restaurant chain plans to file for Chapter 11 bankruptcy protection while it tries to restructure its operations, including nearly 80 movie-themed restaurants. The chain is best known for its hamburgers and its link to celebrity investors Demi Moore, Bruce Willis, Arnold Schwarzenegger, and Sylvester Stallone.

Montel Williams announces he has been diagnosed with multiple sclerosis, a central nervous system degenerative disorder, but says he won't quit his talk show. "This disease is not going to stop me," says Williams, 43. Other celebrities currently battling MS include actress Annette Funicello, comic Richard Pryor, and rock star Ronnie Lane.

SEPTEMBER

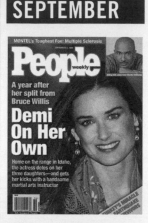

Taking a cue from the summer's surprise hit, *The Blair Witch Project* (which built up an audience on a website), **Adam Sandler** announces that he will take his latest creation directly to his fans on the Net. Sandler's new short film, *The Peeper*, is released Labor Day weekend at www.adamsandler.com. The six-minute animated comedy is viewable on most computer screens.

Ty, the maker of **Beanie Babies**, announces cryptically on its Web site that all Beanie Babies will be retired on New Year's Day. The news causes a frenzy among collectors and parents, but company owner Ty Warner remains mum on the subject.

In a stunning break with tradition, the **Miss America** pageant announces it intends to lift its 49-year-old ban on women who have been married or had abortions. "I'm shocked," says Miss America

1993, Leanza Cornett. Last year's Miss America, Nicole Johnson, and the newly crowned Heather Renee French also join the chorus of critics. Later in the month, the organization's chief executive Robert Beck is released from his contract, and the changes are put on hold pending consultation with state pageant officials.

Tenor **Plácido Domingo** stars in the Metropolitan Opera's season-opening performance for a record-setting 18th time, surpassing the great Enrico Caruso's mark of 17. Domingo sings Canio in "Pagliacci," which was considered Caruso's signature role.

Dutch, the authorized biography of **Ronald Reagan**, causes considerable controversy even before it arrives in stores at the end of the month. The author, Edmund Morris, creates a fictional character—himself—as a childhood friend of Ronald Reagan's—with which to narrate and analyze the former President's life. The book describes Reagan as an "airhead" chief executive whose "hidden depths" are remarkably shallow. Members of Reagan's White House coterie voice strong objections, both to the device and to some of the characterizations.

TRIBUTES

HARRY BLACKMUN

So quiet and unassuming was Supreme Court Justice Harry A. Blackmun that fellow Minnesotan Garrison Keillor once called him "the shy person's justice." It seemed ironic, then, that Blackmun found himself at the center of perhaps the most intractable and heated political debate of the past quarter century. The landmark 1973 *Roe v. Wade* decision, which he wrote for the court's majority, effectively legalized abortion. "I'll carry this one to my grave," he once said of that opinion.

When he died at 90 from complications following hip-replacement surgery, Blackmun, who had also written groundbreaking opinions in the areas of civil rights and free speech, was indeed remembered mostly for *Roe*. But those close to him recalled a modest Minnesota Twins fan who delighted in wiggling his ears for children visiting the court and who brought a deep sense of compassion to the bench.

A grocer's son, born in Nashville, Ill., and raised in St. Paul, Blackmun won a scholarship to Harvard, where he briefly considered medicine before going on to law school. Marrying native Minnesotan Dorothy Clark in 1941—she and three daughters survive him—he spent time in private practice, as counsel for the Mayo Clinic and as a U.S. appeals court judge. President Richard Nixon tapped him for the high court in 1970—his third choice after the Senate rejected nominees Clement Haynsworth and G. Harrold Carswell. "It always kept me a little on the humble side," said Blackmun, who jokingly called himself "Old Number Three." Three years into Blackmun's term, Chief Justice Warren Burger, a childhood friend, asked him to draft *Roe,* which he never regretted. "I think it was right in 1973," he said at his 1994 retirement, "and I think it is right today."

ALLAN CARR

The producer, considered by some to be as over-the-top as his glitzy productions, died at 62 of liver cancer in his Beverly Hills home.

He was best known for turning the Broadway musical *Grease* into a smash 1978 movie and for producing the stage version of *La Cage aux Folles,* which went on to win the 1984 Tony Award for best musical. The only child of a Highland Park, Ill., furniture store owner and an interior decorator, Carr fell in love with theater at an early age. After graduating from Lake Forest College, he moved to L.A. in 1966 and opened a management company with Ann-Margret's husband, Roger Smith. In 1969 he coproduced his first film, the comedy *The First Time.* After seeing *Grease* on Broadway, he bought the movie rights, cowrote the screenplay, and cast John Travolta and Olivia Newton-John. "I was a nerd in high school. Making *Grease* was like being president of your class," Carr once said. Remarking on the twentieth-anniversary rerelease of the now classic film, Carr said: "To have a huge Broadway hit *and* to make this big musical, that's enough. I've made my statement."

PEGGY CASS

Peggy Cass's gift was her gab. So much so that the actress, who died of heart failure at age 74, may be remembered more for her wisecracking chatter on the popular 1960s game show *To Tell the Truth* than for her Tony-winning and Oscar-nominated role of Agnes Gooch in *Auntie Mame.* But the characteristically good-humored Cass didn't mind. "I loved doing it," she told the *St. Petersburg Times* in 1993.

Armed with a brassy voice that, says fellow *Truth* panelist Orson Bean, "could boil the fat off a cabdriver's neck," Cass wielded a razor-sharp wit.

The middle child of a Boston sports promoter and a homemaker, Cass made her stage debut playing a Russian sniper in a 1945 USO show in Australia. She then hit the boards on Broadway in shows such as *Touch and Go.* Though her role in the stage and film versions of *Auntie Mame* won her peer recognition, it wasn't until her first appearance swapping witty repartee with Jack Paar on *The Tonight Show* in 1958, Cass once said, that "all of a sudden, I was famous."

Cass's talents kept her working on quiz shows, in stage productions, and on TV, including the 1995 miniseries *Danielle Steel's Zoya.* But recently she spent much of her time traveling with her husband of 20 years, retired teacher Eugene Feeney, and maintaining ties to those who loved talking to her. "She was always laughing," says Bean. "She was just a joy to be around."

SADIE DELANY

In 1993, when Sarah "Sadie" Delany was 103 years old, she broke her hip and was taken to a hospital. "What a survivor!" writer Amy Hill Hearth remembers thinking. "She was busy comforting all the other patients, who were 40 and 50 years younger. She said, 'Don't worry about me, child. I have a lot to do. I'm not going to die here.'"

In fact, Delany, who died peacefully at age 109 in her home in Mount Vernon, N.Y., had more to do than she might have imagined. The memoir she and her sister

Bessie wrote with Hearth, *Having Our Say: The Delany Sisters' First 100 Years,* was about to become a bestseller and later an acclaimed Broadway play and TV movie starring Diahann Carroll and Ruby Dee. Two years after Bessie's death in 1995, Delany, with Hearth, published *On My Own at 107: Reflections of a Life Without Bessie.* "Sadie missed her terribly," says Hearth. "But it was interesting to see her embrace life again as time went on. She said she'd be with Bessie again."

Born in Virginia, daughters of a former slave who went on to become the first elected black Episcopal bishop, the sisters moved to Harlem during its storied Renaissance and eventually became celebrities together. And yet, says nephew William Murrell, 54, "they were as different as chalk is to cheese." Both earned advanced degrees from Columbia University, but Bessie, who became a dentist, was the sister with attitude; she once told off a "rebby boy" (her term for a Southern white bigot) and feared she would be lynched. Sadie, by contrast, could "sweet-talk the world," Bessie once said, "or play dumb, or whatever it takes to get by without a fuss." Delany landed a job teaching home economics in a white Bronx high school by avoiding an interview, so officials never knew she was "colored," the term she pre-

ferred. "Child, when I showed up," Delany wrote, "they just about died."

The sisters attributed their longevity to a regimen of yoga, cod liver oil, and garlic. And, of course, to staying single. "They said if they got married, they'd have husbands who would worry them to death," says Hearth. "When I met the Delany sisters, I thought, 'This is a treasure.'"

JOE DIMAGGIO

As baseball's enigmatic king of diamonds, he played for the crowd but never to it; in death, he lay surrounded by the very few who were privileged to know him well.

An idol of the American century, Joe DiMaggio might have been buried with great pomp, attended by politicians, performers, and other such lesser lights. But in death, the fisherman's son who so sublimely made center field his green pasture was as restrained as he had been in 84 years of life—and chose his company just as carefully. According to his wishes, DiMaggio's Mass at Saints Peter and Paul Church, in his old North Beach neighborhood of San Francisco, was restricted to family and friends. "It was very dignified," says Father Armand Oliveri, 78, who conducted the service. "The idea was that Joe had achieved a good life and that he had now gone home to his parents."

The Yankee Clipper was above all a family man who

remained devoted to his grandchildren and four great-grandchildren.

The notion of a sentimental DiMaggio may come as a revelation of sorts in light of his meticulously maintained public persona. He came to the Yankees in 1936 as a gawky, toothy high school dropout, but by the time he left the game in 1951, he had become baseball's exemplar of grace. Even more remarkable was the way DiMaggio's legend blossomed in retirement. Rarely granting interviews, he projected an aloof, imperial dignity, even through his nine-month marriage to Marilyn Monroe, whose own celebrity, based on her inescapable sexuality, sometimes made him cringe. He was aware of his status, insisting that he be introduced at Old Timers' games as "baseball's greatest living player," a distinction voted him by sportswriters in 1969.

The enigma of Joseph Paul DiMaggio Jr. began on Nov. 25, 1914, in the fishing village of Martinez, Calif., northeast of San Francisco. The eighth of nine children, he was a baby when his parents, Joseph, a fisherman, and Rosalie, moved the family to San Francisco's North Beach. He played minor league ball for the San Francisco Seals and in 1936 became a rookie sensation for the New York Yankees. Over the next 15 years, he led the Yanks to nine world championships, winning three Most Valuable Player

awards and setting one of baseball's most enduring records with an epic 56-game hitting streak in 1941.

DiMaggio married Hollywood starlet Dorothy Arnold in 1939, and they divorced in 1944. He met Monroe on blind date in 1952. She was impressed, she said, because "he didn't make a pass at me right away," and they married in 1954 at San Francisco's city hall. They were, in some ways, painfully ill-matched. Still, they remained friends until her death in 1962. He never remarried and sent roses to her grave three times a week for 20 years.

Aside from occasional TV commercials, DiMaggio spent most of his post-baseball years simply being Joe DiMaggio, appearing at celebrity golf tournaments and autograph signings. In his last years he raised millions for the Joe DiMaggio Children's Hospital near his Hollywood, Fla., home and visited the 144-bed facility regularly.

JOHN EHRLICHMAN

For many Americans, their names will always be linked—John Ehrlichman and H. R. Haldeman—the scowling, pugnacious aides of President Nixon who, like him, were brought down by Watergate. But while the unrepentant Haldeman, who died in 1993, never lost his brush-cut truculence, Ehrlichman was a different

story. At his death at 73 from the ravages of diabetes, Ehrlichman had gone some way toward contrition. Not only had he grown a beard and settled down to write pulp thrillers, he had publicly expressed his regrets. "I went and lied," he said in 1977 of his role in covering up Watergate crimes. "I abdicated my moral judgments and turned them over to somebody else."

Until his White House years, Ehrlichman had lived what seemed a charmed life. Born in Tacoma, Wash., he was an Eagle Scout who graduated from UCLA—where he met Haldeman—and Stanford University law school. During World War II he served in the Army Air Corps, flying 26 missions as a bomber navigator in Europe and winning the Distinguished Flying Cross. Later, while practicing law in Seattle, he was recruited to work on Nixon's 1960 campaign for the presidency. With Nixon's presidential victory in 1968, Ehrlichman became White House counsel and, afterward, chief domestic policy adviser.

Ehrlichman's duties included overseeing the White House's so-called "plumbers" unit, a team of private operatives whose putative assignment—to trace the origin of leaks to the press—mutated into political espionage and burglary. It was the plumbers' team that bungled the June 17, 1972, break-in at the

Democratic National Committee headquarters in the Watergate complex.

Almost from the first, Ehrlichman was deeply involved in concealing White House ties to the plumbers. But it was Ehrlichman and Haldeman whom Nixon forced to resign in April 1973 in hopes of defusing the scandal. Three years later, Ehrlichman went to prison for 18 months after being convicted of obstruction of justice, conspiracy, and perjury.

Paroled in 1978, he settled in Santa Fe, New Mex. In prison he had written *The Company,* a thinly fictionalized account of his experience in Washington. A series of other novels followed.

Friends tried to burnish Ehrlichman's legacy by stressing his pre-Watergate domestic policy accomplishments. He was widely credited with helping push creation of the Environmental Protection Agency and passage of the Clean Water and Endangered Species acts.

JAMES FARMER

In the years leading up to his death from congestive heart failure at 79, James Farmer lost his sight and his legs to the ravages of diabetes. It seemed a cruelly ironic fate for a founder of the Congress of Racial Equality who, at the height of the civil rights movement, embodied vision and momentum. "He was a real giant," says NAACP chairman Julian Bond, who

earlier told reporters, "He's going to be much missed."

In 1942, the same year he co-founded CORE, Farmer, a Texas-born professor's son, organized one of the early antisegregation sit-ins, at a Chicago coffee shop. By 1961 he was leading the first Freedom Rides. As CORE was eclipsed by more radical black-power groups, Farmer faded from prominence. In 1968, running as a Republican, he lost a Brooklyn congressional race to Shirley Chisholm. He then served as assistant secretary of Health, Education and Welfare in the Nixon Administration, resigning in 1970. In recent years the widowed father of two, who in December retired as a professor at Virginia's Mary Washington College, worried about his place in history. "I have had great anxiety that my people would forget me," Farmer told PEOPLE. Those fears were assuaged in January 1998 when—after a campaign by Bond and other ex-movement leaders—President Clinton awarded him the Medal of Freedom. "James Farmer was one of the founding fathers of the new America, not just the new South," says Rep. John Lewis of Georgia, a friend and civil rights compatriot. "He…made our country a better place."

NORMAN FELL

Nearly 20 years after they parted company, John Ritter still vividly recalls the way

Norman Fell, his old *Three's Company* castmate, would do anything for a laugh. One of Fell's favorite gags was to take off imaginary earrings backstage, hand them to Ritter, and say, "Hold these." Then Fell would rush onto the sitcom's set. "I'd just be standing there," says Ritter, "with my arm outstretched, laughing." Ritter's costar Joyce DeWitt agrees that, unlike Stanley Roper, the crotchety landlord he played on the ABC hit TV show, Fell "was this adorable imp with a glint in his eyes. We were always laughing."

The son of a Philadelphia kosher-restaurant owner and his wife, he was expected to take over the family business. But World War II intervened, and Fell, at 17, saw action as an aerial tail gunner in the South Pacific. Back home, he earned a B.A. in drama from Temple University in 1950. His appetite for acting whetted, Fell struggled to make a go of it in New York City. A chance encounter with Marlon Brando at a deli led to an audition with Brando's mentor, acting teacher Stella Adler, and by 1956, Fell was costarring on Broadway with Edward G. Robinson in *Middle of the Night.*

By then he'd racked up hundreds of roles on live TV, including one as a juror in CBS's 1954 Studio One production of *Twelve Angry Men.* In the late 1950s, Hollywood beckoned, and Fell saw his star rise as a chameleon-like character actor in 36 films.

He was one of Frank Sinatra's casino-heist henchmen in *Ocean's Eleven*, became Dustin Hoffman's exasperated landlord in *The Graduate*, and portrayed military types of every rank in movies such as *Pork Chop Hill*, *PT-109*, and *Catch-22*. He also played TV cops on *87th Precinct* and *Dan August*. With his basset hound face more familiar than his name, Fell in 1974 shot one of American Express's first "Do You Know Me?" commercials. Almost every American did know him five years later after Fell (a last-minute replacement) won the role of Stanley Roper.

Yet, as much as he loved the part, Fell only reluctantly did the spin-off. With good reason: Although *The Ropers* premiered in the spring of 1979 to near-record ratings, viewers lost interest, and a year later the show was canceled.

Witty in public—he was on *The Tonight Show* with Johnny Carson 22 times—Fell kept his most personal travail private. In 1986 he and third wife, Karen Weingard adopted a baby boy, Casey, who at age 5 months was diagnosed with cerebral palsy. For the baby's own health, Weingard placed Casey, now 12, in a private home with five other children who had similarly severe disabilities. "That was hard for Norman," says Weingard.

His friends will miss the fuss that Fell made over them. "Whenever I started to take myself a little seriously,"

says Ritter, "he would tap me on the shoulder and hand me a funhouse mirror and say, 'This is what you really look like,' and I'd laugh. He always made me laugh."

OWEN HART

Hard men with muscled bodies and macho nicknames were rendered powerless, while thousands of fans wondered if the shocking spectacle they had just witnessed was real or part of pro wrestling's over-the-top melodramatics. And in the ring at the Kansas City, Mo., Kemper Arena, Owen Hart—an athlete, a husband, and a father—lay dying.

Hart, known as the "Blue Blazer," had been set to be lowered by cable from high above the ring for a match in an event billed, with unintended prescience, as "Over the Edge." But Hart, 34, became unhooked from his cable (a release mechanism may have been triggered prematurely) and plummeted some 75 feet, hitting his head on one of the ring's padded turnbuckles.

Paramedics tried to revive Hart, who was later pronounced dead of internal bleeding. The youngest of eight wrestling brothers, Hart took to the mat "from the time he was a toddler," says his father, ex-wrestler and promoter Stu Hart, 83, who trained his sons out of the basement of his Calgary home in Alberta, Canada. "Owen had a great outlook

and really enjoyed life."

But Hart, who signed on with the WWF in 1988, had been building a stock portfolio so he could quit wrestling and spend more time with his wife, Martha; son, Oje, 7; and daughter, Athena, 3. On the day he died, Hart donned his mask and told an interviewer, "The Blue Blazer will always triumph over evil forces." Sadly, he could not survive his sport's increasingly surreal showbiz excesses.

DEFOREST KELLEY

DeForest Kelley loved being a part of that pop cultural supernova known as *Star Trek*. The original NBC science fiction series had a mere three-season run, from 1966 to 1969, but lives long in reruns and prospers to this day, having inspired three followup TV series and eight feature films, not to mention millions of rabid fans worldwide. And it made a star of the unassuming Kelley, who died at age 79 after an 18-month struggle with stomach cancer.

Kelley played Dr. Leonard "Bones" McCoy, the cranky but humane physician who served as sounding board for Captain James T. Kirk (William Shatner) and quick-tempered foil for the painfully logical Vulcan, Mr. Spock (Leonard Nimoy). Bones's two signature lines have both become comedy-skit staples. Confronted with a fresh intergalactic crisis, he'd sputter, "Damn it, Jim, I'm just a country doctor!" Or examining a victim of some alien foe, he'd emphatically declare, "He's dead, Jim."

Off-camera the Atlanta native maintained the gentlemanly reserve of his Southern upbringing. "He was a great guy," says James Doohan, *Star Trek*'s Scotty. "But he liked to keep to himself."

The son of Baptist minister, young DeForest sang in his father's church choir and on Atlanta radio shows. In Hollywood, where he moved in 1937, he eventually found a niche as a character actor, playing villains in Westerns such as 1957's *Gunfight at the O.K. Corral* and TV's *Bonanza*. He also became a favorite of ex-cop Roddenberry, then an aspiring producer. "Gene loved working with him," says Roddenberry's widow, Majel Barrett, who played Bones's assistant, Nurse Chapel. "He brought him with him." When it came time to cast *Star Trek*, Roddenberry offered Kelley a choice—Bones or Spock. He never regretted turning down the pointy ears. "I wouldn't have been anywhere near Leonard Nimoy," he once told the *Chicago Tribune*. "He's marvelous."

Kelley all but retired after appearing in 1991's *Star Trek VI: The Undiscovered Country*. He loved mingling with Trekkers at conventions around the world, but he told the *Houston Chronicle* that his greatest legacy was to "have inspired a great number of people to enter the medical world."

RICHARD KILEY

On Valentine's Day 1999, Richard Kiley felt too sick to go out and buy a gift for Patricia, his wife of 31 years. "He hated to shop anyway," she says. So she asked him to do something he loved: to sing. "He was always singing to me, [even] when we were driving in the car," says Patricia, 71. He made her a tape of 1930s romantic ballads, old Irish songs and poems. "I told him it would be something I would treasure," she says.

Kiley—whose 50-plus-year career stretched from his signature role in Broadway's original *Man of La Mancha* to films and Emmy-winning TV turns—died three weeks later at 76 from a bone marrow and blood disorder, at a hospital near his Warwick, N.Y., home. At his funeral, a flutist brought mourners to tears by playing "The Impossible Dream," a tune he had performed over 2,000 times in *La Mancha*.

Born in Chicago, Kiley "was strikingly handsome, and he also had talent," remembers comedian Steve Allen, a high school friend. Breaking into Broadway in the 1950s, Kiley won raves in both dramas and musicals, earning Tonys for 1959's *Redhead* and the long-running *La Mancha*, which opened in 1965. His film credits include *Blackboard Jungle, Looking for Mr. Goodbar*, and, most recently, *Patch Adams*. A

grandfather of 12 (he had six children before splitting with first wife, Mary Bell Wood), Kiley also acted in dozens of TV productions, including 1983's *The Thorn Birds*, and lent his baritone to voice overs. But his passion was the theater. "He made you feel that what you were doing for a living was still an event," says pal Adam Arkin. He loved being on the stage, says Patricia. "That's where Richard's heart was."

STANLEY KUBRICK

His films, bleak yet hugely popular, tackled tough intellectual themes like the tyranny of technology and the power of the state over individuals. His last project, *Eyes Wide Shut*, a psychosexual thriller starring Tom Cruise and Nicole Kidman, took nearly two years to complete. But the 70-year-old Kubrick died unexpectedly of a heart attack in his sleep, shortly before the film's release, never to meet with the public response to what he considered his best work yet. That would be a tall order. A perfectionist who obsessed over every detail of filmmaking, he made only 13 features and just 9 since 1960—most of them masterpieces, including *Dr. Strangelove* (1964); *2001: A Space Odyssey* (1968); and *A Clockwork Orange* (1971).

A common Kubrick theme—man's inability to control his own destiny—seemed to drive his reclusive personal life as well. He stopped giving interviews years ago and shot his films under total secrecy. But friends recall a different Kubrick: gentle, jovial, and ever interested in news of the world—especially his beloved New York Yankees. He worshiped Joe DiMaggio, who outlived him by just one day.

Still, Kubrick wasn't exactly a regular guy—or even a regular director. Despite holding a pilot's license, he loathed flying. Fearing high speeds, he insisted his chauffeur drive his vintage Rolls Royce no faster than 30 mph; on sets, he would shoot as many as 100 takes to perfect a minor scene, but he cared little for his own appearance. The last three of his films were shot within a two-hour drive of the home he shared with his third wife, artist Christiane Harlan, 66 (both of his brief earlier marriages ended in divorce), and he rarely socialized outside its gates.

In fact, the director's 19-bedroom manor was not so much a cocoon as a hive, buzzing with four dogs, five cats, and a constant stream of guests. On their frequent visits, his three daughters—Katharina, 45; Vivian, 38; and Anya, 40—were as likely to find their doting father lunching with pals like novelist John le Carré as with his wife's artist friends.

Kubrick was born in Manhattan, the son of a doctor and his wife. In high school, recalls classmate Eydie Gorme, "the teachers thought he was an idiot because he kept walking around with a box camera." He worked as a magazine photographer after graduating, but soon switched to filmmaking. Despite his fabled artistic temperament, actors were eager to work with him.

2001 author Arthur C. Clarke had recently written a "history" of the twenty-first century for a British newspaper. "I had Stanley receiving a special Oscar for lifetime achievement on his eightieth birthday. Well, I hope it happens posthumously."

VICTOR MATURE

A he-man with a sense of humor, screen hero Victor Mature combined a .45 caliber wit with the 45" chest memorably displayed in such epics as *Samson and Delilah* (with Hedy Lamarr) and *The Robe*.

Many years after he left the restaurant he helped run in his native Louisville, Ky., to go to Hollywood at age 21, Victor Mature admitted, "I was casting about for a job where a guy without brains could make more money than the president."

"He was just this great hunk of sensuality," remembers Piper Laurie, one of his costars, but another, Red Buttons, joked that Mature would shrink from stunts: "He used to say to me, 'Red, I won't take a slippery step.'" The son of an Austrian immigrant, Mature had a knack for a nickel too: He began a profitable business that would endure well past his screen career by selling TVs from his *Samson* dressing room.

Mature, who died of leukemia at age 86 at his home in San Diego, is survived by his fifth wife, Lorey, and their daughter, Victoria, 24. Once dubbed "a beautiful hunk of a man" by publicity agents, Mature found no problem there. "I don't mind being called Glamor Boy," he once cracked, "as long as that check comes on Friday."

IRIS MURDOCH

The celebrated British writer Iris Murdoch died at age 79 in Oxford, England, from complications associated with Alzheimer's disease. A philosopher and the author of 26 novels, Murdoch wrote her highly original works about middle-class Britons, using fiction to probe the nature of good and evil. She was revered and made a Dame of the British Empire in 1987.

Her remarkable 43-year union with husband and literary critic John Bayley was recently recounted by him in *Elegy for Iris,* a tender memoir that one reviewer called "one of the longest love letters ever written."

The couple met in 1953 at evening dinner party; they married in 1956. Disinclined to have children, they both went on to distinguished careers, Bayley making his mark as a professor and critic, with books on Thomas

JOHN F. KENNEDY JR.

Millions followed his story from the beginning. Nearly everyone old enough to have been sentient when President Kennedy was assassinated had expectations for the little boy who had lifted his hand in heartbreaking salute to the passing coffin. As John Jr. proceeded through the ordinary stations of life, the rest of the world looked on, eager to know of it all. But when the single-engine Piper Saratoga that he was piloting plunged into the waters off Martha's Vineyard on the night of July 16, 1999, killing Kennedy, 38, his wife, Carolyn Bessette Kennedy, 33, and her sister Lauren Bessette, 34, it seemed impossible that a life lived so vibrantly could so suddenly end.

Kennedy was proud of his six-seater plane, which he had recently bought second-hand. With 300 hours aloft, he was authorized to pilot the plane only under visual flight rules, having not yet achieved the instrument rating that would allow him to fly in bad weather. That night, the plane was to deliver Lauren to Martha's Vineyard, then continue on to Hyannis where John and Carolyn would be attending the wedding of his cousin, Rory Kennedy. But as the Piper was approaching the Vineyard, a blip on the radar screen at 9:39 p.m., later determined to be his plane, began losing altitude quickly. In the 14 seconds before it went off the radar, the craft fell from 2,600 feet to 1,100 feet—at least eight times faster than a single-engine plane would normally come down for a landing.

By 8 o'clock Saturday morning, dozens of aircraft and ships from all along the coast were deployed in a search that continued through Wednesday, July 21, when word came that John F. Kennedy Jr.'s body had been found a few miles off Gay Head. On Thursday, a small knot of family mourners stood on the stern of the Navy destroyer *Briscoe* for the burial at sea. The following morning, friends and family gathered in Manhattane for a moving memorial to John Jr. and Carolyn at St. Thomas More Catholic Church, where Jacqueline Onassis Kennedy and her children worshipped. The service was attended by President and Mrs. Clinton. Wyclef Jean, of the hip-hop group the Fugees, sang Jimmy Cliff's "Many Rivers to Cross." Ted Kennedy, his voice breaking, eulogized: "Like his father, he had every gift but the length of years."

There's really no parallel to the role John F. Kennedy Jr. played in our public drama. His arrival on November 25, 1960, just 17 days after his father had been elected president of the United States, was a national event. Around the country stories of the first toddlers to career through the White House since the 19th century became a rich part of the Kennedy mystique. With his father's assassination on November 22, 1963, the youngest Kennedy became the focal point, an image sealed in the nation's memory forever.

Despite the attention, Kennedy once said that he "grew up just living a fairly normal life" with his mother, Jacqueline Kennedy Onassis, and his sister, Caroline. John was outgoing and ebullient, while Caroline, like her mother, was poised and controlled. From their earliest years, John and Caroline were kept at a distance from the raucous younger Kennedys by their mother, and the two were unshakably close—a pair of co-conspirators, often caught whispering in the secret language of siblings. As time went on, Caroline, now 41, lived her life privately while John got all the press.

Kennedy always exhibited a healthy skepticism about the mythology surrounding his family, yet with his natural passion, daring, and style, he effortlessly seemed to embody it. He was a free spirit; he partied, in-line skated shirtless on Manhattan streets, kayaked in Vietnam and Iceland, and even sought permission (unsuccessfully) to rappel down the face of Mount Rushmore. Academics were never his strong suit, and he was diagnosed with dyslexia at an early age. In 1979 he enrolled in Rhode Island's tony Brown University (rather than the family alma mater, Harvard), and graduated in 1983 with a B.A. in American history. He showed promise as an actor, but his mother discouraged any thoughts of turning professional. After earning his law degree at New York University, Jackie pulled some strings to get him a job as an assistant district attorney in the office of Manhattan D.A. Robert Morgenthau. But in 1993, after failing the bar exam twice, he eventually passed and successfully prosecuted six cases before tiring of the law.

Although Kennedy doggedly refused to retrace his father's career path, politics was the subtext of his own trajectory, as he took an unlikely turn as a journalist. In September 1995, he and Michael J. Berman launched the lighthearted, lightweight political magazine *George*, and in its fourth year, the magazine had at least defied early predictions of a quick demise. Kennedy had created an utterly public—and at the same time utterly personal—body of work that was certain by its very nature to invite fair criticism. Off the job, he quietly continued the family tradition of service. He founded Reaching Up to provide scholarships to health-care workers and was a member of the President's Committee on Mental Retardation.

Always, there were women. In addition to steadies Sally Munro, a Brown classmate, and actress Christina Haag, there were occasional dates with Madonna and actress Sarah Jessica Parker. More serious was his relationship with Daryl Hannah, which ended in 1994 after five and a half years, amid rumors of an impending marriage.

It was surely not a coincidence that John Kennedy's settling into a real life—not one of soap opera dimensions—occurred in a period framed by the most authentic of life events, his mother's death and his own marriage. On May 20, 1994, it was John who announced that his mother, diagnosed four months earlier with non-Hodgkin's lymphoma, had died. Kennedy was no longer buffered from the glare by the one person upon whom the light of publicity shone more brightly than it did on him.

It wasn't long after his mother's passing that Kennedy proposed to the tall and graceful Carolyn Bessette, a modern American beauty and onetime Calvin Klein staffer. When they wed in 1996, in a small, secret, paparazzi-free affair at Georgia's Cumberland Island, John was not just saying, "This is the woman I love"; he was also saying, "This is who I am." With Carolyn at his side, the man so many expected to be a "Kennedy" found happiness just being *John*.

Like any young couple in love, John and Carolyn Kennedy looked like they had it all figured out. Their home was a cozy loft in New York City's trendy Tribeca, where they entertained friends and frolicked with Friday, their dog. They refused to change their lives because they were "Mr. and Mrs. JFK Jr.," and in their short, sweet time together, Kennedy found the inner peace and confidence to be the regular guy he wanted to be. "John and Carolyn were true soulmates," said a Bessette family spokesperson, "We take solace in the thought that together they will comfort Lauren for eternity." Whatever may have happened on that dark final night, John F. Kennedy Jr. was a man who, in all his full, generous, and adventurous years, rarely lost his bearings in life.

Hardy and Henry James.

The marriage provided them with a haven, a never-never land with naughty rituals like skinny-dipping in rivers while boating parties floated by.

Bayley started seeing signs of his wife's disease about four years ago, during a symposium in Israel. "Things were going very badly," he recalled. "Iris wasn't able to answer or to understand." He took her to a specialist, and a brain scan revealed Alzheimer's. Doctors seemed to give up. "It's not their business anymore; one is on one's own," said Bayley. He bathed her and fed her, choosing not to bring in outside help.

As the end drew near, some of the couple's friends thought that nothing had really changed between them. "John talks about not remembering what 'normal' is," said Lady [Natasha] Spender, widow of the poet Stephen. "When I saw them this past summer pottering off to the agricultural canal, where they bathed, it was like old times. They were chattering away to each other. The conversation made little sense, but it did not matter. The point was their devotion."

Bayley and Iris had arrived at a place beyond fear and hope. A place, he told his visitors, where "a sort of peace descends." He told the newspaper *The Independent*, "She had such a wonderfully good death, so calm."

ANTHONY NEWLEY

Dying didn't sit well with Anthony Newley. "The last days of his life, he was extremely irritable, restless, and kicking a lot," says Sasha Newley, 33, his son with ex-wife Joan Collins. "He was just PO'd he had to die. He quoted Dylan Thomas: 'Do not go gentle into that good night…Rage, rage, against the dying of the light.'"

Newley's courageous war against death proved futile. At age 67 the British born entertainer succumbed to the cancer that had spread to his lungs, liver, and kidney. At his home in Islandia, Fla., he held the hand of Gini Fratini, his companion since 1993, and waited for the pain to pass. "I was stroking his face," says the British designer. Then, she says, "he just went to sleep."

Newley approached his death, life, and work with equal fervor. By age 30, he was a theatrical sensation, writing, directing, and starring in the landmark 1962 Broadway hit *Stop the World, I Want to Get Off*. Though Newley never clicked as a Hollywood actor—his biggest film, 1967's *Dr. Doolittle*, was a flop—the score he cowrote for 1971's *Willy Wonka and the Chocolate Factory* handed Sammy Davis Jr. his signature song, "The Candy Man."

Newley's feverish drive began in Hackney, a working-class London neighborhood, where he was raised by his single mother, Grace (who, at 96, survives him). Newley joined an acting class and at 16 landed the role of the Artful Dodger in the 1948 film classic *Oliver Twist*. For years after, he dabbled in singing, and in 1961 teamed with Leslie Bricusse to write songs and musicals. In 1962's *Stop the World* he played a Chaplinesque everyman buffeted by life.

Afterward, with his career on the wane, Newley relocated to L.A. in 1967 and became a fixture performing on the Las Vegas nightclub scene.

His painful final days were brightened by his 1993 reunion with Gina Fratini, with whom he had had a two-year affair in the 1950s. "We came back together at the perfect time, I suppose," says Fratini. "But it ended too soon."

ANTHONY RADZIWILL

As little boys they played together for hours on end. As adults they served as best man at each other's weddings. And in the early morning hours of July 17, it was Anthony Radziwill who took on the tasks of telephoning Caroline Kennedy Schlossberg, vacationing in Idaho, to tell her that her brother's plane was missing. Technically, the two young men were just cousins. But as anyone who knew Radziwill and John F. Kennedy Jr. understood, they were in truth much more like brothers.

"That's exactly what they were like," says Lee Radziwill Ross, Anthony's mother and Jacqueline Kennedy's younger sister, "Since day one."

Just three weeks after John's funeral, 300 of the Kennedy clan and friends gathered for another painful farewell, this time for Anthony, 40, a TV producer, who died after a decade-long battle with cancer. At a memorial service at Most Holy Trinity Church in East Hampton, NY, his friend Diane Sawyer recalled Radziwill as "a knight who had wandered in from another century, sworn to uphold the codes of beauty, valor, and gallantry."

His cousin Caroline spoke more simply, "Anthony," she said, her voice breaking, "emanated love."

This past July, as his illness progressed, Radziwill and his wife of five years, Carole, 36, an ABC producer, had spent the month at John and wife Carolyn's home on Martha's Vineyard. In the wake of the tragedy that took their best friends' lives, "Anthony and Carole were beyond devastated," says a friend. Still, Radziwill attended John's burial at sea on the Navy destroyer U.S.S. *Briscoe*. "It wasn't easy for him," says a friend, "but he'd never let you know that."

Born in Switzerland to Lee and expatriate Polish Prince Stanislas Radziwill, Anthony spent his childhood in England before moving to the States in 1976. (His parents had divorced in 1974, and Lee married director Herb Ross in 1988.) With a degree from Boston University, Anthony embarked on a broadcasting career that took him to NBC, ABC, and HBO, and earned him three Emmys and a Peabody Award. "I used to tease him about being a prince," says his friend Holly Peterson, "but he was so down-to-earth, he would never have wanted to use that term."

In fact, Radziwill was known as a tireless practical joker. It was that same high spirit, combined with courage, that helped sustain him through his illness. "He knew early on that the prognosis was not encouraging," says ABC's Sam Donaldson. "But after each setback, he simply battled on." Even in the final days of his life, says a friend, "he was still swimming in the ocean."

A small group of friends gathered at a Long Island summer home to belatedly celebrate Radziwill's 40th birthday. "There was a peacefulness about him," says one. Not long after, loved ones met at dusk on an East Hampton beach and, as others had done so recently for his best friend John, cast Radziwill's ashes into the sea.

OLIVER REED

Throughout his life, Oliver Reed was known as much for his drunken exploits as for his roles in films like *Oliver!* No wonder: In 1973, in an all-too-typical display, he inexplicably stripped in the middle of dinner at a Madrid hotel and leaped into a huge tank filled with goldfish.

Reed, 61, spent the final moments of his life doing what he loved best—drinking in a bar. On May 2 at a pub in Malta, where he was working on the film *Gladiator*, Reed suffered a sudden heart attack. "He was one of those great spirits," says actor Michael York. "I'm sure Oliver Reed stories will abound and be celebrated through the centuries."

Born in Wimbledon, England, Reed worked as a boxer and strip-club bouncer before his uncle, director Carol Reed, cast him as villainous Bill Sikes in 1968's *Oliver!* Two years later, Reed's then-shocking nude wrestling scene in *Women in Love* cemented his acting future, and he went on to co-star in 1974's *The Three Musketeers* and 1975's *Tommy* among his roughly 70 films.

Reed had two children, Mark, 38 (with model Kate Byrne, his wife from 1960 to '70), and Sarah, 29 (with dancer Jacquie Daryl, his '70s companion). In 1980, at 42, he began dating Josephine Burge, then 16. Their 1985 marriage lasted until his death.

SHEL SILVERSTEIN

Shel Silverstein was that rare contradiction—a recluse totally engaged in life. He so shunned publicity that he insisted his publisher not give out any biographical information about him. Yet he also said, "I want to go everywhere, look at and listen to everything," and he did. During a career that spanned five decades, Silverstein, 68, left his quirky signature on Nashville, Hollywood, and Broadway—and, most indelibly, on the world of children's literature.

Silverstein, who neither smoked nor drank and stayed fit by practicing yoga and walking everywhere, ironically succumbed to a heart attack at his winter home in Key West, Fla. As friends struggled to fathom his death they remembered his humor, generosity, and utter lack of pretension.

It was *Playboy* founder and editor Hugh Hefner who gave the Chicago-born and -raised Silverstein his first big break, starting in 1956, by featuring his cartoons, stories, and poems in that very adult magazine. Before that, Silverstein's work was known mainly to readers of the Pacific edition of the military newspaper *Stars and Stripes,* where he worked during a hitch in Japan and Korea in the early 1950s. "He was a giant as a talent, a giant as a human being," says Hefner. "He really was a Renaissance man." The

peripatetic Silverstein tickled funny bones of all ages. A prolific, Grammy-winning composer and lyricist, he was the comic whiz behind several hit lyrics, among them "A Boy Named Sue" (recorded by Johnny Cash) and "Cover of the Rolling Stone" (recorded by Dr. Hook). He earned a Best Song Oscar nomination for "I'm Checkin' Out," from the 1990 film *Postcards from the Edge.* He also wrote 10 plays and cowrote the 1988 screenplay *Things Change* with David Mamet.

But the divorced Silverstein, who leaves behind a son, Matthew, 15, will probably be best remembered for his dozen children's books— among them *The Giving Tree* and the bestselling *Where the Sidewalk Ends*—which have been translated into 20 languages and have sold some 14 million hardback copies worldwide. "It is astounding how he crossed over age and gender lines," says Silverstein's editor Robert Warren. Cartoonist Jules Feiffer, a Silverstein friend, understands his gift. "He imagined things the way kids do when they're little, and it goes away when they're older— only in his case it didn't go away," he says. "I admired his line very, very much," he adds, "and stole from it as much as I could."

In his 1981 children's classic, *A Light in the Attic,* which spent 182 weeks on the bestseller list, Silverstein set forth a philosophy that

also makes a most fitting epitaph:

> Draw a crazy picture,
> Write a nutty poem,
> Sing a mumble-gumble song,
> Whistle through your comb.
> Do a loony goony dance,
> Cross the kitchen floor,
> Put something silly in the world
> That ain't been there before.

GENE SISKEL

Whenever Gene Siskel turned to the camera after viewing a movie clip, TV viewers could see from his expression—bursting with excitement—that this was a man in love with movies. He was also in love with the Chicago Bulls. In June, just weeks after flying to New York City for surgery to remove a growth in his brain, he was back home in Chicago, leading a Bulls rally. He had pulled an NBA cap over his head, "and it was clear he wasn't a hundred percent," says his friend Tim Weigel, a local sportscaster. "But he was relishing the moment." Not long afterward, it was the Bulls' turn to pay tribute to Siskel with a minute of silence at the start of their game against the Milwaukee Bucks. Siskel & Ebert's tall, skinny half had died of what his family has described as complications from the surgery the previous May.

The critic, who never gave up his day job reviewing

movies for the *Chicago Tribune,* may have been 53, says columnist and friend Bob Greene, "but, on his best day, he was like an 11-year-old kid. He wanted to see everything the world had to offer." Most of all, he wanted to see movies. For nearly 25 years, he and rival *Chicago Sun Times* critic Roger Ebert, 56, bandied opinions—and occasional sharp words—in their breezy rundown of the week's offerings, graded with their trademark thumbs up or down. They were entertainingly, quirkily stuck with each other—Siskel's Jerry Seinfeld to Ebert's George Costanza.

Their sometimes bristling interactions weren't put on. They even kept track of whose turn it was to sit closest to David Letterman during joint appearances on his show. "We were competitive even right to the end," says Ebert. "We both thought we were the other's older or smarter brother." Though the two rarely socialized, "nobody knew us better," Ebert adds, "except for our wives." Indeed, Siskel was famously close to his family. "Our friendship knew no bounds," says his widow and wife of 19 years, Marlene Iglitzen, 46. "We were buddies, colleagues, and lovers."

Together, Siskel and Ebert were a powerhouse. As their 1970s local public TV hit *Sneak Previews* evolved into the nationally syndicated *At the Movies* and then into *Siskel & Ebert,* they became

America's most watched, most influential film critics, with some 3 million viewers. Very simply, "they connected with the audience," says Kathleen Carroll, former film critic for the *New York Daily News.* In Hollywood, says *Stepmom* executive producer Ron Bass, "theirs were the first reviews you were concerned about."

Siskel's reactions could be unpredictable. His best movie of 1998? *Babe: Pig in the City.* And though he considered *Citizen Kane* the top film of all time, his personal favorite was 1977's *Saturday Night Fever.* "I believe he saw it more than 17 times," says Ebert. A few years later, Siskel even shelled out $2,000 to buy the John Travolta character's white suit, which later fetched $145,500 at auction. Says Marlene, who loved shopping with him for art and antiques: "Gene was just thrilled to be in the presence of inspired work."

Siskel didn't live to review a movie he eagerly looked forward to—May's *Star Wars* prequel. But his health held up long enough for him to praise daughter Callie at her January bat mitzvah. Moving with a walker, "he had difficulty remembering and putting things together in a flow," recalls his friend Bill Kurtis, the former CBS morning anchor. "But it was an emotional little speech. He always seemed to cherish those moments that so many of us take for granted."

A native Chicagoan, Siskel

learned early about life's fragility. Both his father and mother died before he was 10; an aunt and uncle then raised him and his two siblings. After studying philosophy at Yale, he got a reporting job at the *Tribune* in 1969. After just seven months there, he became Ebert's upstart rival.

Not surprisingly, both were wary of the idea, hatched by public station WTTW in 1975, of a show starring competing movie critics. Neither initially liked the "thumb" system, says Thea Flaum, the program's first producer. Siskel also objected to the open-collared shirt and jacket that became his trademark. ("People don't wear ties when they go to the movies," Flaum had chided him.)

After his June surgery, the workaholic Siskel soon returned to his rigorous schedule, taping the show, writing reviews for the *Tribune* and *TV Guide,* and appearing on *CBS This Morning.* His speech was slow. "However," says Bill Kurtis, "we thought it was just a matter of time before 'old Gene will be back.'" Siskel and his wife had made a pact, according to a friend, to keep the news of his worsening condition a secret from virtually everyone outside the family. But when he announced Feb. 4 that he was taking time off, friends grew worried. "He loved his work," says Flaum. "The fact that he would stop gave me a cold, bad feeling." He died 16 days later.

The duo did not get the chance to tape their annual salute to the Oscars, which Siskel attended each year with Marlene. "I'd always look forward to sitting with them," says L.A. screenwriter Nancy De Los Santos, a former *Sneak Previews* producer. "I can't imagine going now. There'll be that empty chair." The one back in the studio, next to Ebert, will be even harder to fill.

DUSTY SPRINGFIELD

Even at the absolute end, Dusty Springfield knew how to dazzle a crowd. On a cold, rainy March day in Henley-on-Thames near London, a horse-drawn hearse bearing her coffin made its way to St. Mary the Virgin Church as nearly 1,000 soaked mourners lined the streets. "I think she was up there laughing," says Pat Rhodes, Springfield's assistant since 1963. "She always said she would love her funeral to stop the traffic in this town, and she did just that."

It wouldn't be the first time Springfield, who died of breast cancer, stopped people cold. Whether it was her taffy blond beehive, panda eyes ringed with makeup, or the smoky, soulful voice behind such 1960s classics as "You Don't Have to Say You Love Me," "I Only Want to Be with You," and "Son of a Preacher Man," Springfield was impossible to miss.

The public thought so too—so much so that she was inducted into the Rock and Roll Hall of Fame. Her friend Elton John gave the induction at ceremonies in New York City on March 15. Sadly, however, Springfield did not live to witness her this last jewel in her crown, having finally succumbed to cancer that was diagnosed in 1994.

Growing up in London, the youngest of two children born to an accountant and a homemaker, Mary Isabel Catherine Bernadette O'Brien overcame natural shyness through her great passion— singing. By 1963 she had also undergone a major makeover, piling on cosmetics, elevating the hair, and renaming herself Dusty Springfield. That year she embarked on a solo career after the breakup of The Springfields, a trio she had formed. She recorded a string of smash singles culminating in her 1969 tour de force album *Dusty in Memphis*.

After that, the never-wed Springfield seemed to lose her way. She developed a drinking and cocaine problem that she didn't curb until the early 1980s. (Later, though, she had a surprise hit single, 1987's "What Have I Done to Deserve This," with the Pet Shop Boys.)

"She left us a legacy of beautiful recordings and fabulous memories," said Elton John. "At her funeral…as the coffin came out of the church, she had a standing ovation." She would have loved it.

SAUL STEINBERG

As an American naval ensign sent to Italy during World War II, Saul Steinberg was given an unusual assignment: Draw Resistance-inspiring cartoons to be dropped behind German lines. His life's work turned out to be no less unlikely. Long before the 84-year-old cartoonist died of cancer at his Manhattan home, his quirky sketches— of a buffoonish Hitler, of Lady Liberty at the Last Supper, of New York City as the center of the universe—had turned doodling into an art form. They had also indelibly altered America's self-image. "His art reshapes the way you think. You can't remember what you thought of something—like the Manhattan view—before he drew it," says Francoise Mouly, Steinberg's good friend and the art editor of *The New Yorker*, which published 727 Steinberg drawings (including 85 magazine covers) in more than 50 years. "I have never depended on art historians or the benediction of museums and critics," Steinberg once said. "I like work to be on the page."

The Romanian-born son of a Jewish box manufacturer father and a baker mother, Steinberg studied sociology and psychology in Bucharest before moving to Milan, where he received a doctoral degree in architecture. In 1942, a year after fleeing Fascist Italy, he arrived in the U.S., where he developed a passion for more blue-plate pleasures: motels, diners, baseball, Nebraska. "He was in awe of America," says Arne Glimcher, chairman of Manhattan's Pace Wildenstein gallery. "He saw with the eyes of a child." Yet Steinberg's awe was tinged with cynicism. "He used to tell me that we all wore masks," says Glimcher. Widely considered aloof, Steinberg "was simply a very private person," says his wife, Hedda Sterne, who was separated from him in the 1970s (they have no children) but remained a friend and was with him when he died. "He just wanted to draw."

SUSAN STRASBERG

When Susan Strasberg was the maid of honor at Cynthia Adler's wedding in 1994, the bride gave her an embroidered pillow that read "Life is uncertain. Eat dessert first." It referred to more than Strasberg's insatiable sweet tooth. The actress, who died of cancer at age 60, had been a Broadway sensation in the title role of *The Diary of Anne Frank* when she was just 17. But despite prodigious talent, the daughter of famous method-acting teachers Lee and Paula Strasberg never replicated that sweet success.

More memorable than most of the movie roles that followed were her famous friendships—Marilyn Monroe was like a sister—and romances with Richard Burton, Warren Beatty, and Cary

Grant. In later years she told all in two well-written books that dealt frankly with her own insecurities and sadly diminished expectations. "There I was, sitting in Hollywood, just waiting for someone to want me," she said in her 1980 autobiography, *Bittersweet*. She died alone in a friend's Manhattan apartment; those close to her say she had no medical insurance. "Sometimes greatness like Susan's gets overlooked in the shuffle," says longtime pal Diane Ladd. "She tried hard to keep the negative out of her life."

That life began in the bustle of Broadway, where Susan's family name was synonymous with serious acting. In 1947 actor Lee Strasberg and his actress wife, Paula, were among the founders of the Actors Studio, where Marlon Brando, James Dean, and Al Pacino trained. In *Bittersweet*, Susan wrote that Lee, who died in 1982, was brilliant but domineering. "She refused to take her [parents'] classes, or their advice," says friend Lee Grant. "She did Anne Frank out of that own instinctive talent of hers."

One guest at the 1955 opening-night party for *Anne Frank* was her parents' student Marilyn Monroe, who had also moved in with Lee, Paula, Susan, and her brother John after her 1954 divorce from Joe DiMaggio. Despite Susan's occasional resentment at the attention her father paid to Monroe,

the two were soul mates, and Strasberg was devastated when Monroe died in 1962. "I blurted out to her, 'Marilyn, I'd give anything to be like you,' " Strasberg wrote in her 1992 book *Marilyn and Me*. "And she said, 'Oh, no, Susie, don't say that. I'd give anything to be like you. People respect you.' "

Not always. At 20 she was heart-broken when her first love, Richard Burton—then 32 and married to actress Sybil Williams—dumped her at the end of the Broadway run of *Time Remembered*, in which they costarred. Her Hollywood career—she moved there in 1964—began with early acclaim in such films as 1955's *Picnic*, but she drifted into lesser roles and endured a disastrous one-year marriage to fellow actor Christopher Jones in 1965. Their daughter, Jennifer, was born with four holes in her heart—a month before Paula Strasberg died—and Susan, who wondered if her experiments with drugs were to blame, cut back on acting to be with the little girl.

Last December the financially strapped Strasberg sold off (for more than $100,000) a cherished possession: a string of pearls that Monroe had given to Paula. "I wear these pearls whenever I need confidence or strength," she told the *Toronto Star* in 1992. "I can feel Marilyn's and Mother's energy, and I can know they are with me."

LIZ TILBERIS

As editor in chief of *Harper's Bazaar,* Liz Tilberis delighted in talking hemlines and haute couture with friends such as Donna Karan and Calvin Klein. But nothing thrilled the sleek arbiter of style more than hearing that her crusade against ovarian cancer, with which she was diagnosed in 1993, had helped someone. A reader called to say that Tilberis's 1998 memoir *No Time to Die* had led to a life-saving early diagnosis. "For Liz," says Jamie Boris, executive director of the Ovarian Cancer Research Fund, of which Tilberis was president, "that was like a dream come true."

Alas, her own dreams of survival did not, and she died in Manhattan after a six-year fight at age 51. Despite the severity of her illness, her death shocked many. "No one in the fashion world thought she was ever going to die—it just wasn't going to happen," says Patrick McCarthy, editor of the *W* magazine. That conviction was a testament to Tilberis's grace: In an industry known more for backbiting than beneficence, she was famous for radiating warmth. "Liz came from one place, and that was love," says Donna Karan. "She made everyone feel good." Not that the British expat was any pushover: She reportedly banged her share of boardroom tables and once even slugged a security guard for shoving one of her editors at a

fashion show. "Liz was the snap, crackle, and pop of the fashion world," says Manhattan socialite Blaine Trump.

In her seven-year reign, Tilberis single-handedly revived the once-struggling *Harper's Bazaar,* introducing a dramatic redesign, increasing circulation by 25 percent, and making dozens of strong alliances along the way. "People who only met her once in the course of business feel they were close friends," says her husband of 27 years, Andrew Tilberis, 56, an artist and father to their sons Robert, 17, and Christopher, 14. "That's the kind of effect Liz had."

Though devoted to her family (she rushed back to their Manhattan home to cook dinner most nights), "work was her passion," says Andrew. When cancer treatments—including a bone-marrow transplant in 1995—intervened, she held meetings at her hospital bed. "For Liz, fashion wasn't simply a career," says *Bazaar*'s fashion director Tonne Goodman. "It was part of her life"

And always had been. "I was interested in fashion from the time I got my first doll," Tilberis told PEOPLE last year. After getting kicked out of Leicester Polytechnic in 1965 for entertaining a boy in her room, she briefly attended art college, where she fell in love with Andrew, who was her tutor, then returned to Leicester and completed her design degree. By the time she and

Andrew wed in July 1971, Tilberis was working her way up as a fashion assistant at *British Vogue.* She was childless in her early 30s, and she underwent unsuccessful fertility treatments before electing to adopt in '81. (Later Tilberis blamed the fertility treatments, which some research has associated with ovarian cancer, for her illness.) In 1987 she was named editor in chief of *British Vogue,* replacing fellow Brit Anna Wintour, who was to take over the U.S. flagship.

Five years later, Tilberis too was lured across the Atlantic. Taking the helm at *Bazaar,* she won a reputation for encouraging young designers and taking artistic risks—and maintaining a stiff upper lip. She was still scrutinizing magazine layouts at home a few days before she died, "If I were to ask her, 'How would you like to be remembered?' " says London PR executive Phyllis Walters, a friend of 27 years, "she would say, 'Don't be silly.' She fought harder than anyone I know."

MEL TORME

Even after he was disabled by a 1996 stroke, Mel Torme never missed a Monday night ritual. With various pals, he'd turn up at L.A. neighbor Hugh Hefner's Playboy Mansion to watch old movies. "We'd run a Jimmy Cagney film or Laurel and Hardy and then an episode of *Flash*

Gordon," says Hefner, a friend since the 1950s. "One time somebody was trying to remember the name of an actor or director: 'Was it so and so?' Mel's speech was impaired. But he was able to confirm the name and got a round of applause from the guys."

For the once robust singer, who died at the UCLA Medical Center at age 73 of complications from the stroke, it may have been his hardest earned ovation. For the past two years, Torme had been confined to a wheel chair and dependent on round-the-clock nursing care. "He did not have a lot of energy," says his son Tracy, 40, a TV writer and producer. "It was very trying for him to sit up, to move, or even to talk for any length of time."

Yet for most of his life, it seemed, Torme had barely paused for breath. In addition to recording dozens of albums, he was an accomplished drummer, pianist, arranger, an occasional actor, and the prolific author of several books and some 300 songs, most notably "Born to Be Blue" and Nat King Cole's 1946 classic "The Christmas Song," both cowritten with Bob Wells. But performing remained his first love. "Not only could he scat sing on a level with Ella Fitzgerald," says jazz critic Neil Tesser, "he could even improvise lyrics because he had such an agile mind."

The elder of two children born in Chicago to Russian immigrant parents, Torme was 4 when he made his professional debut at a local supper club. As the band played, its drummer noticed the tot singing along on his mother's lap and invited him on stage. Young Mel's rendition of "You're Driving Me Crazy" turned into a regular Monday-night gig that paid him $15 a week. By age 9, he was acting on local radio serials, and at 15, after moving with his family to L.A. and enrolling at Hollywood High School, he joined Chico Marx's band. Dropping out of school a year later, he landed a supporting role in *Higher and Higher,* Frank Sinatra's 1943 movie and the first of some 20 films Torme would appear in.

Like Sinatra, he caught fire as a crooner in the 1940s. In the 1960s, though, his voice was all but drowned out by rock and roll, which ruled the airwaves and concert stages. Torme, reduced to playing obscure club gigs, at one point thought of quitting to become an airline pilot. But a 1977 Carnegie Hall concert with pianist George Shearing and saxophone player Gerry Mulligan led to a career revival. And in the '80s, Torme won a whole new audience with his recurring cameos on the NBC sitcom *Night Court.*

Torme's zest extended to his love life. As a bachelor in the late 1940s he had a fling with Ava Gardner, then embarked on marriages to three other actresses—Candy Toxton, Arlene Miles, and Janette Scott, with whom he fathered five children. In 1984 he wed fourth wife, Ali Severson. "Mel did sum it up on a couple of occasions," his longtime manager Dale Sheets says of Torme's divorces. "He'd say, 'Absence makes the heart go wander.' He was traveling a lot."

So much so that son Steve, a swing jazz singer who was 3 when his parents split, says he began bonding with his dad only 15 years ago. Their father son duet of "Straighten Up and Fly Right" was one of the last songs the older Torme recorded. "Two weeks ago, I brought it over to his house because he hadn't heard it yet," says Steve. "He sat there with this smile, and he just had tears running down his cheeks. So I think he liked it."

Torme won a lifetime achievement Grammy in February. He died with his wife and five children at his side. "I used to tell people that he was going to be the George Burns of the music business," says Tracy. "He was going so strong. He hadn't lost any of his voice, and there was no indication that he was going to. That's the real sad irony of the whole thing, that he was cut down right in his prime."

★

Author **Alice Adams**, 72, who wrote the bestselling novel *Superior Women* and was a regular contributor of short stories to *The New Yorker,* in her sleep in San Francisco.

Actor **Kirk Alyn**, 88, who played the first movie Superman, in Houston. After playing the Man of Steel in two 15-part serials in 1948 and 1950, Alyn was courted by producers of the 1951 television series. Already annoyed by the kind of attention the films had brought him, he turned down the part, which then went to George Reeves. Years later Alyn took the uncredited role of Lois Lane's father in the 1978 big-screen version of *Superman,* starring Christopher Reeve.

U.S. Senate clerk **Raymond Scott Bates**, 50, after being struck by a car while crossing a street with his wife in Arlington, Va. Bates's sonorous voice was familiar to Clinton impeachment viewers for calling the roll when senators voted.

English-born actor **Dirk Bogarde**, 78, who was dubbed the "British Rock Hudson" in the 1950s because of his dashing good looks and who starred in 1961's *Victim,* one of the screen's first explorations of the then-taboo subject of homosexuality, of a heart attack in London.

Blues pianist and singer **Charles Brown**, 76, who performed the holiday standard "Merry Christmas, Baby"and helped originate the West Coast "cool blues" sound in the '40s and '50s, of congestive heart failure in Oakland. In March 1999 he was to have been inducted into the Rock and Roll Hall of Fame.

Backlot buckaroo **Rory Calhoun**, 76, who headlined in numerous movie Westerns and starred in TV's *The Texan* from 1958 to '60, of diabetes and emphysema in Burbank, Calif.

Gallery owner **Leo Castelli**, 91, who pushed painters Jasper Johns and Andy Warhol to the forefront of the art world and in so doing helped erase European snobbery about American art, of undisclosed causes in Manhattan.

Hovercraft inventor **Sir Christopher Cockerell**, 88, who in the '50s perfected the means by which even a heavy vehicle could travel on a cushion of air, following complications from a fall in England.

Actor **Iron Eyes Cody**, 94, who memorably shed one single tear in a 1970s antilittering TV commercial, in L.A. Though the public had assumed Iron Eyes to be a Native American, the *New Orleans Times–Picayune* published documentation in

1996 noting he was actually a second-generation Italian-American from Louisiana, but Cody denied the report.

Astronaut **Charles "Pete" Conrad Jr.**, 69, who commanded the *Apollo 12* lunar mission and was the third human being to set foot on the moon—where he literally exclaimed "Whoopee!"—in a low-speed motorcycle accident near Ojai, Calif., ironically, a town named after the Chumash word for *moon.* His death leaves nine living moon walkers, all of whom are in their 60s.

TV and film trouper **Ellen Corby**, 87, best known for playing Grandma on the hit CBS series *The Waltons*—work that won her three Emmys—in Woodland Hills, Calif. Over the course of her six-decade career, she earned an Oscar nomination for her supporting role as the lovelorn aunt in the 1948 film *I Remember Mama.* Before she became a cast member on *The Waltons* in 1972, the character actress was a mainstay on various TV series, often as a persnickety busybody or an adorable old maid.

Stripper **Lili St. Cyr**, 80, who was famous for her onstage bubble baths during the heyday of burlesque and for her dalliances with the rich and famous (Orson Welles and Victor Mature to name but two), in Hollywood. "Sex is currency," she once

46

observed. "What's the use of being beautiful if you can't profit from it?"

Actor and director **Danny Dayton**, 75, who played Archie Bunker's pal Hank Pivnik on *All in the Family* and later on *Archie Bunker's Place* from 1977 to '81, of emphysema in L.A.

Donald Engen, 75, who was the director of the National Air and Space Museum in Washington, D.C., when the glider in which he was a passenger broke apart over Nevada.

Literary lion **Clifton Fadiman**, 95, whose work as an arbiter of the Book-of-the-Month Club selections helped shape the tastes of American readers for more than five decades, on Sanibel Island, Fla.

Retired advertising executive **Christopher Ford**, 92, the father of Harrison Ford, of natural causes in Laguna Hills, Calif.

Big-band belter **Helen Forrest**, 82, who sang with orchestras led by Artie Shaw, Harry James, and Benny Goodman, and whose signature song was "I Had the Craziest Dream," of congestive heart failure in L.A.

TV's most mischievous provocateur, **Allen Funt**, 84, of complications from a 1993 stroke. Between 1960 and 1967, millions of Sunday night viewers tuned in to his *Candid Camera* on CBS to watch the often horrified reactions of unsuspecting passersby, duped by Funt's carefully choreographed ruses.

Actress **Betty Lou Gerson**, 84, who provided the voice of the flamboyant villainess Cruella de Vil in Walt Disney's animated 1961 film *One Hundred and One Dalmatians*, of a stroke in L.A. In addition to extensive radio work and TV appearances, she narrated Disney's *Cinderella* and had a cameo in *Mary Poppins*.

Journalist **Meg Greenfield**, 68, who for the past 20 years presided over the editorial page of the *Washington Post* while also working as a columnist at *Newsweek*, of cancer in Washington, D.C.

Bass singer **Gerald "Bounce" Gregory**, 64, who lent his low notes to the 1950s Spaniels classic "Goodnight Sweetheart, Goodnight," of undisclosed causes in Gary, Ind.

Actress **Sandra Gould**, 78, who played snoopy neighbor Gladys Kravitz on TV's *Bewitched* from 1966 to '72, from a stroke following heart surgery in Burbank, Calif.

Actor **Huntz Hall**, 78, who used a battery of elastic facial expressions playing Dippy in the 60-odd *Bowery Boys* and *Dead End Kids*

films he made from the '30s to the '50s, of heart failure in North Hollywood, Calif.

King Hassan II, 70, Morocco's monarch for 38 years, of a heart attack in Rabat.

Pop music impresario **Bob Herbert**, 57, whose 1994 newspaper ad recruited five unknown singers for a group that came to be known as the Spice Girls, in a car crash in England.

Trumpeter **Al Hirt**, 76, who got his first horn at age 6, blew the bugle in the army, and went on to win some 20 Grammy nominations for his recordings, of liver failure in his native New Orleans. The renowned musician, who honed his robust technique in the clubs of the French Quarter, won one Grammy for the 1963 instrumental "Java."

Jim "Catfish" Hunter, 53, baseball's first free-agent multimillionaire and one of its greatest pitchers, with 224 victories, a perfect game, and five World Series rings, of ALS (Lou Gehrig's disease), in Hertford, N.C.

Pharmacist **Ted Hustead**, 96, whose 60-odd-year policy of handing out free ice water made his Wall Drug Store in Wall, South Dakota (pop. 800), a top tourist attraction, in Philip, South Dakota. Some 2 million thirsty travelers stopped by each year.

Avuncular character actor **Henry Jones**, 86, whose ordinary name contrasted with an extraordinary show-biz career that spanned six decades and included Broadway, film, and some 350 television shows, following complications from a fall in L.A. Among his more familiar roles were the handyman in 1956's *The Bad Seed* and the judge on Cloris Leachman's sitcom *Phyllis* from 1975 to '77.

Writer and director **Garson Kanin**, 86, who with his late wife, the actress-writer Ruth Gordon, scripted two celebrated films pairing Katharine Hepburn and Spencer Tracy (*Adam's Rib* and *Pat and Mike*), in Manhattan. In 1964 Kanin directed Barbra Streisand in her starmaking performance in *Funny Girl* on Broadway.

Daredevil parachutist **Thor Axel Kappfjell**, 32, who made New York City tabloid headlines as Norway's Human Fly by surreptitiously—and illegally—leaping from the top of the Empire State Building and the World Trade Center, after taking a 3,300-feet dive into a fjord in his native country and accidentally slamming into a cliff.

Rockabilly singer/songwriter **Buddy Knox**, 65, who had a string of chart-climbers in the '50s, including "Hula Love," "Rock Your Little Baby to Sleep," and "Party Doll," which hit No. 1 in 1957, of cancer in Bremerton, Wash.

Former clothing salesman **Aaron Lapin**, 85, who came up with the idea of putting whipped cream in a seamless, lined aerosol canister in the late 1940s and made a fortune selling it as Reddi-wip, in L.A.

Basket ace **David Longaberger**, 64, whose zeal for woven containers led him to design the Newark, Ohio, headquarters of his company to look like a seven-story market basket outfitted with a pair of 75-ton handles, of kidney cancer at his home near there. Founded in 1973, Longaberger's basket business turned hardwood maple into highly prized and collectible examples of double-splint weaving, while its overgrown basket building (160 times larger than the standard basket) lured thousands of devoted pilgrims bearing Longaberger baskets.

Forrest Mars Sr., 95, the creator of M&M's candies in 1940, of natural causes in Miami, Fla. At the time of his death, the chocolate mogul was worth an estimated $4 billion.

Author **Helen A. Mayer**, 91, of Parkinson's disease in Manhattan. In 1939 she wrote a children's story about an undersize elephant with oversize ears that Disney turned into the film *Dumbo* in 1941.

Violin virtuoso **Yehudi Menuhin**, 82, praised by fellow fiddle player Itzhak Perlman as "the most phenomenal child prodigy that ever existed, certainly in this century," of heart failure in Berlin. In 1924, at age 8, Menuhin made his professional debut playing Bériot's "Scène de Ballet" with the San Francisco Symphony Orchestra. He went on to conduct classical works around the world, all the while maintaining affection for early Beatles songs, jazz, and the Indian music of Ravi Shankar.

Guy Mitchell, 72, the clean-cut crooner who had nearly 40 hit country and folk records during the '50s, of complications following surgery in Las Vegas. His versions of "Singing the Blues" and "Heartaches by the Numbers" reached No. 1 on the pop charts.

Actor, comedian, and producer **Gary Morton**, 74, of lung cancer outside Palm Springs, Calif. He wed Lucille Ball a year after she divorced Desi Arnaz and was married to her for nearly 28 years until her death in 1989. He oversaw the production of three of Lucy's TV series. He also later had supporting roles in the films *Lenny* and *Postcards from the Edge*.

James (Jimmy) Newman, 36, the son of R&B singer Gladys Knight who also acted as her manager, in Las Vegas of unknown causes.

Madison Avenue magnifico **David Ogilvy**, 88, the founder of the global ad agency Ogilvy & Mather and creator of "Schweppervescence," the eye-patched Hathaway shirt man, and the slogan for Dove soap, at his home in France. In his 1963 bestseller *Confessions of an Advertising Man,* he included his oft-repeated maxim, "The consumer is not a moron; she is your wife. Try not to insult her intelligence."

Women's National Basketball Association player **Kim Perrot**, 32, who overcame the limitations of her size (5'5" and 130 lbs.) to help spur the Houston Comets to consecutive championships in 1997 and 1998, of cancer in Houston.

Forward-thinker **Ed Peterson**, 78, who came up with the idea for the Bac-A-Larm, the device that emits a series of high-pitched beeps when trucks and heavy machinery are moving in reverse, of prostate cancer in Boise, Id.

Female impersonator **Charles Pierce**, 72, who won a devoted following for decades by camping it up as Joan Crawford and Bette Davis in nightclubs, of cancer in L.A.

Trendsetting modiste **Clare Potter**, 95, one of the designers credited with inventing American sportswear, in Fort Ann, N.Y. Her unconventional notions in the 1930s and '40s helped make trousers on women, for example, standard wear today.

Jean Vander Pyl, 79, known to toon aficionados as the voice of Wilma Flintstone; her daughter, Pebbles; and Rosie the Robot on *The Jetsons,* of lung cancer in Dana Point, Calif.

Popular heavyweight **Jerry Quarry**, 53, who went into the ring with Muhammad Ali, Joe Frazier, and Floyd Patterson in the '60s and '70s before eventually lapsing into a state of dementia pugilistica (brain damage caused by repeated blows to the head), in Templeton, Calif., after contracting pneumonia.

Hall of Fame shortstop **Pee Wee Reese**, 80, who in 1955 helped the Brooklyn Dodgers win their only World Series, of lung cancer at his home in Louisville, Ky. Reese was also famous for strength of a different kind: When teammates circulated a petition saying they didn't want to play with blacks, he refused to sign. And when racist fans in Cincinnati taunted Jackie Robinson, Reese, in a gesture both graceful and defiant, stood beside his teammate and put his arm around him.

Character actor **Bert Remsen**, 74, whose credits ranged from *Brewster McCloud* in 1970 to 1999's *Forces of Nature,* of natural causes near L.A.

Popular romance novelist **Nancy Richards-Akers** (*Wild Irish Skies, So Wild a Kiss*), 45, fatally shot twice in the head by Jeremy Akers, her estranged husband, as she sat in her Jeep in Washington, D.C. Several hours later, Akers, 57, an ex-Marine, committed suicide with a shotgun near Washington's Vietnam Veterans Memorial. The couple are survived by three children, ages 9, 11, and 21.

Baseball coach **Cal Ripken Sr.**, 63, the only manager to oversee two sons on the same major-league team (Cal Jr. and Billy of the Orioles), of lung cancer in Baltimore. A chain-smoker of filterless cigarettes, the curmudgeonly Ripken had a voice that one writer said "sounded like the bucket of a backhoe scraping a boulder."

Set decorator **Don Roberts**, 64, whose designs for TV's *The Jeffersons, One Day at a Time,* and *Married . . . with Children* are nearly as familiar to avid viewers as their own homes, of a brain tumor in Woodland Hills, Calif. The chairs that Roberts found for *All in the Family* are now in the Smithsonian.

Actress **Ruth Roman**, 76, a Hollywood screen queen from the late '40s through the '50s whose 30-odd films are relatively unknown today, in her sleep, in Laguna Beach, Calif. Two of her more familiar movies are 1949's *Champion,* in which she played opposite Kik Douglas, and *Strangers on a Train,* the 1951 Hitchcock thriller.

Actor and bandleader **Charles "Buddy" Rogers**, 94, best known for his gutsy performance as a World War I airman in *Wings,* the 1927 silent film that won the first Academy Award for Best Picture, in Rancho Mirage, Calif. In addition to fronting an orchestra on Broadway in the '30s, he was married to "America's Sweetheart," Mary Pickford, and continued to take film roles until 1957.

Ex-pro wrestler **Rick Rood**, 40, who was known for pinning his opponents with a maneuver known as the Rude Awakening, after collapsing at his home in Alpharetta, Ga. The cause of death is unknown, but empty bottles of prescription medicine were found near the body.

Legendary golfer **Gene Sarazen**, 97, who invented the sand wedge in 1931 and was the first in his sport to win the four major championships, in Naples, Fla. His sideline as an apple grower coupled with his habit of dressing to a tee (knickers were de rigueur on the links) earned Sarazen the title "the Squire."

Designer **Altina Schinasi Miranda**, 92, who in the 1930s came up with the pointy-rimmed eyeglass frames she dubbed Harlequins, of a heart attack in Santa Fe, NM.

Chemist **Waldo Semon**, 100, who earned a place in the National Inventors Hall of Fame for creating vinyl in the 1920s, in Hudson, Ohio. He held 116 U.S. patents, including one for bubble gum.

Tenor **Walter Settles**, 71, who at one time led the Grammy-winning gospel group the Fairfield Four, of complications related to a stroke and diabetes in Nashville, Tenn.

Eva Shain, 81, the first woman to judge a heavyweight boxing championship (Muhammad Ali vs. Earnie Shavers in 1977), of cancer in Englewood, N.J.

Photojournalist **Sam Shaw**, 87, the man responsible for the most renowned picture of Marilyn Monroe, in Westwood, N.J. In 1955 the producers of *The Seven Year Itch* hired Shaw to shoot a poster for the film. Before hundreds of onlookers, he photographed Monroe standing on a subway grate as her white pleated chiffon skirt billowed up from the rush of air raised by an oncoming train. (The effect was actually created by a huge electric fan.)

Musician **Bobby Sheehan**, 31, bass player for the Grammy Award–winning band Blues Traveler, from unknown causes, at his home in New Orleans, La.

Actress **Sylvia Sidney**, 88, who played vulnerable heroes in such 1930s films as *An American Tragedy* and *Fury,* of throat cancer in Manhattan. Sidney continued taking acting jobs into the '80s and '90s, including one role as a gravelly-voiced, cigarette-puffing ghost in 1988's *Beetlejuice.*

Horseman **Cecil Smith**, 94, a dirt-poor pony wrangler from Llano, Tex., who went on to become arguably the greatest polo player ever by winning the sport's highest ranking from 1938 to '62, in Boerne, Tex.

Ballplayer **Eddie Stanky**, 83, the contentious infielder nicknamed "the Brat" who helped the Brooklyn Dodgers, the Boston Braves, and the New York Giants win National League pennants, of a heart attack in Fairhope, Ala.

John Stears, 64, the special-effects guru who created James Bond's machine-gun-firing Aston Martin for *Goldfinger* (1964) and the flying cars used in *Chitty Chitty Bang Bang* (1968), of a stroke in L.A. The family waited until memorial services had been held to announce his death. Stears's best-known creations are the affable droids R2-D2 and C-3PO, plus the light sabers he designed for the original *Star Wars*.

Former New York City bus and cab driver **William Stiller**, 102, the father of veteran comic Jerry Stiller and the grandfather of actors Ben and Amy Stiller, in Spring Valley, N.Y.

Zaftig character actress **Shirley Stoler**, 70, who steered clear of typecasting with outré roles ranging from the Nazi concentration camp matron in 1976's *Seven Beauties to Mrs. Steve* to the nutty neighbor on TV's *Pee-wee's Playhouse*, of heart failure in New York City. Songwriter **Jesse Stone**, 97, the grandson of slaves who, in 1954, wrote "Shake, Rattle, and Roll," one of the seminal hits of rock music, in Altamonte Springs, Fla.

Tennis great **Bill Talbert**, 80, who won 33 national titles, including eight U.S. Opens in the '40s, in Manhattan.

Photojournalist **Stanley Tretick**, 77, who took the famous photographs of John F. Kennedy Jr., then almost 3, playing under his father's Oval Office desk, following a series of strokes in a Maryland retirement community,

two days before the young Kennedy's body was found off Martha's Vineyard.

Actor and musician **Bobby Troup**, 80, who wrote the 1946 hit "(Get Your Kicks on) Route 66," and played neurosurgeon Dr. Joe Early on TV's *Emergency!* from 1972 to '77, of a heart attack in L.A.

Real estate developer **Fred C. Trump**, 93, who oversaw the construction of more than 27,000 apartments and row houses in New York City neighborhoods beginning in the late '20s and gave advice (and a small loan) to help son Donald get his start in the same business, in Queens, N.Y.

Character actress **Billye Ree Wallace**, 73, who specialized in playing daffy old biddies on numerous sitcoms (she was Jerry's Nana on *Seinfeld*), of respiratory failure and emphysema in L.A.

Senor Wences, the Spanish-born ventriloquist who delighted *Ed Sullivan Show* audiences in the '50s and '60s with Pedro, his puppet in a box ("S'okay?" "S'all right, s'all right!"), and his falsetto-voiced, bewigged hand-puppet Johnny, in Manhattan on his 103rd birthday.

Announcer **Bill Wendell**, 75, noted for his annunciations of nonsensical *Late Show* sign-ons ("From New

York, mountain fortress of the ancient Incas, it's...Da-aa-vid Letterman!"), of complications from cancer in Boca Raton, Fla.

Sociologist **William H. Whyte**, 81, who bemoaned the button-down conformity of postwar America in his 1956 bestseller *The Organization Man*, of undisclosed causes in New York City.

Jazz and blues baritone **Joe Williams**, 80, renowned for his collaborations with Count Basie and for playing Grandpa Al on *The Cosby Show*, in Las Vegas, while walking home from a hospital where he was being treated for a respiratory ailment.

Country crooner **BoxCar Willie**, 67, of leukemia in Branson, Mo. Born Lecil Martin, he adopted a hobo persona in the '70s to sing about life riding the rails in America.

Magazine trailblazer **Ruth Whitney**, 71, who as editor of *Glamour* from 1967 to '98 helped bring such women's issues as equal pay and the glass ceiling to national attention, of Lou Gehrig's disease in Irvington, N.Y. In 1968 Whitney put a black model on the cover of *Glamour*, a first for a mainstream women's magazine.

MARRIAGES

CNBC financial anchor **Maria Bartiromo**, 31, sometimes known as the "Money Honey," and Jonathan Steinberg, 34, CEO of Individual Investor Group, in Quogue, N.Y.

Princess Caroline of Monaco, 42, and **Prince Ernst of Hanover**, 44, in a civil ceremony that took place in the Salon des Glaces of the principality's pink palace.

Bestselling novelist **Tom Clancy**, 52, and Alexandra Llewellyn, 32, a freelance journalist, in Manhattan. Clancy and first wife, Wanda, had recently ended a 28-year marriage that produced four children.

Actress **Sofia Coppola**, 28, and music video director Spike Jonze, 29, in Napa Valley, Calif. The ceremony was held in a vineyard owned by her dad, director Francis Ford Coppola, and singer Tom Waits sang "Here Comes the Bride."

Courteney Cox, 35, of *Friends* fame, and *Scream* costar **David Arquette**, 27, in San Francisco.
The bride walked down the aisle to Paul McCartney's "Maybe I'm Amazed."

Richard Dreyfuss, 51, and Janelle Lacey, 34, an accountant, in an outdoor ceremony

at his L.A. home, following a year-long engagement.
Emily Erwin, 26, of the Dixie Chicks, and fellow musician Charlie Robison, 34, in their home state of Texas. At the conclusion of the evening ceremony, Erwin joined the Chicks to sing a song written especially for the couple.

Dean Felber, 31, bass player for Hootie and the Blowfish, and Laurie Hutchinson, 25, a magazine editor, in Charleston, S.C. Darius Rucker, whose mellow baritone fronts the group, was the best man.

Former White House press secretary **Marlin Fitzwater**, 56, and his girlfriend of 15 years, Melinda Andrews, 50, an events planner, in an elopement.

Actor **Brad Garrett**, 39, of TV's *Everybody Loves Raymond*, and Jill Diven, 34, at the Beverly Hills Hotel. The couple have an 8-month-old son, Max, who attended the ceremony in a tiny tux.

Helen Hunt, 36, who won the Best Actress Oscar last year for *As Good As It Gets*, and actor **Hank Azaria**, 35, who guest-starred on Hunt's TV series *Mad About You* in a private ceremony at their Los Angeles home. It was the first marriage for both.

Don Johnson, 49, star of *Miami Vice* and recently appearing in CBS's *Nash Bridges*, and Kelley Phleger, 30, a Montessori nursery schoolteacher, in the Getty mansion in San Francisco. This is Johnson's fourth marriage.

Rory Kennedy and **Mark Bailey**, both 30, in a quiet ceremony near Athens, Greece. The ceremony was held 16 days after their original wedding plans were shattered when Rory's cousin John F. Kennedy Jr. died in a plane crash.

Actor **Greg Kinnear**, 35, and his girlfriend of more than six years, Helen Labdon, 29, a British-born former model turned freelance writer, in an 11th-century church in Sussex, Eng.

Actress **Diane Ladd**, 60ish, of *Alice Doesn't Live Here Anymore*, and Robert Hunter, 50ish, a retired businessman, on Valentine's Day in Bel Air, Calif. Ladd was previously married to actor Bruce Dern and stockbroker William Shea Jr.

Baritone belter **Frankie Laine**, 86, who had hits in the '50s like "High Noon" and "Jezebel," and Marcia Kline, 61, a retired real estate agent, near San Diego, Calif.

Actress **Kellie Martin**, 23, and Keith Christian, 25, a law student at New York City's Columbia University, in a garden ceremony near Polson, Mont. The couple, who met as students at Yale, were serenaded by Patti LuPone.

Jailbird **Erik Menendez**, 28, who, with brother Lyle, is serving a life sentence for the murder of their parents in 1989, and Tammi Ruth Saccoman, 37, who is self-employed in the fitness field, at the California State Prison near Sacramento. Menendez does not qualify for conjugal visits, so there was no honeymoon.

Actress **Alyssa Milano**, 26, most recently starring in TV's *Charmed,* and **Cinjun Tate**, singer and guitarist for the rock band Remy Zero in St. Amant, La. The couple said "I do" under a display of dried grapevines and sunflowers.

Actress **Kate Mulgrew**, 44, who captains *Star Trek: Voyager*, and Tim Hagan, 53, a former county commissioner in Ohio, at a ceremony attended only by the bride and groom, the officiant, and a close friend of Mulgrew's. It was the second marriage for both.

Media titan **Rupert Murdoch**, 68, and former TV executive Wendi Deng, 32, aboard *The Morning Glory* in New York City. The cere-

mony took place only 17 days after Murdoch's divorce from his second wife, Anna.

Salt-N-Pepa's **Pepa (née Sandra Denton)**, 34, and fellow rap artist **Treach (Anthony Criss)**, 28, of Naughty by Nature, in Morristown, N.J.

Actress **Rosie Perez**, 34, married her longtime fella, **Seth Zvi Rosenfeld**, 37, a filmmaker, in two ceremonies—a family-only "spiritual" one, followed by a legal one the next day at a chi-chi club in Brooklyn.

Beverly Hills 90210 fixture **Jason Priestley**, 29, and makeup artist Ashlee Peterson, 29, aboard a boat off Miami. It was the first marriage for both.

Waiting to Exhale actress **Lela Rochon**, 35, and **Antoine Fuqua**, director of *The Replacement Killers*, in L.A.

Director **Martin Scorsese**, 56, and book editor Helen Morris in New York City. It was his fifth marriage.

Megamodel **Stella Tennant**, 28, and French photographer David Lasnet in her home village of Oxnam, Scotland. The couple have a 9-month-old son, Marcel.

Musician **Bob Weir**, 51, guitarist for the Grateful Dead, and Natascha Muenter, 32, a former ele-

mentary school teacher, in Mill Valley, Calif. Groom Weir donned a kilt for the occasion.

Raquel Welch, 58, who rose to fame wearing a fur bikini in 1966's *One Million Years B.C.*, to her Bronx-born beau of 2 years, **Richie Palmer**, 44, a owner of a pizza-restaurant-chain, on the back porch of her Beverly Hills mansion. It was her fourth marriage and his second.

Barry Williams, 44, *The Brady Bunch*'s Greg, and Eila Mary Matt, 36, an investment banker. It was his second marriage and her first.

Reese Witherspoon, 23, and *Cruel Intentions* costar **Ryan Phillippe**, 24, in Charleston, S.C.

Olympic ice-skating medalist **Paul Wylie**, 34, and former social worker Katherine Presbrey, 26, in Centerville, Mass. Attending the reception was the skating world's crème de la crème, including Olympic medalists Scott Hamilton, Brian Boitano, Kristi Yamaguchi, Nancy Kerrigan, and Ekaterina Gordeeva.

PARTINGS

Actor and sleight-of-hand man **Harry Anderson**, 46, who presided over TV's *Night Court*, and his wife of 12 years, Leslie Anderson, 46, a magician and an actress, citing irreconcilable differences. She has asked for joint custody of their 13-year-old son, Dashiell.

Actor **Tom Arnold**, 40, with credits in *True Lies* and *Nine Months*, and Beverly Hills hairstylist Julie Champnella, 25, after 3 years of marriage.

The Artist (formerly known as Prince), 40, announced that he is annulling his marriage to Mayte Garcia, 25. The Artist declares he still loves Garcia, a dancer, but that he believes marriage contracts "guarantee the possibility of divorce." The couple plan to renew their vows in an unofficial ceremony on their third anniversary next month.

Bronx-born actress **Ellen Barkin**, 45, and her husband of almost 11 years, Irish actor **Gabriel Byrne**, 48, citing irreconcilable differences. The couple, legally separated for almost six years, have two children, ages 9 and 6.

Actress **Carmen Electra**, 27, and **Dennis Rodman**, the erratic 37-year-old basketball star. The couple, who

wed in Las Vegas six months before, mutually agreed to end their marriage under "amicable circumstances," said their spokesman.

Citing irreconcilable differences, *Lethal Weapon* stalwart **Danny Glover**, 52, and wife Asake Bomani, an art gallery owner, after 18 years of marriage. The couple have one daughter, Mandisa, 23.

Amy Grant, 38, and her husband of 16 years, singer-songwriter **Gary Chapman**. They have three children: Matthew, 11; Millie, 9; and Sarah, 6.

Former Speaker of the House **Newt Gingrich**, 56, and his second wife, Marianne, after 18 years of marriage. When named Speaker in 1994, Newt declared Marianne "his best friend and closet adviser."

Matt Groening, 45, the creator of *The Simpsons,* and his wife, Deborah Groening, 44, citing irreconcilable differences. The couple, who married in 1986, have two sons—Homer (not the cartoon character), 10, and Abraham, 7.

Terminator hero **Linda Hamilton**, 42, and *Titanic* director and self-proclaimed "king of the world" **James Cameron**, 44, after 17

months of marriage. The couple have a daughter, Josephine, 5.

A judge granted an annulment decree to **Mick Jagger**, 56, the endlessly rocking Rolling Stone, and former supermodel **Jerry Hall**, 43, the mother of four of his children. Justice Michael Connell ruled that the pair's 1990 Hindu ceremony on Bali was not a marriage as far as the law is concerned. At the same time he approved a confidential financial settlement between the couple. Hall filed for divorce after reading a tabloid story that pegged Jagger as the father of Brazilian model Luciana Morad's unborn child.

Angelina Jolie, 23, actress daughter of Jon Voight and Golden Globe winner for her role in *Gia,* and husband, **Jonny Lee Miller**, 25, who played Sick Boy in *Trainspotting*. The couple married 22 months earlier.

Stephen Jones, 38, and **Paula Jones**, 32, the former Arkansas state employee who reached an $850,000 settlement with President Clinton in her sexual harassment suit, citing irreconcilable differences. Stephen, an aspiring actor, said he wants alimony. The couple have two sons: Stephen, 6, and Preston, 2.

Ukrainian-born actress **Milla Jovovich**, 23, the exotic-looking heroine who costarred with Bruce Willis in the 1997 sci-fi flick *The Fifth Element*, and **Luc Besson**, 40, the French-born director of the film. Jovovich said the distance between the couple's two residences—hers in L.A., his in France—was more than their 16-month marriage could endure.

Dixie Chicks diva **Natalie Maines**, 24, lead singer for the all-girl group, and Michael Tarabay, 29, a bassist, citing irreconcilable differences. The couple had been married 19 months.

Joe Namath, 55, New York Jets ex-quarterback, and aspiring actress Tatiana Namath (formerly Deborah Mays), 37, after 14 years of wedlock. They have two daughters: Jessica, 13, and Olivia, 8.

Actress **Stefanie Powers**, 56, of *Hart to Hart*, and her husband of six years, agricultural biologist Patrick de la Chesnais, 50, citing irreconcilable differences.

Actress **Lynn Redgrave**, 56, Best Actress Oscar nominee for *Gods and Monsters*, and husband **John Clark**, 66, theater producer, director, and manager of his wife's career, after 32 years. Clark recently revealed that he had fathered a child in 1991 with his then-assistant Nicolette Hannah.

Actor **Ving Rhames**, 39, and his wife, Valerie, 34, after four years of marriage.

Motown diva **Diana Ross**, 55, and husband Arne Naess, 61, a Norwegian shipping tycoon, after 13 years of marriage. Her new album, *Every Day Is a New Day*, is about her struggle with Naess in trying to make a long-distance marriage work. They have two sons: Ross, 11, and Evan, 10.

Brooke Shields, 33, of NBC's *Suddenly Susan*, and husband, tennis champ **Andre Agassi**, 29, after two years. The couple announced that they were ending their marriage with "the utmost love and respect for each other."

Actress **Ione Skye**, 28, the daughter of '60s folk singer Donovan, and her husband of eight years, **Adam Horovitz**, 32, of the rap group the Beastie Boys, citing irreconcilable differences.

Rock star **Rod Stewart**, 54, and his wife, New Zealand-born model **Rachel Hunter**, 29, after 8 years together. Their two children—Renee, 6, and Liam, 4—will stay with Stewart in L.A.

Actor **Kiefer Sutherland**, 32, and his wife of three years, Kelly Winn Sutherland, 38, have separated, though neither has filed for divorce. The couple have no children together, but he has a daughter from his first marriage and she has two sons from a previous relationship.

BIRTHS

Ally McBeal's **Gil Bellows**, 31, and **Rya Kihlstedt**, 29, an actor *(Deep Impact)*; their first child, daughter Ava Emmanuelle. Kihlstedt gave birth in her L.A. home with the help of a midwife.

Actor **Josie Bissett**, 28, and actor **Rob Estes**, 36, who worked together on the late TV series *Melrose Place*; a son, Mason Tru Estes.

Mono-monikered rock-and-roller **Bono**, 39, frontman for the Irish band U2, and Ali Hewson, late 30s, his teenage sweetheart and wife of 17 years, a son, Elijah Bob, their third child.

Monaco's **Princess Caroline**, 42, and her third husband, **Prince Ernst August** of Hanover, 45; their first child, daughter Alexandra.

Actress **Gabrielle Carteris**, 38, who played Andrea Zuckerman on *Beverly Hills, 90210,* before graduating to her own short-lived talk show in 1995, and stockbroker Charles Isaacs, 39; a girl, Mollie Elizabeth. The couple also have a 4-year-old daughter, Kelsey Rose.

Singer-songwriter **Rosanne Cash**, 43, and **John Leventhal**, 46, a producer-songwriter; their first child, Jakob William. Cash has three girls from a previous marriage to musician Rodney Crowell.

Boxing champ **Oscar De La Hoya**, 26, and his fiancée, *The Wedding Singer* actress **Shanna Moakler**, 23; a girl, Atiana Cecilia.

Bill Gates, 43, the Croesus who runs Microsoft, and Melinda, 34; their second child, Rory John.

Actor **Mel Gibson**, 43, and Robyn, 43, his wife of nearly 19 years; a son in L.A., making a grand total of six boys and one girl for the couple.

The male half of TV's *Dharma & Greg,* actor **Thomas Gibson**, 37, who also makes an appearance in the film *Eyes Wide Shut,* and Cristina, 33, a homemaker; their first child, James Parker.

Actress **Tracey Gold**, 29, the former star of *Growing Pains,* who has battled anorexia nervosa, and Roby Marshall, 33, a teacher; their second son, Bailey Vincent.

Law student **Karenna Gore**, 25, daughter of Vice President Al Gore, and Dr. Drew Schiff, 33; a son, Wyatt Gore Schiff, on the Fourth of July.

Actress **Jasmine Guy**, 37, and Terrence Duckette, 37, an investment broker; their first child, a daughter, Imani.

Actress **Patricia Heaton**, 40, of TV's *Everybody Loves Raymond,* and **David Hunt**, 45, an actor; their fourth child, Daniel Patrick.

Latin crooner **Julio Iglesias**, 55, and his Dutch girlfriend, former model Miranda Rijnsburger, 33; their second boy, Rodrigo.

Mick Jagger, 56, and Brazilian model **Luciana Morad**, 29; a son. Jagger has six additional children from three other relationships, including his two marriages.

Playwright-director **David Mamet**, 51, and **Rebecca Pidgeon**, 33, an actress who starred in Mamet's 1998 film *The Spanish Prisoner*; a boy, Noah.

Country singer **John Michael Montgomery**, 34, and his wife, Crystal, 26; a son, Walker Carl. The couple also have a daughter, Madison, 2.

It was seventh heaven for singer and talk show host **Marie Osmond**, 39, and **Brian Blosil**, 46, a record producer, when they gave their brood of six a new baby brother, Matthew R. Blosil.

Cecilia Peck, 40, daughter of Gregory Peck, and writer Daniel Voll, 38; a boy, Harper. He is named after author Harper Lee, whose novel *To Kill a Mockingbird* led to an Oscar-winning role for Gregory Peck in 1962.

Actor **Christian Slater**, 29, and his girlfriend, Ryan Haddon, 28, a television producer; their first child, a son, Jaden Christopher Slater.

Country singer **Travis Tritt**, 36, and Theresa, 26, a homemaker; their first son, Tristan James. The Tritts have a daughter, Tyler, 1.

Tanya Tucker, 40, country queen, and her fiancé, Jerry Laseter, 37, a songwriter; their first child, a baby girl, Layla LaCosta Laseter. Tucker has two kids—daughter Presley, 10, and son Beau, 7—from a previous relationship with actor Ben Reed.

56

THE ONCE MERRY MEN AND WOMEN OF WINDSOR

"I want to be as famous as the queen of England," the ambitious young Andy Warhol proclaimed back in the 1950s. He might as well have said that he wanted to be as famous as the Atlantic Ocean. The current British royal family has something that vast and immemorial about it. In the three centuries of its reign, other crowned families of Europe have been executed or packed off. But the Windsors still occupy the throne—and the public eye—as implacable and seemingly enduring as the planet Jupiter.

It hasn't been easy. The Windsors are expected to behave like the Cleavers even when they're feeling like the Simpsons. Being famous is more than their fate; in a sense it's their job. As the real decision-making power of the monarchy has dwindled, the public symbolism has become more important. On more than one occasion in the past, however, Britons have seemed ready to rid themselves of a dynasty that could look costly, shiftless, and Teutonic. The lessons of the past are not lost on the Windsors, who take their family history not just as a source of pride but also as a series of warnings to the present. Like her father, George VI, Elizabeth II has been a model of dignity and decorum. But a stroll among her ancestors in

the National Portrait Gallery is enough to remind her of any number of hot-blooded blue bloods in her line.

Where does the Windsor saga begin? Actually, with the German Hanoverian kings. The royals like to consider Queen Victoria their matriarch because, while she was from the House of Hanover herself, her marriage to Prince Albert of Saxe-Coburg-Gotha established the present branch of the family tree. So emphasizing Albert's line allows the Windsors to distance themselves from Victoria's Hanoverian predecessors. Starting with **George I**, who was imported to England from Germany in 1714, the five increasingly preposterous rulers had made the British people rue almost the very idea of royalty.

After monarchs who alternated between extravagant skirt-chasing and outright incompetence, **Victoria** acceded to the crown in 1837, the niece of the last Hanoverian king, William IV. Immediately she made it her business to undo their legacy. She brought the monarchy a bit of wholesome romance through a devoted marriage to her German husband, **Prince Albert**. Indeed the transformation of the royal reputation may be Albert's achievement even more than Victoria's. With the middle classes taking

power from the spoiled and lazy aristocrats, Albert gave them a royal family that the common man could both look up to and identify with: wreathed in pomp and ceremony but frugal, sober, dutiful, and monogamous.

Though Victoria's name has come to stand for prudishness, it was as much Albert who brought the moralizing strain to their marriage. As a young woman, the Queen didn't blush to size him up bluntly in her diary. ("Such a pretty mouth," she noted. "A beautiful figure, broad in the shoulders, and a fine waist.") But Albert worried that their children would take after his wayward parents, who had divorced in a tangle of adulteries. Above all he vowed that Edward, heir to the throne, would be raised in an atmosphere of hard schooling and abstinence. Naturally, Edward grew up to be dim, jolly, and goatish.

Upon Albert's death in 1861, Victoria, just 42 years old, plunged down a black hole of widowhood. Albert's bedroom was kept as it was on the day of his death, even to the extent of having fresh bedclothes laid out every night. She eventually roused herself sufficiently to regain the public's affection and lived long enough to see her nine children and forty grandchildren married into most of the royal families of

Europe. On her deathbed she was supported by her grandson Kaiser Wilhelm of Germany, who 13 years later would lead his nation into war against hers.

When Victoria died in 1901, after the longest reign in her nation's history, her reputation for rectitude had become so stultifying that her womanizing heir, son **Edward VII**, found himself lionized for the same habits that had caused so much trouble for so many Hanoverian kings. Throughout his life the insatiable Edward conducted a series of lengthy affairs with some of the most celebrated beauties of the day, including the actresses Lillie Langtry and Sarah Bernhardt. With prosperity at home and a vast empire abroad, the public was willing to overlook the moral lapses of a robust and even randy monarch. After nine popular years on the throne he was followed by **George V**, prim, exacting, and a stickler for impeccable dress. George led the country through World War I when he changed the family name from the Germanic Saxe-Coburg-Gotha to Windsor. He also encouraged closer ties between the royals and the people by allowing the Windsors to marry British nobles and commoners. Indeed among the first to benefit from this new trend was the present Queen Mother, a noblewoman who married George's son Albert, the future George VI.

George VI became the monarch, however, only after his elder brother abdicated. Crowned **Edward VIII** in 1936, the young man was already intent upon marriage to Wallis Warfield Simpson, a divorced American married to a British businessman. But the government would hear nothing of it and presented Edward with a choice—the lady or the land—hoping that he would choose the former and in the process remove a king who showed signs of Nazi sympathies. After a reign of almost a year, he resigned, and bearing the newly invented title of Duke of Windsor, he left England for the Continent and Wallis Simpson. They would return home only for rare visits—and, decades later, to be buried.

England was shaken—indeed on the night of Edward's abdication the sentries around Buckingham Palace were issued live ammunition for the first time in modern history. The public's reaction may have been overestimated, but when Edward's younger brother, Albert, now **George VI**, came to the throne in December 1936, all of Britain was poised for the worst.

For that matter, so was Albert. He had never expected to be king (formal speaking engagements left

The Queen Mother celebrates her ninety-ninth birthday in regal style.

FOLLOW THE ROYAL LINE

The Windsors are but the latest of many families to rule the kingdom. Here is the complete lineage for Britain's crown according to *Whitaker's Almanac*, listed by year of accession.

Saxons and Danes

Egbert	827
Ethelwulf	839
Ethelbald	858
Ethelbert	858
Ethelred	866
Alfred the Great	871
Edward the Elder	899
Athelstan	925
Edmund	940
Edred	946
Edwy	955
Edgar	959
Edward the Martyr	975
Ethelred II	978
Edmund Ironside	1016
Canute the Dane	1017
Harold I	1035
Hardicanute	1040
Edward the Confessor	1042
Harold II	1066

The House of Normandy

William I	1066
William II	1087
Henry I	1100
Stephen	1135

The House of Plantagenet

Henry II	1154
Richard I	1189
John	1199
Henry III	1216
Edward I	1272
Edward II	1307
Edward III	1327
Richard II	1377

The House of Lancaster

Henry IV	1399
Henry V	1413
Henry VI	1422

The House of York

Edward IV	1461
Edward V	1483
Richard II	1483

The House of Tudor

Henry VII	1485
Henry VIII	1509
Edward VI	1547
Jane	1553
Mary I	1553
Elizabeth I	1558

The House of Stuart

James I (VI of Scotland)	1603
Charles I	1625

[Commonwealth declared, 1649]

The House of Stuart (restored)

Charles II	1660
James II (VII of Scotland)	1685
William II and Mary II	1689
Anne	1702

The House of Hanover

George I	1714
George II	1727
George III	1760
George IV	1820
William IV	1830
Victoria	1837

The House of Saxe-Coburg

Edward VII	1901

The House of Windsor

George V	1910
Edward VIII	1936
George VI	1936
Elizabeth II	1952

him shaken and depressed), and when he learned he was suddenly to take the throne, he went to his mother, Queen Mary, and wept for an hour. No wonder it was rumored that George VI was too frail to survive the coronation ceremony.

But his very narrowness and humility turned out to be qualities that were once again in favor among the British people. George VI and his wife, the current **Queen Mother**, Elizabeth, provided Britain with a center of gravity during the grim days of World War II, remaining in Buckingham Palace even when London was being fractured by German bombs and refusing to send Princesses Elizabeth and Margaret out of the country. No wonder Adolf Hitler called her "the most dangerous woman in Europe." King George's family represented what the English wanted during these terrible years: a conscientious and principled king, a winning queen, and two likable young princesses, Elizabeth and Margaret.

Still thriving at 99 after recovering from replacement of her left hip last year (she is now the oldest living British royal ever, having surpassed Queen Victoria's granddaughter Princess Alice), the Queen Mother has become a beloved national institution. Adored for her approachability and cheerful mien, the QM was described by photographer Cecil Beaton as "the great

Queen Elizabeth II takes tea at home with some of her subjects, in Glasgow.

mother figure and nanny of us all." A red-hot number in the '20s, she still likes "drinky-poos" (gin and tonic) before dinner, but she has never forgiven President Jimmy Carter for his shameful breach of etiquette: He kissed her on the lips.

London merchants quake when they see her coming. It's not her taste in tulle, it's that she reportedly rarely pays her accounts. And she's still keen as a tack. Says one old friend about her wicked wit: "She doesn't take prisoners."

Born Lady Elizabeth Bowes-Lyon, the serenely beautiful young woman was the Diana of her day. But fearing life in the royal fishbowl, she twice rejected marriage proposals from the painfully shy, stammering Prince

Albert, who called her "the most wonderful person in the world."

It is amazing that this five-foot-tall aristocrat, the last Empress of India and the honorary colonel of 18 regiments, who has probably never cooked a meal or made a bed, is considered "everybody's mum." But the festivities surrounding her ninetieth birthday in 1990 confirmed the devotion she has long inspired.

When King George, a heavy smoker, died of lung cancer in 1952 at the age of 57, his daughter **Elizabeth II** took up the scepter knowing that her main job would be to preserve the gains her parents had made. Admittedly, Elizabeth is a figurehead, a constitutional monarch who reigns but does not rule. Yet no one trifles with the 72-year-old woman known at Buckingham Palace as The Boss. Part of her power is ex officio: It is bad form to contradict Her Most Excellent Majesty, Elizabeth the Second, by the Grace of God, of the United Kingdom of Great Britain and Northern Ireland and of Her other Realms and Territories, Queen, Head of the Commonwealth, Defender of the Faith. It is also hard to disagree with someone whom *Fortune* magazine reckons as the world's richest woman (though her web site maintains that "the Queen's wealth has often been greatly exaggerated").

But much of Elizabeth's authority arises from the immovable force of her character. This is the monarch who at 27 overrode the objections of advisers and ordered her coronation to be televised because, she said,

THE VULGAR SUBJECT OF MONEY

Loaded as they are, the Windsors prefer not to tarnish themselves so with money. They never carry cash, not a penny. And it's not because they carry American Express, instead. Elizabeth's famous pocketbook is a stage prop. It sometimes contains only mints for her horses. Otherwise, the Windsors come in contact with currency the way other people encounter God—mostly on Sundays. Before church, Charles is reportedly provided with a £5 note for the collection plate; he likes to have it sprayed and ironed by his valet, then neatly creased and left for him beneath his clove box. (You know, the box that holds your before-dinner clove. You probably have one around somewhere.)

The Windsor wealth is complicated. A considerable portion is their own, acquired by them or their ancestors with personal funds. That would include Sandringham and Balmoral, two of the royal country estates, which they own the way the Cartwrights owned the Ponderosa. Both were purchased during Queen Victoria's reign. But the greater part of the wealth that surrounds them is held in trust for the nation. That means the Windsors can wear it, sit on it, eat off it, and go lightheartedly skipping down its glinting corridors. They just can't sew any name tags on it or cart it off to Christie's for auction.

If Britain should ever decide to get rid of the royal family, though, it would be a messy divorce. There's some confusion about which of their property belongs to the state and which is their own. In particular, who rightly possesses the lavish gifts from foreign potentates? Like the 2,000-year-old necklace from Egypt's former King Farouk?

And some of the royals' riches actually do benefit the public. It seems that Windsor Castle, their weekend residence, where construction began in the eleventh century, may be perched atop oil deposits worth an estimated $1 billion. Queen Elizabeth II has given a white-gloved thumbs-up for exploratory drilling on a site somewhere between the royal household golf course and the royal household cricket ground. Any revenue generated will go directly to the Treasury.

By anyone's count, though, the total number is a whopper. *Fortune* magazine has calculated that the Queen is one of the richest people in the world. Recent accounts have reckoned her fortune at anywhere from $450 million to $16 billion (often depending upon whether one includes the property held in trust for the nation). Charles, meanwhile, was believed to be worth about $400 million as of 1991, which would still place him among Britain's 40 wealthiest people. To paraphrase Mel Brooks: It is good to be Queen.

"I have to be seen to be believed." And who continued to appear in public and ride in open cars after her husband's favorite uncle, Lord Mountbatten, was assassinated by an IRA bomb in 1979. And who in 1982 coolly kept a disturbed intruder talking on the edge of her bed until she could summon help.

She grew up during the London blitz and matured in the ensuing period of austerity. The world's wealthiest woman still wanders around Buckingham Palace turning off lights. The heat is kept low and there are no objections; there never are. And when one of her favorite dogs killed a hare, the Queen carefully picked it up and presented it to the kitchen staff. "We can eat this," she announced.

When Elizabeth II rings, a staff of 300 jumps. When she is in London, the prime minister calls on her every Tuesday to brief her on government matters. Though not a quick study, Elizabeth is assiduous, has a phenomenal memory, and often embarrasses ministers by knowing more about issues than they do.

Elizabeth's hold on her subjects begins with her family. When as a 13-year-old she met a dashing cadet, she instantly decided that he was Midshipman Right. Five years later she had not changed her mind, and so in 1947 she married **Prince Philip** of Greece, a great-great-grandchild of Queen Victoria. Queen Elizabeth and Prince Philip celebrated their golden wedding anniversary this year, reminding the world that marital happiness can indeed flourish in a royal family. The two attended a service of thanksgiving at Westminster Abbey, where they were married, and later celebrated the occasion with a garden party at Buckingham Palace. Four thousand couples also marking their fiftieth anniversary were invited to share in the revelry.

Although Elizabeth has inevitably dominated her husband in the public realm, in the world of the Windsor family the Duke of Edinburgh has had authority over educating the children: first Prince Charles and Princess Anne, later Princes Andrew and Edward. But Elizabeth's will is what holds the family and the royal public image together.

Her own image is not universally admired, at least from a fashion point of view. Dressing in a style that can be characterized as pseudo-frumpy, the queen stays out of the tabloids and gets her work done. While her hair is done every Monday at four p.m. by Charles Martyn, her hairdresser for the last two decades, she reads state papers and seldom glances in the mirror. Not everyone is happy about her diffidence. "I sometimes wish she had been a bit more of a clothes person," wistfully admits her couturier of four decades, Sir Hard Amies. "She doesn't care, basically. She listens to our advice, then goes off and wears shabby shoes because they're comfortable." But in fact Elizabeth does care about her appearance. Her outfits—the boxy, brightly colored clothes, clunky handbags, unfashionable reading glasses—are chosen with great deliberation to be unthreatening to women, unobtrusive to men, and easily seen by the crowds that line her path. If she were chic, she would be French, but this queen is British to her bones. That means a love of silver service and afternoon tea, bland food, sweetish wine, jigsaw puzzles, Dick Francis mysteries, and, most of all, tramps in the country amid her Thoroughbreds and her dogs. The Queen herself feeds her six corgis and two dorgis (a mix of dachshund and corgi), cutting up their meat and mixing it with biscuits in their separate bowls set out every afternoon by a footman.

No one takes better care of business than Her Majesty, who has long since realized that her maritally vexed offspring have created a throne-threatening PR problem for the House of Windsor. At the close of 1992, in a now-famous speech, she noted, "It has turned out to be an *annus horribilis*." If not the language of the common man, it was certainly a sentiment commonly understood. And things got even more horrible a few days after that speech.

On the Queen's forty-fifth wedding anniversary, a fire gutted a corner of Windsor Castle, causing damages of up to $60 million. As a debate brewed over who should bear the cost of repairs, Elizabeth, with her unerring sense for image damage control, proclaimed that she would give up a centuries-old royal perk by commencing to pay income tax on her private fortune, as well as pony up $8.5 million toward refurbishing the castle. In 1996 she went one step further, opening 19 state rooms in Buckingham Palace to public tours (leaving 631 rooms still off-limits) while she and the family were taking their annual summer retreat to Balmoral.

Perhaps to counteract an image of the royals as freeloaders, the Queen set up a secret committee in 1996 to consider several astonishing reforms to the monarchy. The most startling change is already in effect. The "Family Firm" pays their own way with the $90 million earned annually from their estates, rather than collecting $12.75 million per year from taxpayers as they did in the past. The Queen tightened the belt even further last year, cutting $8 million in costs for travel

and the upkeep of the Windsor's eight palaces, as part of continuing efforts to make the monarchy less expensive, more open, and more modern. Other proposals include streamlining the royal family to include only the monarch, the consort, and the children; lifting the 295-year-old ban on royals marrying Catholics; and severing the formal links with the Church of England. Many of these progressive suggestions need Parliament's stamp of approval, however, and British politicians' reluctance to tamper with tradition means that the Queen's proposals may remain just that for some time to come. But the government did propose to abolish primogeniture (an eldest son's right to precede an elder sister to the throne) last year and the Queen offered no objection. And, on her own initiative, the Queen pronounced an end to compulsory bowing and curtsying (though they're still appreciated).

Despite her attempts to set things straight with the monarchy, Elizabeth has often been unpopular. In response to public outcry, she appeared on live television in an unprecedented effort to share her family's grief over the death of Princess Diana. And within eight months the Queen could be found on her

first official foray ever to a pub (during a tour of Devon) and riding in a taxi (another first, to promote environmentally friendly liquefied petroleum fuel). This year she has continued to visit more often with her subjects. She is reaching out in other ways, too. Her web site received over 12.5 million hits in its first two months, and a $368,000-a-year communications director, Simon Lewis, 40, joined her staff last year.

Though her popularity with the people took a hit when Diana died, Elizabeth's resolve rarely wavers, and she is always fully aware of her royal responsibilities. As former prime minister Margaret Thatcher said in a televised program screened on the Queen's seventieth birthday, "She is the most conscientious lady. Whatever duty requires, she will do and will go on doing for the rest of her days." The Queen's biographer Ben Pimlott notes, "The monarchy provides the social glue that binds people together." And as the headlines of the past year show, even if they no longer rule the waves, the royals still serve a purpose, and "people remain enormously interested in all things royal."

THE SON ALSO RISES: THE YOUNG WINDSORS

When **Charles, the Prince of Wales**, walked beside his two sons; his father, Duke of Edinburgh; and his former brother-in-law, Charles, Earl Spencer; behind Princess Diana's cortege, savvy observers noticed something extraordinary: The future King of England, usually a pillar of protocol, had parted with tradition by wearing a blue Savile Row suit to the funeral. It was neither a symbol of disrespect nor a fickle fashion statement. Rather, says royal author Brian Hoey, "It was Diana's favorite blue suit, and she helped him choose it. She preferred him in blue [rather] than black or gray. It was a lovely, silent compliment to her."

A more-at-ease Prince Charles enjoys the natural splendor at his Highgrove estate.

The windsurfing-parachuting-scuba-diving Action Prince of the 1970s and the oratorical Philosopher Prince of the 1980s had morphed from the Self-absorbed Prince of the early 1990s. Finally, perhaps, Charles might be finding his true colors. His comportment in the aftermath of Diana's death—tearfully receiving the coffin in France, tenderly consoling his sons, distraughtly walking alone in the misty Scottish highlands outside Balmoral—went a long way toward softening his image as the poster boy for royal stoics, and he is now becoming less formal with his public as well. At the end of last year he cele-

brated his fiftieth birthday in grand style.

Routinely derided as both parent and public figure, he has never quite managed to capture the public's heart, though recent polls indicate Charles is more popular now than he was before Diana's death. "Charles was eclipsed by Diana's dazzle," says Peter Archer, the royals correspondent for the British Press Association. "Now people are taking notice [of him again]."

It's also possible—even likely—that Diana's death has changed him. We've now seen Charles as a doting father, devoted to helping his sons bear the loss of their

mother. He may never match Diana in public displays of affection, but at least there have been some, beginning with his goodbye kiss for William last year before they boarded separate planes for a vacation in Greece. Charles does have much in common with his sons: Both boys are avid huntsmen who love the country life Charles favors, and they are now showing interest in the artistic pursuits that delight their dad. For his part, Charles has indulged in kid-friendly outings, something we never used to see.

The prince has also taken steps to make a place for longtime love Camilla Parker

Bowles in his family life. In January the two made their first public appearance as a couple, exiting the Ritz Hotel after attending a party for Camilla's sister Annabel Elliott's birthday before a crowd of hundreds of photographers. Camilla treated the cheering onlookers to a shaky smile as she accompanied Charles, who gave her elbow the tiniest of proprietary steers, down the steps to the dark green sedan waiting to whisk them to his apartment at St. James's Palace. The next day approving commentary on the milestone dominated Britain's news, and the pair made two more public appearances over the next eight days.

Getting Britons to *support* the union is another matter, though. In one call-in poll, some 75 percent were against the couple's appearing in public together. The Queen, who hasn't formally met Camilla, still isn't issuing any invitations. "Charles wants recognition for Camilla," says Peter Archer, "but he doesn't want to put his mother in a position where they'll meet until the time is right. It's all bound up with sensitive judgments about what the British people are ready to accept." But a first crucial step, an invitation to the Queen Mother's residence in Balmoral, was reportedly planned for the fall.

A lifetime of training, of course, has made him proficient at such judgments. From his early childhood at Buck-ingham Palace, the Queen's eldest son learned that duty always came before pleasure. Until he was 32 years old he lived at home with his parents. Then he found a lovely bride and promptly fulfilled his duty to beget heirs.

Now all he can do is wait for his mother to pass him the scepter. And some recent newspaper articles have depicted his relations with "Mummy" as chronically strained. Meanwhile, Elizabeth is ticking away better than Big Ben, and Charles could end up like his great-great-grandfather King Edward VII, who held the title of Prince of Wales for almost 60 years before his mother, Queen Victoria, passed away.

So much of Charles's behavior, however, is a matter of upbringing and thankless experience. Just weeks after entering the world as heir to the throne in 1948, he was left in the care of nannies while his parents performed their endless royal duties. "There's a famous old photo," says royal author Anthony Holden, "of the Queen arriving home on a train after a coronation tour and greeting her mother and sister [Princess Margaret] with a kiss, then greeting Charles, who was about 4 years old, with a handshake and straightening his collar. That tells the whole story."

In 1971, a year after graduating from Trinity College in Cambridge, the prince enlisted in the Royal Navy, where he served for five years flying helicopters and serving on frigates. Already, at a polo match in the early '70s, he had met Camilla Shand, whose great-grandmother Alice Keppel, had had an affair with Edward VII. Though they hit it off immediately, Camilla, reportedly having no interest in marrying Charles and becoming a public figure, wed cavalry officer Andrew Parker Bowles in 1973.

During the subsequent years, Charles has contributed eloquently and provocatively to the public discourse on the preservation of architecture, the environment, and the language. In 1997 he even fulfilled the grand though slightly depressing role of handing over Hong Kong and its 6.5 million imperial subjects to the Chinese government. On June 30 the prince joined Chinese president Jiang Zemin at a transition ceremony that marked a symbolic sunset over the British empire.

Preparing to ascend to the throne, however, wasn't enough to keep together his marriage with **Lady Diana Spencer**. In his diaries of 1986 and 1987, as reported in *The Prince of Wales,* an authorized biography by Jonathan Dimbleby, he wrote, "How awful incompatibility is…I never thought it would end up like this. How could I have got it all so wrong?"

DIANA, REMEMBERED?

What a difference a year makes. Two years after the tragic death of the "queen of people's hearts" shocked the entire world, the anniversary of Diana's passing was marked in a thoroughly quiet and not-so-reverential fashion. The flag flew at full staff over Buckingham Palace, there was no special prayer service, and her beloved boys spent the day with their father in Balmoral. A French prosecutor concluded there was insufficient evidence to prosecute nine photographers who pursued Diana's car that fateful night and recommended that all charges be dismissed.

Further perspective was added in a new book released to coincide with the anniversary. *Diana in Search of Herself*, by Sally Bedell Smith, portrays Diana as infinitely more troubled than the public realized. Though she radiated grace and poise, Diana suffered acutely from chronic loneliness and an overpowering insecurity. She hated being hounded by the press but at the same time often initiated telephone calls to reporters. "Diana was trapped in a terrible hall of mirrors," writes Smith. "There was a huge disconnect between her public persona and her private life."

Acknowledging that "psychiatrists and psychologists have debated Diana's condition in the British press," Smith argues that Diana suffered from a fairly common but often elusive mental illness called borderline personality disorder, the symptoms of which include impulsiveness, feelings of abandonment, and an inability to sustain relationships. The book covers the last two of these doomed affairs in detail, chronicling Diana's lengthy courtship with Pakistani surgeon Hasnat Khan and underscoring that the romance with Dodi Al Fayed came only weeks after Khan had broken up with her. Smith speculates that Diana wanted to provoke Khan, and notes that she and Dodi were together for barely a month before tragedy struck. Smith extends her revisionist approach to Prince Charles as well: "He probably deserves more credit than he has received for trying to get her into therapy" during their 15-year marriage.

Indeed, as the public gains more distance on Diana's complicated life and her untimely end, Charles, the paradigm of British patience and reserve, is gaining more credit—for everything from his more nurturing care of William and Harry to his slow introduction of Camilla Parker Bowles to public, and royal, life. As for Diana, her legacy is easily found in the young men she bore, who are growing up quickly into the princes she wanted them to be.

As the world celebrated that fairy tale marriage—seen by millions worldwide on July 29, 1981—the seeds of its failure began to become apparent. While the couple was touring Portugal in February 1987, photographers started to notice the first signs of marital strain—topped off by the pair taking separate suites at a palace in Lisbon.

Royal watchers maintain Prince Philip had urged his son to marry a quiet girl and produce an heir. Charles, though less cynical, certainly married a girl—and, at 20, 12 years his junior, that's what she was—for whom he was ill-suited. In December 1992 the Prince and Princess of Wales announced an official separation that finally ended the long charade of their once idealized marriage.

Shortly thereafter, the last hope of a happy ending quickly faded. A racy taped phone chat between Prince Charles and his then confidante and current love interest, Camilla Parker Bowles, was published worldwide. Charles revealed, among other steamy things, his surprising desire to live inside her "trousers or something." He purportedly declared his love for her and gushed, "In the next life, I should like to come back as your knickers."

Then came new revelations of a sexually charged phone conversation in which Diana discussed with *her* confidant, James Gilbey, her fear of getting pregnant. So in December 1993, when the tearful princess announced that she was greatly curtailing her public life, it appeared that the Palace had finally succeeded in reining her in.

"The dream is over. The people's darling will never become queen," proclaimed columnist John Casey in the *Evening Standard.*

In 1994, the second year of their official separation, the union of the prince and princess seemed to unspool with a special savagery and at indecent length in every possible medium. Worse, Charles and the House of Windsor itself seemed to lose in the process the public sympathy they so desperately tried to engender. The fire was fueled by the principals themselves, cooperating with unseemly disclosures and partisan biographies about lovers old and new, alienation of feelings, eating disorders, and suicide attempts. Caught in this murderous crossfire, Charles and Diana found themselves the villains of a klieg-lit reality that had finally, and sadly, overtaken the soft-focus fairy tale. In August of

Prince William emerges proudly from his new car.

1996, after much wrangling on both sides, the fairy tale legally ended in divorce.

Struggling to overcome his image as the diffident twit who allowed his marriage to founder, the prince rolled up his sleeves and wrestled with the demon of publicity. Charles maintained that he remained faithful to Diana "until it became clear that the marriage had irretrievably broken down." (But another '94 tome, *Camilla: The King's Mistress,* claims that Charles spent the night before his wedding with Parker Bowles.)

In January 1995, Camilla and her husband, Andrew, abandoned the charade that their union was intact, ending their 21-year marriage. Palace insiders were convinced that Charles's startling confessions and Camilla's split were part of

an elaborate long-range plan designed to bring their 25-year relationship out of the shadows—and set the stage for another royal marriage.

Before Diana's death, Queen Elizabeth herself demanded that the prince scrap his dream of marrying Parker Bowles, warning him that it could cost him the throne. And in the aftermath of her tragic accident, it appeared highly unlikely that he could marry Camilla in the foreseeable future without deeply offending public opinion.

But now Diana's longtime rival is using the front door again. You've got to hand it to her: Over the past six years, Parker Bowles has been condemned, resurrected, and buried again. Yet she has come through it all with her humor and patience intact.

While marriage is still highly uncertain, Charles's place as future sovereign appears far more secure. "Absolutely, he will be king if he outlives his mother," says Hoey. "There's no question of William bypassing him. William wouldn't want it, the Queen wouldn't want it, and I don't think the country would want it. It's his destiny."

Diana had begun with one overriding duty—to produce an heir, preferably male. And she was fortunate enough within two years of her marriage to produce two towheads (known as the heir and the spare), to whom she referred proudly, proprietarily, as "my boys." Demonstrative where Charles was reserved, preferring fun to formality, she gave **Prince William**, 17, and **Prince Harry**, 15, a sense of childhood that no Windsor would have or could have. By all accounts, William, who lives with the burden of being Charles's heir, felt the pain of his parents breakup, and his mother's death, most acutely. "William already hates press photographers," says Judy Wade, a royals reporter. "This will deepen any anger he has." Harry has seemed positively ebullient on public outings.

William, the boy who seems destined to be king, is leaving childhood behind. A rambunctious toddler who grew into a reserved primary-schooler, he has been learning to cope with the peculiar demands of royal life. He must prepare for a role that will become more public over time, and one that will expose his every misstep. Upon the urging of his grandfather, Wills entered Eton, one of England's most exclusive public (meaning "private") schools, and is the first heir to the British throne to do so. The school has been educational home to many British luminaries since 1440, including Gladstone, Pitt the Elder, and 18 other prime ministers.

Now in his final year, he is both a prefect and captain of the swim team. Earlier this year he quietly visited two Scottish universities, Edinburgh and St. Andrews, as well as checking out his father's alma mater, Cambridge. Brother Harry joined Wills at Eton last year.

Taller than his father at 6' 1½", William has grown into a thoughtful young man with a strong sense of duty and little of the Windsors' emotional detachment. "When you discover you can give joy to people...there is nothing quite like it," Diana once told *The New Yorker*. "William has begun to understand that, too. And I am hoping it will grow in him." Though William could, as one royal watcher suggested half-seriously years ago, "decide to go backpacking in Nepal and not come back," that doesn't seem likely. After all, he is—and always will be—his mother's son. "He knows how much Diana would want him to do the job he was born to do," says Lord Jeffrey Archer, a close friend of Diana's. "He will be conscious of that and, in her memory, do it even better."

Now William's grief is giving way to good times. An excellent student (he won Eton's Sword of Honor, given to the best all-around cadet), he also clocked the school's best times since 1987 in the 50- and 100-meter junior freestyle swims. As avid a country sportsman as his father, he'll be "shooting anything that moves, fishing in

The young princes join in their uncle Edward's wedding ceremony.

the icy River Dee, having what passes for a picnic with footmen serving him," says Brian Hoey.

As his sorrow eases, the young prince is learning to forge a relationship with the press he so abhors. The week before his sixteenth birthday he agreed to answer written questions posed to him by the British Press Association's Peter Archer. His responses were hardly soul-baring, but there were revelations. He shares the royals' love of horses. He like computer games, fast food, techno music, and "modern" clothes that he buys himself. He loves to read, particularly action-adventure fiction and nonfiction; he also likes action movies. He even admitted to a couple of dislikes: the glare of the public spotlight and the adulation of teenage girls.

This year, Wills and Harry appeared together in their first official photo call since the death of their mother—this time to commemorate the happy occasion of William's new wheels, a Volkswagen Golf given to him by Charles for his seventeenth birthday. The modest car was highly customized, with armored windows, roof, doors, and roof panels. Even the tires are bullet-proof and stay inflated when shot at.

The event reinforces the fact that much as he tries, this is no average kid, from his mom's sapphire eyes and his striking physique to the constant companionship of

bodyguards. "William's shoes are always so shiny, his trousers well-pressed," marvels an Eton bookshop owner. "He looks different from the others." Royals author Judy Wade says, "He has replaced his mother as the royal star" and he's not sure he likes it. "William has a hard time with public exposure, let along being a teenager's pinup," she notes.

William is clearly being schooled in the ways of a future monarch. He regularly visits his grandmother at Windsor Castle, across the Thames from Eton. And she has come to see him at school. "The Queen is determined there will be no mistakes with his upbringing or career development," says Hoey. "He's the hope for the future."

Diana, of course, dreamed of nothing less for her son. "She always used to say she wanted William to be happy, and it's quite clear she wanted him to be king," says Archer.

Diana and Charles were not the only royals having trouble making peace with the idea of separate households. Hitched for 16 years, Charles's younger sister, **Princess Anne**, and Captain Mark Phillips were initially drawn together by their passion for horses (both are extraordinary equestrians: Phillips coached America's Olympic team in 1996). But Anne's interests were much broader—she is president of the Save the Children Fund and was even nominated for the Nobel Peace Prize a few

years back. Last year she was the royal family's busiest member, clocking 679 official engagements. Says Anne of her work, "You have to decide at the end of the day if you can live with yourself."

You also have to decide if you can live with your husband, and the affirmative answer increasingly came into doubt. The couple finally separated in 1989, and after divorcing, Anne married longtime love Timothy Laurence, five years her junior, in 1992. As close to her mother as any of her siblings, Anne staged her second wedding as an intimate family affair, attended by only a handful of relatives, including her two children with Phillips, **Peter** and **Zara**. A university student, Peter currently serves as a sporty, down-to-earth role model for William, while his bubbly sister "loves to tease William and make him blush, which he does easily," says Hoey. "She has a wonderful ability to deflate egos."

Anne's second brother, rowdy **Prince Andrew, Duke of York**, has had his fair share of marital bad luck as well. After a plucky performance in the Falklands conflict, helicopter pilot Andy seemed interested mainly in oat-sowing and club-crawling with a string of steamy ladies, culminating with former soft-porn star Koo Stark. What well-bred English girl would marry Andrew and put up with him?

And so, when the prince's

roving eye fell upon Sarah Ferguson in 1985, the nation breathed a collective sigh of relief. A strapping, worldly wench who loved a good time, Fergie seemed perfectly suited to her happy-go-lucky hubby. But while **Sarah, Duchess of York**, produced two lovely daughters, **Princesses Beatrice** and **Eugenie**, she also committed gaffe after gaffe. If the Yorks often struck the public as a pair of heedless hedonists, at least they originally seemed besotted with each other. But Fergie's erratic behavior quickly brought that into doubt as well. After a series of romantic trysts and crass missteps on her part, the duchess was formally separated from the duke in 1992. Later that year London tabs were abrim with graphic photos of Fergie on the Riviera cavorting topless with her American-born "financial

adviser," John Bryan, who was shown smooching the bare instep of her foot while her young daughters looked on. She later confessed that the publication of those photos had been her "most humiliating experience."

Fergie was left scrambling to settle debts reaching more than $6 million by selling off the rights to her children's cartoon character, Budgie the Helicopter, opening a cable television channel, hosting a documentary in the Australian outback, and launching her own perfume.

No stranger to the ups and downs of yo-yo diets, Fergie is well qualified for her current $1.7 million-a-year stint as a Weight Watchers spokeswoman, sharing such confessions as: "My problem, you see, is the bum. My daughters say, 'Give us your wiggle, Mummy.'"

As she admitted on the

Oprah Winfrey Show last year, "I was never cut out for royalty." But she is cut out for celebrity. Her newest role is a stint as a London-based correspondent for the *Today* show in the U.S.

In 1996 the Yorks finally decided to split officially, contending that, unlike the Waleses, their decision was "theirs alone," and not precipitated by a letter from the Queen. According to court insiders, however, Andrew and Fergie are still the closest of friends. They've continued to live on separate floors of Andrew's mansion, Sunninghill, and when Fergie moves it will be to nearby Birch Hall, which the Queen helped purchase. "We have breakfast, lunch, tea, and dinner together," Fergie told *Hello!*, calling her ex "a great man."

Prince Edward, Elizabeth's youngest, was the latest royal to draw the headlines this year. After a quiet five-year courtship, he finally proposed to public relations executive Sophie Rhys-Jones, who noted at their official announcement, "I think I am ready for it."

So in June, 18 years after his eldest brother's wedding amid pomp and pageantry, Edward exchanged vows with Sophie in a ceremony that seemed designed to prove the royals aren't so different from the rest of us.

Instead of a fairy-tale confection, Sophie looked tanned and slim (she had reportedly lost some 10 pounds) and

The newly dubbed (and newly married) Earl and Duchess of Wessex wave to the crowd after their wedding in St. George's Chapel.

wore a sleek, sophisticated coat dress in ivory silk inlaid with 325,000 beads by designer Samantha Shaw, along with a black-and-white pearl necklace designed by her fiancé. Of the 560 guests, most were friends and relatives of the couple, not other crowned heads or dignitaries.

Unlike Diana, who stumbled over Charles's many monikers, Sophie remembered her groom's four names—Edward Antony Richard Louis. The 8,000 ticketed spectators outside cheered as she recited her vows and "it brought a grin to her face," said a guest. Well-wishers 20,000 strong cheered the couple further as they proceeded by horse-drawn carriage to the reception at Windsor Castle.

Newly titled the Earl and Countess of Wessex by the Queen, the couple took only an abbreviated honeymoon. As a pal of Edward's noted, "They're busy people."

Which is what those who know them believe will help make this a lasting union. Though she bears a passing resemblance to the late Diana, Sophie Wessex, as she will be known professionally, plans to continue her PR work, not fill the void left by Diana on the charity circuit. "The royal family [is] doing an exceptional job in the public role," she told the BBC. "I don't see a massive need for me to do the same thing."

An unsurprising characterization from the woman who married the first child of a reigning monarch to—*gulp*—take a real job. Initially employed as a gofer with Andrew Lloyd Webber's Really Useful Theatre Company and eventually rising to overseas manager of *Cats* and *Starlight Express*, Edward left Webber's company and now is joint managing director of a television production company, Ardent Productions. His company produced a game show featuring off-color jokes about his mother, and he lobbied to market the television rights to his wedding but was turned down by the Queen. Currently, he is producing a TV movie about the Queen Mother for NBC. Loyal to his dreams as well as the British ideal of monarchy, the Queen's youngest

child is, ran one editorial, "on the way to becoming the first really modern royal."

Edward's fascination with the theater is hardly unusual among the Windsors. Indeed, if the family reigned in Beverly Hills instead of Westminster, the Queen's younger sister, **Princess Margaret**, would be the family's Elizabeth Taylor. She has been onstage since age six, when she had a walk-on part in her father's coronation. With her theatrical props—a tortoise-shell cigarette holder, a tumbler of Famous Grouse whiskey, and a circle of intimates in the arts—the princess has played varied roles: tragic lover, wife, mother, divorcée, and regal

A ROYAL CALENDAR

A listing of birthdays and other special royal milestones. (Source: *Whitaker's Almanac*)

Lady Wessex (Sophie)	January 20, 1965
Prince Andrew	February 19, 1960
Prince Edward	March 10, 1964
Princess Eugenie	March 23, 1990
Queen Elizabeth	April 21, 1926
The Queen's coronation	June 2, 1953
Prince Philip	June 10, 1921
Prince William	June 21, 1982
Queen Mother	August 4, 1900
Princess Beatrice	August 8, 1988
Princess Anne	August 15, 1950
Princess Margaret	August 21, 1930
Prince Henry	September 15, 1984
Duchess of York (Sarah)	October 15, 1959
Prince Charles	November 14, 1948
The Queen's wedding	November 20, 1947

grand dame. She emanates star quality, complete with romantic intrigues, erratic public behavior, mysterious health problems, and Sunset Boulevard brass. "I can't imagine anything more wonderful," she once said, "than being who I am."

Precocious and irrepressible as a child, the violet-eyed and theatrical Margaret wrapped George VI around her finger. Other men proved harder to keep. As a teenager she fell hard for a dashing fighter pilot, Peter Townsend, 16 years her senior, but finally passed him up at 22 when her union with the divorced Townsend was declared acceptable only if she would give up her claim to the throne and her royal income and if she would spend five years abroad.

Several years later Margaret walked the aisle with photographer Antony Armstrong-Jones (who became **Lord Snowdon** after the wedding). She produced two children with the artistic commoner: **David (Viscount Linley)** and **Lady Sarah Armstrong-Jones**. But their 18-year marriage was not a picture-book affair. Initially rejecting separation as too scandalous, both partners discreetly sizzled with old and new flames until the tabs ran pictures of Margaret and her lover Roddy Llewellyn, a gardener and

CINDERELLA STORY

Don't have a fairy godmother to get you to the ball? Never fear. These days a commoner can snag her prince (or his princess) without magical intervention. Here's a list of royals who married outside of their blue-blood background.

Prince Rainier of Monaco and Grace Kelly
King Edward VIII of England and Wallis Warfield Simpson
King Hussein of Jordan and Queen Noor (née Lisa Najeeb Halaby)
King Harald and Queen Sonja of Norway
Prince Joachim and Princess Alexandra of Denmark (née Alexandra Manley)
Princess Elena of Spain and businessman Jaime de Marichalar
King Carl XVI Gustav of Sweden and Silvia Sommerlath
Crown Prince Alexander of Yugoslavia and Crown Princess Katherine (née Katherine Batis)
Crown Prince Naruhito and Crown Princess Masako of Japan
Emperor Akihito and Empress Michiko of Japan

wannabe pop singer 17 years her junior. An uncontested divorce was granted in 1978.

But Margaret's son, David, did his part to show the happy side of royal life—his marriage in 1993 to Serena Stanhope, a blue blood with cover-girl looks, was a windfall for the monarchy, and their lavish nuptials at St. Margaret's Church were billed as the Wedding of the Year, drawing 650 guests.

Though Margaret suffered a mild stroke last year at a party in Barbados, she does not appear to show any lasting effects—she was in a wheelchair at Edward's wed-

ding, but that was because she had scalded her feet in the bathtub.

As comfortable as the lives of the Windsors seem, ultimately being royal carries with it an incalculable personal price tag. Family members live with constant world scrutiny. And it is an irony of their station that even though they live their whole lives in public, they can barely speak their minds there. But the true value of the royal family lies in the realm of patriotic lumps in the throat. They have, at least until now, given Britain a symbol of nationhood.

SUCCESSION: THE BUCK HOUSE BULLPEN

Under rules codified in the eighteenth century, rightful candidates to the British crown move up inexorably except for two disqualifiers: They cannot be Catholic (or marry into that faith) or be born out of wedlock. Unlike some European monarchies, which abide by the centuries-old Salic law—the exclusion of women from succession—the Court of St. James owes its vitality in great part to females. Victoria and the current queen, for instance, are two of history's longest-reigning sovereigns. This is not to say that Britain's accession rules are not sexist: A monarch is succeeded by his or her eldest son, then by that son's sons in descending order of age, and only then by that son's daughters. The line starts again with the monarch's next youngest son, and so on, ending with the sovereign's daughters and their children. After the offspring are accounted for, the sovereign's brothers come next, followed finally by sisters. From there the line marches through uncles, aunts, and full courts of cousins, including two newborn members of the clan.

Here are the top 25 in the royal bullpen:

1. HRH The Prince of Wales, 51
   (Prince Charles)
2. HRH Prince William of Wales, 17
   (son of Prince Charles)
3. HRH Prince Henry of Wales, 15
   (second son of Prince Charles)
4. HRH The Duke of York (Prince Andrew), 39
   (second son of Queen Elizabeth)
5. HRH Princess Beatrice of York, 11
   (daughter of Prince Andrew)
6. HRH Princess Eugenie of York, 9
   (second daughter of Prince Andrew)
7. HRH Prince Edward, 35
   (third son of Queen Elizabeth)
8. HRH The Princess Royal (Princess Anne), 49
   (daughter of Queen Elizabeth)
9. Peter Phillips, 22
   (the highest-ranking commoner, son of Princess Anne)
10. Zara Phillips, 18
    (daughter of Princess Anne)
11. HRH Princess Margaret, Countess of Snowdon, 69
    (sister of Queen Elizabeth)
12. Viscount Linley (David), 38
    (son of Princess Margaret)
13. Charles Patrick Inigo Armstrong–Jones, (newborn)
    (son of Viscount Linley)
14. Lady Sarah Chatto, 35
    (daughter of Princess Margaret)
15. Samuel David Benedict Chatto, 3
    (son of Lady Sarah Chatto)
16. Arthur David Nathaniel Chatto, (newborn)
    (son of Lady Sarah Chatto)
17. HRH The Duke of Gloucester, 55
    (grandson of King George V, Queen Elizabeth's cousin)
18. The Earl of Ulster (Alexander), 25
    (son of the Duke of Gloucester)
19. Lady Davina Windsor, 22
    (daughter of the Duke of Gloucester)
20. Lady Rose Windsor, 19
    (second daughter of the Duke of Gloucester)
21. HRH The Duke of Kent (Edward), 64
    (cousin to both Queen Elizabeth and Prince Philip and son of George, Duke of Kent, younger brother of Kings Edward VII and George VI)
22. Edward Windsor, Baron Downpatrick, 11
    (son of the Duke of Kent's eldest son, the Earl of St. Andrews, who was dropped from the line when he married a Catholic)
23. Lady Marina Windsor, 7
    (daughter of the Earl of St. Andrews)
24. Lady Amelia Windsor, 4
    (second daughter of the Earl of St. Andrews)
25. Lord Nicholas Windsor, 29
    (second son of the Duke of Kent)

ROYAL HOUSES AROUND THE WORLD

Though they rarely get the tabloid treatment of their British counterparts, less conspicuous royals do reign throughout the world. Here's an international round-up of the places where the crown still glitters.

BELGIUM

Current monarch: King Albert II (crowned 1993)

King Albert II, prince of Liège, was born on June 6, 1934. He is the son of King Leopold III and Queen Astrid, born princess of Sweden, and the brother of the late King Baudouin of Belgium.

The Royal Family:

King Albert II was married to Paola Ruffo di Calabria, the daughter of a princely Italian family, in 1959. The king and queen have three children: Prince Philippe (b. 1960), Princess Astrid (b. 1962), who is now married to the Archduke Lorenz of East Austria, and Prince Laurent (b. 1963). The royal palace is in Brussels.

DENMARK

Current monarch: Queen Margrethe II (crowned 1972)

Margrethe Alexandrine Thorhildur Ingrid, the eldest daughter of King Frederik IX and Queen Ingrid of Denmark, was born on April 16, 1940.

The Royal Family:

Margrethe married French diplomat Henri-Marie-Jean-André, count de Laborde de Monpezat, in 1967 (he changed his name to Prince Henrik upon marriage). The queen and consort have two sons, Prince Frederik (b. 1968) and Prince Joachim (b. 1969; married in 1995 to Princess Alexandra). Crown Prince Frederik, as the official heir to the Danish throne, will eventually become King Frederik X. Besides the official residence in Copenhagen, the family also has a small mansion in southern France at Cahors, the home district of Prince Henrik.

JAPAN

Current monarch: Emperor Akihito (crowned 1989)

Born on December 23, 1933, Emperor Akihito is the eldest son of the late Emperor Hirohito (posthumously known as Emperor Showa) and Empress Nagako.

The Royal Family:

Emperor Akihito married Michiko Shoda in 1959. She is the eldest daughter of the Shoda family, a prominent name in Japanese industrial and academic circles. The emperor and empress live in the imperial palace in Tokyo, and they have three children: Crown Prince Naruhito (b. 1960; married in 1993 to Crown Princess Masako amid much public attention), Prince Akishino (b. 1965; married in 1990 to Princess Kiko), and Princess Sayako (b. 1969).

LIECHTENSTEIN

Current monarch: Prince Hans Adam II (crowned 1989)

His Serene Highness Prince Hans Adam II is the eldest son of the late Prince Franz Josef II of Liechtenstein and Countess Gina von Wilczek. He was born on February 14, 1945.

The Princial Family:

Hans Adam II married Countess Marie Kinsky von Wchinitz and Tettau of Prague in 1967. The couple has four children: Crown Prince Alois (b. 1968; married to Duchess Sophie of Bavaria in 1993; son Joseph Wenzel Maximilian Maria b. 1995; daughter Marie Caroline Immaculata b. 1996), Prince Maximilian (b. 1969), Prince Constantin (b. 1972), and Princess Tatjana (b. 1973). The royal family resides in the Vaduz Castle.

LUXEMBOURG

Current monarch: Grand Duke Jean (crowned 1964)

Grand Duke Jean was born on January 5, 1921. He is the eldest son of the late Grand Duchess Charlotte and Prince Felix of Luxembourg, prince of Bourbon Parma.

The Royal Family:

Grand Duke Jean was married to Princess Joséphine-Charlotte of Belgium in 1953. She is the daughter of Prince Leopold of Belgium and Princess Astrid of Sweden, and the sister of the late King Baudouin of Belgium. The royal couple resides in the Castle of Colmar-Berg in Luxembourg, and they have five children: Princess Marie-Astrid (b. 1954), Prince Henri (b. 1955; the hereditary grand duke of Luxembourg), Prince Jean and his twin sister Princess Margaretha (b. 1957), and Prince Guillaume (b. 1963).

MONACO

Current monarch: Prince Rainier III (crowned 1949)

The Sovereign Prince of Monaco and head of the House of Grimaldi, Prince Rainier III, was born on May 31, 1923. He is the grandson of the late Prince Louis II of Monaco and the son of Princess Charlotte and Prince Pierre, count of Polignac.

The Royal Family:

Prince Rainier III married American actress Grace Kelly (1929–1982) in 1956. She was the daughter of John B. and Margaret Kelly of Philadelphia. The couple had three children: Princess Caroline (b. 1957), married to Prince Ernst August of Hanover; Crown Prince Albert (b. 1958); and Princess Stephanie (b. 1965; married in 1995 to her French-born former bodyguard Daniel Ducruet, 32; now divorced). The Princely Palace is located on the Rock of Monaco, and the family owns a private residence in Paris.

THE NETHERLANDS

Current monarch: Queen Beatrix (crowned 1980)

Beatrix Wilhemina Armgard was born on January 31, 1938, the first child of Queen Juliana and Prince Bernhard of the Netherlands.

The Royal Family:

Queen Beatrix was married to a German diplomat, Claus van Amsberg, prince of the Netherlands, in 1966, and the royal couple now resides in the Huis ten Bosch Palace in the Hague. The queen and prince have three sons: Prince Willem-Alexander Claus Georg Ferdinand (b. 1967),
Prince Johan Friso Bernhard Christiaan David (b. 1968), and Prince Constantijn Christof Frederik Aschwin (b. 1969).

NORWAY

Current monarch: King Harald (crowned 1991)

Born on February 21, 1937, King Harald is the firstborn son of the late King Olav V and Princess Märtha.

The Royal Family:

The announcement that King Harald was to marry commoner Sonja Haraldsen in 1968 triggered much debate about the future of the Norwegian monarchy. Since their marriage, however, Queen Sonja has been accepted by the public. The king and queen, who reside in the royal palace in Oslo, have a daughter, Princess Märtha Louise (b. 1971), and a son, Crown Prince Haakon (b. 1973).

SPAIN

Current monarch: King Juan Carlos (crowned 1975)

Juan Carlos de Borbón y Borbón was born on January 5, 1938. He is the first son of Don Juan de Borbón y Battenberg and Doña María de las Mercedes de Borbón y Orleans, and the grandson of King Alfonso XIII and Queen Victoria Eugenia, who was herself the granddaughter of Queen Victoria of England.

The Royal Family:

King Juan Carlos married Princess Sofía, the daughter of King Paul I and Queen Fredericka of Greece, in 1962. The king and queen have three
children: Princess Elena (b. 1963), Princess Cristina (b. 1965), and Crown Prince Felipe (b. 1968). Princess Elena, second in line for the throne, married banker Jaime de Marichalar, 31, in March 1995. It was Spain's first royal wedding since 1906. The Palacio de La Zarzuela, the family's official residence, is situated five kilometers outside of Madrid. Their summer residence, the Palace of Marivent, is in the city of Palma de Mallorca on the island of Mallorca.

SWEDEN

Current monarch: Carl XVI Gustaf (crowned 1973)

Carl XVI Gustaf was born on April 30, 1946, the youngest child and only son of hereditary Prince Gustaf Adolf of Sweden and Princess Sibylla of Sachsen-Coburg-Gotha.

The Royal Family:

Carl XVI Gustaf married commoner Silvia Renate Sommerlath, daughter of Walther and Alice Sommerlath of the Federal Republic of Germany, in 1976. The king and queen have three children: Princess Victoria (b. 1977), Prince Carl Philip (b. 1979), and Princess Madeleine (b. 1982). In 1980 the Swedish act of succession was changed to allow females the same rights of succession as males; the crown passes to the eldest child regardless of sex. Thus, eldest daughter Victoria has been named the crown princess and successor to Carl XVI Gustaf. The family lived in the royal palace in Stockholm until 1981, when they moved to Drottningholm Palace on the outskirts of the city.

PICKS & PANS 1999

The good, the bad, and the ugly: Here's the year in film as seen by PEOPLE critic Leah Rozen and, where noted, senior writer Tom Gliatto [TG]. Asterisks mark the top choices—like Julia Roberts's *Notting Hill*, worthy family fare like *Tarzan*, and the long-awaited *Star Wars: Episode I—The Phantom Menace*.

*AFFLICTION
Nick Nolte, Sissy Spacek, Willem Dafoe
A part-time cop going nowhere, he has an ex-wife (Mary Beth Hurt), a young daughter he rarely sees, a waitress girlfriend (Spacek), and an abusive, alcoholic father (James Coburn) whom he can't forgive. Nolte is nothing short of perfection in his carefully crafted portrait of a man imploding. (R)

AFTER LIFE
Mochizuki Takashi, Naito Taketoshi
The newly dead must pick a memory to be re-created on film, then head off to eternity with only that memory. A stunningly profound, vital film that makes viewers think long and hard about which memory one would choose. (No rating)

AMERICAN PIE
Jason Biggs, Chris Klein, Thomas Ian Nicholas, Eddie Kaye Thomas
Four male high school seniors make a pact to lose their virginity by graduation in this riotously raunchy adolescent sex comedy that manages to charm as often as it offends. (R)

AMONG GIANTS
Rachel Griffiths, Pete Postlethwaite, James Thornton
In this British import, towers are climbed and painted, many pints are downed, summer passes, the romantic triangle falls into place then disintegrates, and the viewer is left to wonder: What was that all about? [TG] (R)

*ANALYZE THIS
Robert De Niro, Billy Crystal
De Niro gives his screen persona a little spin, a near-imperceptible tweak, and somehow executes a full comic turn. This smart comedy is backed by one of the sharpest ensemble casts in a movie in some time. [TG] (R)

ANOTHER DAY IN PARADISE
James Woods, Melanie Griffith, Vincent Kartheiser, Natasha Gregson Wagner
A drama as violent as it is familiar, *Paradise* plays like too many other on-the-road crime movies. (R)

*ARLINGTON ROAD
Jeff Bridges, Tim Robbins, Joan Cusack, Hope Davis
This thoughtful, provocative thriller about domestic terrorism will have you questioning everything you know or—in the paranoid world the movie inhabits—thought you knew about the folks next door. The gotcha ending will haunt you for days. (R)

AT FIRST SIGHT
Val Kilmer, Mira Sorvino, Kelly McGillis, Nathan Lane
A sluggish, obvious romantic drama. The blind masseur played by Kilmer is such a swell guy that he makes his disability seem, at least initially, as desirable a male attribute as picking up his own dirty socks. (PG-13)

*AUSTIN POWERS: THE SPY WHO SHAGGED ME
Mike Myers, Heather Graham, Michael York, Seth Green, Mindy Sterling, Rob Lowe, Elizabeth Hurley, Verne Troyer
This roisterously ribald sequel is silly fun. Myers will do anything, and does, for a laugh, but the plot is so puny it cries out for steroids. Strong start, baby, but limp finish. (PG-13)

AUTUMN TALE
Marie Rivière, Béatrice Romand
Secretly determined to find a match for a widowed friend, Isabelle (Rivière) takes out a personal ad for herself, a married woman, and meets with the candidates. Pretty, smart, and chatty. [TG] (No rating)

BESIEGED
Thandie Newton, David Thewlis
An African medical student (Newton) lives in Rome and earns her room and board by cleaning the villa of a reclusive English composer (Thewlis), who falls in love with her. But the film is too enigmatically sketchy. (R)

*THE BLAIR WITCH PROJECT
Heather Donahue, Michael Williams, Joshua Leonard
This film purports to be the found footage of three young documentarians who disappeared in the Maryland woods and proves that the horror you never see and can only imagine is way, way scarier than some mask-wearing maniac swinging a bloody axe.(R)

BLAST FROM THE PAST
Brendan Fraser, Alicia Silverstone, Christopher Walken, Sissy Spacek
Parents (Walken and Spacek) give birth to a son (Fraser) in their bomb shelter during the Cuban Missile Crisis and stay below for 35 years before sending him out to investigate. Fraser impresses with his comedic skills and versatility, but once he begins walking the earth, *Blast* suffers from a bad case of the cutes. (PG-13)

BOWFINGER
Steve Martin, Eddie Murphy, Heather Graham, Christine Baranski
Written by Martin and directed with a sure comic touch by Frank Oz (*Dirty Rotten Scoundrels*), *Bowfinger* is a fizzy, funny send-up of the screen trade. Martin, a pathetically desperate but ever optimistic producer, and Murphy, who plays both one of Hollywood's biggest action stars and his bumbling stand-in, make perfect comic foils. (PG-13)

BROKEDOWN PALACE
Claire Danes, Kate Beckinsale, Bill Pullman
In this gritty, often compelling drama about growing up under duress, two teenage girls visiting Bangkok for fun land in a squalid local prison after Thai officials discover heroin in one of their knapsacks (the girls claim not to know it was there). (PG-13)

BUENA VISTA SOCIAL CLUB
Documentary
A glorified promotional video for a sensational album of Cuban music, bringing together more than a dozen great, largely forgotten veteran musicians. Miraculously, the performers are fresh and strong. [TG] (No rating)

THE CASTLE
Michael Caton, Anne Tenney
This appealingly shaggy Australian comedy follows the loopy legal struggle of a dim-witted, family-loving tow-truck driver (Caton) to keep the government from seizing his ramshackle house. (R)

*A CIVIL ACTION
John Travolta, Robert Duvall
This legal drama focuses on an attorney (Travolta) whose unbridled self-confidence brings him to the brink of ruin. The imperfections of Travolta's character keep *Action* going. (PG-13)

*COOKIE'S FORTUNE
Glenn Close, Charles S. Dutton, Liv Tyler, Patricia Neal, Julianne Moore, Chris O'Donnell
There is much to savor in this gently wacky ensemble comedy, with its strongly focused plot and characters who show great depth. (PG-13)

A COOL DRY PLACE
Vince Vaughn, Monica Potter
Vaughn plays a hotshot lawyer who has quit a major Chicago firm to raise his little son in a small town, but just as he gets comfortable, his ex-wife comes back. A dowdy domestic drama, it deserves a quick, quiet burial. [TG] (PG-13)

CRUEL INTENTIONS
Sarah Michelle Gellar, Ryan Phillippe, Reese Witherspoon
This latest adaptation of the classic French tale *Dangerous Liaisons* isn't believable, but it's stylishly shot and full of attractive young people in chic clothes. It's a brainless good time. [TG] (R)

DEEP BLUE SEA
Thomas Jane, Saffron Burrows, Samuel L. Jackson, LL Cool J
This soggy chomp-and-chew action thriller tries to prove that sharks are still scary. *Sea* has enough scares, blood, and action sequences for die-hard shark-flick fans, but neither the script nor the acting ever rise above the routine. (R)

DESERT BLUE
Brendan Sexton III, Kate Hudson, Casey Affleck, Christina Ricci
A disaffected, parentless teen (Sexton III) is stuck in a tiny desert town in California and finds himself surrounded by other bored teens. *Blue* has a talented cast, but it's a shambling bore. (R)

DETROIT ROCK CITY
Edward Furlong, Giuseppe Andrews, James DeBello, Sam Huntington
An energetic if perfunctory coming-of-age comedy, *Detroit* follows four male high school seniors (Furlong and Huntington are best) in 1978 as they take a road trip to the Motor City for a concert by Kiss. The film never transcends its adolescent-guy focus. (R)

DICK
Kirsten Dunst, Michelle Williams, Dan Hedaya, Dave Foley
A hilarious comedy based on the inspired notion that two giggly 15-year-old girls brought about Richard Nixon's downfall, *Dick* has more honest laughs in its first hour than any movie this summer. Smartly directed by Andrew Fleming (*The Craft*). (PG-13)

DOUG'S 1ST MOVIE
Animated
Let this be Doug's last movie. This is an atrociously cheap-looking piece of animation and the story, despite some laudable lessons, climaxes with storm troopers firing off laser guns at a school dance. Charming. [TG] (G)

THE DREAMLIFE OF ANGELS
Elodie Bouchez, Natacha Régnier
A quintessentially European film, tracking the ups and downs in the daily lives of two young women, where nothing much happens and yet everything happens—including something so unexpected and yet so true to the characters and the story that you gasp out loud in the theater. (R)

*DROP DEAD GORGEOUS
Kirstie Alley, Ellen Barkin, Kirsten Dunst, Denise Richards, Allison Janney
As a snarky little satire about beauty pageants, *Gorgeous* doesn't have much new to say but says it with gusto. The movie is too long by a third, but most of the performances are sharp. (PG-13)

DUDLEY DO-RIGHT
Brendan Fraser, Sarah Jessica Parker, Alfred Molina
With Fraser in the title role; Parker as his sweetheart, Nell; and Alfred Molina as Dudley's nemesis, Snidely Whiplash, this live-action sendup of the '60s melodrama cartoon must be judged a disappointment. Not remotely as cute, funny, or smart as Fraser's *George of the Jungle*. (PG) [TG]

EDTV
Matthew McConaughey, Jenna Elfman, Woody Harrelson, Ellen DeGeneres
An affable if less clever satirical comedy that features an eerily similar plot to last year's *Truman Show*, as Ed (McConaughey) knowingly agrees to having his entire life broadcast, 24/7. It lacks an incisive edge, humming along rather than soaring. (PG-13)

EIGHT MILLIMETER
Nicolas Cage, Joaquin Phoenix, Catherine Keener, James Gandolfini
This mirthless but fairly intriguing thriller shows Cage being increasingly drawn into the porn netherworld, alternately attracted and repelled by what he sees. (R)

*ELECTION
Matthew Broderick, Reese Witherspoon
A gloriously goofy comedy, where Broderick plays a civics teacher at war with a student, an ambitious goody-goody named Tracy Flick, in a wonderfully witty performance by Witherspoon. What *Election* does brilliantly is get high school right. (R)

ENTRAPMENT
Sean Connery, Catherine Zeta-Jones, Ving Rhames
A glitzy caper film in which Connery, 68, is awkwardly paired with Zeta-Jones, 29. Zeta-Jones, an insurance investigator, is convinced that Connery, a master thief, has stolen a Rembrandt, and she's hot on his trail—and on his tail. (PG-13)

ETERNITY AND A DAY
Bruno Ganz, Isabelle Renaud
Terminally ill writer (Ganz) sadly, slowly wraps up his affairs before going off to a hospital to die alone. Burdened by artistic self-importance, this Greek import feels like an eternity tacked onto a day and a millennium. [TG] (No rating)

EXISTENZ
Jennifer Jason Leigh, Jude Law
This futuristic thriller with heavy sexual overtones is fascinating and fun in a dark, dark way. A computer-game designer (Leigh) eludes assassins while playing a virtual reality game called eXistenZ. What does it all mean? Beats me. (R)

EYES WIDE SHUT
Tom Cruise, Nicole Kidman, Sydney Pollack, Alan Cumming
Stanley Kubrick's last film should be seen a second time to appreciate its themes of love and lust and trust and truth, but the idea of sitting through it again may be about as alluring as eating a hairball. (R)

*FORCES OF NATURE
Sandra Bullock, Ben Affleck, Maura Tierney, Blythe Danner
A refreshing rethinking of the basic rules of romantic comedy, *Forces* keeps surprising you by being sharper and more entertaining than you might expect. (PG-13)

*THE GENERAL
Brendan Gleeson, Jon Voight
A boisterously funny film about a real-life Irish thief and his criminal career. Gleeson, an Irish stage star, is mesmerizing. (R)

THE GENERAL'S DAUGHTER
John Travolta, Madeleine Stowe, James Cromwell, Timothy Hutton, Clarence Williams III, James Woods, Leslie Stefanson
A heavily contrived and gratuitously sleazy thriller about the murder of a beautiful young female army officer (Stefanson). Travolta adds what zip there is here. (R)

GET REAL
Ben Silverstone
In this small British charmer, 16-year-old Steven (gawky, vulnerably sincere) falls in love with classmate John (strapping, popular, athletic). [TG] (R)

GLORIA
Sharon Stone, Jean-Luke Figueroa
Seen-it-all Gloria (Stone) runs afoul of her mob chums when she protects a little boy whose family has just been iced. Stone's oversize performance seems to have been inspired by…what? *Guys and Dolls?*… as she takes pains to say "dese," "dem," and "dose." (R)

GO
Katie Holmes, Jay Mohr, Sarah Polley, Scott Wolf, Desmond Askew, Taye Diggs
With its hip attitude, overlapping stories, and fractured chronology, *Go* is a kind of *Pulp Fiction* reupholstered in Generations X and Y fabric. Fast, funny, and inventive. (R)

*GOD SAID, "HA!"
Julia Sweeney
Sad, funny, and surprisingly uplifting. Comedian Julia Sweeney, with her lovely comic sensibility, tells a story that would have made Job himself reach for the Kleenex. [TG] (PG-13)

GOODBYE LOVER
Patricia Arquette, Dermot Mulroney, Don Johnson, Mary-Louise Parker
An embarrassingly dull thriller where the plot twists in a mess about brothers, wives, and girlfriends with murder on their minds. (R)

THE HAUNTING
Liam Neeson, Catherine Zeta-Jones, Owen Wilson, Lili Taylor
What starts out as a fun, campy horror film degenerates into a silly special-effects lalapalooza. This *Haunting* has a couple of genuine made-you-jump scares, but viewers will more often titter derisively than nervously. (PG-13)

HIDEOUS KINKY
Kate Winslet, Saïd Taghmaoui
Winslet movingly plays a bohemian English single mother in this poignant character study about seeking adventure on distant shores, but also about knowing when it is time to go home again. (R)

HILARY AND JACKIE
Emily Watson, Rachel Griffiths
A fascinating and frustrating biography tracing the close but often troubled relationship between sisters Hilary and Jacqueline du Pré. Watson and Griffiths both shine. (R)

THE HI-LOW COUNTRY
Woody Harrelson, Billy Crudup, Patricia Arquette, Penelope Cruz
Harrelson gives an exuberant performance in this ruggedly handsome and intelligent Western. (R)

HURLYBURLY
Sean Penn, Kevin Spacey, Meg Ryan, Robin Wright Penn, Chazz Palminteri
Despite sensational performances by Penn, Spacey, and Palminteri as a trio of drugged-out, raging misogynists, the clueless characters are so loathsome and their rants so repetitious that one really doesn't want to spend five minutes in their company. (R)

AN IDEAL HUSBAND
Cate Blanchett, Jeremy Northam, Rupert Everett, Julianne Moore, Minnie Driver, John Wood
This comedy of manners, one of Wilde's better plays, is to be savored for its epigrammatic wit, the crisp, stylish acting of its talented cast, and the ironic parallels between life in the corridors of power, yesterday and today. (PC-13)

IDLE HANDS
Devon Sawa, Seth Green
Hands down awful. This is yet another low-budget splatfest that tries to inject sick humor, but mostly seems just stupidly pointless. (R)

ILLUMINATA
John Turturro, Katherine Borowitz, Susan Sarandon, Christopher Walken
Often amusing but even more often self-indulgent, this comedy-drama cowritten and directed by Turturro lovingly showcases his wife's (Borowitz) superior acting and finely etched beauty. Focusing on a theater company in New York at the turn of the century, it

1999'S TOP TEN GROSSERS

The Force has been with the box office this year, evidenced in the much-anticipated *Star Wars* sequel, the surprising effect of *The Spy Who Shagged Me*, and techno-hit *The Matrix*. Disney had another family hit, and *Mummy* and daddy were also in on the action. As of August 26, these blockbusters lead the pack. (Sources: *Variety*; *Entertainment Weekly*)

1. *Star Wars: Episode I—The Phantom Menace*
2. *Austin Powers 2—The Spy Who Shagged Me*
3. *The Matrix*
4. *Tarzan*
5. *Big Daddy*
6. *The Mummy*
7. *The Blair Witch Project*
8. *The Sixth Sense*
9. *Runaway Bride*
10. *Notting Hill*

proves that artistic crises are better suffered than seen. (R)

IN DREAMS
Annette Bening, Aidan Quinn, Stephen Rea, Robert Downey Jr.
Bening plays an artist tormented by nasty dreams, with images of a murdering maniac, that start coming true. When the maniac (Downey) finally shows up, *Dreams* goes from bad to rotten to the core. (R)

INSPECTOR GADGET
Matthew Broderick, Joely Fisher, Rupert Everett
This uninspired, relentlessly dopey film, based on the TV cartoon, will amuse kids young enough to love any and all jokes involving getting slimed. (PG)

INSTINCT
Anthony Hopkins, Cuba Gooding Jr., Maura Tierney, Donald Sutherland
This half-baked psychological thriller lurches from set piece to set piece without adding up to much. (R)

IN TOO DEEP
Omar Epps, LL Cool J, Nia Long
The tale of an undercover cop (Epps) who finds himself drawn to the thug life, the movie lectures about the evils of drugs and violence while going out of its way to showcase blood-spattered scenes that chronicle everything from sexual assault with a pool cue to the involuntary removal of one character's tongue.Violent, yes, deep, no. (R)

THE IRON GIANT
Animated, with voices by Harry Connick Jr., Jennifer Aniston
Hogarth Hughes, 9, has a secret: His best friend is a 50-foot robot from outer space. A well-told and beautifully drawn tale of friendship and fortitude

based on a novel by British poet Ted Hughes. (PG)

JUST A LITTLE HARMLESS SEX
Alison Eastwood, Robert Mailhouse, Kimberly Williams, Jonathan Silverman
A talky comedy drama in which the hubby whines to his buddies, the missus whines to her gal pals, and everyone ends up at the same bar flirting with one another and with strangers while sorting out their love lives. (R)

THE KING AND I
Animated
Liberties—both big and small, and most of them dumb—have been taken with the plot and the characters of Rodgers and Hammerstein's beloved musical. (G)

LAKE PLACID
Bridget Fonda, Bill Pullman, Oliver Platt, Betty White
This hybrid comedy-horror film about a 30-foot crocodile vacillates uneasily between being funny and scary without fully achieving either. (R)

*LIFE
Eddie Murphy, Martin Lawrence
This prison-buddies comedy is a good, juicy piece of entertainment. Murphy and Lawrence are a well-matched team. [TG] (R)

*LIMBO
Mary Elizabeth Mastrantonio, David Strathairn, Vanessa Martinez
Mother, daughter, and beau become trapped on a deserted island and must depend on each other to survive in this intriguing, if overly deliberate, character drama. (R)

THE LOSS OF SEXUAL INNOCENCE
Julian Sands, Saffron Burrows
The story follows Sands as he matures from an unhappy boy

into a family man who falls for a spiritually restless Italian beauty. If *Innocence* had kept its focus on this relationship, we might have had a movie. [TG] (R)

LOST & FOUND
David Spade, Sophie Marceau
Although Spade can be amusing for five-minute doses on TV, he barely registers during these 98 finger-drumming, leg-jiggling minutes. (PG-13)

THE LOVE LETTER
Kate Capshaw, Ellen DeGeneres, Tom Selleck, Tom Everett Scott
A whimsical romantic comedy with a slender plot that seems stretched even thinner than pulled taffy. Although the energetic cast is willing, *Letter* is ultimately little more than a Post-it note. (PG-13)

LOVERS OF THE ARCTIC CIRCLE
Fele Martinez, Najwa Nimri
One can imagine Martinez and Nimri arranging a weekend getaway, but not to the ends of the earth. *Lovers* may have worked if the couple had seemed genuinely lashed on by passion. [TG] (R)

THE LOVERS ON THE BRIDGE
Juliette Binoche, Denis Lavant
Despite its odd, out-there appeal, this French film about homeless lovers is as overripe as week-old Brie. (R)

LUCIE AUBRAC
Carole Bouquet, Daniel Auteuil
Equal parts World War II thriller and romantic love story, director-writer Claude Berri's film is a stirring reminder of the all-too-human sacrifices made during wartime. Based on the exploits of a real-life heroine of the French Resistance. (R)

*THE MATRIX
Keanu Reeves, Laurence Fishburne
A computer hacker named Neo (Reeves) taps into a mysterious cyberpersonality named Morpheus (Fishburne) in this cyber movie that zips along, fueled by elaborate computer-generated effects. [TG] (R)

MESSAGE IN A BOTTLE
Kevin Costner, Robin Wright Penn, Paul Newman
A sappy romantic drama with a languorous pace. Costner seems to be auditioning here for the title of Mr. Sensitive. (PG-13)

*METROLAND
Emily Watson, Christian Bale
Bale deftly conveys a yearning boy still lurking in his adult self, while Watson radiates wholesome sexiness and smarts in this absorbing and quietly affecting movie. A *Thirtysomething* for Brits. (R)

MICKEY BLUE EYES
Hugh Grant, Jeanne Tripplehorn, James Caan
This tepid romantic comedy of a mob movie is never as wacky or wild as it ought to be. Grant labors hard, and he and Tripplehorn have little romantic chemistry, but Caan is blustery fun. Unless you're feeling generous, fuhgeddaboutit. (PG-13)

MIGHTY JOE YOUNG
Bill Paxton, Charlize Theron
Joe, the 15-foot, 2,000-pound gorilla hero, is pure Saturday-afternoon-movie magic. But *Joe* the film is nothing to go ape over. (PG)

THE MOD SQUAD
Claire Danes, Omar Epps, Giovanni Ribisi, Josh Brolin
Whatever your era and whatever your slang, this movie version of the TV show stinks.

Danes, Epps, and Ribisi, in a barely comprehensible plot, display an energy level as flat as hair after a week without shampooing. (R)

THE MUMMY
Brendan Fraser, Rachel Weisz
This overblown horror movie owes as much to the Indiana Jones franchise as to the 1932 Boris Karloff classic. This Mummy is a truly repulsive decaying frame of mold and gook. [TG] (PG-13)

MUPPETS FROM SPACE
Jeffrey Tambor, Andie MacDowell
Jolly fun for small fries and chaperons. Miss Piggy, as always, steals the show. (G)

THE MUSE
Albert Brooks, Sharon Stone, Andie MacDowell, Jeff Bridges
The latest self-obsessed comedy cowritten, directed by, and starring Brooks starts off sharply entertaining but ends up nearly as vacuous and narcissistic as the Hollywood community it so gleefully lampoons. Funny, but wears out its welcome. (PG-13)

MY FAVORITE MARTIAN
Christopher Lloyd, Jeff Daniels
An uninspired, broad reworking of the '60s television show with the same name. Anyone over the age of 8 will be hard-pressed to find even a few chuckles. (PG)

1998'S OVERSEAS MONEYMAKERS

The world was lovin' Leo in '98; *Titanic* was the tidal wave, but even *The Man in the Iron Mask* more than doubled its domestic haul on foreign screens. *Godzilla* and *The Jackal* also played significantly stronger around the globe than in the U.S. Though action pictures often dominate this list, comedy made a strong showing in both the wry, award-winning *As Good As It Gets* and the raucous *There's Something About Mary*. (Source: *Variety*)

Rank	Title	Gross (in millions)
1.	*Titanic*	1,209
2.	*Armageddon*	263
3.	*Godzilla*	240
4.	*Saving Private Ryan*	235
5.	*Deep Impact*	209
6.	*As Good As It Gets*	166
7.	*Lethal Weapon 4*	155
8.	*There's Something About Mary*	154
9.	*Mulan*	150
10.	*Tomorrow Never Dies*	134
11.	*Dr. Dolittle*	133
12.	*The Man in the Iron Mask*	123
13.	*The Truman Show*	119
14.	*The Mask of Zorro*	112
15.	*The Horse Whisperer*	109
16.	*City of Angels*	105
17.	*The X-Files*	100
18.	*The Jackal*	89
19.	*Good Will Hunting*	88
20.	*Six Days, Seven Nights*	84

MY LIFE SO FAR
Colin Firth, Mary Elizabeth Mastrantonio
Growing up in rural Scotland in the mid-'30s, the 10-year-old (Robert Norman) in this minor coming-of-age movie barely notices that his parents are drifting apart. An elegiac mood piece, as decorative and delicate as fine lace and no less superfluous. (PG-13)

*MY NAME IS JOE
Peter Mullan, Louise Goodall
A blistering drama that will leave viewers as drained as the bottles Joe guzzles during a relapse. Mullan is superb as Joe Kavanagh, the 37-year-old Scotsman who gave up drink 10 months ago but still can't find a job. (R)

MY SON THE FANATIC
Om Puri, Rachel Griffiths, Akbar Kurtha
Parvez's son is slipping ever deeper into Islamic fundamentalism, rejecting all that Parvez (Puri), a hustling Pakistani cab driver, has worked long and hard for. This spiky drama offers an intriguing look at lives that rarely make it to the big screen. (R)

MYSTERY MEN
Ben Stiller, William H. Macy, Hank Azaria, Janeane Garofalo
A motley collection of regular Joes imagine themselves to be superheros fighting evil in their hometown. Despite game efforts by a talented cast, nothing really is at stake here and the film turns into a sprawling mess. (PG-13)

NEVER BEEN KISSED
Drew Barrymore, Molly Shannon, David Arquette, Michael Vartan
This hapless romantic comedy is scene after awkward scene of a hopelessly geeky Barrymore trying too hard to be cool. (PG-13)

*NOTTING HILL
Julia Roberts, Hugh Grant
This sleek, irresistible romantic comedy couldn't be more fun. Movie goddess Anna Scott (Roberts) walks into a London bookstore presided over by Grant and, improbably, romance follows. (PG-13)

*OCTOBER SKY
Jake Gyllenhaal, Chris Cooper, Laura Dern
Based on the memoirs of NASA engineer Homer Hickam Jr., this modest, heartwarming movie tells a story that can't be beat. (PG)

OFFICE SPACE
Ron Livingston, Stephen Root, Gary Cole, Jennifer Aniston
This minor comedy is aimed at a narrow demographic group: guys in their 20s who hate their jobs and the women who love them. Aniston is wasted in a zero role. (R)

THE OTHER SISTER
Diane Keaton, Juliette Lewis
There are amusing and even inspirational moments in Lewis's battle to find a life and love apart from that of her overprotective, disapproving mom (Keaton), but *Sister* is as soft and gooey as a toasted marshmallow. (PG-13)

THE OUT-OF-TOWNERS
Goldie Hawn, Steve Martin
Do we really need to watch Hawn running down an East Village street in ankle boots being chased by an attack dog? Or Martin throwing deli meat to distract it? Not for a New York minute. [TG] (PG-13)

*PAYBACK
Mel Gibson, Gregg Henry, Maria Bello
Payback overflows with attitude and gratuitous violence, with scant help from the overly wiseacre script. But it is always entertaining to watch Gibson shine onscreen. (R)

PEEPING TOM
Carl Boehm, Anna Massey
This perversely fascinating 1960 thriller, now in rerelease, originally left British critics appalled. Although seemingly about a creep who kills (Boehm), it is as much about our own voyeuristic fascination with movies. (No Rating)

PLAYING BY HEART
Sean Connery, Gena Rowlands, Dennis Quaid, Gillian Anderson, Angelina Jolie
The film introduces a series of characters and their romantic dilemmas, and only at the end does it reveal their connection. An impressive cast, but unimpressive results. (R)

PUSHING TIN
John Cusack, Billy Bob Thornton, Cate Blanchett, Angelina Jolie
An anemic comedy about air traffic controllers that fails to stay aloft. Every time *Tin* ventures away from the workplace, it hits turbulence. (R)

THE RED VIOLIN
Samuel L. Jackson, Greta Scacchi
This ambitious, sumptuous-looking drama follows a red violin and its various owners across four centuries, showing how the link between art and life spans the globe, transcending deaths, disastrous love affairs, and political tumult. (No rating)

RETURN WITH HONOR
Documentary
A quarter-century after the Vietnam War, nearly two dozen men tell how they survived life in a North Vietnamese prison, and at what cost. This moving documentary is worth a salute. (No rating)

RUNAWAY BRIDE
Julia Roberts, Richard Gere, Joan Cusack, Rita Wilson
Roberts plays a bride who bolts not just once, but thrice, with Gere as the cynical Manhattan newspaperman who decides to investigate why she is "always a bride, never a bridesmaid." This thoroughly

conventional comedy doesn't disappoint, but neither does it rise above the expected, save for a sassy touch here and there. (PG)

RUN LOLA RUN
Franka Potente, Moritz Bleibtreu
This furiously paced German import leaves an audience spent—but gratefully so. Beyond its dazzling surface and breathless speed, *Lola* is very serious. It stays with you. [TG] (R)

RUSHMORE
Jason Schwartzman, Bill Murray
Bill Murray is marvelous in this quirky comedy about a

hyperactive prep school student (Schwartzman). Fresher and funnier than just about any other movie out there. (R)

THE SCHOOL OF FLESH
Isabelle Huppert, Vincent Martinez
A romantically elegiac French film (with English subtitles) about a Parisian fashion designer (Huppert) and a bartender (Martinez) some 20 years her junior. (No rating)

SHE'S ALL THAT
Freddie Prinze Jr., Rachael Leigh Cook
Prinze, one of the cutest boys in his high school class, will be paired with a female dork for

WORKING TITLES

Would you have seen Travolta and Cage in *Switcheroo*? *Face/Off* kept its original title—but these new releases and old favorites shed previous names on their way to the screen.

What was once...	Eventually became...	What was once...	Eventually became...
Against All Enemies	The Siege	The Kiss	Living Out Loud
Austinpussy	Austin Powers: The Spy Who Shagged Me	The Loners	Easy Rider
		Made Men	GoodFellas
Billy the Third	Tommy Boy	The Magic Hour	Twilight
Black and White	Trading Places	Most Valuable Pooch	Air Bud
Blue Vision	In Dreams	My Posse Don't Do Homework	Dangerous Minds
Bookworm	The Edge		
The Boys in the Bank	Dog Day Afternoon	Navy Cross	G.I. Jane
A Boy's Life	E. T., the Extra-Terrestrial	Paris Match	French Kiss
		The Party	Can't Hardly Wait
Called Home	Witness	People Like Us	Philadelphia
The Colony	Double Team	Prison Rodeo	Stir Crazy
Coma Guy	While You Were Sleeping	The Quest	Coming to America
		The Rainbow Warrior	On Deadly Ground
Daddy's Home	Look Who's Talking	The Rest of Daniel	Forever Young
Extremely Violent	Last Action Hero	Scary Movie	Scream
Father Goose	Fly Away Home	Ship of Fools	The Impostors
Finished with Engines	No Way Out	Simon Says	Die Hard with a Vengeance
The Flood	Hard Rain		
Force Majeure	Return to Paradise	Simple Simon	Mercury Rising
The Forlorn	Addicted to Love	The Soldier's Wife	The Crying Game
Goodnight Moon	Stepmom	Teeny-Weenies	Honey, I Shrunk the Kids
Hot and Cold	Weekend at Bernie's		
An Indian in the City	Jungle 2 Jungle	Ten Soldiers	Red Dawn
I Was a Teenage Teenager	Clueless	3000	Pretty Woman
		Tribulations	Bulworth

his prom date—but even with eyeglasses, flat hair, and paint-splattered overalls, Cook is an ethereal beauty. [TG] (PG-13)

SHILOH 2: SHILOH SEASON
Zachary Browne, Michael Moriarty, Ann Dowd, Scott Wilson, Rod Steiger
This low-key, heartwarming family movie about a boy and his dog emphasizes classic, old-fashioned values and is refreshingly free of special effects. (PG)

SIMPLY IRRESISTIBLE
Sarah Michelle Gellar, Sean Patrick Flanery
A dopey romantic comedy about food-obsessed lovers. Gellar and Flanery have about as much zing as cornstarch. (PG-13)

THE SIXTH SENSE
Bruce Willis, Toni Collette, Olivia Williams, Haley Joel Osment
This psychological thriller with supernatural overtones makes sense only after a humdinger of a final twist. Willis plays a child psychologist trying to help a troubled boy terrorized by ghostly visions. Avoids gory cheap thrills in favor of muted chills. (PG-13)

SOUTH PARK: BIGGER, LONGER, AND UNCUT
Animated
South Park brings back the musical, now with a toilet-paper-thin plot. You might chuckle, but you won't feel good about yourself at the time. (R)

*STAR WARS: EPISODE I—THE PHANTOM MENACE
Liam Neeson, Ewan McGregor, Natalie Portman, Jake Lloyd
While *Menace* delivers myth, imagination, intergalactic travel, and sword fights, its basic plot too closely echoes

that of the original movie. Children will identify with Anakin Skywalker (Lloyd), *Menace*'s 9-year-old slave boy hero, while adult moviegoers will find themselves wishing the human characters were more dynamic. (PG)

STEPMOM
Susan Sarandon, Julia Roberts, Ed Harris
If it didn't star the potent combo of Roberts and Saran-don, and provide a few modest laughs early on, one might quite easily mistake it for a family-therapy training film. (PG-13)

*STILL CRAZY
Stephen Rea, Juliet Aubrey, Billy Connolly, Jimmy Nail, Bill Nighy
This tale of bickering band members trying to recapture the magic twenty years after their breakup is a fond valentine to rock and roll, and to rock and rollers. (R)

SUMMER OF SAM
John Leguizamo, Mira Sorvino, Adrien Brody, Jennifer Esposito
Like a shimmering horizon on a broiling afternoon, *Sam* never quite settles into focus. Despite flashes of brilliance and audacity, director Spike Lee goes overboard with some scenes and is maddeningly elliptical in others. (R)

*TARZAN
Animated, with the voices of Tony Goldwyn, Glenn Close, Minnie Driver
This latest look at the loincloth king explores issues of family and belonging and gives young viewers plenty to mull over afterward. Although its sense of humor and poignancy falter a bit at the end, *Tarzan* comes out swinging. (G)

TEA WITH MUSSOLINI
Cher, Joan Plowright, Maggie Smith, Judi Dench, Lily Tomlin
A dramatically weak story of privileged English expatriates who help raise a motherless Italian youth and survive the Fascists. (PG)

10 THINGS I HATE ABOUT YOU
Julia Stiles, Heath Ledger, Larisa Oleynik, Joseph Gordon-Levitt
This teen film is Shakespeare's *The Taming of the Shrew* plunked down in a contemporary American high school. Though smarter than most adolescent fluff, it never transcends its pre-cap-and-gown concerns. (PG-13)

THE THEORY OF FLIGHT
Kenneth Branagh, Helena Bonham Carter
The kind of picture that gives the ol' unlimited human spirit a bad name. (R)

THE THIN RED LINE
Sean Penn, Nick Nolte, Jim Caviezel, Ben Chaplin, Woody Harrelson
With its meditative exploration of philosophical themes, it follows an army unit in 1942 as it fights the battle of Guadal-canal in the South Pacific. It's beautiful to look at but too often sacrifices characters and plot for flora and fauna. (R)

THE THIRTEENTH FLOOR
Craig Bierko, Gretchen Mol, Vincent D'Onofrio, Dennis Haysbert
This dull sci-fi thriller, about folks who travel back and forth in time in a deadly virtual reality game, is to be avoided. (R)

*THIS IS MY FATHER
Aidan Quinn, James Caan
A powerful drama about a doomed romance and class differences in rural Ireland in 1939. Quinn has never been better, and Moya Farrelly is a find. (R)

THE THOMAS CROWN AFFAIR
Pierce Brosnan, Rene Russo
This is a sleekly entertaining remake of the then ultracool but now hopelessly dated 1968 film. Despite a gutsy performance by Russo and a smoothly competent one by Brosnan, it lacks pizzazz. (R)

*THREE SEASONS
Harvey Keitel, Don Duong
A compelling look at contemporary Vietnam through the interconnected stories of several Saigon residents. (PG-13)

TRICK
Christian Campbell, John Paul Pitoc
A romantic comedy in which Gabriel (Campbell) picks up a muscled dancer, Mark (Pitoc), and spends the evening looking for a place to get more intimate. It's cheerful in a clunky, obvious way as the story becomes not about sex but budding love. [TG] (R)

TRUE CRIME
Clint Eastwood, Isaiah Washington, James Woods, Diane Venora
This crime drama keeps its momentum going until nearly the final stretch, when it becomes too contrived. Given the chance to flex more acting muscles here, Eastwood practically purrs like a contented old tomcat. (R)

THE 24 HOUR WOMAN
Rosie Perez, Marianne Jean-Baptiste, Diego Serrano, Patti LuPone
Although well intentioned, this comedy-drama about a woman (Perez) attempting to balance motherhood and a career is a mess. (R)

TWICE UPON A YESTERDAY
Lena Headey, Douglas Henshall, Penélope Cruz, Elizabeth McGovern
This charming romantic fable puts love on rewind as an unemployed actor (Henshall),

travels back in time to rectify the swinish behavior that caused his longtime sweetie (Headey) to ditch him for another man. (R)

TWIN FALLS IDAHO
Mark Polish, Michael Polish, Michele Hicks
A weird, dreamy, and sentimental film about conjoined twins. As *Idaho* slowly reveals its multiple stories, it takes viewers on a journey that will leave few hearts untouched. (R)

VARSITY BLUES
James Van Der Beek, Jon Voight
A routine high school football drama about a second-string quarterback (Van Der Beek) who gets the touchdowns. (R)

VIRUS
Jamie Lee Curtis, William Baldwin
An uninspired action thriller. Crew members come upon a deserted Russian ship and soon realize that they are being stalked by murderous mechanical robots. Who is behind this evil? Who cares? (R)

A WALK ON THE MOON
Diane Lane, Viggo Mortensen, Anna Paquin, Liev Schreiber
Walk puts characters before period and gets both right. This vividly fresh, romantic drama showcases Diane Lane, making the most of a grown-up, sexy role that lets her really strut her stuff. (R)

WILD WILD WEST
Will Smith, Kevin Kline, Kenneth Branagh, Salma Hayek
A bloated big-screen bore, you'll laugh out loud, if only to exercise those muscles after enforced silence. Smith is eager to please and Kline huffs and puffs mightily, but they can't inflate a lead balloon. (PG-13)

WILLIAM SHAKESPEARE'S A MIDSUMMER NIGHT'S DREAM
Michelle Pfeiffer, Kevin Kline, Calista Flockhart, Rupert Everett, Christian Bale, Stanley Tucci, Sophie Marceau
It is Pfeiffer's good fortune that the majority of her scenes are opposite Kline since the rest of *Dream* is uneven, with the cast mixing and matching acting styles as if fitting together pieces for a crazy quilt. (PG-13)

THE WINSLOW BOY
Jeremy Northam, Nigel Hawthorne, Rebecca Pidgeon, Gemma Jones
A moral drama about a father's fight to clear his son's name after the boy is kicked out of military school on forgery charges. Northam is sexy and sharp as the blue-blooded barrister arguing the boy's case. (G)

THE WOOD
Taye Diggs, Omar Epps, Richard T. Jones
Wedding day, and the groom's two best friends find him drunk at the home of an old girlfriend. En route to the ceremony they lapse in and out of flashback memories that give *Wood* an unfocused glow of nostalgia. [TG] (R)

XIU XIU: THE SENT DOWN GIRL
Lu Lu
Set roughly a quarter-century ago, this hauntingly quiet but powerful tale of girlish innocence destroyed combines the dreamlike simplicity of a fairy tale with the stone-cold bleakness that characterizes Red Chinese history. [TG] (R)

ZERO EFFECT
Bill Pullman, Ben Stiller
This quirky, comedic detective story becomes ever more convoluted, but Pullman's personal charm goes a long way toward keeping one's interest. (R)

THE TOP 100 BOX-OFFICE FILMS OF ALL TIME

This list ranks the largest money-making movies of all time based on domestic (U.S. and Canada) box-office receipts. Figures are accurate through August 26, 1999; summer blockbusters are still earning. (Source: *Variety; ACNielsen EDI*)

Rank Film (year of release)	B.O. Gross
1. Titanic (1997)	$600,788,188
2. Star Wars (1977)	460,947,410
3. Star Wars—The Phantom Menace (1999)	418,513,721
4. E.T., the Extra-Terrestrial (1982)	399,804,539
5. Jurassic Park (1993)	357,067,947
6. Forrest Gump (1994)	329,689,600
7. The Lion King (1994)	312,855,561
8. Return of the Jedi (1983)	309,140,456
9. Independence Day (1996)	306,155,579
10. The Empire Strikes Back (1980)	290,178,670
11. Home Alone (1990)	285,761,243
12. Jaws (1975)	260,000,000
13. Batman (1989)	251,188,924
14. Men in Black (1997)	250,156,830
15. Raiders of the Lost Ark (1981)	242,374,454
16. Twister (1996)	241,721,524
17. Ghostbusters (1984)	238,600,000
18. Beverly Hills Cop (1984)	234,760,478
19. The Lost World: Jurassic Park (1997)	229,086,679
20. Mrs. Doubtfire (1993)	219,195,051
21. Ghost (1990)	217,631,306
22. Aladdin (1992)	217,350,219
23. Saving Private Ryan (1998)	216,173,322
24. Back to the Future (1985)	208,242,016
25. Terminator 2: Judgment Day (1991)	204,843,345
26. Austin Powers 2: The Spy Who Shagged Me (1999)	203,652,820
27. Armageddon (1998)	201,578,182
28. Gone With the Wind (1939)	198,261,470
29. Indiana Jones and the Last Crusade (1989)	197,171,806
30. Toy Story (1995)	191,753,112
31. Dances with Wolves (1990)	184,208,848
32. Batman Forever (1995)	184,031,112
33. The Fugitive (1993)	183,875,760
34. Grease (1978)	181,450,286
35. Liar Liar (1997)	181,410,615
36. Mission: Impossible (1996)	180,981,866
37. Indiana Jones and the Temple of Doom (1984)	179,870,271
38. Pretty Woman (1990)	178,406,268
39. Tootsie (1982)	177,200,000
40. Top Gun (1986)	176,781,728
41. There's Something About Mary (1998)	176,403,287
42. Snow White and the Seven Dwarfs (1937)	175,263,233
43. "Crocodile" Dundee (1986)	174,634,806
44. Home Alone 2: Lost in New York (1992)	173,585,516
45. Rain Man (1988)	172,825,435
46. Air Force One (1997)	172,627,880
47. Apollo 13 (1995)	172,070,496
48. The Matrix (1999)	170,938,928
49. Three Men and a Baby (1987)	167,780,960
50. Tarzan (1999)	165,904,901

Rank Film (year of release)	B.O. Gross
51. Robin Hood: Prince of Thieves (1991)	165,493,908
52. The Exorcist (1973)	165,000,000
53. Batman Returns (1992)	162,831,698
54. A Bug's Life (1998)	162,721,112
55. The Waterboy (1998)	161,468,877
56. The Sound of Music (1965)	160,476,331
57. Big Daddy (1999)	159,025,943
58. The Firm (1993)	158,340,292
59. Fatal Attraction (1987)	156,645,693
60. The Sting (1972)	156,000,000
61. The Mummy (1999)	154,820,855
62. Who Framed Roger Rabbit (1988)	154,112,492
63. Beverly Hills Cop II (1987)	153,665,036
64. Jerry Maguire (1996)	153,658,439
65. Rambo: First Blood Part II (1985)	150,415,432
66. As Good As It Gets (1997)	148,478,011
67. Gremlins (1984)	148,168,459
68. Lethal Weapon 2 (1989)	147,253,986
69. True Lies (1994)	146,282,411
70. Beauty and the Beast (1991)	145,863,363
71. The Santa Clause (1994)	144,833,357
72. Lethal Weapon 3 (1992)	144,731,527
73. Dr. Dolittle (1998)	144,153,418
74. 101 Dalmatians (1961)	143,992,148
75. The Jungle Book (1967)	141,843,612
76. National Lampoon's Animal House (1978)	141,600,000
77. Pocahontas (1995)	141,579,773
78. A Few Good Men (1992)	141,340,178
79. Rush Hour (1998)	141,167,365
80. Deep Impact (1998)	140,464,664
81. Look Who's Talking (1989)	140,088,813
82. Sister Act (1992)	139,605,150
83. The Rocky Horror Picture Show (1975)	138,929,642
84. Good Will Hunting (1997)	138,293,327
85. Platoon (1986)	137,963,328
86. Ransom (1996)	136,458,966
87. Godzilla (1998)	136,314,294
88. 101 Dalmatians (1996)	136,189,294
89. Teenage Mutant Ninja Turtles (1990)	135,265,915
90. Patch Adams (1998)	134,988,003
91. The Godfather (1972)	134,835,055
92. Superman (1978)	134,218,018
93. The Rock (1996)	134,069,511
94. The Silence of the Lambs (1991)	130,726,716
95. Honey, I Shrunk the Kids (1989)	130,724,172
96. The Flintstones (1994)	130,531,208
97. Lethal Weapon 4 (1998)	130,444,603
98. An Officer and a Gentleman (1982)	129,795,549
99. The Nutty Professor (1996)	128,814,019
100. Close Encounters of the Third Kind (1977)	128,290,347

THE TOP 100 BOX-OFFICE FILMS OF 1998

In 1998, *Titanic* continued to sail, while asteroids made a *Deep Impact* on screens and bugs won over the younger set. (Grosses are for U.S. and Canada box office, and are limited to the calendar year; starred films earned additional income in 1997.) (Source: *Variety*)

Rank	Film	B.O. Gross	Rank	Film	B.O. Gross
1.	Titanic*	488,194,015	51.	Pleasantville	38,761,264
2.	Armageddon	201,578,182	52.	How Stella Got Her Groove Back	37,665,439
3.	Saving Private Ryan	190,805,259	53.	Out of Sight	37,562,568
4.	There's Something About Mary	174,422,745	54.	Urban Legend	37,506,463
5.	The Waterboy	147,895,431	55.	Sphere	37,297,851
6.	Dr. Dolittle	144,153,418	56.	Stepmom	35,435,611
7.	Deep Impact	140,464,664	57.	Mouse Hunt*	33,317,341
8.	Godzilla	136,314,294	58.	Mercury Rising	32,983,332
9.	Rush Hour	136,065,335	59.	Bride of Chucky	32,305,400
10.	Good Will Hunting*	134,063,347	60.	A Night at the Roxbury	30,312,145
11.	Lethal Weapon 4	130,444,603	61.	Wild Things	30,147,739
12.	A Bug's Life	127,589,564	62.	Madeline	29,967,750
13.	The Truman Show	125,618,201	63.	Spice World	29,342,592
14.	As Good As It Gets*	124,083,542	64.	The Object of My Affection	29,187,243
15.	Mulan	120,620,254	65.	Grease (reissue)	28,411,018
16.	The Mask of Zorro	93,715,262	66.	Jack Frost	27,986,773
17.	Enemy of the State	92,027,903	67.	Paulie	27,084,499
18.	Antz	88,668,349	68.	The Big Hit	27,066,941
19.	The Rugrats Movie	86,430,992	69.	L.A. Confidential*	27,059,840
20.	The X-Files	83,898,313	70.	Bulworth	26,528,684
21.	The Wedding Singer	80,245,725	71.	Great Expectations	26,420,672
22.	City of Angels	78,892,664	72.	Scream 2	25,731,495
23.	The Horse Whisperer	75,373,563	73.	Can't Hardly Wait	25,605,015
24.	Six Days, Seven Nights	74,339,294	74.	Fallen	25,493,642
25.	Blade	70,095,974	75.	Amistad*	23,582,870
26.	Lost in Space	69,117,629	76.	The Avengers	23,523,710
27.	A Perfect Murder	67,658,331	77.	One True Thing	23,337,196
28.	The Parent Trap	66,308,518	78.	The Players Club	23,047,939
29.	Ever After	65,667,434	79.	Quest for Camelot	22,931,682
30.	You've Got Mail	63,762,374	80.	Rounders	22,921,898
31.	Hope Floats	60,110,313	81.	Beloved	22,747,234
32.	U.S. Marshals	57,833,603	82.	The Borrowers	22,619,589
33.	The Man in the Iron Mask	56,968,169	83.	Jackie Brown*	22,470,563
34.	Everest	55,742,120	84.	He Got Game	21,567,853
35.	Snake Eyes	55,591,409	85.	The Apostle*	20,695,276
36.	What Dreams May Come	55,382,891	86.	Psycho	20,363,450
37.	Small Soldiers	55,143,823	87.	Mighty Joe Young	20,028,356
38.	The Prince of Egypt	55,106,631	88.	John Carpenter's Vampires	19,967,510
39.	Halloween: H20	55,041,738	89.	Jane Austen's Mafia!	19,889,299
40.	Star Trek: Insurrection	53,895,383	90.	Hard Rain	19,870,567
41.	Tomorrow Never Dies*	51,989,026	91.	Species II	19,221,174
42.	Patch Adams	46,444,325	92.	The Replacement Killers	19,204,929
43.	Practical Magic	46,404,796	93.	The Odd Couple II	18,912,328
44.	The Negotiator	44,748,766	94.	The Faculty	18,409,135
45.	Meet Joe Black	43,240,705	95.	Simon Birch	18,253,415
46.	Wag the Dog*	42,869,209	96.	Disturbing Behavior	17,509,368
47.	Ronin	41,552,061	97.	The Big Lebowski	17,498,804
48.	The Siege	39,908,508	98.	Half Baked	17,460,020
49.	Primary Colors	39,299,835	99.	54	16,757,163
50.	I Still Know What You Did Last Summer	38,889,884	100.	Dance with Me	15,923,354

THE TOP 50 FOREIGN-LANGUAGE FILMS

They came, we saw, they conquered: These are the foreign-language films that won North Americans over, subtitles and all. In 1998, we hailed the new emperor (and clown prince), Roberto Benigni, whose *Life Is Beautiful* claimed two Academy Awards and more than doubled the box office of the previous leader, *The Postman*. Also pulling into the list this year was *Central Station*. (Source: *Variety*)

Rank	Film (year of U.S. release, director, country of origin)
1.	*Life Is Beautiful* (1998, Benigni, Italy)
2.	*The Postman (Il Postino)* (1995, Radford, Italy)
3.	*Like Water for Chocolate* (1993, Arau, Mexico)
4.	*I Am Curious (Yellow)* (1969, Sjoman, Sweden)
5.	*La Dolce Vita* (1960, Fellini, Italy)
6.	*La Cage aux folles* (1979, Molinaro, France/Italy)
7.	*Z* (1969, Costa-Gavras, France)
8.	*A Man and a Woman* (1966, Lelouch, France)
9.	*Cinema Paradiso* (1990, Tornatore, Italy/France)
10.	*Emmanuelle* (1975, Jaeckin, France)
11.	*Das Boot* (1982, Peterson, Germany)
12.	*8½* (1963, Fellini, Italy)
13.	*My Life as a Dog* (1987, Hallström, Sweden)
14.	*Elvira Madigan* (1967, Widerberg, Sweden)
15.	*The Story of O* (1975, Jaeckin, France)
16.	*Shall We Dance?* (1997, Suo, Japan)
17.	*Yesterday, Today and Tomorrow* (1964, de Sica, Italy)
18.	*Marriage Italian Style* (1964, de Sica, Italy)
19.	*Dear John* (1964, Lindgren, Sweden)
20.	*Cousin, Cousine* (1976, Tacchella, France)
21.	*Belle de Jour* (1967, Bunuel, France/Italy)
22.	*Women on the Verge of a Nervous Breakdown* (1988, Almodóvar, Spain)
23.	*Fanny and Alexander* (1983, Bergman, Sweden)
24.	*Eat Drink Man Woman* (1994, Lee, Taiwan)
25.	*Two Women* (1961, de Sica, Italy)

Rank	Film (year of U.S. release, director, country of origin)
26.	*The Wedding Banquet* (1993, Lee, Taiwan)
27.	*Diva* (1982, Beineix, France)
28.	*Swept Away* (1975, Wertmüller, Italy)
29.	*Central Station* (1998, Salles, France/Brazil)
30.	*The Garden of the Finzi-Continis* (1971, de Sica, Italy)
31.	*La Cage aux folles II* (1981, Molinaro, France)
32.	*Cyrano de Bergerac* (1990, Rappeneau, France)
33.	*Kolya* (1997, Sverak, Czech Republic)
34.	*King of Hearts* (1967, de Broca, France/England)
35.	*Indochine* (1992, Wargnier, France)
36.	*Europa, Europa* (1991, Holland, France/Germany)
37.	*Belle Epoque* (1993, Trueba, Spain)
38.	*Jean de Florette* (1987, Berri, France)
39.	*Au revoir les enfants* (1988, Malle, France)
40.	*Farewell My Concubine* (1993, Chen, Hong Kong)
41.	*Madame Rosa* (1978, Mizrahi, France)
42.	*Babette's Feast* (1988, Axel, Denmark)
43.	*La Femme Nikita* (1990, Besson, France/Italy)
44.	*Wings of Desire* (1988, Wenders, Germany)
45.	*The Decline of the American Empire* (1986, Arcand, Canada)
46.	*Manon of the Spring* (1987, Berri, France)
47.	*Mediterraneo* (1991, Salvatores, Italy)
48.	*Antonia's Line* (1995, Gorris, Belgium/UK/The Netherlands)
49.	*Tie Me Up! Tie Me Down!* (1990, Almodóvar, Spain)
50.	*Red* (1994, Kieslowski, France)

ALL-TIME INTERNATIONAL BOX-OFFICE CHAMPS

Saving Private Ryan fights its way to the top, as *Armageddon* hurtles on to box-office heights. The question is, how large a universe can *Star Wars—The Phantom Menace* conquer? (Source: *Variety*)

Rank	Film, Year of Release	B.O. Gross (millions)	Rank	Film, Year of Release	B.O. Gross (millions)
1.	*Titanic*, 1997	$1,810	11.	*The Empire Strikes Back*, 1980	528
2.	*Jurassic Park*, 1993	920	12.	*Ghost*, 1990	518
3.	*Independence Day*, 1996	811	13.	*Aladdin*, 1992	497
4.	*Star Wars*, 1977	776	14.	*Indiana Jones and the Last Crusade*, 1989	495
5.	*The Lion King*, 1994	767	15.	*Twister*, 1996	494
6.	*E.T., the Extra-Terrestrial*, 1982	705	16.	*Saving Private Ryan, 1998*	479
7.	*Forrest Gump*, 1994	680	17.	*Terminator 2: Judgment Day*, 1991	517
8.	*Star Wars—The Phantom Menace*, 1999	651	18.	*Home Alone*, 1990	475
9.	*The Lost World: Jurassic Park*, 1997	614	19.	*Return of the Jedi*, 1983	465
10.	*Men in Black*, 1997	577	20.	*Armageddon, 1998*	464

THE AMERICAN FILM INSTITUTE'S TOP 100

To celebrate 100 years of movie making (1896–1996), more than 1,500 ballots were sent to leaders in the industry (and a few outsiders, including President and Mrs. Clinton) to rank the top American films. Controversial outcome? You bet. See how your favorites match up with their list. Those in bold are also among PEOPLE's movie critic Leah Rozen's list of the best (see page 101).

1. **Citizen Kane** (1941)
2. **Casablanca** (1942)
3. **The Godfather** (1972)
4. **Gone With the Wind** (1939)
5. Lawrence of Arabia (1962)
6. **The Wizard of Oz** (1939)
7. **The Graduate** (1967)
8. On the Waterfront (1954)
9. **Schindler's List** (1993)
10. **Singin' in the Rain** (1952)
11. It's a Wonderful Life (1946)
12. **Sunset Boulevard** (1950)
13. The Bridge on the River Kwai (1957)
14. **Some Like It Hot** (1959)
15. Star Wars (1977)
16. **All About Eve** (1950)
17. **The African Queen** (1951)
18. **Psycho** (1960)
19. **Chinatown** (1974)
20. One Flew Over the Cuckoo's Nest (1975)
21. **The Grapes of Wrath** (1940)
22. **2001: A Space Odyssey** (1968)
23. **The Maltese Falcon** (1941)
24. **Raging Bull** (1980)
25. **E.T., the Extra-Terrestrial** (1982)
26. **Dr. Strangelove** (1964)
27. Bonnie and Clyde (1967)
28. Apocalypse Now (1979)
29. Mr. Smith Goes to Washington (1939)
30. The Treasure of Sierra Madre (1948)
31. Annie Hall (1977)
32. The Godfather Part II (1974)
33. **High Noon** (1952)
34. To Kill a Mockingbird (1962)
35. **It Happened One Night** (1934)
36. Midnight Cowboy (1969)
37. **The Best Years of Our Lives** (1946)
38. **Double Indemnity** (1944)
39. Doctor Zhivago (1965)
40. North by Northwest (1959)
41. West Side Story (1961)
42. **Rear Window** (1954)
43. King Kong (1933)
44. **The Birth of a Nation** (1915)
45. A Streetcar Named Desire (1951)
46. A Clockwork Orange (1971)
47. Taxi Driver (1976)
48. **Jaws** (1975)
49. **Snow White and the Seven Dwarfs** (1937)
50. **Butch Cassidy and the Sundance Kid** (1969)

51. The Philadelphia Story (1940)
52. From Here to Eternity (1953)
53. Amadeus (1984)
54. All Quiet on the Western Front (1930)
55. **The Sound of Music** (1965)
56. M*A*S*H (1970)
57. The Third Man (1949)
58. Fantasia (1940)
59. **Rebel Without a Cause** (1955)
60. Raiders of the Lost Ark (1981)
61. Vertigo (1958)
62. Tootsie (1982)
63. Stagecoach (1939)
64. Close Encounters of the Third Kind (1977)
65. The Silence of the Lambs (1991)
66. **Network** (1976)
67. **The Manchurian Candidate** (1962)
68. An American in Paris (1951)
69. **Shane** (1953)
70. The French Connection (1971)
71. Forrest Gump (1994)
72. Ben-Hur (1959)
73. Wuthering Heights (1939)
74. **The Gold Rush** (1925)
75. Dances with Wolves (1990)
76. City Lights (1931)
77. **American Graffiti** (1973)
78. Rocky (1976)
79. The Deer Hunter (1978)
80. **The Wild Bunch** (1969)
81. Modern Times (1936)
82. Giant (1956)
83. Platoon (1986)
84. Fargo (1996)
85. Duck Soup (1933)
86. Mutiny on the Bounty (1935)
87. Frankenstein (1931)
88. Easy Rider (1969)
89. Patton (1970)
90. The Jazz Singer (1927)
91. My Fair Lady (1964)
92. A Place in the Sun (1951)
93. The Apartment (1960)
94. GoodFellas (1990)
95. **Pulp Fiction** (1994)
96. **The Searchers** (1956)
97. **Bringing Up Baby** (1938)
98. Unforgiven (1992)
99. Guess Who's Coming to Dinner (1967)
100. Yankee Doodle Dandy (1942)

THE TOP DOCUMENTARY FILMS

Could there be a new king of the hill? *Everest* climbs steadily to the top of the charts, towering over all docs since the 1980s. *Thrill Ride* also gains height as it continues to give audiences the ride of their lives. Debuting in 1998, *Mysteries of Egypt* joins the ranks as moviegoers show an interest in the world of the unknown and *Africa's Elephant Kingdom* takes a giant step into the winner's circle, stomping out its competitors. (Source: *Variety*)

Rank	Film (year of release)	B.O. Gross
1.	To Fly (1976)	$82,500,000
2.	Everest (1998)	70,500,000
3.	In Search of Noah's Ark (1977)	55,700,000
4.	The Dream Is Alive (1985)	55,200,000
5.	Grand Canyon: The Hidden Secrets (1984)	52,800,000
6.	Raw (1987)	50,500,000
7.	This Is Cinerama (1952)	41,600,000
8.	Richard Pryor Live on the Sunset Strip (1982)	36,300,000
9.	Woodstock (1970)	34,800,000
10.	Seven Wonders of the World (1956)	32,100,000
11.	Cinerama Holiday (1955)	29,600,000
12.	Beavers (1988)	26,400,000
13.	Chariots of the Gods (1973)	25,900,000
14.	Beyond and Back (1978)	23,800,000
15.	To the Limit (1989)	23,500,000

Rank	Film (year of release)	B.O. Gross
16.	Blue Planet (1990)	22,800,000
17.	In Search of Historic Jesus (1980)	22,400,000
18.	The Bermuda Triangle (1978)	22,200,000
19.	The Late Great Planet Earth (1977)	19,500,000
20.	The Vanishing Wilderness (1973)	17,000,000
21.	Richard Pryor Here and Now (1983)	16,200,000
22.	Richard Pryor Live In Concert (1979)	15,800,000
23.	Mysteries of Egypt (1998)	15,100,000
24.	Truth or Dare (1991)	15,000,000
25.	Thrill Ride (1997)	14,400,000
26.	You So Crazy (1994)	10,200,000
27.	Africa's Elephant Kingdom (1998)	9,800,000
28.	Endless Summer (1966)	9,400,000
29.	Dirt (1979)	9,200,000
30.	U2: Rattle and Hum (1988)	8,600,000

OLD MONEY WALLOPS THE NOUVEAU RICHE

The top-grossing movies are nearly all recently released films, due to rising ticket prices. But what if the playing field is leveled? Exhibitor Relations Co., Inc. has compiled the following inflation-adjusted list of the highest-grossing films of all time, including reissues (*). Figures are as of August 31, 1999.

Rank	Title	Opening Date	Adjusted Gross
1.	Gone With the Wind*	1939	$940,838,918
2.	Star Wars*	1977	835,380,901
3.	The Sound of Music*	1965	667,928,113
4.	E.T., the Extra-Terrestrial*	1982	637,783,431
5.	The Ten Commandments	1956	614,390,000
6.	Titanic	1997	613,735,502
7.	Jaws*	1975	600,689,655
8.	Snow White*	1937	511,210,000
9.	101 Dalmatians*	1961	493,423,938
10.	The Empire Strikes Back*	1980	460,117,346
11.	Ben-Hur*	1959	459,620,000
12.	The Exorcist	1973	442,200,000
13.	Return of the Jedi*	1983	440,983,089
14.	The Sting	1973	427,771,756
15.	Star Wars: Episode I—The Phantom Menace	1999	409,084,394
16.	Raiders of the Lost Ark*	1981	408,897,910
17.	Jurassic Park	1993	404,245,969
18.	Fantasia*	1940	389,473,913
19.	The Godfather	1972	372,165,989
20.	Forrest Gump	1994	369,916,428

THE BIGGEST HITS, YEAR BY YEAR

The following are the top five movies of the year based on data from *Variety*, beginning with 1939, when a Hollywood legend, *Gone With the Wind*, hit the theaters. Dollar figures listed are rentals (the amount of money collected by the studio), rather than box-office grosses, a relatively new method of measuring a film's box-office strength. (Figures for 1941 films, with the exception of *Sergeant York*, are rough estimates.)

1939

1. Gone With the Wind	$77,641,106
2. The Wizard of Oz	4,544,851
3. The Hunchback of Notre Dame (tie)	1,500,000
3. Jesse James (tie)	1,500,000
3. Mr. Smith Goes to Washington (tie)	1,500,000

1940

1. Fantasia	$41,660,000
2. Pinocchio	40,442,000
3. Boom Town	4,586,415
4. Rebecca (tie)	1,500,000
4. Santa Fe Trail (tie)	1,500,000

1941

1. Sergeant York	$6,135,707
2. Dive Bomber (tie)	1,500,000
2. Honky Tonk (tie)	1,500,000
2. The Philadelphia Story (tie)	1,500,000
2. A Yank in the R.A.F. (tie)	1,500,000

1942

1. Bambi	$47,265,000
2. Mrs. Miniver	5,390,009
3. Yankee Doodle Dandy	4,719,681
4. Random Harvest	4,665,501
5. Casablanca	4,145,178

1943

1. This Is the Army	$8,301,000
2. For Whom the Bell Tolls	7,100,000
3. The Outlaw	5,075,000
4. The Song of Bernadette	5,000,000
5. Stage Door Canteen	4,339,532

1944

1. Going My Way	$6,500.000
2. Meet Me in St. Louis	5,132,202
3. Since You Went Away	4,924,756
4. 30 Seconds over Tokyo	4,471,080
5. White Cliffs of Dover	4,045,250

1945

1. The Bells of St. Mary's	$8,000,000
2. Leave Her to Heaven	5,500,000
3. Spellbound	4,970,583
4. Anchors Aweigh	4,778,679
5. The Valley of Decision	4,566,374

1946

1. Song of the South	$29,228,717
2. The Best Years of Our Lives (tie)	11,300,000
2. Duel in the Sun (tie)	11,300,000
4. The Jolson Story	7,600,000
5. Blue Skies	5,700,000

1947

1. Welcome Stranger	$6,100,000
2. The Egg and I	5,500,000
3. Unconquered	5,250,000
4. Life with Father	5,057,000
5. Forever Amber	5,000,000

1948

1. The Red Shoes	$5,000,000
2. Red River	4,506,825
3. The Paleface	4,500,000
4. The Three Musketeers	4,306,876
5. Johnny Belinda	4,266,000

1949

1. Samson and Delilah	$11,500,000
2. Battleground	5,051,143
3. Jolson Sings Again (tie)	5,000,000
3. The Sands of Iwo Jima (tie)	5,000,000
5. I Was a Male War Bride	4,100,000

1950

1. Cinderella	$41,087,000
2. King Solomon's Mines	5,586,000
3. Annie Get Your Gun	4,919,394
4. Cheaper by the Dozen	4,425,000
5. Father of the Bride	4,054,405

1951

1. Quo Vadis?	$11,901,662
2. Alice in Wonderland	7,196,000
3. Show Boat	5,533,000
4. David and Bathsheba	4,720,000
5. The Great Caruso	4,531,000

1952

1. This Is Cinerama	$15,400,000
2. The Greatest Show on Earth	14,000,000
3. The Snows of Kilimanjaro	6,500,000
4. Ivanhoe	6,258,000
5. Hans Christian Andersen	6,000,000

1953

1. Peter Pan	$37,584,000
2. The Robe	17,500,000
3. From Here to Eternity	12,200,000
4. Shane	9,000,000
5. How To Marry a Millionaire	7,300,000

1954

1. White Christmas	$12,000,000
2. 20,000 Leagues Under the Sea	11,267,000
3. Rear Window	9,812,271
4. The Caine Mutiny	8,700,000
5. The Glenn Miller Story	7,590,994

1955

1. Lady and the Tramp	$40,249,000
2. Cinerama Holiday	12,000,000
3. Mister Roberts	8,500,000
4. Battle Cry	8,100,000
5. Oklahoma!	7,100,000

1956

1. The Ten Commandments	$43,000,000
2. Around the World in 80 Days	23,120,000
3. Giant	14,000,000
4. Seven Wonders of the World	12,500,000
5. The King and I	8,500,000

1957

1. The Bridge on the River Kwai	$17,195,000
2. Peyton Place	11,500,000
3. Sayonara	10,500,000
4. Old Yeller	10,050,000
5. Raintree County	5,962,839

1958

1. South Pacific	$17,500,000
2. Auntie Mame	9,300,000
3. Cat on a Hot Tin Roof	8,785,162
4. No Time for Sergeants	7,500,000
5. Gigi	7,321.423

1959

1. Ben-Hur	$36,992,088
2. Sleeping Beauty	21,998,000
3. The Shaggy Dog	12,317,000
4. Operation Petticoat	9,321,555
5. Darby O'Gill and the Little People	8,336,000

1960

1. Swiss Family Robinson	$20,178,000
2. Psycho	11,200,000
3. Spartacus	10,300,454
4. Exodus	8,331,582
5. The Alamo	7,918,776

1961

1. 101 Dalmatians	$68,648,000
2. West Side Story	19,645,570
3. The Guns of Navarone	13,000,000
4. El Cid	12,000,000
5. The Absent-Minded Professor	11,426,000

1962

1. How the West Was Won	$20,932,883
2. Lawrence of Arabia	20,310,000
3. The Longest Day	17,600,000
4. In Search of the Castaways	9,975,000
5. The Music Man	8,100,000

1963

1. Cleopatra	$26,000,000
2. It's a Mad, Mad, Mad, Mad World	20,849,786
3. Tom Jones	16,925,988
4. Irma La Douce	11,921,784
5. The Sword in the Stone	10,475,000

1964

1. Mary Poppins	$45,000,000
2. Goldfinger	22,997,706
3. The Carpetbaggers	15,500,000
4. My Fair Lady	12,000,000
5. From Russia with Love	9,924,279

1965

1. The Sound of Music	$79,975,000
2. Doctor Zhivago	47,116,811
3. Thunderball	28,621,434
4. Those Magnificent Men in Their Flying Machines	14,000,000
5. That Darn Cat	12,628,000

1966

1. Hawaii	$15,553,018
2. The Bible	15,000,000
3. Who's Afraid of Virginia Woolf?	14,500,000
4. A Man for All Seasons	12,750,000
5. Lt. Robin Crusoe, USN	10,164,000

1967

1. The Jungle Book	$60,964,000
2. The Graduate	44,090,729
3. Guess Who's Coming to Dinner	25,500,000
4. Bonnie and Clyde	22,800,000
5. The Dirty Dozen	20,403,826

1968

1. Funny Girl	$26,325,000
2. 2001: A Space Odyssey	25,521,917
3. The Odd Couple	20,000,000
4. Bullitt	19,000,000
5. Romeo and Juliet	17,473,000

1969

1. Butch Cassidy and the Sundance Kid	$46,039,000
2. The Love Bug	23,150,000
3. Midnight Cowboy	20,499,282
4. Easy Rider	19,100,000
5. Hello, Dolly!	15,200,000

1970

1. Love Story	$50,000,000
2. Airport	45,220,118
3. M*A*S*H	36,720,000
4. Patton	28,100,000
5. The Aristocats	26,462,000

1971

1. Fiddler on the Roof	$38,251,196
2. Billy Jack	32,500,000
3. The French Connection	26,315,000
4. Summer of '42	20,500,000
5. Diamonds Are Forever	19,726,829

1972

1. The Godfather	$86,691,000
2. The Poseidon Adventure	42,000,000
3. What's Up Doc?	28,000,000
4. Deliverance	22,600,000
5. Jeremiah Johnson	21,900,000

1973

1. The Exorcist	$89,000,000
2. The Sting	78,212,000
3. American Graffiti	55,128,175
4. Papillon	22,500,000
5. The Way We Were	22,457,000

1974

1. The Towering Inferno	$52,000,000
2. Blazing Saddles	47,800,000
3. Young Frankenstein	38,823,000
4. Earthquake	35,849,994
5. The Trial of Billy Jack	31,100,000

1975

1. Jaws	$129,549,325
2. One Flew over the Cuckoo's Nest	59,939,701
3. The Rocky Horror Picture Show	49,782,690
4. Shampoo	23,822,000
5. Dog Day Afternoon	22,500,000

1976

1. Rocky	$56,524,972
2. A Star Is Born	37,100,000
3. King Kong	36,915,000
4. Silver Streak	30,018,000
5. All the President's Men	30,000,000

1977

1. Star Wars	$270,918,000
2. Close Encounters of the Third Kind	82,750,000
3. Saturday Night Fever	74,100,000
4. Smokey and the Bandit	58,949,939
5. The Goodbye Girl	41,839,170

1978

1. Grease	$96,300,000
2. Superman	82,800,000
3. National Lampoon's Animal House	70,826,000
4. Every Which Way but Loose	51,900,000
5. Jaws 2	50,431,964

1979

1. Kramer vs. Kramer	$59,986,335
2. Star Trek: The Motion Picture	56,000,000
3. The Jerk	42,989,656
4. Rocky II	42,169,387
5. Alien	40,300,000

1980

1. The Empire Strikes Back	$173,814,000
2. 9 to 5	59,100,000
3. Stir Crazy	58,364,420
4. Airplane!	40,610,000
5. Any Which Way You Can	40,500,000

1981

1. Raiders of the Lost Ark	$115,598,000
2. Superman II	65,100,000
3. On Golden Pond	61,174,744
4. Arthur	42,000,000
5. Stripes	40,886,589

1982

1. E.T., the Extra-Terrestrial	$228,168,939
2. Tootsie	96,292,736
3. Rocky III	66,262,796
4. An Officer and a Gentleman	55,223,000
5. Porky's	54,000,000

1983

1. Return of the Jedi	$191,648,000
2. Terms of Endearment	50,250,000
3. Trading Places	40,600,000
4. WarGames	38,519,833
5. Superman III	37,200,000

1984

1. Ghostbusters	$130,211,324
2. Indiana Jones and the Temple of Doom	109,000,000
3. Beverly Hills Cop	108,000,000
4. Gremlins	79,500,000
5. The Karate Kid	43,432,881

1985

1. Back to the Future	$104,408,738
2. Rambo: First Blood Part II	78,919,250
3. Rocky IV	76,023,246
4. The Color Purple	47,900,000
5. Out of Africa	43,103,469

1986

1. Top Gun	$79,400,000
2. "Crocodile" Dundee	70,227,000
3. Platoon	69,742,143
4. The Karate Kid, Part II	58,362,026
5. Star Trek IV: The Voyage Home	56,820,071

1987

1. Three Men and a Baby	$81,313,000
2. Beverly Hills Cop II	80,857,776
3. Fatal Attraction	70,000,000
4. Good Morning, Vietnam	58,103,000
5. The Untouchables	36,866,530

1988

1. Rain Man	$86,813,000
2. Who Framed Roger Rabbit	81,244,000
3. Coming to America	65,000,000
4. "Crocodile" Dundee II	57,300,000
5. Twins	57,715,127

1989

1. Batman	$150,500,000
2. Indiana Jones and the Last Crusade	115,500,000
3. Lethal Weapon 2	79,500,000
4. Back to the Future Part II	72,319,630
5. Honey, I Shrunk the Kids	72,007,000

1990

1. Home Alone	$140,099,000
2. Ghost	98,200,000
3. Pretty Woman	81,905,530
4. Dances with Wolves	81,537,971
5. Teenage Mutant Ninja Turtles	67,650,000

1991

1. Terminator 2: Judgment Day	$112,500,000
2. Robin Hood: Prince of Thieves	86,000,000
3. Beauty and the Beast	69,415,000
4. Hook	65,000,000
5. City Slickers	60,750,000

1992

1. Aladdin	$111,740,683
2. Home Alone 2: Lost in New York	103,377,614
3. Batman Returns	100,100,000
4. Lethal Weapon 3	80,000,000
5. A Few Good Men	71,000,000

1993

1. Jurassic Park	$212,953,437
2. Mrs. Doubtfire	111,000,000
3. The Fugitive	97,000,000
4. The Firm	77,047,044
5. Sleepless in Seattle	64,930,137

1994

1. The Lion King	$173,057,366
2. Forrest Gump	156,000,000
3. True Lies	80,000,000
4. The Santa Clause	74,348,689
5. The Flintstones	70,753,383

1995

1. Batman Forever	$105,100,000
2. Toy Story	103,200,000
3. Apollo 13	92,642,370
4. Pocahontas	67,848,010
5. Casper	49,160,810

1996

1. Independence Day	$177,190,000
2. Twister	133,464,330
3. Mission: Impossible	93,067,933
4. Jerry Maguire	74,937,042
5. The Rock	70,600,000

1997

1. The Lost World: Jurassic Park	$130,086,760
2. Men in Black	114,110,497
3. Liar Liar	95,931,900
4. Air Force One	77,734,801
5. Batman & Robin	58,492,667

1998

1. Titanic	$324,425,520
2. Armageddon	104,806,521
3. Saving Private Ryan	89,619,599
4. There's Something About Mary	74,537,493
5. Godzilla	70,850,116

THE 100 BEST MOVIES OF ALL TIME

They are the celluloid touchstones of our inner life, the enduring echoes of various generations, and the most bittersweet of social commentaries played out 10 yards high. PEOPLE's movie critic Leah Rozen has selected 100 of the greatest, an assignment as agonizing as having to pick the 10 greatest home runs ever hit in baseball.

ADAM'S RIB (1949)
Katharine Hepburn and Spencer Tracy as married attorneys on opposite sides of an attempted murder case. The smartest and funniest of their five pairings.

THE ADVENTURES OF ROBIN HOOD (1938)
There have been other Robin Hoods, including Kevin Costner and Sean Connery, but never one as appealingly roguish as Errol Flynn. A rousing adventure.

THE AFRICAN QUEEN (1951)
In a splendidly comic and sweet romance, the mismatched Humphrey Bogart and Katharine Hepburn take a slow love boat up the river in steamy Africa.

ALL ABOUT EVE (1950)
Smart and tart. Director-writer Joseph Mankiewicz's acerbic masterpiece about theater folk, with Bette Davis at her caustic best.

AMERICAN GRAFFITI (1973)
In George Lucas's influential hit film, a group of California teenagers, including Ron Howard and Richard Dreyfuss, spend one long night in 1962 cruising in cars and goofing off.

BACK STREET (1941)
A vintage weepie about a woman who gives up everything for love. This second of three filmed versions of Fannie Hurst's potboiler shines brightly thanks to the incomparable Margaret Sullavan and Charles Boyer.

BADLANDS (1973)
Martin Sheen and Sissy Spacek play a young couple who go on an aimless killing spree in a chilling cult film by director Terence Malick.

BEAUTY AND THE BEAST (1946)
French surrealist Jean Cocteau's sophisticated version of the classic fairy tale *La Belle et la bete* is for grown-up romantics. Then again, the 1991 Disney version, a musical, is pretty swell too.

BELLE DE JOUR (1967)
Director Luis Buñuel's deliciously creepy movie about a bourgeois Paris housewife, a radiant Catherine Deneuve, who spends her days working in a brothel. Or does she?

THE BEST YEARS OF OUR LIVES (1946)
A moving drama about the domestic and occupational difficulties facing three returning World War II vets, with Fredric March, Dana Andrews, and Harold Russell, a real vet who had lost both arms in the war.

THE BICYCLE THIEF (1948)
Director Vittorio de Sica's heartbreaking drama, a linchpin of Italian neo-realism, about a workman who loses everything when his bicycle is stolen.

THE BIRTH OF A NATION (1915)
The first blockbuster. Although parts now seem irredeemably racist, director D. W. Griffith's epic Civil War drama is still a sight to behold.

BLADE RUNNER (1982)
The future as you don't want it to be. Gruff guy Harrison Ford stars in director Ridley Scott's greatlooking sci-fi drama.

BRINGING UP BABY (1938)
A ditzy Katharine Hepburn sets her sights on zoology professor Cary Grant in a delightful screwball comedy. And love that tiger.

BULL DURHAM (1988)
A great romance movie disguised as a baseball picture. Susan Sarandon gets to choose between minor leaguers Kevin Costner and Tim Robbins, both of whom pitch woo her way.

BUTCH CASSIDY AND THE SUNDANCE KID (1969)
In one of the all-time cool buddy movies, Paul Newman and Robert Redford display big star charisma and charm as gallivanting outlaws.

CAGED (1949)
If you see just one women-in-prison film, make it this one. Eleanor Parker stars as the good girl gone wrong.

CASABLANCA (1942)
A kiss is still a kiss, but the ones here have real staying power. This is Hollywood movie-making at its most stylishly satisfying, with Humphrey Bogart and Ingrid Bergman.

CHINATOWN (1974)
Jack Nicholson's nose gets sliced and lots of other nasty things happen in director Roman Polanski's jaundiced thriller set in '30s Los Angeles.

CITIZEN KANE (1941)
The granddaddy of all biopics, though innovative director-star Orson Welles had to change the name from William Randolph Hearst to Charles Foster Kane. A must-see for anyone interested in movies.

THE CROWD (1928)
This silent movie, directed by King Vidor, movingly depicts the everyday life of a young white-collar worker and his wife in New

York City. It shows just how fluid and powerful the images in silent film had become right before sound took over.

DAVID COPPERFIELD (1934)
A perfect film adaptation of Charles Dickens's novel about the adventures of an orphaned youth. W. C. Fields is a hoot as Mr. Micawber.

DAY FOR NIGHT (1973)
French director François Truffaut's valentine to movie-making contains sly references and in-jokes to many of his earlier films. With Jacqueline Bisset and Jean-Pierre Léaud.

DEAD MAN WALKING (1995)
No matter where you stand on the death penalty, this powerful drama scores in telling the story of a nun (Susan Sarandon) who guides a murderer (Sean Penn) to contrition before his execution. Tim Robbins directed.

DO THE RIGHT THING (1989)
Director Spike Lee's street-smart drama about one very hot summer day in a tense Brooklyn neighborhood has plenty to say about race relations and the need for more and better communication.

DOUBLE INDEMNITY (1944)
Barbara Stanwyck, at her bad-girl best, sweet-talks Fred Mac-Murray into helping her kill her husband. Billy Wilder directed.

DR. STRANGELOVE... (1962)
A savagely funny black comedy, though it's a tad dated now, about the nuclear bomb and world politics. Stanley Kubrick directed and Peter Sellers and George C. Scott star.

THE EMPIRE STRIKES BACK (1980)
The best of the *Star Wars* trilogy. Stars Harrison Ford, Carrie Fisher, and Mark Hamill.

E.T., THE EXTRA-TERRESTRIAL (1982)
It may be simple-minded and sentimental, but who can resist this sweet tale of the friendship between a suburban youth and an alien marooned on Earth?

FRANKENSTEIN (1931)
Still the eeriest, and most humane, version of Mary Wollstonecraft Shelley's classic monster tale. With Boris Karloff as the big guy.

THE GENERAL (1926)
Buster Keaton, one of the comic glories of the silent era, piles on brilliant sight gag after sight gag in this Civil War comedy.

THE GODFATHER (1972)
A family drama about the troubled and violent Corleone clan. Director Francis Ford Coppola, with the help of Marlon Brando, James Caan, and a very young Al Pacino, made the ultimate gangster film.

THE GOLD RUSH (1925)
Charlie Chaplin's little tramp seeks his fortune in the Yukon. Watch for the justly famous shoe-eating scene in which Chaplin twirls shoelaces with a fork as if eating spaghetti.

GONE WITH THE WIND (1939)
This Civil War–era drama is big and long and we wouldn't change a minute of it. Except maybe the ending. But, tomorrow's another day, and maybe Rhett will come back then. With Clark Gable and Vivien Leigh.

THE GRADUATE (1968)
In a wonderfully wry comedy, Dustin Hoffman passes his first summer after college floating in his parents' pool and having a desultory affair with Anne Bancroft. Nearly 30 years later, this one still seems fresh.

THE GRAPES OF WRATH (1940)
Director John Ford's masterful adaptation of John Steinbeck's bleak novel about depression-era Oklahomans who head off for what they hope will be a better life in California. With Henry Fonda and Jane Darwell.

A HARD DAY'S NIGHT (1964)
The swinging '60s encapsulated, minus the politics. This first Beatles film is flat-out zany fun.

HIGH NOON (1952)
The Western pared to its bone. With Gary Cooper as the principled lawman who has to go it alone against the bad guys.

HIS GIRL FRIDAY (1940)
Speed is of the essence in this newspaper comedy, with Rosalind Russell and Cary Grant competing to see who can insult the other faster.

HOLIDAY INN (1942)
When Bing Crosby starts singing "White Christmas," you just know it's going to snow in time. Crosby and Fred Astaire costar in this chipper musical as the owners of a hotel where they put on shows with holiday themes.

HUD (1963)
Paul Newman as one of the screen's first anti-heroes, an amoral cowboy who brings no good to all whom he touches. With Melvyn Douglas and Patricia Neal.

INVASION OF THE BODY SNATCHERS (1955)
Low-budget, paranoid '50s sci-fi allegory about aliens taking over residents of a small town. The '78 remake can't hold a pod to it.

IT HAPPENED ONE NIGHT (1934)
Screwball comedy meets road picture in director Frank Capra's jaunty film about a runaway heiress who spars and sparks with a newspaperman. With Claudette Colbert and Clark Gable.

JAWS (1975)
Jumbo shark on the loose. Director Steven Spielberg scored his first blockbuster with this bloody thriller. Dig John Williams's carnivorous score.

THE LADY EVE (1941)

Wickedly entertaining comedy by director Preston Sturges about a con woman (Barbara Stanwyck) who hustles a youthful million-aire (Henry Fonda), only to real-ize almost too late that she's actu-ally in love with the big lug.

THE LAST METRO (1980)

A moving drama about a French theatrical troupe in occupied Paris during World War II. François Truffaut directed, and Catherine Deneuve and Gérard Depardieu star.

LONE STAR (1996)

Director John Sayles's sweeping drama about fathers and sons, the past catching up to us, and cul-tural diversity, all crammed into the lives of folks in one small Texas border town.

LONG DAY'S JOURNEY INTO NIGHT (1962)

Playwright Eugene O'Neill's autobiographical masterpiece, brought to the screen with all the hurt showing. Katharine Hepburn digs deep as the morphine-addicted mother. Also stars Ralph Richardson and Jason Robards.

LONGTIME COMPANION (1990)

An AIDS drama about a tight-knit group of male friends in New York City in the 1980s which poignantly depicts just how devastating the disease is to both those who have it and those they leave behind.

MCCABE AND MRS. MILLER (1971)

Director Robert Altman's lyri-cally haunting look at how the West was wasted, with Warren Beatty as a gunfighter who sets up a brothel and Julie Christie as his opium-addicted madam.

THE MALTESE FALCON (1941)

Love that black bird. With Humphrey Bogart as private eye Sam Spade, who takes no guff from anyone, including conniving Mary Astor.

THE MANCHURIAN CANDIDATE (1962)

A sharp-witted political thriller, from which one suspects Oliver Stone learned much of what he knows. With Frank Sinatra, Laurence Harvey, and Angela Lansbury.

MEAN STREETS (1973)

Loyalty among thieves only goes so far, as a group of boyhood friends in Little Italy discover upon growing up. Martin Scors-ese's breakthrough film, with Robert De Niro and Harvey Keitel.

MILDRED PIERCE (1945)

The ultimate Joan Crawford movie. She plays a suburban divorcée who makes a fortune as a hard-working restaurateur, only to see her spoiled daughter steal her beau.

NETWORK (1976)

Biliousness raised to high art. Paddy Chayefsky's sharp satire about the influence of the media. With Peter Finch, William Holden, and Faye Dunaway.

A NIGHT AT THE OPERA (1935)

The Marx Brothers reek loony havoc when—and before and after—the fat lady sings. Also stars Margaret Dumont, the matronly butt of so many of Groucho's jokes.

NIGHTS OF CABIRIA (1957)

Italian director Federico Fellini, in directing wife Giuletta Masina in her greatest role as a hard-luck prostitute in Rome, made a near-perfect film that will have you laughing one minute, near tears the next. The musical *Sweet Charity* is based on *Cabiria*.

NOTORIOUS (1946)

Alfred Hitchcock at his per-versely romantic best. Sexy and scary, with American agent Cary Grant sending lady love Ingrid Bergman to wed a covert Nazi.

PERSONA (1966)

The personalities of two women, a nurse and the mentally ill patient she is caring for, begin to overlap and mesh in Swedish filmmaker Ingmar Bergman's brooding, disturbing drama. With Liv Ullmann and Bibi Andersson.

PICNIC AT HANGING ROCK (1975)

Spooky goings-on at a girls' school in turn-of-the-century Australia when several of the stu-dents mysteriously vanish, seem-ingly into thin air, while at a pic-nic. Peter Weir directed.

PLACES IN THE HEART (1984)

A lovely movie about human frailty and redemption from director Robert Benton. Sally Field stars as a newly widowed Texas farm woman who perse-veres despite hard times.

THE PLAYER (1992)

Director Robert Altman zings Hollywood in a biting satire about a studio executive who gets away with murder. Tim Robbins has the lead, but masses of other big names show up for cameos.

PSYCHO (1960)

Janet Leigh, get away from that shower. Hitchcock's scalding shocker stars Tony Perkins as a twisted hotel keeper who doesn't like his guests to check out.

PULP FICTION (1994)

Violent, amusing, and cleverly structured, director Quentin Tarantino's movie is vastly more entertaining than the horde of imitations it has spawned. With John Travolta, Bruce Willis, and Samuel L. Jackson.

THE PURPLE ROSE OF CAIRO (1984)

When the hero (Jeff Daniels) of a '30s movie steps out of the screen to begin making time with one of his biggest fans (Mia Farrow), the line between real life during the depression and movie fantasy becomes all too clear in Woody Allen's comic masterpiece.

QUEEN CHRISTINA (1937)

Greta Garbo is at her most androgynously alluring in a romanticized Hollywood biopic about a 17th-century Swedish queen. Check out Garbo's enigmatic expression in the famous final shot.

THE QUIET MAN (1952)

John Wayne and director John Ford left the Wild West behind for the greener fields of Ireland, with splendid results. In this boisterous, appealing love story, Wayne plays an American boxer who woos Irish lass Maureen O'Hara.

RAGING BULL (1980)

Director Martin Scorsese's penetrating look at the troubled life of pugilist Jake La Motta boasts one of Robert De Niro's finest performances.

RASHOMON (1950)

Truth proves elusive as four people involved each give differing accounts of a rape-murder in Japanese director Akira Kurosawa's brilliant drama.

REAR WINDOW (1954)

James Stewart and a sexy Grace Kelly star in Alfred Hitchcock's sophisticated thriller about an invalided photographer who spots a murder across his apartment courtyard.

REBEL WITHOUT A CAUSE (1955)

Alienated teens reign supreme as James Dean—who died before the movie was released—and Natalie Wood express the suffering of their generation.

ROMAN HOLIDAY (1953)

A charming romp with Audrey Hepburn at her most appealingly gamine as a princess who ditches her royal duties and takes up with Gregory Peck, an American newspaperman.

SAVING PRIVATE RYAN (1998)

War is hell, and never more so than in director Steven Spielberg's monumental film about a group of American soldiers who land in France on D-Day. Tom Hanks's final command, "Earn this," haunts us still.

SCHINDLER'S LIST (1983)

Director Steven Spielberg's powerful retelling of the story of businessman Oskar Schindler, who saved hundreds of Jews from the Nazi gas chambers during World War II. With Liam Neeson as Schindler and Ben Kingsley as his Jewish factory foreman.

THE SEARCHERS (1956)

In a multilayered Western by director John Ford, John Wayne spends years searching for his niece, Natalie Wood, after she is captured by Native Americans. One of the most influential films ever made.

SHANE (1953)

A retired gunfighter rides into town and helps out a homesteading couple and their young son. Sounds simple, but it's anything but. With Alan Ladd, Jean Arthur, and Brandon de Wilde.

THE SHOP AROUND THE CORNER (1940)

The famed "Lubitsch Touch," so named for the sophisticated comedy work of director Ernst Lubitsch, shines bright in a charming romance about two bickering shop clerks. With Jimmy Stewart and the matchless Margaret Sullavan.

SHOWBOAT (1936)

This classic musical about life aboard a Mississippi riverboat features dandy Jerome Kern tunes and a glimpse of why Paul Robeson and Helen Morgan were such electrifying performers in their day.

SINGIN' IN THE RAIN (1952)

A musical about Hollywood's awkward transition from silents to talkies, this one can't be beat, especially for Gene Kelly's singing and dancing of the damp title number.

SNOW WHITE AND THE SEVEN DWARFS (1937)

Walt Disney's first feature-length animated feature still shimmers brightly, though Snow White's brusque farewell to the dwarfs at the movie's end seems a mite ungrateful.

SOME LIKE IT HOT (1959)

The funniest movie ever made about cross-dressing. Tony Curtis and Jack Lemmon star as musicians who, after witnessing a mob hit, go undercover with an all-girl band, whose members include Marilyn Monroe. Billy Wilder directed.

THE SOUND OF MUSIC (1965)

Sure, it's sugary, but any time Julie Andrews is on screen in this Rogers and Hammerstein musical about the would-be nun who comes to stay with the Von Trapp family, all is gloriously forgiven.

SULLIVAN'S TRAVELS (1941)

A Hollywood director (Joel McCrea) rediscovers the meaning of life while traveling across America in director Preston Sturges's quick-witted comedy.

SUNSET BOULEVARD (1950)

The original. In director Billy Wilder's savage look at the underbelly of Hollywood, silent star Gloria Swanson made her big comeback playing, appropriately enough, a silent star hoping to make a comeback.

SWEET SMELL OF SUCCESS (1957)

Everyone's corrupt or corruptible in this atmospheric melodrama about nasty dealings between a Broadway press agent (Tony Curtis) and a powerful Manhattan newspaper columnist (Burt Lancaster).

TARZAN AND HIS MATE (1934)

The second of the Johnny Weismuller films about Edgar Rice

Borroughs' ape man, and the best of the series. Maureen O'Sullivan, dressed in next to nothing, makes a perky Jane.

THE TERMINATOR (1984)
Pure nihilistic fun, this sci-fi action thriller deservedly made muscleman Arnold Schwarzenegger, who plays a singularly focused android, into a big star.

THELMA AND LOUISE (1991)
Two good girls go wrong. A feminist firecracker of a movie, with strong performances by Susan Sarandon and Geena Davis. And check out the truly buff Brad Pitt.

THIS IS SPINAL TAP (1984)
This is a blast. Turn your amps up to 11 as you chuckle your way through this comic moc-umentary about a heavy metal rock group and its hangers-on. Rob Reiner directed.

TITANIC (1997)
For sheer scope and size, you gotta love it. Director James Cameron made going to the movies seem like something special again. This water-logged drama turned Leonardo DiCaprio into a household name—at least in households containing teenage girls.

TO HAVE AND HAVE NOT (1944)
Romantic sparks fly in Humprey Bogart and Lauren Bacall's first pairing, a World War II drama that borrows more than a little from *Casablanca* but boasts a comic zing all its own.

TOP HAT (1935)
Fred Astaire and Ginger Rogers dance (and sing) "Cheek to Cheek" and other great Irving Berlin tunes in their most glorious teaming. Keep an eye peeled for a young Lucille Ball in the flower shop.

2001: A SPACE ODYSSEY (1968)
Director Stanley Kubrick's hauntingly beautiful and enormously

TOP FILM SOUNDTRACKS

We love to go to the movies, but a good soundtrack means we can take them home with us, too. And fans do, as this list indicates. (Source: RIAA)

Soundtrack	Sales (in millions)
The Bodyguard	16
Saturday Night Fever	15
Purple Rain	13
Dirty Dancing	11
The Lion King	10
Titanic	10
Footloose	8
Grease	8
Top Gun	7
Waiting to Exhale	7
Flashdance	6
The Big Chill	6
Forrest Gump	5
The Jazz Singer	5
Space Jam	5
Evita	5

influential science fiction thriller. And watch out for HAL.

UNFORGIVEN (1992)
Clint Eastwood directed and stars in a mature, meditative Western about an ex–hired gun turned farmer who goes on one last killing spree.

WHITE HEAT (1949)
Jimmy Cagney at his sinister best as a gangster who can't cut his ties to his mother's apron strings. Great ending.

WHO FRAMED ROGER RABBIT (1988)
It's 'toon time as animated characters and actors interact to solve a crime in a technological bit of trickery that shows just how far animation has come since the days of Gertie the Dinosaur. 'Toon or no 'toon, Jessica Rabbit (voiced by Kathleen Turner) is vavavoom.

THE WILD BUNCH (1969)
Director Sam Pekinpah's violent tale of revenge shakes the good ol' Western by its spurs. With William Holden, Ernest Borgnine, and Robert Ryan.

WITNESS (1985)
Cultures clash as a big-city detective (Harrison Ford) hides out among the Amish in order to protect a young Amish boy who has witnessed a murder.

THE WIZARD OF OZ (1939)
Is once a year often enough? This entertaining children's musical—assuming that the kids are old enough to sit through the flying monkeys—features stellar performances by Judy Garland, Bert Lahr, Ray Bolger, and Jack Haley.

WRITTEN ON THE WIND (1956)
So bad it's good. A steamy melodrama about a very messed-up family, directed by Douglas Sirk, the master of glossy high camp, and starring Rock Hudson, Lauren Bacall, and Dorothy Malone.

HOLLYWOOD'S FOOTPRINTS OF FAME

The first footprints at Grauman's Chinese Theater, as it was originally called, were made by Norma Talmadge in 1927 when, legend holds, she accidentally stepped in wet concrete outside the building. Since then over 190 stars have been immortalized, along with their hands and feet—and sometimes noses (Jimmy Durante), fists (John Wayne), and legs (Betty Grable). Sarandon, Connery, Gere, and Howard all got stuck in cement this year, providing new visual relief to those *Star Wars* fans who spent weeks awaiting the premiere. The full Forecourt of the Stars at Mann's includes:

Abbott & Costello
Don Ameche
Julie Andrews
Edward Arnold
Fred Astaire
Gene Autry
John Barrymore
Freddie Bartholomew
Anne Baxter
Warren Beatty
Wallace Beery
Jack Benny
Edgar Bergen
Joan Blondell
Humphrey Bogart
Charles Boyer
Joe E. Brown
Yul Brynner
George Burns
Cantinflas
Eddie Cantor
Jim Carrey
Jackie Chan
Maurice Chevalier
Sean Connery
Gary Cooper
Jackie Cooper
Jeanne Crain
Joan Crawford
Bing Crosby
Tom Cruise
Bebe Daniels
Linda Darnell
Marion Davies
Bette Davis
Doris Day
Olivia de Havilland
Cecil B. DeMille
The Dionne Quintuplets
Kirk Douglas
Michael Douglas
Marie Dressler
Donald Duck
Irene Dunne
Jimmie Durante
Deanna Durbin
Clint Eastwood
Nelson Eddy
Douglas Fairbanks
Alice Faye
Rhonda Fleming

Henry Fonda
Joan Fontaine
Harrison Ford
Clark Gable
Ava Gardner
Judy Garland
Greer Garson
Janet Gaynor
Richard Gere
Mel Gibson
Danny Glover
Whoopi Goldberg
Betty Grable
Cary Grant
Johnny Grant
Rosa Grauman (founder Sid
   Grauman's mother)
Sid Grauman
Tom Hanks
Ann Harding
Jean Harlow
Rex Harrison
William S. Hart
Susan Hayward
Rita Hayworth
Van Heflin
Sonja Henie
Jean Hersholt
William F. "Bill" Hertz
Charlton Heston
Bob Hope
Ron Howard
Rock Hudson
George Jessel
Van Johnson
Al Jolson
Danny Kaye
Michael Keaton
Gene Kelly
Deborah Kerr
Alan Ladd
Dorothy Lamour
Charles Laughton
Jack Lemmon
Mervyn LeRoy
Harold Lloyd
Sophia Loren
Myrna Loy
George Lucas
William Lundigan
Jeanette MacDonald

Ali MacGraw
Shirley MacLaine
Victor McLaglen
Steve McQueen
Fredric March
Dean Martin
Tony Martin
The Marx Brothers
James Mason
Marcello Mastroianni
Walter Matthau
Lauritz Melchior
Ray Milland
Hayley Mills
Carmen Miranda
Tom Mix
Marilyn Monroe
Colleen Moore
Eddie Murphy
George Murphy
Hildegarde Neff
Pola Negri
Paul Newman
Jack Nicholson
Jack Oakie
Margaret O'Brien
Donald O'Connor
Al Pacino
Louella Parsons
Gregory Peck
Mary Pickford
Ezio Pinza
Sidney Poitier
Dick Powell
Eleanor Powell
William Powell
Tyrone Power
Anthony Quinn
George Raft
Burt Reynolds
Debbie Reynolds
The Ritz Brothers
Edward G. Robinson
May Robson
Ginger Rogers
Roy Rogers
Mickey Rooney
Jane Russell
Rosalind Russell
Susan Sarandon
Arnold Schwarzenegger

Steven Seagal
Peter Sellers
Norma Shearer
Jean Simmons
Frank Sinatra
Red Skelton
Steven Spielberg
Sylvester Stallone
Barbara Stanwyck
Star Trek crew (William
   Shatner, Leonard Nimoy,
   DeForest Kelley, James
   Doohan, Michelle Nichols,
   George Takei, Walter
   Koenig)
Star Wars characters
George Stevens
Jimmy Stewart
Meryl Streep
Gloria Swanson
Constance Talmadge
Norma Talmadge
Elizabeth Taylor
Robert Taylor
Shirley Temple
Danny Thomas
Gene Tierney
John Travolta
Lana Turner
Rudy Vallee
Dick Van Dyke
W. S. Van Dyke
Raoul Walsh
Denzel Washington
John Wayne
Clifton Webb
Oskar Werner
Richard Widmark
Esther Williams
Robin Williams
Bruce Willis
Jane Withers
Natalie Wood
Joanne Woodward
Monty Woolley
Jane Wyman
Diana Wynyard
Loretta Young
Robert Zemeckis
Adolph Zukor

THE BRIGHTEST STARS, BY YEAR

In today's high-pressure movie business, the most valuable commodity is a star who shines so bright that he or she can "open" a movie—filling seats on the basis of pure popularity regardless of the allure of the story line. Every year since 1933, Quigley Publishing has polled more than 500 moviehouse owners nationwide to determine which stars they regarded as the surest-fire box-office draw.

1933

1. Marie Dressler
2. Will Rogers
3. Janet Gaynor
4. Eddie Cantor
5. Wallace Beery
6. Jean Harlow
7. Clark Gable
8. Mae West
9. Norma Shearer
10. Joan Crawford

1934

1. Will Rogers
2. Clark Gable
3. Janet Gaynor
4. Wallace Beery
5. Mae West
6. Joan Crawford
7. Bing Crosby
8. Shirley Temple
9. Marie Dressler
10. Norma Shearer

1935

1. Shirley Temple
2. Will Rogers
3. Clark Gable
4. Fred Astaire & Ginger Rogers
5. Joan Crawford
6. Claudette Colbert
7. Dick Powell
8. Wallace Beery
9. Joe E. Brown
10. James Cagney

1936

1. Shirley Temple
2. Clark Gable
3. Fred Astaire and Ginger Rogers
4. Robert Taylor
5. Joe E. Brown
6. Dick Powell
7. Joan Crawford
8. Claudette Colbert
9. Jeanette MacDonald
10. Gary Cooper

1937

1. Shirley Temple
2. Clark Gable
3. Robert Taylor
4. Bing Crosby
5. William Powell
6. Jane Withers
7. Fred Astaire & Ginger Rogers
8. Sonja Henie
9. Gary Cooper
10. Myrna Loy

1938

1. Shirley Temple
2. Clark Gable
3. Sonja Henie
4. Mickey Rooney
5. Spencer Tracy
6. Robert Taylor
7. Myrna Loy
8. Jane Withers
9. Alice Faye
10. Tyrone Power

1939

1. Mickey Rooney
2. Tyrone Power
3. Spencer Tracy
4. Clark Gable
5. Shirley Temple
6. Bette Davis
7. Alice Faye
8. Errol Flynn
9. James Cagney
10. Sonja Henie

1940

1. Mickey Rooney
2. Spencer Tracy
3. Clark Gable
4. Gene Autry
5. Tyrone Power
6. James Cagney
7. Bing Crosby
8. Wallace Beery
9. Bette Davis
10. Judy Garland

1941

1. Mickey Rooney
2. Clark Gable
3. Abbott & Costello
4. Bob Hope
5. Spencer Tracy
6. Gene Autry
7. Gary Cooper
8. Bette Davis
9. James Cagney
10. Spencer Tracy

1942

1. Abbott & Costello
2. Clark Gable
3. Gary Cooper
4. Mickey Rooney
5. Bob Hope
6. James Cagney
7. Gene Autry
8. Betty Grable
9. Greer Garson
10. Spencer Tracy

1943

1. Betty Grable
2. Bob Hope
3. Abbott & Costello
4. Bing Crosby
5. Gary Cooper
6. Greer Garson
7. Humphrey Bogart
8. James Cagney
9. Mickey Rooney
10. Clark Gable

1944

1. Bing Crosby
2. Gary Cooper
3. Bob Hope
4. Betty Grable
5. Spencer Tracy
6. Greer Garson
7. Humphrey Bogart
8. Abbott & Costello
9. Cary Grant
10. Bette Davis

1945

1. Bing Crosby
2. Van Johnson
3. Greer Garson
4. Betty Grable
5. Spencer Tracy
6. Humphrey Bogart (tie)
6. Gary Cooper (tie)
8. Bob Hope
9. Judy Garland
10. Margaret O'Brien

1946

1. Bing Crosby
2. Ingrid Bergman
3. Van Johnson
4. Gary Cooper
5. Bob Hope
6. Humphrey Bogart
7. Greer Garson
8. Margaret O'Brien
9. Betty Grable
10. Roy Rogers

1947

1. Bing Crosby
2. Betty Grable
3. Ingrid Bergman
4. Gary Cooper
5. Humphrey Bogart
6. Bob Hope
7. Clark Gable
8. Gregory Peck
9. Claudette Colbert
10. Alan Ladd

1948

1. Bing Crosby
2. Betty Grable
3. Abbott & Costello
4. Gary Cooper
5. Bob Hope
6. Humphrey Bogart
7. Clark Gable
8. Cary Grant
9. Spencer Tracy
10. Ingrid Bergman

1949

1. Bob Hope
2. Bing Crosby
3. Abbott & Costello
4. John Wayne
5. Gary Cooper
6. Cary Grant
7. Betty Grable
8. Esther Williams
9. Humphrey Bogart
10. Clark Gable

1950

1. John Wayne
2. Bob Hope
3. Bing Crosby
4. Betty Grable
5. James Stewart
6. Abbott & Costello
7. Clifton Webb
8. Esther Williams
9. Spencer Tracy
10. Randolph Scott

1951

1. John Wayne
2. Dean Martin & Jerry Lewis
3. Betty Grable
4. Abbott & Costello
5. Bing Crosby
6. Bob Hope
7. Randolph Scott
8. Gary Cooper
9. Doris Day
10. Spencer Tracy

1952

1. Dean Martin & Jerry Lewis
2. Gary Cooper
3. John Wayne
4. Bing Crosby
5. Bob Hope
6. James Stewart
7. Doris Day
8. Gregory Peck
9. Susan Hayward
10. Randolph Scott

1953

1. Gary Cooper
2. Dean Martin & Jerry Lewis
3. John Wayne
4. Alan Ladd
5. Bing Crosby
6. Marilyn Monroe
7. James Stewart

8. Bob Hope
9. Susan Hayward
10. Randolph Scott

1954

1. John Wayne
2. Dean Martin & Jerry Lewis
3. Gary Cooper
4. James Stewart
5. Marilyn Monroe
6. Alan Ladd
7. William Holden
8. Bing Crosby
9. Jane Wyman
10. Marlon Brando

1955

1. James Stewart
2. Grace Kelly
3. John Wayne
4. William Holden
5. Gary Cooper
6. Marlon Brando
7. Dean Martin & Jerry Lewis
8. Humphrey Bogart
9. June Allyson
10. Clark Gable

1956

1. William Holden
2. John Wayne
3. James Stewart
4. Burt Lancaster
5. Glenn Ford
6. Dean Martin & Jerry Lewis
7. Gary Cooper
8. Marilyn Monroe
9. Kim Novak
10. Frank Sinatra

1957

1. Rock Hudson
2. John Wayne
3. Pat Boone
4. Elvis Presley
5. Frank Sinatra
6. Gary Cooper
7. William Holden
8. James Stewart
9. Jerry Lewis
10. Yul Brynner

1958

1. Glenn Ford
2. Elizabeth Taylor
3. Jerry Lewis
4. Marlon Brando
5. Rock Hudson
6. William Holden
7. Brigitte Bardot
8. Yul Brynner
9. James Stewart
10. Frank Sinatra

1959

1. Rock Hudson
2. Cary Grant
3. James Stewart
4. Doris Day
5. Debbie Reynolds
6. Glenn Ford
7. Frank Sinatra
8. John Wayne
9. Jerry Lewis
10. Susan Hayward

1960

1. Doris Day
2. Rock Hudson
3. Cary Grant
4. Elizabeth Taylor
5. Debbie Reynolds
6. Tony Curtis
7. Sandra Dee
8. Frank Sinatra
9. Jack Lemmon
10. John Wayne

1961

1. Elizabeth Taylor
2. Rock Hudson
3. Doris Day
4. John Wayne
5. Cary Grant
6. Sandra Dee
7. Jerry Lewis
8. William Holden
9. Tony Curtis
10. Elvis Presley

1962

1. Doris Day
2. Rock Hudson
3. Cary Grant
4. John Wayne
5. Elvis Presley
6. Elizabeth Taylor
7. Jerry Lewis
8. Frank Sinatra
9. Sandra Dee
10. Burt Lancaster

1963

1. Doris Day
2. John Wayne
3. Rock Hudson
4. Jack Lemmon
5. Cary Grant
6. Elizabeth Taylor
7. Elvis Presley
8. Sandra Dee
9. Paul Newman
10. Jerry Lewis

1964

1. Doris Day
2. Jack Lemmon
3. Rock Hudson
4. John Wayne
5. Cary Grant
6. Elvis Presley
7. Shirley MacLaine
8. Ann-Margret
9. Paul Newman
10. Jerry Lewis

1965

1. Sean Connery
2. John Wayne
3. Doris Day
4. Julie Andrews
5. Jack Lemmon
6. Elvis Presley
7. Cary Grant
8. James Stewart
9. Elizabeth Taylor
10. Richard Burton

1966

1. Julie Andrews
2. Sean Connery
3. Elizabeth Taylor
4. Jack Lemmon
5. Richard Burton
6. Cary Grant
7. John Wayne
8. Doris Day
9. Paul Newman
10. Elvis Presley

1967

1. Julie Andrews
2. Lee Marvin
3. Paul Newman
4. Dean Martin
5. Sean Connery
6. Elizabeth Taylor
7. Sidney Poitier
8. John Wayne
9. Richard Burton
10. Steve McQueen

1968

1. Sidney Poitier
2. Paul Newman
3. Julie Andrews
4. John Wayne
5. Clint Eastwood
6. Dean Martin
7. Steve McQueen
8. Jack Lemmon
9. Lee Marvin
10. Elizabeth Taylor

1969

1. Paul Newman
2. John Wayne
3. Steve McQueen
4. Dustin Hoffman
5. Clint Eastwood
6. Sidney Poitier
7. Lee Marvin
8. Jack Lemmon
9. Katharine Hepburn
10. Barbra Streisand

1970

1. Paul Newman
2. Clint Eastwood
3. Steve McQueen
4. John Wayne
5. Elliott Gould
6. Dustin Hoffman
7. Lee Marvin
8. Jack Lemmon
9. Barbra Streisand
10. Walter Matthau

1971

1. John Wayne
2. Clint Eastwood
3. Paul Newman
4. Steve McQueen
5. George C. Scott
6. Dustin Hoffman
7. Walter Matthau
8. Ali MacGraw
9. Sean Connery
10. Lee Marvin

1972

1. Clint Eastwood
2. George C. Scott
3. Gene Hackman
4. John Wayne
5. Barbra Streisand
6. Marlon Brando
7. Paul Newman
8. Steve McQueen
9. Dustin Hoffman
10. Goldie Hawn

1973

1. Clint Eastwood
2. Ryan O'Neal
3. Steve McQueen
4. Burt Reynolds
5. Robert Redford
6. Barbra Streisand
7. Paul Newman
8. Charles Bronson
9. John Wayne
10. Marlon Brando

1974

1. Robert Redford
2. Clint Eastwood
3. Paul Newman
4. Barbra Streisand
5. Steve McQueen
6. Burt Reynolds
7. Charles Bronson
8. Jack Nicholson
9. Al Pacino
10. John Wayne

1975

1. Robert Redford
2. Barbra Streisand
3. Al Pacino
4. Charles Bronson
5. Paul Newman
6. Clint Eastwood
7. Burt Reynolds
8. Woody Allen
9. Steve McQueen
10. Gene Hackman

1976

1. Robert Redford
2. Jack Nicholson
3. Dustin Hoffman
4. Clint Eastwood
5. Mel Brooks
6. Burt Reynolds
7. Al Pacino
8. Tatum O'Neal
9. Woody Allen
10. Charles Bronson

1977

1. Sylvester Stallone
2. Barbra Streisand
3. Clint Eastwood
4. Burt Reynolds
5. Robert Redford
6. Woody Allen
7. Mel Brooks
8. Al Pacino
9. Diane Keaton
10. Robert De Niro

1978

1. Burt Reynolds
2. John Travolta
3. Richard Dreyfuss
4. Warren Beatty
5. Clint Eastwood
6. Woody Allen
7. Diane Keaton
8. Jane Fonda
9. Peter Sellers
10. Barbra Streisand

1979

1. Burt Reynolds
2. Clint Eastwood
3. Jane Fonda
4. Woody Allen
5. Barbra Streisand
6. Sylvester Stallone
7. John Travolta
8. Jill Clayburgh
9. Roger Moore
10. Mel Brooks

1980

1. Burt Reynolds
2. Robert Redford
3. Clint Eastwood
4. Jane Fonda
5. Dustin Hoffman
6. John Travolta
7. Sally Field
8. Sissy Spacek
9. Barbra Streisand
10. Steve Martin

1981

1. Burt Reynolds
2. Clint Eastwood
3. Dudley Moore
4. Dolly Parton
5. Jane Fonda
6. Harrison Ford
7. Alan Alda
8. Bo Derek
9. Goldie Hawn
10. Bill Murray

1982

1. Burt Reynolds
2. Clint Eastwood
3. Sylvester Stallone
4. Dudley Moore
5. Richard Pryor
6. Dolly Parton
7. Jane Fonda
8. Richard Gere
9. Paul Newman
10. Harrison Ford

1983

1. Clint Eastwood
2. Eddie Murphy
3. Sylvester Stallone
4. Burt Reynolds
5. John Travolta
6. Dustin Hoffman
7. Harrison Ford
8. Richard Gere
9. Chevy Chase
10. Tom Cruise

1984

1. Clint Eastwood
2. Bill Murray
3. Harrison Ford
4. Eddie Murphy
5. Sally Field
6. Burt Reynolds
7. Robert Redford
8. Prince
9. Dan Aykroyd
10. Meryl Streep

1985

1. Sylvester Stallone
2. Eddie Murphy
3. Clint Eastwood
4. Michael J. Fox
5. Chevy Chase
6. Arnold Schwarzenegger
7. Chuck Norris
8. Harrison Ford
9. Michael Douglas
10. Meryl Streep

1986

1. Tom Cruise
2. Eddie Murphy
3. Paul Hogan
4. Rodney Dangerfield
5. Bette Midler
6. Sylvester Stallone
7. Clint Eastwood
8. Whoopi Goldberg
9. Kathleen Turner
10. Paul Newman

1987

1. Eddie Murphy
2. Michael Douglas
3. Michael J. Fox
4. Arnold Schwarzenegger
5. Paul Hogan
6. Tom Cruise
7. Glenn Close
8. Sylvester Stallone

9. Cher
10. Mel Gibson

1988
1. Tom Cruise
2. Eddie Murphy
3. Tom Hanks
4. Arnold Schwarzenegger
5. Paul Hogan
6. Danny DeVito
7. Bette Midler
8. Robin Williams
9. Tom Selleck
10. Dustin Hoffman

1989
1. Jack Nicholson
2. Tom Cruise
3. Robin Williams
4. Michael Douglas
5. Tom Hanks
6. Michael J. Fox
7. Eddie Murphy
8. Mel Gibson
9. Sean Connery
10. Kathleen Turner

1990
1. Arnold Schwarzenegger
2. Julia Roberts
3. Bruce Willis
4. Tom Cruise
5. Mel Gibson
6. Kevin Costner

7. Patrick Swayze
8. Sean Connery
9. Harrison Ford
10. Richard Gere

1991
1. Kevin Costner
2. Arnold Schwarzenegger
3. Robin Williams
4. Julia Roberts
5. Macaulay Culkin
6. Jodie Foster
7. Billy Crystal
8. Dustin Hoffman
9. Robert De Niro
10. Mel Gibson

1992
1. Tom Cruise
2. Mel Gibson
3. Kevin Costner
4. Jack Nicholson
5. Macaulay Culkin
6. Whoopi Goldberg
7. Michael Douglas
8. Clint Eastwood
9. Steven Seagal
10. Robin Williams

1993
1. Clint Eastwood
2. Tom Cruise
3. Robin Williams
4. Kevin Costner
5. Harrison Ford

6. Julia Roberts
7. Tom Hanks
8. Mel Gibson
9. Whoopi Goldberg
10. Sylvester Stallone

1994
1. Tom Hanks
2. Jim Carrey
3. Arnold Schwarzenegger
4. Tom Cruise
5. Harrison Ford
6. Tim Allen
7. Mel Gibson
8. Jodie Foster
9. Michael Douglas
10. Tommy Lee Jones

1995
1. Tom Hanks
2. Jim Carrey
3. Brad Pitt
4. Harrison Ford
5. Robin Williams
6. Sandra Bullock
7. Mel Gibson
8. Demi Moore
9. John Travolta
10. Kevin Costner (tie)
10. Michael Douglas (tie)

1996
1. Tom Cruise (tie)
1. Mel Gibson (tie)
3. John Travolta

4. Arnold Schwarzenegger
5. Sandra Bullock
6. Robin Williams
7. Sean Connery
8. Harrison Ford
9. Kevin Costner
10. Michelle Pfeiffer

1997
1. Harrison Ford
2. Julia Roberts
3. Leonardo DiCaprio
4. Will Smith
5. Tom Cruise
6. Jack Nicholson
7. Jim Carrey
8. John Travolta
9. Robin Williams
10. Tommy Lee Jones

1998
1. Tom Hanks
2. Jim Carrey
3. Leonardo DiCaprio
4. Robin Williams
5. Meg Ryan
6. Mel Gibson
7. Adam Sandler
8. Eddie Murphy
9. Cameron Diaz
10. Julia Roberts

STAR LIGHT, STAR BRIGHT

Awarding points on a descending scale of 10, PEOPLE has analyzed Quigley Publishing's yearly film stars rankings to determine the most popular screen actors of all time.

Rank	Actor	Score	Rank	Actor	Score	Rank	Actor	Score
1.	John Wayne	172	17.	Robert Redford (tie)	55	34.	Sean Connery	36
2.	Clint Eastwood	165	19.	Arnold Schwarzenegger	53	35.	Julie Andrews	35
3.	Bing Crosby	111	20.	Sylvester Stallone	50	36.	Humphrey Bogart (tie)	34
4.	Gary Cooper	102	21.	Shirley Temple	49	36.	Gary Cooper (tie)	34
5.	Clark Gable	91	22.	Tom Hanks (tie)	48	36.	Jack Nicholson (tie)	34
6.	Burt Reynolds	90	22.	Barbra Streisand (tie)	48	39.	Kevin Costner (tie)	33
7.	Bob Hope	84	22.	Spencer Tracy (tie)	48	39.	William Holden (tie)	33
8.	Paul Newman	76	22.	Robin Williams (tie)	48	41.	Jim Carrey (tie)	31
9.	Doris Day	72	26.	Steve McQueen	47	41.	Julia Roberts (tie)	31
10.	Rock Hudson	69	27.	Mel Gibson (tie)	46	43.	Elvis Presley	29
11.	Tom Cruise	68	27.	Dean Martin & Jerry Lewis (tie)	46	44.	Jane Fonda (tie)	28
12.	Betty Grable	66	27.	Mickey Rooney (tie)	46	44.	Will Rogers (tie)	28
13.	Cary Grant	62	30.	Elizabeth Taylor	44	46.	Michael Douglas	25
14.	Eddie Murphy	60	31.	Dustin Hoffman	42	47.	Garson Greer	24
15.	Abbott & Costello	57	32.	Jack Lemmon	40	48.	Woody Allen (tie)	22
16.	James Stewart	56	33.	John Travolta	37	48.	Jerry Lewis (tie)	22
17.	Harrison Ford (tie)	55				50.	Glenn Ford	21

THE HOLLYWOOD BLACKLIST

The House Committee on Un-American Activities investigated the entertainment business for subversive activities—i.e., Communist connections—starting in 1947. By the end of the hearings in 1958, roughly 100 film, television, radio, theater, and music industry figures had been questioned. Approximately one-third of them provided the committee with the names of others who were alleged sympathizers. The remainder, insisting that their political beliefs were a private matter, took either the First or the Fifth Amendment and refused to name names; some of these men and women were jailed, almost all were blacklisted, and many had their careers ruined.

The following were some of the most well known of the informers who identified more than 300 supposed Communist sympathizers:

Lee J. Cobb, actor (*On the Waterfront, Twelve Angry Men, Death of a Salesman, Exodus, "The Virginian"*)

Sterling Hayden, actor (*The Asphalt Jungle, Johnny Guitar, Dr. Strangelove*)

Roy Huggins, writer/director/producer ("Cheyenne," "Maverick," "The Rockford Files")

Elia Kazan, director (*Gentleman's Agreement, On the Waterfront, A Streetcar Named Desire*)

Isobel Lennert, screenwriter (*East Side, West Side; Anchors Aweigh; Meet Me in Las Vegas*)

Clifford Odets, playwright (*Waiting for Lefty, Golden Boy*)

Jerome Robbins, dancer/choreographer/assoc. director, New York City Ballet

(*Fancy Free, Interplay, Dances at a Gathering*)

Robert Rossen, director (*Body and Soul, All the King's Men*)

Budd Schulberg, screenwriter/novelist (*On the Waterfront*)

Leo Townsend, screenwriter (*Night and Day, Beach Blanket Bingo, Bikini Beach*)

The following, six of them Oscar winners, refused to incriminate themselves or to inform on others, and as a result were either jailed, blacklisted, or forced to leave the country:

Herschel Bernardi, actor (*The Front*)

Howard Da Silva, actor (*Mommy Dearest*)

Carl Foreman, director/screenwriter (screenwriter, *High Noon*)

Dashiell Hammett, novelist (*The Thin Man, The Maltese Falcon*)

Lillian Hellman, playwright/screenwriter (*The Little Foxes, The Watch on the Rhine*)

Howard Koch, radio writer/screenwriter/playwright ("War of the Worlds," *Casablanca*)

Ring Lardner Jr., screenwriter (*Woman of the Year, Laura, M*A*S*H*)

Philip Loeb, actor ("The Goldbergs")

Joseph Losey, director (*The Concrete Jungle, The Damned, The Servant, Modesty Blaise, Boom!, The Go-Between*)

Albert Maltz, screenwriter/playwright (*This Gun for Hire, Destination Tokyo, The House I Live In, Pride of the Marines, The Robe*)

Arthur Miller, playwright/screenwriter (*The Crucible, Death of a Salesman, The Misfits*)

Zero Mostel, actor/comedian (*A Funny Thing Happened on the Way to the Forum, The Producers, Fiddler on the Roof*)

Dorothy Parker, short-story writer/screenwriter ("Laments for the Living," *A Star Is Born*)

John Randolph, actor (*Come Back, Little Sheba; Serpico*)

Paul Robeson, actor/singer (*Show Boat, The Emperor Jones*)

Waldo Salt, screenwriter (*Midnight Cowboy, Serpico, Coming Home*)

Robert Adrian Scott, screenwriter/producer (producer, *Murder, My Sweet; Crossfire*)

Pete Seeger, musician (coauthor, "If I Had a Hammer")

Gale Sondergaard, actress (*Anthony Adverse, A Night to Remember, The Spider Woman*)

Dalton Trumbo, screenwriter (*Kitty Foyle, Thirty Seconds over Tokyo, The Brave One* [under the name of Robert Rich], *Exodus, Hawaii, Spartacus*)

Sam Wanamaker, actor (*The Spy Who Came in from the Cold, Private Benjamin*)

Nedrick Young, screenwriter (*The Defiant Ones, Inherit the Wind*)

The following have received belated credit from the Writers Guild of America for films previously attributed to other scribes or written under pseudonyms:

Adventures of Robinson Crusoe (1952), screenplay by Hugo Butler and Luis Bunuel. Original credit: screenplay, Philip Ansell Roll and Bunuel

An Affair to Remember (1957), screenplay by Delmer Daves, Donald Ogden Stewart, and Leo McCarey. Original credit: screenplay, Daves and McCarey

Born Free (1966), screenplay by Lester Cole. Original credit: screenplay, Gerald L. C. Copley

The Brave One (1956), screenplay by Harry Franklin and Merrill G. White, story by Dalton Trumbo. Original credit: screenplay, Franklin and White, based on a story by Robert Rich

The Bridge on the River Kwai (1957), screenplay by Carl Foreman and Michael Wilson, based on the novel by Pierre Boulle. Original credit: screenplay, Boulle, from his own novel

Broken Arrow (1950), screenplay by Albert Maltz, based on the novel *Blood Brother* by Elliot Arnold. Original credit: screenplay, Michael Blankfort, based on the novel by Arnold

Cry the Beloved Country (1952), screenplay by Alan Paton and John Howard Lawson. Original credit: screenplay, Alan Paton

The Day of the Triffids (1963), screenplay by Bernard Gordon, based on the novel by John Wyndham. Original credit: screenplay, Philip Yordan, based on the novel by Wyndham

Deadly Is the Female (Gun Crazy) (1950), screenplay by MacKinlay Kantor and Dalton Trumbo, based on a *Saturday Evening Post* story "Gun Crazy" by Kantor. Original credit: screenplay, Kantor and Millard Kaufman, from *Post* story "Gun Crazy" by Kantor

The Defiant Ones (1958), written by Nedrick Young and Harold Jacob Smith. Original credit: screenplay, Nathan E. Douglas and Smith

Earth vs. the Flying Saucers (1956), screenplay by George Worthing Yates and Bernard Gordon. Original credit: screenplay, Yates and Raymond T. Marcus

Friendly Persuasion (1956), screenplay by Michael Wilson, based on the novel by Jessamyn West Original credit: no on-screen writing credits

Hellcats of the Navy (1957), screenplay by David Lang and Bernard Gordon. Original credit: screenplay, Land and Raymond T. Marcus

Inherit the Wind (1960), screenplay by Nedrick Young and Harold Jacob Smith. Original credit: screenplay, Nathan E. Douglas and Smith

Ivanhoe (1952), screenplay by Marguerite Roberts and Noel Langley. Original credit: screenplay, Noel Langley

Lawrence of Arabia (1962), screenplay by Robert Bolt and Michael Wilson, based on the life and writings of T. H. Lawrence. Original credit: screenplay, Robert Bolt

The Misadventures of Merlin Jones (1964), screenplay by Alfred Lewis Levitt and Helen Levitt. Original credit: screenplay, Tom and Helen August

Odds Against Tomorrow (1959), screenplay by Abraham Polonsky and Nelson Gidding, based on the novel by William P. McGivern. Original credit: screenplay, John O. Killens and Gidding, based on the novel by McGivern

The Robe (1953), screenplay by Albert Maltz and Philip Dunne. Original credit: screenplay, Philip Dunne

Roman Holiday (1953), screenplay by Ian McLellan Hunter and John Dighton, story by Dalton Trumbo. Original credit: screenplay, Hunter and Dighton, story by Hunter

SUPERSTAR FILMOGRAPHIES

The filmographies for some of Hollywood's most important, most popular people list only full-length feature films to which these actors and directors contributed significantly. Included are some early works released directly onto video years after completion.

WOODY ALLEN
Director/screenwriter/actor

What's New, Pussycat? (screenwriter/actor, 1965)

What's Up, Tiger Lily? (director/screenwriter/actor, 1966)

Casino Royale (co-screenwriter/actor, 1967)

Take the Money and Run (director/co-screenwriter/actor, 1969)

Bananas (director/screenwriter, 1971)

Play It Again, Sam (screenwriter/actor, 1972)

Everything You Always Wanted To Know About Sex* (*but were afraid to ask) (director/co-screenwriter/actor, 1972)

Sleeper (director/screenwriter/actor, 1973)

Love and Death (director/screenwriter/actor, 1975)

The Front (actor, 1976)

Annie Hall (director/co-screenwriter/actor, 1977; Academy Awards for best picture, best director, best original screenplay)

Interiors (director/screenwriter/ actor, 1978)

Manhattan (director/co-screenwriter/actor, 1979)

Stardust Memories (director/screenwriter/actor, 1980)

A Midsummer Night's Sex Comedy (director/screenwriter/actor, 1982)

Zelig (director/screenwriter/actor, 1983)

Broadway Danny Rose (director/screenwriter/actor, 1984)

The Purple Rose of Cairo (director/screenwriter, 1985)

Hannah and Her Sisters (director/screenwriter/actor, 1986; Academy Award for best original screenplay)

Radio Days (director/screenwriter/actor, 1987)

King Lear (actor, 1987)

September (director/screenwriter, 1987)

Another Woman (director/screenwriter, 1988)

"Oedipus Wrecks," in *New York Stories* (director/co-screenwriter/actor, 1989)

Crimes and Misdemeanors (director/screenwriter/actor, 1989)

Alice (director/screenwriter, 1990)

Scenes from a Mall (actor, 1991)

Shadows and Fog (director/screenwriter/actor, 1992)

Husbands and Wives (director/screenwriter/actor, 1992)

Manhattan Murder Mystery (director/screenwriter/actor, 1993)

Bullets over Broadway (director/co-screenwriter, 1994)

Mighty Aphrodite (director/screenwriter/actor, 1995)

Everyone Says I Love You (director/screenwriter/actor, 1996)

Deconstructing Harry (director/screenwriter/actor, 1997)

Wild Man Blues (documentary subject, 1998)

Antz (cartoon voice, 1998)

Celebrity (director/screenwriter, 1998)

KEVIN BACON
Actor

Animal House (1978)

Friday the 13th (1980)

Only When I Laugh (1981)

Forty Deuces (1982)

Diner (1982)

Enormous Changes at the Last Minute (1983)

Footloose (1984)

Quicksilver (1986)

White Water Summer (a.k.a. *Rites of Summer,* 1987)

End of the Line (1987)

Planes, Trains & Automobiles (1987)

She's Having a Baby (1988)

Criminal Law (1989)

The Big Picture (1989)

Tremors (1990)

Flatliners (1990)

Queens Logic (1991)

Pyrates (1991)

He Said, She Said (1991)

JFK (1991)

A Few Good Men (1992)

The River Wild (1994)

The Air Up There (1994)

Balto (cartoon voice, 1995)

Murder in the First (1995)

Apollo 13 (1995)

Sleepers (1996)

Losing Chase (1996)

Picture Perfect (1997)

Destination Anywhere (1997)

Telling Lies in America (1997)

Digging to China (1998)

Elizabeth Jane (1998)

Wild Things (1998)

Stir of Echoes (1999)

SANDRA BULLOCK
Actor

Who Shot Patakango? (1990)

Religion, Inc. (1990—videotape)

When the Party's Over (1992)

Who Do I Gotta Kill? (1992)

Love Potion No. 9 (1992)

The Vanishing (1993)

Fire on the Amazon (1992—videotape)

Demolition Man (1993)

The Thing Called Love (1993)

Wrestling Ernest Hemingway (1993)

Speed (1994)

While You Were Sleeping (1995)

The Net (1995)

Two If by Sea (1996)

A Time To Kill (1996)

In Love and War (1997)

Speed 2: Cruise Control (1997)

Hope Floats (1998)

Prince of Egypt (cartoon voice, 1998)

Practical Magic (1998)

Forces of Nature (1999)

NICOLAS CAGE
Actor

Fast Times at Ridgemont High (1982)

Valley Girl (1983)

Rumble Fish (1983)

Racing with the Moon (1984)

The Cotton Club (1984)

Birdy (1984)

The Boy in Blue (1986)

Peggy Sue Got Married (1986)

Raising Arizona (1987)

Moonstruck (1987)

Vampire's Kiss (1989)

Wild at Heart (1990)

Time to Kill (1990—videotape)

Fire Birds (1990)

Zandalee (1991)

Honeymoon in Vegas (1992)

Red Rock West (1992)

Amos and Andrew (1993)

Deadfall (1993)

Guarding Tess (1994)

It Could Happen to You (1994)

Trapped in Paradise (1994)

Kiss of Death (1995)

Leaving Las Vegas (1995; Academy Award for best actor)
The Rock (1996)
Con Air (1997)
Face/Off (1997)
City of Angels (1998)
Snake Eyes (1998)
8mm (1999)

JIM CARREY
Actor

Finders Keepers (1984)
Once Bitten (1985)
Peggy Sue Got Married (1986)
The Dead Pool (1988)
Pink Cadillac (1989)
Earth Girls Are Easy (1989)
High Strung (1994—videotape)
Ace Ventura: Pet Detective (1994)
The Mask (1994)
Dumb & Dumber (1994)
Batman Forever (1995)
Ace Ventura: When Nature Calls (1995)
The Cable Guy (1996)
Liar Liar (1997)
The Truman Show (1998)
Simon Birch (1998)
Man on the Moon (1999)

GLENN CLOSE
Actor

The World According to Garp (1982)
The Big Chill (1983)
The Stone Boy (1984)
Greystoke: The Legend of Tarzan, Lord of the Apes (voice, 1984)
The Natural (1984)
Jagged Edge (1985)
Maxie (1985)
Fatal Attraction (1987)
Dangerous Liaisons (1988)
Light Years (cartoon voice, 1988)
Immediate Family (1989)
Hamlet (1990)
Reversal of Fortune (1990)

Meeting Venus (1991)
The Paper (1994)
The House of the Spirits (1994)
Mary Reilly (1996)
101 Dalmatians (1996)
Mars Attacks! (1996)
Paradise Road (1997)
Air Force One (1997)
In & Out (1997)
Cookie's Fortune (1999)
Tarzan (cartoon voice, 1999)

SEAN CONNERY
Actor

No Road Back (1956)
Action of the Tiger (1957)
Another Time, Another Place (1958)
Hell Drivers (1957)
Time Lock (1957)
A Night to Remember (1958)
Tarzan's Greatest Adventure (1959)
Darby O'Gill and the Little People (1959)
On the Fiddle (1961)
The Frightened City (1961)
The Longest Day (1962)
Dr. No (1962)
From Russia with Love (1963)
Goldfinger (1964)
Woman of Straw (1964)
Marnie (1964)
Thunderball (1965)
The Hill (1965)
A Fine Madness (1966)
You Only Live Twice (1967)
Shalako (1968)
Bowler and Bonnet (1969, director)
The Molly Maguires (1970)
The Red Tent (1971)
The Anderson Tapes (1971)
Diamonds Are Forever (1971)
The Offence (or *Something like the Truth*, 1973)
Zardoz (1974)
Murder on the Orient Express (1974)
Ransom (1974)

The Wind and the Lion (1975)
The Man Who Would Be King (1975)
The Terrorists (1975)
Robin and Marian (1976)
The Next Man (1976)
A Bridge Too Far (1977)
The Great Train Robbery (1979)
Meteor (1979)
Cuba (1979)
Outland (1981)
Time Bandits (1981)
Wrong Is Right (1981)
G'ole (1982)
Five Days One Summer (1982)
Never Say Never Again (1983)
Sword of the Valiant (1984)
Highlander (1985)
The Name of the Rose (1986)
The Untouchables (1987; Academy Award for best supporting actor)
The Presidio (1988)
Memories of Me (1988)
Indiana Jones and the Last Crusade (1989)
Family Business (1989)
The Hunt for Red October (1990)
The Russia House (1990)
Highlander II: The Quickening (1991)
Robin Hood: Prince of Thieves (1991)
Medicine Man (1992)
Rising Sun (1993)
A Good Man in Africa (1994)
Just Cause (1995)
First Knight (1995)
Dragonheart (voice, 1996)
The Rock (1996)
The Avengers (1998)
Dancing About Architecture (1998)
Playing by Heart (1998)
Entrapment (1999)

KEVIN COSTNER
Actor/director/producer

Shadows Run Black (1981)
Night Shift (1982)
Stacy's Knights (1982)
The Big Chill (played corpse, all other scenes edited out, 1983)
The Gunrunner (1983)
Table for Five (1983)
Testament (1983)
American Flyers (1985)
Fandango (1985)
Silverado (1985)
Sizzle Beach, U.S.A. (1986)
No Way Out (1987)
The Untouchables (1987)
Bull Durham (1988)
Chasing Dreams (1989)
Field of Dreams (1989)
Dances with Wolves (actor/director/producer, 1990; Academy Awards for best picture, best director)
Revenge (1990)
Robin Hood: Prince of Thieves (1991)
JFK (1991)
The Bodyguard (actor/producer, 1992)
A Perfect World (1993)
Wyatt Earp (actor/producer, 1994)
Rapa Nui (co-producer, 1994)
The War (1994)
Waterworld (actor/producer, 1995)
Tin Cup (1996)
The Postman (actor/director/co-producer, 1997)
Message in a Bottle (1999)
For Love of the Game (1999)

TOM CRUISE
Actor

Endless Love (1981)
Taps (1981)
Losin' It (1983)
The Outsiders (1983)
Risky Business (1983)
All the Right Moves (1983)

Legend (1986)

Top Gun (1986)

The Color of Money (1986)

Cocktail (1988)

Rain Man (1988)

Born on the Fourth of July (1989)

Days of Thunder (1990)

Far and Away (1992)

A Few Good Men (1992)

The Firm (1993)

Interview with the Vampire (1994)

Mission: Impossible (actor/co-producer, 1996)

Jerry Maguire (1996)

Eyes Wide Shut (1999)

CLINT EASTWOOD
Actor/director/producer

Francis in the Navy (1955)

Lady Godiva (1955)

Never Say Goodbye (actor,1955)

Revenge of the Creature (1955)

Tarantula (1955)

The Traveling Saleslady (1956)

Star in the Dust (1956)

Escapade in Japan (1957)

Ambush at Cimarron Pass (1958)

Lafayette Escadrille (1958)

A Fistful of Dollars (1964)

For a Few Dollars More (1965)

The Good, the Bad, and the Ugly (1966)

Coogan's Bluff (1968)

Hang 'Em High (1968)

The Witches (1968)

Where Eagles Dare (1968)

Paint Your Wagon (1969)

Kelly's Heroes (1970)

Two Mules for Sister Sara (1970)

The Beguiled (1971)

Dirty Harry (1971)

Play Misty For Me (actor/director, 1971)

Joe Kidd (1972)

Breezy (1973)

High Plains Drifter (actor/director, 1973)

Magnum Force (1973)

Thunderbolt and Lightfoot (1974)

The Eiger Sanction (actor/director, 1974)

The Outlaw Josey Wales (actor/director, 1975)

The Enforcer (1976)

The Gauntlet (actor/director, 1977)

Every Which Way but Loose (1978)

Escape from Alcatraz (1979)

Any Which Way You Can (1980)

Bronco Billy (actor/director, 1980)

Firefox (actor/director/producer, 1982)

Honkytonk Man (actor/director/producer, 1982)

Sudden Impact (actor/director/producer, 1983)

City Heat (1984)

Tightrope (actor/producer, 1984)

Pale Rider (actor/director/producer, 1985)

Heartbreak Ridge (actor/director/producer, 1986)

Bird (director/producer, 1988)

The Dead Pool (actor/producer, 1988)

Pink Cadillac (1989)

The Rookie (actor/director, 1990)

White Hunter, Black Heart (actor/director/producer, 1990)

Unforgiven (actor/director/producer, 1992; Academy Awards for best director and best film)

In the Line of Fire (actor/producer, 1993)

A Perfect World (actor/director, 1993)

The Bridges of Madison County (actor/director, 1995)

Absolute Power (actor/director, 1997)

Midnight in the Garden of Good and Evil (director/co-producer, 1997)

True Crime (actor/director, 1999)

HARRISON FORD
Actor

Dead Heat on a Merry-Go-Round (1966)

Luv (1967)

A Time for Killing (1967)

Journey to Shiloh (1968)

Getting Straight (1970)

American Graffiti (1973)

The Conversation (1974)

Heroes (1977)

The Possessed (1977)

Star Wars (1977)

The Frisco Kid (1979)

Apocalypse Now (1979)

Hanover Street (1979)

The Empire Strikes Back (1980)

Raiders of the Lost Ark (1981)

Blade Runner (1982)

Return of the Jedi (1983)

Indiana Jones and the Temple of Doom (1984)

Witness (1985)

The Mosquito Coast (1986)

Frantic (1988)

Working Girl (1988)

Indiana Jones and the Last Crusade (1989)

Presumed Innocent (1990)

Regarding Henry (1991)

Patriot Games (1992)

The Fugitive (1993)

Clear and Present Danger (1994)

Sabrina (1995)

Air Force One (1997)

The Devil's Own (1997)

Six Days, Seven Nights (1998)

Random Hearts (1999)

JODIE FOSTER
Actor/director

Napoleon and Samantha (1972)

Kansas City Bomber (1972)

Tom Sawyer (1973)

One Little Indian (1973)

Alice Doesn't Live Here Anymore (1974)

Echoes of a Summer (1976)

Bugsy Malone (1976)

Taxi Driver (1976)

The Little Girl Who Lives Down the Lane (1976)

Freaky Friday (1977)

Candleshoe (1977)

Moi, fleur bleue (1977)

Il Casotto (1977)

Carny (1980)

Foxes (1980)

O'Hara's Wife (1982)

Les Sang des autres (The Blood of Others) (1984)

The Hotel New Hampshire (1984)

Mesmerized (actor/co-producer, 1986)

Siesta (1987)

Five Corners (1988)

The Accused (1988; Academy Award for best actress)

Stealing Home (1988)

Backtrack (1989)

The Silence of the Lambs (1991; Academy Award for best actress)

Little Man Tate (actor/director, 1991)

Shadows and Fog (1992)

Sommersby (1993)

Maverick (1994)

Nell (1994)

Home for the Holidays (director, 1995)

Contact (1997)

Anna and the King (1999)

MEL GIBSON
Actor/director

Summer City (1977)

Tim (1979)

Mad Max (1979)

Attack Force Z (1981)

Gallipoli (1981)

The Road Warrior (1981)

The Year of Living Dangerously (1982)

The Bounty (1984)

Mrs. Soffel (1984)

The River (1984)

Mad Max Beyond Thunderdome (1985)

Lethal Weapon (1987)

Tequila Sunrise (1988)

Lethal Weapon 2 (1989)

Air America (1990)

Bird on a Wire (1990)

Hamlet (1990)

Forever Young (1992)

Lethal Weapon 3 (1992)

The Man Without a Face (actor/director, 1993)

Maverick (1994)

Braveheart (actor/director/producer, 1995; Academy Awards for best director and best picture)

Pocahontas (cartoon voice, 1995)

Ransom (1996)

Conspiracy Theory (1997)

Lethal Weapon 4 (1998)

Payback (1999)

WHOOPI GOLDBERG
Actor

The Color Purple (1985)

Jumpin' Jack Flash (1986)

Burglar (1987)

Fatal Beauty (1987)

Clara's Heart (1988)

The Telephone (1988)

Beverly Hills Brats (1989)

Homer and Eddie (1989)

Ghost (1990; Academy Award for best supporting actress)

The Long Walk Home (1990)

Soapdish (1991)

The Player (1992)

Sarafina! (1992)

Sister Act (1992)

Made in America (1993)

Sister Act 2: Back in the Habit (1993)

Corrina, Corrina (1994)

The Lion King (cartoon voice, 1994)

The Pagemaster (cartoon voice, 1994)

The Little Rascals (1994)

Star Trek: Generations (1994)

Boys on the Side (1995)

Moonlight & Valentino (1995)

Theodore Rex (1996, video)

Eddie (1996)

Bogus (1996)

The Associate (1996)

In & Out (1997)

An Alan Smithee Film: Burn Hollywood Burn (1998)

How Stella Got Her Groove Back (1998)

The Rugrat's Movie (cartoon voice, 1998)

TOM HANKS
Actor

He Knows You're Alone (1980)

Splash (1984)

Bachelor Party (1984)

The Man with One Red Shoe (1985)

Volunteers (1985)

The Money Pit (1986)

Nothing in Common (1986)

Every Time We Say Goodbye (1986)

Dragnet (1987)

Big (1988)

Punchline (1988)

The Burbs (1989)

Turner and Hooch (1989)

Joe Versus the Volcano (1990)

The Bonfire of the Vanities (1990)

Radio Flyer (1992)

A League of Their Own (1992)

Sleepless in Seattle (1993)

Philadelphia (1993; Academy Award for best actor)

Forrest Gump (1994; Academy Award for best actor)

Apollo 13 (1995)

Toy Story (cartoon voice, 1995)

That Thing You Do! (writer/director/actor, 1996)

Saving Private Ryan (1998)

You've Got Mail (1998)

Toy Story 2 (cartoon voice, 1999)

The Green Mile (1999)

ANTHONY HOPKINS
Actor

The Lion in Winter (1968)

Hamlet (1969)

The Looking Glass War (1970)

When Eight Bells Toll (1971)

Young Winston (1972)

A Doll's House (1973)

The Girl From Petrovka (1974)

Juggernaut (1974)

All Creatures Great and Small (1975)

Audrey Rose (1977)

A Bridge Too Far (1977)

International Velvet (1978)

Magic (1978)

A Change of Seasons (1980)

The Elephant Man (1980)

The Bounty (1984)

The Good Father (1986)

84 Charing Cross Road (1987)

The Dawning (1988)

A Chorus of Disapproval (1987)

Desperate Hours (1990)

The Silence of the Lambs (1991; Academy Award for best actor)

Freejack (1992)

Howards End (1992)

The Efficiency Expert (1992)

Bram Stoker's Dracula (1992)

Chaplin (1992)

The Remains of the Day (1993)

Shadowlands (1993)

The Trial (1993)

The Road to Wellville (1994)

Legends of the Fall (1994)

The Innocent (1995)

Nixon (1995)

August (actor/director, 1996)

Surviving Picasso (1996)

The Edge (1997)

Amistad (1997)

The Mask of Zorro (1998)

Meet Joe Black (1998)

Instinct (1999)

HELEN HUNT
Actor

Rollercoaster (1977)

Girls Just Want to Have Fun (1985)

Trancers (a.k.a. Future Cop) (1985)

Peggy Sue Got Married (1986)

Project X (1987)

Stealing Home (1988)

Miles from Home (1988)

Next of Kin (1989)

The Waterdance (1992)

Only You (1992)

Bob Roberts (1992)

Mr. Saturday Night (1992)

Kiss of Death (1995)

Twister (1996)

As Good As It Gets (1997; Academy Award for best actress)

NICOLE KIDMAN
Actor

Bush Christmas (1983)

BMX Bandits (1983)

Archer's Adventure (1985)

The Wacky World of Wills and Burke (1985)

Windrider (1986)

Nightmaster (1987)

The Bit Part (1987)

Emerald City (1988)

Dead Calm (1989)

Days of Thunder (1990)

Flirting (1991)

Billy Bathgate (1991)

Far and Away (1992)

My Life (1993)

Malice (1993)

To Die For (1994)

Batman Forever (1995)

The Portrait of a Lady (1996)

The Peacemaker (1997)

Practical Magic (1998)

Eyes Wide Shut (1999)

SPIKE LEE
Director/producer/screen-
writer/actor

She's Gotta Have It
(director/producer/screen-
writer/actor, 1986)

School Daze (director/pro-
ducer/screenwriter/actor,
1988)

Do the Right Thing
(director/producer/screen-
writer/actor, 1989)

Mo' Better Blues
(director/producer/screen-
writer/actor, 1990)

Lonely in America, (actor,
1990)

Jungle Fever (director/pro-
ducer/screenwriter/actor,
1991)

Malcolm X (director/producer/
co-screenwriter/actor, 1992)

Crooklyn (director/producer/
co-screenwriter/actor, 1994)

Clockers (director/co-?pro-
ducer/co-screenwriter, 1995)

Girl 6 (director/producer,
1996)

Get On The Bus (director/pro-
ducer, 1996)

When We Were Kings
(interviewee, 1996)

4 Little Girls (director/pro-
ducer, 1997)

He Got Game (director/pro-
ducer/screenwriter, 1998)

Summer of Sam (director/co-
producer/co-screenwriter,
1999)

DEMI MOORE
Actor/Producer

Choices (1981)

Parasite (1982)

Young Doctors in Love (1982)

Blame It on Rio (1984)

No Small Affair (1984)

St. Elmo's Fire (1985)

About Last Night (1986)

One Crazy Summer (1986)

Wisdom (1986)

The Seventh Sign (1988)

We're No Angels (1989)

Ghost (1990)

Mortal Thoughts (actor/co-
producer, 1991)

Nothing but Trouble (1991)

The Butcher's Wife (1991)

A Few Good Men (1992)

Indecent Proposal (1993)

Disclosure (1994)

The Scarlet Letter (1995)

Now and Then (1995)

The Juror (1996)

The Hunchback of Notre Dame
(cartoon voice, 1996)

Striptease (1996)

Beavis and Butt-Head Do
America (cartoon voice, 1996)

Austin Powers: International
Man of Mystery (co-producer,
1997)

G.I. Jane (1997)

Deconstructing Harry (1997)

JACK NICHOLSON
Actor/producer/screenwriter/
director

Cry Baby Killer (1958)

Studs Lonigan (1960)

Too Soon to Love (1960)

The Wild Ride (1960)

Little Shop of Horrors (1961)

The Broken Land (1962)

The Raven (1963)

The Terror (1963)

Thunder Island (screenwriter,
1963)

Ensign Pulver (1964)

Back Door to Hell (1964)

The Fortune (1965)

Flight to Fury (actor/screen-
writer, 1966)

Ride in the Whirlwind
(actor/producer/screenwriter,
1966)

Hell's Angels on Wheels
(1966)

The Shooting (actor/producer,
1967)

The Trip (screenwriter, 1967)

St. Valentine's Day Massacre
(1967)

Head (actor/producer/screen-
writer, 1968)

Psych-Out (1968)

Easy Rider (1969)

Five Easy Pieces (1970)

On a Clear Day You Can See
Forever (1970)

Rebel Rousers (1970)

Carnal Knowledge (1971)

Drive, He Said (director/pro-
ducer/screenwriter, 1971)

A Safe Place (1971)

The King of Marvin Gardens
(1972)

The Last Detail (1973)

Chinatown (1974)

The Fortune (1975)

One Flew over the Cuckoo's
Nest (1975; Academy Award
for best actor)

The Passenger (1975)

Tommy (1975)

The Last Tycoon (1976)

The Missouri Breaks (1976)

Goin' South (actor/director,
1978)

The Shining (1980)

The Border (1981)

The Postman Always Rings
Twice (1981)

Reds (1981)

Terms of Endearment (1983;
Academy Award for best supporting actor)

Prizzi's Honor (1985)

Heartburn (1986)

Broadcast News (1987)

Ironweed (1987)

The Witches of Eastwick
(1987)

Batman (1989)

The Two Jakes (actor/director,
1990)

Man Trouble (1992)

A Few Good Men (1992)

Hoffa (1992)

Wolf (1994)

The Crossing Guard (1995)

Mars Attacks! (1996)

The Evening Star (1996)

Blood and Wine (1997)

As Good As It Gets (1997;
Academy Award for best
actor)

GWYNETH PALTROW
Actor

Shout (1991)

Hook (1991)

Flesh and Bone (1993)

Malice (1993)

Mrs. Parker and the Vicious
Circle (1994)

Seven (1995)

Moonlight and Valentino
(1995)

Jefferson in Paris (1995)

The Pallbearer (1996)

Emma (1996)

Hard Eight (1997)

A Perfect Murder (1997)

Sliding Doors (1998)

Hush (1998)

Great Expectations (1998)

Shakespeare in Love (1998;
Academy Award for best
actress)

The Talented Mr. Ripley (1999)

MICHELLE PFEIFFER
Actor

The Hollywood Knights (1980)

Falling in Love Again (1980)

Charlie Chan and the Curse of
the Dragon Queen (1981)

Grease 2 (1982)

Scarface (1983)

Into the Night (1985)

Ladyhawke (1985)

Sweet Liberty (1986)

Amazon Women on the Moon
(1987)

The Witches of Eastwick
(1987)

Dangerous Liaisons (1988)

Married to the Mob (1988)

Tequila Sunrise (1988)

The Fabulous Baker Boys
(1989)

The Russia House (1990)

Frankie and Johnny (1991)

Batman Returns (1992)

Love Field (1992)

The Age of Innocence (1993)

Wolf (1994)

Dangerous Minds (1995)

Up Close and Personal (1996)

To Gillian on Her 37th Birthday (1996)

One Fine Day (1996)

A Thousand Acres (1997)

Prince of Egypt (cartoon voice, 1998)

William Shakespeare's A Midsummer Night's Dream (1999)

The Story of Us (1999)

BRAD PITT
Actor

Cutting Class (1989)

Happy Together (1989)

Across the Tracks (1991)

Thelma & Louise (1991)

Johnny Suede (1991)

Cool World (1992)

A River Runs Through It (1992)

True Romance (1993)

Kalifornia (1993)

The Favor (1994)

Interview with the Vampire (1994)

Legends of the Fall (1994)

Seven (1995)

Twelve Monkeys (1995)

Sleepers (1996)

The Devil's Own (1997)

Seven Years in Tibet (1997)

Meet Joe Black (1998)

Fight Club (1999)

JULIA ROBERTS
Actor

Satisfaction (1988)

Mystic Pizza (1988)

Blood Red (1989)

Steel Magnolias (1989)

Pretty Woman (1990)

Flatliners (1990)

Sleeping with the Enemy (1991)

Dying Young (1991)

Hook (1991)

The Player (1992)

The Pelican Brief (1993)

I Love Trouble (1994)

Ready to Wear (1994)

Something to Talk About (1995)

Mary Reilly (1996)

Everyone Says I Love You (1996)

My Best Friend's Wedding (1997)

Conspiracy Theory (1997)

Stepmom (1998)

Notting Hill (1999)

Runaway Bride (1999)

MEG RYAN
Actor

Rich and Famous (1981)

Amityville 3-D (1983)

Armed and Dangerous (1986)

Top Gun (1986)

Innerspace (1987)

Promised Land (1987)

D.O.A. (1988)

The Presidio (1988)

When Harry Met Sally... (1989)

Joe Versus the Volcano (1990)

The Doors (1991)

Prelude to a Kiss (1992)

Sleepless in Seattle (1993)

Flesh and Bone (1993)

When a Man Loves a Woman (1994)

I.Q. (1994)

French Kiss (actor/co-producer, 1995)

Restoration (1995)

Courage Under Fire (1996)

Addicted to Love (1997)

Anastasia (cartoon voice, 1997)

City of Angels (1998)

Hurlyburly (1998)

You've Got Mail (1998)

Hanging Up (1999)

WINONA RYDER
Actor

Lucas (1986)

Square Dance (1987)

Beetlejuice (1988)

1969 (1988)

Heathers (1989)

Great Balls of Fire! (1989)

Welcome Home, Roxy Carmichael (1990)

Mermaids (1990)

Edward Scissorhands (1990)

Night on Earth (1991)

Bram Stoker's Dracula (1992)

The Age of Innocence (1993)

Reality Bites (1994)

The House of the Spirits (1994)

Little Women (1994)

How to Make an American Quilt (1995)

Boys (1996)

Looking for Richard (1996)

The Crucible (1996)

Alien Resurrection (1997)

Celebrity (1998)

Lost Souls (1999)

SUSAN SARANDON
Actor

Joe (1970)

Lady Liberty (a.k.a. Mortadella) (1972)

Lovin' Molly (1974)

The Front Page (1974)

The Rocky Horror Picture Show (1975)

The Great Waldo Pepper (1975)

Dragonfly (1976)

The Great Smokey Roadblock (actor/co-producer, 1976)

Checkered Flag or Crash (1977)

The Other Side of Midnight (1977)

Pretty Baby (1978)

King of the Gypsies (1978)

Something Short of Paradise (1979)

Loving Couples (1980)

Atlantic City (1981)

Tempest (1982)

The Hunger (1983)

The Buddy System (1984)

Compromising Positions (1985)

The Witches of Eastwick (1987)

Bull Durham (1988)

Sweet Hearts Dance (1988)

The January Man (1989)

A Dry White Season (1989)

White Palace (1990)

Thelma & Louise (1991)

Bob Roberts (1992)

Light Sleeper (1992)

Lorenzo's Oil (1992)

The Client (1994)

Safe Passage (1994)

Little Women (1994)

Dead Man Walking (1995)

James and the Giant Peach (cartoon voice, 1996)

Twilight (1998)

Stepmom (1998)

Anywhere But Here (1999)

Cradle Will Rock (1999)

ARNOLD SCHWARZENEGGER
Actor

Hercules in New York (1974)

Stay Hungry (1976)

Pumping Iron (1977)

The Villain (1979)

Conan the Barbarian (1982)

Conan the Destroyer (1984)

The Terminator (1984)

Commando (1985)

Red Sonja (1985)

Raw Deal (1986)

Predator (1987)

The Running Man (1987)

Red Heat (1988)

Twins (1988)

Total Recall (1989)

Kindergarten Cop (1990)

Terminator 2: Judgment Day (1991)

Last Action Hero (1993)

True Lies (1994)

Junior (1994)

Eraser (1996)

Jingle All the Way (1996)

Batman & Robin (1997)

End of Days (1999)

MARTIN SCORSESE
Director/producer/screen-writer

Who's That Knocking at My Door? (director/screenwriter/actor, 1969)

Street Scenes 1970 (director/actor, 1970)

Boxcar Bertha (director, 1972)

Mean Streets (director/screenwriter, 1973)

Alice Doesn't Live Here Anymore (director, 1974)

Taxi Driver (director, 1976)

New York, New York (director, 1977)

American Boy: A Profile of Steven Prince (director, 1978)

The Last Waltz (director/actor, 1978)

Raging Bull (director/actor, 1980)

The King of Comedy (director/actor, 1983)

After Hours (director, 1985)

The Color of Money (director, 1986)

The Last Temptation of Christ (director, 1988)

"Life Lessons" in *New York Stories* (director, 1989)

GoodFellas (director/co-screenwriter, 1990)

Made in Milan (director, 1990)

The Grifters (producer, 1990)

Cape Fear (director, 1991)

The Age of Innocence (director/co-screenwriter, 1993)

Clockers (co-producer, 1995)

Casino (director/co-screenwriter, 1995)

Kundun (director, 1997)

Bringing Out the Dead (director, 1999)

STEVEN SPIELBERG
Director/producer/screen-writer

Duel (director, telefilm, 1971; U.S. theatrical release, 1984)

The Sugarland Express (director/co-screenwriter, 1974)

Jaws (director, 1975)

Close Encounters of the Third Kind (director/screenwriter, 1977)

1941 (director, 1979)

Raiders of the Lost Ark (director, 1981)

E.T., the Extra-Terrestrial (director/co-producer, 1982)

Poltergeist (co-producer/co-screenwriter, 1982)

"Kick the Can," in *Twilight Zone — The Movie* (director/co-producer, 1983)

Indiana Jones and the Temple of Doom (director, 1984)

The Color Purple (director/co-producer, 1985)

Empire of the Sun (director/co-producer, 1987)

Always (director/co-producer, 1989)

Indiana Jones and the Last Crusade (director, 1989)

Hook (director, 1991)

An American Tail II: Fievel Goes West (co-producer, 1991)

Jurassic Park (director, 1993)

Schindler's List (director/producer, 1993; Academy Awards for best director, best picture)

The Lost World: Jurassic Park (director, 1997)

Amistad (director/co-producer, 1997)

Saving Private Ryan (director/co-producer, 1998; Academy Award for best director)

SYLVESTER STALLONE
Actor/director/screenwriter

A Party at Kitty and Stud's (reissued as *The Italian Stallion*) (1970)

Bananas (1971)

The Lords of Flatbush (actor/co-screenwriter, 1974)

Capone (1975)

Death Race 2000 (1975)

Farewell, My Lovely (1975)

No Place to Hide (1975)

The Prisoner of Second Avenue (1975)

Cannonball (1976)

Rocky (actor/screenwriter/fight choreographer, 1976)

F.I.S.T. (actor/co-screenwriter, 1978)

Paradise Alley (actor/director/screenwriter, 1978)

Rocky II (actor/director/screenwriter/fight choreographer, 1979)

Victory (1981)

Nighthawks (1981)

First Blood (actor/co-screenwriter, 1982)

Rocky III (actor/director/screenwriter/fight choreographer, 1982)

Staying Alive (director/co-producer/co-screenwriter, 1983)

Rhinestone (actor/co-screenwriter, 1984)

Rambo: First Blood, Part II (actor/co-screenwriter, 1985)

Rocky IV (actor/director/screenwriter, 1985)

Cobra (actor/screenwriter, 1986)

Over the Top (actor/co-screenwriter, 1987)

Rambo III (actor/co-screenwriter, 1988)

Lock Up (1989)

Tango and Cash (1989)

Rocky V (actor/screenwriter, 1990)

Oscar (1991)

Stop! or My Mom Will Shoot (1992)

Cliffhanger (actor/co-screenwriter, 1993)

Demolition Man (1993)

The Specialist (1994)

Judge Dredd (1995)

Assassins (1995)

Daylight (1996)

Cop Land (1997)

An Alan Smithee Film: Burn Hollywood Burn (1998)

Antz (cartoon voice, 1998)

SHARON STONE
Actor

Stardust Memories (1980)

Deadly Blessing (1981)

Bolero (1981)

Irreconcilable Differences (1984)

King Solomon's Mines (1985)

Allan Quartermain and the Lost City of Gold (1987)

Action Jackson (1988)

Above the Law (1988)

Personal Choice (a.k.a. *Beyond the Stars*) (1989)

Blood and Sand (1989)

Total Recall (1990)

He Said, She Said (1991)

Scissors (1991)

Year of the Gun (1991)

Basic Instinct (1992)

Where Sleeping Dogs Lie (1992)

Diary of a Hitman (1992)

Sliver (1993)

Intersection (1994)

The Specialist (1994)

The Quick and the Dead (1995)

Casino (1995)

Diabolique (1996)

Last Dance (1996)

Sphere (1998)

Antz (cartoon voice, 1998)

The Mighty (1998)

The Muse (1999)

MERYL STREEP
Actor

Julia (1977)

The Deer Hunter (1978)

Manhattan (1979)

The Seduction of Joe Tynan (1979)

Kramer vs. Kramer (1979; Academy Award for best supporting actress)

The French Lieutenant's Woman (1981)

Sophie's Choice (1982; Academy Award for best actress)

Still of the Night (1982)
Silkwood (1983)
Falling in Love (1984)
Plenty (1985)
Out of Africa (1985)
Heartburn (1986)
Ironweed (1987)
A Cry in the Dark (1988)
She-Devil (1989)
Postcards from the Edge (1990)
Defending Your Life (1991)
Death Becomes Her (1992)
The House of the Spirits (1994)
The River Wild (1994)
The Bridges of Madison County (1995)
Before and After (1996)
Marvin's Room (1996)
One True Thing (1998)
Antz (cartoon voice, 1998)
Dancing with Lughnasa (1998)
Music of the Heart (1999)

EMMA THOMPSON
Actor/screenwriter

Henry V (1989)
The Tall Guy (1989)
Impromptu (1990)
Dead Again (1991)
Howard's End (1992)
Peter's Friends (1992)
Much Ado About Nothing (1993)
The Remains of the Day (1993)
In the Name of the Father (1993)
Junior (1994)

Carrington (1995)
Sense and Sensibility (actor/screenwriter, 1995; Academy Award for best adapted screenplay)
The Winter Guest (1997)
Primary Colors (1998)

JOHN TRAVOLTA
Actor

The Devil's Rain (1975)
Carrie (1976)
Saturday Night Fever (1977)
Grease (1978)
Moment by Moment (1978)
Urban Cowboy (1980)
Blow Out (1981)
Staying Alive (1983)
Two of a Kind (1983)
Perfect (1985)
The Experts (1989)
Look Who's Talking (1989)
Look Who's Talking Too (1990)
Shout (1991)
Eyes of an Angel (1991)
Look Who's Talking Now (1993)
Pulp Fiction (1994)
Get Shorty (1995)
White Man's Burden (1995)
Broken Arrow (1996)
Phenomenon (1996)
Michael (1996)
Face/Off (1997)
She's So Lovely (1997)
Mad City (1997)
Primary Colors (1998)
A Civil Action (1998)
The Thin Red Line (1998)
The General's Daughter (1999)

DENZEL WASHINGTON
Actor

Carbon Copy (1981)
A Soldier's Story (1984)
Power (1986)
Cry Freedom (1987)
Glory (1989; Academy Award for best supporting actor)
For Queen and Country (1989)
Reunion (1989)
The Mighty Quinn (1989)
Mo' Better Blues (1990)
Heart Condition (1990)
Ricochet (1991)
Mississippi Masala (1991)
Malcolm X (1992)
Much Ado About Nothing (1993)
The Pelican Brief (1993)
Philadelphia (1993)
Crimson Tide (1995)
Virtuosity (1995)
Devil in a Blue Dress (1995)
Courage Under Fire (1996)
The Preacher's Wife (1996)
Fallen (1998)
He Got Game (1998)
The Siege (1998)
The Bone Collector (1999)

ROBIN WILLIAMS
Actor

Can I Do It...Til I Need Glasses? (1977)
Popeye (1980)
The World According to Garp (1982)
The Survivors (1983)
Moscow on the Hudson (1984)

Seize the Day (1986)
The Best of Times (1986)
Club Paradise (1986)
Good Morning, Vietnam (1987)
The Adventures of Baron Munchausen (1989)
Dead Poets Society (1989)
Cadillac Man (1990)
Awakenings (1990)
Dead Again (1991)
Shakes the Clown (1991)
Hook (1991)
The Fisher King (1991)
FernGully: The Last Rainforest (cartoon voice, 1992)
Aladdin (cartoon voice, 1992)
Toys (1992)
Mrs. Doubtfire (1993)
Being Human (1994)
Nine Months (1994)
To Wong Foo, Thanks for Everything, Julie Newmar (1994)
Jumanji (1995)
The Birdcage (1996)
Jack (1996)
The Secret Agent (1996)
Hamlet (1996)
Fathers' Day (1997)
Flubber (1997)
Good Will Hunting (1997; Academy Award for best supporting actor)
Deconstructing Harry (1997)
What Dreams May Come (1998)
Home Fries (1998)
Patch Adams (1998)
Jacob the Liar (1999)
Bicentennial Man (1999)

THE TOP VIDEOS, YEAR BY YEAR

Billboard magazine has been tracking video sales since 1980 and rentals since 1982. First we bought Jane Fonda workout tapes, then cartoon classics. Now *Austin Powers's* shagadelic video performance has boosted the sequel to new box-office heights, far outpacing the original. Is it a trend, or a one-time trip, baby?

1980

Sales
1. *The Godfather*
2. *Saturday Night Fever*
3. *Superman*
4. *M*A*S*H*
5. *The Godfather, Part II*
6. *Blazing Saddles*
7. *10*
8. *Grease*
9. *The Sound of Music*
10. *Halloween*

1981

Sales
1. *Airplane!*
2. *Caddyshack*
3. *9 to 5*
4. *Superman*
5. *Alien*
6. *Star Trek*
7. *Fame*
8. *Ordinary People*
9. *The Elephant Man*
10. *Popeye*

1982

Sales
1. *Clash of the Titans*
2. *An American Werewolf in London*
3. *Atlantic City*
4. *Stir Crazy*
5. *The Jazz Singer*
6. *The Blue Lagoon*
7. *Kramer vs. Kramer*
8. *Casablanca*
9. *Raging Bull*
10. *Jane Fonda's Workout*

Rentals
1. *Clash of the Titans*
2. *An American Werewolf in London*
3. *Arthur*
4. *Star Wars*
5. *Fort Apache, the Bronx*
6. *For Your Eyes Only*
7. *On Golden Pond*
8. *Stripes*
9. *The Cannonball Run*
10. *Superman II*

1983

Sales
1. *Jane Fonda's Workout*
2. *Star Trek II: The Wrath of Khan*
3. *An Officer and a Gentleman*
4. *The Compleat Beatles*
5. *Rocky III*
6. *Playboy Vol. I*
7. *Poltergeist*
8. *Star Wars*
9. *Blade Runner*
10. *The Road Warrior*

Rentals
1. *An Officer and a Gentleman*
2. *Star Trek II: The Wrath of Khan*
3. *The Road Warrior*
4. *Rocky III*
5. *Poltergeist*
6. *First Blood*
7. *Das Boot*
8. *Night Shift*
9. *Blade Runner*
10. *Sophie's Choice*

1984

Sales
1. *Jane Fonda's Workout*
2. *Raiders of the Lost Ark*
3. *Making Michael Jackson's "Thriller"*
4. *Flashdance*
5. *Duran Duran*
6. *Risky Business*
7. *48 Hrs.*
8. *Do It Debbie's Way*
9. *Trading Places*
10. *The Jane Fonda Workout Challenge*

Rentals
1. *Raiders of the Lost Ark*
2. *Risky Business*
3. *Flashdance*
4. *48 Hrs.*
5. *Tootsie*
6. *Mr. Mom*
7. *Sudden Impact*
8. *Trading Places*
9. *Blue Thunder*
10. *Making Michael Jackson's "Thriller"*

1985

Sales
1. *Jane Fonda's Workout*
2. *Jane Fonda's Prime Time Workout*
3. *Making Michael Jackson's "Thriller"*
4. *Purple Rain*
5. *Gone with the Wind*
6. *The Jane Fonda Workout Challenge*
7. *Raiders of the Lost Ark*
8. *Raquel, Total Beauty and Fitness*
9. *We Are the World—The Video Event*
10. *Wham! The Video*

Rentals
1. *The Karate Kid*
2. *The Terminator*
3. *Police Academy*
4. *Romancing the Stone*
5. *Revenge of the Nerds*
6. *The Natural*
7. *Starman*
8. *The Empire Strikes Back*
9. *Bachelor Party*
10. *Splash*

1986

Sales
1. *Jane Fonda's New Workout*
2. *Jane Fonda's Workout*
3. *Pinocchio*
4. *Beverly Hills Cop*
5. *The Sound of Music*
6. *Jane Fonda's Prime Time Workout*
7. *Casablanca*
8. *Gone With the Wind*
9. *The Wizard of Oz*
10. *The Best of John Belushi*

Rentals
1. *Back to the Future*
2. *Beverly Hills Cop*
3. *Prizzi's Honor*
4. *Witness*
5. *Ghostbusters*
6. *Rambo: First Blood Part II*
7. *Return of the Jedi*
8. *Cocoon*
9. *Mask*
10. *Gremlins*

1987

Sales
1. Jane Fonda's Low Impact Aerobic Workout
2. Jane Fonda's New Workout
3. Sleeping Beauty
4. Top Gun
5. Callanetics
6. The Sound of Music
7. Kathy Smith's Body Basics
8. Indiana Jones and the Temple of Doom
9. Star Trek III: The Search for Spock
10. Star Trek II: The Wrath of Khan

Rentals
1. Short Circuit
2. Top Gun
3. Back to School
4. Indiana Jones and the Temple of Doom
5. Down and Out in Beverly Hills
6. The Color of Money
7. Ferris Bueller's Day Off
8. Stand By Me
9. Ruthless People
10. Aliens

1988

Sales
1. Lady and the Tramp
2. Callanetics
3. Jane Fonda's Low Impact Aerobic Workout
4. Star Trek IV: The Voyage Home
5. Start Up with Jane Fonda
6. An American Tail
7. Jane Fonda's New Workout
8. Pink Floyd: The Wall
9. Dirty Dancing
10. Sleeping Beauty

Rentals
1. Dirty Dancing
2. Lethal Weapon
3. Fatal Attraction
4. The Untouchables
5. The Witches of Eastwick
6. No Way Out
7. Outrageous Fortune
8. Robocop
9. Stakeout
10. Tin Men

1989

Sales
1. Cinderella
2. E.T., the Extra-Terrestrial
3. Jane Fonda's Complete Workout
4. Moonwalker
5. Callanetics
6. Dirty Dancing
7. The Wizard of Oz: The Fiftieth Anniversary Edition
8. Lethal Weapon
9. U2 Rattle and Hum
10. Pink Floyd: The Delicate Sound of Thunder

Rentals
1. Big
2. Die Hard
3. A Fish Called Wanda
4. Three Men and a Baby
5. Beetlejuice
6. Coming to America
7. Cocktail
8. Twins
9. Bull Durham
10. "Crocodile" Dundee II

1990

Sales
1. Bambi
2. New Kids on the Block: Hangin' Tough Live
3. The Little Mermaid
4. Lethal Weapon 2
5. The Wizard of Oz: The Fiftieth Anniversary Edition
6. Batman
7. Honey, I Shrunk the Kids
8. The Land Before Time
9. Who Framed Roger Rabbit
10. Teenage Mutant Ninja Turtles: Cowabunga, Shredhead

Rentals
1. Look Who's Talking
2. When Harry Met Sally
3. Parenthood
4. K-9
5. Dead Poets Society
6. Steel Magnolias
7. Sea of Love
8. Turner & Hooch
9. Black Rain
10. Internal Affairs

1991

Sales
1. Pretty Woman
2. The Little Mermaid
3. Peter Pan
4. The Jungle Book
5. The Three Tenors in Concert
6. Richard Simmons: Sweatin' to the Oldies
7. Teenage Mutant Ninja Turtles: The Movie
8. The Terminator
9. Ducktales: The Movie
10. Total Recall

Rentals
1. Ghost
2. Pretty Woman
3. GoodFellas
4. Bird on a Wire
5. Flatliners
6. The Hunt for Red October
7. Kindergarten Cop
8. Total Recall
9. Sleeping with the Enemy
10. Another 48 Hrs.

1992

Sales
1. Fantasia
2. 101 Dalmations
3. The Jungle Book
4. Robin Hood: Prince of Thieves
5. Cherfitness: A New Attitude
6. Fievel Goes West
7. 1992 Playboy Video Playmate Calendar
8. Home Alone
9. The Rescuers Down Under
10. Playboy: Sexy Lingerie IV

Rentals
1. Thelma and Louise
2. The Silence of the Lambs
3. The Fisher King
4. City Slickers
5. Backdraft
6. Cape Fear
7. The Hand That Rocks the Cradle
8. Father of the Bride
9. Deceived
10. What About Bob?

1993

Sales
1. Beauty and the Beast
2. Pinocchio
3. 101 Dalmatians
4. Playboy Celebrity Centerfold: Jessica Hahn
5. Sister Act
6. Playboy Playmate of the Year 1993: Anna Nicole Smith
7. Cindy Crawford/Shape Your Body Workout
8. Home Alone 2: Lost in New York
9. Disney's Sing Along Songs: Friend Like Me
10. Beethoven

Rentals
1. Sister Act
2. Patriot Games
3. Under Siege
4. A League of Their Own
5. A Few Good Men
6. Scent of a Woman
7. Unforgiven
8. Sneakers
9. Passenger 57
10. The Bodyguard

1994

Sales
1. Aladdin
2. Playboy Celebrity Centerfold: Dian Parkinson
3. Yanni: Live at the Acropolis
4. Free Willy
5. Mrs. Doubtfire
6. The Fugitive
7. The Return of Jafar
8. The Fox and the Hound
9. Ace Ventura: Pet Detective
10. Beauty and the Beast

Rentals
1. Sleepless in Seattle
2. Philadelphia
3. In the Line of Fire
4. The Pelican Brief
5. The Fugitive
6. The Firm
7. Carlito's Way
8. Sliver
9. Ace Ventura: Pet Detective
10. Mrs. Doubtfire

1995

Sales
1. The Lion King
2. Forrest Gump
3. Speed
4. Jurassic Park
5. The Mask
6. Playboy: The Best of Pamela Anderson
7. Snow White and the Seven Dwarfs
8. The Crow
9. Pink Floyd: Pulse
10. Yanni: Live at the Acropolis

Rentals
1. The Shawshank Redemption
2. True Lies
3. Disclosure
4. Speed
5. The Client
6. Clear and Present Danger
7. When a Man Loves a Woman
8. Dumb and Dumber
9. Just Cause
10. Outbreak

1996

Sales
1. Babe
2. Apollo 13
3. Pulp Fiction
4. Playboy: The Best of Jenny McCarthy
5. The Aristocats
6. Batman Forever
7. Jumanji
8. Pocahontas
9. Cinderella
10. Heavy Metal

Rentals
1. Braveheart
2. The Usual Suspects
3. Seven
4. Heat
5. Twelve Monkeys
6. Get Shorty
7. Crimson Tide
8. Casino
9. Executive Decision
10. The Net

1997

Sales
1. Riverdance—The Show
2. Lord of the Dance
3. Independence Day
4. Jerry Maguire
5. 101 Dalmatians
6. Space Jam
7. Toy Story
8. Bambi
9. Star Wars Trilogy— Special Edition
10. The Hunchback of Notre Dame

Rentals
1. Fargo
2. Scream
3. Donnie Brasco
4. Sling Blade
5. Absolute Power
6. The First Wives Club
7. Sleepers
8. Phenomenon
9. Ransom
10. Jerry Maguire

1998

Sales
1. Austin Powers
2. Hercules
3. As Good As It Gets
4. Men in Black
5. Spice World
6. The Little Mermaid: The Special Edition
7. My Best Friend's Wedding
8. Grease: 20th Anniversary Edition
9. Air Force One
10. Titanic

Rentals
1. L.A. Confidential
2. Face/Off
3. As Good As It Gets
4. Good Will Hunting
5. The Devil's Advocate
6. Boogie Nights
7. The Full Monty
8. The Game
9. Wag the Dog
10. Austin Powers

EXTRA! EXTRA! HOW TO GET IN THE BIG PICTURE

Can you pretend to see Godzilla *and* drop your jaw? Or is normalcy in the presence of stars more your forté? Either way, don't sit around waiting to be discovered. Here's how to get your face on the silver screen (or at least in a car commercial). (For more detailed information, check *Back to One,* by Cullen Chambers.)

CASTING AGENCIES

The easiest way to land a bit part in the movies, on TV, or on the radio is to register with a casting agency. There are hundreds of these in the L.A. area. Most charge a modest registration fee of $20 or under, or no fee at all. The following are some of the best known and reputed. The proper registration procedure is noted at the end of each entry.

Academy Kids Management
(casts children and young adults only)
Vineland Studios
4942 Vineland Ave. #200
N. Hollywood, CA 91601
(818) 769-8091
Walk-ins on selected Sundays

Anna Miller Casting
P.O. Box 66
Sunland, CA 91041
(323) 957-4696

Walk-in dates, times, and locations updated on the fourth of each month

Bill Dance Casting
(must be 18 or older)
3518 W. Cahuenga Blvd. #210
Los Angeles, CA 90068
(323) 878-1131
Walk-ins Monday through Thursday from noon to 1 p.m.

Cast of Thousands
(must be 18 or older)
P.O. Box 1899
Burbank, CA 91507
(818) 985-9995
Send a photograph—along with your height, weight, age, and telephone number—to the address above.

Central/Cenex Casting
The largest casting agency in the entertainment industry. Central Casting handles union actors; Cenex handles nonunion actors.
Central: 2835 N. Naomi St.
Burbank, CA 91504-2024

(818) 562-2700
Walk-ins on Tuesdays and Thursdays from 2 to 3:30 p.m.
Cenex: 1700 W. Burbank Blvd.
Burbank, CA 91504
(818) 562-2800
Walk-ins Mondays, Wednesdays, and Fridays from 10 to 11:30 a.m.(must be 18 or older)

Lane Model and Talent Agency
14071 Windsor Place
Santa Ana, CA 92705
(714) 731-1420 or
(714) 731-4560
Send photo and résumé with self-addressed stamped envelope.

Messenger Associates Casting
P.O. Box 2380
Toluca Lake, CA 91610
(818) 760-3696
Call to find out registration times between 10:00 and 10:30 a.m. on weekdays.

HOW THE MIGHTY HAVE RISEN

They're big stars now—but they weren't born that way. These Hollywood idols began their movie careers as lowly extras.

Lucille Ball
Gary Cooper
Bill Cosby
Kevin Costner
Robert De Niro
Robert Duvall
Clark Gable
Teri Garr
Janet Gaynor

Whoopi Goldberg
Mark Harmon
Dustin Hoffman
Bob Hope
Casey Kasem
Michael Landon
Sophia Loren
Marilyn Monroe
Mary Tyler Moore

Ronald Reagan
Burt Reynolds
Tom Selleck
Suzanne Somers
Sylvester Stallone
Donald Sutherland
John Wayne

Rainbow Casting
12501 Chandler Blvd. #204
N. Hollywood, CA 91607
(818) 752-2278
Walk-ins Monday through Thursday from 11 a.m. to 2 p.m.

Screen Children Agency
(casts children and young adults only)
4000 Riverside Drive
Suite A
Burbank, CA 91505
(818) 846-4300
Send photo and résumé with a self-addressed stamped envelope

TRADE SOURCES

These magazines list casting calls and give up-to-the-minute facts on current films and theater productions.

Back Stage
1515 Broadway 14th floor
New York, NY 10036-8986
(212) 764-7300
Published: weekly
Cost per issue: $2.50

*Back Stage West/
Drama-logue*
5055 Wilshire Blvd.
Los Angeles, CA 90036
(323) 525-2356
Published: weekly
Cost per issue: $2.00

Hollywood Reporter
5055 Wilshire Blvd.
Los Angeles, CA 90036
(323) 525-2000
Published: weekdays
Cost per issue: $1.75 every day
except Tuesday
Cost per Tuesday issue: $2.50

Daily Variety
5700 Wilshire Blvd.
Suite 120
Los Angeles, CA 90036
(310) 978-6911
(800) 552-3632
Published: weekdays
Cost per issue: $1.75

Daily Variety Gotham
245 W. 17th St.
New York, NY 10011
(212) 645-0067
Published: weekdays
Cost per issue: $1.75

PAYMENT

Extra work may be a rich experience, but it's not a very lucrative one. A typical salary for eight hours is $40; children can claim somewhat higher wages. The money's a little better if you're in Actors Equity, Screen Actors Guild, or the American Federation of Television and Radio Artists—yet you needn't join a union to get in on the action, and you'll still get salary "bumps" for almost anything you do beyond standing around in a crowd scene. Time-and-a-half is paid for shifts between eight and 10 hours; double time is paid for anything over 10 hours.

TALKING THE TALK

On the set, what separates the men from the boys (or the women from the girls) is whether they truly know how to separate the "gaffer" from the "flipper."

craft services
on-set catering

flipper
cosmetic false teeth for children

gaffer
lighting and electrical equipment crew member

golden time
overtime after the 16th hour for theatrical talent

honey wagon
truck or towed vehicle containing dressing rooms, production offices, and/or mobile restrooms

hot set
a set that is ready for use and is not to be disturbed

P&G
performers with a clean-cut, all-American look like; favored by Proctor & Gamble for its ads

sight-and-sound
parents' right under union contract to be within sight and sound of their child performer at all times

wild track
soundtrack with no apparent relationship to the picture it accompanies

OSCAR—DECADE BY DECADE

For 71 years Oscar has been handed out—now he's at an age for savoring life's achievements. "He rattles," says Olivia de Havilland, holding her 1949 Oscar to the phone receiver and shaking him to illustrate. Ernest Borgnine, a 1955 winner, complains that his Oscar "flakes." Jack Lemmon, who took his *Mr. Roberts* Oscar home in 1956, says the statue rusted: "I had to send him back to the Academy to be redipped." But, ah, how nice to have the old guy around.

Sure, like any sexagenarian, Oscar has taken his lumps. He's been called "a cruel joke" (Marion Davies), "a heartbreaker" (Orson Welles), and "something to be feared" (George C. Scott). But don't count him out. Oscar's imprimatur can add $25 million or more to a winning film's gross, double an actor's salary, and at least triple the size of his ego.

What a shock, then, to learn that Oscar started life as a patsy. In 1927, MGM kingpin Louis B. Mayer and 35 cronies decided to form an Academy of Motion Picture Arts and Sciences. Forget the high-toned blather of the first charter seeking "the improvement and advancement of the…profession." What Mayer really wanted was to stop the advance of film unions. An Academy would keep labor disputes in the hands of the studios. As a carrot to actors, writers, directors, and technicians, Mayer formed a committee to find "some little way" of rewarding merit in film.

While Mayer finagled, MGM art director Cedric Gibbons doodled a sketch of a naked man with a sword, standing on a reel of film. Today Oscar is a thirteen-and-a-half inch, eight-and-a-half pound trophy cast in a metal alloy, then plated in turn with copper, nickel, silver, and finally gold. At Oscar's debut in 1929, some laughed. Screenwriter Frances (*The Champ*) Marion believed Hollywood had found its ideal symbol, "an athletic body…with half his head, that part which held his brains, completely sliced off."

But, hey, Oscar didn't need brains. The studio bosses controlled the nominations and virtually hand-picked the winners. It took years for Oscar to clean house—the Academy did not even start using sealed envelopes until 1941. Since then the Academy, which has grown from a scant 36 members in 1927 to the 4,523 voting members of today, has tried to discourage machinations, especially ad campaigns, to influence voting. It hasn't succeeded, of course. But Oscar, by dint of sheer perseverance, has become, in the words of 1957 winner Alec (*The Bridge on the River Kwai*) Guinness, "the most highly prized [award] of all." At this point, the grandstanding and costuming have become as much a reason for tuning in the Oscars as finding out the winners. "Well, hell—let's face it," says Katharine Hepburn, recipient of a record four Oscars for acting, "It's our track meet. It's painful but it's thrilling."

THE FIRST DECADE

1927–1936

Oscar threw his first party in 1929. The press stayed away. A black-tie crowd clapped politely as all 12 awards were distributed in under five minutes. The three Best Actor nominees didn't bother to show up. Janet Gaynor, first Best Actress winner, gamely tried to act thrilled. "Had I known what it would come to mean in the next few years," she said later, "I'm sure I'd have been overwhelmed." It was the first and last Oscar bust. The Depression and the sound era soon made movies into the ideal escapism, and Oscar's touch came to mean box-office gold. Some aspired to win. Others conspired. As ever in Hollywood, greed, jealousy, and raw ambition added up to a helluva show.

The first Best Actor winner, Emil Jannings, had scooted home to Germany before collecting his Oscar scroll. His later Nazi propaganda films—

done, he said, under duress—made him a favorite with Hitler. Marlene Dietrich disputed the Führer on the talents of her *Blue Angel* costar: "He was a terrible ham."

★

First ceremony: Hollywood's elite jammed the Roosevelt Hotel to hear Al Jolson put down the Oscar as a "paperweight." Jolie's film, *The Jazz Singer*—an early talkie—had been disqualified; only silent films were eligible. The Academy was suspicious of new trends. Some things never change.

★

The WWI air extravaganza *Wings*, starring Buddy Rogers, Clara Bow, and Richard Arlen, was the first Best Picture winner. With tinted color in the battle scenes and noise machines in the theaters to simulate plane crashes, here was a primitive *Top Gun* that showed the Academy's early fondness for spectacle.

★

In 1930, Norma Shearer, winner for *The Divorcée*, posed for a photograph with Oscar two days *before* the ceremony. "She sleeps with the boss," sniped Joan Crawford. Rumor had it that MGM's Irving Thalberg pressured employees to vote for his wife.

★

Oscar's first tie: Fredric March (*Dr. Jekyll and Mr. Hyde*) and Wallace Beery (*The Champ*) shared the 1931 gold. Both had recently adopted children. "Odd," said March, "that Wally and I were given awards for best male performance."

★

Clark Gable and Claudette Colbert both took Oscars for Frank Capra's 1934 comedy, *It Happened One Night*, as did Capra and the film—the only clean sweep in Academy history until *One Flew over the Cuckoo's Nest* duplicated the feat in 1975. No one expected it. Everybody still thinks Gable won for *Gone With the Wind*.

★

The Academy invented a new category, Best Song, prompted by Fred Astaire & Ginger Rogers's dancing and singing of "The Continental" in 1934's *The Gay Divorcee*.

★

Bette Davis collected an award for 1935's *Dangerous*, and gave the statue its name. Reflecting that the trophy "resembled the backside" of her first husband, bandleader Harmon Oscar Nelson Jr., she dubbed her prize Oscar. The moniker stuck.

THE SECOND DECADE

1937–1946

The Oscar ceremony was establishment now, broadcast on radio. In 1939 Gone with the Wind *became the most popular and profitable film ever. But this was also a time of war, as reflected in movies from* Mrs. Miniver *to* The Best Years of Our Lives. *Winston Churchill hailed* Miniver *as "propaganda worth a hundred battleships." As a wartime cost-cutting measure, the Academy ended its elaborate banquets and took the show inside a theater, where food and drink could no longer distract from the ego battles.*

Walt Disney is given a special honorary award for 1938's *Snow White and the Seven Dwarfs*, featuring one large Oscar and seven tiny ones.

★

Gone With the Wind, then the costliest movie in history ($3,957,000) wins eight Oscars, a record not broken until 1958's *Gigi*. Leigh was the triumphant victor, Gable the disgruntled loser. "This was my last chance," he groaned. He was right.

Hattie McDaniel, Miss Scarlett's maid, was the first black actor to win an Oscar. Hattie sobbed on accepting her plaque (supporting players didn't receive full statues until 1943).

★

Playing George M. Cohan in 1942, James Cagney—America's favorite tough guy—became the first actor to win an Oscar for a musical. "Don't forget," said Jimmy in his acceptance speech, "it was a pretty good part."

★

Bogie told Ingrid Bergman in *Casablanca* that their wartime love story "didn't amount to a hill of beans in this crazy world." Except for winning the Best Picture

Oscar of 1943 and the hearts of all romantics.

★

Barry Fitzgerald's role as a twinkly old priest in 1944's *Going My Way* made him a popular winner. But at home a few days later, he forgot that wartime Oscars were made of plaster instead of bronze and decapitated his prize with a golf club.

★

The Lost Weekend, the Best Picture of 1945, offered an unsparing portrait of an alcoholic, by Ray Milland. "I gave it everything I had," said the actor. He must have. Accepting the Oscar, a speechless Milland simply bowed and departed.

THE THIRD DECADE

1947–1956
No sooner had the war ended over there than the Academy embarked on its own war at home. The enemy? Television. The little black box was emptying movie theaters at an alarming rate. The studios retaliated at first with sex, violence and Cinemascope, then gave in. So did Oscar. The Academy Awards were telecast for the first time in 1953. Variety's headline heralded a new era: "1ST MAJOR PIX— TV WEDDING BIG CLICK."

Many years prior, actor Walter Huston said he asked his son, John, "If you ever become a writer or director, please find a good part for your old man." John complied with *The Treasure of the*

Sierra Madre and won 1948 Oscars for them both.

★

Joseph Mankiewicz's crackerjack 1950 comedy *All About Eve* still holds the record—14 nominations. Though *Eve* won six Oscars, including Best Picture, co-stars Bette Davis and Anne Baxter both lost to *Born Yesterday*'s Judy Holliday.

★

Vivien Leigh copped her second Best Actress Oscar in 1951 for *A Streetcar Named Desire*. When the award was announced in Hollywood, Leigh was in New York starring in *Antony and Cleopatra* with then-husband Laurence Olivier.

★

In Hollywood, Donald O'Connor watched Shirley Booth's reaction in New York on being named 1952's Best Actress for *Come Back, Little Sheba*. Meanwhile, the largest single audience (about 80 million) in TV's five-year history saw the first Oscarcast.

★

Having fought to play Maggio in 1953's *From Here to Eternity*, Frank Sinatra triumphed. Said the Best Supporting Actor, "I ducked the party and took a walk. Just me and Oscar." The salty version of James Jones's Army-barracks novel won a whopping eight Oscars, including Best Picture. And Deborah Kerr's sexy roll on the sand with Burt Lancaster cracked her saintly image.

★

A year before her royal wedding in 1956, *The Country Girl*'s Grace Kelly scored an upset victory over Judy Garland in *A Star is Born*. Kelly confided: "I wanted to win so badly, I was afraid that I would stand up no matter which name was read out."

★

First-time film producer Michael Todd nabbed the 1956 Best Picture Oscar with his star-studded *Around the World in 80 Days*. "Imagine this—and being married to Liz, too," he enthused.

THE FOURTH DECADE

1957–1966
The times they were a-changing. Drugs, hippies, the youth movement, civil rights demonstrations, the Kennedy assassination: Many films dealt with these social and political upheavals. But you couldn't tell by Oscar. Relevant was out; big was in. The Academy awarded either historical epics (Ben-Hur, The Bridge on the River Kwai, Lawrence of Arabia, A Man for All Seasons) or blockbuster musicals (Gigi, West Side Story, My Fair Lady, The Sound of Music). The most controversial move on the Academy's part was to issue a formal slap to those who tried to "buy" Oscar nominations by purchasing self-congratulatory ads in the trade papers. Few paid heed.

Joanne Woodward, the new Mrs. Paul Newman, collected her 1957 Oscar for *The Three*

Faces of Eve in a $100 dress she made herself. Joan Crawford claimed Hollywood glamour "had been set back twenty years." When Paul finally won his Oscar, twenty-nine years later, clothes weren't a problem. He didn't show up at all.

★

In 1959, Best Picture *Ben-Hur* took a record eleven Oscars, including Best Actor for Charlton Heston, who got the part after Burt Lancaster dropped out. "It was hard work," said Chuck, who drove a mean chariot. But some questioned his talents. "That Heston," said actor Aldo Ray, "what a hamola."

★

Denounced in Congress in 1950 for her adulterous affair with Roberto Rossellini, Ingrid Bergman ended her decade-long Hollywood exile by presenting a 1959 Best Picture Oscar to *Gigi* producer Arthur Freed. She said her recipe for happiness was "good health and a poor memory."

★

Sporting a tracheotomy scar from a near-fatal bout of pneumonia, Liz Taylor scored a sympathy Oscar for 1960's *Butterfield 8*. In 1966 Liz won Oscar No. 2 for *Who's Afraid of Virginia Woolf?*, but railed at the Academy when fifth husband Richard Burton failed to win too.

★

"I'd like to think it will help," said Sidney Poitier after Anne Bancroft opened the envelope and, for 1963's *Lilies of the Field*, he became

the first black Best Actor winner. "But I don't believe my Oscar will be a magic wand that will wipe away the restrictions on job opportunities for Negro actors."

★

Sisters and Best Actress nominees Lynn and Vanessa Redgrave, cited respectively for 1966's *Georgy Girl* and *Morgan!*, were only the second sister nominees in Oscar history. And they came from a notable British acting family to boot. Maybe so. But Liz Taylor still whupped them both.

THE FIFTH DECADE

1967–1976

Oscar neared its half-century mark in a reactionary mood. Breakthrough films such as Bonnie and Clyde, The Graduate, *and* Easy Rider *ended up losers. In 1968, the year of* 2001: A Space Odyssey, Oliver! *won the Best Picture prize. Yikes. No wonder a streaker felt the need to defame one of the decade's Academy telecasts. Then, a rebel cry was heard in filmland. Newcomers Dustin Hoffman and Jon Voight dared to duke it out with the Duke, John Wayne, for the statue. They failed, but their X-rated* Midnight Cowboy *took the Best Picture prize in 1969. Jane Fonda raised hackles with her Vietnam views and won anyway. The warring factions of the Academy were creating sparks.*

For the second time in Oscar history, a tie was declared.

Funny Girl's Barbra Streisand and *The Lion in Winter's* Katharine Hepburn received the same number of votes from the 1968 Academy's 3,030 members. Designer Edith Head was "shocked," not by the tie but by Streisand's tacky peeka-boo pantsuit.

★

John Wayne had to let it all hang out in 1969 as bloated, one-eyed Rooster Cogburn to finally collect his first Oscar at 62 after 250 movies. "Wow," drawled the Duke, "if I had known, I would have put that eye patch on 35 years earlier."

★

Deriding the Oscars as a "meat parade," George C. Scott declined his nomination as 1970's Best Actor. "My God!" exclaimed Goldie Hawn as she opened the envelope and read the winner's name, "It's George C. Scott."

★

When Marlon Brando was voted 1972's Best Actor, he sent Apache Sacheen Little-feather to reject the Oscar for all the Native Americans Hollywood had demeaned. "Childish," scowled Charlton Heston. "Wonderful," gushed Jane Fonda.

★

Would-be comic Robert Opel snuck backstage at the 1974 Oscars ceremony, flustering emcee David Niven as the cameras cut away to spare home viewers the streaker's shortcomings. The hit of a dull show, Opel was found murdered five years later in his San Francisco sex shop.

★

Struggling actor Sylvester Stallone took half a week to write a script for himself about an underdog fighter. He lost the Best Actor Oscar, but the sleeper film won the title as Best Picture of 1976. "Rocky will be remembered," said Sly with typical modesty.

THE SIXTH DECADE

1977–1986

Oscar had a goal now. Ignoring the films of George Lucas and Steven Spielberg became a full-time job. The Hardy Boys of the zap-happy set combined their youthful fantasies with dazzling special effects to create eight of the top 10 box office hits of all time (E.T., Star Wars, Return of the Jedi, The Empire Strikes Back, Jaws, Raiders of the Lost Ark, Indiana Jones, and Back to the Future). Not a Best Picture winner in the bunch. The Academy, doing penance for scorning Vietnam in the previous decade, anointed politically themed films from The Deer Hunter to Platoon. A vote for Gandhi, the movie, was a vote for Gandhi, the man. Oscar, typically late, began sporting a social conscience.

Accepting her Best Supporting Actress Oscar for 1976's Julia, Vanessa Redgrave dismissed as "Zionist hoodlums" those who showed up to protest her politics. The audience booed, Vanessa had to dine later with her two bodyguards, and a confused Jack Nicholson cracked, "What are these Zionists? I've been skiing."

★

"It's simply terrific. This is something," sputtered Diane Keaton after accepting the

IN THE NAME OF PRODUCTION

More and more celebrity actors are starting their own production companies. But how did they get such funny names? Here's a list of some luminary-owned companies and the inspiration behind their appellations.

Actor	Production Company	Where the Name Came From
Tim Allen	Boxing Cats Prods.	A memorable image from one of Mr. Allen's dreams
Antonio Banderas	Green Moon LLC	Federico García Lorca's poetry attributes Andalusians' dark skin not to the sun but to the light of the green moon
Kevin Costner	TIG Productions	The nickname of his grandmother
Clint Eastwood	Malpaso Productions	A creek in Carmel, Calif., and a Spanish expression meaning "dangerous step," which critics mistakenly assumed he made in forming the company
Jodie Foster	Egg Pictures	The egg as a symbol of protection
Tom Hanks	Clavius Base	The otherworldly planet in Stanley Kubrick's 2001: A Space Odyssey
Dustin Hoffman	Punch Productions	After the Punchinello character in Punch and Judy shows
Elizabeth Hurley and Hugh Grant	Simian Productions	Inspired by Ms. Hurley's affection for and preservation efforts toward chimps
Meg Ryan	Prufrock Pictures	Alluding to one of her favorite poems, T. S. Eliot's "Love Song of J. Alfred Prufrock"
Wesley Snipes	Amen Ra Films	Has been roughly translated to "an unseen source of all creation"; also a reference to the Egyptian sun god, and reportedly an acronym for "Africans Minds Engaged 'N Royal Affairs"
Denzel Washington	Mundy Lane Entertainment	The street he grew up on in Mount Vernon, New York
Sigourney Weaver	Goatcay Prods.	The name of a favorite island retreat

1977 Best Actress prize for *Annie Hall* from first winner Janet Gaynor. Her co-star and former boyfriend Woody Allen stayed home and shrugged off the Academy as meaningless: "I just don't think they know what they're doing."

★

Robert Redford and Warren Beatty have never won Oscars for their acting. That might make sense. Instead, each (Redford for 1980's *Ordinary People* and Beatty for 1981's *Reds*) took the prize as Best Director—a pinnacle Hitchcock, Bergman, Fellini, and Welles never reached. Go figure.

★

Jane Fonda rushed from the 1982 Academy Awards show to present her ailing father and *On Golden Pond* costar, Henry, with the long-overdue first Oscar of his 47-year career. "Hell, if I hadn't won, I wouldn't be able to walk with my head up anymore," Fonda said to his wife, Shirlee. He died five months later.

★

Gidget gets respect: For 1984's *Places in the Heart*, Sally Field won a second Oscar and spoke the words that will haunt her forever: "You like me! You like me!"

★

Perennial also-ran Paul Newman won for reprising his 1961 *Hustler* role in 1986's *The Color of Money*. "After losing six times, I felt it cruel and unusual punishment to attend," said the no-show.

★

Writer-director Oliver Stone took the 1986 Best Picture Oscar for *Platoon*, based on his wartime experiences in Vietnam—a film almost no studio wanted to make.

★

In 1987 Marlee Matlin of *Children of a Lesser God* became the first hearing-impaired Best Actress winner. "After I'm alone I'm going to scream," she said.

THE SEVENTH DECADE

1987–1996

Oscar continues his old traditions by heaping awards on elder statesmen—from Clint Eastwood, Paul Newman, and Sean Connery to Jack Palance, Jessica Tandy, and Martin Landau—who should have been recognized long before. Best Director continues to be a fickle category—how could Oscar recognize Apollo 13 *for seemingly everything except Ron Howard's direction? But the drought finally ends for traditional punching bag Steven Spielberg. Of course it took the culturally significant* Schindler's List *to get the Oscar monkey off of Spielberg's back (after three previous Best Director nominations), rather than his second-highest grossing movie of all time,* Jurassic Park— *making it clear that he was chosen as best director, not most successful. In 1995,* Forrest Gump *bucks the conventional wisdom that box-office favorites don't play well in Academy-land, becoming the highest-grossing picture ever to claim the Best Picture Award.*

In 1988, a barely dressed, slightly tattooed Cher wins Best Actress and announces, "I don't think that this means I am somebody, but I guess I'm on my way."

★

The telecast hits new lows in production values in 1989, with the dreadful Snow White musical opening giving Oscar a black eye.

★

Whoopi Goldberg becomes only the second African-American woman to claim an acting award, as Best Supporting Actress for her role in 1990's *Ghost*.

★

Jack Palance shows he's no old-timer by performing one-handed push-ups by way of accepting his Best Supporting Actor statuette for *City Slickers*. And he provides Oscar host Billy Crystal with a year's worth of material.

★

Lizzy Gardiner, the winner for best costume design on *Priscilla, Queen of the Desert*, makes a memorable imprint on the 1995 ceremonies in her dress fashioned from American Express gold cards.

★

Jessica Lange is 1995's Best Actress for a 1991 performance: Trapped for years by Orion Pictures' financial woes, her *Blue Sky* languished on a bank vault's floor.

★

In 1996, actors get tougher to categorize. Mel Gibson wins trophies for producing and directing—but not acting in—*Braveheart*. Similarly, first-time scripter Emma Thompson takes Best Adapted Screenplay honors for her *Sense and Sensibility*.

★

As Decade Seven closes, the academy's love for independent film burns brighter than ever. *The English Patient*'s sweep makes it an all-time champ; trophies not taken by the big-studio rejects go to the off-Hollywood likes of *Fargo, Sling Blade*, and *Shine*. Were it not for Cuba Gooding Jr.'s *Jerry Maguire* win, no major Oscar would have stayed in Tinseltown.

THE EIGHTH DECADE

1997 and counting

It's too early to note trends for Decade Eight—especially considering how quickly the Academy's tastes turn—but at least the signs are getting clearer. Titanic's *record-tying cruise aside, small films continue to lead the charge, and the big studios' fretting becomes louder. For 1998,* Shakespeare in Love *claims a striking 13 nominations and 7 statuettes, overtaking the early front-runner and box-office leader,* Saving Private Ryan. *Even though Spielberg is recognized for his directing talents for only the second time, it still looks as if he is passed over again. As the promotional drumbeats of Miramax and others become louder, it's unclear how much longer Oscar will shine on the culturally accomplished over box-office favorites.*

At the 70th Academy Awards, Oscar offers a "family portrait," filling the stage with past acting honorees. Though the segment's appeal was tested by appearing over three hours into the ceremony, star power works its magic, with particularly strong applause for Gregory Peck and Shirley Temple Black.

★

Oscar moves to Sunday night for the first time in its history in 1999, and the telecast is marked as the longest ever. The surest sign of life comes from two-time winner Italian actor/director/writer Roberto Benigni, who literally jumps for joy on his way to the podium and exclaims, "I want to kiss everybody because you are the measure of joy." And he means it.

THE ACADEMY AWARDS

	1927–28	1928–29	1929–30
Picture	Wings	Broadway Melody	All Quiet on the Western Front
Actor	Emil Jannings, The Last Command; The Way of All Flesh	Warner Baxter, In Old Arizona	George Arliss, Disraeli
Actress	Janet Gaynor, Seventh Heaven; Street Angel; Sunrise	Mary Pickford, Coquette	Norma Shearer, The Divorcée
Director	Frank Borzage, Seventh Heaven; Lewis Milestone, Two Arabian Knights	Frank Lloyd, The Divine Lady; Weary River; Drag	Lewis Milestone, All Quiet on the Western Front
Adapted Screenplay	Benjamin Glazer, Seventh Heaven	—	—
Original Story	Ben Hecht, Underworld	Hans Kraly, The Patriot	Frances Marion, The Big House
Cinematography	Sunrise	White Shadows in the South Seas	With Byrd at the South Pole
Interior Decoration	The Dove and The Tempest	The Bridge of San Luis Rey	King of Jazz
Sound	—	—	The Big House

OSCAR RECORDS

Most awards in any category: Walt Disney, 27 regular and six special

Most honored films: Ben-Hur in 1959 and Titanic in 1997, with 11 each, and West Side Story in 1961, with 10

Most nominated films: All About Eve and Titanic, with 14 each, and Gone With the Wind, From Here to Eternity, Mary Poppins, Who's Afraid of Virginia Woolf?, Forrest Gump, and Shakespeare in Love, with 13 each

Most nominated films to receive no awards: The Turning Point and The Color Purple, with 11 each

Most Best Actor awards: Spencer Tracy, Fredric March, Gary Cooper, Marlon Brando, Dustin Hoffman, Tom Hanks, and Jack Nicholson, with two each

Most Best Director awards: John Ford with four, for The Informer, The Grapes of Wrath, How Green Was My Valley, and The Quiet Man

Most Best Actress awards: Katharine Hepburn with four, for Morning Glory, Guess Who's Coming to Dinner, The Lion in Winter, and On Golden Pond

Best Actress awards for debut performances: Shirley Booth for Come Back, Little Sheba, Barbra Streisand for Funny Girl, and Marlee Matlin for Children of a Lesser God

First African-American Oscar winner: Hattie McDaniel, Best Supporting Actress, in Gone With the Wind

	1930–31	1931–32	1932–33
Picture	*Cimarron*	*Grand Hotel*	*Cavalcade*
Actor	Lionel Barrymore, *A Free Soul*	Wallace Beery, *The Champ;* Fredric March, *Dr. Jekyll and Mr. Hyde*	Charles Laughton, *The Private Life of Henry VIII*
Actress	Marie Dressler, *Min and Bill*	Helen Hayes, *The Sin of Madelon Claudet*	Katharine Hepburn, *Morning Glory*
Supporting Actor	—	—	—
Supporting Actress	—	—	—
Director	Norman Taurog, *Skippy*	Frank Borzage, *Bad Girl*	Frank Lloyd, *Cavalcade*
Adapted Screenplay/ Screenplay	Howard Estabrook, *Cimarron*	Edwin Burke, *Bad Girl*	Victor Heerman and Sarah Y. Mason, *Little Women*
Original Story	John Monk Saunders, *The Dawn Patrol*	Francis Marion, *The Champ*	Robert Lord, *One Way Passage*
Song	—	—	—
Score	—	—	—
Cinematography	*Tabu*	*Shanghai Express*	*A Farewell to Arms*
Interior Decoration	*Cimarron*	*Transatlantic*	*Cavalcade*
Film Editing	—	—	—
Sound	Paramount Studio Sound Department	Paramount Studio Sound Department	*A Farewell to Arms*
Short Films	—	*Flower and Trees* (Cartoons); *The Music Box* (Comedy); *Wrestling Swordfish* (Novelty)	*The Three Little Pigs* (Cartoons); *So This Is Harris* (Comedy); *Krakatoa* (Novelty)

POPULAR AND PRAISED

Few films claim the hearts of both the moviegoing public and the majority of the Academy of Motion Picture Arts and Sciences. In fact, only 10 of the top 100 moneymakers of all time have won best-picture Oscars. Those films are listed below, ranked in order of amount grossed. (Source: *Variety*)

1.	*Titanic*	1997
2.	*Forrest Gump*	1994
3.	*Gone With the Wind*	1939
4.	*Dances with Wolves*	1990
5.	*Rain Man*	1988
6.	*The Sound of Music*	1965
7.	*The Sting*	1973
8.	*Platoon*	1986
9.	*The Godfather*	1972
10.	*The Silence of the Lambs*	1991

1934	1935	1936	1937
It Happened One Night	*Mutiny on the Bounty*	*The Great Ziegfeld*	*The Life of Emile Zola*
Clark Gable, *It Happened One Night*	Victor McLaglen, *The Informer*	Paul Muni, *The Story of Louis Pasteur*	Spencer Tracy, *Captains Courageous*
Claudette Colbert, *It Happened One Night*	Bette Davis, *Dangerous*	Luise Rainer, *The Great Ziegfeld*	Luise Rainer, *The Good Earth*
—	—	Walter Brennan, *Come and Get It*	Joseph Schildkraut, *The Life of Emile Zola*
—	—	Gale Sondergaard, *Anthony Adverse*	Alice Brady, *In Old Chicago*

1934	1935	1936	1937
Frank Capra, *It Happened One Night*	John Ford, *The Informer*	Frank Capra, *Mr. Deeds Goes to Town*	Leo McCarey, *The Awful Truth*
Robert Riskin, *It Happened One Night*	Dudley Nichols, *The Informer*	Pierre Collings and Sheridan Gibney, *The Story of Louis Pasteur*	Heinz Herald, Geza Herczeg, and Norman Reilly Raine, *The Life of Emile Zola*
Arthur Caesar, *Manhattan Melodrama*	Ben Hecht and Charles MacArthur, *The Scoundrel*	Pierre Collings and Sheridan Gibney, *The Story of Louis Pasteur*	William A. Wellman and Robert Carson, *A Star is Born*
"The Continental" *(The Gay Divorcée)*	"Lullaby of Broadway" *(Gold Diggers of 1935)*	"The Way You Look Tonight" *(Swing Time)*	"Sweet Leilani" *(Waikiki Wedding)*
One Night of Love	*The Informer*	*Anthony Adverse*	*100 Men and a Girl*
Cleopatra	*A Midsummer Night's Dream*	*Anthony Adverse*	*The Good Earth*

1934	1935	1936	1937
The Merry Widow	*The Dark Angel*	*Dodsworth*	*Lost Horizon*
Eskimo	*A Midsummer Night's Dream*	*Anthony Adverse*	*Lost Horizon*
One Night of Love	*Naughty Marietta*	*San Francisco*	*The Hurricane*
The Tortoise and the Hare (Cartoons); *La Cucaracha* (Comedy); *City of Wax* (Novelty)	*Three Orphan Kittens* (Cartoons); *How To Sleep* (Comedy); *Wings over Mt. Everest* (Novelty)	*Country Cousin* (Cartoons); *Bored of Education* (One-Reel); *The Public Pays* (Two-Reel); *Give Me Liberty* (Color)	*The Old Mill* (Cartoons); *Private Life of the Gannetts* (One-Reel); *Torture Money* (Two-Reel); *Penny Wisdom* (Color)

DISNEY'S WINNING TUNES

Disney has dominated the Oscar Best Song category in recent years, winning seven times in the last nine years. In total, the studio has won 10 times in this category; Paramount still leads with 16 wins, while 20th Century Fox's 10 wins tie it with Disney for second place.

Song	Film	Year
"When You Wish Upon a Star"	*Pinocchio*	1940
"Zip-a-Dee-Doo-Dah"	*Song of the South*	1947
"Chim Chim Cher-ee"	*Mary Poppins*	1964
"Under the Sea"	*The Little Mermaid*	1989
"Sooner or Later"	*Dick Tracy*	1990
"Beauty and the Beast"	*Beauty and the Beast*	1991
"A Whole New World"	*Aladdin*	1992
"Can You Feel the Love Tonight"	*The Lion King*	1994
"Colors of the Wind"	*Pocahontas*	1995
"You Must Love Me"	*Evita*	1996

	1938	1939	1940
Picture	You Can't Take It with You	Gone With the Wind	Rebecca
Actor	Spencer Tracy, Boys Town	Robert Donat, Goodbye, Mr. Chips	James Stewart, The Philadelphia Story
Actress	Bette Davis, Jezebel	Vivien Leigh, Gone With the Wind	Ginger Rogers, Kitty Foyle
Supporting Actor	Walter Brennan, Kentucky	Thomas Mitchell, Stagecoach	Walter Brennan, The Westerner
Supporting Actress	Fay Bainter, Jezebel	Hattie McDaniel, Gone With the Wind	Jane Darwell, The Grapes of Wrath
Director	Frank Capra, You Can't Take It with You	Victor Fleming, Gone With the Wind	John Ford, The Grapes of Wrath
Screenplay	Ian Dalrymple, Cecil Lewis, and W. P. Lipscomb, Pygmalion	Sidney Howard, Gone With the Wind	Donald Ogden Stewart, The Philadelphia Story
Original Screenplay/ Original Story	Eleanore Griffin and Dore Schary, Boys Town	Lewis R. Foster, Mr. Smith Goes to Washington	Preston Sturges, The Great McGinty; Benjamin Glazer and John S. Toldy, Arise, My Love
Song	"Thanks for the Memory" (Big Broadcast of 1938)	"Over the Rainbow" (The Wizard of Oz)	"When You Wish upon a Star" (Pinocchio)
Score/Original Score	Alexander's Ragtime Band; The Adventures of Robin Hood	Stagecoach; The Wizard of Oz	Tin Pan Alley; Pinocchio
Cinematography	The Great Waltz	Wuthering Heights (B&W); Gone With the Wind (Color)	Rebecca (B&W); The Thief of Bagdad (Color)
Interior Decoration	The Adventures of Robin Hood	Gone With the Wind	Pride and Prejudice (B&W); The Thief of Bagdad (Color)
Film Editing	The Adventures of Robin Hood	Gone With the Wind	North West Mounted Police
Sound	The Cowboy and the Lady	When Tomorrow Comes	Strike Up the Band
Special Effects	—	The Rains Came	The Thief of Bagdad
Short Films	Ferdinand the Bull (Cartoons); That Mothers Might Live (One-Reel); Declaration of Independence (Two-Reel)	The Ugly Duckling (Cartoons); Busy Little Bears (One-Reel); Sons of Liberty (Two-Reel)	Milky Way (Cartoons); Quicker 'N a Wink (One-Reel); Teddy, the Rough Rider (Two-Reel)
Documentaries	—	—	—

> 66 I'm lucky my grandmother was such a terrible driver. 99
> —Alfred Uhry, winner for Best Original Screenplay, *Driving Miss Daisy*, 1989

1941	1942	1943	1944
How Green Was My Valley	Mrs. Miniver	Casablanca	Going My Way
Gary Cooper, Sergeant York	James Cagney, Yankee Doodle Dandy	Paul Lukas, Watch on the Rhine	Bing Crosby, Going My Way
Joan Fontaine, Suspicion	Greer Garson, Mrs. Miniver	Jennifer Jones, The Song of Bernadette	Ingrid Bergman, Gaslight
Donald Crisp, How Green Was My Valley	Van Heflin, Johnny Eager	Charles Coburn, The More the Merrier	Barry Fitzgerald, Going My Way
Mary Astor, The Great Lie	Teresa Wright, Mrs. Miniver	Katina Paxinou, For Whom the Bell Tolls	Ethel Barrymore, None but the Lonely Heart
John Ford, How Green Was My Valley	William Wyler, Mrs. Miniver	Michael Curtiz, Casablanca	Leo McCarey, Going My Way
Sidney Buchman and Seton I. Miller, Here Comes Mr. Jordan	George Froeschel, James Hilton, Claudine West, and Arthur Wimperis, Mrs. Miniver	Julius J. Epstein, Philip G. Epstein, and Howard Koch, Casablanca	Frank Butler and Frank Cavett, Going My Way
Harry Segall, Here Comes Mr. Jordan; Herman J. Mankiewicz and Orson Welles, Citizen Kane	Michael Kanin and Ring Lardner Jr., Woman of the Year; Emeric Pressburger, The Invaders	Norman Krasna, Princess O'Rourke; William Saroyan, The Human Comedy	Lamar Trotti, Wilson; Leo McCarey, Going My Way
"The Last Time I Saw Paris" (Lady Be Good)	"White Christmas" (Holiday Inn)	"You'll Never Know" (Hello, Frisco, Hello)	"Swinging on a Star" (Going My Way)
All That Money Can Buy (Dramatic); Dumbo (Musical)	Now, Voyager (Dramatic or Comedy); Yankee Doodle Dandy (Musical)	The Song of Bernadette (Dramatic or Comedy); This Is the Army (Musical)	Since You Went Away (Dramatic or Comedy); Cover Girl (Musical)
How Green Was My Valley (B&W); Blood and Sand (Color)	Mrs. Miniver (B&W); The Black Swan (Color)	The Song of Bernadette (B&W); The Phantom of the Opera (Color)	Laura (B&W); Wilson (Color)
How Green Was My Valley (B&W); Blossoms in the Dust (Color)	This Above All (B&W); My Gal Sal (Color)	The Song of Bernadette (B&W); The Phantom of the Opera (Color)	Gaslight (B&W); Wilson (Color)
Sergeant York	The Pride of the Yankees	Air Force	Wilson
That Hamilton Woman	Yankee Doodle Dandy	This Land Is Mine	Wilson
I Wanted Wings	Reap the Wild Wind	Crash Dive	Thirty Seconds over Tokyo
Lend a Paw (Cartoons); Of Pups and Puzzles (One-Reel); Main Street on the March (Two-Reel)	Der Fuehrer's Face (Cartoons); Speaking of Animals and Their Families (One-Reel); Beyond the Line of Duty (Two-Reel)	Yankee Doodle Mouse (Cartoons); Amphibious Fighters (One-Reel); Heavenly Music (Two-Reel)	Mouse Trouble (Cartoons); Who's Who in Animal Land (One-Reel); I Won't Play (Two-Reel)
Churchill's Island	Battle of Midway; Kokoda Front Line; Moscow Strikes Back; Prelude to War	December 7th (Short); Desert Victory (Feature)	With the Marines at Tarawa (Short); The Fighting Lady (Feature)

	1945	1946	1947
Picture	*The Lost Weekend*	*The Best Years of Our Lives*	*Gentleman's Agreement*
Actor	Ray Milland, *The Lost Weekend*	Fredric March, *The Best Years of Our Lives*	Ronald Colman, *A Double Life*
Actress	Joan Crawford, *Mildred Pierce*	Olivia de Havilland, *To Each His Own*	Loretta Young, *The Farmer's Daughter*
Supporting Actor	James Dunn, *A Tree Grows in Brooklyn*	Harold Russell, *The Best Years of Our Lives*	Edmund Gwenn, *Miracle on 34th Street*
Supporting Actress	Anne Revere, *National Velvet*	Anne Baxter, *The Razor's Edge*	Celeste Holm, *Gentleman's Agreement*
Director	Billy Wilder, *The Lost Weekend*	William Wyler, *The Best Years of Our Lives*	Elia Kazan, *Gentleman's Agreement*
Screenplay	Charles Brackett and Billy Wilder, *The Lost Weekend*	Robert E. Sherwood, *The Best Years of Our Lives*	George Seaton, *Miracle on 34th Street*
Original Screenplay/Original Story	Richard Schweizer, *Marie-Louise*; Charles G. Booth, *The House on 92nd Street*	Muriel and Sydney Box, *The Seventh Veil*; Clemence Dane, *Vacation from Marriage*	Sidney Sheldon, *The Bachelor and the Bobby-Soxer*; Valentine Davies, *Miracle on 34th Street*
Song	"It Might As Well Be Spring" *(State Fair)*	"On the Atchison, Topeka and Santa Fe" *(The Harvey Girls)*	"Zip-A-Dee-Doo-Dah" *(Song of the South)*
Score—Dramatic or Comedy/Musical	*Spellbound; Anchors Aweigh*	*The Best Years of Our Lives; The Jolson Story*	*A Double Life; Mother Wore Tights*
Cinematography	*The Picture of Dorian Gray* (B&W); *Leave Her to Heaven* (Color)	*Anna and the King of Siam* (B&W); *The Yearling* (Color)	*Great Expectations* (B&W); *Black Narcissus* (Color)
Costume Design	—	—	—
Interior Decoration, through 1946; Art Direction—Set Decoration, from 1947	*Blood on the Sun* (B&W); *Frenchman's Creek* (Color)	*Anna and the King of Siam* (B&W); *The Yearling* (Color)	*Great Expectations* (B&W); *Black Narcissus* (Color)
Film Editing	*National Velvet*	*The Best Years of Our Lives*	*Body and Soul*
Sound	*The Bells of St. Mary's*	*The Jolson Story*	*The Bishop's Wife*
Special Effects	*Wonder Man*	*Blithe Spirit*	*Green Dolphin Street*
Short Films	*Quiet Please* (Cartoons); *Stairway to Light* (One-Reel); *Star in the Night* (Two-Reel)	*The Cat Concerto* (Cartoons); *Facing Your Danger* (One-Reel); *A Boy and His Dog* (Two-Reel)	*Tweetie Pie* (Cartoons); *Goodbye Miss Turlock* (One-Reel); *Climbing the Matterhorn* (Two-Reel)
Documentaries	*Hitler Lives?* (Short); *The True Glory* (Feature)	*Seeds of Destiny* (Short)	*First Steps* (Short); *Design for Death* (Feature)

66 I do feel like the Academy is slacking off in the class quotient—after all, I won. 99

—Sally Field, Best Actress, 1979
Best Actress, 1984

1948	1949	1950	1951
Hamlet	All the King's Men	All About Eve	An American in Paris
Laurence Olivier, Hamlet	Broderick Crawford, All the King's Men	José Ferrer, Cyrano de Bergerac	Humphrey Bogart, The African Queen
Jane Wyman, Johnny Belinda	Olivia de Havilland, The Heiress	Judy Holliday, Born Yesterday	Vivien Leigh, A Streetcar Named Desire
Walter Huston, The Treasure of the Sierra Madre	Dean Jagger, Twelve O'Clock High	George Sanders, All About Eve	Karl Malden, A Streetcar Named Desire
Claire Trevor, Key Largo	Mercedes McCambridge, All the King's Men	Josephine Hull, Harvey	Kim Hunter, A Streetcar Named Desire
John Huston, The Treasure of the Sierra Madre	Joseph L. Mankiewicz, A Letter to Three Wives	Joseph L. Mankiewicz, All About Eve	George Stevens, A Place in the Sun
John Huston, The Treasure of the Sierra Madre	Joseph L. Mankiewicz, A Letter to Three Wives	Joseph L. Mankiewicz, All About Eve	Michael Wilson and Harry Brown, A Place in the Sun
Richard Schweizer and David Wechsler, The Search	Douglas Morrow, The Stratton Story (Motion Picture Story); Robert Pirosh, Battleground (Story and Screenplay)	Edna & Edward Anhalt, Panic in the Streets (Motion Picture Story); Charles Brackett, Billy Wilder, and D.M. Marshman Jr., Sunset Boulevard (Story and Screenplay)	Paul Dehn and James Bernard, Seven Days to Noon (Motion Picture Story); Alan Jay Lerner, An American in Paris (Story and Screenplay)
"Buttons and Bows" (The Paleface)	"Baby, It's Cold Outside" (Neptune's Daughter)	"Mona Lisa" (Captain Carey, USA)	"In the Cool, Cool, Cool of the Evening" (Here Comes the Groom)
The Red Shoes; Easter Parade	The Heiress; On the Town	Sunset Boulevard; Annie Get Your Gun	A Place in the Sun; An American in Paris
The Naked City (B&W); Joan of Arc (Color)	Battleground (B&W); She Wore a Yellow Ribbon (Color)	The Third Man (B&W); King Solomon's Mines (Color)	A Place in the Sun (B&W); An American in Paris (Color)
Hamlet (B&W); Joan of Arc (Color)	The Heiress (B&W); Adventures of Don Juan (Color)	All About Eve (B&W); Samson and Delilah (Color)	A Place in the Sun (B&W); An American in Paris (Color)
Hamlet (B&W); The Red Shoes (Color)	The Heiress (B&W); Little Women (Color)	Sunset Boulevard (B&W); Samson and Delilah (Color)	A Streetcar Named Desire (B&W); An American in Paris (Color)
The Naked City	Champion	King Solomon's Mines	A Place in the Sun
The Snake Pit	Twelve O'Clock High	All About Eve	The Great Caruso
Portrait of Jennie	Mighty Joe Young	Destination Moon	When Worlds Collide
The Little Orphan (Cartoons); Symphony of a City (One-Reel); Seal Island (Two-Reel)	For Scent-imental Reasons (Cartoons); Aquatic House Party (One-Reel); Van Gogh (Two-Reel)	Gerald McBoing-Boing (Cartoons); Grandad of Races (One-Reel); In Beaver Valley (Two-Reel)	Two Mouseketeers (Cartoons); World of Kids (One-Reel); Nature's Half Acre (Two-Reel)
Toward Independence (Short); The Secret Land (Feature)	A Chance To Live and So Much for So Little (Short); Daybreak in Udi (Feature)	Why Korea? (Short); The Titan: Story of Michelangelo (Feature)	Benjy (Short); Kon-Tiki (Feature)

> 66 I just drove up to be in the pre-Oscar show. 99
>
> —Steve Martin, 1984

	1952	1953	1954
Picture	*The Greatest Show on Earth*	*From Here to Eternity*	*On the Waterfront*
Actor	Gary Cooper, *High Noon*	William Holden, *Stalag 17*	Marlon Brando, *On the Waterfront*
Actress	Shirley Booth, *Come Back, Little Sheba*	Audrey Hepburn, *Roman Holiday*	Grace Kelly, *The Country Girl*
Supporting Actor	Anthony Quinn, *Viva Zapata!*	Frank Sinatra, *From Here to Eternity*	Edmond O'Brien, *The Barefoot Contessa*
Supporting Actress	Gloria Grahame, *The Bad and the Beautiful*	Donna Reed, *From Here to Eternity*	Eva Marie Saint, *On the Waterfront*
Director	John Ford, *The Quiet Man*	Fred Zinnemann, *From Here to Eternity*	Elia Kazan, *On the Waterfront*
Screenplay	Charles Schnee, *The Bad and the Beautiful*	Daniel Taradash, *From Here to Eternity*	George Seaton, *The Country Girl*
Story/Story and Screenplay	Frederic M. Frank, Theodore St. John, and Frank Cavett, *The Greatest Show on Earth;* T.E.B. Clarke, *The Lavender Hill Mob*	Ian McLellan Hunter, *Roman Holiday;* Charles Brackett, Walter Reisch, and Richard Breen, *Titanic*	Philip Yordan, *Broken Lance;* Budd Schulberg, *On the Waterfront*
Song	"High Noon (Do Not Forsake Me, Oh My Darlin')" *(High Noon)*	"Secret Love" *(Calamity Jane)*	"Three Coins in the Fountain" *(Three Coins in the Fountain)*
Score—Dramatic or Comedy/Musical	*High Noon; With a Song in My Heart*	*Lili; Call Me Madam*	*The High and the Mighty; Seven Brides for Seven Brothers*
Cinematography	*The Bad and the Beautiful* (B&W); *The Quiet Man* (Color)	*From Here to Eternity* (B&W); *Shane* (Color)	*On the Waterfront* (B&W); *Three Coins in the Fountain* (Color)
Costume Design	*The Bad and the Beautiful* (B&W); *Moulin Rouge* (Color)	*Roman Holiday* (B&W); *The Robe* (Color)	*Sabrina* (B&W); *Gate of Hell* (Color)
Art Direction—Set Decoration	*The Bad and the Beautiful* (B&W); *Moulin Rouge* (Color)	*Julius Caesar* (B&W); *The Robe* (Color)	*On the Waterfront* (B&W); *20,000 Leagues Under the Sea* (Color)
Film Editing	*High Noon*	*From Here to Eternity*	*On the Waterfront*
Foreign Language Film	—	—	—
Sound	*Breaking the Sound Barrier*	*From Here to Eternity*	*The Glenn Miller Story*
Special Effects	*Plymouth Adventure*	*The War of the Worlds*	*20,000 Leagues Under the Sea*
Short Films	*Johann Mouse* (Cartoons); *Light in the Window* (One-Reel); *Water Birds* (Two-Reel)	*Toot, Whistle, Plunk and Boom* (Cartoons); *The Merry Wives of Windsor Overture* (One-Reel); *Bear Country* (Two-Reel)	*When Magoo Flew* (Cartoons); *This Mechanical Age* (One-Reel); *A Time Out of War* (Two-Reel)
Documentaries	*Neighbours* (Short); *The Sea Around Us* (Feature)	*The Alaskan Eskimo* (Short); *The Living Desert* (Feature)	*Thursday's Children* (Short); *The Vanishing Prairie* (Feature)

1955	1956	1957	1958
Marty	*Around the World in 80 Days*	*The Bridge on the River Kwai*	*Gigi*
Ernest Borgnine, *Marty*	Yul Brynner, *The King and I*	Alec Guinness, *The Bridge on the River Kwai*	David Niven, *Separate Tables*
Anna Magnani, *The Rose Tattoo*	Ingrid Bergman, *Anastasia*	Joanne Woodward, *The Three Faces of Eve*	Susan Hayward, *I Want to Live!*
Jack Lemmon, *Mister Roberts*	Anthony Quinn, *Lust for Life*	Red Buttons, *Sayonara*	Burl Ives, *The Big Country*
Jo Van Fleet, *East of Eden*	Dorothy Malone, *Written on the Wind*	Miyoshi Umeki, *Sayonara*	Wendy Hiller, *Separate Tables*
Delbert Mann, *Marty*	George Stevens, *Giant*	David Lean, *The Bridge on the River Kwai*	Vincente Minnelli, *Gigi*
Paddy Chayefsky, *Marty*	James Poe, John Farrow, and S.J. Perelman, *Around the World in 80 Days* (Adapted)	Pierre Boulle, *The Bridge on the River Kwai* (Adapted)	Alan Jay Lerner, *Gigi* (Adapted)
Daniel Fuchs, *Love Me or Leave Me*; William Ludwig and Sonya Levien, *Interrupted Melody*	Dalton Trumbo (aka Robert Rich), *The Brave One*; Albert Lamorisse, *The Red Balloon* (Original)	George Wells, *Designing Woman*	Nathan E. Douglas and Harold Jacob Smith, *The Defiant Ones*
"Love is a Many-Splendored Thing" *(Love Is a Many-Splendored Thing)*	"Whatever Will Be, Will Be (Que Será, Será)" *(The Man Who Knew Too Much)*	"All the Way" *(The Joker Is Wild)*	"Gigi" *(Gigi)*
Love is a Many-Splendored Thing, Oklahoma!	*Around the World in 80 Days*; *The King and I*	*The Bridge on the River Kwai*	*The Old Man and the Sea*; *Gigi*
The Rose Tattoo (B&W); *To Catch a Thief* (Color)	*Somebody up There Likes Me* (B&W); *Around the World in 80 Days* (Color)	*The Bridge on the River Kwai*	*The Defiant Ones* (B&W); *Gigi* (Color)
I'll Cry Tomorrow (B&W); *Love Is a Many-Splendored Thing* (Color)	*The Solid Gold Cadillac* (B&W); *The King and I* (Color)	*Les Girls*	*Gigi*
The Rose Tattoo (B&W); *Picnic* (Color)	*Somebody up There Likes Me* (B&W); *The King and I* (Color)	*Sayonara*	*Gigi*
Picnic	*Around the World in 80 Days*	*The Bridge on the River Kwai*	*Gigi*
—	*La Strada* (Italy)	*The Nights of Cabiria* (Italy)	*My Uncle* (France)
Oklahoma!	*The King and I*	*Sayonara*	*South Pacific*
The Bridges at Toko-Ri	*The Ten Commandments*	*The Enemy Below*	*tom thumb*
Speedy Gonzales (Cartoon); *Survival City* (One-Reel); *The Face of Lincoln* (Two-Reel)	*Mister Magoo's Puddle Jumper* (Cartoons); *Crashing the Water Barrier* (One-Reel); *The Bespoke Overcoat* (Two-Reel)	*Birds Anonymous* (Cartoons); *The Wetback Hound* (Live Action)	*Knighty Knight Bugs* (Cartoons); *Grand Canyon* (Live Action)
Men Against the Arctic (Short); *Helen Keller in Her Story* (Feature)	*The True Story of the Civil War* (Short); *The Silent World* (Feature)	*Albert Schweitzer* (Feature)	*AMA Girls* (Short); *White Wilderness* (Feature)

	1959	1960	1961
Picture	Ben-Hur	The Apartment	West Side Story
Actor	Charlton Heston, Ben-Hur	Burt Lancaster, Elmer Gantry	Maximilian Schell, Judgment at Nuremburg
Actress	Simone Signoret, Room at the Top	Elizabeth Taylor, Butterfield 8	Sophia Loren, Two Women
Supporting Actor	Hugh Griffith, Ben-Hur	Peter Ustinov, Spartacus	George Chakiris, West Side Story
Supporting Actress	Shelley Winters, The Diary of Anne Frank	Shirley Jones, Elmer Gantry	Rita Moreno, West Side Story
Director	William Wyler, Ben-Hur	Billy Wilder, The Apartment	Robert Wise and Jerome Robbins, West Side Story
Adapted Screenplay	Neil Paterson, Room at the Top	Richard Brooks, Elmer Gantry	Abby Mann, Judgment at Nuremberg
Story and Screenplay	Russell Rouse and Clarence Greene, story; Stanley Shapiro and Maurice Richlin, screenplay, Pillow Talk	Billy Wilder and I.A.L. Diamond, The Apartment	William Inge, Splendor in the Grass
Song	"High Hopes" (A Hole in the Head)	"Never on Sunday" (Never on Sunday)	"Moon River" (Breakfast at Tiffany's)
Score	Ben-Hur (Dramatic or Comedy); Porgy and Bess (Musical)	Exodus (Dramatic or Comedy); Song Without End (The Story of Franz Liszt) (Musical)	Breakfast at Tiffany's (Dramatic or Comedy); West Side Story (Musical)
Cinematography	The Diary of Anne Frank (B&W); Ben-Hur (Color)	Sons and Lovers (B&W); Spartacus (Color)	The Hustler (B&W); West Side Story (Color)
Costume Design	Some Like It Hot (B&W); Ben-Hur (Color)	The Facts of Life (B&W); Spartacus (Color)	La Dolce Vita (B&W); West Side Story (Color)
Art Direction—Set Decoration	The Diary of Anne Frank (B&W); Ben-Hur (Color)	The Apartment (B&W); Spartacus (Color)	The Hustler (B&W); West Side Story (Color)
Film Editing	Ben-Hur	The Apartment	West Side Story
Foreign Language Film	Black Orpheus (France)	The Virgin Spring (Sweden)	Through a Glass Darkly (Sweden)
Sound	Ben-Hur	The Alamo	West Side Story
Sound Effects (Editing)	—	—	—
Visual Effects	—	—	—
Special Effects	Ben-Hur	The Time Machine	The Guns of Navarone
Short Films	Moonbird (Cartoons); The Golden Fish (Live Action)	Munro (Cartoons); Day of the Painter (Live Action)	Ersatz (The Substitute) (Cartoons); Seawards the Great Ships (Live Action)
Documentaries	Glass (Short); Serengeti Shall Not Die (Feature)	Giuseppina (Short); The Horse with the Flying Tail (Feature)	Project Hope (Short); Le Ciel et la boue (Sky Above and Mud Beneath) (Feature)

1962 | 1963 | 1964 | 1965

1962	1963	1964	1965
Lawrence of Arabia	*Tom Jones*	*My Fair Lady*	*The Sound of Music*
Gregory Peck, *To Kill a Mockingbird*	Sidney Poitier, *Lilies of the Field*	Rex Harrison, *My Fair Lady*	Lee Marvin, *Cat Ballou*
Anne Bancroft, *The Miracle Worker*	Patricia Neal, *Hud*	Julie Andrews, *Mary Poppins*	Julie Christie, *Darling*
Ed Begley, *Sweet Bird of Youth*	Melvyn Douglas, *Hud*	Peter Ustinov, *Topkapi*	Martin Balsam, *A Thousand Clowns*
Patty Duke, *The Miracle Worker*	Margaret Rutherford, *The V.I.P.s*	Lila Kedrova, *Zorba the Greek*	Shelley Winters, *A Patch of Blue*
David Lean, *Lawrence of Arabia*	Tony Richardson, *Tom Jones*	George Cukor, *My Fair Lady*	Robert Wise, *The Sound of Music*
Horton Foote, *To Kill a Mockingbird*	John Osborne, *Tom Jones*	Edward Anhalt, *Beckett*	Robert Bolt, *Doctor Zhivago*
Ennio de Concini, Alfredo Giannetti, and Pietro Germi, *Divorce—Italian Style*	James R. Webb, *How the West Was Won*	S. H. Barnett, story; Peter Stone and Frank Tarloff, screenplay, *Father Goose*	Frederic Raphael, *Darling*
"Days of Wine and Roses" *(Days of Wine and Roses)*	"Call Me Irresponsible" *(Papa's Delicate Condition)*	"Chim Chim Cher-ee" *(Mary Poppins)*	"The Shadow of Your Smile" *(The Sandpiper)*
Lawrence of Arabia (Original); *The Music Man* (Adaptation)	*Tom Jones* (Original); *Irma La Douce* (Adaptation)	*Mary Poppins* (Original); *My Fair Lady* (Adaptation)	*Doctor Zhivago* (Original); *The Sound of Music* (Adaptation)
The Longest Day (B&W); *Lawrence of Arabia* (Color)	*Hud* (B&W); *Cleopatra* (Color)	*Zorba the Greek* (B&W); *My Fair Lady* (Color)	*Ship of Fools* (B&W); *Doctor Zhivago* (Color)
Whatever Happened to Baby Jane? (B&W); *The Wonderful World of the Brothers Grimm* (Color)	*8½* (B&W); *Cleopatra* (Color)	*The Night of the Iguana* (B&W); *My Fair Lady* (Color)	*Darling* (B&W); *Doctor Zhivago* (Color)
To Kill a Mockingbird (B&W); *Lawrence of Arabia* (Color)	*America America* (B&W); *Cleopatra* (Color)	*Zorba the Greek* (B&W); *My Fair Lady* (Color)	*Ship of Fools* (B&W); *Doctor Zhivago* (Color)
Lawrence of Arabia	*How the West Was Won*	*Mary Poppins*	*The Sound of Music*
Sundays and Cybèle (France)	*8½* (Italy)	*Yesterday, Today and Tomorrow* (Italy)	*The Shop on Main Street* (Czechoslovakia)
Lawrence of Arabia	*How the West Was Won*	*My Fair Lady*	*The Sound of Music*
—	*It's a Mad, Mad, Mad, Mad World*	*Goldfinger*	*The Great Race*
—	*Cleopatra*	*Mary Poppins*	*Thunderball*
The Longest Day	—	—	—
The Hole (Cartoons); *Heureux Anniversaire* (Live Action)	*The Critic* (Cartoons); *An Occurrence at Owl Creek Bridge* (Live Action)	*The Pink Phink* (Cartoons); *Casals Conducts: 1964* (Live Action)	*The Dot and the Line* (Cartoons); *The Chicken (Le Poulet)* (Live Action)
Dylan Thomas (Short); *Black Fox* (Feature)	*Chagall* (Short); *Robert Frost: A Lover's Quarrel with the World* (Feature)	*Nine from Little Rock* (Short); *Jacques-Yves Cousteau's World Without Sun* (Feature)	*To Be Alive!* (Short); *The Eleanor Roosevelt Story* (Feature)

	1966	**1967**	**1968**
Picture	*A Man for All Seasons*	*In the Heat of the Night*	*Oliver!*
Actor	Paul Scofield, *A Man for All Seasons*	Rod Steiger, *In the Heat of the Night*	Cliff Robertson, *Charly*
Actress	Elizabeth Taylor, *Who's Afraid of Virginia Woolf?*	Katharine Hepburn, *Guess Who's Coming to Dinner*	Katharine Hepburn, *The Lion in Winter;* Barbra Streisand, *Funny Girl*
Supporting Actor	Walter Matthau, *The Fortune Cookie*	George Kennedy, *Cool Hand Luke*	Jack Albertson, *The Subject Was Roses*
Supporting Actress	Sandy Dennis, *Who's Afraid of Virginia Woolf?*	Estelle Parsons, *Bonnie and Clyde*	Ruth Gordon, *Rosemary's Baby*
Director	Fred Zinnemann, *A Man for All Seasons*	Mike Nichols, *The Graduate*	Carol Reed, *Oliver!*
Adapted Screenplay	Robert Bolt, *A Man for All Seasons*	Stirling Silliphant, *In the Heat of the Night*	James Goldman, *The Lion in Winter*
Story and Screenplay	Claude Lelouch, story; Pierre Uytterhoeven and Claude Lelouch, screenplay, *A Man and a Woman*	William Rose, *Guess Who's Coming to Dinner?*	Mel Brooks, *The Producers*
Song	"Born Free" *(Born Free)*	"Talk to the Animals" *(Doctor Dolittle)*	"The Windmills of Your Mind" *(The Thomas Crown Affair)*
Score	*Born Free* (Original); *A Funny Thing Happened on the Way to the Forum* (Adaptation)	*Thoroughly Modern Millie* (Original); *Camelot* (Adaptation)	*The Lion in Winter* (Nonmusical); *Oliver!* (Musical)
Cinematography	*Who's Afraid of Virginia Woolf?* (B&W); *A Man for All Seasons*	*Bonnie and Clyde*	*Romeo and Juliet*
Costume Design	*Who's Afraid of Virginia Woolf?* (B&W); *A Man for All Seasons* (Color)	*Camelot*	*Romeo and Juliet*
Art Direction—Set Decoration	*Who's Afraid of Virginia Woolf?* (B&W); *Fantastic Voyage* (Color)	*Camelot*	*Oliver!*
Film Editing	*Grand Prix*	*In the Heat of the Night*	*Bullitt*
Foreign Language Film	*A Man and a Woman* (France)	*Closely Watched Trains* (Czechoslovakia)	*War and Peace* (U.S.S.R.)
Sound	*Grand Prix*	*In the Heat of the Night*	*Oliver!*
Sound Effects (Editing)	*Grand Prix*	*The Dirty Dozen*	—
Visual Effects	*Fantastic Voyage*	*Doctor Dolittle*	*2001: A Space Odyssey*
Short Films	*Herb Alpert and the Tijuana Brass Double Feature* (Cartoons); *Wild Wings* (Live Action)	*The Box* (Cartoons); *A Place to Stand* (Live Action)	*Winnie the Pooh and the Blustery Day* (Cartoons); *Robert Kennedy Remembered* (Live Action)
Documentaries	*A Year Toward Tomorrow* (Short); *The War Game* (Feature)	*The Redwoods* (Short); *The Anderson Platoon* (Feature)	*Why Man Creates* (Short); *Journey into Self* (Feature)

1969	1970	1971	1972
Midnight Cowboy	Patton	The French Connection	The Godfather
John Wayne, True Grit	George C. Scott, Patton	Gene Hackman, The French Connection	Marlon Brando, The Godfather
Maggie Smith, The Prime of Miss Jean Brodie	Glenda Jackson, Women in Love	Jane Fonda, Klute	Liza Minnelli, Cabaret
Gig Young, They Shoot Horses, Don't They?	John Mills, Ryan's Daughter	Ben Johnson, The Last Picture Show	Joel Grey, Cabaret
Goldie Hawn, Cactus Flower	Helen Hayes, Airport	Cloris Leachman, The Last Picture Show	Eileen Heckart, Butterflies Are Free
John Schlesinger, Midnight Cowboy	Franklin J. Schaffner, Patton	William Friedkin, The French Connection	Bob Fosse, Cabaret
Waldo Salt, Midnight Cowboy	Ring Lardner Jr., M*A*S*H	Ernest Tidyman, The French Connection	Mario Puzo and Francis Ford Coppola, The Godfather
William Goldman, Butch Cassidy and the Sundance Kid	Francis Ford Coppola and Edmund H. North, Patton	Paddy Chayefsky, The Hospital	Jeremy Larner, The Candidate
"Raindrops Keep Fallin' on My Head" (Butch Cassidy and the Sundance Kid)	"For All We Know" (Lovers and Other Strangers)	"Theme from Shaft" (Shaft)	"The Morning After" (The Poseidon Adventure)
Butch Cassidy and the Sundance Kid (Nonmusical); Hello Dolly! (Musical)	Love Story (Original Score); Let It Be (Original Song Score)	Summer of '42 (Dramatic); Fiddler on the Roof (Adapted)	Limelight (Dramatic); Cabaret (Adapted)
Butch Cassidy and the Sundance Kid	Ryan's Daughter	Fiddler on the Roof	Cabaret
Anne of the Thousand Days	Cromwell	Nicholas and Alexandra	Travels with My Aunt
Hello Dolly!	Patton	Nicholas and Alexandra	Cabaret
Z	Patton	The French Connection	Cabaret
Z (Algeria)	Investigation of a Citizen Above Suspicion (Italy)	The Garden of the Finzi-Continis (Italy)	The Discreet Charm of the Bourgeoisie (France)
Hello Dolly!	Patton	Fiddler on the Roof	Cabaret
—	—	—	—
Marooned	Tora! Tora! Tora!	Bedknobs and Broomsticks	—
It's Tough to Be a Bird (Cartoons); The Magic Machines (Live Action)	Is It Always Right To Be Right? (Cartoons); The Resurrection of Broncho Billy (Live Action)	The Crunch Bird (Animated); Sentinels of Silence (Live Action)	A Christmas Carol (Animated); Norman Rockwell's World...An American Dream (Live Action)
Czechoslovakia 1968 (Short); Arthur Rubinstein—The Love of Life (Feature)	Interviews with My Lai Veterans (Short); Woodstock (Feature)	Sentinels of Silence (Short); The Hellstrom Chronicle (Feature)	This Tiny World (Short); Marjoe (Feature)

	1973	**1974**	**1975**
Picture	The Sting	The Godfather Part II	One Flew over the Cuckoo's Nest
Actor	Jack Lemmon, Save the Tiger	Art Carney, Harry and Tonto	Jack Nicholson, One Flew over the Cuckoo's Nest
Actress	Glenda Jackson, A Touch of Class	Ellen Burstyn, Alice Doesn't Live Here Anymore	Louise Fletcher, One Flew over the Cuckoo's Nest
Supporting Actor	John Houseman, The Paper Chase	Robert De Niro, The Godfather Part II	George Burns, The Sunshine Boys
Supporting Actress	Tatum O'Neal, Paper Moon	Ingrid Bergman, Murder on the Orient Express	Lee Grant, Shampoo
Director	George Roy Hill, The Sting	Francis Ford Coppola, The Godfather Part II	Milos Forman, One Flew over the Cuckoo's Nest
Adapted Screenplay	William Peter Blatty, The Exorcist	Francis Ford Coppola and Mario Puzo, The Godfather Part II	Lawrence Hauben and Bo Goldman, One Flew over the Cuckoo's Nest
Original Screenplay	David S. Ward, The Sting	Robert Towne, Chinatown	Frank Pierson, Dog Day Afternoon
Song	"The Way We Were" (The Way We Were)	"We May Never Love Like This Again" (The Towering Inferno)	"I'm Easy" (Nashville)
Score	The Way We Were (Original); The Sting (Adaptation)	The Godfather Part II (Original); The Great Gatsby (Adaptation)	Jaws (Original); Barry Lyndon (Adaptation)
Cinematography	Cries and Whispers	The Towering Inferno	Barry Lyndon
Costume Design	The Sting	The Great Gatsby	Barry Lyndon
Art Direction—Set Decoration	The Sting	The Godfather Part II	Barry Lyndon
Film Editing	The Sting	The Towering Inferno	Jaws
Foreign Language Film	Day for Night (France)	Amarcord (Italy)	Dersu Uzala (U.S.S.R.)
Sound	The Exorcist	Earthquake	Jaws
Visual Effects	—	—	—
Short Films	Frank Film (Animated); The Bolero (Live Action)	Closed Mondays (Animated); One-Eyed Men Are Kings (Live Action)	Great (Animated); Angel and Big Joe (Live Action)
Documentaries	Princeton: A Search for Answers (Short); The Great American Cowboy (Feature)	Don't (Short); Hearts and Minds (Feature)	The End of the Game (Short); The Man Who Skied down Everest (Feature)

> 66 All I got was free champagne at restaurants for two weeks and then that stopped. 99
>
> —Dianne Wiest
> Best Supporting Actress, 1986

1976	1977	1978	1979
Rocky	*Annie Hall*	*The Deer Hunter*	*Kramer vs. Kramer*
Peter Finch, *Network*	Richard Dreyfuss, *The Goodbye Girl*	Jon Voight, *Coming Home*	Dustin Hoffman, *Kramer vs. Kramer*
Faye Dunaway, *Network*	Diane Keaton, *Annie Hall*	Jane Fonda, *Coming Home*	Sally Field, *Norma Rae*
Jason Robards, *All the President's Men*	Jason Robards, *Julia*	Christopher Walken, *The Deer Hunter*	Melvyn Douglas, *Being There*
Beatrice Straight, *Network*	Vanessa Redgrave, *Julia*	Maggie Smith, *California Suite*	Meryl Streep, *Kramer vs. Kramer*
John G. Avildsen, *Rocky*	Woody Allen, *Annie Hall*	Michael Cimino, *The Deer Hunter*	Robert Benton, *Kramer vs. Kramer*
William Goldman, *All the President's Men*	Alvin Sargent, *Julia*	Oliver Stone, *Midnight Express*	Robert Benton, *Kramer vs. Kramer*
Paddy Chayefsky, *Network*	Woody Allen and Marshall Brickman, *Annie Hall*	Nancy Dowd, story; Waldo Salt and Robert C. Jones, screenplay, *Coming Home*	Steve Tesich, *Breaking Away*
"Evergreen" *(A Star Is Born)*	"You Light Up My Life" *(You Light Up My Life)*	"Last Dance" *(Thank God It's Friday)*	"It Goes Like It Goes" *(Norma Rae)*
The Omen (Original); *Bound for Glory* (Adaptation)	*Star Wars* (Original); *A Little Night Music* (Adaptation)	*Midnight Express* (Original); *The Buddy Holly Story* (Adaptation)	*A Little Romance* (Original); *All That Jazz* (Adaptation)
Bound for Glory	*Close Encounters of the Third Kind*	*Days of Heaven*	*Apocalypse Now*
Fellini's Casanova	*Star Wars*	*Death on the Nile*	*All That Jazz*
All the President's Men	*Star Wars*	*Heaven Can Wait*	*All That Jazz*
Rocky	*Star Wars*	*The Deer Hunter*	*All That Jazz*
Black and White in Color (Ivory Coast)	*Madame Rosa* (France)	*Get Out Your Handkerchiefs* (France)	*The Tin Drum* (Federal Republic of Germany)
All the President's Men	*Star Wars*	*The Deer Hunter*	*Apocalypse Now*
—	*Star Wars*	—	*Alien*
Leisure (Animated); *In the Region of Ice* (Live Action)	*Sand Castle* (Animated); *I'll Find a Way* (Live Action)	*Special Delivery* (Animated); *Teenage Father* (Live Action)	*Every Child* (Animated); *Board and Care* (Live Action)
Number Our Days (Short); *Harlan County, U.S.A.* (Feature)	*Gravity Is My Enemy* (Short); *Who Are the DeBolts? And Where Did They Get Nineteen Kids?* (Feature)	*The Flight of the Gossamer Condor* (Short); *Scared Straight!* (Feature)	*Paul Robeson: Tribute to an Artist* (Short); *Best Boy* (Feature)

> 66 If we didn't honor backstabbers in this town, there would be no awards ceremony. 99
>
> —Tom Arnold, on the honorary Oscar presentation to Elia Kazan, 1999

	1980	1981	1982
Picture	*Ordinary People*	*Chariots of Fire*	*Gandhi*
Actor	Robert De Niro, *Raging Bull*	Henry Fonda, *On Golden Pond*	Ben Kingsley, *Gandhi*
Actress	Sissy Spacek, *Coal Miner's Daughter*	Katharine Hepburn, *On Golden Pond*	Meryl Streep, *Sophie's Choice*
Supporting Actor	Timothy Hutton, *Ordinary People*	John Gielgud, *Arthur*	Louis Gossett Jr., *An Officer and a Gentleman*
Supporting Actress	Mary Steenburgen, *Melvin and Howard*	Maureen Stapleton, *Reds*	Jessica Lange, *Tootsie*
Director	Robert Redford, *Ordinary People*	Warren Beatty, *Reds*	Richard Attenborough, *Gandhi*
Adapted Screenplay	Alvin Sargent, *Ordinary People*	Ernest Thompson, *On Golden Pond*	Costa-Gavras and Donald Stewart, *Missing*
Original Screenplay	Bo Goldman, *Melvin and Howard*	Colin Welland, *Chariots of Fire*	John Briley, *Gandhi*
Song	"Fame" *(Fame)*	"Arthur's Theme (Best That You Can Do)" *(Arthur)*	"Up Where We Belong" *(An Officer and a Gentleman)*
Original Score	*Fame*	*Chariots of Fire*	*E.T., the Extra-Terrestrial; Victor/Victoria* (Song Score/Adaptation)
Cinematography	*Tess*	*Reds*	*Gandhi*
Costume Design	*Tess*	*Chariots of Fire*	*Gandhi*
Art Direction—Set Decoration	*Tess*	*Raiders of the Lost Ark*	*Gandhi*
Film Editing	*Raging Bull*	*Raiders of the Lost Ark*	*Gandhi*
Foreign Language Film	*Moscow Does Not Believe in Tears* (U.S.S.R.)	*Mephisto* (Hungary)	*Volver A Empezar (To Begin Again)* (Spain)
Sound	*The Empire Strikes Back*	*Raiders of the Lost Ark*	*Gandhi*
Sound Effects (Editing)	—	—	*E.T., the Extra-Terrestrial*
Makeup	—	*An American Werewolf in London*	*Quest for Fire*
Visual Effects	—	*Raiders of the Lost Ark*	*E.T., the Extra-Terrestrial*
Short Films	*The Fly* (Animated); *The Dollar Bottom* (Live Action)	*Crac* (Animated); *Violet* (Live Action)	*Tango* (Animated); *A Shocking Accident* (Live Action)
Documentaries	*Karl Hess: Toward Liberty* (Short); *From Mao to Mozart: Isaac Stern in China* (Feature)	*Genocide* (Short); *Close Harmony* (Feature)	*If You Love This Planet* (Short); *Just Another Missing Kid* (Feature)

1983	1984	1985	1986
Terms of Endearment	Amadeus	Out of Africa	Platoon
Robert Duvall, Tender Mercies	F. Murray Abraham, Amadeus	William Hurt, Kiss of the Spider Woman	Paul Newman, The Color of Money
Shirley MacLaine, Terms of Endearment	Sally Field, Places in the Heart	Geraldine Page, The Trip to Bountiful	Marlee Matlin, Children of a Lesser God
Jack Nicholson, Terms of Endearment	Haing S. Ngor, The Killing Fields	Don Ameche, Cocoon	Michael Caine, Hannah and Her Sisters
Linda Hunt, The Year of Living Dangerously	Peggy Ashcroft, A Passage to India	Anjelica Huston, Prizzi's Honor	Dianne Wiest, Hannah and Her Sisters
James L. Brooks, Terms of Endearment	Milos Forman, Amadeus	Sydney Pollack, Out of Africa	Oliver Stone, Platoon
James L. Brooks, Terms of Endearment	Peter Shaffer, Amadeus	Kurt Luedtke, Out of Africa	Ruth Prawer Jhabvala, A Room with a View
Horton Foote, Tender Mercies	Robert Benton, Places in the Heart	William Kelley, Pamela Wallace, and Earl W. Wallace, Witness	Woody Allen, Hannah and Her Sisters
"Flashdance...What a Feeling" (Flashdance)	"I Just Called To Say I Love You" (The Woman in Red)	"Say You, Say Me" (White Nights)	"Take My Breath Away" (Top Gun)
The Right Stuff; Yentl (Song Score/Adaptation)	A Passage to India; Purple Rain (Song Score)	Out of Africa	'Round Midnight
Fanny & Alexander	The Killing Fields	Out of Africa	The Mission
Fanny & Alexander	Amadeus	Ran	A Room with a View
Fanny & Alexander	Amadeus	Out of Africa	A Room with a View
The Right Stuff	The Killing Fields	Witness	Platoon
Fanny & Alexander (Sweden)	Dangerous Moves (Switzerland)	The Official Story (Argentina)	The Assault (The Netherlands)
The Right Stuff	Amadeus	Out of Africa	Platoon
The Right Stuff	—	Back to the Future	Aliens
—	Amadeus	Mask	The Fly
Return of the Jedi	Indiana Jones and the Temple of Doom	Cocoon	Aliens
Sundae in New York (Animated); Boys and Girls (Live Action)	Charade (Animated); Up (Live Action)	Anna & Bella (Animated); Molly's Pilgrim (Live Action)	A Greek Tragedy (Animated); Precious Images (Live Action)
Flamenco at 5:15 (Short); He Makes Me Feel Like Dancin' (Feature)	The Stone Carvers (Short); The Times of Harvey Milk (Feature)	Witness to War: Dr. Charlie Clements (Short); Broken Rainbow (Feature)	Women—For America, for the World (Short); Artie Shaw: Time Is All You've Got and Down and out in America (Feature)

145

	1987	1988	1989
Picture	The Last Emperor	Rain Man	Driving Miss Daisy
Actor	Michael Douglas, Wall Street	Dustin Hoffman, Rain Man	Daniel Day-Lewis, My Left Foot
Actress	Cher, Moonstruck	Jodie Foster, The Accused	Jessica Tandy, Driving Miss Daisy
Supporting Actor	Sean Connery, The Untouchables	Kevin Kline, A Fish Called Wanda	Denzel Washington, Glory
Supporting Actress	Olympia Dukakis, Moonstruck	Geena Davis, The Accidental Tourist	Brenda Fricker, My Left Foot
Director	Bernardo Bertolucci, The Last Emperor	Barry Levinson, Rain Man	Oliver Stone, Born on the Fourth of July
Adapted Screenplay	Mark Peploe and Bernardo Bertolucci, The Last Emperor	Christopher Hampton, Dangerous Liaisons	Tom Schulman, Dead Poets Society
Original Screenplay	John Patrick Shanley, Moonstruck	Ronald Bass and Barry Morrow, Rain Man	Alfred Uhry, Driving Miss Daisy
Song	"(I've Had) The Time of My Life" (Dirty Dancing)	"Let the River Run" (Working Girl)	"Under the Sea" (The Little Mermaid)
Original Score	The Last Emperor	The Milagro Beanfield War	The Little Mermaid
Cinematography	The Last Emperor	Mississippi Burning	Glory
Costume Design	The Last Emperor	Dangerous Liaisons	Henry V
Art Direction—Set Decoration	The Last Emperor	Dangerous Liaisons	Batman
Film Editing	The Last Emperor	Who Framed Roger Rabbit	Born on the Fourth of July
Foreign Language Film	Babette's Feast (Denmark)	Pelle the Conqueror (Denmark)	Cinema Paradiso (Italy)
Sound	The Last Emperor	Bird	Glory
Sound Effects (Editing)	—	Who Framed Roger Rabbit	Indiana Jones and the Last Crusade
Makeup	Harry and the Hendersons	Beetlejuice	Driving Miss Daisy
Visual Effects	Innerspace	Who Framed Roger Rabbit	The Abyss
Short Films	The Man Who Planted Trees (Animated); Ray's Male Heterosexual Dance Hall (Live Action)	Tin Toy (Animated); The Appointments of Dennis Jennings (Live Action)	Balance (Animated); Work Experience (Live Action)
Documentaries	Young at Heart (Short); The Ten-Year Lunch: The Wit and the Legend of the Algonquin Round Table (Feature)	You Don't Have To Die (Short); Hotel Terminus: The Life and Times of Klaus Barbie (Feature)	The Johnstown Flood (Short); Common Threads: Stories from the Quilt (Feature)

> 66 This is a terrible mistake because I have used up all my English...now my body is in tumult because it's a colossal moment of joy. 99
> —Roberto Benigni, Best Actor, 1998
> Best Foreign Film, 1998

1990	1991	1992	1993
Dances with Wolves	The Silence of the Lambs	Unforgiven	Schindler's List
Jeremy Irons, Reversal of Fortune	Anthony Hopkins, The Silence of the Lambs	Al Pacino, Scent of a Woman	Tom Hanks, Philadelphia
Kathy Bates, Misery	Jodie Foster, The Silence of the Lambs	Emma Thompson, Howards End	Holly Hunter, The Piano
Joe Pesci, GoodFellas	Jack Palance, City Slickers	Gene Hackman, Unforgiven	Tommy Lee Jones, The Fugitive
Whoopi Goldberg, Ghost	Mercedes Ruehl, The Fisher King	Marisa Tomei, My Cousin Vinny	Anna Paquin, The Piano
Kevin Costner, Dances with Wolves	Jonathan Demme, The Silence of the Lambs	Clint Eastwood, Unforgiven	Steven Spielberg, Schindler's List
Michael Blake, Dances with Wolves	Ted Tally, The Silence of the Lambs	Ruth Prawer Jhabvala, Howards End	Steven Zaillian, Schindler's List
Bruce Joel Rubin, Ghost	Callie Khouri, Thelma & Louise	Neil Jordan, The Crying Game	Jane Campion, The Piano
"Sooner or Later (I Always Get My Man)" (Dick Tracy)	"Beauty and the Beast" (Beauty and the Beast)	"A Whole New World" (Aladdin)	"Streets of Philadelphia" (Philadelphia)
Dances with Wolves	Beauty and the Beast	Aladdin	Schindler's List
Dances with Wolves	JFK	A River Runs Through It	Schindler's List
Cyrano de Bergerac	Bugsy	Bram Stoker's Dracula	The Age of Innocence
Dick Tracy	Bugsy	Howards End	Schindler's List
Dances with Wolves	JFK	Unforgiven	Schindler's List
Journey of Hope (Switzerland)	Mediterraneo (Italy)	Indochine (France)	Belle Epoque (Spain)
Dances with Wolves	Terminator 2: Judgment Day	The Last of the Mohicans	Jurassic Park
The Hunt for Red October	Terminator 2: Judgment Day	Bram Stoker's Dracula	Jurassic Park
Dick Tracy	Terminator 2: Judgment Day	Bram Stoker's Dracula	Mrs. Doubtfire
Total Recall	Terminator 2: Judgment Day	Death Becomes Her	Jurassic Park
Creature Comforts (Animated); The Lunch Date (Live Action)	Manipulation (Animated); Session Man (Live Action)	Mona Lisa Descending a Staircase (Animated); Omnibus (Live Action)	The Wrong Trousers (Animated); Black Rider (Live Action)
Days of Waiting (Short); American Dream (Feature)	Deadly Deception: General Electric, Nuclear Weapons and Our Environment (Short); In the Shadow of the Stars (Feature)	Educating Peter (Short); The Panama Deception (Feature)	Defending Our Lives (Short); I Am a Promise: The Children of Stanton Elementary School (Feature)

> 66 I think they gave it to me because I'm the oldest. 99
>
> —Jessica Tandy, Best Actress, 1989

	1994	1995	1996
Picture	Forrest Gump	Braveheart	The English Patient
Actor	Tom Hanks, Forrest Gump	Nicolas Cage, Leaving Las Vegas	Geoffrey Rush, Shine
Actress	Jessica Lange, Blue Sky	Susan Sarandon, Dead Man Walking	Frances McDormand, Fargo
Supporting Actor	Martin Landau, Ed Wood	Kevin Spacey, The Usual Suspects	Cuba Gooding Jr., Jerry Maguire
Supporting Actress	Dianne Wiest, Bullets over Broadway	Mira Sorvino, Mighty Aphrodite	Juliette Binoche, The English Patient
Director	Robert Zemeckis, Forrest Gump	Mel Gibson, Braveheart	Anthony Minghella, The English Patient
Adapted Screenplay	Eric Roth, Forrest Gump	Emma Thompson, Sense and Sensibility	Billy Bob Thornton, Sling Blade
Original Screenplay	Roger Avary and Quentin Tarantino, Pulp Fiction	Christopher McQuarrie, The Usual Suspects	Ethan Coen & Joel Coen, Fargo
Best Song	"Can You Feel the Love Tonight" (The Lion King)	"Colors of the Wind" (Pocahontas)	"You Must Love Me" (Evita)
Original Score	The Lion King	The Postman (Il Postino)	Emma (Musical or Comedy); The English Patient (Drama)
Cinematography	Legends of the Fall	Braveheart	The English Patient
Costume Design	The Adventures of Priscilla, Queen of the Desert	Restoration	The English Patient
Art Direction—Set Decoration	The Madness of King George	Restoration	The English Patient
Film Editing	Forrest Gump	Apollo 13	The English Patient
Foreign Language Film	Burnt by the Sun	Antonia's Line	Kolya
Sound	Speed	Apollo 13	The English Patient
Sound Effects (Editing)	Speed	Braveheart	The Ghost and the Darkness
Makeup	Ed Wood	Braveheart	The Nutty Professor
Visual Effects	Forrest Gump	Babe	Independence Day
Short Films	Bob's Birthday (Animated); Franz Kafka's It's a Wonderful Life and Trevor (Live Action)	A Close Shave (Animated); Lieberman in Love (Live Action)	Quest (Animated); Dear Diary (Live Action)
Documentaries	A Time for Justice (Short); Maya Lin: A Strong Clear Vision (Feature)	One Survivor Remembers (Short); Anne Frank Remembered (Feature)	Breathing Lessons: The Life and Work of Mark O'Brien (Short); When We Were Kings (Feature)

1997   1998

1997	1998
Titanic	*Shakespeare in Love*
Jack Nicholson, *As Good As It Gets*	Roberto Benigni, *Life Is Beautiful*
Helen Hunt, *As Good As It Gets*	Gwyneth Paltrow, *Shakespeare in Love*
Robin Williams, *Good Will Hunting*	James Coburn, *Affliction*
Kim Basinger, *L.A. Confidential*	Judi Dench, *Shakespeare in Love*

James Cameron, *Titanic*	Steven Spielberg, *Saving Private Ryan*
Brian Helgeland and Curtis Hanson, *L.A. Confidential*	Bill Condon, *Gods and Monsters*
Ben Affleck and Matt Damon, *Good Will Hunting*	Marc Norman and Tom Stoppard, *Shakespeare in Love*
"My Heart Will Go On" *(Titanic)*	"When You Believe" *(Prince of Egypt)*
The Full Monty (Musical or Comedy); *Titanic* (Drama)	*Shakespeare in Love* (Musical or Comedy); *Life Is Beautiful* (Drama)
Titanic	*Saving Private Ryan*

Titanic	*Shakespeare in Love*
Titanic	*Shakespeare in Love*
Titanic	*Saving Private Ryan*
Character	*Life Is Beautiful*
Titanic	*Saving Private Ryan*
Titanic	*Saving Private Ryan*

Men in Black	*Elizabeth*
Titanic	*What Dreams May Come*
Geri's Game (Animated); *Visas and Virtue* (Live Action)	*Bunny* (Animated); *Election Night (Valgaften)* (Live Action)
A Story of Healing (Short); *The Long Way Home* (Feature)	*The Personals: Improvisations on Romance in the Golden Years* (Short); *The Last Days* (Feature)

FILM AWARDS

NATIONAL SOCIETY OF FILM CRITICS

Annual Award for Best Film

1966	Blow-Up
1967	Persona
1968	Shame
1969	Z
1970	M*A*S*H
1971	Claire's Knee
1972	The Discreet Charm of the Bourgeoisie
1973	Day for Night
1974	Scenes from a Marriage
1975	Nashville
1976	All The President's Men
1977	Annie Hall
1978	Get Out Your Handkerchiefs
1979	Breaking Away
1980	Melvin and Howard
1981	Atlantic City
1982	Tootsie
1983	Night of the Shooting Stars
1984	Stranger Than Paradise
1985	Ran
1986	Blue Velvet
1987	The Dead
1988	The Unbearable Lightness of Being
1989	Drugstore Cowboy
1990	GoodFellas
1991	Life Is Sweet
1992	Unforgiven
1993	Schindler's List
1994	Pulp Fiction
1995	Babe
1996	Breaking the Waves
1997	L.A. Confidential
1998	Out of Sight

SUNDANCE FILM FESTIVAL

GRAND JURY PRIZE

1978	Girlfriends
1979	Spirit in the Wind
1981	Heartland
	Gal Young Un

Dramatic

1982	Street Music
1983	Purple Haze
1984	Old Enough
1985	Blood Simple
1986	Smooth Talk
1987	Waiting for the Moon
	Trouble with Dick
1988	Heat and Sunlight
1989	True Love
1990	Chameleon Street
1991	Poison

1992	In the Soup
1993	Ruby in Paradise
	Public Access
1994	What Happened Was . . .
1995	The Brothers McMullen
1996	Welcome to the Dollhouse
1997	Sunday
1998	Slam
1999	Three Seasons

FILMMAKERS TROPHY
Dramatic

1989	Powwow Highway
1990	House Party
1991	Privilege
1992	Zebrahead
1993	Fly By Night
1994	Clerks
1995	Angela
1996	Girls Town
1997	In the Company of Men
1998	Smoke Signals
1999	Tumbleweeds

AUDIENCE AWARD
Dramatic

1989	sex, lies and videotape
1990	Longtime Companion
1991	One Cup of Coffee (released as "Pastime")
1992	The Waterdance
1993	El Mariachi
1994	Spanking the Monkey
1995	Picture Bride
1996	Care of the Spitfire Grill (released as "The Spitfire Grill")
1997	Hurricane (released as "Hurricane Streets")
	love jones
1998	Smoke Signals
1999	Three Seasons

CANNES FILM FESTIVAL

Palme d'Or for Best Film

1946	La Bataille du rail (France)
1947	Antoine et Antoinette (France)
1948	No festival
1949	The Third Man (G.B.)
1950	No festival
1951	Miracle in Milan (Italy)
	Miss Julie (Sweden)
1952	Othello (Morocco)
	Two Cents Worth of Hope (Italy)
1953	Wages of Fear (France)
1954	Gate of Hell (Japan)
1955	Marty (U.S.)
1956	World of Silence (France)

1957	Friendly Persuasion (U.S.)
1958	The Cranes are Flying (U.S.S.R.)
1959	Black Orpheus (France)
1960	La Dolce Vita (Italy)
1961	Viridiana (Spain)
	Une Aussi longue absence (France)
1962	The Given Word (Brazil)
1963	The Leopard (Italy)
1964	The Umbrellas of Cherbourg (France)
1965	The Knack (G.B.)
1966	A Man and a Woman (France)
	Signore e Signori (Italy)
1967	Blow-Up (G.B.)
1968	Festival disrupted; no awards
1969	If . . . (G.B.)
1970	M*A*S*H (U.S.)
1971	The Go-Between (G.B.)
1972	The Working Class Goes to Paradise (Italy)
	The Mattei Affair (Italy)
1973	Scarecrow (U.S.)
	The Hireling (G.B.)
1974	The Conversation (U.S.)
1975	Chronicle of the Burning Years (Algeria)
1976	Taxi Driver (U.S.)
1977	Padre Padrone (Italy)
1978	L'Albero Degli Zoccoli (Italy)
1979	The Tin Drum (Germany)
	Apocalypse Now (U.S.)
1980	All That Jazz (U.S.)
	Kagemusha (Japan)
1981	Man of Iron (Poland)
1982	Missing (U.S.)
	Yol (Turkey)
1983	The Ballad of Narayama (Japan)
1984	Paris, Texas (Germany)
1985	When Father Was Away On Business (Yugoslavia)
1986	The Mission (G.B.)
1987	Under the Sun of Satan (France)
1988	Pelle the Conqueror (Denmark)
1989	sex, lies and videotape (U.S.)
1990	Wild at Heart (U.S.)
1991	Barton Fink (U.S.)
1992	The Best Intentions (Denmark)
1993	The Piano (New Zealand)
	Farewell My Concubine (Hong Kong)
1994	Pulp Fiction (U.S.)
1995	Underground (Bosnia)
1996	Secrets and Lies (G.B.)
1997	The Taste of Cherry (Iran)
	The Eel (Japan)
1998	Eternity and a Day (Greece-Italy-France)
1999	Rosetta (Belgium)

VENICE FILM FESTIVAL

Golden Lion [for Best Film or Best Foreign Film]

1932	No official award
1933	No festival
1934	Man of Aran (G.B.)
1935	Anna Karenina (U.S.)
1936	Der Kaiser von Kalifornien (Germany)
1937	Un Carnet debal (France)
1938	Olympia (Germany)
1939	No award given
1940	Der Postmeister (Germany)
1941	Ohm Kruger (Germany)
1942	Der grosse König (Germany)
1943	No festival
1944	No festival
1945	No festival
1946	The Southerner (U.S.)
1947	Sirena (Czechoslovakia)
1948	Hamlet (G.B.)
1949	Manon (France)
1950	Justice is Done (France)
1951	Rashomon (Japan)
1952	Forbidden Games (France)
1953	No award given
1954	Romeo and Juliet (Italy/G.B.)
1955	Ordet (Denmark)
1956	No award given
1957	Aparajito (India)
1958	Muhomatsu no Issho (Japan)
1959	Il Generale della Rovere (Italy)
1960	Le Passage du Rhin (France)
1961	Last Year at Marienbad (France)
1962	Childhood of Ivan (U.S.S.R.)
1963	Le Mani sulla città (Italy)
1964	Red Desert (Italy)
1965	Of a Thousand Delights (Italy)
1966	Battle of Algiers (Italy)
1967	Belle de Jour (France)
1968	Die Aristen in der Zirkuskuppel (Germany)

Jury and award system discontinued 1969–79

1980	Gloria (U.S.)
	Atlantic City (France/Canada)
1981	Die Bleierne Zeit (Germany)
1982	The State of Things (Germany)
1983	Prénom Carmen (France/Switzerland)
1984	Year of the Quiet Sun (Poland)
1985	Sans toit ni loi (Vagabonde) (France)
1986	Le Rayon vert (France)
1987	Au revoir, les enfants (France)
1988	The Legend of the Holy Drinker (Italy)
1989	A City of Sadness (Taiwan)
1990	Rosencrantz and Guildenstern Are Dead (G.B.)
1991	Urga (U.S.S.R./France)
1992	The Story of Qiu Ju (China)
1993	Blue (France)
	Short Cuts (U.S.)
1994	Before the Rain (Macedonia)
	Vive L'Amour (Taiwan)
1995	Cyclo (France-Vietnam)
1996	Michael Collins (Great Britain-U.S.)
1997	Hana-bi (Fireworks) (Japan)
1998	The Way We Laughed (Italy)

BERLIN FILM FESTIVAL AWARD

Golden Bear Award for Best Film

1953	The Wages of Fear (France)
1954	Hobson's Choice (G.B.)
1955	The Rats (Germany)
1956	Invitation to the Dance (G.B.)
1957	Twelve Angry Men (U.S.)
1958	The End of the Day (Sweden)
1959	The Cousins (France)
1960	Lazarillo de Tormes (Spain)
1961	La Notte (Italy)
1962	A Kind of Loving (G.B.)
1963	Oath of Obedience (Germany)
	The Devil (Italy)
1964	Dry Summer (Turkey)
1965	Alphaville (France)
1966	Cul-de-Sac (G.B.)
1967	Le Depart (Belgium)
1968	Ole Dole Duff (Sweden)
1969	Early Years (Yugoslavia)
1970	No award
1971	The Garden of the Finzi-Continis (Italy)
1972	The Canterbury Tales (Italy)
1973	Distant Thunder (India)
1974	The Apprenticeship of Duddy Kravitz (Canada)
1975	Orkobefogadas (Hungary)
1976	Buffalo Bill and the Indians (U.S.) [award declined]
1977	The Ascent (U.S.S.R.)
1978	The Trouts (Spain)
	The Words of Max (Spain)
1979	David (Germany)
1980	Heartland (U.S.)
	Palermo Oder Wolfsburg (Germany)
1981	Di Presa Di Presa (Spain)
1982	Die Sehnsucht der Veronica Voss (Germany)
1983	Ascendancy (G.B.)
	The Beehive (Spain)
1984	Love Streams (U.S.)
1985	Wetherby (G.B.)
	Die Frau und der Fremde (Germany)
1986	Stammhein (Germany)
1987	The Theme (U.S.S.R.)
1988	Red Sorghum (China)
1989	Rain Man (U.S.)
1990	Music Box (U.S.)
	Larks on a String (Czechoslovakia)
1991	House of Smiles (Italy)
1992	Grand Canyon (U.S.)
1993	The Woman from the Lake of Scented Souls (China)
	The Wedding Banquet (Taiwan/U.S.)
1994	In the Name of the Father (UK/Ireland)
1995	Live Bait (France)
1996	Sense and Sensibility (G.B.)
1997	The People vs. Larry Flynt (U.S.)
1998	Central do Brasil (Brazil)
1999	The Thin Red Line (U.S.)

INDEPENDENT SPIRIT AWARDS

These prizes are considered the Oscars of the independent film world.

Best Feature

1986	After Hours
1987	Platoon
1988	River's Edge
1989	Stand and Deliver
1990	sex, lies and videotape
1991	The Grifters
1992	Rambling Rose
1993	The Player
1994	Short Cuts
1995	Pulp Fiction
1996	Leaving Las Vegas
1997	Fargo
1998	The Apostle

Best First Feature

1987	Spike Lee, director *She's Gotta Have It*
1988	Emile Ardolino, director *Dirty Dancing*
1989	Donald Petrie, director *Mystic Pizza*
1990	Michael Lehmann, director *Heathers*
1991	Whit Stillman, producer/director *Metropolitan*
1992	Matty Rich, director *Straight Out of Brooklyn*
1993	Neal Jimenez and Michael Steinberg, directors *The Waterdance*
1994	Robert Rodriguez, director *El Mariachi*
1995	David O. Russell, director *Spanking the Monkey*
1996	Edward Burns, director *The Brothers McMullen*
1997	Billy Bob Thornton, director *Sling Blade*
1998	Kasi Lemmons, director *Eve's Bayou*

Best Director

1986 Martin Scorsese
After Hours
1987 Oliver Stone
Platoon
1988 John Huston
The Dead
1989 Ramon Menendez
Stand and Deliver
1990 Steven Soderbergh
sex, lies and videotape
1991 Charles Burnett
To Sleep with Anger
1992 Martha Coolidge
Rambling Rose
1993 Carl Franklin
One False Move
1994 Robert Altman
Short Cuts
1995 Quentin Tarantino
Pulp Fiction
1996 Mike Figgis
Leaving Las Vegas
1997 Joel Coen
Fargo
1998 Robert Duvall
The Apostle

Best Screenplay

1986 Horton Foote
The Trip to Bountiful
1987 Oliver Stone
Platoon
1988 Neal Jimenez
River's Edge
1989 Ramon Menendez and Tom
Musca
Stand and Deliver
1990 Gus Van Sant Jr. and Daniel Yost
Drugstore Cowboy
1991 Charles Burnett
To Sleep with Anger
1992 Gus Van Sant Jr.
My Own Private Idaho
1993 Neal Jimenez
The Waterdance
1994 Robert Altman and Frank
Barhydt
Short Cuts
1995 David O. Russell
Spanking the Monkey
1996 Christopher McQuarrie
The Usual Suspects
1997 Joel Coen and Ethan Coen
Fargo
1998 Kevin Smith
Chasing Amy

Best Cinematographer

1986 Toyomichi Kurita
Trouble In Mind

1987 Bob Richardson
Platoon
1988 Haskell Wexler
Matewan
1989 Sven Nykvist
*The Unbearable Lightness of
Being*
1990 Robert Yeoman
Drugstore Cowboy
1991 Fred Elmes
Wild at Heart
1992 Walt Lloyd
Kafka
1993 Frederick Elmes
Night on Earth
1994 Lisa Rinzler
Menace II Society
1995 John Thomas
Barcelona
1996 Declan Quinn
Leaving Las Vegas
1997 Roger Deakins
Fargo
1998 Declan Quinn
Kama Sutra

Best Actor

1986 M. Emmet Walsh
Blood Simple
1987 James Woods
Salvador
1988 Dennis Quaid
The Big Easy
1989 Edward James Olmos
Stand and Deliver
1990 Matt Dillon
Drugstore Cowboy
1991 Danny Glover
To Sleep with Anger
1992 River Phoenix
My Own Private Idaho
1993 Harvey Keitel
Bad Lieutenant
1994 Jeff Bridges
American Heart
1995 Samuel L. Jackson
Pulp Fiction
1996 Sean Penn
Dead Man Walking
1997 William H. Macy
Fargo
1998 Robert Duvall
The Apostle

Best Actress

1986 Geraldine Page
The Trip to Bountiful
1987 Isabella Rossellini
Blue Velvet
1988 Sally Kirkland
Anna

1989 Jodie Foster
Five Corners
1990 Andie MacDowell
sex, lies, and videotape
1991 Anjelica Huston
The Grifters
1992 Judy Davis
Impromptu
1993 Fairuza Balk
Gas, Food, Lodging
1994 Ashley Judd
Ruby in Paradise
1995 Linda Fiorentino
The Last Seduction
1996 Elisabeth Shue
Leaving Las Vegas
1997 Frances McDormand
Fargo
1998 Julie Christie
Afterglow

Best Supporting Actor

1988 Morgan Freeman
Street Smart
1989 Lou Diamond Phillips
Stand and Deliver
1990 Max Perlich
Drugstore Cowboy
1991 Bruce Davison
Longtime Companion
1992 David Strathairn
City of Hope
1993 Steve Buscemi
Reservoir Dogs
1994 Christopher Lloyd
Twenty Bucks
1995 Chazz Palminteri
Bullets over Broadway
1996 Benicio Del Toro
The Usual Suspects
1997 Benecio Del Toro
Basquiat
1998 Jason Lee
Chasing Amy

Best Supporting Actress

1988 Anjelica Huston
The Dead
1989 Rosanna De Soto
Stand and Deliver
1990 Laura San Giacomo
sex, lies, and videotape
1991 Sheryl Lee Ralph
To Sleep with Anger
1992 Diane Ladd
Rambling Rose
1993 Alfre Woodard
Passion Fish
1994 Lili Taylor
Household Saints
1995 Dianne Wiest
Bullets over Broadway

1996 Mare Winningham
Georgia
1997 Elizabeth Pena
Lone Star
1998 Debbi Morgan
Eve's Bayou

Best Foreign Film

1986 Kiss of the Spider Woman
1987 A Room with a View
1988 My Life as a Dog
1989 Wings of Desire
1990 My Left Foot
1991 Sweetie
1992 An Angel at My Table
1993 The Crying Game
1994 The Piano
1995 Red
1996 Before the Rain
1997 Secrets and Lies
1998 The Sweet Hereafter

MTV MOVIE AWARDS

Best Movie

1992 Terminator 2: Judgment Day
1993 A Few Good Men
1994 Menace II Society
1995 Pulp Fiction
1996 Seven
1997 Scream
1998 Titanic
1999 There's Something About Mary

Best Male Performance

1992 Arnold Schwarzenegger
Terminator 2: Judgment Day
1993 Denzel Washington
Malcolm X
1994 Tom Hanks
Philadelphia
1995 Brad Pitt
Interview with the Vampire
1996 Jim Carrey
Ace Ventura: When Nature Calls
1997 Tom Cruise
Jerry Maguire
1998 Leonardo DiCaprio
Titanic
1999 Jim Carrey
The Truman Show

Best Female Performance

1992 Linda Hamilton
Terminator 2: Judgment Day
1993 Sharon Stone
Basic Instinct
1994 Janet Jackson
Poetic Justice
1995 Sandra Bullock
Speed

1996 Alicia Silverstone
Clueless
1997 Claire Danes
William Shakespeare's Romeo and Juliet
1998 Neve Campbell
Scream 2
1999 Cameron Diaz
There's Something About Mary

Breakthrough Performance

1992 Edward Furlong
Terminator 2: Judgment Day
1993 Marisa Tomei
My Cousin Vinny
1994 Alicia Silverstone
The Crush
1995 Kirsten Dunst
Interview with the Vampire
1996 George Clooney
From Dusk Till Dawn
1997 Matthey McConaughey
A Time To Kill
1998 Heather Graham
Boogie Nights
1999 James Van Der Beek
Varsity Blues
Katie Holmes
Disturbing Behavior

Best Comedic Performance

1992 Billy Crystal
City Slickers
1993 Robin Williams
Aladdin
1994 Robin Williams
Mrs. Doubtfire
1995 Jim Carrey
Dumb and Dumber
1996 Jim Carrey
Ace Ventura: When Nature Calls
1997 Jim Carrey
The Cable Guy
1998 Jim Carrey
Liar, Liar

Best Villain

1992 Rebecca DeMornay
The Hand That Rocks the Cradle
1993 Jennifer Jason Leigh
Single White Female
1994 Alicia Silverstone
The Crush
1995 Dennis Hopper
Speed
1996 Kevin Spacey
Seven
1997 Jim Carrey
The Cable Guy
1998 Mike Myers
Austin Powers: International Man of Mystery

1999 Matt Dillon
There's Something About Mary
Stephen Dorff
Blade

Best On-Screen Duo

1992 Mike Myers and Dana Carvey
Wayne's World
1993 Mel Gibson and Danny Glover
Lethal Weapon 3
1994 Harrison Ford and Tommy Lee Jones
The Fugitive
1995 Keanu Reeves and Sandra Bullock
Speed
1996 Chris Farley and David Spade
Tommy Boy
1997 Sean Connery and Nicolas Cage
The Rock
1998 John Travolta and Nicolas Cage
Face/Off
1999 Jackie Chan and Chris Tucker
Rush Hour

Most Desirable Male

1992 Keanu Reeves
Point Break
1993 Chistian Slater
Untamed Heart
1994 William Baldwin
Sliver
1995 Brad Pitt
Legends of the Fall
1996 Brad Pitt
Seven

Most Desirable Female

1992 Linda Hamilton
Terminator 2: Judgment Day
1993 Sharon Stone
Basic Instinct
1994 Janet Jackson
Poetic Justice
1995 Sandra Bullock
Speed
1996 Alicia Silverstone
Clueless

Best Song

1992 Bryan Adams
"(Everything I Do) I Do It For You"
(Robin Hood: Prince of Thieves)
1993 Whitney Houston
"I Will Always Love You" *(The Bodyguard)*
1994 Michael Jackson
"Will You Be Thorc" *(Frcc Willy)*
1995 Stone Temple Pilots
"Big Empty" *(The Crow)*

1996	Brandy
	"Sittin' up in My Room"
	(Waiting to Exhale)
1997	Bush
	"Machinehead" *(Fear)*
1998	Will Smith
	"Men in Black" *(Men in Black)*
1999	Aerosmith
	"I Don't Want to Miss a Thing"
	(Armageddon)

Best Kiss

1992	Macaulay Culkin and Anna
	Chlumsky
	My Girl
1993	Marisa Tomei and Christian
	Slater
	Untamed Heart
1994	Woody Harrelson and Demi Moore
	Indecent Proposal
1995	Jim Carrey and Lauren Holly
	Dumb and Dumber
1996	Natasha Henstridge and Anthony
	Guidere
	Species
1997	Will Smith and Vivica A. Fox
	Independence Day
1998	Adam Sandler and Drew
	Barrymore
	The Wedding Singer
1999	Gwyneth Paltrow and Joseph
	Fiennes
	Shakespeare In Love

Best Action Sequence

1992	Terminator 2: Judgment Day
1993	Lethal Weapon 3
1994	The Fugitive
1995	Speed
1996	Braveheart
1997	Twister
1998	Face/Off
1999	Armageddon

Best New Filmmaker Award

1992	John Singleton
	Boyz N the Hood
1993	Carl Franklin
	One False Move
1994	Steven Zaillian
	Searching for Bobby Fischer
1995	Steve James
	Hoop Dreams
1996	Wes Anderson
	Bottle Rocket
1997	Doug Liman
	Swingers
1998	Peter Cattaneo
	The Full Monty
1999	Guy Ritchie
	Lock, Stock & Two Smoking
	Barrels

Best Fight

1996	Adam Sandler and Bob Barker
	Happy Gilmore
1997	Fairuza Balk and Robin Tunney
	The Craft
1998	Will Smith and Cockroach
	Men in Black
1999	Ben Stiller and Puffy the Dog
	There's Something About Mary

Lifetime Achievement Award

1992	Jason Voorhees
	Friday the 13th
1993	The Three Stooges
1994	Richard Roundtree
	Shaft film series
1995	Jackie Chan
1996	Godzilla
1997	Chewbacca
1998	Clint Howard

DIRECTOR'S GUILD AWARDS

1948–49	*A Letter to Three Wives*
	Joseph Mankiewicz
1949–50	*All the King's Men*
	Robert Rossen
1950–51	*All About Eve*
	Joseph Mankiewicz
1951	*A Place in the Sun*
	George Stevens
1952	*The Quiet Man*
	John Ford
1953	*From Here to Eternity*
	Fred Zinnemann
1954	*On the Waterfront*
	Elia Kazan
1955	*Marty*
	Delbert Mann
1956	*Giant*
	George Stevens
1957	*Bridge on the River Kwai*
	David Lean
1958	*Gigi*
	Vincente Minnelli
1959	*Ben-Hur*
	William Wyler
1960	*The Apartment*
	Billy Wilder
1961	*West Side Story*
	Robert Wise and Jerome
	Robbins
1962	*Lawrence of Arabia*
	David Lean
1963	*Tom Jones*
	Tony Richardson
1964	*My Fair Lady*
	George Cukor
1965	*The Sound of Music*
	Robert Wise
1966	*A Man for All Seasons*
	Fred Zinnemann
1967	*The Graduate*
	Mike Nichols

1968	*The Lion in Winter*
	Anthony Harvey
1969	*Midnight Cowboy*
	John Schlesinger
1970	*Patton*
	Franklin J. Schaffner
1971	*The French Connection*
	William Friedkin
1972	*The Godfather*
	Francis Ford Coppola
1973	*The Sting*
	George Roy Hill
1974	*The Godfather Part II*
	Francis Ford Coppola
1975	*One Flew over the*
	Cuckoo's Nest
	Milos Forman
1976	*Rocky*
	John G. Avildsen
1977	*Annie Hall*
	Woody Allen
1978	*The Deer Hunter*
	Michael Cimino
1979	*Kramer vs. Kramer*
	Robert Benton
1980	*Ordinary People*
	Robert Redford
1981	*Reds*
	Warren Beatty
1982	*Gandhi*
	Richard Attenborough
1983	*Terms of Endearment*
	James L. Brooks
1984	*Amadeus*
	Milos Forman
1985	*The Color Purple*
	Steven Spielberg
1986	*Platoon*
	Oliver Stone
1987	*The Last Emperor*
	Bernardo Bertolucci
1988	*Rain Man*
	Barry Levinson
1989	*Born on the Fourth of July*
	Oliver Stone
1990	*Dances with Wolves*
	Kevin Costner
1991	*The Silence of the Lambs*
	Jonathan Demme
1992	*Unforgiven*
	Clint Eastwood
1993	*Schindler's List*
	Steven Spielberg
1994	*Forrest Gump*
	Robert Zemeckis
1995	*Apollo 13*
	Ron Howard
1996	*The English Patient*
	Anthony Minghella
1997	*Titanic*
	James Cameron
1998	*Saving Private Ryan*
	Steven Spielberg

PICKS & PANS 1998-1999

You know the refrain: more channels, more programs, more "news magazines," and fewer shows worth watching. *The Sopranos* stood out and animation continued to bloom, but, otherwise, *Felicity* did not abound. PEOPLE's TV critic Terry Kelleher appraises the new and revisits some old favorites.

BECKER
CBS
Ted Danson plays an abrasive but dedicated physician in a Bronx general practice. The problem here is not the star's performance but the writers' unwillingness to take the character far enough.

BRIMSTONE
FOX
A dead cop, serving an afterlife sentence in hell for murdering his wife's rapist, must track down 113 dangerously evil souls who are wreaking havoc on earth. This erratic drama ranges from rather clever to awfully grisly.

BROTHER'S KEEPER
ABC
A trouble-prone pro-football player moves in with his older brother, a widower with an 8-year-old son. Tough to believe but not so to enjoy.

BUDDY FARO
CBS
Dennis Farina is perfect as fabled L.A. private eye Buddy Faro, a missing person since '78 who teams up with the young P.I. who has been hired to find him. Fast-paced and full of funny asides.

CHARMED
The WB
Shannen Doherty, Holly Marie Combs, and Alyssa Milano are a trio of sisters and witches who employ their powers for the betterment of humanity. Wavering between frightening and funny, this show is watchable but not spellbinding.

CONRAD BLOOM
NBC
Mark Feuerstein is mildly appealing as an advertising copywriter who is the kind of guy women just love. A little too reminiscent of other shows about New York City singles with media-related jobs.

COSTELLO
FOX
Though her acting skills are rudimentary, Sue Costello is likable as Sue Murphy, a woman in her 20s who works in a south Boston bah. This show needs to smahten up and tone it down.

COUSIN SKEETER
Nickelodeon
This sitcom centers on a shy 13-year-old who is constantly dragged into mischief by his cousin, who is a puppet. On paper this probably looked great; onscreen it's an awkward, if amiable, hybrid.

CUPID
ABC
Playing a guy who claims to be the Roman god of love, Jeremy Piven is an irresistible force—mercurial, mischievous, and impossibly glib. You may fall for this one.

THE DAILY SHOW WITH JON STEWART
Comedy Central
Stewart is more likable than Craig Kilborn as host of this half-hour news-spoof talk show, and the show's satire is smart enough to have real sting.

DILBERT
UPN
Animated sitcom based on a Scott Adams's comic strip, including well-cast voices Daniel Stern, Chris Elliott, and Larry Miller. Some dull moments, but fills its quota of office comedy.

ENCORE! ENCORE!
NBC
The often hilarious Nathan Lane plays a washed-up bachelor opera star forced to return home to California and make himself useful around the family winery. Unlikely to yield any vintage comedy.

FAMILY GUY
FOX
In this sitcom, animation lends itself particularly well to the free-association comedy of creator Seth MacFarlane.

FANTASY ISLAND
ABC
Malcolm McDowell, playing the mysterious, imperious hotelier who makes guests' dreams come true, is a far more intriguing innkeeper than Ricardo Montalban in the original series. Not a five-star resort, but the host is first-class.

FELICITY
The WB
Keri Russell draws us to her character, a freshman at the fictional equivalent of New York University. May seem implausible, except to viewers who are in their youth or haven't forgotten it. Sensitive without being soapy.

FOX FILES
FOX

A weekly network newsmagazine that tends to punch up a story even when the facts are strong enough to speak for themselves.

FUTURAMA
FOX

In what looks like another clever, irreverent, cutting-edge animated comedy from creator Matt Groening, a frustrated pizza deliverer time-trips 1,000 years forward and teams up with a one-eyed female alien and a hard-drinking robot.

GvsE
USA

This goofy show features two dead dudes working as undercover agents for the Almighty, saving souls and battling a bunch of demons called Morlocks. Overly violent, it has some trouble being gritty and crazy at the same time, but the G in it outweighs the E.

HOLDING THE BABY
FOX

Call it *Two Guys, a Girl, and a Baby*. By any name, this banal new sitcom is nothing you haven't seen before.

HOME MOVIES
UPN

Home Movies uses the Squiggle-Vision Process—minimalist drawings wobbly animated. The show meanders, but patient viewers will be amused by the disheveled single mother.

THE HOWARD STERN RADIO SHOW
Syndicated

Imagine our disappointment when Howard Stern unveiled an alternative to *Saturday Night Live* that was lazy, old, and tiresome, featuring videotaped highlights from his radio show as well as a few made-for-TV segments.

THE HUGHLEYS
ABC

This is the familiar story of a husband and father who is less intelligent than his wife and less mature than his young children. For this series to work, the main character must show signs of growth.

JESSE
NBC

Call this middling sitcom *UN-Married . . . with Child*. Christina Applegate plays Jesse Warner, a single mother who desperately needs to relax; otherwise, she's so normal that the supporting cast must bear much of the comedy load.

THE KING OF QUEENS
CBS

Not too original, but the cast, including Kevin James and Leah Remini as a married couple and Jerry Stiller as their eccentric live-in father-in-law, makes this King more than a commoner.

L.A. DOCTORS
CBS

Four ambitious Los Angeles internists balance trendiness, dedication, and the business end of medicine. Worth an office visit for fans of the hospital dramas *ER* and *Chicago Hope*.

THE LATE LATE SHOW WITH CRAIG KILBORN
CBS

Can we all assume that he really is a vain, cocksure guy who is too stuck on himself—not just playing one on TV? On Kilborn's new show, which includes a few old *Daily Show* features, the attitude never stops.

THE LATE LATE SHOW WITH TOM SNYDER
CBS

Snyder's interviews are actual conversations, a television rarity. The silver-haired Snyder is a TV personality with personality, and

late night will seem gray when he's gone.

LIVING IN CAPTIVITY
FOX

This uneven comedy of suburban eccentricity is in need of fine-tuning.

MAD ABOUT YOU
NBC

Paul Reiser and Helen Hunt are still terrific as married New Yorkers Paul and Jamie Buchman, but this season the writers failed to get the most out of some promising situations.

MAD TV
FOX

Has the virtues and the defects that *Saturday Night Live* has. Earns the most laughs when mining the rich territory of pop-culture parody but puts recurring characters through the same tired paces.

MAGGIE WINTERS
CBS

Faith Ford's character returns home after leaving her philandering husband in Chicago. Life in her little hometown is, uh, slow—for the viewers, too.

THE MAGNIFICENT SEVEN
CBS

Michael Biehn leads a group of gunslingers who are hired to protect a town. Loosely based on the 1960 movie, it offers decent entertainment for fans of the genre.

THE MAN SHOW
Comedy Central

Think *Animal House 1999* or *Howard Stern Lite*. Jimmy Kimmel and Adam Carolla have potential, but their show is mostly low-class gags for guys.

MARTIAL LAW
CBS

A tongue-in-cheek cop show. The comedic appeal lies largely in the contrast between Sammy

Hung's doughy appearance and his awesome, destructive power as a Shanghai policeman and martial artist who is assigned to the LAPD.

MERCY POINT
UPN

Familiar medical drama in a sci-fi setting. Its strongest point is the skillful performance of Joe Morton as a doctor who is totally dedicated and—though expert in alien physiology—totally human.

MILLENNIUM
FOX

What began in '96 as a dank, depressing, yet authentically atmospheric serial-killer-of-the-week thriller has grown more pretentious and less coherent with each new installment.

NEWSRADIO
NBC

Max Lewis, played by Jon Lovitz, has earned his share of laughs with familiar tics and off-beat timing. This show is still on the right frequency.

THE NORM SHOW
ABC

As a law-breaking ex-hockey player sentenced to perform community service as a social worker, Norm Macdonald comes across better when he's part of a team instead of smirking solo.

NYPD BLUE
ABC

When Jimmy Smits left the show, Rick Schroder's character became Andy Sipowicz's (Dennis Franz) new partner in the New York Police Department. The show has its petty irritations, but with Bobby's death, it seems revitalized.

OH BABY
Lifetime

Cynthia Stevenson is engaging as an unmarried software executive in her 30s who decides to

have a child by artificial insemination. Funny and surprisingly truthful, with supporting roles, including Joanna Gleason as Stevenson's best friend, that are exceptionally well cast.

PAYNE
CBS

This Americanization of the British series *Fawlty Towers* stars John Larroquette, a master of supercilious attitude, in the John Cleese role of the less-than-hospitable hotelier. The situations are still farcical, but it's slow-paced and low-energy.

PENN & TELLER'S SIN CITY SPECTACULAR
FX

The gross-out kings of magic, Penn & Teller, now have a splashy Las Vegas variety series. For P&T fans, a spectacular; for others, an oddity.

THE PJs
FOX

Employing stop-motion animation with foam-latex puppets against the backdrop of an inner-city housing project, this show, whose creators include Eddie Murphy, marries cartoon whimsy and harsh reality. Can be plenty funny when it isn't crude and offensive—and even when it is.

PROVIDENCE
NBC

An L.A. plastic surgeon returns to her native Providence, Rhode Island, and goes to work in a family-practice clinic. This drama is implausible at every turn.

ROCK CANDY
VH1

The cable music channel's first newsmagazine is a hoot: video liner notes with attitude.

THE SECRET DIARY OF DESMOND PFEIFFER
UPN

A black nobleman booted out of England becomes the butler-confidant of President Abraham Lincoln. Controversial but not thought-provoking, this sitcom is unabashedly dumb, farcical, tasteless, and sophomoric.

THE SECRET LIVES OF MEN
ABC

Three divorced males in their 30s hang out, play golf, and kvetch. Walks a fine line between funny and annoying.

SEX AND THE CITY
HBO

Sarah Jessica Parker stars as a sex columnist in Manhattan. An improving chronicle of sexual misadventures.

60 MINUTES II
CBS

Dan Rather, Bob Simon, Charlie Rose, and Vicki Mabrey report on a well-mixed batch of fresh stories and recycled items. May the stopwatch tick on.

THE SOPRANOS
HBO

James Gandolfini gives a superb performance as a gangster trying to get in touch with his feelings. Engrossing portrait of the Mafioso as everyman in a series that offers more than laughs.

SPIN CITY
ABC

Michael J. Fox stars in this fast-paced, clever sitcom set in the offices of New York's City Hall, but the writers need to be reminded that there's more to politics than sex.

SPORTS NIGHT
ABC

A comedy about the people who put together a fictional show similar to ESPN's *SportsCenter*. We're betting that with experience, this inconsistent show can find a way to win.

THE STEVE HARVEY SHOW
The WB
Harvey stars as a high school music teacher and former member of a popular '70s R&B group. The writers' apparent priority is to place the adults in trite situations with sexual overtones.

STRANGE WORLD
ABC
From ex–*X-Files* producer Howard Gordon comes this murky and derivative sci-fi series about a Gulf War veteran who is now a civilian medical investigator for the army. Enter this in the Y-Bother Files.

SUNSET BEACH
NBC
The show's trite plots feature sex and scheming in Southern California.

TRINITY
NBC
It's hard, at first, to sort out the characters in this close-knit Irish-American New York family, but what redeems the soap opera stereotypes is the spirited, engaging young cast, including the beguiling Tate Donovan.

TURKS
CBS
The cast is solid, but this police drama seems tame compared to the likes of *NYPD Blue.*

TWO OF A KIND
ABC
A contrived, formulaic sitcom starring Mary-Kate and Ashley Olsen, 11-year-old twins who are identical but distinguishable. The redeeming feature is the free-spirited babysitter, played by Sally Wheeler.

V.I.P.
Syndicated
Pamela Anderson Lee plays a small-town innocent who saves a movie star's life and winds up as front woman for a bodyguard agency. Agreeably tongue-in-cheek, but there's nothing important about *V.I.P.*

WELCOME TO PARADOX
Sci-Fi Channel
These weekly dramas, all based on short stories, are set in Betaville, a future city filled with ultrahigh technology and perennial human unhappiness. Happily, this series is not unworthy to be mentioned in the same sentence as Rod Sterling's classic show, *The Twilight Zone.*

WHERE ARE THEY NOW?
VH1
Offers current snapshots of rock stars who have flamed out. The show has attitude all right, but it leaves us wondering what our own attitudes should be toward irresponsible and/or illegal conduct by the likes of Billy Idol.

THE WILD THORNBERRYS
Nickelodeon
This skewed, funny, animated show from the creators of Rugrats, featuring voices by Tim Curry, Danielle Harris, Lacey Chabert, and Tom Kane, concerns a family that travels the world to film nature documentaries.

WILL & GRACE
NBC
Will, a gay lawyer, and Grace, a straight interior designer, are best friends, soulmates, and roommates. The show needs to guard against the cutesies, but Eric McCormack and Debra Messing convey the warmth and fun in their characters' relationship.

ZOE, DUNCAN, JACK & JANE
The WB
A comedy version of *Dawson's Creek*, except it doesn't earn many laughs.

THE TOP INFOMERCIALS

This unique form of advertising—in the guise of programming—was first seen on American television in 1984 when advertising was deregulated, and the affliction has metastasized since. The following is a list of 1998's 10 most profitable infomercials, based exclusively on the shows' sales. (Source: *Steve Dworman's Infomercial Marketing Report*)

1. Bioslim (diet)
2. George Foreman's Lean Grilling Machine
3. Total Gym (fitness machine)
4. Larry North's North American Slim Down (diet)
5. Dalton McCry's How to Hit the Golf Ball As Straight As You Can, Point Guaranteed
6. Red Devil Grill
7. Dr. Morter's Dynamic Health
8. Epilstop (hair removal)
9. Timeworks (fitness)
10. Ingenio—T-Fal (cookware)

THE CABLE DIRECTORY

The following is a complete list of all national cable television networks, as of our press date, according to the National Cable Television Association. In many cases, the networks on the air are also online.

A&E TELEVISION NETWORKS (A&E)
Original biographies, mysteries, and specials
www.biography.com

ADAM & EVE
Adult movies
www.cyberspice.com

ADULTVISION
Erotic movies

ALL NEWS CHANNEL
Continuous newscasts
www.allnews.com

AMC (AMERICAN MOVIE CLASSICS)
Hollywood's greatest films
www.amctv.com

AMERICA'S HEALTH NETWORK
Health information, using call-in format
www.ahn.com

AMERICA'S VOICE
Links Washington leaders with citizens in on-air forums, in-depth reports
www.americasvoice.com

ANA TELEVISION
Programming in Arabic and English for Arab-Americans

ANIMAL PLANET
Varied animal and natural history programming
www.animalplanet.com

ASIAN AMERICAN SATELLITE TV
Chinese-language news, drama, movies, sports, education, and entertainment
www.scea.org/aatv.html

BBC AMERICA
British TV, with comedies, dramas, news, and documentaries

BET (BLACK ENTERTAINMENT TELEVISION)
Music videos, sports, family sitcoms, concerts, specials, talk

shows, gospel, news
www.msbet.com

BET ACTION PAY PER VIEW
Action, sci-fi, and thriller movies
www.msbet.com

BET MOVIES/ STARZ!3
Films with Afro-American themes and perspectives

BET ON JAZZ: THE CABLE JAZZ CHANNEL
Jazz productions, films, and documentaries
www.msbet.com

BLOOMBERG INFORMATION TELEVISION
Financial markets, news, sports, and weather in "multiscreen" format
www.bloomberg.com

THE BOX
Viewer-programmed music videos of all types

BRAVO CABLE NETWORK
Cultural offerings, including films, arts specials, interviews
www.bravotv.com

C-SPAN (CABLE SATELLITE PUBLIC AFFAIRS NETWORK)
Straight news from Washington and around the nation
www.c-span.org

C-SPAN2
Live coverage of the U.S. Senate and BOOK TV
www.c-span.org

C/NET: THE COMPUTER NETWORK
News, information, and resources related to computers
www.cnet.com

CABLE VIDEO STORE
Pay-per-view movies and special events

CANAL SUR
Latin American newscasts, entertainment, and sports

CARTOON NETWORK
Cartoons and animation

CBS EYE ON PEOPLE
Entertainment and information focusing on people/personalities

CBS TELENOTICIAS
Spanish-language news network on Latin America, 24 hours a day

CELTICVISION
Alternative English-language programming with a distinct Celtic flavor

CINE LATINO
Original Spanish-language movies

CINEMAX
Variety of film entertainment
www.cinemax.com

CLASSIC ARTS SHOWCASE
Nonprofit arts programming
www.classicartsshowcase.org

CMT: COUNTRY MUSIC TELEVISION
Country music videos
www.country.com

CNBC
Business, money, and talk programming
www.cnbc.com

CNN (CABLE NEWS NETWORK)
Business, news, weather, sports
www.cnn.com

CNN HEADLINE NEWS
News updates, 24 hours a day
www.cnn.com/HLN

CNNFN (THE FINANCIAL NETWORK)
Market and business news
www.cnnfn.com

CNNI (CNN INTERNATIONAL)
Global news, business, weather,

and sports, 24 hours a day
www.cnn.com/CNNI

CNN/SI
Sports news, 24 hours a day

COMEDY CENTRAL
All-comedy programming
www.comedycentral.com

COURTROOM TELEVISION NETWORK (COURT TV)
Live trial coverage and legal features
www.courttv.com

THE CRIME CHANNEL
Crime-related programming, including series, movies, and news

DEEP DISH TV
Educational programming
www.igc.org/deepdish

DISCOVERY CHANNEL
Informative entertainment
www.discovery.com

DISCOVERY CIVILIZATION CHANNEL
Documentaries on the people, places, and events from prehistory to the 21st century

DISCOVERY HEALTH CHANNEL
Health trends, news, and information in the world of medicine

DISCOVERY HOME & LEISURE
Guide to better living and home how-to

DISCOVERY KIDS CHANNEL
Educational entertainment

DISCOVERY SCIENCE CHANNEL
High tech and how things work

DISCOVERY WINGS CHANNEL
For flight enthusiasts

DISNEY CHANNEL
Family entertainment
www.disneychannel.com

THE DREAM NETWORK
Late-night feel-good message and inspirational music
www.thedreamnetwork.com

E! ENTERTAINMENT TELEVISION
All about celebrities
www.eonline.com

ECOLOGY COMMUNICATIONS
Trends, news, fiction, and non-fiction about the environment
www.ecology.com

ENCORE THEMATIC MULTIPLEX SM
Movies, with "mood on demand" viewing options

ENCORE
Premium movie service

ESPN
Sports programming
ESPNet.SportsZone.com

ESPN CLASSIC
Classic sports programming

ESPN2
Live and original sports programming
ESPNet.SportsZone.com

ESPNEWS
Continuous scores, highlights, analyses, interviews, press conferences, statistics, and news
ESPNet.SportsZone.com

ETHNIC-AMERICAN BROADCASTING CO. L.P.
Foreign-language ethnic programming
www.eabc.com

EWTN
Religious programming in English and Spanish
www.etwn.com

THE FILIPINO CHANNEL
All-Filipino news, drama, sitcoms, sports, musicals, and cultural programs
www.abs-cbni.com/tfcdir.html

FIT TV
Health and fitness
www.fittv.com

FLIX
Movies from the '60s to the '90s

FOOD NETWORK
All facets of food, fitness, health, nutrition
www.foodtv.com

FOX FAMILY CHANNEL
Family-oriented series, specials, and movies

www.foxfamilychannel.com

FOX NEWS CHANNEL
General news service
www.foxnews.com

FOX SPORTS AMÉRICAS
Spanish-language sports

FOXNET
Regular Fox network programs
www.foxnetwork.com

FREE SPEECH TV (FSTV)
Experimental media and progressive programming
www.freespeech.org

FX (FOX BASIC CABLE)
General entertainment

FXM: MOVIES FROM FOX
Films and original programming

GALAVISIÓN
Spanish-language movies, sports, news
www.galavision.com

GAME SHOW NETWORK
Play-along games and classic game show episodes
www.sony.com

GAY ENTERTAINMENT TELEVISION
Gay talk, style, and variety programming

GEMS INTERNATIONAL TELEVISION
Spanish-language women's programming

THE GOLF CHANNEL
Golf coverage, news stats, and instruction
www.thegolfchannel.com

GOODLIFE TV NETWORK
Mixed programming for post-49 audience
www.goodtv.com

GREAT AMERICAN COUNTRY (GAC)
Country music videos
www.countrystars.com

HBO (HOME BOX OFFICE)
Films, specials, sports
www.hbo.com

THE HISTORY CHANNEL
Historical documentaries, movies, and miniseries

www.historychannel.com

HOME & GARDEN TELEVISION
Lifestyle programming
www.hgtv.com

HOME SHOPPING NETWORK (HSN)
Live, 24-hour video retailing

HOME SHOPPING SPREE (SPREE!)
More shopping at home

HOT CHOICE
Action-adventure and "adult
appeal" movies
www.ppv.com

HTV
Spanish-language music videos
www.htv.com

THE IDEA CHANNEL
Leading scholars in discussions
on a variety of topics
www.ideachannel.com

THE INDEPENDENT FILM CHANNEL
Independent films
www.ifctv.com

**THE INSPIRATIONAL NETWORK
(INSP)**
Ministry programs, family-
oriented movies, dramas, music,
children's programs, and specials

INTERNATIONAL CHANNEL
Multinational programming in
more than 20 languages
www.I-channel.com

KALEIDOSCOPE NETWORK, INC.
Programming by and for people
with disabilities

KNOWLEDGE TV
Programming for personal
growth
www.jec.edu

LADBROKE RACING CHANNEL
Live Thoroughbred and harness
racing

LAS VEGAS TELEVISION NETWORK
News, subscription gaming, and
subscription adult

THE LEARNING CHANNEL (TLC)
Educational programming for all
www.discovery.com

LIFETIME TELEVISION (LIFE)
Entertainment and information
programming for women
www.lifetimetv.com

THE LOCOMOTION CHANNEL
24-hour network for teens and
young adults with worldwide
animation of every form

M2: MUSIC TELEVISION
Music videos

MILITARY CHANNEL, INC.
Military theme programming
www.militarytv.com

MOR GALLERIA
Shopping channel

THE MOVIE CHANNEL
High-appeal genre movies

MOVIEPLEX
Seven movie channels in one

MSNBC
All-news network
www.msnbc.com

MTV: MUSIC TELEVISION
Music videos and pop culture
programming
www.mtv.com

MTV NETWORKS LATIN AMERICA
Spanish-language music videos

MUCHMUSIC USA
Interactive music programming
www.muchmusic.com/usa

MY PET TV
Animal info and entertainment

NASA TELEVISION
Space program coverage and
other educational material
www.nasa.gov/ntv

NATIONAL JEWISH TELEVISION
Religious and cultural programming

NESHAMA
Universal Torah Broadcasting
Network

NEWSWORLD INTERNATIONAL
Alternative perspective on world
news

**NICK AT NITE/NICK AT NITE'S TV
LAND**
America's favorite classic televi-
sion programs

NICKELODEON/NICK AT NITE
Kids' programming during the
day; TV classics afterhours
www.nick-at-nite.viacom.com

OASIS TV, INC.
Holistic lifestyles, human-
potential, health, environment,
visionary-arts, metaphysics, and
world-peace programming
www.oasistv.com

ODYSSEY CHANNEL
Interfaith and values-based programming
www.odysseychannel.com

THE OUTDOOR CHANNEL
Outdoor lifestyle programming
www.outdoorchannel.com

OUTDOOR LIFE NETWORK
Outdoor recreation, conserva-
tion, wilderness, and adventure
programming
www.greatoutdoors.com

THE OUTLET MALL NETWORK
TV home shopping and internet
shopping

OVATION—THE ARTS NETWORK
Visual and performing arts
www.ovationtv.com

PAX TV
Family-oriented programming
with minimal violence and sexual themes, and no foul language
www.paxtv.com

PLAYBOY TV
Adult entertainment
www.playboy.com

PRAISE TELEVISION
Christian music-video
entertainment

**PRODUCT INFORMATION NETWORK
(PIN)**
Infomercials

PROTO X
Unfiltered programming by

young voices, 18–34 years old

QVC
Home-shopping service
www.qvc.com

ROMANCE CLASSICS
Romance programming

THE SCI-FI CHANNEL
Original and classic science fiction fare
www.sci-fi.com

SCOLA
International TV news, broadcast to schools

SHOP AT HOME
Electronic retailing

SHOWTIME
Movies, series, specials, boxing, other entertainment
www.showtimeonline.com

SINGLEVISION
Personal ads
www.singlevision.com

SPEEDVISION NETWORK
Automotive, marine, aviation, and motorcycle programming
www.speedvision.com

SPICE
Subscription service adult movies
www.cyberspice.com

SPICE HOT
Same movies as Spice, only "hotter" versions
www.cyberspice.com

STARZ!
First-run premium movies

STUDENT FILM NETWORK
Short-length films, alternative and experimental works

STYLE
24-hour style, fashion, and design programming
www.eonline.com

SUN TV
News, sports, entertainment shows from the Caribbean, and Central and South America

CABLE'S BIGGEST NETWORKS

Ranked by number of subscribers, these cable channels are found in the most American homes. (Source: National Cable Television Association)

1. Discovery Channel
2. TBS Superstation
3. C-SPAN (Cable Satellite Public Affairs Network)
4. FOX Family Channel
5. ESPN
6. CNN (Cable News Network)
7. Lifetime Television (LIFE)
8. TNN: The Nashville Network
9. A&E Television Networks (A&E)
10. The Weather Channel
11. CNN Headline News
12. USA Network
13. MTV: Music Television
14. AMC (American Movie Classics)
15. The Learning Channel (TLC)
16. QVC
17. Nickelodeon/Nick at Nite
18. TNT (Turner Network Television)
19. VH1 (Music First)
20. CNBC

SUNDANCE CHANNEL
Independent film and documentary works
www.sundancechannel.com

TBS SUPERSTATION
Movies, sports, comedies, original programming

TELEMUNDO
Spanish-language programming, with movies, game shows, news, music, soap operas, kids' shows, and sports

TNN: THE NASHVILLE NETWORK
Country music and lifestyle programming
www.country.com

TNT (TURNER NETWORK TELEVISION)
Vintage and original films, sports, kids' shows, specials

TOON DISNEY
Disney animation, 24 hours daily
www.disneychannel.com

TOTAL COMMUNICATION NETWORK
For deaf, hard-of-hearing, and hearing audiences

THE TRAVEL CHANNEL
Travel ideas, dream vacations, and money-saving information
www.travelchannel.com

TRINITY BROADCASTING NETWORK
Religious programming
www.tbn.org

TRIO
General entertainment for all

TURNER CLASSIC MOVIES (TCM)
Nearly 400 movies per month
www.tcm.turner.com

TV 5-LA TELEVISION INTERNATIONALE
French-language programming from France, Switzerland, Belgium, and Canada
www.tv5.org

TV ASIA
Programming from the Asian subcontinent, mostly in Hindi and English

TV-JAPAN
News, sports, drama, education, and kids' shows from Japan

U NETWORK
Student-produced programming in all genres

UNIVISION
Spanish-speaking programs, with movies, novelas, sports, news
www.univision.net

USA NETWORK
All-entertainment network

UVTV/KTLA
Los Angeles station featuring Dodgers baseball

UVTV/WGN
Chicago station featuring Cubs and White Sox baseball, Bulls and NCAA basketball

UVTV/WPIX
New York station featuring New York Yankees baseball and preseason Giants and Jets football

VALUEVISION
Home shopping
www.vvtv.com

VH1 (MUSIC FIRST)
Music videos targeted to the 25- to 44-year-old audience
www.vh1.com

VIDEO CATALOG CHANNEL
Antique and collectible shopping

VIEWER'S CHOICE
Films, sports, musical events
www.ppv.com

WAM! AMERICA'S KIDZ NETWORK
Commercial-free, socially responsible programming for 8- to 16-year-olds

WISDOM NETWORK
Holistic health and self-development
www.wisdomnetwork.com

THE WEATHER CHANNEL
24-hour local, national, and international weather information
www.weather.com

WORLDJAZZ
National and international jazz

THE WORSHIP NETWORK
Christian worship and music set to scenic videos

WSBK
Boston station offering movies, specials, and local sports

Z MUSIC TELEVISION
Christian music videos with no sex, drugs, or violence

ZDTV
Help and how-to news and business about technology and the internet
www.zdtv.com

WHAT'S IN A NAME?

Is a favorite show any less sweet by a different name? The creators often thought so. And so many of the most popular shows of all time began with names other than those that became familiar to millions. A sampling follows (when a show had multiple names, they are listed in sequence).

Original Name	Final Name	Original Name	Final Name
The Alley Cats	Charlie's Angels	Mr. Solo/Solo	The Man From U.N.C.L.E.
The Brady Brood	The Brady Bunch		
45 Minutes from Harlem	Diff'rent Strokes	Occupation Unknown	What's My Line?
Country Cousins/ The Eddie Albert Show	Green Acres	Oil	Dynasty
		Ozark Widow/Dern Tootin'/ Whistle Stop	Petticoat Junction
Cyborg	The Six Million Dollar Man	The Rise and Shine Revue	Today
Danny Doyle	I Spy		
Eye-Opener	CBS Morning Show	Spencer's Mountain	The Waltons
Family Business	The Partridge Family	Sunset 77	77 Sunset Strip
The Flagstones	The Flintstones	Those Were the Days	All in the Family
McHale's Men	McHale's Navy	Wally and the Beaver	Leave It to Beaver
Head of the Family	The Dick Van Dyke Show		

THE MOST POPULAR SHOWS ON TV

The following chart shows America's TV favorites every year beginning in 1949.
(Sources: *Variety* and, after 1949–50, Nielsen Media Research)

1949–50

1. The Texaco Star Theater — NBC
2. Toast of the Town (Ed Sullivan) — CBS
3. Arthur Godfrey's Talent Scouts — CBS
4. Fireball Fun for All — NBC
5. Philco Television Playhouse — NBC
6. Fireside Theatre — NBC
7. The Goldbergs — CBS
8. Suspense — CBS
9. The Ford Television Theater — CBS
10. Cavalcade of Stars — DUMONT

1950–51

1. The Texaco Star Theater — NBC
2. Fireside Theatre — NBC
3. Your Show of Shows — NBC
4. Philco Television Playhouse — NBC
5. The Colgate Comedy Hour — NBC
6. Gillette Cavalcade of Sports — NBC
7. Arthur Godfrey's Talent Scouts — CBS
8. Mama — CBS
9. Robert Montgomery Presents — NBC
10. Martin Kane, Private Eye — NBC
11. Man Against Crime — CBS
12. Somerset Maugham Theatre — NBC
13. Kraft Television Theatre — NBC
14. Toast of the Town (Ed Sullivan) — CBS
15. The Aldrich Family — NBC
16. You Bet Your Life — NBC
17. Armstrong Circle Theater (tie) — NBC
17. Big Town (tie) — CBS
17. Lights Out (tie) — NBC
20. The Alan Young Show — CBS

1951–52

1. Arthur Godfrey's Talent Scouts — CBS
2. The Texaco Star Theater — NBC
3. I Love Lucy — CBS
4. The Red Skelton Show — NBC
5. The Colgate Comedy Hour — NBC
6. Fireside Theatre — NBC
7. The Jack Benny Program — CBS
8. Your Show of Shows — NBC
9. You Bet Your Life — NBC
10. Arthur Godfrey and His Friends — CBS
11. Mama — CBS
12. Philco Television Playhouse — NBC
13. Amos 'n' Andy — CBS
14. Big Town — CBS
15. Pabst Blue Ribbon Bouts — CBS
16. Gillette Cavalcade of Sports — NBC
17. The Alan Young Show — CBS
18. All-Star Revue (tie) — NBC
18. Dragnet (tie) — NBC
20. Kraft Television Theatre — NBC

1952–53

1. I Love Lucy — CBS
2. Arthur Godfrey's Talent Scouts — CBS
3. Arthur Godfrey and His Friends — CBS
4. Dragnet — NBC
5. The Texaco Star Theater — NBC
6. The Buick Circus Hour — NBC
7. The Colgate Comedy Hour — NBC
8. Gangbusters — NBC
9. You Bet Your Life — NBC
10. Fireside Theatre — NBC
11. The Red Buttons Show — CBS
12. The Jack Benny Program — CBS
13. Life with Luigi — CBS
14. Pabst Blue Ribbon Bouts — CBS
15. Goodyear Television Playhouse — NBC
16. The Life of Riley — NBC
17. Mama — CBS
18. Your Show of Shows — NBC
19. What's My Line? — CBS
20. Strike It Rich — CBS

1953–54

1. I Love Lucy — CBS
2. Dragnet — NBC
3. Arthur Godfrey's Talent Scouts (tie) — CBS
3. You Bet Your Life (tie) — NBC
5. The Bob Hope Show — NBC
6. The Buick-Berle Show — NBC
7. Arthur Godfrey and His Friends — CBS
8. The Ford Television Theater — NBC
9. The Jackie Gleason Show — CBS
10. Fireside Theatre — NBC
11. The Colgate Comedy Hour (tie) — NBC
11. This Is Your Life (tie) — NBC
13. The Red Buttons Show — CBS
14. The Life of Riley — NBC
15. Our Miss Brooks — CBS
16. Treasury Men in Action — NBC
17. All-Star Revue (Martha Raye) — NBC
18. The Jack Benny Program — CBS
19. Gillette Cavalcade of Sports — NBC
20. Philco Television Playhouse — NBC

1954–55

1. I Love Lucy — CBS
2. The Jackie Gleason Show — CBS
3. Dragnet — NBC
4. You Bet Your Life — NBC
5. Toast of the Town (Ed Sullivan) — CBS
6. Disneyland — ABC
7. The Bob Hope Show — NBC
8. The Jack Benny Program — CBS
9. The Martha Raye Show — NBC
10. The George Gobel Show — NBC
11. The Ford Television Theater — NBC
12. December Bride — CBS
13. The Buick-Berle Show — NBC
14. This Is Your Life — NBC
15. I've Got a Secret — CBS
16. Two for the Money — CBS
17. Your Hit Parade — NBC
18. The Millionaire — CBS
19. General Electric Theater — CBS
20. Arthur Godfrey's Talent Scouts — CBS

1955–56

1.	The $64,000 Question	CBS
2.	I Love Lucy	CBS
3.	The Ed Sullivan Show	CBS
4.	Disneyland	ABC
5.	The Jack Benny Program	CBS
6.	December Bride	CBS
7.	You Bet Your Life	NBC
8.	Dragnet	NBC
9.	I've Got a Secret	CBS
10.	General Electric Theater	CBS
11.	Private Secretary (tie)	CBS
11.	The Ford Television Theater (tie)	NBC
13.	The Red Skelton Show	CBS
14.	The George Gobel Show	NBC
15.	The $64,000 Challenge	CBS
16.	Arthur Godfrey's Talent Scouts	CBS
17.	The Lineup	CBS
18.	Shower of Stars	CBS
19.	The Perry Como Show	NBC
20.	The Honeymooners	CBS

1957–58

1.	Gunsmoke	CBS
2.	The Danny Thomas Show	CBS
3.	Tales of Wells Fargo	NBC
4.	Have Gun, Will Travel	CBS
5.	I've Got a Secret	CBS
6.	The Life and Legend of Wyatt Earp	ABC
7.	General Electric Theater	CBS
8.	The Restless Gun	NBC
9.	December Bride	CBS
10.	You Bet Your Life	NBC
11.	Alfred Hitchcock Presents (tie)	CBS
11.	Cheyenne (tie)	ABC
13.	The Tennessee Ernie Ford Show	NBC
14.	The Red Skelton Show	CBS
15.	Wagon Train (tie)	NBC
15.	Sugarfoot (tie)	ABC
15.	Father Knows Best (tie)	CBS
18.	Twenty-One	NBC
19.	The Ed Sullivan Show	CBS
20.	The Jack Benny Program	CBS

1959–60

1.	Gunsmoke	CBS
2.	Wagon Train	NBC
3.	Have Gun, Will Travel	CBS
4.	The Danny Thomas Show	CBS
5.	The Red Skelton Show	CBS
6.	Father Knows Best (tie)	CBS
6.	77 Sunset Strip (tie)	ABC
8.	The Price Is Right	NBC
9.	Wanted: Dead or Alive	CBS
10.	Perry Mason	CBS
11.	The Real McCoys	ABC
12.	The Ed Sullivan Show	CBS
13.	The Bing Crosby Show	ABC
14.	The Rifleman	ABC
15.	The Tennessee Ernie Ford Show	NBC
16.	The Lawman	ABC
17.	Dennis the Menace	CBS
18.	Cheyenne	ABC
19.	Rawhide	CBS
20.	Maverick	ABC

1956–57

1.	I Love Lucy	CBS
2.	The Ed Sullivan Show	CBS
3.	General Electric Theater	CBS
4.	The $64,000 Question	CBS
5.	December Bride	CBS
6.	Alfred Hitchcock Presents	CBS
7.	I've Got a Secret (tie)	CBS
7.	Gunsmoke (tie)	CBS
9.	The Perry Como Show	NBC
10.	The Jack Benny Program	CBS
11.	Dragnet	NBC
12.	Arthur Godfrey's Talent Scouts	CBS
13.	The Millionaire (tie)	CBS
13.	Disneyland (tie)	ABC
15.	Shower of Stars	CBS
16.	The Lineup	CBS
17.	The Red Skelton Show	CBS
18.	You Bet Your Life	NBC
19.	The Life and Legend of Wyatt Earp	ABC
20.	Private Secretary	CBS

1958–59

1.	Gunsmoke	CBS
2.	Wagon Train	NBC
3.	Have Gun, Will Travel	CBS
4.	The Rifleman	ABC
5.	The Danny Thomas Show	CBS
6.	Maverick	ABC
7.	Tales of Wells Fargo	NBC
8.	The Real McCoys	ABC
9.	I've Got a Secret	CBS
10.	Wyatt Earp	ABC
11.	The Price Is Right	NBC
12.	The Red Skelton Show	CBS
13.	Zane Grey Theater (tie)	CBS
13.	Father Knows Best (tie)	CBS
15.	The Texan	CBS
16.	Wanted: Dead or Alive (tie)	CBS
16.	Peter Gunn (tie)	NBC
18.	Cheyenne	ABC
19.	Perry Mason	CBS
20.	The Tennessee Ernie Ford Show	NBC

1960–61

1.	Gunsmoke	CBS
2.	Wagon Train	NBC
3.	Have Gun, Will Travel	CBS
4.	The Andy Griffith Show	CBS
5.	The Real McCoys	ABC
6.	Rawhide	CBS
7.	Candid Camera	CBS
8.	The Untouchables (tie)	ABC
8.	The Price Is Right (tie)	NBC
10.	The Jack Benny Program	CBS
11.	Dennis the Menace	CBS
12.	The Danny Thomas Show	CBS
13.	My Three Sons (tie)	ABC
13.	77 Sunset Strip (tie)	ABC
15.	The Ed Sullivan Show	CBS
16.	Perry Mason	CBS
17.	Bonanza	NBC
18.	The Flintstones	ABC
19.	The Red Skelton Show	CBS
20.	Alfred Hitchcock Presents	CBS

1961–62

1. Wagon Train — NBC
2. Bonanza — NBC
3. Gunsmoke — CBS
4. Hazel — NBC
5. Perry Mason — CBS
6. The Red Skelton Show — CBS
7. The Andy Griffith Show — CBS
8. The Danny Thomas Show — CBS
9. Dr. Kildare — NBC
10. Candid Camera — CBS
11. My Three Sons — ABC
12. The Garry Moore Show — CBS
13. Rawhide — CBS
14. The Real McCoys — ABC
15. Lassie — CBS
16. Sing Along with Mitch — NBC
17. Dennis the Menace (tie) — CBS
17. Marshal Dillon (tie)
    (Gunsmoke reruns) — CBS
19. Ben Casey — ABC
20. The Ed Sullivan Show — CBS

1962–63

1. The Beverly Hillbillies — CBS
2. Candid Camera (tie) — CBS
2. The Red Skelton Show (tie) — CBS
4. Bonanza (tie) — NBC
4. The Lucy Show (tie) — CBS
6. The Andy Griffith Show — CBS
7. Ben Casey (tie) — ABC
7. The Danny Thomas Show (tie) — CBS
9. The Dick Van Dyke Show — CBS
10. Gunsmoke — CBS
11. Dr. Kildare (tie) — NBC
11. The Jack Benny Program (tie) — CBS
13. What's My Line? — CBS
14. The Ed Sullivan Show — CBS
15. Hazel — NBC
16. I've Got a Secret — CBS
17. The Jackie Gleason Show — CBS
18. The Defenders — CBS
19. The Garry Moore Show (tie) — CBS
19. To Tell the Truth (tie) — CBS

1963–64

1. The Beverly Hillbillies — CBS
2. Bonanza — NBC
3. The Dick Van Dyke Show — CBS
4. Petticoat Junction — CBS
5. The Andy Griffith Show — CBS
6. The Lucy Show — CBS
7. Candid Camera — CBS
8. The Ed Sullivan Show — CBS
9. The Danny Thomas Show — CBS
10. My Favorite Martian — CBS
11. The Red Skelton Show — CBS
12. I've Got a Secret (tie) — CBS
12. Lassie (tie) — CBS
12. The Jack Benny Program (tie) — CBS
15. The Jackie Gleason Show — CBS
16. The Donna Reed Show — ABC
17. The Virginian — NBC
18. The Patty Duke Show — ABC
19. Dr. Kildare — NBC
20. Gunsmoke — CBS

1964–65

1. Bonanza — NBC
2. Bewitched — ABC
3. Gomer Pyle, U.S.M.C. — CBS
4. The Andy Griffith Show — CBS
5. The Fugitive — ABC
6. The Red Skelton Hour — CBS
7. The Dick Van Dyke Show — CBS
8. The Lucy Show — CBS
9. Peyton Place (II) — ABC
10. Combat — ABC
11. Walt Disney's Wonderful
    World of Color — NBC
12. The Beverly Hillbillies — CBS
13. My Three Sons — ABC
14. Branded — NBC
15. Petticoat Junction (tie) — CBS
15. The Ed Sullivan Show (tie) — CBS
17. Lassie — CBS
18. The Munsters (tie) — CBS
18. Gilligan's Island (tie) — CBS
20. Peyton Place (V) — ABC

1965–66

1. Bonanza — NBC
2. Gomer Pyle, U.S.M.C. — CBS
3. The Lucy Show — CBS
4. The Red Skelton Hour — CBS
5. Batman (II) — ABC
6. The Andy Griffith Show — CBS
7. Bewitched (tie) — ABC
7. The Beverly Hillbillies (tie) — CBS
9. Hogan's Heroes — CBS
10. Batman (I) — ABC
11. Green Acres — CBS
12. Get Smart — NBC
13. The Man from U.N.C.L.E. — NBC
14. Daktari — CBS
15. My Three Sons — CBS
16. The Dick Van Dyke Show — CBS
17. Walt Disney's Wonderful
    World of Color (tie) — NBC
17. The Ed Sullivan Show (tie) — CBS
19. The Lawrence Welk Show (tie) — ABC
19. I've Got a Secret (tie) — CBS

1966–67

1. Bonanza — NBC
2. The Red Skelton Hour — CBS
3. The Andy Griffith Show — CBS
4. The Lucy Show — CBS
5. The Jackie Gleason Show — CBS
6. Green Acres — CBS
7. Daktari (tie) — CBS
7. Bewitched (tie) — ABC
7. The Beverly Hillbillies (tie) — CBS
10. Gomer Pyle, U.S.M.C. (tie) — CBS
10. The Virginian (tie) — NBC
10. The Lawrence Welk Show (tie) — ABC
10. The Ed Sullivan Show (tie) — CBS
14. The Dean Martin Show (tie) — CBS
14. Family Affair (tie) — CBS
16. Smothers Brothers
    Comedy Hour — CBS
17. The CBS Friday Night
    Movie (tie) — CBS
17. Hogan's Heroes (tie) — CBS
19. Walt Disney's Wonderful
    World of Color — NBC
20. Saturday Night at the
    Movies — NBC

1967–68

1. The Andy Griffith Show — CBS
2. The Lucy Show — CBS
3. Gomer Pyle, U.S.M.C. — CBS
4. Gunsmoke (tie) — CBS
4. Family Affair (tie) — CBS
4. Bonanza (tie) — NBC
7. The Red Skelton Hour — CBS
8. The Dean Martin Show — NBC
9. The Jackie Gleason Show — CBS
10. Saturday Night at the Movies — NBC
11. Bewitched — ABC
12. The Beverly Hillbillies — CBS
13. The Ed Sullivan Show — CBS
14. The Virginian — NBC
15. The CBS Friday Night Movie (tie) — CBS
15. Green Acres (tie) — CBS
17. The Lawrence Welk Show — ABC
18. Smothers Brothers Comedy Hour — CBS
19. Gentle Ben — CBS
20. Tuesday Night at the Movies — NBC

1968–69

1. Rowan and Martin's Laugh-In — NBC
2. Gomer Pyle, U.S.M.C. — CBS
3. Bonanza — NBC
4. Mayberry R.F.D. — CBS
5. Family Affair — CBS
6. Gunsmoke — CBS
7. Julia — NBC
8. The Dean Martin Show — NBC
9. Here's Lucy — CBS
10. The Beverly Hillbillies — CBS
11. Mission: Impossible (tie) — CBS
11. Bewitched (tie) — ABC
11. The Red Skelton Hour (tie) — CBS
14. My Three Sons — CBS
15. The Glen Campbell Goodtime Hour — CBS
16. Ironside — NBC
17. The Virginian — NBC
18. The F.B.I. — ABC
19. Green Acres — CBS
20. Dragnet — NBC

1969–70

1. Rowan and Martin's Laugh-In — NBC
2. Gunsmoke — CBS
3. Bonanza — NBC
4. Mayberry R.F.D. — CBS
5. Family Affair — CBS
6. Here's Lucy — CBS
7. The Red Skelton Hour — CBS
8. Marcus Welby, M.D. — ABC
9. The Wonderful World of Disney — NBC
10. The Doris Day Show — CBS
11. The Bill Cosby Show — NBC
12. The Jim Nabors Hour — CBS
13. The Carol Burnett Show — CBS
14. The Dean Martin Show — NBC
15. My Three Sons (tie) — CBS
15. Ironside (tie) — NBC
15. The Johnny Cash Show (tie) — ABC
18. The Beverly Hillbillies — CBS
19. Hawaii Five-O — CBS
20. Glen Campbell Goodtime Hour — CBS

1970–71

1. Marcus Welby, M.D. — ABC
2. The Flip Wilson Show — NBC
3. Here's Lucy — CBS
4. Ironside — NBC
5. Gunsmoke — CBS
6. The ABC Movie of the Week — ABC
7. Hawaii Five-O — CBS
8. Medical Center — CBS
9. Bonanza — NBC
10. The F.B.I. — ABC
11. The Mod Squad — ABC
12. Adam-12 — NBC
13. Rowan and Martin's Laugh-In (tie) — NBC
13. The Wonderful World of Disney (tie) — NBC
15. Mayberry R.F.D. — CBS
16. Hee Haw — CBS
17. Mannix — CBS
18. The Men from Shiloh — NBC
19. My Three Sons — CBS
20. The Doris Day Show — CBS

1971–72

1. All in the Family — CBS
2. The Flip Wilson Show — NBC
3. Marcus Welby, M.D. — ABC
4. Gunsmoke — CBS
5. The ABC Movie of the Week — ABC
6. Sanford and Son — NBC
7. Mannix — CBS
8. Funny Face (tie) — CBS
8. Adam-12 (tie) — NBC
10. The Mary Tyler Moore Show — CBS
11. Here's Lucy — CBS
12. Hawaii Five-O — CBS
13. Medical Center — CBS
14. The NBC Mystery Movie — NBC
15. Ironside — NBC
16. The Partridge Family — ABC
17. The F.B.I. — ABC
18. The New Dick Van Dyke Show — CBS
19. The Wonderful World of Disney — NBC
20. Bonanza — NBC

1972–73

1. All in the Family — CBS
2. Sanford and Son — NBC
3. Hawaii Five-O — CBS
4. Maude — CBS
5. Bridget Loves Bernie (tie) — CBS
5. The NBC Sunday Mystery Movie (tie) — NBC
7. The Mary Tyler Moore Show (tie) — CBS
7. Gunsmoke (tie) — CBS
9. The Wonderful World of Disney — NBC
10. Ironside — NBC
11. Adam-12 — NBC
12. The Flip Wilson Show — NBC
13. Marcus Welby, M.D. — ABC
14. Cannon — CBS
15. Here's Lucy — CBS
16. The Bob Newhart Show — CBS
17. ABC Tuesday Movie of the Week — ABC
18. NFL Monday Night Football — ABC
19. The Partridge Family (tie) — ABC
19. The Waltons (tie) — CBS

1973–74

1. All in the Family — CBS
2. The Waltons — CBS
3. Sanford and Son — NBC
4. M*A*S*H — CBS
5. Hawaii Five-O — CBS
6. Maude — CBS
7. Kojak (tie) — CBS
7. The Sonny and Cher Comedy Hour (tie) — CBS
9. The Mary Tyler Moore Show (tie) — CBS
9. Cannon (tie) — CBS
11. The Six Million Dollar Man — ABC
12. The Bob Newhart Show (tie) — CBS
12. The Wonderful World of Disney (tie) — NBC
14. The NBC Sunday Mystery Movie — NBC
15. Gunsmoke — CBS
16. Happy Days — ABC
17. Good Times (tie) — CBS
17. Barnaby Jones (tie) — CBS
19. NFL Monday Night Football (tie) — ABC
19. The CBS Friday Night Movie (tie) — CBS

1974–75

1. All in the Family — CBS
2. Sanford and Son — NBC
3. Chico and the Man — NBC
4. The Jeffersons — CBS
5. M*A*S*H — CBS
6. Rhoda — CBS
7. Good Times — CBS
8. The Waltons — CBS
9. Maude — CBS
10. Hawaii Five-O — CBS
11. The Mary Tyler Moore Show — CBS
12. The Rockford Files — NBC
13. Little House on the Prairie — NBC
14. Kojak — CBS
15. Police Woman — NBC
16. S.W.A.T. — ABC
17. The Bob Newhart Show — CBS
18. The Wonderful World of Disney (tie) — NBC
18. The Rookies (tie) — ABC
20. Mannix — CBS

1975–76

1. All in the Family — CBS
2. Rich Man, Poor Man — ABC
3. Laverne and Shirley — ABC
4. Maude — CBS
5. The Bionic Woman — ABC
6. Phyllis — CBS
7. Sanford and Son (tie) — NBC
7. Rhoda (tie) — CBS
9. The Six Million Dollar Man — ABC
10. The ABC Monday Night Movie — ABC
11. Happy Days — ABC
12. One Day at a Time — CBS
13. The ABC Sunday Night Movie — ABC
14. The Waltons (tie) — CBS
14. M*A*S*H (tie) — CBS
16. Starsky and Hutch (tie) — ABC
16. Good Heavens (tie) — ABC
18. Welcome Back, Kotter — ABC
19. The Mary Tyler Moore Show — CBS
20. Kojak — CBS

1976–77

1. Happy Days — ABC
2. Laverne and Shirley — ABC
3. The ABC Monday Night Movie — ABC
4. M*A*S*H — CBS
5. Charlie's Angels — ABC
6. The Big Event — NBC
7. The Six Million Dollar Man — ABC
8. The ABC Sunday Night Movie (tie) — ABC
8. Baretta (tie) — ABC
8. One Day at a Time (tie) — CBS
11. Three's Company — ABC
12. All in the Family — CBS
13. Welcome Back, Kotter — ABC
14. The Bionic Woman — ABC
15. The Waltons (tie) — CBS
15. Little House on the Prairie (tie) — NBC
17. Barney Miller — ABC
18. 60 Minutes (tie) — CBS
18. Hawaii Five-O (tie) — CBS
20. NBC Monday Night at the Movies — NBC

1977–78

1. Laverne and Shirley — ABC
2. Happy Days — ABC
3. Three's Company — ABC
4. Charlie's Angels (tie) — ABC
4. All in the Family (tie) — CBS
4. 60 Minutes (tie) — CBS
7. Little House on the Prairie — NBC
8. M*A*S*H (tie) — CBS
8. Alice (tie) — CBS
10. One Day at a Time — CBS
11. How the West Was Won — ABC
12. Eight Is Enough — ABC
13. Soap — ABC
14. The Love Boat — ABC
15. NBC Monday Night Movie — NBC
16. NFL Monday Night Football — ABC
17. Barney Miller (tie) — ABC
17. Fantasy Island (tie) — ABC
19. The Amazing Spider-Man (tie) — CBS
19. Project U.F.O. (tie) — NBC

1978–79

1. Laverne and Shirley — ABC
2. Three's Company — ABC
3. Mork & Mindy — ABC
4. Happy Days (tie) — ABC
4. The Ropers (tie) — ABC
6. What's Happening!! (tie) — ABC
6. Alice (8:30) (tie) — CBS
8. M*A*S*H — CBS
9. One Day at a Time (Monday) — CBS
10. Taxi — ABC
11. 60 Minutes (tie) — CBS
11. Charlie's Angels (tie) — ABC
13. Angie — ABC
14. Alice (9:30) — CBS
15. All in the Family — CBS
16. WKRP in Cincinnati (tie) — CBS
16. Soap (tie) — ABC
18. Eight Is Enough — ABC
19. All in the Family — CBS
20. Barney Miller (tie) — ABC
20. CBS Sunday Night Movie (tie) — CBS

1979–80

1.	60 Minutes	CBS
2.	Three's Company	ABC
3.	That's Incredible	ABC
4.	M*A*S*H	CBS
5.	Alice	CBS
6.	Dallas	CBS
7.	Flo	CBS
8.	The Jeffersons	CBS
9.	The Dukes of Hazzard	CBS
10.	One Day at a Time	CBS
11.	WKRP in Cincinnati	CBS
12.	Goodtime Girls	ABC
13.	Archie Bunker's Place	CBS
14.	Taxi	ABC
15.	Eight Is Enough	ABC
16.	Little House on the Prairie	NBC
17.	House Calls	CBS
18.	Real People	NBC
19.	CHiPs	NBC
20.	Happy Days	ABC

1980–81

1.	Dallas	CBS
2.	60 Minutes	CBS
3.	The Dukes of Hazzard	CBS
4.	Private Benjamin	CBS
5.	M*A*S*H	CBS
6.	The Love Boat	ABC
7.	The NBC Tuesday Night Movie	NBC
8.	House Calls	CBS
9.	The Jeffersons (tie)	CBS
9.	Little House on the Prairie (tie)	NBC
11.	The Two of Us	CBS
12.	Alice	CBS
13.	Real People (tie)	NBC
13.	Three's Company (tie)	ABC
15.	The NBC Movie of the Week (tie)	NBC
15.	One Day at a Time (tie)	CBS
17.	Too Close for Comfort (tie)	ABC
17.	Magnum, P.I. (tie)	CBS
19.	Diff'rent Strokes (tie)	NBC
19.	NFL Monday Night Football (tie)	ABC

1981–82

1.	Dallas (9:00)	CBS
2.	Dallas (10:00)	CBS
3.	60 Minutes	CBS
4.	Three's Company (tie)	ABC
4.	CBS NFL Football Post 2 (tie)	CBS
6.	The Jeffersons	CBS
7.	Joanie Loves Chachi	ABC
8.	The Dukes of Hazzard (9:00)	CBS
9.	Alice (tie)	CBS
9.	The Dukes of Hazzard (8:00) (tie)	CBS
11.	The ABC Monday Night Movie (tie)	ABC
11.	Too Close for Comfort (tie)	ABC
13.	M*A*S*H	CBS
14.	One Day at a Time	CBS
15.	NFL Monday Night Football	ABC
16.	Falcon Crest	CBS
17.	Archie Bunker's Place (tie)	CBS
17.	The Love Boat (tie)	ABC
19.	Hart to Hart	ABC
20.	Trapper John, M.D.	CBS

1982–83

1.	60 Minutes	CBS
2.	Dallas	CBS
3.	M*A*S*H (tie)	CBS
3.	Magnum, P.I. (tie)	CBS
5.	Dynasty	ABC
6.	Three's Company	ABC
7.	Simon & Simon	CBS
8.	Falcon Crest	CBS
9.	NFL Monday Night Football	ABC
10.	The Love Boat	ABC
11.	One Day at a Time (Sunday)	CBS
12.	Newhart (Monday)	CBS
13.	The Jeffersons (tie)	CBS
13.	The A Team (tie)	NBC
15.	The Fall Guy (9:00)	ABC
16.	Newhart (Sunday, 9:30)	CBS
17.	The Mississippi	CBS
18.	9 to 5	ABC
19.	The Fall Guy	ABC
20.	The ABC Monday Night Movie	ABC

1983–84

1.	Dallas	CBS
2.	Dynasty	ABC
3.	The A Team	NBC
4.	60 Minutes	CBS
5.	Simon & Simon	CBS
6.	Magnum, P.I.	CBS
7.	Falcon Crest	CBS
8.	Kate & Allie	CBS
9.	Hotel	ABC
10.	Cagney & Lacey	CBS
11.	Knots Landing	CBS
12.	The ABC Sunday Night Movie (tie)	ABC
12.	The ABC Monday Night Movie (tie)	ABC
14.	TV's Bloopers & Practical Jokes	NBC
15.	AfterMASH	CBS
16.	The Fall Guy	ABC
17.	The Four Seasons	CBS
18.	The Love Boat	ABC
19.	Riptide	NBC
20.	The Jeffersons	CBS

1984–85

1.	Dynasty	ABC
2.	Dallas	CBS
3.	The Cosby Show	NBC
4.	60 Minutes	CBS
5.	Family Ties	NBC
6.	The A Team (tie)	NBC
6.	Simon & Simon (tie)	CBS
8.	Knots Landing	CBS
9.	Murder, She Wrote	CBS
10.	Falcon Crest (tie)	CBS
10.	Crazy Like a Fox (tie)	CBS
12.	Hotel	ABC
13.	Cheers	NBC
14.	Riptide (tie)	NBC
14.	Who's the Boss? (tie)	ABC
16.	Magnum, P.I.	CBS
17.	Hail to the Chief	ABC
18.	Newhart	CBS
19.	Kate & Allie	CBS
20.	The NBC Monday Night Movie	NBC

1985–86

1. The Cosby Show — NBC
2. Family Ties — NBC
3. Murder, She Wrote — CBS
4. 60 Minutes — CBS
5. Cheers — NBC
6. Dallas (tie) — CBS
6. Dynasty (tie) — ABC
6. The Golden Girls (tie) — NBC
9. Miami Vice — NBC
10. Who's the Boss? — ABC
11. Perfect Strangers — ABC
12. Night Court — NBC
13. The CBS Sunday
    Night Movie — CBS
14. Highway to Heaven (tie) — NBC
14. Kate & Allie (tie) — CBS
16. NFL Monday Night
    Football — ABC
17. Newhart — CBS
18. Knots Landing (tie) — CBS
18. Growing Pains (tie) — ABC
20. 227 — NBC

1986–87

1. The Cosby Show — NBC
2. Family Ties — NBC
3. Cheers — NBC
4. Murder, She Wrote — CBS
5. Night Court — NBC
6. The Golden Girls — NBC
7. 60 Minutes — CBS
8. Growing Pains — ABC
9. Moonlighting — ABC
10. Who's the Boss? — ABC
11. Dallas — CBS
12. Nothing in Common — NBC
13. Newhart — CBS
14. Amen — NBC
15. 227 — NBC
16. Matlock (tie) — NBC
16. CBS Sunday Night
    Movie (tie) — CBS
16. NBC Monday Night
    Movie (tie) — NBC
19. NFL Monday Night
    Football (tie) — ABC
19. Kate & Allie (tie) — CBS

1987–88

1. The Cosby Show — NBC
2. A Different World — NBC
3. Cheers — NBC
4. Growing Pains (Tuesday) — ABC
5. Night Court — NBC
6. The Golden Girls — NBC
7. Who's the Boss? — ABC
8. 60 Minutes — CBS
9. Murder, She Wrote — CBS
10. The Wonder Years — ABC
11. Alf — NBC
12. Moonlighting (tie) — ABC
12. L.A. Law (tie) — NBC
14. NFL Monday Night
    Football — ABC
15. Matlock (tie) — NBC
15. Growing Pains
    (Wednesday) (tie) — ABC
17. Amen — NBC
18. Family Ties — NBC
19. Hunter — NBC
20. The CBS Sunday
    Night Movie — CBS

1988–89

1. Roseanne (9:00) (tie) — ABC
1. The Cosby Show (tie) — NBC
3. Roseanne (8:30) (tie) — ABC
3. A Different World (tie) — NBC
5. Cheers — NBC
6. 60 Minutes — CBS
7. The Golden Girls — NBC
8. Who's the Boss? — ABC
9. The Wonder Years — ABC
10. Murder, She Wrote — CBS
11. Empty Nest — NBC
12. Anything but Love — ABC
13. Dear John — NBC
14. Growing Pains — ABC
15. Alf (tie) — NBC
15. L.A. Law (tie) — NBC
17. Matlock — NBC
18. Unsolved Mysteries (tie) — NBC
18. Hunter (tie) — NBC
20. In the Heat of the Night — NBC

1989–90

1. Roseanne — ABC
2. The Cosby Show — NBC
3. Cheers — NBC
4. A Different World — NBC
5. America's Funniest
   Home Videos — ABC
6. The Golden Girls — NBC
7. 60 Minutes — CBS
8. The Wonder Years — ABC
9. Empty Nest — NBC
10. Chicken Soup — ABC
11. NFL Monday Night Football — ABC
12. Unsolved Mysteries — NBC
13. Who's the Boss? — ABC
14. L.A. Law (tie) — NBC
14. Murder, She Wrote (tie) — CBS
16. Grand — NBC
17. In the Heat of the Night — NBC
18. Dear John — NBC
19. Coach — ABC
20. Matlock — NBC

1990–91

1. Cheers — NBC
2. 60 Minutes — CBS
3. Roseanne — ABC
4. A Different World — NBC
5. The Cosby Show — NBC
6. NFL Monday Night
   Football — ABC
7. America's Funniest
   Home Videos — ABC
8. Murphy Brown — CBS
9. America's Funniest
   People (tie) — ABC
9. Designing Women (tie) — CBS
9. Empty Nest (tie) — NBC
12. Golden Girls — NBC
13. Murder, She Wrote — CBS
14. Unsolved Mysteries — NBC
15. Full House — ABC
16. Family Matters — ABC
17. Coach (tie) — ABC
17. Matlock (tie) — NBC
19. In the Heat of the Night — NBC
20. Major Dad — CBS

1991–92

1.	60 Minutes	CBS
2.	Roseanne	ABC
3.	Murphy Brown	CBS
4.	Cheers	NBC
5.	Home Improvement	ABC
6.	Designing Women	CBS
7.	Coach	ABC
8.	Full House	ABC
9.	Murder, She Wrote (tie)	CBS
9.	Unsolved Mysteries (tie)	NBC
11.	Major Dad (tie)	CBS
11.	NFL Monday Night Football (tie)	ABC
13.	Room For Two	ABC
14.	The CBS Sunday Night Movie	CBS
15.	Evening Shade	CBS
16.	Northern Exposure	CBS
17.	A Different World	NBC
18.	The Cosby Show	NBC
19.	Wings	NBC
20.	America's Funniest Home Videos (tie)	ABC
20.	Fresh Prince of Bel Air (tie)	NBC

1992–93

1.	60 Minutes	CBS
2.	Roseanne	ABC
3.	Home Improvement	ABC
4.	Murphy Brown	CBS
5.	Murder, She Wrote	CBS
6.	Coach	ABC
7.	NFL Monday Night Football	ABC
8.	The CBS Sunday Night Movie (tie)	CBS
8.	Cheers (tie)	NBC
10.	Full House	ABC
11.	Northern Exposure	CBS
12.	Rescue: 911	CBS
13.	20/20	ABC
14.	The CBS Tuesday Night Movie (tie)	CBS
14.	Love & War (tie)	CBS
16.	Fresh Prince of Bel Air (tie)	NBC
16.	Hangin' with Mr. Cooper (tie)	ABC
16.	The Jackie Thomas Show (tie)	ABC
19.	Evening Shade	CBS
20.	Hearts Afire (tie)	CBS
20.	Unsolved Mysteries (tie)	NBC

1993–94

1.	Home Improvement	ABC
2.	60 Minutes	CBS
3.	Seinfeld	NBC
4.	Roseanne	ABC
5.	Grace Under Fire	ABC
6.	These Friends of Mine	ABC
7.	Frasier	NBC
8.	Coach (tie)	ABC
8.	NFL Monday Night Football (tie)	ABC
10.	Murder, She Wrote	CBS
11.	Murphy Brown	CBS
12.	Thunder Alley	ABC
13.	The CBS Sunday Night Movie	CBS
14.	20/20	ABC
15.	Love & War	CBS
16.	Primetime Live (tie)	ABC
16.	Wings (tie)	NBC
18.	NYPD Blue	ABC
19.	Homicide: Life on the Street	NBC
20.	Northern Exposure	CBS

1994–95

1.	Seinfeld	NBC
2.	ER	NBC
3.	Home Improvement	ABC
4.	Grace Under Fire	ABC
5.	NFL Monday Night Football	ABC
6.	60 Minutes	CBS
7.	NYPD Blue	ABC
8.	Friends	NBC
9.	Roseanne (tie)	ABC
9.	Murder, She Wrote (tie)	CBS
11.	Mad About You	NBC
12.	Madman of the People	NBC
13.	Ellen	ABC
14.	Hope & Gloria	NBC
15.	Frasier	NBC
16.	Murphy Brown	CBS
17.	20/20	ABC
18.	CBS Sunday Movie	CBS
19.	NBC Monday Night Movies	NBC
20.	Dave's World	CBS

1995–96

1.	ER	NBC
2.	Seinfeld	NBC
3.	Friends	NBC
4.	Caroline in the City	NBC
5.	NFL Monday Night Football	ABC
6.	The Single Guy	NBC
7.	Home Improvement	ABC
8.	Boston Common	NBC
9.	60 Minutes	CBS
10.	NYPD Blue	ABC
11.	Frasier (tie)	NBC
11.	20/20 (tie)	ABC
13.	Grace Under Fire	ABC
14.	Coach (tie)	ABC
14.	NBC Monday Night Movies (tie)	NBC
16.	Roseanne	ABC
17.	The Nanny	CBS
18.	Murphy Brown (tie)	CBS
18.	Primetime Live (tie)	ABC
18.	Walker, Texas Ranger (tie)	CBS

1996–97

1.	ER	NBC
2.	Seinfeld	NBC
3.	Suddenly Susan	NBC
4.	Friends (tie)	NBC
4.	The Naked Truth (tie)	NBC
6.	Fired Up	NBC
7.	NFL Monday Night Football	ABC
8.	The Single Guy	NBC
9.	Home Improvement	ABC
10.	Touched by an Angel	CBS
11.	60 Minutes	CBS
12.	20/20	ABC
13.	NYPD Blue	ABC
14.	CBS Sunday Movie	CBS
15.	Primetime Live	ABC
16.	Frasier	NBC
17.	Spin City	ABC
18.	NBC Sunday Night Movie (tie)	NBC
18.	The Drew Carey Show (tie)	ABC
20.	The X-Files	FOX

1997–98

1. Seinfeld — NBC
2. ER — NBC
3. Veronica's Closet — NBC
4. Friends — NBC
5. NFL Monday Night Football — ABC
6. Touched by an Angel — CBS
7. 60 Minutes — CBS
8. Union Square — NBC
9. CBS Sunday Movie — CBS
10. Frasier (tie) — NBC
10. Home Improvement (tie) — ABC
10. Just Shoot Me (tie) — NBC
13. Dateline NBC–Tuesday — NBC
14. NFL Monday Showcase — ABC
15. Dateline NBC–Monday — NBC
16. The Drew Carey Show (tie) — ABC
16. Fox NFL Sunday Post-Game Show (tie) — FOX
18. 20/20 — ABC
19. NYPD Blue (tie) — ABC
19. Primetime Live (tie) — ABC
19. The X-Files (tie) — FOX

1998–1999

1. ER — NBC
2. Friends — NBC
3. Frasier — NBC
4. NFL Monday Night Football — ABC
5. Jesse (tie) — NBC
5. Veronica's Closet (tie) — NBC
7. 60 Minutes — CBS
8. Touched by an Angel — CBS
9. CBS Sunday Movie — CBS
10. 20/20–Wednesday — ABC
11. Home Improvement — ABC
12. Everybody Loves Raymond — CBS
13. NYPD Blue — ABC
14. Law and Order — NBC
15. The Drew Carey Show (tie) — ABC
15. 20/20–Friday (tie) — ABC
17. Jag (tie) — CBS
17. NFL Monday Night Showcase (tie) — ABC
17. Providence (tie) — NBC
17. Dateline Friday (tie) — NBC

1998-99 SPECIAL RATINGS

The following are Nielsen ratings for a variety of special categories for the most recent season. (Source: Nielsen Media Research)

SYNDICATED TALK SHOWS

1. Jerry Springer, Studios USA
2. The Oprah Winfrey Show, Kingworld
3. The Rosie O'Donnell Show, Warner Brothers
4. The Montel Williams Show, Paramount
5. Sally Jessy Raphael, Studios USA
6. Live with Regis and Kathie Lee, Buena Vista
7. Ricki Lake, Columbia Tristar
8. The Jenny Jones Show, Warner Brothers
9. Maury, Studios USA
10. The Maury Povich Show, Paramount

SOAPS

1. The Young and the Restless, CBS
2. The Bold and the Beautiful, CBS
3. Days of Our Lives, NBC
4. General Hospital, ABC
5. As the World Turns, CBS
6. All My Children, ABC
7. Guiding Light, CBS
8. One Life to Live, ABC
9. Another World, NBC
10. Port Charles, ABC

QUIZ AND GAME SHOWS

1. Wheel of Fortune, KingWorld
2. Jeopardy!, KingWorld
3. The Price Is Right, CBS (11:30–12:00 p.m.)
4. Wheel of Fortune (weekend), KingWorld
5. The Price Is Right, CBS (11:00–11:30 a.m.)
6. Hollywood Squares, KingWorld
7. Change of Heart, Warner Brothers
8. Love Connection, Warner Brothers
9. Match Game, Pearson Television
10. Newlywed Game/Dating Game Hour, Columbia Tristar

SATURDAY MORNING CHILDREN'S PROGRAMS

1. Batman Beyond, WB
2. Disney's One Saturday Morning, ABC (9:30–10:00 a.m.) (tie)
2. Hang Time, NBC (10:30–11:00 a.m.) (tie)
2. Pokémon, WB (tie)
5. Saved by the Bell, NBC
6. City Guys, NBC (tie)
6. Disney's One Saturday Morning, ABC (9:00–9:30 a.m.) (tie)
6. Disney's One Saturday Morning, ABC (10:00–10:30 a.m.) (tie)
6. One World, NBC (tie)
10. Power Rangers: Lost Galaxy, FOX

PBS'S MOST POPULAR PROGRAMS

Viewers often associate PBS with children's programming, but in fact PBS is a variety service offering a mix of nature, history, arts, news, and public affairs programming. It is PBS's diverse schedule that draws the viewers, driven this year by the burgeoning and top-rated *Antiques Roadshow*. (Source: PBS)

1. *Antiques Roadshow*
2. *"Cats"* (*Great Performances* special)
3. *Frank Lloyd Wright* (Ken Burns miniseries) (tie)
3. *A Capitol Fourth* (tie)
3. *Championship Ballroom Dancing 1998* (tie)
6. *Antiques Roadshow, Jr.* (tie)
6. *Championship Ballroom Dancing 1999* (tie)
6. *The Rockies by Rail* (tie)
9. *Savage Earth*

10. *The Farmer's Wife* (*Frontline* special miniseries) (tie)
10. *NOVA* (tie)
10. *This Old House* (tie)
13. *Escape! Because Accidents Happen* (*NOVA* special miniseries)
14. *The American Experience* (tie)
14. *Nature* (tie)
16. *Africans in America*

GOING TO THE ROADSHOW

Want to know how much that china dish from Aunt Edna is actually worth? It could have more than just sentimental value. At the *Antiques Roadshow*, you'll learn whether your antiques are valuable collector's items or just conversation pieces. Here is how you can attend—and maybe even end up on TV.

While no one is guaranteed air-time, everyone with a ticket will be seen by an appraiser at PBS's popular *Antiques Roadshow*. For tour sites and dates, check www.pbs.org. Tickets are distributed on site, on a first-come–first-served basis at 7:30 a.m. on the day of the event (though you may line up at any time earlier than 7:30 that feels reasonable to you). Each ticket specifies one of three shifts for entry into the production area: 8:00 a.m., 11:00 a.m., or 2:00 p.m. You have the option of waiting outside the hall or returning at the time designated on your ticket. Everyone who attends must have an item for appraisal or accompany someone who does. When you enter the production area, a generalist appraiser will examine your items and direct you to the appropriate specialist appraiser for your item. If your item is selected and you agree to be taped, you will be escorted to the waiting room for makeup and then be asked to wait your turn to be on camera. Good Luck!

THE TOP 50 TELEVISION SHOWS

These single broadcasts drew the largest percentages of the viewing public. Disappointed *Seinfeld* fans can take heart that while its finale attracted only about 41% of TV homes to place 64th, its audience of 40.5 million viewers makes it the 12th-most-watched broadcast in history. (Source: Nielsen Media Research)

Rank	Program	Date
1.	M*A*S*H	February 28, 1983
2.	Dallas ("Who Shot J.R.?")	November 21, 1980
3.	Roots, Part 8 (conclusion)	January 30, 1977
4.	Super Bowl XVI	January 24, 1982
5.	Super Bowl XVII	January 30, 1983
6.	Winter Olympics	February 23, 1994
7.	Super Bowl XX	January 26, 1986
8.	Gone With the Wind, Part 1	November 7, 1976
9.	Gone With the Wind, Part 2	November 8, 1976
10.	Super Bowl XII	January 15, 1978
11.	Super Bowl XIII	January 21, 1979
12.	Bob Hope Christmas Show	January 15, 1970
13.	Super Bowl XVIII (tie)	January 22, 1984
13.	Super Bowl XIX (tie)	January 20, 1985
15.	Super Bowl XIV	January 20, 1980
16.	Super Bowl XXX	January 28, 1996
17.	ABC Theater ("The Day After")	November 20, 1983
18.	Roots, Part 6 (tie)	January 28, 1977
18.	The Fugitive (tie)	August 29, 1967
20.	Super Bowl XXI	January 25, 1987
21.	Roots, Part 5	January 27, 1977
22.	Super Bowl XXVIII (tie)	January 30, 1994
22.	Cheers (tie)	May 20, 1993
24.	The Ed Sullivan Show (TV debut of The Beatles)	February 9, 1964
25.	Super Bowl XXVII	January 31, 1993

Rank	Program	Date
26.	Bob Hope Christmas Show	January 14, 1971
27.	Roots, Part 3	January 25, 1977
28.	Super Bowl XXXII	January 23, 1998
29.	Super Bowl XI (tie)	January 9, 1977
29.	Super Bowl XV (tie)	January 25, 1981
31.	Super Bowl VI	January 16, 1972
32.	Winter Olympics (tie)	February 25, 1994
33.	Roots, Part 2 (tie)	January 24, 1977
34.	The Beverly Hillbillies	January 8, 1964
35.	Roots, Part 4 (tie)	January 26, 1977
35.	The Ed Sullivan Show (with The Beatles) (tie)	February 16, 1964
37.	Super Bowl XXIII	January 22, 1989
38.	The 43rd Academy Awards	April 7, 1970
39.	Super Bowl XXXI	January 26, 1997
40.	The Thorn Birds, Part 3	March 29, 1983
41.	The Thorn Birds, Part 4	March 30, 1983
42.	NFC championship game	January 10, 1982
43.	The Beverly Hillbillies	January 15, 1964
44.	Super Bowl VII	January 14, 1973
45.	Thorn Birds, Part 2	March 28, 1983
46.	Super Bowl IX (tie)	January 12, 1975
46.	The Beverly Hillbillies (tie)	February 26, 1964
48.	Super Bowl X (tie)	January 18, 1976
48.	Airport (tie)	November 11, 1973
48.	Love Story (tie)	October 1, 1972
48.	Cinderella (tie)	February 22, 1965

MOST-WATCHED MOVIES ON TELEVISION

This list includes network prime-time feature films, both those made for theaters and those (including miniseries) made specifically for TV (*). Although *The Wizard of Oz*'s best showing misses our list at No. 34, many years of high ratings have made it, overall, the most popular movie ever shown on TV. (Source: Nielsen Media Research)

Rank	Movie	Air Date
1.	Roots, Part 8*	January 30, 1977
2.	Gone With the Wind, Part 1	November 7, 1976
3.	Gone With the Wind, Part 2	November 8, 1976
4.	The Day After*	November 20, 1983
5.	Roots, Part 6*	January 28, 1977
6.	Roots, Part 5*	January 27, 1977
7.	Roots, Part 3*	January 25, 1977
8.	Roots, Part 2*	January 24, 1977
9.	Roots, Part 4*	January 26, 1977
10.	The Thorn Birds, Part 3*	March 29, 1983
11.	The Thorn Birds, Part 4*	March 30, 1983
12.	The Thorn Birds, Part 2*	March 28, 1983
13.	Love Story (tie)	October 1, 1972
13.	Airport (tie)	November 11, 1973
13.	Roots, Part 7* (tie)	January 29, 1977

Rank	Movie	Air Date
16.	The Winds of War, Part 7*	February 13, 1983
17.	Roots, Part 1	January 23, 1977
18.	The Winds of War, Part 2*	February 7, 1983
19.	The Thorn Birds, Part 1*	March 27, 1983
20.	The Godfather, Part 2	November 18, 1974
21.	Jaws	November 4, 1979
22.	The Poseidon Adventure	October 27, 1974
23.	The Birds (tie)	January 16, 1968
23.	True Grit (tie)	November 12, 1972
25.	Patton	November 19, 1972
26.	The Bridge on the River Kwai	September 25, 1966
27.	Jeremiah Johnson (tie)	January 18, 1976
27.	Helter Skelter, Part 2 (tie)*	April 2, 1976
29.	Rocky (tie)	February 4, 1979
29.	Ben-Hur (tie)	February 14, 1971

PEOPLE'S FAVORITE 50 TV STARS

The most popular TV personalities are not necessarily the most influential, but rather the sort of folks you'd like to know in real life. This year PEOPLE's Michael A. Lipton stands pat on his timeless list of tube all-stars:

TIM ALLEN
It's so nice to have a klutz around the house, but nobody could screw up as hilariously or nail the punchlines as deftly as Allen, *Home Improvement*'s hammer-handed dufus dad.

JAMES ARNESS
With his weatherbeaten face, loping gait, and laconic delivery, he stood alone as TV's last—and best—Western hero.

BEA ARTHUR
The first sitcom feminist: her foghorn voice, bristly authority, and, er, Maude-lin wit reduced mere men to spineless jellyfish.

LUCILLE BALL
Those lips (pouting ruefully), those eyes (pop-eyed with surprise), that voice ("Rick-kyyyyy!") always delivered 24-karat comedy.

JACK BENNY
Well! He got more laughs with That Look than Uncle Miltie ever did in a dress or Benny's old crony Burns did waving his cigar.

ANDRE BRAUGHER
On the strength of his performance in *Homicide* detective Frank Pemberton, Braugher defined steely urban cool, world-wise sadness, and integrity.

RAYMOND BURR
With his imposing baritone and X-ray eyes that penetrated the most ingenious alibis, Burr's Perry Mason never rested his defense till the guilty party (never, of course, his poor, framed client) confessed on the stand.

JOHNNY CARSON
Silver-haired, silver-tongued paterfamilias to Jay and Dave, this wise old night owl could give a hoot about returning to the throne he held for four glorious decades.

RICHARD CHAMBERLAIN
Let's see: '60s dreamboat Dr. Kildare leaves TV to Hamlet it up on the British stage, then triumphantly returns as the King of the Miniseries. There's gotta be a movie of the week here...

GEORGE CLOONEY
A Kildare for the '90s—and *ER*'s first breakout star—Clooney, more magnetic than an MRI scan, could set pulses fluttering with just a cocked head, a raised brow, and a sly grin.

KATIE COURIC
She's your tomboyish kid sister all grown up, and while there's a mule-like kick to her interviews, her big heart and feisty twinkle keep her warm.

WALTER CRONKITE
America's most trusted anchor earned the nickname "Old Iron-pants" through his marathon coverage of conventions, assassinations, and resignations, but it was his gosh-darn, oh-boyish enthusiasm that made him the man to watch reporting the moon shots.

ROMA DOWNEY
All angels should be as radiantly wholesome as this fetching yet feisty Irish-born actress, who, with a lilt in her voice—and her heart—gives prime-time do-goodism a good name.

PHIL DONAHUE
"Caller, are you there?" Earnest, excitable, daring, and dashing (literally, into the audience), the snow-thatched maestro of day-time talk left no taboo unturned, no trauma untreated.

DAVID DUCHOVNY
A minimalist actor with sad, basset eyes and a sly-like-a-fox humor, he is the exemplar of '90s cool and cynicism.

LINDA EVANS
Prime-time soaps' poor little rich girl, she more than held her own against mean old Alexis. Even while (literally) slinging mud, her wholesome sexiness remained Krystle-clear.

PETER FALK
As the raincoat-rumpled detective with the frog-horn voice, Falk brought an ironic sense of mischief to his role as a regular guy besting the arrogant elites.

DENNIS FRANZ
The blustery, beer-bellied blue-collar joe as macho sex symbol. You got a problem with dat?

JAMES GARNER
Despite a body wracked by wear and tear, and a face etched with wisdom and woe, Garner remains TV's most credible—and comedic—action star.

JACKIE GLEASON
How sweet it was to see The Great One storm, scheme, and suffer as Ralph Kramden, the Willy Loman of bus drivers.

JOHN GOODMAN
As Roseanne's better—and slightly bigger—half, he was in many ways Gleason's heir as the hearty har-har working stiff, only blessed with an earthy realism.

KELSEY GRAMMER
Portraying TV's favorite shrink, the pompous yet endearing

Dr. Frasier Crane, in the two hit series (*Cheers* and *Frasier*), Grammer has managed to balance his character's comic bluster with the sort of wry, deadpan wit that's all too rare in prime-time sitcoms.

LARRY HAGMAN

So gleefully villainous, he made the viewer his grinning accomplice. We were completely in thrall of devilish J.R., TV's most hissable, kissable anti-hero.

ALFRED HITCHCOCK

TV transformed the film name into a household face—an erudite gargoyle whose drollery and drop-dead delivery made for a murderously marvelous one-man-show-within-the-show.

DAVID JANSSEN

A haggard, haunted underdog whose raspy voice and soulful brow served him brilliantly, whether playing fugitives or feds.

MICHAEL LANDON

From Little Joe Cartwright to big man on the prairie to angelic emissary, Landon made sentimentality a virtue, wrung drama out of decency, and rang true.

ANGELA LANSBURY

How did Cabot Cove manage to rack up the nation's highest murder rate? Ask this nebbishy doyenne of TV crimesolvers.

LASSIE

The wonder dog of our childhoods.

JAY LENO

The hardest-working man in showbiz sweated bullets to show us he was as good as—or, as his ratings would indicate, better than—Letterman.

HEATHER LOCKLEAR

Her simultaneous stints as *Dynasty*'s vixenette and *T.J. Hooker*'s rookie cop in the '80s gave no hint she'd blossom (like poison ivy) into *Melrose Place*'s mellifluous villainess.

ELIZABETH MONTGOMERY

Sure, she bewitched us with that wiggly nose, but beyond the levity (and levitation), a serious TV-movie actress was in the wings.

MARY TYLER MOORE

She can still turn the world on with her smile. Yet for most of us, she'll always remain winsome single girl Mary Richards, her cap forever aloft, frozen in time.

LEONARD NIMOY

Who says a pointy-eared intellectual can't be a sex symbol? Star Trekkers melded their minds with Spock's and became one with the sci-fi universe.

ROSIE O'DONNELL

Okay, so she's no Oprah. But with her showbiz connections, breezy banter, and self-effacing, seat-of-the-pants wit, O'Donnell revitalized daytime talk.

REGIS PHILBIN

Morning TV's twinkle-eyed curmudgeon, the perfect complement (and, perhaps, antidote) to self-absorbed Kathie Lee.

GILDA RADNER

The madcap heart and soul of the original *Saturday Night Live*.

DONNA REED

A suburban TV mom for the ages —smart, beautiful, and sunny.

MICHAEL RICHARDS

A maniac for all seasons: All he had to do to get laughs was walk/stagger/glide/boogie/tumble through Seinfeld's door.

FRED ROGERS

It really was a beautiful day in the neighborhood when this genial, sweet, pro176tective grown-up first sat down 30 years ago, laced up his sneakers, and became every kid's best friend.

ROY ROGERS

The quintessential TV cowboy, tall in the saddle, handy with a six-shooter, yet for the most part, just plain Trigger-happy.

FRED SAVAGE

The joys and agonies of adolescence were wonderfully expressed in Savage's tender, perpetually wide-eyed visage.

TOM SELLECK

TV's merriest manchild, he spent his Magnum opus living out every guy's fantasies—and has a bright new career in sitcoms.

PHIL SILVERS

Ten-HUT! His Sgt. Bilko was a fast-squawking, never-balking con artist supreme who tweaked authority and energized '50s TV.

HOMER SIMPSON

Slobbus americanus, he eclipses his bratty son Bart, and has even been known to dispense pearls of Homer-spun wisdom.

SUZANNE SOMERS

A sitcom sexpot turned infomericial empress—no ifs, ands, or buttmasters about it.

RICHARD THOMAS

Forever boyish, dreamy-eyed, sensitively staring out moonlit windows, pen held to lips: the good son, the stalwart sib.

DICK VAN DYKE

Limber-limbed, rubber-faced, G-rated precursor to Jim Carrey, he could trip the light fantastic (even while tripping over an ottoman).

VANNA WHITE

She turns letters—and heads— with a sensual body language all her own.

OPRAH WINFREY

So empathetic is this talk-show tsarina with her guests—and so upfront about herself it's scary— that she could be having a ball one day, and bawling the next.

HENRY WINKLER

Aaaaaaay! This retro '70s-cum-'50s sitcom star exuded the cool we all wished we'd had in our not-so-happy high school days.

PEOPLE'S 50 FORMATIVE SHOWS

The mark of all great series is their profound, or at least pervasive, impact on pop culture. No sooner are they on the air—like this season's *The Sopranos*—than it's impossible to remember how we got along without them. Here are PEOPLE's shows of shows.

THE ADVENTURES OF SUPERMAN
More than 40 years later, this show starring George Reeves as the Man of Steel is still the only good superhero series TV has ever produced.

ALL IN THE FAMILY
At the heart of this epochal sitcom were the corrosive working-class prejudices of Archie Bunker, a Northern redneck. His political arguments with his liberal live-in son-in-law make *Crossfire* seem tame.

ALL MY CHILDREN
The soap trend-setter has tackled big social and medical issues without ever losing a grip on its primary imperative: addictive story-telling.

AN AMERICAN FAMILY
In their time (the 1970s), the exhibitionistic Loud family opened themselves up to freak-show derision. But they paved the way for the current rage of reality-based shows, from MTV's *The Real World* to Fox's *Cops* and all those voyeuristic video-clip shows.

THE ANDY GRIFFITH SHOW
The precursor of the so-called rusticoms of the '60s, this quiet masterpiece had heart, humor, wisdom, and—often over-looked— an outstanding cast. The launching pad for *Gomer Pyle, U.S.M.C* and *Mayberry R.F.D.*

THE BEVERLY HILLBILLIES
Yee ha! The most outrageous yokel yuk-fest this side of *Li'l Abner*. Bonus points for TV's most recognizable theme song.

BONANZA
It was that larger-than-life clan, the Cartwrights, that made the Ponderosa worth visiting every week.

THE BULLWINKLE SHOW
Jay Ward's kaleidoscopic, pun-crammed cartoon about a dense moose and a plucky flying squirrel delighted kids of all ages.

BURNS AND ALLEN
This iconoclastic '50s show gleefully disregarded TV tradition, including the observance of "the fourth wall." The comic chemistry between this old vaudeville team has never been duplicated.

CANDID CAMERA
"When you least expect it / You're elected / You're the star today." Alan Funt milked hilarious results from simply filming people in situations when they thought no one was watching.

CHARLIE'S ANGELS
A brilliant TV concept: staff a standard detective show with a gorgeous trio (Farrah Fawcett, Kate Jackson, and Jaclyn Smith) in sausage-skin clothing. This was producer Aaron Spelling's first megahit and his finest hour.

CHEERS
The pluperfect pinnacle of the sitcom genre.

THE COSBY SHOW
Witty, warm, and winning, the domestic experiences of the Huxtables touted family values without sermonizing.

THE DICK VAN DYKE SHOW
The first TV comedy to thoroughly exploit dual settings. For the first half of the '60s, the only place on the planet funnier than the Petrie household was Rob's office at the apocryphal *Alan Brady Show.*

DRAGNET
The show's deliberately laconic style ("Just the facts, ma'am") only underscored the gritty power of its tales of cops and miscreants.

DYNASTY
The squabbles of the Carringtons proved that the rich really are different than you and me: They dress swankily while hatching Byzantine plots of revenge against one another.

GUNSMOKE
TV's archetypal and longest running Western.

HILL STREET BLUES
Creator Steven Bochco spiced up his precinct house gumbo with a rich slate of characters, multi-tiered narratives, wry humor and a dash of fatalism.

THE HONEYMOONERS
The antics of a bus driver and a sewer worker in a Brooklyn tenement yielded a priceless vein of American humor. Jackie Gleason and Art Carney were sublime.

JEOPARDY!
The thinking person's game show.

L.A. LAW
A powerhouse legal drama complex, unpredictable, imaginative and always rewarding.

THE LARRY SANDERS SHOW
This sardonic backstage tour of a talk show is TV's funniest satire, perhaps because we love to see the medium mock itself.

LEAVE IT TO BEAVER
Took the familiar family sitcom formula of the '50s and gave it a devious adolescent twist. Show stealer: Eddie Haskell

MARY HARTMAN, MARY HARTMAN

And now for something completely different. This soap opera spoof presented everyday life in Fernwood, Ohio, as a pastiche of country song, floor-wax commercial, and Kurt Vonnegut novel.

THE MARY TYLER MOORE SHOW

A magical confluence of concept, cast, and material made this the high watermark of '70s television.

M*A*S*H

Hands-down, the most successful series ever spun off from a feature film. The comedy lasted eight years longer than the Korean War had.

MIAMI VICE

Against a gaudy SoFlo backdrop of neon and pastels, cute cops chase after well-armed cocaine cowboys in flashy sport scars and cigarette boats. The only reason TV has ever furnished to stay home on Friday nights.

MISSION: IMPOSSIBLE

Your mission, should you decide to accept it, is to name a better adventure series than this taut, gripping espionage exercise.

NIGHTLINE

A provident opportunity to hash out the day's big news event.

N.Y.P.D. BLUE

The most electrifying cop show since *Naked City* (1958–63). Acute and suspenseful, *N.Y.P.D. Blue* roars by like a runaway train.

THE ODD COUPLE

Opposites amuse, but never so much as in this impeccably cast, tone-perfect comedy about a pair of mismatched, middle-aged, Manhattan neo-bachelors.

THE ROCKFORD FILES

The couch potato's choice: a sly, undemanding, endlessly entertaining delight.

ROSEANNE

An adventurous, abrasive, authentic and always amusing examination of the struggles of a working-class family.

ROWAN AND MARTIN'S LAUGH-IN

With zany banter, double entendres, and go-go dancers (including Goldie Hawn), this late-'60s comedy cavalcade nudged TV into the age of hipsters.

ST. ELSEWHERE

Piquant and volatile, this Jack-in-the-box drama about a lesser Boston hospital ran from intense tragedy to bawdy comedy.

SEINFELD

An hermetic, exquisitely maintained comedy of contemporary urban manners and mores.

SESAME STREET

This jauntily educational PBS series for pre-schoolers is culturally diverse, inventive and altogether admirable.

77 SUNSET STRIP

The most influential of the Sputnik-era private eye series was this ultra-cool conceit which starred Efrem Zimbalist Jr. and Roger Smith as a pair of suave, college-educated judo experts.

THE SIMPSONS

You'd need a shelf full of books like this Almanac and a crack research staff to run down all the pop culture references in a single episode of this puckish cartoon about the post-nuclear family.

60 MINUTES

The ultimate news magazine.

STAR TREK

This notorious cult favorite was little-honored during its original '60s run but became a rerun staple and has launched a thriving industry of spin-offs.

THE SOPRANOS

Only on cable could you get away with this profane, violent, sexy, and satiric profile of an angst-ridden, shrink-wrapped New Jersey Mafia family man—and his dysfunctional domestic clan. An offer the networks could refuse—to their everlasting regret.

THIRTYSOMETHING

Though dismissed by cynics as yuppie whining, this was in fact a drama of rare pathos, complexity and insight.

TODAY

The oldest, and in our book, the best of the matinal infotainment bandwagons.

THE TONIGHT SHOW

It's a tradition as comfortable as flannel pajamas: awaiting the Sandman while watching Johnny's (and now Jay's) guests play musical chairs.

THE TWILIGHT ZONE

This spine-tingling supernatural anthology was penetrating, often profound, but above all, singularly spooky.

WALT DISNEY PRESENTS

Over four decades, under a variety of banners and working alternately for each of the three major networks, the Disney studio consistently turned out the tube's finest, most indelible family fare.

THE X-FILES

"The truth is out there." Really out there. But week after week, this suspenseful series transforms paranormal and outright bizarre concepts into gripping, credible drama.

YOU BET YOUR LIFE

This '50s series was ostensibly a quiz show, but in fact that was merely a pretext for host Groucho Marx to sharpen his legendary wit on a succession of contestants.

YOUR SHOW OF SHOWS

The apex of the variety show, this '50s favorite thrived on the versatile comedic talents of Sid Caesar and Imogene Coca and a stable of writers, including Mel Brooks, Larry Gelbart, Neil Simon, and Woody Allen.

SOME OF THE GOOD DIE YOUNG

Everyone remembers the long-running hits, but what about the quality shows that disappeared before they were old enough to walk? Of the countless shows that died after one season or less, here are 30 that PEOPLE critic Terry Kelleher misses the most.

THE ASSOCIATES
ABC, 1979
Effervescent sitcom set at a law firm. An early showcase for a major talent named Martin Short.

BEACON HILL
CBS, 1975
Derided as an expensive American imitation of *Upstairs, Downstairs*, this drama never got a chance to prove its worth.

THE BEN STILLER SHOW
FOX, 1992–93
Before he got hot on the big screen, Stiller starred in a hip half-hour sketch series with rock-bottom ratings.

THE BOB NEWHART SHOW
NBC, 1961–62
Not Newhart's first sitcom—or his second, third, or fourth. We're talking about his very first series, an acclaimed comedy-variety show that lasted just one season.

BUFFALO BILL
NBC, 1983–84
Dabney Coleman was an egotistical local TV personality in this unusually pungent sitcom. Geena Davis and Max Wright stood out in a strong supporting cast.

CALL TO GLORY
ABC, 1984–85
Craig T. Nelson starred as an Air Force officer and family man caught up in the historic events of the 1960s. Soared briefly but failed to maintain altitude.

CALUCCI'S DEPARTMENT
CBS, 1973
We still have a soft spot for this forgotten sitcom starring James Coco as the head of a New York City unemployment office. Sadly, the show got fired.

EAST SIDE, WEST SIDE
CBS, 1963–64
George C. Scott played a social worker (who later became a congressional aide) in a serious-minded drama that didn't shy away from controversial subjects.

EZ STREETS
CBS, 1996–97
Not your standard cops and crooks show, but rather a moody drama of moral ambiguity in a decaying city. In other words, it had "low ratings" written all over it.

THE FAMOUS TEDDY Z
CBS, 1989–90
Smart sitcom set at a Hollywood talent agency featured Alex Rocco's fabulous characterization of super-pushy Al Floss.

FOR THE PEOPLE
CBS, 1965
William Shatner, before *Star Trek,* starred in this classy drama about a New York City prosecutor. This line on his resume almost makes up for *T. J. Hooker.*

FRANK'S PLACE
CBS, 1987–88
Tim Reid played a New Orleans restaurateur in a low-key comedy with some serious moments and no annoying laugh track.

Too few viewers sampled this delectation.

GUN
ABC, 1997
Top-notch, Robert Altman–produced anthology that followed a gun from owner to owner. Shot blanks in the ratings.

HE & SHE
CBS, 1967–68
Real-life husband and wife Richard Benjamin and Paula Prentiss were the nominal stars, but Jack Cassidy stole the show as a vain actor with a superhero complex.

THE LAW AND MR. JONES
ABC, 1960–61
Not a Hall of Fame show, really, but James Whitmore may have been the most likable lawyer in TV history.

LIFELINE
NBC, 1978
Documentary series with a strong, simple concept: Follow one doctor each week. Twenty years later, in the age of "reality" shows, it might have been a hit.

MAX HEADROOM
ABC, 1987
Heady combination of sci-fi and TV satire. Not a smash, but quite a conversation piece.

MIDDLE AGES
CBS, 1992
Peter Riegert headed a fine ensemble cast in this short-lived drama about a group of guys on the cusp of 40.

MY WORLD AND WELCOME TO IT
NBC, 1969–70
A James Thurber–like cartoonist (William Windom) had Walter Mittyish dreams depicted through animation. Maybe it was too imaginative for a mass audience.

NICHOLS
NBC, 1971–72
James Garner took a laudable gamble with this offbeat Western about a reluctant sheriff trying to keep order without carrying a gun.

THE NIGHT STALKER
ABC, 1974–75
Humor and horror combined, with Darren McGavin as a rough-around-the-edges reporter covering vampires, werewolves, and other undesirables.

NOTHING SACRED
ABC, 1997–98
An unorthodox Catholic priest (Kevin Anderson) in a poor urban parish. A good idea bravely executed. No wonder it was canceled.

POLICE SQUAD!
ABC, 1982
Yes, those successful Naked Gun movies with Leslie Nielsen were based on a zany comedy series that ABC axed after a handful of episodes. One of the all-time least brilliant network decisions.

PROFIT
FOX, 1996
Daring drama about a frighteningly enterprising young man (Adrian Pasdar) clawing his way toward the top of the corporate ladder.

THE RICHARD BOONE SHOW
NBC, 1963–64
Fresh from *Have Gun Will Travel*, Boone starred in an anthology series with a regular repertory company (including Harry Morgan and Robert Blake). Will someone please resurrect this concept?

SHANNON'S DEAL
NBC, 1990 and 1991
Filmmaker John Sayles created this well-crafted series about a flawed lawyer (Jamey Sheridan).

SKAG
NBC, 1980
Gutsy drama starred Karl Malden as an old-fashioned blue-collar breadwinner trying to adjust to new realities.

SQUARE PEGS
CBS, 1982–83
Enjoyably quirky sitcom about two misfit high school girls, one of whom was the delightful Sarah Jessica Parker.

TRIALS OF O'BRIEN
CBS, 1965–66
The pre-Columbo Peter Falk was a defense lawyer with a disordered personal life in this drama with a light touch. Saturday-night viewers preferred Lawrence Welk. Go figure.

A YEAR IN THE LIFE
NBC, 1987–88
Intelligent extended-family drama with the reliable Richard Kiley in the patriarch's role.

TRIVIAL TRIUMPHS

The answer: See below. The question? Who are *Celebrity Jeopardy!*'s all-time highest earners? These totals reflect the winnings donated to each celeb's charity or charities of choice. (P.S. Former L.A. Lakers player Kareem Abdul-Jabbar won the 1998 tourney.) (Source: *Jeopardy!*)

Jerry Orbach	$34,000	Jeff Greenfield	$23,000
Charles Shaughnessy	$31,800	Wallace Langham	$21,800
Norman Schwarzkopf	$28,000	Gil Bellows	$21,200
Kareem Abdul-Jabbar	$27,000	Michael McKean	$20,400
Mark McEwen	$26,700	Robin Quivers	$19,500
Bob Costas	$25,000	Jodi Applegate	$19,401
Cheech Marin	$25,000	Jim Lampley	$19,200
Thomas Gibson	$24,400	Mike Piazza	$17,900
Laura Innes	$24,400	Fred Savage	$17,100
Sam Waterston	$23,800	Dee Dee Myers	$15,900

NICK AT NITE'S CLASSIC TV COUNTDOWN, 1998

Nick at Nite and its sister network, TV Land, joined forces to create the "Top 25" slate of honorees in the tenth annual rerun countdown to usher in 1999, hosted by Casey Kasem. As always, the selections are based on viewer requests, ratings, critical commentary, pre-fame celebrity guest stars, show landmarks (first episodes, marriages, and births), and quintessential moments or bizarre plot twists.

1 *The Brady Bunch*
"The Subject Was Noses"

"Something suddenly came up"…to the top of the charts! A stray football, a date with Doug, plenty of the innocent teenage angst that made the Bradys so ineffably Brady, and it all added up to a classic episode, indeed.

2 *The Dick Van Dyke Show*
"Coast to Coast Big Mouth"

A perennial on the countdown charts, this masterpiece features Laura Petrie's accidental revelation on national TV that Alan Brady wears a toupee and the hilarious apology scene that is perhaps writer-producer-actor Carl Reiner's single finest on-screen performance.

3 *Dobie Gillis*
"The Best-Dressed Man"

A definitive chapter in Dobie's endless quest for the heart of the money-grubbing but beautiful Thalia Menninger. Guest stars Warren Beatty as Dobie's archrival, Milton Armitage; Tuesday Weld as Thalia; and Mel Blanc as the manager of the clothing store who spurs Dobie to compete with Milton's sartorial verve.

4 *The Bob Newhart Show*
"Death Be My Destiny"

The elevators behind Carol's reception area were often used as comic props, opening to reveal surprises, closing to end conversations abruptly, but in this episode they took center stage. Bob steps into the open elevator shaft, and his close call with "Mr.

Death" creates a phobia that Bob can't beat. It's a case of "psychologist, analyze thyself," and a memorable episode.

5 *I Love Lucy*
"Lucy Makes a TV Commercial"

It's "Vitameatavegamin" (in case you've always wondered how to spell it) and perhaps the most memorable individual performance in TV history, as Lucy rehearses her role as a television spokesperson. This was the first show ever to finish No. 1 three times—it garnered the top spot in 1997, 1995, and 1994.

6 *Laverne and Shirley*
"The Dating Game"

When Laverne and Shirley moved from Milwaukee to Los Angeles, we all knew the end was near. But the move did breathe new life into some episodes—and brought us the finest Lenny and Squiggy episode of them all, as the boys end up as Bachelors Number Two and Three on *The Dating Game*. Michael McKean and David Lander took their absurdist vision of perennial losers to new lows in this episode.

7 *The Mary Tyler Moore Show*
"Chuckles Bites the Dust"

Chuckles the Clown is the host of a kiddy show on WJM-TV. In a terrible accident while dressed as a Peanut, Chuckles is shucked—and killed—by a rogue elephant. Mary can't believe how quickly people begin making sick jokes about the tragedy…until the classic funeral scene.

8 *Bewitched*
"Divided He Falls"

Dick York at his gawky, sputtering best—split into two Darrins—the fun-loving one who suggests that Sam "whap up some champagne"and the hardworking one who bores poor Larry Tate to tears with his unrelenting marketing suggestions.

9 *Dragnet*
"The LSD Story, AKA Blue Boy"

This episode is more popularly known as "Blue Boy," named for its antagonist, a teenage boy who has painted his face blue and yellow and buried his head in the ground on an acid trip. Blue Boy's lunatic ravings and Joe Friday's moralizing have made this episode one of TV Land's all-time most requested.

10 *The Brady Bunch*
"Johnny Bravo"

Marcia's most memorable episode may have out-ranked Greg's, but this episode has plenty of fans who will argue it was every bit as good. As if that isn't enough, Barry "Greg Brady" Williams released a 1999 single entitled "Johnny's Back," heralding his character's return.

11 *Alfred Hitchcock Presents*
"Lamb to the Slaughter"

A true classic, starring Barbara Bel Geddes, who offs her offending hubbie using a leg of lamb as the proverbial "blunt instrument." The twist? She serves the "evidence" to the investigating officers.

12 The Mary Tyler Moore Show
"Love Is All Around"

The episode that started it all, as Mary flees from a broken engagement to a fresh start in Minneapolis. In quick order she "steals" Rhoda's apartment and interviews with Lou Grant at WJM-TV. In that classic encounter she orders a Brandy Alexander and, most important, displays "spunk."

13 The Mary Tyler Moore Show
"Ted Baxter's Famous Broadcasters School"

The pompous newscaster is talked into a money-making scheme and drags the entire newsroom down with him. As the "school song" puts it: "We have no gym, we have no pool, but we have heart, at Ted Baxter's Famous Broadcasters School."

14 The Dick Van Dyke Show
"It May Look Like a Walnut"

An atypical episode of a series, but a memorable one. Rob and Laura stay up watching an old horror movie, and Rob soon finds himself living out the strange invasion of the Twyloites and their leader—who looks exactly like Danny Thomas. The highlight is Laura spilling forth in a cascade of walnuts from the closet.

15 I Love Lucy
"Job Switching"

With I Love Lucy running in syndication ever since it went off the air—and in countries around the world—we estimate there are approximately 1 billion people alive today who will know which episode you mean when you say "the chocolate factory."

16 Taxi
"Fantasy Borough, Pt. 2"

The gang is comparing their unfulfilled dreams and wishes, and Lassie turns up in a rare but memorable guest-starring role.

17 Laverne and Shirley
"Why Did the Fireman...?"

The end of the unfinished title question is the surprising "...have to die." In an unusual but moving episode, Laverne finds true love at last, in the person of a fireman played by Ted Danson. But on the verge of proposing, he is called away to his last fire. Laverne lives in haunted denial but learns to accept that he is gone.

18 Newhart
"The Last Newhart"

Though the episode itself is a strange and uneven one—including a number of inscrutable references to Fiddler on the Roof—it is all redeemed by the greatest series finale of all time: A golf ball knocks Dick Loudon senseless, and Dr. Bob Hartley awakens to find that it was all a dream.

19 Green Acres
"Never Trust a Little Old Lady"

Green Acres combined surrealism and nonsense that Salvador Dali and Lewis Carroll would have admired, and never more so than in this episode. A little old lady's weather predictions lead to many strange things, none more strange than the haunting final scene: Oliver and Lisa at night out in the field among tomato plants that are being warmed by flaming stacks of pancakes.

20 The Brady Bunch
"Amateur Night"

Sure you know a lot of the words to "Sunshine Day," but can you also do the Silver Platters dance? And most important of all, "Can You Dig the Sunshine?"

21 Taxi
"Reverend Jim: A Space Odyssey"

The very very Reverend Jim—Christopher Lloyd—had made an earlier appearance in the garage

(to marry Latka to a lady of the evening so that he could avoid deportation), but this was the episode in which he became a permanent member of the gang and took his legendary driver's exam and answers the question "What does a yellow light mean?"

22 I Dream of Jeannie
"Mrs. Djinn Djinn"

An invisible dog wreaks havoc, but most important of all, this is one of only two episodes in which Jeannie accidentally reveals her navel, which was ordered by network censors to be covered.

23 My Three Sons
"The Triplets"

After Mike left for college, adopting Ernie was only a stop-gap measure. They knew that eventually the title of the long-running series would no longer ring true, so when Robby got married and started a family of his own—lo and behold, he had three boys, all at once!

24 The Brady Bunch
"Eenie Meenie, Mommy Daddy"

Incredible but true: An episode centered around Cindy made the charts in 1998! It's that bizarre story about the cruel elementary school that gives every child one ticket to the school play, so that each child must face the horrible choice of one of the two parents.

25 Happy Days
"Richie Fights Back"

You can only be so tough with a "Howdy-Doody" face—but classic performances by Ron Howard and Henry Winkler created a quintessential episode as Richie attempts to remake himself in the Fonz's image.

HOW TO GET TICKETS TO TELEVISION SHOWS

Say what you want about television, but at least it's free (more or less). Not only that, but you can also obtain free tickets to see talk shows, game shows, and situation comedies, most of which tape in New York, Chicago, or Los Angeles. Here's how.

NEW YORK

THE DAILY SHOW

Call (212) 586-2477, visit www.comedycentral.com/dailyshow, or send a postcard with your name, address, phone number, and the number of tickets desired to The Daily Show, 13 West 54th St., New York, NY 10019. The Daily Show generally tapes in the evening, Monday through Thursday. You may request up to four tickets; a ticket does not guarantee admission. You must be 18 or older to attend.

LATE NIGHT WITH CONAN O'BRIEN

Mail one postcard per show with your name, address, phone number, preferred show date (optional), and number of tickets desired (max of five) to *Late Night* Tickets, c/o NBC, 30 Rockefeller Plaza, New York, NY 10112. Tickets are also available by phone request. Call (212) 664-3057 for more information. The waiting list is about 4 to 6 weeks, and the ticket office will try to accommodate specific requests. A limited number of day-of-taping general admission and standby tickets are available Tuesday through Friday at 9 a.m. on the 49th Street side of the building (same address as above). Standbys are distributed one per person on a first-come–first-served basis and, like called-in tickets, do not guarantee admission. Minimum age is 16. Call (212) 664-3057 for details or (212) 664-3056 for an updated show schedule.

EMERIL LIVE

The Food Network conducts a ticket lottery in New York and Chicago, and sign-up occurs once or twice a year. Entry dates are posted on www.foodtv.com before each lottery period begins. To sign up, you may send an email to Webmaster@NewYorkShow.Com or a post card to Food Network, 1177 Ave. of the Americas, 31st Fl., New York NY 10036. Winners are picked in groups throughout the year and are informed by phone 15 to 30 days before the taping date. Food Network does not accept phone calls regarding ticket requests or the ticket lottery.

THE LATE SHOW WITH DAVID LETTERMAN

To request two tickets, send a postcard with your name, address, and daytime and evening phone numbers to *Late Show* Tickets, The Ed Sullivan Theater, 1697 Broadway, New York, NY 10019. Waiting time may be in excess of nine months, and specific dates generally cannot be accommodated. Tapings are Monday through Thursday. Standby tickets are available on the day of the show by calling (212) 247-6497 at 11:00 a.m. The ticket recipient must have ID to match the name given when calling in. It is advised that you dress warmly as the studio is kept cold. Minimum age is 18. For more information, call (212) 975-5300, or visit www.cbs.com.

LIVE WITH REGIS AND KATHIE LEE

Send a postcard with your name, address, phone number, and the desired number of tickets (limit of four per request) to *Live* Tickets, Ansonia Station, P.O. Box 777, New York, NY 10023-0777. There is a twelve-month wait for tickets. On show days, standby numbers may be requested at 8 a.m. on West 67th Street and Columbus Avenue. Receiving a number does not guarantee admission. Standbys will be seated on a first-come–first-served basis after ticketholders have been seated. Minimum age is 10. Ticket holders may be required to show ID before entering the studio, and it is suggested that you dress warmly to attend the taping, as the studio is kept cold. For more ticket and taping information, call (212) 456-3537.

THE MAURY SHOW

For ticket information and taping schedules, call the ticket line, (212) 547-8400, and leave a message, recording your name, address, and phone number. A representative will contact you. Tickets can also be reserved by postcard. Write to: The Maury Show, 15 Penn Plaza, New York, NY 10001. Standby tickets are available starting at 9:15 a.m. on the day of the taping at Hotel Pennsylvania, Grand Ballroom, 15 Penn Plaza, New York. To reserve by email, write to: audience@themauryshow.com. Minimum age is 16.

THE MONTEL WILLIAMS SHOW

To request reservations up to three weeks in advance of the show date, call the ticket line at (212) 989-8101 or (212) 830-0365 and leave a message, recording your full name and day and evening phone numbers. Call no later than the day before the show date. Whether you request tickets by phone or mail, a representative must speak with you to confirm dates and times of taping, which vary from show to show. To confirm reservations, call (212) 830-0364. For air date information only, call (212) 830-0300. The studio is located at 433 West 53rd St., New York, NY 10019. There is a minimum age of 17 and a dressy-casual dress code; no white shirts, black shirts, hats, sunglasses, or scarves on the head are permitted. The studio is kept cool, so dress accordingly.

RICKI LAKE

Send a postcard with your address and number of tickets (maximum of four) desired to *The Ricki Lake Show*, Ticket Office, 226 W. 26th St., 4th Fl., New York, NY 10001. Tickets are distributed on a first-come–first-served basis two to three weeks before the show and do not guarantee admission. Standby tickets are available at the studio (above address) one hour before taping. Minimum age is 18. For more information, call (212) 352-3322.

THE ROSIE O'DONNELL SHOW

Requests (maximum of 2 tickets) are accepted only during March, April, May, and June preceding the season. Send a postcard to NBC Tickets, c/o *The Rosie O'Donnell Show*, 30 Rockefeller Plaza, New York, NY 10112. There is a twelve-month wait for tickets, and representatives cannot honor requests for specific dates. Standby tickets are available on the day of the show at the NBC Page Desk on the West 49th Street side of the studio lobby, opposite the Rockefeller Center Garage. These tickets are distributed at 8 a.m. but do not guarantee admission. Call (212) 664-4000 for information. Minimum age is five years old.

SALLY JESSY RAPHAEL

Send a postcard with your address and the number of tickets desired to *Sally Jessy Raphael* Tickets, P.O. Box 1400, Radio City Station, New York, NY 10101. For standby tickets, available at 515 West 57th St., arrive at 8:30 a.m. on taping days.

SATURDAY NIGHT LIVE

To obtain tickets for next season, send one postcard with your name and address to NBC Tickets, *Saturday Night Live*, 30 Rockefeller Plaza, New York, NY 10112. NBC accepts postcards during the month of August only, and these requests will be entered into a lottery drawing. If you are selected, you will be notified by mail two weeks in advance that you have received two tickets to either the dress rehearsal or the live broadcast. *SNL* tapes from September to May only. It is not possible to request specific dates, but standby tickets are available on the Saturdays of original shows at 9:15 a.m. at the side entrance of the GE Building on West 49th Street, opposite the Rockefeller Center garage. Standbys are given on a first-come–first-served basis, and only one per person; they do not guarantee admission. Minimum age is 16. For more information, call (212) 664-4000. Phone reservations are not available.

CHICAGO

THE JENNY JONES SHOW

For tickets, call (312) 836-9485 at least three weeks in advance. When calling, you must have a local Chicago phone number where you will be staying. The show is taped on Tuesday, Thursday, and Friday, at 9:45 a.m. and 1:45 p.m. If you do not have tickets, you may arrive at the studio at 9:45 a.m. on the day of taping for possible seating. The studio is located at the NBC Tower, 454 North Columbus Dr., Chicago, IL 60611. Minimum age is 18.

JERRY SPRINGER

Write to *The Jerry Springer Show* (Tickets), 454 N. Columbus Dr., 2nd Fl., Chicago, IL 60611, with your name, address, local phone number, number of tickets, and date desired, or call (312) 321-5365 or (800) 96-JERRY. Requests should be made at least one month in advance. Tickets are generally mailed out one to three weeks before the taping, and there is a minimum age of 10 required to attend. Audience members may not wear shorts and must present proper ID before entering the studio.

OPRAH

Tickets are not available by mail, but reservations to appear in the studio audience can be made by calling (312) 591-9222. These lines are often busy as soon as the caller line opens at 9 a.m.

Central Time. Reservations are taken no more than 30 days in advance of the show. Audience members must be 18 years old or over with a photo ID. Children 16 and 17 may attend only if accompanied by a parent with birth certificate identification.

LOS ANGELES

THE LATE LATE SHOW WITH CRAIG KILBORN

Call On-Camera Audiences at (213) 833-6469 or write to them at *The Late Late Show with Craig Kilborn*, c/o On-Camera Audiences, 224 East Olive Ave., #205, Burbank, CA 91502. Tapings are Monday through Friday at CBS Television City in Los Angeles.

POLITICALLY INCORRECT WITH BILL MAHER

Call the ticket line at (323) 575-4321 to make a reservation, or email a ticket request at http://abc.go.com/pi/tickets/index/ html. All reservations, which you must have before coming to the studio, are taken on a first-come–first-served basis. If you do not receive a confirmation call, you do not have a reservation. The studio is located at CBS Television City, 7800 Beverly Blvd., Los Angeles, CA, at the corner of Beverly and Fairfax. Arrival time is 4:00 on Monday, Tuesday, and Thursday. The studio is kept cold, so dress accordingly. Minimum age is 18.

THE TONIGHT SHOW WITH JAY LENO

Send a self-addressed, stamped envelope with the date of the show you would like to see and the number of tickets desired (maximum of four) to NBC Tickets, 3000 W. Alameda Ave., Burbank, CA 91523. Tickets will be mailed two to three weeks before the show. On the day of tapings, tickets are available at the Burbank ticket counter off the California Street side of the studio facility. Hours are 8 a.m. to 5 p.m., Monday through Friday, but arrive early as tickets are distributed on a first-come–first-served basis and do not guarantee admission. The minimum age to attend is 16 and photo ID is required. For recorded ticket information, taping schedules, group bookings, and directions to the Burbank, CA, studios, call NBC Studios at (818) 840-3537.

FRASIER, MOESHA, *AND MORE*

Paramount Guest Relations handles the reservations for shows such as *Frasier*; *Moesha*; *Two Guys and a Girl*; and *Dharma & Greg*. You may request tickets by calling Paramount Guest Relations at (323) 956-1777 between 9 a.m. and 6 p.m., Monday through Friday. Reservations become available five working days before each scheduled show and are taken on a first-come–first-served basis while the supply lasts. A limited number of standby tickets are available by phone but do not guarantee admission. Production schedules vary from week to week. For recorded ticket and taping information, call the Paramount Guest Relations line at (323) 956-5575.

FRIENDS *AND OTHER SERIES*

Audiences Unlimited distributes limited numbers of tickets for many of the situation comedies shot before live audiences in the Los Angeles area. They have tickets for favorites such as *Friends, Everybody Loves Raymond,* and *The Drew Carey Show,* as well as award shows, new programs like *Donny and Marie,* and programs on Nickelodeon.

For schedule information, studio locations, age restrictions, a list of shows with available tickets, and to order tickets up to 60 days in advance, call (818) 753-3470. A one-month advance show taping–filming schedule is available by calling (818) 753-3470, ext. 802, or by sending a self-addressed, stamped envelope to Audiences Unlimited, 100 Universal City Plaza, Building 153, Universal City, CA 91608. Tickets are available by mail from the same address.

Tickets may be requested on line at www.tvtickets.com up to 30 days before the show date. Your computer will print out your tickets, which will only be activated after you leave a voice-mail at (818) 753-3470 with the name of the show, show date and time, the number of tickets, and your name.

If you are visiting Universal Studios Hollywood, you may stop by the TV ticket booth located in the Entertainment Center to get tickets for selected shows filming that week.

Tickets to some shows, such as *Friends,* are only available by mail order, and there is typically a four- to six-month wait. Tickets are limited for all shows, so include alternate choices. There is a six-ticket maximum per request.

HOW TO GET ON AUDIENCE-PARTICIPATION SHOWS

We all play along with the game shows when we watch at home, but only a few of us make it on to the air to play the games for real. Here are the wheres and hows on becoming a contestant on some of the leading shows.

JEOPARDY!

Every year, over 15,000 trivia buffs apply for some 400 contestant slots. All contestants must first pass a 50-question test. Los Angeles test dates are available from the *Jeopardy!* contestant line, (310) 244-5367, Monday through Friday, from 10:00 to 4:30. The test dates are scheduled intermittently throughout the year, so call two to three weeks prior to being in the Los Angeles area to schedule an appointment. For information about out-of-town and tournament contestant searches, watch your local *Jeopardy!* station for announcements. Successful test-takers are invited to play a mock version of the game. If that goes well, they may be called to be scheduled as contestants, from one month to one year after the tryout.

To participate in the studio audience, send a self-addressed stamped envelope to *Jeopardy!* Tickets, P.O. Box 3763, Hollywood, CA 90028, or call 800-482-9840. *Jeopardy!* is generally taped Tuesdays and Wednesdays, with five shows each day.

MTV SHOWS

MTV airs several shows with audience participants, contestants, and dancers, among them *FANatic, The Cut*, and the annual spring break and summertime specials. Many of these shows require auditions and/or advance reservations. MTV sets up individual audience participation hot lines for each show that will be taped. Hotline num-

bers are broadcast on MTV and on local radio stations approximately one month to two weeks before each event. Information and phone numbers for individual shows are available on the MTV website (www.mtv.com). Shows involving extensive participation, such as *Real World* and *Road Rules*, generally require a five-minute audition video and often hold open casting calls around the country. Check the website at www.bunim-murray.com for further details. For more MTV casting information, call the Viewer Service Hotline at (212) 258-8700.

THE PRICE IS RIGHT

Since all of the contestants on *The Price Is Right* are selected from the audience, call the 24-hour ticket hotline number at (323) 575-2449 for the most up-to-date taping schedule and ticket information, or (323) 575-2458 for information about individual tickets. Tickets can be requested by sending a note specifying your preferred date and number of tickets (the maximum is ten) and a self-addressed, stamped envelope to *The Price Is Right*, CBS Television City, 7800 Beverly Blvd., Los Angeles, CA 90036. Allow four to six weeks for a response. Tickets are also available from the ticket window at the above address starting one week prior to the date of taping up to the day before taping. The office is open from 9:00 to 5:00 on business days, except Mondays through Thursdays of taping,

when it is open from 6:30 a.m. to 5:00 p.m. No tickets are available on the day of taping, but you may request a "Nonticket slip," which, like priority and standby tickets, does not guarantee admission. Priority numbers are distributed starting at 7:30 a.m. Admission to the studio is on a first-come–first-serve basis for ticket-holders. *The Price Is Right* is usually taped on Mondays at 1:15 and 4:30 and on Tuesdays, Wednesdays, and Thursdays at 2:30. Ticket-holders are processed several hours before each taping begins for name-tag distribution, interviews, and admission to the studio. Minimum age is 18. Photo ID and a document with your Social Security number are required at the taping.

WHEEL OF FORTUNE

To audition as a contestant, send a postcard with your name, address, nearest major city, and phone number to *Wheel of Fortune*, 10202 W. Washington Blvd., Rm. 5300, Culver City, CA 90232. Candidates whose postcards are randomly selected will be given auditions. Contestant auditions are held sporadically throughout the year, both in Los Angeles and during contestant searches around the U.S. Auditions involve a fill-in-the-blank test and a mock game. The most up-to-date information on auditions is available by calling (213) 520-5555, Monday through Friday, from 10:00 a.m. to 6:00 p.m., Pacific Standard Time. For information on attending the show as an audience member, call (800) 482-9840.

STARS WITH SOAPY ROOTS

Ricky Martin, Usher, and Sarah Michelle Gellar are just a few of the many who were big on daytime before they became bigtime. Test your soap-opera memory against our list.

Actor	Character	Soap
Richard Dean Anderson	Dr. Jeff Webber	General Hospital
Armand Assante	Dr. Mike Powers	The Doctors
Kevin Bacon	Tim Werner	Guiding Light
Alec Baldwin	Billy Allison Aldrich	The Doctors
Bonnie Bedelia	Sandy Porter	Love of Life
Tom Berenger	Timmy Siegel	One Life to Live
Corbin Bernsen	Kenny Graham	Ryan's Hope
Yasmine Bleeth	Ryan Fenelli	Ryan's Hope
Carol Burnett	Verla Grubbs	All My Children
Ellen Burstyn	Dr. Kate Bartok	The Doctors
Kate Capshaw	Jinx Avery Mallory	The Edge of Night
Tia Carrere	Jade Soong	General Hospital
Dixie Carter	Olivia Brandeis "Brandy" Henderson	The Edge of Night
Nell Carter	Ethel Green	Ryan's Hope
Gabrielle Carteris	Tracy Julian	Another World
Shaun Cassidy	Dusty Walker	General Hospital
Lacey Chabert	Bianca Montgomery	All My Children
Jill Clayburgh	Grace Bolton	Search for Tomorrow
Dabney Coleman	Dr. Tracy Brown	Bright Promise
Courteney Cox	Bunny	As the World Turns
Ted Danson	Tim Conway	Somerset
Olympia Dukakis	Barbara Moreno	Search for Tomorrow
Morgan Fairchild	Jennifer Phillips	Search for Tomorrow
Laurence Fishburne	Joshua West	One Life to Live
Faith Ford	Julia Shearer	Another World
Vivica A. Fox	Dr. Stephanie Simmons	The Young and the Restless
Morgan Freeman	Roy Bingham	Another World
Sarah Michelle Gellar	Kendall Hart	All My Children
Thomas Gibson	Samuel R. "Sam" Fowler	Another World
Kelsey Grammer	Dr. Canard	Another World
Charles Grodin	Matt Crane	The Young Marrieds
Larry Hagman	Ed Gibson	The Edge of Night
Mark Hamill	Kent Murray	General Hospital
David Hasselhoff	Bill "Snapper" Foster	The Young and the Restless
Anne Heche	Marley Hudson	Another World
Lauren Holly	Julie Chandler	All My Children
Kate Jackson	Daphne Harridge	Dark Shadows
James Earl Jones	Dr. Jim Frazier	Guiding Light

Actor	Character	Soap
Tommy Lee Jones	Dr. Mark Toland	One Life to Live
Raul Julia	Miguel Garcia	Love of Life
Kevin Kline	Woody Reed	Search for Tomorrow
Don Knotts	Wilbur Peabody	Search for Tomorrow
Téa Leoni	Lisa Di Napoli	Santa Barbara
Judith Light	Karen Martin	One Life to Live
Hal Linden	Larry Carter	Search for Tomorrow
Ray Liotta	Joey Perini	Another World
Ricky Martin	Miguel Morez	General Hospital
Marsha Mason	Judith Cole	Love of Life
Demi Moore	Jackie Templeton	General Hospital
Kate Mulgrew	Mary Ryan Fenelli	Ryan's Hope
Luke Perry	Ned Bates	Loving
Regis Philbin	Malachy Malone	Ryan's Hope
Phylicia Rashad	Courtney Wright	One Life to Live
Christopher Reeve	Benno ("Beanie" or "Ben") Harper	Love of Life
Ving Rhames	Czaja Carnek	Another World
Eric Roberts	Ted Bancroft	Another World
Meg Ryan	Betsy Stewart	As the World Turns
Pat Sajak	Kevin Hathaway	Days of Our Lives
Susan Sarandon	Sarah	Search for Tomorrow
Kyra Sedgwick	Julia Shearer	Another World
Tom Selleck	Jed Andrews	The Young and the Restless
Christian Slater	D. J. LaSalle	Ryan's Hope
Rick Springfield	Dr. Noah Drake	General Hospital
John Stamos	Blackie Parrish	General Hospital
Marisa Tomei	Marcy Thompson	As the World Turns
Janine Turner	Laura Templeton	General Hospital
Kathleen Turner	Nola Dancy Aldrich	The Doctors
Cicely Tyson	Martha Frazier	Guiding Light
Blair Underwood	Bobby Blue	One Life to Live
Usher	Raymond	The Bold and the Beautiful
Jack Wagner	Frisco Jones	General Hospital
Christopher Walken	Michael Bauer	Guiding Light
Sigourney Weaver	Avis Ryan	Somerset
Billy Dee Williams	Dr. Jim Frazier	Guiding Light
JoBeth Williams	Brandy Sheloo	Guiding Light
Robin Wright	Kelly Capwell	Santa Barbara

PRIME TIME'S TOP 40

There's something infectious about television theme songs. Here are the ones that hit highest on the *Billboard* charts. (The list excludes songs that were hits prior to their adoption as television anthems.)

Song	Show	Performer	Chart Position/Year
I'll Be There for You*	Friends	The Rembrandts	1/1995
S.W.A.T.	S.W.A.T.	Rhythm Heritage	1/1975
Welcome Back	Welcome Back, Kotter	John Sebastian	1/1976
Miami Vice	Miami Vice	Jan Hammer	1/1985
Believe It or Not	The Greatest American Hero	Joey Scarbury	2/1981
Dragnet	Dragnet	Ray Anthony Orchestra	3/1953
Secret Agent Man	Secret Agent Man	Johnny Rivers	3/1966
Hawaii Five-O	Hawaii Five-O	The Ventures	4/1969
Happy Days	Happy Days	Pratt and McClain	5/1976
Makin' It	Makin' It	David Naughton	5/1979
Peter Gunn	Peter Gunn	Ray Anthony Orchestra	8/1959
Three Stars Will Shine Tonight	Dr. Kildare	Richard Chamberlain	10/1962
The Rockford Files	The Rockford Files	Mike Post	10/1975
Hill Street Blues	Hill Street Blues	Mike Post and Larry Carlton	10/1981
Closer to Free	Party of Five	The BoDeans	16/1996
Zorro	Zorro	The Chordettes	17/1958
Batman	Batman	The Marketts	17/1966
Different Worlds	Angie	Maureen McGovern	18/1979
Bonanza	Bonanza	Al Caiola	19/1961
Keep Your Eye on the Sparrow	Baretta	Rhythm Heritage	20/1976
Mr. Lucky	Mr. Lucky	Henry Mancini Orchestra	21/1960
The Dukes of Hazzard	The Dukes of Hazzard	Waylon Jennings	21/1980
Moonlighting	Moonlighting	Al Jarreau	23/1987
Making Our Dreams Come True	Laverne and Shirley	Cyndi Grecco	25/1976
Magnum, P.I.	Magnum, P.I.	Mike Post	25/1982
Ben Casey	Ben Casey	Valjean	28/1962
Blue Star	Medic	Felicia Sanders	29/1955
Route 66	Route 66	Nelson Riddle Orchestra	30/1962
Ballad of Paladin	Have Gun Will Travel	Duane Eddy	33/1962
Seattle	Here Come the Brides	Perry Como	38/1969
The Men	The Men	Isaac Hayes	38/1972
Mission: Impossible	Mission: Impossible	Lalo Schifrin	41/1968
Those Were the Days	All in the Family	Carroll O'Connor and Jean Stapleton	43/1971
The Ballad of Jed Clampett	Beverly Hillbillies	Lester Flatt and Earl Scruggs	44/1962
Charlie's Angels	Charlie's Angels	Henry Mancini	45/1977
Dynasty	Dynasty	Bill Conti	52/1982
My Three Sons	My Three Sons	Lawrence Welk Orchestra	55/1961

*Reached No. 1 on *Billboard*'s Hot 100 Airplay Chart before release as an A-side single; upon release, reached No. 17 on *Billboard*'s Hot 100 Singles Chart.

YADA, YADA, YADA

From *spongeworthy* to *shiksappeal*, *Seinfeld* wallowed in a giddy love of language. Jerry and the gang left us with more than memories—here's a short *Seinfeld* vocabulary builder, featuring perfect terms learned from the show and practiced at the water cooler. Giddyup!

Anti-Dentite Someone who hates dentists; Kramer castigates Jerry for being one.

B.B.O. Smell on wheels: tenacious car stink Beyond Body Odor.

Buck Naked The stage name George says he'd use if he became a porn star.

Change Teams What Elaine wants a handsome gay man to do; he stays with his team—not that there's anything wrong with that.

Close-Talker He's polite, he's charming, he's in your face—so close you can feel his tonsils vibrate.

Deaf Date Opposite of blind date: rendezvous with someone you've seen but not heard.

Double Dipping The chip hits the fan when George's snack-table faux pas—redipping a chip after taking a bite—casts a pall over an otherwise convivial funeral.

Festivus A festival for the rest of us, invented by George's father, Frank, as an alternative holiday. Requires an aluminum pole and a father-son wrestling match before dinner.

Friends-in-law Hand-me-down acquaintances; friends of friends.

"Get out!" Elaine's term when she's incredulous and doesn't believe the speaker.

"Giddyup!" Kramer's exclamation of enthusiasm, with spastic head gestures.

High-Talker Vocal she-man whose voice registers as a woman's over the phone.

"Hoochie Mama!" Kramer's favorite term to use when shocked.

Kavorka Animal attraction possessed by Kramer; seems to work only on Latvian Orthodox nuns.

Leave-Behind, The Lame Costanzian attempt to put a down payment on a second date by hiding an object at a woman's apartment during first date.

Low-Talker Someone as whispery-voiced as Kramer's clothing-designer girlfriend, whose lack of volume resulted in Jerry agreeing to wear her puffy shirt on national TV.

Make-Up Sex Spectacular sometime by-product of breaking up. Trumped only by conjugal-visit sex or fugitive sex.

Manssière, a.k.a. The Bro Chestal support for the over-endowed male, invented by Kramer and modeled by Frank Costanza.

Master of Your Domain Title acquired after completing a period of bodily self-denial in "The Contest."

Mimbo A male bimbo; Elaine's interest in one proves females are as superficial as Jerry.

Must-Lie Situation Typified by viewing an ugly baby whose parents ask, "Isn't he gorgeous?"

"Not that there's anything wrong with that" Open-minded footnote that is perpetually appended to George and Jerry's insistence that they're not gay lovers.

Pop-In, The Dreaded, potentially awkward impromptu visit from love interest.

Pre-Emptive Breakup A strategic split launched solely to acquire the upper hand (a.k.a. "hand") in a relationship.

Re-Gifter One who gives as a gift something he received as a gift—such as a label maker.

Schmoopie Cloying term of endearment ("You're *Schmoopie!*" "No, you're *Schmoopie!*"), which, when used by couples in public, causes friends to run screaming.

Sexual perjury Call it lying in bed: Jerry's term for Elaine's faked enthusiasm during sex.

Shiksappeal Mysterious power that attracts Jewish men to non-Jewish women like Elaine, especially at bar mitzvahs.

Shrinkage George's ego, and more, recedes after he takes a dip in cold water, and Jerry's girlfriend sees him buck naked.

Sidler A guy who sneaks up behind Elaine to share credit for her accomplishments; the Stealth fighter of office politics.

Spongeworthy Elaine's criterion for whether to sleep with a guy in the face of a shortage of her favorite contraceptive.

Stabworthy Spongeworthy's *Fatal Attraction*–like cousin: Elaine is turned on when she finds out a guy stood her up because he was knifed by his girlfriend.

Switch, The Theoretically possible (say George and Jerry), practically suicidal idea of breaking up with one woman in order to date her roommate.

Yada, yada, yada To cut a long story short; an ellipsis. Advantage: Succinctness. Disadvantage: Crucial information may be left out (e.g., George was engaged to Susan, *yada, yada, yada,* George is no longer engaged).

THE EMMY AWARDS

As the television industry has developed over the years, so has the business of television awards—so much so that the Emmys are now presented in two separate ceremonies to accommodate the growth of categories. The following presents a wide selection of winners in major areas throughout Emmy's history.

	1949	1950
Actor	—	Alan Young
Actress	—	Gertrude Berg
Drama	—	Pulitzer Prize Playhouse, ABC
Variety Program	—	The Alan Young Show, CBS
Game Show	—	Truth or Consequences, CBS
Children's Show	Time for Beany, KTLA	Time for Beany, KTLA

	1951	1952	1953
Actor	Sid Caesar	Thomas Mitchell	Donald O'Connor, Colgate Comedy Hour, NBC
Actress	Imogene Coca	Helen Hayes	Eve Arden, Our Miss Brooks, CBS
Drama	Studio One, CBS	Robert Montgomery Presents, NBC	U.S. Steel Hour, ABC
Mystery, Action, or Adventure	—	Dragnet, NBC	Dragnet, NBC
Comedy	Red Skelton Show, NBC	I Love Lucy, CBS	I Love Lucy, CBS
Comedian	Red Skelton, NBC	Lucille Ball, CBS; Jimmy Durante, NBC	—
Variety Program	Your Show of Shows, NBC	Your Show of Shows, NBC	Omnibus, CBS
Game Show	—	What's My Line?, CBS	This is Your Life, NBC; What's My Line?, CBS
Children's Program	—	Time for Beany, KTLA	Kukla, Fran & Ollie, NBC

	1954	1955	1956
Actor	Danny Thomas, Make Room for Daddy, ABC	Phil Silvers, The Phil Silvers Show, CBS	Robert Moss, Father Knows Best, NBC
Actress	Loretta Young, The Loretta Young Show, NBC	Lucille Ball, I Love Lucy, CBS	Loretta Young, The Loretta Young Show, NBC
Drama	U.S. Steel Hour, ABC	Producers' Showcase, NBC	Playhouse 90, CBS
Mystery, Action, or Adventure	Dragnet, NBC	Disneyland, ABC	—
Comedy	Make Room for Daddy, ABC	The Phil Silvers Show, CBS	—
Comedian	—	Phil Silvers, CBS; Nanette Fabray, NBC	Sid Caesar, Caesar's Hour, NBC; Nanette Fabray, Caesar's Hour, NBC
Variety Series	Disneyland, ABC	The Ed Sullivan Show, CBS	
Game Show	This Is Your Life, NBC	The $64,000 Question, CBS	—
Children's Program	Lassie, CBS	Lassie, CBS	—

	1957	1958–59	1959–60
Drama	*Gunsmoke*, CBS	*The Alcoa Hour/Goodyear Playhouse*, NBC; *Playhouse 90*, CBS	*Playhouse 90*, CBS
Actor—Series	—	Raymond Burr, *Perry Mason*, CBS (Drama)	Robert Stack, *The Untouchables*, ABC
Actress—Series	—	Loretta Young, *The Loretta Young Show*, NBC (Drama)	Jane Wyatt, *Father Knows Best*, CBS
Supporting Actor—Series	—	Dennis Weaver, *Gunsmoke*, CBS	—
Supporting Actress—Drama Series	—	Barbara Hale, *Perry Mason*, CBS	—
Director—Drama	—	George Schaefer, *Little Moon of Aloban*, NBC; Jack Smight, *Eddie*, NBC	Robert Mulligan, *The Moon and Sixpence*, NBC
Writer—Drama	—	James Costigan, *Little Moon of Alban*, NBC; Alfred Brenner and Ken Hughes, *Eddie*, NBC	Rod Serling, *The Twilight Zone*, CBS
Comedy	*The Phil Silvers Show*, CBS	*The Jack Benny Show*, CBS	*Art Carney Special*, NBC
Actor—Comedy Series	Robert Young, *Father Knows Best*, NBC	Jack Benny, *The Jack Benny Show*, CBS	Dick Van Dyke, *The Dick Van Dyke Show*, CBS
Actress—Comedy Series	Jane Wyatt, *Father Knows Best*, NBC	Jane Wyatt, *Father Knows Best*, CBS & NBC	Jane Wyatt, *Father Knows Best*, CBS
Supporting Actor—Comedy Series	Carl Reiner, *Caesar's Hour*, NBC	Tom Poston, *The Steve Allen Show*, NBC	
Supporting Actress—Comedy Series	Ann B. Davis, *The Bob Cummings Show*, CBS and NBC	Ann B. Davis, *The Bob Cummings Show*, NBC	—
Director—Comedy/Comedy Series	—	Peter Tewksbury, *Father Knows Best*, CBS	Ralph Levy and Bud Yorkin, *The Jack Benny Hour Specials*, CBS
Writer—Comedy/Comedy Series	Nat Hiken, Billy Friedberg, Phil Sharp, Terry Ryan, Coleman Jacoby, Arnold Rosen, Sidney Zelinko, A.J. Russell, and Tony Webster, *The Phil Silvers Show*, CBS	Sam Perrin, George Balzer, Hal Goldman, and Al Gordon, *The Jack Benny Show*, CBS	Sam Perrin, George Balzer, Hal Goldman, and Al Gordon, *The Jack Benny Show*, CBS
Variety Program	*The Dinah Shore Chevy Show*, NBC	*The Dinah Shore Chevy Show*, NBC	*The Fabulous Fifties*, CBS
Game Show	—	*What's My Line?*, CBS	—
Children's Program	—	—	*Huckleberry Hound*, SYN

	1960–61	1961–62	1962–63
Actor	Raymond Burr, *Perry Mason*, CBS	E.G. Marshall, *The Defenders*, CBS	E.G. Marshall, *The Defenders*, CBS
Actress	Barbara Stanwyck, *The Barbara Stanwyck Show*, NBC	Shirley Booth, *Hazel*, NBC	Shirley Booth, *Hazel*, NBC
Drama	*Macbeth*, NBC	*The Defenders*, CBS	*The Defenders*, CBS
Director—Drama	George Schaefer, *Macbeth*, NBC	Franklin Schaffner, *The Defenders*, CBS	Stuart Rosenberg, *The Defenders*, CBS
Writer—Drama	Rod Serling, *The Twilight Zone*, CBS	Reginald Rose, *The Defenders*, CBS	Robert Thorn, Reginald Rose, *The Defenders*, CBS
Comedy	*The Jack Benny Show*, CBS	*The Bob Newhart Show*, NBC	*The Dick Van Dyke Show*, CBS
Director—Comedy	Sheldon Leonard, *The Danny Thomas Show*, CBS	Nat Hiken, *Car 54, Where Are You?*, NBC	John Rich, *The Dick Van Dyke Show*, CBS
Writer—Comedy	Sherwood Schwartz, Dave O'Brien, Al Schwartz, Martin Ragaway, and Red Skelton, *The Red Skelton Show*, CBS	Carl Reiner, *The Dick Van Dyke Show*, CBS	Carl Reiner, *The Dick Van Dyke Show*, CBS
Variety Program	*Astaire Time*, NBC	*The Garry Moore Show*, CBS	*The Andy Williams Show*, NBC
Individual Performance—Variety or Music Program/Series	Fred Astaire, *Astaire Time*, NBC	Carol Burnett, *The Garry Moore Show*, CBS	Carol Burnett, *Julie and Carol at Carnegie Hall*, CBS; *Carol and Company*, CBS
Panel, Quiz or Audience Participation	—	—	*College Bowl*, CBS
Children's Program	*Young People's Concert: Aaron Copland's Birthday Party*, CBS	*New York Philharmonic Young People's Concerts with Leonard Bernstein*, CBS	*Walt Disney's Wonderful World of Color*, NBC

THE RATINGS CONNECTION

Having the No. 1 rated show for a season doesn't necessarily guarantee Emmy success…or does it? Here is a list of the No. 1 shows that have also won the top honors—along with those that have achieved the dubious distinction of winning the ratings race but losing the Emmy battle.

EMMY WINNERS
Texaco Star Theatre
I Love Lucy
The $64,000 Question
Gunsmoke
Rowan and Martin's Laugh-In
All in the Family
60 Minutes
The Cosby Show
Cheers
Seinfeld
ER

EMMY LOSERS
Arthur Godfrey's Talent Scouts
Wagon Train
The Beverly Hillbillies
Bonanza
The Andy Griffith Show
Marcus Welby, M.D.
Happy Days
Laverne and Shirley
Three's Company
Dallas
Dynasty
Roseanne
Home Improvement

	1963–64	1964–65	1965–66
Drama	*The Defenders*, CBS	In 1964–65 the entire award system was changed for one year, and there were no awards given in individual categories that in any way match the categories from other years.	*The Fugitive*, ABC
Actor—Drama Series	Jack Klugman, *The Defenders*, CBS		Bill Cosby, *I Spy*, NBC
Actress—Drama Series	Shelley Winters, *Two Is The Number*, NBC		Barbara Stanwyck, *The Big Valley*, ABC
Supporting Actor—Drama Series	Albert Parker, *One Day In The Life of Ivan Denisovich*, NBC	—	James Daly, *Eagle in a Cage*, NBC
Supporting Actress—Drama Series	Ruth White, *Little Moon of Alban*, NBC	—	Lee Grant, *Peyton Place*, ABC
Writer—Drama	Ernest Kinay, *The Defenders*, CBS	—	Sydney Pollack, *The Game*, NBC
Director—Drama	Tom Gries, *East Side/West Side*, CBS	—	Millard Lampell, *Eagle in a Cage*, NBC
Comedy	*The Dick Van Dyke Show*, CBS	—	*The Dick Van Dyke Show*, CBS
Actor—Comedy Series	Dick Van Dyke, *The Dick Van Dyke Show*, CBS	—	Dick Van Dyke, *The Dick Van Dyke Show*, CBS
Actress—Comedy Series	Mary Tyler Moore, *The Dick Van Dyke Show*, CBS	—	Mary Tyler Moore, *The Dick Van Dyke Show*, CBS
Supporting Actor—Comedy Series	—	—	Don Knotts, *The Andy Griffith Show*, CBS
Supp. Actress—Comedy Series	—	—	Alice Pearce, *Bewitched*, ABC
Director—Comedy	Jerry Paris, *The Dick Van Dyke Show*, CBS	—	William Asher, *Bewitched*, ABC
Writer—Comedy	Carl Reiner, Sam Denoff, and Bill Penky, *The Dick Van Dyke Show*, CBS		Bill Persky, Sam Denoff, *The Dick Van Dyke Show*, CBS
Variety Program	*The Danny Kaye Show*, CBS	—	*The Andy Williams Show*, NBC
Director—Variety or Music	Robert Scheerer, *The Danny Kaye Show*, CBS	—	Alan Handley, *The Julie Andrews Show*, NBC
Writer—Variety	—	—	Al Gordon, Hal Goldman, and Sheldon Keller, *An Evening with Carol Channing*, CBS
Children's Program	*Discovery '63-'64*, ABC	—	*A Charlie Brown Christmas*, CBS

WINNING TEAMS

Looking for a rare wedding gift? Consider his-and-hers Emmies: Only seven married couples have ever sported matching trophies. One duo, *St. Elsewhere*'s Daniels and Bartlett, won for playing a husband and wife onscreen.

Hume Cronyn & Jessica Tandy
William Daniels & Bonnie Bartlett
Danny DeVito & Rhea Perlman
Phil Donahue & Marlo Thomas
Alfred Lunt & Lynn Fontanne
George C. Scott & Colleen Dewhurst
Christine Lahti & Thomas Schlamme

	1966–67	**1967–68**	**1968–69**
Drama Series	*Mission: Impossible,* CBS	*Mission: Impossible,* CBS	*NET Playhouse,* NET
Actor—Drama Series	Bill Cosby, *I Spy,* NBC	Bill Cosby, *I Spy,* NBC	Carl Betz, *Judd, for the Defense,* ABC
Actress—Drama Series	Barbara Bain, *Mission: Impossible,* CBS	Barbara Bain, *Mission: Impossible,* CBS	Barbara Bain, *Mission: Impossible,* CBS
Supporting Actor— Drama	Eli Wallach, *The Poppy Is Also a Flower,* ABC	Milburn Stone, *Gunsmoke,* CBS	—
Supporting Actress— Drama	Agnes Moorehead, *The Wild, Wild West,* CBS	Barbara Anderson, *Ironside,* NBC	Susan Saint James, *The Name of the Game,* NBC
Director—Drama	Alex Segal, *Death of a Salesman,* CBS	Paul Bogart, *Dear Friends,* CBS	David Green, *The People Next Door,* CBS
Writer—Drama	Bruce Geller, *Mission: Impossible,* CBS	Loring Mandel, *Do Not Go Gentle into That Good Night,* CBS	J. P. Miller, *The People Next Door,* CBS
Comedy	*The Monkees,* NBC	*Get Smart,* NBC	*Get Smart,* NBC
Actor—Comedy Series	Don Adams, *Get Smart,* NBC	Don Adams, *Get Smart,* NBC	Don Adams, *Get Smart,* NBC
Actress—Comedy Series	Lucille Ball, *The Lucy Show,* CBS	Lucille Ball, *The Lucy Show,* CBS	Hope Lange, *The Ghost and Mrs. Muir,* NBC
Supporting Actor— Comedy Series	Don Knotts, *The Andy Griffith Show,* CBS	Werner Klemperer, *Hogan's Heroes,* CBS	Werner Klemperer, *Hogan's Heroes,* CBS
Supporting Actress— Comedy Series	Frances Bavier, *The Andy Griffith Show,* CBS	Marion Lorne, *Bewitched,* ABC	—
Director—Comedy/ Comedy Series	James Frawley, *The Monkees,* NBC	Bruce Bilson, *Get Smart,* NBC	—
Writer—Comedy/ Comedy Series	Buck Henry and Leonard Stern, *Get Smart,* NBC	Allan Burns and Chris Hayward, *He and She,* CBS	Alan Blye, Bob Einstein, Murray Roman, Carl Gottlieb, Jerry Music, Steve Martin, Cecil Tuck, Paul Wayne, Cy Howard, and Mason Williams, *The Smothers Brothers Comedy Hour,* CBS
Variety Program	*The Andy Williams Show,* NBC	*Rowan and Martin's Laugh-In,* NBC	*Rowan and Martin's Laugh-In,* NBC
Director—Variety or Music	Fielder Cook, *Brigadoon,* ABC	Jack Haley, Jr., *Movin' with Nancy,* NBC	—
Writer—Variety or Music	Mel Brooks, Sam Denoff, Bill Persky, Carl Reiner, and Mel Tolkin, *The Sid Caesar, Imogene Coca, Carl Reiner, Howard Morris Special,* CBS	Chris Beard, Phil Hahn, Jack Hanrahan, Coslough Johnson, Paul Keyes, Marc London, Allan Manings, David Panich, Hugh Wedlock, and Digby Wolfe, *Rowan and Martin's Laugh-In,* NBC	—
Children's Program	*Jack and the Beanstalk,* NBC	—	—

	1969–70	**1970–71**	**1971–72**
Drama	*Marcus Welby, M.D.*, ABC	*The Bold Ones: The Senator,* NBC	*Elizabeth R,* PBS
Actor—Drama Series	Robert Young, *Marcus Welby, M.D.*, ABC	Hal Holbrook, *The Bold Ones: The Senator,* NBC	Peter Falk, *Columbo,* NBC
Actress—Drama Series	Susan Hampshire, *The Forsyte Saga*, NET	Susan Hampshire, *The First Churchills,* PBS	Glenda Jackson, *Elizabeth R.,* PBS
Supporting Actor—Drama Series	James Brolin, *Marcus Welby, M.D.*, ABC	David Burns, *The Price,* NBC	Jack Warden, *Brian's Song,* ABC
Supporting Actress—Drama Series	Gail Fisher, *Mannix,* CBS	Margaret Leighton, *Hamlet,* NBC	Jenny Agutter, *The Snow Goose,* NBC
Director—Drama Series	—	Daryl Duke, *The Bold Ones: The Senator,* NBC	Alexander Singer, *The Bold Ones: The Lawyers,* NBC
Writer—Drama	Richard Levinson and William Link, *My Sweet Charlie,* NBC	Joel Oliansky, *The Bold Ones: The Senator,* NBC	Richard L. Levinson and William Link, *Columbo,* NBC
Comedy	*My World and Welcome to It,* NBC	*All in the Family,* CBS	*All in the Family,* CBS
Actor—Comedy Series	William Windom, *My World and Welcome to It,* NBC	Jack Klugman, *The Odd Couple,* ABC	Carroll O'Connor, *All in the Family,* CBS
Actress—Comedy Series	Hope Lange, *The Ghost and Mrs. Muir,* ABC	Jean Stapleton, *All in the Family,* CBS	Jean Stapleton, *All in the Family,* CBS
Supporting Actor—Comedy Series	Michael Constantine, *Room 222,* ABC	Edward Asner, *The Mary Tyler Moore Show,* CBS	Edward Asner, *The Mary Tyler Moore Show,* CBS
Supporting Actress—Comedy Series	Karen Valentine, *Room 222,* ABC	Valerie Harper, *The Mary Tyler Moore Show,* CBS	Valerie Harper, *The Mary Tyler Moore Show,* CBS; Sally Struthers, *All in the Family, CBS*
Director—Comedy Series	—	Jay Sandrich, *The Mary Tyler Moore Show,* CBS	John Rich, *All in the Family,* CBS
Writer—Comedy Series	—	James L. Brooks and Allan Burns, *The Mary Tyler Moore Show,* CBS	Burt Styler, *All in the Family,* CBS
Drama/Comedy Special	—	—	*Brian's Song,* ABC
Variety or Music Series	*The David Frost Show,* SYN	*The David Frost Show,* SYN (Talk); *The Flip Wilson Show,* NBC (Music)	*The Dick Cavett Show,* ABC (Talk), *The Carol Burnett Show,* CBS (Music)
Director—Variety or Music	—	Mark Warren, *Rowan and Martin's Laugh-In,* NBC	Art Fisher, *The Sonny & Cher Comedy Hour,* CBS
Writer—Variety or Music	—	Herbert Baker, Hal Goodman, Larry Klein, Bob Weiskopf, Bob Schiller, Norman Steinberg, and Flip Wilson, *The Flip Wilson Show,* NBC	Don Hinkley, Stan Hart, Larry Siegel, Woody Kling, Roger Beatty, Art Baer, Ben Joelson, Stan Burns, Mike Marmer, and Arnie Rosen, *The Carol Burnett Show,* CBS
Daytime Drama Series	—	—	*The Doctors,* NBC
Children's Program	*Sesame Street,* NET	*Sesame Street,* PBS	*Sesame Street,* PBS

	1972–73	1973–74	1974–75
Drama	*The Waltons*, CBS	*Upstairs, Downstairs*, PBS	*Upstairs, Downstairs*, PBS
Actor—Drama Series	Richard Thomas, *The Waltons*, CBS	Telly Savalas, *Kojak*, CBS	Robert Blake, *Baretta*, ABC
Actress—Drama Series	Michael Learned, *The Waltons*, CBS	Michael Learned, *The Waltons*, CBS	Jean Marsh, *Upstairs, Downstairs*, PBS
Supporting Actor—Drama/Drama Series	Scott Jacoby, *That Certain Summer*, ABC	Michael Moriarty, *The Glass Menagerie*, ABC	Will Geer, *The Waltons*, CBS
Supporting Actress—Drama/Drama Series	Ellen Corby, *The Waltons*, CBS	Joanna Miles, *The Glass Menagerie*, ABC	Ellen Corby, *The Waltons*, CBS
Director—Drama	Joseph Sargent, *The Marcus Nelson Murders*, CBS	John Korty, *The Autobiography of Miss Jane Pittman*, CBS	George Cukor, *Love Among the Ruins*, ABC
Director—Drama Series	Jerry Thorpe, *Kung Fu*, ABC	Robert Butler, *The Blue Knight*, NBC	Bill Bain, *Upstairs, Downstairs*, PBS
Writer—Drama Series	John McGreevey, *The Waltons*, CBS	Joanna Lee, *The Waltons*, CBS	Howard Fast, *Benjamin Franklin*, CBS
Comedy	*All in the Family*, CBS	*M*A*S*H*, CBS	*The Mary Tyler Moore Show*, CBS
Actor—Comedy Series	Jack Klugman, *The Odd Couple*, ABC	Alan Alda, *M*A*S*H*, CBS	Tony Randall, *The Odd Couple*, ABC
Actress—Comedy Series	Mary Tyler Moore, *The Mary Tyler Moore Show*, CBS	Mary Tyler Moore, *The Mary Tyler Moore Show*, CBS	Valerie Harper, *Rhoda*, CBS
Supporting Actor—Comedy Series	Ted Knight, *The Mary Tyler Moore Show*, CBS	Rob Reiner, *All in the Family*, CBS	Ed Asner, *The Mary Tyler Moore Show*, CBS
Supporting Actress—Comedy Series	Valerie Harper, *The Mary Tyler Moore Show*, CBS	Cloris Leachman, *The Mary Tyler Moore Show*, CBS	Betty White, *The Mary Tyler Moore Show*, CBS
Director—Comedy Series	Jay Sandrich, *The Mary Tyler Moore Show*, CBS	Jackie Cooper, *M*A*S*H*, CBS	Gene Reynolds, *M*A*S*H*, CBS
Writer—Comedy Series	Michael Ross, Bernie West, and Lee Kalcheim, *All in the Family*, CBS	Treva Silverman, *The Mary Tyler Moore Show*, CBS	Ed. Weinberger and Stan Daniels, *The Mary Tyler Moore Show*, CBS
Drama/Comedy Special	*A War of Children*, CBS	*The Autobiography of Miss Jane Pittman*, CBS	*The Law*, NBC
Variety Series	*The Julie Andrews Hour*, ABC	*The Carol Burnett Show*, CBS	*The Carol Burnett Show*, CBS
Director—Variety or Music	Bill Davis, *The Julie Andrews Hour*, ABC	Dave Powers, *The Carol Burnett Show*, CBS	Dave Powers, *The Carol Burnett Show*, CBS

1972–73   1973–74   1974–75

	1972–73	1973–74	1974–75
Writer—Variety or Music Series	Stan Hart, Larry Siegel, Gail Parent, Woody Kling, Roger Beatty, Tom Patchett, Jay Tarses, Robert Hilliard, Arnie Kogen, Bill Angelos, and Buz Kohan, *The Carol Burnett Show*, CBS	Ed Simmons, Gary Belkin, Roger Beatty, Arnie Kogen, Bill Richmond, Gene Perret, Rudy De Luca, Barry Levinson, Dick Clair, Jenna McMahon, and Barry Harman, *The Carol Burnett Show*, CBS	Ed Simmons, Gary Belkin, Roger Beatty, Arnie Kogen, Bill Richmond, Gene Perret, Rudy De Luca, Barry Levinson, Dick Clair, and Jenna McMahon, *The Carol Burnett Show*, CBS
Variety, Music, or Comedy Special	*Singer Presents Liza with a "Z,"* CBS	*Lily Tomlin*, CBS	*An Evening with John Denver*, ABC
Miniseries/Limited Series	*Tom Brown's Schooldays*, PBS	*Columbo*, NBC	*Benjamin Franklin*, CBS
Actor—Miniseries/Limited Series	Anthony Murphy, *Tom Brown's Schooldays*, PBS	William Holden, *The Blue Knight*, NBC	Peter Falk, *Columbo*, NBC
Actress—Miniseries/Limited Series	Susan Hampshire, *Vanity Fair*, PBS	Mildred Natwick, *The Snoop Sisters*, NBC	Jessica Walter, *Amy Prentiss*, NBC
Daytime Drama Series	*The Edge of Night*, CBS	*The Doctors*, NBC	*The Young and the Restless*, CBS
Actor—Daytime Drama Series	—	Macdonald Carey, *Days of Our Lives*, NBC	Macdonald Carey, *Days of Our Lives*, NBC
Actress—Daytime Drama Series	—	Elizabeth Hubbard, *The Doctors*, NBC	Susan Flannery, *Days of Our Lives*, NBC
Host—Game Show	—	Peter Marshall, *The Hollywood Squares*, NBC	Peter Marshall, *The Hollywood Squares*, NBC
Host—Talk or Service	—	Dinah Shore, *Dinah's Place*, NBC	Barbara Walters, *Today*, NBC
Game Show	—	*Password*, ABC	*Hollywood Squares*, NBC
Talk, Service or Variety Series	—	*The Merv Griffin Show*, SYN	*Dinah!*, SYN
Children's Special	—	*Marlo Thomas and Friends in Free To Be…You and Me*, ABC	*Yes, Virginia, There Is a Santa Claus*, ABC
Children's Entertainment Series	—	*Zoom*, PBS	*Star Trek*, NBC

1975–76   1976–77   1977–78

	1975–76	1976–77	1977–78
Drama	*Police Story*, NBC	*Upstairs, Downstairs*, PBS	*The Rockford Files*, NBC
Actor—Drama Series	Peter Falk, *Columbo*, NBC	James Garner, *The Rockford Files*, NBC	Edward Asner, *Lou Grant*, CBS
Actress—Drama Series	Michael Learned, *The Waltons*, CBS	Lindsay Wagner, *The Bionic Woman*, ABC	Sada Thompson, *Family*, ABC
Supporting Actor—Drama Series	Anthony Zerbe, *Harry-O*, ABC	Gary Frank, *Family*, ABC	Robert Vaughn, *Washington: Behind Closed Doors*, ABC
Supp. Actress—Drama Series	Ellen Corby, *The Waltons*, CBS	Kristy McNichol, *Family*, ABC	Nancy Marchand, *Lou Grant*, CBS
Director—Drama Series	David Greene, *Rich Man, Poor Man*, ABC	David Greene, *Roots*, ABC	Marvin J. Chomsky, *Holocaust*, NBC
Writer—Drama Series	Sherman Yellen, *The Adams Chronicles*, PBS	Ernest Kinoy and William Blinn, *Roots*, ABC	Gerald Green, *Holocaust*, NBC
Comedy	*The Mary Tyler Moore Show*, CBS	*The Mary Tyler Moore Show*, CBS	*All in the Family*, CBS
Actor—Comedy Series	Jack Albertson, *Chico and the Man*, NBC	Carroll O'Connor, *All in the Family*, CBS	Carroll O'Connor, *All in the Family*, CBS
Actress—Comedy Series	Mary Tyler Moore, *The Mary Tyler Moore Show*, CBS	Beatrice Arthur, *Maude*, CBS	Jean Stapleton, *All in the Family*, CBS

	1975–76	1976–77	1977–78
Supporting Actor— Comedy Series	Ted Knight, *The Mary Tyler Moore Show*, CBS	Gary Burghoff, *M*A*S*H*, CBS	Rob Reiner, *All in the Family*, CBS
Supporting Actress—Comedy Series	Betty White, *The Mary Tyler Moore Show*, CBS	Mary Kay Place, *Mary Hartman, Mary Hartman*, SYN	Julie Kavner, *Rhoda*, CBS
Director—Comedy/ Comedy Series	Gene Reynolds, *M*A*S*H*, CBS	Alan Alda, *M*A*S*H*, CBS	Paul Bogart, *All in the Family*, CBS
Writer— Comedy Series	David Lloyd, *The Mary Tyler Moore Show*, CBS	Allan Burns, James L. Brooks, Ed. Weinberger, Stan Daniels, David Lloyd, and Bob Ellison, *The Mary Tyler Moore Show*, CBS	Bob Weiskopf and Bob Schiller (Teleplay); Barry Harman and Harve Brosten (Story), *All in the Family*, CBS
Drama/Comedy Special	*Eleanor and Franklin*, ABC	*Eleanor and Franklin: The White House Years*, ABC	*The Gathering*, ABC
Variety Series	*NBC's Saturday Night*, NBC	*Van Dyke and Company*, NBC	*The Muppet Show*, SYN
Limited Series	*Upstairs, Downstairs*, PBS	*Roots*, ABC	*Holocaust*, NBC
Actor— Limited Series	Hal Holbrook, *Sandburg's Lincoln*, NBC	Christopher Plummer, *The Moneychangers*, NBC	Michael Moriarty, *Holocaust*, NBC
Actress— Limited Series	Rosemary Harris, *Notorious Women*, PBS	Patty Duke Astin, *Captains and the Kings*, NBC	Meryl Streep, *Holocaust*, NBC
Daytime Drama Series	*Another World*, NBC	*Ryan's Hope*, ABC	*Days of Our Lives*, NBC
Actor—Daytime Drama Series	Larry Haines, *Search for Tomorrow*, CBS	Val Dufour, *Search for Tomorrow*, CBS	James Pritchett, *The Doctors*, NBC
Actress—Daytime Drama Series	Helen Gallagher, *Ryan's Hope*, ABC	Helen Gallagher, *Ryan's Hope*, ABC	Laurie Heinemann, *Another World*, NBC
Host—Game Show	Allen Ludden, *Password*, ABC	Bert Convy, *Tattletales*, CBS	Richard Dawson, *Family Feud*, ABC
Host—Talk or Service Series	Dinah Shore, *Dinah!*, SYN	Phil Donahue, *Donahue*, SYN	Phil Donahue, *Donahue*, SYN
Game Show	*The $20,000 Pyramid*, ABC	*Family Feud*, ABC	*The Hollywood Squares*, NBC
Talk, Service or Variety Series	*Dinah!*, SYN	*The Merv Griffin Show*, SYN	*Donahue*, SYN
Children's Entertainment Series	*Big Blue Marble*, SYN	*Zoom*, PBS	*Captain Kangaroo*, CBS

	1978–79	1979–80	1980–81
Drama	*Lou Grant*, CBS	*Lou Grant*, CBS	*Hill Street Blues*, NBC
Actor—Drama Series	Ron Leibman, *Kaz*, CBS	Ed Asner, *Lou Grant*, CBS	Daniel J. Travanti, *Hill Street Blues*, NBC
Actress—Drama Series	Mariette Hartley, *The Incredible Hulk*, CBS	Barbara Bel Geddes, *Dallas*, CBS	Barbara Babcock, *Hill Street Blues*, NBC
Supporting Actor— Drama Series	Stuart Margolin, *The Rockford Files*, NBC	Stuart Margolin, *The Rockford Files*, NBC	Michael Conrad, *Hill Street Blues*, NBC
Supporting Actress— Drama Series	Kristy McNichol, *Family*, ABC	Nancy Marchand, *Lou Grant*, CBS	Nancy Marchand, *Lou Grant*, CBS
Director—Drama Series	Jackie Cooper, *The White Shadow*, CBS	Roger Young, *Lou Grant*, CBS	Robert Butler, *Hill Street Blues*, NBC
Writer—Drama Series	Michele Gallery, *Lou Grant*, CBS	Seth Freeman, *Lou Grant*, CBS	Michael Kozoll and Steven Bochco, *Hill Street Blues*, NBC
Comedy	*Taxi*, ABC	*Taxi*, ABC	*Taxi*, ABC
Actor—Comedy Series	Carroll O'Connor, *All in the Family*, CBS	Richard Mulligan, *Soap*, ABC	Judd Hirsch, *Taxi*, ABC
Actress—Comedy Series	Ruth Gordon, *Taxi*, ABC	Cathryn Damon, *Soap*, ABC	Isabel Sanford, *The Jeffersons*, CBS
Supporting Actor—Comedy Series	Robert Guillaume, *Soap*, ABC	Harry Morgan, *M*A*S*H*, CBS	Danny De Vito, *Taxi*, ABC
Supporting Actress—Comedy Series	Sally Struthers, *All in the Family*, CBS	Loretta Swit, *M*A*S*H*, CBS	Eileen Brennan, *Private Benjamin*, CBS
Director—Comedy Series	Noam Pitlik, *Barney Miller*, ABC	James Burrows, *Taxi*, ABC	James Burrows, *Taxi*, ABC
Writer—Comedy Series	Alan Alda, *M*A*S*H*, CBS	Bob Colleary, *Barney Miller*, ABC	Michael Leeson, *Taxi*, ABC
Drama/Comedy Special	*Friendly Fire*, ABC	*The Miracle Worker*, NBC	*Playing for Time*, CBS
Variety Program	*Steve & Eydie Celebrate Irving Berlin*, NBC	*Baryshnikov on Broadway*, ABC	*Lily: Sold Out*, CBS
Director—Variety or Music	—	Dwight Hemion, *Baryshnikov on Broadway*, ABC	Don Mischer, *The Kennedy Center Honors: A National Celebration of the Performing Arts*, CBS

	1978–79	1979–80	1980–81
Writer—Variety or Music	—	Buz Kohan, *Shirley MacLaine… Every Little Movement*, CBS	Jerry Juhl, David Odell, Chris Langham, *The Muppet Show*, SYN
Limited Series	*Roots: The Next Generations*, ABC	*Edward & Mrs. Simpson*, SYN	*Shogun*, NBC
Actor—Limited Series	Peter Strauss, *The Jericho Mile*, ABC	Powers Boothe, *Guyana Tragedy: The Story of Jim Jones*, CBS	Anthony Hopkins, *The Bunker*, CBS
Actress—Limited Series	Bette Davis, *Strangers: The Story of a Mother and Daughter*, CBS	Patty Duke Astin, *The Miracle Worker*, NBC	Vanessa Redgrave, *Playing for Time*, CBS
Supporting Actor— Limited Series or Special	Marlon Brando, *Roots: The Next Generations*, ABC	George Grizzard, *The Oldest Living Graduate*, NBC	David Warner, *Masada*, ABC
Supporting Actress— Limited Series or Special	Esther Rolle, *Summer of My German Soldier*, NBC	Mare Winningham, *Amber Waves*, ABC	Jane Alexander, *Playing for Time*, CBS
Director—Limited Series or Special	David Greene, *Friendly Fire*, ABC	Marvin J. Chomsky, *Attica*, ABC	James Goldstone, *Kent State*, NBC
Writer—Limited Series or Special	Patrick Nolan and Michael Mann, *The Jericho Mile*, ABC	David Chase, *Off the Minnesota Strip*, ABC	Arthur Miller, *Playing for Time*, CBS
Daytime Drama Series	*Ryan's Hope*, ABC	*Guiding Light*, CBS	*General Hospital*, ABC
Actor—Daytime Drama Series	Al Freeman, Jr., *One Life to Live*, ABC	Douglass Watson, *Another World*, NBC	Douglass Watson, *Another World*, NBC
Actress—Daytime Drama Series	Irene Dailey, *Another World*, NBC	Judith Light, *One Life to Live*, ABC	Judith Light, *One Life to Live*, ABC
Supporting Actor— Daytime Drama Series	Peter Hansen, *General Hospital*, ABC	Warren Burton, *All My Children*, ABC	Larry Haines, *Search for Tomorrow*, CBS
Supporting Actress— Daytime Drama Series	Suzanne Rogers, *Days of Our Lives*, NBC	Francesca James, *All My Children*, ABC	Jane Elliot, *General Hospital*, ABC
Host—Game Show	Dick Clark, *The $20,000 Pyramid*, ABC	Peter Marshall, *The Hollywood Squares*, NBC	Peter Marshall, *The Hollywood Squares*, NBC
Host—Talk or Service	Phil Donahue, *Donahue*, SYN	Phil Donahue, *Donahue*, SYN	Hugh Downs, *Over Easy*, PBS
Game Show	*The Hollywood Squares*, NBC	*The Hollywood Squares*, NBC; *The $20,000 Pyramid*, ABC	*The $20,000 Pyramid*, ABC
Talk, Service or Variety Series	*Donahue*, SYN	*Donahue*, SYN	*Donahue*, SYN
Children's Special	*Christmas Eve on Sesame Street*, PBS	—	*Donahue and Kids*, NBC
Children's Entertainment Series	*Kids Are People Too*, ABC	*Hot Hero Sandwich*, NBC	*Captain Kangaroo*, CBS

	1981–82	1982–83	1983–84
Drama	*Hill Street Blues,* NBC	*Hill Street Blues,* NBC	*Hill Street Blues,* NBC
Actor—Drama Series	Daniel J. Travanti, *Hill Street Blues,* NBC	Ed Flanders, *St. Elsewhere,* NBC	Tom Selleck, *Magnum, P.I.,* CBS
Actress—Drama Series	Michael Learned, *Nurse,* CBS	Tyne Daly, *Cagney & Lacey,* CBS	Tyne Daly, *Cagney & Lacey,* CBS
Supporting Actor—Drama Series	Michael Conrad, *Hill Street Blues,* NBC	James Coco, *St. Elsewhere,* NBC	Bruce Weitz, *Hill Street Blues,* NBC
Supporting Actress—Drama Series	Nancy Marchand, *Lou Grant,* CBS	Doris Roberts, *St. Elsewhere,* NBC	Alfre Woodard, *Hill Street Blues,* NBC
Director—Drama Series	Harry Harris, *Fame,* NBC	Jeff Bleckner, *Hill Street Blues,* NBC	Corey Allen, *Hill Street Blues,* NBC
Writer—Drama Series	Steven Bochco, Anthony Yerkovich, Jeffrey Lewis and Michael Wagner (Teleplay); Michael Kozoll, and Steven Bochco (Story), *Hill Street Blues,* NBC	David Milch, *Hill Street Blues,* NBC	John Ford Noonan (Teleplay); John Masius and Tom Fontana (Story), *St. Elsewhere,* NBC
Comedy	*Barney Miller,* ABC	*Cheers,* NBC	*Cheers,* NBC
Actor—Comedy Series	Alan Alda, *M*A*S*H,* CBS	Judd Hirsch, *Taxi,* NBC	John Ritter, *Three's Company,* ABC
Actress—Comedy Series	Carol Kane, *Taxi,* ABC	Shelley Long, *Cheers,* NBC	Jane Curtin, *Kate & Allie,* CBS
Supporting Actor—Comedy Series	Christopher Lloyd, *Taxi,* ABC	Christopher Lloyd, *Taxi,* NBC	Pat Harrington, Jr., *One Day at a Time,* CBS
Supp. Actress—Comedy Series	Loretta Swit, *M*A*S*H,* CBS	Carol Kane, *Taxi,* NBC	Rhea Perlman, *Cheers,* NBC
Director—Comedy Series	Alan Rafkin, *One Day at a Time,* CBS	James Burrows, *Cheers,* NBC	Bill Persky, *Kate & Allie,* CBS
Writer—Comedy Series	Ken Estin, *Taxi,* ABC	Glen Charles, Les Charles, *Cheers,* NBC	David Angel, *Cheers,* NBC
Drama/Comedy Special	*A Woman Called Golda,* SYN	*Special Bulletin,* NBC	*Something About Amelia,* ABC
Variety, Music, or Comedy Program	*Night of 100 Stars,* ABC	*Motown 25: Yesterday, Today, Forever,* NBC	*The 6th Annual Kennedy Center Honors: A Celebration of the Performing Arts,* CBS
Individual Performance—Variety or Music Program	—	Leontyne Price, *Live From Lincoln Center: Leontyne Price, Zubin Mehta, and the New York Philharmonic,* PBS	Cloris Leachman, *Screen Actors Guild 50th Anniversary Celebration,* CBS
Director—Variety or Music	Dwight Hemion, *Goldie and Kids Listen to Us,* ABC	Dwight Hemion, *Sheena Easton Act I,* NBC	Dwight Hemion, *Here's Television Entertainment,* NBC
Writer—Variety or Music	John Candy, Joe Flaherty, Eugene Levy, Andrea Martin, Rick Moranis, Catherine O'Hara, Dave Thomas, Dick Blasucci, Paul Flaherty, Bob Dolman, John McAndrew, Doug Steckler, M. Bert Rich, Jeffrey Barron, Michael Short, Chris Cluess, Stuart Kreisman, and Brian McConnachie, *SCTV Comedy Network,* NBC	John Candy, Joe Flaherty, Eugene Levy, Andrea Martin, Martin Short, Dick Blasucci, Paul Flaherty, John McAndrew, Doug Steckler, Bob Dolman, Michael Short, and Mary Charlotte Wilcox, *SCTV Network,* NBC	Steve O'Donnell, Gerard Mulligan, Sanford Frank, Joseph E. Toplyn, Christopher Elliott, Matt Wickline, Jeff Martin, Ted Greenberg, David Yazbek, Merrill Markoe, and David Letterman, *Late Night with David Letterman,* NBC

	1981–82	1982–83	1983–84
Limited Series	*Marco Polo*, NBC	*Nicholas Nickleby*, SYN	*Concealed Enemies*, PBS
Actor—Limited Series or Special	Mickey Rooney, *Bill*, CBS	Tommy Lee Jones, *The Executioner's Song*, NBC	Laurence Olivier, *King Lear*, SYN
Actress—Limited Series or Special	Ingrid Bergman, *A Woman Called Golda*, SYN	Barbara Stanwyck, *The Thorn Birds*, ABC	Jane Fonda, *The Dollmaker*, ABC
Supporting Actor—Limited Series or Special	Laurence Olivier, *Brideshead Revisited*, PBS	Richard Kiley, *The Thorn Birds*, ABC	Art Carney, *Terrible Joe Moran*, CBS
Supporting Actress—Limited Series or Special	Penny Fuller, *Elephant Man*, ABC	Jean Simmons, *The Thorn Birds*, ABC	Roxana Zal, *Something About Amelia*, ABC
Director—Limited Series or Special	Marvin J. Chomsky, *Inside the Third Reich*, ABC	John Erman, *Who Will Love My Children?*, ABC	Jeff Bleckner, *Concealed Enemies*, PBS
Writer—Limited Series or Special	Corey Blechman (Teleplay); Barry Morrow (Story), *Bill*, CBS	Marshall Herskovitz (Teleplay); Edward Zwick, Marshall Herskovitz (Story), *Special Bulletin*, NBC	William Hanley, *Something About Amelia*, ABC
Daytime Drama Series	*Guiding Light*, CBS	*The Young & The Restless*, CBS	*General Hospital*, ABC
Actor—Daytime Drama Series	Anthony Geary, *General Hospital*, ABC	Robert S. Woods, *One Life to Live*, ABC	Larry Bryggman, *As the World Turns*, CBS
Actress—Daytime Drama Series	Robin Strasser, *One Life To Live*, ABC	Dorothy Lyman, *All My Children*, ABC	Erika Slezak, *One Life To Live*, ABC
Supporting Actor—Daytime Drama Series	David Lewis, *General Hospital*, ABC	Darnell Williams, *All My Children*, ABC	Justin Deas, *As the World Turns*, CBS
Supporting Actress—Daytime Drama Series	Dorothy Lyman, *All My Children*, ABC	Louise Shaffer, *Ryan's Hope*, ABC	Judi Evans, *The Guiding Light*, CBS
Host—Game Show	Bob Barker, *The Price Is Right*, CBS	Betty White, *Just Men!*, NBC	Bob Barker, *The Price Is Right*, CBS
Host—Talk or Service	Phil Donahue, *Donahue*, SYN	Phil Donahue, *Donahue*, SYN	Gary Collins, *Hour Magazine*, SYN
Game Show	*Password Plus*, NBC	*The New $25,000 Pyramid*, CBS	*The $25,000 Pyramid*, CBS
Talk or Service Series	*The Richard Simmons Show*, SYN	*This Old House*, PBS	*Woman to Woman*, SYN
Children's Special	*The Wave*, ABC	*Big Bird in China*, NBC	*He Makes Me Feel Like Dancin'*, NBC
Children's Series	*Captain Kangaroo*, CBS	*Smurfs*, NBC	*Captain Kangaroo*, CBS

	1984–85	1985–86	1986–87
Drama	*Cagney and Lacey,* CBS	*Cagney & Lacey,* CBS	*L. A. Law,* NBC
Actor—Drama Series	William Daniels, *St. Elsewhere,* NBC	William Daniels, *St. Elsewhere,* NBC	Bruce Willis, *Moonlighting,* ABC
Actress—Drama Series	Tyne Daly, *Cagney & Lacey,* CBS	Sharon Gless, *Cagney & Lacey,* CBS	Sharon Gless, *Cagney & Lacey,* CBS
Supporting Actor—Drama Series	Edward James Olmos, *Miami Vice,* NBC	John Karlen, *Cagney & Lacey,* CBS	John Hillerman, *Magnum, P.I.,* CBS
Supporting Actress—Drama Series	Betty Thomas, *Hill Street Blues,* NBC	Bonnie Bartlett, *St. Elsewhere,* NBC	Bonnie Bartlett, *St. Elsewhere,* NBC
Director—Drama Series	Karen Arthur, *Cagney & Lacey,* CBS	Georg Stanford Brown, *Cagney & Lacey,* CBS	Gregory Hoblit, *L.A. Law,* NBC
Writer—Drama Series	Patricia M. Green, *Cagney & Lacey,* CBS	Tom Fontana, John Tinker, and John Masius, *St. Elsewhere,* NBC	Steven Bochco, Terry Louise Fisher, *L.A. Law,* NBC
Comedy	*The Cosby Show,* NBC	*The Golden Girls,* NBC	*The Golden Girls,* NBC
Actor—Comedy Series	Robert Guillaume, *Benson,* ABC	Michael J. Fox, *Family Ties,* NBC	Michael J. Fox, *Family Ties,* NBC
Actress—Comedy Series	Jane Curtin, *Kate & Allie,* CBS	Betty White, *The Golden Girls,* NBC	Rue McClanahan, *The Golden Girls,* NBC
Supporting Actor—Comedy Series	John Larroquette, *Night Court,* NBC	John Larroquette, *Night Court,* NBC	John Larroquette, *Night Court,* NBC
Supporting Actress—Comedy Series	Rhea Perlman, *Cheers,* NBC	Rhea Perlman, *Cheers,* NBC	Jackée Harry, *227,* NBC
Director—Comedy Series	Jay Sandrich, *The Cosby Show,* NBC	Jay Sandrich, *The Cosby Show,* NBC	Terry Hughes, *The Golden Girls,* NBC
Writer—Comedy Series	Ed. Weinberger, Michael Leeson, *The Cosby Show,* NBC	Barry Fanaro and Mort Nathan, *The Golden Girls,* NBC	Gary David Goldberg, Alan Uger, *Family Ties,* NBC
Drama/Comedy Special	*Do You Remember Love,* CBS	*Love Is Never Silent,* NBC	*Promise,* CBS
Variety, Music, or Comedy Program	*Motown Returns to the Apollo,* NBC	*The Kennedy Center Honors: A Celebration of the Performing Arts,* CBS	*The 1987 Tony Awards,* CBS
Individual Performance—Variety or Music Program	George Hearn, *Sweeney Todd,* PBS	Whitney Houston, *The 28th Annual Grammy Awards,* CBS	Robin Williams, *A Carol Burnett Special: Carol, Carl, Whoopi & Robin,* ABC
Director—Variety or Music	Terry Hughes, *Sweeney Todd,* PBS	Waris Hussein, *Copacabana,* CBS	Don Mischer, *The Kennedy Center Honors: A Celebration of the Performing Arts,* CBS
Writer—Variety or Music	Gerard Mulligan, Sandy Frank, Joe Toplyn, Chris Elliott, Matt Wickline, Jeff Martin, Eddie Gorodetsky, Randy Cohen, Larry Jacobson, Kevin Curran, Fred Graver, Merrill Markoe, and David Letterman, *Late Night with David Letterman,* NBC	David Letterman, Steve O'Donnell, Sandy Frank, Joe Toplyn, Chris Elliott, Matt Wickline, Jeff Martin, Gerard Mulligan, Randy Cohen, Larry Jacobson, Kevin Curran, Fred Graver, and Merrill Markoe, *Late Night with David Letterman,* NBC	Steve O'Donnell, Sandy Frank, Joe Toplyn, Chris Elliott, Matt Wickline, Jeff Martin, Gerard Mulligan, Randy Cohen, Larry Jacobson, Kevin Curran, Fred Graver, Adam Resnick, and David Letterman, *Late Night with David Letterman,* NBC

	1984–85	1985–86	1986–87
Miniseries	The Jewel in the Crown, PBS	Peter the Great, NBC	A Year in the Life, NBC
Actor—Miniseries	Richard Crenna, The Rape of Richard Beck, ABC	Dustin Hoffman, Death of a Salesman, CBS	James Woods, Promise, CBS
Actress—Miniseries	Joanne Woodward, Do You Remember Love, CBS	Marlo Thomas, Nobody's Child, CBS	Gena Rowlands, The Betty Ford Story, ABC
Supporting Actor—Miniseries or Special	Karl Malden, Fatal Vision, NBC	John Malkovich, Death of a Salesman, CBS	Dabney Coleman, Sworn to Silence, ABC
Supporting Actress—Miniseries/ Limited Series or Special	Kim Stanley, Cat on a Hot Tin Roof, PBS	Colleen Dewhurst, Between Two Women, ABC	Piper Laurie, Promise, CBS
Director—Miniseries or Special	Lamont Johnson, Wallenberg: A Hero's Story, NBC	Joseph Sargent, Love Is Never Silent, NBC	Glenn Jordan, Promise, CBS
Writer—Miniseries or Special	Vickie Patik, Do You Remember Love, CBS	Ron Cowen and Daniel Lipman (Teleplay); Sherman Yellen (Story), An Early Frost, NBC	Richard Friedenberg (Teleplay); Kenneth Blackwell, Tennyson Flowers, and Richard Frieden- berg (Story), Promise, CBS
Daytime Drama Series	The Young and the Restless, CBS	The Young and the Restless, CBS	As the World Turns, CBS
Actor—Daytime Drama Series	Darnell Williams, All My Children, ABC	David Canary, All My Children, ABC	Larry Bryggman, As the World Turns, CBS
Actress—Daytime Drama Series	Kim Zimmer, Guiding Light, CBS	Erika Slezak, One Life To Live, ABC	Kim Zimmer, Guiding Light, CBS
Supporting Actor—Daytime Drama Series	Larry Gates, Guiding Light, CBS	John Wesley Shipp, As the World Turns, CBS	Gregg Marx, As the World Turns, CBS
Supporting Actress—Daytime Drama Series	Beth Maitland, The Young and the Restless, CBS	Leann Hunley, Days of Our Lives, NBC	Kathleen Noone, All My Children, ABC
Ingenue— Daytime Drama Series	Tracey E. Bregman, The Young and the Restless, CBS	Ellen Wheeler, Another World, NBC	Martha Byrne, As the World Turns, CBS
Younger Leading Man— Daytime Drama Series	Brian Bloom, As the World Turns, CBS	Michael E. Knight, All My Children, ABC	Michael E. Knight, All My Children, ABC
Host—Game Show	Dick Clark, The $25,000 Pyramid, CBS	Dick Clark, The $25,000 Pyramid, CBS	Bob Barker, The Price Is Right, CBS
Host—Talk or Service	Phil Donahue, Donahue, SYN	Phil Donahue, Donahue, SYN	Oprah Winfrey, The Oprah Winfrey Show, SYN
Game Show	The $25,000 Pyramid, CBS	The $25,000 Pyramid, CBS	The $25,000 Pyramid, CBS
Talk, Service or Variety Series	Donahue, SYN	Donahue, SYN	The Oprah Winfrey Show, SYN
Children's Special	Displaced Person, PBS	Anne of Green Gables, PBS	Jim Henson's The Storyteller: Hans My Hedgehog, NBC
Children's Series	Sesame Street, PBS	Sesame Street, PBS	Sesame Street, PBS

	1987–88	**1988–89**	**1989–90**
Drama	*thirtysomething*, ABC	*L.A. Law*, NBC	*L.A. Law*, NBC
Actor—Drama Series	Richard Kiley, *A Year in the Life*, NBC	Carroll O'Connor, *In the Heat of the Night*, NBC	Peter Falk, *Columbo*, ABC
Actress—Drama Series	Tyne Daly, *Cagney & Lacey*, CBS	Dana Delany, *China Beach*, ABC	Patricia Wettig, *thirtysomething*, ABC
Supporting Actor—Drama Series	Larry Drake, *L.A. Law*, NBC	Larry Drake, *L.A. Law*, NBC	Jimmy Smits, *L.A. Law*, NBC
Supporting Actress—Drama Series	Patricia Wettig, *thirtysomething*, ABC	Melanie Mayron, *thirtysomething*, ABC	Marg Helgenberger, *China Beach*, ABC
Director—Drama Series	Mark Tinker, *St. Elsewhere*, NBC	Robert Altman, *Tanner '88*, HBO	Thomas Carter, *Equal Justice*, ABC; Scott Winant, *thirtysomething*, ABC
Writer—Drama Series	Paul Haggis, Marshall Herskovitz, *thirtysomething*, ABC	Joseph Dougherty, *thirtysomething*, ABC	David E. Kelley, *L.A. Law*, NBC
Comedy	*The Wonder Years*, ABC	*Cheers*, NBC	*Murphy Brown*, CBS
Actor—Comedy Series	Michael J. Fox, *Family Ties*, NBC	Richard Mulligan, *Empty Nest*, NBC	Ted Danson, *Cheers*, NBC
Actress—Comedy Series	Beatrice Arthur, *The Golden Girls*, NBC	Candice Bergen, *Murphy Brown*, CBS	Candice Bergen, *Murphy Brown*, CBS
Supporting Actor—Comedy Series	John Larroquette, *Night Court*, NBC	Woody Harrelson, *Cheers*, NBC	Alex Rocco, *The Famous Teddy Z*, CBS
Supporting Actress—Comedy Series	Estelle Getty, *The Golden Girls*, NBC	Rhea Perlman, *Cheers*, NBC	Bebe Neuwirth, *Cheers*, NBC
Director—Comedy Series	Gregory Hoblit, *Hooperman*, ABC	Peter Baldwin, *The Wonder Years*, ABC	Michael Dinner, *The Wonder Years*, ABC
Writer—Comedy Series	Hugh Wilson, *Frank's Place*, CBS	Diane English, *Murphy Brown*, CBS	Bob Brush, *The Wonder Years*, ABC
Drama/Comedy Special	*Inherit the Wind*, NBC	*Day One*, CBS	*Caroline?*, CBS; *The Incident*, CBS
Variety, Music, or Comedy Program	*Irving Berlin's 100th Birthday Celebration*, CBS	*The Tracey Ullman Show*, FOX	*In Living Color*, FOX
Individual Performance—Variety or Music Program	Robin Williams, *ABC Presents a Royal Gala*, ABC	Linda Ronstadt, *Canciones de Mi Padre*, PBS	Tracey Ullman, *The Best of the Tracey Ullman Show*, FOX
Director—Variety or Music	Patricia Birch and Humphrey Burton, *Celebrating Gershwin*, PBS	Jim Henson, *The Jim Henson Hour*, NBC	Dwight Hemion, *The Kennedy Center Honors: A Celebration of the Performing Arts*, CBS

	1987–88	**1988–89**	**1989–90**
Writer—Variety or Music	Jackie Mason, *Jackie Mason on Broadway*, HBO	James Downey, head writer; John Bowman, A. Whitney Brown, Gregory Daniels, Tom Davis, Al Franken, Shannon Gaughan, Jack Handey, Phil Hartman, Lorne Michaels, Mike Myers, Conan O'Brien, Bob Odenkirk, Herb Sargent, Tom Schiller, Robert Smigel, Bonnie Turner, Terry Turner, and Christine Zander, writers; George Meyer, additional sketches, *Saturday Night Live*, NBC	Billy Crystal, *Billy Crystal: Midnight Train to Moscow*, HBO; James L. Brooks, Heide Perlman, Sam Simon, Jerry Belson, Marc Flanagan, Dinah Kirgo, Jay Kogen, Wallace Wolodarsky, Ian Praiser, Marilyn Suzanne Miller, and Tracey Ullman, *The Tracey Ullman Show*, FOX
Miniseries	*The Murder of Mary Phagan*, NBC	*War and Remembrance*, ABC	*Drug Wars: The Camarena Story*, NBC
Actor—Miniseries or Special	Jason Robards, *Inherit the Wind*, NBC	James Woods, *My Name is Bill W.*, ABC	Hume Cronyn, *Age-Old Friends*, HBO
Actress—Miniseries or Special	Jessica Tandy, *Foxfire*, CBS	Holly Hunter, *Roe vs. Wade*, NBC	Barbara Hershey, *A Killing in a Small Town*, NBC
Supporting Actor—Miniseries or Special	John Shea, *Baby M*, ABC	Derek Jacobi, *The Tenth Man*, CBS	Vincent Gardenia, *Age-Old Friends*, HBO
Supporting Actress—Miniseries or Special	Jane Seymour, *Onassis: The Richest Man in the World*, ABC	Colleen Dewhurst, *Those She Left Behind*, NBC	Eva Marie Saint, *People Like Us*, NBC
Director—Miniseries or Special	Lamont Johnson, *Gore Vidal's Lincoln*, NBC	Simon Wincer, *Lonesome Dove*, CBS	Joseph Sargent, *Caroline?*, CBS
Writer—Miniseries or Special	William Hanley, *The Attic: The Hiding of Anne Frank*, CBS	Abby Mann, Robin Vote, and Ron Hutchison, *Murderers Among Us: The Simon Wiesenthal Story*, HBO	Terrence McNally, *Andre's Mother*, PBS
Daytime Drama Series	*Santa Barbara*, NBC	*Santa Barbara*, NBC	*Santa Barbara*, NBC
Actor—Daytime Drama Series	David Canary, *All My Children*, ABC	David Canary, *All My Children*, ABC	A Martinez, *Santa Barbara*, NBC
Actress—Daytime Drama Series	Helen Gallagher, *Ryan's Hope*, ABC	Marcy Walker, *Santa Barbara*, NBC	Kim Zimmer, *Guiding Light*, CBS
Supp. Actor—Daytime Drama	Justin Deas, *Santa Barbara*, NBC	Justin Deas, *Santa Barbara*, NBC	Henry Darrow, *Santa Barbara*, NBC
Supporting Actress—Daytime Drama Series	Ellen Wheeler, *All My Children*, ABC	Debbi Morgan, *All My Children*, ABC; Nancy Lee Grahn, *Santa Barbara*, NBC	Julia Barr, *All My Children*, ABC
Ingenue—Daytime Drama Series	Julianne Moore, *As the World Turns*, CBS	Kimberly McCullough, *General Hospital*, ABC	Cady McClain, *All My Children*, ABC
Younger Leading Man—Daytime Drama Series	Billy Warlock, *Days of Our Lives*, NBC	Justin Gocke, *Santa Barbara*, NBC	Andrew Kavovit, *As the World Turns*, CBS
Host—Game Show	Bob Barker, *The Price Is Right*, CBS	Alex Trebek, *Jeopardy!*, SYN	Alex Trebek, *Jeopardy!*, SYN; Bob Barker, *The Price Is Right*, CBS
Host—Talk or Service Show	Phil Donahue, *Donahue*, SYN	Sally Jessy Raphael, *Sally Jessy Raphael*, SYN	Joan Rivers, *The Joan Rivers Show*, SYN
Game Show	*The Price Is Right*, CBS	*The $25,000 Pyramid*, CBS	*Jeopardy!*, SYN
Talk, Service, or Variety Series	*The Oprah Winfrey Show*, SYN	*The Oprah Winfrey Show*, SYN	*Sally Jessy Raphael*, SYN
Children's Special	*The Secret Garden*, CBS	*Free To Be...A Family*, ABC	*A Mother's Courage: The Mary Thomas Story*, NBC
Children's Series	*Sesame Street*, PBS	*Newton's Apple*, PBS	*Reading Rainbow*, PBS

	1990–91	1991–92	1992–93
Drama	*L.A. Law*, NBC	*Northern Exposure*, CBS	*Picket Fences*, CBS
Actor—Drama Series	James Earl Jones, *Gabriel's Fire*, ABC	Christopher Lloyd, *Avonlea*, DIS	Tom Skerritt, *Picket Fences*, CBS
Actress—Drama Series	Patricia Wettig, *thirtysomething*, ABC	Dana Delany, *China Beach*, ABC	Kathy Baker, *Picket Fences*, CBS
Supporting Actor—Drama Series	Timothy Busfield, *thirtysomething*, ABC	Richard Dysart, *L.A. Law*, NBC	Chad Lowe, *Life Goes On*, ABC
Supporting Actress—Drama Series	Madge Sinclair, *Gabriel's Fire*, ABC	Valerie Mahaffey, *Northern Exposure*, CBS	Mary Alice, *I'll Fly Away*, NBC
Director—Drama Series	Thomas Carter, *Equal Justice*, ABC	Eric Laneuville, *I'll Fly Away*, NBC	Barry Levinson, *Homicide—Life on the Street*, NBC
Writer—Drama Series	David E. Kelley, *L.A. Law*, NBC	Andrew Schneider and Diane Frolov, *Northern Exposure*, CBS	Tom Fontana, *Homicide—Life on the Street*, NBC
Comedy	*Cheers*, NBC	*Murphy Brown*, CBS	*Seinfeld*, NBC
Actor—Comedy Series	Burt Reynolds, *Evening Shade*, CBS	Craig T. Nelson, *Coach*, ABC	Ted Danson, *Cheers*, NBC
Actress—Comedy Series	Kirstie Alley, *Cheers*, NBC	Candice Bergen, *Murphy Brown*, CBS	Roseanne Arnold, *Roseanne*, ABC
Supporting Actor—Comedy Series	Jonathan Winters, *Davis Rules*, ABC	Michael Jeter, *Evening Shade*, CBS	Michael Richards, *Seinfeld*, NBC
Supp. Actress—Comedy Series	Bebe Neuwirth, *Cheers*, NBC	Laurie Metcalf, *Roseanne*, ABC	Laurie Metcalf, *Roseanne*, ABC
Director—Comedy Series	James Burrows, *Cheers*, NBC	Barnet Kellman, *Murphy Brown*, CBS	Betty Thomas, *Dream On*, HBO
Writer—Comedy Series	Gary Dontzig and Steven Peterman, *Murphy Brown*, CBS	Elaine Pope and Larry Charles, *Seinfeld*, NBC	Larry David, *Seinfeld*, NBC
Variety, Music, or Comedy Program	*The 63rd Annual Academy Awards*, ABC	*The Tonight Show Starring Johnny Carson*, NBC	*Saturday Night Live*, NBC
Individual Performance—Variety or Music Program	Billy Crystal, *The 63rd Annual Academy Awards*, ABC	Bette Midler, *The Tonight Show Starring Johnny Carson*, NBC	Dana Carvey, *Saturday Night Live*, NBC
Director—Variety or Music	Hal Gurnee, *Late Night with David Letterman*, NBC	Patricia Birch, *Unforgettable with Love: Natalie Cole Sings the Songs of Nat King Cole*, PBS	Walter C. Miller, *The 1992 Tony Awards*, CBS
Writer—Variety or Music	Hal Kanter and Buz Kohan, writers; Billy Crystal, David Steinberg, Bruce Vilanch, and Robert Wuhl (Special Material), *The 63rd Annual Academy Awards*, ABC	Hal Kanter and Buz Kohan, writers); Billy Crystal, Marc Shaiman, David Steinberg, Robert Wuhl, and Bruce Vilanch, special material, *The 64rd Annual Academy Awards*, ABC	Judd Apatow, Robert Cohen, David Cross, Brent Forrester, Jeff Kahn, Bruce Kirschbaum, Bob Odenkirk, Sultan Pepper, Dino Stamatopoulos, and Ben Stiller, *The Ben Stiller Show*, FOX
Made for Television Movie	—	*Miss Rose White*, Hallmark Hall of Fame, NBC	*Barbarians at the Gate*, HBO; *Stalin*, HBO
Miniseries	*Separate but Equal*, ABC	*A Woman Named Jackie*, NBC	*Prime Suspect 2*, PBS

	1990–91	1991–92	1992–93
Actor—Miniseries or Special	John Gielgud, *Summer's Lease*, PBS	Beau Bridges, *Without Warning: The James Brady Story*, HBO	Robert Morse, *Tru*, PBS
Actress—Miniseries or Special	Lynn Whitfield, *The Josephine Baker Story*, HBO	Gena Rowlands, *Face of a Stranger*, CBS	Holly Hunter, *The Positively True Adventures of the Alleged Texas Cheerleader-Murdering Mom*, HBO
Supporting Actor—Miniseries or Special	James Earl Jones, *Heat Wave*, TNT	Hume Cronyn, *Neil Simon's Broadway Bound*, ABC	Beau Bridges, *The Positively True Adventures of the Alleged Texas Cheerleader-Murdering Mom*, HBO
Supporting Actress—Miniseries or Special	Ruby Dee, *Decoration Day*, NBC	Amanda Plummer, *Miss Rose White*, NBC	Mary Tyler Moore, *Stolen Babies*, LIF
Director—Miniseries or Special	Brian Gibson, *The Josephine Baker Story*, HBO	Daniel Petrie, *Mark Twain and Me*, DIS	James Sadwith, *Sinatra*, CBS
Writer—Miniseries or Special	Andrew Davies, *House of Cards*, PBS	John Falsey and Joshua Brand, *I'll Fly Away*, NBC	Jane Anderson, *The Positively True Adventures of the Alleged Texas Cheerleader-Murdering Mom*, HBO
Daytime Drama Series	*As the World Turns*, CBS	*All My Children*, ABC	*The Young and the Restless*, CBS
Actor—Daytime Drama Series	Peter Bergman, *The Young and the Restless*, CBS	Peter Bergman, *The Young and the Restless*, CBS	David Canary, *All My Children*, ABC
Actress—Daytime Drama Series	Finola Hughes, *General Hospital*, ABC	Erika Slezak, *One Life to Live*, ABC	Linda Dano, *Another World*, NBC
Supporting Actor—Daytime Drama Series	Bernie Barrow, *Loving*, ABC	Thom Christopher, *One Life to Live*, ABC	Gerald Anthony, *General Hospital*, ABC
Supporting Actress—Daytime Drama Series	Jess Walton, *The Young and the Restless*, CBS	Maeve Kinkead, *Guiding Light*, CBS	Ellen Parker, *Guiding Light*, CBS
Younger Actress—Daytime Drama Series	Anne Heche, *Another World*, NBC	Tricia Cast, *The Young and the Restless*, CBS	Heather Tom, *The-Young and the Restless*, CBS
Younger Leading Man—Daytime Drama Series	Rick Hearst, *Guiding Light*, CBS	Kristoff St. John, *The Young and the Restless*, CBS	Monti Sharp, *Guiding Light*, CBS
Host—Game Show	Bob Barker, *The Price Is Right*, CBS	Bob Barker, *The Price Is Right*, CBS	Pat Sajak, *Wheel of Fortune*, SYN
Host—Talk or Service Show	Oprah Winfrey, *The Oprah Winfrey Show*, SYN	Oprah Winfrey, *The Oprah Winfrey Show*, SYN	Oprah Winfrey, *The Oprah Winfrey Show*, SYN
Game Show	*Jeopardy!*, SYN	*Jeopardy!*, SYN	*Jeopardy!*, SYN
Talk, Service, or Variety Series	*The Oprah Winfrey Show*, SYN	*The Oprah Winfrey Show*, SYN	*Good Morning America*, ABC
Children's Special	*You Can't Grow Home Again: A 3-2-1 Contact Extra*, PBS	*Mark Twain and Me*, DIS	*Shades of a Single Protein*, ABC
Children's Series	*Sesame Street*, PBS	*Sesame Street*, PBS	*Reading Rainbow*, PBS; *Tiny Toon Adventures*, SYN (Animated)

	1993-94	1994-95	1995-96
Drama	*Picket Fences*, CBS	*NYPD Blue*, ABC	*ER*, NBC
Actor—Drama Series	Dennis Franz, *NYPD Blue*, ABC	Mandy Patinkin, *Chicago Hope*, CBS	Dennis Franz, *NYPD Blue*, ABC
Actress—Drama Series	Sela Ward, *Sisters*, NBC	Kathy Baker, *Picket Fences*, CBS	Kathy Baker, *Picket Fences*, CBS
Supporting Actor—Drama Series	Fyvush Finkel, *Picket Fences*, CBS	Ray Walston, *Picket Fences*, CBS	Ray Walston, *Picket Fences*, CBS
Supporting Actress—Drama Series	Leigh Taylor-Young, *Picket Fences*, CBS	Julianna Margulies, *ER*, NBC	Tyne Daly, *Christy*, CBS
Director—Drama Series	Daniel Sackheim, *NYPD Blue*, ABC	Mimi Leder, *ER*, NBC	Jeremy Kagan, *Chicago Hope*, CBS
Writer—Drama Series	Ann Biderman, *NYPD Blue*, ABC	Michael Crichton, *ER*, NBC	Darin Morgan, *The X-Files*, Fox
Comedy	*Frasier*, NBC	*Frasier*, NBC	*Frasier*, NBC
Actor—Comedy Series	Kelsey Grammer, *Frasier*, NBC	Kelsey Grammer, *Frasier*, NBC	John Lithgow, *3rd Rock from the Sun*, NBC
Actress—Comedy Series	Candice Bergen, *Murphy Brown*, CBS	Candice Bergen, *Murphy Brown*, CBS	Helen Hunt, *Mad About You*, NBC
Supporting Actor—Comedy Series	Michael Richards, *Seinfeld*, NBC	David Hyde Pierce, *Frasier*, NBC	Rip Torn, *The Larry Sanders Show*, HBO
Supp. Actress—Comedy Series	Laurie Metcalf, *Roseanne*, ABC	Christine Baranski, *Cybill*, CBS	Julia Louis-Dreyfuss, *Seinfeld*, NBC
Director—Comedy Series	James Burrows, *Frasier*, NBC	David Lee, *Frasier*, NBC	Michael Lembeck, *Friends*, NBC
Writer—Comedy Series	David Angel, Peter Casey, and David Lee, *Frasier*, NBC	Chuck Ranberg, Anne Flett-Giordano, *Frasier*, NBC	Joe Keenan, Christopher Lloyd, Rob Greenberg, Jack Burditt, Chuck Ranberg, Anne Flett-Giordano, Linda Morris, and Vic Rauseo, *Frasier*, NBC
Variety, Music, or Comedy Program	*Late Show With David Letterman*, CBS	*The Tonight Show with Jay Leno*, NBC	*Dennis Miller Live*, HBO
Individual Performance—Variety or Music Program	Tracey Ullman, *Tracey Ullman Takes On New York*, HBO	Barbra Streisand, *Barbra Streisand: The Concert*, HBO	Tony Bennett, *Tony Bennett Live by Request: A Valentine Special*, A&E
Director—Variety or Music	Walter C. Miller, *The Tony Awards*, CBS	Jeff Margolis, *The 67th Annual Academy Awards*, ABC	Louis J. Horvitz, *The Kennedy Center Honors*, CBS
Writer—Variety or Music	Jeff Cesario, Mike Dugan, Eddie Feldmann, Gregory Greenberg, Dennis Miller, Kevin Rooney, *Dennis Miller Live*, HBO	Jeff Cesario, Ed Driscoll, David Feldman, Eddie Feldmann, Gregory Greenberg, Dennis Miller, Kevin Rooney, *Dennis Miller Live*, HBO	Eddie Feldmann, David Feldmann, Mike Gandolfini, Tom Hertz, Leah Krinsky, Dennis Miller, Rick Overton, *Dennis Miller Live*, HBO
Made for Television Movie	*And the Band Played On*, HBO	*Indictment: The McMartin Trial*, HBO	*Truman*, HBO
Miniseries	*Mystery: Prime Suspect 3*, PBS	*Joseph*, TNT	*Gulliver's Travels*, NBC

	1993-94	1994-95	1995-96
Actor—Miniseries or Special	Hume Cronyn, *Hallmark Hall of Fame: To Dance With the White Dog*, CBS	Raul Julia, *The Burning Season*, HBO	Alan Rickman, *Rasputin*, HBO
Actress—Miniseries or Special	Kirstie Alley, *David's Mother*, CBS	Glenn Close, *Serving in Silence: The Margarethe Cammemeyer Story*, NBC	Helen Mirren, *Prime Suspect: Scent of Darkness*, PBS
Supporting Actor—Miniseries or Special	Michael Goorjian, *David's Mother*, CBS	Donald Sutherland, *Citizen X*, HBO	Tom Hulce, *The Heidi Chronicles*, TNT
Supporting Actress—Miniseries or Special	Cicely Tyson, *Oldest Living Confederate Widow Tells All*, CBS	Judy Davis, *Serving in Silence: The Margarethe Cammemeyer Story*, NBC	Greta Scacchi, *Rasputin*, HBO
Director—Miniseries or Special	John Frankenheimer, *Against the Wall*, HBO	John Frankenheimer, *The Burning Season*, HBO	John Frankenheimer, *Andersonville*, TNT
Writer—Miniseries or Special	Bob Randall, *David's Mother*, CBS	Alison Cross, *Serving in Silence: The Margarethe Cammermeyer Story*, NBC	Simon Moore, *Gulliver's Travels*, NBC
Daytime Drama Series	*All My Children*, ABC	*General Hospital*, ABC	*General Hospital*, ABC
Actor—Daytime Drama Series	Michael Zaslow, *Guiding Light*, CBS	Justin Deas, *Guiding Light*, CBS	Charles Keating, *Another World*, NBC
Actress—Daytime Drama Series	Hillary B. Smith, *One Life to Live*, ABC	Erika Slezak, *One Life to Live*, ABC	Erika Slezak, *One Life to Live*, ABC
Supporting Actor—Daytime Drama Series	Justin Deas, *Guiding Light*, CBS	Jerry Ver Dorn, *Guiding Light*, CBS	Jerry Ver Dorn, *Guiding Light*, CBS
Supporting Actress—Daytime Drama Series	Susan Haskell, *One Life to Live*, ABC	Rena Sofer, *General Hospital*, ABC	Anna Holbrook, *Another World*, NBC
Younger Actress—Daytime Drama Series	Melissa Hayden, *Guiding Light*, CBS	Sarah Michelle Gellar, *All My Children*, ABC	Kimberly McCullough, *General Hospital*, ABC
Younger Leading Man—Daytime Drama Series	Roger Howarth, *One Life to Live*, ABC	Jonathan Jackson, *General Hospital*, ABC	Kevin Mambo, *Guiding Light*, CBS
Host—Talk or Service Show	Oprah Winfrey, *The Oprah Winfrey Show*, SYN	Oprah Winfrey, *The Oprah Winfrey Show*, SYN	Montel Williams, *The Montel Williams Show*, SYN
Game Show	*Jeopardy!*, SYN	*Jeopardy!*, SYN	*The Price Is Right*, CBS
Talk, Service, or Variety Series	*The Oprah Winfrey Show*, SYN-	*The Oprah Winfrey Show*, SYN	*The Oprah Winfrey Show*, SYN
Children's Special	*Dead Drunk: The Kevin Tunell Story*, HBO	*A Child Betrayed: The Calvin Mire Story*, HBO	*Stand Up*, CBS
Children's Series	*Sesame Street*, PBS; *Rugrats*, Nick (Animated)	*Nick News*, Nickelodeon; *Where on Earth is Carmen San Diego?*, Fox (Animated)	*Sesame Street*, PBS; *Animaniacs*, WB (Animated)

	1996-97	**1997-98**	**1998-99**
Drama	*Law & Order,* NBC	*The Practice,* ABC	*The Practice,* ABC
Actor—Drama Series	Dennis Franz, *NYPD Blue,* ABC	Andre Braugher, *Homicide: Life on the Street,* NBC	Dennis Franz, *NYPD Blue,* ABC
Actress—Drama Series	Gillian Anderson, *The X-Files,* Fox	Christine Lahti, *Chicago Hope,* CBS	Edie Falco, *The Sopranos,* HBO
Supporting Actor—Drama Series	Hector Elizondo, *Chicago Hope,* CBS	Gordon Clapp, *NYPD Blue,* ABC	Michael Badalucco, *The Practice,* ABC
Supporting Actress—Drama Series	Kim Delaney, *NYPD Blue,* ABC	Camryn Manheim, *The Practice,* ABC	Holland Taylor, *The Practice,* ABC
Director—Drama Series	Mark Tinker, *NYPD Blue,* ABC	Mark Tinker, *Brooklyn South,* CBS and Paris Barclay, *NYPD Blue,* ABC	Paris Barclay, *NYPD Blue,* ABC
Writer—Drama Series	David Milch, Stephen Gaghan, Michael R. Perry, *NYPD Blue,* ABC	Bill Clark, Nicholas Wooton, David Milch, *NYPD Blue,* ABC	James Manos, Jr., David Chase, *The Sopranos,* HBO
Comedy	*Frasier,* NBC	*Frasier,* NBC	*Ally McBeal,* FOX
Actor—Comedy Series	John Lithgow, *3rd Rock from the Sun,* NBC	Kelsey Grammer, *Frasier,* NBC	John Lithgow, *3rd Rock from the Sun,* NBC,
Actress—Comedy Series	Helen Hunt, *Mad About You,* NBC	Helen Hunt, *Mad About You,* NBC	Helen Hunt, *Mad About You,* NBC
Supporting Actor—Comedy Series	Michael Richards, *Seinfeld,* NBC	David Hyde Pierce, *Frasier,* NBC	David Hyde Pierce, *Frasier,* NBC
Supporting Actress—Comedy Series	Kristen Johnston, *3rd Rock from the Sun,* NBC	Lisa Kudrow, *Friends,* NBC	Kristen Johnston, *3rd Rock from the Sun,* NBC
Director—Comedy Series	David Lee, *Frasier,* NBC	Todd Holland, *The Larry Sanders Show,* HBO	Thomas Schlamme, *Will & Grace,* NBC
Writer—Comedy Series	Ellen DeGeneres, Mark Driscoll, Dava Savel, Tracy Newman, and Jonathan Stark, *Ellen,* ABC	Peter Tolan, Garry Shandling, *The Larry Sanders Show,* HBO	Jay Kogen, *Frasier,* NBC
Variety, Music, or Comedy Program	*Tracey Takes On...,* HBO (series) *Chris Rock: Bring the Pain,* HBO (special)	*Late Show with David Letterman,* CBS (series); *The 1997 Tony Awards* (special)	*Late Show With David Letterman,* CBS (series); *1998 Tony Awards,* CBS (special)
Individual Performance—Variety or Music Program	Bette Midler, *Bette Midler: Diva Las Vegas,* HBO	Billy Crystal, *The 70th Annual Academy Awards,* ABC	*John Leguizamo's Freak,* HBO,
Director—Variety or Music	Don Mischer, *Centennial Olympic Games, Opening Ceremonies,* NBC	Louis J. Horvitz, *The 70th Annual Academy Awards,* ABC	Paul Miller, *1998 Tony Awards,* CBS,
Writer—Variety or Music	Chris Rock, *Chris Rock: Bring the Pain,* HBO	Eddie Feldmann, Dennis Miller, David Feldman, Leah Krinsky, Jim Hanna, David Weiss, and Jose Arroyo, *Dennis Miller Live,* HBO	Tom Agna, Vernon Chatman, Louis CK, Lance Crouther, Gregory Greenberg, Ali LeRoi, Steve O'Donnell, Chris Rock, Frank Sebastiano, Chuck Sklar, Jeff Stilson, Wanda Sykes-Hall, Mike Upchurch, *The Chris Rock Show,* HBO
Made for Television Movie	*Miss Evers' Boys,* HBO	*Don King: Only in America,* HBO	*A Lesson Before Dying,* HBO
Miniseries	*Prime Suspect 5: Errors of Judgment,* PBS	*From the Earth to the Moon,* HBO	*Horatio Hornblower,* A&E

	1996-97	1997-98	1998-99
Actor—Miniseries or Special	Armand Assante, *Gotti*, HBO	Gary Sinise, *George Wallace*, TNT	Stanley Tucci, *Winchell*, HBO
Actress—Miniseries or Special	Alfre Woodard, *Miss Evers' Boys*, HBO	Ellen Barkin, *Before Women Had Wings*, ABC	Helen Mirren, *The Passion Of Ayn Rand*, SHO
Supporting Actor—Miniseries or Special	Beau Bridges, *The Second Civil War*, HBO	George C. Scott, *12 Angry Men*, SHO	Peter O'Toole, *Joan Of Arc*, CBS,
Supporting Actress—Miniseries or Special	Diana Rigg, *Rebecca*, PBS	Mare Winningham, *George Wallace*, TNT	Anne Bancroft, *Deep In My Heart*, CBS
Director—Miniseries or Special	Andrei Konchalovsky, *The Odyssey, Parts I and II*, NBC	John Frankenheimer, *George Wallace*, TNT	Allan Arkush, *The Temptations*, NBC
Writer—Miniseries or Special	Horton Foote, *William Faulkner's Old Man*, CBS	Kario Salem, *Don King: Only in America*, HBO	Ann Peacock, *A Lesson Before Dying*, HBO
Daytime Drama Series	*General Hospital*, ABC	*All My Children*, ABC	*General Hospital*, ABC
Actor—Daytime Drama Series	Justin Deas, *Guiding Light*, CBS	Eric Braeden, *The Young and the Restless*, CBS	Anthony Geary, *General Hospital*, ABC
Actress—Daytime Drama Series	Jess Walton, *The Young and the Restless*, CBS	Cynthia Watros, *Guiding Light*	Susan Lucci, *All My Children*, ABC
Supporting Actor—Daytime Drama Series	Ian Buchanan, *The Bold and the Beautiful*, CBS	Steve Burton, *General Hospital*, ABC	Stuart Damon, *General Hospital*, ABC
Supporting Actress—Daytime Drama Series	Michelle Stafford, *The Young and the Restless*, CBS	Julia Barr, *All My Children*, ABC	Sharon Case, *The Young and the Restless*, CBS
Younger Actress—Daytime Drama Series	Sarah Brown, *General Hospital*, ABC	Sarah Brown, *General Hospital*, ABC	Heather Tom, *The Young and the Restless*, CBS
Younger Leading Man—Daytime Drama Series	Kevin Mambo, *Guiding Light*, CBS	Jonathan Jackson, *General Hospital*, ABC	Jonathan Jackson, *General Hospital*, ABC
Talk Show Host	Rosie O'Donnell, *The Rosie O'Donnell Show*, SYN	Rosie O'Donnell, *The Rosie O'Donnell Show*, SYN; and Oprah Winfrey, *The Oprah Winfrey Show*, SYN (tie)	Rosie O'Donnell, *The Rosie O'Donnell Show*, SYN
Game Show	*The Price Is Right*, CBS	*Jeopardy!*, SYN	*Win Ben Stein's Money*, COM
Talk Show	*The Oprah Winfrey Show*, SYN	*The Rosie O'Donnell Show*, SYN	*The Rosie O'Donnell Show*, SYN
Children's Series	*Reading Rainbow*, PBS; *Animaniacs*, WB (Animated)	*Sesame Street*, PBS	*Sesame Street*, PBS (pre-school); *Disney Presents "Bill Nye The Science Guy,"* SYN

PICKS & PANS 1999

The loudest sounds from the world of pop music concern cute boys, girl power, and MP3, but the PEOPLE playlist is brimming with a far greater variety of sounds to download or disregard. Asterisks denote our reviewers' "pick of the week" selections during the year.

TWENTIETH CENTURY
Alabama

Don't expect anything revolutionary. Here Alabama gives more of the same, and their fans will thank them for it.

TAL BACHMAN
Tal Bachman

Multi-instrumentalist singer-songwriter son of guitar hero Randy (the Guess Who; Bachman-Turner Overdrive) eschews Dad's heavy metal for an appealing pop sound on this debut.

MILLENNIUM
Backstreet Boys

A schmaltzy collection of yearning ballads and formulaic dance numbers, much of this album sounds like an updated, techno-kissed copy of a New Kids on the Block CD. But at least these lads can sing—their vocal interplay creates harmonic magic as their voices soar and intertwine.

I'VE GOT A RIGHT TO CRY
Mandy Barnett

Nashville finds its newest diva. Barnett, with her hearty, bluesy voice and blend of sensuality and natural musicality, is equally comfortable with swing music, ballads, and old standards.

A DAY IN THE LIFE
Eric Benét

Benét shoots for a broader audience with songs that look at the spiritual side of love instead of simply its sweaty sexuality. Thanks to his inviting rich tenor, shaded with hints of jazz and hip hop, and songs that feel like songs rather than merely catchy hooks, Benét shows that he's a contender.

*THE UNAUTHORIZED BIOGRAPHY OF REINHOLD MESSNER
Ben Folds Five

Despite its heroic, rock operatic overtones, Messner is not a rock opera but a mock opera. Folds, Jessee, and Sledge have fashioned a wall of orchestral sound to accompany Folds's witty, autobiographical tunes about mundane tragedies like being dumped by bands and girlfriends.

BETTY3
Betty

Known originally for their intricate vocal harmonies and bawdy good humor, this trio has morphed from a mostly a cappella group into a hard-rocking guitar band. Betty's best yet.

*B*WITCHED
*B*Witched*

It's hard to listen to the peppy, dance-inducing arrangements and party-girl harmonies of this button-cute quartet of teen singers without thinking that these tunes rolled right off the Spice rack. But the B*Witched crew not only have stronger voices than their famous doppelgirls, they actually play their own instruments.

*BY YOUR SIDE
The Black Crowes

The Atlanta-based band seems to recycle classic rock and roll whole—a few cuts sound like old Rolling Stones outtakes and vocals as if done by Rod Stewart—but unreconstructed rock fans will be happy that music like this is being made at all these days.

MARY
Mary J. Blige

With her husky, often raw, always richly expressive voice, Blige brings soulful passion to modern R&B. Another jewel in a soul royal's crown.

*NO EXIT
Blondie

A viable, vibrant album by a group of enduring innovators. Blondie, now back after 17 years, is funny, funky, sexy, and filled with the sort of verve and attitude that their younger counterparts can only dream of.

SOGNO
Andrea Bocelli

With the Orchestra Filarmonica Italiana, the irresistible tenor brings operatic power (and holds the schmaltz) on romantic ballads, including the *Quest for Camelot* opus "The Prayer," with Celine Dion.

DESTINY
Jim Brickman

Brickman's tendency to play the piano with all deliberate speed makes him sound at times like a new student rushing through his afternoon keyboard exercises. A good demonstration of why some regard his keyboard doodling as vapid and boring New Age white noise.

EDEN
Sarah Brightman
The former Mrs. Andrew Lloyd Webber gives baroque-pop treatment to 15 tunes made for classical style.

JONATHA BROOKE LIVE
Jonatha Brooke
A voice certain to appeal to Joni Mitchell fans. Her intelligent, jazz-inflected tunes are a hit on this compilation of live performances.

TROUBLE
Buckwheat Zydeco
For 20 years, Stanley "Buckwheat" Dural Jr. has been dishing up zydeco's musical gumbo—gobs of Creole accordion music mixed with Afro-Cuban rhythms and Southern rock-and-soul. Here, Dural and his band deliver 10 tracks of propulsive, rollicking dance-party music.

BEACH HOUSE ON THE MOON
Jimmy Buffett
Pascagoula, Mississippi's native son may be getting just a bit cranky. Having expressed his views on aging in his 1998 best-seller, *A Pirate Looks at 50*, Buffett elaborates on the theme here. Happily, his easygoing humor keeps him from seeming as down in the mouth as he is as long in the tooth.

BLUE'S BIG TREASURE: A MUSICAL ADVENTURE
Steve Burns and Friends
Burns and a lively group of musicians present an audio version of the popular TV show *Blues Clues*, which introduces young listeners to a broad range of musical styles, from blues to bluegrass.

*PRESS ON
June Carter Cash
Joined here by her ailing husband, Johnny Cash; daughter Rosie; ex-sons-in-law Marty Stuart and Rodney Crowell; and son John Carter Cash, June takes a welcome step into the limelight with wistful humor and a warm, family-sing spirit.

TAILGATE PARTY
The Charlie Daniels Band
Satisfying and consistent but about as full of surprises as a box of saltines, Daniels provides a mixed bag of original tunes and country-rock covers. His limitations as a lead vocalist make him a less-than-ideal singer for Lynyrd Skynyrd's "Freebird."

SURRENDER
The Chemical Brothers
This album triggers exciting performances from big-name singers (like Noel Gallagher of Oasis) and delivers a canny mix of dreamy soundscapes and Star Wars–like aural effects.

I DON'T WANT TO MISS A THING
Mark Chesnutt
One reason Mark Chesnutt has moved into the ranks of Nashville's most entertaining male singers is that he and producer Mark Wright are so adept at finding good and varied songs. (The album includes the title ballad of the action movie *Armageddon*.)

RESURRECTION
Chris Perez Band
Guitarist Perez (widower of murdered Tejano star Selena), with ex-Selena bandmate Joe Ojeda and vocalist John Garza, bows with this impressive bilingual album of emotion-packed guitar rock.

CLAUDIA CHURCH
Claudia Church
It's probably a coincidence that Church sounds so much like the early Rosanne Cash—having acceded to the title of Mrs. Rodney Crowell after Cash relinquished it. Her debut, produced and cowritten by Crowell, shifts effectively from emotional, cerebral tunes to peppy, rhythm-driven material with a versatile sound that proves that she's the real goods.

STEREOTYPE A
Cibo Matto
This delightfully eclectic Japanese-born pop duo with the funny Italian name incorporates bossa nova, heavy metal, and even hip hop into their music. As weirdly diverse as all this sounds, Stereotype A sparkles with bright harmonies, clever lyrics, and dance-friendly rhythms.

SONG FOR THE YEAR 2000
David Allan Coe
While most of the songs have his familiar, country-boy slant, this sudden embrace of the politically correct will surely seem a bit calculated to some. There's always the feeling that he's trying to be something he isn't.

SNOWFALL ON THE SAHARA
Natalie Cole
Cole, a larger-than-life pop presence who possesses the true diva's grandeur of talent and history, returns with this unlikely mix of tunes that keep the bombast to a minimum and allow her artfully restrained vocals to shine.

DOSAGE
Collective Soul
Despite the refreshing features, such as string sections, hip-hop rhythms, and ringing guitars, these Southern rockers stick to the tried and true. Singer-songwriter Roland has honed his pleasantly raspy voice, but no amount of craft can mask his generally hollow lyrics.

TARZAN
Phil Collins, Mark Mancina
Of the five new songs composed for this soundtrack, only one has much zippity doo-dah. Included is Mancina's dramatic score, along with multiple, nearly identical alternate versions of Collins's tunes.

*COME BY ME
Harry Connick Jr.
Connick, the out-of-time crooner and big-band leader, is alive and swinging with compositions that would have shone in Sinatra's songbook half a century ago. Here, Connick boldly alternates his own tunes with gems by Cole Porter and Irving Berlin, a risky trick that he pulls off nicely.

TALK ON CORNERS: SPECIAL EDITION
The Corrs
A collection of pretty, pop-lite tunes that could use more Celtic flavoring and less studio gloss. The album is best when harking back to the sounds of the Old Sod: reeling fiddles, soaring harmonies, and the haunting tin whistle.

BURY THE HATCHET
The Cranberries
Recently regrouped, brothers Mike and Noel Hogan, drummer Fergal Lawler, and new mom O'Riordan return with lame lyrics and sleepy arrangements so bland they sound as if recorded in a Prozac haze.

COME ON DOWN TO MY WORLD
J. D. Crowe and the New South
Crowe's band sounds a little like Flatt & Scruggs, a little like Ricky Skaggs, and a big lump like the Nitty Gritty Dirt Band. A bonanza for bluegrass fans, this album reaches back to traditional blues and places it alongside tunes by more contemporary songwriters.

*HALF MAD MOON
The Damnations TX
Sisters Deborah Kelly and Amy Boone, raised in Schoharie, New York, join the proud tradition of authentic-seeming country folks who aren't really from the country. With this fun and fiery major-label debut, the two singers combine irresistible harmonies with a raucous, whiskey-soaked sound to make true mountain music.

UNFINISHED BUSINESS
Dave Davies
Long relegated to big brother Ray's shadow, Davies compiles a double CD of old Kinks songs and solo tunes that finally place him in the spotlight and prove that he is a talented composer in his own right.

THE COMPLETE BITCHES BREW SESSIONS
Miles Davis
Davis first showcased his fusion of jazz and rock on 1970's *Bitches Brew*, now rereleased with outtakes.

A NIGHT TO REMEMBER
Joe Diffie
Diffie has a gritty voice, a sturdy, macho style and a slew of No. 1 country hits on his résumé. Here he sings angst-ridden songs with energy in the good-ol'-boy tradition.

*UP UP UP UP UP UP
Ani DiFranco
A performer before she was 10, DiFranco is an independent folkie with a passion for funky rhythms and lefty politics. Her twelfth album is a spare, mesmerizing batch of treats.

FLY
Dixie Chicks
Just as full of down-home Texas twang as their first, *Fly* is a sophomore album that soars. Neither pop nor corn, just deep-fried country with lots of snap.

GET SKINTIGHT
The Donnas
Four female garage rockers raise a Ramones-style ruckus with these punk rock party tunes. Their music is a timeless burst of renegade teen spirit.

THE MOUNTAIN
Steve Earle and the Del McCoury Band
This tribute to bluegrass icon Bill Monroe comes close to his musical standards: The mandolin playing is especially lively, and the fiddler saws away nicely—but the vocals truly suffer by comparison and most of the tunes have a self-consciously artsy quality.

THE DUKE ELLINGTON CENTENNIAL EDITION: THE COMPLETE RCA VICTOR RECORDINGS, 1927–1973
Duke Ellington
Exhaustive but never tiring; the composer's genius shines on 24 CDs.

DA REAL WORLD
Missy "Misdemeanor" Elliot
On this fierce and furious album, Missy and guests Aaliyah and Lil' Kim testify about shady friends, shifty men, and the down-and-dirty ins and outs of relationships.

DANCE HALL DREAMS
Rosie Flores
While the lively, sturdy-voiced Flores has long since demonstrated her mastery of country rock and western swing, it is a pleasure to hear how movingly she sings the more emotional songs on this CD.

*UTOPIA PARKWAY
Fountains of Wayne
From the sheer exuberance of the opening title track to its wistful closing tune, the album is a slice of pop-rock heaven. A fountain of melody, harmony, and hooks, the lyrics live up to promising titles like "Red Dragon Tattoo" and "The Valley of Malls."

MINOR CHORDS AND MAJOR THEMES
Gigolo Aunts
This mop-topped quartet caught a break when one of their tunes appeared, fittingly, in a homage to '60s pop. Bristling with bright, instantly appealing pop hooks, *Minor Chords* hearkens back to that distant epoch when songs were tailored to keep listeners from surfing the AM radio dial.

ON HOW LIFE IS
Macy Gray
Macy Gray scores with an eclectic and soulful debut, mixing rock, soul, and the blues with a wit and a creativity that is joyously refreshing. Count this among the year's most promising debuts.

DO THE COLLAPSE
Guided By Voices
Robert Pollard steers Guided By Voices to heady pop heights and pays homage to the 1960s and '70s pop music he was weaned on with these 16 two- and three-minute symphonies.

SCHIZOPHONIC
Geri Halliwell
Mine the best bits from the Spice Girls' two-album canon and you will have the basic ingredients for this good-humored pop confection from Spice World's lone escapee.

TRIO II
Emmylou Harris, Linda Ronstadt, Dolly Parton
The trio's sound is bright, fresh, and harmonically rich. Even the dullest tunes are redeemed by the sound of these three marvelous voices blending into something greater than the very substantial sum of its parts.

TIMBRE
Sophie Hawkins
Hawkins offers a gloomy world view with strings attached on this uniformly dreary album. The cello adds an appropriate dirge-like quality while Hawkins's voice is frail, sounding like a depressed Ricky Lee Jones.

THICKER THAN WATER
Mike Henderson and The Bluebloods
The best part of this country blues band is its piano player, John Jarvis, whose richly layered, hard-driving solos enliven the band's otherwise routine blues music.

LIVE AT WOODSTOCK
Jimi Hendrix
On August 18, 1969, after most of the audience had dispersed at the scheduled end of the three-day Aquarian Exposition, the headliner finally played. We're still listening.

FUSE
Joe Henry
Henry stays as far from his old honky-tonk style as he can get, employing sampled sounds and other studio effects. The result, happily, is a moody, mesmerizing album.

SKY MOTEL
Kristin Hersh
Hersh creates a spare but sharp setting for her unsettling, vividly literate lyrics, whose images can be as frightening as they are fascinating, belying her soft appearance and sweet soprano. The album is as enthralling as it is unnerving.

LOVE THINKETH NO EVIL
Peter Himmelman
After 18 years of eluding stardom, Bob Dylan's son-in-law may win mainstream recognition with this virtuoso performance of lovely melodies and intelligent, imagery-rich songs.

GREATEST HITS
Billie Holiday
A golden baker's dozen: a collection of tunes sung by Lady Day in her 1935–41 prime, with a jaw-dropping all-star roster of accompanists.

GHETTO HYMNS
Dave Hollister
Tough meets tender in the solo debut CD from Hollister, who dresses his old-school soul crooning in street-smart beats on

"My Favorite Girl" and other tuneful tracks.

IT'S YOUR THING: THE STORY OF THE ISLEY BROTHERS
The Isley Brothers
From their 1950s rock classic "Shout (Parts 1& 2)" to their polished R&B hits of the '90s, the Isleys have been shakin' it up, baby, for more than 40 years.

SYNKRONIZED
Jamiroquai
Along with the usual funky jazz-pop tunes, Kay—who writes and arranges the group's music—adds an even greater dose of '60s- and '70s-style funk to the mix, owing heavy debts to R&B stars of yore: Stevie Wonder, Curtis Mayfield, and Sly and the Family Stone.

BLUES BLUES BLUES
The Jimmy Rogers All-Stars
Just before he died in 1997 at age 73, Rogers and fans Eric Clapton, Keith Richards, and Stephen Stills jam on tunes like Rogers's own "Sweet Home Chicago."

ELTON JOHN AND TIM RICE'S AIDA
Elton John and Various Artists
Not to be confused with Verdi's 1871 opera, this album was written for Disney's new Broadway version. Though this features performances by artists such as Sting, Lenny Kravitz, and Janet Jackson, it unfolds as one long—very long—ballad.

MAYBE NOT TONIGHT
Sammy Kershaw
Kershaw's rugged voice blends perfectly with Lorrie Morgan's smooth, sweet style on the romantic but bittersweet song that opens this up-tempo country album.

REALLY ROSIE
Carole King
New to CD, King's classic 1975 kids' album, with lyrics (and pictures) by Maurice Sendak, captivates taller listeners as well.

MANY DIFFERENT ROADS
Gladys Knight
On her first-ever soul-stirring gospel album Knight celebrates a half century in showbiz. With her husky alto sounding as supple as ever, she turns this collection of originals and revival-meeting standards into a lilting and heartfelt testament of faith.

*PEASANTS, PIGS AND ASTRONAUTS
Kula Shaker
With richly textured melodies and ringing vocal harmonies, Kula Shaker masters all manners of pop styles, from rave-up psychedelia to smokey blues and exotic Delhi-flavored soundscapes.

PHOTOGRAPH SMILE
Julian Lennon
After eight years, John Lennon's son still sounds like a chip off the old block—albeit a relatively lightweight, sentimental one. Most of these tunes are watery, vaguely worded love ballads with melodies as sweet as Julian's baby photo on the cover.

SINGIN' IN THE BATHTUB
John Lithgow
Backed alternately by a sparse rhythm section and a 30-piece big band, Lithgow sings for the small fry on this often charming CD. Mostly the tunes are glib, silly, and child-friendly, and Lithgow, to his credit, sings with kids, not at them.

GOD IS REAL
Little Richard
Dropping the giddy falsetto with which he belted the lascivious lyrics of his rockin' early gems, Richard sings in a deeper but no less ecstatic baritone. He rips it up in the name of the Lord.

BUZZ ME IN
Jack Logan
The Georgia lo-fi rocker (with backing by his band the Liquor Cabinet) goes hi-fi, adding

(yikes!) strings without doing harm to his tuneful world-gone-wrong songs.

*HEAD MUSIC
The London Suede
More fun and friskier than a fresh batch of cookie-cutter boy groups and overflowing with throbbing bass lines, hip-swaying tempos, and romantic melodies you can sing along with, this British quintet releases an old-fashioned rock album with plenty of new sparkle.

THIS WORLD IS NOT MY HOME
Lone Justice
Honky-tonk waif goddess Maria McKee's duet with U2's Bono is one highlight of this compilation disc featuring the music of Lone Justice, the sadly short-lived 1980s Los Angeles cow-punk band.

ON THE 6
Jennifer Lopez
This Bronx-born Puerto Rican dancer, actress, and sex symbol has added pop singer to her already impressive résumé. Here Lopez offers a seamless blend of hip hop, pop, soul, dance, and Latin genres, and though her voice is a bit thin, she has definite flair and musicality.

THE McGARRIGLE HOUR
Kate and Anna McGarrigle
The singing sisters, along with Kate's ex (Loudon Wainwright), their son (Rufus), and friends like Emmylou Harris and Linda Ronstadt, achieve true harmonic convergence.

A PLACE IN THE SUN
Tim McGraw
Nashville veteran McGraw shows new promise, getting a boost from background vocals by Patty Loveless and the distinctive Kim Carnes. Put these elements together and there seems to be more to this guy than has met the ear so far.

STAY THE SAME
Joey McIntyre
With this debut solo collection of love ballads and Stevie Wonder–influenced dance tunes, Joey just may give the Backstreet Boys, 'N Sync and the rest of this year's New Kids a run for the teenybopper bucks.

BEAUTIFUL DISEASE
Duff McKagen
An endangered rocker is alive and banging his head. McKagen works the same middle ground between punk and heavy metal that he and former Guns N' Roses members first detonated on *Appetite*.

UNIVERSAL MADNESS
Madness
Hailed by young admirers, 1980s British invaders return with this rousing CD, recorded live in L.A.

THE FEELING'S BACK
Chuck Mangione
Resonant and autumnal, the flugelhorn maestro's CD sounds like it was recorded in a church…and it was.

*DESTINY: RARE SKA SIDES FROM STUDIO ONE
Bob Marley and the Wailers
This album reprises tunes recorded between 1963 and 1966, a full decade before Marley rode his reggae beat to world stardom. Marley and his mates are joined on some tracks by Junior Braithwaite and Beverley Kelso, and sing simply about

love and loss in voices of pure, sweet yearning.

BIG TRAIN
Wynton Marsalis and the Lincoln Center Jazz Orchestra
One of six CDs in his astounding Swinging into the 21st series of jazz and classical compositions set for release in 1999, this Train roars.

RICKY MARTIN
Ricky Martin
And they said it would all be downhill after Menudo. Now 27, big Ricky is enjoying the kind of crossover success many performers only dream about. While the bulk of the album's tracks tends toward balladry, the up-tempo tunes are best.

*HEY! ALBUM
Marvelous 3
You may find it tough to resist the word games played by newcomer Butch Walker, lead scribe, singer, and guitarist for this Atlanta-based trio. Despite Walker's habit of singing with a phony British accent, the combination of lively backup vocals and chunky power chords make marvelous Top 40–style pop.

LIVE AT LUTHER COLLEGE
Dave Matthews/Tim Reynolds
On this acoustic double CD, Matthews is accompanied only by guitarist Tim Reynolds. Despite virtuoso guitar interplay, the album may be hailed by fans but probably not by those unfamiliar with Matthews's odd vocal calisthenics and repetitive arrangements.

HOME TO YOU
John Michael Montgomery
This country-music album sounds as if someone said "Loosen up!" to John Michael and he listened. The picked-up pace puts more demands on his backup musicians, who propel things along.

*TATTOOS & SCARS
Montgomery Gentry
The title of their first CD may sound like the billing for a TV wrestling show, but Eddie Montgomery and Troy Gentry are a first-rate country duo with the rough-and-tumble energy of Brooks & Dunn and a sweet, two-part harmony that often recalls the Everly Brothers.

MY HEART
Lorrie Morgan
Morgan's sultry, honey-smoked voice is tailor-made for those good old country tunes of heartache and regret. On this solid but not spectacular effort, she wrings drama and emotion out of merely average songs.

*BACK ON TOP
Van Morrison
This may well be his most accessible, entertaining work since the Belfast soul man sang of moondance nights and brown-eyed girls. From the rocking boogie of the opening number to the aching, bittersweet beauty of his ballads, Morrison mixes gospel and R&B into a soaring style that's all his own.

CONTINENTAL DRIFTER
Charlie Musselwhite
The harmonica great drifts way south, adding Brazilian and Cuban flavorings to his blues with a little help from amigo Eliades Ochoa and his Cuban band, Cuarteto Patria.

CHEATING AT SOLITAIRE
Mike Ness
With his band Social Distortion on hiatus, punk folkie Ness gets

helping hands from Bruce Springsteen, Brian Setzer, and X's Billy Zoom for this album of original and cover tunes.

VALENCE STREET
The Neville Brothers
Oldest brother Art stars on four tunes, Aaron can make classifieds sound like scripture, and Cyril proves himself a soul crooner in his own right. Brother Charles keeps his vocals in the background but shines on saxophone and as a composer in this zesty musical gumbo.

BAD LOVE
Randy Newman
If you like your romance laced with irony and whimsy, Newman is the Man. Anyone who stumbles upon these shrewd, tuneful numbers in this collection of far-from-conventional love songs should consider himself fortunate indeed.

BANG BANG BANG
Nitty Gritty Dirt Band
Twenty-seven years after their classic "Will the Circle Be Unbroken" helped make traditional country hip, the enduring Nashville rockers pop up with this appealing, dance-friendly offering.

THE REAL ¡SOCK RAY BLUE!
Mojo Nixon & the Toadliquors
The author of "Don Henley Must Die" is back with more funny, politically incorrect rockabilly.

BEST OF THE VANGUARD YEARS
Odetta
Veteran 1960s folk balladeer Odetta Felious sings blues, gospel, and civil rights anthems in a selection of tracks from three early albums.

FIGHT SONGS
Old 97's
Pealing guitars, appealing vocals, and surprisingly world-weary lyrics animate a self-assured fourth album from a group of young Texas twangers.

THROUGH A GLASS DARKLY
David Olney
This neofolk album of morbid, pretentious songs and toneless droning suggests the kind of drivel Lisa Kudrow screeches on *Friends* for laughs.

THE OMD SINGLES
Orchestral Manoeuvres in the Dark
Twenty years after Brits Andy McCluskey and Paul Humphreys began turning out catchy synth-pop hits like "If You Leave" and "Dreaming," their seminal '80s band takes a final bow with this retrospective best-of compilation.

CENTRAL RESERVATION
Beth Orton
Orton's midtempo music is filled with catchy dance beats, gorgeous folk guitars, and haunting string sections. Although most of the lyrics focus on life's more painful moments, the effect of her music is both jubilant and timeless.

OWSLEY
Owsley
After years of waiting, Owsley finally releases an album shimmering with pop craft and chock-full of engaging vocals, ringing harmonies, and terrific airplay-ready tunes that have him poised for overnight success.

LEGENDS
Pinetop Perkins and Hubert Sumlin
Perkins, longtime pianist in Muddy Waters's blues band, and Sumlin, whose electric guitar put the sting in Howlin' Wolf's gritty blues sound, have influenced three generations of players. In this collaborative effort, guitars talk, the piano vamps, and the interplay between these fine old bluesmen makes these tunes swing.

ON THE GOOD SHIP LOLLIPOP
The Persuasions
As adept at percussive vocal

effects as they are at soaring quartet-style gospel harmonies, the singers make instrumentation superfluous. Here the quintet aims to entertain a new generation, and kids will need no persuading to play this.

ECHO
Tom Petty and the Heartbreakers
Although Petty still wears his influences of his rock elders on his sleeve, this album is unmistakably his own. No tape loops, drum programs, or other studio gimmickry here; just Petty's trademark power chords and wry story songs, with stellar play by founding Heartbreakers.

I'D RATHER EAT GLASS
Bijou Phillips
Bijou opts for a harsh sound in her debut, displaying her skewed, adolescent lyric poetry in a hard-rock setting. Don't expect to hear any of her father's sunny California tunes—she sings with an annoying mix of anger and self-pity but not nearly enough pathos.

ZERO ZERO ZERO
Sam Phillips
Phillips presents her own "director's cut" of affecting songs from her past four albums.

SAM PREKOP
Sam Prekop
With his seductively whispered vocals, Chicago art-rocker Sam Prekop mixes romantic, melancholy lyrics with bossa nova and samba rhythms, soft guitars, and

even a cornet in his winning solo debut.

ARTIST OF THE CENTURY
Elvis Presley
"Hearing him for the first time," Bob Dylan says of His Rock Highness in liner notes to this unarguably titled 3-CD, 75-track collection, "was like busting out of jail."

SUNRISE
Elvis Presley
Until Elvis first walked into Sam Phillips's Memphis Recording Service, the studio's motto ("We record Anything—Anywhere—Anytime") had been a beacon only to black musicians in segregated Memphis. This collection of Elvis's entire output on Sun Records, including his unreleased tracks and outtakes, is a doubly historic collection that marks the arrival of the rock King and a vital bridge across pop music's racial divide.

*¡VIVA EL AMOR!
Pretenders
They sure don't make 'em like femme rock pioneer Chrissie Hynde. It is heartening to find that she has weathered tragedy—two founding Pretenders died of drug overdoses in the early '80s, and her pal Linda McCartney shot this CD's cover photo a month before she died of cancer last year—with her musical verve intact.

*CALIFORNICATION
Red Hot Chili Peppers
The rejuvenated group celebrates lead guitarist Frusciante's return with this explosive stew of hard funk, hip hop, and heavy metal. The result is hot and savory.

*IT'S ABOUT TIME
Julie Reeves
With a bright, plaintive voice and a seductive, energetic style, Reeves makes you think of a much younger Kitty Wells or a slightly younger Patty Loveless. This newest Nashville talent seems perfectly capable of making it big on her own.

*TAKE YOUR SHOES OFF
The Robert Cray Band
A sheer blast of rocking good times, Cray and his band perform with a newfound intensity and playfulness. This is a head-first dive into the familiar waters of '60s and '70s soul music, with its gospel-flavored vocals and funky rhythms in the tradition of Otis Redding and Al Green.

LONG WAY HOME FROM ANYWHERE
Bruce Robison
Robison tempers his country music with generous dashes of the blues and Western swing. This rich and varied debut solo album displays Robison's Texas roots while branching out into more traditional country material.

WESTERN WALL: THE TUCSON SESSIONS
Linda Ronstadt and Emmylou Harris
Harmonizing like a twang and a tear, Ronstadt's earthy lead blends with Harris's airy soprano to heavenly effect. Tender, mournful, and winning.

EVERY DAY IS A NEW DAY
Diana Ross
The queen of sheen emerges again with an album that melds her enduring style with fresh substance. Ross succeeds in celebrating pop's recent developments without abandoning her strong R&B roots.

702
702
Though difficult to distinguish from any number of sexy, soulful acts, 702 has appeal and pure singing skills. Despite their affinity for thumping grooves and drum-driven rhythm, their smooth, subtle approach is just as seductive.

BY 7:30
Vonda Shepard
Filled with tunes that tell of personal struggles, such as low self-esteem and unrequited love, Shepard sings with folksy passion. Although the piano and guitar arrangements mark an improvement over her last album, many of the lyric constructions are wacky.

LEARN TO CROON
Frank Sinatra and Tommy Dorsey and His Orchestra
Rare 1940s radio broadcasts sound like brand-new studio recordings by the crooner and his big-band mentor.

THE SUMMIT: IN CONCERT
Frank Sinatra, Dean Martin, Sammy Davis Jr.
This 1962 concert album includes way too many relaxed moments and too little serious singing. The first of a collection of remastered and unreleased Sinatra material, there must be a lot more worthwhile than this.

ANCIENT TONES
Ricky Skaggs
Country musicians don't come any rootsier than Skaggs. This is an invigorating celebration of bluegrass music's timelessness, wisely mixing an array of classics with new tunes written by himself and others.

ASTRO LOUNGE
Smash Mouth
If these smart-alecky rockers aren't careful, they could be accused of fashioning a concept album. Astro Lounge is full of free-floating whimsy and smart pop-rock hooks lifted from sources as diverse as Phil Spector and ? and the Mysterians, and sounds variously like Madness, Elvis Costello, and those contemporary masters of derivation, Oasis.

223

…BABY ONE MORE TIME
Britney Spears

Though she is peppy and enthusiastic, this 17-year-old is not quite precocious enough. Her debut, complete with a suggestive title and in-a-rush-to-grow-up tunes, seems inappropriately mature. An unpolished singer, Spears could use more voice training.

KARMA
Rick Springfield

"Resurrect" seems an appropriate word, since Springfield's first studio album in 11 years is so heavily freighted with religious overtones. But Springfield might be pushing his luck—even the less explicitly reverential tracks are on the heavy side.

FEARLESS
Karen Staley

Here the best country singer-songwriter you probably never heard of shows she can sing with the tops in the biz. As a singer, Staley's tough-but-vulnerable style allows her to tackle everything, from bluesy, honky-tonk romps to sentimental ballads.

QUINTESSENCE VOL. 1
The Stan Getz Quartet with Chet Baker

Saxophonist jazzmen Getz and trumpeter Chet Baker play it oh-so-cool during a 1983 live concert in Norway.

SWING
Lisa Stansfield

Fans of Britain's hazel-eyed soul

princess may have been pining for more of her lush, R&B-flavored pop tunes. Instead, the 33-year-old singer and songwriter jumps on the big-band wagon with an album of supper club music from a film of the same name, possessing the nimble vocal chops that the jump-jiving genre demands.

ALWAYS NEVER THE SAME
George Strait

Strait is an always warm, always graceful singer with a shrewd ear for tasteful country melodies that suit his style—and what his twenty-fourth album lacks in pleasant surprises, it more than makes up for in reliability.

THE PILGRIM
Marty Stuart

Stuart brings his usual energy and rough-hewn appeal to his tunes and enlists such talent as Emmylou Harris, Earl Scruggs, and Pam Tillis to help tell the tale of a Mississippi man who gets involved with a married woman, is rejected, and then wanders off cross-country looking for a poetic place to kill himself before finding redemption.

*14:59
Sugar Ray

This cleverly named album, aimed at critics convinced that the band's 15 minutes of fame are over, combines witty tunes with driving pop, ska, thrash metal, and surf-rock rhythms.

CHALEE TENNISON
Chalee Tennison

Tennison's rich sturdy voice and heartfelt intensity is reminiscent of Loretta Lynn or Tammy Wynette. Her appropriate set of women-done-wrong songs, along with a more urban country sound (a bit like K. T. Oslin), brings uncommon maturity to her music.

THE HUSH
Texas

This all-around solid album could well bring the Scottish quintet closer to the American spotlight. Here they display a rare inventiveness and a soulful rock sound, making the most of what is not an especially literate set of 12 songs.

MOCK TUDOR
Richard Thompson

Troubadour Richard Thompson strums up tunes both searing and poetical. Though Thompson still sometimes indulges his quiet, folkish side, he mostly turns up the volume here. This is the real deal.

*FANMAIL
TLC

Cyber Supremes for a new generation, TLC is back with their sexy combo of vulnerability and in-your-face attitude. The trio blends old-style girl-group harmonies with edgy, electronic background noise and more subdued, acoustic, midtempo ballads for a modern sound with sass.

THE COMPLETE LIVE 1965 SHOW
Ernest Tubb and the Texas Troubadours

A rare treasure, this double CD documents a special era when country stars performed long sets in small clubs just for the love of it. It captures Tubb, who died in 1984, in peak form and clearly enjoying the intimate interaction with his audience.

USHER LIVE
Usher
Silky, funkified croonings from Usher Raymond, with vocal assists from R&B starlets Faith Evans, Lil' Kim, and Shanice Wilson.

AUSTIN POWERS: THE SPY WHO SHAGGED ME
Various Artists
Miss Behave herself, Madonna, not only stars on this soundtrack CD along with R.E.M. and Green Day, she also cashes in: The disc is released on her own thriving label.

DIVAS EXOTICA
Various Artists
These aren't your children's divas. Full-time pros such as Billie Holiday, Edith Piaf, and Nina Simone are joined by Marilyn Monroe, Jayne Mansfield, and Ann Margaret, who contribute amateur performances of novelty material.

FISH TREE WATER BLUES
Various Artists
Grateful Dead alum Bob Weir, R&B icons Ruth Brown and Etta James, and '90s folkie Ani DiFranco celebrate Earth Day with this benefit compilation CD.

GAGA FOR YA-YA: ZYDECO MADNESS
Various Artists
The bestseller *Divine Secrets of the Ya-Ya Sisterhood* inspired this collection of leap-froggin' Louisiana Zydeco by many of its top practitioners.

LILITH FAIR: A CELEBRATION OF WOMEN IN MUSIC, VOL. 2, VOL. 3
Various Artists
These volumes showcase Lilith's more ethnically diverse and musically muscular lineup. *Volume 2* features powerhouse performances by Sinead O'Connor, Queen Latifah, Tracy Bonham, and Holly McNarland. Sold separately, *Volume 3* features quieter performers such as Suzanne

Vega and the Indigo Girls along with rockers like Luscious Jackson.

*MALI TO MEMPHIS: AN AFRICAN-AMERICAN ODYSSEY
Various Artists
This fascinating compilation celebrates the musical kinship between American blues and African rhythm with songs of praise and mourning from both modern American and West African performers.

THE MISSISSIPPI: RIVER OF SONG
Various Artists
The contemporary sound of gritty performers, alternative-rock bands, and a three-minute chant by a group of Ojibwe musicians make for a disappointing tribute to the Mighty Mississippi.

NO BOUNDARIES: A BENEFIT FOR THE KOSOVAR REFUGEES
Various Artists
Pearl Jam's cover of "Last Kiss," about a teen killed in a car wreck, has ironic resonance on this benefit CD for war victims. Oasis and the Wallflowers also contribute.

THE ORLEANS RECORDS STORY
Various Artists
Combing Louisiana's bayous and barrooms for acts from R&B's colorful past, Orleans's Carlo Ditta presents a sampler of tracks by artists such as Roland Stone and Blue Lu Barker.

PEACOCK GOSPEL CLASSICS
Various Artists
Popular soloists, talented groups, and rocking church choirs are represented on the latest release in this ongoing, wondrous black gospel series.

PEARLS IN THE SNOW: THE SONGS OF KINKY FRIEDMAN
Various Artists
Willie Nelson, Lyle Lovett, Dwight Yoakam, and others help pay tribute to the quirky 1970s country rocker turned mystery novelist.

RETURN OF THE GRIEVOUS ANGEL: A TRIBUTE TO GRAM PARSONS
Various Artists
The late country rock pioneer's songs are covered by Wilco, the Pretenders, and Beck, among other disciples.

SONGS AND BALLADS OF AMERICAN HISTORY AND OF THE ASSASSINATION OF PRESIDENTS
Various Artists
From the Library of Congress folk archive, chilling Civil War–era news delivered in song.

ULTIMATE DIVAS
Various Artists
The first six artists on this collection compiled by label president Clive Davis are as heavenly as musical creatures get. But record buyers will wonder if Whitney Houston, Dionne Warwick, Annie Lennox, and Toni Braxton are included because they are among the greatest of our time or because all have been at one time or another Arista artists.

LIVE, LAUGH, LOVE
Clay Walker
Walker's warm voice is still true and steady, and he is more energetic and musically upbeat than ever before.

SOCIAL STUDIES
Loudon Wainwright III
Wainwright first performed many of these topical zingers on National Public Radio. Here he aims witty, observant broadsides at music industry greed, urban paranoia, compulsive smokers, and millennial madness.

MULE VARIATIONS
Tom Waits
Although the blues inform most tracks, Waits, a charmingly eccentric songwriter with the jagged-as-broken-glass voice, distinguishes his meat-and-potatoes rock arrangements and proves again why he deserves an audience.

THE DEFINITIVE COLLECTION
Dionne Warwick
Twenty luminous vocals, including her Burt Bacharach–penned hits. Whatever you do, do not "Walk On By."

THIRD GENERATION BLUES
Doc and Richard Watson
American music's walking folk treasure, Doc Watson returns with a rich baritone and renowned flat-pick guitar style undiminished by age, while Richard complements his grandpa with playing that would make Merle (whose accidental death spurred Doc's retreat) proud.

EXTREMELY COOL
Chuck E. Weiss
Several of the tunes on this album are done in a gravelly voiced, finger-poppin', 1950s black-hipster-beatnik style reminiscent of the early style of its producer, Tom Waits. Others sound like they were sung through a megaphone and all that raspy-voiced patois does get annoying after prolonged exposure.

*SUICAINE GRATIFACTION
Paul Westerberg
A collection of dark band-on-the-run songs that sound as if they were composed after an especially grueling tour. Although his lyrics are both sad and unsettling, the minimalist melodies he ekes out are lovely and packed with feeling.

STAYING POWER
Barry White
Is there anything in creation quite as low-down, soothing, and sexy as Barry White's elemental basso aphrodisia? Here he serves up another steamy collection of music with assists from duet partners Chaka Khan and Lisa Stansfield, as well as a cameo rap from guest Sean "Puffy" Combs.

*SUMMER TEETH
Wilco
An ambitious, beautifully crafted and almost twang-free album. With his knack for sing-along melodies, rocking arrangements, and decidedly noncountry studio effects, founder Tweedy has strayed far from the fold—to winning effect.

THE EGO HAS LANDED
Robbie Williams
Booted out of the British boy-band Take That in 1995 and plagued by substance-abuse, Williams is now being hailed in the U.K. as the Great Pop Hope. This U.S. debut best-of compilation, culled from his two British albums, proves that the hype is justified.

WHAT I DESERVE
Kelly Willis
When Hollywood powers finally get around to making a movie about the tribulations of Fleetwood Mac, Willis would be a good choice to play the early Stevie Nicks. Willis has a tremolo-tinged, emotionally potent voice that's as musical in her country idiom as Nicks's is in rock, and her songs are consistently well done.

LIVE AT MCCABE'S GUITAR SHOP
Nancy Wilson
This charming but lightweight solo acoustic album contains a few forgettable Wilson originals, some recycled Heart tunes, and some of Nancy's faves. Wilson is in fine voice, but unfortunately, her songwriting and persona simply aren't strong enough to stand alone.

ANYWAY THE WIND BLOWS
Bill Wyman & the Rhythm Kings
Former Rolling Stoner Bill Wyman along with the Rhythm Kings play an appealing form of R&B, supper-club swing, and even the occasional jug-band ditty with the help of some sterling sidemen.

ROCK AND ROLL HALL OF FAME

The Rock and Roll Hall of Fame in Cleveland continues to select the greatest rock and roll musicians for inclusion. A nominee must have released a record at least 25 years prior to induction; Early Influences honors the formative figures in rock.

1986

Chuck Berry
James Brown
Ray Charles
Sam Cooke
Fats Domino
The Everly Brothers
Buddy Holly
Jerry Lee Lewis
Elvis Presley
Little Richard

Early Influences
Robert Johnson
Jimmie Rodgers
Jimmy Yancey

Nonperformers
Alan Freed
Sam Phillips

Lifetime Achievement
John Hammond

1987

The Coasters
Eddie Cochran
Bo Diddley
Aretha Franklin
Marvin Gaye
Bill Haley
B. B. King
Clyde McPhatter
Ricky Nelson
Roy Orbison
Carl Perkins
Smokey Robinson
Big Joe Turner
Muddy Waters
Jackie Wilson

Early Influences
Louis Jordan
T-Bone Walker
Hank Williams

Nonperformers
Leonard Chess
Ahmet Ertegun
Jerry Leiber and Mike Stoller
Jerry Wexler

1988

The Beach Boys
The Beatles
The Drifters
Bob Dylan
The Supremes

Early Influence
Woody Guthrie

Leadbelly
Les Paul

Nonperformer
Berry Gordy Jr.

1989

Dion
Otis Redding
The Rolling Stones
The Temptations
Stevie Wonder

Early Influences
The Ink Spots
Bessie Smith
The Soul Stirrers

Nonperformer
Phil Spector

1990

Hank Ballard
Bobby Darin
The Four Seasons
The Four Tops
The Kinks
The Platters
Simon and Garfunkel
The Who

Early Influences
Louis Armstrong
Charlie Christian
Ma Rainey

Nonperformers
Lamont Dozier
Gerry Goffin and Carole King
Brian Holland and Eddie Holland

1991

LaVern Baker
The Byrds
John Lee Hooker
The Impressions
Wilson Pickett
Jimmy Reed
Ike and Tina Turner

Early Influence
Howlin' Wolf

Nonperformers
Dave Bartholomew
Ralph Bass

Lifetime Achievement
Nesuhi Ertegun

1992

Bobby "Blue" Bland
Booker T. and the MG's
Johnny Cash
Jimi Hendrix Experience
The Isley Brothers
Sam and Dave
The Yardbirds

Early Influences
Elmore James
Professor Longhair

Nonperformers
Leo Fender
Doc Pomus
Bill Graham

1993

Ruth Brown
Cream
Creedence Clearwater Revival
The Doors
Etta James
Frankie Lymon and the Teenagers
Van Morrison
Sly and the Family Stone

Early Influence
Dinah Washington

Nonperformers
Dick Clark
Milt Gabler

1994

The Animals
The Band
Duane Eddy
Grateful Dead
Elton John
John Lennon
Bob Marley
Rod Stewart

Early Influence
Willie Dixon

Nonperformer
Johnny Otis

1995

The Allman Brothers Band
Al Green
Janis Joplin
Led Zeppelin
The Vandellas
Neil Young
Frank Zappa

Early Influence
The Orioles

Nonperformer
Paul Ackerman

1996

David Bowie
Gladys Knight and the Pips
Jefferson Airplane
Little Willie John
Pink Floyd
The Shirelles
The Velvet Underground

Early Influence
Pete Seeger

Nonperformer
Tom Donahue

1997

Joni Mitchell
Buffalo Springfield
The Young Rascals
Parliament/Funkadelic
The Jackson Five
The Bee Gees
Crosby, Stills and Nash

Early Influence
Bill Monroe
Mahalia Jackson

Nonperformer
Syd Nathan

1998

The Eagles
Fleetwood Mac
The Mamas and the Papas
Lloyd Price
Santana
Gene Vincent

Early Influence
J. R. Morton

Nonperformer
Allen Toussaint

1999

Billy Joel
Paul McCartney
Curtis Mayfield
Del Shannon
Dusty Springfield
Bruce Springsteen
The Staple Singers

Early Influences
Charles Brown
Bob Willis and His Texas Playboys

Nonperformer
George Martin

JAZZ HALL OF FAME

Down Beat magazine, America's leading jazz publication, conducts an annual poll of both readers and critics to determine the greatest luminaries of the jazz world. The honorees:

	Readers poll	Critics poll			Readers poll	Critics poll
1952	Louis Armstrong	—		1975	Cannonball Adderley	Cecil Taylor
1953	Glenn Miller	—		1976	Woody Herman	King Oliver
1954	Stan Kenton	—		1977	Paul Desmond	Benny Carter
1955	Charlie Parker	—		1978	Joe Venuti	Rahsaan Roland Kirk
1956	Duke Ellington	—		1979	Ella Fitzgerald	Lennie Tristano
1957	Benny Goodman	—		1980	Dexter Gordon	Max Roach
1958	Count Basie	—		1981	Art Blakey	Bill Evans
1959	Lester Young	—		1982	Art Pepper	Fats Navarro
1960	Dizzy Gillespie	—		1983	Stephane Grappelli	Albert Ayler
1961	Billie Holiday	Coleman Hawkins		1984	Oscar Peterson	Sun Ra
1962	Miles Davis	Bix Beiderbecke		1985	Sarah Vaughan	Zoot Sims
1963	Thelonious Monk	Jelly Roll Morton		1986	Stan Getz	Gil Evans
1964	Eric Dolphy	Art Tatum		1987	Lionel Hampton	Johnny Dodds, Thad Jones,
1965	John Coltrane	Earl Hines				Teddy Wilson
1966	Bud Powell	Charlie Christian		1988	Jaco Pastorius	Kenny Clarke
1967	Billy Strayhorn	Bessie Smith		1989	Woody Shaw	Chet Baker
1968	Wes Montgomery	Sidney Bechet,		1990	Red Rodney	Mary Lou Williams
		Fats Waller		1991	Lee Morgan	John Carter
1969	Ornette Coleman	Pee Wee Russell,		1992	Maynard Ferguson	James P. Johnson
		Jack Teagarden		1993	Gerry Mulligan	Edward Blackwell
1970	Jimi Hendrix	Johnny Hodges		1994	Dave Brubeck	Frank Zappa
1971	Charles Mingus	Roy Eldridge,		1995	J. J. Johnson	Julius Hemphill
		Django Reinhardt		1996	Horace Silver	Artie Shaw
1972	Gene Krupa	Clifford Brown		1997	Nat King Cole	Tony Williams
1973	Sonny Rollins	Fletcher Henderson		1998	Frank Sinatra	Elvin Jones
1974	Buddy Rich	Ben Webster		1999		Betty Carter

COUNTRY MUSIC HALL OF FAME

Located in Nashville along with everything else in country music, the Country Music Hall of Fame inducts its honorees each autumn. The enshrined elite:

1962	Roy Acuff	1975	Minnie Pearl	1990	Tennessee Ernie Ford
1963	(elections held but no one candidate received enough votes)	1976	Paul Cohen, Kitty Wells	1991	Boudleaux and Felice Bryant
		1977	Merle Travis	1992	George Jones, Frances Preston
1964	Tex Ritter	1978	Grandpa Jones	1993	Willie Nelson
1965	Ernest Tubb	1979	Hubert Long, Hank Snow	1994	Merle Haggard
1966	James R. Denny, George D. Hay, Uncle Dave Macon, Eddy Arnold	1980	Connie B. Gay, Original Sons of the Pioneers, Johnny Cash	1995	Roger Miller and Jo Walker-Meador
1967	Red Foley, J. L. Frank, Jim Reeves, Stephen H. Sholes	1981	Vernon Dalhart, Grant Turner	1996	Patsy Montana, Buck Owens, Ray Price
		1982	Lefty Frizzell, Marty Robbins, Roy Horton	1997	Harlan Howard, Brenda Lee, Cindy Walker
1968	Bob Wills	1983	Little Jimmy Dickens	1998	George Morgan, Elvis Presley, Tammy Wynette, E. W. "Bud" Wendell
1969	Gene Autry	1984	Ralph Peer, Floyd Tillman		
1970	Original Carter Family (A. P. Carter, Maybelle Carter, Sara Carter), Bill Monroe	1985	Lester Flatt and Earl Scruggs		
		1986	Wesley Rose, The Duke of Paducah	1999	Dolly Parton, Johnny Bond, Conway Twitty
1971	Arthur Edward Satherley	1987	Rod Brasfield		
1972	Jimmie Davis	1988	Roy Rogers, Loretta Lynn		
1973	Patsy Cline, Chet Atkins	1989	Jack Stapp, Hank Thompson, Cliffie Stone		
1974	Owen Bradley, Frank "Pee Wee" King				

TOP CONCERT APPEARANCES

The following survey lists the most successful North American individual concert appearances, based on box-office grosses, for 1998 and for all time. A concert appearance is defined here as all performances in a visit to a single town. (Source: Pollstar)

1998

1. The Rolling Stones/ — New York City
   Fiona Apple
2. Billy Joel — Uniondale, New York
3. Billy Joel — New York City
4. Billy Joel — Philadelphia, Pennsylvania
5. Yanni — New York City
6. "Lemonwheel"/Phish — Limestone, Maine
7. The Rolling Stones — Mexico City, Mexico
8. Elton John — New York City
9. Garth Brooks/ — Minneapolis, Minnesota
   Trisha Yearwood
10. Tibetan Freedom Concert — Washington, D.C.
    (Red Hot Chili Peppers, Dave Matthews Band, R.E.M., Herbie Hancock, Live, Pearl Jam, Blues Traveler, Wallflowers)
11. The Rolling Stones/ — Honolulu, Hawaii
    Jonny Lang
12. Eric Clapton/ — New York City
    Distant Cousins
13. The Rolling Stones/ — San Diego, California
    Santana
14. AIDS Project Los Angeles — Universal City, California
    Benefit (Natalie Cole, Boyz II Men)
15. The Rolling Stones/ — Portland, Oregon
    Jonny Lang
16. George Strait Country — Columbus, Ohio
    Music Festival (Tim McGraw, John Michael Montgomery, Faith Hill, Lee Ann Womack, Asleep At The Wheel)
17. Garth Brooks/ — San Antonio, Texas
    Trisha Yearwood/ Steve Wariner
18. Garth Brooks/ — Philadelphia, Pennsylvania
    Trisha Yearwood
19. Celine Dion/ — Chicago, Illinois
    Andre Phillppe Gagnon
20. George Strait Country — Tempe, Arizona
    Music Festival (Tim McGraw, John Michael Montgomery, Faith Hill, Lee Ann Womack, Lia McCann)

ALL TIME

1. Barbra Streisand — New York City, 1994
2. Elton John/Billy Joel — East Rutherford, New Jersey, 1994
3. Barbra Streisand — Las Vegas, 1993
4. 3 Tenors (Jose Carreras/ Placido Domingo/ Luciano Pavarotti) — East Rutherford, New Jersey, 1996
5. Barbra Streisand — Anaheim, California, 1994
6. The Rolling Stones — Mexico City, 1995
7. The Rolling Stones/ Living Colour/ Mar & Magette/ Dou Dov n' Diaye Rose — New York City, 1989
8. Bette Midler — New York City, 1993
9. The Rolling Stones/ Pearl Jam — Oakland, California, 1997
10. The Rolling Stones — East Rutherford, New Jersey, 1994
11. The Rolling Stones/ Seal — Oakland, California, 1994
12. The Rolling Stones/ Guns N' Roses/ Living Colour — Los Angeles, 1989
13. Madonna — Mexico City, 1993
14. Paul Simon/Simon & Garfunkel — New York City, 1993
15. 3 Tenors (Jose Carreras/ Placido Domingo/ Luciano Pavarotti) — Toronto, Ontario, Canada, 1997
16. Barbra Streisand — Auburn Hills, Michigan, 1994
17. Elton John/Billy Joel — Philadelphia, 1994
18. Bruce Springsteen & the E Street Band — East Rutherford, New Jersey, 1985
19. The Rolling Stones/ Foo Fighters — East Rutherford, New Jersey, 1997
20. Luis Miguel — Mexico City, Mexico, 1997

TOP CONCERT TOURS

These are the most successful North American tours of all time, along with year-by-year leaders since 1988. The rankings are based on grosses rather than attendance. (Source: Pollstar)

ALL TIME

Rank	Artist	Year of tour
1.	The Rolling Stones	1994
2.	Pink Floyd	1994
3.	The Rolling Stones	1989
4.	The Rolling Stones	1997
5.	U2	1997
6.	The Eagles	1994
7.	New Kids on the Block	1990
8.	U2	1992
9.	The Eagles	1995
10.	Barbra Streisand	1994
11.	Grateful Dead	1994
12.	Elton John/Billy Joel	1994
13.	Elton John	1998
14.	Grateful Dead	1993
15.	KISS	1996
16.	Boyz II Men	1995
17.	Billy Joel	1990
18.	The Who	1989
19.	Dave Matthews Band	1998
20.	Bruce Springsteen & the E Street Band	1985

1988

Rank	Artist	Cities/Shows
1.	Pink Floyd	23/35
2.	Van Halen's "Monsters of Rock"	23/26
3.	Def Leppard	94/112
4.	Grateful Dead	33/80
5.	Aerosmith	96/105
6.	Michael Jackson	19/54
7.	AC/DC	105/110
8.	Rod Stewart	82/88
9.	Rat Pack/Ultimate Event	23/41
10.	George Michael	32/46
11.	Whitesnake	83/84
12.	Bruce Springsteen & the E Street Band	21/43
13.	Robert Plant	88/92
14.	Luther Vandross/Anita Baker	26/42
15.	INXS	75/81

16.	John Cougar Mellencamp	45/54
17.	Kenny Rogers	88/167
18.	New Edition	67/70
19.	Randy Travis	98/119
20.	Sting	75/79

1989

Rank	Artist	Cities/Shows
1.	The Rolling Stones	33/60
2.	The Who	27/39
3.	Bon Jovi	129/143
4.	Grateful Dead	33/73
5.	New Kids on the Block	112/143
6.	Neil Diamond	29/69
7.	Metallica	134/140
8.	Elton John	32/47
9.	Rod Stewart	61/71
10.	Beach Boys/Chicago	57/59
11.	Poison	82/83
12.	R.E.M.	84/87
13.	Cinderella	135/136
14.	Barry Manilow	44/123
15.	George Strait	90/104
16.	New Edition	48/49
17.	Kenny Rogers	85/115
18.	Alabama	77/79
19.	Reba McEntire	111/126
20.	Randy Travis	88/105

1990

Rank	Artist	Cities/Shows
1.	New Kids on the Block	122/152
2.	Billy Joel	53/95
3.	Paul McCartney	21/32
4.	Grateful Dead	27/63
5.	Janet Jackson	62/89
6.	Aerosmith	92/101
7.	M. C. Hammer	132/138
8.	Mötley Crüe	103/108
9.	Phil Collins	27/56
10.	Eric Clapton	48/57
11.	David Bowie	41/51
12.	Madonna	12/32
13.	KISS	121/121
14.	Rush	56/63
15.	Depeche Mode	32/33

16.	Randy Travis	98/125
17.	Whitesnake	99/101
18.	Fleetwood Mac	54/62
19.	Kenny Rogers	66/105
20.	Alabama	102/103

1991

Rank	Artist	Cities/Shows
1.	Grateful Dead	27/76
2.	ZZ Top	85/106
3.	The Judds	116/126
4.	Rod Stewart	47/59
5.	Paul Simon	72/76
6.	Guns N' Roses	30/43
7.	Bell Biv Devoe/Johnny Gill/Keith Sweat	66/72
8.	Michael Bolton	70/103
9.	Garth Brooks	94/111
10.	Clint Black	92/100
11.	AC/DC	57/60
12.	Sting	64/81
13.	Luther Vandross	50/60
14.	Scorpions	90/93
15.	Van Halen	42/46
16.	Frank Sinatra	30/53
17.	Randy Travis	93/107
18.	Jimmy Buffett	37/51
19.	Jane's Addiction (includes Lollapalooza)	56/66
20.	Yes	55/57

1992

Rank	Artist	Cities/Shows
1.	U2	61/73
2.	Grateful Dead	23/55
3.	Guns N' Roses/Metallica	25/25
4.	Neil Diamond	26/69
5.	Bruce Springsteen	36/59
6.	Genesis	24/28
7.	Elton John	32/49
8.	Metallica	87/102
9.	Eric Clapton	30/37
10.	Hammer	123/130
11.	Bryan Adams	92/94
12.	Jimmy Buffett	43/64
13.	Lollapalooza II	29/35
14.	Garth Brooks	78/79

		Cities/Shows
15.	Reba McEntire	102/111
16.	Ozzy Osbourne	80/88
17.	John Mellencamp	44/55
18.	Harry Connick Jr.	43/87
19.	Def Leppard	72/77
20.	Rush	52/55

1993

Rank	Artist	Cities/Shows
1.	Grateful Dead	29/81
2.	Rod Stewart	54/68
3.	Neil Diamond	43/75
4.	Paul McCartney	23/23
5.	Bette Midler	29/71
6.	Billy Joel	22/39
7.	Garth Brooks	29/54
8.	Jimmy Buffett	32/52
9.	Reba McEntire	97/105
10.	Kenny G	82/97
11.	"Lollapalooza III"	29/34
12.	Aerosmith	61/66
13.	Clint Black/Wynonna	70/73
14.	Van Halen	32/40
15.	Alan Jackson	98/105
16.	Luther Vandross	42/49
17.	Peter Gabriel	31/38
18.	Def Leppard	90/91
19.	Depeche Mode	40/49
20.	Elton John	27/34

1994

Rank	Artist	Cities/Shows
1.	The Rolling Stones	43/60
2.	Pink Floyd	39/59
3.	The Eagles	32/54
4.	Barbra Streisand	6/22
5.	Grateful Dead	29/84
6.	Elton John/Billy Joel	14/21
7.	Aerosmith	71/76
8.	Lollapalooza IV	33/43
9.	Phil Collins	41/59
10.	Reba McEntire	96/102
11.	Bette Midler	44/54
12.	Billy Joel	40/49
13.	Michael Bolton	84/93
14.	Metallica	49/50
15.	ZZ Top	93/96
16.	Janet Jackson	63/72
17.	Brooks & Dunn	95/99
18.	Alan Jackson	93/99
19.	Jimmy Buffett	25/43
20.	Rod Stewart	33/34

1995

Rank	Artist	Cities/Shows
1.	The Eagles	46/58
2.	Boyz II Men	133/134
3.	R.E.M.	63/81
4.	Grateful Dead	20/45
5.	Jimmy Page/Robert Plant	56/68
6.	Van Halen	85/94
7.	Tom Petty and the Heartbreakers	80/89
8.	Reba McEntire	91/101
9.	Elton John	27/41
10.	Elton John/Billy Joel	10/12
11.	Alan Jackson	95/97
12.	Jimmy Buffett	37/52
13.	Yanni	50/59
14.	Vince Gill	82/90
15.	Phish	67/79
16.	Brooks & Dunn	91/91
17.	George Strait	48/49
18.	Live	79/81
19.	Lollapalooza '95	26/29
20.	Amy Grant	79/80

1996

Rank	Artist	Cities/Shows
1.	KISS	75/92
2.	Garth Brooks	41/121
3.	Neil Diamond	49/72
4.	Rod Stewart	62/65
5.	Bob Seger	57/64
6.	Jimmy Buffett	28/44
7.	Reba McEntire	83/86
8.	Alanis Morissette	88/98
9.	Hootie & The Blowfish	73/80
10.	Ozzy Osbourne	100/100
11.	AC/DC	74/81
12.	Dave Matthews Band	78/81
13.	George Strait	53/58
14.	Sting	51/56
15.	The Smashing Pumpkins	68/79
16.	The H.O.R.D.E. Festival	40/42
17.	The Who	22/31
18.	Phish	42/50
19.	Lollapallooza '96	20/22
20.	Alan Jackson	71/71

1997

Rank	Artist	Cities/Shows
1.	The Rolling Stones	26/33
2.	U2	37/46
3.	Fleetwood Mac	40/44
4.	Metallica	65/77
5.	Brooks & Dunn/ Reba McEntire	66/69
6.	Garth Brooks	28/110
7.	Tina Turner	56/70
8.	The Artist Formerly Known As Prince	71/73
9.	Jimmy Buffett	31/44
10.	Aerosmith	60/63
11.	Phish	34/45
12.	Phil Collins	32/35
13.	Alan Jackson	66/67
14.	ZZ Top	93/94
15.	Bush	69/69
16.	Lilith Fair	36/38
17.	Barry Manilow	72/103
18.	Kenny G/Toni Braxton	40/45
19.	Puff Daddy & The Family	35/37
20.	Vince Gill	76/77

1998

Rank	Artist	Cities/Shows
1.	Elton John	52/63
2.	Dave Matthews Band	76/85
3.	Celine Dion	31/43
4.	Yanni	82/93
5.	Garth Brooks	27/99
6.	Eric Clapton	42/45
7.	Shania Twain	87/92
8.	Janet Jackson	56/60
9.	George Strait Country Music Festival	18/18
10.	The Rolling Stones	13/20
11.	Jimmy Buffett	32/44
12.	Lillith Fair	46/56
13.	Billy Joel	15/38
14.	Aerosmith	67/70
15.	Page/Plant	50/52
16.	Metallica	42/44
17.	Phish	40/56
18.	Rod Stewart	40/42
19.	Pearl Jam	40/44
20.	The Spice Girls	39/39

BILLBOARD'S TOP 10 SINGLES

As the century ends, the most popular songs have a much different beat, with country and rap artists holding numerous spots on the pop charts—but the lyrics still explore the timeless themes of boys and love. (Source: *Billboard*)

1946

1. "Prisoner of Love," Perry Como
2. "To Each His Own," Eddy Howard
3. "The Gypsy," Ink Spots
4. "Five Minutes More," Frank Sinatra
5. "Rumors Are Flying," Frankie Carle
6. "Oh! What It Seemed To Be," Frankie Carle
7. "Personality," Johnny Mercer & The Pied Pipers
8. "South America, Take It Away," Bing Crosby & The Andrews Sisters
9. "The Gypsy," Dinah Shore
10. "Oh! What It Seemed To Be," Frank Sinatra

1947

1. "Near You," Francis Craig
2. "Peg O' My Heart," Harmonicats
3. "Heartaches," Ted Weems
4. "Linda," Ray Noble Orchestra & Buddy Clark (tie)
4. "Smoke, Smoke, Smoke (That Cigarette)," Tex Williams (tie)
6. "I Wish I Didn't Love You So," Vaughn Monroe
7. "Peg O' My Heart," Three Suns
8. "Anniversary Song," Al Jolson
9. "Near You," Larry Green Orchestra
10. "That's My Desire," Sammy Kaye

1948

1. "Twelfth Street Rag," Pee Wee Hunt
2. "Mañana (Is Good Enough for Me)," Peggy Lee
3. "Now Is the Hour," Bing Crosby
4. "A Tree in the Meadow," Margaret Whiting
5. "My Happiness," Jon & Sandra Steele
6. "You Can't Be True, Dear," Ken Griffin & Jerry Wayne
7. "Little White Lies," Dick Haymes
8. "You Call Everybody Darlin'," Al Trace
9. "My Happiness," Pied Pipers
10. "I'm Looking Over a Four Leaf Clover," Art Mooney

1949

1. "Riders in the Sky," Vaughn Monroe Orchestra
2. "That Lucky Old Sun," Frankie Laine

3. "You're Breaking My Heart," Vic Damone
4. "Some Enchanted Evening," Perry Como
5. "Slipping Around," Jimmy Wakely & Margaret Whiting
6. "I Can Dream, Can't I?" Andrews Sisters & Gordon Jenkins
7. "Cruising Down the River," Russ Morgan Orchestra
8. "A Little Bird Told Me," Evelyn Knight & The Stardusters
9. "Mule Train," Frankie Laine
10. "Jealous Heart," Al Morgan

1950

1. "Goodnight Irene," Gordon Jenkins & The Weavers
2. "Mona Lisa," Nat King Cole
3. "Third Man Theme," Anton Karas
4. "Sam's Song," Gary & Bing Crosby
5. "Simple Melody," Gary & Bing Crosby
6. "Music, Music, Music," Teresa Brewer
7. "Third Man Theme," Guy Lombardo
8. "Chattanoogie Shoe Shine Boy," Red Foley
9. "Harbor Lights," Sammy Kaye
10. "It Isn't Fair," Sammy Kaye & Don Cornell

1951

1. "Too Young," Nat King Cole
2. "Because of You," Tony Bennett
3. "How High the Moon," Les Paul & Mary Ford
4. "Come On-A My House," Rosemary Clooney
5. "Be My Love," Mario Lanza
6. "On Top of Old Smoky," Weavers
7. "Cold, Cold Heart," Tony Bennett
8. "If," Perry Como
9. "Loveliest Night of the Year," Mario Lanza
10. "Tennessee Waltz," Patti Page

1952

1. "Blue Tango," Leroy Anderson
2. "Wheel of Fortune," Kay Starr
3. "Cry," Johnnie Ray
4. "You Belong to Me," Jo Stafford
5. "Auf Wiederseh'n, Sweetheart," Vera Lynn

6. "I Went to Your Wedding," Patti Page
7. "Half as Much," Rosemary Clooney
8. "Wish You Were Here," Eddie Fisher & Hugo Winterhalter
9. "Here in My Heart," Al Martino
10. "Delicado," Percy Faith

1953

1. "Song From Moulin Rouge," Percy Faith
2. "Vaya con Dios," Les Paul & Mary Ford
3. "Doggie in the Window," Patti Page
4. "I'm Walking Behind You," Eddie Fisher
5. "You, You, You," Ames Brothers
6. "Till I Waltz Again with You," Teresa Brewer
7. "April in Portugal," Les Baxter
8. "No Other Love," Perry Como
9. "Don't Let the Stars Get in Your Eyes," Perry Como
10. "I Believe," Frankie Laine

1954

1. "Little Things Mean a Lot," Kitty Kallen
2. "Wanted," Perry Como
3. "Hey, There," Rosemary Clooney
4. "Sh-Boom," Crew Cuts
5. "Make Love to Me," Jo Stafford
6. "Oh! My Pa-Pa," Eddie Fisher
7. "I Get So Lonely," Four Knights
8. "Three Coins in the Fountain," Four Aces
9. "Secret Love," Doris Day
10. "Hernando's Highway," Archie Bleyer

1955

1. "Cherry Pink and Apple Blossom White," Perez Prado
2. "Rock Around the Clock," Bill Haley & His Comets
3. "The Yellow Rose of Texas," Mitch Miller
4. "Autumn Leaves," Roger Williams
5. "Unchained Melody," Les Baxter
6. "The Ballad of Davy Crockett," Bill Hayes
7. "Love Is a Many-Splendored Thing," Four Aces

8. "Sincerely," McGuire Sisters
9. "Ain't That a Shame," Pat Boone
10. "Dance with Me Henry," Georgia Gibbs

1956

1. "Heartbreak Hotel," Elvis Presley
2. "Don't Be Cruel," Elvis Presley
3. "Lisbon Antigua," Nelson Riddle
4. "My Prayer," Platters
5. "The Wayward Wind," Gogi Grant
6. "Hound Dog," Elvis Presley
7. "The Poor People of Paris," Les Baxter
8. "Whatever Will Be Will Be (Que Sera Sera)," Doris Day
9. "Memories Are Made of This," Dean Martin
10. "Rock and Roll Waltz," Kay Starr

1957

1. "All Shook Up," Elvis Presley
2. "Love Letters in the Sand," Pat Boone
3. "Little Darlin'," Diamonds
4. "Young Love," Tab Hunter
5. "So Rare," Jimmy Dorsey
6. "Don't Forbid Me," Pat Boone
7. "Singing the Blues," Guy Mitchell
8. "Young Love," Sonny James
9. "Too Much," Elvis Presley
10. "Round and Round," Perry Como

1958

1. "Volare (Nel Blu Dipinto Di Blu)," Domenico Modugno
2. "All I Have To Do Is Dream"/ "Claudette," Everly Brothers
3. "Don't"/"I Beg of You," Elvis Presley
4. "Witch Doctor," David Seville
5. "Patricia," Perez Prado
6. "Sail Along Silvery Moon"/ "Raunchy," Billy Vaughn
7. "Catch a Falling Star"/"Magic Moments," Perry Como
8. "Tequila," Champs
9. "It's All in the Game," Tommy Edwards
10. "Return to Me," Dean Martin

1959

1. "The Battle of New Orleans," Johnny Horton
2. "Mack the Knife," Bobby Darin
3. "Personality," Lloyd Price
4. "Venus," Frankie Avalon
5. "Lonely Boy," Paul Anka
6. "Dream Lover," Bobby Darin

7. "The Three Bells," Browns
8. "Come Softly to Me," Fleetwoods
9. "Kansas City," Wilbert Harrison
10. "Mr. Blue," Fleetwoods

1960

1. "Theme from A Summer Place," Percy Faith
2. "He'll Have To Go," Jim Reeves
3. "Cathy's Clown," Everly Brothers
4. "Running Bear," Johnny Preston
5. "Teen Angel," Mark Dinning
6. "It's Now or Never," Elvis Presley
7. "Handy Man," Jimmy Jones
8. "I'm Sorry," Brenda Lee
9. "Stuck on You," Elvis Presley
10. "The Twist," Chubby Checker

1961

1. "Tossin' and Turnin'," Bobby Lewis
2. "I Fall to Pieces," Patsy Cline
3. "Michael," Highwaymen
4. "Cryin'," Roy Orbison
5. "Runaway," Del Shannon
6. "My True Story," Jive Five
7. "Pony Time," Chubby Checker
8. "Wheels," String-a-Longs
9. "Raindrops," Dee Clark
10. "Wooden Heart (Muss I Denn)," Joe Dowell

1962

1. "Stranger on the Shore," Mr. Acker Bilk
2. "I Can't Stop Loving You," Ray Charles
3. "Mashed Potato Time," Dee Dee Sharp
4. "Roses Are Red," Bobby Vinton
5. "The Stripper," David Rose
6. "Johnny Angel," Shelley Fabares
7. "Loco-motion," Little Eva
8. "Let Me In," Sensations
9. "The Twist," Chubby Checker
10. "Soldier Boy," Shirelles

1963

1. "Sugar Shack," Jimmy Gilmer & The Fireballs
2. "Surfin' USA," Beach Boys
3. "The End of the World," Skeeter Davis
4. "Rhythm of the Rain," Cascades
5. "He's So Fine," Chiffons
6. "Blue Velvet," Bobby Vinton
7. "Hey Paula," Paul & Paula
8. "Fingertips II," Little Stevie Wonder

9. "Washington Square," Village Stompers
10. "It's All Right," Impressions

1964

1. "I Want To Hold Your Hand," Beatles
2. "She Loves You," Beatles
3. "Hello, Dolly!" Louis Armstrong
4. "Oh, Pretty Woman," Roy Orbison
5. "I Get Around," Beach Boys
6. "Everybody Loves Somebody," Dean Martin
7. "My Guy," Mary Wells
8. "We'll Sing in the Sunshine," Gale Garnett
9. "Last Kiss," J. Frank Wilson & The Cavaliers
10. "Where Did Our Love Go," Supremes

1965

1. "Wooly Bully," Sam the Sham & The Pharaohs
2. "I Can't Help Myself," Four Tops
3. "(I Can't Get No) Satisfaction," Rolling Stones
4. "You Were on My Mind," We Five
5. "You've Lost That Lovin' Feelin'," Righteous Brothers
6. "Downtown," Petula Clark
7. "Help!," Beatles
8. "Can't You Hear My Heartbeat," Herman's Hermits
9. "Crying in the Chapel," Elvis Presley
10. "My Girl," Temptations

1966

1. "The Ballad of the Green Berets," S/Sgt. Barry Sadler
2. "Cherish," Association
3. "(You're My) Soul and Inspiration," Righteous Brothers
4. "Reach Out I'll Be There," Four Tops
5. "96 Tears," ? & the Mysterians
6. "Last Train to Clarksville," Monkees
7. "Monday, Monday," Mamas & the Papas
8. "You Can't Hurry Love," Supremes
9. "Poor Side of Town," Johnny Rivers
10. "California Dreamin'," Mamas & the Papas

1967

1. "To Sir with Love," Lulu
2. "The Letter," Box Tops
3. "Ode to Billie Joe," Bobby Gentry
4. "Windy," Association
5. "I'm a Believer," Monkees
6. "Light My Fire," Doors

7. "Somethin' Stupid," Nancy Sinatra & Frank Sinatra
8. "Happy Together," Turtles
9. "Groovin'," Young Rascals
10. "Can't Take My Eyes Off You," Frankie Valli

1968

1. "Hey Jude," Beatles
2. "Love Is Blue (L'Amour Est Blue)," Paul Mauriat
3. "Honey," Bobby Goldsboro
4. "(Sittin' on) The Dock of the Bay," Otis Redding
5. "People Got To Be Free," Rascals
6. "Sunshine of Your Love," Cream
7. "This Guy's in Love with You," Herb Alpert
8. "The Good, the Bad and the Ugly," Hugo Montenegro
9. "Mrs. Robinson," Simon & Garfunkel
10. "Tighten Up," Archie Bell & The Drells

1969

1. "Sugar, Sugar," Archies
2. "Aquarius/Let the Sunshine In," Fifth Dimension
3. "I Can't Get Next to You," Temptations
4. "Honky Tonk Women," Rolling Stones
5. "Everyday People," Sly & the Family Stone
6. "Dizzy," Tommy Roe
7. "Hot Fun in the Summertime," Sly & the Family Stone
8. "I'll Never Fall in Love Again," Tom Jones
9. "Build Me Up Buttercup," Foundations
10. "Crimson and Clover," Tommy James & The Shondells

1970

1. "Bridge over Troubled Water," Simon & Garfunkel
2. "(They Long To Be) Close to You," Carpenters
3. "American Woman"/"No Sugar Tonight," Guess Who
4. "Raindrops Keep Fallin' on My Head," B. J. Thomas
5. "War," Edwin Starr
6. "Ain't No Mountain High Enough," Diana Ross
7. "I'll Be There," Jackson 5
8. "Get Ready," Rare Earth
9. "Let It Be," Beatles
10. "Band of Gold," Freda Payne

1971

1. "Joy to the World," Three Dog Night
2. "Maggie May"/"Reason To Believe," Rod Stewart
3. "It's Too Late"/"I Feel the Earth Move," Carole King
4. "One Bad Apple," Osmonds
5. "How Can You Mend a Broken Heart," Bee Gees
6. "Indian Reservation," Raiders
7. "Go Away Little Girl," Donny Osmond
8. "Take Me Home, Country Roads," John Denver with Fat City
9. "Just My Imagination (Running Away with Me)," Temptations
10. "Knock Three Times," Dawn

1972

1. "The First Time Ever I Saw Your Face," Roberta Flack
2. "Alone Again (Naturally)," Gilbert O'Sullivan
3. "American Pie," Don McLean
4. "Without You," Nilsson
5. "Candy Man," Sammy Davis Jr.
6. "I Gotcha," Joe Tex
7. "Lean on Me," Bill Withers
8. "Baby Don't Get Hooked on Me," Mac Davis
9. "Brand New Key," Melanie
10. "Daddy Don't You Walk So Fast," Wayne Newton

1973

1. "Tie a Yellow Ribbon 'Round the Ole Oak Tree," Tony Orlando & Dawn
2. "Bad, Bad Leroy Brown," Jim Croce
3. "Killing Me Softly with His Song," Roberta Flack
4. "Let's Get It On," Marvin Gaye
5. "My Love," Paul McCartney & Wings
6. "Why Me," Kris Kristofferson
7. "Crocodile Rock," Elton John
8. "Will It Go Round in Circles," Billy Preston
9. "You're So Vain," Carly Simon
10. "Touch Me in the Morning," Diana Ross

1974

1. "The Way We Were," Barbra Streisand
2. "Seasons in the Sun," Terry Jacks
3. "Love's Theme," Love Unlimited Orchestra
4. "Come and Get Your Love," Redbone
5. "Dancing Machine," Jackson 5
6. "The Loco-motion," Grand Funk Railroad
7. "TSOP," MFSB

8. "The Streak," Ray Stevens
9. "Bennie and the Jets," Elton John
10. "One Hell of a Woman," Mac Davis

1975

1. "Love Will Keep Us Together," Captain & Tennille
2. "Rhinestone Cowboy," Glen Campbell
3. "Philadelphia Freedom," Elton John
4. "Before the Next Teardrop Falls," Freddy Fender
5. "My Eyes Adored You," Frankie Valli
6. "Shining Star," Earth, Wind & Fire
7. "Fame," David Bowie
8. "Laughter in the Rain," Neil Sedaka
9. "One of These Nights," Eagles
10. "Thank God I'm a Country Boy," John Denver

1976

1. "Silly Love Songs," Wings
2. "Don't Go Breaking My Heart," Elton John & Kiki Dee
3. "Disco Lady," Johnnie Taylor
4. "December, 1963 (Oh, What a Night)," Four Seasons
5. "Play That Funky Music," Wild Cherry
6. "Kiss and Say Goodbye," Manhattans
7. "Love Machine, Pt. 1," Miracles
8. "50 Ways To Leave Your Lover," Paul Simon
9. "Love Is Alive," Gary Wright
10. "A Fifth of Beethoven," Walter Murphy & The Big Apple Band

1977

1. "Tonight's the Night (Gonna Be Alright)," Rod Stewart
2. "I Just Want To Be Your Everything," Andy Gibb
3. "Best of My Love," Emotions
4. "Love Theme from *A Star Is Born* (Evergreen)" Barbra Streisand
5. "Angel in Your Arms," Hot
6. "I Like Dreamin'," Kenny Nolan
7. "Don't Leave Me This Way," Thelma Houston
8. "(Your Love Has Lifted Me) Higher and Higher," Rita Coolidge
9. "Undercover Angel," Alan O'Day
10. "Torn Between Two Lovers," Mary MacGregor

1978

1. "Shadow Dancing," Andy Gibb
2. "Night Fever," Bee Gees
3. "You Light Up My Life," Debby Boone
4. "Stayin' Alive," Bee Gees
5. "Kiss You All Over," Exile

6. "How Deep Is Your Love," Bee Gees
7. "Baby Come Back," Player
8. "Love Is Thicker Than Water," Andy Gibb
9. "Boogie Oogie Oogie," A Taste of Honey
10. "Three Times a Lady," Commodores

1979

1. "My Sharona," Knack
2. "Bad Girls," Donna Summer
3. "Le Freak," Chic
4. "Do Ya Think I'm Sexy," Rod Stewart
5. "Reunited," Peaches & Herb
6. "I Will Survive," Gloria Gaynor
7. "Hot Stuff," Donna Summer
8. "Y.M.C.A.," Village People
9. "Ring My Bell," Anita Ward
10. "Sad Eyes," Robert John

1980

1. "Call Me," Blondie
2. "Another Brick in the Wall," Pink Floyd
3. "Magic," Olivia Newton-John
4. "Rock with You," Michael Jackson
5. "Do That to Me One More Time," Captain & Tennille
6. "Crazy Little Thing Called Love," Queen
7. "Coming Up," Paul McCartney
8. "Funkytown," Lipps, Inc.
9. "It's Still Rock and Roll to Me," Billy Joel
10. "The Rose," Bette Midler

1981

1. "Bette Davis Eyes," Kim Carnes
2. "Endless Love," Diana Ross & Lionel Richie
3. "Lady," Kenny Rogers
4. "(Just Like) Starting Over," John Lennon
5. "Jessie's Girl," Rick Springfield
6. "Celebration," Kool & the Gang
7. "Kiss on My List," Daryl Hall & John Oates
8. "I Love a Rainy Night," Eddie Rabbitt
9. "9 to 5," Dolly Parton
10. "Keep On Loving You," REO Speedwagon

1982

1. "Physical," Olivia Newton-John
2. "Eye of the Tiger," Survivor
3. "I Love Rock 'n' Roll," Joan Jett & the Blackhearts
4. "Ebony and Ivory," Paul McCartney & Stevie Wonder

5. "Centerfold," The J. Geils Band
6. "Don't You Want Me," Human League
7. "Jack and Diane," John Cougar
8. "Hurts So Good," John Cougar
9. "Abracadabra," Steve Miller Band
10. "Hard To Say I'm Sorry," Chicago

1983

1. "Every Breath You Take," The Police
2. "Billie Jean," Michael Jackson
3. "Flashdance…What a Feeling," Irene Cara
4. "Down Under," Men at Work
5. "Beat It," Michael Jackson
6. "Total Eclipse of the Heart," Bonnie Tyler
7. "Maneater," Daryl Hall & John Oates
8. "Baby Come to Me," Patti Austin with James Ingram
9. "Maniac," Michael Sembello
10. "Sweet Dreams (Are Made of This)," Eurythmics

1984

1. "When Doves Cry," Prince
2. "What's Love Got To Do with It," Tina Turner
3. "Say Say Say," Paul McCartney & Michael Jackson
4. "Footloose," Kenny Loggins
5. "Against All Odds (Take a Look at Me Now)," Phil Collins
6. "Jump," Van Halen
7. "Hello," Lionel Richie
8. "Owner of a Lonely Heart," Yes
9. "Ghostbusters," Ray Parker Jr.
10. "Karma Chameleon," Culture Club

1985

1. "Careless Whisper," Wham! featuring George Michael
2. "Like a Virgin," Madonna
3. "Wake Me Up Before You Go-Go," Wham!
4. "I Want To Know What Love Is," Foreigner
5. "I Feel for You," Chaka Khan
6. "Out of Touch," Daryl Hall & John Oates
7. "Everybody Wants To Rule the World," Tears for Fears
8. "Money for Nothing," Dire Straits
9. "Crazy for You," Madonna
10. "Take on Me," a-ha

1986

1. "That's What Friends Are For," Dionne & Friends
2. "Say You, Say Me," Lionel Richie

3. "I Miss You," Klymaxx
4. "On My Own," Patti LaBelle & Michael McDonald
5. "Broken Wings," Mr. Mister
6. "How Will I Know," Whitney Houston
7. "Party All the Time," Eddie Murphy
8. "Burning Heart," Survivor
9. "Kyrie," Mr. Mister
10. "Addicted to Love," Robert Palmer

1987

1. "Walk Like an Egyptian," Bangles
2. "Alone," Heart
3. "Shake You Down," Gregory Abbott
4. "I Wanna Dance with Somebody (Who Loves Me)," Whitney Houston
5. "Nothing's Gonna Stop Us Now," Starship
6. "C'est La Vie," Robbie Nevil
7. "Here I Go Again," Whitesnake
8. "The Way It Is," Bruce Hornsby & the Range
9. "Shakedown," Bob Seger
10. "Livin' On a Prayer," Bon Jovi

1988

1. "Faith," George Michael
2. "Need You Tonight," INXS
3. "Got My Mind Set on You," George Harrison
4. "Never Gonna Give You Up," Rick Astley
5. "Sweet Child o' Mine," Guns N' Roses
6. "So Emotional," Whitney Houston
7. "Heaven Is a Place on Earth," Belinda Carlisle
8. "Could've Been," Tiffany
9. "Hands to Heaven," Breathe
10. "Roll with It," Steve Winwood

1989

1. "Look Away," Chicago
2. "My Prerogative," Bobby Brown
3. "Every Rose Has Its Thorn," Poison
4. "Straight Up," Paula Abdul
5. "Miss You Much," Janet Jackson
6. "Cold Hearted," Paula Abdul
7. "Wind Beneath My Wings," Bette Midler
8. "Girl You Know It's True," Milli Vanilli
9. "Baby, I Love Your Way/Freebird Medley," Will to Power
10. "Giving You the Best That I Got," Anita Baker

1990

1. "Hold On," Wilson Phillips
2. "It Must Have Been Love," Roxette
3. "Nothing Compares 2 U," Sinéad O'Connor

4. "Poison," Bell Biv Devoe
5. "Vogue," Madonna
6. "Vision of Love," Mariah Carey
7. "Another Day in Paradise," Phil Collins
8. "Hold On," En Vogue
9. "Cradle of Love," Billy Idol
10. "Blaze of Glory," Jon Bon Jovi

1991

1. "(Everything I Do) I Do It for You," Bryan Adams
2. "I Wanna Sex You Up," Color Me Badd
3. "Gonna Make You Sweat," C+C Music Factory
4. "Rush Rush," Paula Abdul
5. "One More Try," Timmy T.
6. "Unbelievable," EMF
7. "More Than Words," Extreme
8. "I Like the Way (The Kissing Game)," Hi-Five
9. "The First Time," Surface
10. "Baby Baby," Amy Grant

1992

1. "End of the Road," Boyz II Men
2. "Baby Got Back," Sir Mix-A-Lot
3. "Jump," Kris Kross
4. "Save the Best for Last," Vanessa Williams
5. "Baby-Baby-Baby," TLC
6. "Tears in Heaven," Eric Clapton
7. "My Lovin' (You're Never Gonna Get It)," En Vogue
8. "Under the Bridge," Red Hot Chili Peppers
9. "All 4 Love," Color Me Badd
10. "Just Another Day," Jon Secada

1993

1. "I Will Always Love You," Whitney Houston
2. "Whoomp! (There It Is)," Tag Team

3. "Can't Help Falling in Love," UB40
4. "That's the Way Love Goes," Janet Jackson
5. "Freak Me," Silk
6. "Weak," SWV
7. "If I Ever Fall in Love," Shai
8. "Dreamlover," Mariah Carey
9. "Rump Shaker," Wreckx-N-Effect
10. "Informer," Snow

1994

1. "The Sign," Ace of Base
2. "I Swear," All-4-One
3. "I'll Make Love to You," Boyz II Men
4. "The Power of Love," Celine Dion
5. "Hero," Mariah Carey
6. "Stay (I Missed You)," Lisa Loeb & Nine Stories
7. "Breathe Again," Toni Braxton
8. "All for Love," Bryan Adams/Rod Stewart/Sting
9. "All That She Wants," Ace of Base
10. "Don't Turn Around," Ace of Base

1995

1. "Gangsta's Paradise," Coolio featuring L.V.
2. "Waterfalls," TLC
3. "Creep," TLC
4. "Kiss from a Rose," Seal
5. "On Bended Knee," Boyz II Men
6. "Another Night," Real McCoy
7. "Fantasy," Mariah Carey
8. "Take A Bow," Madonna
9. "Don't Take It Personal (Just One of Dem Days)," Monica
10. "This Is How We Do It," Montell Jordan

1996

1. "Macarena (Bayside Boys Mix)," Los Del Rio
2. "One Sweet Day," Mariah Carey & Boyz II Men
3. "Because You Loved Me," Celine Dion

4. "Nobody Knows," The Tony Rich Project
5. "Always Be My Baby," Mariah Carey
6. "Give Me One Reason," Tracy Chapman
7. "Tha Crossroads," Bone Thugs-N-Harmony
8. "I Love You Always Forever," Donna Lewis
9. "You're Makin' Me High/Let It Flow," Toni Braxton
10. "Twisted," Keith Sweat

1997

1. "Candle in the Wind 1997"/"Something About the Way You Look Tonight," Elton John
2. "You Were Meant for Me"/"Foolish Games," Jewel
3. "I'll Be Missing You," Puff Daddy & Faith Evans (Featuring 112)
4. "Un-Break My Heart," Toni Braxton
5. "Can't Nobody Hold Me Down," Puff Daddy (featuring Mase)
6. "I Believe I Can Fly," R. Kelly
7. "Don't Let Go (Love)," En Vogue
8. "Return of the Mack," Mark Morrison
9. "How Do I Live," LeAnn Rimes
10. "Wannabe," Spice Girls

1998

1. "The Boy Is Mine," Brandy & Monica
2. "Too Close," Next
3. "You're Still the One," Shania Twain
4. "Candle in the Wind 1997"/"Something About the Way You Look Tonight," Elton John
5. "Been Around the World," Puff Daddy & The Family
6. "How Do I Live," LeAnn Rimes
7. "Nice & Slow," Usher
8. "No, No, No," Destiny's Child
9. "My Way," Usher
10. "My All," Mariah Carey

BILLBOARD'S TOP 10 ALBUMS

For the first nine years, soundtracks and cast albums topped the annual chart. In 1998, a *Titanic* wave rolled the classical-sounding soundtrack to No. 1, for only the second time in the last 20 years. Our hearts do go on. (Source: *Billboard*)

1957

1. *My Fair Lady,* original cast
2. *Hymns,* Tennessee Ernie Ford
3. *Oklahoma!,* soundtrack
4. *Around the World in 80 Days,* soundtrack
5. *The King and I,* soundtrack
6. *Calypso,* Harry Belafonte
7. *Love Is the Thing,* Nat King Cole
8. *The Eddy Duchin Story,* soundtrack
9. *Songs of the Fabulous Fifties,* Roger Williams
10. *Film Encores,* Mantovani

1958

1. *My Fair Lady,* original cast
2. *The Music Man,* original cast
3. *Johnny's Greatest Hits,* Johnny Mathis
4. *South Pacific,* soundtrack
5. *Come Fly with Me,* Frank Sinatra
6. *Around the World in 80 Days,* soundtrack
7. *Warm,* Johnny Mathis
8. *South Pacific,* original cast
9. *Ricky,* Ricky Nelson
10. *The King and I,* soundtrack

1959

1. *Music from "Peter Gunn,"* Henry Mancini
2. *Gigi,* soundtrack
3. *South Pacific,* soundtrack
4. *From the Hungry i,* Kingston Trio
5. *The Kingston Trio at Large,* Kingston Trio
6. *Sing Along with Mitch,* Mitch Miller
7. *Inside Shelley Berman,* Shelley Berman
8. *Exotica, Vol. 1,* Martin Denny
9. *My Fair Lady,* original cast
10. *Flower Drum Song,* original cast

1960

1. *The Sound of Music,* original cast
2. *Inside Shelley Berman,* Shelley Berman
3. *The Button-Down Mind of Bob Newhart,* Bob Newhart
4. *Sixty Years of Music America Loves Best, Vol. I,* various artists
5. *Here We Go Again,* Kingston Trio
6. *Sold Out,* Kingston Trio
7. *Heavenly,* Johnny Mathis

8. *South Pacific,* soundtrack
9. *Faithfully,* Johnny Mathis
10. *Outside Shelley Berman,* Shelley Berman

1961

1. *Camelot,* original cast
2. *Great Motion Picture Themes,* various artists
3. *Never on Sunday,* soundtrack
4. *The Sound of Music,* original cast
5. *Exodus,* soundtrack
6. *Knockers Up,* Rusty Warren
7. *G.I. Blues,* Elvis Presley/soundtrack
8. *Sing Along with Mitch,* Mitch Miller
9. *Calcutta,* Lawrence Welk
10. *Tonight in Person,* Limeliters

1962

1. *West Side Story,* soundtrack
2. *Breakfast at Tiffany's,* Henry Mancini
3. *Blue Hawaii,* Elvis Presley/soundtrack
4. *West Side Story,* original cast
5. *The Sound of Music,* original cast
6. *Time Out,* Dave Brubeck
7. *Camelot,* original cast
8. *Your Twist Party,* Chubby Checker
9. *Knockers Up,* Rusty Warren
10. *Judy at Carnegie Hall,* Judy Garland

1963

1. *West Side Story,* soundtrack
2. *Peter, Paul and Mary,* Peter, Paul and Mary
3. *Moving,* Peter, Paul and Mary
4. *Joan Baez in Concert,* Joan Baez
5. *I Left My Heart in San Francisco,* Tony Bennett
6. *Moon River and Other Great Movie Themes,* Andy Williams
7. *Lawrence of Arabia,* soundtrack
8. *Days of Wine and Roses,* Andy Williams
9. *Oliver,* original cast
10. *Modern Sounds in Country and Western Music, Vol. 2,* Ray Charles

1964

1. *Hello, Dolly!,* original cast
2. *In the Wind,* Peter, Paul and Mary
3. *Honey in the Horn,* Al Hirt

4. *The Barbra Streisand Album,* Barbra Streisand
5. *West Side Story,* soundtrack
6. *Peter, Paul and Mary,* Peter, Paul & Mary
7. *The Second Barbra Streisand Album,* Barbra Streisand
8. *Meet the Beatles,* Beatles
9. *The Third Barbra Streisand Album,* Barbra Streisand
10. *Moon River and Other Great Movie Themes,* Andy Williams

1965

1. *Mary Poppins,* soundtrack
2. *Beatles '65,* Beatles
3. *The Sound of Music,* soundtrack
4. *My Fair Lady,* soundtrack
5. *Fiddler on the Roof,* original cast
6. *Goldfinger,* soundtrack
7. *Hello, Dolly!,* original cast
8. *Dear Heart,* Andy Williams
9. *Introducing Herman's Hermits,* Herman's Hermits
10. *Beatles VI,* Beatles

1966

1. *Whipped Cream and Other Delights,* Herb Alpert & the Tijuana Brass
2. *The Sound of Music,* soundtrack
3. *Going Places,* Herb Alpert & the Tijuana Brass
4. *Rubber Soul,* Beatles
5. *What Now My Love,* Herb Alpert & the Tijuana Brass
6. *If You Can Believe Your Eyes and Ears,* Mamas & the Papas
7. *Dr. Zhivago,* soundtrack
8. *Revolver,* Beatles
9. *Color Me Barbra,* Barbra Streisand
10. *Ballad of the Green Berets,* S/Sgt. Barry Sadler

1967

1. *More of the Monkees,* Monkees
2. *The Monkees,* Monkees
3. *Dr. Zhivago,* soundtrack
4. *The Sound of Music,* soundtrack
5. *The Temptations' Greatest Hits,* Temptations
6. *A Man and a Woman,* soundtrack
7. *S.R.O.,* Herb Alpert & the Tijuana Brass

8. *Whipped Cream and Other Delights*, Herb Alpert & the Tijuana Brass
9. *Going Places*, Herb Alpert & the Tijuana Brass
10. *Sgt. Pepper's Lonely Hearts Club Band*, Beatles

1968

1. *Are You Experienced?*, Jimi Hendrix Experience
2. *The Graduate*, Simon & Garfunkel/soundtrack
3. *Disraeli Gears*, Cream
4. *Magical Mystery Tour*, Beatles/soundtrack
5. *Diana Ross and the Supremes' Greatest Hits*, Diana Ross & The Supremes
6. *Sgt. Pepper's Lonely Hearts Club Band*, Beatles
7. *The Doors*, The Doors
8. *Parsley, Sage, Rosemary and Thyme*, Simon & Garfunkel
9. *Vanilla Fudge*, Vanilla Fudge
10. *Blooming Hits*, Paul Mauriat & His Orchestra

1969

1. *In-a-Gadda-Da-Vida*, Iron Butterfly
2. *Hair*, original cast
3. *Blood, Sweat and Tears*, Blood, Sweat and Tears
4. *Bayou Country*, Creedence Clearwater Revival
5. *Led Zeppelin*, Led Zeppelin
6. *Johnny Cash at Folsom Prison*, Johnny Cash
7. *Funny Girl*, soundtrack
8. *The Beatles (The White Album)*, Beatles
9. *Donovan's Greatest Hits*, Donovan
10. *The Association's Greatest Hits*, Association

1970

1. *Bridge over Troubled Water*, Simon & Garfunkel
2. *Led Zeppelin II*, Led Zeppelin
3. *Chicago*, Chicago
4. *Abbey Road*, Beatles
5. *Santana*, Santana
6. *Get Ready*, Rare Earth
7. *Easy Rider*, soundtrack
8. *Butch Cassidy and the Sundance Kid*, soundtrack
9. *Joe Cocker!*, Joe Cocker
10. *Three Dog Night Was Captured Live at the Forum*, Three Dog Night

1971

1. *Jesus Christ Superstar*, various artists
2. *Tapestry*, Carole King
3. *Close to You*, Carpenters
4. *Pearl*, Janis Joplin
5. *Abraxas*, Santana
6. *The Partridge Family Album*, Partridge Family
7. *Sweet Baby James*, James Taylor
8. *Tea for the Tillerman*, Cat Stevens
9. *Greatest Hits*, Sly & the Family Stone
10. *Chicago III*, Chicago

1972

1. *Harvest*, Neil Young
2. *Tapestry*, Carole King
3. *American Pie*, Don McLean
4. *Teaser and the Firecat*, Cat Stevens
5. *Hot Rocks, 1964–71*, Rolling Stones
6. *Killer*, Alice Cooper
7. *First Take*, Roberta Flack
8. *America*, America
9. *Music*, Carole King
10. *Madman Across the Water*, Elton John

1973

1. *The World Is a Ghetto*, War
2. *Summer Breeze*, Seals & Crofts
3. *Talking Book*, Stevie Wonder
4. *No Secrets*, Carly Simon
5. *Lady Sings the Blues*, Diana Ross
6. *They Only Come Out at Night*, Edgar Winter Group
7. *I Am Woman*, Helen Reddy
8. *Don't Shoot Me, I'm Only the Piano Player*, Elton John
9. *I'm Still in Love with You*, Al Green
10. *Seventh Sojourn*, Moody Blues

1974

1. *Goodbye Yellow Brick Road*, Elton John
2. *John Denver's Greatest Hits*, John Denver
3. *Band on the Run*, Paul McCartney & Wings
4. *Innervisions*, Stevie Wonder
5. *You Don't Mess Around with Jim*, Jim Croce
6. *American Graffiti*, soundtrack
7. *Imagination*, Gladys Knight & The Pips
8. *Behind Closed Doors*, Charlie Rich
9. *The Sting*, soundtrack
10. *Tres Hombres*, ZZ Top

1975

1. *Elton John—Greatest Hits*, Elton John
2. *John Denver's Greatest Hits*, John Denver
3. *That's the Way of the World*, Earth, Wind & Fire
4. *Back Home Again*, John Denver
5. *Phoebe Snow*, Phoebe Snow
6. *Heart Like a Wheel*, Linda Ronstadt
7. *Captain Fantastic and the Brown Dirt Cowboy*, Elton John
8. *An Evening with John Denver*, John Denver
9. *AWB*, Average White Band
10. *On the Border*, Eagles

1976

1. *Frampton Comes Alive*, Peter Frampton
2. *Fleetwood Mac*, Fleetwood Mac
3. *Wings at the Speed of Sound*, Wings
4. *Greatest Hits, 1971–1975*, Eagles
5. *Chicago IX—Chicago's Greatest Hits*, Chicago
6. *The Dream Weaver*, Gary Wright
7. *Desire*, Bob Dylan
8. *A Night at the Opera*, Queen
9. *History—America's Greatest Hits*, America
10. *Gratitude*, Earth, Wind & Fire

1977

1. *Rumours*, Fleetwood Mac
2. *Songs in the Key of Life*, Stevie Wonder
3. *A Star Is Born*, Barbra Streisand/Kris Kristofferson/soundtrack
4. *Hotel California*, Eagles
5. *Boston*, Boston
6. *A New World Record*, Electric Light Orchestra
7. *Part 3*, K.C. & the Sunshine Band
8. *Silk Degrees*, Boz Scaggs
9. *Night Moves*, Bob Seger & the Silver Bullet Band
10. *Fleetwood Mac*, Fleetwood Mac

1978

1. *Saturday Night Fever*, Bee Gees/various artists/soundtrack
2. *Grease*, John Travolta/Olivia Newton-John/soundtrack
3. *Rumours*, Fleetwood Mac
4. *The Stranger*, Billy Joel
5. *Aja*, Steely Dan
6. *Feels So Good*, Chuck Mangione
7. *The Grand Illusion*, Styx
8. *Simple Dreams*, Linda Ronstadt
9. *Point of Know Return*, Kansas
10. *Slowhand*, Eric Clapton

1979

1. *52nd Street*, Billy Joel
2. *Spirits Having Flown*, Bee Gees
3. *Minute by Minute*, Doobie Brothers
4. *The Cars*, The Cars
5. *Breakfast in America*, Supertramp
6. *Live and More*, Donna Summer
7. *Pieces of Eight*, Styx
8. *Bad Girls*, Donna Summer
9. *Parallel Lines*, Blondie
10. *Blondes Have More Fun*, Rod Stewart

1980

1. *The Wall*, Pink Floyd
2. *The Long Run*, Eagles
3. *Off the Wall*, Michael Jackson
4. *Glass Houses*, Billy Joel
5. *Damn the Torpedoes*, Tom Petty & the Heartbreakers
6. *Against the Wind*, Bob Seger & the Silver Bullet Band
7. *In the Heat of the Night*, Pat Benatar
8. *Eat to the Beat*, Blondie
9. *In Through the Out Door*, Led Zeppelin
10. *Kenny*, Kenny Rogers

1981

1. *Hi Infidelity*, REO Speedwagon
2. *Double Fantasy*, John Lennon & Yoko Ono
3. *Greatest Hits*, Kenny Rogers
4. *Christopher Cross*, Christopher Cross
5. *Crimes of Passion*, Pat Benatar
6. *Paradise Theatre*, Styx
7. *Back in Black*, AC/DC
8. *Voices*, Daryl Hall & John Oates
9. *Zenyatta Mondatta*, The Police
10. *The River*, Bruce Springsteen

1982

1. *Asia*, Asia
2. *Beauty and the Beat*, The Go-Go's
3. *4*, Foreigner
4. *American Fool*, John Cougar
5. *Freeze-Frame*, The J. Geils Band
6. *Escape*, Journey
7. *Get Lucky*, Loverboy
8. *Bella Donna*, Stevie Nicks
9. *Chariots of Fire*, Vangelis/soundtrack
10. *Ghost in the Machine*, The Police

1983

1. *Thriller*, Michael Jackson
2. *Business as Usual*, Men at Work
3. *Synchronicity*, The Police
4. *H2O*, Daryl Hall & John Oates
5. *1999*, Prince
6. *Lionel Richie*, Lionel Richie

7. *Jane Fonda's Workout Record*, Jane Fonda
8. *Pyromania*, Def Leppard
9. *Kissing To Be Clever*, Culture Club
10. *Olivia's Greatest Hits, Vol. 2*, Olivia Newton-John

1984

1. *Thriller*, Michael Jackson
2. *Sports*, Huey Lewis & the News
3. *Can't Slow Down*, Lionel Richie
4. *An Innocent Man*, Billy Joel
5. *Colour by Numbers*, Culture Club
6. *1984*, Van Halen
7. *Eliminator*, ZZ Top
8. *Synchronicity*, The Police
9. *Footloose*, soundtrack
10. *Seven and the Ragged Tiger*, Duran Duran

1985

1. *Born in the U.S.A.*, Bruce Springsteen
2. *Reckless*, Bryan Adams
3. *Like a Virgin*, Madonna
4. *Make It Big*, Wham!
5. *Private Dancer*, Tina Turner
6. *No Jacket Required*, Phil Collins
7. *Beverly Hills Cop*, soundtrack
8. *Suddenly*, Billy Ocean
9. *Purple Rain*, Prince & the Revolution
10. *Songs from the Big Chair*, Tears for Fears

1986

1. *Whitney Houston*, Whitney Houston
2. *Heart*, Heart
3. *Scarecrow*, John Cougar Mellencamp
4. *Afterburner*, ZZ Top
5. *Brothers in Arms*, Dire Straits
6. *Control*, Janet Jackson
7. *Welcome to the Real World*, Mr. Mister
8. *Promise*, Sade
9. *No Jacket Required*, Phil Collins
10. *Primitive Love*, Miami Sound Machine

1987

1. *Slippery When Wet*, Bon Jovi
2. *Graceland*, Paul Simon
3. *Licensed To Ill*, Beastie Boys
4. *The Way It Is*, Bruce Hornsby & the Range
5. *Control*, Janet Jackson
6. *The Joshua Tree*, U2
7. *Fore!*, Huey Lewis & the News
8. *Night Songs*, Cinderella
9. *Rapture*, Anita Baker
10. *Invisible Touch*, Genesis

1988

1. *Faith*, George Michael
2. *Dirty Dancing*, soundtrack
3. *Hysteria*, Def Leppard
4. *Kick*, INXS
5. *Bad*, Michael Jackson
6. *Appetite for Destruction*, Guns N' Roses
7. *Out of the Blue*, Debbie Gibson
8. *Richard Marx*, Richard Marx
9. *Tiffany*, Tiffany
10. *Permanent Vacation*, Aerosmith

1989

1. *Don't Be Cruel*, Bobby Brown
2. *Hangin' Tough*, New Kids on the Block
3. *Forever Your Girl*, Paula Abdul
4. *New Jersey*, Bon Jovi
5. *Appetite for Destruction*, Guns N' Roses
6. *The Raw & the Cooked*, Fine Young Cannibals
7. *GNR Lies*, Guns N' Roses
8. *Traveling Wilburys*, Traveling Wilburys
9. *Hysteria*, Def Leppard
10. *Girl You Know It's True*, Milli Vanilli

1990

1. *Janet Jackson's Rhythm Nation 1814*, Janet Jackson
2. *...But Seriously*, Phil Collins
3. *Soul Provider*, Michael Bolton
4. *Pump*, Aerosmith
5. *Please Hammer Don't Hurt 'Em*, M.C. Hammer
6. *Forever Your Girl*, Paula Abdul
7. *Dr. Feelgood*, Mötley Crüe
8. *The End of the Innocence*, Don Henley
9. *Cosmic Thing*, The B-52's
10. *Storm Front*, Billy Joel

1991

1. *Mariah Carey*, Mariah Carey
2. *No Fences*, Garth Brooks
3. *Shake Your Money Maker*, The Black Crowes
4. *Gonna Make You Sweat*, C+C Music Factory
5. *Wilson Phillips*, Wilson Phillips
6. *To the Extreme*, Vanilla Ice
7. *Please Hammer Don't Hurt 'Em*, M.C. Hammer
8. *The Immaculate Collection*, Madonna
9. *Empire*, Queensryche
10. *I'm Your Baby Tonight*, Whitney Houston

1992

1. *Ropin' the Wind*, Garth Brooks
2. *Dangerous*, Michael Jackson

3. *Nevermind*, Nirvana
4. *Some Gave All*, Billy Ray Cyrus
5. *Achtung Baby*, U2
6. *No Fences*, Garth Brooks
7. *Metallica*, Metallica
8. *Time, Love, & Tenderness*, Michael Bolton
9. *Too Legit To Quit*, Hammer
10. *Totally Krossed Out*, Kris Kross

1993

1. *The Bodyguard*, soundtrack
2. *Breathless*, Kenny G
3. *Unplugged*, Eric Clapton
4. *janet.*, Janet Jackson
5. *Some Gave All*, Billy Ray Cyrus
6. *The Chronic*, Dr. Dre
7. *Pocket Full of Kryptonite*, Spin Doctors
8. *Ten*, Pearl Jam
9. *The Chase*, Garth Brooks
10. *Core*, Stone Temple Pilots

1994

1. *The Sign*, Ace of Base
2. *Music Box*, Mariah Carey
3. *Doggystyle*, Snoop Doggy Dogg
4. *The Lion King*, soundtrack
5. *August & Everything After*, Counting Crows
6. *VS.*, Pearl Jam

7. *Toni Braxton*, Toni Braxton
8. *janet.*, Janet Jackson
9. *Bat out of Hell II: Back into Hell*, Meat Loaf
10. *The One Thing*, Michael Bolton

1995

1. *Cracked Rear View*, Hootie & The Blowfish
2. *The Hits*, Garth Brooks
3. *II*, Boyz II Men
4. *Hell Freezes Over*, Eagles
5. *Crazysexycool*, TLC
6. *Vitalogy*, Pearl Jam
7. *Dookie*, Green Day
8. *Throwing Copper*, Live
9. *Miracles: The Holiday Album*, Kenny G
10. *The Lion King* soundtrack

1996

1. *Jagged Little Pill*, Alanis Morissette
2. *Daydream*, Mariah Carey
3. *Falling into You*, Celine Dion
4. *Waiting to Exhale*, soundtrack
5. *The Score*, Fugees
6. *The Woman in Me*, Shania Twain
7. *Fresh Horses*, Garth Brooks
8. *Anthology 1*, The Beatles
9. *Cracked Rear View*, Hootie & The Blowfish

10. *Mellon Collie and the Infinite Sadness*, The Smashing Pumpkins

1997

1. *Spice*, Spice Girls
2. *Tragic Kingdom*, No Doubt
3. *Falling into You*, Celine Dion
4. *Space Jam*, soundtrack
5. *Pieces of You*, Jewel
6. *Blue*, LeAnn Rimes
7. *Bringing Down the Horse*, The Wallflowers
8. *Life After Death*, The Notorious B.I.G.
9. *Secrets*, Toni Braxton
10. *No Way Out*, Puff Daddy & The Family

1998

1. *Titanic*, soundtrack
2. *Let's Talk About Love*, Celine Dion
3. *Sevens*, Garth Brooks
4. *Backstreet Boys*, Backstreet Boys
5. *Come On Over*, Shania Twain
6. *Yourself or Someone Like You*, Matchbox 20
7. *City of Angels*, soundtrack
8. *Big Willie Style*, Will Smith
9. *Savage Garden*, Savage Garden
10. *Spiceworld*, Spice Girls

DESERT ISLAND DISCS

Since 1983, *Pulse!* (the magazine published by Tower Records/Video) has been asking major recording artists, "If you were stranded on a desert island, what 10 records would you want with you?" The following is a sampling from its archives.

BECK

Dust Bowl Ballads	Woody Guthrie
Outer Space	Toby Rean and the Common People
The Flasher	Soundtrack
Getz/Gilberto	Stan Getz and Joao Gilberto
Moog: The Eclectic Electrics of	Dick Hyman
Any compilation by	Carter Family
Any compilation by	Mississippi Fred McDowell
Comic Strip	Serge Gainsbourg
Songs From a Room	Leonard Cohen
Right Now!	Pussy Galore

TOM PETTY

Good Vibrations: Thirty Years of The Beach Boys	The Beach Boys
The Byrds	The Byrds
Greatest Hits	The Searchers
Rainin' in My Heart	Slim Harpo
The Chess Box	Howlin' Wolf
Elvis—The King of Rock & Roll:The Complete '50s Masters	Elvis Presley
Grevious Angel	Gram Parsons
Greatest Hits	Wilson Pickett
$1,000,000 Worth of Twang	Duane Eddy
A Date With the Everly Brothers	The Everly Brothers

ANTHONY KIEDIS (RED HOT CHILI PEPPERS)

I Against I	Bad Brains
Talking Book	Stevie Wonder
Anything by	Bob Marley and the Wailers
Hardcore Jollies	Funkadelic
Greatest Hits	James Brown
Greatest Hits	Marvin Gaye
Greatest Hits	Billie Holiday
Are You Experienced?	Jimi Hendrix Experience

BILLY JOEL

Take Five	Dave Brubeck
Rubber Soul	The Beatles
Hot Rocks, 1964–69	The Rolling Stones
Adagio for Strings	Samuel Barber, performed by Leonard Bernstein and the New York Philharmonic
Led Zeppelin	Led Zeppelin

Axis: Bold As Love	Jimi Hendrix Experience
The Complete Tatum Solo Masterpieces, Volumes 1–9	Art Tatum
John Barleycorn Must Die	Traffic
Otis Redding's Greatest Hits	Otis Redding
The Genius of Ray Charles	Ray Charles

NOEL GALLAGHER (OASIS)

"Pretty Vacant"	The Sex Pistols
"Paperback Writer"	The Beatles
"I Can See for Miles"	The Who
"Tin Soldier"	Small Faces
"You Really Got Me"	The Kinks
"Smells Like Teen Spirit"	Nirvana
"I Wanna Be Your Dog"	The Stooges
"Mirror Man"	Captain Beefheart
"Subterranean Homesick Blues"	Bob Dylan
"One"	U2

CARLY SIMON

Tea for the Tillerman	Cat Stevens
Caverna Magica	Andreas Vollenweider
Midnight Love	Marvin Gaye
Alchemy—Live	Dire Straits
Winter	George Winston
Water Music	George Frideric Handel
Porgy and Bess	any version
Puccini Arias	Kiri Te Kanawa
Paradise and Lunch	Ry Cooder
Greatest Hits	The Temptations
I Musici, Concerto in A Minor, Concerto in D Minor, Brandenburg Concertos	Johann Sebastian Bach

K.D. LANG

The Patsy Cline Story	Patsy Cline
Hard Hitting Songs for Hard Hit People	Hazel Dickens
Season of Glass	Yoko Ono
Country Hits, Vol. 7 (K-Tel)	various artists
Mingus	Joni Mitchell
Latin à la Lee	Peggy Lee
Any album by	Kate Bush
Wild, Wild Young Women	various artists
Ella and Oscar	Ella Fitzgerald and Oscar Peterson
Rickie Lee Jones	Rickie Lee Jones

DWIGHT YOAKAM

The Best of Buck Owens, Vols. I, II, III	Buck Owens
Buckaroo	Buck Owens
The Songs That Made Him Famous	Johnny Cash
The Columbia Sessions	Stanley Brothers
The Best of Merle Haggard	Merle Haggard
The Georgia Satellites	The Georgia Satellites
Can't Stand the Weather	Stevie Ray Vaughan
...And a Time To Dance	Los Lobos
Rockin' George Jones	George Jones
Get Yer Ya-Ya's Out	The Rolling Stones
Green River	Creedence Clearwater Revival
Riptide	Robert Palmer

KEITH RICHARDS (ROLLING STONES)

"Little Queenie"	Chuck Berry
Any album of	Johann Sebastian Bach
Any album of	Wolfgang Amadeus Mozart
"Key to the Highway"	Little Walter with Jimmy Rogers
"Still a Fool"	Muddy Waters
"Reach Out"	Four Tops
"Mystery Train"	Elvis Presley
"Come on Everybody"	Eddie Cochran
"That'll Be the Day"	Buddy Holly

Some doo-wop by the Jive Five, or maybe a bit of Segovia.

AIMEE MANN

Plants & Birds & Rocks & Things	The Loud Family
Mellow Gold	Beck
Exile in Guyville	Liz Phair
Frosting on the Beater	The Posies
Odessey & Oracle	The Zombies
Sgt. Pepper's Lonely Hearts Club Band	The Beatles
Good Old Boys	Randy Newman
Straight Up	Badfinger
Imperial Bedroom	Elvis Costello
Walk Across the Rooftops	The Blue Nile

PORTISHEAD

"In Bloom"	Nirvana
"Superstition"	Stevie Wonder
"Lucky"	Radiohead
"Please Don't Let Me Be Misunderstood"	Nina Simone
"Georgia on My Mind"	Ray Charles
"Black Steel in the Hour of Chaos"	Public Enemy
"Love Will Tear Us Apart"	Joy Division

"Scenario"	A Tribe Called Quest
"It's a Man's Man's Man's World"	James Brown
"Psychomania"	theme music from the film

ICE CUBE

To the East, Blackwards	X-Clan
Fear of a Black Planet	Public Enemy
Any album by	K-Solo
Holy Intellect	Poor Righteous Teachers
Greatest Hits	Marvin Gaye
Greatest Hits	Harold Melvin and the Blue Notes
Greatest Hits	Parliament
Greatest Hits	James Brown
AmeriKKKa's Most Wanted	Ice Cube

SUZANNE VEGA

Eli and the 13th Confession	Laura Nyro
Songs of Leonard Cohen	Leonard Cohen
The Velvet Underground and Nico	The Velvet Underground
Sounds of Silence	Simon and Garfunkel
Synchronicity (side 2)	The Police
Hatful of Hollow	The Smiths
Somebody's Got To Do It	Frank Christian
Working on Wings to Fly	Cindy Kallet
2	Cindy Kallet

DAVE PIRNER (SOUL ASYLUM)

Bitches Brew	Miles Davis
The Complete Recordings	Robert Johnson
Out of Step	Minor Threat
Exile on Main Street	The Rolling Stones
Loaded	The Velvet Underground
Horses	Patti Smith
The Stooges	The Stooges
Poor Boy	Woodie Guthrie
Pearl	Janis Joplin
Up on the Sun	Meat Puppets

BRIAN SETZER

The Sun Sessions	Elvis Presley
"Mac the Knife"	Bobby Darin
"Blue Jean Bop"	Gene Vincent
"Something Else"	Eddie Cochran
Live at the Sands	Count Basie Orchestra
Ultra Lounge series	Various artists
One Mo Time	Louis Jordan
The Genius Of...	Chet Atkins
Original Sun Greatest Hits	Carl Perkins
Let Me Off Uptown	Gene Krupa

THE BESTSELLING ALBUMS OF ALL TIME

The Recording Industry Association of America tracks monthly album sales and awards gold and platinum certification based on the sale of 500,000 units for gold, one million units for platinum, and two million units or more for multiplatinum. Here are the albums that top the lists, organized by category, as of August 1999.

ROCK/POP

25 million
Michael Jackson, *Thriller*, 1982
Eagles, *Their Greatest Hits, 1971–1975*, 1977

23 million
Pink Floyd, *The Wall*, 1979

21 million
Led Zeppelin, *Led Zeppelin IV*, 1971

20 million
Billy Joel, *Greatest Hits, Volumes I & II*, 1985

18 million
Fleetwood Mac, *Rumours*, 1977

17 million
The Beatles, *The Beatles*, 1968

16 million
AC/DC, *Back in Black*, 1980
Boston, *Boston*, 1976
Hootie & The Blowfish, *Cracked Rear View*, 1994

Whitney Houston/various artists, *The Bodyguard* soundtrack, 1992
Alanis Morissette, *Jagged Little Pill*, 1995

15 million
Bee Gees/various artists, *Saturday Night Fever* soundtrack, 1977
Eagles, *Hotel California*, 1976
Guns N' Roses, *Appetite for Destruction*, 1987
Led Zeppelin, *Physical Graffiti*, 1975
Elton John, *Greatest Hits*, 1974
Pink Floyd, *The Dark Side of the Moon*, 1973
Bruce Springsteen, *Born in the U.S.A.*, 1984

14 million
The Beatles, *1967–1970*, 1993

13 million
The Beatles, *1962–1966*, 1993
Whitney Houston, *Whitney Houston*, 1985
Meat Loaf, *Bat out of Hell*, 1977

Prince and the Revolution, *Purple Rain*, 1984
Bruce Springsteen, *Bruce Springsteen & the E Street Band Live, 1975–1985*, 1986

12 million
Bon Jovi, *Slippery When Wet*, 1986
Boyz II Men, *II*, 1994
Def Leppard, *Hysteria*, 1987

11 million
The Beatles, *Abbey Road*, 1969
The Beatles, *Sgt. Pepper's Lonely Hearts Club Band*, 1967
Led Zeppelin, *Led Zeppelin II*, 1969
Metallica, *Metallica*, 1991
James Taylor, *Greatest Hits*, 1976
various artists, *Dirty Dancing* soundtrack, 1987

10 million
Backstreet Boys, *Backstreet Boys*, 1997
Mariah Carey, *Music Box*, 1993
Mariah Carey, *Daydream*, 1995

RAP WRAPPED UP

Twenty years after its commercial breakthrough, rap has become a dominant part of the pop music landscape. Here, selected by PEOPLE music critic Jeremy Helligar, are some of the genre's essential albums.

1. Arrested Development, *3 Years, 5 Months and 2 Days in the Life of...* (1992)
2. Beastie Boys, *Licensed to Ill* (1986)
3. Beastie Boys, *Paul's Boutique* (1989)
4. De La Soul, *3 Feet High & Rising* (1989)
5. Digable Planets, *Blowout Comb* (1994)
6. Dr. Dre, *The Chronic* (1993)
7. Missy "Misdemeanor" Elliot, *Supa Dupa Fly* (1997)
8. Fugees, *The Score* (1996)
9. Grandmaster Flash & The Furious Five, *Greatest Messages* (1987)
10. Lil' Kim, *Hard Core* (1996)
11. L.L. Cool J, *All World* (1996)
12. Naughty By Nature, *Poverty's Paradise* (1995)
13. N.W.A., *Straight Outta Compton* (1989)
14. Public Enemy, *Fear of a Black Planet* (1990)
15. Run-D.M.C., *Together Forever: Greatest Hits 1983–1991* (1991)
16. Salt-N-Pepa, *Black's Magic* (1990)
17. A Tribe Called Quest, *Beats, Rhymes and Life* (1996)
18. Notorious B.I.G., *Ready to Die* (1994)
19. Lauryn Hill, *The Miseducation of Lauryn Hill* (1998)
20. Wu-Tang Clan, *Enter the Wu-Tang (36 Chambers)* (1994)

Eric Clapton, *Unplugged,* 1992
Phil Collins, *No Jacket Required,* 1985
Celine Dion, *Falling into You,* 1996
Doobie Brothers, *Best of the Doobies,* 1976
Green Day, *Dookie,* 1994
Journey, *Journey's Greatest Hits,* 1988
Carole King, *Tapestry,* 1971
Led Zeppelin, *Houses of the Holy,* 1973
Madonna, *Like a Virgin,* 1984
Bob Marley and the Wailers, *Legend,* 1984
George Michael, *Faith,* 1987
Nirvana, *Nevermind,* 1991
No Doubt, *Tragic Kingdom,* 1995
Pearl Jam, *Ten,* 1991
Lionel Richie, *Can't Slow Down,* 1984
TLC, *CrazySexyCool,* 1994
U2, *The Joshua Tree,* 1987
Van Halen, *Van Halen,* 1978
various artists, *The Lion King* soundtrack, 1994
ZZ Top, *Eliminator,* 1983

9 million

Ace of Base, *The Sign,* 1993
Aerosmith, *Greatest Hits,* 1980
Boyz II Men, *Cooleyhighharmony,* 1991
Def Leppard, *Pyromania,* 1983
Celine Dion, *Let's Talk About Love,* 1997
Dire Straits, *Brothers in Arms,* 1985
Eagles, *Eagles Greatest Hits Volume II,* 1982
Whitney Houston, *Whitney,* 1987
Jewel, *Pieces of You,* 1995
Billy Joel, *The Stranger,* 1977
Journey, *Escape,* 1981
R.E.O. Speedwagon, *Hi-Infidelity,* 1982
Van Halen, *1984,* 1984
various artists, *The Great Band Era,* 1965

8 million

The Beatles, *The Beatles Anthology Volume 1,* 1995
Michael Bolton, *Time, Love and Tenderness,* 1991

Toni Braxton, *Toni Braxton,* 1993
Mariah Carey, *Mariah Carey,* 1991
Led Zeppelin, *Led Zeppelin I,* 1969
Michael Jackson, *Bad,* 1987
New Kids on the Block, *Hangin' Tough,* 1988
Olivia Newton-John/John Travolta, *Grease* soundtrack, 1972
Tom Petty and the Heartbreakers, *Greatest Hits,* 1993
Smashing Pumpkins, *Mellon Collie and the Infinite Sadness,* 1996
various artists, *Footloose* soundtrack, 1984
U2, *Achtung Baby,* 1991
Whitesnake, *Whitesnake,* 1987

COUNTRY

16 million

Garth Brooks, *No Fences,* 1990

14 million

Garth Brooks, *Ropin' the Wind,* 1991

12 million

Garth Brooks, *Double Live,* 1998
Kenny Rogers, *Greatest Hits,* 1980
Shania Twain, *Come On Over,* 1997

11 million

Shania Twain, *The Woman in Me,* 1995

10 million

Garth Brooks, *The Hits,* 1994

9 million

Garth Brooks, *Garth Brooks,* 1989
Billy Ray Cyrus, *Some Gave All,* 1992

8 million

Garth Brooks, *The Chase,* 1991
Garth Brooks, *In Pieces,* 1993
Patsy Cline, *Greatest Hits,* 1967

6 million

Garth Brooks, *Fresh Horses,* 1995
Dixie Chicks, *Wide Open Spaces,* 1998
Alan Jackson, *A Lot About Livin' (And a Little About Love),* 1992
LeAnn Rimes, *Blue,* 1996

5 million

Alabama, *Alabama's Greatest Hits,* 1986

Alabama, *Mountain Music,* 1982
Brooks & Dunn, *Brand New Man,* 1991
Garth Brooks, *Sevens,* 1997
Reba McEntire, *Greatest Hits, Vol. 2,* 1993
Tim McGraw, *Not a Moment Too Soon,* 1994
Bonnie Raitt, *Luck of the Draw,* 1991
Kenny Rogers, *The Gambler,* 1978
George Strait, *Pure Country,* 1992
George Strait, *Strait out of the Box,* 1995
Randy Travis, *Always and Forever,* 1987
Wynonna, *Wynonna,* 1992

4 million

Alabama, *Feels So Right,* 1981
Alabama, *Roll On,* 1984
Brooks & Dunn, *Hard Workin' Man,* 1993
Deana Carter, *Did I Shave My Legs For This?,* 1996
Vince Gill, *When Love Finds You,* 1994
Alan Jackson, *Don't Rock the Jukebox,* 1991
Alan Jackson, *Who I Am,* 1994
Alan Jackson, *Greatest Hits Collection,* 1995
Waylon Jennings, *Greatest Hits,* 1979
John Michael Montgomery, *Kickin' It Up,* 1994
Anne Murray, *Greatest Hits,* 1980
Willie Nelson, *Willie and Family Live,* 1978
Willie Nelson, *Always on My Mind,* 1982
Willie Nelson, *Stardust,* 1990
Bonnie Raitt, *Nick of Time,* 1989
LeAnn Rimes, *You Light Up My Life–Inspirational Songs,* 1997
Kenny Rogers, *Ten Years of Gold,* 1978
Kenny Rogers, *20 Greatest Hits,* 1983
Shania Twain, *Come On Over,* 1997
various artists, *Take Me Home Country Roads,* 1973

3 million

Alabama, *The Closer You Get,* 1983

Clint Black, *Killin' Time,* 1989

Clint Black, *Put Yourself in My Shoes,* 1990

Garth Brooks, *Beyond the Season,* 1992

Garth Brooks, *The Garth Brooks Collection,* 1994

Charlie Daniels Band, *Million Mile Reflections,* 1978

Vince Gill, *I Still Believe in You,* 1992

Alan Jackson, *Greatest Hits Collection,* 1995

Reba McEntire, *For My Broken Heart,* 1991

Reba McEntire, *Greatest Hits,* 1987

Reba McEntire, *Rumor Has It,* 1990

Reba McEntire, *It's Your Call,* 1992

Reba McEntire, *Read My Mind,* 1994

Tim McGraw, *Everywhere,* 1997

John Michael Montgomery, *John Michael Montgomery,* 1995

John Michael Montgomery, *Life's a Dance,* 1992

Kenny Rogers, *Kenny,* 1979

The Statler Brothers, *Best of The Statler Brothers,* 1975

George Strait, *Carryin' Your Love With Me,* 19

Randy Travis, *Storms of Life,* 1992

Travis Tritt, *It's All About To Change,* 1991

Dwight Yoakam, *This Time,* 1994

JAZZ

12 million

Kenny G, *Breathless,* 1992

8 million

Kenny G, *Miracles,* 1994

5 million

Kenny G, *Duotones,* 1986

4 million

Kenny G, *Silhouette,* 1988

3 million

George Benson, *Breezin',* 1984

Kenny G, *Kenny G Live,* 1989

Kenny G, *The Moment,* 1996

2 million

Kenny G, *Greatest Hits,* 1997

Platinum

George Benson, *Give Me the Night,* 1980

George Benson, *In Flight,* 1977

George Benson, *Weekend in L.A.,* 1978

Kenny G, *Gravity,* 1985

Herbie Hancock, *Future Shock,* 1983

Bob James/David Sanborn, *Double Vision,* 1991

Al Jarreau, *Breakin' Away,* 1982

Chuck Mangione, *Feels So Good,* 1977

Spyro Gyra, *Morning Dance,* 1979

RAP / HIP-HOP

11 million

TLC, *CrazySexyCool,* 1994

10 million

M.C. Hammer, *Please Hammer Don't Hurt 'Em,* 1990

9 million

2Pac, *All Eyez On Me,* 1996

8 million

Beastie Boys, *Licensed To Ill,* 1986

Notorious B.I.G., *Life After Death,* 1997

7 million

Vanilla Ice, *To the Extreme,* 1990

6 million

Fugees, *The Score,* 1996

Puff Daddy and The Family, *No Way Out,* 1997

5 million

2Pac, *Greatest Hits,* 1998

Lauryn Hill, *The Miseducation of Lauryn Hill,* 1998

Salt-N-Pepa, *Very Necessary,* 1993

4 million

2Pac, *R U Still Down? (Remember Me),* 1997

Arrested Development, *3 Years, 5 Months and 2 Days in the Life of...,* 1992

Bone Thugs-N-Harmony, *E. 1999 Eternal,* 1995

Bone Thugs-N-Harmony, *The Art of War,* 1997

Fugees, *The Score,* 1996

Kris Kross, *Totally Krossed Out,* 1992

Master P, *MP Da Last Don,* 1998

Will Smith, *Big Willie Style,* 1997

Snoop Doggy Dogg, *Doggystyle,* 1993

TLC, *Fanmail,* 1999

Wu-Tang Clan, *Wu-Tang Forever,* 1997

3 million

Beastie Boys, *Hello Nasty,* 1998

Beastie Boys, *Ill-Communication,* 1994

D.J. Jazzy Jeff and The Fresh Prince, *He's the D.J., I'm the Rapper,* 1988

Dr. Dre, *The Chronic,* 1992

Warren G., *Regulate...G Funk Era,* 1994

Hammer, *Too Legit to Quit,* 1992

Jay-Z, *Hard Knock Life, Volume 2* 1998

Mase, *Harlem World,* 1997

Run-D.M.C., *Raising Hell,* 1986

CLASSICAL

10 million

Titanic soundtrack, 1997

2 million

Benedictine Monks of Santo Domingo de Silos, *Chant,* 1994

Andrea Bocelli, *Romanza,* 1997

Carreras, Domingo, Pavarotti, *The Three Tenors in Concert,* 1990

1 Million

Back to Titanic soundtrack, 1998

Andrea Bocelli, *Sogno,* 1999

Wendy Carlos, *Switched on Bach,* 1986

Carreras, Domingo, Pavarotti with Mehta, *The Three Tenors in Concert 1994,* 1994

Luciano Pavarotti, *O Holy Night,* London, 1985

Royal Philharmonic Orchestra, *Hooked on Classics,* 1982

Piotr Tchaikovsky performed by Van Cliburn with the RCA Symphony Orchestra/Kirill Kondrashin, *Piano Concerto No. 1 in B-flat Minor, Op. 23,* 1982

Various artists, *250 Years of Great Music—Bach to Bernstein,* 1992

THE ROCK OF AGES: PEOPLE'S FAVORITE 50

Steve Dougherty has been PEOPLE's chief music writer since 1985. Here is his completely subjective list of the 50 albums he'd stock in his personal jukebox.

ATLANTIC R&B 1947–1974 (1991)
Various artists
Before they named it Rock, it was spelled R&B. A chest of pop's buried treasures.

AT THE FILMORE EAST (1979)
The Allman Brothers Band
Soulful sibs Duane and Gregg Allman unveil their new invention, Southern Rock, before a crowd of appreciative Yankees in a watershed New York City live show.

THE BAND (1969)
The Band
Rock 'n' roll's Great American Novel came with a backbeat and Robbie Robertson's story songs, as told by Richard Manuel, Levon Helm, and Rick Danko.

THE BEATLES (1968)
The Beatles
From the classic rock of the opening track to the electronica precursor "Revolution No. 9," the legendary White Album plays like a modern pop history lesson taught by four Fab profs.

ODELAY (1996)
Beck
An album from pop's beat-crazy, wordy rapping kid, Beck Hansen

(no relation to the Oklahoma teen trio), that shows off his heightened senses of rhythm and humor.

CHUCK BERRY'S GOLDEN HITS (1967)
Chuck Berry
The brown-eyed handsome man told Tchaikovsky the news: There is indeed such a thing as a three-minute masterpiece.

MERMAID AVENUE (1998)
Billy Bragg & Wilco
Brit singer Bragg and the country punks of Wilco give a posthumous present to folk icon Woodie Guthrie: a sparkling pop album of the troubadour's wondrous, and previously unsung, songs.

THE RISE AND FALL OF ZIGGY STARDUST AND THE SPIDERS FROM MARS (1972)
David Bowie
Music had never glittered quite like this before and glam rock never sounded so good again.

20 ALL-TIME GREATEST HITS! (1991)
James Brown
You'll feel good! But then, you knew that you would.

LONDON CALLING (1979)
The Clash
They pronounced rock dead,

then celebrated its resurrection on this, a double album without a lame cut in the lot.

MY AIM IS TRUE (1977)
Elvis Costello
He looked punk, acted mean, sounded nasty, and hit right on target in his album debut.

LAYLA AND OTHER ASSORTED LOVE SONGS (1970)
Derek and the Dominoes
Eric Clapton and Duane Allman. 'Nuff said.

THE CHRONIC (1992)
Dr. Dre (with Snoop Doggy Dogg)
Hip-hop's auteur and his pet rapper share their bemused family values.

BRINGING IT ALL BACK HOME (1965),
HIGHWAY 61 REVISITED (1965),
TIME OUT OF MIND (1997)
Bob Dylan
For all who question the lasting fuss over the rheumy rock laureate, three masterworks.

I NEVER LOVED A MAN (THE WAY I LOVE YOU) (1967)
Aretha Franklin
They invented soul so she could be queen.

Beck, *Odelay*

Nirvana, *Nevermind*

U2, *Achtung Baby*

WHAT'S GOING ON (1971)
Marvin Gaye
Motown's sex star made hearts and minds quicken with this ambitious song cycle.

ARE YOU EXPERIENCED? (1967)
Jimi Hendrix Experience
That voice. Those songs. That guitar. We're still asking, "Where did this guy come from?"

ARTHUR (DECLINE AND FALL OF THE BRITISH EMPIRE) (1969), **MUSWELL HILLBILLIES** (1971)
The Kinks
Tommy without the pretensions: these are two of plaintive mod genius Ray Davies's brilliantly realized theme albums.

ORIGINAL GOLDEN HITS, VOLS. 1 AND 2 (1969)
Jerry Lee Lewis
Killer tracks from The Killer: All is forgiven.

GROOVIEST 17 ORIGINAL HITS (1959)
Little Richard
"Good Golly Miss Molly," "Tutti Fruiti," "Lucille," "Long Tall Sally," "Rip It Up." Macon, Ga.'s absolutely fabulous former dishwasher screamed 'em all to life at New Orleans's Specialty Records studio.

COURT AND SPARK (1974)
Joni Mitchell
The ultimate chick singer whips one on the boys.

MOBY GRAPE (1967)
Moby Grape
San Francisco's one-masterpiece wonder squeezed all their juice into this ignored collection.

AMERICAN BEAUTY (1970)
The Grateful Dead
Haight-Ashbury's free-form improvisational space cowboys shelve the jams and craft an aptly titled musical masterpiece.

THE BEST OF VAN MORRISON (1990)
Van Morrison
Romance for the soul.

NEVERMIND (1991)
Nirvana
Full of as much old-fashioned tube amplifier feedback as neo-

THE 10 MOST OVERRATED ALBUMS

For those contrarians who would rather smash discs than play them, here is a flip-side list of legendary nonlegends in the annals of rock.

SLIPPERY WHEN WET (1986)
Bon Jovi
Hair metal pin-up star Jon Bon Jovi's was the pretty face that helped sell many millions of copies of a mediocre album filled with lyric clichés and generic power chords.

4 WAY STREET (1971)
Crosby, Stills, Nash and Young
They could have used a stop sign.

THE DOORS (1967)
The Doors
As an icon, Jim Morrison can't be beat; but his great looks, leather pants, and lucrative afterlife make people forget he was a mediocre singer and pretentious poet masquerading as a rock star.

USE YOUR ILLUSION I & II (1991)
Guns N' Roses
Out the year punk pretender Axl Rose was rendered irrelevant by the real thing (Kurt Cobain), these two simultaneously released, gibberishly titled albums smelled like a teen record buyer rip-off.

UNTITLED (1971)
Led Zeppelin
The album that gave us "Stairway to Heaven" and other artifacts of arena-ready blowhard rock.

(WHAT'S THE STORY) MORNING GLORY? (1995)
Oasis
They like to compare themselves to the Beatles and Stones but prove with this album's lame lyrics and hand-me-down sound to be in the same league with neither.

ELVIS (TV SPECIAL) (1968)
Elvis Presley
The gig that was trumpeted as his return to '50s form. Leatherclad in Vegas a year after the Summer of Love, The King was already out of touch with current culture and his music.

THE DREAM OF THE BLUE TURTLES (1985)
Sting
The Police man lured listeners with his pop status, then stung them with stingy jazz.

TOMMY (1969)
The Who
Maybe if Pete had left it to critics to call his own composition "A Rock Opera," it wouldn't make us want to gag.

MODERN R&B
Soulful self-expression is the creed of the great R&B singers of yore. Today's poor imitators, from Mariah Carey to the Backstreet Boys, caterwaul trite lyrics over clichéd arrangements to achieve the appearance, but not the true grit, of emotion. Call it artificial soul.

punk martyr Kurt Cobain's fabled rage, this is a call to get with it for all classic rock-fixated geezers who insist that the music ain't what it used to be.

TEAR THE ROOF OFF (1993)
Parliament Funkadelic
So they did, and something memorable was born.

THE SUN SESSIONS (1987), ELVIS' GOLDEN RECORDS, VOL. 1 (1958)
Elvis Presley
Rock and roll at its best.

1999 (1982)
Prince
From when he had a name and all the critics loved him in New York, and everywhere else.

MURMUR (1983)
R.E.M.
The debut album that brought "Radio Free Europe" to the promised land. What's it about? Who knows? Who cares?

HISTORY OF OTIS REDDING (1968)
Otis Redding
The greatest soul ever told.

TIM (1985)
The Replacements
Put "Swingin' Party" on replay, never let it stop.

BEGGAR'S BANQUET (1968), STICKY FINGERS (1971), THE SINGLES COLLECTION (1989)
The Rolling Stones
The first two are mid-career classics. In the last, an obscure collection of mostly mono, many never released in the U.S. singles, finds the Stones paying tribute to their black American heroes.

NEVER MIND THE BOLLOCKS, HERE'S THE SEX PISTOLS (1977)
Sex Pistols
Unlistenable then, unbeatable now, it mocks, it taunts, it screams, and you can dance to it!

BACK TO MONO (1991)
Phil Spector
Actually four CDs, offering unforgettable visits by (mostly) girl groups to the little man's Great Wall of Sound.

BORN TO RUN (1975)
Bruce Springsteen
The Boss as rock and roll tradesman, redefining the exuberant yearning to get out on the highway with a guitar strapped 'cross his back.

STORYTELLER (Boxed Set, 1992)
Rod Stewart
Remember that before he turned out the lights and cuddled up to the Manilow inside him, Rod the mod was an underrated lyricist who rivaled Van Morrison in the U.K. soul crooner department.

HITSVILLE USA: THE MOTOWN SINGLES COLLECTION (1992)
The Supremes, The Four Tops, Smokey Robinson and The Miracles, The Jackson Five, The Temptations, et al.
The soundtrack of the '60s, courtesy of Detroit's big wheel, Berry Gordy. (And it's got Mary Wells and Marvin Gaye, too.)

TALKING HEADS 77 (1977)
Talking Heads
Leading the punk revolt from these shores, art school misfit David Byrne makes his bow as one of rock's strangest, and most talented, characters.

ACHTUNG BABY (1991)
U2
The Dubliners finally drop the earnest façade, as well as the endlessly repeated rhythm guitar riff that launched them and deliver a sonic treat recorded in the cold war capital of Berlin.

MEATY BEATY BIG AND BOUNCY (1971)
The Who
Known for their big productions, including the overrated *Tommy* and underrated *Quadrophenia*, the London mods rocked Top 40 radio with these high explosives.

SUMMER TEETH (1999)
Wilco
Pop go the country rockers and craft an edgy masterpiece.

CAR WHEELS ON A GRAVEL ROAD (1998)
Lucinda Williams
The Lake Charles, Louisiana, native takes listeners on a musically and emotionally rich journey through the scarred by-ways of her heartland.

AFTER THE GOLD RUSH (1970)
Neil Young
One nugget from four brilliant decades of work by the once and current rocker.

THE NAME OF THIS BAND IS …

From Abba to ZZ Top, here's the scoop on how some leading bands came up with their famous names.

Abba: An acronym made up of the first initials of the band members' names—Agnetha Fältskog, Benny Andersson, Björn Ulvaeus, and Anni-Frid Lyngstad.

Ben Folds Five: This three-membered band chose to use "five" for alliterative effect.

Black Sabbath: An occult thriller by novelist Denis Wheatley.

Depeche Mode: A French magazine, translating to "fast fashion."

Duran Duran: The villain's name in the 1967 sci-fi film *Barbarella*.

Bob Dylan: Robert Zimmerman took his new last name not from Dylan Thomas, as is often assumed, but from an uncle "Dillion."

Eurythmics: The word is defined in the *American Heritage Dictionary* as "the choreographic art of interpreting musical composition by a rhythmical, free-style graceful movement of the body in response to the rhythm of the music."

Grateful Dead: An English folk ballad archetype involving karma and the life cycle.

Hole: Band leader Courtney Love chose the name after a line in the Greek tragedy *Medea*: "There's a hole burning deep inside of me." She says she picked it because "I knew it would confuse people."

Jane's Addiction: Allegedly, Jane is a Hollywood hooker through whom the band members met in Los Angeles.

Led Zeppelin: Keith Moon, drummer for The Who, predicted Jimmy Page's heavy blues-rock sound would "go over like a lead zeppelin."

Living Colour: Inspired by the introduction to the old Walt Disney TV show: "The following program is brought to you in living color."

The Meat Puppets: From the idea that the musicians are only vehicles of their music's will.

Pearl Jam: Named after Eddie Vedder's grandmother Pearl, who was married to a Native American and made hallucinogenic preserves from peyote.

Pink Floyd: A combination of the names of two Georgia bluesmen, Pink Anderson and Floyd Council.

The Police: An ironic reference to drummer Stewart Copeland's father, former chief of the CIA's Political Action Staff.

Soundgarden: Named after a beach sculpture that hums in the wind by Lake Washington in Seattle.

They Might Be Giants: A 1971 film title cribbed from *Don Quixote*; band members liked its curiosity and paranoia.

UB40: Since the band members were all unemployed, they chose the name of the British unemployment benefit card.

Velvet Underground: From the title of an obscure book about sadomasochism.

ZZ Top: After Texas bluesman Z. Z. Hill.

CHANGE OF TUNE

Like the best-laid plans, the best-named bands often went astray before deciding on a final moniker. Here are some enduring groups with their long-lost early names.

Final Name	Original Name	Final Name	Original Name
The Bangles	Supersonic Bangs; Bangs	Journey	Golden Gate Rhythm Section
The Beach Boys	Carl and the Passions	Led Zeppelin	New Yardbirds
The Beatles	Johnny and the Moondogs	Lynyrd Skynyrd	My Backyard
The Bee Gees	Rattlesnakes	The Mamas and the Papas	New Journeymen
Black Sabbath	Earth	The Righteous Brothers	Paramours
Buffalo Springfield	The Herd	Salt-N-Pepa	Supernature
The Byrds	Beefeaters	Simon and Garfunkel	Tom and Jerry
Creedence Clearwater Revival	The Golliwogs	Styx	Trade Winds; TW4
Culture Club	Praise of Lemmings	Sonny and Cher	Caesar and Cleo
The Cure	Obelisk; Goat Band	Steppenwolf	Sparrow
Depeche Mode	Composition of Sound	The Supremes	Primettes
Dire Straits	Cafe Racers	Talking Heads	Artistics
Earth Wind & Fire	Salty Peppers	The Temptations	The Elgins
Grateful Dead	Warlocks	U2	Feedback; the Hype

THE 50 BEST COUNTRY ALBUMS

PEOPLE's Randy Vest touts this country-album starter set, with additional tips of the Stetson to Webb Pierce, Ernest Tubb, Kitty Wells, Bob Wills, and many others.

THE BEST OF EDDY ARNOLD (1967)
Eddy Arnold
The Tennessee Plowboy shows his smoother side on these (mostly) '60s tracks.

THINKIN' PROBLEM (1994)
David Ball
Among a sea of hat acts, Ball's topper stands out in the crowd, thanks to this twangy tour de force.

KILLIN' TIME (1989)
Clint Black
An incredible, play-it-over-and-over-again debut that garnered Black five No. 1 singles.

NO FENCES (1990)
Garth Brooks
Pure, heartfelt songs recorded just before Garth became GARTH.

HIGH AND DRY (1991)
Marty Brown
Of all the pretenders to Hank's throne, Brown is the real deal.

COME ON COME ON (1992)
Mary Chapin Carpenter
A blissful fusion of country, folk, and rock from the "hometown girl."

I FELL IN LOVE (1990)
Carlene Carter
After years of dabbling in rock, June Carter and Carl Smith's little girl finds her roots in country.

JOHNNY CASH AT FOLSOM PRISON (1968)
Johnny Cash
Cash's live performance for a throng of inmates remains a milestone. "Folsom Prison Blues" can still evoke chills.

KING'S RECORD SHOP (1987)
Rosanne Cash
Produced by then hubby Rodney Crowell, this Grammy-winning album is right on the money.

THE PATSY CLINE STORY (1963)
Patsy Cline
Sublime sounds from country's high priestess of female vocalists.

DIAMONDS AND DIRT (1988)
Rodney Crowell
Singer-songwriter Crowell hit a home run with this critically lauded and commercially successful release.

GUITAR TOWN (1986)
Steve Earle
Rough-housin' Earle found himself a spot on country's crowded map with this inspired outing.

THE BEST OF LEFTY FRIZZELL (1991)
Lefty Frizzell
His style influenced everyone from Willie to Merle to George Jones. Here's the evidence.

WHEN I CALL YOUR NAME (1989)
Vince Gill
The sweetest pipes this side of heaven, caressing material that's just as heavenly.

CHISELED IN STONE (1987)
Vern Gosdin
A hard-edged voice that's packed with pathos.

TRIO (1987)
Emmylou Harris, Dolly Parton, Linda Ronstadt
Three distinct song stylists in a perfect, harmonious blend.

DOWN EVERY ROAD 1962–1994 (1996)
Merle Haggard
A four-disc anthology shows why the Hag is one of country's enduring legends.

HIGHWAYMAN (1985)
The Highwaymen (Johnny Cash, Waylon Jennings, Kris Kristofferson, Willie Nelson)
An inspired collaboration between some of country's elder statesmen.

ROCKIN' IN THE COUNTRY: THE BEST OF WANDA JACKSON (1990)
Wanda Jackson
From rockabilly to Nash-pop, Jackson growls and purrs up a storm.

SHE THINKS I STILL CARE: THE GEORGE JONES COLLECTION (1997)
George Jones
A two-disc set chronicling Jones's often overlooked years with the United Artists label in the '60s.

THE JUDDS (WYNONNA & NAOMI) (1984)
The Judds
Wynonna and her mater never sounded quite as honest or engaging after this memorable debut.

PICKIN' ON NASHVILLE (1989)
Kentucky Headhunters
Raucous rock from the Bluegrass State's (and Arkansas') impish, redneck sons.

SHADOWLAND (1988)
k.d. lang
Lang teams up with legendary producer Owen Bradley to create studio magic.

ANTHOLOGY 1956–80 (1991)
Brenda Lee
The songs are mostly pop, but the pipes are pure country all the way.

20 GREATEST HITS (1987)
Loretta Lynn
From givin' a carousin' hubby what-fer to wardin' off a would-be man-stealer, the coal miner's daughter is a tough lady to top.

GOLDEN HITS (1965)
Roger Miller
The King of the Road's loopy takes on booze, buffalo, and Britain.

COUNTRY MUSIC HALL OF FAME (1991)
Bill Monroe
The father of bluegrass and his mandolin. Need we say more?

LEAVE THE LIGHT ON (1989)
Lorrie Morgan
George Morgan's daughter takes center stage and stakes a claim on country's landscape.

WHY LADY WHY (1983)
Gary Morris
A voice of operatic strength surrounding some mighty sturdy songs.

JUST LIKE OLD TIMES (1992)
Heather Myles
A rousing, Bakersfield-influenced sleeper by a dynamic singer.

RED HEADED STRANGER (1975)
Willie Nelson
Bare-bones country by the genre's celebrated redneck outlaw.

WILL THE CIRCLE BE UNBROKEN (1972)
The Nitty Gritty Dirt Band
An historic summit with the likes of Roy Acuff and Mother Maybelle Carter.

THE NEW NASHVILLE CATS (1991)
Mark O'Connor
The country fiddler/classical composer is joined by some 50 heavyweight pickers on this Grammy-winning set.

'80S LADIES (1987)
K. T. Oslin
Sassy and bittersweet songs truthfully sung by a seasoned survivor.

THE BUCK OWENS COLLECTION, 1959–1990 (1992)
Buck Owens
Three CDs worth of classic tunes from the king of the Bakersfield sound and his stalwart Buckaroos.

THE COMPLETE '50S MASTERS (1992)
Elvis Presley
The King's earliest sides (8 CDs!) before Hollywood and mediocrity beckoned.

THE ESSENTIAL RAY PRICE, 1951–62 (1991)
Ray Price
Raw performances from the man once known as the "Cherokee Cowboy" who later found success crooning pop-styled ballads.

FOUR WALLS: THE LEGEND BEGINS (1991)
Jim Reeves
An early, mostly harder-edged Reeves, already showing signs of that vocal "touch of velvet."

THE ESSENTIAL MARTY ROBBINS, 1951–82 (1991)
Marty Robbins
The King of the Balladeers lends his distinct tenor to storytelling songs and country-pop.

WHAT A WOMAN WANTS TO HEAR (1991)
Dawn Sears
Shamefully overlooked powerhouse vocalist whose followup, *Nothin' but Good*, was equally as memorable.

THE ESSENTIAL CONNIE SMITH (1996)
Connie Smith
One of country's greatest female singers of the '60s, '70s, or for that matter, any decade.

STRAIT OUT OF THE BOX (1995)
George Strait
From a winning 16-year career, here are the cream of the crop.

STORMS OF LIFE (1986)
Randy Travis
With this debut album, Travis helped to restore country music's heart and soul. He's never equalled it.

THE VERY BEST OF CONWAY TWITTY (1978)
Conway Twitty
Once called "the best friend a song ever had," Twitty put his own indelible stamp on the country genre.

KEVIN WELCH (1990)
Kevin Welch
Call it alterna-country. This singer-songwriter from Oklahoma brings a poet's sensibility to his work.

THE ESSENTIAL DOTTIE WEST (1996)
Dottie West
West's husky vocals were never better than on these defining 1960s and '70s tracks.

I WONDER DO YOU THINK OF ME (1989)
Keith Whitley
The title cut alone by the late, lamented Whitley will break your heart.

40 GREATEST HITS (1978)
Hank Williams
The Daddy...the King... the Master.

ANNIVERSARY: TWENTY YEARS OF HITS (1987)
Tammy Wynette
Wynette conveys more pain in "Til I Get it Right" than most artists can in their entire repertoire.

GUITARS, CADILLACS, ETC., ETC. (1986)
Dwight Yoakam
California honky-tonk collides with Nashville tradition. A rouser of a debut.

GREAT TITLES TO COUNTRY SONGS

A case could be made that the aptest aphorists of pop culture are country songwriters. Here are some of C&W's quirkier titles.

"All My Exes Live in Texas," George Strait

"Divorce Me C.O.D.," Merle Travis

"Don't You Think This Outlaw Bit's Done Got Out of Hand," Waylon Jennings

"Heaven's Just a Sin Away," The Kendells

"I Cheated Me Right Out of You," Moe Bandy

"I Forgot More Than You'll Ever Know," Davis Sisters

"I Gave Her the Ring, She Gave Me the Finger," Kinchafoonee Cowboys

"I'll Never Get Out of This World Alive," Hank Williams Sr.

"I'm Gonna Hire a Wino to Decorate Our Home," David Frizzell

"I'm the Only Hell (Mama Ever Raised)," Johnny Paycheck

"It's Not Love (But It's Not Bad)," Merle Haggard

"I've Enjoyed About as Much of This as I Can Stand," Porter Wagoner

"The Lord Knows I'm Drinkin'," Cal Smith

"Mama's in the Graveyard, Papa's in the Pen (Papa Loved Mama and Mama Loved Men)," Garth Brooks

"Marriage Has Ruined More Good Love Affairs," Jan Howard

"Maximum Security to Minimum Wage," Don King

"Now I Lay Me Down To Cheat," David Allan Coe

"She's Actin' Single (I'm Drinkin' Doubles)," Gary Stewart

"She Got the Goldmine (I Got the Shaft)," Jerry Reed

"She Was Bitten on the Udder by an Adder," Jethro Burns

"Sleeping Single (in a Double Bed)," Barbara Mandrell

"Take an Old Cold Tater and Wait," Little Jimmy Dickens

"Take This Job and Shove It," Johnny Paycheck

"Two of a Kind, Workin' on a Full House," Garth Brooks

"Waitin' in Your Welfare Line," Buck Owens

"What's Made Milwaukee Famous (Has Made a Loser Out of Me)," Jerry Lee Lewis

"When It's Springtime in Alaska (It's Forty Below)," Johnny Horton

"Yonder Comes a Sucker," Jim Reeves

"You Just Hurt My Last Feeling," Sammi Smith

"You're Gonna Ruin My Bad Reputation," Ronnie McDowell

"You're Out Doing What I'm Here Doing Without," Gene Watson

"You're the Reason Our Kids Are Ugly," Loretta Lynn

PEOPLE'S 20 TRAILBLAZERS OF COUNTRY MUSIC

Many of these legendary divas and dudes of the Grand Ole Opry are now dead, but their music and influence live forever—from Nashville to Austin to Bakersfield, wherever country artists are at work.

Roy Acuff	Tennessee Ernie Ford	Roy Rogers
Eddy Arnold	Lefty Frizzell	Hank Snow
Gene Autry	Bill Monroe	Ernest Tubb
Boudleaux Bryant	Minnie Pearl	Kitty Wells
The Carter Family	Tex Ritter	Hank Williams Sr.
Patsy Cline	Marty Robbins	Bob Wills
Spade Cooley	Jimmie Rodgers	

JAZZ: ESSENTIAL LISTENING

Not encyclopedic or definitive, this is simply a list of 50 marvelous jazz albums. The recordings here date from the '20s to the '90s, and they cover a range of styles. Any jazz purist, or for that matter, impurist, will find sins of omission and commission on this list. All we—the jazz jury at PEOPLE—can say is that these albums have enriched our lives immeasurably and given us an almost embarrassing amount of pleasure. To us, these recordings are the easiest sort of listening, full of wit, passion, invention, and beauty.

Louis Armstrong	*Hot Fives and Sevens,* Vol. II or III (1926–27)
Chet Baker	*My Funny Valentine* (1954)
Count Basie	*The Original American Decca Recordings* (1937–39)
Bix and Tram Beiderbecke	*The Bix Beiderbecke Story,* Vol. II (1927–28)
Art Blakey & The Jazz Messengers	*Buhaina's Delight* (1961)
Clifford Brown and Max Roach	*Clifford Brown and Max Roach* (1954–55)
Betty Carter	*Betty Carter* (1966)
Ornette Coleman	*The Shape of Jazz to Come* (1959–60)
Ornette Coleman	*Free Jazz* (1960)
John Coltrane	*Coltranc* (1957)
John Coltrane	*Meditations* (1965)
Miles Davis	*Kind of Blue* (1959)
Miles Davis and Gil Evans	*Porgy and Bess* (1958)
Paul Desmond and Gerry Mulligan	*Two of a Mind* (1962)
Eric Dolphy	*Out to Lunch* (1964)
Duke Ellington	*The Blanton-Webster Band* (1940-42)
Duke Ellington & The Jungle Band	*Rockin' in Rhythm,* Vol. III (1929–31)
Bill Evans	*The Village Vanguard Sessions* (1961)
Art Farmer	*Something to Live For* (1987)
Ella Fitzgerald	*The Gershwin Songbook* (1959)
Ella Fitzgerald	*The Intimate Ella* (1960)

Stan Getz	*The Roost Quartets 1950-51* (1950–51)
Benny Goodman	*Carnegie Hall Concert* (1938)
Charlie Haden & Quartet	*Haunted Heart* (1990)
Lionel Hampton	*The Complete Lionel Hampton* (1937–41)
Herbie Hancock	*Maiden Voyage* (1965)
Coleman Hawkins	*Body and Soul: The Complete Coleman Hawkins,* Vol. I (1929–40)
Coleman Hawkins	*The Complete Coleman Hawkins* (1944)
Fletcher Henderson and Don Redman	*Developing an American Orchestra, 1923 1937* (1923–37)
Billie Holiday	*The Quintessential Billie Holiday,* Vol. III, IV, or V (1937–39)
James P. Johnson	*Snowy Morning Blues* (1930, 1944)
Abbey Lincoln	*The World Is Falling Down* (1990)
Charles Mingus	*New Tijuana Moods* (1957)
Thelonious Monk	*The Unique Thelonious Monk* (1956)
Thelonious Monk	*Alone in San Francisco* (1959)
Thelonious Monk	*Monk's Dream* (1962)
Gerry Mulligan	*What Is There to Say?* (1958–59)
Oliver Nelson	*Blues and the Abstract Truth* (1961)
King Oliver	*King Oliver's Jazz Band 1923* (1923)

Charlie Parker — *The Charlie Parker Story* (1945)

Charlie Parker (with Dizzy Gillespie, Max Roach, Bud Powell, and Charles Mingus) — *The Greatest Jazz Concert Ever* (1953)

Bud Powell — *The Amazing Bud Powell*, Vol. I (1949–51)

Bud Powell — *The Genius of Bud Powell* (1951)

Sonny Rollins — *A Night at the Village Vanguard*, Vols. I and II (1957)

John Scofield — *Time on My Hands* (1989)

Art Tatum — *The Tatum Solo Masterpieces*, Vol. III (1953–55)

Cecil Taylor — *Unit Structures* (1966)

Sarah Vaughan and Clifford Brown — *Sarah Vaughan with Clifford Brown* (1954)

Fats Waller — *The Joint Is Jumpin'* (1929–43)

Lester Young — *The Complete Lester Young* (1943–44)

JAZZ TODAY

A new generation of stars is emerging in jazz. Steeped in tradition, technically prodigious, often daring, and always fired by the energy and passion of youth, they are a formidable lot, as varied in style as they are united in their allegiance to the verities of swing, the blues, and improvisation. Here are some standout albums by the the new school.

Geri Allen, *Twenty One* (1994)
(piano)

James Carter, *The Real Quietstorm* (1995)
(saxophone/flute/clarinet)

Marty Ehrlich, *Can You Hear a Motion?* (1994)
(various instruments)

Kenny Garrett, *Triology* (1995)
(alto sax)

Javon Jackson, *For One Who Knows* (1995)
(saxophone)

Hank Jones and Charlie Haden, *Steal Away: Spirituals, Hymns, and Folk Songs* (1995)
(piano; bass)

Leroy Jones, *Mo' Cream from the Crop* (1994)
(trumpet)

Keb' Mo', *Keb' Mo'* (1994)
(guitar)

Abbey Lincoln, *A Turtle's Dream* (1994)
(vocals)

Marcus Printup, *Song for the Beautiful Woman* (1995)
(trumpet)

Eric Reed, *The Swing and I* (1995)
(piano)

Jacky Terrasson, *Jacky Terrasson* (1995)
(piano)

Steve Turre, *Rhythm Within* (1995)
(trombone)

Cassandra Wilson, *Blue Skies* (1988)
(vocals)

50 GREAT CLASSICAL RECORDINGS

We can't really presume to pick a classical library for all tastes, but PEOPLE's editors will hazard this tendentious consensus of outstanding recordings.

Johann Sebastian Bach	*Brandenburg Concertos*, Munich Bach Orchestra/Karl Richter
Johann Sebastian Bach	*The Well-Tempered Clavier*, BWV 846-893, Davitt Moroney
Samuel Barber	*Adagio for Strings*, Saint Louis Symphony Orchestra/Leonard Slatkin
Béla Bartók	*String Quartets Nos. 1–6*, Emerson Quartet
Ludwig van Beethoven	*Symphonies Nos. 1–9, Complete Cycles*, Berlin Philharmonic/Herbert von Karajan
Ludwig van Beethoven	*Piano Sonata in C Minor, Op. 13, "Pathétique,"* Wilhelm Kempff
Ludwig van Beethoven	*Piano Sonata in C-sharp Minor, Op. 27, No. 2, "Moonlight,"* Wilhelm Kempff
Hector Berlioz	*Symphonie fantastique*, French National Radio Orchestra/Sir Thomas Beecham
Leonard Bernstein	*Chichester Psalms*, John Paul Bogart; Camerata Singers, New York Philharmonic/ Leonard Bernstein
Georges Bizet	*Carmen*, Agnes Baltsa, José Carreras; Chorus of the Paris Opéra, Berlin Philharmonic/Herbert von Karajan
Johannes Brahms	*Violin Concerto in D, Op. 77*, Itzhak Perlman; Chicago Symphony Orchestra/Carlo Maria Giulini
Benjamin Britten	*War Requiem, Op. 66*, Lorna Haywood, Anthony Rolfe Johnson, Benjamin Luxon; Atlanta Boy Choir, Atlanta Symphony Orchestra & Chorus/Robert Shaw
Frédéric Chopin	*26 Preludes*, Dmitri Alexeev
Aaron Copland	*Appalachian Spring*, New York Philharmonic/Leonard Bernstein
Claude Debussy	*Images*, Claudio Arrau
Antonín Dvořák	*Symphony No. 9 in E Minor, Op. 95, "From the New World,"* London Symphony Orchestra/István Kertész
César Franck	*Symphony in D Minor*, Berlin Radio Symphony Orchestra/Vladimir Ashkenazy
George Gershwin	*Rhapsody in Blue*, Columbia Symphony Orchestra, New York Philharmonic/ Leonard Bernstein
George Gershwin	*Porgy and Bess,* Willard White, Leona Mitchell; Cleveland Orchestra & Chorus/ Lorin Maazel
George Frideric Handel	*Messiah*, Heather Harper, Helen Watts, John Wakefield, John Shirley-Quirk; London Symphony Orchestra & Choir/Sir Colin Davis
Joseph Haydn	*Symphonies Nos. 93-104, "London,"* Royal Concertgebouw Orchestra/Sir Colin Davis
Joseph Haydn	*String Quartets, Op. 76, "Erdödy,"* Takács Quartet
Charles Ives	*Three Places in New England*, Boston Symphony Orchestra/Michael Tilson Thomas
Franz Liszt	*Les Préludes*, Philadelphia Orchestra/Riccardo Muti
Gustav Mahler	*Symphony No. 9 in D*, Vienna Philharmonic/Bruno Walter
Felix Mendelssohn	*Violin Concerto in E Minor, Op. 64,* Kyung Wha Chung; Montreal Symphony Orchestra/ Charles Dutoit

Wolfgang Amadeus Mozart	*Symphony No. 41 in C, K. 551, "Jupiter,"* Columbia Symphony Orchestra/Bruno Walter
Wolfgang Amadeus Mozart	*A Little Night Music, K. 525*, Prague Chamber Orchestra/Sir Charles Mackerras
Wolfgang Amadeus Mozart	*The Marriage of Figaro*, Samuel Ramey, Lucia Popp; London Opera Chorus, London Philharmonic Orchestra/Sir George Solti
Wolfgang Amadeus Mozart	*Don Giovanni,* Eberhard Wächter, Joan Sutherland, Elisabeth Schwarzkopf; Philharmonia Orchestra & Chorus/Carlo Maria Giulini
Modest Mussorgsky	*Pictures at an Exhibition*, Montreal Symphony Orchestra/Charles Dutoit
Giacomo Puccini	*La Bohème,* Mirella Freni, Luciano Pavarotti; Chorus of the Deutsche Oper Berlin, Berlin Philharmonic/Herbert von Karajan
Sergei Prokofiev	*Symphony No. 1 in D, Op. 25, "Classical,"* Berlin Philharmonic/Herbert von Karajan
Sergei Rachmaninoff	*Piano Concerto No. 2 in C Minor, Op. 18*, Vladimir Ashkenazy; London Symphony Orchestra/André Previn
Nikolai Rimsky-Korsakov	*Scheherazade, Op. 35*, Royal Concertgebouw Orchestra/Kirill Kondrashin
Gioacchino Rossini	*The Barber of Seville*, Leo Nucci, William Matteuzzi, Cecilia Bartoli; Chorus & Orchestra of the Teatro Comunale di Bologna/Giuseppe Patanè
Camille Saint-Saëns	*The Carnival of the Animals*, Montreal Symphony Orchestra, London Sinfonietta/ Charles Dutoit
Domenico Scarlatti	*Keyboard Sonatas*, Vladimir Horowitz
Arnold Schoenberg	*Verklärte Nacht (Transfigured Night), Op. 4*, Jiri Najnar, Vaclav Bernasek; Talich Quartet
Franz Schubert	*Die Schöne Müllerin, D. 795; Winterreise, D. 911*, Dietrich Fischer-Dieskau, Gerald Moore
Robert Schumann	*Op. 19, "Carnaval: Pretty Scenes on Four Notes,"* Artur Rubinstein
Dmitri Shostakovich	*Symphony No. 5 in D Minor, Op. 47*, Royal Concertgebouw Orchestra/Bernard Haitink
Jean Sibelius	*Symphony No. 5 in E-flat, Op. 82*, Boston Symphony Orchestra/Sir Colin Davis
Igor Stravinsky	*The Rite of Spring*, New York Philharmonic, Cleveland Orchestra/Pierre Boulez
Piotr Ilyich Tchaikovsky	*Symphony No. 6 in B Minor, Op. 74, "Pathétique,"* Leningrad Philharmonic/Evgeny Mravinsky
Piotr Ilyich Tchaikovsky	*Piano Concerto No. 1 in B-flat Minor, Op. 23*, Van Cliburn; RCA Symphony Orchestra/Kirill Kondrashin
Giuseppe Verdi	*Requiem*, Elisabeth Schwarzkopf, Christa Ludwig, Nicolai Gedda, Nicolai Ghiaurov; Philharmonia Orchestra & Chorus/Carlo Maria Giulini
Giuseppe Verdi	*La Traviata*, Joan Sutherland, Luciano Pavarotti; London Opera Chorus, National Philharmonic Orchestra/Richard Bonynge
Antonio Vivaldi	*Concertos for Violin, Strings, and Continuo, Op. 8, Nos. 1–4, "The Four Seasons,"* Alan Loveday; Academy of St. Martin-in-the-Fields/Sir Neville Marriner
Richard Wagner	*The Ring of the Nibelung*, Birgit Nilsson, Wolfgang Windgassen; Chorus & Orchestra of the Bayreuth Festival/Karl Böhm

THE 50 GREATEST CLASSICAL COMPOSERS

They're all dead white men, but they sure could write a tune. Here are the classics of the classical composers as selected by PEOPLE.

Johann Sebastian Bach (German, 1685–1750)

Samuel Barber (American, 1910–81)

Béla Bartók (Hungarian, 1881–1945)

Ludwig van Beethoven (German, 1770–1827)

Hector Berlioz (French, 1803–69)

Leonard Bernstein (American, 1918–90)

Georges Bizet (French, 1838–75)

Johannes Brahms (German, 1833–97)

Benjamin Britten (British, 1913–76)

John Cage (American, 1912–92)

Elliott Carter (American, b. 1908)

Frédéric Chopin (Polish, 1810–49)

Aaron Copland (American, 1900–90)

François Couperin (French, 1668–1733)

Claude Debussy (French, 1862–1918)

Antonín Dvořák (Czech, 1841–1904)

Gabriel Fauré (French, 1845–1924)

César Franck (Belgian/French, 1822–90)

George Gershwin (American, 1898–1937)

George Frideric Handel (German/British, 1685–1759)

Franz Joseph Haydn (Austrian, 1732–1809)

Paul Hindemith (German, 1895–1963)

Charles Ives (American, 1874–1954)

Leos Janácek (Czech, 1854–1928)

Franz Liszt (Hungarian, 1811–86)

Gustav Mahler (Bohemian/Austrian, 1860–1911)

Felix Mendelssohn (German, 1809–47)

Claudio Monteverdi (Italian, 1567–1643)

Wolfgang Amadeus Mozart (Austrian, 1756–91)

Giovanni da Palestrina (Italian, c. 1525–94)

Sergei Prokofiev (Russian, 1891–1953)

Giacomo Puccini (Italian, 1858–1924)

Sergei Rachmaninoff (Russian, 1873–1943)

Jean-Philippe Rameau (French, 1683–1764)

Maurice Ravel (French, 1875–1937)

Camille Saint-Saëns (French, 1835–1921)

Domenico Scarlatti (Italian, 1685–1757)

Arnold Schoenberg (Austrian, 1874–1951)

Franz Schubert (Austrian, 1797–1828)

Dmitri Shostakovich (Russian, 1906–75)

Jean Sibelius (Finnish, 1865–1957)

Johann Strauss (Austrian, 1825–99)

Richard Strauss (German, 1864–1949)

Igor Stravinsky (Russian, 1882–1971)

Piotr Ilyitch Tchaikovsky (Russian, 1840–93)

Georg Philipp Telemann (German, 1681–1767)

Ralph Vaughan Williams (British, 1872–1958)

Giuseppe Verdi (Italian, 1813–1901)

Antonio Vivaldi (Italian, 1678–1741)

Richard Wagner (German, 1813–83)

MUSICAL PERIODS

As it turns out, classical music isn't all classical. To help you sort out baroque quartets and romantic symphonies from classical sonatas and modern operas, here's the chronological breakdown of musical periods:

PERIOD	DATES
Renaissance	1450–1600
Baroque	1600–1750
Classical	1750–1825
Romantic	1825–1910
Modern	1910–present

MAJOR AMERICAN SYMPHONY ORCHESTRAS

From Miami to Seattle, American cities are supporting some of the finest symphonies in the world. The following orchestras, 25 of the most important in the U.S., are listed with their conductors or music directors.

Atlanta Symphony Orchestra	Yoel Levi	Atlanta, GA
Baltimore Symphony Orchestra	Yuri Temirkanov	Baltimore, MD
Boston Symphony Orchestra	Seiji Ozawa	Boston, MA
Chicago Symphony Orchestra	Daniel Barenboim	Chicago, IL
Cincinnati Symphony Orchestra	Jesús Lopez-Cobos	Cincinnati, OH
Cleveland Orchestra	Christoph von Dohnányi	Cleveland, OH
Columbus Symphony	Alessandro Siciliani	Columbus, OH
Dallas Symphony Orchestra	Andrew Litton	Dallas, TX
Detroit Symphony Orchestra	Neeme Järvi	Detroit, MI
Florida Philharmonic Orchestra	James Judd	Fort Lauderdale, FL
Houston Symphony	Christoph Eschenbach	Houston, TX
Indianapolis Symphony Orchestra	Raymond Leppard	Indianapolis, IN
Los Angeles Philharmonic	Esa-Pekka Salonen	Los Angeles, CA
Milwaukee Symphony Orchestra	Andreas Delfs	Milwaukee, WI
Minnesota Orchestra	Eiji Oue	Minneapolis, MN
National Symphony Orchestra	Leonard Slatkin	Washington, DC
New World Symphony	Michael Tilson Thomas	Miami Beach, FL
New York Philharmonic	Kurt Masur	New York, NY
Oregon Symphony	James DePreist	Portland, OR
Philadelphia Orchestra	Wolfgang Sawallisch	Philadelphia, PA
Pittsburgh Symphony Orchestra	Mariss Jansons	Pittsburgh, PA
St. Louis Symphony Orchestra	Hans Vonk	St. Louis, MO
San Francisco Symphony	Michael Tilson Thomas	San Francisco, CA
Seattle Symphony	Gerard Schwarz	Seattle, WA
Utah Symphony Orchestra	Keith Lockhart	Salt Lake City, UT

CLIFFS' CLUES TO OPERA PLOTS

Opera is drama expressed musically, verbally, and visually—the ultimate experience for ears, eyes, and emotions. If you're intimidated by the prospect of sitting through three or more hours of heightened drama in a foreign language, but are intrigued by the passionate, mysterious world of divas and Don Juans, start here, with our summaries of 10 classics. (Dates given indicate the first staged production.)

THE BARBER OF SEVILLE (1782)
Composed by Gioacchino Rossini, text by Sterbini. Based on the novel by Beaumarchais. Set in Seville, Spain, in the 17th century.

Count Almaviva, a Grandee of Spain, loves Rosina, the young ward and bride-to-be of Dr. Bartolo. With the help of Figaro, the town barber and busybody, the Count enters his rival's home disguised as a drunken soldier, then as a music teacher. Having gained access to Rosina, he easily persuades her to take his hand. Almaviva then convinces a notary, procured by Bartolo for his own marriage to Rosina, to marry him to Rosina in Bartolo's absence.

LA BOHÈME (1896)
Composed by Giacomo Puccini, text by Luigi Illica and Giuseppe Giacosa. Based on the novel Scènes de la vie de Bohème *by Henri Murger. Set in Paris, France, in the 17th century.*

Rodolfo, a poet, lives in the Latin Quarter of Paris with his dear friends—a painter, a philosopher, and a musician—who defy their hunger with cheerfulness and pranks. The quartet of friends is so poor that they resort to burning Rodolfo's poetry to keep warm. But Rodolfo's heart is soon warmed by the frail and consumptive Mimi, who knocks on his door one night, her candle extinguished by a winter draft. The two fall in love, but Mimi grows weaker and weaker. Eventually, her sickness and Rodolfo's overprotectiveness drive the two apart. Mimi's last request is to return to Rodolfo's attic room, where they first met, and where she will die in his arms.

DON CARLOS (1867)
Composed by Giuseppe Verdi, text by G. Méry and C. du Locle. Based on the play by Friedrich von Schiller. Set in France and Spain, during the Spanish Inquisition.

Don Carlos, infante of Spain, is torn between a futile love for Queen Elizabeth, his stepmother, to whom he was once engaged, and a fierce desire to bring freedom to Flanders, a Protestant country under Spanish (Catholic) domain. The queen's attendant, who is deeply in love with Carlos, tells the king, untruthfully, that Carlos and Elizabeth have been unfaithful to him. Carlos is sent to death, ostensibly for demanding to be let go to Flanders. Elizabeth remains at her husband's side, and Carlos escapes his death in the last moments of the opera, saved by the King's father, who takes Carlos into the cloister.

DON GIOVANNI (1787)
Composed by Wolfgang Amadeus Mozart, text by Lorenzo da Ponte. Based on the text Il Convitato *by Giovanni Bertati. Set in Seville at the end of the 18th century.*

The insatiable lover, Don Juan, jaunts from lass to lass, breaking hearts and wreaking havoc before he is finally dragged into Hell by the statue of the Commendatore who he killed in a duel after attempting to seduce his daughter, Doña Anna.

ELEKTRA (1909)
Composed by Richard Strauss, text by Hugo von Hofmannsthal. Adapted from the play by Sophocles. Set in ancient Mycenae.

Her soul withered by grief, Elektra is bent on avenging the seven-year-old murder of her father, Agamemnon, at the hands of her mother, Klytämnestra, and her mother's lover, Aegisth. Elektra persuades her brother Orest to murder Klytämnestra and Aegisth. The murders send Elektra into a dance of joy that becomes a frenzied dance of death, ending in the explosion of her heart.

LUCIA DI LAMMERMOOR (1835)
Composed by Gaetano Donizetti, text by Salvatore Cammarano. Based on the novel The Bride of Lammermoor *by Sir Walter Scott. Set in Scotland in 1700.*

Her mother's death is slowly but inexorably driving the tragic Lucia to madness. She loves Edgardo, but their promised union is sabotaged by her brother, who forces her to marry Arturo, a wealthy man she does not love. Tormented by visions of ghosts and spirits and devastated over the loss of Edgardo, Lucia murders her groom on their wedding night, then experiences a series of hallucinations before collapsing and dying of a broken heart.

RIGOLETTO (1851)

Composed by Giuseppe Verdi, text by Francesco Maria Piave. Based on Victor Hugo's Le Roi s'amuse. *Set Mantua, Italy, in the 16th century.*

Rigoletto, a court jester, intends to have the Duke of Mantua murdered for seducing his daughter, Gilda, but brings about the murder of the girl, instead.

The first of a "romantic trilogy," *Rigoletto* is followed by *Il Trovotore* and *La Traviata.*

TOSCA (1900)

Composed by Giacomo Puccini, text by Giuseppe Giacosa and Luigi Illica. Based on the play La Tosca *by Victorien Sardou. Set in Rome, in 1800.*

Floria Tosca, a prima donna, is passionately pursued by the evil Scarpia, chief of the Roman police. Yet Tosca loves Cavara-dossi, a painter and a liberal patriot. She attempts to save her lover from execution when he is accused of aiding a fugitive, by pretending to yield to Scarpia's wishes, then killing him. But her actions unwittingly help to destroy her true love, Cavara-dossi.

LA TRAVIATA (1853)

Composed by Giuseppe Verdi, text by Francesco Maria Piave. Based on Alexandre Dumas's play La Tame aux Camélias. *Set in Paris and vicinity in 1850.*

Violetta, a courtesan, renounces her life of pleasure in order to be with her gentlemanly lover, Alfredo. But Alfredo's father persuades Violetta that she is a blight on his family and that she must leave Alfredo for the good of his career. She returns to her former protector, with whom Alfredo fights a duel. Alfredo is subsequently forced to flee the country, and will return only to find Violetta dying of consumption.

TRISTAN AND ISOLDE (1865)

Composed and written by Richard Wagner. Set in a ship at sea, in England, and in Ireland, in a legendary time.

Tristan is dispatched to Ireland by his uncle, King Marke, to win him Isolde's hand. Yet Tristan and Isolde have long loved one another, each believing their love to be unrequited. On board the vessel that brings them to Cornwall, they drink what they believe to be a death potion, but is in fact a love potion. King Marke later discovers them in a midnight embrace. Tristan, wounded by one of the king's knights, flees to France. Isolde follows, finds him dying, and she too dies by his side.

THE WORLD'S LARGEST OPERA HOUSES

These houses showcase the world's best singers and stand as monuments to the grandeur of opera.

Opera House	Location	Total Capacity
The Metropolitan Opera	New York, NY	4,065
Cincinnati Opera	Cincinnati, OH	3,630
Lyric Opera of Chicago	Chicago, IL	3,563
San Francisco Opera	San Francisco, CA	3,476
The Dallas Opera	Dallas, TX	3,420

MTV VIDEO MUSIC AWARDS

BEST VIDEO OF THE YEAR
1984	The Cars	You Might Think
1985	Don Henley	The Boys of Summer
1986	Dire Straits	Money for Nothing
1987	Peter Gabriel	Sledgehammer
1988	INXS	Need You Tonight/Mediate
1989	Neil Young	This Note's for You
1990	Sinead O'Connor	Nothing Compares 2 U
1991	R.E.M.	Losing My Religion
1992	Van Halen	Right Now
1993	Pearl Jam	Jeremy
1994	Aerosmith	Cryin'
1995	TLC	Waterfalls
1996	The Smashing Pumpkins	Tonight, Tonight
1997	Jamiroquai	Virtual Insanity
1998	Madonna	Ray of Light
1999	Lauryn Hill	Doo Wop (That Thing)

BEST MALE VIDEO
1984	David Bowie	China Girl
1985	Bruce Springsteen	I'm on Fire
1986	Robert Palmer	Addicted to Love
1987	Peter Gabriel	Sledgehammer
1988	Prince	U Got the Look
1989	Elvis Costello	Veronica
1990	Don Henley	The End of the Innocence
1991	Chris Isaak	Wicked Game (Concept)
1992	Eric Clapton	Tears in Heaven (Performance)
1993	Lenny Kravitz	Are You Gonna Go My Way
1994	Tom Petty and the Heartbreakers	Mary Jane's Last Dance
1995	Tom Petty and the Heartbreakers	You Don't Know How It Feels
1996	Beck	Where It's At
1997	Beck	The Devil's Haircut
1998	Will Smith	Just the Two of Us
1999	Will Smith	Miami

BEST FEMALE VIDEO
1984	Cyndi Lauper	Girls Just Want To Have Fun
1985	Tina Turner	What's Love Got To Do with It
1986	Whitney Houston	How Will I Know
1987	Madonna	Papa Don't Preach
1988	Suzanne Vega	Luka
1989	Paula Abdul	Straight Up
1990	Sinead O'Connor	Nothing Compares 2 U
1991	Janet Jackson	Love Will Never Do Without You
1992	Annie Lennox	Why
1993	k.d. lang	Constant Craving
1994	Janet Jackson	If
1995	Madonna	Take a Bow
1996	Alanis Morissette	Ironic
1997	Jewel	You Were Meant for Me
1998	Madonna	Ray of Light
1999	Lauryn Hill	Doo Wop (That Thing)

BEST CONCEPT VIDEO
1984	Herbie Hancock	Rockit
1985	Glenn Frey	Smuggler's Blues
1986	a-ha	Take On Me
1987	Peter Gabriel/ Stephen Johnson	Sledgehammer
1988	Pink Floyd	Learning to Fly

BEST GROUP VIDEO
1984	ZZ Top	Legs
1985	USA for Africa	We Are the World
1986	Dire Straits	Money for Nothing
1987	Talking Heads	Wild Wild Life
1988	INXS	Need You Tonight/Mediate
1989	Living Colour	Cult of Personality
1990	The B-52's	Love Shack
1991	R.E.M.	Losing My Religion
1992	U2	Even Better Than the Real Thing
1993	Pearl Jam	Jeremy
1994	Aerosmith	Cryin'
1995	TLC	Waterfalls
1996	Foo Fighters	Big Me
1997	No Doubt	Don't Speak
1998	Backstreet Boys	Everybody (Backstreet's Back)
1999	TLC	No Scrubs

BEST NEW ARTIST IN A VIDEO
1984	Eurythmics	Sweet Dreams (Are Made of This)
1985	'Til Tuesday	Voices Carry
1986	a-ha	Take On Me
1987	Crowded House	Don't Dream It's Over
1988	Guns N' Roses	Welcome to the Jungle
1989	Living Colour	Cult of Personality
1990	Michael Penn	No Myth
1991	Jesus Jones	Right Here, Right Now
1992	Nirvana	Smells Like Teen Spirit
1993	Stone Temple Pilots	Plush
1994	Counting Crows	Mr. Jones
1995	Hootie & The Blowfish	Hold My Hand
1996	Alanis Morissette	Ironic
1997	Fiona Apple	Sleep to Dream
1998	Natalie Imbruglia	Torn
1999	Eminem	My Name Is

BEST RAP VIDEO
1989	D.J. Jazzy Jeff & The Fresh Prince	Parents Just Don't Understand
1990	M.C. Hammer	U Can't Touch This
1991	L.L. Cool J	Mama Said Knock You Out
1992	Arrested Development	Tennessee
1993	Arrested Development	People Everyday
1994	Snoop Doggy Dogg	Doggy Dogg World
1995	Dr. Dre	Keep Their Heads Ringin'
1996	Coolio featuring LV	Gangsta's Paradise

1997	The Notorious B.I.G.	Hypnotize
1998	Will Smith	Gettin' Jiggy Wit It
1999	Jay-Z featuring Ja Rule/Amil-lion	Can I Get a...

BEST DANCE VIDEO

1989	Paula Abdul	Straight Up
1990	M.C. Hammer	U Can't Touch This
1991	C+C Music Factory	Gonna Make You Sweat (Everybody Dance Now)
1992	Prince & the New Power Generation	Cream
1993	En Vogue	Free Your Mind
1994	Salt-N-Pepa w/ En Vogue	Whatta Man
1995	Michael and Janet Jackson	Scream
1996	Coolio	1, 2, 3, 4 (Sumpin' New)
1997	Spice Girls	Wannabe
1998	Prodigy	Smack My Bitch Up
1999	Ricky Martin	Livin' la Vida Loca

BEST METAL/HARD ROCK VIDEO

1989	Guns N' Roses	Sweet Child o' Mine
1990	Aerosmith	Janie's Got a Gun
1991	Aerosmith	The Other Side
1992	Metallica	Enter Sandman
1993	Pearl Jam	Jeremy
1994	Soundgarden	Black Hole Sun
1995	White Zombie	More Human Than Human
1996	Metallica	Until It Sleeps
1997	Aerosmith	Falling in Love (Is Hard on the Knees)
1998	Aerosmith	Pink
1999	Korn	Freak on a Leash

BEST R&B VIDEO

1993	En Vogue	Free Your Mind
1994	Salt-N-Pepa w/ En Vogue	Whatta Man
1995	TLC	Waterfalls
1996	The Fugees	Killing Me Softly
1997	Puff Daddy and the Family	I'll Be Missing You
1998	Wyclef Jean featuring Refugee Allstars	Gone 'Till November
1999	Lauryn Hill	Doo Wop (That Thing)

BEST POP VIDEO

| 1999 | Ricky Martin | Livin' la Vida Loca |

BEST VIDEO FROM A FILM

1987	Talking Heads	Wild Wild Life [True Stories]
1988	Los Lobos	La Bamba [La Bamba]
1989	U2 with B.B. King	When Love Comes to Town [U2 Rattle and Hum]
1990	Billy Idol	Cradle of Love [The Adventures of Ford Fairlaine]
1991	Chris Isaak	Wicked Game [Wild at Heart]
1992	Queen	Bohemian Rhapsody [Wayne's World]
1993	Alice in Chains	Would? [Singles]

1994	Bruce Springsteen	Streets of Philadelphia [Philadelphia]
1995	Seal	Kiss from a Rose [Batman Forever]
1996	Coolio	Gangsta's Paradise [Dangerous Minds]
1997	Will Smith	Men in Black [Men in Black]
1998	Aerosmith	I Don't Want to Miss a Thing [Armageddon]
1999	Madonna	Beautiful Stranger [Austin Powers: The Spy Who Shagged Me]

BEST CHOREOGRAPHY IN A VIDEO

1994	Salt-N-Pepa w/ En Vogue	Whatta Man
1995	Michael and Janet Jackson	Scream
1996	Bjork	It's Oh So Quiet
1997	Beck	The New Pollution
1998	Madonna	Ray of Light
1999	Fatboy Slim	Praise You

BEST ALTERNATIVE VIDEO

1991	Jane's Addiction	Been Caught Stealing
1992	Nirvana	Smells Like Teen Spirit
1993	Nirvana	In Bloom (Version 1—Dresses)
1994	Nirvana	Heart-Shaped Box
1995	Weezer	Buddy Holly
1996	The Smashing Pumpkins	1979
1997	Sublime	What I Got
1998	Green Day	Time of Your Life (Good Riddance)

BEST SPECIAL EFFECTS IN A VIDEO

1984	Herbie Hancock	Rockit
1985	Tom Petty & the Heartbreakers	Don't Come Around Here No More
1986	a-ha	Take On Me
1987	Peter Gabriel	Sledgehammer
1988	Squeeze	Hourglass
1989	Michael Jackson	Leave Me Alone
1990	Tears For Fears	Sowing the Seeds of Love
1991	Faith No More	Falling to Pieces
1992	U2	Even Better Than the Real Thing
1993	Peter Gabriel	Steam
1994	Peter Gabriel	Kiss That Frog
1995	The Rolling Stones	Love Is Strong
1996	The Smashing Pumpkins	Tonight, Tonight
1997	Jamiroquai	Virtual Insanity
1998	Madonna	Frozen
1999	Garbage	Special

BEST DIRECTION IN A VIDEO

1984	ZZ Top	Sharp Dressed Man
1985	Don Henley	The Boys of Summer
1986	a-ha	Take On Me
1987	Peter Gabriel	Sledgehammer
1988	George Michael	Father Figure
1989	Madonna	Express Yourself
1990	Madonna	Vogue
1991	R.E.M.	Losing My Religion

1992	Van Halen	Right Now
1993	Pearl Jam	Jeremy
1994	R.E.M.	Everybody Hurts
1995	Weezer	Buddy Holly
1996	The Smashing Pumpkins	Tonight, Tonight
1997	Beck	The New Pollution
1998	Madonna	Ray of Light
1999	Fatboy Slim	Praise You

BREAKTHROUGH VIDEO

1988	INXS	Need You Tonight/Mediate
1989	Art of Noise, featuring Tom Jones	Kiss
1990	Tears for Fears;	Sowing the Seeds of Love
1991	R.E.M.	Losing My Religion
1992	Red Hot Chili Peppers	Give It Away
1993	Los Lobos	Kiko & The Lavender Moon
1994	R.E.M.	Everybody Hurts
1995	Weezer	Buddy Holly
1996	The Smashing Pumpkins	Tonight, Tonight
1997	Jamiroquai	Virtual Insanity
1998	Prodigy	Smack My Bitch Up
1999	Fatboy Slim	Praise You

BEST WEB SITE
1999   www.redhotchilipeppers.com

VIDEO VANGUARD AWARD

1984	The Beatles, David Bowie, Richard Lester
1985	David Byrne, Kevin Godley and Lol Creme, Russell Mulcahy
1986	Madonna and Zbigniew Rybeznski
1987	Julien Temple and Peter Gabriel
1988	Michael Jackson
1989	George Michael
1990	Janet Jackson
1991	(see below)
1992	(see below)
1993	no award given
1994	Tom Petty
1995	R.E.M.
1996	no award given
1997	Mark Romanek, L.L. Cool J
1998	The Beastie Boys

MICHAEL JACKSON VIDEO VANGUARD AWARD

1991	Bon Jovi, Wayne Isham
1992	Guns N' Roses

VIEWER'S CHOICE AWARD

1984	Michael Jackson	Thriller
1985	USA for Africa	We Are the World
1986	a-ha	Take On Me
1987	U2	With or Without You
1988	INXS	Need You Tonight/Mediate
1989	Madonna	Like a Prayer
1990	Aerosmith	Janie's Got a Gun
1994	Aerosmith	Cryin'
1995	TLC	Waterfalls
1996	Bush	Glycerine
1997	Prodigy	Breathe
1998	Puff Daddy & The Family featuring The Lox, Lil' Kim, The Notorious B.I.G., and fuzzbubble	It's All About the Benjamins (Rock Remix)
1999	Backstreet Boys	I Want It That Way

THE GRAMMY AWARDS

Even more so than most award-giving bodies, the National Academy of Recording Arts and Sciences has switched, added, deleted, and renamed its various award categories on a regular basis. The following chart gathers the majority of continuing categories that honor mainstream musical achievement. This means you won't find the awards for polka or jacket liner notes, but you will find years of musical greats (and electorate gaffes) in an easy-to-follow format.

	1958	1959	1960
Record of the Year	Domenico Modugno, "Nel Blu Dipinto Di Blu (Volare)"	Bobby Darin, "Mack the Knife"	Percy Faith, "Theme from *A Summer Place*"
Album of the Year	Henry Mancini, *The Music from Peter Gunn*	Frank Sinatra, *Come Dance with Me*	Bob Newhart, *Button Down Mind*
Song of the Year	Domenico Modugno, "Nel Blu Dipinto Di Blu (Volare)"	Jimmy Driftwood, "The Battle of New Orleans"	Ernest Gold, "Theme from *Exodus*"
Pop Vocal, Female	Ella Fitzgerald, *Ella Fitzgerald Sings the Irving Berlin Song Book*	Ella Fitzgerald, "But Not for Me"	Ella Fitzgerald, *Mack the Knife, Ella in Berlin*
Pop Vocal, Male	Perry Como, "Catch a Falling Star"	Frank Sinatra, *Come Dance with Me*	Ray Charles, *Genius of Ray Charles*
New Artist	—	Bobby Darin	Bob Newhart
Pop Vocal, Duo or Group with Vocal	Louis Prima and Keely Smith, "That Old Black Magic"	Mormon Tabernacle Choir, "Battle Hymn of the Republic"	Eydie Gormé and Steve Lawrence, "We Got Us"
Rhythm and Blues Song	Champs, "Tequila"	Dinah Washington, "What a Diff'rence a Day Makes"	Ray Charles, "Let the Good Times Roll"
Jazz, Soloist	—	Ella Fitzgerald, *Ella Swings Lightly*	—
Jazz, Group	Count Basie, *Basie*	Jonah Jones, *I Dig Chicks*	André Previn, *West Side Story*
Jazz, Big Band/ Large Ensemble Performance	—	—	Henry Mancini, *The Blues and the Beat*
Folk Recording	—	Kingston Trio, *The Kingston Trio at Large*	Harry Belafonte, *Swing Dat Hammer*
Cast Show Album	*The Music Man*	*Porgy and Bess*	*The Sound of Music*
Comedy Recording (Spoken Word/Musical)	David Seville, "The Chipmunk Song"	Shelley Berman, *Inside Shelley Berman*; Homer & Jethro, *The Battle of Kookamonga*	Bob Newhart, *Button Down Mind Strikes Back*; Paul Weston and Jo Stafford, *Jonathan and Darlene Edwards in Paris*
Classical Orchestral Performance	Felix Slatkin, Hollywood Bowl Symphony, *Gaîeté Parisienne*	Charles Munch, conductor, Boston Symphony, *Debussy: Images for Orchestra*	Fritz Reiner, conductor, Chicago Symphony, *Bartók: Music for Strings, Percussion and Celeste*
Opera Recording	Roger Wagner Chorale, *Virtuoso*	Erich Leinsdorf, conductor, Vienna Philharmonic, *Mozart: The Marriage of Figaro*	Erich Leinsdorf, conductor, Rome Opera House Chorus and Orchestra, *Puccini: Turandot* (Solos: Tebaldi, Nilsson, Bjoerling, Tozzi)
Chamber Music Performance	Hollywood String Quartet, *Beethoven: Quartet 130*	Artur Rubinstein, *Beethoven: Sonata No. 21 in C, Op. 53; "Waldstein" Sonata No. 18 in E Flat, Op. 53, No. 3*	Laurindo Almeida, *Conversations with the Guitar*

	1961	**1962**	**1963**
Record of the Year	Henry Mancini, "Moon River"	Tony Bennett, "I Left My Heart in San Francisco"	Henry Mancini, "The Days of Wine and Roses"
Album of the Year	Judy Garland, *Judy at Carnegie Hall*	Vaughn Meader, *The First Family*	Barbra Streisand, *The Barbra Streisand Album*
Song of the Year	Henry Mancini and Johnny Mercer, "Moon River"	Leslie Bricusse and Anthony Newley, "What Kind of Fool Am I"	Johnny Mercer and Henry Mancini, "The Days of Wine and Roses"
(Pop) Vocal, Female	Judy Garland, *Judy at Carnegie Hall*	Ella Fitzgerald, *Ella Swings Brightly with Nelson Riddle*	Barbra Streisand, *The Barbra Streisand Album*
(Pop) Vocal, Male	Jack Jones, "Lollipops and Roses"	Tony Bennett, "I Left My Heart in San Francisco"	Jack Jones, "Wives and Lovers"
New Artist	Peter Nero	Robert Goulet	Swingle Singers
Pop Vocal, Duo or Group with Vocal	Lambert, Hendricks & Ross, *High Flying*	Peter, Paul & Mary, "If I Had a Hammer"	Peter, Paul & Mary, "Blowin' in the Wind"
Rhythm and Blues Song	Ray Charles, "Hit the Road, Jack"	Ray Charles, "I Can't Stop Loving You"	Ray Charles, "Busted"
Jazz, Soloist/Small Group	André Previn, *André Previn Plays Harold Arlen*	Stan Getz, *Desafinado*	Bill Evans, *Conversations with Myself*
Jazz, Big Band/Large Ensemble Performance	Stan Kenton, *West Side Story*	Stan Kenton, *Adventures in Jazz*	Woody Herman Band, *Encore: Woody Herman, 1963*
Contemporary Folk	Belafonte Folk Singers, *Belafonte Folk Singers at Home and Abroad*	Peter, Paul & Mary, "If I Had a Hammer"	Peter, Paul & Mary, "Blowin' in the Wind"
Cast Show Album	*How To Succeed in Business Without Really Trying*	*No Strings*	*She Loves Me*
Comedy Recording	Mike Nichols and Elaine May, *An Evening with Mike Nichols and Elaine May*	Vaughn Meader, *The First Family*	Allen Sherman, *Hello Mudduh, Hello Faddah*
Classical Album	Igor Stravinsky, conductor, Columbia Symphony, *Stravinsky Conducts, 1960: Le Sacre du Printemps; Petruchka*	Vladimir Horowitz, *Columbia Records Presents Vladimir Horowitz*	Benjamin Britten, conductor, London Symphony Orchestra and Chorus, *Britten: War Requiem*
Classical Orchestral Performance	Charles Munch, conductor, Boston Symphony, *Ravel: Daphnis et Chloe*	Igor Stravinsky, conductor, Columbia Symphony, *Stravinsky: The Firebird Ballet*	Erich Leinsdorf, conductor, Boston Symphony, *Bartók: Concerto for Orchestra*
Opera Recording	Gabriele Santini, conductor, Rome Opera Chorus and Orchestra, *Puccini: Madama Butterfly*	Georg Solti, conductor, Rome Opera House Orchestra and Chorus (Solos: Price, Vickers, Gorr, Merrill, Tozzi), *Verdi: Aïda*	Erich Leinsdorf, conductor, RCA Italiana Orchestra and Chorus (Solos: Price, Tucker, Elias), *Puccini: Madama Butterfly*
Chamber Music Performance	Jascha Heifetz, Gregor Piatigorsky, William Primrose, *Beethoven: Serenade, Op. 8; Kodaly: Duo for Violin & Cello, Op. 7*	Jascha Heifetz, Gregor Piatigorsky, William Primrose, *The Heifetz-Piatigorsky Concerts with Primrose, Pennario and Guests*	Julian Bream Consort, *An Evening of Elizabethan Music*

	1964	1965	1966
Record of the Year	Stan Getz and Astrud Gilberto, "The Girl from Ipanema"	Herb Alpert & The Tijuana Brass, "A Taste of Honey"	Frank Sinatra, "Strangers in the Night"
Album of the Year	Stan Getz and Joao Gilberto, *Getz/Gilberto*	Frank Sinatra, *September of My Years*	Frank Sinatra, *Sinatra: A Man & His Music*
Song of the Year	Jerry Herman, "Hello, Dolly!"	Paul Francis Webster and Johnny Mandel, "The Shadow of Your Smile (Love Theme from *The Sandpiper*)"	John Lennon and Paul McCartney, "Michelle"
Pop Vocal, Female	Barbra Streisand, "People"	Barbra Streisand, *My Name Is Barbra*	Eydie Gorme, "If He Walked into My Life"
Pop Vocal, Male	Louis Armstrong, "Hello, Dolly!"	Frank Sinatra, "It Was a Very Good Year"	Frank Sinatra, "Strangers in the Night"
Rock Vocal Female, Male	Petula Clark, "Downtown"	Petula Clark, "I Know a Place"; Roger Miller, "King of the Road"	Paul McCartney, "Eleanor Rigby"
New Artist	The Beatles	Tom Jones	—
Pop Vocal, Duo or Group	The Beatles, *A Hard Day's Night*	Anita Kerr Quartet, *We Dig Mancini*	Anita Kerr Quartet, "A Man and a Woman"
Rock Performance, Duo or Group with Vocal	—	Statler Brothers, "Flowers on the Wall"	The Mamas & The Papas, "Monday, Monday"
Rhythm and Blues Song	Nancy Wilson, "How Glad I Am"	James Brown, "Papa's Got a Brand New Bag"	Ray Charles, "Crying Time"
R&B Vocal	—	—	Ray Charles, "Crying Time"
R&B Duo or Group with Vocal	—	—	Ramsey Lewis, "Hold It Right There"
Country Song	Roger Miller, "Dang Me"	Roger Miller, "King of the Road"	Bill Sherrill and Glenn Sutton, "Almost Persuaded"
Country Vocal, Female	Dottie West, "Here Comes My Baby"	Jody Miller, "Queen of the House"	Jeannie Seely, "Don't Touch Me"
Country Vocal, Male	Roger Miller, "Dang Me"	Roger Miller, "King of the Road"	David Houston, "Almost Persuaded"
Jazz, Group	Stan Getz, *Getz/Gilberto*	Ramsey Lewis Trio, *The "In" Crowd*	Wes Montgomery, *Goin' Out of My Head*
Jazz, Big Band/ Large Ensemble Performance	Laurindo Almeida, *Guitar from Ipanema*	Duke Ellington Orchestra, *Ellington '66*	—
Gospel Performance, Duo, Group, Choir or Chorus	—	George Beverly Shea and Anita Ker Quartet, *Southland Favorites*	Porter Wagoner & the Blackwood Bros., *Grand Old Gospel*
Folk Recording	Gale Garnett, *We'll Sing in the Sunshine*	Harry Belafonte, Miriam Makeba, *An Evening with Belafonte/Makeba*	Cortelia Clark, *Blues in the Street*
Cast Show Album	*Funny Girl*	*On a Clear Day You Can See Forever*	*Mame*
Comedy Recording	Bill Cosby, *I Started Out as a Child*	Bill Cosby, *Why Is There Air?*	Bill Cosby, *Wonderfulness*

1964 | 1965 | 1966

	1964	1965	1966
Classical Album	Leonard Bernstein, conductor, New York Philharmonic, *Bernstein: Symphony No. 3*	Vladimir Horowitz, *Horowitz at Carnegie Hall: An Historic Return*	Morton Gould conductor, Chicago Symphony, *Ives: Symphony No. 1 in D Minor*
Classical Orchestral Performance	Erich Leinsdorf, conductor, Boston Symphony, *Mahler: Symphony No. 5 in C Sharp Minor;* Berg: *Wozzeck Excerpts*	Leopold Stokowski, conductor, American Symphony, *Ives: Symphony No. 4*	Erich Leinsdorf, conductor, Boston Symphony, *Mahler: Symphony No. 6 in A Minor*
Opera Recording	Herbert von Karajan, conductor, Vienna Philharmonic and Chorus (Solos: Price, Corelli, Merrill, Freni), *Bizet: Carmen*	Karl Bohm, conductor, Orchestra of German Opera, Berlin, (Solos: Fischer-Dieskau, Lear, Wunderlich), *Berg: Wozzeck*	Georg Solti, conductor, Vienna Philharmonic (Solos: Nilsson, Crespin, Ludwig, King, Hotter), *Wagner: Die Walküre*
Chamber Music Performance	Jascha Heifetz, Gregor Piatigorsky (Jacob Lateiner, piano), *Beethoven: Trio No. 1 in E Flat, Op. 1, No. 1*	Juilliard String Quartet, *Bartók: The Six String Quartets*	Boston Symphony Chamber Players, *Boston Symphony Chamber Players*

1967 | 1968 | 1969

	1967	1968	1969
Record of the Year	5th Dimension, "Up, Up and Away"	Simon & Garfunkel, "Mrs. Robinson"	5th Dimension, "Aquarius/Let the Sunshine In"
Album of the Year	The Beatles, *Sgt. Pepper's Lonely Hearts Club Band*	Glen Campbell, *By the Time I Get to Phoenix*	Blood, Sweat & Tears, *Blood, Sweat & Tears*
Song of the Year	Jim Webb, "Up, Up and Away"	Bobby Russell, "Little Green Apples"	Joe South, "Games People Play"
Pop Vocal, Female	Bobbie Gentry, "Ode to Billie Joe"	Dionne Warwick, "Do You Know the Way To San Jose"	Peggy Lee, "Is That All There Is"
Pop Vocal, Male	Glen Campbell, "By the Time I Get to Phoenix"	José Feliciano, "Light My Fire"	Harry Nilsson, "Everybody's Talkin"
New Artist	Bobbie Gentry	José Feliciano	Crosby, Stills & Nash
Pop Vocal	5th Dimension, "Up, Up and Away"	Simon & Garfunkel, "Mrs. Robinson"	5th Dimension, "Aquarius/Let the Sunshine In"
Rock Performance, Duo or Group	5th Dimension, "Up, Up and Away"	—	—
Rhythm and Blues Song	Aretha Franklin, "Respect"	Otis Redding and Steve Cropper, "(Sittin' On) the Dock of the Bay"	Richard Spencer, "Color Him Father"
R&B Vocal, Female	Aretha Franklin, "Respect"	Aretha Franklin, "Chain of Fools"	Aretha Franklin, "Share Your Love With Me"
R&B Vocal, Male	Lou Rawls, "Dead End Street"	Otis Redding, "(Sittin' On) the Dock of the Bay"	Joe Simon, "The Chokin' Kind"

	1967	1968	1969
R&B Duo or Group with Vocal	Sam & Dave, "Soul Man"	The Temptations, "Cloud Nine"	The Isley Brothers, "It's Your Thing"
Country Song	John Hartford, "Gentle on My Mind"	Bobby Russell, "Little Green Apples"	Shel Silverstein, "A Boy Named Sue"
Country Vocal, Female	Tammy Wynette, "I Don't Wanna Play House"	Jeannie C. Riley, "Harper Valley P.T.A."	Tammy Wynette, "Stand By Your Man"
Country Vocal, Male	Glen Campbell, "Gentle on My Mind"	Johnny Cash, "Folsom Prison Blues"	Johnny Cash, "A Boy Named Sue"
Country Performance, Duo or Group with Vocal	Johnny Cash and June Carter, "Jackson"	Flatt & Scruggs, "Foggy Mountain Breakdown"	Waylon Jennings & The Kimberlys, "MacArthur Park"
Jazz, Group	Cannonball Adderley Quintet, *Mercy, Mercy, Mercy*	Bill Evans Trio, *Bill Evans at the Montreux Jazz Festival*	Wes Montgomery, *Willow Weep For Me*
Jazz, Big Band/ Large Ensemble Performance	Duke Ellington, *Far East Suite*	Duke Ellington, *And His Mother Called Him Bill*	Quincy Jones, "Walking in Space"
Gospel Performance, Duo, Group, Choir or Chorus	Porter Wagoner & The Blackwood Bros. Quartet, *More Grand Old Gospel*	Happy Goodman Family, *The Happy Gospel of the Happy Goodmans*	Porter Wagoner & the Blackwood Bros., *In Gospel Country*
Folk Recording	John Hartford, "Gentle on My Mind"	Judy Collins, "Both Sides Now"	Joni Mitchell, *Clouds*
Cast Show Album	*Cabaret*	*Hair*	*Promises, Promises*
Comedy Recording	Bill Cosby, *Revenge*	Bill Cosby, *To Russell, My Brother, Whom I Slept With*	Bill Cosby, *The Best of Bill Cosby*
Classical Album	Pierre Boulez, conductor, Orchestra and Chorus of Paris National Opera (Solos: Berry, Strauss, Uhl, Doench), *Berg: Wozzeck;* Leonard Berstein, conductor, London Symphony, *Mahler: Symphony No. 8 in E Flat Major ("Symphony of a Thousand")*	—	Walter Carlos, *Switched-On Bach*
Classical Orchestral Performance	Igor Stravinsky, conductor, Columbia Symphony, *Stravinsky: Firebird & Petrouchka Suites*	Pierre Boulez, conductor, New Philharmonic Orchestra, *Boulez Conducts Debussy*	Pierre Boulez, conductor, Cleveland Orchestra, *Boulez Conducts Debussy, Vol. 2: "Images Pour Orchestre"*
Opera Recording	Pierre Boulez, conductor, Orchestra and Chorus of Paris National Opera (Solos: Berry, Strauss, Uhl, Doench), *Berg: Wozzeck*	Erich Leinsdorf, conductor, New Philharmonic Orchestra and Ambrosian Opera Chorus (Soloists: Price, Troyanos, Raskin, Milnes, Shirley, Flagello), *Mozart: Cosi fan tutte*	Herbert von Karajan, conductor, Berlin Philharmonic (Soloists: Thomas, Stewart, Stolze, Dernesch, Keleman, Dominguez, Gayer, Ridderbusch), *Wagner: Siegfried*
Chamber Music Performance	Ravi Shankar and Yehudi Menuhin, *West Meets East*	E. Power Biggs with Edward Tarr Brass Ensemble and Gabrieli Consort, Vittorio Negri, conductor, *Gabrieli: Canzoni for Brass, Winds, Strings & Organ*	The Philadelphia, Cleveland, and Chicago Brass Ensembles, *Gabrieli: Antiphonal Music of Gabrieli (Canzoni for Brass Choirs)*

	1970	1971	1972
Record of the Year	Simon & Garfunkel, "Bridge Over Troubled Water"	Carole King, "It's Too Late"	Roberta Flack, "The First Time Ever I Saw Your Face"
Album of the Year	Simon & Garfunkel, *Bridge Over Troubled Water*	Carole King, *Tapestry*	George Harrison and Friends (Ravi Shankar, Bob Dylan, Leon Russell, Ringo Starr, Billy Preston, Eric Clapton, Klaus Voorman, others), *The Concert for Bangladesh*
Song of the Year	Paul Simon, "Bridge Over Troubled Water"	Carole King, "You've Got a Friend"	Ewan MacColl, "The First Time Ever I Saw Your Face"
Pop Vocal, Female	Dionne Warwick, "I'll Never Fall In Love Again"	Carole King, "Tapestry"	Helen Reddy, "I Am Woman"
Pop Vocal, Male	Ray Stevens, "Everything Is Beautiful"	James Taylor, "You've Got a Friend"	Nilsson, "Without You"
New Artist	The Carpenters	Carly Simon	America
Pop Vocal, Duo or Group with Vocal	Carpenters, "Close to You"	Carpenters, *Carpenters*	Roberta Flack and Donny Hathaway, "Where Is the Love"
Rhythm and Blues Song	Ronald Dunbar, General Johnson, "Patches"	Bill Withers, "Ain't No Sunshine"	Barrett Strong and Norman Whitfield, "Papa Was a Rolling Stone"
R&B Vocal, Female	Aretha Franklin, "Don't Play That Song"	Aretha Franklin, "Bridge Over Troubled Water"	Aretha Franklin, "Young, Gifted & Black"
R&B Vocal, Male	B.B. King, "The Thrill Is Gone"	Lou Rawls, "A Natural Man"	Billy Paul, "Me and Mrs. Jones"
R&B Duo or Group with Vocal	The Delfonics, "Didn't I (Blow Your Mind This Time)"	Ike and Tina Turner, "Proud Mary"	The Temptations, "Papa Was a Rolling Stone"
Country Song	Marty Robbins, "My Woman, My Woman, My Wife"	Kris Kristofferson, "Help Me Make It Through the Night"	Ben Peters, "Kiss an Angel Good Mornin' "
Country Vocal, Female	Lynn Anderson, "Rose Garden"	Sammi Smith, "Help Me Make It Through the Night"	Donna Fargo, "Happiest Girl in the Whole U.S.A."
Country Vocal, Male	Ray Price, "For the Good Times"	Jerry Reed, "When You're Hot, You're Hot"	Charley Pride, *Charley Pride Sings Heart Songs*
Country Performance, Duo or Group with Vocal	Johnny Cash and June Carpenter, "If I Were a Carpenter"	Conway Twitty and Loretta Lynn, "After the Fire Is Gone"	The Statler Brothers, "Class of '57"
Traditional Blues Recording	T-Bone Walker, "Good Feelin' "	Muddy Waters, *They Call Me Muddy Waters*	Muddy Waters, *The London Muddy Waters Session*
Jazz, Soloist	—	Bill Evans, *The Bill Evans Album*	Gary Burton, *Alone at Last*
Jazz, Group	Bill Evans, *Alone*	Bill Evans Trio, *The Bill Evans Album*	Freddie Hubbard, *First Light*
Jazz, Big Band/ Large Ensemble Performance	Miles Davis, *Bitches Brew*	Duke Ellington, *New Orleans Suite*	Duke Ellington, *Togo Brava Suite*
Gospel Performance, Duo, Group, Choir or Chorus	Oak Ridge Boys, "Talk About the Good Times"	Charley Pride, "Let Me Live"	Blackwood Brothers, *L-O-V-E*
Cast Show Album	*Company*	*Godspell*	*Don't Bother Me, I Can't Cope*
Comedy Recording	Flip Wilson, *The Devil Made Me Buy This Dress*	Lily Tomlin, *This Is a Recording*	George Carlin, *FM & AM*

	1970	**1971**	**1972**
Classical Album	Colin Davis, conductor, Royal Opera House Orchestra and Chorus (Solos: Vickers, Veasey Lindholm), *Berlioz: Les Troyens*, Philips	Vladimir Horowitz, *Horowitz Plays Rachmaninoff*	Georg Solti, conductor, Chicago Symphony, Vienna Boys Choir, Vienna State Opera Chorus, Vienna Singverein Chorus and soloists, *Mahler: Symphony No. 8 in E Flat Major (Symphony of a Thousand)*
Classical Orchestral Performance	Pierre Boulez, conductor, Cleveland Orchestra, *Stravinsky: Le Sacre du printemps*	Carlo Maria Giulini, conductor, Chicago Symphony, *Mahler: Symphony No. 1 in D Major*	Georg Solti, conductor, Chicago Symphony, *Mahler: Symphony No. 7 in E Minor*
Opera Recording	Colin Davis, conductor, Royal Opera House Orchestra and Chorus (Solos: Vickers, Veasey, Lindholm), *Berlioz: Les Troyens*	Erich Leinsdorf, conductor, London Symphony and John Alldis Choir (Solos: Price, Domingo, Milnes, Bumbry, Raimondi), *Verdi: Aïda*	Colin Davis, conductor, BBC Symphony/Chorus of Covent Garden (Solos: Gedda, Eda-Pierre, Soyer, Berbie), *Berlioz: Benvenuto Cellini*
Chamber Music Performance	Eugene Istomin, Isaac Stern, Leonard Rose, *Beethoven: The Complete Piano Trios*	Juilliard Quartet, *Debussy: Quartet in G Minor/Ravel: Quartet in F Major*	Julian Bream and John Williams, *Julian & John*

	1973	**1974**	**1975**
Record of the Year	Roberta Flack, "Killing Me Softly with His Song"	Olivia Newton-John, "I Honestly Love You"	Captain & Tennille, "Love Will Keep Us Together"
Album of the Year	Stevie Wonder, *Innervisions*	Stevie Wonder, *Fulfillingness' First Finale*	Paul Simon, *Still Crazy After All These Years*
Song of the Year	Norman Gimbel and Charles Fox, "Killing Me Softly with His Song"	Marilyn and Alan Bergman, Marvin Hamlisch, "The Way We Were"	Stephen Sondheim, "Send In the Clowns"
Pop Vocal, Female	Roberta Flack, "Killing Me Softly with His Song"	Olivia Newton-John, "I Honestly Love You"	Janis Ian, "At Seventeen"
Pop Vocal, Male	Stevie Wonder, "You Are the Sunshine of My Life"	Stevie Wonder, *Fulfillingness' First Finale*	Paul Simon, *Still Crazy After All These Years*
New Artist	Bette Midler	Marvin Hamlisch	Natalie Cole
Pop Vocal, Duo or Group with Vocal	Gladys Knight & The Pips, "Neither One of Us (Wants To Be the First To Say Goodbye)"	Paul McCartney & Wings, "Band on the Run"	Eagles, "Lyin' Eyes"
Rhythm and Blues Song	Stevie Wonder, "Superstition"	Stevie Wonder, "Living for the City"	H. W. Casey, Richard Finch, Willie Clarke, and Betty Wright, "Where Is the Love"
R&B Vocal, Female	Aretha Franklin, "Master of Eyes"	Aretha Franklin, "Ain't Nothing Like the Real Thing"	Natalie Cole, "This Will Be"
R&B Vocal, Male	Stevie Wonder, "Superstition"	Stevie Wonder, "Boogie On Reggae Woman"	Ray Charles, "Living for the City"

	1973	1974	1975
R&B Duo or Group with Vocal	Gladys Knight & The Pips, "Midnight Train to Georgia"	Rufus, "Tell Me Something Good"	Earth, Wind & Fire, "Shining Star"
Country Song	Kenny O'Dell, "Behind Closed Doors"	Norris Wilson and Bill Sherrill, "A Very Special Love Song"	Chips Moman and Larry Butler, "(Hey Won't You Play) Another Somebody Done Somebody Wrong Song"
Country Vocal, Female	Olivia Newton-John, "Let Me Be There"	Anne Murray, "Love Song"	Linda Ronstadt, "I Can't Help It (If I'm Still in Love with You)"
Country Vocal, Male	Charlie Rich, "Behind Closed Doors"	Ronnie Milsap, "Please Don't Tell Me How the Story Ends"	Willie Nelson, "Blue Eyes Crying in the Rain"
Country Performance, Duo or Group with Vocal	Kris Kristofferson and Rita Coolidge, "From the Bottle to the Bottom"	The Pointer Sisters, "Fairytale"	Kris Kristofferson and Rita Coolidge, "Lover Please"
Traditional Blues Recording	Doc Watson, *Then and Now*	Doc and Merle Watson, *Two Days in November*	Muddy Waters, *The Muddy Waters Woodstock Album*
Jazz, Soloist	Art Tatum, *God Is in the House*	Charlie Parker, *First Recordings!*	Dizzy Gillespie, *Oscar Peterson and Dizzy Gillespie*
Jazz, Group	Supersax, *Supersax Plays Bird*	Oscar Peterson, Joe Pass, and Niels Pedersen, *The Trio*	Return to Forever featuring Chick Corea, *No Mystery*
Jazz, Big Band/ Large Ensemble Performance	Woody Herman, *Giant Steps*	Woody Herman, *Thundering Herd*	Phil Woods with Michel Legrand & His Orchestra, *Images*
Cast Show Album	*A Little Night Music*	*Raisin*	*The Wiz*
Comedy Recording	Cheech & Chong, *Los Cochinos*	Richard Pryor, *That Nigger's Crazy*	Richard Pryor, *Is It Something I Said?*
Classical Album	Pierre Boulez, conductor, New York Philharmonic, *Bartók: Concerto for Orchestra*	Georg Solti, conductor, Chicago Symphony, *Berlioz: Symphonie Fantastique*	Georg Solti, conductor, Chicago Symphony, *Beethoven: Symphonies (9) Complete*
Classical Orchestral Performance	Pierre Boulez, conductor, New York Philharmonic, *Bartók: Concerto for Orchestra*	Georg Solti, conductor, Chicago Symphony, *Berlioz: Symphonie Fantastique*	Pierre Boulez, conductor, New York Philharmonic, *Ravel: Daphnis et Chloë*
Opera Recording	Leonard Bernstein, conductor, Metropolitan Opera Orchestra and Manhattan Opera Chorus (Solos: Horne, McCracken, Maliponte, Krause), *Bizet: Carmen*	Georg Solti, conductor, London Philharmonic (Soloists: Caballé, Domingo, Milnes, Blegen, Raimondi), *Puccini: La Bohème*	Colin Davis, conductor, Royal Opera House, Covent Garden (Solos: Caballé, Baker, Gedda, Ganzarolli, Van Allen, Cotrubas), *Mozart: Cosi fan tutte*
Chamber Music Performance	Gunther Schuller and New England Ragtime Ensemble, *Joplin: The Red Back Book*	Artur Rubinstein, Henryk Szeryng, and Pierre Fournier, *Brahms: Trios (complete)/ Schumann: Trio No. 1 in D Minor*	Artur Rubinstein, Henryk Szeryng, and Pierre Fournier, *Shubert: Trios Nos. 1 in B Flat Major Op. 99 & 2 in E Flat Major Op. 100*

	1976	**1977**	**1978**
Record of the Year	George Benson, "This Masquerade"	Eagles, "Hotel California"	Billy Joel, "Just the Way You Are"
Album of the Year	Stevie Wonder, *Songs in the Key of Life*	Fleetwood Mac, *Rumours*	The Bee Gees and others, *Saturday Night Fever*
Song of the Year	Bruce Johnston, "I Write the Songs"	Joe Brooks, "You Light Up My Life"; Barbra Streisand, "Love Theme from *A Star Is Born* (Evergreen)"	Billy Joel, "Just the Way You Are"
(Pop) Vocal, Female	Linda Ronstadt, *Hasten Down the Wind*	Barbra Streisand, "Love Theme from *A Star Is Born* (Evergreen)"	Anne Murray, "You Needed Me"
(Pop) Vocal, Male	Stevie Wonder, *Songs in the Key of Life*	James Taylor, "Handy Man"	Barry Manilow, "Copacabana (At the Copa)"
New Artist	Starland Vocal Band	Debby Boone	A Taste of Honey
Pop Vocal, Duo or Group with Vocal	Chicago, "If You Leave Me Now"	The Bee Gees, "How Deep Is Your Love"	The Bee Gees, *Saturday Night Fever*
Rhythm and Blues Song	Boz Scaggs and David Paich, "Lowdown"	Leo Sayer and Vini Poncia, "You Make Me Feel Like Dancing"	Paul Jabara, "Last Dance"
R&B Vocal, Female	Natalie Cole, "Sophisticated Lady (She's a Different Lady)"	Thelma Houston, "Don't Leave Me This Way"	Donna Summer, "Last Dance"
R&B Vocal, Male	Stevie Wonder, "I Wish"	Lou Rawls, *Unmistakably Lou*	George Benson, "On Broadway"
R&B Duo or Group with Vocal	Marilyn McCoo and Billy Davis, Jr., "You Don't Have To Be a Star (To Be in My Show)"	Emotions, "Best of My Love"	Earth, Wind & Fire, "All 'n All"
Country Song	Larry Gatlin, "Broken Lady"	Richard Leigh, "Don't It Make My Brown Eyes Blue"	Don Schlitz, "The Gambler"
Country Vocal, Female	Emmylou Harris, *Elite Hotel*	Crystal Gayle, "Don't It Make My Brown Eyes Blue"	Dolly Parton, *Here You Come Again*
Country Vocal, Male	Ronnie Milsap, "(I'm a) Stand by My Woman Man"	Kenny Rogers, "Lucille"	Willie Nelson, "Georgia on My Mind"
Country Performance, Duo or Group with Vocal	Amazing Rhythm Aces, "The End Is Not in Sight (The Cowboy Tune)"	The Kendalls, "Heaven's Just a Sin Away"	Waylon Jennings and Willie Nelson, "Mamas Don't Let Your Babies Grow Up To Be Cowboys"
Ethnic or Traditional Recording	John Hartford, *Mark Twang*	Muddy Waters, *Hard Again*	Muddy Waters, *I'm Ready*
Jazz, Soloist	Count Basie, *Basie & Zoot*	Oscar Peterson, *The Giants*	Oscar Peterson, *Montreux '77, Oscar Peterson Jam*
Jazz, Group	Chick Corea, *The Leprechaun*	Phil Woods, *The Phil Woods Six—Live from the Showboat*	Chick Corea, *Friends*
Jazz, Big Band/ Large Ensemble Performance	Duke Ellington, *The Ellington Suites*	Count Basie & His Orchestra, *Prime Time*	Thad Jones and Mel Lewis, *Live in Munich*
Cast Show Album	*Bubbling Brown Sugar*	*Annie*	*Ain't Misbehavin'*
Comedy Recording	Richard Pryor, *Bicentennial Nigger*	Steve Martin, *Let's Get Small*	Steve Martin, *A Wild and Crazy Guy*
Classical Album	Artur Rubinstein with Daniel Barenboim, conductor, London Philharmonic, *Beethoven: The Five Piano Concertos*	Leonard Bernstein, Vladimir Horowitz, Isaac Stern, Mstislav Rostropovich, Dietrich Fischer-Dieskau, Yehudi Menuhin, Lyndon Woodside, *Concert of the Century* (recorded live at Carnegie Hall May 18, 1976)	Itzhak Perlman with Carlo Maria Giulini, conductor, Chicago Symphony, *Brahms: Concerto for Violin in D Major*

272

	1976	1977	1978
Classical Orchestral Performance	Georg Solti, conductor, Chicago Symphony, *Strauss: Also Sprach Zarathustra*	Carlo Maria Giulini, conductor, Chicago Symphony, *Mahler: Symphony No. 9 in D Major*	Herbert von Karajan, conductor, Berlin Philharmonic, *Beethoven: Symphonies (9) Complete*
Opera Recording	Lorin Maazel conductor, Cleveland Orchestra and Chorus (Solos: Mitchell, White), *Gershwin: Porgy & Bess*	John De Main, conductor, Houston Grand Opera Production (Solos: Albert, Dale, Smith, Shakesnider, Lane, Brice, Smalls), *Gershwin: Porgy & Bess*	Julius Rudel, conductor, New York City Opera Orchestra and Chorus (Solos: Sills, Titus), *Lehar: The Merry Widow*
Chamber Music Performance	David Munrow, conductor, The Early Music Consort of London, *The Art of Courtly Love*	Juilliard Quartet, *Schöenberg: Quartets for Strings*	Itzhak Perlman and Vladimir Ashkenazy, *Beethoven: Sonatas for Violin and Piano*

GRAMMY AWARD RECORDS

In 1957, the newly formed National Academy of Recording Arts & Sciences first conceived of a peer award to recognize outstanding achievement in the recording field. The Grammys, named after the gramophone statuette, have since expanded from 28 categories to 95. The following artists have all set records in the annals of Grammy history:

Youngest "Album of the Year" winner:
Alanis Morissette, age 21, when *Jagged Little Pill* was named 1995's best LP

Winningest winner:
Georg Solti, the conductor of the Chicago Symphony, has won 31 awards

Winningest female:
Aretha Franklin, with 15 awards (and an uninterrupted winning streak from 1967 to 1974)

Most awards in a single year:
Michael Jackson in 1983, with seven for Album of the Year, *Thriller*, and one for *E.T., the Extra-Terrestrial* as Best Recording for Children

Most country awards:
Chet Atkins with 14

Most jazz awards:
Ella Fitzgerald with 13

Most comedy awards:
Bill Cosby with 9

Most opera awards:
Leontyne Price with 13

	1979	1980	1981
Record of the Year	The Doobie Brothers, "What a Fool Believes"	Christopher Cross, "Sailing"	Kim Carnes, "Bette Davis Eyes"
Album of the Year	Billy Joel, *52nd Street*	Christopher Cross, *Christopher Cross*	John Lennon and Yoko Ono, *Double Fantasy*
Song of the Year	Kenny Loggins and Michael McDonald, "What a Fool Believes"	Christopher Cross, "Sailing"	Donna Weiss and Jackie DeShannon, "Bette Davis Eyes"
Pop Vocal, Female	Dionne Warwick, "I'll Never Love This Way Again"	Bette Midler, "The Rose"	Lena Horne, *Lena Horne: The Lady and Her Music Live on Broadway*
Pop Vocal, Male	Billy Joel, *52nd Street*	Kenny Loggins, "This Is It"	Al Jarreau, *Breakin' Away*
Rock Vocal, Female	Donna Summer, "Hot Stuff"	Pat Benatar, *Crimes of Passion*	Pat Benatar, "Fire and Ice"
Rock Vocal, Male	Bob Dylan, "Gotta Serve Somebody"	Billy Joel, *Glass Houses*	Rick Springfield, "Jessie's Girl"
New Artist	Rickie Lee Jones	Christopher Cross	Sheena Easton
Pop Vocal, Duo or Group with Vocal	The Doobie Brothers, *Minute by Minute*	Barbra Streisand and Barry Gibb, "Guilty"	The Manhattan Transfer, "Boy from New York City"
Rock Performance, Duo or Group with Vocal	The Eagles, "Heartache Tonight"	Bob Seger & the Silver Bullet Band, *Against the Wind*	The Police, "Don't Stand So Close to Me"
Rhythm and Blues Song	David Foster, Jay Graydon, and Bill Champlin, "After the Love Has Gone"	Reggie Lucas and James Mtume, "Never Knew Love Like This Before"	Bill Withers, William Salter, and Ralph MacDonald, "Just the Two of Us"
R&B Vocal, Female	Dionne Warwick, "Déjà Vu"	Stephanie Mills, "Never Knew Love Like This Before"	Aretha Franklin, "Hold On, I'm Comin' "
R&B Vocal, Male	Michael Jackson, "Don't Stop 'Til You Get Enough"	George Benson, *Give Me the Night*	James Ingram, "One Hundred Ways"
R&B Duo or Group with Vocal	Earth, Wind & Fire, "After the Love Has Gone"	Manhattans, "Shining Star"	Quincy Jones, *The Dude*
Country Song	Bob Morrison and Debbie Hupp, "You Decorated My Life"	Willie Nelson, "On the Road Again"	Dolly Parton, "9 to 5"
Country Vocal, Female	Emmylou Harris, *Blue Kentucky Girl*	Anne Murray, "Could I Have This Dance"	Dolly Parton, "9 to 5"
Country Vocal, Male	Kenny Rogers, "The Gambler"	George Jones, "He Stopped Loving Her Today"	Ronnie Milsap, "(There's) No Gettin' Over Me"
Country Performance, Duo or Group with Vocal	Charlie Daniels Band, "The Devil Went Down to Georgia"	Roy Orbison and Emmylou Harris, "That Lovin' You Feelin' Again"	Oak Ridge Boys, "Elvira"
Ethnic or Traditional Recording	Muddy Waters, *Muddy "Mississippi" Waters Live*	Dr. Isaiah Ross, Maxwell Street Jimmy, Big Joe William, Son House, Rev. Robert Wilkins, Little Brother Montgomery, and Sunnyland Slim, *Rare Blues*	B. B. King, *There Must Be a Better World Somewhere*
Jazz Vocal, Female	Ella Fitzgerald, *Fine and Mellow*	Ella Fitzgerald, *A Perfect Match/Ella & Basie*	Ella Fitzgerald, *Digital III at Montreux*
Jazz Vocal, Male	—	George Benson, "Moody's Mood"	Al Jarreau, "Blue Rondo à la Turk"
Jazz, Soloist	Oscar Peterson, *Jousts*	Bill Evans, *I Will Say Goodbye*	John Coltrane, *Bye, Bye Blackbird*

	1979	1980	1981
Jazz, Group	Gary Burton and Chick Corea, Duet	Bill Evans, We Will Meet Again	Chick Corea and Gary Burton, Chick Corea and Gary Burton in Concert, Zurich, October 28, 1979
Jazz, Big Band/ Large Ensemble Performance	Duke Ellington, At Fargo, 1940 Live	Count Basie and Orchestra, On the Road	Gerry Mulligan & His Orchestra, Walk on the Water
Jazz Fusion Performance, Vocal or Instrumental	Weather Report, 8:30	Manhattan Transfer, "Birdland"	Grover Washington Jr., Winelight
Cast Show Album	Sweeney Todd	Evita	Lena Horne: The Lady and Her Music Live on Broadway
Comedy Recording	Robin Williams, Reality...What a Concept	Rodney Dangerfield, No Respect	Richard Pryor, Rev. Du Rite
Classical Album	Georg Solti, conductor, Chicago Symphony Orchestra, Brahms: Symphonies (4) Complete	Pierre Boulez, conductor, Orchestre d l'Opera de Paris (Solos: Stratas, Minton, Mazura, Toni Blankenheim), Berg: Lulu	Georg Solti, conductor, Chicago Symphony Orchestra and Chorus (Solos: Buchanan, Zakai), Mahler: Symphony No. 2 in C Minor
Classical Orchestral Performance	Georg Solti, conductor, Chicago Symphony, Brahms: Symphonies (4) Complete	Georg Solti, conductor, Chicago Symphony, Bruckner: Symphony No. 6 in A Major	Georg Solti, conductor, Chicago Symphony, Mahler: Symphony No. 2 in C Minor
Opera Recording	Colin Davis, conductor, Orchestra and Chorus of the Royal Opera House, Covent Garden (Solos: Vickers, Harper, Summers), Britten: Peter Grimes	Pierre Boulez, conductor, Orchestre d l'Opera de Paris (Solos: Stratas, Minton, Mazura, Blankenheim), Berg: Lulu	Charles Mackerras, conductor, Vienna Philharmonic (Solos: Zahradnicek, Zitek, Zidek), Janacek: From the House of the Dead
Chamber Music Performance	Dennis Russel Davies, conductor, St. Paul Chamber Orchestra, Copland: Appalachian Spring	Itzhak Perlman and Pinchas Zukerman, Music for Two Violins (Moszkowski: Suite for Two Violins/Shostakovich: Duets/ Prokofiev: Sonata for Two Violins)	Itzhak Perlman, Lynn Harrell, and Vladimir Ashkenazy, Tchaikovsky: Piano Trio in A Minor

FAMOUS LOSERS

The following artists have never won a Grammy in a competitive category, although many have been nominated. Asterisks indicate that the performers have, however, belatedly received the NARAS Lifetime Achievement Award.

AC/DC	Fats Domino*	Little Richard
Beach Boys	The Doors	Pretenders
Chuck Berry*	The Drifters	Queen
Jackson Browne	The Four Tops	Cat Stevens
The Byrds	Peter Frampton	Diana Ross
Cher	Benny Goodman*	Lawrence Welk
Patsy Cline*	Grateful Dead	Kitty Wells*
Sam Cooke	Jimi Hendrix*	The Who
Creedence Clearwater Revival	The Jackson 5	Hank Williams, Sr.*
Cream	Janis Joplin	Neil Young
Bing Crosby*	Led Zeppelin	

	1982	1983	1984
Record of the Year	Toto, "Rosanna"	Michael Jackson, "Beat It"	Tina Turner, "What's Love Got To Do with It"
Album of the Year	Toto, *Toto IV*	Michael Jackson, *Thriller*	Lionel Richie, *Can't Slow Down*
Song of the Year	Johnny Christopher, Mark James, and Wayne Thompson, "Always on My Mind"	Sting, "Every Breath You Take"	Graham Lyle and Terry Britten, "What's Love Got To Do with It"
Pop Vocal, Female	Melissa Manchester, "You Should Hear How She Talks About You"	Irene Cara, "Flashdance...What a Feeling"	Tina Turner, "What's Love got To Do with It"
Pop Vocal, Male	Lionel Richie, "Truly"	Michael Jackson, *Thriller*	Phil Collins, "Against All Odds (Take a Look at Me Now)"
Rock Vocal, Female	Pat Benatar, "Shadows of the Night"	Pat Benatar, "Love Is a Battlefield"	Tina Turner, "Better Be Good to Me"
Rock Vocal, Male	John Cougar, "Hurts So Good"	Michael Jackson, "Beat It"	Bruce Springsteen, "Dancing in the Dark"
New Artist	Men at Work	Culture Club	Cyndi Lauper
Pop Vocal, Duo or Group with Vocal	Joe Cocker and Jennifer Warnes, "Up Where We Belong"	The Police, "Every Breath You Take"	Pointer Sisters, "Jump (For My Love)"
Rock Performance, Duo or Group with Vocal	Survivor, "Eye of the Tiger"	The Police, *Synchronicity*	Prince and the Revolution, *Purple Rain*
Rhythm and Blues Song	Jay Graydon, Steve Lukather, and Bill Champlin, "Turn Your Love Around"	Michael Jackson, "Billie Jean"	Prince, "I Feel for You"
R&B Vocal, Female	Jennifer Holliday, "And I Am Telling You I'm Not Going"	Chaka Khan, *Chaka Khan*	Chaka Khan, "I Feel for You"
R&B Vocal, Male	Marvin Gaye, "Sexual Healing"	Michael Jackson, "Billie Jean"	Billy Ocean, "Caribbean Queen (No More Love on the Run)"
R&B Duo or Group with Vocal	Dazz Band,"Let It Whip"; Earth, Wind & Fire, "Wanna Be With You"	Rufus & Chaka Khan, "Ain't Nobody"	James Ingram and Michael McDonald, "Yah Mo B There"
Country Song	Johnny Christopher, Wayne Thompson, and Mark James, "Always on My Mind"	Mike Reed, "Stranger in My House"	Steve Goodman, "City of New Orleans"
Country Vocal, Female	Juice Newton, "Break It To Me Gently"	Anne Murray, "A Little Good News"	Emmylou Harris, "In My Dreams"
Country Vocal, Male	Willie Nelson, "Always on My Mind"	Lee Greenwood, "I.O.U."	Merle Haggard, "That's the Way Love Goes"
Country Performance, Group	Alabama, *Mountain Music*	Alabama, *The Closer You Get*	The Judds, "Mama He's Crazy"
Traditional Blues Recording	Clarence "Gatemouth" Brown, *Alright Again*	B. B. King, *Blues 'n' Jazz*	John Hammond, Stevie Ray Vaughan & Double Trouble, Sugar Blue, Koko Taylor & The Blues Machine, Luther "Guitar Junior" Johnson, and J. B. Hutto & The New Hawks, *Blues Explosion*
Reggae Recording	—	—	Black Uhuru, *Anthem*
Jazz Vocal, Female	Sarah Vaughan, *Gershwin Live!*	Ella Fitzgerald, *The Best Is Yet to Come*	—
Jazz Vocal, Male	Mel Torme, *An Evening with George Shearing and Mel Torme*	Mel Torme, *Top Drawer*	Joe Williams, *Nothin' but the Blues*
Jazz, Soloist	Miles Davis, *We Want Miles*	Wynton Marsalis, *Think of One*	Wynton Marsalis, *Hot House Flowers*

	1982	1983	1984
Jazz, Group	Phil Woods Quartet, *"More" Live*	The Phil Woods Quartet, *At the Vanguard*	Art Blakey & The Jazz Messengers, *New York Scene*
Jazz, Big Band/ Large Ensemble Performance	Count Basie & His Orchestra, *Warm Breeze*	Rob McConnell and The Boss Brass, *All in Good Time*	Count Basie & His Orchestra, *88 Basie Street*
Jazz Fusion Performance	Pat Metheny Group, *Offramp*	Pat Metheny Group, *Travels*	Pat Metheny Group, *First Circle*
Gospel Performance, Female	—	Amy Grant, "Ageless Medley"	Amy Grant, "Angels"
Gospel Performance, Male	—	Russ Taff, *Walls of Glass*	Michael W. Smith, *Michael W. Smith 2*
Gospel Performance, Duo, Group, Choir or Chorus	—	Sandi Patti and Larnelle Harris, "More Than Wonderful"	Debby Boone and Phil Driscoll, "Keep the Flame Burning"
Ethnic or Traditional Folk Recording	Queen Ida, *Queen Ida and the Bon Temps Zydeco Band on Tour*	Clifton Chenier & His Red Hot Louisiana Band, *I'm Here*	Elizabeth Cotten, *Elizabeth Cotten Live!*
Cast Show Album	*Dreamgirls*	*Cats (Complete Original Broadway Cast Recording)*	*Sunday in the Park with George*
Comedy Recording	Richard Pryor, *Live on the Sunset Strip*	Eddie Murphy, *Eddie Murphy: Comedian*	"Weird Al" Yankovic, "Eat It"
Classical Album	Glenn Gould, *Bach: The Goldberg Variations*	Georg Solti, conductor, Chicago Symphony, *Mahler: Symphony No. 9 in D Major*	Neville Marriner, conductor, Academy of St. Martin-in-the-Fields/Ambrosian Opera Chorus/Choristers of Westminster Abbey, *Amadeus (Original Soundtrack)*
Classical Orchestral Performance	James Levine, conductor, Chicago Symphony, *Mahler: Symphony No. 7 in E Minor (Song of the Night)*	Georg Solti, conductor, Chicago Symphony, *Mahler: Symphony No. 9 in D Major*	Leonard Slatkin, conductor, St. Louis Symphony, *Prokofiev: Symphony No. 5 in B Flat, Op. 100*
Opera Recording	Pierre Boulez, conductor, Bayreuth Festival Orchestra (Solos: Jones, Altmeyer, Wenkel, Hofmann, Jung, Jerusalem, Zednik, McIntyre, Salminen, Becht), *Wagner: Der Ring des Nibelungen*	James Levine, conductor, The Metropolitan Opera Orchestra and Chorus (Solos: Stratas, Domingo, MacNeill), *Verdi: La Traviata*	Lorin Maazel, conductor, Orchestre National de France/Choeurs et Maitrise de Radio France (Solos: Johnson, Esham, Domingo, Raimondi), *Bizet: Carmen*
Chamber Music Performance	Richard Stoltzman and Richard Goode, *Brahms: The Sonatas for Clarinet & Piano, Op. 120*	Mstislav Rostropovich and Rudolph Serkin, *Brahms: Sonata for Cello & Piano in E Minor, Op. 38 & Sonata in F Major, Op. 99*	Juilliard String Quartet, *Beethoven: The Late String Quartets*

	1985	1986	1987
Record of the Year	USA for Africa, "We Are the World"	Steve Winwood, "Higher Love"	Paul Simon, "Graceland"
Album of the Year	Phil Collins, *No Jacket Required*	Paul Simon, *Graceland*	U2, *The Joshua Tree*
Song of the Year	Michael Jackson and Lionel Richie, "We Are the World"	Burt Bacharach and Carole Bayer Sager, "That's What Friends Are For"	James Horner, Barry Mann, and Cynthia Weil, "Somewhere Out There"
Pop Vocal, Female	Whitney Houston, "Saving All My Love for You"	Barbra Streisand, *The Broadway Album*	Whitney Houston, "I Wanna Dance with Somebody (Who Loves Me)"
Pop Vocal, Male	Phil Collins, *No Jacket Required*	Steve Winwood, "Higher Love"	Sting, *Bring on the Night*
Rock Vocal, Female	Tina Turner, "One of the Living"	Tina Turner, "Back Where You Started"	—
Rock Vocal, Male	Don Henley, "The Boys of Summer"	Robert Palmer, "Addicted to Love"	Bruce Springsteen, *Tunnel of Love*
New Artist	Sade	Bruce Hornsby and the Range	Jody Watley
Pop Vocal, Duo or Group with Vocal	USA for Africa, "We Are the World"	Dionne Warwick & Friends featuring Elton John, Gladys Knight, and Stevie Wonder, "That's What Friends Are For"	Bill Medley and Jennifer Warnes, "(I've Had) The Time of My Life"
Rock Performance, Group	Dire Straits, "Money for Nothing"	Eurythmics, "Missionary Man"	U2, *The Joshua Tree*
New Age Recording	—	Andreas Vollenweider, *Down to the Moon*	Yusef Lateef, *Yusef Lateef's Little Symphony*
Rhythm and Blues Song	Narada Michael Walden and Jeffrey Cohen, "Freeway of Love"	Anita Baker, Louis A. Johnson, Gary Bias, "Sweet Love"	Bill Withers, "Lean on Me"
R&B Vocal, Female	Aretha Franklin, "Freeway of Love"	Anita Baker, *Rapture*	Aretha Franklin, *Aretha*
R&B Vocal, Male	Stevie Wonder, *In Square Circle*	James Brown, "Living in America"	Smokey Robinson, "Just To See Her"
R&B Duo or Group with Vocal	Commodores, "Nightshift"	Prince & The Revolution, "Kiss"	Aretha Franklin and George Michael, "I Knew You Were Waiting (For Me)"
Country Song	Jimmy L. Webb, "Highwayman"	Jamie O'Hara, "Grandpa (Tell Me 'Bout the Good Old Days)"	Paul Overstreet and Don Schlitz, *Forever and Ever, Amen*
Country Vocal, Female	Rosanne Cash, "I Don't Know Why You Don't Want Me"	Reba McEntire, "Whoever's in New England"	K. T. Oslin, "80's Ladies"
Country Vocal, Male	Ronnie Milsap, "Lost in the Fifties Tonight (In the Still of the Night)"	Ronnie Milsap, *Lost in the Fifties Tonight*	Randy Travis, *Always & Forever*
Country Performance, Duo or Group with Vocal	The Judds, *Why Not Me*	The Judds, "Grandpa (Tell Me 'Bout the Good Old Days)"	Dolly Parton, Linda Ronstadt, and Emmylou Harris, *Trio*
Country Vocal, Collaboration	—	—	Ronnie Milsap and Kenny Rogers, "Make No Mistake, She's Mine"
Traditional Blues Recording	B. B. King, "My Guitar Sings the Blues"	Albert Collins, Robert Cray, and Johnny Copeland, *Showdown*	Professor Longhair, *Houseparty New Orleans Style*
Contemporary Blues	—	—	Robert Cray Band, *Strong Persuader*

1985 | 1986 | 1987

	1985	1986	1987
Reggae Recording	Jimmy Cliff, *Cliff Hanger*	Steel Pulse, *Babylon the Bandit*	Peter Tosh, *No Nuclear War*
Jazz Vocal, Female	Cleo Laine, *Cleo at Carnegie, the 10th Anniversary Concert*	Diane Schuur, *Timeless*	Diane Schuur, *Diane Schuur & The Count Basie Orchestra*
Jazz Vocal, Male	Jon Hendricks and Bobby McFerrin, "Another Night in Tunisia"	Bobby McFerrin, " 'Round Midnight"	Bobby McFerrin, "What Is This Thing Called Love"
Jazz, Soloist	Wynton Marsalis, *Black Codes from the Underground*	Miles Davis, *Tutu*	Dexter Gordon, *The Other Side of 'Round Midnight*
Jazz, Group	Wynton Marsalis Group, *Black Codes from the Underground*	Wynton Marsalis, *J Mood*	Wynton Marsalis, *Marsalis Standard Time, Volume I*
Jazz, Big Band/ Large Ensemble Performance	John Barry and Bob Wilber, *The Cotton Club*	The Tonight Show Band with Doc Severinsen, *The Tonight Show Band with Doc Severinsen*	The Duke Ellington Orchestra, conducted by Mercer Ellington, *Digital Duke*
Jazz Fusion Performance, Vocal or Instrumental	David Sanborn, *Straight to the Heart*	Bob James and David Sanborn, *Double Vision*	Pat Metheny Group, *Still Life (Talking)*
Gospel Performance, Female	Amy Grant, *Unguarded*	Sandi Patti, *Morning Like This*	Deniece Williams, "I Believe in You"
Gospel Performance, Male	Larnelle Harris, "How Excellent Is Thy Name"	Philip Bailey, *Triumph*	Larnelle Harris, *The Father Hath Provided*
Gospel Performance, Duo, Group, Choir or Chorus	Larnelle Harris and Sandi Patti, "I've Just Seen Jesus"	Sandi Patti & Deniece Williams, "They Say"	Mylon LeFevre & Broken Heart, *Crack the Sky*
Traditional Folk Recording	Rockin' Sidney, "My Toot Toot"	Doc Watson, *Riding the Midnight Train*	Ladysmith Black Mambazo, *Shaka Zulu*
Contemporary Folk Recording	—	Arlo Guthrie, John Hartford, Richie Havens, Bonnie Koloc, Nitty Gritty Dirt Band, John Prine and others, *Tribute to Steve Goodman*	Steve Goodman, *Unfinished Business*
Cast Show Album	*West Side Story*	*Follies in Concert*	*Les Misérables*
Comedy Recording	Whoopi Goldberg, *Whoopi Goldberg*	Bill Cosby, *Those of You With or Without Children, You'll Understand*	Robin Williams, *A Night at the Met*
Classical Album	Robert Shaw, conductor, Atlanta Symphony Orchestra and Chorus, (Solo: Aler) *Berlioz: Requiem*	Vladimir Horowitz, *Horowitz: The Studio Recordings, New York 1985*	Vladimir Horowitz, *Horowitz in Moscow*
Classical Orchestral Performance	Robert Shaw, conductor, Atlanta Symphony Orchestra, *Fauré: Pelléas et Mélisande*	Georg Solti, conductor, Chicago Symphony Orchestra, *Liszt: A Faust Symphony*	Georg Solti, conductor, Chicago Symphony Orchestra, *Beethoven: Symphony No. 9 in D Minor*
Opera Recording	Georg Solti, conductor, Chicago Symphony Orchestra and Chorus (Solos: Mazura, Langridge), *Schoenberg: Moses und Aaron*	John Mauceri, conductor, New York City Opera Chorus and Orchestra (Solos: Mills, Clement, Eisler, Lankston, Castle, Reeve, Harrold, Billings), *Bernstein: Candide*	James Levine, conductor, Vienna Philharmonic (Solos: Tomowa-Sintow, Battle, Baltsa, Lakes, Prey), *R. Strauss: Ariadne auf Naxos*
Chamber Music Performance	Emanuel Ax and Yo-Yo Ma, *Brahms: Cello and Piano Sonatas in E Major & F Major*	Yo-Yo Ma and Emanuel Ax, *Beethoven: Cello & Piano Sonata No. 4 in C and Variations*	Itzhak Perlman, Lynn Harrell, and Vladimir Ashkenazy, *Beethoven: The Complete Piano Trios*

	1988	1989	1990
Record of the Year	Bobby McFerrin, "Don't Worry, Be Happy"	Bette Midler, "Wind Beneath My Wings"	Phil Collins, "Another Day in Paradise"
Album of the Year	George Michael, *Faith*	Bonnie Raitt, *Nick of Time*	Quincy Jones, *Back on the Block*
Song of the Year	Bobby McFerrin, "Don't Worry, Be Happy"	Larry Henley and Jeff Silbar, "Wind Beneath My Wings"	Julie Gold, "From a Distance"
Pop Vocal, Female	Tracy Chapman, "Fast Car"	Bonnie Raitt, "Nick of Time"	Mariah Carey, "Vision of Love"
Pop Vocal, Male	Bobby McFerrin, "Don't Worry, Be Happy"	Michael Bolton, "How Am I Supposed to Live Without You"	Roy Orbison, "Oh, Pretty Woman"
Rock Vocal, Female	Tina Turner, *Tina Live in Europe*	Bonnie Raitt, *Nick of Time*	Alannah Myles, "Black Velvet"
Rock Vocal, Male	Robert Palmer, "Simply Irresistible"	Don Henley, *The End of the Innocence*	Eric Clapton, "Bad Love"
New Artist	Tracy Chapman	No award (Milli Vanilli)	Mariah Carey
Pop Vocal, Duo or Group with Vocal	The Manhattan Transfer, *Brasil*	Linda Ronstadt and Aaron Neville, "Don't Know Much"	Linda Ronstadt with Aaron Neville, "All My Life"
Rock Performance, Duo or Group with Vocal	U2, "Desire"	Traveling Wilburys, *Traveling Wilburys, Volume I*	Aerosmith, "Janie's Got a Gun"
New Age Recording	Shadowfax, *Folksongs for a Nuclear Village*	Peter Gabriel, *Passion (Music from The Last Temptation of Christ)*	Mark Isham, *Mark Isham*
Hard Rock	Jethro Tull, *Crest of a Knave*	Living Colour, "Cult of Personality"	Living Colour, *Time's Up*
Metal	—	Metallica, "One"	Metallica, "Stone Cold Crazy"
Alternative	—	—	Sinéad O'Connor, *I Do Not Want What I Haven't Got*
Rap Performance, Solo	D.J. Jazzy Jeff & The Fresh Prince, "Parents Just Don't Understand"	Young MC, "Bust a Move"	M.C. Hammer, "U Can't Touch This"
Rap Performance by a Duo or Group	—	—	Ice-T, Melle Mel, Big Daddy Kane, Kool Moe Dee, and Quincy Jones III, "Back on the Block"
Rhythm and Blues Song	Anita Baker, Skip Scarborough, and Randy Holland, "Giving You the Best That I Got"	Kenny Gamble and Leon Huff, "If You Don't Know Me By Now"	Rick James, Alonzo Mille, and M.C. Hammer, "U Can't Touch This"
R&B Vocal, Female	Anita Baker, "Giving You the Best That I Got"	Anita Baker, *Giving You the Best That I Got*	Anita Baker, *Compositions*
R&B Vocal, Male	Terence Trent D'Arby, *Introducing the Hardline According to Terence Trent D'Arby*	Bobby Brown, "Every Little Step"	Luther Vandross, "Here and Now"
R&B Duo or Group with Vocal	Gladys Knight & The Pips, "Love Overboard"	Soul II Soul featuring Caron Wheeler, "Back to Life"	Ray Charles and Chaka Khan, "I'll Be Good to You"
Country Song	K. T. Oslin, "Hold Me"	Rodney Crowell, "After All This Time"	Jon Vezner and Don Henry, "Where've You Been"

	1988	1989	1990
Country Vocal, Female	K. T. Oslin, "Hold Me"	k.d. lang, *Absolute Torch and Twang*	Kathy Mattea, "Where've You Been"
Country Vocal, Male	Randy Travis, *Old 8 x 10*	Lyle Lovett, *Lyle Lovett and His Large Band*	Vince Gill, "When I Call Your Name"
Country Performance, Duo or Group with Vocal	The Judds, "Give a Little Love"	The Nitty Gritty Dirt Band, *Will the Circle Be Unbroken, Volume 2*	The Kentucky Headhunters, *Pickin' on Nashville*
Country Vocal, Collaboration	Roy Orbison and k.d. lang, "Crying"	Hank Williams Jr. and Hank Williams Sr., "There's a Tear in My Beer"	Chet Atkins and Mark Knopfler, "Poor Boy Blues"
Traditional Blues Recording	Willie Dixon, *Hidden Charms*	John Lee Hooker and Bonnie Raitt, "I'm in the Mood"	B.B. King, *Live at San Quentin*
Contemporary Blues	The Robert Cray Band, "Don't Be Afraid of the Dark"	Stevie Ray Vaughan & Double Trouble, *In Step*	The Vaughan Brothers, *Family Style*
Reggae Recording	Ziggy Marley & The Melody Makers, *Conscious Party*	Ziggy Marley & The Melody Makers, *One Bright Day*	Bunny Wailer, *Time Will Tell—A Tribute to Bob Marley*
Jazz Vocal, Female	Betty Carter, *Look What I Got!*	Ruth Brown, *Blues on Broadway*	Ella Fitzgerald, *All That Jazz*
Jazz Vocal, Male	Bobby McFerrin, "Brothers"	Harry Connick Jr., *When Harry Met Sally...*	Harry Connick Jr., *We Are in Love*
Jazz, Soloist	Michael Brecker, *Don't Try This at Home*	Miles Davis, *Aura*	Oscar Peterson, *The Legendary Oscar Peterson Trio Live at the Blue Note*
Jazz, Group	McCoy Tyner, Pharaoh Sanders, David Murray, Cecil McBee, and Roy Haynes, *Blues for Coltrane: A Tribute to John Coltrane*	Chick Corea Akoustic Band, *Chick Corea Akoustic Band*	Oscar Peterson Trio, *The Legendary Oscar Peterson Trio Live at the Blue Note*
Jazz, Big Band/ Large Ensemble Performance	Gil Evans & The Monday Night Orchestra, *Bud & Bird*	Miles Davis, *Aura*	George Benson featuring the Count Basie Orchestra; Frank Foster, conductor, "Basie's Bag"
Jazz Fusion Performance, Vocal or Instrumental	Yellowjackets, *Politics*	Pat Metheny Group, *Letter from Home*	Quincy Jones, "Birdland"
Gospel Performance, Female	Amy Grant, *Lead Me On*	CeCe Winans, "Don't Cry"	—
Gospel Performance, Male	Larnelle Harris, *Christmas*	BeBe Winans, "Meantime"	—
Gospel Performance, Duo, Group, Choir or Chorus	The Winans, *The Winans Live at Carnegie Hall*	Take 6, "The Savior Is Waiting"	Rev. James Cleveland, *Having Church*
Traditional Folk Recording	Various artists, *Folkways: A Vision Shared—A Tribute to Woody Guthrie and Leadbelly*	Bulgarian State Female Vocal Choir, *Le Mystère des voix bulgares, Vol. II*	Doc Watson, *On Praying Ground*
Contemporary Folk Recording	Tracy Chapman, *Tracy Chapman*	Indigo Girls, *Indigo Girls*	Shawn Colvin, *Steady On*
Cast Show Album	*Into the Woods*	*Jerome Robbins' Broadway*	*Les Misérables, The Complete Symphonic Recording*

	1988	**1989**	**1990**
Comedy Recording	Robin Williams, *Good Morning, Vietnam*	"Professor" Peter Schickele, *P.D.Q. Bach: 1712 Overture and Other Musical Assaults*	"Professor" Peter Schickele, *P.D.Q. Bach: Oedipus Tex & Other Choral Calamities*
Classical Album	Robert Shaw, conductor, Atlanta Symphony Orchestra and Chorus, *Verdi: Requiem and Operatic Choruses*	Emerson String Quartet, *Bartók: 6 String Quartets*	Leonard Bernstein, conductor, New York Philharmonic, *Ives: Symphony No. 2 (and Three Short Works)*
Classical Orchestral Performance	Robert Shaw, conductor, Atlanta Symphony Orchestra, *Rorem: String Symphony*; Louis Lane, conductor, Atlanta Symphony Orchestra, *Sunday Morning* and *Eagles*	Leonard Bernstein, conductor, New York Philharmonic, *Mahler: Sym. No. 3 in D Min.*	Leonard Bernstein, conductor, Chicago Symphony, *Shostakovich: Symphonies No. 1, Op. 10, and No. 7, Op. 60*
Opera Recording	Georg Solti, conductor, Vienna State Opera Choir & Vienna Philharmonic (Solos: Domingo, Norman, Randova, Nimsgern, Sotin, Fischer-Dieskau), *Wagner: Lohengrin*	James Levine, conductor, Metropolitan Opera Orchestra (Solos: Lakes, Moll, Morris, Norman, Behrens, Ludwig), *Wagner: Die Walküre*	James Levine, conductor, Metropolitan Opera Orchestra (Solos: Morris, Ludwig, Jerusalem, Wlaschiha, Moll, Zednik, Rootering), *Wagner: Das Rheingold*
Chamber Music Performance	Murray Perahia and Sir Georg Solti, pianos, with David Corkhill and Evelyn Glennie, percussion, *Bartók: Sonata for Two Pianos and Percussion; Brahms: Variations on a Theme by Joseph Haydn for Two Pianos*	Emerson String Quartet, *Bartók: 6 String Quartets*	Itzhak Perlman, violin; Daniel Barenboim, piano, *Brahms: The Three Violin Sonatas*

GRAMMY CHAMPS

Sir Georg Solti still reigns supreme as the National Academy of Recording Arts and Sciences' most honored musician, though Robert Shaw, Pat Metheny, and Vince Gill all made advances towards the late conductor's mark.

Sir Georg Solti	31	Ray Charles	12
Quincy Jones	26	Eric Clapton	12
Vladimir Horowitz	25	Vince Gill	12
Pierre Boulez	20	Yo-Yo Ma	12
Henry Mancini	20	Thomas Z. Shepard	12
Stevie Wonder	20	Sting (including The Police)	12
Leonard Bernstein	16	Duke Ellington	11
Paul Simon (including Simon & Garfunkel)	16	James Mallinson	11
John T. Williams	16	Pat Metheny (including Pat Metheny Group)	11
Aretha Franklin	15	Roger Miller	11
Itzhak Perlman	15	Kenneth "Babyface" Edmonds	10
Chet Atkins	14	George Harrison (including The Beatles and Travelling Wilburys)	10
Robert Shaw (including Robert Shaw Chorale)	14		
Ella Fitzgerald	13	John Lennon (including The Beatles)	10
David Foster	13	Bobby McFerrin	10
Michael Jackson	13	Alan Menken	10
Paul McCartney (including The Beatles and Wings)	13	Artur Rubinstein	10
Leontyne Price	13	Robert Woods	10

	1991	1992	1993
Record of the Year	Natalie Cole (with Nat "King" Cole), "Unforgettable"	Eric Clapton, "Tears in Heaven"	Whitney Houston, "I Will Always Love You"
Album of the Year	Natalie Cole, *Unforgettable*	Eric Clapton, *Unplugged*	Whitney Houston and others, *The Bodyguard—Original Soundtrack*
Song of the Year	Irving Gordon, "Unforgettable"	Eric Clapton and Will Jennings, "Tears in Heaven"	Alan Menken and Tim Rice, "A Whole New World"
Pop Vocal, Female	Bonnie Raitt, "Something to Talk About"	k.d. lang, "Constant Craving"	Whitney Houston, "I Will Always Love You"
Pop Vocal, Male	Michael Bolton, "When a Man Loves a Woman"	Eric Clapton, "Tears in Heaven"	Sting, "If I Ever Lose My Faith In You"
Rock Vocal, Female	Bonnie Raitt, *Luck of the Draw*	Melissa Etheridge, "Ain't It Heavy"	—
Rock Vocal, Male	—	Eric Clapton, *Tears in Heaven*	—
Rock Song/ Rock Vocal Performance, Solo	Sting, "Soul Cages"	Eric Clapton and Jim Gordon, "Layla"	Meat Loaf, "I'd Do Anything for Love (But I Won't Do That)"
New Artist	Mark Cohn	Arrested Development	Toni Braxton
Pop Vocal, Duo or Group with Vocal	R.E.M., "Losing My Religion"	Celine Dion and Peabo Bryson, "Beauty and the Beast"	Peabo Bryson and Regina Belle, "A Whole New World"
Rock Performance, Duo or Group with Vocal	Bonnie Raitt and Delbert McClinton, "Good Man, Good Woman"	U2, *Achtung Baby*	Aerosmith, "Living on the Edge"
New Age Recording	Mannheim Steamroller, *Fresh Aire 7*	Enya, *Sheperd Moons*	Paul Winter Consort, *Spanish Angel*
Hard Rock	Van Halen, *For Unlawful Carnal Knowledge*	Red Hot Chili Peppers, "Give It Away"	Stone Temple Pilots, "Plush"
Metal	Metallica, *Metallica*	Nine Inch Nails, "Wish"	Ozzy Ozbourne, "I Don't Want To Change the World"
Alternative	R.E.M., *Out of Time*	Tom Waits, *Bone Machine*	U2, *Zooropa*
Rap Performance, Solo	L.L. Cool J, "Mama Said Knock You Out"	Sir Mix-A-Lot, "Baby Got Back"	Dr. Dre, "Let Me Ride"
Rap Performance by a Duo or Group	D.J. Jazzy Jeff & The Fresh Prince, "Summertime"	Arrested Development, "Tennessee"	Digable Planets, "Rebirth of Slick (Cool Like Dat)"
Rhythm and Blues Song	Luther Vandross, Marcus Miller, and Teddy Vann, "Power of Love/Love Power"	L.A. Reid, Babyface, and Daryl Simmons, "End of the Road"	Janet Jackson, James Harris III, and Terry Lewis, "That's the Way Love Goes"
R&B Vocal, Female	Patti LaBelle, *Burnin'*; Lisa Fischer; "How Can I Ease the Pain"	Chaka Khan, *The Woman I Am*	Toni Braxton, "Another Sad Love Song"
R&B Vocal, Male	Luther Vandross, *Power of Love*	Al Jarreau, *Heaven and Earth*	Ray Charles, "A Song For You"
R&B Duo or Group with Vocal	Boyz II Men, *Cooleyhighharmony*	Boyz II Men, "End of the Road"	Sade, "No Ordinary Love"
Country Song	Naomi Judd, John Jarvis, and Paul Overstreet, "Love Can Build a Bridge"	Vince Gill and John Barlow Jarvis, "I Still Believe in You"	Lucinda Williams, "Passionate Kisses"
Country Vocal, Female	Mary-Chapin Carpenter, "Down at the Twist and Shout"	Mary-Chapin Carpenter, "I Feel Lucky"	Mary-Chapin Carpenter, "Passionate Kisses"
Country Vocal, Male	Garth Brooks, *Ropin' the Wind*	Vince Gill, *I Still Believe in You*	Dwight Yoakam, "Ain't That Lonely Yet"

	1991	1992	1993
Country Performance, Duo or Group with Vocal	The Judds, "Love Can Build a Bridge"	Emmylou Harris & The Nash Ramblers, *Emmylou Harris & The Nash Ramblers at the Ryman*	Brooks & Dunn, "Hard Workin' Man"
Country Vocal, Collaboration	Steve Wariner, Ricky Skaggs, and Vince Gill, "Restless"	Travis Tritt and Marty Stuart, "The Whiskey Ain't Workin' "	Reba McEntire and Linda Davis, "Does He Love You"
Traditional Blues Recording	B. B. King, *Live at the Apollo*	Dr. John, *Goin' Back to New Orleans*	B.B. King, *Blues Summit*
Contemporary Blues	Buddy Guy, *Damn Right, I've Got the Blues*	Stevie Ray Vaughan & Double Trouble, *The Sky Is Crying*	Buddy Guy, *Feels Like Rain*
Reggae Recording	Shabba Ranks, *As Raw as Ever*	Shabba Ranks, *X-tra Naked*	Inner Circle, *Bad Boys*
Jazz, Soloist	Stan Getz, "I Remember You"	Joe Henderson, "Lush Life"	Joe Henderson, "Miles Ahead"
Jazz, Group	Oscar Peterson Trio, *Saturday Night at the Blue Note*	Branford Marsalis, *I Heard You Twice the First Time*	Joe Henderson, *So Near, So Far (Musings for Miles)*
Jazz, Big Band/ Large Ensemble Performance	Dizzy Gillespie & The United Nation Orchestra, *Live at the Royal Festival Hall*	McCoy Tyner Big Band, *The Turning Point*	Miles Davis and Quincy Jones, *Miles and Quincy Live at Montreaux*
Jazz Fusion Performance	—	Pat Metheny, *Secret Story*	—
Gospel Performance, Duo, Group, Choir or Chorus	Sounds of Blackness, *The Evolution of Gospel*	Music & Arts Seminar Mass Choir; Edwin Hawkins, choir director, *Edwin Hawkins Music & Arts Seminar Mass Choir: Recorded Live in Los Angeles*	Brooklyn Tabernacle Choir; Carol Cymbala, choir director, *Live...We Come Rejoicing*
Traditional Folk Recording	Ken Burns and John Colby, *The Civil War*	The Chieftains, *Another Country*	The Chieftains, *The Celtic Harp*
Contemporary Folk Recording	John Prine, *The Missing Years*	The Chieftains, *An Irish Evening Live at the Grand Opera House, Belfast*	Nanci Griffith, *Other Voices/Other Rooms*
Cast Show Album	*The Will Rogers Follies*	*Guys and Dolls*	*The Who's Tommy*
Comedy Recording	"Professor" Peter Schickele, *P.D.Q. Bach: WTWP Classical Talkity-Talk Radio*	"Professor" Peter Schickele, *P.D.Q. Bach: Music for an Awful Lot of Winds & Percussion*	George Carlin, *Jammin' in New York*
Classical Album	Leonard Bernstein, conductor, London Symphony Orchestra (Solos: Hadley, Anderson, Ludwig, Green, Gedda, Jones), *Bernstein: Candide*	Leonard Bernstein, conductor, Berlin Philharmonic Orchestra, *Mahler: Symphony No. 9*	Pierre Boulez, conductor, Chicago Symphony Orchestra and Chorus; John Alen John Tomlinson, baritone, *Bartók: The Wooden Prince & C*
Classical Orchestral Performance	Daniel Barenboim, conductor, Chicago Symphony Orchestra, *Corigliano: Symphony No. 1*	Leonard Bernstein, conductor, Berlin Philharmonic Orchestra, *Mahler: Symphony No. 9*	Pierre Boulez, conductor, Chicago Symphony, *Bartók: The Wooden Prince*
Opera Recording	James Levine, conductor, Metropolitan Opera Orchestra and Chorus (Solos: Behrens, Studer, Schwarz, Goldberg, Weikl, Wlaschiha, Salminen), *Wagner: Götterdämmerung*	Georg Solti conductor, Vienna Philharmonic (Solos: Domingo, Varady, Van Dam, Behrens, Runkel, Jo), *R. Strauss: Die Frau Ohne Schatten*	John Nelson, conductor, English Chamber Orchestra and Ambrosian Opera Chorus (Solos: Battle, Horne, Ramey, Aler, McNair, Chance, Mackie, Doss); *Handel: Semele*
Chamber Music Performance	Isaac Stern and Jamie Laredo, violins; Yo-Yo Ma, cello; Emanuel Ax, piano, *Brahms: Piano Quartets*	Yo-Yo Ma, cello; Emanuel Ax, piano, *Brahms: Sonatas for Cello & Piano*	Anne-Sophie Mutter, violin, and James Levine, conductor, Chicago Symphony, *Berg: Violin Concerto/Rihm: Time Chant*

	1994	**1995**	**1996**
Record of the Year	Sheryl Crow, "All I Wanna Do"	Seal, "Kiss From a Rose"	Eric Clapton, "Change the World"
Album of the Year	Tony Bennett, *MTV Unplugged*	Alanis Morissette, *Jagged Little Pill*	Celine Dion, *Falling Into You*
Song of the Year	Bruce Springsteen, "Streets of Philadelphia"	Seal, "Kiss From a Rose"	Gordon Kennedy, Wayne Kirkpatrick & Tommy Sims, "Change the World"
Pop Vocal, Female	Sheryl Crow, "All I Wanna Do"	Annie Lennox, "No More 'I Love You's' "	Toni Braxton, "Un-Break My Heart"
Pop Vocal, Male	Elton John, "Can You Feel the Love Tonight"	Seal, "Kiss From a Rose"	Eric Clapton, "Change the World"
Rock Vocal, Female	Melissa Etheridge, "Come to My Window"	Alanis Morissette, "You Oughta Know"	Sheryl Crow, "If It Makes You Happy"
Rock Vocal, Male	Bruce Springsteen, "Streets of Philadelphia"	Tom Petty, "You Don't Know How It Feels"	Beck, "Where It's At"
Rock Song/ Rock Vocal Performance, Solo	Bruce Springsteen, "Streets of Philadelphia"	Glen Ballard and Alanis Morissette, "You Oughta Know"	Tracy Chapman, "Give Me One Reason"
New Artist	Sheryl Crow	Hootie & The Blowfish	LeAnn Rimes
Pop Vocal, Duo or Group with Vocal	All-4-One, "I Swear"	Hootie & The Blowfish, "Let Her Cry"	The Beatles, "Free As a Bird"
Rock Performance, Duo or Group with Vocal	Aerosmith, "Crazy"	Blues Traveler, "Run-Around"	Dave Matthews Band, "So Much To Say"
New Age Recording	Paul Winter, "Prayer for the Wild Thing"	George Winston, *Forest*	Enya, *The Memory of Trees*
Hard Rock	Soundgarden, "Black Hole Sun"	Pearl Jam, "Spin the Black Circle"	The Smashing Pumpkins, "Bullet with Butterfly Wings"
Metal	Soundgarden, "Spoonman"	Nine Inch Nails, "Happiness in Slavery"	Rage Against the Machine, "Tire Me"
Alternative	Green Day, *Dookie*	Nirvana, *MTV Unplugged in New York*	Beck, *Odelay*
Rap Performance, Solo	Queen Latifah, "U.N.I.T.Y."	Coolio, "Gangsta's Paradise"	L.L. Cool J, "Hey Lover"
Rap Performance by a Duo or Group	Salt-N-Pepa, "None of Your Business"	Method Man Featuring Mary J. Blige, "I'll Be There for You"/ "You're All I Need to Get By"	Bone Thugs-N-Harmony, "Tha Crossroads"
Rhythm and Blues Song	Babyface, "I'll Make Love to You"	Stevie Wonder, "For Your Love"	Babyface, "Exhale (Shoop Shoop)"
R&B Vocal, Female	Toni Braxton, "Breathe Again"	Anita Baker, "I Apologize"	Toni Braxton, "You're Makin' Me High"
R&B Vocal, Male	Babyface, "When Can I See You"	Stevie Wonder, "For Your Love"	Luther Vandross, "Your Secret Love"
R&B Duo or Group with Vocal	Boyz II Men, "I'll Make Love to You"	TLC, "Creep"	The Fugees, "Killing Me Softly"
Country Song	Gary Baker and Frank J. Myers, "I Swear"	Vince Gill, "Go Rest High on That Mountain"	Bill Mack, "Blue"
Country Vocal, Female	Mary Chapin Carpenter, "Shut Up and Kiss Me"	Alison Krauss, "Baby, Now That I've Found You"	LeAnn Rimes, "Blue"
Country Vocal, Male	Vince Gill, "When Love Finds You"	Vince Gill, "Go Rest High on That Mountain"	Vince Gill, "Worlds Apart"

	1994	1995	1996
Country Performance, Duo or Group with Vocal	Asleep at the Wheel with Lyle Lovett, "Blues for Dixie"	The Mavericks, "Here Comes the Rain"	Brooks & Dunn, "My Maria"
Country Vocal, Collaboration	Aaron Neville and Trisha Yearwood, "I Fall to Pieces"	Shenandoah & Alison Krauss, "Somewhere in the Vicinity of the Heart"	Vince Gill featuring Alison Krauss & Union Station, "High Lonesome Sound"
Traditional Blues Recording	Eric Clapton, *From the Cradle*	John Lee Hooker, *Chill Out*	James Cotton, *Deep in the Blues*
Contemporary Blues	Pops Staples, *Father Father*	Buddy Guy, *Slippin' In*	Keb' Mo', *Just Like You*
Reggae Recording	Bunny Wailer, *Crucial! Roots Classics*	Shaggy, *Boombastic*	Bunny Wailer, *Hall of Fame—A Tribute to Bob Marley's 50th Anniversary*
Jazz, Soloist	Benny Carter, "Prelude to a Kiss"	Lena Horne, *An Evening With Lena Horne* (vocals); Michael Brecker, *Impressions* (instrumental)	Cassandra Wilson, *New Moon Daughter* (vocals); Michael Brecker, "Cabin Fever" (instrumental)
Jazz, Group/ Jazz, Instrumental Performance, Individual or Group	Ron Carter, Herbie Hancock, Wallace Roney, Wayne Shorter & Tony Williams, *A Tribute to Miles*	McCoy Tyner Trio Featuring Michael Brecker, *Infinity*	Michael Brecker, *Tales from the Hudson*
Jazz, Big Band/ Large Ensemble Performance	McCoy Tyner Big Band, *Journey*	GRP All-Star Big Band & Tom Scott, "All Blues"	Count Basie Orchestra (with The New York Voices), *Live at Manchester Craftsmen's Guild*
Contemporary Jazz Performance	—	Pat Metheny Group, *We Live Here*	Wayne Shorter, *High Life*
Gospel Performance, Duo, Group, Choir or Chorus	The Thompson Community Singers, Rev. Milton Brunson, choir director, *Through God's Eyes* and The Love Fellowship Crusade Choir, Hezekiah Walker, choir director, *Live in Atlanta at Morehouse College* (tie)	The Brooklyn Tabernacle Choir, *Praise Him...Live!*	Shirley Caesar's Outreach Convention Choir, *Just a Word*
Traditional Folk Recording	Bob Dylan, *World Gone Wrong*	Ramblin' Jack Elliott, *South Coast*	Pete Seeger, *Pete*
Contemporary Folk Recording	Johnny Cash, *American Recordings*	Emmylou Harris, *Wrecking Ball*	Bruce Springsteen, *The Ghost of Tom Joad*
Cast Show Album	*Passion*	*Smokey Joe's Cafe—The Songs of Leiber and Stoller*	*Riverdance*
Comedy Recording	Sam Kinison, *Live From Hell*	Jonathan Winters, *Crank Calls*	Al Franken, *Rush Limbaugh Is a Big Fat Idiot*
Classical Album	Pierre Boulez, conductor, Chicago Symphony Orchestra, *Bartok: Concerto for Orch.; Four Orchestral Pieces, Op. 12*	Pierre Boulez, conductor, Cleveland Orchestra and Chorus, *Debussy: La Mer; Nocturnes; Jeux, etc.*	Leonard Slatkin, conductor, various Artists, *Corigliano: Of Rage and Remembrance*
Classical Orchestral Performance	Pierre Boulez, conductor, Chicago Symphony Orchestra, *Bartok: Concerto for Orch.; Four Orchestral Pieces, Op. 12*	Pierre Boulez, conductor, Cleveland Orchestra and Chorus, *Debussy: La Mer; Nocturnes; Jeux, etc.*	Michael Tilson Thomas, conductor, San Francisco Symphony, *Prokofiev: Romeo and Juliet (Scenes from the Ballet)*
Opera Recording	Kent Nagano, conductor, Orchestra and Chorus of Opera de Lyon (Solos: Cheryl Struder, Jerry Hadley, Samuel Ramey, Kenn Chester), *Floyd: Susannah*	Charles Dutoit, conductor, Montreal Symphony Orchestra & Chorus, *Berlioz: Les Troyens*	Richard Hickox, conductor, Opera London, London Symphony Chorus, City of London Sinfonia (Solos: Philip Langridge, Alan Opie, Janice Watson), *Britten: Peter Grimes*
Chamber Music Performance	Daniel Barenboim, piano; Dale Clevenger, horn; Larry Combs, clarinet (Chicago Symphony), Daniele Damiano, bassoon; Hansjorg Schellenberger, oboe (Berlin Philharmonic), *Beethoven/Mozart: Quintets*	Emanuel Ax, piano; Yo-Yo Ma, cello; Richard Stoltzman, clarinet, *Brahms/Beethoven/Mozart: Clarinet Trios*	Cleveland Quartet, *Corigliano: String Quartet*

1997 1998

	1997	1998
Record of the Year	Shawn Colvin, "Sunny Came Home"	Celine Dion, "My Heart Will Go On"
Album of the Year	Bob Dylan, *Time Out of Mind*	Lauryn Hill, *The Miseducation Of Lauryn Hill*
Song of the Year	Shawn Colvin, "Sunny Came Home"	James Horner and Will Jennings, "My Heart Will Go On"
Pop Vocal, Female	Sarah McLachlan, "Building a Mystery"	Celine Dion, "My Heart Will Go On"
Pop Vocal, Male	Elton John, "Candle in the Wind 1997"	Eric Clapton, "My Father's Eyes"
Rock Vocal, Female	Fiona Apple, "Criminal"	Alanis Morissette, "Uninvited"
Rock Vocal, Male	Bob Dylan, "Cold Irons Bound"	Lenny Kravitz, "Fly Away"
Rock Song	Jakob Dylan, "One Headlight"	Alanis Morissette, "Uninvited"
New Artist	Paula Cole	Lauryn Hill
Pop Performance, Duo or Group with Vocal	Jamiroquai, "Virtual Insanity"	The Brian Setzer Orchestra, "Jump Jive An' Wail"
Rock Performance, Duo or Group with Vocal	The Wallflowers, "One Headlight"	Aerosmith, "Pink"
New Age Album	Michael Hedges, *Oracle*	Clannad, *Landmarks*
Hard Rock Performance	The Smashing Pumpkins, "The End Is the Beginning Is the End"	Jimmy Page and Robert Plant, "Most High"
Metal Performance	Tool, *Aenema*	Metallica, *Better Than You*
Alternative Performance	Radiohead, *OK Computer*	Beastie Boys, *Hello Nasty*
Rap Performance, Solo	Will Smith, "Men in Black"	Will Smith, "Gettin' Jiggy Wit It"
Rap Performance by a Duo or Group	Puff Daddy & Faith Evans featuring 112, "I'll Be Missing You"	Beastie Boys, "Intergalactic"
R&B Song	R. Kelly, "I Believe I Can Fly"	Lauryn Hill, "Doo Wop (That Thing)"
R&B Vocal, Female	Erykah Badu, "On & On"	Lauryn Hill, "Doo Wop (That Thing)"
R&B Vocal, Male	R. Kelly, "I Believe I Can Fly"	Stevie Wonder, "St. Louis Blues"
R&B Performance, Duo or Group with Vocal	Blackstreet, "No Diggity"	Brandy and Monica, "The Boy Is Mine"
Country Song	Bob Carlisle & Randy Thomas, "Butterfly Kisses"	Robert John "Mutt" Lange and Shania Twain, "You're Still the One "
Country Vocal, Female	Trisha Yearwood, "How Do I Live"	Shania Twain, "You're Still the One"
Country Vocal, Male	Vince Gill, "Pretty Little Adriana"	Vince Gill, "If You Ever Have Forever in Mind"
Country Performance, Duo or Group with Vocal	Allison Krauss & Union Station, "Looking in the Eyes of Love"	Dixie Chicks, "There's Your Trouble"

ALL THE REST

Ninety-five categories strong, here are all the other Grammy winners from 1998.

Best Pop Collaboration with Vocals: "I Still Have That Other Girl," Elvis Costello & Burt Bacharach

Best Pop Instrumental Performance: "Sleepwalk," The Brian Setzer Orchestra

Best Dance Recording: "Ray of Light," Madonna

Best Pop Album: *Ray of Light,* Madonna

Best Traditional Pop Vocal Performance: *Live at Carnegie Hall—The 50th Anniversary Concert,* Patti Page

Best Rock Instrumental Performance: "The Roots of Coincidence," Pat Metheny Group

Best Rock Album: *The Globe Sessions,* Sheryl Crow

Best R&B Album: *The Miseducation of Lauryn Hill,* Lauryn Hill

Best Traditional R&B Vocal Performance: *Live! One Night Only,* Patti LaBelle

Best Rap Album: *Vol. 2...Hard Knock Life,* Jay-Z

Best Country Instrumental Performance: "A Soldier's Joy," Randy Scruggs and Vince Gill

Best Country Album: *Wide Open Spaces,* Dixie Chicks

Best Bluegrass Album: *Bluegrass Rules,* Ricky Skaggs and Kentucky Thunder

Best Latin Jazz Performance: *Hot House,* Arturo Sandoval

Best Latin Pop Performance: *Vuelve,* Ricky Martin

Best Latin Rock/Alternative Performance: *Suenos Liquidos,* Mana

Best Tropical Latin Performance: *Contra la Corriente,* Marc Anthony

Best Mexican-American Music Performance: *Los Super Seven,* Los Super Seven

Best Tejano Music Performance: *Said and Done,* Flaco Jimenez

Best World Music Album: *Quanta Live,* Gilberto Gil

Best Polka Album: *Dance with Me,* Jimmy Sturr and His Orchestra

Best Musical Album for Children: *Elmopalooza!,* The Sesame Street Muppets with Various Artists

Best Spoken Word Album for Children: *The Children's Shakespeare,* Various Artists (including Jim Belushi and Linda Hamilton)

Best Spoken Word Album: *Still Me,* Christopher Reeve

Best Instrumental Composition: "Almost 12," Bela Fleck, Future Man and Victor Lemonte Wooten, composers (Bela Fleck and The Flecktones)

Best Instrumental Composition Written for a Motion Picture or for Television: *Saving Private Ryan,* John Williams, composer

(continued on next page)

287

1997   1998

	1997	1998
Country Vocal, Collaboration	Trisha Yearwood & Garth Brooks, "In Another's Eyes"	Clint Black, Joe Diffie, Merle Haggard, Emmylou Harris, Alison Krauss, Patty Loveless, Earl Scruggs, Ricky Skaggs, Marty Stuart, Pam Tillis, Randy Travis, Travis Tritt, and Dwight Yoakam, *Same Old Train*
Traditional Blues Album	John Lee Hooker, *Don't Look Back*	Otis Rush, *Any Place I'm Going*
Contemporary Blues Album	Taj Mahal, *Senor Blues*	Keb' Mo', *Slow Down*
Reggae Album	Ziggy Marley & The Melody Makers, *Fallen Is Babylon*	Sly and Robbie, *Friends*
Jazz, Soloist	Dee Dee Bridgewater, *Dear Ella* (vocals); Doc Cheatham & Nicholas Payton, "Stardust" (instrumental)	Shirley Horn, *I Remember Miles* (vocals); Chick Corea and Gary Burton, "Rhumbata" (instrumental)
Jazz, Instrumental Performance, Individual or Group	Charlie Haden & Pat Metheny, *Beyond the Missouri Sky*	Herbie Hancock, *Gershwin's World*
Jazz, Large Ensemble Performance	Joe Henderson Big Band, *Joe Henderson Big Band*	Count Basie Orchestra; Grover Mitchell, Director, *Count Plays Duke*
Contemporary Jazz Performance	Randy Brecker, *Into the Sun*	Pat Metheny Group, *Imaginary Day*
Gospel Album	dc Talk, *Welcome to the Freak Show: dc Talk* (rock); Jars of Clay, *Much Afraid* (pop/contemp.); The Fairfield Four, *I Couldn't Hear Nobody Pray* (trad. soul); Take 6, *Brothers* (contemp. soul); God's Property, *God's Property from Kirk Franlin's Nu Nation* (choir/chorus)	Ashley Cleveland, *You Are There* (rock); Deniece Williams, *This Is My Song* (pop/contemp); Cissy Houston, *He Leadeth Me* (trad. soul); Kirk Franklin, *The Nu Nation Project* (contemp. soul); The Associates; O'Landa Draper, Choir Director, *Reflections* (choir/chorus)
Traditional Folk Album	BeauSoleil, *L'Amour ou La Folie*	The Chieftains with Various Artists, *Long Journey Home*
Contemporary Folk Album	Bob Dylan, *Time Out of Mind*	Lucinda Williams, *Car Wheels on a Gravel Road*
Cast Show Album	*Chicago: The Musical*	*The Lion King*
Comedy Album	Chris Rock, *Roll with the New*	Mel Brooks & Carl Reiner, *The 2000 Year Old Man in the Year 2000*
Classical Album	Yo-Yo Ma, violincello; David Zinman, conductor, Philadelphia Orchestra, *Premieres—Cello Concertos (Works of Danielpour, Kirchner, Rouse)*	Robert Shaw, conductor, Atlanta Sym. Orch. Cho.; Atlanta Sym. Orch., *Barber: Prayers of Kierkegaard/Vaughan Williams: Dona Nobis Pacem/Bartok: Cantata Profana*
Classical Orchestral Performance	Pierre Boulez, conductor, The Cleveland Orchestra, The Cleveland Orchestra Chorus, *Berlioz: Symphonie Fantastique; Tristia*	Pierre Boulez, conductor, Chicago Sym. Orch, *Mahler: Sym. No. 9*
Opera Recording	Sir Georg Solti, conductor; Ben Heppner, Herbert Lippert, Karita Mattila, Alan Opie, Rene Pape, Iris Vermillion, Chicago Symphony Chorus, Chicago Symphony Orchestra, *Wagner: Die Meistersinger Von Nurnberg*	Pierre Boulez, conductor; Jessye Norman; Laszlo Polgar; Chicago Symphony Orchestra, *Bartók: Bluebeard's Castle*
Chamber Music Performance	Emerson String Quartet, *Beethoven: The String Quartets*	André Previn, piano; Gil Shaham, violin, *American Scenes*

Best Song Written for a Motion Picture or for Television: "My Heart Will Go On" (from *Titanic*), James Horner and Will Jennings, songwriters (Celine Dion)

Best Instrumental Arrangement: "Waltz for Debby," Don Sebesky, arranger (Don Sebesky)

Best Instrumental Arrangement Accompanying Vocal(s): "St. Louis Blues," Herbie Hancock, Robert Sadin, and Stevie Wonder, arrangers (Herbie Hancock)

Best Recording Package: *Ray of Light*, Kevin Reagan, art director (Madonna)

Best Boxed Recording Package: *The Complete Hank Williams*, Jim Kemp and Virginia Team, art directors

Best Album Notes: *Miles Davis Quintet 1965–1968*

Best Historical Album: *The Complete Hank Williams*

Best Engineered Album, Non-Classical: *The Globe Sessions*

Producer of the Year, Non-Classical: Rob Cavallo

Remixer of the Year, Non-Classical: David Morales

Best Engineered Album, Classical: *Barber: Prayers of Kierkegaard/Vaughan Williams: Dona Nobis Pacem/Bartók: Cantata Profana*

Producer of the Year, Classical: Steven Epstein

Best Choral Performance: *Barber: Prayers of Kierkegaard/Vaughan Williams: Dona Nobis Pacem/Bartók: Cantata Profana*

Best Instrumental Soloist(s) Performance (with Orchestra): "Penderecki: Violin Con. No. 2 'Metamorphosen,'" Anne-Sophie Mutter, violin; Krzysztof Penderecki, conductor (London Sym. Orch.)

Best Instrumental Soloist Performance (without Orchestra): *Bach: English Suites Nos. 1, 3 & 6*, Murray Perahia, piano

Best Small Ensemble Performance (with or without Conductor): *Reich: Music for 18 Musicians*, Steve Reich and Musicians

Best Classical Vocal Performance: *The Beautiful Voice* (Works of Charpentier, Gounod, Massenet, Flotow, etc.), Renee Fleming, soprano

Best Classical Contemporary Composition: "Penderecki: Violin Con. No. 2 'Metamorphosen,'" Krzysztof Penderecki, composer (Anne-Sophie Mutter, violin; Krzysztof Penderecki, conductor; London Sym. Orch.)

Best Classical Crossover Album: *Soul of the Tango—The Music of Astor Piazzolla* (Libertango; Mumuki; Milonga Del Angel, etc.), Yo-Yo Ma, cello; Jorge Calandrelli, conductor

Best Short Form Music Video: *Ray of Light*, Madonna

Best Long Form Music Video: *American Masters: Lou Reed: Rock & Roll Heart*, Lou Reed

THE COUNTRY MUSIC ASSOCIATION AWARDS

	1967	**1968**	**1969**
Entertainer	Eddy Arnold	Glen Campbell	Johnny Cash
Song	Dallas Frazier, "There Goes My Everything"	Bobby Russell, "Honey"	Bob Ferguson, "Carroll County Accident"
Female Vocalist	Loretta Lynn	Tammy Wynette	Tammy Wynette
Male Vocalist	Jack Greene	Glen Campbell	Johnny Cash
Album	Jack Greene, *There Goes My Everything*	Johnny Cash, *Johnny Cash at Folsom Prison*	Johnny Cash, *Johnny Cash at San Quentin Prison*
Single	Jack Greene, "There Goes My Everything"	Jeannie C. Riley, "Harper Valley P.T.A."	Johnny Cash, "A Boy Named Sue"
Vocal Group	The Stoneman Family	Porter Wagoner and Dolly Parton	Johnny Cash and June Carter
Musician	Chet Atkins	Chet Atkins	Chet Atkins

	1970	**1971**	**1972**
Entertainer	Merle Haggard	Charley Pride	Loretta Lynn
Song	Kris Kristofferson, "Sunday Morning Coming Down"	Freddie Hart, "Easy Loving"	Freddie Hart, "Easy Loving"
Female Vocalist	Tammy Wynette	Lynn Anderson	Loretta Lynn
Male Vocalist	Merle Haggard	Charley Pride	Charley Pride
Album	Merle Haggard, *Okie from Muskogee*	Ray Price, *I Won't Mention It Again*	Merle Haggard, *Let Me Tell You About a Song*
Single	Merle Haggard, "Okie From Muskogee"	Sammi Smith, "Help Me Make It Through the Night"	Donna Fargo, "The Happiest Girl in the Whole U.S.A."
Vocal Group	The Glaser Brother	The Osborne Brothers	The Statler Brothers
Vocal Duo	Porter Wagoner and Dolly Parton	Porter Wagoner and Dolly Parton	Conway Twitty and Loretta Lynn
Musician	Jerry Reed	Jerry Reed	Charlie McCoy

	1973	**1974**	**1975**
Entertainer	Roy Clark	Charlie Rich	John Denver
Song	Kenny O'Dell, "Behind Closed Doors"	Don Wayne, "Country Bumpkin"	John Denver, "Back Home Again"
Female Vocalist	Loretta Lynn	Olivia Newton-John	Dolly Parton
Male Vocalist	Charlie Rich	Ronnie Milsap	Waylon Jennings
Album	Charlie Rich, *Behind Closed Doors*	Charlie Rich, *A Very Special Love Song*	Ronnie Milsap, *A Legend in My Time*
Single	Charlie Rich, "Behind Closed Doors"	Cal Smith, "Country Bumpkin"	Freddy Fender, "Before the Next Teardrop Falls"
Vocal Group	The Statler Brothers	The Statler Brothers	The Statler Brothers
Vocal Duo	Conway Twitty and Loretta Lynn	Conway Twitty and Loretta Lynn	Conway Twitty and Loretta Lynn
Musician	Charlie McCoy	Don Rich	Johnny Gimble

	1976	**1977**	**1978**
Entertainer	Mel Tillis	Ronnie Milsap	Dolly Parton
Song	Larry Weiss, "Rhinestone Cowboy"	Roger Bowling & Hal Bynum, "Lucille"	Richard Leigh, "Don't It Make My Brown Eyes Blue"
Female Vocalist	Dolly Parton	Crystal Gayle	Crystal Gayle
Male Vocalist	Ronnie Milsap	Ronnie Milsap	Don Williams
Album	Waylon Jennings, Willie Nelson, Tompall Glaser, Jessi Colter, *Wanted—The Outlaws*	Ronnie Milsap, *Ronnie Milsap Live*	Ronnie Milsap, *It Was Almost Like a Song*
Single	Waylon Jennings & Willie Nelson, "Good Hearted Woman"	Kenny Rogers, "Lucille"	The Kendalls, "Heaven's Just a Sin Away"
Vocal Group	The Statler Brothers	The Statler Brothers	The Oak Ridge Boys
Vocal Duo	Waylon Jennings & Willie Nelson	Jim Ed Brown & Helen Cornelius	Kenny Rogers and Dottie West
Musician	Hargus "Pig" Robbins	Roy Clark	Roy Clark

1979 | 1980 | 1981

	1979	1980	1981
Entertainer	Willie Nelson	Barbara Mandrell	Barbara Mandrell
Song	Don Schlitz, "The Gambler"	Bobby Braddock & Curly Putman, "He Stopped Loving Her Today"	Bobby Braddock & Curly Putman, "He Stopped Loving Her Today"
Female Vocalist	Barbara Mandrell	Emmylou Harris	Barbara Mandrell
Male Vocalist	Kenny Rogers	George Jones	George Jones
Album	Kenny Rogers, *The Gambler*	Original Motion Picture Soundtrack, *Coal Miner's Daughter*	Don Williams, *I Believe in You*
Single	Charlie Daniels Band, "The Devil Went Down to Georgia"	George Jones, "He Stopped Loving Her Today"	Oak Ridge Boys, "Elvira"
Vocal Group	The Statler Brothers	The Statler Brothers	Alabama
Horizon Award	—	—	Terri Gibbs
Vocal Duo	Kenny Rogers and Dottie West	Moe Bandy and Joe Stampley	David Frizzell and Shelly West
Musician	Charlie Daniels	Roy Clark	Chet Atkins

1982 | 1983 | 1984

	1982	1983	1984
Entertainer	Alabama	Alabama	Alabama
Song	Johnny Christopher, Wayne Carson, Mark James, "Always On My Mind"	Johnny Christopher, Wayne Carson, Mark James, "Always On My Mind"	Larry Henley, Jeff Silbar, "Wind Beneath My Wings"
Female Vocalist	Janie Fricke	Janie Fricke	Reba McEntire
Male Vocalist	Ricky Skaggs	Lee Greenwood	Lee Greenwood
Album	Willie Nelson, *Always on My Mind*	Alabama, *The Closer You Get*	Anne Murray, *A Little Good News*
Single	Willie Nelson, "Always on My Mind"	John Anderson, "Swingin' "	Anne Murray, "A Little Good News"
Vocal Group	Alabama	Alabama	The Statler Brothers
Horizon Award	Ricky Skaggs	John Anderson	The Judds
Vocal Duo	David Frizzell and Shelly West	Merle Haggard and Willie Nelson	Willie Nelson & Julio Iglesias
Musician	Chet Atkins	Chet Atkins	Chet Atkins

	1985	**1986**	**1987**
Entertainer	Ricky Skaggs	Reba McEntire	Hank Williams Jr.
Song	Lee Greenwood, "God Bless the USA"	Paul Overstreet, Don Schlitz, "On the Other Hand"	Paul Overstreet, Don Schlitz, "Forever and Ever, Amen"
Female Vocalist	Reba McEntire	Reba McEntire	Reba McEntire
Male Vocalist	George Strait	George Strait	Randy Travis
Album	George Strait, *Does Fort Worth Ever Cross Your Mind*	Ronnie Milsap, *Lost in the Fifties Tonight*	Randy Travis, *Always and Forever*
Single	The Judds, "Why Not Me"	Dan Seals, "Bop"	Randy Travis, "Forever and Ever, Amen"
Vocal Group	The Judds	The Judds	The Judds
Horizon Award	Sawyer Brown	Randy Travis	Holly Dunn
Vocal Duo	Anne Murray and Dave Loggins	Dan Seals and Marie Osmond	Ricky Skaggs and Sharon White
Musician	Chet Atkins	Johnny Gimble	Johnny Gimble
Music Video	Hank Williams Jr., *All My Rowdy Friends Are Comin' Over Tonight*	George Jones, *Who's Gonna Fill Their Shoes*	Hank Williams Jr., *My Name Is Bocephus*

	1988	**1989**	**1990**
Entertainer	Hank Williams Jr.	George Strait	George Strait
Song	K.T. Oslin, "80's Ladies"	Max D. Barnes, Vern Gosdin, "Chiseled in Stone"	Jon Vezner, Don Henry, "Where've You Been"
Female Vocalist	K.T. Oslin	Kathy Mattea	Kathy Mattea
Male Vocalist	Randy Travis	Ricky Van Shelton	Clint Black
Album	Hank Williams Jr., *Born to Boogie*	Nitty Gritty Dirt Band, *Will the Circle Be Unbroken, Vol. II*	Kentucky HeadHunters, *Pickin' on Nashville*
Single	Kathy Mattea, "Eighteen Wheels and a Dozen Roses"	Keith Whitley, "I'm No Stranger to the Rain"	Vince Gill, "When I Call Your Name"
Vocal Group	Highway 101	Highway 101	Kentucky HeadHunters
Vocal Event	Dolly Parton, Emmylou Harris, Linda Ronstadt, *Trio*	Hank Williams Jr., Hank Williams Sr.	Lorrie Morgan, Keith Whitley
Horizon Award	Ricky Van Shelton	Clint Black	Garth Brooks
Vocal Duo	The Judds	The Judds	The Judds
Musician	Chet Atkins	Johnny Gimble	Johnny Gimble
Music Video	—	Hank Williams Jr., Hank Williams Sr., *There's a Tear in My Beer*	Garth Brooks, *The Dance*

1991 | 1992 | 1993

	1991	1992	1993
Entertainer	Garth Brooks	Garth Brooks	Vince Gill
Song	Vince Gill, Tim DuBois, "When I Call Your Name"	Vince Gill, Max D. Barnes, "Look at Us"	Vince Gill, John Barlow Jarvis, "I Still Believe in You"
Female Vocalist	Tanya Tucker	Mary-Chapin Carpenter	Mary-Chapin Carpenter
Male Vocalist	Vince Gill	Vince Gill	Vince Gill
Album	Garth Brooks, *No Fences*	Garth Brooks, *Ropin' the Wind*	Vince Gill, *I Still Believe in You*
Single	Garth Brooks, "Friends in Low Places"	Billy Ray Cyrus, "Achy Breaky Heart"	Alan Jackson, "Chattahoochee"
Vocal Group	Kentucky HeadHunters	Diamond Rio	Diamond Rio
Vocal Event	Mark O'Connor & The New Nashville Cats (featuring Vince Gill, Ricky Skaggs, and Steve Wariner)	Marty Stuart, Travis Tritt	George Jones with Vince Gill, Mark Chesnutt, Garth Brooks, Travis Tritt, Joe Diffie, Alan Jackson, Pam Tillis, T. Graham Brown, Patty Loveless, Clint Black, *I Don't Need Your Rockin' Chair*
Horizon Award	Travis Tritt	Suzy Bogguss	Mark Chesnutt
Vocal Duo	The Judds	Brooks & Dunn	Brooks & Dunn
Musician	Mark O'Connor	Mark O'Connor	Mark O'Connor
Music Video	Garth Brooks, *The Thunder Rolls*	Alan Jackson, *Midnight in Montgomery*	Alan Jackson, *Chattahoochee*

1994 | 1995 | 1996

	1994	1995	1996
Entertainer	Vince Gill	Alan Jackson	Brooks & Dunn
Song	Alan Jackson, Jim McBride, "Chattahoochee"	Gretchen Peters, "Independence Day"	Vince Gill, "Go Rest High on That Mountain"
Female Vocalist	Pam Tillis	Alison Krauss	Patty Loveless
Male Vocalist	Vince Gill	Vince Gill	George Strait
Album	*Common Thread: The Songs of the Eagles*	Patty Loveless, *When Fallen Angels Fly*	George Strait, *Blue Clear Sky*
Single	John Michael Montgomery, "I Swear"	Alison Krauss and the Union Station, "When You Say Nothing at All"	George Strait, "Check Yes or No"
Vocal Group	Diamond Rio	The Mavericks	The Mavericks
Vocal Event	Reba McEntire with Linda Davis, "Does He Love You"	Shenandoah with Alison Krauss, "Somewhere in the Vicinity of the Heart"	Dolly Parton with Vince Gill, "I Will Always Love You"
Horizon Award	John Michael Montgomery	Alison Krauss	Bryan White
Vocal Duo	Brooks & Dunn	Brooks & Dunn	Brooks & Dunn
Musician	Mark O'Connor	Mark O'Connor	Mark O'Connor
Music Video	Martina McBride, *Independence Day*	The Tractors, *Baby Likes to Rock It*	Junior Brown, *My Wife Thinks You're Dead*

	1997	1998	1999
Entertainer	Garth Brooks	Garth Brooks	Shania Twain
Song	Matraca Berg, Gary Harrison, "Strawberry Wine"	Billy Kirsch, Steve Wariner, "Holes in the Floor of Heaven"	Annie Roboff, Robin Lerner, Beth Nielsen Chapman, "This Kiss"
Female Vocalist	Trisha Yearwood	Trisha Yearwood	Martina McBride
Male Vocalist	George Strait	George Strait	Tim McGraw
Album	George Strait, *Carrying Your Love With Me*	Tim McGraw, *Everywhere*	Tim McGraw, *A Place in the Sun*
Single	Deana Carter, "Strawberry Wine"	"Holes in the Floor of Heaven," Steve Wariner	"Wide Open Spaces," Dixie Chicks
Vocal Group	Diamond Rio	Dixie Chicks	Dixie Chicks
Vocal Event	Tim McGraw with Faith Hill, "It's Your Love"	Patty Loveless with George Jones, "You Don't Seem to Miss Me"	Vince Gill and Patty Loveless, "My Kind of Woman/My Kind of Man"
Horizon Award	LeAnn Rimes	Dixie Chicks	Jo Dee Messina
Vocal Duo	Brooks & Dunn	Brooks & Dunn	Brooks & Dunn
Musician	Brent Mason	Brent Mason	Randy Scruggs
Music Video	Kathy Mattea, *455 Rocket*	Faith Hill, *This Kiss*	Dixie Chicks, "Wide Open Spaces"

QUEENS OF COUNTRY

Critically lauded and popularly applauded, women crooners were and are fundamental to the success of country music. Here are the genre's leading ladies:

Mary Chapin Carpenter
With over 8 million albums sold worldwide, five Grammy Awards, and two CMA Awards, Carpenter is one of the preeminent singer-songwriters in the business.

Deana Carter
The child of session-guitarist extraordinaire Fred Carter Jr. sings with a frankness that transforms her music into profound poetry.

Patsy Cline
Though she was killed in a 1963 plane crash at age 30, her *Greatest Hits* went multiplatinum in 1992.

Patty Loveless
Patty's music is about emotion. She exposes her rawest nerves, bruises, and doubts for the sake of reaching the core of her songs.

Loretta Lynn
Moving to Nashville in 1961, this "coal miner's daughter" from Butcher's Hollow, Kentucky, subsequently turned out 16 No.1 singles and was immortalized on the silver screen with a 1980 film bio starring Sissy Spacek.

Tammy Wynette
A former hairdresser, Wynette topped the charts in 1968 with her now-signature songs, "D-I-V-O-R-C-E" and "Stand by Your Man." Never before or since has country music experienced such pain and heartache in one distinct voice.

Shania Twain
Critics carped when sexy, Canadian-born Twain twanged her way up the country and pop charts with her fresh fusion of rural and rock. Three Grammys and some 20 million album sales later, Twain's still laughing.

Reba McEntire
As the seller of more than 35 million records, the star of country music's greatest roadshow, and five triple platinum albums to her credit, Reba is the most successful female country star in history.

LeAnn Rimes
The Patsy Cline reincarnation was the youngest singer, at age 13, to debut in the country chart's Top 50.

Kitty Wells
Country's first major female star, she was the first woman to have a No. 1 country single in 1952, with the song "It Wasn't God Who Made Honky Tonk Angels."

Trisha Yearwood
One of music's finest interpretive vocalists, Trisha worked her way up from an intern to multiple platinum–selling albums.

PICKS & PANS 1999

It was a year of storytelling, with John le Carré, Salman Rushdie, and Thomas Harris delivering much-anticipated new works of fiction, and Monica and George revealing their own storied tales. Titles marked with an asterisk are the critics' picks of the year.

FICTION

TURN OF THE CENTURY
Kurt Andersen
The cofounder of *Spy* magazine deconstructs the New York City–centered media conglomerates of 2000. With microchip-thin characters and weak storytelling, this book is millennial mainly in the sense that centuries seem to go by while you're reading it.

GIDEON
Russell Andrews
Under the nom de plume Russell Andrews, writer-editor Peter Andrew Gethers and mystery novelist David Russell Handler serve up a saucy thriller that has some peppery fun with the literary scene.

DREAMLAND
Kevin Baker
Historical figures mingle with imaginary characters in this epic re-creation of an era. Romance and intrigue keep the plot moving briskly, but Baker shows more imagination than depth, with multiple plots and high spirits that can be a little wearying.

GIRLS' GUIDE TO HUNTING AND FISHING
Melissa Bank
Though set on swank beaches and in the glitzy Manhattan publishing scene, this funny fictional report on the dating wars is refreshingly down to earth.

LINK
Walt Becker
An irresistible sci-fi thriller that smoothly mixes Indiana Jones–style adventure with *X-Files* spookiness. Despite wordy scientific soliloquies, the awe-inspiring premise makes for a close encounter of a very cool kind.

CITY OF LIGHT
Lauren Belfer
Despite some far-fetched plot turns, this ambitious, cleanly written novel keeps the reader's attention firmly focused on its well-drawn characters' personal dramas and their struggle to save the grandeur of Niagara Falls. A suspenseful historical novel set in Buffalo in 1901.

UNTIL THE REAL THING COMES ALONG
Elizabeth Berg
Real estate agent Patty Anne Murphy is 36, single, and wants a baby more than anything, so she convinces her gay best friend to play daddy. A tough premise for any writer to pull off, but Berg is up to the challenge. Warmly told tale of off-beat motherhood.

TARA ROAD
Maeve Binchy
The Irish author of bestseller *Circle of Friends* tells the story of a woman who needs time away when her husband gets a younger girlfriend pregnant. Binchy makes us feel utterly involved, and her enormous appeal to American readers shouldn't diminish a bit with this.

THE BROKEN HEARTS CLUB
Ethan Black
A dark thriller in which a romantically bitter NYPD detective hunts down love-spurned men suspected of murdering their former mates.

DARKNESS PEERING
Alice Blanchard
What make this mystery truly haunting are Blanchard's deft portrait of a town; her blighted, dead-on characters; and the evocative style. A heartrending suspense debut.

THE ELEANOR ROOSEVELT GIRLS
Bonnie Bluh
In this funny and poignant tale, seven bosom buddies draw strength from their friendship as they navigate the decades.

THE LAW OF SIMILARS
Chris Bohjalian
A warm yet uncloying evocation of a deeply rooted Yankee community torn between old virtues and New Age remedies. Unlike his powerful novel *Midwives*, however, it ends with a disappointing whimper.

A SUDDEN CHANGE OF HEART
Barbara Taylor Bradford
A sudsy saga of two women whose lifelong friendship outlasts their marriages. The predictable plot twists and cardboard characters may not trouble fans and those who enjoy the undemanding pleasures of fantasy and bathos.

THE HOUSE THAT ATE THE HAMPTONS
James Brady
The real-life monument to excess now rising in Sagaponack, NY, a 100,000-square-foot residential monstrosity, is a subject ripe for fictionalization, but Brady proves not to be the man for the job. His muddled plot, procession of one-note characters, and New York name-dropping make a silly satire.

THE CAT WHO SAW STARS
Lilian Jackson Braun
While on vacation at Moose Lake, Jim Qwilleran and his beloved Siamese cats, Koko and Yum Yum, dig up a dead backpacker and stumble into a somewhat jumbled—but thoroughly entertaining—murder mystery.

CAT ON THE SCENT
Rita Mae Brown and Sneaky Pie Brown
Intrepid cats Mrs. Murphy and Pewter—with interspecies cooperation from Tucker, a corgi—uncover evidence, solve a murder, and stage a rescue. Too precious at times but ultimately charming.

*LITTLE GREEN MEN
Christopher Buckley
Imagine *Independence Day* as rewritten by H. L. Mencken and you've got this hilarious novel by the author of *Thank You for Smoking*. Close encounter of the funniest kind.

IN THE DRINK
Kate Christensen
In this wry first novel, a boozy female ghostwriter stumbles into pricey bars and bad sex in glamour-choked New York City.

WE'LL MEET AGAIN
Mary Higgins Clark
The bestselling author returns with a knuckle-biting mystery about murder, suicide, revenge, and other low deeds among the swells of Greenwich, Connecticut.

DANGEROUS KISS
Jackie Collins
In this winning sequel, Lucky Santangelo, who has starred in four of Collins's 17 bestsellers, is ready to give up her career until teenage thugs kill her half-brother's wife and shoot her husband.

*ANGELS FLIGHT
Michael Connelly
Harry Bosch investigates the murder of an attorney who represents alleged victims of police brutality. Compelling reading, though not with quite the haunting power of the author's previous *Blood Work*.

BLACK NOTICE
Patricia Cornwell
Although the plot never achieves the flash point of last year's *Point of Origin*, its intriguing premise, notably restrained writing, and the promise of a new romance for forensic pathologist Kay Scarpetta make this hair-raising tale worthy of attention.

SOUTHERN CROSS
Patricia Cornwell
The second installment of her new police series puts laughs ahead of logic. Cornwell has done better.

L.A. REQUIEM
Robert Crais
Elvis Cole and Joe Pike are challenged as never before when Pike's former lover is murdered and the ex-cop is now suspected, by an LAPD investigator who hates him, of killing her. A whodunit with salsa and soul.

THE TRIALS OF NIKKI HILL
Christopher Darden and Dick Lochte
A high-profile crime. A celebrity defendant. An earnest young deputy district attorney. Though he stretches the limits of credibility, O.J.'s prosecutor proves to be a very entertaining author.

THE EXPERIMENT
John Darnton
This sizzling technocaper can take a ghoulish turn at times, but *The Experiment* bubbles along with nary a mistake.

IRIS RAINER DART

WHEN I FALL IN LOVE

By the bestselling author of BEACHES

*WHEN I FALL IN LOVE
Iris Rainer Dart
Quick pacing, economically sketched characters, and some genuinely amusing jokes allow readers to overcome the gooey message about loving a guy for "his perfect and beautiful soul," not his damaged body. A guilty pleasure by the author of *Beaches*.

LAKE NEWS
Barbara Delinsky
From the author of Coast Road— the engaging tale of a cabaret singer who retreats to her small hometown after being accused of romancing a cardinal.

SISTER OF MY HEART
Chitra Banerjee Divakaruni
Award-winning author of 1997's bestselling *The Mistress of Spices* offers an irresistible novel about two Indian cousins, bound forever by their special entrance into the world, who find their love tested.

CAT IN AN INDIGO MOOD
Carole Nelson Douglas
Feline P.I. Midnight Louie prowls the alleys of Las Vegas, solving crimes and romancing runaways like a furry Sam Spade. This time out, his quick-thinking daughter, Midnight Louise, lends a paw as the always engaging Louie stalks a serial killer.

GLAMORAMA
Bret Easton Ellis
This satire of an actor-model in Manhattan is initially clever and the observations wicked fun, but it lurches into a ridiculous, gory, and tiresome Euro-anarchist terror plot.

JUNETEENTH
Ralph Ellison
Left unfinished at Ellison's death, to be later edited and assembled by John F. Callahan, this novel begins in the 1950s, when a racist senator is shot and the preacher who raised him is summoned to his bedside. This successor to *Invisible Man* combines the beauty of a lyric poem with the soaring force of a sermon.

*HIGH FIVE
Janet Evanovich
In this fifth comic thriller featuring Stephanie Plum, the sassy hero is drawn into a crime involving bank-account skimming and some body parts in a garbage bag. Steph has a spunky, earthy appeal—like a hot dog at the beach with a few grains of sand.

OTHERWISE ENGAGED
Suzanne Finnamore
This amusing debut novel is a spare, comic tale of prenuptial jitters. Unfortunately, it never transcends protagonist Eve's commitment worries.

WHITE OLEANDER
Janet Fitch

Adolescent girls with unstable mothers are a familiar theme in fiction today, but there's nothing derivative about this overnight bestseller. First-time novelist Fitch is overly fond of bad similes and contrived poet-speak, but this book will seduce you.

THE KIND I'M LIKELY TO GET
Ken Foster

From a divorced bookstore clerk to a drug dealer for movie stars, the characters in this collection grapple, ineptly and often amusingly, with their baroque, twisted fates.

WHY NOT ME?: THE INSIDE STORY OF THE MAKING AND UNMAKING OF THE FRANKEN PRESIDENCY
Al Franken

The former *Saturday Night Live* writer, one of our savviest satirists, chronicles his own fanciful bid for the White House in 2000, with hilarious spoofs of campaign ads, memos, news clips, and the candidate's diary.

*KILLING ME SOFTLY
Nicci French

A research scientist has increasingly dark suspicions about her mountain-climbing mystery man in this story of peak psychological suspense. Sleek prose and convincing characters make for a compulsive read.

SOAP OPERA
Eileen Fulton

The actor who played As The World Turns's Lisa Miller for forty years puts her dramatic experience to delightfully entertaining use in her first romance novel, set on the fictional soap Another Life.

THE TESSERACT
Alex Garland

This story, which examines how easily the connections between people can be broken, lacks the shock value of *The Beach*, but Garland's skill at creating tension drives this mature, intelligent, and rewarding novel forward with the force of a thriller.

VITA NOVA
Louise Glück

In her best book since winning the Pulitzer Prize six years ago, Glück explores that terrible interval between the loss of a love and the stirrings of new life and new emotions.

EVENSONG
Gail Godwin

A sequel to 1991's *Father Melancholy's Daughter*, *Evensong* is thoughtful, deliberately paced, and meticulous in its attentions to the subtleties of character and the meaning of religious faith.

THE WHITE BONE
Barbara Gowdy

Told from the point of view of three pachyderms struggling to survive in drought-stricken, hunter-ridden Africa, this captivating novel portrays elephants who have complex relationships and petty squabbles just like people.

THE GAZEBO
Emily Grayson

Two lovers torn apart by family duties as teens reunite every May 27 for 50 years—as friends—at the town gazebo. The story is often touching, but it's hard to warm up to characters who seem so determined to be martyrs and leave us feeling so manipulated.

THE TESTAMENT
John Grisham

The story of an old business tycoon, his six greedy heirs, and the lawyers eager to carve up his $11 billion estate comes to life with engagingly crooked characters and juicy legal twists, but it lacks the tautness and intrigue of earlier bestsellers.

SUCH A PRETTY, PRETTY GIRL
Winston Groom

A woman who's not very good at relationships enlists her ex-boyfriend to find the man who's blackmailing her. The author of *Forrest Gump* has created a masterfully suspenseful tale, but don't expect to feel good.

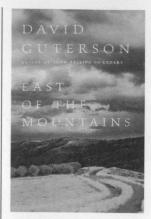

EAST OF THE MOUNTAINS
David Guterson

A man with terminal cancer prepares to commit suicide but reconsiders due to unexpected events. Lacks the underlying drama and social commentary that energized 1995's *Snow Falling on Cedars*, but it's just right if you're in the mood for lyrical images.

THE POYSON GARDEN
Karen Harper

This novel finds Queen-to-be Elizabeth Tudor in a web of romantic and murderous intrigue, set long before her *Shakespeare in Love* heyday.

HANNIBAL
Thomas Harris

This long-awaited sequel to The Silence of the Lambs, which was as deep and disturbing a thriller as has ever been written, is a truly scary book; it's just not the kind of five-star fare its demon, erudite flesh-eater Hannibal Lector deserves.

MOTHER OF PEARL
Melinda Haynes

Touches on all the themes that Oprah Winfrey delights in, but other readers may find themselves less enchanted by the novel's implausible characters, preposterous dialogue, and overwrought prose style. Turgid melodrama of smalltown Southern life.

*SIS BOOM BAH
Jane Heller
Two sisters, whose feelings for each other are beyond contempt, fall for their mother's cardiologist and become prime suspects when he is murdered. Heller, with a breezy, lighthearted touch and an ironic sense of humor, concocts another delightful summer read.

TRUE AT FIRST LIGHT: A FICTIONAL MEMOIR
Ernest Hemingway
This absorbing but hardly profound account of Hemingway's life in Kenya in the early 1950s was reconstituted by his son Patrick from a longer manuscript. Not the master's best, but still the master's.

*EMPRESS OF THE SPLENDID SEASON
Oscar Hijuelos
Lydia Espana cleans the homes of affluent New Yorkers but clings proudly to memories of her privileged childhood in Cuba. In this simply splendid novel, Hijuelos lovingly suggests that true beauty lies in the small moments of a "decent, genteel, low-key" life.

*ASHES TO ASHES
Tami Hoag
FBI profiler John Quinn and victims' advocate Kate Conlan try to push aside an old animus and focus on a serial killer who gets wilier with each murder. This smoldering mystery demonstrates why Hoag is one of the hottest names in the suspense game.

LOCAL GIRLS
Alice Hoffman
From the author of Practical Magic, a series of stories on how four Long Island, New York, women—mother, daughter, daughter's cousin, and friend—navigate family bonds, binds, and betrayals.

MUSIC FOR TORCHING
A. M. Homes
A haunting tale of suburban ennui. It's no small achievement that the author of the controversial (and similarly disturbing) *In a Country of Mothers* manages to portray this blighted couple as people more to be pitied than loathed.

A CERTAIN AGE
Tama Janowitz
Queen of the '80s literary brat pack reemerges with a trenchant novel about urban (bad) manners in the '90s. Though the premise wears thin, her story amuses to the end.

ABUNDANTLY SIMPLE
Helen Kafka and Laura Hellen
You'd expect this parody of Simple Abundance—that annoying 1995 collection of homespun homilies—to be satisfyingly sardonic, but most of these pseudo-journal entries come off as unfunny, insulting, or just plain sick.

THE PRODIGAL SPY
Joseph Kanon
The latest political thriller from a publishing executive reheats the Cold War with history, mystery, and a blast from the political past. Kanon's witty, tense, and vivid prose cements the reputation he built with *Los Alamos*.

NO ONE YOU KNOW
Bruce Eric Kaplan
Droll, sharp-eyed cartoons, mostly from *The New Yorker*, about couples, kids, and the absurdities they create, by a former writer for *Seinfeld*.

A NEW SONG
Jan Karon
Karon has downsized Father Tim Kavanagh, the mainstay of four previous bestselling novels, and abandoned the charming small town of Mitford, North Carolina. This shift in locale benefits no one.

*HART'S WAR
John Katzenbach
When the only African-American in a WWII German prison camp is arrested for murdering a belligerent racist, Tommy Hart must defend the black flier against growing odds. Electrifying courtroom drama framed by a fascinating chapter of history.

TRUMPET
Jackie Kay
In this captivating first novel, the celebrated Scottish poet echoes the true story of American pianist

Billy Tipton with the story of jazzman Joss Moody, who is discovered by his mortician to be a woman.

ME, BY JIMMY (BIG BOY) VALENTE
Garrison Keillor
A satire of Minnesota governor Jesse "the Body" Ventura. But satire requires knowledge, and Keillor knows neither Ventura's old profession, wrestling, nor his new one, politics, and it seems that he's not above lifting old *SNL* bits, either.

*JUPITER'S BONES
Faye Kellerman
Though this is Kellerman's eleventh Peter Decker/Rina Lazarus novel, it doesn't disappoint. Mystery shrouded in skin-crawling suspense.

*BILLY STRAIGHT
Jonathan Kellerman
Petra Connor must solve the murder of the former wife of a football-player-turned-TV-star and protect the homeless twelve-year-old boy who witnessed it. A first-rate thriller.

THE SECOND ANGEL
Philip Kerr
In 2069, Earth has been ravaged by a devastating virus for which the only cure is a complete transfusion of uninfected blood. Kerr backs up his plot with plenty of science, but anemic characters and lengthy footnotes slowly drain the life from this would-be thriller.

LUCY SULLIVAN IS GETTING MARRIED
Marion Keyes
This simple tale of looking for Mr. Right has a distinctly unsophisticated feel to it and all the nuance of an after-school special.

THE GIRL WHO LOVED TOM GORDON
Stephen King
Our top yarn-spinner serves up an absorbing tale about a 9-year-old girl who gets lost in the Maine woods, where she is stalked by some fiendish creature and hallucinates about meeting her idol, Boston Red Sox relief pitcher Tom "Flash" Gordon.

*HUNTING DOWN AMANDA
Andrew Klavan

Plucky characters, gut-churning danger, and a gifted little girl are at the heart of this brilliantly conceived page-turner. A smart, gritty thriller.

SEIZE THE NIGHT
Dean Koontz

In this sequel to the popular *Fear Nothing*, Christopher Snow gets caught up in some hellish interspecies genetic experiments and kidnapping. The plot is ludicrous, but this kind of suspense will raise goosebumps on your goosebumps.

THE SABBATHDAY RIVER
Jean Hanff Korelitz

Well-meaning but unconvincing suspense tale of a left-wing New Yorker who struggles to fit into a conservative New Hampshire town and becomes even more estranged upon discovering an infant's corpse in a nearby river.

COLD HEART
Lynda La Plante

This devious, miniseries-ready mystery has come up with a match for *Prime Suspect*'s memorable detective Jane Tennison in the tough but vulnerable Lorraine Page. La Plante's clinches may leave you lukewarm, but her plotting sizzles.

SINGLE & SINGLE
John le Carré

Le Carré reveals a world at once deeply disquieting and oddly reassuring in this story of a son who betrays his father then repents his treason, spending the second half of the book in action-hero mode. Where's the fun in that? This is far from his finest.

*PRAYERS FOR RAIN
Dennis Lehane

In the fifth mystery of a celebrated series, the author of *Gone, Baby, Gone* shows a gift for stringing out scenes and creating tension as a Boston PI puzzles his way toward a sadistic killer.

*BE COOL
Elmore Leonard

This new novel with Chili Palmer, the Miami Beach shylock seen in the 1995 film *Get Shorty*, murders the competition with its spot-on detail about the music business, language sharp enough to mince a coconut, and real heat between believable men and women.

JOINING
Johanna Lindsey

In her 35th romance novel—the first 34 have been *New York Times* bestsellers—Lindsey again creates intriguing characters and weaves mini history lessons into her storytelling. An entertaining read.

AMSTERDAM
Ian McEwan

Two friends make a pact that if either one should deteriorate, the other will swiftly and painlessly end his suffering while dignity remains. This stylishly entertaining farce, recipient of the Booker Prize, is flawlessly executed.

PSI/NET
Rob MacGregor and Billy Dee Williams

Psychic espionage thriller about a former agent in a CIA-sponsored program to use telepathy and telekinesis to attack foreign enemies. Despite its sprightly pace and credible dialogue, the novel just doesn't add up—too many coincidences and too much hocus-pocus.

*DUANE'S DEPRESSED
Larry McMurtry

The hero struggles with depression in this picture-perfect final novel of the Duane Moore trilogy. In bare and beautiful prose, McMurtry makes his characters our friends and their crises our own.

NIGHT WHISPERS
Judith McNaught

A fast-paced romantic thriller in which a small-town Florida policewoman investigates her tony Palm Beach relatives.

NEUROTICA
Sue Margolis

Anna Shapiro embarks on a shagathon as she tries to decide between mind-blowing sex and marriage to a husband with whom she hasn't felt the earth move in three years. Can be wickedly funny, but veers into kinky subplots she should have left alone.

THE DROWNING PEOPLE
Richard Mason

He seems to have cribbed his plotlines from *Victorian Novels for Dummies*. Amid much brooding on love, loss, and windswept-castle maintenance, various people die of unnatural plot twists—Mason is lucky his characters don't sue him for inducing logic whiplash.

*SPLIT IMAGE
Judy Mercer

Ariel Gold, the spunky reporter-sleuth who starred in Mercer's *Double Take* and *Fast Forward*, gets caught in a cunning game of truth or consequences that keeps you guessing until the final pages.

WHILE I WAS GONE
Sue Miller

Jo Becker contemplates an affair with a man who has a chilling secret. A love story with brains and a gripping plot, it raises fascinating questions about identity and forgiveness.

CRY DANCE
Kirk Mitchell

In the series opener of this exciting new competitor for the best-selling Jim Chee–Joe Leaphorn

Navajo mysteries, Bureau of Indian Affairs agent Emmett Parker is called to investigate after a body is found at a remote outpost in the Grand Canyon.

BASILICA
William D. Montalbano
No ordinary whodunit, this mystery—in which a former Miami homicide cop investigates a murder in the Vatican sometime in the near future—explores conscience as well as crime.

THE LUST LIZARD OF MELANCHOLY COVE
Christopher Moore
Moore's fifth novel is a funny tale about psychopharmaceuticals, a sea monster, and "l'amour" in a nutty California town.

BLUE LIGHT
Walter Mosley
Crime-fiction master Mosley turns a large cast, fantastic elements, biblical allusions, and talk of Thucydides into an abstract sci-fi novel about community and identity. Though it's engaging, this tale fails to shine.

THE LOVE OF A GOOD WOMAN
Alice Munro
In these eight jewellike stories, the grande dame of Canadian fiction explores love, passion, and the surprising paths that emerge from both.

THE LONG SANDY HAIR OF NEFTOON ZAMORA
Michael Nesmith
A former Monkee's debut novel, in which a musician is on a quest to confirm the existence of a legendary New Mexican character. Apart from an ace vocabulary and some dazzling Joycean flashbacks, Nesmith's prose is dull, dull, dull.

HUSH MONEY
Robert B. Parker
In the 26th Spenser mystery, the popular Boston PI courts danger when he agrees to take on two cases for loved ones.

SMOKE SCREEN
Vincent Patrick
A twisting, expertly crafted thriller in which a high-stakes jewel theft

gone wrong is actually the first stage in an even more complex struggle against a political terrorist with a deadly secret.

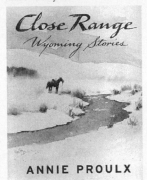

CLOSE RANGE: WYOMING STORIES
Annie Proulx
In 11 powerful stories, Proulx, who won the 1994 Pulitzer Prize for *The Shipping News*, rips away our romantic notions of the West and asks how capable any of us are of outrunning our origins. Her fatalistic answer adds up to some breathtaking reading.

I THEE WED
Amanda Quick
In this 15th tale from Jayne Ann Krentz's alter ego, a lady evades a villain's potion by aiding his would-be captor.

COME TOGETHER
Emlyn Rees and Josie Lloyd
Commitment-averse Jack meets nice girl Amy and is transformed into a sensitive guy. Chapters alternate between Amy's point of view (written by Lloyd with deft British wit) and Jack's (Rees's jarring look at the single-male psyche). Page-turning fun.

DEATH DU JOUR
Kathy Reichs
A forensic anthropologist examines the corpses found at a torched Quebec farmhouse. As in her knockout 1997 debut, *Déjà Dead*, forensics expert Reichs spins an atmospheric, suspensefully paced yarn. Bone-chilling prime crime.

VITTORIO THE VAMPIRE
Anne Rice
Alas, this teenage vampire's story reads too much like a dime-store bodice-ripper crossed with a low-budget horror flick. Though we are well bathed in the Italian Renaissance atmosphere and devilish details, neither frills nor tricks can rescue this tedious tale.

CLOUD NINE
Luanne Rice
From the author of *Crazy in Love,* a novel about a woman whose brush with death awakens her to an entirely new life.

THE MIDNIGHT HOUR
Karen Robards
A tale of stalking and romantic intrigue set in a placid Ohio suburb, from the bestselling author of *Hunter's Moon* and *The Senator's Wife.*

THE GROUND BENEATH HER FEET
Salman Rushdie
This engaging yet unsatisfying and gruelingly uninvolving novel variously suggests Norman Mailer, Harold Robbins, the Greek myth of Orpheus, and the kind of pop novel Stephen King might write if he abandoned the horror business.

THE HANDYMAN
Carolyn See
This charming, often hilarious novel whisks us back to the time before Bob Hampton became a renowned painter, when his job as an L.A. handyman had him repairing and rearranging the lives of everyone around him.

WELCOME TO PARADISE
Laurence Shames
From the author of *Mangrove Squeeze,* a darkly comic tale of vacationing Mafiosi and the havoc they wreak in Key West.

A CELIBATE SEASON
Carol Shields and Blanche Howard
Two friends team up to craft a poignant epistolary tale about a couple who learn the limits of their marriage during a 10-month separation.

THE MARCHING SEASON
Daniel Silva
The spy-fiction ace unspools his latest thriller amid the tangled and bloody conflicts of Northern Ireland.

JACKSTRAWS
Charles Simic
A master of the surreal, Simic packs his poems full of horror movies, bleak jokes, savage ironies, and the things an insomniac notices on the ceiling

*I LEFT MY BACK DOOR OPEN
April Sinclair
This entertaining tale about an overweight incest survivor who's looking for love is light and quick and packed with enough issues to keep a daytime talk-show host busy. Readers who can withstand the clichés about a good man being hard to find will enjoy it.

HAVANA BAY
Martin Cruz Smith
Though engrossing, this police procedural, which brings back the cohero of *Gorky Park*, gets bogged down by too many characters, too much untranslated Spanish dialogue, and too much convoluted subplot.

RUN CATCH KISS
Amy Sohn
Paralleling the life of its young author, an ex-sex columnist in New York City, this wry novel details the exploits of a recent college grad who finds her bliss as—surprise!—a sex columnist.

*GRANNY DAN
Danielle Steel
An unnamed narrator discovers that her deceased grandmother was a prima ballerina who fell in love with the czar's family doctor on the eve of the Russian Revolution. Despite its lack of realism, even Lenin would be touched.

THE FIRES
René Steinke
Already snapped up by aspiring movie producer Madonna, this debut novel generates lots of heat with its story of a woman, once disfigured in a fire, with a compulsive need to set blazes.

AMY AND ISABELLE
Elizabeth Strout
First-time novelist's moving story of bashful women who open up to love. Strout, whose style has been compared to Anne Tyler's and Alice Hoffman's, writes with abundant warmth, illustrating how a tragedy can be just what folks need to thaw their hearts.

ACT OF REVENGE
Robert K. Tanenbaum
In their 11th adventure, the gunslinging Karps race to solve four murders before their 12-year-old daughter gets caught in the crossfire.

*FACE-TIME
Erik Tarloff
A thought-provoking and entertaining piece of political fiction, by turns psychodrama and meditation on the allure of power. Insightful, well-crafted tale of inside-the-beltway cuckoldry in the White House.

BLUE BLOOD
Pamela Thomas-Graham
When the wife of a white college buddy is murdered, the cops think that one of Nicci Chase's black male students did it. Chase, a black Harvard professor, thinks she knows better. Loaded with familiar social commentary, this formulaic saga stalls as coincidence too often substitutes for craft.

THE TRAVELLING HORN PLAYER
Barbara Trapido
A woman's death exposes the lives of everyone she knew in this novel by a British author called a "latter-day Jane Austen."

OTHER PEOPLE'S CHILDREN
Joanna Trollope
The popular British author portrays the tangled lives and emotions of two families forced together when a couple try marriage for the second time.

THE BEST AMERICAN SHORT STORIES OF THE CENTURY
Edited by John Updike and Katrina Kenison
Lorrie Moore and Annie Proulx join the select company of Ernest Hemingway and F. Scott Fitzgerald in this collection of 55 masterful short takes.

BAGOMBO SNUFF BOX
Kurt Vonnegut
Though there are some clunkers in this collection of 23 irony-drenched short stories first published in the '50s—lines that sound painfully naive; a cranky and humorless epilogue—it's, all in all, a good showing.

*THE BREAKER
Minette Walters
In this tantalizing psychological thriller, Nick Ingram must solve a homicide while distracted by a witness, someone for whom he's long had an unrequited crush. Gives the English village mystery a fine new spin.

GETTING OVER JOHN DOE
Suzanne Yalof
Think you've met the perfect guy? A *Glamour* editor recounts her own ill-fated quest in this slim, stylishly illustrated satire.

NONFICTION

WEAR CLEAN UNDERWEAR: BUSINESS WISDOM FROM MOM
Rhonda Abrams
Abrams spouts irritatingly folksy advice for corporate managers, but there are some fascinating profiles of companies that have played nice and reaped rewards.

BARKITECTURE
Fred Albert
A photographic look at state-of-the-arf doghouses that will leave you panting for more.

SALINGER: A BIOGRAPHY
Paul Alexander
Slim pickings bio of America's most famous literary hermit. Since those close to Salinger have all clammed up, you won't learn anything important here.

AHS GREAT PLANT GUIDE
American Horticultural Society
This fact-crammed guide to more than 2,000 plants is small enough to fit in a big pocket.

BILL AND HILLARY: THE MARRIAGE
Christopher Andersen
Andersen, clearly no fan of the First Couple, seizes on sleaze too much and with too little attribution. Titillating, perhaps, but in the end the book is merely banal, as the mystery of what keeps Bill and Hillary together remains largely unanswered.

*WOMAN: AN INTIMATE GEOGRAPHY
Natalie Angier
With a true passion for science and a poet's linguistic flair, Pulitzer-winning *New York Times* reporter Angier offers surprising and fascinating tidbits in this lively dissection of womanhood.

RED FLAGS! HOW TO KNOW WHEN YOU'RE DATING A LOSER
Gary S. Aumiller and Daniel A. Goldfarb
Here's a concept! Within three dates, you can use the telltale signs provided here by FBI consultants to see if your guy is one of 25 loser types. Once the perp is on your most-unwanted list, dump him by following the technique specific to his type.

THE GOOD BLACK
Paul M. Barrett
A tense, true story about an ambitious African-American lawyer who files a discrimination suit when his career goes awry.

THE ART OF MEHNDI
Sumita Batra with Liz Wilde
The latest fashion fad, Mehndi is the centuries-old practice in India of applying temporary henna tattoos. The painter of choice for many celebs shares history and how-to guidance on applying the tattoos at home.

JOY SCHTICK
Joy Behar
This collection of essays and "random thoughts" by the stand-up member of ABC's talk show *The View* reads like a tryout of comic material, hastily thrown together and carelessly edited.

UFOS, JFK, AND ELVIS
Richard Belzer
Belzer embraces so many explanations of JFK's assassination that his cockeyed thesis seems to be: Have it your way—just don't believe anything the government tells you.

LOVE OF GOLDENS
Edited by Todd R. Berger
This anthology of stories and glowing photographs pays tribute to golden retrievers.

MAY I KISS YOU ON THE LIPS, MISS SANDRA?
Sandra Bernhard
In this collection of musings and poems, the comedian has traded in her signature spitefulness for a calm and centered spirituality. She weaves in a message of love, truth,

patience, and, yes, kindness, without sounding sappy.

THE 50 FUNNIEST MOVIES OF ALL TIME
Kathryn Bernheimer
The writing of Denver critic Bernheimer is all too dry, but the best part of books such as these is that they serve as starting points for good arguments. Let the popcorn fly. Good fun, but how could she possibly have overlooked…?

BOUND BY HONOR
Bill Bonanno
Salvatore "Bill" Bonanno—whose father, Joe "Bananas," was reputedly the model for Mario Puzo's Don Corleone—delivers a fascinating first-hand account of what it's like to be born into the Mafia.

VALUES OF THE GAME
Bill Bradley
The former U.S. senator and basketball Hall of Famer offers some slamdunk life lessons in teamwork and character.

LOVE LESSONS: TWELVE REAL-LIFE LOVE STORIES
Lois Smith Brady
Even cynics might be charmed by these tales, but the stories become boring when overplayed and peppered with trite truisms from *New York Times* wedding columnist Brady.

*THE EMPERORS OF CHOCOLATE: INSIDE THE SECRET WORLD OF HERSHEY AND MARS
Joël Glenn Brenner
A former *Washington Post* reporter

offers a remarkable new look at two of the world's largest candy kingdoms and the eccentric visionaries who built them up.

INDIANA GOTHIC
Pope Brock

Brock uncovers his upstanding family's big secret: that his great-grandfather was shockingly murdered.

ALLEGORY OF THE SUPERMARKET
Stephanie Brown

In witty poems like "I Was a Phony Baloney!" and "Marriage," Brown's tart insights show that humor can sting as well as beguile.

THE SWEET POTATO QUEENS' BOOK OF LOVE
Jill Conner Browne

Yet another bevy of warm-hearted, tough-minded Southern belles to follow Rebecca Well's *Ya-Ya Sisterhood*. Some will be inspired by the quick wit and high spirits in this collection of advice, but others may feel a bit wearied by all this blue-eyed Southern soul.

BARBECUE AMERICA
Rick Browne and Jack Bettridge

There are exotic recipes, great tips, fascinating glimpses into the mania of barbecue nuts, and photos that all but drip off the page in this awesome homage to backyard cuisine.

I'M A STRANGER HERE MYSELF
Bill Bryson

The bestselling author of *A Walk in the Woods*, an Iowan who moved back to America after 20 years in England, is funnier than almost anyone on either side of the pond. This collection of Bryson's newspaper columns explains his new life in New Hampshire to the British.

A SHORT HISTORY OF RUDENESS
Mark Caldwell

To literary critic Caldwell, this is the Age of the Breakdown of Common Courtesy. While his book admirably calls attention to a troubling aspect of the American culture, it does so with surprisingly little passion. Too nice, waffling analysis of a worrisome trend.

NOTE FOUND IN A BOTTLE: MY LIFE AS A DRINKER
Susan Cheever

Cheever is unable to convey the emotional and physical price she paid for sipping too many martinis as she focuses on recounting her numerous relationships rather than her drinking problem.

EDUCATING ESME
Esmé Raji Codell

The often hilarious diary of a newly minted fifth-grade teacher's struggles against student apathy and bureaucratic red tape.

ONE YEAR OFF: LEAVING IT ALL BEHIND FOR A ROUND-THE-WORLD JOURNEY WITH OUR CHILDREN
David Elliot Cohen

Oh, no, not another book about some guy's midlife crisis. Wrong. Cohen set off on a voyage of self-discovery with his wife and three children, and he got a pretty entertaining book out of it, compiled from e-mails sent regularly to friends back home in California.

THE ART OF HAPPINESS
His Holiness the Dalai Lama and Howard C. Cutler, M.D.

The spiritual leader of the Tibetan people and a psychiatrist share a joyous, life-affirming philosophy.

FROM MOTHER GOOSE TO DR. SEUSS: CHILDREN'S BOOK COVERS, 1860–1960
Harold Darling

These 250 colorful examples of book covers will delight any parent who has ever picked out a volume for a child.

IN THE WINGS
Diana Douglas Darrid

In this frank yet soft-hearted memoir, Diana Douglas Darrid shines the light on her first husband, Kirk Douglas; their first son, Michael; and her beloved second husband, writer and producer Bill Darrid. But the drama wears thin in this front-row seat.

COWBOY: A LOVE STORY
Sara Davidson

A divorced mother approaching 50, Davidson meets a chap who seems a very unlikely partner for a supersophisticated L.A. TV writer. She executes what is a rather cheesy concept for a book with intelligence, candor, and humor.

DON'T KNOW MUCH ABOUT THE BIBLE
Kenneth C. Davis

Davis again shows a knack for making esoteric ideas understandable. Reading him is like returning to the classroom of the best teacher you ever had.

LOVE, ELLEN: A MOTHER/DAUGHTER JOURNEY
Betty DeGeneres

Granted, this national spokeswoman for parental acceptance of gay children is famous because her daughter is the first star of a network series to come out of the closet, but her story is worthwhile, and instructive for parents with similar issues.

THE PROMISE OF SLEEP
Dr. William C. Dement, with Christopher Vaughan

An expert in sleep therapy traces the connection between restful nights and healthy days.

LAST SUPPERS
James L. Dickerson

Celebrities reveal what they would choose for their last meal if the world were to end tomorrow. While some readers may find the exercise tasteless and some of the dishes cheesy, most will relish the book's enticing recipes.

MADELEINE ALBRIGHT: A TWENTIETH-CENTURY ODYSSEY
Michael Dobbs
In this inspiring biography, *Washington Post* reporter Dobbs offers an intimate look at Madeleine Albright's journey from poor refugee to our first female Secretary of State.

ON THE BUS WITH ROSA PARKS
Rita Dove
The former U.S. poet laureate, best known for *Thomas and Beulah,* movingly honors the woman who set off a civil rights revolution when she refused to move to the back of a Montgomery, Alabama, bus in 1955.

THIS OLD FARM: A TREASURY OF FAMILY FARM MEMORIES
Edited by Michael Dregni
This touching, nostalgic album of rural Americana includes photographs, advertisements, paintings, essays, and recollections that are vivid enough to draw in the most citified of city slickers.

*SCARS OF SWEET PARADISE: THE LIFE AND TIMES OF JANIS JOPLIN
Alice Echols
Historian Echols presents over 100 interviews with the singer's friends and acquaintances, offering information and insight into a generation's cultural upheaval, the price it exacted, and the carving out of a legend's niche in history.

MOON: THE LIFE AND DEATH OF A ROCK LEGEND
Tony Fletcher
In the skilled hands of a British-born music journalist, this richly anecdotal biography of The Who's notorious drummer is a terrific read, despite flaws.

FAREWELL: A MEMOIR OF A TEXAS CHILDHOOD
Horton Foote
Reminscences of Depression-era Texas by a playwright and veteran screenwriter of Oscar-winning scripts for *To Kill a Mockingbird, The Trip to Bountiful,* and *Tender Mercies.* Hollywood writer's tedium vitae.

MADE FOR THE SHADE
Judy Glattstein
Here are a bunch of ways in which the artful deployment of shrubs, flowers and ferns can bring life and contrasting color to pretty places where the sun is stingy.

BALANCING ACT
Martin Gottfried
There is a story to tell about Angela Lansbury, but author Gottfried, drama critic for the *New York Law Journal,* doesn't seem up to the job. This authorized biography is tediously written.

OUR KIND OF PEOPLE
Lawrence Otis Graham
Debutante balls. Arranged marriages. The obsession with "good" hair. Graham (author of *Member of the Club*) offers an insider's view of the black upper class.

THE NICHOLAS EFFECT: A BOY'S GIFT TO THE WORLD
Reg Green
When Nicholas Green was murdered by highway robbers, his parents donated his organs to save five lives. In this affecting memoir, the boy's father, a journalist, shows what it's like to go from an ordinary family of four to international advocates for organ donation.

THE HUNGRY OCEAN
Linda Greenlaw
The Perfect Storm may have thrilled you, but in this New England sea captain's taut, funny memoir, it's another day at the office.

*PLAYING FOR KEEPS: MICHAEL JORDAN AND THE WORLD HE MADE
David Halberstam
A thoughtful and fascinating study of Jordan's far-reaching impact on American culture. Halberstam the historian can be windy, but his illuminating insights condense into a surprisingly fresh portrait.

GO FOR THE GOAL
Mia Hamm
From the star of the charming U.S. squad that won the Women's World Cup, this is must reading for any girl (or boy, for that matter) serious about soccer. A mix of aphorisms, no-nonsense advice, and instructional tips, Hamm's authoritative insights mirror her wholesome, hardworking image. She shoots, she scores.

THEY CAN'T HIDE US ANYMORE
Richie Havens with Steve Davidowitz
Once the opening act at Woodstock, folksinger Richie Havens writes tales of the people he met in New York City during the 1960s. Despite the nostalgic appeal, he grows wearisome fast.

REBELS IN WHITE GLOVES: COMING OF AGE WITH HILLARY'S CLASS— WELLESLEY '69
Miriam Horn
Familiar but engaging tales of coming of age in the 1960s with Hillary Rodham's college class.

BRAVE DAMES AND WIMPETTES
Susan Isaacs
Engaging analysis of women's roles and images on page and screen.

GARCIA: AN AMERICAN LIFE
Blair Jackson
This reverential biography of Jerry Garcia, the leader of the iconic '60s rock band the Grateful Dead, lionizes its subject in a wealth of detail, including an almost note-by-note history of the band.

ALL I NEED TO KNOW IN LIFE I LEARNED FROM ROMANCE NOVELS
Victoria M. Johnson
Finally, a self-help book that reveals how an ordinary person can achieve all the heat, passion, and moral fervor of a dime-store novel. Really.

NASHVILLE WIVES
Mrs. George Jones and Tom Carter
Interviews with the wives of Garth Brooks, Billy Ray Cyrus, Kenny Rogers, Glen Campbell, and a dozen other Nashville stars. There's too much standing by their men, not enough insight.

ROLLING STONE: THE '70S
Edited by Ashley Kahn, Holly George-Warren, Shawn Dahl
Original and vintage essays and illustrations recapture the decade that gave us Watergate, disco, and Star Wars, and continues to exert a strong hold.

*HOUSE BROKEN
Richard Karn with George Mair
The man who plays Al Borland on the TV sitcom *Home Improvement* describes his real-life experiences remodeling his Hollywood hacienda in this nicely constructed memoir and how-to guide.

CLARA: THE EARLY YEARS
Margo Kaufman
With charm and ample wit, journalist Kaufman counts the ways a demanding, 12-pound glossy black pug with Bette Davis eyes taught her how to be a mother.

GOLDEN BOY: THE FAME, MONEY, AND MYSTERY OF OSCAR DE LA HOYA
Tim Kawakami
Kawakami, a sportswriter for the *Los Angeles Times*, writes a 320-page valentine disguised as a sports biography to welterweight boxing champ Oscar De La Hoya.

LEARNING TO FLY TRAPEZE—REFLECTIONS ON FEAR, TRUST, AND THE JOY OF LETTING GO
Sam Keen
This invigorating memoir by the author of the 1991 bestseller *Fire in the Belly* lays on the spiritualism a bit heavily at times. In the end, however, Keen's Roberto Benigni–like sense of wonder is as winning as a flawless triple spiral.

*AUDREY STYLE
Pamela Clarke Keogh
A former magazine journalist for *British Vogue* and *Self,* Keogh packs wonderful pictures and homage-paying service into a book that brims with style and substance, like Hepburn herself.

HOME TOWN
Tracy Kidder
The Pulitzer Prize–winning author sets out to take a broad view of Northampton, Massachusetts, a kind of New Age Pleasantville that Kidder brings movingly to life.

THE DUCHESS OF WINDSOR
Greg King
This uneven new biography aims to rehabilitate the good name of a woman the author calls one of our century's "most reviled."

WOMEN & LOVE
Mira Kirshenbaum
Go on enough "love adventures," says the author, and you're bound to find joy. Though sprinkled with some rather strange similes ("Love is like deep-sea diving"..."Sex is like cooking chicken"), the examination of what women really want is insightful.

SINGLE NO MORE
Ellen Kreidman
Some tips are too obvious, but the encouragement is heartfelt, especially for the older set and single parents.

THE COMPLETE IDIOT'S GUIDE TO DATING
Dr. Judy Kuriansky
This funny and comprehensive guide will wise up the love-lorn of any age and gender. Shunning sexual stereotypes and acknowledging that gays and lesbians also have love lives, it is thorough, progressive, and very refreshing.

LABELLE CUISINE
Patti LaBelle
Soul diva tells stories about cooking for family and friends. Despite LaBelle's promise to reveal "my ancestors' treasured recipes," most of these dishes can be found in standard American cookbooks.

TRAVELING MERCIES: SOME THOUGHTS ON FAITH
Anne Lamott
In this irreverent spiritual journal, an unmarried mother with dreadlocks and a healthy sense of irony explains how she found God.

DINNER AT MISS LADY'S: MEMORIES AND RECIPES FROM A SOUTHERN CHILDHOOD
Luann Landon
Half family memoir, half cookbook. Landon's stories in languid prose, like her artery-clogging recipes, are meant to be savored.

UPPITY WOMEN OF THE RENAISSANCE
Vicki Léon
A witty look at an epoch's disorderly dames and soulful femmes, like the woman who rebuffed King Henry VIII—and lived.

I WISH I WERE THIN, I WISH I WERE FAT
Michelle Joy Levine
A psychotherapist explains why even the most diet-aware women can be subconsciously compelled to remain fat.

DEAR EXILE
Hilary Liftin and Kate Montgomery
Letters between two former college roommates—separated by the Atlantic Ocean—show the lasting power of friendship.

GET SMART WITH YOUR HEART
Suzanne Lopez
Even Cupid can be stupid at times, which is why this psychotherapist turns love into an exact science. Complex quizzes and charts show that if you're an outgoing "type-three personality," like Brooke Shields, you may find Johnny Depp, a "four," too moody.

FOR THE LIFE OF YOUR DOG
Greg Louganis and Betsy Sikora Siino
After his stellar Olympic career, Louganis began training and showing dogs. His advice about caring for four-legged family members is

as carefully balanced as his spectacular dives.

GODFORSAKEN SEA
Derek Lundy

An account of a 1996–97 around-the-world solo sailing race. The lack of word definition makes it hard to understand what's happening, let alone muster sympathy for people who have gotten themselves into life-threatening situations.

RAY CHARLES: MAN AND MUSIC
Michael Lydon

An exhaustively researched, movingly written biography of Brother Ray, the man Frank Sinatra once called "the only genius in our business."

THE FREE-SPIRITED GARDEN
Susan McClure

Lush meadows and cozy little Edens can be grown with creeping plants and flowers that reseed themselves.

CLIMBING ROSES
Elvin McDonald

This is one of four charming volumes in *The Rose Garden Series*. Here, the garden editor of *Traditional Home* celebrates the ones that ramble and climb untidily on walls, trellises, and arbors.

COMFORT FROM A COUNTRY QUILT
Reba McEntire

Less a quilt than a series of Post-it notes, this book by the 44-year-old country singer is from the Robert Fulghum, fortune-cookie school of literature. But her fans will likely be forgiving enough to enjoy it.

LIFE STRATEGIES
Phillip C. McGraw, Ph.D.

The Dallas psychologist and legal strategist who helped Oprah Winfrey through a hard time explains how to achieve personal goals with planning.

CRAZY HORSE
Larry McMurtry

This book on the great Sioux warrior is the first in a series of short biographies that pair some of our finest writers with history's most compelling figures.

THE SKINNY: WHAT EVERY SKINNY WOMAN KNOWS ABOUT DIETING (AND WON'T TELL YOU!)
Patricia Marx and Susan Sistrom

Here are the hottest secrets, tips, and extreme measures—mostly tongue in cheek—from a pair of New York City freelance writers who regularly lunch bigtime yet still squeeze into a size 4.

THE MASK OF MOTHERHOOD
Susan Maushart

She writes engagingly and persuasively about the fact that, with so many options open to them, today's mothers feel more pressure than ever to defend their choices by donning a happy face.

BELLA TUSCANY
Frances Mayes

Return to sunny Italy, where asparagus grow wild and olive trees are sacred. Fall in love again with the charming people and countryside of Cortona in this evocative follow-up to the surprise hit *Under the Tuscan Sun*.

ENCORE PROVENCE
Peter Mayle

This series of essays skips merrily from the art of the shrug to truffle poaching to the Citröen parked neatly in someone's living room. The ground may be a bit well worn, but the bestselling Mayle is the antidote to an overwired age and its dot-commandos.

SHOW ME THE MAGIC
Paul Mazursky

This Hollywood memoir by the director of *An Unmarried Woman* is sporadically amusing but also burdened by pretension and needs more direction at times.

THE FIRST PARTNER: HILLARY RODHAM CLINTON
Joyce Milton

The most ravenous curiosity about Bill and Hillary Clinton's marriage is likely to be satisfied by this gossipy, well-written, and finally devastating biography of the woman in the White House.

IN THE BLINK OF AN EYE
Pat Milton

TWA Flight 800, which exploded off the coast of Long Island on July 17, 1996, continues to fascinate. A correspondent for the Associated Press, Milton chillingly recounts the flight's final moments and the FBI's quest for the truth. Heartbreaking yet inspiring disaster story.

MONICA'S
STORY

ANDREW MORTON
Author of the #1 *New York Times* bestseller *Diana: Her True Story*

MONICA'S STORY
Andrew Morton

Thanks to Monica's appealing immaturity and appalling self-absorption, our costly, deeply destructive recent political crisis is finally revealed for what it was: an Oval Office teen romance.

FOOD AND WHINE
Jennifer Moses

Part memoir and part cookbook, this diary of a young mother serves up sardonic Erma Bombeck–style observations about the pains of starting a family.

CINDERELLA STORY: MY LIFE IN GOLF
Bill Murray with George Peper

In this genial if wispy memoir, Murray tells how his love of the game began. Despite a few bogeys, his wit is par for the course.

THE ORCHID THIEF
Susan Orlean

The delicate beauty of exotic blossoms inspires eccentric collectors and swamp-smart suppliers alike in this true-life South Florida smuggling mystery.

VULGAR FAVORS
Maureen Orth
This book delves into the life and crimes of Andrew Cunanan, the man who murdered Gianni Versace, but doesn't substantially alter our understanding of either.

KEEPING FAITH
Jodi Picoult
This tale of a young girl who talks to God and heals people—inciting a media riot in the process—raises significant questions about faith, religion, and society.

LADIES FIRST
Queen Latifah with Karen Hunter
This uplifting if somewhat superficial book tells the tale of a strong, young African-American who grew up around poverty, drugs, and prejudice, and followed her head and heart to become a successful, humane woman and rap artist.

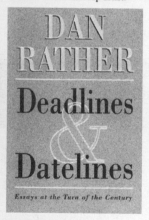

DEADLINES AND DATELINES
Dan Rather
Weekly syndicated newspaper columns by CBS newsman Rather form the basis of this odds-and-ends collection. His musty prose style could use some freshening, but he reveals a beguiling sense of humor.

THE ROSE BIBLE
Rayford Clayton Reddell
Garden columnist Ray Reddell has more than 8,000 rose bushes at his California ranch and is an expert on all matters rosarian.

SEE JANE WIN
Dr. Sylvia Rimm
The *Today* show's resident parenting expert surveys successful women to learn how childhood experiences such as team sports and travel inspired role models in fields like law, education, and the arts.

DON'T COUNT THE CANDLES—JUST KEEP THE FIRE LIT!
Joan Rivers
Comedian Joan Rivers gives tips on coping with aging that are mostly fortune-cookie platitudes, when they're not obvious or shamelessly shallow.

SHY BOY
Monty Roberts
With help from stunning photos by Christopher Dydyk, the author of *The Man Who Listens to Horses* recounts his gentling of a wild mustang.

BARBARA JORDAN
Mary Beth Rogers
From preacher's daughter to civil rights champion, this engaging bio charts the inspiring rise of the first black woman elected to Congress from the South.

REAL AGE
Michael F. Roizen, M.D.
An internist tells how to gauge your true age and learn to feel younger—and live longer—by minimizing stress.

LIVE NOW, AGE LATER
Isadore Rosenfeld, M.D.
Pointing to golden-oldie dynamos like Sean Connery and Senator John Glenn, a seasoned physician explains how good habits, a healthy diet, and the right medical care can keep you youthful and energetic.

ONE MORE TIME
Mike Royko
In this posthumous collection of his columns, journalist Royko displays the breezy wit that made him so beloved in the Windy City.

ROAD SWING
Steve Rushin
A *Sports Illustrated* writer takes a laugh-a-mile journey to the soul of American sports, including bowling night in St. Louis and small-town Iowa baseball.

DIETING WITH THE DUCHESS
Sarah, the Duchess of York, and Weight Watchers
From the woman who was once maligned as the Duchess of Pork, a memoir of her personal battle of the bulge, plus her own diet tips and fave recipes.

MORRIE: IN HIS OWN WORDS
Morrie Schwartz
Lessons on life and death from the college professor who became the subject of the bestselling *Tuesdays with Morrie.*

GET A LIFE!
William Shatner with Chris Kreski
The actor who played Captain Kirk investigates *Star Trek's* cult following, but despite its rich subject, the book is disappointingly skimpy on detail and insight.

BEAUTY FADES, DUMB IS FOREVER: THE MAKING OF A HAPPY WOMAN
Judge Judy Sheindlin
The tips in this book aren't surprising or subtle, but her message bears repeating, and the book is worth reading if only for its wacky glimpses into the judge's life.

ON SUNSET BOULEVARD
Ed Sikov
Engaging bio of Billy Wilder, the brilliant screenwriter and director who gave us *Some Like It Hot* and *Double Indemnity.*

DANCING WITH CATS
Burton Silver and Heather Busch
Cleverly mixes mock-pretentious writing with whimsical, entertaining photographs of cat-human paws de deux.

NUREYEV: HIS LIFE
Diane Solway
Nureyev, not exactly a noble fellow, nonetheless remains a fascinating one in this vivid portrait of ballet's first pop star.

BREASTS
Meema Spadola
Inspired by the 1996 Cinemax documentary of the same name, a collection of interviews with women on the physical and emotional significance of their most public private parts.

ALTHORP: THE STORY OF AN ENGLISH HOUSE
Charles Spencer
Princess Diana's younger brother offers an extraordinarily dry look at his family's ancestral home.

THE BUZZWORD BINGO BOOK
Lara Stein and Benjamin Yoskovitz
This guidebook to Tom Davis's popular new bingo spinoff may help you actualize your dream, conceive killer apps, and climb up the org chart.

*ALL TOO HUMAN: A POLITICAL EDUCATION
George Stephanopoulos
This much-anticipated, entertaining memoir from Clinton's former senior aide and confidant is a briskly paced, PG-rated insider's take on Clinton's political prowess.

TWO PUPPIES
Jane and Michael Stern
Veteran husband-and-wife authors write a compare-and-contrast account of two newborn pooches. Though the book is at times both moving and amusing, it reads like one tale (or tail) too many.

FEEL THIS BOOK
Ben Stiller and Janeane Garofalo
In this neurotic, how-not-to guide to romance, Stiller conveys a touching pathos, but Garofalo's caustic humor does not translate as well to the page.

HOW MEN HAVE BABIES
Alan Thicke
From the star of *Growing Pains,* a part-serious, part-comic guide for the man who needs to know what to expect when the woman in his life is expecting.

YESTERDAY, I CRIED
Iyanla Vanzant
The bestselling minister and spiritual guide mines her own troubled past to teach life's healing lessons.

CATS INTO EVERYTHING
Bob Walker
These photographs of Walker's nine feline friends, in all their moods and activities, is a perfect gift for cat lovers.

BOOTLEG
Damon Wayans
At his best—which is to say laugh-out-loud funny—Wayans deftly skewers celebs and has-beens, husbands and wives, and blacks and whites with equal politically-incorrect abandon, revealing a fierce, fearless, and funky comic sensibility.

FIRST PERSON PLURAL: MY LIFE AS A MULTIPLE
Cameron West, Ph.D.
In this memoir, bought by Hollywood for actor Robin Williams, a man struggles to stay sane when he develops 24 different personalities.

CONSUMING PASSIONS
Michael Lee West
From the acclaimed author of *She Flew the Coop* comes this scrumptiously witty memoir about family, food, and the American South.

THE CALLING: A YEAR IN THE LIFE OF AN ORDER OF NUNS
Catherine Whitney
Journalist and author Whitney gives an inside view of the Sisters of Saint Dominic of the Holy Cross. This is all great material, but the poor organization and sloppy writing don't do it justice.

THE TAO OF BOW WOW
Deborah Wood
This accessible manual offers an alternative, loving approach to raising and training your pooch and forging a unique human-canine bond.

SPAM: A BIOGRAPHY
Carolyn Wyman
Syndicated newspaper columnist Wyman's witty, extensively illustrated overview playfully mixes Spam's history with examples of its use and abuse. An unexpectedly tasty dish.

FICTION AND NONFICTION BESTSELLERS

Publishers Weekly began charting the nation's top-selling hardcover fiction in 1895. The first nonfiction lists were published regularly beginning in 1917, and during World War I the trade magazine even tracked the most popular war books. (The Winston Churchill on the fiction lists, by the way, was an American novelist who died in 1947; his British statesman namesake was, of course, a bestselling and Nobel Prize–winning writer of nonfiction.) These rankings are not based on net sales figures but rather on publishers' reports of copies shipped and billed.

1900

Fiction
1. *To Have and To Hold*, Mary Johnston
2. *Red Pottage*, Mary Cholmondeley
3. *Unleavened Bread*, Robert Grant
4. *The Reign of Law*, James Lane Allen
5. *Eben Holden*, Irving Bacheller
6. *Janice Meredith*, Paul Leicester Ford
7. *The Redemption of David Corson*, Charles Frederic Goss
8. *Richard Carvel*, Winston Churchill
9. *When Knighthood Was in Flower*, Charles Major
10. *Alice of Old Vincennes*, Maurice Thompson

1901

Fiction
1. *The Crisis*, Winston Churchill
2. *Alice of Old Vincennes*, Maurice Thompson
3. *The Helmet of Navarre*, Bertha Runkle
4. *The Right of Way*, Gilbert Parker
5. *Eben Holden*, Irving Bacheller
6. *The Visits of Elizabeth*, Elinor Glyn
7. *The Puppet Crown*, Harold MacGrath
8. *Richard Yea-and-Nay*, Maurice Hewlett
9. *Graustark*, George Barr McCutcheon
10. *D'ri and I*, Irving Bacheller

1902

Fiction
1. *The Virginian*, Owen Wister
2. *Mrs. Wiggs of the Cabbage Patch*, Alice Caldwell Hegan
3. *Dorothy Vernon of Haddon Hall*, Charles Major
4. *The Mississippi Bubble*, Emerson Hough
5. *Audrey*, Mary Johnston
6. *The Right of Way*, Gilbert Parker
7. *The Hound of the Baskervilles*, A. Conan Doyle
8. *The Two Vanrevels*, Booth Tarkington
9. *The Blue Flower*, Henry van Dyke
10. *Sir Richard Calmady*, Lucas Malet

1903

Fiction
1. *Lady Rose's Daughter*, Mary Augusta Ward
2. *Gordon Keith*, Thomas Nelson Page
3. *The Pit*, Frank Norris
4. *Lovey Mary*, Alice Hegan Rice
5. *The Virginian*, Owen Wister
6. *Mrs. Wiggs of the Cabbage Patch*, Alice Hegan Rice
7. *The Mettle of the Pasture*, James Lane Allen
8. *Letters of a Self-Made Merchant to His Son*, George Horace Lorimer
9. *The One Woman*, Thomas Dixon Jr.
10. *The Little Shepherd of Kingdom Come*, John Fox Jr.

1904

Fiction
1. *The Crossing*, Winston Churchill
2. *The Deliverance*, Ellen Glasgow
3. *The Masquerader*, anonymous (Katherine Cecil Thurston)
4. *In the Bishop's Carriage*, Miriam Michelson
5. *Sir Mortimer*, Mary Johnston
6. *Beverly of Graustark*, George Barr McCutcheon
7. *The Little Shepherd of Kingdom Come*, John Fox Jr.
8. *Rebecca of Sunnybrook Farm*, Kate Douglas Wiggin
9. *My Friend Prospero*, Henry Harland
10. *The Silent Places*, Stewart Edward White

1905

Fiction
1. *The Marriage of William Ashe*, Mary Augusta Ward
2. *Sandy*, Alice Hegan Rice
3. *The Garden of Allah*, Robert Hichens
4. *The Clansman*, Thomas Dixon Jr.
5. *Nedra*, George Barr McCutcheon
6. *The Gambler*, Katherine Cecil Thurston
7. *The Masquerader*, anonymous (Katherine Cecil Thurston)
8. *The House of Mirth*, Edith Wharton
9. *The Princess Passes*, C. N. and A. M. Williamson
10. *Rose o' the River*, Kate Douglas Wiggin

1906

Fiction
1. *Coniston*, Winston Churchill
2. *Lady Baltimore*, Owen Wister
3. *The Fighting Chance*, Robert W. Chambers
4. *The House of a Thousand Candles*, Meredith Nicholson
5. *Jane Cable*, George Barr McCutcheon
6. *The Jungle*, Upton Sinclair
7. *The Awakening of Helena Ritchie*, Margaret Deland
8. *The Spoilers*, Rex Beach
9. *The House of Mirth*, Edith Wharton
10. *The Wheel of Life*, Ellen Glasgow

1907

Fiction
1. *The Lady of the Decoration*, Frances Little
2. *The Weavers*, Gilbert Parker
3. *The Port of Missing Men*, Meredith Nicholson
4. *The Shuttle*, Frances Hodgson Burnett
5. *The Brass Bowl*, Louis J. Vance
6. *Satan Sanderson*, Hallie Erminie Rives
7. *The Daughter of Anderson Crow*, George Barr McCutcheon
8. *The Younger Set*, Robert W. Chambers
9. *The Doctor*, Ralph Connor
10. *Half a Rogue*, Harold MacGrath

1908

Fiction
1. *Mr. Crewe's Career*, Winston Churchill
2. *The Barrier*, Rex Beach
3. *The Trail of the Lonesome Pine*, John Fox Jr.
4. *The Lure of the Mask*, Harold MacGrath

5. *The Shuttle*, Frances Hodgson Burnett
6. *Peter*, F. Hopkinson Smith
7. *Lewis Rand*, Mary Johnston
8. *The Black Bag*, Louis J. Vance
9. *The Man from Brodney's*, George Barr McCutcheon
10. *The Weavers*, Gilbert Parker

1909

Fiction
1. *The Inner Shrine*, anonymous (Basil King)
2. *Katrine*, Elinor Macartney Lane
3. *The Silver Horde*, Rex Beach
4. *The Man in Lower Ten*, Mary Roberts Rinehart
5. *The Trail of the Lonesome Pine*, John Fox Jr.
6. *Truxton King*, George Barr McCutcheon
7. *54–40 or Fight*, Emerson Hough
8. *The Goose Girl*, Harold MacGrath
9. *Peter*, F. Hopkinson Smith
10. *Septimus*, William J. Locke

1910

Fiction
1. *The Rosary*, Florence Barclay
2. *A Modern Chronicle*, Winston Churchill
3. *The Wild Olive*, anonymous (Basil King)
4. *Max*, Katherine Cecil Thurston
5. *The Kingdom of Slender Swords*, Hallie Erminie Rives
6. *Simon the Jester*, William J. Locke
7. *Lord Loveland Discovers America*, C. N. and A. M. Williamson
8. *The Window at the White Cat*, Mary Roberts Rinehart
9. *Molly Make-Believe*, Eleanor Abbott
10. *When a Man Marries*, Mary Roberts Rinehart

1911

Fiction
1. *The Broad Highway*, Jeffrey Farnol
2. *The Prodigal Judge*, Vaughan Kester
3. *The Winning of Barbara Worth*, Harold Bell Wright
4. *Queed*, Henry Sydnor Harrison
5. *The Harvester*, Gene Stratton Porter
6. *The Iron Woman*, Margaret Deland
7. *The Long Roll*, Mary Johnston
8. *Molly Make-Believe*, Eleanor Abbott
9. *The Rosary*, Florence Barclay
10. *The Common Law*, Robert W. Chambers

1912

Fiction
1. *The Harvester*, Gene Stratton Porter
2. *The Street Called Straight*, Basil King
3. *Their Yesterdays*, Harold Bell Wright
4. *The Melting of Molly*, Maria Thompson Daviess
5. *A Hoosier Chronicle*, Meredith Nicholson
6. *The Winning of Barbara Worth*, Harold Bell Wright
7. *The Just and the Unjust*, Vaughan Kester
8. *The Net*, Rex Beach
9. *Tante*, Anne Douglas Sedgwick
10. *Fran*, J. Breckenridge Ellis

Nonfiction
1. *The Promised Land*, Mary Antin
2. *The Montessori Method*, Maria Montessori

3. *South America*, James Bryce
4. *A New Conscience and an Ancient Evil*, Jane Addams
5. *Three Plays*, Eugène Brieux
6. *Your United States*, Arnold Bennett
7. *Creative Evolution*, Henri Bergson
8. *How to Live on Twenty-four Hours a Day*, Arnold Bennett
9. *Woman and Labor*, Olive Schreiner
10. *Mark Twain*, Albert Bigelow Paine

1913

Fiction
1. *The Inside of the Cup*, Winston Churchill
2. *V.V.'s Eyes*, Henry Sydnor Harrison
3. *Laddie*, Gene Stratton Porter
4. *The Judgment House*, Sir Gilbert Parker
5. *Heart of the Hills*, John Fox Jr.

MOST CHALLENGED (NOT BANNED) BOOKS

Books enrich our lives, but to a certain vocal part of the population they can enrage as well. While the intention of those challenging these books *was* to ban them, most of the books stayed on the shelves because of the efforts of librarians, teachers, parents, and students. Here are the most challenged books in school libraries and curriculums, in the last year, according to the American Library Association's Office for Intellectual Freedom (Jan. 1–Dec. 31, 1998) and between 1982 and 1996 according to People for the American Way.

1982–96
1. *Of Mice and Men*, John Steinbeck
2. *The Catcher in the Rye*, J. D. Salinger
3. *The Chocolate War*, Robert Cormier
4. *I Know Why the Caged Bird Sings*, Maya Angelou
5. *Scary Stories to Tell in the Dark*, Alvin Schwartz
6. *The Adventures of Huckleberry Finn*, Mark Twain
7. *More Scary Stories to Tell in the Dark*, Alvin Schwartz
8. *Go Ask Alice*, anonymous
9. *Bridge to Terabithia*, Katherine Paterson
10. *The Witches*, Roald Dahl

1998
1. *The Chocolate War*, Robert Cormier
2. *It's Perfectly Normal*, Robbie Harris
3. *Of Mice and Men*, John Steinbeck
4. *Goosebumps* series, R. L. Stine
5. *Fear Street*, R. L. Stine
6. *I Know Why the Caged Bird Sings*, Maya Angelou
7. *The Giver*, Lois Lowry
8. *Always Running*, Luis Rodriguez
9. *Crazy Boy*, Jane Leslie Conly
10. *Blubber*, Judy Blume

6. *The Amateur Gentleman*, Jeffrey Farnol
7. *The Woman Thou Gavest Me*, Hall Caine
8. *Pollyanna*, Eleanor H. Porter
9. *The Valiants of Virginia*, Hallie Erminie Rives
10. *T. Tembarom*, Frances Hodgson Burnett

Nonfiction
1. *Crowds*, Gerald Stanley Lee
2. *Germany and the Germans*, Price Collier
3. *Zone Policeman 88*, Harry A. Franck
4. *The New Freedom*, Woodrow Wilson
5. *South America*, James Bryce
6. *Your United States*, Arnold Bennett
7. *The Promised Land*, Mary Antin
8. *Auction Bridge To-Day*, Milton C. Work
9. *Three Plays*, Eugène Brieux
10. *Psychology and Industrial Efficiency*, Hugo Munsterberg

1914

Fiction
1. *The Eyes of the World*, Harold Bell Wright
2. *Pollyanna*, Eleanor H. Porter
3. *The Inside of the Cup*, Winston Churchill
4. *The Salamander*, Owen Johnson
5. *The Fortunate Youth*, William J. Locke
6. *T. Tembarom*, Frances Hodgson Burnett
7. *Penrod*, Booth Tarkington
8. *Diane of the Green Van*, Leona Dalrymple
9. *The Devil's Garden*, W. B. Maxwell
10. *The Prince of Graustark*, George Barr McCutcheon

1915

Fiction
1. *The Turmoil*, Booth Tarkington
2. *A Far Country*, Winston Churchill
3. *Michael O'Halloran*, Gene Stratton Porter
4. *Pollyanna Grows Up*, Eleanor H. Porter
5. *K*, Mary Roberts Rinehart
6. *Jaffery*, William J. Locke
7. *Felix O'Day*, F. Hopkinson Smith
8. *The Harbor*, Ernest Poole
9. *The Lone Star Ranger*, Zane Grey
10. *Angela's Business*, Henry Sydnor Harrison

1916

Fiction
1. *Seventeen*, Booth Tarkington
2. *When a Man's a Man*, Harold Bell Wright

3. *Just David*, Eleanor H. Porter
4. *Mr. Britling Sees It Through*, H. G. Wells
5. *Life and Gabriella*, Ellen Glasgow
6. *The Real Adventure*, Henry Kitchell Webster
7. *Bars of Iron*, Ethel M. Dell
8. *Nan of Music Mountain*, Frank H. Spearman
9. *Dear Enemy*, Jean Webster
10. *The Heart of Rachael*, Kathleen Norris

1917

Fiction
1. *Mr. Britling Sees It Through*, H. G. Wells
2. *The Light in the Clearing*, Irving Bacheller
3. *The Red Planet*, William J. Locke
4. *The Road to Understanding*, Eleanor H. Porter
5. *Wildfire*, Zane Grey
6. *Christine*, Alice Cholmondeley
7. *In the Wilderness*, Robert S. Hichens
8. *His Family*, Ernest Poole
9. *The Definite Object*, Jeffrey Farnol
10. *The Hundredth Chance*, Ethel M. Dell

General Nonfiction
1. *Rhymes of a Red Cross Man*, Robert W. Service
2. *The Plattsburg Manual*, O. O. Ellis and E. B. Garey
3. *Raymond*, Sir Oliver Lodge
4. *Poems of Alan Seeger*, Alan Seeger
5. *God the Invisible King*, H. G. Wells
6. *Laugh and Live*, Douglas Fairbanks
7. *Better Meals for Less Money*, Mary Green

War Books
1. *The First Hundred Thousand*, Ian Hay
2. *My Home in the Field of Honor*, Frances W. Huard
3. *A Student in Arms*, Donald Hankey
4. *Over the Top*, Arthur Guy Empey
5. *Carry On*, Coningsby Dawson
6. *Getting Together*, Ian Hay
7. *My Second Year of the War*, Frederick Palmer
8. *The Land of Deepening Shadow*, D. Thomas Curtin
9. *Italy, France and Britain at War*, H. G. Wells
10. *The Worn Doorstep*, Margaret Sherwood

1918

Fiction
1. *The U. P. Trail*, Zane Grey

2. *The Tree of Heaven*, May Sinclair
3. *The Amazing Interlude*, Mary Roberts Rinehart
4. *Dere Mable*, Edward Streeter
5. *Oh, Money! Money!*, Eleanor H. Porter
6. *Greatheart*, Ethel M. Dell
7. *The Major*, Ralph Connor
8. *The Pawns Count*, E. Phillips Oppenheim
9. *A Daughter of the Land*, Gene Stratton Porter
10. *Sonia*, Stephen McKenna

General Nonfiction
1. *Rhymes of a Red Cross Man*, Robert W. Service
2. *Treasury of War Poetry*, G. H. Clark
3. *With the Colors*, Everard J. Appleton
4. *Recollections*, Viscount Morley
5. *Laugh and Live*, Douglas Fairbanks
6. *Mark Twain's Letters*, Albert Bigelow Paine, editor
7. *Adventures and Letters of Richard Harding Davis*, Richard Harding Davis
8. *Over Here*, Edgar Guest
9. *Diplomatic Days*, Edith O'Shaughnessy
10. *Poems of Alan Seeger*, Alan Seeger

War Books
1. *My Four Years in Germany*, James W. Gerard
2. *The Glory of the Trenches*, Coningsby Dawson
3. *Over the Top*, Arthur Guy Empey
4. *A Minstrel in France*, Harry Lauder
5. *Private Peat*, Harold R. Peat
6. *Outwitting the Hun*, Lieut. Pat O'Brien
7. *Face to Face with Kaiserism*, James W. Gerard
8. *Carry On*, Coningsby Dawson
9. *Out to Win*, Coningsby Dawson
10. *Under Fire*, Henri Barbusse

1919

Fiction
1. *The Four Horsemen of the Apocalypse*, V. Blasco Ibañez
2. *The Arrow of Gold*, Joseph Conrad
3. *The Desert of Wheat*, Zane Grey
4. *Dangerous Days*, Mary Roberts Rinehart
5. *The Sky Pilot in No Man's Land*, Ralph Connor
6. *The Re-creation of Brian Kent*, Harold Bell Wright
7. *Dawn*, Gene Stratton Porter
8. *The Tin Soldier*, Temple Bailey
9. *Christopher and Columbus*, "Elizabeth"

10. *In Secret*, Robert W. Chambers

Nonfiction
1. *The Education of Henry Adams*, Henry Adams
2. *The Years Between*, Rudyard Kipling
3. *Belgium*, Brand Whitlock
4. *The Seven Purposes*, Margaret Cameron
5. *In Flanders Fields*, John McCrae
6. *Bolshevism*, John Spargo

1920

Fiction
1. *The Man of the Forest*, Zane Grey
2. *Kindred of the Dust*, Peter B. Kyne
3. *The Re-creation of Brian Kent*, Harold Bell Wright
4. *The River's End*, James Oliver Curwood
5. *A Man for the Ages*, Irving Bacheller
6. *Mary-Marie*, Eleanor H. Porter
7. *The Portygee*, Joseph C. Lincoln
8. *The Great Impersonation*, E. Phillips Oppenheim
9. *The Lamp in the Desert*, Ethel M. Dell
10. *Harriet and the Piper*, Kathleen Norris

Nonfiction
1. *Now It Can Be Told*, Philip Gibbs
2. *The Economic Consequences of the Peace*, John M. Keynes
3. *Roosevelt's Letters to His Children*, Joseph B. Bishop, editor
4. *Theodore Roosevelt*, William Roscoe Thayer
5. *White Shadows in the South Seas*, Frederick O'Brien
6. *An American Idyll*, Cornelia Stratton Parker

1921

Fiction
1. *Main Street*, Sinclair Lewis
2. *The Brimming Cup*, Dorothy Canfield
3. *The Mysterious Rider*, Zane Grey
4. *The Age of Innocence*, Edith Wharton
5. *The Valley of Silent Men*, James Oliver Curwood
6. *The Sheik*, Edith M. Hull
7. *A Poor Wise Man*, Mary Roberts Rinehart
8. *Her Father's Daughter*, Gene Stratton Porter
9. *The Sisters-in-Law*, Gertrude Atherton
10. *The Kingdom Round the Corner*, Coningsby Dawson

Nonfiction
1. *The Outline of History*, H. G. Wells
2. *White Shadows in the South Seas*, Frederick O'Brien

3. *The Mirrors of Downing Street, A Gentleman with a Duster* (pseudonym for Harold Begbie)
4. *The Autobiography of Margot Asquith*, Margot Asquith
6. *Peace Negotiations*, Robert Lansing

1922

Fiction
1. *If Winter Comes*, A. S. M. Hutchinson
2. *The Sheik*, Edith M. Hull
3. *Gentle Julia*, Booth Tarkington
4. *The Head of the House of Coombe*, Frances Hodgson Burnett
5. *Simon Called Peter*, Robert Keable
6. *The Breaking Point*, Mary Roberts Rinehart
7. *This Freedom*, A. S. M. Hutchinson
8. *Maria Chapdelaine*, Louis Hémon
9. *To the Last Man*, Zane Grey
10. *Babbitt*, Sinclair Lewis (tie)
10. *Helen of the Old House*, Harold Bell Wright (tie)

Nonfiction
1. *The Outline of History*, H. G. Wells
2. *The Story of Mankind*, Hendrik Willem Van Loon
3. *The Americanization of Edward Bok*, Edward Bok
4. *Diet and Health*, Lulu Hunt Peters
5. *The Mind in the Making*, James Harvey Robinson
6. *The Outline of Science*, J. Arthur Thomson
7. *Outwitting Our Nerves*, Josephine A. Jackson and Helen M. Salisbury
8. *Queen Victoria*, Lytton Strachey
9. *Mirrors of Washington*, anonymous (Clinton W. Gilbert)
10. *Painted Windows*, A Gentleman with a Duster (pseudonym for Harold Begbie)

1923

Fiction
1. *Black Oxen*, Gertrude Atherton
2. *His Children's Children*, Arthur Train
3. *The Enchanted April*, "Elizabeth"
4. *Babbitt*, Sinclair Lewis
5. *The Dim Lantern*, Temple Bailey
6. *This Freedom*, A. S. M. Hutchinson
7. *The Mine with the Iron Door*, Harold Bell Wright
8. *The Wanderer of the Wasteland*, Zane Grey
9. *The Sea-Hawk*, Rafael Sabatini
10. *The Breaking Point*, Mary Roberts Rinehart

Nonfiction
1. *Etiquette*, Emily Post
2. *The Life of Christ*, Giovanni Papini
3. *The Life and Letters of Walter H. Page*, Burton J. Hendrick, editor
4. *The Mind in the Making*, James Harvey Robinson
5. *The Outline of History*, H. G. Wells
6. *Diet and Health*, Lulu Hunt Peters
7. *Self-Mastery Through Conscious Auto-Suggestion*, Emile Coué
8. *The Americanization of Edward Bok*, Edward Bok
9. *The Story of Mankind*, Hendrik Willem Van Loon
10. *A Man from Maine*, Edward Bok

1924

Fiction
1. *So Big*, Edna Ferber
2. *The Plastic Age*, Percy Marks
3. *The Little French Girl*, Anne Douglas Sedgwick
4. *The Heirs Apparent*, Philip Gibbs
5. *A Gentleman of Courage*, James Oliver Curwood
6. *The Call of the Canyon*, Zane Grey
7. *The Midlander*, Booth Tarkington
8. *The Coast of Folly*, Coningsby Dawson
9. *Mistress Wilding*, Rafael Sabatini
10. *The Homemaker*, Dorothy Canfield Fisher

Nonfiction
1. *Diet and Health*, Lulu Hunt Peters
2. *The Life of Christ*, Giovanni Papini
3. *The Boston Cooking School Cook Book*, rev. ed., Fannie Farmer, editor
4. *Etiquette*, Emily Post
5. *Ariel*, André Maurois
6. *The Cross Word Puzzle Books*, Prosper Buranelli, et al.
7. *Mark Twain's Autobiography*, Mark Twain
8. *Saint Joan*, Bernard Shaw
9. *The New Decalogue of Science*, Albert E. Wiggam
10. *The Americanization of Edward Bok*, Edward Bok

1925

Fiction
1. *Soundings*, A. Hamilton Gibbs
2. *The Constant Nymph*, Margaret Kennedy
3. *The Keeper of the Bees*, Gene Stratton Porter
4. *Glorious Apollo*, E. Barrington
5. *The Green Hat*, Michael Arlen

6. *The Little French Girl*, Anne Douglas Sedgwick
7. *Arrowsmith*, Sinclair Lewis
8. *The Perennial Bachelor*, Anne Parrish
9. *The Carolinian*, Rafael Sabatini
10. *One Increasing Purpose*, A. S. M. Hutchinson

Nonfiction

1. *Diet and Health*, Lulu Hunt Peters
2. *The Boston Cooking School Cook Book*, rev. ed., Fannie Farmer, editor
3. *When We Were Very Young*, A. A. Milne
4. *The Man Nobody Knows*, Bruce Barton
5. *The Life of Christ*, Giovanni Papini
6. *Ariel*, André Maurois
7. *Twice Thirty*, Edward Bok
8. *Twenty-five Years*, Lord Grey
9. *Anatole France Himself*, J. J. Brousson
10. *The Cross Word Puzzle Books*, Prosper Buranelli, et al.

1926

Fiction

1. *The Private Life of Helen of Troy*, John Erskine
2. *Gentlemen Prefer Blondes*, Anita Loos
3. *Sorrell and Son*, Warwick Deeping
4. *The Hounds of Spring*, Sylvia Thompson
5. *Beau Sabreur*, P. C. Wren
6. *The Silver Spoon*, John Galsworthy
7. *Beau Geste*, P. C. Wren
8. *Show Boat*, Edna Ferber
9. *After Noon*, Susan Ertz
10. *The Blue Window*, Temple Bailey

Nonfiction

1. *The Man Nobody Knows*, Bruce Barton
2. *Why We Behave Like Human Beings*, George A. Dorsey
3. *Diet and Health*, Lulu Hunt Peters
4. *Our Times*, Vol. I, Mark Sullivan
5. *The Boston Cooking School Cook Book*, rev. ed., Fannie Farmer, editor
6. *Auction Bridge Complete*, Milton C. Work
7. *The Book Nobody Knows*, Bruce Barton
8. *The Story of Philosophy*, Will Durant
9. *The Light of Faith*, Edgar A. Guest
10. *Jefferson and Hamilton*, Claude G. Bowers

1927

Fiction

1. *Elmer Gantry*, Sinclair Lewis
2. *The Plutocrat*, Booth Tarkington
3. *Doomsday*, Warwick Deeping
4. *Sorrell and Son*, Warwick Deeping
5. *Jalna*, Mazo de la Roche
6. *Lost Ecstasy*, Mary Roberts Rinehart
7. *Twilight Sleep*, Edith Wharton

8. *Tomorrow Morning*, Anne Parrish
9. *The Old Countess*, Anne Douglas Sedgwick
10. *A Good Woman*, Louis Bromfield

Nonfiction

1. *The Story of Philosophy*, Will Durant
2. *Napoleon*, Emil Ludwig
3. *Revolt in the Desert*, T. E. Lawrence
4. *Trader Horn*, Vol. I, Alfred Aloysius Horn and Ethelreda Lewis
5. *We*, Charles A. Lindbergh
6. *Ask Me Another*, Julian Spafford and Lucien Esty
7. *The Royal Road to Romance*, Richard Halliburton
8. *The Glorious Adventure*, Richard Halliburton
9. *Why We Behave Like Human Beings*, George A. Dorsey
10. *Mother India*, Katherine Mayo

1928

Fiction

1. *The Bridge of San Luis Rey*, Thornton Wilder
2. *Wintersmoon*, Hugh Walpole
3. *Swan Song*, John Galsworthy
4. *The Greene Murder Case*, S. S. Van Dine
5. *Bad Girl*, Viña Delmar
6. *Claire Ambler*, Booth Tarkington
7. *Old Pybus*, Warwick Deeping
8. *All Kneeling*, Anne Parrish
9. *Jalna*, Mazo de la Roche
10. *The Strange Case of Miss Annie Spragg*, Louis Bromfield

Nonfiction

1. *Disraeli*, André Maurois
2. *Mother India*, Katherine Mayo
3. *Trader Horn*, Vol. I, Alfred Aloysius Horn and Ethelreda Lewis
4. *Napoleon*, Emil Ludwig
5. *Strange Interlude*, Eugene O'Neill
6. *We*, Charles A. Lindbergh
7. *Count Luckner, the Sea Devil*, Lowell Thomas
8. *Goethe*, Emil Ludwig
9. *Skyward*, Richard E. Byrd
10. *The Intelligent Woman's Guide to Socialism and Capitalism*, George Bernard Shaw

1929

Fiction

1. *All Quiet on the Western Front*, Erich Maria Remarque
2. *Dodsworth*, Sinclair Lewis
3. *Dark Hester*, Anne Douglas Sedgwick

4. *The Bishop Murder Case*, S. S. Van Dine
5. *Roper's Row*, Warwick Deeping
6. *Peder Victorious*, O. E. Rölvaag
7. *Mamba's Daughters*, DuBose Heyward
8. *The Galaxy*, Susan Ertz
9. *Scarlet Sister Mary*, Julia Peterkin
10. *Joseph and His Brethren*, H. W. Freeman

Nonfiction

1. *The Art of Thinking*, Ernest Dimnet
2. *Henry the Eighth*, Francis Hackett
3. *The Cradle of the Deep*, Joan Lowell
4. *Elizabeth and Essex*, Lytton Strachey
5. *The Specialist*, Chic Sale
6. *A Preface to Morals*, Walter Lippmann
7. *Believe It or Not*, Robert L. Ripley
8. *John Brown's Body*, Stephen Vincent Benét
9. *The Tragic Era*, Claude G. Bowers
10. *The Mansions of Philosophy*, Will Durant

1930

Fiction

1. *Cimarron*, Edna Ferber
2. *Exile*, Warwick Deeping
3. *The Woman of Andros*, Thornton Wilder
4. *Years of Grace*, Margaret Ayer Barnes
5. *Angel Pavement*, J. B. Priestley
6. *The Door*, Mary Roberts Rinehart
7. *Rogue Herries*, Hugh Walpole
8. *Chances*, A. Hamilton Gibbs
9. *Young Man of Manhattan*, Katharine Brush
10. *Twenty-four Hours*, Louis Bromfield

Nonfiction

1. *The Story of San Michele*, Axel Munthe
2. *The Strange Death of President Harding*, Gaston B. Means and May Dixon Thacker
3. *Byron*, André Maurois
4. *The Adams Family*, James Truslow Adams
5. *Lone Cowboy*, Will James
6. *Lincoln*, Emil Ludwig
7. *The Story of Philosophy*, Will Durant
8. *The Outline of History*, H. G. Wells
9. *The Art of Thinking*, Ernest Dimnet
10. *The Rise of American Civilization*, Charles and Mary Beard

1931

Fiction

1. *The Good Earth*, Pearl S. Buck
2. *Shadows on the Rock*, Willa Cather
3. *A White Bird Flying*, Bess Streeter Aldrich

4. *Grand Hotel*, Vicki Baum
5. *Years of Grace*, Margaret Ayer Barnes
6. *The Road Back*, Erich Maria Remarque
7. *The Bridge of Desire*, Warwick Deeping
8. *Back Street*, Fannie Hurst
9. *Finch's Fortune*, Mazo de la Roche
10. *Maid in Waiting*, John Galsworthy

Nonfiction
1. *Education of a Princess*, Grand Duchess Marie
2. *The Story of San Michele*, Axel Munthe
3. *Washington Merry-Go-Round*, anonymous (Drew Pearson and Robert S. Allen)
4. *Boners: Being a Collection of Schoolboy Wisdom, or Knowledge as It Is Sometimes Written*, compiled by Alexander Abingdon; illustrated by Dr. Seuss
5. *Culbertson's Summary*, Ely Culbertson
6. *Contract Bridge Blue Book*, Ely Culbertson
7. *Fatal Interview*, Edna St. Vincent Millay
8. *The Epic of America*, James Truslow Adams
9. *Mexico*, Stuart Chase
10. *New Russia's Primer*, Mikhail Ilin

1932

Fiction
1. *The Good Earth*, Pearl S. Buck
2. *The Fountain*, Charles Morgan
3. *Sons*, Pearl S. Buck
4. *Magnolia Street*, Louis Golding
5. *The Sheltered Life*, Ellen Glasgow
6. *Old Wine and New*, Warwick Deeping
7. *Mary's Neck*, Booth Tarkington
8. *Magnificent Obsession*, Lloyd C. Douglas
9. *Inheritance*, Phyllis Bentley
10. *Three Loves*, A. J. Cronin

Nonfiction
1. *The Epic of America*, James Truslow Adams
2. *Only Yesterday*, Frederick Lewis Allen
3. *A Fortune to Share*, Vash Young
4. *Culbertson's Summary*, Ely Culbertson
5. *Van Loon's Geography*, Hendrik Willem Van Loon
6. *What We Live By*, Ernest Dimnet
7. *The March of Democracy*, James Truslow Adams
8. *Washington Merry-Go-Round*, anonymous (Drew Pearson and Robert S. Allen)

9. *The Story of My Life*, Clarence Darrow
10. *More Merry-Go-Round*, anonymous (Drew Pearson and Robert S. Allen)

1933

Fiction
1. *Anthony Adverse*, Hervey Allen
2. *As the Earth Turns*, Gladys Hasty Carroll
3. *Ann Vickers*, Sinclair Lewis
4. *Magnificent Obsession*, Lloyd C. Douglas
5. *One More River*, John Galsworthy
6. *Forgive Us Our Trespasses*, Lloyd C. Douglas
7. *The Master of Jalna*, Mazo de la Roche
8. *Miss Bishop*, Bess Streeter Aldrich
9. *The Farm*, Louis Bromfield
10. *Little Man, What Now?*, Hans Fallada

Nonfiction
1. *Life Begins at Forty*, Walter B. Pitkin
2. *Marie Antoinette*, Stefan Zweig
3. *British Agent*, R. H. Bruce Lockhart
4. *100,000,000 Guinea Pigs*, Arthur Kallet and F. J. Schlink
5. *The House of Exile*, Nora Waln
6. *Van Loon's Geography*, Hendrik Willem Van Loon
7. *Looking Forward*, Franklin D. Roosevelt
8. *Contract Bridge Blue Book of 1933*, Ely Culbertson
9. *The Arches of the Years*, Halliday Sutherland
10. *The March of Democracy*, Vol. II, James Truslow Adams

1934

Fiction
1. *Anthony Adverse*, Hervey Allen
2. *Lamb in His Bosom*, Caroline Miller
3. *So Red the Rose*, Stark Young
4. *Good-Bye, Mr. Chips*, James Hilton
5. *Within This Present*, Margaret Ayer Barnes
6. *Work of Art*, Sinclair Lewis
7. *Private Worlds*, Phyllis Bottome
8. *Mary Peters*, Mary Ellen Chase
9. *Oil for the Lamps of China*, Alice Tisdale Hobart
10. *Seven Gothic Tales*, Isak Dinesen

Nonfiction
1. *While Rome Burns*, Alexander Woollcott
2. *Life Begins at Forty*, Walter B. Pitkin
3. *Nijinsky*, Romola Nijinsky

4. *100,000,000 Guinea Pigs*, Arthur Kallet and F. J. Schlink
5. *The Native's Return*, Louis Adamic
6. *Stars Fell on Alabama*, Carl Carmer
7. *Brazilian Adventure*, Peter Fleming
8. *Forty-two Years in the White House*, Ike Hoover
9. *You Must Relax*, Edmund Jacobson
10. *The Life of Our Lord*, Charles Dickens

1935

Fiction
1. *Green Light*, Lloyd C. Douglas
2. *Vein of Iron*, Ellen Glasgow
3. *Of Time and the River*, Thomas Wolfe
4. *Time Out of Mind*, Rachel Field
5. *Good-Bye, Mr. Chips*, James Hilton
6. *The Forty Days of Musa Dagh*, Franz Werfel
7. *Heaven's My Destination*, Thornton Wilder
8. *Lost Horizon*, James Hilton
9. *Come and Get It*, Edna Ferber
10. *Europa*, Robert Briffault

Nonfiction
1. *North to the Orient*, Anne Morrow Lindbergh
2. *While Rome Burns*, Alexander Woollcott
3. *Life with Father*, Clarence Day
4. *Personal History*, Vincent Sheean
5. *Seven Pillars of Wisdom*, T. E. Lawrence
6. *Francis the First*, Francis Hackett
7. *Mary Queen of Scotland and the Isles*, Stefan Zweig
8. *Rats, Lice and History*, Hans Zinsser
9. *R. E. Lee*, Douglas Southall Freeman
10. *Skin Deep*, M. C. Phillips

1936

Fiction
1. *Gone with the Wind*, Margaret Mitchell
2. *The Last Puritan*, George Santayana
3. *Sparkenbroke*, Charles Morgan
4. *Drums Along the Mohawk*, Walter D. Edmonds
5. *It Can't Happen Here*, Sinclair Lewis
6. *White Banners*, Lloyd C. Douglas
7. *The Hurricane*, Charles Nordhoff and James Norman Hall
8. *The Thinking Reed*, Rebecca West
9. *The Doctor*, Mary Roberts Rinehart
10. *Eyeless in Gaza*, Aldous Huxley

Nonfiction
1. *Man the Unknown*, Alexis Carrel
2. *Wake Up and Live!*, Dorothea Brande

3. *The Way of a Transgressor*, Negley Farson
4. *Around the World in Eleven Years*, Patience, Richard, and Johnny Abbe
5. *North to the Orient*, Anne Morrow Lindbergh
6. *An American Doctor's Odyssey*, Victor Heiser
7. *Inside Europe*, John Gunther
8. *Live Alone and Like It*, Marjorie Hillis
9. *Life with Father*, Clarence Day
10. *I Write As I Please*, Walter Duranty

1937

Fiction
1. *Gone with the Wind*, Margaret Mitchell
2. *Northwest Passage*, Kenneth Roberts
3. *The Citadel*, A. J. Cronin
4. *And So—Victoria*, Vaughan Wilkins
5. *Drums Along the Mohawk*, Walter D. Edmonds
6. *The Years*, Virginia Woolf
7. *Theatre*, W. Somerset Maugham
8. *Of Mice and Men*, John Steinbeck
9. *The Rains Came*, Louis Bromfield
10. *We Are Not Alone*, James Hilton

Nonfiction
1. *How to Win Friends and Influence People*, Dale Carnegie
2. *An American Doctor's Odyssey*, Victor Heiser
3. *The Return to Religion*, Henry C. Link
4. *The Arts*, Hendrik Willem Van Loon
5. *Orchids on Your Budget*, Marjorie Hillis
6. *Present Indicative*, Noel Coward
7. *Mathematics for the Million*, Lancelot Hogben
8. *Life with Mother*, Clarence Day
9. *The Nile*, Emil Ludwig
10. *The Flowering of New England*, Van Wyck Brooks

1938

Fiction
1. *The Yearling*, Marjorie Kinnan Rawlings
2. *The Citadel*, A. J. Cronin
3. *My Son, My Son!*, Howard Spring
4. *Rebecca*, Daphne du Maurier
5. *Northwest Passage*, Kenneth Roberts
6. *All This, and Heaven Too*, Rachel Field
7. *The Rains Came*, Louis Bromfield
8. *And Tell of Time*, Laura Krey
9. *The Mortal Storm*, Phyllis Bottome
10. *Action at Aquila*, Hervey Allen

Nonfiction
1. *The Importance of Living*, Lin Yutang
2. *With Malice Toward Some*, Margaret Halsey
3. *Madame Curie*, Eve Curie
4. *Listen! The Wind*, Anne Morrow Lindbergh
5. *The Horse and Buggy Doctor*, Arthur E. Hertzler
6. *How to Win Friends and Influence People*, Dale Carnegie
7. *Benjamin Franklin*, Carl Van Doren
8. *I'm a Stranger Here Myself*, Ogden Nash
9. *Alone*, Richard E. Byrd
10. *Fanny Kemble*, Margaret Armstrong

1939

Fiction
1. *The Grapes of Wrath*, John Steinbeck
2. *All This, and Heaven Too*, Rachel Field
3. *Rebecca*, Daphne du Maurier
4. *Wickford Point*, John P. Marquand
5. *Escape*, Ethel Vance
6. *Disputed Passage*, Lloyd C. Douglas
7. *The Yearling*, Marjorie Kinnan Rawlings
8. *The Tree of Liberty*, Elizabeth Page
9. *The Nazarene*, Sholem Asch
10. *Kitty Foyle*, Christopher Morley

Nonfiction
1. *Days of Our Years*, Pierre van Paassen
2. *Reaching for the Stars*, Nora Waln
3. *Inside Asia*, John Gunther
4. *Autobiography with Letters*, William Lyon Phelps
5. *Country Lawyer*, Bellamy Partridge
6. *Wind, Sand and Stars*, Antoine de Saint-Exupéry
7. *Mein Kampf*, Adolf Hitler
8. *A Peculiar Treasure*, Edna Ferber
9. *Not Peace but a Sword*, Vincent Sheean
10. *Listen! The Wind*, Anne Morrow Lindbergh

1940

Fiction
1. *How Green Was My Valley*, Richard Llewellyn
2. *Kitty Foyle*, Christopher Morley
3. *Mrs. Miniver*, Jan Struther
4. *For Whom the Bell Tolls*, Ernest Hemingway
5. *The Nazarene*, Sholem Asch
6. *Stars on the Sea*, F. van Wyck Mason
7. *Oliver Wiswell*, Kenneth Roberts
8. *The Grapes of Wrath*, John Steinbeck
9. *Night in Bombay*, Louis Bromfield
10. *The Family*, Nina Fedorova

Nonfiction
1. *I Married Adventure*, Osa Johnson
2. *How to Read a Book*, Mortimer Adler
3. *A Smattering of Ignorance*, Oscar Levant
4. *Country Squire in the White House*, John T. Flynn
5. *Land Below the Wind*, Agnes Newton Keith
6. *American White Paper*, Joseph W. Alsop Jr. and Robert Kintnor
7. *New England: Indian Summer*, Van Wyck Brooks
8. *As I Remember Him*, Hans Zinsser
9. *Days of Our Years*, Pierre van Paassen
10. *Bet It's a Boy*, Betty B. Blunt

1941

Fiction
1. *The Keys of the Kingdom*, A. J. Cronin
2. *Random Harvest*, James Hilton
3. *This Above All*, Eric Knight
4. *The Sun Is My Undoing*, Marguerite Steen
5. *For Whom the Bell Tolls*, Ernest Hemingway
6. *Oliver Wiswell*, Kenneth Roberts
7. *H. M. Pulham, Esquire*, John P. Marquand
8. *Mr. and Mrs. Cugat*, Isabel Scott Rorick
9. *Saratoga Trunk*, Edna Ferber
10. *Windswept*, Mary Ellen Chase

Nonfiction
1. *Berlin Diary*, William L. Shirer
2. *The White Cliffs*, Alice Duer Miller
3. *Out of the Night*, Jan Valtin
4. *Inside Latin America*, John Gunther
5. *Blood, Sweat and Tears*, Winston S. Churchill
6. *You Can't Do Business with Hitler*, Douglas Miller
7. *Reading I've Liked*, Clifton Fadiman, editor
8. *Reveille in Washington*, Margaret Leech
9. *Exit Laughing*, Irvin S. Cobb
10. *My Sister and I*, Dirk van der Heide

1942

Fiction
1. *The Song of Bernadette*, Franz Werfel
2. *The Moon Is Down*, John Steinbeck
3. *Dragon Seed*, Pearl S. Buck
4. *And Now Tomorrow*, Rachel Field
5. *Drivin' Woman*, Elizabeth Pickett
6. *Windswept*, Mary Ellen Chase
7. *The Robe*, Lloyd C. Douglas
8. *The Sun Is My Undoing*, Marguerite Steen
9. *Kings Row*, Henry Bellamann

10. *The Keys of the Kingdom*, A. J. Cronin

Nonfiction

1. *See Here, Private Hargrove*, Marion Hargrove
2. *Mission to Moscow*, Joseph E. Davies
3. *The Last Time I Saw Paris*, Elliot Paul
4. *Cross Creek*, Marjorie Kinnan Rawlings
5. *Victory Through Air Power*, Major Alexander P. de Seversky
6. *Past Imperfect*, Ilka Chase
7. *They Were Expendable*, W. L. White
8. *Flight to Arras*, Antoine de Saint-Exupéry
9. *Washington Is Like That*, W. M. Kiplinger
10. *Inside Latin America*, John Gunther

1943

Fiction

1. *The Robe*, Lloyd C. Douglas
2. *The Valley of Decision*, Marcia Davenport
3. *So Little Time*, John P. Marquand
4. *A Tree Grows in Brooklyn*, Betty Smith
5. *The Human Comedy*, William Saroyan
6. *Mrs. Parkington*, Louis Bromfield
7. *The Apostle*, Sholem Asch
8. *Hungry Hill*, Daphne du Maurier
9. *The Forest and the Fort*, Hervey Allen
10. *The Song of Bernadette*, Franz Werfel

Nonfiction

1. *Under Cover*, John Roy Carlson
2. *One World*, Wendell L. Willkie
3. *Journey Among Warriors*, Eve Curie
4. *On Being a Real Person*, Harry Emerson Fosdick
5. *Guadalcanal Diary*, Richard Tregaskis
6. *Burma Surgeon*, Lt. Col. Gordon Seagrave
7. *Our Hearts Were Young and Gay*, Cornelia Otis Skinner and Emily Kimbrough
8. *U. S. Foreign Policy*, Walter Lippmann
9. *Here Is Your War*, Ernie Pyle
10. *See Here, Private Hargrove*, Marion Hargrove

1944

Fiction

1. *Strange Fruit*, Lillian Smith
2. *The Robe*, Lloyd C. Douglas
3. *A Tree Grows in Brooklyn*, Betty Smith
4. *Forever Amber*, Kathleen Winsor
5. *The Razor's Edge*, W. Somerset Maugham
6. *The Green Years*, A. J. Cronin
7. *Leave Her to Heaven*, Ben Ames Williams

8. *Green Dolphin Street*, Elizabeth Goudge
9. *A Bell for Adano*, John Hersey
10. *The Apostle*, Sholem Asch

Nonfiction

1. *I Never Left Home*, Bob Hope
2. *Brave Men*, Ernie Pyle
3. *Good Night, Sweet Prince*, Gene Fowler
4. *Under Cover*, John Roy Carlson
5. *Yankee from Olympus*, Catherine Drinker Bowen
6. *The Time for Decision*, Sumner Welles
7. *Here Is Your War*, Ernie Pyle
8. *Anna and the King of Siam*, Margaret Landon
9. *The Curtain Rises*, Quentin Reynolds
10. *Ten Years in Japan*, Joseph C. Grew

1945

Fiction

1. *Forever Amber*, Kathleen Winsor
2. *The Robe*, Lloyd C. Douglas
3. *The Black Rose*, Thomas B. Costain
4. *The White Tower*, James Ramsey Ullman
5. *Cass Timberlane*, Sinclair Lewis
6. *A Lion Is in the Streets*, Adria Locke Langley
7. *So Well Remembered*, James Hilton
8. *Captain from Castile*, Samuel Shellabarger
9. *Earth and High Heaven*, Gwethalyn Graham
10. *Immortal Wife*, Irving Stone

Nonfiction

1. *Brave Men*, Ernie Pyle
2. *Dear Sir*, Juliet Lowell
3. *Up Front*, Bill Mauldin
4. *Black Boy*, Richard Wright
5. *Try and Stop Me*, Bennett Cerf
6. *Anything Can Happen*, George and Helen Papashvily
7. *General Marshall's Report*, U.S. War Department General Staff
8. *The Egg and I*, Betty MacDonald
9. *The Thurber Carnival*, James Thurber
10. *Pleasant Valley*, Louis Bromfield

1946

Fiction

1. *The King's General*, Daphne du Maurier
2. *This Side of Innocence*, Taylor Caldwell
3. *The River Road*, Frances Parkinson Keyes
4. *The Miracle of the Bells*, Russell Janney
5. *The Hucksters*, Frederic Wakeman

6. *The Foxes of Harrow*, Frank Yerby
7. *Arch of Triumph*, Erich Maria Remarque
8. *The Black Rose*, Thomas B. Costain
9. *B.F.'s Daughter*, John P. Marquand
10. *The Snake Pit*, Mary Jane Ward

Nonfiction

1. *The Egg and I*, Betty MacDonald
2. *Peace of Mind*, Joshua L. Liebman
3. *As He Saw It*, Elliott Roosevelt
4. *The Roosevelt I Knew*, Frances Perkins
5. *Last Chapter*, Ernie Pyle
6. *Starling of the White House*, Thomas Sugrue and Col. Edmund Starling
7. *I Chose Freedom*, Victor Kravchenko
8. *The Anatomy of Peace*, Emery Reves
9. *Top Secret*, Ralph Ingersoll
10. *A Solo in Tom-Toms*, Gene Fowler

1947

Fiction

1. *The Miracle of the Bells*, Russell Janney
2. *The Moneyman*, Thomas B. Costain
3. *Gentleman's Agreement*, Laura Z. Hobson
4. *Lydia Bailey*, Kenneth Roberts
5. *The Vixens*, Frank Yerby
6. *The Wayward Bus*, John Steinbeck
7. *House Divided*, Ben Ames Williams
8. *Kingsblood Royal*, Sinclair Lewis
9. *East Side, West Side*, Marcia Davenport
10. *Prince of Foxes*, Samuel Shellabarger

Nonfiction

1. *Peace of Mind*, Joshua L. Liebman
2. *Information Please Almanac, 1947*, John Kieran, editor
3. *Inside U.S.A.*, John Gunther
4. *A Study of History*, Arnold J. Toynbee
5. *Speaking Frankly*, James F. Byrnes
6. *Human Destiny*, Pierre Lecomte du Noüy
7. *The Egg and I*, Betty MacDonald
8. *The American Past*, Roger Butterfield
9. *The Fireside Book of Folk Songs*, Margaret B. Boni, editor
10. *Together*, Katharine T. Marshall

1948

Fiction

1. *The Big Fisherman*, Lloyd C. Douglas
2. *The Naked and the Dead*, Norman Mailer
3. *Dinner at Antoine's*, Frances Parkinson Keyes
4. *The Bishop's Mantle*, Agnes Sligh Turnbull
5. *Tomorrow Will Be Better*, Betty Smith

6. *The Golden Hawk*, Frank Yerby
7. *Raintree County*, Ross Lockridge Jr.
8. *Shannon's Way*, A. J. Cronin
9. *Pilgrim's Inn*, Elizabeth Goudge
10. *The Young Lions*, Irwin Shaw

Nonfiction
1. *Crusade in Europe*, Dwight D. Eisenhower
2. *How to Stop Worrying and Start Living*, Dale Carnegie
3. *Peace of Mind*, Joshua L. Liebman
4. *Sexual Behavior in the Human Male*, A. C. Kinsey, et al.
5. *Wine, Women and Words*, Billy Rose
6. *The Life and Times of the Shmoo*, Al Capp
7. *The Gathering Storm*, Winston Churchill
8. *Roosevelt and Hopkins*, Robert E. Sherwood
9. *A Guide to Confident Living*, Norman Vincent Peale
10. *The Plague and I*, Betty MacDonald

1949

Fiction
1. *The Egyptian*, Mika Waltari
2. *The Big Fisherman*, Lloyd C. Douglas
3. *Mary*, Sholem Asch
4. *A Rage to Live*, John O'Hara
5. *Point of No Return*, John P. Marquand
6. *Dinner at Antoine's*, Frances Parkinson Keyes
7. *High Towers*, Thomas B. Costain
8. *Cutlass Empire*, Van Wyck Mason
9. *Pride's Castle*, Frank Yerby
10. *Father of the Bride*, Edward Streeter

Nonfiction
1. *White Collar Zoo*, Clare Barnes Jr.
2. *How to Win at Canasta*, Oswald Jacoby
3. *The Seven Storey Mountain*, Thomas Merton
4. *Home Sweet Zoo*, Clare Barnes Jr.
5. *Cheaper by the Dozen*, Frank B. Gilbreth Jr. and Ernestine Gilbreth Carey
6. *The Greatest Story Ever Told*, Fulton Oursler
7. *Canasta, the Argentine Rummy Game*, Ottilie H. Reilly
8. *Canasta*, Josephine Artayeta de Viel and Ralph Michael
9. *Peace of Soul*, Fulton J. Sheen
10. *A Guide to Confident Living*, Norman Vincent Peale

1950

Fiction
1. *The Cardinal*, Henry Morton Robinson
2. *Joy Street*, Frances Parkinson Keyes
3. *Across the River and into the Trees*, Ernest Hemingway
4. *The Wall*, John Hersey
5. *Star Money*, Kathleen Winsor
6. *The Parasites*, Daphne du Maurier
7. *Floodtide*, Frank Yerby
8. *Jubilee Trail*, Gwen Bristow
9. *The Adventurer*, Mika Waltari
10. *The Disenchanted*, Budd Schulberg

Nonfiction
1. *Betty Crocker's Picture Cook Book*
2. *The Baby*
3. *Look Younger, Live Longer*, Gayelord Hauser

THE LONGEST WORDS

Though most of us will never attempt to use them, these are the longest unhyphenated words in that linguists' Bible, the *Oxford English Dictionary.*

WORD		LETTERS
1.	pneumonoultramicroscopicsilicovolcanoconiosis	45
2.	supercalifragilisticexpialidocious	34
3.	pseudopseudohypoparathyroidism	30
4.	floccinaucinihilipilification	29
4.	triethylsulphonemethylmethane	29
6.	antidisestablishmentarianism	28
6.	octamethylcyclotetrasiloxane	28
6.	tetrachlorodibenzoparadioxin	28
9.	hepaticocholangiogastronomy	27
10.	radiommunoelectrophoresis	26
10.	radioimmunoelectrophoretic	26

4. *How I Raised Myself from Failure to Success in Selling*, Frank Bettger
5. *Kon-Tiki*, Thor Heyerdahl
6. *Mr. Jones, Meet the Master*, Peter Marshall
7. *Your Dream Home*, Hubbard Cobb
8. *The Mature Mind*, H. A. Overstreet
9. *Campus Zoo*, Clare Barnes Jr.
10. *Belles on Their Toes*, Frank Gilbreth Jr. and Ernestine Gilbreth Carey

1951

Fiction
1. *From Here to Eternity*, James Jones
2. *The Caine Mutiny*, Herman Wouk
3. *Moses*, Sholem Asch
4. *The Cardinal*, Henry Morton Robinson
5. *A Woman Called Fancy*, Frank Yerby
6. *The Cruel Sea*, Nicholas Monsarrat
7. *Melville Goodwin, U.S.A.*, John P. Marquand
8. *Return to Paradise*, James A. Michener
9. *The Foundling*, Cardinal Spellman
10. *The Wanderer*, Mika Waltari

Nonfiction
1. *Look Younger, Live Longer*, Gayelord Hauser
2. *Betty Crocker's Picture Cook Book*
3. *Washington Confidential*, Jack Lait and Lee Mortimer
4. *Better Homes and Gardens Garden Book*
5. *Better Homes and Gardens Handyman's Book*
6. *The Sea Around Us*, Rachel L. Carson
7. *Thorndike-Barnhart Comprehensive Desk Dictionary*, Clarence L. Barnhart, editor
8. *Pogo*, Walt Kelly
9. *Kon-Tiki*, Thor Heyerdahl
10. *The New Yorker Twenty-fifth Anniversary Album*

1952

Fiction
1. *The Silver Chalice*, Thomas B. Costain
2. *The Caine Mutiny*, Herman Wouk
3. *East of Eden*, John Steinbeck
4. *My Cousin Rachel*, Daphne du Maurier
5. *Steamboat Gothic*, Frances Parkinson Keyes
6. *Giant*, Edna Ferber
7. *The Old Man and the Sea*, Ernest Hemingway
8. *The Gown of Glory*, Agnes Sligh Turnbull
9. *The Saracen Blade*, Frank Yerby
10. *The Houses in Between*, Howard Spring

Nonfiction

1. *The Holy Bible: Revised Standard Version*
2. *A Man Called Peter*, Catherine Marshall
3. *U.S.A. Confidential*, Jack Lait and Lee Mortimer
4. *The Sea Around Us*, Rachel L. Carson
5. *Tallulah*, Tallulah Bankhead
6. *The Power of Positive Thinking*, Norman Vincent Peale
7. *This I Believe*, Edward P. Morgan, editor; Edward R. Murrow, foreword
8. *This Is Ike*, Wilson Hicks, editor
9. *Witness*, Whittaker Chambers
10. *Mr. President*, William Hillman

1953

Fiction

1. *The Robe*, Lloyd C. Douglas
2. *The Silver Chalice*, Thomas B. Costain
3. *Désirée*, Annemarie Selinko
4. *Battle Cry*, Leon M. Uris
5. *From Here to Eternity*, James Jones
6. *The High and the Mighty*, Ernest K. Gann
7. *Beyond This Place*, A. J. Cronin
8. *Time and Time Again*, James Hilton
9. *Lord Vanity*, Samuel Shellabarger
10. *The Unconquered*, Ben Ames Williams

Nonfiction

1. *The Holy Bible: Revised Standard Version*
2. *The Power of Positive Thinking*, Norman Vincent Peale
3. *Sexual Behavior in the Human Female*, Alfred C. Kinsey, et al.
4. *Angel Unaware*, Dale Evans Rogers
5. *Life Is Worth Living*, Fulton J. Sheen
6. *A Man Called Peter*, Catherine Marshall
7. *This I Believe*, Edward P. Morgan, editor; Edward R. Murrow, foreword
8. *The Greatest Faith Ever Known*, Fulton Oursler and G. A. O. Armstrong
9. *How to Play Your Best Golf*, Tommy Armour
10. *A House Is Not a Home*, Polly Adler

1954

Fiction

1. *Not as a Stranger*, Morton Thompson
2. *Mary Anne*, Daphne du Maurier
3. *Love Is Eternal*, Irving Stone
4. *The Royal Box*, Frances Parkinson Keyes
5. *The Egyptian*, Mika Waltari
6. *No Time for Sergeants*, Mac Hyman
7. *Sweet Thursday*, John Steinbeck

8. *The View from Pompey's Head*, Hamilton Basso
9. *Never Victorious, Never Defeated*, Taylor Caldwell
10. *Benton's Row*, Frank Yerby

Nonfiction

1. *The Holy Bible: Revised Standard Version*
2. *The Power of Positive Thinking*, Norman Vincent Peale
3. *Better Homes and Gardens New Cook Book*
4. *Betty Crocker's Good and Easy Cook Book*
5. *The Tumult and the Shouting*, Grantland Rice
6. *I'll Cry Tomorrow*, Lillian Roth, Gerold Frank, and Mike Connolly
7. *The Prayers of Peter Marshall*, Catherine Marshall, editor
8. *This I Believe, 2*, Raymond Swing, editor
9. *But We Were Born Free*, Elmer Davis
10. *The Saturday Evening Post Treasury*, Roger Butterfield, editor

1955

Fiction

1. *Marjorie Morningstar*, Herman Wouk
2. *Auntie Mame*, Patrick Dennis
3. *Andersonville*, MacKinlay Kantor
4. *Bonjour Tristesse*, Françoise Sagan
5. *The Man in the Gray Flannel Suit*, Sloan Wilson
6. *Something of Value*, Robert Ruark
7. *Not As a Stranger*, Morton Thompson
8. *No Time for Sergeants*, Mac Hyman
9. *The Tontine*, Thomas B. Costain
10. *Ten North Frederick*, John O'Hara

Nonfiction

1. *Gift from the Sea*, Anne Morrow Lindbergh
2. *The Power of Positive Thinking*, Norman Vincent Peale
3. *The Family of Man*, Edward Steichen
4. *A Man Called Peter*, Catherine Marshall
5. *How to Live 365 Days a Year*, John A. Schindler
6. *Better Homes and Gardens Diet Book*
7. *The Secret of Happiness*, Billy Graham
8. *Why Johnny Can't Read*, Rudolf Flesch
9. *Inside Africa*, John Gunther
10. *Year of Decisions*, Harry S Truman

1956

Fiction

1. *Don't Go Near the Water*, William Brinkley
2. *The Last Hurrah*, Edwin O'Connor
3. *Peyton Place*, Grace Metalious
4. *Auntie Mame*, Patrick Dennis
5. *Eloise*, Kay Thompson
6. *Andersonville*, MacKinlay Kantor
7. *A Certain Smile*, Françoise Sagan
8. *The Tribe That Lost Its Head*, Nicholas Monsarrat
9. *The Mandarins*, Simone de Beauvoir
10. *Boon Island*, Kenneth Roberts

Nonfiction

1. *Arthritis and Common Sense*, rev. ed., Dan Dale Alexander
2. *Webster's New World Dictionary of the American Language*, concise ed., David B. Guralnik
3. *Betty Crocker's Picture Cook Book*, 2nd. ed.
4. *Etiquette*, Frances Benton
5. *Better Homes and Gardens Barbecue Book*
6. *The Search for Bridey Murphy*, Morey Bernstein
7. *Love or Perish*, Smiley Blanton, M.D.
8. *Better Homes and Gardens Decorating Book*
9. *How to Live 365 Days a Year*, John A. Schindler
10. *The Nun's Story*, Kathryn Hulme

1957

Fiction

1. *By Love Possessed*, James Gould Cozzens
2. *Peyton Place*, Grace Metalious
3. *Compulsion*, Meyer Levin
4. *Rally Round the Flag, Boys!*, Max Shulman
5. *Blue Camellia*, Frances Parkinson Keyes
6. *Eloise in Paris*, Kay Thompson
7. *The Scapegoat*, Daphne du Maurier
8. *On the Beach*, Nevil Shute
9. *Below the Salt*, Thomas B. Costain
10. *Atlas Shrugged*, Ayn Rand

Nonfiction

1. *Kids Say the Darndest Things!*, Art Linkletter
2. *The FBI Story*, Don Whitehead
3. *Stay Alive All Your Life*, Norman Vincent Peale
4. *To Live Again*, Catherine Marshall
5. *Better Homes and Gardens Flower Arranging*

6. *Where Did You Go? Out. What Did You Do? Nothing*, Robert Paul Smith
7. *Baruch: My Own Story*, Bernard M. Baruch
8. *Please Don't Eat the Daisies*, Jean Kerr
9. *The American Heritage Book of Great Historic Places*
10. *The Day Christ Died*, Jim Bishop

1958

Fiction

1. *Doctor Zhivago*, Boris Pasternak
2. *Anatomy of a Murder*, Robert Traver
3. *Lolita*, Vladimir Nabokov
4. *Around the World with Auntie Mame*, Patrick Dennis
5. *From the Terrace*, John O'Hara
6. *Eloise at Christmastime*, Kay Thompson
7. *Ice Palace*, Edna Ferber
8. *The Winthrop Woman*, Anya Seton
9. *The Enemy Camp*, Jerome Weidman
10. *Victorine*, Frances Parkinson Keyes

Nonfiction

1. *Kids Say the Darndest Things!*, Art Linkletter
2. *'Twixt Twelve and Twenty*, Pat Boone
3. *Only in America*, Harry Golden
4. *Masters of Deceit*, Edgar Hoover
5. *Please Don't Eat the Daisies*, Jean Kerr
6. *Better Homes and Gardens Salad Book*
7. *The New Testament in Modern English*, J. P. Phillips, trans.
8. *Aku-Aku*, Thor Heyerdahl
9. *Dear Abby*, Abigail Van Buren
10. *Inside Russia Today*, John Gunther

1959

Fiction

1. *Exodus*, Leon Uris
2. *Doctor Zhivago*, Boris Pasternak
3. *Hawaii*, James Michener
4. *Advise and Consent*, Allen Drury
5. *Lady Chatterley's Lover*, D. H. Lawrence
6. *The Ugly American*, William J. Lederer and Eugene L. Burdick
7. *Dear and Glorious Physician*, Taylor Caldwell
8. *Lolita*, Vladimir Nabokov
9. *Mrs. 'Arris Goes to Paris*, Paul Gallico
10. *Poor No More*, Robert Ruark

Nonfiction

1. *'Twixt Twelve and Twenty*, Pat Boone
2. *Folk Medicine*, D. C. Jarvis

3. *For 2¢ Plain*, Harry Golden
4. *The Status Seekers*, Vance Packard
5. *Act One*, Moss Hart
6. *Charley Weaver's Letters from Mamma*, Cliff Arquette
7. *The Elements of Style*, William Strunk Jr. and E. B. White
8. *The General Foods Kitchens Cookbook*
9. *Only in America*, Harry Golden
10. *Mine Enemy Grows Older*, Alexander King

1960

Fiction

1. *Advise and Consent*, Allen Drury
2. *Hawaii*, James A. Michener
3. *The Leopard*, Giuseppe di Lampedusa
4. *The Chapman Report*, Irving Wallace
5. *Ourselves to Know*, John O'Hara
6. *The Constant Image*, Marcia Davenport
7. *The Lovely Ambition*, Mary Ellen Chase
8. *The Listener*, Taylor Caldwell
9. *Trustee from the Toolroom*, Nevil Shute
10. *Sermons and Soda-Water*, John O'Hara

Nonfiction

1. *Folk Medicine*, D. C. Jarvis
2. *Better Homes and Gardens First Aid for Your Family*
3. *The General Foods Kitchens Cookbook*
4. *May This House Be Safe from Tigers*, Alexander King
5. *Better Homes and Gardens Dessert Book*
6. *Better Homes and Gardens Decorating Ideas*
7. *The Rise and Fall of the Third Reich*, William L. Shirer
8. *The Conscience of a Conservative*, Barry Goldwater
9. *I Kid You Not*, Jack Paar
10. *Between You, Me and the Gatepost*, Pat Boone

1961

Fiction

1. *The Agony and the Ecstasy*, Irving Stone
2. *Franny and Zooey*, J. D. Salinger
3. *To Kill a Mockingbird*, Harper Lee
4. *Mila 18*, Leon Uris
5. *The Carpetbaggers*, Harold Robbins
6. *Tropic of Cancer*, Henry Miller
7. *Winnie Ille Pu*, Alexander Lenard, trans.
8. *Daughter of Silence*, Morris West

9. *The Edge of Sadness*, Edwin O'Connor
10. *The Winter of Our Discontent*, John Steinbeck

Nonfiction

1. *The New English Bible: The New Testament*
2. *The Rise and Fall of the Third Reich*, William Shirer
3. *Better Homes and Gardens Sewing Book*
4. *Casserole Cook Book*
5. *A Nation of Sheep*, William Lederer
6. *Better Homes and Gardens Nutrition for Your Family*
7. *The Making of the President, 1960*, Theodore H. White
8. *Calories Don't Count*, Dr. Herman Taller
9. *Betty Crocker's New Picture Cook Book: New Edition*
10. *Ring of Bright Water*, Gavin Maxwell

1962

Fiction

1. *Ship of Fools*, Katherine Anne Porter
2. *Dearly Beloved*, Anne Morrow Lindbergh
3. *A Shade of Difference*, Allen Drury
4. *Youngblood Hawke*, Herman Wouk
5. *Franny and Zooey*, J. D. Salinger
6. *Fail-Safe*, Eugene Burdick and Harvey Wheeler
7. *Seven Days in May*, Fletcher Knebel and Charles W. Bailey II
8. *The Prize*, Irving Wallace
9. *The Agony and the Ecstasy*, Irving Stone
10. *The Reivers*, William Faulkner

Nonfiction

1. *Calories Don't Count*, Dr. Herman Taller
2. *The New English Bible: The New Testament*
3. *Better Homes and Gardens Cook Book: New Edition*
4. *O Ye Jigs & Juleps!*, Virginia Cary Hudson
5. *Happiness Is a Warm Puppy*, Charles M. Schulz
6. *The Joy of Cooking: New Edition*, Irma S. Rombauer and Marion Rombauer Becker
7. *My Life in Court*, Louis Nizer
8. *The Rothschilds*, Frederic Morton
9. *Sex and the Single Girl*, Helen Gurley Brown
10. *Travels with Charley*, John Steinbeck

1963

Fiction

1. *The Shoes of the Fisherman*, Morris L. West
2. *The Group*, Mary McCarthy
3. *Raise High the Roof Beam, Carpenters, and Seymour—An Introduction*, J. D. Salinger
4. *Caravans*, James A. Michener
5. *Elizabeth Appleton*, John O'Hara
6. *Grandmother and the Priests*, Taylor Caldwell
7. *City of Night*, John Rechy
8. *The Glass-Blowers*, Daphne du Maurier
9. *The Sand Pebbles*, Richard McKenna
10. *The Battle of the Villa Fiorita*, Rumer Godden

Nonfiction

1. *Happiness Is a Warm Puppy*, Charles M. Schulz
2. *Security Is a Thumb and a Blanket*, Charles M. Schulz

3. *J.F.K.: The Man and the Myth*, Victor Lasky
4. *Profiles in Courage: Inaugural Edition*, John F. Kennedy
5. *O Ye Jigs & Juleps!*, Virginia Cary Hudson
6. *Better Homes and Gardens Bread Cook Book*
7. *The Pillsbury Family Cookbook*
8. *I Owe Russia $1200*, Bob Hope
9. *Heloise's Housekeeping Hints*
10. *Better Homes and Gardens Baby Book*

1964

Fiction

1. *The Spy Who Came in from the Cold*, John le Carré
2. *Candy*, Terry Southern and Mason Hoffenberg
3. *Herzog*, Saul Bellow
4. *Armageddon*, Leon Uris
5. *The Man*, Irving Wallace
6. *The Rector of Justin*, Louis Auchincloss

7. *The Martyred*, Richard E. Kim
8. *You Only Live Twice*, Ian Fleming
9. *This Rough Magic*, Mary Stewart
10. *Convention*, Fletcher Knebel and Charles W. Bailey II

Nonfiction

1. *Four Days*, American Heritage and United Press International
2. *I Need All the Friends I Can Get*, Charles M. Schulz
3. *Profiles in Courage: Memorial Edition*, John F. Kennedy
4. *In His Own Write*, John Lennon
5. *Christmas Is Together-Time*, Charles M. Schulz
6. *A Day in the Life of President Kennedy*, Jim Bishop
7. *The Kennedy Wit*, compiled by Bill Adler
8. *A Moveable Feast*, Ernest Hemingway
9. *Reminiscences*, General Douglas MacArthur
10. *The John F. Kennedys*, Mark Shaw

LITERATURE GOES TO THE MOVIES

It's no secret that many movies, both good and bad, are based on books. This list presents a small sampling of unusual, delightful, and surprising books by leading writers that were turned into well-known movies. (The dates after the titles indicate the year of the film version's release.)

American Hero (released as *Wag the Dog*, 1997), Larry Beinhart
Awakenings (1990), Oliver Sacks
The Blue Angel (1930, 1959), Heinrich Mann
The Body Snatcher (1945), Robert Louis Stevenson
Breakfast at Tiffany's (1961), Truman Capote
Burning Patience (released as *Il Postino (The Postman)*, 1995), Antonio Skarmeta
Chitty, Chitty, Bang, Bang (1968), Ian Fleming
The Death and Life of Dith Pran (released as *The Killing Fields*, 1984), Sidney Schanberg
Deliverance (1972), James Dickey
Do Androids Dream of Electric Sheep? (released as *Blade Runner*, 1982), Philip K. Dick
Donnie Brasco: My Undercover Life in the Mafia (released as *Donnie Brasco*, 1997), Joseph D. Pistone with Richard Woodley
Don't Look Now (1971), Daphne du Maurier
Dream Story (released as *Eyes Wide Shut*, 1999), Arthur Schnitzler
The Executioners (released as *Cape Fear*, 1962, 1991), J. D. MacDonald
The Grifters (1990), Jim Thompson
The Hamlet (originally *The Long, Hot Summer*, 1957) William Faulkner
Jumanji (1995), Chris Van Allsburg

The Killer Angels (released as *Gettysburg*, 1993), Michael Shaara
L.A. Confidential (1997), James Ellroy
The Last Picture Show (1971), Larry McMurtry
Legends of the Fall (1994), Jim Harrison
Lost Moon (released as *Apollo 13*, 1995), Jim Lovell and Jeffrey Kluger
The Magnificent Ambersons (1942), Booth Tarkington
The Maltese Falcon (1941; also released as *Satan Met a Lady*, 1937), Dashiell Hammett
Mildred Pierce (1945), James M. Cain
The Natural (1984), Bernard Malamud
The Postman Always Rings Twice (1946, 1981), James M. Cain
Psycho (1960), Robert Bloch
Rum Punch (released as *Jackie Brown*, 1997), Elmore Leonard
The Seven Pillars of Wisdom (released as *Lawrence of Arabia*, 1962), T. E. Lawrence
Seven Years in Tibet (1997), Heinrich Harrar
Starship Troopers (1997), Robert A. Heinlein
Tales from the South Pacific (produced as the musical *South Pacific* and later released as a film, 1958), James Michener
The Turn of the Screw (released as *The Innocents*, 1961), Henry James
Two Hours to Doom (released as *Dr. Strangelove*, 1964), Peter George

1965

Fiction
1. *The Source*, James A. Michener
2. *Up the Down Staircase*, Bel Kaufman
3. *Herzog*, Saul Bellow
4. *The Looking Glass War*, John le Carré
5. *The Green Berets*, Robin Moore
6. *Those Who Love*, Irving Stone
7. *The Man with the Golden Gun*, Ian Fleming
8. *Hotel*, Arthur Hailey
9. *The Ambassador*, Morris West
10. *Don't Stop the Carnival*, Herman Wouk

Nonfiction
1. *How to Be a Jewish Mother*, Dan Greenburg
2. *A Gift of Prophecy*, Ruth Montgomery
3. *Games People Play*, Eric Berne, M.D.
4. *World Aflame*, Billy Graham
5. *Happiness Is a Dry Martini*, Johnny Carson
6. *Markings*, Dag Hammarskjöld
7. *A Thousand Days*, Arthur Schlesinger Jr.
8. *My Shadow Ran Fast*, Bill Sands
9. *Kennedy*, Theodore C. Sorensen
10. *The Making of the President, 1964*, Theodore H. White

1966

Fiction
1. *Valley of the Dolls*, Jacqueline Susann
2. *The Adventurers*, Harold Robbins
3. *The Secret of Santa Vittoria*, Robert Crichton
4. *Capable of Honor*, Allen Drury
5. *The Double Image*, Helen MacInnes
6. *The Fixer*, Bernard Malamud
7. *Tell No Man*, Adela Rogers St. Johns
8. *Tai-Pan*, James Clavell
9. *The Embezzler*, Louis Auchincloss
10. *All in the Family*, Edwin O'Connor

Nonfiction
1. *How to Avoid Probate*, Norman F. Dacey
2. *Human Sexual Response*, William Howard Masters and Virginia E. Johnston
3. *In Cold Blood*, Truman Capote
4. *Games People Play*, Eric Berne, M.D.
5. *A Thousand Days*, Arthur M. Schlesinger Jr.
6. *Everything but Money*, Sam Levenson
7. *The Random House Dictionary of the English Language*
8. *Rush to Judgment*, Mark Lane
9. *The Last Battle*, Cornelius Ryan
10. *Phyllis Diller's Housekeeping Hints*, Phyllis Diller

1967

Fiction
1. *The Arrangement*, Elia Kazan
2. *The Confessions of Nat Turner*, William Styron (tie)
2. *The Chosen*, Chaim Potok (tie)
4. *Topaz*, Leon Uris
5. *Christy*, Catherine Marshall
6. *The Eighth Day*, Thornton Wilder
7. *Rosemary's Baby*, Ira Levin
8. *The Plot*, Irving Wallace
9. *The Gabriel Hounds*, Mary Stewart
10. *The Exhibitionist*, Henry Sutton

Nonfiction
1. *Death of a President*, William Manchester
2. *Misery Is a Blind Date*, Johnny Carson
3. *Games People Play*, Eric Berne, M.D.
4. *Stanyan Street and Other Sorrows*, Rod McKuen
5. *A Modern Priest Looks at His Out-dated Church*, Father James Kavanaugh
6. *Everything but Money*, Sam Levenson
7. *Our Crowd*, Stephen Birmingham
8. *Edgar Cayce—The Sleeping Prophet*, Jess Stearn (tie)
8. *Better Homes and Gardens Favorite Ways with Chicken* (tie)
8. *Phyllis Diller's Marriage Manual*, Phyllis Diller (tie)

1968

Fiction
1. *Airport*, Arthur Hailey
2. *Couples*, John Updike
3. *The Salzburg Connection*, Helen MacInnes
4. *A Small Town in Germany*, John Le Carré
5. *Testimony of Two Men*, Taylor Caldwell
6. *Preserve and Protect*, Allen Drury
7. *Myra Breckinridge*, Gore Vidal
8. *Vanished*, Fletcher Knebel
9. *Christy*, Catherine Marshall
10. *The Tower of Babel*, Morris L. West

Nonfiction
1. *Better Homes and Gardens New Cook Book*
2. *The Random House Dictionary of the English Language: College Edition*, Laurence Urdang, editor
3. *Listen to the Warm*, Rod McKuen
4. *Between Parent and Child*, Haim G. Ginott
5. *Lonesome Cities*, Rod McKuen

6. *The Doctor's Quick Weight Loss Diet*, Erwin M. Stillman and Samm Sinclair Baker
7. *The Money Game*, Adam Smith
8. *Stanyan Street and Other Sorrows*, Rod McKuen
9. *The Weight Watcher's Cook Book*, Jean Nidetch
10. *Better Homes and Gardens Eat and Stay Slim*

1969

Fiction
1. *Portnoy's Complaint*, Philip Roth
2. *The Godfather*, Mario Puzo
3. *The Love Machine*, Jacqueline Susann
4. *The Inheritors*, Harold Robbins
5. *The Andromeda Strain*, Michael Crichton
6. *The Seven Minutes*, Irving Wallace
7. *Naked Came the Stranger*, Penelope Ashe
8. *The Promise*, Chaim Potok
9. *The Pretenders*, Gwen Davis
10. *The House on the Strand*, Daphne du Maurier

Nonfiction
1. *American Heritage Dictionary of the English Language*, William Morris, editor
2. *In Someone's Shadow*, Rod McKuen
3. *The Peter Principle*, Laurence J. Peter and Raymond Hull
4. *Between Parent and Teenager*, Dr. Haim G. Ginott
5. *The Graham Kerr Cookbook*, The Galloping Gourmet
6. *The Selling of the President, 1968*, Joe McGinniss
7. *Miss Craig's 21-Day Shape-Up Program for Men and Women*, Marjorie Craig
8. *My Life and Prophecies*, Jeane Dixon with René Noorbergen
9. *Linda Goodman's Sun Signs*, Linda Goodman
10. *Twelve Years of Christmas*, Rod McKuen

1970

Fiction
1. *Love Story*, Erich Segal
2. *The French Lieutenant's Woman*, John Fowles
3. *Islands in the Stream*, Ernest Hemingway
4. *The Crystal Cave*, Mary Stewart
5. *Great Lion of God*, Taylor Caldwell
6. *QB VII*, Leon Uris

7. *The Gang That Couldn't Shoot Straight*, Jimmy Breslin
8. *The Secret Woman*, Victoria Holt
9. *Travels with My Aunt*, Graham Greene
10. *Rich Man, Poor Man*, Irwin Shaw

Nonfiction

1. *Everything You Always Wanted to Know About Sex but Were Afraid to Ask*, David Reuben, M.D.
2. *The New English Bible*
3. *The Sensuous Woman*, "J"
4. *Better Homes and Gardens Fondue and Tabletop Cooking*
5. *Up the Organization*, Robert Townsend
6. *Ball Four*, Jim Bouton
7. *American Heritage Dictionary of the English Language*, William Morris
8. *Body Language*, Julius Fast
9. *In Someone's Shadow*, Rod McKuen
10. *Caught in the Quiet*, Rod McKuen

1971

Fiction

1. *Wheels*, Arthur Hailey
2. *The Exorcist*, William P. Blatty
3. *The Passions of the Mind*, Irving Stone
4. *The Day of the Jackal*, Frederick Forsyth
5. *The Betsy*, Harold Robbins
6. *Message from Malaga*, Helen MacInnes
7. *The Winds of War*, Herman Wouk
8. *The Drifters*, James A. Michener
9. *The Other*, Thomas Tryon
10. *Rabbit Redux*, John Updike

Nonfiction

1. *The Sensuous Man*, "M"
2. *Bury My Heart at Wounded Knee*, Dee Brown
3. *Better Homes and Gardens Blender Cook Book*
4. *I'm O.K., You're O.K.*, Thomas Harris
5. *Any Woman Can!*, David Reuben, M.D.
6. *Inside the Third Reich*, Albert Speer
7. *Eleanor and Franklin*, Joseph P. Lash
8. *Wunnerful, Wunnerful!*, Lawrence Welk
9. *Honor Thy Father*, Gay Talese
10. *Fields of Wonder*, Rod McKuen

1972

Fiction

1. *Jonathan Livingston Seagull*, Richard Bach
2. *August, 1914*, Alexander Solzhenitsyn
3. *The Odessa File*, Frederick Forsyth

4. *The Day of the Jackal*, Frederick Forsyth
5. *The Word*, Irving Wallace
6. *The Winds of War*, Herman Wouk
7. *Captains and the Kings*, Taylor Caldwell
8. *Two from Galilee*, Marjorie Holmes
9. *My Name Is Asher Lev*, Chaim Potok
10. *Semi-Tough*, Dan Jenkins

Nonfiction

1. *The Living Bible*, Kenneth Taylor
2. *I'm O.K., You're O.K.*, Thomas Harris
3. *Open Marriage*, Nena and George O'Neill
4. *Harry S. Truman*, Margaret Truman
5. *Dr. Atkins' Diet Revolution*, Robert C. Atkins
6. *Better Homes and Gardens Menu Cook Book*
7. *The Peter Prescription*, Laurence J. Peter
8. *A World Beyond*, Ruth Montgomery
9. *Journey to Ixtlan*, Carlos Castaneda
10. *Better Homes and Gardens Low-Calorie Desserts*

1973

Fiction

1. *Jonathan Livingston Seagull*, Richard Bach
2. *Once Is Not Enough*, Jacqueline Susann
3. *Breakfast of Champions*, Kurt Vonnegut
4. *The Odessa File*, Frederick Forsyth
5. *Burr*, Gore Vidal
6. *The Hollow Hills*, Mary Stewart
7. *Evening in Byzantium*, Irwin Shaw
8. *The Matlock Paper*, Robert Ludlum
9. *The Billion Dollar Sure Thing*, Paul E. Erdman
10. *The Honorary Consul*, Graham Greene

Nonfiction

1. *The Living Bible*, Kenneth Taylor
2. *Dr. Atkins' Diet Revolution*, Robert C. Atkins
3. *I'm O.K., You're O.K.*, Thomas Harris
4. *The Joy of Sex*, Alex Comfort
5. *Weight Watchers Program Cookbook*, Jean Nidetch
6. *How to Be Your Own Best Friend*, Mildred Newman, et al.
7. *The Art of Walt Disney*, Christopher Finch
8. *Better Homes and Gardens Home Canning Cookbook*
9. *Alistair Cooke's America*, Alistair Cooke
10. *Sybil*, Flora R. Schreiber

1974

Fiction

1. *Centennial*, James A. Michener
2. *Watership Down*, Richard Adams
3. *Jaws*, Peter Benchley
4. *Tinker, Tailor, Soldier, Spy*, John le Carré
5. *Something Happened*, Joseph Heller
6. *The Dogs of War*, Frederick Forsyth
7. *The Pirate*, Harold J. Robbins
8. *I Heard the Owl Call My Name*, Margaret Craven
9. *The Seven-Per-Cent Solution*, John H. Watson, M.D., Nicholas Meyer, editor
10. *The Fan Club*, Irving Wallace

Nonfiction

1. *The Total Woman*, Marabel Morgan
2. *All the President's Men*, Carl Bernstein and Bob Woodward
3. *Plain Speaking: An Oral Biography of Harry S. Truman*, Merle Miller
4. *More Joy: A Lovemaking Companion to The Joy of Sex*, Alex Comfort
5. *Alistair Cooke's America*, Alistair Cooke
6. *Tales of Power*, Carlos A. Castaneda
7. *You Can Profit from a Monetary Crisis*, Harry Browne
8. *All Things Bright and Beautiful*, James Herriot
9. *The Bermuda Triangle*, Charles Berlitz with J. Manson Valentine
10. *The Memory Book*, Harry Lorayne and Jerry Lucas

1975

Fiction

1. *Ragtime*, E. L. Doctorow
2. *The Moneychangers*, Arthur Hailey
3. *Curtain*, Agatha Christie
4. *Looking for Mister Goodbar*, Judith Rossner
5. *The Choirboys*, Joseph Wambaugh
6. *The Eagle Has Landed*, Jack Higgins
7. *The Greek Treasure: A Biographical Novel of Henry and Sophia Schliemann*, Irving Stone
8. *The Great Train Robbery*, Michael Crichton
9. *Shogun*, James Clavell
10. *Humboldt's Gift*, Saul Bellow

Nonfiction

1. *Angels: God's Secret Agents*, Billy Graham
2. *Winning Through Intimidation*, Robert Ringer

3. *TM: Discovering Energy and Overcoming Stress*, Harold H. Bloomfield
4. *The Ascent of Man*, Jacob Bronowski
5. *Sylvia Porter's Money Book*, Sylvia Porter
6. *Total Fitness in 30 Minutes a Week*, Laurence E. Morehouse and Leonard Gross
7. *The Bermuda Triangle*, Charles Berlitz with J. Manson Valentine
8. *The Save-Your-Life Diet*, David Reuben
9. *Bring on the Empty Horses*, David Niven
10. *Breach of Faith: The Fall of Richard Nixon*, Theodore H. White

1976

Fiction
1. *Trinity*, Leon Uris
2. *Sleeping Murder*, Agatha Christie
3. *Dolores*, Jacqueline Susann
4. *Storm Warning*, Jack Higgins
5. *The Deep*, Peter Benchley
6. *1876*, Gore Vidal
7. *Slapstick: or, Lonesome No More!*, Kurt Vonnegut
8. *The Lonely Lady*, Harold Robbins
9. *Touch Not the Cat*, Mary Stewart
10. *A Stranger in the Mirror*, Sidney Sheldon

Nonfiction
1. *The Final Days*, Bob Woodward and Carl Bernstein
2. *Roots*, Alex Haley
3. *Your Erroneous Zones*, Dr. Wayne W. Dyer
4. *Passages: The Predictable Crises of Adult Life*, Gail Sheehy

AMERICA'S POETS LAUREATE

To honor America's greatest poets, the Librarian of Congress names a poet laureate. The anointed:

Robert Penn Warren	1986–87
Richard Wilbur	1987–88
Howard Nemerov	1988–90
Mark Strand	1990–91
Joseph Brodsky	1991–92
Mona Van Duyn	1992–93
Rita Dove	1993–95
Robert Hass	1995–97
Robert Pinsky	1997–

5. *Born Again*, Charles W. Colson
6. *The Grass Is Always Greener over the Septic Tank*, Erma Bombeck
7. *Angels: God's Secret Agents*, Billy Graham
8. *Blind Ambition: The White House Years*, John Dean
9. *The Hite Report: A Nationwide Study of Female Sexuality*, Shere Hite
10. *The Right and the Power: The Prosecution of Watergate*, Leon Jaworski

1977

Fiction
1. *The Silmarillion*, J. R. R. Tolkien; Christopher Tolkien
2. *The Thorn Birds*, Colleen McCullough
3. *Illusions: The Adventures of a Reluctant Messiah*, Richard Bach
4. *The Honourable Schoolboy*, John le Carré
5. *Oliver's Story*, Erich Segal
6. *Dreams Die First*, Harold Robbins
7. *Beggarman, Thief*, Irwin Shaw
8. *How to Save Your Own Life*, Erica Jong
9. *Delta of Venus: Erotica*, Anaïs Nin
10. *Daniel Martin*, John Fowles

Nonfiction
1. *Roots*, Alex Haley
2. *Looking Out for #1*, Robert Ringer
3. *All Things Wise and Wonderful*, James Herriot
4. *Your Erroneous Zones*, Dr. Wayne W. Dyer
5. *The Book of Lists*, David Wallechinsky, Irving Wallace, and Amy Wallace
6. *The Possible Dream: A Candid Look at Amway*, Charles Paul Conn
7. *The Dragons of Eden: Speculations on the Evolution of Human Intelligence*, Carl Sagan
8. *The Second Ring of Power*, Carlos Castaneda
9. *The Grass Is Always Greener over the Septic Tank*, Erma Bombeck
10. *The Amityville Horror*, Jay Anson

1978

Fiction
1. *Chesapeake*, James A. Michener
2. *War and Remembrance*, Herman Wouk
3. *Fools Die*, Mario Puzo
4. *Bloodlines*, Sidney Sheldon
5. *Scruples*, Judith Krantz
6. *Evergreen*, Belva Plain
7. *Illusions: The Adventures of a Reluctant Messiah*, Richard Bach
8. *The Holcroft Covenant*, Robert Ludlum

9. *Second Generation*, Howard Fast
10. *Eye of the Needle*, Ken Follett

Nonfiction
1. *If Life Is a Bowl of Cherries—What Am I Doing in the Pits?*, Erma Bombeck
2. *Gnomes*, Wil Huygen and Rien Poortvliet
3. *The Complete Book of Running*, James Fixx
4. *Mommie Dearest*, Christina Crawford
5. *Pulling Your Own Strings*, Dr. Wayne W. Dyer
8. *RN: The Memoirs of Richard Nixon*, Richard Nixon
7. *A Distant Mirror: The Calamitous Fourteenth Century*, Barbara Tuchman
8. *Faeries*, Brian Froud and Alan Lee
9. *In Search of History: A Personal Adventure*, Theodore H. White
10. *The Muppet Show Book*, The Muppet People

1979

Fiction
1. *The Matarese Circle*, Robert Ludlum
2. *Sophie's Choice*, William Styron
3. *Overload*, Arthur Hailey
4. *Memories of Another Day*, Harold Robbins
5. *Jailbird*, Kurt Vonnegut
6. *The Dead Zone*, Stephen King
7. *The Last Enchantment*, Mary Stewart
8. *The Establishment*, Howard Fast
9. *The Third World War: August 1985*, Gen. Sir John Hackett, et al.
10. *Smiley's People*, John le Carré

Nonfiction
1. *Aunt Erma's Cope Book*, Erma Bombeck
2. *The Complete Scarsdale Medical Diet*, Herman Tarnower, M.D., and Samm Sinclair Baker
3. *How to Prosper During the Coming Bad Years*, Howard J. Ruff
4. *Cruel Shoes*, Steve Martin
5. *The Pritikin Program for Diet and Exercise*, Nathan Pritikin and Patrick McGrady Jr.
6. *White House Years*, Henry Kissinger
7. *Lauren Bacall: By Myself*, Lauren Bacall
8. *The Brethren: Inside the Supreme Court*, Bob Woodward and Scott Armstrong
9. *Restoring the American Dream*, Robert J. Ringer
10. *The Winner's Circle*, Charles Paul Conn

1980

Fiction

1. *The Covenant*, James A. Michener
2. *The Bourne Identity*, Robert Ludlum
3. *Rage of Angels*, Sidney Sheldon
4. *Princess Daisy*, Judith Krantz
5. *Firestarter*, Stephen King
6. *The Key to Rebecca*, Ken Follett
7. *Random Winds*, Belva Plain
8. *The Devil's Alternative*, Frederick Forsyth
9. *The Fifth Horseman*, Larry Collins and Dominique Lapierre
10. *The Spike*, Arnaud de Borchgrave and Robert Moss

Nonfiction

1. *Crisis Investing: Opportunities and Profits in the Coming Great Depression*, Douglas R. Casey
2. *Cosmos*, Carl Sagan
3. *Free to Choose: A Personal Statement*, Milton and Rose Friedman
4. *Anatomy of an Illness as Perceived by the Patient*, Norman Cousins
5. *Thy Neighbor's Wife*, Gay Talese
6. *The Sky's the Limit*, Dr. Wayne W. Dyer
7. *The Third Wave*, Alvin Toffler
8. *Craig Claiborne's Gourmet Diet*, Craig Claiborne with Pierre Franey
9. *Nothing Down*, Robert Allen
10. *Shelley: Also Known as Shirley*, Shelley Winters

1981

Fiction

1. *Noble House*, James Clavell
2. *The Hotel New Hampshire*, John Irving
3. *Cujo*, Stephen King
4. *An Indecent Obsession*, Colleen McCullough
5. *Gorky Park*, Martin Cruz Smith
6. *Masquerade*, Kit Williams
7. *Goodbye, Janette*, Harold Robbins
8. *The Third Deadly Sin*, Lawrence Sanders
9. *The Glitter Dome*, Joseph Wambaugh
10. *No Time for Tears*, Cynthia Freeman

Nonfiction

1. *The Beverly Hills Diet*, Judy Mazel
2. *The Lord God Made Them All*, James Herriot
3. *Richard Simmons' Never-Say-Diet Book*, Richard Simmons
4. *A Light in the Attic*, Shel Silverstein
5. *Cosmos*, Carl Sagan
6. *Better Homes & Gardens New Cook Book*

1982

Fiction

1. *E.T., the Extra-Terrestrial Storybook*, William Kotzwinkle
2. *Space*, James A. Michener
3. *The Parsifal Mosaic*, Robert Ludlum
4. *Master of the Game*, Sidney Sheldon
5. *Mistral's Daughter*, Judith Krantz
6. *The Valley of Horses*, Jean M. Auel
7. *Different Seasons*, Stephen King
8. *North and South*, John Jakes
9. *2010: Odyssey Two*, Arthur C. Clarke
10. *The Man from St. Petersburg*, Ken Follett

Nonfiction

1. *Jane Fonda's Workout Book*, Jane Fonda
2. *Living, Loving and Learning*, Leo Buscaglia
3. *And More by Andy Rooney*, Andrew A. Rooney
4. *Better Homes & Gardens New Cookbook*
5. *Life Extension: Adding Years to Your Life and Life to Your Years—A Practical Scientific Approach*, Durk Pearson and Sandy Shaw
6. *When Bad Things Happen to Good People*, Harold S. Kushner
7. *A Few Minutes with Andy Rooney*, Andrew A. Rooney
8. *The Weight Watchers Food Plan Diet Cookbook*, Jean Nidetch
9. *Richard Simmons' Never-Say-Diet Cookbook*, Richard Simmons
10. *No Bad Dogs: The Woodhouse Way*, Barbara Woodhouse

1983

Fiction

1. *Return of the Jedi Storybook*, Joan D. Vinge, adapt.
2. *Poland*, James A. Michener
3. *Pet Sematary*, Stephen King
4. *The Little Drummer Girl*, John le Carré
5. *Christine*, Stephen King
6. *Changes*, Danielle Steel
7. *The Name of the Rose*, Umberto Eco
8. *White Gold Wielder: Book Three of The Second Chronicles of Thomas Covenant*, Stephen R. Donaldson
9. *Hollywood Wives*, Jackie Collins
10. *The Lonesome Gods*, Louis L'Amour

Nonfiction

1. *In Search of Excellence: Lessons from America's Best-Run Companies*, Thomas J. Peters and Robert H. Waterman Jr.
2. *Megatrends: Ten New Directions Transforming Our Lives*, John Naisbitt
3. *Motherhood: The Second Oldest Profession*, Erma Bombeck
4. *The One Minute Manager*, Kenneth Blanchard and Spencer Johnson
5. *Jane Fonda's Workout Book*, Jane Fonda
6. *The Best of James Herriot*, James Herriot
7. *The Mary Kay Guide to Beauty: Discovering Your Special Look*
8. *On Wings of Eagles*, Ken Follett
9. *Creating Wealth*, Robert G. Allen
10. *The Body Principal: The Exercise Program for Life*, Victoria Principal

1984

Fiction

1. *The Talisman*, Stephen King and Peter Straub
2. *The Aquitaine Progression*, Robert Ludlum
3. *The Sicilian*, Mario Puzo
4. *Love and War*, John Jakes
5. *The Butter Battle Book*, Dr. Seuss
6. *". . . And the Ladies of the Club,"* Helen Hooven Santmyer
7. *The Fourth Protocol*, Frederick Forsyth
8. *Full Circle*, Danielle Steel
9. *The Life and Hard Times of Heidi Abromowitz*, Joan Rivers
10. *Lincoln: A Novel*, Gore Vidal

Nonfiction

1. *Iacocca: An Autobiography*, Lee Iacocca with William Novak
2. *Loving Each Other*, Leo Buscaglia
3. *Eat to Win: The Sports Nutrition Bible*, Robert Haas, M.D.
4. *Pieces of My Mind*, Andrew A. Rooney
5. *Weight Watchers Fast and Fabulous Cookbook*
6. *What They Don't Teach You at Harvard Business School: Notes from a Street-Smart Executive*, Mark H. McCormack
7. *Women Coming of Age*, Jane Fonda with Mignon McCarthy
8. *Moses the Kitten*, James Herriot
9. *The One Minute Salesperson*, Spencer Johnson, M.D., and Larry Wilson
10. *Weight Watchers Quick Start Program Cookbook*, Jean Nidetch

1982 — continued from column

7. *Miss Piggy's Guide to Life*, Miss Piggy as told to Henry Beard
8. *Weight Watchers 365-Day Menu Cookbook*
9. *You Can Negotiate Anything*, Herb Cohen
10. *A Few Minutes with Andy Rooney*, Andrew A. Rooney

1985

Fiction
1. *The Mammoth Hunters*, Jean M. Auel
2. *Texas*, James A. Michener
3. *Lake Wobegon Days*, Garrison Keillor
4. *If Tomorrow Comes*, Sidney Sheldon
5. *Skeleton Crew*, Stephen King
6. *Secrets*, Danielle Steel
7. *Contact*, Carl Sagan
8. *Lucky*, Jackie Collins
9. *Family Album*, Danielle Steel
10. *Jubal Sackett*, Louis L'Amour

Nonfiction
1. *Iacocca: An Autobiography*, Lee Iacocca with William Novak
2. *Yeager: An Autobiography*, Gen. Chuck Yeager and Leo Janos
3. *Elvis and Me*, Priscilla Beaulieu Presley with Sandra Harmon
4. *Fit for Life*, Harvey and Marilyn Diamond
5. *The Be-Happy Attitudes*, Robert Schuller
6. *Dancing in the Light*, Shirley MacLaine
7. *A Passion for Excellence: The Leadership Difference*, Thomas J. Peters and Nancy K. Austin
8. *The Frugal Gourmet*, Jeff Smith
9. *I Never Played the Game*, Howard Cosell with Peter Bonventre
10. *Dr. Berger's Immune Power Diet*, Stuart M. Berger, M.D.

1986

Fiction
1. *It*, Stephen King
2. *Red Storm Rising*, Tom Clancy
3. *Whirlwind*, James Clavell
4. *The Bourne Supremacy*, Robert Ludlum
5. *Hollywood Husbands*, Jackie Collins
6. *Wanderlust*, Danielle Steel
7. *I'll Take Manhattan*, Judith Krantz
8. *Last of the Breed*, Louis L'Amour
9. *The Prince of Tides*, Pat Conroy
10. *A Perfect Spy*, John le Carré

Nonfiction
1. *Fatherhood*, Bill Cosby
2. *Fit for Life*, Harvey and Marilyn Diamond
3. *His Way: The Unauthorized Biography of Frank Sinatra*, Kitty Kelley
4. *The Rotation Diet*, Martin Katahn
5. *You're Only Old Once*, Dr. Seuss
6. *Callanetics: Ten Years Younger in Ten Hours*, Callan Pinckney
7. *The Frugal Gourmet Cooks with Wine*, Jeff Smith
8. *Be Happy—You Are Loved!*, Robert H. Schuller
9. *Word for Word*, Andrew A. Rooney
10. *James Herriot's Dog Stories*, James Herriot

1987

Fiction
1. *The Tommyknockers*, Stephen King
2. *Patriot Games*, Tom Clancy
3. *Kaleidoscope*, Danielle Steel
4. *Misery*, Stephen King
5. *Leaving Home: A Collection of Lake Wobegon Stories*, Garrison Keillor
6. *Windmills of the Gods*, Sidney Sheldon
7. *Presumed Innocent*, Scott Turow
8. *Fine Things*, Danielle Steel
9. *Heaven and Hell*, John Jakes
10. *The Eyes of the Dragon*, Stephen King

Nonfiction
1. *Time Flies*, Bill Cosby
2. *Spycatcher: The Candid Autobiography of a Senior Intelligence Officer*, Peter Wright with Paul Greengrass
3. *Family: The Ties That Bind . . . and Gag!*, Erma Bombeck
4. *Veil: The Secret Wars of the CIA, 1981–1987*, Bob Woodward
5. *A Day in the Life of America*, Rick Smolan and David Cohen
6. *The Great Depression of 1990*, Ravi Batra
7. *It's All in the Playing*, Shirley MacLaine
8. *Man of the House: The Life and Political Memoirs of Speaker Tip O'Neill*, Thomas P. O'Neill Jr. with William Novak
9. *The Frugal Gourmet Cooks American*, Jeff Smith
10. *The Closing of the American Mind*, Allan Bloom

1988

Fiction
1. *The Cardinal of the Kremlin*, Tom Clancy
2. *The Sands of Time*, Sidney Sheldon
3. *Zoya*, Danielle Steel
4. *The Icarus Agenda*, Robert Ludlum
5. *Alaska*, James A. Michener
6. *Till We Meet Again*, Judith Krantz
7. *The Queen of the Damned*, Anne Rice
8. *To Be the Best*, Barbara Taylor Bradford
9. *One: A Novel*, Richard Bach
10. *Mitla Pass*, Leon Uris

Nonfiction
1. *The 8-Week Cholesterol Cure*, Robert E. Kowalski
2. *Talking Straight*, Lee Iacocca with Sonny Kleinfield
3. *A Brief History of Time: From the Big Bang to Black Holes*, Steven W. Hawking
4. *Trump: The Art of the Deal*, Donald J. Trump with Tony Schwartz
5. *Gracie: A Love Story*, George Burns
6. *Elizabeth Takes Off*, Elizabeth Taylor
7. *Swim with the Sharks Without Being Eaten Alive*, Harvey MacKay
8. *Christmas in America*, David Cohen, editor
9. *Weight Watchers Quick Success Program Book*, Jean Nidetch
10. *Moonwalk*, Michael Jackson

1989

Fiction
1. *Clear and Present Danger*, Tom Clancy
2. *The Dark Half*, Stephen King
3. *Daddy*, Danielle Steel
4. *Star*, Danielle Steel
5. *Caribbean*, James A. Michener
6. *The Satanic Verses*, Salman Rushdie
7. *The Russia House*, John le Carré
8. *The Pillars of the Earth*, Ken Follet
9. *California Gold*, John Jakes
10. *While My Pretty One Sleeps*, Mary Higgins Clark

Nonfiction
1. *All I Really Need to Know I Learned in Kindergarten: Uncommon Thoughts on Common Things*, Robert Fulghum
2. *Wealth Without Risk: How to Develop a Personal Fortune Without Going Out on a Limb*, Charles J. Givens
3. *A Woman Named Jackie*, C. David Heymann
4. *It Was on Fire When I Lay Down on It*, Robert Fulghum
5. *Better Homes and Gardens New Cook Book*
6. *The Way Things Work*, David Macaulay
7. *It's Always Something*, Gilda Radner
8. *Roseanne: My Life as a Woman*, Roseanne Barr
9. *The Frugal Gourmet Cooks Three Ancient Cuisines: China, Greece, and Rome*, Jeff Smith
10. *My Turn: The Memoirs of Nancy Reagan*, Nancy Reagan with William Novak

1990

Fiction

1. *The Plains of Passage*, Jean M. Auel
2. *Four Past Midnight*, Stephen King
3. *The Burden of Proof*, Scott Turow
4. *Memories of Midnight*, Sidney Sheldon
5. *Message from Nam*, Danielle Steel
6. *The Bourne Ultimatum*, Robert Ludlum
7. *The Stand: The Complete and Uncut Edition*, Stephen King
8. *Lady Boss*, Jackie Collins
9. *The Witching Hour*, Anne Rice
10. *September*, Rosamunde Pilcher

Nonfiction

1. *A Life on the Road*, Charles Kuralt
2. *The Civil War*, Geoffrey C. Ward with Ric Burns and Ken Burns
3. *The Frugal Gourmet on Our Immigrant Heritage: Recipes You Should Have Gotten from Your Grandmother*, Jeff Smith
4. *Better Homes and Gardens New Cook Book*
5. *Financial Self-Defense: How to Win the Fight for Financial Freedom*, Charles J. Givens
6. *Homecoming: Reclaiming and Championing Your Inner Child*, John Bradshaw
7. *Wealth Without Risk: How to Develop a Personal Fortune Without Going Out on a Limb*, Charles J. Givens
8. *Bo Knows Bo*, Bo Jackson and Dick Schaap
9. *An American Life: An Autobiography*, Ronald Reagan
10. *Megatrends 2000: Ten New Directions for the 1990s*, John Naisbitt and Patricia Aburdene

1991

Fiction

1. *Scarlett: The Sequel to Margaret Mitchell's "Gone with the Wind,"* Alexandra Ripley
2. *The Sum of All Fears*, Tom Clancy
3. *Needful Things*, Stephen King
4. *No Greater Love*, Danielle Steel
5. *Heartbeat*, Danielle Steel
6. *The Doomsday Conspiracy*, Sidney Sheldon
7. *The Firm*, John Grisham
8. *Night Over Water*, Ken Follet
9. *Remember*, Barbara Taylor Bradford
10. *Loves Music, Loves to Dance*, Mary Higgins Clark

Nonfiction

1. *Me: Stories of My Life*, Katharine Hepburn

2. *Nancy Reagan: The Unauthorized Biography*, Kitty Kelley
3. *Uh-Oh: Some Observations from Both Sides of the Refrigerator Door*, Robert Fulghum
4. *Under Fire: An American Story*, Oliver North with William Novak
5. *Final Exit: The Practicalities of Self-Deliverance and Assisted Suicide for the Dying*, Derek Humphry
6. *When You Look Like Your Passport Photo, It's Time to Go Home*, Erma Bombeck
7. *More Wealth Without Risk*, Charles J. Givens
8. *Den of Thieves*, James B. Stewart
9. *Childhood*, Bill Cosby
10. *Financial Self-Defense*, Charles J. Givens

1992

Fiction

1. *Dolores Claiborne*, Stephen King
2. *The Pelican Brief*, John Grisham
3. *Gerald's Game*, Stephen King
4. *Mixed Blessings*, Danielle Steel
5. *Jewels*, Danielle Steel
6. *The Stars Shine Down*, Sidney Sheldon
7. *Tale of the Body Thief*, Anne Rice
8. *Mexico*, James A. Michener
9. *Waiting to Exhale*, Terry McMillan
10. *All Around the Town*, Mary Higgins Clark

Nonfiction

1. *The Way Things Ought to Be*, Rush Limbaugh
2. *It Doesn't Take a Hero: The Autobiography*, Gen. H. Norman Schwarzkopf
3. *How to Satisfy a Woman Every Time*, Naura Hayden
4. *Every Living Thing*, James Herriot
5. *A Return to Love*, Marianne Williamson
6. *Sam Walton: Made in America*, Sam Walton
7. *Diana: Her True Story*, Andrew Morton
8. *Truman*, David McCullough
9. *Silent Passage*, Gail Sheehy
10. *Sex*, Madonna

1993

Fiction

1. *The Bridges of Madison County*, Robert James Waller
2. *The Client*, John Grisham
3. *Slow Waltz at Cedar Bend*, Robert James Waller
4. *Without Remorse*, Tom Clancy
5. *Nightmares and Dreamscapes*, Stephen King

6. *Vanished*, Danielle Steel
7. *Lasher*, Anne Rice
8. *Pleading Guilty*, Scott Turow
9. *Like Water for Chocolate*, Laura Esquivel
10. *The Scorpio Illusion*, Robert Ludlum

Nonfiction

1. *See, I Told You So*, Rush Limbaugh
2. *Private Parts*, Howard Stern
3. *Seinlanguage*, Jerry Seinfeld
4. *Embraced by the Light*, Betty J. Eadie with Curtis Taylor
5. *Ageless Body, Timeless Mind*, Deepak Chopra
6. *Stop the Insanity*, Susan Powter
7. *Women Who Run with the Wolves*, Clarissa Pinkola Estes
8. *Men Are from Mars, Women Are from Venus*, John Gray
9. *The Hidden Life of Dogs*, Elizabeth Marshall Thomas
10. *And If You Play Golf, You're My Friend*, Harvey Penick with Bud Shrake

1994

Fiction

1. *The Chamber*, John Grisham
2. *Debt of Honor*, Tom Clancy
3. *The Celestine Prophecy*, James Redfield
4. *The Gift*, Danielle Steel
5. *Insomnia*, Steven King
6. *Politically Correct Bedtime Stories*, James Finn Garner
7. *Wings*, Danielle Steel
8. *Accident*, Danielle Steel
9. *The Bridges of Madison County*, Robert James Waller
10. *Disclosure*, Michael Crichton

Nonfiction

1. *In the Kitchen with Rosie*, Rosie Daley
2. *Men Are from Mars, Women Are from Venus*, John Gray
3. *Crossing the Threshold of Hope*, John Paul II.
4. *Magic Eye I*, N.E. Thing Enterprises
5. *The Book of Virtues*, William J. Bennett
6. *Magic Eye II*, N.E. Thing Enterprises
7. *Embraced by the Light*, Betty J. Eadie with Curtis Taylor
8. *Don't Stand Too Close to a Naked Man*, Tim Allen
9. *Couplehood*, Paul Reiser
10. *Magic Eye III*, N.E. Thing Enterprises

1995

Fiction

1. *The Rainmaker*, John Grisham
2. *The Lost World*, Michael Crichton

3. *Five Days in Paris*, Danielle Steel
4. *The Christmas Box*, Richard Paul Evans
5. *Lightning*, Danielle Steel
6. *The Celestine Prophecy*, James Redfield
7. *Rose Madder*, Stephen King
8. *Silent Night*, Mary Higgins Clark
9. *Politically Correct Holiday Stories*, James Finn Garner
10. *The Horse Whisperer*, Nicholas Evans

Nonfiction

1. *Men Are from Mars, Women Are from Venus*, John Gray
2. *My American Journey*, Colin Powell with Joseph Perisco
3. *Miss America*, Howard Stern
4. *The Seven Spiritual Laws of Success*, Deepak Chopra
5. *The Road Ahead*, Bill Gates
6. *Charles Kuralt's America*, Charles Kuralt
7. *Mars and Venus in the Bedroom*, John Gray
8. *To Renew America*, Newt Gingrich
9. *My Point...and I Do Have One*, Ellen DeGeneres
10. *The Moral Compass*, William J. Bennett

1996

Fiction

1. *The Runaway Jury*, John Grisham
2. *Executive Orders*, Tom Clancy
3. *Desperation*, Stephen King
4. *Airframe*, Michael Crichton
5. *The Regulators*, Richard Bachman
6. *Malice*, Danielle Steele
7. *Silent Honor*, Danielle Steel
8. *Primary Colors*, anonymous
9. *Cause of Death*, Patricia Cornwell
10. *The Tenth Insight*, James Redfield

Nonfiction

1. *Make the Connection*, Oprah Winfrey and Bob Greene
2. *Men Are from Mars, Women Are from Venus*, John Gray
3. *The Dilbert Principle*, Scott Adams
4. *Simple Abundance*, Sarah Ban Breathnach
5. *The Zone*, Barry Sears with Bill Lawren
6. *Bad As I Wanna Be*, Dennis Rodman
7. *In Contempt*, Christopher Darden
8. *A Reporter's Life*, Walter Cronkite
9. *Dogbert's Top Secret Management Handbook*, Scott Adams
10. *My Sergei: A Love Story*, Ekaterina Gordeeva with E. M. Swift

1997

Fiction

1. *The Partner*, John Grisham
2. *Cold Mountain*, Charles Frazier
3. *The Ghost*, Danielle Steel
4. *The Ranch*, Danielle Steel
5. *Special Delivery*, Danielle Steel
6. *Unnatural Exposure*, Patricia Cornwell
7. *The Best Laid Plans*, Sidney Sheldon
8. *Pretend You Don't See Her*, Mary Higgins Clark
9. *Cat & Mouse*, James Patterson
10. *Hornet's Nest*, Patricia Cornwell

Nonfiction

1. *Angela's Ashes*, Frank McCourt
2. *Simple Abundance*, Sarah Ban Breathnach
3. *Midnight in the Garden of Good and Evil*, John Berendt
4. *The Royals*, Kitty Kelley
5. *Joy of Cooking*, Irma S. Rombauer, Marion Rombauer Becker, and Ethan Becker
6. *Diana: Her True Story*, Andrew Morton
7. *Into Thin Air*, Jon Krakauer

8. *Conversations with God, Book I*, Neale Donald Walsch
9. *Men Are from Mars, Women Are from Venus*, John Gray
10. *Eight Weeks to Optimum Health*, Andrew Weil

1998

Fiction

1. *The Street Lawyer*, John Grisham
2. *Rainbow Six*, Tom Clancy
3. *Bag of Bones*, Stephen King
4. *A Man in Full*, Tom Wolfe
5. *Mirror Image*, Danielle Steel
6. *The Long Road Home*, Danielle Steel
7. *The Klone and I*, Danielle Steel
8. *Point of Origin*, Patricia Cornwell
9. *Paradise*, Toni Morrison
10. *All Through the Night*, Mary Higgins Clark

Nonfiction

1. *The 9 Steps to Financial Freedom*, Suze Orman
2. *The Greatest Generation*, Tom Brokaw
3. *Sugar Busters!*, H. Leighton Steward, Morrison C. Bethea, Sam S. Andrews, and Luis A. Balart
4. *Tuesdays with Morrie*, Mitch Albom
5. *The Guinness Book of Records 1999*
6. *Talking to Heaven*, James Van Praagh
7. *Something More: Excavating Your Authentic Self*, Sarah Ban Breathnach
8. *In the Meantime*, Iyanla Vanzant
9. *A Pirate Looks at Fifty*, Jimmy Buffett
10. *If Life Is a Game These Are the Rules*, Cherie Carter-Scott, Ph.D.

TRY ANOTHER TITLE

A title can make or break a book. Had these literary masterpieces gone to press with their original tags, who knows where they, or we, would be now.

The Title That Made History

All Things Bright and Beautiful, James Harriot
East of Eden, John Steinbeck
The Mill on the Floss, George Eliot
Moby Dick, Herman Melville
Roots, Alex Haley
The Rose Tattoo, Tennessee Williams
Valley of the Dolls, Jacqueline Susann
War and Peace, Leo Tolstoy

The Rejected Title

It Shouldn't Happen to a Vet
The Salinas Valley
St. Ogg's on the Floss; The House of Tullever; Sister Maggie
The Whale
Before This Anger
The Eclipse of May 29, 1919
They Don't Build Statues to Businessmen
All's Well That Ends Well

BESTSELLING CHILDREN'S BOOKS

Publishers Weekly recently started a sales list devoted solely to children's books. Here are the bestselling hardcovers introduced during the last four years.

1995

1. *Pocahontas (Classic)*, Disney/Mouse Works
2. *Pocahontas*, Justine Korman, illustrated by D. Williams
3. *The Children's Book of Virtues*, William J. Bennett, illustrated by Michael Hague
4. *Guess How Much I Love You*, Sam McBratney, illustrated by Anita Jeram
5. *Pocahontas: Wind's Lullaby*, Justine Korman, illustrated by Peter Emslie and D. Williams
6. *Daisy-Head Mayzie*, Dr. Seuss
7. *Winnie the Pooh: The Grand and Wonderful Day*, Mary Packard, illustrated by Darrell Baker
8. *Rainbow Fish to the Rescue!*, Marcus Pfister
9. *Hide & Squeak, Meeko!*, Disney/Mouse Works
10. *Pocahontas (Sturdy Shape)*, Mary Packard, illustrated by Darrell Baker

1996

1. *Falling Up*, Shel Silverstein
2. *The Hunchback of Notre Dame*, Disney/Mouse Works
3. *Disney's Hunchback of Notre Dame*, adapted by Justine Korman, illustrated by Don Williams
4. *My Many Colored Days*, Dr. Seuss, illustrated by Steve Johnson and Lou Fancher
5. *Disney's Hunchback of Notre Dame: Quasimodo the Hero*, Barbara Bazaldua, illustrated by Don Williams
6. *Disney's 101 Dalmatians: Snow Puppies*, Barbara Bazaldua, illustrated by Don Williams
7. *Disney's Winnie the Pooh: The Sweetest Christmas*, Ann Braybrooks, illustrated by Josie Yee
8. *Guess How Much I Love You*, Sam McBratney, illustrated by Anita Jeram
9. *The Hunchback of Notre Dame*, Disney/Mouse Works
10. *Djali's Jolly Day*, Disney/Mouse Works

1997

1. *Hercules (Classic)*, Disney/Mouse Works
2. *Anastasia (Little Golden Book)*, Golden
3. *Disney: Pooh's Grand Adventure*, Golden
4. *Disney: Pooh and the Dragon*, Golden
5. *Sesame Street: Tickle Me: My Name Is Elmo*, Golden
6. *Disney's Hercules*, Golden
7. *The Children's Book of Heroes*, edited by William J. Bennett, illustrated by Michael Hague
8. *Disney's Pooh: Eeyore, Be Happy!*, Golden
9. *Disney's Pooh: Happy Easter*, Golden
10. *Disney's 101 Dalmatians*, Golden

1998

1. *Blue's Clues: The Shape Detective*, Simon Spotlight
2. *Blue's Clues: Blue's #1 Picnic*, Simon Spotlight
3. *Barney's Twinkle, Twinkle Little Star*, Lyrick/Barney
4. *Disney's Mulan*, Golden Books
5. *If You Give a Pig a Pancake*, Laura Numeroff, illustrated by Felicia Bond
6. *A Bug's Life: Classic Storybook*, Disney/Mouseworks
7. *Blue's Clues: Blue's Big Birthday*, Simon Spotlight
8. *The 20th-Century Children's Book Treasury*, edited by Janet Schulman
9. *Teletubbies: The Magic String*, Scholastic
10. *Teletubbies Play Hide-and-Seek*, Scholastic

LITERARY LISTENING

Americans have been doing a lot of reading behind the wheel, and as this list of bestselling audio books reveals, our tastes are pretty broad. Based on 1998's most successful books to tape at Waldenbooks, this list gives us a good gauge of the year's most popular listening.

1. *Men Are from Mars, Women Are from Venus*, John Gray
2. *The Street Lawyer*, John Grisham
3. *Rainbow Six*, Tom Clancy
4. *Don't Sweat the Small Stuff... and It's All Small Stuff*, Richard Carlson
5. *The Horse Whisperer*, Nicholas Evans
6. *The Seven Habits of Highly Effective People*, Stephen R. Covey
7. *The 9 Steps to Financial Freedom*, Suze Orman
8. *The Street Lawyer (Unabridged)*, John Grisham
9. *You Belong to Me*, Mary Higgins Clark
10. *Cold Mountain*, Charles Frazier
11. *Dirty Jokes and Beer*, Drew Carey
12. *Spectre (Star Trek)*, William Shatner
13. *A Prairie Home Companion 20th Anniversary Collection*, Garrison Keillor
14. *Midnight in the Garden of Good and Evil*, John Berendt
15. *Angela's Ashes*, Frank McCourt

BESTSELLING CHILDREN'S BOOKS OF ALL TIME

The following is a list of the 100 bestselling hardcover children's books. The figures reflect domestic sales from the original date of publication through the end of 1996. (Source: *Publishers Weekly*)

Rank Book, Author (original publication date)

1. *The Poky Little Puppy*, Janette Sebring Lowrey (1942)
2. *The Tale of Peter Rabbit*, Beatrix Potter (1902)
3. *Tootle*, Gertrude Crampton (1945)
4. *Saggy Baggy Elephant*, Kathryn and Byron Jackson (1947)
5. *Scuffy the Tugboat*, Gertrude Crampton (1955)
6. *Pat the Bunny*, Dorothy Kunhardt (1940)
7. *Green Eggs and Ham*, Dr. Seuss (1960)
8. *The Cat in the Hat*, Dr. Seuss (1957)
9. *The Littlest Angel*, Charles Tazewell (1946)
10. *One Fish, Two Fish, Red Fish, Blue Fish*, Dr. Seuss (1960)
11. *Where the Sidewalk Ends*, Shel Silverstein (1974)
12. *Hop on Pop*, Dr. Seuss (1963)
13. *Dr. Seuss's ABC*, Dr. Seuss (1960)
14. *The Tale of Benjamin Bunny*, Beatrix Potter (1904)
15. *The Giving Tree*, Shel Silverstein (1964)
16. *The Children's Bible* (1965)
17. *Disney's The Lion King*, adapted by Justine Korman (1994)
18. *The Tale of Jemima Puddle-Duck*, Beatrix Potter (1908)
19. *Richard Scarry's Best Word Book Ever*, Richard Scarry (1963)
20. *The Real Mother Goose*, illus. by Blanche F. Wright (1989)
21. *The Cat in the Hat Comes Back*, Dr. Seuss (1958)
22. *A Light in the Attic*, Shel Silverstein (1981)
23. *Are You My Mother?*, P.D. Eastman (1960)
24. *The Tale of Squirrel Nutkin*, Beatrix Potter (1903)
25. *The Tale of Tom Kitten*, Beatrix Potter (1907)
26. *Fox In Socks*, Dr. Seuss (1965)
27. *Where's Waldo*, Martin Handford (1987)
28. *The Great Waldo Search*, Martin Handford (1989)
29. *The Polar Express*, Chris Van Allsburg (1985)
30. *Winnie-the-Pooh*, A.A. Milne, illus. by Ernest Shepard (1926)
31. *Find Waldo Now*, Martin Handford (1989)
32. *Go, Dog Go!*, P.D. Eastman (1961)
33. *Oh, the Places You'll Go!*, Dr. Seuss (1990)
34. *Macmillan Dictionary for Children*, edited by Judith Levey (1975)
35. *My Book About Me (by Me, Myself)*, Dr. Seuss, illus. by Roy McKie (1969)
36. *Walt Disney's Storyland*, Walt Disney (1962)
37. *The Cat in the Hat Beginner Book Dictionary*, P.D. Eastman (1964)
38. *How the Grinch Stole Christmas*, Dr. Seuss (1957)
39. *The Rainbow Fish*, Marcus Pfister (1992)
40. *Richard Scarry's Best Mother Goose Ever*, Richard Scarry (1964)
41. *The Touch Me Book*, Pat and Eve Witte (1961)
42. *Goodnight Moon*, Margaret Wise Brown, illus. by Clement Hurd (1947)
43. *I Am a Bunny*, Ole Risom, illus. by Richard Scarry (1963)
44. *The Little Engine That Could*, Watty Piper (1930)
45. *Charlotte's Web*, E.B. White, illus. by Garth Williams (1952)
46. *Never Talk to Strangers*, Irma Joyce (1967)
47. *When We Were Very Young*, A.A. Milne, illus. by Ernest Shepard (1924)
48. *Richard Scarry's Best Storybook Ever*, Richard Scarry (1968)
49. *Barney's Magical Picnic*, Stephen White (1993)
50. *I Can Read with My Eyes Shut*, Dr. Seuss (1978)

51. *The Secret of the Old Clock* (Nancy Drew #1), Carolyn Keene (1930)
52. *The Tower Treasure* (Hardy Boys #1), Franklin Dixon (1927)
53. *Just Imagine* (1992)
54. *Put Me In the Zoo*, Robert Lopshire (1960)
55. *Disney's 101 Dalmations*, adapted by Ronald Kidd (1991)
56. *The Very Hungry Caterpillar*, Eric Carle (1969)
57. *Barney's Farm Animals* (1993)
58. *Where the Wild Things Are*, Maurice Sendak (1964)
59. *Richard Scarry's Cars and Trucks and Things That Go*, Richard Scarry (1968)
60. *Disney's Beauty and the Beast*, adapted by Ronald Kidd (1992)
61. *The Little Prince*, Antoine de Saint Exupery (1943)
62. *Eloise Wilkin's Mother Goose*, Eloise Wilkin (1961)
63. *Disney's The Little Mermaid*, adapted by Ronald Kidd (1991)
64. *Oh, The Things You Can Think!*, Dr. Seuss (1975)
65. *Love Is a Special Way of Feeling*, Joan Walsh Anglund (1960)
66. *Big Bird's Color Game*, Children's Television Workshop (1980)
67. *Disney's Aladdin*, adapted by Ronald Kidd (1992)
68. *The Hidden Staircase* (Nancy Drew #2), Carolyn Keene (1930)
69. *The House on the Cliff* (Hardy Boys #2), Franklin Dixon (1927)
70. *Meet Samantha*, Susan Adler (1986)
71. *Animalia*, Graeme Base (1987)
72. *Barney's Favorite Mother Goose Rhymes Vol. 1* (1993)
73. *Disney's The Lion King*, adapted by Ronald Kidd (1994)
74. *Meet Andy*, Connie Porter (1993)
75. *Oh Say Can You Say?*, Dr. Seuss (1979)
76. *Barney's Color Surprise* (1993)
77. *The Way Things Work*, David Macaulay (1988)
78. *Tawny Scrawny Lion*, Kathryn Jackson (1952)
79. *Make Way for Ducklings*, Robert McCloskey (1941)
80. *Meet Kirsten*, Janet Shaw (1986)
81. *There's A Wocket in My Pocket*, Dr. Seuss (1974)
82. *Millions of Cats*, Wanda Gag (1928)
83. *E.T., the Extra-Terrestrial Story Book*, William Kotzwinkle (1992)
84. *A Fly Went By*, Mike McClintock (1958)
85. *The Bungalow Mystery* (Nancy Drew #3), Carolyn Keene (1930)
86. *Santa Mouse*, Elfrieda Dewitt (1966)
87. *The Magic Locket*, Elizabeth Koda-Callan (1988)
88. *The Secret of the Old Mill* (Hardy Boys #3), Franklin Dixon (1930)
89. *Mr. Brown Can Moo! Can You?*, Dr. Seuss (1970)
90. *If You Give a Mouse a Cookie*, Laura Numeroff, illus. by Felicia Bond (1985)
91. *Richard Scarry's What Do People Do All Day?*, Richard Scarry (1968)
92. *Where's Spot?*, Eric Hill (1980)
93. *House at Pooh Corner*, A.A. Milne, illus: by Ernest Shepard (1928)
94. *The Tall Book of Nursery Tales*, illus. by Feodor Rojankovsky (1944)
95. *Yertle the Turtle and Other Stories*, Dr. Seuss (1958)
96. *Richard Scarry's Early Words*, Richard Scarry (1976)
97. *The Jolly Postman*, Janet and Allan Ahlberg (1986)
98. *The Mystery of Lilac Inn* (Nancy Drew #4), Carolyn Keene (1930)
99. *Dr. Seuss's Sleep Book*, Dr. Seuss (1962)
100. *Baby Bop's Counting Book* (1993)

THE PEOPLE BOOKSHELF

PEOPLE hasn't been reviewing books long enough to hazard a best-of-the-century list, but here are the books we loved the most over the past 25 years.

FICTION

Absolute Power, David Baldacci
The Accidental Tourist, Anne Tyler
All the Pretty Horses, Cormac McCarthy
Anagrams, Lorrie Moore
Anton the Dove Fancier, Bernard Gotfryd
August, Judith Rossner
Before and After, Rosellen Brown
Beloved, Toni Morrison
Birds of America, Lorrie Moore
Birdy, William Wharton
The Blooding, Joseph Wambaugh
The Blue Afternoon, William Boyd
Body and Soul, Frank Conroy
The Bonfire of the Vanities, Tom Wolfe
Breathing Lessons, Anne Tyler
Bridget Jones's Diary, Helen Fielding
Cat's Eye, Margaret Atwood
Clockers, Richard Price
The Cloister Walk, Kathleen Norris
Cold Mountain, Charles Frazier
Collaborators, Janet Kauffman
The Collected Stories, Isaac Bashevis Singer
The Color Purple, Alice Walker
Come to Grief, Dick Francis
A Confederacy of Dunces, John Kennedy Toole
Damascus Gate, Robert Stone
Dinner at the Homesick Restaurant, Anne Tyler
The Dragons of Eden, Carl Sagan
Dutch Shea Jr., John Gregory Dunne
East Is East, T. Coraghessan Boyle
Ellis Island, Mark Helprin
Enchantment, Daphne Merkin
Eye of the Needle, Ken Follett
Fanny, Erica Jong
The Farming of Bones, Edwidge Danticat
Final Payments, Mary Gordon
The Firm, John Grisham

The First Man in Rome, Colleen McCullough
For Love, Sue Miller
Foreign Affairs, Alison Lurie
Get Shorty, Elmore Leonard
The Glass House, Laura Furman
The God of Small Things, Arundhati Roy
Gone, Baby, Gone, Dennis Lehane
The Good Mother, Sue Miller
Gorky Park, Martin Cruz Smith
The Green Mile, Stephen King
Happy to Be There, Garrison Keillor
Her First American, Lore Segal
The Honourable Schoolboy, John Le Carré
The House of the Spirits, Isabel Allende
Illumination Night, Abbie Hoffman
An Indecent Obsession, Colleen McCollough
Independence Day, Richard Ford
Kolymsky Heights, Lionel Davidson
Krik? Krak!, Edwidge Danticat
Labrava, Elmore Leonard
Lake Wobegon Days, Garrison Keillor
Lancelot, Walker Percy
A Lesson Before Dying, Ernest J. Gaines
The Liar's Club, Mary Karr
Libra, Don DeLillo
A Light in the Attic, Shel Silverstein
Life Its Ownself, Dan Jenkins
Love in the Time of Cholera, Gabriel García Márquez
The Love Letter, Cathleen Schine
Machine Dreams, Jayne Anne Phillips
The Mambo Kings Play Songs of Love, Oscar Hijuelos
A Man in Full, Tom Wolfe
A Map of the World, Jane Hamilton
Maus: A Survivor's Tale, II: And Here My Troubles Begin, Art Spiegelman
Me and My Baby View the Eclipse, Lee Smith

Memoirs of an Invisible Man, H. F. Saint
Monkeys, Susan Minot
Monsignor Quixote, Graham Greene
More Die of Heartbreak, Saul Bellow
Music for Chameleons, Truman Capote
The Natural Man, Ed McClanahan
Noble House, James Clavell
Owning Jolene, Shelby Hearon
The Palace Thief, Ethan Canin
Patrimony, Philip Roth
Perfume, Patrick Süskind
Poodle Springs, Raymond Chandler and Robert B. Parker
The Pope of Greenwich Village, Vincent Park
Presumed Innocent, Scott Turow
The Progress of Love, Alice Munro
Quinn's Book, William Kennedy
Rabbit at Rest, John Updike
The Robber Bride, Margaret Atwood
Roger's Version, John Updike
Rose, Martin Cruz Smith
The Russia House, John Le Carré
Salvador, Joan Didion
The Secret History, Donna Tartt
Seventh Heaven, Alice Hoffman
She's Come Undone, Wally Lamb
The Sicilian, Mario Puzo
Smilla's Sense of Snow, Peter Hoeg
A Soldier of the Great War, Mark Helprin
Sophie's Choice, William Styron
Stormy Weather, Carl Hiaasen
Talking to the Dead, Sylvia Watanabe
Tooth Imprints on a Corn Dog, Mark Leyner
Tracks, Louise Erdrich
The Tree of Life, Hugh Nissenson
True Confessions, John Gregory Dunne
The Twenty-Seventh City, Jonathan Franzen
Typical American, Gish Jen
Underworld, Don Delillo

Waiting to Exhale, Terry McMillan
The White Hotel, D. M. Thomas
Who Will Run the Frog Hospital?, Lorrie Moore
Winter's Tale, Mark Helprin
World's Fair, E. L. Doctorow
The Yellow Wind, David Grossman

NONFICTION

All Over But the Shoutin', Rick Bragg
American Caesar, William Manchester
American Prospects, Joel Sternfeld
Backlash, Susan Faludi
Best Intentions, Robert Sam Anson
The Best of Dear Abby, Abigail Van Buren
Blood Sport, James B. Stewart
Blue Highways, William Least Heat Moon
The Bookmakers's Daughter, Shirley Abbott
The Box: An Oral History of Television 1920–61, Jeff Kisseloff
Cameraworks, David Hockney
The Chimpanzees of Gombe, Jane Goodall
A Civil Action, Jonathan Harr
Colored People: A Memoir, Henry Louis Gates Jr.
The Culture of Narcissism, Christopher Lasch
Dave Barry Is Not Making This Up, Dave Barry
Dave Barry Slept Here, Dave Barry
Den of Thieves, James B. Stewart
The Devil's Candy, Julie Salamon
A Distant Mirror, Barbara Tuchman
Dreaming: Hard Luck and Good Times in America, Carolyn See
The Duke of Deception, Geoffrey Wolff
Edie, Jean Stein, edited with George Plimpton
Edith Sitwell, Victoria Glendinning
The Fatal Shore, Robert Hughes
Fatal Vision, Joe McGinniss
Fatherhood, Bill Cosby
The Forbidden Experiment, Roger Shattuck

Fungus the Bogeyman, Raymond Briggs
Gal, Ruthie Bolton
The Girl I Left Behind, Jane O'Reilly
The Glass House, Laura Furman
Goldwyn: A Biography, A. Scott Berg
A Good Life, Ben Bradlee
"The Good War," Studs Terkel
The Hidden Life of Dogs, Elizabeth Marshall
Home Before Dark, Susan Cheever
Hometown, Peter Davis
The Hot Zone, Richard Preston
House, Tracy Kidder
I Dream a World, Brian Lanker
In and Out of the Garden, Sara Midda
In Contempt, Christopher Darden
Ingrid Bergman: My Story, Ingrid Bergman and Alan Burgess
Inside Edge: A Revealing Journey into the Secret World of Figure Skating, Christine Brennan
Into the Wild, Jon Krakauer
Into Thin Air, Jon Krakauer
Jackie Robinson: A Biography, Arnold Rampersad
January Sun, Richard Stengel
The Kennedys: An American Dream, Peter Collier and David Horowitz
Kissinger, Walter Isaacson
The Knife and Gun Club, Eugene Richards
The Last Lion, William Manchester
Laura Z.: A Life, Laura Z. Hobson
Lauren Bacall: By Myself, Lauren Bacall
Lenin's Tomb, David Remnick
A Life of Picasso, John Richardson
Lindbergh, A. Scott Berg
Little League Confidential, Bill Geist
The Lives of John Lennon, Albert Goldman
Loitering with Intent, Peter O'Toole
Maida Heatter's Book of Great Chocolate Desserts, Maida Heatter
The Man Who Mistook His Wife for a Hat, Oliver Sacks
Means of Ascent, Robert A. Caro
The Medusa and the Snail, Lewis Thomas

Midair, Frank Conroy
Miss Manners' Guide to Excruciatingly Correct Behavior, Judith Martin
Mister Rogers Talks with Parents, Fred Rogers and Barry Head
Moonshine, Alec Wilkinson
The Non-Runner's Book, Vic Ziegel and Lewis Grossberger
No Ordinary Time, Doris Kearns Goodwin
On Boxing, Joyce Carol Oates
On Photography, Susan Sontag
Outrage, Vincent Bugliosi
Pablo Picasso: A Retrospective, edited by William Rubin
Payback, Joe Klein
Personal History, Katharine Graham
Photoportraits, Henri Cartier-Bresson
President Kennedy, Richard Reeves
The Ragman's Son, Kirk Douglas
The Rise of Theodore Roosevelt, Edmund Morris
A Rumor of War, Philip Caputo
Saul Steinberg, Harold Rosenberg
Serpentine, Thomas Thompson
Side Effects, Woody Allen
The Sketchbooks of Picasso, Pablo Picasso
The Snow Leopard, Peter Mathiessen
The Spirit Catches You and You Fall Down, Anne Fadiman
The Story of English, Robert McCrum, William Cran, and Robert MacNeil
Still Me, Christopher Reeve
Sylvia Plachy's Unguided Tour, Sylvia Plachy
The Teamsters, Steven Brill
Thank You for Smoking, Christopher Buckley
Truman, David McCullough
What Falls Away, Mia Farrow
Why Are They Weeping?, photographed by David C. Turnley and written by Alan Cowell
Workers, Sebastião Salgado
A Writer's Beginnings, Eudora Welty
The Years of Lyndon Johnson: The Path to Power, Robert A. Caro

THE PEOPLE TRASH HEAP

PEOPLE's reviewers read these books because they had to—it's their job. But you have a choice. Here are the works Picks & Pans' critics dumped on as the worst—or most over-rated—since the magazine began publishing 25 years ago.

FICTION

Alnilam, James Dickey

American Psycho, Bret Easton Ellis

Ancient Evenings, Norman Mailer

Answer as a Man, Taylor Caldwell

Any Woman's Blues, Erica Jong

Ascent into Hell, Andrew M. Greeley

Beast, Peter Benchley

The Big Hype, Avery Corman

A Bloodsmoor Romance, Joyce Carol Oates

The Bourne Ultimatum, Robert Ludlum

Brain, Robin Cook

By the Light of My Father's Smile, Alice Walker

Children of Light, Robert Stone

The Children's Story, James Clavell

Christine, Stephen King

The Coup, John Updike

Daddy, Danielle Steel

The Devil's Alternative, Frederick Forsyth

Doctors, Erich Segal

Empress, Sylvia Wallace

Fever, Robin Cook

Floating Dragon, Peter Straub

.44, Jimmy Breslin and Dick Schaap

Free to Love, Ivana Trump

Friends in High Places, John Weitz

The Girl of the Sea of Cortez, Peter Benchley

Godplayer, Robin Cook

Gumpisms, Winston Groom

Happy Endings, Sally Quinn

Heartburn, Nora Ephron

The Holcroft Covenant, Robert Ludlum

Hollywood Kids, Jackie Collins

Home Front, Patti Davis with Maureen Strange Foster

The Hope, Herman Wouk

A House of Secrets, Patti Davis

I Dream a World, Brian Lanker

Illusions: The Adventures of a Reluctant Messiah, Richard Bach

In Praise of the Stepmother, Mario Vargas Llosa

Inside, Outside, Herman Wouk

The Island, Peter Benchley

Lace, Shirley Conran

Lasher, Anne Rice

The Last Days of America, Paul Erdman

Legion, William Peter Blatty

Life After God, Douglas Coupland

Lord of the Dance, Andrew M. Greeley

Love and War, John Jakes

Lucky, Jackie Collins

Lust, Susan Minot

The Mammoth Hunters, Jean M. Auel

Manhattan, Neal Travis

A Matter of Honor, Jeffrey Archer

Maybe, Lillian Hellman

Megan's Book of Divorce, Erica Jong

Memories of Another Day, Harold Robbins

Men in Love, Nancy Friday

The Men's Club, Leonard Michaels

Message from Nam, Danielle Steel

Mindbend, Robin Cook

The Minstrel, Bernard Benson

Model Behavior, Jay McInerney

Monimbo, Robert Moss and Arnaud de Borchgrave

The Mosquito Coast, Paul Theroux

The Mummy, Anne Rice

Murder in the White House, Margaret Truman

Nature's End, Whitley Streiber and James Kunetka

The Ninth Configuration, William Peter Blatty

Of Love and Shadows, Isabel Allende

The Old Neighborhood, Avery Corman

Oliver's Story, Erich Segal

The Origin, Irving Stone

Outbreak, Robin Cook

Pandora, Anne Rice

The Paper Men, William Golding

Parachutes and Kisses, Erica Jong

The Pigeon, Patrick Süskind

The Pillars of the Earth, Ken Follett

Pinball, Jerzy Kosinski

The Plagiarist, Benjamin Cheever

Postcards from the Edge, Carrie Fisher

A Prayer for Owen Meany, John Irving

Prime Time, Joan Collins

"Q" Clearance, Peter Benchley

Queen of the Damned, Anne Rice

Regrets Only, Sally Quinn

Rock Star, Jackie Collins

The Runaway Soul, Harold Brodkey

S., John Updike

Sailor Song, Ken Kesey

Savages, Shirley Conran

Scruples, Judith Krantz

See You Later, Alligator, William F. Buckley Jr.

Singing Songs, Meg Tilly

Slaves of New York, Tama Janowitz

Slow Waltz at Cedar Bend, Robert James Waller

Smart Women, Judy Blume

Spellbinder, Harold Robbins

Sphinx, Robin Cook

Spring Collection, Judith Krantz

Star, Danielle Steel

The Story of Henri Todd, William F. Buckley Jr.

Story of My Life, Jay McInerney

The Student Body, Jane Harvard

The Talisman, Stephen King and Peter Straub

The Temple of My Familiar, Alice Walker

Texas, James Michener

Timequake, Kurt Vonnegut

Tinsel, William Goldman

Toward the End of Time, John Updike

The Vampire Armand, Anne Rice

Vox, Nicholson Baker

The Walnut Door, John Hersey

West of Sunset, Dirk Bogarde

Where Love Goes, Joyce Maynard

Whirlwind, James Clavell

The Winners, Dominick Dunne

NONFICTION

An Affair to Remember, Maureen Donaldson and William Royce

Among the Porcupines, Carol Matthau

Andrew Wyeth: The Helga Pictures, John Wilmerding

Bardot, Deneuve, Fonda, Roger Vadim

Been There, Haven't Done That, Tara Fitzgerald

Better than Sex, Hunter Thompson

The Beverly Hills Diet, Judy Mazel

Beyond Reason, Margaret Trudeau

The Bible Code, Michael Drosnin

Bitch, Elizabeth Wurtzel

Blown Away, A. E. Hotchner

Book, Whoopi Goldberg

The Book of Lists, David Wallechinsky, Irving Wallace, and Amy Wallace

Brando for Breakfast, Anna Kashfi and E. P. Stein

Brother Billy, Ruth Carter Stapleton

Bus 9 to Paradise, Leo Buscaglia

Cary Grant: The Lonely Heart, Charles Higham and Roy Moseley

Character: America's Search for Leadership, Gail Sheehy

Cruel Shoes, Steve Martin

Dance with the Devil, Kirk Douglas

Dancing in the Light, Shirley MacLaine

Dave Barry Turns 50, Dave Barry

Diana Alone, Nicholas Davies

Driving Under the Affluence, Julia Phillips

Elizabeth Taylor: The Last Star, Kitty Kelley

Elvis, Albert Goldman

Elvis Aaron Presley: Revelations from the Memphis Mafia, Alanna Nash, with Billy Smith, Marty Lacker and Lamar Fike

Enter Whining, Fran Drescher

Family—The Ties That Bind . . . and Gag!, Erma Bombeck

Feminine Force: Release the Power Within to Create the Life You Deserve, Georgette Mosbacher

Find O.J.: The Juice Is Loose, Peter Wood and Jeff Vaughn

Flight of the Avenger: George Bush at War and in Love, Joe Hyams

Garbo: Her Story, Antoni Gronowicz

Give War a Chance, P. J. O'Rourke

Glory Days: Bruce Springsteen in the 1980s, Dave Marsh

Good Guys, Bad Guys, Shere Hite and Kate Colleran

Having It All, Helen Gurley Brown

The Hite Report on Male Sexuality, Shere Hite

How to Take Charge of Your Life, Bernard Berkowitz and Mildred Newman

In the American West, Richard Avedon

The Informers, Bret Easton Ellis

I Remember, Dan Rather

It's All in the Playing, Shirley MacLaine

I Want to Tell You, O. J. Simpson

Jack and Jackie: Portrait of an American Marriage, Christopher Andersen

The Jackson Phenomenon, Elizabeth O. Colton

Just Between Us Girls, Sydney Biddle Barrows

Just Enough Rope, Joan Braden

The Killing of the Unicorn, Peter Bogdanovich

The Kiss, Kathryn Harrison

The Last Brother, Joe McGinniss

Laurence Olivier: A Biography, Donald Spoto

Life's Little Instruction Book, H. Jackson Brown Jr.

The Linda Evans Beauty and Exercise Book, Linda Evans

The Lives of John Lennon, Albert Goldman

The Long Road Out of Hell, Marilyn Manson with Neil Strauss

Marcia Clark: Her Private Trials and Public Triumphs, Clifford L. Linedecker

Metropolitan Life, Fran Lebowitz

Mistrial of the Century, Tracy Kennedy

More Memories, Ralph Emery

Mountain, Get Out of My Way, Montel Williams with Daniel Paisner

Mutant Message Down Under, Marlo Morgan

My Lives, Roseanne

Nice Work If You Can Get It, Michael Feinstein

1945, Newt Gingrich and William R. Forstchen

Not That You Asked, Andrew A. Rooney

Now You Know, Kitty Dukakis

Number One, Billy Martin and Peter Golenboch

O.J.: 101 Theories, Conspiracies, and Alibis, Peter Roberts

On Your Own, Brooke Shields

The One-Minute Father, Spencer Johnson, M.D.

The One-Minute Mother, Spencer Johnson, M.D.

Out on a Limb, Shirley MacLaine

A Place at the Table, Bruce Bawer

The Power to Heal, edited by Rick Smolan, Phillip Moffitt, and Matthew Naythons, M.D.

Princess in Love, Anna Pasternak

Promiscuities, Naomi Wolf

Pulling Your Own Strings, Dr. Wayne Dyer

The Rants, Dennis Miller

Real Moments, Barbara DeAngelis

Restoring the American Dream, Robert Ringer

Revolution from Within, Gloria Steinem

RN: The Memoirs of Richard Nixon, Richard Nixon

The Royals, Kitty Kelley

Running and Being, Dr. George Sheehan

The Second Seduction, Frances Lear

Secrets of a Sparrow, Diana Ross

Sex, Madonna

The Search for Justice, Robert Shapiro with Larkin Warren

Shelley: Also Known As Shirley, Shelley Winters

Social Studies, Fran Lebowitz

Spice World, The Spice Girls

The Starr Report, Kenneth Starr

Tennessee: Cry of the Heart, Dotson Rader

Thy Neighbor's Wife, Gay Talese

Transformation, Whitley Streiber

Uh-Oh, Robert Fulghum

Wasted: The Preppie Murder, Linda Wolfe

Welcome to Your Facelift, Helen Bransford

Without a Doubt, Marcia Clark and Teresa Carpenter

Willie, Willie Nelson with Bud Shrake

Women and Love, Shere Hite

Women's Work, Anne Tolstoi Wallach

Woody Allen: A Biography, Eric Lax

You Have to Stand for Something, or You'll Fall for Anything, Star Jones with Daniel Paisner

BIBLIOGRAPHIES OF LEADING AUTHORS

These are complete listings for a broad selection of the most popular, most admired, most discussed, and most eagerly devoured authors today. For each, all full-length works, poetry, and plays are listed, followed by the year of publication.

ISABEL ALLENDE

Fiction
The House of the Spirits (1985)
Eva Luna (1988)
Of Love and Shadows (1988)
The Infinite Plan (1993)
Paula (1995)

Nonfiction
Aphrodite: A Memoir of the Senses (1998)

MARGARET ATWOOD

Fiction
The Edible Woman (1969)
Surfacing (1972)
Lady Oracle (1976)
Dancing Girls (1977)
Life Before Man (1979)
Bodily Harm (1981)
Murder in the Dark (1983)
Bluebeard's Egg (1983)
The Handmaid's Tale (1985)
Cat's Eye (1988)
Wilderness Tips (1991)
Good Bones and Simple Murders (1992)
The Robber Bride (1993)
Alias Grace (1996)

Poetry
The Circle Game (1964)
The Animals in That Country (1968)
The Journals of Susanna Moodie (1970)
Procedures for Underground (1970)
Power Politics (1971)
You Are Happy (1974)
Two-Headed Poems (1978)
True Stories (1981)
Snake Poems (1983)
Interlunar (1984)
Morning in the Burned House (1995)

Children's books
Up in the Tree (1978)
Anna's Pet (1980)
For the Birds (1990)
Princess Prunella and the Purple Peanut (1995)

Nonfiction
Survival: A Thematic Guide to Canadian Literature (1972)
Days of the Rebels, 1815–1840 (1977)
Second Words (1982)
Strange Things: The Malevolent North in Canadian Literature (1996)

SAUL BELLOW

Fiction
Dangling Man (1944)
The Victim (1947)
The Adventures of Augie March (1953; National Book Award)
Seize the Day (1956)
Henderson the Rain King (1959)
Herzog (1964; National Book Award)
Mr. Sammler's Planet (1970; National Book Award)
Humbolt's Gift (1975; Pulitzer Prize)
The Dean's December (1982)
Mosby's Memoirs & Other Stories (1984)
A Theft (1989)
Something to Remember Me By (1991)
More Die of Heartbreak (1987)
The Actual (1997)
Him with His Foot in His Mouth and Other Stories (1998)

Nonfiction
To Jerusalem and Back: A Personal Account (1976)
It All Adds Up (1994)

Play
The Last Analysis, a Play (produced 1964)

Nobel Prize for Literature, 1976

TOM CLANCY

Fiction
The Hunt for Red October (1984)
Red Storm Rising (1986)
Patriot Games (1987)
The Cardinal of the Kremlin (1988)
Clear and Present Danger (1989)
The Sum of All Fears (1991)
Without Remorse (1993)
Debt of Honor (1994)
Executive Orders (1996)
Rainbow Six (1998)

Nonfiction
Submarine: A Guided Tour Inside a Nuclear Warship (1993)
Armored Cav: A Guided Tour of an Armored Cavalry Regiment (1994)
Fighter Wing: A Guided Tour of an Air Force Combat Wing (1995)
Reality Check: What's Going On Out There? (1995)
Marine: A Guided Tour of a Marine Expeditionary Unit (1996)
Airborne: A Guided Tour of an Airborne Taskforce (1997)
Into the Storm: A Study in Command (coauthor, 1997)
Carrier: A Guided Tour of an Aircraft Carrier (1998)
Every Man a Tiger (coauthor, 1999)

PAT CONROY

Fiction
The Boo (1970)
The Water Is Wide (1972)
The Great Santini (1976)
The Lords of Discipline (1980)
The Prince of Tides (1986)
Beach Music (1995)

MICHAEL CRICHTON

Fiction
The Andromeda Strain (1969)
The Terminal Man (1972)
Westworld (screenplay, 1975)
The Great Train Robbery (1975)
Eaters of the Dead (1976)
Congo (1980)
Sphere (1987)
Jurassic Park (1990)
Rising Sun (1992)
Disclosure (1994)
The Lost World (1995)
Airframe (1996)

Fiction written as John Lange
Odds On (1966)
Scratch One (1967)
Easy Go (1968; republished as The Last Tomb, 1974)
The Venom Business (1969)
Zero Cool (1970)
Drug of Choice (1970)
Grave Descend (1970)
Binary (1972)

Fiction written as Jeffrey Hudson
A Case of Need (1968)

Fiction written as Michael Douglas (with brother Douglas Crichton)
Dealing, Or the Berkeley-to-Boston Forty-Brick Lost-Bag Blues (1971)

Nonfiction
Five Patients: The Hospital Explained (1970)
Jasper Johns (1977)
Electronic Life: How to Think about Computers (1983)
Travels (autobiography, 1988)

DON DELILLO

Fiction
Americana (1971)
End Zone (1972)
Great Jones Street (1973)

Ratner's Star (1976)

Players (1977)

Running Dog (1978)

The Names (1982)

White Noise (1985; National Book Award)

Libra (1988)

Mao II (1991; PEN/Faulkner Award)

Underworld (1997)

Fiction written as Cleo Birdwell

Amazons (1980)

Play

Valparaiso: A Play in Two Acts (1999)

E. L. DOCTOROW

Fiction

Welcome to Hard Times (1960)

Big as Life (1966)

The Book of Daniel (1971)

Ragtime (1975; National Book Critics Circle Award)

Loon Lake (1980)

World's Fair (1985; National Book Award)

Billy Bathgate (1989; National Book Critics Circle Award; PEN/Faulkner Award)

The Waterworks (1994)

Nonfiction

Jack London, Hemingway, and the Constitution: Selected Writings, 1977–1992 (1993)

The Lives of Poets (1997)

Play

Drinks Before Dinner (1979)

LOUISE ERDRICH

Fiction

Love Medicine (1984; National Book Critics Circle Award)

The Beet Queen (1986)

Tracks (1988)

The Crown of Columbus (co-author, 1991)

The Bingo Palace (1994)

The Blue Jay's Dance (1995)

Tales of Burning Love (1996)

The Antelope Wife (1998)

Poetry

Jacklight (1984)

Baptism of Desire (1989)

Children's books

Grandmother's Pigeon (1996)

The Birchbark House (1999)

JOHN GRISHAM

Fiction

A Time to Kill (1988)

The Firm (1990)

The Pelican Brief (1990)

The Client (1993)

The Chamber (1994)

The Rainmaker (1995)

The Runaway Jury (1996)

The Partner (1997)

The Street Lawyer (1998)

The Testament (1999)

MARK HELPRIN

Fiction

Winter's Tale (1983)

Refiner's Fire (1990)

Dove of the East and Other Stories (1990)

Ellis Island and Other Stories (1990)

A Soldier of the Great War (1991)

Memoir from Antproof Case (1995)

Children's books

Swan Lake (1989)

A City in Winter (1996)

The Veil of Snows (1997)

STEPHEN KING

Fiction

Carrie (1975)

Salem's Lot (1976)

The Shining (1977)

Night Shift (1978)

The Stand (1978)

The Dead Zone (1979)

Firestarter (1980)

Cujo (1981)

The Dark Tower: The Gunslinger (1982)

Christine (1983)

Pet Sematary (1983)

The Talisman (coauthor, 1984)

Cycle of the Werewolf (1985)

It (1986)

The Eyes of the Dragon (1987)

Misery (1987)

The Tommyknockers (1987)

The Dark Half (1989)

The Dark Tower II: The Drawing of Three (1989)

Four Past Midnight (1990)

The Dark Tower III: The Waste Lands (1991)

Needful Things (1991)

Gerald's Game (1992)

Dolores Claiborne (1992)

Nightmares and Dreamscapes (1993)

Insomnia (1994)

Rose Madder (1995)

The Green Mile (serial novel, 1996)

Desperation (1996)

The Dark Tower IV: Wizards and Glass (1997)

Bag of Bones (1998)

Apt Pupil: A Novella in Different Seasons (1998)

The Girl Who Loved Tom Gordon (1999)

Storm of the Century (teleplay, 1999)

Hearts in Atlantis (1999; novellas)

Fiction written as Richard Bachman

Rage (1977)

The Long Walk (1979)

Roadwork: A Novel of the First Energy Crisis (1981)

The Running Man (1982)

Thinner (1984)

The Regulators (1996)

Nonfiction

Danse Macabre (1981)

JOHN LE CARRÉ
(nom de plume of David Cornwell)

Fiction

Call for the Dead (1960)

A Murder of Quality (1962)

The Spy Who Came In from the Cold (1964)

The Incongruous Spy (1964)

The Looking Glass War (1965)

A Small Town in Germany (1968)

The Naive and Sentimental Lover (1971)

Tinker, Tailor, Soldier, Spy (1977)

Smiley's People (1980)

The Honourable Schoolboy (1982)

The Little Drummer Girl (1983)

A Perfect Spy (1986)

The Russia House (1989)

The Secret Pilgrim (1991)

The Night Manager (1993)

Our Game (1995)

The Tailor of Panama (1996)

Single & Single (1999)

ROBERT LUDLUM

Fiction

The Scarlatti Inheritance (1971)

The Osterman Weekend (1972)

The Matlock Paper (1973)

The Rhineman Exchange (1974)

The Gemini Contenders (1976)

The Chancellor Manuscript (1977)

The Holcroft Covenant (1978)

The Matarese Circle (1979)

The Bourne Identity (1980)

The Parsifal Mosaic (1982)

The Aquitaine Progression (1984)

The Bourne Supremacy (1986)

The Icarus Agenda (1988)

The Bourne Ultimatum (1990)

The Road to Omaha (1992)

The Scorpio Illusion (1993)

The Apocalypse Watch (1995)

The Matarese Countdown (1997)

Fiction written as Jonathan Ryder

Trevayne (1973; reissued under Robert Ludlum, 1992)

The Cry of the Halidon (1974; reissued under Robert Ludlum, 1996)

Fiction written as Michael Shepherd

The Road to Gandolfo (1975; reissued under Robert Ludlum, 1992)

NORMAN MAILER

Fiction

The Naked and the Dead (1948)

Barbary Shore (1951)

The Deer Park (1955; screenplay, Wild 90, 1967)

Deaths for the Ladies (1962)

The Presidential Papers (1963)

An American Dream (1965)

Cannibals and Christians (1966)

Existential Errands (1972)

Genius and Lust (1976)

The Executioner's Song (1979; Pulitzer Prize; screenplay 1982)

Ancient Evenings (1983)

Tough Guys Don't Dance (1984; screenplay 1987)

Huckleberry Finn, Alive at One Hundred (1984)

Harlot's Ghost (1992)

The Gospel According to the Son (1996)

Nonfiction

Advertisements for Myself (1959)

Why Are We in Vietnam? (1967)

The Armies of the Night: History as a Novel, the Novel as History (1968; Pulitzer Prize; National Book Award)

Miami and the Siege of Chicago (1968; National Book Award)

Of a Fire on the Moon (1970)

King of the Hill: On the Fight of the Century (1971)

St. George and the Godfather (1971)

The Prisoner of Sex (1971)

Marilyn: A Biography (1973)

The Faith of Graffiti (1974)

The Fight (1975)

Of Women and Their Elegance (1980)

Of a Small and Modest Malignancy, Wicked and Bristling with Dots (1980)

Pieces and Pontifications (1982)

Oswald's Tale (1995)

Portrait of Picasso as a Young Man (1995)

The Time of Our Time (1998)

TONI MORRISON

Fiction

The Bluest Eye (1969)

Sula (1973)

Song of Solomon (1977; National Book Critics Circle Award)

Tar Baby (1981)

Beloved (1987; Pulitzer Prize)

Jazz (1992)

Paradise (1998)

Nonfiction

Playing in the Dark: Whiteness and the Literary Imagination (1992)

The Dancing Mind (1996)

Children's Book

The Big Box (1999)

Play

Dreaming Emmett (1986)

Nobel Prize for Literature, 1993

THOMAS PYNCHON

Fiction

V (1963)

The Crying of Lot 49 (1965)

Gravity's Rainbow (1973; National Book Award)

Vineland (1990)

Mason & Dixon (1997)

ANNE RICE

Fiction

Interview with the Vampire (1976)

The Feast of All Saints (1980)

Cry to Heaven (1982)

The Vampire Lestat (1985)

The Queen of the Damned (1988)

The Mummy, or Ramses the Damned (1989)

The Witching Hour (1990)

Tale of the Body Thief (1992)

Lasher (1993)

Taltos (1994)

Memnoch the Devil (1995)

Servant of the Bones (1996)

Violin (1997)

Pandora (1998)

The Vampire Armand (1998)

Vittorio the Vampire (1999)

Fiction written as A. N. Roquelaure

The Claiming of Sleeping Beauty (1983)

Beauty's Punishment (1984)

Beauty's Release: The Continued Erotic Adventures of Sleeping Beauty (1985)

Fiction written as Anne Rampling

Exit to Eden (1985)

Belinda (1986)

PHILIP ROTH

Fiction

Goodbye, Columbus (1959; National Book Award)

Letting Go (1962)

When She Was Good (1967)

Portnoy's Complaint (1969)

Our Gang (1971)

The Breast (1972)

The Great American Novel (1973)

My Life as a Man (1974)

Reading Myself and Others (1975)

The Professor of Desire (1977)

The Ghost Writer (1979)

Zuckerman Unbound (1981)

The Anatomy Lesson (1983)

Zuckerman Bound (1985)

The Counterlife (1987; National Book Critics Circle Award)

Deception (1990)

Operation Shylock (1993; PEN/Faulkner Award)

Sabbath's Theater (1995; National Book Award)

The Prague Orgy (1996)

American Pastoral (1997)

I Married a Communist (1998)

Nonfiction

The Facts: A Novelist's Autobiography (1988)

Patrimony: A True Story (memoirs, 1991; National Book Critics Circle Award)

SALMAN RUSHDIE

Fiction

Grimus (1975)

Midnight's Children (1981; Booker Prize)

Shame (1983)

The Satanic Verses (1989)

Haroun and the Sea of Stories (1991)

East, West: Stories (1995)

The Moor's Last Sigh (1996)

The Ground Beneath Her Feet (1999)

Nonfiction

The Jaguar Smile: A Nicaraguan Journey (1987)

Imaginary Homelands (1992)

MAURICE SENDAK

Children's books

Kenny's Window (1956)

Very Far Away (1957)

The Sign on Rosie's Door (1960)

Chicken Soup with Rice (1962)

One Was Johnny (1962)

Alligators All Around (1962)

Pierre (1962)

Where the Wild Things Are (1963; Caldecott Medal)

Hector Protector [and] As I Went Over the Water (1965)

Higglety Pigglety Pop! or, There Must Be More to Life (1967)

In the Night Kitchen (1970)

Ten Little Rabbits: A Counting Book with Mino the Magician (1970)

Maurice Sendak's Really Rosie (1975)

Some Swell Pup; or Are You Sure You Want a Dog? (1976)

Seven Little Monsters (1977)

Outside Over There (1981)

We Are All in the Dumps with Jack and Guy (1993)

Bernard (1994)

Max (1994)

Moishe (1994)

Tsippi (1994)

The Miami Giant (coauthor, 1995)

Swine Lake (coauthor, 1999)

Fly By Night (coauthor, 1999)

Hans Christian Anderson Award, 1970

Nonfiction

Worlds of Childhood: The Art and Craft of Writing for Children (coeditor, 1998)

DANIELLE STEEL

Fiction

Going Home (1973)

Passion's Promise (1977)

Now and Forever (1978)

The Promise (1978)

Season of Passion (1979)

Summer's End (1979)

To Love Again (1980)

The Ring (1980)

Loving (1980)

Remembrance (1981)

PAGES

Palomino (1981)
Once in a Lifetime (1982)
Crossings (1982)
A Perfect Stranger (1982)
Thurston House (1983)
Changes (1983)
Full Circle (1984)
Family Album (1985)
Secrets (1985)
Wanderlust (1986)
Fine Things (1987)
Kaleidoscope (1987)
Zoya (1988)
Star (1989)
Daddy (1989)
Message from Nam (1990)
Heartbeat (1991)
No Greater Love (1991)
Jewels (1992)
Mixed Blessings (1992)
Vanished (1993)
Accident (1994)
The Gift (1994)
Wings (1994)
Silent Honor (1995)
Lightning (1995)
Five Days in Paris (1995)
Malice (1996)
The Ranch (1997)
Special Delivery (1997)
The Ghost (1997)
The Long Road Home (1998)
The Klone and I (1998)
Mirror Image (1998)
Bittersweet (1999)
Granny Dan (1999)

Children's books
Max and the Babysitter (1989)
Martha's Best Friend (1989)
Max's Daddy Goes to the
  Hospital (1989)
Martha's New Daddy (1989)

Max's New Baby (1989)
Martha's New School (1989)
Max Runs Away (1990)
Martha's New Puppy (1990)
Max and Grandma and Grandpa
  Winky (1991)
Martha and Hilary and the
  Stranger (1991)
Freddie's Trip (1992)
Freddie's First Night Away
  (1992)
Freddie and the Doctor (1992)
Freddie's Accident (1992)
Poetry
Love Poems by Danielle Steel
  (1981)

Nonfiction
Having a Baby (1984)
His Bright Light (1998)

ANNE TYLER

Fiction
If Morning Ever Comes (1964)
The Tin Can Tree (1965)
A Slipping-Down Life (1970)
The Clock Winder (1972)
Celestial Navigation (1974)
Searching for Caleb (1976)
Earthly Possessions (1977)
Morgan's Passing (1980)
Dinner at the Homesick
  Restaurant (1982)
The Accidental Tourist (1985;
  National Book Critics Circle
  Award)
Breathing Lessons (1988;
  Pulitzer Prize)
Saint Maybe (1991)
Ladder of Years (1995)
A Slipping-Down Life (1997)
A Patchwork Planet (1998)

Children's book
Tumble Tower (1993)

JOHN UPDIKE

Fiction
The Poorhouse Fair (1959)
Rabbit, Run (1960)
The Centaur (1963; National
  Book Award)
Of the Farm (1965)
Couples (1968)
Bech: A Book (1970)
Rabbit Redux (1971)
A Month of Sundays (1975)
Marry Me: A Romance (1976)
The Coup (1978)
Rabbit Is Rich (1981; Pulitzer
  Prize; National Book Award;
  National Book Critics Circle
  Award)
Bech Is Back (1982)
The Witches of Eastwick (1984)
Roger's Version (1986)
S. (1988)
Rabbit at Rest (1990; Pulitzer
  Prize; National Book Critics
  Circle Award)
Memoirs of the Ford
  Administration (1992)
Brazil (1994)
In the Beauty of the Lilies
  (1996)
Toward the End of Time (1997)
Bech at Bay (1998)
The Best American Short Stories
  of the Century (coeditor,
  1999)

Nonfiction
Self Consciousness (memoirs,
  1989)
Golf Dreams (1996)

Play
Buchanan Dying (1974)

Children's books
The Magic Flute (1962)
The Ring (1964)

A Child's Calendar (1965)
Bottom's Dream (1969)

ALICE WALKER

Fiction
The Third Life of Grange
  Copeland (1970)
Meridian (1976)
The Color Purple (1982; Pulitzer
  Prize; National Book Award)
The Temple of My Familiar (1989)
Possessing the Secret of Joy
  (1992)
By the Light of My Father's Smile
  (1998)

Nonfiction
Warrior Marks (1993)
The Same River Twice (memoirs,
  1996)
Anything We Love Can Be Saved:
  A Writer's Activism (1998)

Poetry
Once (1976)
Revolutionary Petunias and
  Other Poems (1973)
Goodnight, Willie Lee, I'll See
  You in the Morning (1984)
Horses Make a Landscape Look
  More Beautiful (1984)
Her Blue Body Everything We
  Know: Earthling Poems,
  1965–1990 (1990)

Children's books
Langston Hughes, American
  Poet (1974)
To Hell with Dying (1988)
Finding the Green Stone (1991)

BOOKS OF THE CENTURY

To commemorate the New York Public Library's 100th anniversary, the librarians of this venerable institution identified books that, from their varying perspectives, have played defining roles in the making of the 20th century. Included are books that influenced the course of events, for good and for bad; books that interpreted new worlds; and books that simply delighted millions of patrons.

LANDMARKS OF MODERN LITERATURE
The Three Sisters, Anton Chekhov (1901)
Remembrance of Things Past, Marcel Proust (1913-27)
Tender Buttons, Gertrude Stein (1914)
The Metamorphosis, Franz Kafka (1915)
Renascence and Other Poems, Edna St. Vincent Millay (1917)
The Wild Swans at Coole, William Butler Yeats (1917)
Six Characters in Search of an Author, Luigi Pirandello (1921)
The Waste Land, T. S. Eliot (1922)
Ulysses, James Joyce (1922)
The Magic Mountain, Thomas Mann (1924)
The Great Gatsby, F. Scott Fitzgerald (1925)
To the Lighthouse, Virginia Woolf (1927)
Gypsy Ballads, Frederico García Lorca (1928)
Native Son, Richard Wright (1940)
The Age of Anxiety: A Baroque Eclogue, W. H. Auden (1947)
Invisible Man, Ralph Ellison (1952)
Lolita, Vladimir Nabokov (1955)
Fictions, Jorge Luis Borges (1944; 2nd augmented edition 1956)
One Hundred Years of Solitude, Gabriel García Márquez (1967)
Song of Solomon, Toni Morrison (1977)

PROTEST AND PROGRESS
The Battle with the Slum, Jacob Ritts (1902)
The Souls of Black Folk, W. E. B. Du Bois (1903)
The Jungle, Upton Sinclair (1906)
Twenty Years at Hull-House, Jane Addams (1910)

The House on Henry Street, Lillian Wald (1915)
The Autobiography of Lincoln Steffens, Lincoln Steffens (1931)
U.S.A., John Dos Passos (1937)
The Grapes of Wrath, John Steinbeck (1939)
Let Us Now Praise Famous Men, James Agee and Walker Evans (1941)
Strange Fruit, Lillian Smith (1944)
Growing Up Absurd, Paul Goodman (1960)
The Fire Next Time, James Baldwin (1963)
The Autobiography of Malcolm X, Malcolm X (1965)
And the Band Played On, Randy Shilts (1987)
There Are No Children Here, Alex Kotlowitz (1991)

POPULAR CULTURE & MASS ENTERTAINMENT
Dracula, Bram Stoker (1897)
The Turn of the Screw, Henry James (1898)
The Hound of the Baskervilles, Arthur Conan Doyle (1902)
Tarzan of the Apes, Edgar Rice Burroughs (1912)
Riders of the Purple Sage, Zane Grey (1912)
The Mysterious Affair at Styles, Agatha Christie (1920)
How to Win Friends and Influence People, Dale Carnegie (1936)
Gone with the Wind, Margaret Mitchell (1936)
The Big Sleep, Raymond Chandler (1939)
The Day of the Locust, Nathanael West (1939)

Peyton Place, Grace Metalious (1956)
The Cat in the Hat, Dr. Seuss (1957)
Stranger in a Strange Land, Robert A. Heinlein (1961)
Catch-22, Joseph Heller (1961)
In Cold Blood: A True Account of a Multiple Murder and Its Consequences, Truman Capote (1965)
Ball Four: My Life and Times Throwing the Knuckleball in the Big Leagues, Jim Bouton (1970)
Carrie, Stephen King (1974)
The Bonfire of the Vanities, Tom Wolfe (1987)

WOMEN RISE
The Age of Innocence, Edith Wharton (1920)
Woman Suffrage and Politics: The Inner Story of the Suffrage Movement, Carrie Chapman Catt and Nettie Rogers Shuler (1923)
My Fight for Birth Control, Margaret Sanger (1931)
Dust Tracks on a Dirt Road, Zora Neale Hurston (1942)
The Second Sex, Simone de Beauvoir (1949)
The Golden Notebook, Doris Lessing (1962)
The Feminine Mystique, Betty Friedan (1963)
I Know Why the Caged Bird Sings, Maya Angelou (1969)
Sisterhood Is Powerful: An Anthology of Writings from the Women's Liberations Movement, edited by Robin Morgan (1970)
Against Our Will: Men, Women and Rape, Susan Brownmiller (1975)
The Color Purple, Alice Walker (1982)

ECONOMICS & TECHNOLOGY

The Theory of the Leisure Class: An Economic Study of Institutions, Thorstein Veblen (1899)

The Protestant Ethic and the Spirit of Capitalism, Max Weber (1904–1905)

The Education of Henry Adams, Henry Adams (1907)

The General Theory of Employment, Interest and Money, John Meynard Keynes (1936)

A Theory of the Consumption Function, Milton Friedman (1957)

The Affluent Society, John Kenneth Galbraith (1958)

The Death and Life of Great American Cities, Jane Jacobs (1961)

Superhighway—Super Hoax, Helen Leavitt (1970)

Small Is Beautiful: A Study of Economics As If People Mattered, E. F. Schumacher (1973)

The Whole Internet: User's Guide and Catalogue, Ed Krol (1992)

MIND & SPIRIT

Suicide: A Study in Sociology, Emile Durkheim (1897)

The Interpretation of Dreams, Sigmund Freud (1900)

Studies in the Psychology of Sex, Havelock Ellis (1901–28)

The Varieties of Religious Experience: A Study in Human Nature, Wiilliam James (1902)

The Prophet, Kahlil Gibran (1923)

Why I Am Not a Christian, Bertrand Russell (1927)

Coming of Age in Samoa, Margaret Mead (1928)

Being and Nothingness, Jean-Paul Sartre (1943)

The Common Sense Book of Baby Care, Dr. Benjamin Spock (1946)

The Holy Bible, Revised Standard Version (1952)

The Courage to Be, Paul Tillich (1952)

One Flew over the Cuckoo's Nest, Ken Kesey (1962)

The Politics of Ecstasy, Timothy Leary (1968)

On Death and Dying, Elisabeth Kübler-Ross (1969)

The Uses of Enchantment, Bruno Bettelheim (1976)

MORE BOOKS THAT SHAPE LIVES

The Library of Congress established its Center for the Book in 1977 to stimulate public interest in books, reading, and libraries. Here is its list of the 25 books that have had the greatest impact on readers' lives.

The Adventures of Huckleberry Finn, Mark Twain
Atlas Shrugged, Ayn Rand
The Autobiography of Benjamin Franklin
The Bible
The Catcher in the Rye, J. D. Salinger
Charlotte's Web, E. B. White
The Diary of a Young Girl, Anne Frank
Don Quixote, Miguel de Cervantes
Gone with the Wind, Margaret Mitchell
Hiroshima, John Hersey
How to Win Friends and Influence People, Dale Carnegie

I Know Why the Caged Bird Sings, Maya Angelou
Invisible Man, Ralph Ellison
The Little Prince, Antoine de Saint-Exupéry
Little Women, Louisa May Alcott
The Lord of the Rings, J. R. R. Tolkien
Roots, Alex Haley
The Secret Garden, Frances Hodgson Burnett
To Kill a Mockingbird, Harper Lee
Treasure Island, Robert Louis Stevenson
Walden, Henry David Thoreau
War and Peace, Leo Tolstoy
What Color Is Your Parachute? Richard Nelson Bolles

THE MODERN LIBRARY FICTION LIST

Get out your pencils and get ready to quibble. Last year the Modern Library released its list of the top 100 English-language novels of the century (so never mind that manuscript in progress), 59 of which happen to be available in Modern Library editions. The hue and cry was heard even in hushed libraries. Objectors noted the panel of 10 was 90% male, all white, with an average age of just under 69, and a clear distaste for the contemporary. But at least they got us talking—and reading.

Rank	Book, Author (original publication date)
1.	*Ulysses*, James Joyce (1922)
2.	*The Great Gatsby*, F. Scott Fitzgerald (1925)
3.	*A Portrait of the Artist as a Young Man*, James Joyce (1916)
4.	*Lolita*, Vladimir Nabokov (1955)
5.	*Brave New World*, Aldous Huxley (1932)
6.	*The Sound and the Fury*, William Faulkner (1929)
7.	*Catch-22*, Joseph Heller (1961)
8.	*Darkness at Noon*, Arthur Koestler (1941)
9.	*Sons and Lovers*, D. H. Lawrence (1913)
10.	*The Grapes of Wrath*, John Steinbeck (1939)
11.	*Under the Volcano*, Malcolm Lowry (1947)
12.	*The Way of All Flesh*, Samuel Butler (1903)
13.	*1984*, George Orwell (1949)
14.	*I, Claudius*, Robert Graves (1934)
15.	*To the Lighthouse*, Virginia Woolf (1927)
16.	*An American Tragedy*, Theodore Dreiser (1925)
17.	*The Heart Is a Lonely Hunter*, Carson McCullers (1940)
18.	*Slaughterhouse Five*, Kurt Vonnegut, Jr. (1969)
19.	*Invisible Man*, Ralph Ellison (1952)
20.	*Native Son*, Richard Wright (1940)
21.	*Henderson the Rain King*, Saul Bellow (1959)
22.	*Appointment in Samarra*, John O'Hara (1934)
23.	*U.S.A.* (trilogy), John Dos Passos (1936)
24.	*Winesburg, Ohio*, Sherwood Anderson (1919)
25.	*A Passage to India*, E. M. Forster (1924)
26.	*The Wings of the Dove*, Henry James (1902)
27.	*The Ambassadors*, Henry James (1903)
28.	*Tender Is the Night*, F. Scott Fitzgerald (1934)
29.	*Studs Lonigan* (trilogy), James T. Farrell (1935)
30.	*The Good Soldier*, Ford Madox Ford (1915)
31.	*Animal Farm*, George Orwell (1945)
32.	*The Golden Bowl*, Henry James (1904)
33.	*Sister Carrie*, Theodore Dreiser (1900)
34.	*A Handful of Dust*, Evelyn Waugh (1934)
35.	*As I Lay Dying*, William Faulkner (1934)
36.	*All the King's Men*, Robert Penn Warren (1946)
37.	*The Bridge of San Luis Rey*, Thornton Wilder (1927)
38.	*Howards End*, E. M. Forster (1910)
39.	*Go Tell It on the Mountain*, James Baldwin (1953)
40.	*The Heart of the Matter*, Graham Greene (1948)
41.	*Lord of the Flies*, William Golding (1954)
42.	*Deliverance*, James Dickey, (1970)
43.	*A Dance to the Music of Time* (series), Anthony Powell (1975)
44.	*Point Counter Point*, Aldous Huxley (1928)
45.	*The Sun Also Rises*, Ernest Hemingway (1926)
46.	*The Secret Agent*, Joseph Conrad (1907)
47.	*Nostromo*, Joseph Conrad (1904)
48.	*The Rainbow*, D. H. Lawrence (1915)
49.	*Women in Love*, D. H. Lawrence (1920)
50.	*Tropic of Cancer*, Henry Miller (1934)

Rank	Book, Author (original publication date)
51.	*The Naked and the Dead*, Norman Mailer (1948)
52.	*Portnoy's Complaint*, Philip Roth (1969)
53.	*Pale Fire*, Vladimir Nabokov (1962)
54.	*Light in August*, William Faulkner (1932)
55.	*On the Road*, Jack Kerouac (1957)
56.	*The Maltese Falcon*, Dashiell Hammett (1930)
57.	*Parade's End*, Ford Madox Ford (1928)
58.	*The Age of Innocence*, Edith Wharton (1920)
59.	*Zuleika Dobson*, Max Beerbohm (1911)
60.	*The Moviegoer*, Walker Percy (1961)
61.	*Death Comes for the Archbishop*, Willa Cather (1927)
62.	*From Here to Eternity*, James Jones (1951)
63.	*The Wapshot Chronicle*, John Cheever (1957)
64.	*The Catcher in the Rye*, J. D. Salinger (1951)
65.	*A Clockwork Orange*, Anthony Burgess (1962)
66.	*Of Human Bondage*, W. Somerset Maugham (1915)
67.	*Heart of Darkness*, Joseph Conrad (1902)
68.	*Main Street*, Sinclair Lewis (1920)
69.	*The House of Mirth*, Edith Wharton (1905)
70.	*The Alexandria Quartet*, Lawrence Durrell (1960)
71.	*A High Wind in Jamaica*, Richard Hughes (1929)
72.	*A House for Mr. Biswas*, V. S. Naipaul (1961)
73.	*The Day of the Locust*, Nathanael West (1939)
74.	*A Farewell to Arms*, Ernest Hemingway (1929)
75.	*Scoop*, Evelyn Waugh (1938)
76.	*The Prime of Miss Jean Brodie*, Muriel Spark (1961)
77.	*Finnegans Wake*, James Joyce (1939)
78.	*Kim*, Rudyard Kipling (1901)
79.	*A Room with a View*, E. M. Forster (1908)
80.	*Brideshead Revisited*, Evelyn Waugh (1945)
81.	*The Adventures of Augie March*, Saul Bellow (1971)
82.	*Angle of Repose*, Wallace Stegner (1971)
83.	*A Bend in the River*, V. S. Naipaul (1979)
84.	*The Death of the Heart*, Elizabeth Bowen (1938)
85.	*Lord Jim*, Joseph Conrad (1900)
86.	*Ragtime*, E. L. Doctorow (1975)
87.	*The Old Wives' Tale*, Arnold Bennett (1908)
88.	*The Call of the Wild*, Jack London (1903)
89.	*Loving*, Henry Green (1945)
90.	*Midnight's Children*, Salman Rushdie (1981)
91.	*Tobacco Road*, Erskine Caldwell (1932)
92.	*Ironweed*, William Kennedy (1983)
93.	*The Magus*, John Fowles (1966)
94.	*Wide Sargasso Sea*, Jean Rhys (1966)
95.	*Under the Net*, Iris Murdoch (1954)
96.	*Sophie's Choice*, William Styron (1979)
97.	*The Sheltering Sky*, Paul Bowles (1949)
98.	*The Postman Always Rings Twice*, James M. Cain (1934)
99.	*The Ginger Man*, J. P. Donleavy (1955)
100.	*The Magnificent Ambersons*, Booth Tarkington (1918)

THE MODERN LIBRARY NONFICTION LIST

This year the Modern Library struck again, with a selection of the century's best nonfiction. The panel was slightly younger and a little more balanced for gender and race, and the final results were a tad less controversial. The primary dispute was whether these books are important to read or just plain important (case in point, Whitehead and Russell's *Principia Mathematica*). Read, and judge, for yourself.

Rank	Book, Author
1.	*The Education of Henry Adams*, Henry Adams
2.	*The Varieties of Religious Experience*, William James
3.	*Up from Slavery*, Booker T. Washington
4.	*A Room of One's Own*, Virginia Woolf
5.	*Silent Spring*, Rachel Carson
6.	*Selected Essays, 1917–1932*, T. S. Eliot
7.	*The Double Helix*, James D. Watson
8.	*Speak, Memory*, Vladimir Nabokov
9.	*The American Language*, H. L. Mencken
10.	*The General Theory of Employment, Interest, and Money*, John Maynard Keynes
11.	*The Lives of a Cell*, Lewis Thomas
12.	*The Frontier in American History*, Frederick Jackson Turner
13.	*Black Boy*, Richard Wright
14.	*Aspects of the Novel*, E. M. Forster
15.	*The Civil War*, Shelby Foote
16.	*The Guns of August*, Barbara Tuchman
17.	*The Proper Study of Mankind*, Isaiah Berlin
18.	*The Nature and Destiny of Man*, Reinhold Niebuhr
19.	*Notes of a Native Son*, James Baldwin
20.	*The Autobiography of Alice B. Toklas*, Gertrude Stein
21.	*The Elements of Style*, William Strunk and E. B. White
22.	*An American Dilemma*, Gunnar Myrdal
23.	*Principia Mathematica*, Alfred North Whitehead and Bertrand Russell
24.	*The Mismeasure of Man*, Stephen Jay Gould
25.	*The Mirror and the Lamp*, Meyer Howard Abrams
26.	*The Art of the Soluble*, Peter B. Medawar
27.	*The Ants*, Bert Hölldobler and Edward O. Wilson
28.	*A Theory of Justice*, John Rawls
29.	*Art and Illusion*, Ernest H. Gombrich
30.	*The Making of the English Working Class*, E. P. Thompson
31.	*The Souls of Black Folk*, W. E. B. Du Bois
32.	*Principia Ethica*, G. E. Moore
33.	*Philosophy and Civilization*, John Dewey
34.	*On Growth and Form*, D'Arcy Thompson
35.	*Ideas and Opinions*, Albert Einstein
36.	*The Age of Jackson*, Arthur Schlesinger Jr.
37.	*The Making of the Atomic Bomb*, Richard Rhodes
38.	*Black Lamb and Grey Falcon*, Rebecca West
39.	*Autobiographies*, W. B. Yeats
40.	*Science and Civilization in China*, Joseph Needham
41.	*Goodbye to All That*, Robert Graves
42.	*Homage to Catalonia*, George Orwell
43.	*The Autobiography of Mark Twain*, Mark Twain
44.	*Children of Crisis*, Robert Coles
45.	*A Study of History*, Arnold J. Toynbee
46.	*The Affluent Society*, John Kenneth Galbraith
47.	*Present at the Creation*, Dean Acheson
48.	*The Great Bridge*, David McCullough
49.	*Patriotic Gore*, Edmund Wilson
50.	*Samuel Johnson*, Walter Jackson Bate
51.	*The Autobiography of Malcolm X*, Alex Haley and Malcolm X
52.	*The Right Stuff*, Tom Wolfe
53.	*Eminent Victorians*, Lytton Strachey
54.	*Working*, Studs Terkel
55.	*Darkness Visible*, William Styron
56.	*The Liberal Imagination*, Lionel Trilling
57.	*The Second World War*, Winston Churchill
58.	*Out of Africa*, Isak Dinesen
59.	*Jefferson and His Time*, Dumas Malone
60.	*In the American Grain*, William Carlos Williams
61.	*Cadillac Desert*, Marc Reisner
62.	*The House of Morgan*, Ron Chernow
63.	*The Sweet Science*, A. J. Liebling
64.	*The Open Society and Its Enemies*, Karl Popper
65.	*The Art of Memory*, Frances A. Yates
66.	*Religion and the Rise of Capitalism*, R. H. Tawney
67.	*A Preface to Morals*, Walter Lippmann
68.	*The Gate of Heavenly Peace*, Jonathan D. Spence
69.	*The Structure of Scientific Revolutions*, Thomas S. Kuhn
70.	*The Strange Career of Jim Crow*, C. Vann Woodward
71.	*The Rise of the West*, William H. McNeill
72.	*The Gnostic Gospels*, Elaine Pagels
73.	*James Joyce*, Richard Ellmann
74.	*Florence Nightingale*, Cecil Woodham-Smith
75.	*The Great War and Modern Memory*, Paul Fussell
76.	*The City in History*, Lewis Mumford
77.	*Battle Cry of Freedom*, James M. McPherson
78.	*Why We Can't Wait*, Martin Luther King Jr.
79.	*The Rise of Theodore Roosevelt*, Edmund Morris
80.	*Studies in Iconography*, Erwin Panofsky
81.	*The Face of Battle*, John Keegan
82.	*The Strange Death of Liberal England*, George Dangerfield
83.	*Vermeer*, Lawrence Gowing
84.	*A Bright Shining Lie*, Neil Sheehan
85.	*West with the Night*, Beryl Markham
86.	*This Boy's Life*, Tobias Wolff
87.	*A Mathematician's Apology*, G. H. Hardy
88.	*Six Easy Pieces*, Richard P. Feynman
89.	*Pilgrim at Tinker Creek*, Annie Dillard
90.	*The Golden Bough*, James George Frazer
91.	*Shadow and Act*, Ralph Ellison
92.	*The Power Broker*, Robert A. Caro
93.	*The American Political Tradition*, Richard Hofstadter
94.	*The Contours of American History*, William Appleman Williams
95.	*The Promise of American Life*, Herbert Croly
96.	*In Cold Blood*, Truman Capote
97.	*The Journalist and the Murderer*, Janet Malcolm
98.	*The Taming of Chance*, Ian Hacking
99.	*Operating Instructions*, Anne Lamott
100.	*Melbourne*, Lord David Cecil

LITERARY AWARDS

NATIONAL BOOK AWARDS

Fiction

1950 Nelson Algren
The Man with the Golden Arm
1951 William Faulkner
The Collected Stories of William Faulkner
1952 James Jones
From Here to Eternity
1953 Ralph Ellison
Invisible Man
1954 Saul Bellow
The Adventures of Augie March
1955 William Faulkner
A Fable
1956 John O'Hara
Ten North Frederick
1957 Wright Morris
The Field of Vision
1958 John Cheever
The Wapshot Chronicle
1959 Bernard Malamud
The Magic Barrel
1960 Philip Roth
Goodbye, Columbus
1961 Conrad Richter
The Waters of Kronos
1962 Walker Percy
The Moviegoer
1963 J. F. Powers
Morte D'Urban
1964 John Updike
The Centaur
1965 Saul Bellow
Herzog
1966 Katherine Anne Porter
The Collected Stories of Katherine Anne Porter
1967 Bernard Malamud
The Fixer
1968 Thornton Wilder
The Eighth Day
1969 Jerzy Kosinski
Steps
1970 Joyce Carol Oates
Them
1971 Saul Bellow
Mr. Sammler's Planet
1972 Flannery O'Connor
The Complete Stories of Flannery O'Connor
1973 John Barth
Chimera
John Williams
Augustus
1974 Thomas Pynchon
Gravity's Rainbow
Isaac Bashevis Singer
A Crown of Feathers and Other Stories

1975 Robert Stone
Dog Soldiers
Thomas Williams
The Hair of Harold Roux
1976 William Gaddis
JR
1977 Wallace Stegner
The Spectator Bird
1978 Mary Lee Settle
Blood Ties
1979 Tim O'Brien
Going After Cacciato
1980 William Styron (hardcover)
Sophie's Choice
John Irving (paperback)
The World According to Garp
1981 Wright Morris (hardcover)
Plains Song
John Cheever (paperback)
The Stories of John Cheever
1982 John Updike (hardcover)
Rabbit Is Rich
William Maxwell (paperback)
So Long, See You Tomorrow
1983 Alice Walker (hardcover)
The Color Purple
Eudora Welty (paperback)
Collected Stories of Eudora Welty
1984 Ellen Gilchrist
Victory over Japan: A Book of Stories
1985 Don DeLillo
White Noise
1986 E. L. Doctorow
World's Fair
1987 Larry Heinemann
Paco's Story
1988 Pete Dexter
Paris Trout
1989 John Casey
Spartina
1990 Charles Johnson
Middle Passage
1991 Norman Rush
Mating
1992 Cormac McCarthy
All the Pretty Horses
1993 E. Annie Proulx
The Shipping News
1994 William Gaddis
A Frolic of His Own
1995 Philip Roth
Sabbath's Theater
1996 Andrea Barrett
Ship Fever and Other Stories
1997 Charles Frazier
Cold Mountain
1998 Alice McDermott
Charming Billy

Nonfiction

1950 Ralph L. Rusk
Ralph Waldo Emerson
1951 Newton Arvin
Herman Melville
1952 Rachel Carson
The Sea Around Us
1953 Bernard A. De Voto
The Course of an Empire
1954 Bruce Catton
A Stillness at Appomattox
1955 Joseph Wood Krutch
The Measure of Man
1956 Herbert Kubly
An American in Italy
1957 George F. Kennan
Russia Leaves the War
1958 Catherine Drinker Bowen
The Lion and the Throne
1959 J. Christopher Herold
Mistress to an Age: A Life of Madame de Stael
1960 Richard Ellmann
James Joyce
1961 William L. Shirer
The Rise and Fall of the Third Reich
1962 Lewis Mumford
The City in History: Its Origins, Its Transformations and Its Prospects
1963 Leon Edel
Henry James, Vol. II: The Conquest of London. Henry James, Vol. III: The Middle Years
No general nonfiction prize awarded 1964–79
1980 Tom Wolfe (hardcover)
The Right Stuff
Peter Matthiessen (paperback)
The Snow Leopard
1981 Maxine Hong Kingston (hardcover)
China Men
Jane Kramer (paperback)
The Last Cowboy
1982 Tracy Kidder (hardcover)
The Soul of a New Machine
Victor S. Navasky (paperback)
Naming Names
1983 Fox Butterfield (hardcover)
China: Alive in the Bitter Sea
James Fallows (paperback)
National Defense
1984 Rovert V. Remini
Andrew Jackson and the Course of American Democracy, 1833–1845
1985 J. Anthony Lukas
Common Ground: A Turbulent Decade in the Lives of Three American Families

1986	Barry Lopez *Arctic Dreams*	1962	Alan Dugan *Poems*	1995	Stanley Kunitz *Passing Through: The Later*
1987	Richard Rhodes *The Making of the Atom Bomb*	1963	William Strafford *Traveling Through the Dark*	1996	*Poems New and Selected* Hayden Carruth
1988	Neil Sheehan *A Bright Shining Lie: John Paul* *Vann and America in Vietnam*	1964	John Crowe Ransom *Selected Poems*	1997	*Scrambled Eggs and Whiskey* William Meredith *Effort at Speech: New and*
1989	Thomas L. Friedman *From Beirut to Jerusalem*	1965	Theodore Roethke *The Far Field*	1998	*Selected Poems* Gerald Stern
1990	Ron Chernow *The House of Morgan: An Ameri-* *can Banking Dynasty and the*	1966	James Dickey *Buckdancer's Choice: Poems*		*This Time: New and Selected* *Poems*
	Rise of Modern Finance	1967	James Merrill *Nights and Days*		

Young People's Literature

1991	Orlando Patterson *Freedom*
1992	Paul Monette *Becoming a Man: Half a Life* *Story*

1968	Robert Bly *The Light Around the Body*
1969	John Berryman *His Toy, His Dream, His Rest*
1970	Elizabeth Bishop *The Complete Poems*

1996	Victor Martinez *Parrot in the Oven: Mi Vida*
1997	Han Dolan *Dancing on the Edge*
1998	Louis Sachar *Holes*

1993	Gore Vidal *United States: Essays* *1952–1992*
1994	Sherwin B. Nuland *How We Die: Reflections on Life's* *Final Chapter*
1995	Tina Rosenberg *The Haunted Land: Facing* *Europe's Ghosts After* *Communism*
1996	James Caroll *An American Requiem*
1997	Joseph J. Ellis *American Sphinx: The Character* *of Thomas Jefferson*
1998	Edward Ball *Slaves in the Family*

1971	Mona Van Duyn *To See, To Take*
1972	Howard Moss *Selected Poems* Frank O'Hara *The Collected Poems of* *Frank O'Hara*
1973	A. R. Ammons *Collected Poems, 1951–1971*
1974	Allen Ginsberg *The Fall of America: Poems of* *These States* Adrienne Rich *Diving into the Wreck: Poems* *1971–1972*
1975	Marilyn Hacker *Presentation Piece*
1976	John Ashbery *Self-Portrait in a Convex Mirror*

NEWBERY MEDAL BOOKS

For children's literature

1922	Hendrik van Loon *The Story of Mankind*
1923	Hugh Lofting *The Voyages of Doctor Dolittle*
1924	Charles Hawes *The Dark Frigate*
1925	Charles Finger *Tales from Silver Lands*
1926	Arthur Chrisman *Shen of the Sea*
1927	Will James *Smoky, the Cowhorse*
1928	Dhan Mukerji *Gay Neck, the Story of a Pigeon*

Poetry

1950	William Carlos Williams *Paterson: Book III and Selected* *Poems*
1951	Wallace Stevens *The Auroras of Autumn*
1952	Marianne Moore *Collected Poems*
1953	Archibald MacLeish *Collected Poems, 1917–1952*
1954	Conrad Aiken *Collected Poems*
1955	Wallace Stevens *The Collected Poems of Wallace* *Stevens*
1956	W. H. Auden *The Shield of Achilles*
1957	Richard Wilbur *Things of This World*
1958	Robert Penn Warren *Promises: Poems, 1954–1956*
1959	Theodore Roethke *Words for the Wind*
1960	Robert Lowell *Life Studies*
1961	Randall Jarrell *The Woman at the* *Washington Zoo*

1977	Richard Eberhart *Collected Poems, 1930–1976*
1978	Howard Nemerov *The Collected Poems of Howard* *Nemerov*
1979	James Merrill *Mirabell: Book of Numbers*
1980	Philip Levine *Ashes*
1981	Lisel Mueller *The Need to Hold Still*
1982	William Bronk *Life Supports: New and* *Collected Poems*
1983	Galway Kinnell *Selected Poems* Charles Wright *Country Music: Selected Early* *Poems*
1991	Philip Levine *What Work Is*
1992	Mary Oliver *New and Selected Poems*
1993	A. R. Ammons *Garbage*
1994	James Tate *A Worshipful Company of Fletchers*

1929	Eric P. Kelly *The Trumpeter of Krakow*
1930	Rachel Field *Hitty, Her First Hundred Years*
1931	Elizabeth Coatsworth *The Cat Who Went to Heaven*
1932	Laura Armer *Waterless Mountain*
1933	Elizabeth Lewis *Young Fu of the Upper Yangtze*
1934	Cornelia Meigs *Invincible Louisa*
1935	Monica Shannon *Dobry*
1936	Carol Brink *Caddie Woodlawn*
1937	Ruth Sawyer *Roller Skates*
1938	Kate Seredy *The White Stag*
1939	Elizabeth Enright *Thimble Summer*
1940	James Daugherty *Daniel Boone*
1941	Armstrong Sperry *Call It Courage*

1942	Walter Edmonds
	The Matchlock Gun
1943	Elizabeth Gray
	Adam of the Road
1944	Esther Forbes
	Johnny Tremain
1945	Robert Lawson
	Rabbit Hill
1946	Lois Lenski
	Strawberry Girl
1947	Carolyn Bailey
	Miss Hickory
1948	William Pène du Bois
	The Twenty-One Balloons
1949	Marguerite Henry
	King of the Wind
1950	Marguerite de Angeli
	The Door in the Wall
1951	Elizabeth Yates
	Amos Fortune, Free Man
1952	Eleanor Estes
	Ginger Pye
1953	Ann Nolan Clark
	Secret of the Andes
1954	Joseph Krumgold
	...And Now Miguel
1955	Meindert DeJong
	The Wheel on the School
1956	Jean Lee Latham
	Carry On, Mr. Bowditch
1957	Virginia Sorenson
	Miracles on Maple Hill
1958	Harold Keith
	Rifles for Watie
1959	Elizabeth George Speare
	The Witch of Blackbird Pond
1960	Joseph Krumgold
	Onion John
1961	Scott O'Dell
	Island of the Blue Dolphins
1962	Elizabeth George Speare
	The Bronze Bow
1963	Madeleine L'Engle
	A Wrinkle in Time
1964	Emily Neville
	It's Like This, Cat
1965	Maia Wojciechowska
	Shadow of a Bull
1966	Elizabeth Borton de Trevino
	I, Juan de Pareja
1967	Irene Hunt
	Up a Road Slowly
1968	E. L. Konigsburg
	From the Mixed-Up Files of Mrs. Basil E. Frankweiler
1969	Lloyd Alexander
	The High King
1970	William H. Armstrong
	Sounder
1971	Betsy Byars
	Summer of the Swans
1972	Robert C. O'Brien
	Mrs. Frisby and the Rats of NIMH

1973	Jean Craighead George
	Julie of the Wolves
1974	Paula Fox
	The Slave Dancer
1975	Virginia Hamilton
	M. C. Higgins, the Great
1976	Susan Cooper
	The Grey King
1977	Mildred D. Taylor
	Roll of Thunder, Hear My Cry
1978	Katherine Paterson
	Bridge to Terabithia
1979	Ellen Raskin
	The Westing Game
1980	Joan W. Blos
	A Gathering of Days
1981	Katherine Paterson
	Jacob Have I Loved
1982	Nancy Willard
	A Visit to William Blake's Inn: Poems for Innocent and Experienced Travelers
1983	Cynthia Voight
	Dicey's Song
1984	Beverly Cleary
	Dear Mr. Henshaw
1985	Robin McKinley
	The Hero and the Crown
1986	Patricia MacLachlan
	Sarah, Plain and Tall
1987	Sid Fleischman
	The Whipping Boy
1988	Russell Freedman
	Lincoln: A Photobiography
1989	Paul Fleischman
	Joyful Noise: Poems for Two Voices
1990	Lois Lowry
	Number the Stars
1991	Jerry Spinelli
	Maniac Magee
1992	Phyllis Reynolds Naylor
	Shiloh
1993	Cynthia Rylant
	Missing May
1994	Lois Lowry
	The Giver
1995	Sharon Creech
	Walk Two Moons
1996	Karen Cushman
	The Midwife's Apprentice
1997	E. L. Konigsburg
	The View from Saturday
1998	Karen Hesse
	Out of Dust
1999	Louis Sachar
	Holes

CALDECOTT MEDAL BOOKS

For children's picture books

1938	Helen Dean Fish, ill. by Dorothy P. Lathrop
	Animals of the Bible
1939	Thomas Handforth
	Mei Li
1940	Ingri and Edgar Parin d'Aulaire
	Abraham Lincoln
1941	Robert Lawson
	They Were Strong and Good
1942	Robert McCloskey
	Make Way for Ducklings
1943	Virginia Lee Burton
	The Little House
1944	James Thurber, ill. by Louis Slobodkin
	Many Moons
1945	Rachel Field, ill. by Elizabeth Orton Jones
	Prayer for a Child
1946	Maude and Mishka Petersham
	The Rooster Crows
1947	Golden MacDonald, ill. by Leonard Weisgard
	The Little Island
1948	Alvin Tresselt, ill. by Roger Duvoisin
	White Snow, Bright Snow
1949	Berta and Elmer Hader
	The Big Snow
1950	Leo Politi
	Song of the Swallows
1951	Katherine Milhous
	The Egg Tree
1952	Will Lipkind, ill. by Nicolas Mordvinoff
	Finders Keepers
1953	Lynd Ward
	The Biggest Bear
1954	Ludwig Bemelmans
	Madeline's Rescue
1955	Marcia Brown
	Cinderella
1956	John Langstaff, ill. by Feodor Rojankovsky
	Frog Went A-Courtin'
1957	Janice Udry, ill. by Marc Simont
	A Tree Is Nice
1958	Robert McCloskey
	Time of Wonder
1959	Barbara Cooney
	Chanticleer and the Fox
1960	Marie Hall Ets and Aurora Labastida
	Nine Days to Christmas
1961	Ruth Robbins, ill. by Nicolas Sidjakov
	Baboushka and the Three Kings
1962	Marcia Brown
	Once a Mouse
1963	Ezra Jack Keats
	The Snowy Day

1964 Maurice Sendak
Where the Wild Things Are
1965 Beatrice Schenk de Regniers, ill.
by Beni Montresor
May I Bring a Friend?
1966 Sorche Nic Leodhas, ill. by Nonny
Hogrogian
Always Room for One More
1967 Evaline Ness
Sam, Bangs & Moonshine
1968 Barbara Emberley, ill. by Ed
Emberley
Drummer Hoff
1969 Arthur Ransome, ill. by Uri
Shulevitz
*The Fool of the World and the
Flying Ship*
1970 William Steig
Sylvester and the Magic Pebble
1971 Gail E. Haley
A Story a Story
1972 Nonny Hogrogian
One Fine Day
1973 Lafcadio Hearn, retold by Arlene
Mosel, ill. by Blair Lent
The Funny Little Woman
1974 Harve Zemach, picts. by Margot
Zemach
Duffy and the Devil
1975 Gerald McDermott
Arrow to the Sun
1976 Verna Aardema, picts. by Leo
and Diane Dillon
*Why Mosquitoes Buzz in People's
Ears*
1977 Margaret Musgrove, picts. by Leo
and Diane Dillon
Ashanti to Zulu
1978 Peter Spier
Noah's Ark
1979 Paul Goble
The Girl Who Loved Wild Horses
1980 Donald Hall, picts. by Barbara
Cooney
Ox-Cart Man
1981 Arnold Lobel
Fables
1982 Chris Van Allsburg
Jumanji
1983 Blaise Cendrars, trans. and ill.
by Marcia Brown
Shadow
1984 Alice and Martin Provensen
*The Glorious Flight: Across the
Channel with Louis Blériot*
1985 Margaret Hodges, ill. by Trina
Schart Hyman
Saint George and the Dragon
1986 Chris Van Allsburg
The Polar Express

1987 Arthur Yorinks, ill. by Richard
Egielski
Hey, Al
1988 Jane Yolen, ill. by John Schoenherr
Owl Moon
1989 Karen Ackerman, ill. by Stephen
Gammell
Song and Dance Man
1990 Ed Young
Lon Po Po
1991 David Macaulay
Black and White
1992 David Wiesner
Tuesday
1993 Emily Arnold McCully
Mirette on the High Wire
1994 Allen Say
Grandfather's Journey
1995 Eve Bunting, ill. by David Diaz
Smoky Night
1996 Peggy Rathmann
Officer Buckle and Gloria
1997 David Wisniewski
Golem
1998 Paul O. Zelinsky
Rapunzel
1999 Mary Azarian
Snowflake Bentley

BOLLINGEN PRIZE IN POETRY

1949 Wallace Stevens
1950 John Crowe Ransom
1951 Marianne Moore
1952 Archibald MacLeish
William Carlos Williams
1953 W. H. Auden
1954 Leonie Adams
Louise Bogan
1955 Conrad Aiken
1956 Allen Tate
1957 E. E. Cummings
1958 Theodore Roethke
1959 Delmore Schwartz
1960 Yvor Winters
1961 Richard Eberhart
John Hall Wheelock
1962 Robert Frost
1965 Horace Gregory
1967 Robert Penn Warren
1969 John Berryman
Karl Shapiro
1971 Richard Wilbur
Mona Van Duyn
1973 James Merrill
1975 A. R. Ammons
1977 David Ignatow
1979 W. S. Merwin
1981 May Swenson
Howard Nemerov
1983 Anthony E. Hecht
John Hollander

1985 John Ashbery
Fred Chappell
1987 Stanley Kunitz
1989 Edgar Bowers
1991 Laura (Riding) Jackson
Donald Justice
1993 Mark Strand
1995 Kenneth Koch
1997 Gary Snyder
1999 Robert White Creeley

PEN/FAULKNER AWARD

Best American work of fiction

1981 Walter Abish
How German Is It?
1982 David Bradley
The Chaneysville Incident
1983 Toby Olson
Seaview
1984 John Edgar Wideman
Sent for You Yesterday
1985 Tobias Wolff
The Barracks Thief
1986 Peter Taylor
The Old Forest
1987 Richard Wiley
Soldiers in Hiding
1988 T. Coraghessan Boyle
World's End
1989 James Salter
Dusk
1990 E. L. Doctorow
Billy Bathgate
1991 John Edgar Wideman
Philadelphia Fire
1992 Don DeLillo
Mao II
1993 E. Annie Proulx
Postcards
1994 Philip Roth
Operation Shylock
1995 David Guterson
Snow Falling on Cedars
1996 Richard Ford
Independence Day
1997 Gina Berriault
Women in Their Beds
1998 Rafi Zabor
The Bear Comes Home
1999 Michael Cunningham
The Hours

BOOKER PRIZE

British award for fiction

1969 P. H. Newby
Something to Answer For
1970 Bernice Rubens
The Elected Member
1971 V. S. Naipaul
In a Free State
1972 John Berger
G
1973 J. G. Farrell
The Siege of Krishnapur
1974 Nadine Gordimer
The Conservationist
1975 Ruth Prawer Jhabvala
Heat and Dust
1976 David Storey
Saville
1977 Paul Scott
Staying On
1978 Iris Murdoch
The Sea, the Sea
1979 Penelope Fitzgerald
Offshore
1980 William Golding
Rites of Passage
1981 Salman Rushdie
Midnight's Children
1982 Thomas Keneally
Schindler's Ark
1983 J. M. Coetzee
Life and Times of Michael K
1984 Anita Brookner
Hotel du Lac
1985 Keri Hulme
The Bone People
1986 Kingsley Amis
The Old Devils
1987 Penelope Lively
Moon Tiger
1988 Peter Carey
Oscar and Lucinda
1989 Kazuo Ishiguro
The Remains of the Day
1990 A. S. Byatt
Possession
1991 Ben Okri
The Famished Road
1992 Michael Ondaatje
The English Patient
Barry Unsworth
Sacred Hunger
1993 Roddy Doyle
Paddy Clark Ha Ha Ha
1994 James Kelman
How Late It Was, How Late
1995 Pat Barker
The Ghost Road
1996 Graham Swift
Last Orders
1997 Arundhati Roy
The God of Small Things
1998 Ian McEwan
Amsterdam

NOBEL PRIZE FOR LITERATURE

1901 Rene-Francois-Armend Prudhomme
France
1902 Bjornstjerne Bjornson
Norway
1903 Christian Mommsen
Germany
1904 Jose Echegaray y Eizaguirre
Spain
Frederic Mistral
France
1905 Henryk Sienkiewicz
Poland
1906 Giosue Carducci
Italy
1907 Joseph Rudyard Kipling
Great Britain
1908 Rudolph Eucker
Germany
1909 Selma Lagerlof
Sweden
1910 Paul Ludwig von Heyse
Germany
1911 Maurice Maeterlinck
Belgium
1912 Gerhart Hauptmann
Germany
1913 Sir Rabindranath Tagore
India
1915 Roland Romain
France
1916 Carl Gustof Verner Von
Heidenstam
Sweden
1917 Karl Adolph Gjellerup
Denmark
Henrik Pontoppidan
Denmark
1918 Erik Axel Karlfeldt
Sweden
1919 Carl Spitteler
Switzerland
1920 Knut Hamsun
Norway
1921 Anatole France
France
1922 Jacinto Benaventi y Martinez
Spain
1923 William Butler Yeats
Ireland
1924 Wladylaw Reymont
Poland
1925 George Bernard Shaw
Ireland
1926 Grazia Deledda
Italy
1927 Henri Bergson
France
1928 Sigrid Undset
Norway
1929 Paul Mann
Germany

1930 Henry Sinclair Lewis
United States
1931 Erik Axel Karlfeldt
Sweden
1932 John Galsworthy
Great Britain
1933 Ivan Bunin
Russia
1934 Luigi Pirandello
Italy
1936 Eugene O'Neill
United States
1937 Roger Martin du Gard
France
1938 Pearl S. Buck
United States
1939 Frans Sillanpaa
Finland
1944 Johannes Jensen
Denmark
1945 Gabriela Mistral
Chile
1946 Herman Hesse
Germany
1947 Andre Gide
France
1948 Thomas Stearns Eliot
United States
Isaac Singer
Poland
1949 William Faulkner
United States
1950 Bertrand Russell
Great Britain
1951 Par Fabian Lagerkirst
Sweden
1952 Francois Mauriac
France
1953 Sir Winston Churchill
Great Britain
1954 Ernest Hemingway
United States
1955 Halldor Laxness
Iceland
1956 Juan Jimenez
Spain
1957 Albert Camus
France
1958 Boris Pasternak
Russia
1959 Salvatore Quasimodo
Italy
1960 Saint-John Perse
France
1961 Ivo Andric
Yugoslavia
1962 John Steinbeck
United States
1963 Giorgos Seferis
Greece
1964 Jean-Paul Sartre
France
1965 Mikhail Sholokov
Russia

1966	Shmuel Agnon Austria		1997	Dario Fo Italy		1976	Horticulture

1966 Shmuel Agnon
      Austria
      Leonie Sachs
      Germany
1967 Miguel Asturias
      Guatemala
1968 Yasunari Kawabata
      Japan
1969 Samuel Beckett
      Ireland
1970 Alexander Solzhenitsyn
      Russia
1971 Pablo Neruda
      Chile
1972 Heinrich Boll
      Germany
1973 Patrick White
      Australia
1974 Euyind Johnson
      Sweden
1975 Eugenio Montale
      Italy
1976 Saul Bellow
      United States
1977 Vicente Aleixandre y Merlo
      Spain
1978 Isaac Bashevis Singer
      United States
1979 Odysseus Elytis
      Greece
1980 Czeslaw Milosz
      Poland
1981 Elias Canetti
      Bulgaria
1982 Gabriel Jose García Márquez
      Colombia
1983 William Golding
      Great Britain
1984 Jaroslav Seifert
      Czechoslovakia
1985 Claude Simon
      France
1986 Wole Soyinka
      Nigeria
1987 Joseph Brodsky
      Russia
1988 Naguib Mahfouz
      Egypt
1989 Camilo Jose Cela
      Spain
1990 Octavio Paz
      Mexico
1991 Nadine Gordimer
      South Africa
1992 Derek Walcott
      St. Lucia
1993 Toni Morrison
      United States
1994 Kenzaburo Oe
      Japan
1995 Seamus Heaney
      Ireland
1996 Wislawa Szymborska
      Poland

1997 Dario Fo
      Italy
1998 José Saramago
      Portugal
1999 Günter Grass
      Germany

NATIONAL MAGAZINE AWARD

Public Service/Public Interest

1970 Life
1971 The Nation
1972 Philadelphia
1973 [not awarded]
1974 Scientific American
1975 Consumer Reports
1976 Business Week
1977 Philadelphia
1978 Mother Jones
1979 New West
1980 Texas Monthly
1981 Reader's Digest
1982 The Atlantic Monthly
1983 Foreign Affairs
1984 The New Yorker
1985 The Washingtonian
1986 Science 85
1987 Money
1988 The Atlantic Monthly
1989 California
1990 Southern Exposure
1991 Family Circle
1992 Glamour
1993 The Family Therapy Network
1994 Philadelphia
1995 The New Republic
1996 Texas Monthly
1997 Fortune
1998 The Atlantic Monthly
1999 Time

Specialized Journalism

1970 Philadelphia
1971 Rolling Stone
1972 Architectural Record
1973 Psychology Today
1974 Texas Monthly
1975 Medical Economics
1976 United Mine Workers Journal
1977 Architectural Record
1978 Scientific American
1979 National Journal
1980 IEEE Spectrum

Design/Visual Excellence

1970 Look
1971 Vogue
1972 Esquire
1973 Horizon
1974 Newsweek
1975 Country Journal
      National Lampoon

1976 Horticulture
1977 Rolling Stone
1978 Architectural Digest
1979 Audubon
1980 GEO
1981 Attenzione
1982 Nautical Quarterly
1983 New York
1984 House & Garden
1985 Forbes
1986 Time
1987 Elle
1988 Life
1989 Rolling Stone
1990 Esquire
1991 Condé Nast Traveler
1992 Vanity Fair
1993 Harper's Bazaar
1994 Allure
1995 Martha Stewart Living
1996 Wired
1997 I.D. Magazine
1998 Entertainment Weekly
1999 ESPN: The Magazine

Reporting (Excellence)/News Reporting

1970 The New Yorker
1971 The Atlantic Monthly
1972 The Atlantic Monthly
1973 New York
1974 The New Yorker
1975 The New Yorker
1976 Audubon
1977 Audubon
1978 The New Yorker
1979 Texas Monthly
1980 Mother Jones
1981 National Journal
1982 The Washingtonian
1983 Institutional Investor
1984 Vanity Fair
1985 Texas Monthly
1986 Rolling Stone
1987 Life
1988 Baltimore Magazine
      The Washingtonian
1989 The New Yorker
1990 The New Yorker
1991 The New Yorker
1992 The New Republic
1993 IEEE Spectrum
1994 The New Yorker
1995 The Atlantic Monthly
1996 The New Yorker
1997 Outside
1998 Rolling Stone
1999 Newsweek

General Excellence
(Under 100,000 circulation)

1981 ARTnews
1982 Camera Arts
1983 Louisiana Life

1984	The American Lawyer
1985	Manhattan, inc.
1986	New England Monthly
1987	New England Monthly
1988	The Sciences
1989	The Sciences
1990	7 Days
1991	The New Republic
1992	The New Republic
1993	Lingua Franca
1994	Print
1995	I.D. Magazine
1996	The Sciences
1997	I.D. Magazine
1998	DoubleTake
1999	I.D. Magazine

General Excellence (100,000–400,000)

1981	Audubon
1982	Rocky Mountain Magazine
1983	Harper's Magazine
1984	Outside
1985	American Heritage
1986	3-2-1 Contact
1987	Common Cause
1988	Hippocrates
1989	American Heritage
1990	Texas Monthly
1991	Interview
1992	Texas Monthly
1993	American Photo
1994	Wired
1995	Men's Journal
1996	Civilization
1997	Wired
1998	Preservation
1999	Fast Company

General Excellence (400,000–1,000,000)

1981	Business Week
1982	Science 81
1983	Science 82
1984	House & Garden
1985	American Health
1986	Discover
1987	Elle
1988	Fortune
1989	Vanity Fair
1990	Metropolitan Home
1991	Condé Nast Traveler
1992	Mirabella
1993	The Atlantic Monthly
1994	Health
1995	The New Yorker
1996	Outside
1997	Outside
1998	Outside
1999	Condé Nast Traveler

General Excellence (over 1,000,000)

1981	Glamour
1982	Newsweek

1983	Life
1984	National Geographic
1985	Time
1986	Money
1987	People Weekly
1988	Parents
1989	Sports Illustrated
1990	Sports Illustrated
1991	Glamour
1992	National Geographic
1993	Newsweek
1994	Business Week
1995	Entertainment Weekly
1996	Business Week
1997	Vanity Fair
1998	Rolling Stone
1999	Vanity Fair

Essays and Criticism

1978	Esquire
1979	Life
1980	Natural History
1981	Time
1982	The Atlantic Monthly
1983	The American Lawyer
1984	The New Republic
1985	Boston
1986	The Sciences
1987	Outside
1988	Harper's Magazine
1989	Harper's Magazine
1990	Vanity Fair
1991	The Sciences
1992	The Nation
1993	The American Lawyer
1994	Harper's Magazine
1995	Harper's Magazine
1996	The New Yorker
1997	The New Yorker
1998	The New Yorker
1999	The Atlantic Monthly

Fiction

1978	The New Yorker
1979	The Atlantic Monthly
1980	Antaeus
1981	The North American Review
1982	The New Yorker
1983	The North American Review
1984	Seventeen
1985	Playboy
1986	The Georgia Review
1987	Esquire
1988	The Atlantic
1989	The New Yorker
1990	The New Yorker
1991	Esquire
1992	Story
1993	The New Yorker
1994	Harper's Magazine
1995	Story
1996	Harper's Magazine

1997	The New Yorker
1998	The New Yorker
1999	Harper's Magazine

Single Topic Issue

1979	Progressive Architecture
1980	Scientific American
1981	Business Week
1982	Newsweek
1983	IEEE Spectrum
1984	Esquire
1985	American Heritage
1986	IEEE Spectrum
1987	Bulletin of the Atomic Scientists
1988	Life
1989	Hippocrates
1990	National Geographic
1991	The American Lawyer
1992	Business Week
1993	Newsweek
1994	Health
1995	Discover
1996	Bon Appétit
1997	Scientific American
1998	The Sciences
1999	The Oxford American

Personal Service/Service to the Individual

1974	Sports Illustrated
1975	Esquire
1976	Modern Medicine
1977	Harper's Magazine
1978	Newsweek
1979	The American Journal of Nursing
1980	Saturday Review
1982	Philadelphia
1983	Sunset
1984	New York
1985	The Washingtonian
1986	Farm Journal
1987	Consumer Reports
1988	Money
1989	Good Housekeeping
1990	Consumer Reports
1991	New York
1992	Creative Classroom
1993	Good Housekeeping
1994	Fortune
1995	SmartMoney
1996	SmartMoney
1997	Glamour
1998	Men's Journal
1999	Good Housekeeping

Special Interests

1986	Popular Mechanics
1987	Sports Afield
1988	Condé Nast Traveler
1989	Condé Nast Traveler
1990	Arts & Antiques
1991	New York
1992	Sports Afield

1993 Philadelphia
1994 Outside
1995 Gentlemen's Quarterly
1996 Saveur
1997 Smithsonian Magazine
1998 Entertainment Weekly
1999 PC Computing

Photography

1985 Life
1986 Vogue
1987 National Geographic
1988 Rolling Stone
1989 National Geographic
1990 Texas Monthly
1991 National Geographic
1992 National Geographic
1993 Harper's Bazaar
1994 Martha Stewart Living
1995 Rolling Stone
1996 Saveur
1997 National Geographic
1998 W
1999 Martha Stewart Living

Feature Writing

1988 The Atlantic Monthly
1989 Esquire
1990 The Washingtonian
1991 U.S. News & World Report
1992 Sports Illustrated
1993 The New Yorker
1994 Harper's Magazine
1995 Gentlemen's Quarterly
1996 Gentlemen's Quarterly
1997 Sports Illustrated
1998 Harper's Magazine
1999 The American Scholar

New Media

1999 Cigar Aficionado

PULITZER PRIZE

Fiction

1918 Ernest Poole
His Family
1919 Booth Tarkington
The Magnificent Ambersons
1920 No award
1921 Edith Wharton
The Age of Innocence
1922 Booth Tarkington
Alice Adams
1923 Willa Cather
One of Ours
1924 Margaret Wilson
The Able McLaughlins
1925 Edna Ferber
So Big
1926 Sinclair Lewis (refused prize)
Arrowsmith

1927 Louis Bromfield
Early Autumn
1928 Thornton Wilder
Bridge of San Luis Rey
1929 Julia M. Peterkin
Scarlet Sister Mary
1930 Oliver LaFarge
Laughing Boy
1931 Margaret Ayer Barnes
Years of Grace
1932 Pearl S. Buck
The Good Earth
1933 T. S. Stribling
The Store
1934 Caroline Miller
Lamb in His Bosom
1935 Josephine W. Johnson
Now in November
1936 Harold L. Davis
Honey in the Horn
1937 Margaret Mitchell
Gone with the Wind
1938 John P. Marquand
The Late George Apley
1939 Marjorie Kinnan Rawlings
The Yearling
1940 John Steinbeck
The Grapes of Wrath
1941 No award
1942 Ellen Glasgow
In This Our Life
1943 Upton Sinclair
Dragon's Teeth
1944 Martin Flavin
Journey in the Dark
1945 John Hersey
A Bell for Adano
1946 No award
1947 Robert Penn Warren
All the King's Men
1948 James A. Michener
Tales of the South Pacific
1949 James Gould Cozzens
Guard of Honor
1950 A. B. Guthrie, Jr.
The Way West
1951 Conrad Richter
The Town
1952 Herman Wouk
The Caine Mutiny
1953 Ernest Hemingway
The Old Man and the Sea
1954 No award
1955 William Faulkner
A Fable
1956 MacKinlay Kantor
Andersonville
1957 No award
1958 James Agee
A Death in the Family
1959 Robert Lewis Taylor
The Travels of Jaimie McPheeters
1960 Allen Drury
Advise and Consent

1961 Harper Lee
To Kill a Mockingbird
1962 Edwin O'Connor
The Edge of Sadness
1963 William Faulkner
The Reivers
1964 No award
1965 Shirley Ann Grau
The Keepers of the House
1966 Katherine Anne Porter
The Collected Stories of Katherine Anne Porter
1967 Bernard Malamud
The Fixer
1968 William Styron
The Confessions of Nat Turner
1969 N. Scott Momaday
House Made of Dawn
1970 Jean Stafford
Collected Stories
1971 No award
1972 Wallace Stegner
Angle of Repose
1973 Eudora Welty
The Optimist's Daughter
1974 No award
1975 Michael Shaara
The Killer Angels
1976 Saul Bellow
Humboldt's Gift
1977 No award
1978 James Alan McPherson
Elbow Room
1979 John Cheever
The Stories of John Cheever
1980 Norman Mailer
The Executioner's Song
1981 John Kennedy Toole
A Confederacy of Dunces
1982 John Updike
Rabbit Is Rich
1983 Alice Walker
The Color Purple
1984 William Kennedy
Ironweed
1985 Alison Lurie
Foreign Affairs
1986 Larry McMurtry
Lonesome Dove
1987 Peter Taylor
A Summons to Memphis
1988 Toni Morrison
Beloved
1989 Anne Tyler
Breathing Lessons
1990 Oscar Hijuelos
The Mambo Kings Play Songs of Love
1991 John Updike
Rabbit at Rest
1992 Jane Smiley
A Thousand Acres
1993 Robert Olen Butler
A Good Scent from a Strange Mountain

1994 E. Annie Proulx
The Shipping News
1995 Carol Shields
The Stone Diaries
1996 Richard Ford
Independence Day
1997 Steven Millhauser
*Martin Dressler: The Tale of an
American Dreamer*
1998 Philip Roth
American Pastoral
1999 Michael Cunningham
The Hours

Nonfiction

1962 Theodore H. White
The Making of the President, 1960
1963 Barbara W. Tuchman
The Guns of August
1964 Richard Hofstadter
*Anti-Intellectualism in
American Life*
1965 Howard Mumford Jones
O Strange New World
1966 Edwin Way Teale
Wandering Through Winter
1967 David Brion Davis
*The Problem of Slavery in
Western Culture*
1968 Will Durant and Ariel Durant
*Rousseau and Revolution: The
Tenth and Concluding Volume of
The Story of Civilization*
1969 Norman Mailer
The Armies of the Night
Rene Jules Dubos
So Human an Animal
1970 Erik H. Erikson
Gandhi's Truth
1971 John Toland
The Rising Sun
1972 Barbara W. Tuchman
*Stilwell and the American Expe-
rience in China, 1911–1945*
1973 Robert Coles
Children of Crisis, Vols. II and III
Francis FitzGerald
*Fire in the Lake: The Vietnamese
and the Americans in Vietnam*
1974 Ernest Becker
The Denial of Death
1975 Annie Dillard
Pilgram at Tinker Creek
1976 Robert N. Butler
Why Survive?: Being Old in America
1977 William W. Warner
Beautiful Swimmers
1978 Carl Sagan
The Dragons of Eden
1979 Edward O. Wilson
On Human Nature
1980 Douglas R. Hofstadter
*Gödel, Escher, Bach: An Eternal
Golden Braid*

1981 Carl E. Schorske
*Fin-de-Siecle Vienna: Politics
and Culture*
1982 Tracy Kidder
The Soul of a New Machine
1983 Susan Sheehan
Is There No Place on Earth for Me ?
1984 Paul Starr
*The Social Transformation of
American Medicine*
1985 Studs Terkel
*The Good War: An Oral History of
World War Two*
1986 J. Anthony Lukas
*Common Ground: A Turbulent
Decade in the Lives of
Three American Families*
Joseph Lelyveld
Move Your Shadow
1987 David K. Shipler
*Arab and Jew: Wounded Spirits
in a Promised Land*
1988 Richard Rhodes
The Making of the Atomic Bomb
1989 Neil Sheehan
*A Bright Shining Lie: John Paul
Vann and America in Vietnam*
1990 Dale Maharidge and
Michael Williamson
And Their Children After Them
1991 Bert Holdobler and
Edward O. Wilson
The Ants
1992 Daniel Yergin
*The Prize: The Epic Quest for Oil,
Money, and Power*
1993 Garry Wills
Lincoln at Gettysburg
1994 David Remnick
Lenin's Tomb
1995 Jonathan Weiner
*The Beak of the Finch: A Story of
Evolution in Our Time*
1996 Tina Rosenberg
*The Haunted Land: Facing
Europe's Ghosts After Communism*
1997 Richard Kluger
*Ashes to Ashes: America's
Hundred-Year Cigarette War, the
Public Health, and the
Unabashed Triumph of Philip
Morris*
1998 Jared Diamond
*Guns, Germs, and Steel: The Fates
of Human Societies*
1999 John A. McPhee
Annals of the Former World

Poetry

1918 Sara Teasdale
Love Songs
1919 Carl Sandburg
Corn Huskers
Margaret Widemer
Old Road to Paradise

1920 No award
1921 No award
1922 Edwin Arlington Robinson
Collected Poems
1923 Edna St. Vincent Millay
*The Ballad of the Harp-Weaver;
A Few Figs from Thistles;
Eight Sonnets in American
Poetry, 1922; A Miscellany*
1924 Robert Frost
*New Hampshire: A Poem with
Notes and Grace Notes*
1925 Edwin Arlington Robinson
The Man Who Died Twice
1926 Amy Lowell
What's O'Clock
1927 Leonora Speyer
Fiddler's Farewell
1928 Edwin Arlington Robinson
Tristram
1929 Stephen Vincent Benet
John Brown's Body
1930 Conrad Aiken
Selected Poems
1931 Robert Frost
Collected Poems
1932 George Dillon
The Flowering Stone
1933 Archibald MacLeish
Conquistador
1934 Robert Hillyer
Collected Verse
1935 Audrey Wurdemann
Bright Ambush
1936 Robert P. Tristram Coffin
Strange Holiness
1937 Robert Frost
A Further Range
1938 Marya Zaturenska
Cold Morning Sky
1939 John Gould Fletcher
Selected Poems
1940 Mark Van Doren
Collected Poems
1941 Leonrard Bacon
Sunderland Capture
1942 William Rose Benet
The Dust Which Is God
1943 Robert Frost
A Witness Tree
1944 Stephen Vincent Benet
Western Star
1945 Karl Shapiro
V-Letter and Other Poems
1946 No award
1947 Robert Lowell
Lord Weary's Castle
1948 W. H. Auden
The Age of Anxiety
1949 Peter Viereck
Terror and Decorum
1950 Gwendolyn Brooks
Annie Allen

1951 Carl Sandburg
Complete Poems
1952 Marianne Moore
Collected Poems
1953 Archibald MacLeish
Collected Poems 1917–1952
1954 Theodore Roethke
The Waking
1955 Wallace Stevens
Collected Poems
1956 Elizabeth Bishop
Poems, North and South
1957 Richard Wilbur
Things of This World
1958 Robert Penn Warren
Promises: Poems 1954–1956
1959 Stanley Kunitz
Selected Poems 1928–1958
1960 W. D. Snodgrass
Heart's Needle
1961 Phyllis McGinley
Times Three: Selected Verse from Three Decades
1962 Alan Dugan
Poems
1963 William Carlos Williams
Pictures from Breughel
1964 Louis Simpson
At the End of the Open Road
1965 John Berryman
77 Dream Songs
1966 Richard Eberhart
Selected Poems

1967 Anne Sexton
Live or Die
1968 Anthony Hecht
The Hard Hours
1969 George Oppen
Of Being Numerous
1970 Richard Howard
Untitled Subjects
1971 W. S. Merwin
The Carrier of Ladders
1972 James Wright
Collected Poems
1973 Maxine Kumin
Up Country
1974 Robert Lowell
The Dolphin
1975 Gary Snyder
Turtle Island
1976 John Ashbery
Self-Portrait in a Convex Mirror
1977 James Merrill
Divine Comedies
1978 Howard Nemerov
Collected Poems
1979 Robert Penn Warren
Now and Then
1980 Donald Justice
Selected Poems
1981 James Schuyler
The Morning of the Poem
1982 Sylvia Plath
The Collected Poems
1983 Galway Kinnell
Selected Poems

1984 Mary Oliver
American Primitive
1985 Carolyn Kizer
Yin
1986 Henry Taylor
The Flying Change
1987 Rita Dove
Thomas and Beulah
1988 William Meredith
Partial Accounts: New and Selected Poems
1989 Richard Wilbur
New and Collected Poems
1990 Charles Simic
The World Doesn't End
1991 Mona Van Duyn
Near Changes
1992 James Tate
Selected Poems
1993 Louise Gluck
The Wild Iris
1994 Yusef Komunyakaa
Neon Vernacular
1995 Philip Levine
The Simple Truth
1996 Jorie Graham
The Dream of the Unified Field
1997 Lisel Mueller
Alive Together
1998 Charles Wright
Black Zodiac
1999 Mark Strand
Blizzard of One

BROADWAY SHOWS OF THE 1998–1999 SEASON

With naked stars, retiring comics, and prominent imports (both actors and plays), Broadway was the star of the Times Square revival. For the second year in a row, the public's regard meant record ticket sales. Here's what filled the houses. (Source: *Variety*)

NEW PRODUCTIONS
Amy's View
An Evening with Jerry Herman (M-Rev)
Annie Get Your Gun (M-R)
Aznavour (Sp-So)
Band in Berlin (M)
The Blue Room
The Civil War (M)
Closer
Colin Quinn: An Irish Awake (So)
Death of a Salesman (P-R)
Electra
Fool Moon (Sp)
Footloose (M)
Fosse (M)
The Gershwins' Fascinating Rhythm (M-Rev)
Getting and Spending
Jerry Seinfeld: I'm Telling You for the Last Time—Live On Broadway (Sp-So)
The Iceman Cometh (P-R)
It Ain't Nothin' but the Blues (M)
The Lion in Winter (P-R)
Little Me (M-R)
The Lonesome West
Mandy Patinkin in Concert: Mamaloshen (Sp-So)

More to Love: A Big Fat Comedy
Night Must Fall (P-R)
Not About Nightingales
On the Town (M-R)
Parade (M)
Peter Pan (M-R)
Ring Round the Moon (P-R)
Rollin' on the T.O.B.A. (M-Rev)
Sandra Bernhard: I'm Still Here...Damn It! (Sp-So)
Side Man
Swan Lake (M-R)
Via Dolorosa
The Weir
Twelfth Night (P-R-Sub)
You're a Good Man, Charlie Brown (M-R)

HOLDOVERS
Art
Beauty and the Beast (M)
The Beauty Queen of Leenane
Bring in 'Da Noise, Bring in 'Da Funk (M)
Cabaret (M-R)
Cats (M)
The Chairs (P-R)
Chicago (M-R)
The Diary of Anne Frank (P-R)

Forever Tango (Sp)
Freak (Sp)
High Society (M)
Honour
Jekyll & Hyde (M)
The Judas Kiss
The Last Night of Ballyhoo
Les Misérables (M)
The Lion King (M)
Miss Saigon (M)
The Phantom of the Opera (M)
Ragtime (M)
Rent (M)
The Scarlet Pimpernel (M)
1776 (M-R)
Smokey Joe's Cafe (M-Rev)
The Sound of Music (M-R)
The Sunshine Boys (P-R)
Titanic (M)
A View from the Bridge (P-R)
Wait Until Dark (P-R)

(M) denotes musical
(R) denotes revival
(So) denotes solo performance
(Rev) denotes revue
(Sp) denotes special attraction

THAT'S SHOW BIZ

Despite a significant drop in road receipts, the Great White Way still lags far behind the provinces in producing revenue. Out-of-town demand for hits (plus a few Broadway fizzlers) means the show must go on...on tour. (Source: *Variety*)

Season	Broadway box office/ total shows during most profitable week	Road box office/ total shows during most profitable week
1982–83	$203.1 million/27 shows	$184.3 million/24 shows
1987–88	$253.5 million/21 shows	$223.0 million/24 shows
1992–93	$327.7 million/21 shows	$620.6 million/34 shows
1993–94	$356.0 million/21 shows	$687.7 million/30 shows
1994–95	$406.3 million/23 shows	$694.6 million/33 shows
1995–96	$436.1 million/28 shows	$762.3 million/27 shows
1996–97	$499.4 million/27 shows	$752.9 million/27 shows
1997–98	$557.3 million/32 shows	$794.1 million/26 shows
1998–99	$588.1 million/30 shows	$711.4 million/26 shows

LONGEST-RUNNING SHOWS ON BROADWAY

The following is a list of the longest-running shows on Broadway (as of September 12, 1999) based on the number of performances. (M) stands for musical and (R) for revival. (Source: *Variety*)

Cats (M) (1982–)	7,069
A Chorus Line (M) (1975–90)	6,137
Oh! Calcutta! (M-R) (1976–89)	5,852
Les Misérables (M) (1987–)	5,151
The Phantom of the Opera (M) (1988–)	4,881
Miss Saigon (M) (1991–)	3,492
42nd Street (M) (1980–89)	3,486
Grease (M) (1972–80)	3,388
Fiddler on the Roof (M) (1964–72)	3,242
Life with Father (1939–47)	3,224
Tobacco Road (1933–41)	3,182
Hello, Dolly! (M) (1964–70)	2,844
My Fair Lady (M) (1956–62)	2,717
Annie (M) (1977–83)	2,377
Man of La Mancha (M) (1965–71)	2,328
Abie's Irish Rose (1922–27)	2,327
Beauty and the Beast (M) (1994–)	2,250
Oklahoma! (M) (1943–48)	2,212
Pippin (M) (1972–77)	1,944
South Pacific (M) (1949–54)	1,925
The Magic Show (M) (1974–78)	1,920
Smokey Joe's Cafe (M) (1995–)	1,893
Deathtrap (1978–82)	1,792
Gemini (1977–81)	1,788
Harvey (1944–49)	1,775
Dancin' (M) (1978–82)	1,774
La Cage aux folles (M) (1983–87)	1,761
Hair (M) (1968–72)	1,750
The Wiz (M) (1975–79)	1,672
Born Yesterday (1946–49)	1,642
Crazy for You (1992-96)	1,622
Ain't Misbehavin' (M) (1978–82)	1,604
Best Little Whorehouse in Texas (M) (1978–82)	1,584
Mary, Mary (1961–64)	1,572
Evita (M) (1979–83)	1,567
Voice of the Turtle (1943–48)	1,557
Barefoot in the Park (1963–64)	1,530
Brighton Beach Memoirs (1983–86)	1,530
Dreamgirls (M) (1981–85)	1,521
Mame (M) (1966–70)	1,508

Grease (M-R) (1993–98)	1,503
Same Time, Next Year (1976–78)	1,453
Arsenic and Old Lace (1941–44)	1,444
The Sound of Music (M) (1959–63)	1,443
How to Succeed in Business Without Really Trying (M) (1961–65)	1,417
Rent (M) (1996–)	1,408
Hellzapoppin (M) (1938–41)	1,404
The Music Man (M) (1957–61)	1,375
Funny Girl (M) (1964–67)	1,348
Mummenschanz (M) (1977–80)	1,326
Oh! Calcutta! (M) (1969–72)	1,314
Angel Street (1941–44)	1,295
Lightnin' (1918–21)	1,291
Promises, Promises (M) (1968–72)	1,281
The King and I (M) (1951–54)	1,246
Cactus Flower (1965–68)	1,234
Torch Song Trilogy (1982–85)	1,222
Sleuth (1970–73)	1,222
1776 (M) (1969–72)	1,217
Equus (1974–77)	1,209
Sugar Babies (M) (1979–82)	1,208
Guys and Dolls (M) (1950–53)	1,200
Amadeus (1980–83)	1,181
Chicago (M-R) (1996–)	1,178
Cabaret (M) (1966–69)	1,165
Mister Roberts (1948–51)	1,157
Annie Get Your Gun (M) (1946–49)	1,147
Guys and Dolls (M-R) (1992–95)	1,143
The Seven Year Itch (1952–55)	1,141
Butterflies Are Free (1969–72)	1,128
Pins and Needles (M) (1937–40)	1,108
Plaza Suite (1968–70)	1,097
They're Playing Our Song (M) (1979–81)	1,082
Kiss Me, Kate (M) (1948–51)	1,070
Don't Bother Me, I Can't Cope (M) (1972–74)	1,065
The Pajama Game (M) (1954–56)	1,063
Shenandoah (M) (1975–77)	1,050
Teahouse of the August Moon (1953–56)	1,027

BROADWAY'S FAVORITES: PLACE THAT TUNE

Know the song but can't place the musical in which it originally appeared? Here is a checklist of some Great White Way melodies that linger on.

SONG	SHOW
"Almost Like Being in Love"	Brigadoon
"And I Am Telling You I'm Not Going"	Dreamgirls
"Anything You Can Do"	Annie Get Your Gun
"Bali Ha'i"	South Pacific
"The Ballad of Mack the Knife"	The Threepenny Opera
"Bewitched, Bothered, and Bewildered"	Pal Joey
"A Bushel and a Peck"	Guys and Dolls
"Climb Ev'ry Mountain"	The Sound of Music
"Everything's Coming Up Roses"	Gypsy
"Getting to Know You"	The King and I
"I Am What I Am"	La Cage aux folles
"I Cain't Say No"	Oklahoma!
"I Could Have Danced All Night"	My Fair Lady
"I Don't Know How to Love Him"	Jesus Christ Superstar
"I Feel Pretty"	West Side Story
"I Get a Kick Out of You"	Anything Goes
"I Got Plenty o' Nothin' "	Porgy and Bess
"I Got Rhythm"	Girl Crazy
"I Got the Sun in the Morning"	Annie Get Your Gun
"I Whistle a Happy Tune"	The King and I
"If Ever I Would Leave You"	Camelot
"It Ain't Necessarily So"	Porgy and Bess
"I've Grown Accustomed to Her Face"	My Fair Lady
"Let the Sunshine In"	Hair
"Lover, Come Back to Me"	The New Moon
"Luck Be a Lady"	Guys and Dolls
"Maria"	West Side Story
"Memory"	Cats

SONG	SHOW
"The Music of the Night"	The Phantom of the Opera
"My Favorite Things"	The Sound of Music
"Oh, What a Beautiful Mornin' "	Oklahoma!
"Ol' Man River"	Show Boat
"One Night in Bangkok"	Chess
"On the Street Where You Live"	My Fair Lady
"The Quest (The Impossible Dream)"	Man of La Mancha
"Seasons of Love"	Rent
"Seventy-Six Trombones"	The Music Man
"Shall We Dance?"	The King and I
"Smoke Gets in Your Eyes"	Roberta
"Some Enchanted Evening"	South Pacific
"The Sound of Music"	The Sound of Music
"Summertime"	Porgy and Bess
"Sunrise, Sunset"	Fiddler on the Roof
"Tea for Two"	No, No, Nanette
"Thank Heaven for Little Girls"	Gigi
"There Is Nothin' Like a Dame"	South Pacific
"There's No Business Like Show Business"	Annie Get Your Gun
"This Is the Army, Mr. Jones"	This Is the Army
"This is the Moment"	Jekyll & Hyde
"Till There Was You"	The Music Man
"Tomorrow"	Annie
"Tonight"	West Side Story
"You'll Never Walk Alone"	Carousel
"You're the Top"	Anything Goes
"We Need a Little Christmas"	Mame
"What I Did for Love"	A Chorus Line

SCHOOLS FOR STARS

Even some of the most talented thespians have honed their gifts in the classroom, as indicated by the alumni rolls of these five career-nurturing institutions.

CARNEGIE MELLON SCHOOL OF DRAMA

Shari Belafonte, actor
Steven Bochco, producer
Albert Brooks, actor/director
Ted Danson, actor
Iris Rainier Dart, novelist
Barbara Feldon, actor
Mark Frost, producer
Mariette Hartley, actor
Holly Hunter, actor
Jack Klugman, actor
Judith Light, actor
Burke Moses, actor
John Pasquin, director
George Peppard, actor
George Romero, director
Laura San Giacomo, actor
Ellen Travolta, actor
Michael Tucker, actor
Blair Underwood, actor
John Wells, producer

JUILLIARD SCHOOL DRAMA DIVISION

Christine Baranski, actor
Andre Braugher, actor
Kelsey Grammer, actor
William Hurt, actor
Laura Linney, actor
Patti LuPone, actor/singer
Val Kilmer, actor
Kevin Kline, actor/director
Linda Kozlowski, actor
Kelly McGillis, actor
Elizabeth McGovern, actor
Mandy Patinkin, actor/singer
Christopher Reeve, actor
Ving Rhames, actor
Kevin Spacey, actor
Jeanne Tripplehorn, actor
Robin Williams, actor

NEW YORK UNIVERSITY, TISCH SCHOOL OF THE ARTS

Alec Baldwin, actor
Barry Bostwick, actor
Joel Coen, screenwriter
Billy Crudup, actor
Kathryn Erbe, actor
Bridget Fonda, actor
Lisa Gay Hamilton, actor
Marcia Gay Harden, actor
Kristen Johnston, actor
Tony Kushner, playwright
Eriq LaSalle, actor
Spike Lee, director/screenwriter/actor
Camryn Manheim, actor
Andrew McCarthy, actor
Jerry O'Connell, actor
Adam Sandler, actor
Kevin Spacey, actor
Stephen Spinella, actor
D. B. Sweeney, actor
Skeet Ulrich, actor
George C. Wolfe, director

NORTHWESTERN UNIVERSITY SCHOOL OF SPEECH

Ann-Margret, actor/dancer
Warren Beatty, actor
Richard Benjamin, actor
Karen Black, actor
Brad Hall, actor
Charlton Heston, actor
Sherry Lansing, producer
Shelly Long, actor
Julia Louis-Dreyfus, actor
Dermot Mulroney, actor
Patricia Neal, actor
Jerry Orbach, actor
Paula Prentiss, actor
Tony Randall, actor
Tony Roberts, actor
David Schwimmer, actor
Peter Strauss, actor
Kimberly Williams, actor

YALE SCHOOL OF DRAMA

Angela Bassett, actor
Robert Brustein, director/writer
David Duchovny, actor
Christopher Durang, playwright
Charles S. Dutton, actor
Jill Eikenberry, actor
David Alan Grier, actor
John Guare, playwright
A. R. Gurney, playwright
Julie Harris, actor
Tama Janowitz, writer
Elia Kazan, director
Stacy Keach, actor
Mark Linn-Baker, actor
Santo Loquasto, set designer
Frances McDormand, actor
Paul Newman, actor
Carrie Nye, actor
Tony Shalhoub, actor
Talia Shire, actor
Meryl Streep, actor
Ted Tally, playwright/screenwriter
John Turturro, actor/director
Joan Van Ark, actor
Courtney B. Vance, actor
Wendy Wasserstein, playwright
Sigourney Weaver, actor
Edmund Wilson, writer
Henry Winkler, actor/director

THEATER'S LEADING LIGHTS

Selected for their contributions to today's theater, the following artists are responsible for many of the most important and popular plays currently being produced in the English language. Each list of works notes every play, screenplay, or teleplay created by the artist (aside from one acts), as well as major awards won by the work and the year of its first production.

BETH HENLEY
playwright/screenwriter

Parade (1975)

Crimes of the Heart (1979; Pulitzer Prize; screenplay, 1986)

The Moon Watch (screenplay, 1983)

The Miss Firecracker Contest (1984; screenplay, 1986)

The Wake of Jamey Foster (1984)

The Debutante Ball (1985)

The Lucky Spot (1986)

True Stories (coauthor, screenplay, 1986)

Nobody's Fool (screenplay, 1987)

Abundance (1989; screenplay [*Come West with Me*], 1998)

Signature (1990)

Control Freaks (1992)

Revelers (1994)

L-Play (1995)

Impossible Marriage (1998)

TONY KUSHNER
playwright

A Bright Room Called Day (1986)

The Illusion (adaptor, 1987)

Angels in America Part I: Millennium Approaches (1990; Tony Award; Pulitzer Prize)

Angels in America Part II: Perestroika (1993; Tony Award)

Slavs! (1994)

Dybbuk (adaptor, 1995)

Hydriotaphia (1997)

ANDREW LLOYD WEBBER
composer

Joseph and the Amazing Technicolor Dreamcoat (1968)

Jesus Christ Superstar (1971)

Jeeves (1974; revision *By Jeeves*, 1996)

Evita (1976; Tony Award)

Cats (1982; Tony Award; Grammy Award)

Song and Dance (1982)

Starlight Express (1984)

The Phantom of the Opera (1986)

Aspects of Love (1989)

Sunset Boulevard (1993; Tony Award)

Whistle Down the Wind (1996)

DAVID MAMET
playwright/screenwriter

The Duck Variations (1972)

Mackinac (1974)

Squirrels (1974)

Sexual Perversity in Chicago (1974)

American Buffalo (1975; screenplay, 1996)

The Poet and the Rent (1975)

Marranos (1975)

Reunion (1976)

The Woods (1977)

The Revenge of the Space Pandas, or Binky Rudich and the Two-Speed Clock (1977)

The Water Engine: An American Fable (1977)

A Life in the Theatre (1977; teleplay, 1993)

Lone Canoe, or, The Explorer (1979)

Lakeboat (1980)

The Postman Always Rings Twice (screenplay, 1981)

The Verdict (screenplay, 1982)

Edmond (1982)

Glengarry Glen Ross (1983; Pulitzer Prize; screenplay, 1992)

Red River (adaptor, 1983)

The Cherry Orchard (adaptor, 1985)

The Shawl (1985)

Three Sisters (adaptor, 1985)

The Untouchables (screenplay, 1987)

House of Games (screenplay, 1987)

Things Change (coauthor screenplay, 1987)

Speed-the-Plow (1988)

We're No Angels (screenplay, 1989)

Homicide (screenplay, 1991)

Oleanna (1992; screenplay, 1994)

Hoffa (screenplay, 1992)

The Cryptogram (1994)

Vanya on 42nd Street (coadaptor, screenplay, 1994)

The Edge (screenplay, 1997)

The Old Neighborhood (1997)

Wag the Dog (coadaptor, screenplay, 1997)

The Spanish Prisoner (screenplay, 1998)

Boston Marriage (1999)

The Winslow Boy (screenplay, 1999)

Lansky (teleplay; 1999)

TERRENCE MCNALLY
playwright

And Things That Go Bump in the Night (1964)

Next (1967)

Where Has Tommy Flowers Gone (1971)

Whiskey (1973)

Bad Habits (1974)

The Ritz (1974)

It's Only a Play (1985)

The Rink (1985)

Frankie and Johnny in the Claire de Lune (1987; screenplay, *Frankie and Johnny,* 1991)

The Lisbon Traviata (1989)

Andre's Mother (teleplay, 1990; Emmy Award)

Lips Together, Teeth Apart (1991)

Prelude and Liebestod (1991)

A Perfect Ganesh (1993)

Kiss of the Spider Woman (book, 1993; Tony Award)

Love! Valour! Compassion! (1994; Tony Award; screenplay, 1997)

Master Class (1995; Tony Award)

Ragtime (book, 1996; Tony Award)

Corpus Christi (1998)

House (1998)

ARTHUR MILLER
playwright/screenwriter

Honors at Dawn (1936)

No Villain (1936)

The Half-Bridge (written 1943, never produced)

The Pussycat and the Expert Plumber Who Was a Man (radio play, 1943)

William Ireland's Confession (radio play, 1942)

The Man Who Had All the Luck (1944)

That They May Win (1944)

The Story of G.I. Joe (screenplay, 1945)

Grandpa and the Statue (radio play, 1942)

The Story of Gus (radio play, 1942)

All My Sons (1947)

Death of a Salesman (1948; Pulitzer Prize)

An Enemy of the People (adaptor, 1950)

The Crucible (1953; Tony Award; screenplay, 1996)

A View from the Bridge (1955)

A Memory of Two Mondays (1955)

The Witches of Salem (screenplay, 1958)

The Misfits (screenplay, 1961)

After the Fall (1964)

Incident at Vichy (1964)

The Price (1968)

Fame (1971)

The Creation of the World and Other Business (1972; musical version, *Up from Paradise,* 1982)

The Archbishop's Ceiling (1977)

The American Clock (adaptor, 1979)

Playing for Time (adaptor, teleplay, 1981)

Two-Way Mirror (1982)

Danger: Memory (1987)

The Golden Years (radio play, 1987)

Everybody Wins (screenplay, 1990)

The Ride Down Mt. Morgan (1991)

The Last Yankee (1993)

Broken Glass (1994)

Mr. Peter's Connections (1998)

MARSHA NORMAN
playwright/screenwriter

Getting Out (1977)

The Pool Hall (1978)

It's the Willingness (teleplay, 1978)

Third and Oak: The Laundromat (1978)

Circus Valentine (1979)

In Trouble at Fifteen (teleplay, 1980)

The Holdup (1980)

'Night, Mother (1983; Pulitzer Prize; screenplay, 1984)

Traveler in the Dark (1984)

The Fortune Teller (novel, 1988)

Sarah and Abraham (1988)

The Secret Garden (book and lyrics, 1991; Tony Award)

Face of a Stranger (teleplay, 1992)

Loving Daniel Boone (1992)

The Red Shoes (book and lyrics, 1993)

Trudy Blue (1995)

HAROLD PINTER
playwright/screenwriter

The Room (1957)

The Birthday Party (1958; screenplay, 1968; teleplay, 1987)

The Dumb Waiter (1960)

The Caretaker (1960)

A Night Out (radio play, 1960)

The Collection (teleplay, 1961)

The Servant (screenplay, 1963)

The Lover (1963)

The Pumpkin Eater (screenplay, 1964)

The Tea Party (1965)

The Quiller Memorandum (screenplay, 1966)

Accident (screenplay, 1967)

The Basement (radio 1967; stage 1969)

Landscape (1968)

The Homecoming (screenplay, 1973)

Silence (1969)

The Go-Between (screenplay, 1970)

The Last Tycoon (screenplay, 1971)

Old Times (1971)

The Proust Screenplay: A la Recherche du temps perdu (screenplay, 1973)

No Man's Land (1975)

Players (radio play, 1975)

Betrayal (1978; screenplay, 1982)

Langrishe, Go Down (adaptor, screenplay, 1978)

The Hothouse (1980)

The French Lieutenant's Woman (screenplay, 1981)

Other Places (1982)

Turtle Diary (screenplay, 1985)

Reunion (screenplay, 1989)

The Comfort of Strangers (screenplay, 1990)

The Handmaid's Tale (adaptor, screenplay, 1990)

Moonlight (1993)

The Trial (screenplay, 1993)

Ashes to Ashes (1996)

SAM SHEPARD
playwright/screenwriter

Up to Thursday (1965)

Dog (1965)

Rocking Chair (1965)

4-H Club (1965)

La Turista (1967)

Forensic and the Navigators (1967)

Me and My Brother (coauthor, screenplay, 1967)

Operation Sidewinder (1969)

The Unseen Hand (1969)

Zabriskie Point (coauthor, screenplay, 1970)

Cowboy Mouth (coauthor, 1971)

Ringaleenio (screenplay, 1971)

The Tooth of Crime (1972)

Blue Bitch (1973)

Nightwalk (coauthor, 1973)

Little Ocean (1974)

Geography of a Horse Dreamer (1974)

The Sad Lament of Pecos Bill on the Eve of Killing His Wife (1976)

Suicide in B Flat (1976)

Angel City (1977)

Curse of the Starving Class (1977)

Inacoma (1977)

Buried Child (1978; Pulitzer Prize)

Seduced (1978)

Tongues (coauthor, 1979)

Savage/Love (coauthor, 1979)

Jackson's Dance (coauthor, 1980)

True West (1980)

Black Bart and the Sacred Hills (1981)

Fool for Love (1983; screenplay, 1985)

Superstitions (1983)

Paris, Texas (coauthor, screenplay, 1984)

A Lie of the Mind (1985)

The War in Heaven: Angel's Monologue (coauthor, teleplay, 1985)

States of Shock (1989)

Far North (screenplay, 1992)

Silent Tongue (screenplay, 1993)

Simpatico (1994)

When the World Was Green (A Chef's Fable) (coauthor, 1996)

Eyes for Consuela (1998)

NEIL SIMON
playwright/screenwriter

Adventures of Marco Polo: A Musical Fantasy (book, 1959)

Heidi (book, 1959)

Come Blow Your Horn (1961)

Little Me (book, 1962; revised version, 1982)

Barefoot in the Park (originally Nobody Loves Me, 1963; screenplay, 1967)

The Odd Couple (1965; Tony Award; screenplay, 1968; female version, 1985)

Sweet Charity (book, 1966)

The Star-Spangled Girl (1966)

After the Fox (screenplay, 1966)

Promises, Promises (book, 1968)

Plaza Suite (1968; screenplay, 1971)

The Last of the Red-Hot Lovers (1969; screenplay, 1972)

The Gingerbread Lady (1970; revised as Only When I Laugh, screenplay, 1982)

The Out-of-Towners (screenplay, 1970)

The Prisoner of Second Avenue (1971; screenplay, 1975)

The Heartbreak Kid (screenplay, 1973)

The Sunshine Boys (1972; screenplay, 1975; teleplay, 1997)

The Good Doctor (1973)

God's Favorite (1974)

California Suite (1976; screenplay, 1978)

Murder by Death (screenplay, 1976)

The Goodbye Girl (screenplay, 1977; book, 1993)

Chapter Two (1977; screenplay, 1979)

The Cheap Detective (screenplay, 1978)

They're Playing Our Song (book, 1979)

I Ought to Be in Pictures (1980; screenplay, 1982)

Seems Like Old Times (screenplay, 1980)

Fools (1981)

Max Dugan Returns (screenplay, 1983)

Brighton Beach Memoirs (1983; Pulitzer Prize; screenplay, 1986)

The Slugger's Wife (screenplay, 1984)

Biloxi Blues (1985; Tony Award; screenplay, 1988)

Broadway Bound (1986)

Rumors (1988)

Lost in Yonkers (1991; Tony Award; Pulitzer Prize; screenplay, 1993)

The Marrying Man (screenplay, 1991)

Broadway Bound (screenplay, teleplay, 1992)

Jake's Women (1992; teleplay, 1996)

Laughter on the 23rd Floor (1993)

London Suite (1995)

Proposals (1997)

Neil Simon's The Odd Couple II (screenplay, 1998)

A special Tony was awarded to Mr. Simon in 1975 for overall contribution to the theater.

STEPHEN SONDHEIM
composer/lyricist

West Side Story (lyrics, 1957)

Gypsy (lyrics, 1959)

A Funny Thing Happened on the Way to the Forum (music and lyrics, 1962)

Anyone Can Whistle (music and lyrics, 1964)

Do I Hear a Waltz? (lyrics, 1965)

The Mad Show (co-lyricist, 1966)

Company (music and lyrics, 1970; Tony Award)

Follies (music and lyrics, 1971; Tony Award)

A Little Night Music (music and lyrics, 1973; Tony Award)

Candide (revival, co-lyricist, 1973)

The Frogs (music and lyrics, 1974)

Pacific Overtures (music and lyrics, 1976)

Sweeney Todd (music and lyrics, 1979; Tony Award)

Merrily We Roll Along (music and lyrics, 1981)

Sunday in the Park with George (music and lyrics, 1984; Pulitzer Prize)

Into the Woods (music and lyrics, 1987; Tony Award)

Assassins (music and lyrics, 1991)

Passion (music and lyrics, 1994; Tony Award)

Getting Away with Murder (coauthor, 1996)

Putting It Together (1998)

Wise Guys (1999)

TOM STOPPARD
playwright

A Walk on the Water (1960)

The Dissolution of Dominic Boot (radio play, 1964)

"M" Is for Moon Among Other Things (radio play, 1964)

The Gamblers (1965)

If You're Glad I'll Be Frank (radio play, 1966)

Rosencrantz and Guildenstern Are Dead (1966; Tony Award; screenplay, 1990)

Tango (adaptor, 1966)

A Separate Peace (teleplay, 1966)

Lord Malquist and Mr. Moon (novel, 1966)

Albert's Bridge (radio play, 1967)

Teeth (teleplay, 1967)

Another Moon Called Earth (teleplay, 1967)

Neutral Ground (teleplay, 1968)

The Real Inspector Hound (1968)

After Magritte (1970)

Where Are They Now? (radio play, 1970)

Dogg's Our Pet (1971)

Jumpers (1972)

Artist Descending a Staircase (radio play, 1972; stage, 1988)

The House of Bernarda Alba (adaptor, 1973)

Travesties (1974; Tony Award)

Dirty Linen, and Newfound-land (1976)

The Fifteen Minute Hamlet (1976)

Professional Foul (teleplay, 1977)

Every Good Boy Deserves Favour: A Play for Actors and Orchestra (1977)

Night and Day (1978)

Undiscovered Country (1979)

Dogg's Hamlet, Cahoot's MacBeth (1979)

On the Razzle (adaptor, 1981)

The Real Thing (1982; Tony Award)

The Dog It Was That Died (radio play, 1982)

The Love for Three Oranges (adaptor, 1983)

Rough Crossing (adaptor, 1984)

Squaring the Circle: Poland 1980–81 (TV docudrama, 1984)

Dalliance (adaptor, 1986)

Largo Desolato (adaptor, 1986)

Brazil (screenplay, 1987)

Empire of the Sun (adaptor, screenplay, 1987)

Hapgood (1988)

The Dog It Was That Died (adaptor, 1989)

The Russia House (1989)

Billy Bathgate (film, 1990)

In the Native State (radio play, 1991)

Arcadia (1993)

Indian Ink (1995)

The Invention of Love (1997)

Shakespeare in Love (coauthor, screenplay, 1998; Academy Award)

TOMMY TUNE
director/choreographer/performer

Baker Street (actor, 1965)

A Joyful Noise (actor, 1967)

How Now Dow Jones (actor, 1968)

Seesaw (actor, 1973; Tony)

The Club (director, 1976)

Sunset (director, 1977)

The Best Little Whorehouse in Texas (co-director and choreographer, 1978)

A Day in Hollywood/A Night in the Ukraine (director and choreographer, 1980; Tony Award for best choreographer)

Cloud 9 (director, 1981)

Nine (director and choreographer, 1982; Tony Award for best director)

My One and Only (actor, co-director, co-choreographer, 1983; Tony Awards for best

MUSICAL THEATER HALL OF FAME

The Musical Theater Hall of Fame, organized by a committee from New York University, announced its first set of inductees (greats from the past) and honorees (still-active legends) in 1993.

INDUCTEES
Jerome Kern
George and Ira Gershwin
Richard Rodgers
Oscar Hammerstein II
Alan Jay Lerner
Frederick Loewe
Ethel Merman
Irving Berlin
Cole Porter
E. Y. "Yip" Harburg
Mary Martin
Frank Loesser
Dorothy Fields
Abe Burrows
Harold Rome
George M. Cohan
Ella Fitzgerald
Harold Arlen
Leonard Bernstein
Eubie Blake
Lorenz Hart
Jerome Robbins

HONOREES
Carol Channing
Jule Styne
George Abbott
Gwen Verdon
Betty Comden
Adolph Green
Jerry Herman
Burton Lane
John Kander
Fred Ebb

choreographer and best actor)

Stepping Out (director, 1987)

Grand Hotel (1989; Tony Awards for best director and best choreographer)

The Will Rogers Follies (director, choreographer, 1991; Tony Awards for best director and best choreographer)

The Best Little Whorehouse Goes Public (co-director, 1994)

Busker Alley (actor, 1995)

WENDY WASSERSTEIN
playwright/screenwriter

Any Woman Can't (1973)

When Dinah Shore Ruled the Earth (coauthor, 1977)

Uncommon Women and Others (teleplay, 1978)

The Sorrows of Gin (adaptor, teleplay, 1981)

Hard Sell (1980)

Isn't It Romantic? (1981)

Tender Offer (1983)

The Man in a Case (adaptor, 1985)

Miami (coauthor, book, 1985)

Drive, She Said (1988)

The Heidi Chronicles (1988; Pulitzer Prize, Tony Award)

Kiss, Kiss Darling (1991)

The Sisters Rosenzweig (1993)

An American Daughter (1997)

The Object of My Affection (adaptor, screenplay, 1998)

AUGUST WILSON
playwright

Black Bart and the Sacred Hills (1981)

Jitney (1982)

Joe Turner's Come and Gone (1983)

Ma Rainey's Black Bottom (1984)

Fences (1985; Pulitzer, Tony)

The Piano Lesson (1987; Pulitzer)

Two Trains Running (1990)

Seven Guitars (1995)

MAJOR SHOWS THAT BEGAN IN REGIONAL THEATERS

Beginning in the '70s, the creative impetus in American drama began to shift away from the increasingly expensive Broadway venues and toward regional and nonprofit theaters. While most major playwrights once wrote directly for Broadway production, regional theaters have more commonly become the place of origination for America's most important plays. The following productions may have gone on to national and even international fame, but they all began in regional theaters.

American Buffalo, by David Mamet, Goodman Theater, Chicago

Angels in America, by Tony Kushner, Eureka Theatre Company, San Francisco

Annie, by Thomas Meehan, Martin Charnin, and Charles Strouse, Goodspeed Opera House, East Haddam, Connecticut

Big River, adapted by William Hauptman from Mark Twain, La Jolla Playhouse, La Jolla, California

Buried Child, by Sam Shepard, Magic Theater, San Francisco

California Suite, by Neil Simon, Hartman Theatre, Stamford, Connecticut

Children of a Lesser God, by Mark Medoff, Mark Taper Forum, Los Angeles

The Colored Museum, by George C. Wolfe, Crossroads Theatre Company, New Brunswick, New Jersey

Conversations with My Father, by Herb Gardner, Seattle Repertory Theatre

Crimes of the Heart, by Beth Henley, Actors Theatre of Louisville

Eastern Standard, by Richard Greenberg, Seattle Repertory Theatre

Fences, by August Wilson, Yale Repertory Theatre, New Haven, Connecticut

The Gin Game, by D. L. Coburn, Long Wharf Theatre, New Haven, Connecticut

Glengarry Glen Ross, by David Mamet, Goodman Theatre, Chicago

The Heidi Chronicles, by Wendy Wasserstein, Seattle Repertory Theatre

How to Succeed in Business Without Really Trying, La Jolla Playhouse, La Jolla, California

BROADWAY: PRICEY, DICEY, BUT FILLING SEATS

Theater attendance is still reaching new highs, increasing for the fourth year in a row. The prices listed below represent the net collected by management after taxes and various deductions; showgoers actually paid about 10% more. (Source: *Variety*)

Year	Average Ticket Price	Attendance	Year	Average Ticket Price	Attendance
1975-76	$9.86	7,181,898	1987-88	$31.65	8,142,722
1976-77	10.60	8,815,095	1988-89	32.88	7,968,273
1977-78	12.05	8,621,262	1989-90	35.24	8,039,106
1978-79	14.02	9,115,613	1990-91	36.53	7,314,138
1979-80	15.29	9,380,648	1991-92	39.69	7,365,528
1980-81	17.97	10,822,324	1992-93	41.71	7,856,727
1981-82	22.07	10,025,788	1993-94	43.87	8,116,031
1982-83	25.07	8,102,262	1994-95	44.92	9,044,763
1983-84	28.68	7,898,765	1995-96	46.06	9,468,210
1984-85	29.06	7,156,683	1996-97	48.40	10,318,217
1985-86	29.20	6,527,498	1997-98	49.39	11,283,378
1986-87	29.74	6,968,277	1998-99	50.68	11,605,278

I'm Not Rappaport, by Herb Gardner, Seattle Repertory Theatre

In the Belly of the Beast, adapted by Adrian Hall from Jack Henry Abbott, Trinity Repertory Company, Providence, Rhode Island

Into the Woods, by James Lapine and Stephen Sondheim, Old Globe Theatre, San Diego

Jekyll & Hyde, by Frank Wildhorn, Alley Theatre, Houston, Texas

Jelly's Last Jam, by George C. Wolfe, Jelly Roll Morton, and Susan Birkenhead, Mark Taper Forum, Los Angeles

Joe Turner's Come and Gone, by August Wilson, Yale Repertory Theatre, New Haven, Connecticut

Love Letters, by A. R. Gurney, Long Wharf Theatre, New Haven, Connecticut

Ma Rainey's Black Bottom, by August Wilson, Yale Repertory Theatre, New Haven, Connecticut

Master Class, by Terrence McNally, Philadelphia Theater Company, Pennsylvania

"Master Harold"...and the Boys, by Athol Fugard, Yale Repertory Theatre, New Haven, Connecticut

'Night, Mother, by Marsha Norman, American Repertory Theatre, Cambridge, Massachusetts

Prelude to a Kiss, by Craig Lucas, South Coast Repertory, Costa Mesa, California

Quilters, by Molly Newman and Barbara Damashek, Denver Center Theatre Company

Streamers, by David Rabe, Long Wharf Theatre, New Haven, Connecticut

Twilight, by Anna Deavere Smith, Mark Taper Forum, Los Angeles, California

True West, by Sam Shepard, Steppenwolf Theatre Company, Chicago

Two Trains Running, by August Wilson, Yale Repertory Theatre, New Haven, Connecticut

The Wake of Jamey Foster, by Beth Henley, Hartford Stage Company, Hartford, Connecticut

The Who's "Tommy," by Pete Townshend and Wayne Cilento, La Jolla Playhouse, La Jolla, California

MAJOR REGIONAL THEATERS AND THEIR DIRECTORS

Far from the bright lights of Broadway, vibrant regional theater companies can be found in rural communities, urban neighborhoods, metropolitan centers, and suburbs around the U.S. Their repertoire ranges from the classics to musicals to modern plays to experimental, multi-media, and solo-performance works. Despite deeply felt cuts in government funding, these shining companies continue to cast their light from every corner of the country.

Actors Theatre of Louisville, Louisville, Kentucky, Jon Jory, producing director

Alley Theatre, Houston, Gregory Boyd, artistic director

Alliance Theatre Company, Atlanta, Kenny Leon, artistic director

American Conservatory Theater, San Francisco, Carey Perloff, artistic director

American Repertory Theatre, Cambridge, Massachusetts, Robert Brustein, artistic director

Arena Stage, Washington, D.C., Molly D. Smith, artistic director

Center Stage, Baltimore, Irene Lewis, artistic director

Dallas Theater Center, Dallas, Richard Hamburger, artistic director

Goodman Theatre, Chicago, Robert Falls, artistic director

Goodspeed Opera House, East Haddam, Connecticut, Michael P. Price, executive director

Guthrie Theater, Minneapolis, Joe Dowling, artistic director

Hartford Stage Company, Hartford, Connecticut, Michael Wilson, artistic director

La Jolla Playhouse, La Jolla, California, Anne Hamburger, artistic director

Long Wharf Theatre, New Haven, Connecticut, Douglas Hughes, artistic director

Mark Taper Forum, Los Angeles, Gordon Davidson, artistic director

McCarter Theatre Center for the Performing Arts, Princeton, New Jersey, Emily Mann, artistic director

Milwaukee Repertory Theater, Milwaukee, Joseph Hanreddy, artistic director

Old Globe Theatre, San Diego, Jack O'Brien, artistic director

Oregon Shakespeare Festival, Ashland, Oregon, Libby Appel, artistic director

Seattle Repertory Theatre, Seattle, Sharon Ott, artistic director

Shakespeare Theatre, Washington, D.C., Michael Kahn, artistic director

South Coast Repertory, Costa Mesa, California, David Emmes, producing artistic director

Steppenwolf Theatre Company, Chicago, Martha Lavey, artistic director

Trinity Repertory Company, Providence, Rhode Island, Oscar Eustis, artistic director

Yale Repertory Theatre, New Haven, Connecticut, Stan Wojewodski Jr., artistic director

THE TONY AWARDS

	1947	1948	1949
Actor (Dramatic)	Fredric March, *Years Ago;* José Ferrer, *Cyrano de Bergerac*	Basil Rathbone, *The Heiress;* Henry Fonda, *Mister Roberts;* Paul Kelly, *Command Decision*	Rex Harrison, *Anne of the Thousand Days*
Actress (Dramatic)	Helen Hayes, *Happy Birthday;* Ingrid Bergman, *Joan of Lorraine*	Jessica Tandy, *A Streetcar Named Desire;* Judith Anderson, *Medea;* Katharine Cornell, *Antony and Cleopatra*	Martita Hunt, *The Madwoman of Chaillot*
Supporting Actor (Dramatic)	—	—	Arthur Kennedy, *Death of a Salesman*
Supporting Actress (Dramatic)	Patricia Neal, *Another Part of the Forest*	—	Shirley Booth, *Goodbye, My Fancy*
Play	—	*Mister Roberts*	*Death of a Salesman*
Actor (Musical)	—	Paul Hartman, *Angel in the Wings*	Ray Bolger, *Where's Charley?*
Actress (Musical)	—	Grace Hartman, *Angel in the Wings*	Nanette Fabray, *Love Life*
Supporting Actor (Musical)	David Wayne, *Finian's Rainbow*	—	—
Supporting Actress (Musical)	—	—	—
Musical	—	—	*Kiss Me Kate*
Director	Elia Kazan, *All My Sons*	—	Elia Kazan, *Death of a Salesman*
Score	—	—	Cole Porter, *Kiss Me Kate*
Author (Dramatic)	—	Thomas Heggen and Joshua Logan, *Mister Roberts*	Arthur Miller, *Death of a Salesman*
Author (Musical)	—		Bella and Samuel Spewack, *Kiss Me Kate*
Scenic Designer	—	Horace Armistead, *The Medium*	Jo Mielziner, *Sleepy Hollow; Summer and Smoke; Anne of the Thousand Days; Death of a Salesman; South Pacific*
Costume Designer	—	—	Lemuel Ayers, *Kiss Me Kate*
Choreographer	Agnes de Mille, *Brigadoon;* Michael Kidd, *Finian's Rainbow*	Jerome Robbins, *High Button Shoes*	Gower Champion, *Lend an Ear*
Producer (Dramatic)	—	Leland Hayward, *Mister Roberts*	Kermit Bloomgarden and Walter Fried, *Death of a Salesman*
Producer (Musical)	—	—	Saint-Subber and Lemuel Ayers, *Kiss Me Kate*
Conductor and Musical Director	—	—	Max Meth, *As the Girls Go*
Stage Technician	—	George Gebhardt; George Pierce	—

1950	1951	1952	1953
Sydney Blackmer, *Come Back, Little Sheba*	Claude Rains, *Darkness at Noon*	Jose Ferrer, *The Shrike*	Tom Ewell, *The Seven Year Itch*
Shirley Booth, *Come Back, Little Sheba*	Uta Hagen, *The Country Girl*	Julie Harris, *I Am a Camera*	Shirley Booth, *Time of the Cuckoo*
—	Eli Wallach, *The Rose Tattoo*	John Cromwell, *Point of No Return*	John Williams, *Dial M for Murder*
—	Maureen Stapleton, *The Rose Tattoo*	Marian Winters, *I Am a Camera*	Beatrice Straight, *The Crucible*
The Cocktail Party	*The Rose Tattoo*	*The Fourposter*	*The Crucible*
Ezio Pinza, *South Pacific*	Robert Alda, *Guys and Dolls*	Phil Silvers, *Top Banana*	Thomas Mitchell, *Hazel Flagg*
Mary Martin, *South Pacific*	Ethel Merman, *Call Me Madam*	Gertrude Lawrence, *The King and I*	Rosalind Russell, *Wonderful Town*
Myron McCormick, *South Pacific*	Russell Nype, *Call Me Madam*	Yul Brynner, *The King and I*	Hiram Sherman, *Two's Company*
Juanita Hall, *South Pacific*	Isabel Bigley, *Guys and Dolls*	Helen Gallagher, *Pal Joey*	Sheila Bond, *Wish You Were Here*
South Pacific	*Guys and Dolls*	*The King and I*	*Wonderful Town*
Joshua Logan, *South Pacific*	George S. Kaufman, *Guys and Dolls*	Jose Ferrer, *The Shrike; The Fourposter; Stalag 17*	Joshua Logan, *Picnic*
Richard Rodgers, *South Pacific*	Frank Loesser, *Guys and Dolls*	—	Leonard Bernstein, *Wonderful Town*
T.S. Eliot, *The Cocktail Party*	Tennessee Williams, *The Rose Tattoo*	—	Arthur Miller, *The Crucible*
Oscar Hammerstein II and Joshua Logan, *South Pacific*	Jo Swerling and Abe Burrows, *Guys and Dolls*	—	Joseph Fields and Jerome Chodorov, *Wonderful Town*
Jo Mielziner, *The Innocents*	Boris Aronson, *The Rose Tattoo; The Country Girl; Season in the Sun*	Jo Mielziner, *The King and I*	Raoul Pene du Bois, *Wonderful Town*
Aline Bernstein, *Regina*	Miles White, *Bless You All*	Irene Sharaff, *The King and I*	Miles White, *Hazel Flagg*
Helen Tamiris, *Touch and Go*	Michael Kidd, *Guys and Dolls*	Robert Alton, *Pal Joey*	Donald Saddler, *Wonderful Town*
Gilbert Miller, *The Cocktail Party*	Cheryl Crawford, *The Rose Tattoo*	—	Kermit Bloomgarden, *The Crucible*
Richard Rodgers, Oscar Hammerstein II, Leland Hayward, and Joshua Logan, *South Pacific*	Cy Feuer and Ernest H. Martin, *Guys and Dolls*	—	Robert Fryer, *Wonderful Town*
Maurice Abravanel, *Regina*	Lehman Engel, *The Consul*	Max Meth, *Pal Joey*	Lehman Engel, *Wonderful Town; Gilbert and Sullivan Season*
Joe Lynn, master propertyman, *Miss Liberty*	Richard Raven, *The Autumn Garden*	Peter Feller, master carpenter, *Call Me Madam*	Abe Kurnit, *Wish You Were Here*

	1954	1955	1956
Actor (Dramatic)	David Wayne, *The Teahouse of the August Moon*	Alfred Lunt, *Quadrille*	Paul Muni, *Inherit the Wind*
Actress (Dramatic)	Audrey Hepburn, *Ondine*	Nancy Kelly, *The Bad Seed*	Julie Harris, *The Lark*
Featured/Supporting Actor (Dramatic)	John Kerr, *Tea and Sympathy*	Francis L. Sullivan, *Witness for the Prosecution*	Ed Begley, *Inherit the Wind*
Featured/Supporting Actress (Dramatic)	Jo Van Fleet, *The Trip to Bountiful*	Patricia Jessel, *Witness for the Prosecution*	Una Merkel, *The Ponder Heart*
Play	*The Teahouse of the August Moon*	*The Desperate Hours*	*The Diary of Anne Frank*
Actor (Musical)	Alfred Drake, *Kismet*	Walter Slezak, *Fanny*	Ray Walston, *Damn Yankees*
Actress (Musical)	Dolores Gray, *Carnival in Flanders*	Mary Martin, *Peter Pan*	Gwen Verdon, *Damn Yankees*
Featured/Supporting Actor Role (Musical)	Harry Belafonte, *John Murray Anderson's Almanac*	Cyril Ritchard, *Peter Pan*	Russ Brown, *Damn Yankees*
Featured/Supporting Actress (Musical)	Gwen Verdon, *Can-Can*	Carol Haney, *The Pajama Game*	Lotte Lenya, *The Threepenny Opera*
Musical	*Kismet*	*The Pajama Game*	*Damn Yankees*
Director	Alfred Lunt, *Ondine*	Robert Montgomery, *The Desperate Hours*	Tyrone Guthrie, *The Matchmaker; Six Characters in Search of an Author; Tamburlaine the Great*
Director (Dramatic)	—	—	—
Director (Musical)	—	—	—
Score	Alexander Borodin, *Kismet*	Richard Adler and Jerry Ross, *The Pajama Game*	Richard Adler and Jerry Ross, *Damn Yankees*
Author (Dramatic)	John Patrick, *The Teahouse of the August Moon*	Joseph Hayes, *The Desperate Hours*	Frances Goodrich and Albert Hackett, *The Diary of Anne Frank*
Author (Musical)	Charles Lederer and Luther Davis, *Kismet*	George Abbott and Richard Bissell, *The Pajama Game*	George Abbott and Douglass Wallop, *Damn Yankees*
Scenic Designer	Peter Larkin, *Ondine; The Teahouse of the August Moon*	Oliver Messel, *House of Flowers*	Peter Larkin, *Inherit the Wind; No Time for Sergeants*
Costume Designer	Richard Whorf, *Ondine*	Cecil Beaton, *Quadrille*	Alvin Colt, *The Lark/Phoenix '55/Pipe Dream*
Choreographer	Michael Kidd, *Can-Can*	Bob Fosse, *The Pajama Game*	Bob Fosse, *Damn Yankees*
Producer (Dramatic)	Maurice Evans and George Schaefer, *The Teahouse of the August Moon*	Howard Erskine and Joseph Hayes, *The Desperate Hours*	Kermit Bloomgarden, *The Diary of Anne Frank*
Producer (Musical)	Charles Lederer, *Kismet*	Frederick Brisson, Robert Griffith, and Harold S. Prince, *The Pajama Game*	Frederick Brisson, Robert Griffith, Harold S. Prince in association with Albert B. Taylor, *Damn Yankees*
Conductor and Musical Director	Louis Adrian, *Kismet*	Thomas Schippers, *The Saint of Bleecker Street*	Hal Hastings, *Damn Yankees*
Stage Technician	John Davis, *Picnic*	Richard Rodda, *Peter Pan*	Harry Green, electrician and sound man, *The Middle of the Night; Damn Yankees*

1957	1958	1959	1960
Fredric March, *Long Day's Journey into Night*	Ralph Bellamy, *Sunrise at Campobello*	Jason Robards Jr., *The Disenchanted*	Melvyn Douglas, *The Best Man*
Margaret Leighton, *Separate Tables*	Helen Hayes, *Time Remembered*	Gertrude Berg, *A Majority of One*	Anne Bancroft, *The Miracle Worker*
Frank Conroy, *The Potting Shed*	Henry Jones, *Sunrise at Campobello*	Charlie Ruggles, *The Pleasure of His Company*	Roddy McDowall, *The Fighting Cock*
Peggy Cass, *Auntie Mame*	Anne Bancroft, *Two for the Seesaw*	Julie Newmar, *The Marriage-Go-Round*	Anne Revere, *Toys in the Attic*
Long Day's Journey into Night	*Sunrise at Campobello*	*J.B.*	*The Miracle Worker*
Rex Harrison, *My Fair Lady*	Robert Preston, *The Music Man*	Richard Kiley, *Redhead*	Jackie Gleason, *Take Me Along*
Judy Holliday, *Bells Are Ringing*	Gwen Verdon, *New Girl in Town;* Thelma Ritter, *New Girl in Town*	Gwen Verdon, *Redhead*	Mary Martin, *The Sound of Music*
Sydney Chaplin, *Bells Are Ringing*	David Burns, *The Music Man*	Russell Nype, *Goldilocks;* cast of *La Plume de ma tante*	Tom Bosley, *Fiorello!*
Edith Adams, *Li'l Abner*	Barbara Cook, *The Music Man*	Pat Stanley, *Goldilocks;* cast of *La Plume de ma tante*	Patricia Neway, *The Sound of Music*
My Fair Lady	*The Music Man*	*Redhead*	*Fiorello!*
Moss Hart, *My Fair Lady*	—	Elia Kazan, *J.B.*	—
—	Vincent J. Donehue, *Sunrise at Campobello*	—	Arthur Penn, *The Miracle Worker*
—	—	—	George Abbott, *Fiorello!*
Frederick Loewe, *My Fair Lady*	Meredith Willson, *The Music Man*	Albert Hague, *Redhead*	Jerry Bock, *Fiorello!;* Richard Rodgers, *The Sound of Music*
Eugene O'Neill, *Long Day's Journey into Night*	Dore Schary, *Sunrise at Campobello*	Archibald MacLeish, *J.B.*	William Gibson, *The Miracle Worker*
Alan Jay Lerner, *My Fair Lady*	Meredith Willson and Franklin Lacey, *The Music Man*	Herbert and Dorothy Fields, Sidney Sheldon, and David Shaw, *Redhead*	Jerome Weidman and George Abbott, *Fiorello!;* Howard Lindsay and Russel Crouse, *The Sound of Music*
Oliver Smith, *A Clearing in the Woods; Candide; Auntie Mame; My Fair Lady; Eugenia; A Visit to a Small Planet*	Oliver Smith, *West Side Story*	Donald Oenslager, *A Majority of One*	Howard Bey, *Toys in the Attic* (Dramatic); Oliver Smith, *The Sound of Music* (Musical)
Cecil Beaton, *Little Glass Clock/ My Fair Lady*	Motley, *The First Gentleman*	Robert Ter-Arutunian, *Redhead*	Cecil Beaton, *Saratoga*
Michael Kidd, *Li'l Abner*	Jerome Robbins, *West Side Story*	Bob Fosse, *Redhead*	Michael Kidd, *Destry Rides Again*
Leigh Connell, Theodore Mann, and Jose Quintero, *Long Day's Journey into Night*	Lawrence Langner, Theresa Helburn, Armina Marshall, and Dore Schary, *Sunrise at Campobello*	Alfred de Liagre, Jr., *J.B.*	Fred Coe, *The Miracle Worker*
Herman Levin, *My Fair Lady*	Kermit Bloomgarden, Herbert Greene, Frank Productions, *The Music Man*	Robert Fryer and Lawrence Carr, *Redhead*	Robert Griffith and Harold Prince, *Fiorello!;* Leland Hayward and Richard Halliday, *The Sound of Music*
Franz Allers, *My Fair Lady*	Herbert Greene, *The Music Man*	Salvatore Dell'Isola, *Flower Drum Song*	Frederick Dvonch, *The Sound of Music*
Howard McDonald (posthumous), carpenter, *Major Barbara*	Harry Romar, *Time Remembered*	Sam Knapp, *The Music Man*	John Walters, chief carpenter, *The Miracle Worker*

	1961	1962	1963
Actor (Dramatic)	Zero Mostel, *Rhinoceros*	Paul Scofield, *A Man for All Seasons*	Arthur Hill, *Who's Afraid of Virginia Woolf?*
Actress (Dramatic)	Joan Plowright, *A Taste of Honey*	Margaret Leighton, *Night of the Iguana*	Uta Hagen, *Who's Afraid of Virginia Woolf?*
Featured/Supporting Actor (Dramatic)	Martin Gabel, *Big Fish, Little Fish*	Walter Matthau, *A Shot in the Dark*	Alan Arkin, *Enter Laughing*
Featured/Supporting Actress (Dramatic)	Colleen Dewhurst, *All the Way Home*	Elizabeth Ashley, *Take Her, She's Mine*	Sandy Dennis, *A Thousand Clowns*
Play	*Becket*	*A Man for All Seasons*	*Who's Afraid of Virginia Woolf?*
Actor (Musical)	Richard Burton, *Camelot*	Robert Morse, *How to Succeed in Business Without Really Trying*	Zero Mostel, *A Funny Thing Happened on the Way to the Forum*
Actress (Musical)	Elizabeth Seal, *Irma La Douce*	Anna Maria Alberghetti, *Carnival*	Vivien Leigh, *Tovarich*
Featured/Supporting Actor (Musical)	Dick Van Dyke, *Bye, Bye Birdie*	Charles Nelson Reilly, *How to Succeed in Business Without Really Trying*	David Burns, *A Funny Thing Happened on the Way to the Forum*
Featured/Supporting Actress (Musical)	Tammy Grimes, *The Unsinkable Molly Brown*	Phyllis Newman, *Subways Are for Sleeping*	Anna Quayle, *Stop the World—I Want to Get Off*
Musical	*Bye, Bye Birdie*	*How to Succeed in Business Without Really Trying*	*A Funny Thing Happened on the Way to the Forum*
Director (Dramatic)	John Gielgud, *Big Fish, Little Fish*	Noel Willman, *A Man for All Seasons*	Alan Schneider, *Who's Afraid of Virginia Woolf?*
Director (Musical)	Gower Champion, *Bye, Bye Birdie*	Abe Burrows, *How to Succeed in Business Without Really Trying*	George Abbott, *A Funny Thing Happened on the Way to the Forum*
Score	—	Richard Rodgers, *No Strings*	Lionel Bart, *Oliver!*
Author (Dramatic)	Jean Anouilh, *Becket*	Robert Bolt, *A Man for All Seasons*	—
Author (Musical)	Michael Stewart, *Bye, Bye Birdie*	Abe Burrows, Jack Weinstock, and Willie Gilbert, *How to Succeed in Business Without Really Trying*	Burt Shevelove and Larry Gelbart, *A Funny Thing Happened on the Way to the Forum*
Scenic Designer	Oliver Smith, *Becket* (Dramatic); Oliver Smith, *Camelot* (Musical)	Will Steven Armstrong, *Carnival*	Sean Kenny, *Oliver!*
Costume Designer	Motley, *Becket;* Adrian and Tony Duquette, *Camelot*	Lucinda Ballard, *The Gay Life*	Anthony Powell, *The School for Scandal*
Choreographer	Gower Champion, *Bye, Bye Birdie*	Agnes de Mille, *Kwamina;* Joe Layton, *No Strings*	Bob Fosse, *Little Me*
Producer (Dramatic)	David Merrick, *Becket*	Robert Whitehead and Roger L. Stevens, *A Man for All Seasons*	Richard Barr and Clinton Wilder, Theatre 1963, *Who's Afraid of Virginia Woolf?*
Producer (Musical)	Edward Padula, *Bye, Bye Birdie*	Cy Feuer and Ernest Martin, *How to Succeed in Business Without Really Trying*	Harold Prince, *A Funny Thing Happened on the Way to the Forum*
Conductor and Musical Director	Franz Allers, *Camelot*	Elliot Lawrence, *How to Succeed in Business Without Really Trying*	Donald Pippin, *Oliver!*
Stage Technician	Teddy Van Bemmel, *Becket*	Michael Burns, *A Man for All Seasons*	—

1964	1965	1966	1967
Alec Guinness, *Dylan*	Walter Matthau, *The Odd Couple*	Hal Holbrook, *Mark Twain Tonight!*	Paul Rogers, *The Homecoming*
Sandy Dennis, *Any Wednesday*	Irene Worth, *Tiny Alice*	Rosemary Harris, *The Lion in Winter*	Beryl Reid, *The Killing of Sister George*
Hume Cronyn, *Hamlet*	Jack Albertson, *The Subject Was Roses*	Patrick Magee, *Marat/Sade*	Ian Holm, *The Homecoming*
Barbara Loden, *After the Fall*	Alice Ghostley, *The Sign in Sidney Brustein's Window*	Zoe Caldwell, *Slapstick Tragedy*	Marian Seldes, *A Delicate Balance*
Luther	*The Subject Was Roses*	*Marat/Sade*	*The Homecoming*
Bert Lahr, *Foxy*	Zero Mostel, *Fiddler on the Roof*	Richard Kiley, *Man of La Mancha*	Robert Preston, *I Do! I Do!*
Carol Channing, *Hello, Dolly!*	Liza Minnelli, *Flora, the Red Menace*	Angela Lansbury, *Mame*	Barbara Harris, *The Apple Tree*
Jack Cassidy, *She Loves Me*	Victor Spinetti, *Oh, What a Lovely War!*	Frankie Michaels, *Mame*	Joel Grey, *Cabaret*
Tessie O'Shea, *The Girl Who Came to Supper*	Maria Karnilova, *Fiddler on the Roof*	Beatrice Arthur, *Mame*	Peg Murray, *Cabaret*
Hello, Dolly!	*Fiddler on the Roof*	*Man of La Mancha*	*Cabaret*
Mike Nichols, *Barefoot in the Park*	Mike Nichols, *Luv; The Odd Couple*	Peter Brook, *Marat/Sade*	Peter Hall, *The Homecoming*
Gower Champion, *Hello, Dolly!*	Jerome Robbins, *Fiddler on the Roof*	Albert Marre, *Man of La Mancha*	Harold Prince, *Cabaret*
Jerry Herman, *Hello, Dolly!*	Jerry Bock and Sheldon Harnick, *Fiddler on the Roof*	Mitch Leigh and Joe Darion, *Man of La Mancha*	John Kander and Fred Ebb, *Cabaret*
John Osborne, *Luther*	Neil Simon, *The Odd Couple*	—	—
Michael Stewart, *Hello, Dolly!*	Joseph Stein, *Fiddler on the Roof*	—	—
Oliver Smith, *Hello, Dolly!*	Oliver Smith, *Baker Street; Luv; The Odd Couple*	Howard Bay, *Man of La Mancha*	Boris Aronson, *Cabaret*
Freddy Wittop, *Hello, Dolly!*	Patricia Zipprodt, *Fiddler on the Roof*	Gunilla Palmstierna-Weiss, *Marat/Sade*	Patricia Zipprodt, *Cabaret*
Gower Champion, *Hello, Dolly!*	Jerome Robbins, *Fiddler on the Roof*	Bob Fosse, *Sweet Charity*	Ronald Field, *Cabaret*
Herman Shumlin, *The Deputy*	Claire Nichtern, *Luv*	—	—
David Merrick, *Hello, Dolly!*	Harold Prince, *Fiddler on the Roof*	—	—
Shepard Coleman, *Hello, Dolly!*	—	—	—
—	—	—	—

	1968	1969	1970
Actor (Dramatic)	Martin Balsam, *You Know I Can't Hear You When the Water's Running*	James Earl Jones, *The Great White Hope*	Fritz Weaver, *Child's Play*
Actress (Dramatic)	Zoe Caldwell, *The Prime of Miss Jean Brodie*	Julie Harris, *Forty Carats*	Tammy Grimes, *Private Lives*
Featured/Supporting Actor (Dramatic)	James Patterson, *The Birthday Party*	Al Pacino, *Does a Tiger Wear a Necktie?*	Ken Howard, *Child's Play*
Featured/Supporting Actress (Dramatic)	Zena Walker, *Joe Egg*	Jane Alexander, *The Great White Hope*	Blythe Danner, *Butterflies Are Free*
Play	*Rosencrantz and Guildenstern Are Dead*	*The Great White Hope*	*Borstal Boy*
Actor (Musical)	Robert Goulet, *The Happy Time*	Jerry Orbach, *Promises, Promises*	Cleavon Little, *Purlie*
Actress (Musical)	Leslie Uggams, *Hallelujah, Baby!*; Patricia Routledge, *Darling of the Day*	Angela Lansbury, *Dear World*	Lauren Bacall, *Applause*
Featured/Supporting Actor (Musical)	Hiram Sherman, *How Now, Dow Jones*	Ronald Holgate, *1776*	Rene Auberjonois, *Coco*
Featured/Supporting Actress (Musical)	Lillian Hayman, *Hallelujah, Baby!*	Marian Mercer, *Promises, Promises*	Melba Moore, *Purlie*
Musical	*Hallelujah, Baby!*	*1776*	*Applause*
Director (Dramatic)	Mike Nichols, *Plaza Suite*	Peter Dews, *Hadrian VII*	Joseph Hardy, *Child's Play*
Director (Musical)	Gower Champion, *The Happy Time*	Peter Hunt, *1776*	Ron Field, *Applause*
Book (Musical)	—	—	—
Score	Jule Styne, Betty Comden, and Adolph Green, *Hallelujah, Baby!*	—	—
Scenic Designer	Desmond Heeley, *Rosencrantz and Guildenstern Are Dead*	Boris Aronson, *Zorba*	Howard Bay, *Cry for Us All*; Jo Mielziner, *Child's Play*
Costume Designer	Desmond Heeley, *Rosencrantz and Guildenstern Are Dead*	Louden Sainthill, *Canterbury Tales*	Cecil Beaton, *Coco*
Lighting Designer	—	—	Jo Mielziner, *Child's Play*
Choreographer	Gower Champion, *The Happy Time*	Joe Layton, *George M!*	Ron Field, *Applause*
Producer (Dramatic)	The David Merrick Arts Foundation, *Rosencrantz and Guildenstern Are Dead*	—	—
Producer (Musical)	Albert Selden, Hal James, Jane C. Nusbaum, and Harry Rigby, *Hallelujah, Baby!*	—	—

1971	1972	1973	1974
Brian Bedford, *The School for Wives*	Cliff Gorman, *Lenny*	Alan Bates, *Butley*	Michael Moriarty, *Find Your Way Home*
Maureen Stapleton, *The Gingerbread Lady*	Sada Thompson, *Twigs*	Julie Harris, *The Last of Mrs. Lincoln*	Colleen Dewhurst, *A Moon for the Misbegotten*
Paul Sand, *Story Theatre*	Vincent Gardenia, *The Prisoner of Second Avenue*	John Lithgow, *The Changing Room*	Ed Flanders, *A Moon for the Misbegotten*
Rae Allen, *And Miss Reardon Drinks a Little*	Elizabeth Wilson, *Sticks and Bones*	Leora Dana, *The Last of Mrs. Lincoln*	Frances Sternhagen, *The Good Doctor*
Sleuth	*Sticks and Bones*	*That Championship Season*	*The River Niger*
Hal Linden, *The Rothschilds*	Phil Silvers, *A Funny Thing Happened on the Way to the Forum* (Revival)	Ben Vereen, *Pippin*	Christopher Plummer, *Cyrano*
Helen Gallagher, *No, No, Nanette*	Alexis Smith, *Follies*	Glynis Johns, *A Little Night Music*	Virginia Capers, *Raisin*
Keene Curtis, *The Rothschilds*	Larry Blyden, *A Funny Thing Happened on the Way to the Forum* (Revival)	George S. Irving, *Irene*	Tommy Tune, *Seesaw*
Patsy Kelly, *No, No, Nanette*	Linda Hopkins, *Inner City*	Patricia Elliot, *A Little Night Music*	Janie Sell, *Over Here!*
Company	*Two Gentlemen of Verona*	*A Little Night Music*	*Raisin*
Peter Brook, *Midsummer Night's Dream*	Mike Nichols, *The Prisoner of Second Avenue*	A. J. Antoon, *That Championship Season*	Jose Quintero, *A Moon for the Misbegotten*
Harold Prince, *Company*	Harold Prince and Michael Bennett, *Follies*	Bob Fosse, *Pippin*	Harold Prince, *Candide*
George Furth, *Company*	John Guare and Mel Shapiro, *Two Gentlemen of Verona*	Hugh Wheeler, *A Little Night Music*	Hugh Wheeler, *Candide*
Stephen Sondheim, *Company*	Stephen Sondheim, *Follies*	Stephen Sondheim, *A Little Night Music*	Frederick Loewe (Music); Alan Jay Lerner (Lyrics), *Gigi*
Boris Aronson, *Company*	Boris Aronson, *Follies*	Tony Walton, *Pippin*	Franne and Eugene Lee, *Candide*
Raoul Pene du Bois, *No, No, Nanette*	Florence Klotz, *Follies*	Florence Klotz, *A Little Night Music*	Franne Lee, *Candide*
H. R. Poindexter, *Story Theatre*	Tharon Musser, *Follies*	Jules Fisher, *Pippin*	Jules Fisher, *Ulysses in Nighttown*
Donald Saddler, *No, No, Nanette*	Michael Bennett, *Follies*	Bob Fosse, *Pippin*	Michael Bennett, *Seesaw*
Helen Bonfils, Morton Gottlieb, and Michael White, *Sleuth*	—	—	—
Harold Prince, *Company*	—	—	—

	1975	**1976**	**1977**
Actor (Dramatic)	John Kani and Winston Ntshona, *Sizwe Banzi Is Dead & The Island*	John Wood, *Travesties*	Al Pacino, *The Basic Training of Pavlo Hummel*
Actress (Dramatic)	Ellen Burstyn, *Same Time, Next Year*	Irene Worth, *Sweet Bird of Youth*	Julie Harris, *The Belle of Amherst*
Featured Actor (Dramatic)	Frank Langella, *Seascape*	Edward Herrmann, *Mrs. Warren's Profession*	Jonathan Pryce, *Comedians*
Featured Actress (Dramatic)	Rita Moreno, *The Ritz*	Shirley Knight, *Kennedy's Children*	Trazana Beverley, *For Colored Girls Who Have Considered Suicide/When the Rainbow Is Enuf*
Play	*Equus*	*Travesties*	*The Shadow Box*
Actor (Musical)	John Cullum, *Shenandoah*	George Rose, *My Fair Lady*	Barry Bostwick, *The Robber Bridegroom*
Actress (Musical)	Angela Lansbury, *Gypsy*	Donna McKechnie, *A Chorus Line*	Dorothy Loudon, *Annie*
Featured Actor (Musical)	Ted Ross, *The Wiz*	Sammy Williams, *A Chorus Line*	Lenny Baker, *I Love My Wife*
Featured Actress (Musical)	Dee Dee Bridgewater, *The Wiz*	Carole Bishop, *A Chorus Line*	Delores Hall, *Your Arms Too Short to Box with God*
Musical	*The Wiz*	*A Chorus Line*	*Annie*
Director (Dramatic)	John Dexter, *Equus*	Ellis Rabb, *The Royal Family*	Gordon Davidson, *The Shadow Box*
Director (Musical)	Geoffrey Holder, *The Wiz*	Michael Bennett, *A Chorus Line*	Gene Saks, *I Love My Wife*
Book (Musical)	James Lee Barrett, *Shenandoah*	James Kirkwood and Nicholas Dante, *A Chorus Line*	Thomas Meehan, *Annie*
Score	Charlie Smalls (Music & Lyrics), *The Wiz*	Marvin Hamlisch (Music); Edward Kleban (Lyrics), *A Chorus Line*	Charles Strouse (Music); Martin Charnin (Lyrics), *Annie*
Scenic Designer	Carl Toms, *Sherlock Holmes*	Boris Aronson, *Pacific Overtures*	David Mitchell, *Annie*
Costume Designer	Geoffrey Holder, *The Wiz*	Florence Klotz, *Pacific Overtures*	Theoni V. Aldredge, *Annie;* Santo Loquasto, *The Cherry Orchard*
Lighting Designer	Neil Patrick Jampolis, *Sherlock Holmes*	Tharon Musser, *A Chorus Line*	Jennifer Tipton, *The Cherry Orchard*
Choreographer	George Faison, *The Wiz*	Michael Bennett and Bob Avian, *A Chorus Line*	Peter Gennaro, *Annie*
Reproduction of a Play or Musical	—	—	*Porgy and Bess*

1978

Barnard Hughes, *Da*

Jessica Tandy, *The Gin Game*

Lester Rawlins, *Da*

Ann Wedgeworth, *Chapter Two*

Da

John Cullum, *On the Twentieth Century*

Liza Minnelli, *The Act*

Kevin Kline, *On the Twentieth Century*

Nell Carter, *Ain't Misbehavin'*

Ain't Misbehavin'

Melvin Bernhardt, *Da*

Richard Maltby Jr., *Ain't Misbehavin'*

Betty Comden and Adolph Green, *On the Twentieth Century*

Cy Coleman (Music); Betty Comden and Adolph Green (Lyrics), *On the Twentieth Century*

Robin Wagner, *On the Twentieth Century*

Edward Gorey, *Dracula*

Jules Fisher, *Dancin'*

Bob Fosse, *Dancin'*

Dracula

1979

Tom Conti, *Whose Life Is It Anyway?*

Constance Cummings, *Wings;* Carole Shelley, *The Elephant Man*

Michael Gough, *Bedroom Farce*

Joan Hickson, *Bedroom Farce*

The Elephant Man

Len Cariou, *Sweeney Todd*

Angela Lansbury, *Sweeney Todd*

Henderson Forsythe, *The Best Little Whorehouse in Texas*

Carlin Glynn, *The Best Little Whorehouse in Texas*

Sweeney Todd

Jack Hofsiss, *The Elephant Man*

Harold Prince, *Sweeney Todd*

Hugh Wheeler, *Sweeney Todd*

Stephen Sondheim (Music & Lyrics), *Sweeney Todd*

Eugene Lee, *Sweeney Todd*

Franne Lee, *Sweeney Todd*

Roger Morgan, *The Crucifer of Blood*

Michael Bennett and Bob Avian, *Ballroom*

—

1980

John Rubinstein, *Children of a Lesser God*

Phyllis Frelich, *Children of a Lesser God*

David Rounds, *Morning's at Seven*

Dinah Manoff, *I Ought to Be in Pictures*

Children of a Lesser God

Jim Dale, *Barnum*

Patti LuPone, *Evita*

Mandy Patinkin, *Evita*

Priscilla Lopez, *A Day in Hollywood, a Night in the Ukraine*

Evita

Vivian Matalon, *Morning's at Seven*

Harold Prince, *Evita*

Tim Rice, *Evita*

Andrew Lloyd Webber (Music); Tim Rice (Lyrics), *Evita*

John Lee Beatty, *Talley's Folly;* David Mitchell, *Barnum*

Theoni V. Aldredge, *Barnum*

David Hersey, *Evita*

Tommy Tune and Thommie Walsh, *A Day in Hollywood, a Night in the Ukraine*

Elizabeth I. McCann, Nelle Nugent, Ray Larsen, producers, *Morning's at Seven*

1981

Ian McKellen, *Amadeus*

Jane Lapotaire, *Piaf*

Brian Backer, *The Floating Light Bulb*

Swoosie Kurtz, *Fifth of July*

Amadeus

Kevin Kline, *The Pirates of Penzance*

Lauren Bacall, *Woman of the Year*

Hinton Battle, *Sophisticated Ladies*

Marilyn Cooper, *Woman of the Year*

42nd Street

Peter Hall, *Amadeus*

Wilford Leach, *The Pirates of Penzance*

Peter Stone, *Woman of the Year*

John Kander (Music); Fred Ebb (Lyrics), *Woman of the Year*

John Bury, *Amadeus*

Willa Kim, *Sophisticated Ladies*

John Bury, *Amadeus*

Gower Champion, *42nd Street*

Joseph Papp, producer, *The Pirates of Penzance*

	1982	1983	1984
Actor (Dramatic)	Roger Rees, *The Life and Adventures of Nicholas Nickleby*	Harvey Fierstein, *Torch Song Trilogy*	Jeremy Irons, *The Real Thing*
Actress (Dramatic)	Zoë Caldwell, *Medea*	Jessica Tandy, *Foxfire*	Glenn Close, *The Real Thing*
Featured Actor (Dramatic)	Zakes Mokae, *"Master Harold"...and the Boys*	Matthew Broderick, *Brighton Beach Memoirs*	Joe Mantegna, *Glengarry Glen Ross*
Featured Actress (Dramatic)	Amanda Plummer, *Agnes of God*	Judith Ivey, *Steaming*	Christine Baranski, *The Real Thing*
Play	*The Life and Adventures of Nicholas Nickleby*	*Torch Song Trilogy*	*The Real Thing*
Actor (Musical)	Ben Harney, *Dreamgirls*	Tommy Tune, *My One and Only*	George Hearn, *La Cage aux folles*
Actress (Musical)	Jennifer Holliday, *Dreamgirls*	Natalia Makarova, *On Your Toes*	Chita Rivera, *The Rink*
Featured Actor (Musical)	Cleavant Derricks, *Dreamgirls*	Charles "Honi" Coles, *My One and Only*	Hinton Battle, *The Tap Dance Kid*
Featured Actress (Musical)	Liliane Montevecchi, *"Nine"*	Betty Buckley, *Cats*	Lila Kedrova, *Zorba*
Musical	*"Nine"*	*Cats*	*La Cage aux folles*
Director (Dramatic)	Trevor Nunn and John Caird, *The Life and Adventures of Nicholas Nickleby*	Gene Saks, *Brighton Beach Memoirs*	Mike Nichols, *The Real Thing*
Director (Musical)	Tommy Tune, *"Nine"*	Trevor Nunn, *Cats*	Arthur Laurents, *La Cage aux folles*
Book (Musical)	Tom Eyen, *Dreamgirls*	T. S. Eliot, *Cats*	Harvey Fierstein, *La Cage aux folles*
Score	Maury Yeton (Music & Lyrics), *"Nine"*	Andrew Lloyd Webber (Music); T. S. Eliot (Lyrics), *Cats*	Jerry Herman (Music & Lyrics), *La Cage aux folles*
Scenic Designer	John Napier and Dermot Hayes, *The Life and Adventures of Nicholas Nickleby*	Ming Cho Lee, *K2*	Tony Straiges, *Sunday in the Park with George*
Costume Designer	William Ivey Long, *"Nine"*	John Napier, *Cats*	Theoni V. Aldredge, *La Cage aux folles*
Lighting Designer	Tharon Musser, *Dreamgirls*	David Hersey, *Cats*	Richard Nelson, *Sunday in the Park with George*
Choreographer	Michael Bennett and Michael Peters, *Dreamgirls*	Thommie Walsh and Tommy Tune, *My One and Only*	Danny Daniels, *The Tap Dance Kid*
Reproduction of a Play or Musical	Barry and Fran Weissler, CBS Video Enterprises, Don Gregory, producers, *Othello*	Alfred De Liagre Jr., Roger L. Stevens, John Mauceri, Donald R. Seawell, Andre Pastoria, producers, *On Your Toes*	Robert Whitehead, Roger L. Stevens, producers, *Death of a Salesman*

1985	1986	1987	1988
Derek Jacobi, *Much Ado About Nothing*	Judd Hirsch, *I'm Not Rappaport*	James Earl Jones, *Fences*	Ron Silver, *Speed-the-Plow*
Stockard Channing, *Joe Egg*	Lily Tomlin, *The Search for Signs of Intelligent Life in the Universe*	Linda Lavin, *Broadway Bound*	Joan Allen, *Burn This*
Barry Miller, *Biloxi Blues*	John Mahoney, *The House of Blue Leaves*	John Randolph, *Broadway Bound*	B. D. Wong, *M. Butterfly*
Judith Ivey, *Hurlyburly*	Swoosie Kurtz, *The House of Blue Leaves*	Mary Alice, *Fences*	L. Scott Caldwell, *Joe Turner's Come and Gone*
Biloxi Blues	*I'm Not Rappaport*	*Fences*	*M. Butterfly*
—	George Rose, *The Mystery of Edwin Drood*	Robert Lindsay, *Me and My Girl*	Michael Crawford, *The Phantom of the Opera*
—	Bernadette Peters, *Song & Dance*	Maryann Plunkett, *Me and My Girl*	Joanna Gleason, *Into the Woods*
Ron Richardson, *Big River*	Michael Rupert, *Sweet Charity*	Michael Maguire, *Les Misérables*	Bill McCutcheon, *Anything Goes*
Leilani Jones, *Grind*	Bebe Neuwirth, *Sweet Charity*	Frances Ruffelle, *Les Misérables*	Judy Kaye, *The Phantom of the Opera*
Big River	*The Mystery of Edwin Drood*	*Les Misérables*	*The Phantom of the Opera*
Gene Saks, *Biloxi Blues*	Jerry Zaks, *The House of Blue Leaves*	Lloyd Richards, *Fences*	John Dexter, *M. Butterfly*
Des McAnuff, *Big River*	Wilford Leach, *The Mystery of Edwin Drood*	Trevor Nunn and John Caird, *Les Misérables*	Harold Prince, *The Phantom of the Opera*
William Hauptman, *Big River*	Rupert Holmes, *The Mystery of Edwin Drood*	Alain Boublil and Claude-Michel Schönberg, *Les Misérables*	James Lapine, *Into the Woods*
Roger Miller (Music & Lyrics), *Big River*	Rupert Holmes (Music & Lyrics), *The Mystery of Edwin Drood*	Claude-Michel Schönberg (Music); Herbert Kretzmer, and Alain Boublil (Lyrics), *Les Misérables*	Stephen Sondheim (Music & Lyrics), *Into the Woods*
Heidi Landesman, *Big River*	Tony Walton, *The House of Blue Leaves*	John Napier, *Les Misérables*	Maria Bjornson, *The Phantom of the Opera*
Florence Klotz, *Grind*	Patricia Zipprodt, *Sweet Charity*	John Napier, *Starlight Express*	Maria Bjornson, *The Phantom of the Opera*
Richard Riddell, *Big River*	Pat Collins, *I'm Not Rappaport*	David Hersey, *Starlight Express*	Andrew Bridge, *The Phantom of the Opera*
—	Bob Fosse, *Big Deal*	Gillian Gregory, *Me and My Girl*	Michael Smuin, *Anything Goes*
The Shubert Organization, Emanuel Azenberg, Roger Berlind, Ivan Bloch, MTM Enterprises, Inc., producers, *Joe Egg*	Jerome Minskoff, James M. Nederlander, Arthur Rubin, Joseph Harris, producers, *Sweet Charity*	Jay H. Fuchs, Steven Warnick, Charles Patsos, producers, *All My Sons*	Lincoln Center Theater, Gregory Mosher, Bernard Gersten, producers, *Anything Goes*

	1989	1990	1991
Actor (Dramatic)	Philip Bosco, *Lend Me a Tenor*	Robert Morse, *Tru*	Nigel Hawthorne, *Shadowlands*
Actress (Dramatic)	Pauline Collins, *Shirley Valentine*	Maggie Smith, *Lettice & Lovage*	Mercedes Ruehl, *Lost in Yonkers*
Featured Actor (Dramatic)	Boyd Gaines, *The Heidi Chronicles*	Charles Durning, *Cat on a Hot Tin Roof*	Kevin Spacey, *Lost in Yonkers*
Featured Actress (Dramatic)	Christine Baranski, *Rumors*	Margaret Tyzack, *Lettice & Lovage*	Irene Worth, *Lost in Yonkers*
Play	*The Heidi Chronicles*	*The Grapes of Wrath*	*Lost in Yonkers*
Actor (Musical)	Jason Alexander, *Jerome Robbins' Broadway*	James Naughton, *City of Angels*	Jonathan Pryce, *Miss Saigon*
Actress (Musical)	Ruth Brown, *Black and Blue*	Tyne Daly, *Gypsy*	Lea Salonga, *Miss Saigon*
Featured Actor (Musical)	Scott Wise, *Jerome Robbins' Broadway*	Michael Jeter, *Grand Hotel, the Musical*	Hinton Battle, *Miss Saigon*
Featured Actress (Musical)	Debbie Shapiro, *Jerome Robbins' Broadway*	Randy Graff, *City of Angels*	Daisy Eagan, *The Secret Garden*
Musical	*Jerome Robbins' Broadway*	*City of Angels*	*The Will Rogers Follies*
Director (Dramatic)	Jerry Zaks, *Lend Me a Tenor*	Frank Galati, *The Grapes of Wrath*	Jerry Zaks, *Six Degrees of Separation*
Director (Musical)	Jerome Robbins, *Jerome Robbins' Broadway*	Tommy Tune, *Grand Hotel, the Musical*	Tommy Tune, *The Will Rogers Follies*
Book (Musical)	—	Larry Gelbart, *City of Angels*	Marsha Norman, *The Secret Garden*
Score	—	Cy Coleman (Music); David Zippel (Lyrics), *City of Angels*	Cy Coleman (Music); Betty Comden and Adolph Green (Lyrics), *The Will Rogers Follies*
Scenic Designer	Santo Loquasto, *Cafe Crown*	Robin Wagner, *City of Angels*	Heidi Landesman, *The Secret Garden*
Costume Designer	Claudio Segovia, Hector Orezzoli, *Black and Blue*	Santo Loquasto, *Grand Hotel, the Musical*	Willa Kim, *The Will Rogers Follies*
Lighting Design	Jennifer Tipton, *Jerome Robbins' Broadway*	Jules Fisher, *Grand Hotel, the Musical*	Jules Fisher, *The Will Rogers Follies*
Choreographer	Cholly Atkins, Henry LeTang, Frankie Manning, Fayard Nicholas, *Black and Blue*	Tommy Tune, *Grand Hotel, the Musical*	Tommy Tune, *The Will Rogers Follies*
Reproduction of a Play or Musical	Lincoln Center Theater, Gregory Mosher, Bernard Gersten, producers, *Our Town*	Barry and Fran Weissler, Kathy Levin, Barry Brown, producers, *Gypsy*	Barry and Fran Weissler, Pace Theatrical Group, producers, *Fiddler on the Roof*

1992	1993	1994	1995
Judd Hirsch, *Conversations with My Father*	Ron Leibman, *Angels in America: Millennium Approaches*	Stephen Spinella, *Angels in America: Perestroika*	Ralph Fiennes, *Hamlet*
Glenn Close, *Death and the Maiden*	Madeline Kahn, *The Sisters Rosensweig*	Diana Rigg, *Medea*	Cherry Jones, *The Heiress*
Larry Fishburne, *Two Trains Running*	Stephen Spinella, *Angels in America: Millennium Approaches*	Jeffrey Wright, *Angels in America: Perestroika*	John Glover, *Love! Valour! Compassion!*
Brid Brennan, *Dancing at Lughnasa*	Debra Monk, *Redwood Curtain*	Iane Adams, *An Inspector Calls*	Frances Sternhagen, *The Heiress*
Dancing at Lughnasa	*Angels in America: Millennium Approaches*	*Angels in America: Perestroika*	*Love! Valour! Compassion!*
Gregory Hines, *Jelly's Last Jam*	Brent Carver, *Kiss of the Spider Woman—The Musical*	Boyd Gaines, *She Loves Me*	Matthew Broderick, *How to Succeed in Business Without Really Trying*
Faith Prince, *Guys and Dolls*	Chita Rivera, *Kiss of the Spider Woman—The Musical*	Donna Murphy, *Passion*	Glenn Close, *Sunset Boulevard*
Scott Waara, *The Most Happy Fella*	Anthony Crivello, *Kiss of the Spider Woman—The Musical*	Jarrod Emick, *Damn Yankees*	George Hearn, *Sunset Boulevard*
Tonya Pinkins, *Jelly's Last Jam*	Andrea Martin, *My Favorite Year*	Audra Ann McDonald, *Carousel*	Gretha Boston, *Show Boat*
Crazy for You	*Kiss of the Spider Woman—The Musical*	*Passion*	*Sunset Boulevard*
Patrick Mason, *Dancing at Lughnasa*	George C. Wolfe, *Angels in America: Millennium Approaches*	Stephen Daldry, *An Inspector Calls*	Gerald Gutierrez, *The Heiress*
Jerry Zaks, *Guys and Dolls*	Des McAnuff, *The Who's Tommy*	Nicholas Hynter, *Carousel*	Harold Prince, *Show Boat*
William Finn and James Lapine, *Falsettos*	Terrence McNally, *Kiss of the Spider Woman—The Musical*	James Lapine, *Passion*	Christopher Hampton and Don Black, *Sunset Boulevard*
William Finn, *Falsettos*	John Kander (Music), Fred Ebb (Lyrics), *Kiss of the Spider Woman—The Musical;* Pete Townshend (Music and Lyrics), *The Who's Tommy*	Stephen Sondheim, *Passion*	Andrew Lloyd Webber (music), Christopher Hampton and Don Black (lyrics), *Sunset Boulevard*
Tony Walton, *Guys and Dolls*	John Arnone, *The Who's Tommy*	Bob Crowley, *Carousel*	John Napier, *Sunset Boulevard*
William Ivey Long, *Crazy for You*	Florence Klotz, *Kiss of the Spider Woman—The Musical*	Ann Hould-Ward, *Beauty and the Beast*	Florence Klotz, *Show Boat*
Jules Fisher, *Jelly's Last Jam*	Chris Parry, *The Who's Tommy*	Rick Fisher, *An Inspector Calls*	Andrew Bridge, *Sunset Boulevard*
Susan Stroman, *Crazy for You*	Wayne Cilento, *The Who's Tommy*	Kenneth McMillan, *Carousel*	Susan Stroman, *Show Boat*
Dodger Productions, Roger Berlind, Jujamcyn Theaters/TV Asahi, Kardana Productions, John F. Kennedy Center for the Performing Arts, producers, *Guys and Dolls*	Roundabout Theatre Company, Todd Haimes, producers, *Anna Christie*	Noel Pearson, the Shubert Organization, Capital Cities/ABC, Joseph Harris, producers, *An Inspector Calls* (Dramatic); Lincoln Center Theater, Andre Bishop, Bernard Gersten, the Royal National Theater, Cameron Mackintosh, the Rodgers & Hammerstein Organization, producers, *Carousel* (Musical)	Lincoln Center Theater, Andre Bishop, Bernard Gersten, producers, *The Heiress* (Dramatic); Livent (U.S.) Inc., producer, *Show Boat* (Musical)

	1996	1997	1998
Actor (Dramatic)	George Grizzard, *A Delicate Balance*	Christopher Plummer, *Barrymore*	Anthony LaPaglia, *A View from the Bridge*
Actress (Dramatic)	Zoë Caldwell, *Master Class*	Janet McTeer, *A Doll's House*	Marie Mullen, *The Beauty Queen of Leenane*
Featured Actor (Dramatic)	Ruben Santiago-Hudson, *Seven Guitars*	Owen Teale, *A Doll's House*	Tom Murphy, *The Beauty Queen of Leenane*
Featured Actress (Dramatic)	Audra McDonald, *Master Class*	Lynne Thigpen, *An American Daughter*	Anna Manahan, *The Beauty Queen of Leenane*
Play	*Master Class*	*The Last Night of Ballyhoo*	*Art*
Actor (Musical)	Nathan Lane, *A Funny Thing Happened on the Way to the Forum*	James Naughton, *Chicago*	Alan Cumming, *Cabaret*
Actress (Musical)	Donna Murphy, *Passion*	Bebe Neuwirth, *Chicago*	Natasha Richardson, *Cabaret*
Featured Actor (Musical)	Wilson Jermain Heredia, *Rent*	Chuck Cooper, *The Life*	Ron Rifkin, *Cabaret*
Featured Actress (Musical)	Ann Duquesnay, *Bring in 'Da Noise, Bring in 'Da Funk*	Lillias White, *The Life*	Audra McDonald, *Ragtime*
Musical	*Rent*	*Titanic*	*The Lion King*
Director (Dramatic)	Gerald Gutierrez, *A Delicate Balance*	Anthony Page, *A Doll's House*	Garry Hynes, *The Beauty Queen of Leenane*
Director (Musical)	George C. Wolfe, *Bring in 'Da Noise, Bring in 'Da Funk*	Walter Bobbie, *Chicago*	Julie Taymor, *The Lion King*
Book (Musical)	Jonathan Larson, *Rent*	Peter Stone, *Titanic*	Terrence McNally, *Ragtime*
Score	Jonathan Larson, *Rent*	Maury Yeston, *Titanic*	Stephen Flaherty (music); Lynn Ahrens (lyrics), *Ragtime*
Scenic Designer	Brian Thomson, *The King and I*	Stewart Laing, *Titanic*	Richard Hudson, *The Lion King*
Costume Designer	Roger Kirk, *The King and I*	Judith Dolan, *Candide*	Julie Taymor, *The Lion King*
Lighting Designer	Jules Fisher and Peggy Eisenhauer, *Bring in 'Da Noise, Bring in 'Da Funk*	Ken Billington, *Chicago*	Donald Holder, *The Lion King*
Choreographer	Savion Glover, *Bring in 'Da Noise, Bring in 'Da Funk*	Ann Reinking, *Chicago*	Garth Fagan, *The Lion King*
Orchestration	—	Jonathan Tunick, *Titanic*	William David Brohn, *Ragtime*
Reproduction of a Play or Musical	Lincoln Center Theater, producer, *A Delicate Balance* (Dramatic); Dodger Productions, the John F. Kennedy Center for the Performing Arts, James M. Nederlander, Perseus Productions, John Frost, The Adelaide Festival Center, the Rodgers and Hammerstein Organization, producers, *The King and I* (Musical)	Bill Kenwright, Thelma Holt, producers, *A Doll's House* (Dramatic); Barry Weissler, Fran Weissler, Kardana Prods. Inc., producers, *Chicago* (Musical)	Roundabout Theater Co., Todd Haimes, Ellen Richard, Roger Berlind, James M. Nederlander, Nathaniel Kramer, Elizabeth Ireland McCann, Roy Gabay, Old Ivy Prods., producers, *A View from the Bridge* (Dramatic); Roundabout Theater Co., Todd Haimes, Ellen Richard, *Cabaret* (Musical)

1999

Brian Dennehy, *Death of a Salesman*

Judi Dench, *Amy's View*

Frank Wood, *Side Man*

Elizabeth Franz, *Death of a Salesman;* Claire Bloom, *Electra*

Side Man

Martin Short, *Little Me*

Bernadette Peters, *Annie Get Your Gun*

Roger Bart, *You're a Good Man, Charlie Brown*

Kristin Chenoweth, *You're a Good Man, Charlie Brown*

Fosse

Robert Falls, *Death of a Salesman*

Matthew Bourne, *Swan Lake*

Alfred Uhry, *Parade*

Jason Robert Brown, *Parade*

Richard Hoover, *Not About Nightingales*

Lez Brotherston, *Swan Lake*

Andrew Bridge, *Fosse*

Matthew Bourne, *Swan Lake*

Ralph Burns & Douglas Besterman, *Fosse*

Death of a Salesman (Dramatic); *Annie Get Your Gun* (Musical)

A POP CULTURE TIMELINE OF THE 20TH CENTURY

Here is a selective chronicle of the events and inventions, milestones and hallmarks, people and productions that have entertained us and changed life in our century.

1900

THE BROWNIE BOX CAMERA, the first consumer-oriented camera, is introduced by Eastman Kodak. It sells for $1.

PHILOSOPHER FRIEDRICH NIETZSCHE dies after 11 years of madness.

THE HOT DANCE around the nation is the cake walk, invented by African Americans in the late 18th century.

STAGE ACTRESS SARAH BERNHARDT, 56, makes her film debut in *Hamlet's Duel.* She plays Hamlet.

BOOKER T. WASHINGTON publishes his autobiography, *Up from Slavery.*

FERDINAND VON ZEPPELIN'S famous airship makes its first flight on July 20.

1901

VICTORIA, Queen of England and Ireland, and Empress of India, dies on January 22 at age 82, marking the end of the Victorian Era.

THE VICTOR TALKING MACHINE COMPANY is formed by Emile Berliner and Eldridge Johnson. "His Master's Voice" is the registered trademark for their gramophones, called Victrolas.

1902

BEATRIX POTTER creates the first of her legendary Peter Rabbit children's stories.

1903

THE GREAT TRAIN ROBBERY, starring Max Anderson, is released, marking the debut of the first male movie star.

THE WORLD SERIES is launched, pitting the winners of the National and the American Leagues against each other: this year, the Boston Red Stockings triumph over the Pittsburgh Pirates.

ORVILLE AND WILBUR WRIGHT fly the first powered, heavier-than-air airplane at Kitty Hawk, N.C., on December 17.

1904

HELEN KELLER graduates with honors from Radcliffe, thanks to years of devoted assistance from Anne Sullivan, who will go down in history as the Miracle Worker.

FREUD introduces the idea of neuroses in *The Psychopathology of Everyday Life,* his first major work on psychoanalysis.

THE TEDDY BEAR makes its debut. Created by the German Richard Sterb, it is inspired by President Theodore Roosevelt, who refused to kill a bear cub on a hunting trip.

1905

THE WORLD'S FIRST all-motion picture theater opens in Pittsburgh. The cost is 10¢ for a showing of *Poor But Honest.*

ALBERT EINSTEIN publishes his theory of the photoelectric effect, which is later essential in the development of the TV camera.

Sarah Bernhardt.

1906

Jelly Roll Morton at the piano.

FERDINAND "JELLY ROLL" MORTON, jazz's first great composer, writes "The King Porter Stomp."

THE SAN FRANCISCO EARTHQUAKE kills hundreds on April 18 and causes hundreds of millions of dollars in damage throughout the Bay Area as the city crashes and burns.

UPTON SINCLAIR publishes *The Jungle,* his exposé of the meat-packing industry, which prompts Congress to pass labor reform laws in addition to the Pure Food and Drug Act and the Meat Packing Act of 1906.

1907

FLORENZ ZIEGFELD offers his first version of the *Ziegfeld Follies,* an extravaganza that will continue for 24 years.

HENRY ADAMS'S masterful autobiography, *The Education of Henry Adams,* is published privately; the Nobel Prize for Biography will be awarded to Adams posthumously in 1919.

COLOR PHOTOGRAPHY becomes practical for the first time due to the development of a new method by the brothers Auguste and Louis Lumière.

THE FIRST MOTION PICTURE with both sound and color is shown in Cleveland.

THE RINGLING BROTHERS buy out their archrivals, Barnum and Bailey, although the two circuses will be operated separately until 1919.

1908

A L'ECU D'OR becomes the earliest dated pornographic film.

THE FIRST MODEL T, known as the Tin Lizzy, is produced on October 1 at Ford's Detroit plant.

THE FIRST COMMERCIAL COLOR FILM, G. A. Smith's *A Visit to the Seaside* (Britain), is released.

1909

ROLLER COASTERS become increasingly popular in amusement parks all over the country.

VITAGRAPH'S *Les Misérables* becomes the first feature film produced in the United States.

THE FIRST ANIMATED CARTOON, *Gertie the Dinosaur,* is released.

ROBERT EDWIN PEARY becomes the first person ever to reach the North Pole.

1910

AUTHOR MARK TWAIN (Samuel Longhorne Clemens) dies at 74.

Mark Twain.

THOMAS EDISON demonstrates his "kinetophone," which successfully displays talking motion pictures.

THE BOY SCOUTS OF AMERICA is founded by William D. Boyce, who takes his inspiration from the English program started by Sir Robert Baden-Powell.

T. S. ELIOT writes *Love Song of J. Alfred Prufrock* while a Harvard undergraduate; it becomes one of the seminal works of the Modernist movement when it is published in 1915.

1911

JEAN, Larry Trimble's pet collie, becomes the first canine star on the big screen. Hired by Vitagraph, she earns $10 more per week than Trimble earns as an actor-writer.

IRVING BERLIN writes "Alexander's Ragtime Band," melding the rhythms of black ragtime into American popular music.

1912

SEIZING ON A CRAZE that has millions of Americans doing the tango, the turkey trot, the hesitation waltz, and the one-step, Victor releases a series of recordings intended for dancing.

THE *TITANIC* sinks after hitting an iceberg on April 14, drowning 1,595 people.

ZANE GREY publishes his most famous Western, *Riders of the Purple Sage*.

THE FIRST BLUES SONG is published by W. C. Handy. Originally called "Memphis Blues," it becomes a hit as "Mr. Crump."

PERHAPS THE BEST ALL-AROUND ATHLETE in history, Native American track-and-field star Jim Thorpe dominates the Olympics, winning gold medals for both the pentathlon and the decathlon. But his medals are taken away from him when it is discovered that he played semi-pro baseball two years before.

STUNT FLYING becomes a staple across the country, taking a terrible toll on pioneering aviators.

1913

DUKE ELLINGTON writes his first song, "Soda Fountain Rag," at the age of 14.

BILLBOARD magazine publishes its first song-popularity chart by listing leading songs in vaudeville as well as bestselling sheet music.

THE FIRST CROSSWORD puzzle is published in the *New York World*.

1914

CHARLIE CHAPLIN creates the legendary Little Tramp in his second film, *Kid's Auto Races*.

BERT WILLIAMS, a popular vaudevillian, stars in *Darktown Jubilee*, one of the first movies to use an African American actor rather than white actors in blackface. The movie causes a riot in Brooklyn, N.Y.

THE TARZAN SAGA begins with the publication of *Tarzan of the Apes* by Edgar Rice Burroughs.

ASCAP—the American Society of Composers, Authors, and Publishers—is formed to empower artists to collect fees for the performances and use of their work.

THE PANAMA CANAL opens on May 18.

WORLD WAR I breaks out on July 28. One of the many consequences is that movie production outside of the United States will be suspended, allowing American filmmakers to dominate the industry.

1915

ALBERT EINSTEIN proposes the General Theory of Relativity.

AUDREY MUNSON reveals all as she becomes the first leading lady to appear on the screen nude in *Inspiration*.

MARGARET SANGER is jailed for writing about birth control in her book *Family Limitation*.

THE MOST FAMOUS MOVIE of the silent era, D. W. Griffith's *The Birth of a Nation*, opens in New York City to great success, but is bitterly criticized for its racism.

THE DIVINE Sarah Bernhardt finally faces what appears to be the end of her stage career when her leg is amputated at the age of 71; the next year, however, she stages what proves at last to be her final one-for-the-road, this time playing Portia in *The Merchant of Venice* with an artificial leg.

THE PROVINCETOWN PLAYERS are organized in Massa-chusetts and become the first to present the works of playwright Eugene O'Neill. The next year the group moves its already highly influential theater to New York where it begins the off-Broadway theater movement.

USING VACUUM TUBES, AT&T introduces long-distance service between New York and San Francisco.

THE MOVIE BUSINESS takes root in Hollywood, California, land of good weather and cheap labor. By 1915, half of all American films are made there.

1916

NOTORIOUS SIBERIAN MONK GRIGORY RASPUTIN is murdered. Rasputin had been a confidant and

Grigory Rasputin.

advisor to the Czarina after using his hypnotic powers to "cure" the Empress's heir, Alexis, of hemophilia.

TWO VERY DIFFERENT major American writers die—action-adventure writer Jack London, author of *Call of the Wild*, and expatriate novelist Henry James, author of *Portrait of a Lady*.

THE DADA MOVEMENT is founded in Zurich as an anti-art, anti-literature protest against the atrocities of the Great War.

1917

"THE DIXIE JAZZ BAND ONE-STEP" by Nick LaRocca's Original Dixieland Jazz Band, a group of white musicians, is the first jazz record to be released in the United States.

MATA HARI, a Dutch dancer, is executed by the French as a spy for Germany.

THE FIRST PULITZER PRIZES are awarded, in the categories of biography, history, and journalism. The award for drama is added the following year.

1918

PRESIDENT WOODROW WILSON proclaims his Fourteen Points for world peace; World War I comes to an end on November 11.

DAYLIGHT SAVINGS TIME is introduced in America.

1919

JACK DEMPSEY, known as the Manassa Mauler, wins the world heavyweight boxing championship.

Mata Hari.

1920

PROHIBITION begins with the enactment of the Eighteenth Amendment, which makes it illegal to produce, sell, or drink alcoholic beverages.

HERCULE POIROT is introduced in Agatha Christie's first novel, *The Mysterious Affair at Styles.*

MAMIE SMITH becomes the first African-American singer to record a vocal blues performance with "Crazy Blues."

THE NATION'S FIRST RADIO stations— KDKA, Pittsburgh and WWJ, Detroit— hit the airwaves.

1921

THE FIRST MISS AMERICA pageant is held on September 9, won by Margaret Gorman, Miss Washington, D.C.

READER'S DIGEST begins publication.

1922

THE FIRST 3-D feature film is released when Nat Deverich creates *Power of Love.*

NANOOK OF THE NORTH by Robert J. Flaherty is released and comes to be regarded as one of the greatest documentaries ever filmed.

THE TECHNICOLOR film process makes its initial successful run.

JAMES JOYCE'S *Ulysses* is published in Paris by the expatriate American Sylvia Beach; though one of the greatest novels of the century, it remains banned in the United States until December 6, 1933, when a judge rules that the book does not contain "the leer of a sensualist."

1923

LEE DEFOREST devises a method of recording sound directly on film. Producers utilize the technology to create vaudeville shorts.

THE COVERED WAGON, the first of the great Western epics, is released to huge success.

TIME magazine begins publication, providing the news in a flavorful, succinct format.

1924

STAGE LEGENDS Alfred Lunt and Lynn Fontanne first appear together as a team in a play called *The Guardsman.*

THE FIRST MILLION-SELLERS in America are instrumentals: Paul Whiteman's *Whispering* and Ben Selvin's *Dardanella.*

NATHAN LEOPOLD and Richard Loeb are tried for the "thrill killing" of 14-year-old Robert Franks; Clarence Darrow's pioneering insanity plea saves them from execution.

THE LITTLE ORPHAN ANNIE comic strip is created by Harold Gray.

1925

THE FIRST national spelling bee is held.

THE AGE OF THE CHARLESTON bounces into dancehalls across America.

THE NEW YORKER is founded on February 21, edited by Harold Ross. The first issue bears the image of Eustace Tilley, who will come to serve as the magazine's unofficial symbol and patriarch.

THE WSM BARN DANCE—renamed the *Grand Ole Opry* in 1928—premieres in November.

THE CLASSIC NOVEL of the Jazz Age, *The Great Gatsby* by F. Scott Fitzgerald, is published.

1926

TELEVISION is invented in Scotland by John Logie Baird, but the Depression and World War II stifle development of the industry until the '50s.

DEFORD BAILEY is the first African American musician to appear on Nashville's *Grand Ole Opry* show. He becomes nationally known as "The Harmonica Wizard,"

and remains a regular until 1941.

RUDOLPH VALENTINO, the most popular of all male silent film stars and a worldwide sex symbol, dies at age 31 of a ruptured appendix and a gastric ulcer.

Rudolph Valentino.

NBC RADIO is founded.

NEW YORK talks to London in the first successful transatlantic radiotelephone conversation.

MAE WEST writes and stars in a play called *Sex*; the performance that launches her

Mae West.

career as the greatest sex symbol of the era also inspires the police to close the show and sentence West to 10 days in a workhouse.

THE BOOK-OF-THE-MONTH CLUB is founded, the first of the mail-order book programs. The first offering is Sylvia Townsend Warner's novel, *Lolly Willowes.*

MINIATURE GOLF is introduced in Lookout Mountain, Tenn., and from there it expands to over 40,000 courses within three years.

THE SUN ALSO RISES, the classic novel of disillusionment in the postwar years, is written by Ernest Hemingway.

1927

THE AGE OF THE TALKIES arrives with the Warner Bros. release of the wildly successful film *The Jazz Singer,* starring Al Jolson.

THE FIRST CAR RADIOS are introduced.

CHARLES LINDBERGH makes the first nonstop solo flight across the Atlantic, from New York to Paris.

Charles Lindbergh and his famous plane.

1928

TELEVISION comes to a home in Schenectady, N.Y., and begins receiving regularly scheduled broadcasts, three afternoons a week, on its one and one-half-inch screen.

WOMEN COMPETE in the Olympics (in Amsterdam) for the first time.

AMELIA EARHART becomes the first woman to fly across the Atlantic Ocean when she lands in London.

MICKEY MOUSE debuts in Walt Disney's first cartoon, *Plane Crazy*. The public however, first meets him in *Steamboat Willie*, which is released before its progenitor.

1929

THE FIRST ACADEMY AWARDS are presented at the Hollywood Roosevelt Hotel in Los Angeles, May 16. Douglas Fairbanks Sr. presents all of the awards in five minutes. The first winner for Best Picture is the now-forgotten Clara Bow vehicle, *Wings*.

VIRGINIA WOOLF publishes her feminist classic, *A Room of One's Own*.

CBS (Columbia Broadcasting System) is founded by William S. Paley, age 27.

THE MUSEUM OF MODERN ART (MOMA) opens in New York with an exhibition of works by Cezanne, Gaugin, Seurat, and Van Gogh.

ON BLACK THURSDAY, October 24, the stock market crashes, abruptly beginning the transition from the Roaring Twenties to the Great Depression.

KODAK introduces 16mm color movie film.

1930

SINCLAIR LEWIS becomes the first American to win the Nobel Prize for Literature.

THE FIRST SUPERMARKET opens in Queens, N.Y., offering low prices, and a huge selection; it achieves tremendous success overnight.

THE HAYS OFFICE creates a production code to enforce self-censorship in the film business. **GRANT WOOD** paints *American Gothic*.

GARBO TALKS, in Eugene O'Neill's *Anna Christie*, her first speaking role.

Garbo poses.

1931

THE WORLD'S TALLEST BUILDING, the Empire State Building, is opened to the public. RCA and NBC install a TV transmitter atop the building.

AL "SCARFACE" CAPONE, all-time great American gangster, goes to jail for tax evasion.

THE WHITNEY MUSEUM, founded by sculptor and railroad heiress Gertrude Vanderbilt Whitney, opens in New York City.

SCRABBLE is invented by New York architect Alfred Butts, but the game is turned down by every manufacturer; not until 1948 is Scrabble widely distributed, and not until 1952 does word of mouth turn it into a bonanza.

1932

THE LINDBERGH BABY is kidnapped on May 1, only to be discovered dead 12 days later, after the parents pay a $50,000 ransom.

OF THEE I SING, a musical comedy written by George and Ira Gershwin with book by George S.

Kaufman and Morrie Ryskind, becomes the first musical to win a Pulitzer Prize.

BIG-TIME VAUDEVILLE begins its final fadeout as the last two-a-day show opens at the Palace on Broadway.

ECSTASY, in which Hedy Lamarr appears nude, becomes the first film in which a sexual experience is depicted.

FRANCES PERKINS becomes the first woman to hold a Cabinet post when she is appointed secretary of labor by Franklin Delano Roosevelt.

THE FIRST DRIVE-IN cinema is built in Camden, N.J., accommodating 400 cars, and opens with *Wife Beware*.

PRESIDENT ROOSEVELT holds the first Fireside Chat on March 12, a radio address to the entire nation.

PROHIBITION is repealed with the ratification of the 21st Amendment on December 5. The watering holes that soon cover the country—bars, saloons, cocktail lounges—have a new feature, the jukebox.

THE FIRST NATIONAL FOOTBALL LEAGUE championship playoff pits the Chicago Bears against the New York Giants on December 17. The Bears win, 23–21.

THE APOLLO THEATRE stages its first live show in Harlem.

BENNY GOODMAN begins his radio show *Let's Dance*, establishing himself as the "King of Swing."

JOHN DILLINGER, Public Enemy No. 1, is gunned down in chicago by FBI agents.

THE FEDERAL THEATRE PROJECT is instituted by Congress as part of the Works Progress Administration. An attempt to assist an ailing theater community hit badly by the Depression, it is disbanded in 1939.

BECKY SHARP, the first full-length color feature film, opens.

THE FIRST NIGHT BASEBALL game in the major leagues is played between the Cincinnati Reds and

the Philadelphia Phillies. Cincinnati wins, 2–1.

GEORGE AND DOROTHY GERSHWIN'S opera *Porgy and Bess* opens at Boston's Colonial Theater.

JESSE OWENS wins four gold medals in track events at the Berlin Olympics, infuriating German Chancellor Adolf Hitler,who preaches the mental and physical supremacy of Aryan whites over all other races.

MARGARET MITCHELL'S *Gone with the Wind*

is published, selling a million copies in six months and winning the Pulitzer Prize in 1937. It will be her only book.

FRANKLIN DELANO ROOSEVELT is reelected president in the greatest Democratic landslide ever, carrying 48 states.

EUGENE O'NEILL, the great American dramatist, is awarded the Nobel Prize for Literature.

Jesse Owens in gold-medal form.

1937

VENTRILOQUIST EDGAR BERGEN and Charlie McCarthy premiere on NBC. They will remain hugely popular with audiences when the show makes the move from radio to TV.

JOHN STEINBECK'S *Of Mice and Men* is published.

THE FIRST worldwide radio broadcast to be received in the United States brings us the coronation of King George VI of England on May 12.

1938

WALT DISNEY'S *Snow White and the Seven Dwarfs* tops the movie charts, making Disney internationally famous, and goes on to become an all-time classic.

OUR TOWN, by Thornton Wilder, is produced (and not in a high school theater). It wins a Pulitzer.

HEAVYWEIGHT BOXING champion Joe Louis defends his title with a first-round knockout of German boxer Max Schmeling, a Nazi hero who symbolizes the notion of Aryan superiority. His victory is viewed as a triumph both for African Americans and for democracy.

THE DIRIGIBLE *Hindenburg* bursts into flames as it lands in New Jersey on May

Joe Louis.

6, marking the virtual end of lighter-than-air transportation. Simultaneously, the first coast-to-coast radio broadcast is conducted by Herbert Morrison, who reports on the disaster.

THE RADIO PLAY *War of the Worlds* (based on the novel by H.G. Wells) is broadcast on October 30 by Orson Welles, causing widespread panic among listeners who believe its story of an invasion from Mars.

1939

THE FIRST GOLDFISH is swallowed by a Harvard undergrad, beginning a fad that quickly sweeps across the nation and sets off such variations on the theme as eating light bulbs and biting snakes' heads off.

MARIAN ANDERSON, world-famous African American contralto, is denied permission to sing in Washington D.C.'s Constitution Hall by the Daughters of the American Revolution. Undaunted, she is sponsored by Eleanor Roosevelt in a triumphant performance on the steps of the Lincoln Memorial in front of 75,000 fans.

ROBERT KANE creates the cartoon character Batman.

THE GOLDEN GATE Exposition is held in San Francisco.

LOU NOVA squares off against Max Baer in the first televised prizefight, direct from Yankee Stadium. Nova wins in 11 rounds.

RHETT BUTLER'S infamous declaration in the film version of *Gone with the Wind*, "Frankly, my dear, I don't give a damn," breaks the taboo against cursing in the movies.

AT THE NEW YORK WORLD'S FAIR thousands ogle RCA TV sets featuring a 12-inch screen reflected in a cabinet-lid mirror.

1940

RICHARD WRIGHT'S masterpiece, *Native Son*, is published to wide acclaim; it is later adapted for a successful Broadway run.

A WORKABLE COLOR TV is announced by Peter Goldmark, chief television engineer at CBS.

THE COTTON CLUB, Harlem's famous jazz nightclub, closes down.

CONGRESS passes the Selective Service Act, the first U.S. peacetime draft law ever.

1941

THE FIRST TV AD comes on the air, marking the advent of commercial television; the spot, for Bulova watches, lasts 10 seconds and costs the company $9.

PEARL HARBOR is bombed by Japan on December 7, a day of infamy that ushers the U.S. into World War II.

1942

RODGERS AND HAMMERSTEIN transform the musical comedy

with their production of *Oklahoma!*

PHYSICISTS John Atanasoff and Clifton Berry develop the first fully electronic computer.

CAPITOL RECORDS is launched by Glenn Wallichs, who invents the art of record promotion by sending copies of new record releases to prominent disc jockeys.

BING CROSBY releases "White Christmas," from the film *Holiday Inn,* and it becomes the biggest-selling song from a movie in history.

1943

FRANK LLOYD WRIGHT begins work on the Solomon R. Guggenheim Museum in New York. Founded in 1939 as the Museum of Non-Objective Painting, the building opens its doors in 1959.

GEORGE WASHINGTON CARVER, 81, dies in Tuskegee, Ala. Born into slavery, he developed inventive uses for peanuts, soybeans, and other traditional Southern crops, which proved to be a boon to agriculture in the region.

1944

BILLBOARD introduces the first country music charts, first called "Most-Played Juke Box Hillbilly Records" and then changed to "Folk Records" before being relabeled "Country & Western" in 1949.

PAPER SHORTAGES during World War II force the publishing business to experiment with softcover bindings for its books, with stunning success.

1945

SMELL-O-VISION is created by Swiss inventor Hans E. Laube, who develops a "smell pack" that is stimulated by TV waves to produce an odor to accompany what is being shown on the screen.

WORLD WAR II comes to an end. Germany surrenders on May 8 (V-E Day). The only atomic bombs ever to be used in war are dropped by the U.S. on Hiroshima on August 6 and Nagasaki three days later, leading to the surrender of Japan on August 15 (V-J Day).

1946

DR. BENJAMIN SPOCK revolutionizes the way Americans raise their families with his *Common Sense Book of Baby and Child Care.*

WINSTON CHURCHILL coins the term "iron curtain" in a speech at Westminster College in Missouri.

THE U.S. detonates a nuclear bomb on Bikini Atoll on July 5 in the South Pacific. Five days later, designer Louis Reard commemorates the blast at a fashion show in Paris, where a certain itsy-bitsy, teeny-weeny two-piece bathing suit makes its first appearance.

THE CANNES FILM FESTIVAL premieres in September.

THE FIRST TV SOAP OPERA, *Faraway Hill,* debuts on the DuMont network.

CONSUMERS RUSH to buy the new 10-inch RCA TV set for $375. This "Model T of television" ushers in the TV age.

1947

THE POLAROID Land camera is patented by Dr. Edwin Land,

providing prints that develop inside the camera within a minute. It enters the market the following year, selling for $90.

JACKIE ROBINSON becomes the first African American to sign with a major-league baseball team. His first game with the Brooklyn Dodgers is an exhibition game against the New York Yankees.

NBC'S *KRAFT TELEVISION THEATRE* introduces serious drama. Overnight, cheese sales soar and Madison Avenue melts.

FLYING SAUCER! The first sighting is reported on June 25, according to one source.

THE WORLD SERIES is broadcast on TV for the first time and four million baseball fans watch the New York Yankees and the Brooklyn Dodgers battle it out. The Yanks go on to win the series.

THE FIRST ANTOINETTE PERRY (TONY) AWARDS for excellence in theater are handed out. No best play award is included, but José Ferrer wins as Best Actor, and Best Actress awards go to Ingrid Bergman and Helen Hayes.

THE TRANSISTOR is invented by Bell

Telephone Laboratories; it becomes one of the most significant advances in the history of consumer electronics, paving the way for miniature TV sets, radios, and gear like CD players that haven't yet been invented.

1948

TED MACK'S *THE ORIGINAL AMATEUR HOUR* premieres in January. By year's end the first "ratings sweep" declares it the most popular show on TV.

THE PHONOGRAPH RECORDING market is fraught with competition as companies come up with improvements on the old 78 rpm disks. Columbia introduces the first long-playing commercial record, the 33⅓ rpm disk, and RCA releases the 45.

LEE STRASBERG takes over the Actors Studio, introducing the Method acting techniques that will profoundly influence such students as Marlon Brando, Paul Newman, James Dean, and Marilyn Monroe.

THE MOTORCYCLE CLAN Hell's Angels is formed.

THE ED SULLIVAN SHOW premiers to an initially poor viewer response. The influential variety program will stay on the air until 1971.

THE TERM "COLD WAR" is popularized by a speech before the Senate War Investigation Committee.

TV SET SALES skyrocket, with an estimated 250,000 sets installed every month.

NORMAN MAILER'S first novel, *The Naked and the Dead*, comes out. It remains one of the most important fictional works about World War II.

1949

CHIC YOUNG'S *BLONDIE* is the most popular comic strip in the world.

THE FIRST CABLE television systems go into homes.

ARTHUR MILLER'S play *Death of a Salesman*, the first dramatic tragedy to feature a common man as a protagonist, wins a Pulitzer Prize.

UNERRING *CRUSADER RABBIT* debuts as the first made-for-TV animated cartoon.

1950

GWENDOLYN BROOKS is the first African American to win a Pulitzer Prize, for her work *Annie Allen*.

MCCARTHYISM begins in February when the obscure U.S. senator Joseph McCarthy alleges that the federal government is infested with Communists.

GOOD OL' CHARLIE BROWN enters American culture as Charles Schulz creates the legendary comic strip *Peanuts*.

TELEVISION takes it first late-night variety plunge with *Broadway Open House*, and "dumb blonde" Dagmar (Jennie Lewis) becomes the first boob-tube sex symbol.

THE FIRST AMERICAN TROOPS land in Korea on July 1 after soldiers from North Korea invade South Korea. Although the move is described as a United Nations action, American soldiers comprise the vast majority of foreign troops. With news footage being aired on American TVs, it is also the first living-room war.

HOLLYWOOD buys its first million-dollar property: Columbia

acquires the rights to the successful Broadway play *Born Yesterday* from the writer Garson Kanin.

A. C. NIELSEN begins gathering ratings data for TV, employing electronic viewing records along with written logs to determine the popularity of shows.

BELL LABORATORIES and Western Electric create the first telephone answering machine.

THE SITCOM laugh track is introduced on *The Hank McCune Show*, a program that has the added distinction of being canceled midseason.

THE FIRST CREDIT CARD is introduced through the Diners Club.

THE CISCO KID, starring Duncan Renaldo and Leo Carillo, is the first TV series filmed in color. At the time, there are fewer than 100 experimental sets in the U.S.

THE 1949 NOBEL PRIZE for Literature is retroactively awarded to William Faulkner. No prize had been awarded the previous year because none of the candidates had won a majority of the votes.

1951

PAY-PER-VIEW dies a premature death after Zenith begins testing its "Phonevision" in Chicago. Viewers can dial a phone number and watch a recent feature film for $1. But skittish movie studios decide not to make first-run films available, fearing the consequences.

SENATE HEARINGS on organized crime rivet the nation. Mobster Frank Costello allows only his hands to be shown.

UNIVAC I, the first commercially built computer, goes into operation at the Census Bureau in Philadelphia.

CBS broadcasts the first commercial color telecast on June 25 with a one-hour special from New York to four other cities.

NBC begins the first network coast-to-coast programming.

AMOS 'N' ANDY bows with TV's first all-black cast. Though canceled in 1953, reruns air until 1966, when protests about racial stereotyping force withdrawal of the show from syndication.

I LOVE LUCY debuts to tremendous success,

creating the mold for TV sitcoms.

CLEVELAND DJ Alan Freed, the first to introduce black R&B to a white audience on station WJW, coins the term "rock and roll."

CBS debuts its "unblinking eye," which evolves into TV's most famous logo.

GIAN CARLO MENOTTI'S *Amahl and the Night Visitors* becomes the first made-for-TV opera on Christmas Eve. It becomes a perennial seasonal favorite.

1952

THE REVISED STANDARD edition of the Old Testament, only the third authorized Protestant revision in 341 years, becomes a No. 1 bestseller and sets records by selling 1.6 million copies in eight weeks; the old record was held by *Gone with the Wind,* which sold 1 million books in six months.

THE MOUSETRAP, originally a play created by Agatha Christie for the 80th birthday of Britain's Queen Mary, premieres in London. It will become the longest-

running theatrical work of all time.

MAD **MAGAZINE** and the *National Enquirer* make their debuts.

UNIDENTIFIED FLYING OBJECTS capture the imagination of Americans. No longer looked on as simply science fiction, the national fascination with UFOs even prompts the U.S. Air Force to publish possible photographs of the phenomena.

THE FIRST HYDROGEN BOMB is detonated on November 1, and Americans' fear of complete annihilation intensifies.

BWANA DEVIL leads a resurgence of popularity for 3-D movies, Hollywood's attempt to combat the appeal of "free" TV.

PANTY RAIDS occur in epic proportions at college sororities across the nation.

TWO OF TELEVISION'S biggest all-time hits—*Today,* hosted by Dave Garroway, and *Guiding Light*—begin broadcasting on NBC and CBS, respectively; both programs are still going strong today.

THE MARILYN MONROE image crystallizes with four film releases, helping movie theaters draw

Marilyn Monroe.

Americans away from their TV sets.

ART LINKLETTER tosses a *House Party* on September 1, and the bash lasts longer (17 years) than any daytime variety show.

VEEP HOPEFUL Richard Nixon makes a politician's first direct TV appeal on September 23, citing his dog, Checkers, in his successful quest to beat fund-misuse charges and save his career.

CHRISTINE JORGENSON returns from Denmark where she had undergone the first publicized sex-change operation.

1953

I LOVE LUCY features the birth of Little Ricky on January 19 as the real Lucille Ball gives birth to Desi Arnaz Jr. The landmark show draws a 92 percent share of TV sets in use, or 44 million viewers—a record to date. Turns out the "dual birth" was no happy accident, since Desi Junior was born by a scheduled caesarean section. The event received more media attention than Dwight Eisenhower's inauguration, which took place the following day. Eisenhower and Nixon form the first Republican administration in 24 years.

DESI JR. scores again when the first issue of *TV Guide* is published, featuring him on the cover.

AT AGE 27, Queen Elizabeth II is crowned as England's monarch.

JULIUS AND ETHEL ROSENBERG are executed, the only American civilians ever to receive such a penalty for espionage.

THE DISC JOCKEY Top 40 radio format is established on KOWH, an Omaha station. It features a limited number of records played over and over, hourly news breaks, and sporadic chatter from the announcer.

CINEMASCOPE premieres with *The Robe,* and its wide-screen format becomes a huge hit with filmgoers.

***PLAYBOY* MAGAZINE** is founded by 27-year-old Hugh Hefner with a first issue featuring the nude Marilyn Monroe on its cover.

THE FIRST ROCK AND ROLL song hits the Billboard charts: Bill Haley and His Comets' "Crazy, Man, Crazy."

THE RCA compatible color television is approved by the FCC and becomes the industry standard.

HOUSTON'S KUHT debuts as the country's first noncommercial educational TV station; within 10 years there will be 75 other such stations.

Hugh Hefner.

inspiring a groundswell of support for the senator's critics and ultimately precipitating his downfall.

SEGREGATION in schools is declared unconstitutional on May 14 in the landmark case, *Brown vs. Board of Education.*

ELVIS PRESLEY cuts his first record, the double-sided 45 "That's All Right (Mama)"/"Blue Moon of Kentucky."

THE FIRST COLOR TV sets and the first

transistor radios are marketed.

TONIGHT!, later known as *The Tonight Show,* premieres with Steve Allen as host.

SWANSON brings out the very first TV dinners—ominously, turkey—for 69¢.

1954

MARILYN MONROE marries former New York Yankees star Joe DiMaggio, a second marriage for both. Alas, the match is not meant to be—Marilyn files for divorce nine months later.

TELEVISION JOURNALIST Edward R. Murrow launches the first major attack on Joseph McCarthy's witch-hunt tactics on CBS's *See It Now,*

1955

CONTRALTO MARIAN ANDERSON becomes the first African American to sing a major role at the Metropolitan Opera, appearing as Ulrica in Verdi's *Masked Ball.*

A NEW ERA in domestic politics is launched with the first filmed presidential press conference. Both TV and motion picture newsreel photographers cover the event.

Elvis Presley.

WALT DISNEY'S TV show, *Disneyland*, first appears on ABC and quickly becomes one of the most successful programs on the tube. One segment, "Davy Crockett, Indian Fighter," instigates a full-blooded Davy Crockett mania, which sweeps the country. Over 3,000 Crockett-related items sell in crazy numbers, from coonskin caps to Bill Hayes's song "Ballad of Davy Crockett," which rises to the top of the charts.

ANN LANDERS launches her advice column in the *Chicago Sun-Times*.

BILL HALEY and His Comets' "Rock Around the Clock" goes to No. 1 on *Billboard*'s charts on June 6, marking the indisputable ascent of rock and roll.

DISNEYLAND, the first theme amusement park, opens south of Los Angeles in Anaheim.

JAMES DEAN stars in *Rebel Without a Cause,* his second and penultimate starring role before crashing his Porsche later in the year and dying at age 26. His death gives rise to his enduring status as a cult hero, embodying the spirit of rebelliousness so sought after by America's younger generation.

BOB KEESHAN debuts as the Captain on *Captain Kangaroo,* which goes on to become the longest-running kids' show. *The Mickey Mouse Club* begins as well.

IN ONE OF THE greatest record deals of all time, RCA buys Elvis's contract—for an unprecedented $40,000—from Sam Phillips's Sun Records.

COMIC BOOK popularity reaches unprecedented heights, with sales soaring beyond a billion copies. Concern over their violent content increases in due measure, prompting New York State to ban the sale of certain graphic comics to minors.

1956

ACTOR GRACE KELLY retires from Hollywood and marries Prince Rainier III of Monaco, a member of the thousand-year-old Grimaldi dynasty, in one of the most publicized marriages of the century.

BEAT POET ALAN GINSBERG'S *"Howl" and Other Poems* is released and its publisher is promptly brought up on obscenity charges that are later successfully defended in court.

MARILYN MONROE weds husband No. 3, Pulitzer- and Tony Award-winning playwright Arthur Miller (it's his second marriage). The two are divorced in 1961.

DEAN MARTIN and Jerry Lewis are a team no more. They split on July 25, exactly 10 years after they first appeared together in Atlantic City.

NBC'S Huntley and Brinkley are TV's first co-anchors: "Goodnight, Chet." "Goodnight, David."

IN HIS FIRST YEAR OF stardom, Elvis releases "Don't Be Cruel"/ "Hound Dog," a 45 that becomes the biggest hit of all time on *Billboard*'s charts. His appearance on Ed Sullivan's *Toast of the Town* on September 9, shot discreetly above the pelvis, earns the highest rating for any regularly scheduled program, drawing an estimated audience of 50 million people. He also appears in his first movie, *Love Me Tender.*

1957

LEONARD BERNSTEIN is named the first American musical director of the New York Philharmonic.

Slick Jerry Lee Lewis.

JERRY LEE LEWIS scandalizes the nation when he marries his 13-year-old cousin, Myra Gale Brown—also committing bigamy by failing to divorce wife, Jane Mitcham.

BOBBY FISCHER, 14, wins the U.S. chess championship.

THE HULA HOOP is introduced and takes America by storm, selling over 45 million by 1958.

DICK CLARK'S *American Bandstand* moves from a local Philadelphia station to its national debut on ABC. It becomes TV's longest-running variety show.

THE SOVIET UNION launches *Sputnik*, and the space race.

LEAVE IT TO BEAVER debuts on CBS, presenting the audience with the most typically American family to date.

THE NAT "KING" COLE SHOW, the first major series with an African American host, is canceled after a year, for lack of a national sponsor.

1958

ALVIN AILEY founds the American Dance Theatre.

BILLBOARD begins its Hot 100 chart; the first No. 1 record is "Poor Little Fool" by Ricky Nelson.

VLADIMIR NABOKOV'S sensational novel *Lolita* is published by Putnam after being rejected as too obscene by four other American publishers.

DEEJAYS AT ST. LOUIS' KWK radio station complete their "Record Breaking Week" when, at the insistence of the management, "undesirable" records are given a final play on the airwaves and then ceremoniously destroyed. Most of the sacrificed recordings are of rock and roll music.

SCIENTISTS at the ESSO Gas Research Center—now EXXON—announce on July 28 that they have found that drivers waste gas when they listen to rock and roll because they tend to jiggle the pedals in time with the beat.

VAN CLIBURN becomes the first American to win a gold medal at the Tchaikovsky International Piano Festival. His subsequent recording of the composer's *Piano Concerto No. 1* is the first classical record to go gold.

THE BROOKLYN DODGERS and the New York Giants move to California, bringing major-league baseball to the West Coast.

THE GRAMMY AWARDS are launched. Ignoring the rising predominance of rock and roll, the organizers present Best Album of the Year to Henry Mancini and name "Volaré" by Domenico Modugno as Best Song.

QUIZ SHOW scandals erupt with an initial investigation of answer-feeding on a program called *Dotto* prompted by a complaint by contestant Eddie Hilgemeier. By the end of the year most quiz shows are pulled off the air.

1959

BUDDY HOLLY, Ritchie Valens, and The Big Bopper are tragically killed in February when their single-engine light aircraft crashes in a snow-storm about 10 minutes after takeoff.

BARBIE is introduced to the toy world, created by Ruth and Elliot Handler, who founded Mattel in 1945. The doll's proportions, if copied on a human scale, would be 33-18-28. Barbie was named for the Handlers' daughter, Barbara, just as their son, Ken, was later honored when his parents created a male companion doll.

ISLAND IN THE SUN, starring James Mason, Dorothy Dandridge, Harry Belafonte, and Joan Fontaine, becomes the first film to portray interracial romance.

THE U.S. POSTMASTER GENERAL bans *Lady Chatterley's Lover* by D. H. Lawrence, but sales skyrocket after courts hold that the book is not obscene.

AMERICANS SEE THE WORLD from a new perspective as *Explorer VI* sends down the first photograph of Earth taken from outer space.

THE TELEPHONE-BOOTH JAMMING fad hits this year and fades almost as quickly. The fad first catches hold on the West Coast and moves quickly across the country, the record being set with 32 squashed students at Modesto Junior College in California.

MOTOWN RECORDS is founded in Detroit by songwriter Berry Gordy Jr.

IS TELEVISION KING? In December, for the first time, TV rings up more in commercial sales ($1.24 billion) than Hollywood cashes in box-office receipts ($1.235 billion).

1960

ELVIS PRESLEY'S army career, which began in March of 1958, comes to a close.

A CONGRESSIONAL investigation into payola determines that radio deejays have been receiving payments from record companies to play their disks. Dick Clark and Alan Freed are the particular focus of allegations, and Freed eventually loses his job.

SMELL-O-VISION hits theaters as Michael

Todd Jr.'s film *Scent of Mystery* is released to general indifference.

Master director Alfred Hitchcock.

PSYCHO, directed by Alfred Hitchcock, sets new movie attendance records and earns a mint as one of the most frightening films ever made.

THE TWIST is introduced by 19-year-old Chubby Checker.

BEN-HUR collects a record 11 Oscars out of 12 nominations.

THE FANTASTICKS debuts May 3. It will become the longest-running off-Broadway show ever, hitting its 14,000th performance on March 2, 1994—and still going strong at the Sullivan Street Playhouse in Greenwich Village. Since its beginning, notable performers have included Kevin Kline, Richard Chamberlain, and Jerry Orbach.

THE FLINTSTONES debuts as prime time's first animated sitcom.

BIRTH CONTROL PILLS become available for widespread use as the FDA approves the public sale of Enovid at $10 to $11 for a month's supply.

1961

THE FIRST FRENCH KISS on the Hollywood big screen takes place between Natalie Wood and Warren Beatty in *Splendor in the Grass.*

SOPRANO LEONTYNE PRICE, 34, debuts at New York's Metropolitan Opera House in *Il Trovatore* and receives a 45-minute ovation.

BOB DYLAN gives his first solo performance, opening for blues musician John Lee Hooker in New York City's Gerde's Folk City.

ABC'S WIDE WORLD OF SPORTS with Jim McKay is introduced and runs on Saturday afternoons, showing us "the thrill of victory and the agony of defeat."

ALAN B. SHEPARD JR. becomes the first American astronaut

Jacqueline Kennedy lights up the White House.

to go into space on May 5.

SATURDAY NIGHT AT THE MOVIES debuts as the first regular TV showcase for major motion pictures.

1962

JACQUELINE KENNEDY takes the country on a televised tour of the White House.

THE FIRST USE OF NUDITY in advertising appears in *Harper's Bazaar* in a bare-breasted photo by Richard Avedon.

THE FIRST JAMES BOND movie, *Dr. No,* is released. Starring as

007 is Sean Connery, 32.

DIRECT-DIAL long-distance telephone service begins in the United States.

MARILYN MONROE dies of a barbiturate overdose at age 36 on August 5.

THE VIRGINIAN makes its debut as the first 90-minute TV series. In a nine-year run, its cast includes Lee Majors, David Hartman, and Lee J. Cobb as a frontier judge.

JOHNNY CARSON takes over *The Tonight Show* where he will reign as King of Television until he retires in 1992.

1963

WEIGHT WATCHERS enters the market, turning dieting into big business.

POP ART is given its first major show at the Guggenheim Museum in New York. Artists include Andy Warhol, Jasper Johns, and Roy Lichtenstein.

BETTY FRIEDAN publishes her landmark feminist tract, *The Feminine Mystique*.

JULIA CHILD bubbles up on *The French Chef* and becomes public TV's first star; she'll keep TV cooking for the next 10 years.

WHISKEY A-GO-GO opens in Los Angeles, beginning its tenure as Hollywood's longest-lived club devoted to cutting-edge rock music.

THE BEATLES release their first single in the U.S., "Please Please Me," in February along with their LP *Introducing The Beatles*.

CLEOPATRA, with Elizabeth Taylor and Richard Burton, scores as both the top money-maker of the year and one of the biggest flops in movie history as its vast costs far overrun its huge budget; Tay-

lor alone receives $1.75 million for her participation.

PEBBLES FLINTSTONE is born to parents Wilma and Fred on February 22 at the Bedrock Rockapedia Hospital.

TROLLS are introduced. Billed as good-luck charms, their ugliness is a charm indeed, producing sales in the millions.

THE FUGITIVE debuts September 17; David Janssen runs. He'll catch the one-armed man—and a then record prime-time audience—in the '67 finale. That episode still ranks as the third-most-watched episode of a television series ever.

PRESIDENT JOHN F. KENNEDY, 46, is assassinated in

Elizabeth Taylor as Cleopatra.

Dallas on November 22. The immediacy of television's coverage of the surrounding events transforms TV into a witness to history and binds together a nation in mourning.

1964

FIVE THOUSAND SCREAMING FANS greet The Beatles at Kennedy Airport in New York on February 7, when the band arrives for its first American tour. Two days later the Fab Four appear on *The Ed Sullivan Show*. They draw an estimated 75 percent of all TV viewers, making it the most-watched hour of television to date. Songs include "All My Loving," "She Loves You," and "I Want To Hold Your Hand."

THE MOOG, the first commercial music synthesizer, is developed.

ELIZABETH TAYLOR finally meets her match, again, as she marries husband No. 5, Richard Burton, just 10 days after getting a divorce from Eddie Fisher. The two had met on the set of *Cleopatra*.

THE HOME VIDEO RECORDER is invented in Japan by the Sony Corporation.

MARSHALL MCLUHAN declares that the "medium is the message" in his book *Understanding Media*. Nobody gets it, but everybody talks about it.

LYNDON B. JOHNSON'S "daisy" campaign spot airs once on September 7, suggesting that Republican opponent Goldwater is nuke-happy. Fallout: LBJ wins in a landslide.

PEYTON PLACE airs September 15 as the first prime-time soap and becomes a smash hit.

G.I. JOE is introduced by Hasbro and sells for $4.

MARTIN LUTHER KING JR. receives the Nobel Peace Prize. Jean-Paul Sartre is awarded the Nobel Prize for Literature and becomes the first person to reject the honor.

1965

SOUPY SALES asks his loyal young viewers to send him "those little green pieces of paper" from dad's wallet, "and I'll send you a postcard from

Puerto Rico." The January 1 stunt draws a big enough response to get Sales suspended by the station, but viewers protest and he is reinstated.

BELL-BOTTOMS grace the nation's hips, and lava lamps make a splash, selling 2.5 million units this year alone.

THE FIRST AMERICAN COMBAT TROOPS not deployed in an advisory capacity land in South Vietnam, turning a local conflict into an undeclared large-scale international war.

THE NATIONAL ENDOWMENT for the Arts and Humanities is established by Congress.

"(I CAN'T GET NO) SATISFACTION," the classic Rolling Stones tune, becomes a No. 1 hit in the United States, sealing the British invasion as one of the dominant musical developments of the decade.

THE BEATLES play before 55,000 fans at New York's Shea Stadium on August 15 to open their third U.S. tour.

THE SOUND OF MUSIC is released, eventually overtaking *Gone With the Wind* to rank for a time as the top box-office earner ever.

GO-GO DANCING and its accompanying little white boots quickly wax and then wane in popularity among discotheque goers.

CINEMA'S 34-year rule against nudity is broken when a scene in *The Pawnbroker* is approved by the ratings board as essential to the plot.

CBS AND NBC adopt virtually all-color formats starting with the fall season.

BILL COSBY becomes the first African American TV star, in *I Spy*.

SONY introduces the first commercial home video tape recorder. The size of an overnight bag, it costs $995.

1966

"YESTERDAY," the most recorded song in the history of popular music, is released by Paul McCartney in the first solo by a Beatle. The record label, however, still reads "Beatles."

CINEMA'S BLUE LANGUAGE ban finally falls with *Who's Afraid of Virginia Woolf?*

THE SUPREMES become the first female group to top the U.S. album chart with *Supremes a Go Go.*

JOHN LENNON makes his most infamous remark on August 5 by saying that he and his Beatles bandmembers are "more popular than Jesus." Subsequently radio stations across the country take Beatles songs off the air.

LSD is pulled off the market by its manufacturer, Sandoz Pharmaceuticals, after being banned by the government in response to controversy over the hallucinogen's recreational uses.

STAR TREK is launched in September 8 and remains on the air until 1969. It will become one of the few series to be more popular in syndication than in its network run.

"PAUL IS DEAD." For those who believe, November 9 marks the date of the Beatle's supposed decapitation.

STEREO CASSETTE TAPE RECORDERS are introduced, a breakthrough for tape cartridges.

1967

THE FIRST SUPER BOWL is held on January 15, broadcast in color on both CBS and NBC; setting a model for future contests, the Green Bay Packers defeat the Kansas City Chiefs in a lopsided game, 35–10.

THE BLACK PANTHER PARTY is founded in Oakland by Huey Newton and Bobby Seale.

OTIS REDDING, 26, dies in a plane crash in December. One month later, his biggest hit, the chart-topping "Sittin' on the Dock of the Bay," is released.

ELVIS PRESLEY weds Priscilla Beaulieu on May 1 at the Aladdin Hotel in Las Vegas.

THE MONTEREY INTERNATIONAL POP FESTIVAL in California features such performers as Janis Joplin, Jimi Hendrix, and the Grateful Dead.

RIOTING breaks out in Detroit as racial tension builds; over 17,000 people are arrested in what proves to be the worst U.S. riot of the century.

FOLKSINGER PETE SEEGER is finally allowed to appear on

TV (on *The Smothers Brothers Comedy Hour*) after having been blacklisted for 17 years for his leftist politics.

HAIR has its off-Broadway premiere at the Public Theatre in New York.

ROLLING STONE magazine begins publication under the direction of 21-year-old Jann Wenner.

PRESIDENT LYNDON B. JOHNSON signs a law insuring federal support for public TV, and the Corporation for Public Broadcasting is created.

THE FIRST WITH SO-CALLED SPAGHETTI WESTERN, Sergio Leone's *A Fistful of Dollars*, is released in the United States. Filmed in 1964, it stars Clint Eastwood.

INTERRACIAL ROMANCE unfolds on TV as Mia and Paul fall for each other on *Love Is a Many Splendored Thing*.

BOXER MUHAMMAD ALI is stripped of his heavyweight title after refusing to serve in the army during the Vietnam War.

THE FIRST HUMAN HEART TRANSPLANT is performed by Dr. Christiaan Barnard in South Africa on Louis Washkansky, who lives for 18 days.

Martin Luther King Jr. giving his famous "I have a dream" speech in Washington, D.C.

MAO TSE-TUNG'S QUOTATIONS, better known as the Red Book, is the biggest-selling read in the world this year.

1968

CARDIGAN-CARRYING MISTER ROGERS opens his Neighborhood February 19, beginning a 27-year run that will establish a PBS record.

MOVIE RATINGS are introduced by the Motion Picture Association of America. The original classifications are G, M (mature audience), R, and X. M is changed to GP two years later, and then PG (parental guidance) a year after that. PG-13 is invented in 1984 as the result of a dispute over the vio-

lence in *Gremlins* and *Indiana Jones and the Temple of Doom*, and in 1990 the nefarious X is replaced by NC-17.

ARTHUR CLARKE and Stanley Kubrick's *2001: A Space Odyssey* is released, introducing the evil computer, Hal, an antihero who becomes a cultural icon.

THE EARLIEST-KNOWN HEIDI scandal: With 50 seconds left and the New York Jets leading the Oakland Raiders, NBC cuts from the game to the movie *Heidi*. The Raiders go on to win by scoring two touchdowns in nine seconds.

CIVIL RIGHTS LEADER Martin Luther King Jr. is assassinated on April 4 at age 39 on the balcony outside of his motel room in

Memphis, Tenn. Many American cities erupt in riots.

ROBERT F. KENNEDY, 42, is assassinated June 5 by Sirhan Sirhan in a Los Angeles hotel after winning the California presidential primary. In response, David Crosby writes "A Long Time Coming."

AT THE SUMMER OLYMPIC GAMES in Mexico City, American runners Tommy Smith and John Carlos give the black power salute as they receive their gold and bronze medals, resulting in their suspension from competition.

PRESIDENTIAL CANDIDATE Richard Nixon appears on *Laugh-In* and says, "Sock it to me!"

JULIA, premiering September 17, is the first TV series to star a black woman in a non-menial role as Diahann Carroll plays a nurse who is also a single parent.

MIKE WALLACE and Harry Reasoner start grilling as *60 Minutes* starts ticking on September 24; the news program will eventually top the ratings.

1969

THE BEATLES stage their last public performance on January 30 from a rooftop in London.

JIM MORRISON, lead singer for The Doors, is arrested for lewd and lascivious behavior after exposing himself at a concert in Miami.

DIANA ROSS invites 350 special guests to the trendy Daisy Club in Beverly Hills to see the new Motown act, The Jackson Five.

JOHN LENNON and Yoko Ono tie the knot on Gibraltar March 20.

THE FIRST FULL-FRONTAL male nudity appears in film with Alan Bates and Oliver Reed in Ken Russell's *Women in Love.*

THE ALTAMONT FESTIVAL—starring such acts as The Rolling Stones, Santana, Jefferson Airplane, and Crosby, Stills, Nash & Young—is struck by tragedy when the Hell's Angels security force beats to death an 18-year-old boy.

CAST MEMBERS of the play *Oh! Calcutta!* are arrested for indecent exposure in Los Angeles.

THE SUPREME COURT rules that laws prohibiting the private possession of obscene material by adults are unconstitutional.

PRINCE CHARLES is officially titled Prince of Wales.

UPON WALKING ON THE MOON on July 20, Neil Armstrong proclaims, "That's one small step for a man, one giant leap for mankind."

ACTRESS SHARON TATE, wife of director Roman Polanski, is found murdered along with four others—victims of Charles Manson's cult, known as The Family. Although not present at the house that night, would-be rock musician and psychopath Manson is convicted of the grisly killings and imprisoned.

THE WOODSTOCK Music and Art Festival is held August 15–17 in upstate New York. Playing before an audience of around 400,000, featured performers include The Who, Grateful Dead, Janis Joplin, Joe Cocker, Santana, Jimi Hendrix, Jefferson Airplane, and Crosby, Stills, Nash & Young.

SESAME STREET debuts, starring Big Bird, Oscar, Bert,

Jimi Hendrix.

Ernie, Cookie Monster, Grover, and Kermit; it marks a radical breakthrough for children's TV programming.

TINY TIM marries Miss Vickie before 45 million witnesses on *The Tonight Show.*

1970

RECORDING TOGETHER for the last time, the Beatles cut "I Me Mine" on January 3. The historic breakup happens on April 10, when Paul McCartney announces that he will not record with John Lennon again. By the end of the year, John, Paul, George, and Ringo have all released albums of their own.

EVERYTHING *You Always Wanted to Know About Sex, but Were Afraid To Ask* by Dr. David Reuben becomes a No. 1 bestseller.

JIMI HENDRIX and Janis Joplin both die drug-related deaths this year at age 27.

THE FILM VERSION OF *M*A*S*H,* with Elliott Gould and Donald Sutherland, is officially banned from military installations for "reducing the conventions and paraphernalia of war to total idiocy."

MIDNIGHT COWBOY is the first and only X-rated film to win Best Picture at the Academy Awards.

MASTERPIECE THEATRE is introduced on National Educational Television, hosted by Alistair Cooke, featuring BBC dramas.

TV'S PARTRIDGE FAMILY records "I Think I Love You," which becomes a smash hit first in the show's story line and then in real life, and makes David Cassidy a teen idol.

WATERBEDS hit the market, and although technical problems often produce flooding, sales skyrocket.

MONDAY NIGHT FOOTBALL takes its bow September 21 (with the New York Jets vs. the Cleveland Browns) and strains U.S. marriages, but Don Meredith, Howard Cosell, and Frank Gifford will boost ABC's ratings.

1971

CIGARETTE ADS are banned January 2 and TV networks lose $200 million in annual advertising.

CBS'S controversial *All in the Family* is introduced, featuring the bigoted Archie Bunker, whose offensive diatribes and hilarious family members drive the show's great popularity.

EXCERPTS FROM THE PENTAGON PAPERS, leaked by Daniel Ellsberg, are published in the *New York Times*, showing that presidential administrations had indeed recognized the futility of the Vietnam War but escalated involvement anyway and then lied about it. The Nixon administration attempts to block publication but the Supreme Court rules in favor of the newspaper on First Amendment grounds.

BILL GRAHAM closes down Fillmore East in New York City and Fillmore West in San Francisco, unable to pay the increasing prices charged by the musicians he has showcased for so long.

MUHAMMAD ALI'S conviction for draft evasion is overturned by the Supreme Court, which rules that the boxer's pacifist religious convictions were sincere.

JIM MORRISON, 27, dies in a bathtub in Paris on July 3.

HOSTED BY GEORGE HARRISON, the Concert for Bangladesh initiates the rise of the celebrity fundraiser. The concert features Ringo Starr, Eric Clapton, and Bob Dylan, but while its success is great, only a small fraction of its proceeds ever reach the starving people of Bangladesh.

LEGENDARY ALLMAN BROTHERS Band member Duane Allman is killed on October 29 in a motorcycle accident near Macon, Ga.

1972

MS., edited by Gloria Steinem, publishes its premiere issue in January.

RECLUSIVE MULTIMILLIONAIRE Howard Hughes exposes as a hoax an upcoming "autobiography" supposedly written with, but actually forged by, author Clifford Irving.

PONG, the first commercial computer game, is created by Atari.

BURT REYNOLDS poses nude for the centerfold of *Cosmopolitan*.

AT THE SUMMER OLYMPICS in Munich, 11 Israeli Olympians are killed by Arab terrorists, and the games are suspended for the first time in history.

JONATHAN LIVINGSTON SEAGULL establishes itself as the best-selling book since *Gone with the Wind*.

DEEP THROAT becomes one of the most successful porn films ever made; produced on a budget of $40,000, it goes on to gross around $40 million.

THE HOME BOX OFFICE cable channel goes on the air in Wilkes-Barre, Pa., with 365 subscribers. The first offering is a Paul Newman movie, *Sometimes a Great Notion*.

1973

ROE V. WADE is upheld by the Supreme Court, legalizing unrestricted abortion in the first trimester of pregnancy.

A CEASE-FIRE agreement is signed on January 27 that essentially ends the Vietnam War.

Marlon Brando as the Godfather.

SACHEEN LITTLEFEATHER refuses Marlon Brando's Oscar for Best Actor on his behalf to protest the treatment of Native Americans. (Brando had been nominated for *The Godfather*.)

PBS'S *STEAMBATH* takes on a taboo as Valerie Perrine becomes the first woman to bare her breasts in a dramatic TV program.

AT THE AGE OF 38, Seiji Ozawa becomes the youngest permanent conductor of the Boston Symphony.

A BREAK-IN at Democratic party headquarters at the Watergate Hotel is discovered, eventually leading to the only resignation of a sitting president in American history when Richard Nixon is forced to leave office on August 9 of the following year.

PUNK/NEW WAVE club CBGB and OMFUG (which stands for Country, Bluegrass, Blues, and Other Music for Uplifting Gourmandizers) opens its doors on Manhattan's divey Bowery, becoming home to such performers as Blondie, Talking Heads, Patti Smith, The Ramones, The Police, Joan Jett, and Sid Vicious. As Joey Ramone put it 20 years later, "It's a birthplace. It's like a big womb there. It's very primitive, very primal."

BILLIE JEAN KING trounces male chauvinist Bobby Riggs in tennis's ballyhooed "Battle of the Sexes."

THE AMERICAN PSYCHIATRIC ASSOCIATION reverses its traditional position and declares that homosexuality is not a mental illness.

1974

THE AUTOBIOGRAPHY OF MISS JANE PITTMAN, starring Cicely Tyson, becomes one of TV's most highly praised and successful special programs, going on to win nine Emmys.

HEIRESS PATRICIA HEARST is kidnapped by the Symbionese Liberation Army, which she later joins and with which she commits a robbery. Nineteen months after her kidnapping, Hearst is captured and convicted.

AFTER 10 YEARS OF MARRIAGE, Cher files for divorce from her husband and performing partner Sonny Bono. She marries Gregg Allman of the Allman Brothers Band only four days after the divorce is finalized.

PEOPLE magazine, featuring Mia Farrow on the cover, is launched by Time, Inc., in February.

EVEL KNIEVEL fails his attempt to jump the

Snake River Canyon on his motorcycle, but survives.

ONE THOUSAND FANS at a David Cassidy concert in London are injured during a frenzy following the teen idol's appearance. One concertgoer dies.

FLORIDA TV commentator Chris Chubbuck announces her own suicide at the end of the news broadcast, and proceeds to shoot herself in the head on the air.

ALEKSANDR SOLZHENITSYN is expelled from Russia for his dissident writings; this year *The Gulag Archipelago* is also published in the West.

STREAKING becomes a momentary fad, primarily on college campuses, although the madness eventually extends to telecasts of the Academy Awards and *The Tonight Show.*

RUSSIAN DANCER EXTRAORDINAIRE Mikhail Barishnikov defects to the West, electrifying the American dance scene.

KAREN SILKWOOD is killed in a suspicious car crash on November 13. A laboratory worker at the Kerr-McGee plutonium plant, she dies on her way to meet with a reporter to discuss safety hazards at her workplace.

Sonny and Cher, before the divorce.

1975

THE VIETNAM WAR officially comes to an end.

JOHN LENNON wins a four-year-long battle against American immigration authorities when they drop his case for humanitarian reasons due to the pregnancy of Yoko Ono.

SATURDAY NIGHT LIVE hits the airwaves from New York City, with guest host George Carlin.

RICHARD BURTON and Elizabeth Taylor marry for the second time, only a year after their divorce.

THE VIDEOCASSETTE recorder/player is introduced by Sony.

MOOD RINGS are introduced and reach their peak in only a few months, selling more than 20 million before passing from popular fancy. Meanwhile, maintenance-free pet rocks also hit the short-term big time.

1976

THE MINISERIES comes to commercial TV, as *Rich Man, Poor Man* airs, starring Peter Strauss,

Susan Blakely, and Nick Nolte.

BRITAIN'S PRINCESS MARGARET scandalizes the world with an illicit liaison on the island of Mustique with brewery heir Roddy Llewellyn. She and her husband, Lord Snowdon, separate later this year.

GONE WITH THE WIND is telecast over two evenings on NBC, earning the highest ratings to date.

1977

ALEX HALEY'S novel *Roots*, a story of his quest for his ancestors in Africa and America, is made into the most successful miniseries in history. It wins a record nine Emmys, and mesmerizes the country for over a week, drawing approximately 130 million people to watch at least one of its eight episodes.

STUDIO 54 opens its doors in New York, becoming the quintessential glamorous nightclub until owners Steve Rubell and Ian Shrager are arrested for tax evasion in 1980.

GEORGE LUCAS releases *Star Wars*, which becomes the highest-grossing movie of all time until

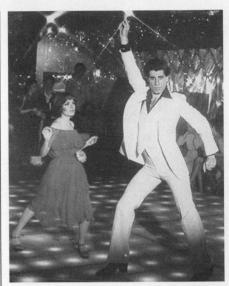

John Travolta strikes the pose that made him famous.

dethroned by *E. T., the Extra-Terrestrial* five years later.

THE KING IS DEAD: Elvis Presley, 42, passes on at Graceland, his palatial estate in Memphis, Tenn., on August 16.

SOAP introduces prime time's first gay character–Billy Crystal as Jodie Dallas.

RONALD ZAMORA, 15, confesses to murder and claims TV made him do it; he will be convicted in the first televised trial.

SATURDAY NIGHT FEVER premieres in New York on December 14, launching the disco era.

1978

FORMER FIRST LADY Betty Ford helps break the stigma of addiction by entering a rehabilitation clinic.

THE WORLD'S FIRST test-tube baby, Louise Brown, is born July 25 in England.

AT 25 HOURS and $25 million, the dramatization of James Michener's *Centennial* is the most outsized program yet produced for TV.

JIM JONES leads his followers to a mass death in Jonestown, Guyana, on November 18. 1,914 of his cult commit suicide or kill each other.

SONY invents the revolutionary Walkman, the first portable cassette player.

1979

RAP MUSIC is ushered into the commercial age when the Sugarhill Gang releases "Rapper's Delight." Earlier in the year a Brooklyn group called The Fatback Band had produced "King Tim III (Personality Jock)," a disk widely regarded as the first rap record.

WHILE THE WOMEN on TV's *Charlie's Angels* changed outfits on average eight times per show, a guest appearance this year by Farrah Fawcett (who left the show in 1977) easily breaks the record: In one hour-long program she changes clothes 12 times.

1980

THE U.S. HOCKEY TEAM beats the Soviet Union during the Winter Olympics at Lake Placid, on their way to winning their first gold medal since 1960—and only their second gold since the Olympics began.

President Ronald Reagan.

POST-IT NOTES enter the market, revolutionizing the office and the refrigerator.

TED KOPPEL'S *Nightline*, begun as an ABC series following the status of U.S. hostages in Iran, brings hard news in the wee hours.

COMEDIAN RICHARD PRYOR is badly burned when a flammable drug mixture used to make "freebase," a cocaine derivative, explodes in his face.

WITH SUCH BLOCKBUSTER musicals as *A Chorus Line, Oh! Calcutta!,* and *Evita* on the boards, Broadway box offices collect almost $200 million, a dramatic increase over a five-year period. Road shows during this period experience an even greater success.

TV'S FIRST ALL-NEWS SERVICE begins with Ted Turner's Cable News Network on June 1. Broadcasting 24 hours a day, the network loses $16 million in a year, but grabs seven million viewers.

HALF THE NATION'S VIEWERS tune in to *Dallas* on November 21 to find out "Who Shot J.R.?," more viewers than for any other single TV show in history.

MARK DAVID CHAPMAN shoots and kills John Lennon on December 8 outside the singer's apartment in New York City.

1981

HOMOSEXUAL MEN across the country are struck down by a wave of cancer and pneumonia that is traced to a mysterious breakdown in the body's disease-fighting system. It will be referred to later as Acquired Immune Deficiency Syndrome, or AIDS.

HILL STREET BLUES premieres.

TICKETS TO BROADWAY'S *The Life and Adventures of Nicholas Nickleby* go on sale at the Plymouth Theatre for a record-setting $100 each.

PRESIDENT RONALD REAGAN is shot in an assassination attempt on March 30 that leaves his press secretary, James Brady, paralyzed for life. John Hinckley apparently undertakes the assassination in an attempt to impress Jodie Foster.

THE VIDEO GAME PAC MAN devours the market as young people everywhere are seized with acute Pacmania.

CHARLES, PRINCE OF WALES, and Lady Diana Spencer are married on July 29 at Saint Paul's Cathedral in London.

MTV unveils music for your eyes on August 1. The channel's opener: "Video Killed the Radio Star," by The Buggles.

SANDRA DAY O'CONNOR becomes the first woman Supreme Court justice in U.S. history.

PRIVATE SATELLITE DISHES sprout after the FCC gives them the okay. By the end of the '80s, there will be two million nationwide.

1982

OZZY OSBOURNE bites the head off a live bat thrown at him during a performance on January 20, a moment that is immortalized in heavy metal chronicles.

THE REVEREND SUN MYUNG MOON performs a mass ceremony at Madison Square Garden, marrying some 4,150 of his followers, the "Moonies."

MICHAEL JACKSON'S *Thriller* is released. Selling over 20 million copies in 1983 and 1984 alone, it becomes the biggest-selling album in history.

JOHN BELUSHI dies March 5 of an overdose of cocaine and heroin in a Hollywood hotel room.

CHARLES AND DI produce their first offspring, Prince William, on June 21, the latest heir to the British throne.

PRINCESS GRACE dies on September 14 after an automobile accident.

THE WATCHMAN, Sony's portable microtelevision, is invented.

THE FIRST ARTIFICIAL HEART is transplanted into Barney C. Clark, age 61, in Utah. He lives for 112 days.

1983

CABLE TV subscribers reach the 30 million mark.

SINGER KAREN CARPENTER dies of anorexia nervosa on February 4.

M*A*S*H ends its 11-year, 14-Emmy run with the largest audi-

ence ever to watch a single TV show.

ASTRONAUT SALLY RIDE becomes the first american woman in space as she blasts off on June 18 with four colleagues aboard the space shuttle *Challenger*.

VANESSA WILLIAMS becomes the first African American to win the Miss America pageant. She relinquishes her title two months before her term ends in 1984, when it is discovered that revealing nude photos of the singer are going to be published in *Penthouse*.

THE CHILLING TV DRAMA *The Day After*, with Jason Robards, explores the aftermath of nuclear war, harden-

ing both pro- and anti-freeze positions.

CABBAGE PATCH DOLLS, introduced by Coleco Industries, become the holy grail of the holiday season.

1984

HOME TAPING OF TV programming is held not to be in violation of copyright law by the Supreme Court, which throws out a suit brought against Sony by MCA and Walt Disney.

SURROGATE CONCEPTION is successful for the first time in California.

GERALDINE FERRARO becomes the first woman to run for vice president as presidential candidate Walter Mondale names the Queens congresswoman as his running mate; the pair lose the election to President Reagan and Vice President George Bush in a landslide.

GYMNAST MARY LOU RETTON wins two gold, two silver, and two bronze Olympic medals for the U.S.

SIDNEY BIDDLE BARROWS is arrested. Known as the Mayflower Madam, she included numerous famous and pow-

Vice-presidential candidate Geraldine Ferraro.

erful people among her clients.

THE COSBY SHOW premieres, becoming the most popular series of the decade before going off the air in 1993.

THE FIRST ALL-RAP RADIO format is introduced by KDAY in Los Angeles.

RUN-DMC becomes the first rap group to have an album—*Run-DMC*—certified gold.

BOB GELDOF and Band Aid's "Do They Know It's Christmas" raise money to help feed the starving people of Africa.

1985

"WE ARE THE WORLD" is recorded by 45 pop music superstars under the auspices of USA for Africa.

CRACK COCAINE hits the streets, further devastating already blighted urban areas.

PIANO MAN BILLY JOEL and supermodel Christie Brinkley tie the knot.

MADONNA begins her road debut, The Virgin Tour, on April 10.

THE MUSIC INDUSTRY'S benefit for African famine relief, Live Aid, is staged in London and Philadelphia

and beamed all over the world.

ROCK HUDSON becomes the first major public figure to die of AIDS, at 59, on October 2.

1986

THE SPACE SHUTTLE *CHALLENGER* explodes January 28 shortly after launching, killing everyone on board, including schoolteacher Christa McAuliffe, the first private citizen to go into space.

FILIPINO FIRST LADY Imelda Marcos is found to possess 2,700 pairs of shoes.

ARNOLD SCHWARZENEGGER and Maria Shriver are married.

JOHNNY CARSON stops talking to Joan Rivers when she accepts an offer to host a late-night show on the Fox network.

CAROLINE KENNEDY marries artist-designer Edwin Schlossberg.

PRINCE ANDREW marries Sarah Ferguson in London on July 23.

THE OPRAH WINFREY SHOW, originally a local program called *A.M. Chicago*, goes

national on September 8. Its host soon establishes herself as one of the most successful personalities in show business.

TURNER BROADCASTING colorizes black-and-white classics and directors, stars and movie buffs see red. First to run: Jimmy Cagney's *Yankee Doodle Dandy*.

1987

JESSICA HAHN is implicated in a scandal with TV evangelist Jim Bakker.

VAN GOGH'S "Irises" is auctioned at $53.9 million, the highest price ever paid for a painting at the time.

PRINCE CHARLES and Diana begin leading separate lives in March as their marriage starts to deteriorate.

PRESIDENTIAL CANDIDATE Gary Hart's connection with model Donna Rice destroys his political aspirations, and he is forced to withdraw from the race.

GARRISON KEILLOR broadcasts his last radio show, *A Prairie Home Companion*, from Lake Wobegon on June 13 and moves to New York City.

PORN QUEEN CICCIOLINA wins a seat in the Italian parliament on June 16.

BRUCE WILLIS and Demi Moore are married November 21 in Las Vegas.

1988

TV PREACHER JIMMY SWAGGART admits his involvement with pornography and prostitutes. His February 21 statement, "I have sinned," deals a serious setback to electronic evangelism.

COMPACT DISCS outsell vinyl albums for the first time: the Recording Industry Association of America reports unit sales of 149.7 million CDs to 72.4 million records.

SONNY BONO is elected mayor of Palm Springs, California.

THE VERY LAST Playboy Club in America closes July 30 in Lansing, Mich.

ACTRESS ROBIN GIVENS files for divorce on October 7 from world heavyweight champion Mike Tyson, claiming that the fighter is violent.

TALK SHOW HOST Phil Donahue wears a

dress on November 18 to boost his ratings.

BENAZIR BHUTTO of Pakistan becomes the first woman to lead an Islamic nation.

PAN AM FLIGHT 103 explodes over Lockerbie, Scotland, killing all 259 passengers.

THE ERA of the personal video arrives when Sony introduces the Video Walkman, an ultracompact VCR with a three-inch color screen.

1989

LATE-NIGHT TV gets its first regular African-American host on January 3 with comedian Arsenio Hall.

VIRTUAL REALITY, the term as well as the equipment to achieve it, is invented by Jaron Lanier.

NOVELIST SALMAN RUSHDIE is forced into hiding after a death threat is issued by Islamic militants angry over what they see as sacrilege in his book *The Satanic Verses.*

KIM BASINGER steps in to rescue near-bankrupt Braselton, Ga., by buying the town for a reported $20 million.

LUCILLE BALL, perhaps the most beloved television star in history, dies on April 26.

ACTOR ROB LOWE is identified by Fulton County, Ga. officials in a homemade porn video with an under-aged girl.

PLAYBOY **FOUNDER** Hugh Hefner marries former *Playboy* Playmate Kimberley Conrad.

JOSE MENENDEZ AND his wife, Kitty, are found murdered August 20 in their $4 million Beverly Hills mansion. Their sons, Lyle and Erik, will later be accused of murdering their parents for money, though at their trials the brothers claim that years of sexual and psychological abuse by their parents drove them to kill in self-defense.

PETE ROSE, Cincinnati Reds manager and one of the greatest baseball players in history, is banned from the game for life for gambling.

TV GUIDE boasts a picture on the cover of the newly slim Oprah Winfrey, but the image turns out to be a composite of Oprah's head and Ann-Margret's body.

PRINCESS ANNE issues a palace statement

on August 31 that she is officially separating from her husband, Mark Phillips.

THE BERLIN WALL falls on November 9.

SAN FRANCISCO GIANTS pitcher Dave Dravecky retires after an aborted comeback attempt from cancer in his pitching arm.

1990

THE SIMPSONS spins off from *The Tracey Ullman Show* and makes the fledgling Fox network a real contender as a fourth network.

NELSON MANDELA is released from prison after 27 years of incarceration for leading a campaign against the South African government.

"ICE ICE BABY" by Vanilla Ice becomes the first rap record to top the U.S. singles chart.

SONY creates the first portable compact disc player, the Discman.

M. C. HAMMER releases *Please Hammer Don't Hurt 'Em,* which becomes the biggest-selling rap record in history.

DONALD AND IVANA TRUMP divorce.

MILLI VANILLI is accused of fraud for using voices other than its own on its Grammy-winning album, *Girl You Know It's True.* The group is forced to surrender the award.

IN THE FIRST such ruling against a music group in the U. S., a Florida judge declares 2 Live Crew's album *As Nasty As They Wanna Be* obscene and bans all sales of the rap recording to minors. The move ignites a campaign against censorship in the music business.

TWIN PEAKS debuts on ABC as a two-hour movie with limited commercial interruption.

SEINFELD, a show about "nothing," quietly debuts on May 31.

AMERICA RELIVES the war between the states with Ken Burns's indelible PBS documentary *The Civil War.*

IN AN EFFORT to raise money for AIDS research, the *Red Hot & Blue* album is released on October 30, featuring such stars as U2, David Byrne, and The Neville Brothers performing Cole Porter songs.

1991

OPERATION DESERT SHIELD turns into Desert Storm on January 16 as the Allied forces attack Iraq to liberate Kuwait. CNN's Bernard Shaw, Peter Arnett, and John Holliman broadcast live to the world from downtown Baghdad.

THE GODFATHER OF SOUL, James Brown, is released from a Georgia prison after serving two years of a six-year sentence for aggravated assault, not stopping for police, and carrying a gun.

RODNEY KING'S beating by Los Angeles police is recorded by an observer with a home video camera on March 3.

DR. JACK KEVORKIAN'S attempts to help people commit suicide first come to light.

WILLIAM KENNEDY SMITH, nephew of Ted Kennedy, is accused of rape by a Florida woman; after a harrowing trial, he is exonerated.

PAUL REUBENS, creator of the much-admired *Pee-wee's Playhouse* and the character Pee-wee Herman, is busted in Florida for indecent exposure.

Paul Reubens, a.k.a. Pee-wee Herman, after his infamous arrest.

LIZ TAYLOR marries husband number seven, 39-year-old Larry Fortensky, a carpenter she met at the Betty Ford Center. The wedding, held on Michael Jackson's estate, draws such guests as Nancy Reagan.

THE ANITA HILL/ CLARENCE THOMAS hearings galvanize the nation with charges of sexual harassment against the Supreme Court nominee; Thomas is narrowly approved for the post.

MAGIC JOHNSON announces his retirement from professional basketball because he has tested positive for the HIV virus.

MEDIA MOGUL Ted Turner and actress-cum-fitness-guru Jane Fonda are married.

1992

ARTHUR ASHE, tennis star and beloved public figure, dies of AIDS.

MIKE TYSON is convicted of raping beauty contestant Desiree Washington and is jailed in the Indiana Youth Center in Plainfield, Ohio until 1995. While in prison, Tyson studied the Koran intensely, and has embraced its teachings.

TAMMY FAYE BAKKER files for divorce from husband Jim, who's still in prison on a fraud conviction and not eligible for parole for another three years.

FERGIE AND ANDY separate after six years of marriage.

A *MURPHY BROWN* segment in which the unmarried Murphy gives birth, spurs the wrath of Vice President Dan Quayle and instigates a nation-wide debate over family values.

LONG ISLAND TEENAGER Amy Fisher shoots Mary Jo Buttafuoco.

JOHNNY CARSON ends his reign over late-night talk shows on May 22 with his last appearance on *The Tonight Show.*

CANDIDATE BILL CLINTON appears on *The Arsenio Hall Show,* complete with dark shades and saxophone, to perform "Heartbreak Hotel" with the show's "posse."

WOODY ALLEN AND MIA FARROW begin a bitter custody battle over their son Satchel, 4, and two children they adopted together, Moses, 14, and daughter Dylan, 7. The dispute is fueled by Allen's affair with Farrow's adopted daughter Soon-Yi Previn.

THE TORONTO BLUE JAYS become the first non-American team to win that most American of sports championships, the World Series, with a 4–2 series win over Ted Turner's Atlanta Braves.

PRINCE CHARLES and Princess Diana formally serparate.

1993

THE U.S. POSTAL SERVICE releases its commemorative Elvis stamp, featuring the youthful Elvis, the overwhelming selection of the voting public.

BILL WYMAN leaves The Rolling Stones in January. He is 56.

DR. DRE'S album *The Chronic* (named after a very potent form of marijuana) reaches No. 1 on the *Billboard* charts and becomes the most successful hard-core rap album to date.

MICHAEL JACKSON tells interviewer Oprah Winfrey that his lightened skin color is due to a rare skin disease, and says that he is in love with Brooke Shields. Later in the year Jackson is accused of having fondled a 13-year-old Los Angeles boy.

PRINCE, born Prince Rogers Nelson, turns 35 and, in a most confusing commemoration, changes his name to a symbol that no one knows how to pronounce, He is now "The Artist Formally Known as Prince.".

JULIA ROBERTS, 25, and Lyle Lovett, 35, wed.

ACTOR RIVER PHOENIX, 23, dies on October 31. The young actor had a reputation for clean living, but coroners find high levels of cocaine and morphine as well as Valium and marijuana in Phoenix's system.

1994

NANCY KERRIGAN is attacked in January by a club-wielding assailant, but battles back from the resulting knee injury to win a silver medal in the Winter Olympics.

MICHAEL JORDAN quits basketball and signs with the Chicago White Sox, fulfilling his childhood dream of becoming a baseball player. Playing for the Birmingham Barons, a Class AA team, he hits .202 for the season.

STEVEN SPIELBERG finally claims Oscars for Best Picture and Best Director with *Schindler's List*, which receives a total of seven awards. *Jurassic Park* wins another three. Later in the year, Spielberg forms Dreamworks SKG, the first new major studio in 55 years, with record mogul David Geffen and former Disney executive Jeffrey Katzenberg.

KURT COBAIN takes his own life with a shotgun on April 8 in his Seattle-area lakeside home. He joins a long and sad list of fellow rock stars: Janis Joplin, Jimi Hendrix, Jim Morrison—all dead at 27.

JACQUELINE BOUVIER KENNEDY ONASSIS dies at age 64 on May 19. She had been diagnosed just four months before with non-Hodgkin's lymphoma, a cancer of the lymphatic system.

NICOLE BROWN SIMPSON, 35, and Ronald Goldman, 25, are brutally murdered in front of Simpson's Brentwood condominium. After an eerie low-speed chase watched live on television by 95 million people, Nicole's ex-husband O.J. Simpson surrenders to police and is charged with the murders.

NEVERLAND meets Graceland as Michael Jackson and Lisa Marie Presley get hitched in a secret ceremony in the Dominican Republic.

WOODSTOCK '94 is held on the 25th anniversary of the original with acts old (the Allman Brothers Band, Bob Dylan) and new (Green Day, Nine Inch Nails).

GEORGE FOREMAN, 45, recaptures the heavyweight title he lost to Muhammad Ali 20 years ago. He defeats Michael Moore in Las Vegas with a 10th-round knockout.

1995

O.J. SIMPSON is found not guilty of the murders of Nicole Brown Simpson and Ronald Goldman.

OLYMPIC DIVER GREG LOUGANIS discloses to Barbara Walters and readers of his memoirs that "I do have AIDS."

EAZY-E, (a.k.a. Eric Wright), 31, the founder of rap group N.W.A. and president of Ruthless Records, dies of AIDS.

MICHAEL JORDAN resumes his basketball career. Dismayed by the baseball strike, he dons a new basketball jersey, #45, and leads the Chicago Bulls to another run of three straight championships.

TOUTED AS LATIN MUSIC'S Madonna, the Texas-born singer Selena is killed by her fan club president Yolanda Saldvar, 34, whom she was about to confront for embezzling funds.

CHRISTOPHER REEVE suffers a tragic accident on a cross-country jumping course, when his 7-year-old chestnut Thoroughbred Eastern Express refuses a fence. Though he is wearing a protective vest and helmet, the fall causes multiple fractures in his spinal column, leaving the actor paralyzed.

THE KING OF POP and his princess go live with Diane Sawyer and draw over 60 million viewers. The combination inter-

O. J. Simpson tries on the infamous black glove in his 1995 murder trial.

view/publicity opportunity includes an answer to fans' most frequently asked question: Do Lisa-Marie and Michael have sex? The answer: "Yes, yes, yes," answers the Mrs. Presley-Jackson.

HUGH GRANT is arrested for engaging in a "lewd act" with Sunset Strip prostitute Divine Brown. Grant soon begins his tour of contrition with a *Tonight Show* appearance that draws the show its third-highest ratings ever.

THE WALT DISNEY COMPANY announces that it's buying Capital Cities/ABC for $19 million. The day after Disney's acquisition, Westinghouse Electric announces its agreement to pur-

chase CBS for $5.4 billion.

LEGENDARY GRATEFUL DEAD guru Jerry Garcia, 53, dies of an apparent heart attack. To many who have idolized the band from its formation in 1966, it is a sad ending to the "feel good" era that the Dead carried well into the '90s with their record-grossing tours.

NEW YORK YANKEE GREATS gather in Dallas to lay to rest Mickey Mantle, dead of cancer, in a funeral filled with warm memories.

AFTER 10 YEARS IN THE PLANNING, the $92 million I. M. Pei–designed Rock and Roll Hall of Fame and Museum opens in Cleveland, Ohio, paying tribute to 40 years of rock

and to the jazz, blues, and gospel artists who laid down the roots of the genre.

HE WAS THE FIRST TALK show host to invite the audience into the act, but after 29 years, Phil Donahue calls it quits. He was seen in 200 television markets at the height of his popularity, winning 20 Emmys along the way.

MAYBE IT WAS JUST A matter of time: Lisa Marie Presley files for divorce from husband of 20 months, Michael Jackson.

AFTER TWO HOURS of deliberation, a jury rules that Random

House owes Joan Collins further payment on her book contract for *A Ruling Passion.* Saying her 690-page manuscript was unpublishable, Random House had sued Collins, and the *Dynasty* actress had countersued for the balance of her contract, $3.6 million.

THEODORE JOHN KACZYNSKI, 53, the former Berkeley math professor suspected of being the Unabomber, is charged with possessing a partially completed pipe bomb.

JACKIE KENNEDY ONASSIS'S belongings are auctioned off during a four-day sale at Sotheby's New York. The least expensive item, an etching of Washington, D.C., valued no higher than $30, sells for $2,070. A walnut cigar humidor smokes out $574,500.

EIGHT CLIMBERS ON MOUNT EVEREST become victims in one of the worst tragedies to strike the 29,028-foot Himalayan peak since it was first scaled in 1953.

GYMNAST KERRI STRUG, 18, limps to the gold after her heart-stopping final vault clinches top honors—the first ever— for the U.S.

women's team. The Tucson, Arizona, native had to be carried to the medal stand by coach Bela Karolyi.

PRINCESS DIANA and Prince Charles's divorce becomes official in late August.

JOHN F. KENNEDY JR. and Calvin Klein publicist Carolyn Bessette surprise everyone with a secret wedding on Cumberland Island, off the Georgia coast.

THE MATERNAL GIRL'S newest release, born in October, is a daughter: Lourdes Maria Ciccone Leon. Her father is Carlos Leon, Madonna's personal trainer and companion.

A SANTA MONICA CIVIL JURY finds O. J. Simpson liable in the 1994 deaths of Ron Goldman and Nicole Brown Simpson. According to Goldman's father, the family—which is awarded $8.5 million—"is grateful for a verdict of responsibility."

TARA LIPINSKI, 14, becomes the youngest U.S. figure skating champion ever.

SCOTTISH RESEARCHERS introduce a new star to biology—Dolly, a 7-month-old Finn-Dorset lamb that began life not like any other lamb but as a speck of DNA from a mature female sheep, of which she is now a perfect copy.

MEMBERS OF THE HEAVEN'S GATE CULT, who believed their deaths would give them passage aboard a UFO trailing the Hale-Bopp Comet, commit mass suicide.

TIGER WOODS, 21, becomes the youngest golfer to win the Masters and the first African American to win a major golf championship—while breaking the tournament record at 18 under par.

FRANK GIFFORD, 66, is caught on hidden video in an intimate encounter with a flight attendant, tarnishing the image of an idyllic marriage put forth by his wife, talk show queen Kathie Lee Gifford.

ELLEN DEGENERES and her character on ABC's *Ellen* both come out of the closet.

TIMOTHY MCVEIGH is found guilty on 11 federal charges, including seven

counts of murder, relating to 1995's Oklahoma City blast. He is sentenced to death.

CATS becomes the longest-running show in Broadway history.

MIKE TYSON is banned from the ring after biting off part of heavyweight champion Evander Holyfield's earlobe during a bout.

ITALIAN DESIGNER GIANNI VERSACE, 50, is shot to death outside his South Beach mansion in Miami Beach, Florida. He is gunned down by suspected gay serial killer Andrew Philip Cunanan, 27, who later shoots himself to death.

THE WORLD MOURNS the death of Princess Diana, victim of an early morning car crash in a tunnel below Paris's Seine River. Her funeral at Westminster Abbey is watched by 2 billion viewers.

CHRIS FARLEY, 33, is found dead in his Chicago condominium. An autopsy reports the death is from an accidental cocaine overdose.

LOUISE WOODWARD, 19, a British au pair, is convicted of the second degree murder of 8-month-

old Matthew Eappen. Her conviction is reduced to manslaughter by the judge, who sentences her to 279 days, the time already served while awaiting trial.

1998

ALLEGATIONS FIRST COME TO LIGHT in early January that President Clinton, 51, engaged in an affair with a White House intern, Monica Lewinsky, 24. In September, special prosecutor Kenneth Starr provides Congress with a shockingly detailed account of the President's alleged trespasses, and a videotape of Clinton's grand jury testimony is televised nationwide.

ER, prime time's No. 1–rated TV show, is renewed by NBC for a reported record $13 million an episode.

RANDOM HOUSE book publishers is sold by tycoon Si Newhouse to the giant German media company Bertelsmann, for a reported $1.5 billion.

FRANK SINATRA, the 82-year-old singer, movie actor, producer, record and casino mogul, and controversial figure, considered by many to be the Voice of the Century, dies on May 14.

SEINFELD, the hit sitcom of the decade, signs off the air, but only after much hype.

PHIL HARTMAN, 50, the *NewsRadio* actor-comedian, is shot multiple times and killed by his wife, Brynn, as he sleeps. After confessing to a friend, Brynn, 40, returns home and

shoots herself in the head.

GERI "GINGER SPICE" HALLIWELL, 25, announces she is leaving the Spice Girls, just before the group begins a sold-out U.S. tour.

HIGH-PROFILE COUPLE Bruce Willis, 41, and Demi Moore, 35, split up after 11 years of marriage. Moore will have custody of the couple's three daughters, ages 4 to 9.

BARBRA STREISAND, 56, and actor James Brolin, 57, tie the knot on the second anniversary of their first date. They are married at her Malibu estate, among a glittering background of stars.

NEW YORKER **MAGAZINE EDITOR** (since 1992) Tina Brown, 44, leaves her post to start a co-venture with Miramax Films that will launch *Talk*

magazine, produce feature films and TV programs, and publish books.

ST. LOUIS CARDINAL MARK MCGWIRE, 34, breaks Roger Maris's home-run record for the most home runs hit in a single baseball season, finishing with 70 homers.

PEOPLE
EXTRAS

THE MOST INTRIGUING PEOPLE: 1974–PRESENT

Every December, in the Christmas double issue, the PEOPLE editors single out the 25 most intriguing people of the past year. We reprint here the complete roll of honorees, with a brief description for each, to remind readers of the notable and notorious from the past 25 years.

1974

Gerald Ford—The president copes with an office he didn't seek and savage inflation.

Patty Hearst—The kidnapped newspaper heiress turned terrorist might be another face in the crowd—but in disguise.

Joe Hirshhorn—He heaps the land with beauty by donating 2,000 sculptures and 4,000 paintings to Smithsonian's new Hirshhorn Museum.

Kay Graham—The publisher of the *Washington Post* emerges as the big winner of Watergate.

Yasir Arafat—A tough soldier takes the point for Palestine and addresses the United Nations.

Faye Dunaway—A panther of an actress springs back to the top in *Chinatown, The Towering Inferno,* and *Three Days of the Condor.*

Alexander Solzhenitsyn—The Russian exile's Nobel honors are late but sweet.

Nelson Rockefeller—The vice president–elect has his finances questioned by Congress; being rich turns out to be a problem.

Leon Jaworski—The Watergate prosecutor knew Nixon was lying, but couldn't say it.

Erica Jong—A hit author who is like her uninhibited heroine in *Fear of Flying.*

Francis Ford Coppola—*Godfather II* confirms him as cinema's creative king.

Muhammad Ali—The title isn't enough for the world heavyweight champ—he wants another son.

Pat Nixon—The former First Lady deals stoically with her husband's fall from grace.

John Glenn—Could the Ohio senator and former astronaut be the Ike of the '70s?

Sherlock Holmes—He emerges from Victorian England as the most omnipresent literary figure of 1974.

Carter Heyward—One of 11 women ordained as Episcopal priests (the ordinations were later declared invalid) defies her church to serve her God.

Stevie Wonder—A blind artist brings soul to all his music.

Alexander Calder—Now it seems every U.S. city must have one of his mobiles.

Charlie Finley—The owner of the Oakland A's doesn't win friends, just the World Series.

Ella Grasso—The first woman in American history to capture a governorship without inheriting the office from her husband. In this year of political women, Conn.'s governor–elect is the biggest name of all.

J. Kenneth Jamieson—Exxon's chief has big profits and big problems.

Jimmy Connors—He catches fire; his romance catches cold.

Gunnar Myrdal—Nobel Prize winner in economics is honored for his "pioneering work in the theory of money and economic fluctuations."

Valerie Harper—*Rhoda*'s a winner on her own, and so much for TV taboos.

Mikhail Baryshnikov—The former Kirov Ballet star defects to Toronto, and ballet is changed forever.

1975

Betty Ford—The president's secret weapon is a refreshing First Lady high on being herself.

Richard Zanuck—Son of Darryl F., he makes his own name coproducing Hollywood's most toothsome grosser ever (*Jaws*).

Frank E. Fitzsimmons—The boss of 2.2 million teamsters is Nixon's buddy and shows he is "not Hoffa's puppet."

Charles Manson—He's in prison, but may have influenced Squeaky Fromme in her failed assassination attempt on President Ford.

Daniel Patrick Moynihan—Fighting Irishman at the U.N. talks tough—and, many Americans feel, talks sense too.

James Coleman—The University of Chicago professor blamed for busing says it backfired.

Indira Gandhi—After six months of rule in India, her popularity soars.

Cher Bono Allman—Move over Liz 'n' Dick, this ricochet bride is the new First Lady of splitsville.

Andrei Sakharov—The Nobel Peace Prize winner is a man under siege in his own country.

Teng Hsiao-Ping—After years of obscurity, a tough, blunt, outspoken man steps into the big shoes of Chinese leadership.

Patty Hearst—Was she a volunteer terrorist or a victim of her captors?

Christina Onassis—The only daughter of the late shipping magnate Aristotle Onassis has the ships and the gold, and marries her father's rival.

Leonard Matlovich—The ex–Air Force sergeant is discharged after admitting his homosexuality and sets up the Matlovich Foundation for Civil Rights.

Dolly Parton—There's a brain under that beehive of Nashville's new queen-in-waiting.

Fred Lynn—An all-American boy dazzles Boston and baseball in his miraculous rookie year.

Frank Borman—An ex-astronaut takes the controls of a company in a financial tailspin and gets Eastern Airlines off the ground.

Rosemary Rogers—The master of the erotic gothic takes her readers past the bedroom door.

Werner Erhard—In the wake of TM and Zen, a former encyclopedia huckster is the smooth guru of est.

Woody Allen—A winning klutz moves from snappy one-liners to triple creative threat— actor, director, and author with his latest, *Without Feathers*.

Marabel Morgan—The Florida housewife behind *The Total Woman* cashes in on the antifeminist backlash.

Jerry Brown—California loves its young governor who avoids the mansion, limos, and labels.

Don King—A flashy ex-con turned promoter is the new lord of the rings.

Hercule Poirot—Who kills the famed Belgian detective after 55 years? No, not the butler, but Dame Agatha Christie.

Anwar Sadat—The president of Egypt opens the Suez Canal, closed since the Six Day War in 1967.

Gelsey Kirkland—The prima ballerina of the American Ballet dances a triumphant *Giselle*, highlighting a great year in ballet.

1976

Jimmy Carter—The president-elect wants to be the "citizen president."

Farrah Fawcett-Majors—The shape of things to come? The nation watches an "Angel" turn into a star.

Andrew Wyeth—Is he America's most popular painter? The thought grieves some critics, who see him as "the rich man's Norman Rockwell."

Betty Williams—After seven bloody years, an anguished mother whose three children were killed starts her own movement and asks Ulster to give peace a chance.

Andrew Young—The first black ambassador to the United Nations. When this former congressman speaks, Jimmy Carter listens.

Juan Carlos I—The new Spanish king takes aim at Franco's fascist legacy and hands power to the people.

Linda Ronstadt—A vagabond grows into country rock's First Lady.

Reverend Sun Myung Moon—Troubles build up for the mysterious head of the Unification Church.

Bert Jones—A cool, calm Colt is pro football's man with the golden arm.

Julius Nyerere—Tanzania's superstar of black African diplomacy acts as a buffer between ruling white Ian Smith's government and the black nationalists of Rhodesia.

Carl Sagan—The Viking I expedition on Mars provides vicarious adventure for a would-be space explorer.

Fred Silverman—Since TV's superprogrammer switched channels, ABC enjoys Happy Days and Mashes CBS.

Liz Ray—The woman whose affair with Representative Wayne Hays set off the steamiest Washington sex scandal in years brings out a book and gets religion.

C. W. McCall—After "Convoy," the year's bestselling single, Rubberduck is king of the road.

Shere Hite—That report on women's sexuality becomes a bestseller, and its author moves on to men.

PEOPLE'S COVER CHAMPS

Their fame far exceeded the usual 15 minutes. The saga of their lives held readers rapt. Here are the titleholders for the most times featured on the cover of PEOPLE.

Personality	Number of Covers
Princess Diana	51
Elizabeth Taylor	14
Sarah Ferguson	13
Michael Jackson	13
Jacqueline Kennedy Onassis	13
Cher	11

Donald Kendall—With the Soviets part of the Pepski Generation, Pepsico's chief is now waging war on Coke.

Vivian Reed—The star of Broadway's *Bubbling Brown Sugar* proves that black is beautiful at the box office.

Ron Kovic—Disabled Vietnam veteran turned antiwar activist and author of *Born on the Fourth of July* sells movie rights for $150,000—and is a new breed of Yankee Doodle Dandy.

Chevy Chase—He's hot and you're not: *Saturday Night*'s stumblebum says so much for tepid TV.

Regine—The queen mother of the disco craze opens clubs all over the globe.

Har Gobind Khorana—A shy genius gives the world its first man-made working gene.

Nadia Comaneci—The Rumanian Olympic champion prepares for the 1980 games in Moscow. In Montreal she was just about perfect—now she wants even more.

Robert Redford—The actor turns producer with *All the President's Men* and shows he's not just a pretty face.

Don Shomron—The Israeli general who led the Entebbe raid to save 105 hostages is a global hero and can't understand why.

King Kong—Producer Dino De Laurentis sees and monkey does—$200 million, he hopes.

Jimmy Carter—The first year at 1600: he likes it, Rosalynn is chilly, and Amy's adjusting.

Diane Keaton—Her gamble on *Looking for Mr. Goodbar* put Woody Allen's flaky foil in the Hollywood catbird seat.

General Omar Torrijos—Ratify the canal treaties or bring in the marines, says Panama's strongman.

Steven Ross—An impresario of all parlors (originally funeral), the founder-chairman of Warner Communications is the greatest showman on earth.

Midge Costanza—Assertive and quick-tongued, she's Carter's pipeline to the people as the assistant for public liaison.

Anwar Sadat and Menachem Begin—Is it a possible secret weapon of peace that the president of Egypt and the prime minister of Israel are so much alike?

Ted Turner—After the Americas Cup the sea gets a little choppy for the cable entrepreneur and baseball team owner.

Margaret Trudeau—The runaway wife of Canada's prime minister, Pierre Trudeau, says of her old life, "Politics is an ugly and thankless role. What I did was never really appreciated."

Robert Byrd—A self-made fiddler calls the tunes in the world's most exclusive club.

Susanne Albrecht—A brutal murder of an old friend makes her the dark queen of German terrorism.

Lily Tomlin—The actress/comedian won a Tony for her one-woman show *Appearing Nitely*. "Is this the country to whom I'm speaking?" Happily for America the answer is yes.

Billy Carter—President Carter's baby brother and typical southern "sly ole boy" has an agent and a career as spokesman for products such as Billy Beer. He may be a royal pain to some, but his brother is still amused.

Anita Bryant—After a *très* un-gay year, she's still praising God and passing the orange juice.

Shaun Cassidy—The star of *The Hardy Boys* moonlights as a pop star, and preadolescent America is swooning.

Jacqueline Onassis—Quits her editor's job at Viking and gets $25 million from step-daughter Christina Onassis.

Jasper Johns—The enigmatic master of pop art—known for depictions of the stars and stripes, targets, alphabets, and lightbulbs—stays on target.

Toni Morrison—"O-o-o-ooh she done fly" into the literary top rank with *Song of Solomon*.

Dr. Robert Linn—His liquid protein diet has him in fat city, but some unexplained deaths worry the FDA.

Tracy Austin—Out of the cradle and onto the courts comes a new tennis wunderkind, at 14 the youngest player ever to be invited to Wimbledon.

Rosalyn Yalow—All this: winner of the 1977 Nobel Prize for medicine, first laureate educated only in the United States, sixth woman science winner, second woman medicine winner.

Reggie Jackson—Once just a hot dog; now he's a candy bar and a millionaire Yankee hero.

Stevie Nicks—A songwriting soprano with fragile vocal cords casts her sexy spell on rock.

George Lucas—From the void he created the droid and a new "force" in film.

Princess Caroline—Grace and Rainier's grown-up little girl will wed Junot next July.

Jimmy Carter—At Camp David he negotiates peace between Egypt and Israel, but back in the White House he looks for antidotes to rising inflation and helps Amy practice her pitch on the violin.

Pope John Paul II—A tough Polish priest molds the papacy to his own ebullient personality.

Queen Noor al-Hussein—The blue-jeaned American queen says of her king, "I'd be delighted to have his child."

G. William Miller—The chairman of the Federal Reserve says of inflation, in effect, "We have nothing to fear but fear itself."

Teng Hsiao-Ping—The tough vice-premier gives China less of Mao, and more of himself.

Brooke Shields—Pretty baby at 13: One horse, three movies, beaucoup bucks, but no beau.

Melvin Gottlieb—The dream this Princeton physicist pursues is limitless energy from nuclear fusion.

Louise Brown—The first test-tube baby is doing just fine, thank you, but the fuss is far from over.

Reverend Jim Jones—When this religious demagogue felt his encampment was threatened by Congress and newsmen, he offered a deadly communion to his followers.

John Belushi—With the hit movie *Animal House*, TV's man of mugs is becoming a hard act to outgross—in every way.

Jim Fixx—His *The Complete Book of Running*, a how-to book on the simplest sport in the world, is the year's runaway bestseller.

Garry Marshall—TV writer and producer of the hits *Laverne and Shirley* and *Happy Days* continues his successful career with *Mork and Mindy*.

Arlene Blum—The University of California biochemist who led the first all-woman expedition up Annapurna, the tenth highest peak in the world, loses two fellow climbers.

Howard Jarvis—The crusader against high property taxes may have changed the future of U.S. politics following the endorsement of his Proposition 13 by California voters in June.

Miss Piggy—The famed Muppet pig states, "I want children, my career, and the frog—not necessarily in that order."

Luciano Pavarotti—It's supertenor, opera's newest sex symbol.

Cheryl Tiegs—This model's photos still bring out the beast, and earn her $2,000 for a day's work, but her new goal is survival in the TV jungle.

Meat Loaf—Rock's newest (and heftiest) hero takes a Texas-size bite into the music biz.

Sir Freddie Laker—The founder of the Skytrain revolutionized air fares with cheap transatlantic flights and has a knighthood to prove his success.

Nancy Lopez—The golfer has a fantastic year, finishing first in nine out of 25 tournaments and is named Rookie Player and Golfer of the Year.

John Travolta—Stayin' Alive is the word for the solitary new superstar besieged by his fans.

James Crosby—The man who brought big-time gambling to Atlantic City hopes for the city's economic rebirth.

John Irving—His novel *The World According to Garp* is on the bestseller list and revenues allow the down-to-earth Vermonter to work full-time on his upcoming work, *The Hotel New Hampshire*.

Donna Summer—The queen of disco is softening her act, but she'd still love to love you, baby.

Burt Reynolds—Life isn't always easy for a star working on a new image: sensitivity.

1979

Rosalynn Carter—The First Lady skirts the charge that she is involved in government policy formation, and instead emphasizes the Carters as a family.

Aleksandr Godunov—The Russian danseur defects to the United States "to dance more often," but his volatile personality may be the reason he has yet to perform.

Marvin Mitchelson—The millionaire divorce lawyer makes "palimony" a household threat.

Bo Derek—Shows the world that she's a 10 as costar to Dudley Moore, and is credited with bringing sex back to films.

Lee Iacocca—Struggles valiantly to get Chrysler into gear under the threat of bankruptcy.

Sly Stallone—Comes off the canvas for the biggest movie purse of the year, *Rocky II*, and is already thinking ahead to *Rocky III*.

Megan Marshack—After a year of seclusion, former vice president Nelson Rockefeller's secretary and companion on the night of his death is back in New York.

Mani Said al-Otaiba—Leader of OPEC, he writes poetry and tames his Arab colleagues with cordial threats.

Joan Kennedy—Impressing the nation, she sobers up to be at Ted's side for the campaign.

Johnny Carson—Carson announces that he plans to give up his 17-year reign and $2.5-million contract at NBC and may entertain offers from ABC.

Ayatollah Khomeini—The fate of the hostages is still unknown, but Iran's fanatic ruler leads his nation toward chaos with growing social and economic problems.

Tom Wolfe—After six years of writer's block, his latest, *The*

Right Stuff, is his biggest seller.

Joan Baez—The brave anti-warrior raises her voice for the boat people and refugees of Cambodia and is accused of changing her tune on Vietnam.

Sebastian Coe—After setting three world records, this British runner takes time out to prepare for the Olympics in Moscow, complete his postgraduate studies, and take a break from all the "razzmatazz."

Gloria Vanderbilt—Living up to her genes, the poor little rich girl brings new chic to a bottom line with her top-grossing designer jeans.

Bruce Babbitt—The Arizona governor and member of the presidential commission to investigate Three Mile Island believes nuclear power is a necessary evil.

Meryl Streep—A big year for the most intelligent actress now at work, with *Manhattan, Kramer vs. Kramer,* and *The Deer Hunter.*

Willie Stargell—Captain of the Pittsburgh Pirates, voted MVP this year, but didn't need an award to get the respect and love of his team.

Pope John Paul II—Good receptions all over the world indicate a fine first year for the new pope, although his message is often a bitter pill to swallow.

Paul Volcker—The chairman of the Federal Reserve leads an exemplary frugal life, which he brings to the office.

Jesse Jackson—Reverend Jackson jets around the world offering support and often inflammatory statements.

Dan Aykroyd—*Saturday Night Live* loses the brilliant actor/writer, who is moving on to make more movies.

Margaret Thatcher—The first female prime minister of England is not a promotion for feminist ideals but advocates a nostalgic return "to economic Calvinism: hard work, self reliance, and upward mobility."

William Webster—America's top cop takes aim at a tough target: modernizing and de-Hooverizing the FBI.

Deborah Harry—Gentlemen and record buyers prefer this platinum blondie: she switches disco to a new wavelength.

PEOPLE'S BEST AND WORST DRESSED

Who are the biggest fashion victors and victims? The following celebrities found themselves on PEOPLE's Best Dressed and Worst Dressed lists most often.

ALL-TIME WINNERS	ALL-TIME SINNERS	1999'S BEST AND WORST
3 Times	**6 Times**	**10 Best Dressed**
Princess Caroline	Madonna	Candice Bergen
Princess Diana		Sophia Loren
Kevin Costner	**5 Times**	Camryn Manheim
Jackie Onassis	Sarah Ferguson	Ricky Martin
Gwyneth Paltrow		Gwyneth Paltrow
Julia Roberts	**4 Times**	Brad Pitt
Prince William	Arsenio Hall	Julia Roberts
	Daryl Hannah	Diane Sawyer
2 Times	Cher	Will Smith
Corbin Bernsen		Catherine Zeta-Jones
Brandy	**3 Times**	
Sandra Bullock	Paula Abdul	
Delta Burke	Rosanna Arquette	**10 Worst Dressed**
Cher	The Artist Formerly Known As Prince	David Arquette
George Clooney	Kim Basinger	Mariah Carey
Tom Cruise	Demi Moore	Lisa Nicole Carson
Mel Gibson	Roseanne	Cher
Don Johnson		Val Kilmer
Michael Jordan	**2 Times**	Madonna
Angela Lansbury	Justine Bateman	Nick Nolte
Cyndi Lauper	Geena Davis	Caroline Rhea
Donna Mills	Princess Diana	Adam Sandler
Liz Taylor	Andrea Evans	Shania Twain
Bruce Willis	Goldie Hawn	
	Elton John	
	Cybill Shepherd	
	Princess Stephanie	
	Liz Taylor	
	Ivana Trump	
	Raquel Welch	

1980

Ronald Reagan—He wins the presidency by a landslide.

Goldie Hawn—*Private Benjamin* liberates a beloved ding-a-ling, promoting her to captain of her soul.

Lech Walesa—An unemployed electrician becomes a working-class hero to Poland and the free world.

Colonel Charlie Beckwith—The commander of the failed mission to rescue American hostages in Iran emerges as a quiet hero.

Herbert Boyer—If nothing else, his forays into genetic engineering can turn this scientist into a multimillionaire.

Mary Cunningham—Blond, beautiful, and no longer at Bendix, she's looking for room at the top.

Fidel Castro—He grinned after solving 125,000 problems, but now he faces a new one: Reagan.

Mel Weinberg—A king con artist sets up Abscam for the FBI and snares some unsuspecting politicians.

Sugar Ray Leonard—Who is the greatest? A tough little man wins the boxing championship and the title.

Robert Redford—First time behind the scenes, a superstar directs a fine film and says, "I'll phase out acting."

Jean Harris—Was the death of Scarsdale Diet's Dr. Tarnower an accident or murder? Only the quiet headmistress knows.

Stephen King—A mild downeaster discovers terror is the ticket.

Grete Waitz—A swift Norwegian teacher gives the cold shoulder to the other women runners in the world.

Baron St. Helens—An English diplomat's name lives on as a killer volcano.

The Reverend Jerry Falwell—A TV preacher sells America on flag, family, and freedom, of sorts.

Pat Benatar—Rock finds its missing lynx: she's doing time in the top 10 for what she calls *Crimes of Passion.*

Lee Rich—Like J. R. Ewing's assailant, the producer behind *Dallas* aims to please, and does.

Sonia Johnson—In the battle for the Equal Rights Amendment, a Mormon feminist waits for the balloon to go up.

Sam Shepard—Mr. Funk of off-Broadway may be the Redford of the '80s—if he can play his way.

Richard Pryor—Having been through the fire, he's back with a new self and, he says, no bad habits.

Eudora Welty—The critics bow before the small-town tales of a masterly Southern writer.

Soichiro Honda—The Henry Ford of the Japanese auto industry is known as "Pop" to his workers.

Beverly Sills—Bubbles from Brooklyn has stopped singing and begun bossing the company she once graced, the New York City Opera.

Dan Rather—When asked if he can hold Walter Cronkite's audience, the new CBS Atlas shrugs.

Brooke Shields—From *Blue Lagoon* to blue ads for blue jeans, nothing is coming between her and success.

1981

Ronald Reagan—The president survives an assassination attempt, promises 25% tax cuts over the next three years, and says time will tell if he'll run again in '84.

Elizabeth Taylor—Old Violet Eyes gets a Tony nomination for her first Broadway performance, in *The Little Foxes.*

Lech Walesa—Poland's patriarch of Solidarity is a man of faith and bold deeds, organizing 10 million Poles to stand up to their government.

Bradford Smith—Though his Voyager project took us to the planets, he may face a permanent grounding from Reagan's budget axe.

Bryant Gumbel—The new *Today* show host aims to be king of the mountain on morning TV.

Crown Prince Fahd—The Saudi heir-apparent works to preserve peace between Israel and radical Arab nations.

Rabbit Angstrom—John Updike's fictional hero returns fat, rich, and ready for the '80s.

Ted Turner—In his one-man air war, cable's Captain Courageous stares down the big guns of network TV.

Princess Diana—A kindergarten teacher becomes a princess, beguiles the world, and produces an heir.

Gloria Monty—Producing ABC's *General Hospital,* she's behind the biggest bubble in showbiz: soap operas.

David Stockman—Reagan's budget director is nearly done in by his own hand, the one that would tighten the nation's belt.

Lena Horne—A glamorous grandmother wants audiences to wonder, "how does the old broad do it?"

John McEnroe—He's number one in tennis, but superbrat's score with the public is still love-hate.

Edgar Bronfman—Seagram's liquor baron enlivens a year of corporate merger mania.

Barbara Mandrell—No hee-haw, a new country queen takes on TV and wins.

Thomas Sowell—Ronald Reagan's favorite black intellectual attracts attention and decides he doesn't like it.

Wolfgang Amadeus Mozart—After two centuries, Austria's child prodigy has become the world's favorite composer.

Tom Selleck—More modest than macho, he's the hot-as-a-pistol heartthrob of *Magnum P.I.*

Mick Jagger—Mr. Rolling Stone finds sweet satisfaction with rock's richest tour ever.

Richard Viguerie—The New Right's buoyant fundraiser helps purge the Senate of four of its most powerful Democrats.

Nicholas Nickleby—At $100 a seat it could have been a bleak house on Broadway, but Dickens proved a smash.

Sandra Day O'Connor—Up at 4 a.m. to read briefs, she learns that a woman justice's work is never done.

Harrison Ford—He's the new breed of action star—little ego, medium fame, big bucks.

Fernando Valenzuela—Baseball almost struck out, but a Mexican rookie conjures up a magical season.

Elizabeth McGovern—A talented beauty soars from high school to stardom as a dippy sex kitten in *Ragtime*.

YEAR-BY-YEAR, THE BEST- (AND WORST-) SELLING PEOPLE ISSUES

Here are the regular weekly issues that fared best and worst at the newsstand in our first 25 years.

	Best Seller	Worst Seller
1974	The Johnny Carsons	J. Paul Getty
1975	Cher & Gregg Allman	Liv Ullmann
1976	Cher, Gregg, & Baby	Nancy Reagan
1977	Tony Orlando's Breakdown	Julie Andrews
1978	Olivia Newton-John	Vice President & Mrs. Mondale
1979	A Readers' Poll/5th Anniversary	Fleetwood Mac
1980	John Lennon, A Tribute	Paul Simon
1981	Charles & Diana's Wedding	Justice Sandra Day O'Connor
1982	Princess Grace, A Tribute	*Annie,* the musical
1983	Karen Carpenter's Death	Sally Ride, America's First Woman in Space
1984	Michael Jackson	How To Make Your Kid a Star
1985	The Other Life of Rock Hudson	Bisset & Godunov
1986	Andrew & Fergie's Wedding	The Raid on Libya
1987	The Follies of Fergie & Di	Michael Caine
1988	Burt & Loni's Wedding	Our American Hostages
1989	Lucy, A Tribute	Abbie Hoffman, Death of a Radical
1990	Patrick Swayze	Campus Rape
1991	Jeffrey Dahmer	Richard & Jeramie Dreyfuss
1992	Princess Diana	Betty Rollin: "I Helped My Mother Die"
1993	Julia Robert's Wedding Album	Hillary Clinton
1994	The Nicole Simpson Murders	Kelsey Grammer
1995	David Smith	Larry Hagman
1996	Margaux Hemingway's Death	Audrey Meadows and Gene Kelly: Tributes
1997	Goodbye Diana	The Fight Against Child Abuse
1998	Barbra's Wedding Album	Emmy's 50th Birthday

1982

Ronald Reagan—Two years into his term, the president enjoys his "confinement" in the White House.

Joan Jett—Rock's latest leading lady earns her stripes with a hard look and her hit song, *I Love Rock and Roll.*

Ariel Sharon—Stunned by backlash from the Beirut massacre, the defiant Israeli defense minister battles on.

Princess Stephanie—Numbed by her mother's death, a sad teenager has lost her zest for life.

Jessica Lange—A talented beauty gets a monkey off her back with two major films, *Tootsie* and *Frances.*

Herschel Walker—Forget the Heisman—Georgia's got the trophy that counts: the best running back in football, bar none.

Larry Gelbart—After 10 years, *M*A*S*H* departs, but the man who wrote the show has a wacky new hit called *Tootsie.*

Margaret Thatcher—With Churchill to inspire her, a dogged prime minister triumphs in a nasty little war in the Falkland Islands.

Dr. William DeVries—A surgeon touches the soul with a new machine, the artificial heart.

Princess Diana—She may have those newlywed blues, but she's still Britain's darling.

Yuri Andropov—Emerging from the shadows of the Soviet KGB, a master spy takes over Brezhnev's Kremlin.

George Wallace—Politically recast as a friend of blacks, he seeks their votes and forgiveness—and gets both.

Paolo Rossi—A handsome soccer hero leads Italy to the World Cup and wins back the hearts of his countrymen.

Randall Forsberg—A Massachusetts scholar sounds a nationwide call to (freeze) arms.

Norma Kamali—Wowing Seventh Avenue has been no sweat for fashion's Greta Garbo.

E.T.—An alien finds his home in Hollywood.

Richard Gere—*Officer* makes a star, if not quite a gentleman, out of a movie maverick.

Sam Knox—An authority on the scourge of the sexes offers some consoling facts to legions of herpes victims.

Andrew Lloyd Webber—From the Bible to back alleys, Broadway's hottest composer strikes all the right notes.

Evelyn Waugh—A curmudgeon's elegy for England's upper crust, *Brideshead Revisited* becomes the TV event of 1982.

Barbra Streisand—At 40, the Brooklyn songbird returns to the Old World to conquer a new one—directing *Yentl*.

Ted Koppel—A clear-eyed shark surveys war and peace and revolutionizes night-owl journalism on *Nightline*.

Kiri Te Kanawa—New Zealand's diva hits the top in opera and wins a royal title by acting nothing like a dame.

Reverend Sun Myung Moon—The Unification Church's controversial leader is convicted of tax evasion, but he still wins converts.

Paul Newman—*The Verdict* is in: a risky role may win Blue Eyes that elusive Oscar gold.

Bill Agee and Mary Cunningham—The Bendix takeover didn't take, but this famous couple makes one merger that works.

1983

Ronald Reagan—After harrowing events in Granada and Lebanon, the president finishes a tough year on a tougher note with the bombing of Syrian anti-aircraft nests in the mountains east of Beirut.

Debra Winger—A Hollywood sexpot turns serious actress and scores on her own *Terms*.

Fidel Castro—The aging lion of revolution in Latin America gets savvy—and pulls in his claws.

The Cabbage Patch Kids—Glassy of eye and poker of face, this chubby, alien horde masks a plot to take over the planet.

Jesse Jackson—An explosive orator's campaign breeds fusion and fission for the Democrats.

William Gates—Dropping out of Harvard pays off for a computer whiz kid who's making hard cash from Microsoft software.

Sam Shepard—He has it all as a laureate of stage and screen but just wants anonymity.

Chun Byung In—The career of an "infallible" pilot ends in the debris of Korean Air Lines flight 007, shot down over Soviet airspace in August.

Mr. T—The terror of *The A-Team* is indisputably the show-business maniac of the year.

Ben Lexcen—An impish Aussie designer and his magic keel haul the America's Cup Down Under after 132 years of U.S. ownership.

Joan Rivers—Where's Johnny Carson? Home, watching a *Tonight Show* guest host skewer guests and boost his ratings.

Robert Mastruzzi—A Bronx high school principal won't let his school be less than the best.

Eddie Murphy—He makes folks mad, but he's got it made.

Matthew Broderick—Oh, to be young and hot in Hollywood; yet instead of acting up, the leader of the brat pack is buttoned-down.

Barbara McClintock—After six decades of research, the shy discoverer of biology's "jumping genes" wins her Nobel Prize.

Harvey Fierstein—Brooklyn's funny boy takes Broadway on a gay mad whirl with *La Cage aux folles*.

Philip Johnson—The grand old man of architecture comes full circle, designing the downfall of his own glass box.

Vanessa Williams—A thorny crown goes with the job of being the first black Miss America.

Richard Chamberlain—He gets no awards from his peers, but the public hails the king of miniseries.

Michael Jackson—Thanks to a *Thriller* album, the former small fry of the Jacksons becomes the biggest star in pop.

Rei Kawakubo—Japan's Stravinsky of fashion rocks the West with her atonal, asymmetric sad rags.

Konrad Kujau—A Nazi-obsessed amateur forger fakes the Führer's diaries and nearly fools the world.

Alice Walker—*The Color Purple*, her protagonist's letters to God, bring her a bestseller and a Pulitzer.

Alfred Hitchcock—Three years after his death, five buried treasures from the master of suspense prove to be the movie event of 1983.

Jennifer Beals—Dazzling looks and a ripped wardrobe turn a dancing Yalie into a flashy star.

1984

Geraldine Ferraro—A tough, savvy, political pioneer loses the battle for vice president but wins a historic war for women.

Bruce Springsteen—*Born in the U.S.A.* reaches for 5 million sales and the Boss transcends mere legend to become a symbol of all that once was right about America.

Andrei Gromyko—For nearly half a century, this most durable diplomat has been the poker face of Soviet foreign policy.

José Napoleón Duarte—On the broad shoulders of this gutsy president rest El Salvador's hopes of emerging from a nightmare civil war.

Mary Lou Retton—L.A.'s golden girl Olympian marches to a new beat as Madison Avenue's million-dollar baby.

Richard Gere—This elusive screen actor seems bent on preserving the silence that marks him as a Hollywood enigma.

Peter Ueberroth—An organizational wizard turns the L.A. Olympic Games into a glowing personal triumph.

Joe Kittinger—In the year's greatest adventure, a hard-nosed pilot transforms a POW fantasy into a dream come true with a solo flight across the Atlantic in a hot-air balloon.

Farrah Fawcett—With *The Burning Bed*, her career surges, and at 37 she's a happy mother-to-be—proud papa Ryan O'Neal hopes they're altar-bound.

Clint Eastwood—As *Tightrope*'s kinky cop he reveals new and darker dimensions that leave astonished critics cheering.

Betty Ford—The former First Lady publicly tackles her problems with alcohol and painkillers—and helps cure a nation's ills.

John Malkovich—A versatile young Chicago actor storms Broadway in *Death of a Salesman* and stakes a claim on Oscar in two of the year's best movies, *Places in the Heart* and *The Killing Fields*.

John Henry—This equine geriatric marvel has traveled from coast to coast and convincingly proved that the race is not always to the youngest.

Sparky Anderson—He managed the Detroit Tigers to victory in the World Series and also leads the league in rough-hewn rhetoric.

Tina Turner—After eight years of deep rivers and high mountains, a self-professed "Soul Survivor" strides back into the rock and roll promised land with her new album, *Private Dancer*.

William Kennedy—At 56, Albany's patient author watches the work of a lifetime pay off with a Pulitzer Prize, *The Cotton Club*, movie deals, and a $264,000 MacArthur "genius grant."

Lee Iacocca—With his autobiography riding atop the bestseller list, Chrysler's blunt shirt-sleeve philosopher offers a plan to fix the sputtering economy.

Vanessa Williams—The first black Miss America's reign is distinguished by dignity, delight,

and talent—until the discovery that she had posed nude forces her resignation.

Kathleen Turner—The star of *Romancing the Stone* mixes sex and sensitivity to become the hottest actress since Streep.

James Baker—President Ronald Reagan remains curiously ageless as his chief of staff grows older quickly—could there be a connection?

Kathleen Morris—A controversial Minnesota prosecutor vows to continue the legal fight against sexual abuse of children.

John Torrington—From his ice-shrouded tomb in the Canadian Arctic, a 19th-century explorer sheds new light on the chilling fate of Britain's ill-fated Franklin expedition.

Bill Murray—This ghostbuster is the comedy star of the year's biggest box-office hit ($220 million), but if you think it's gone to his head—get outta here.

Baby Fae—A wondering world watches as a child with a transplanted baboon heart fights for life.

Michael Jackson—PEOPLE ran five covers, 73 photos, and 33,205 words on the singer during 1984—what more is there to say?

1985

Bob Geldof—Moved by scenes of mass starvation, this scruffy Irishman raises a cry with a song and rouses the world to save the hungry.

Joe Kennedy—The best-known name in American politics surfaces again as Bobby's eldest son announces for the congressional seat once held by his Uncle Jack.

Corazon Aquino—As the ghost of her assassinated husband haunts the rule of Philippine president Ferdinand Marcos, a housewife rides an emotional swell to political prominence.

Steven Rosenberg—By energizing the body's natural defenses, a surgeon at the National Cancer Institute may have made the biggest step in 30 years toward a cancer cure.

Rambo—His deeds are the stuff of cinema legend from here to Haiphong, but to the folks of one small western town, he's just a local boy with a preposterous set of pecs.

Akira Kurosawa—Japan's feisty grand old man of the movies comes back from despair to film *Ran*, a feudal version of *King Lear* that may turn out to be his greatest triumph.

Nelson Mandela—Banished behind prison walls since 1964, a legendary black leader may yet save South Africa from the horror of racial war.

William Perry—He can block, run, and do endorsements. The 308-pound Refrigerator is the big surprise of the football season.

Uli Derickson—TWA Flight 847's flight attendant becomes the heroine of a hijacking.

Bernhard Goetz—New York's subway vigilante acted out our angriest fantasies, but a year later the questions remain—is he a hero or a villain, a victim or a criminal?

William Hurt—His risky transvestite role in *Kiss of the Spider Woman* makes him an Oscar favorite as Best Actor, but he'd rather hide from the world than try to be world-famous.

Hulk Hogan—The World Wrestling Federation's heavyweight champion's favorite subjects are his biceps, his California home, and milk, his breakfast of champions.

PEOPLE'S MOST BEAUTIFUL PEOPLE

Every year PEOPLE faces the difficult task of choosing only 50 of the most stunning celebrities we've seen all year. Here is the face of beauty in 1999, lead by new and undisputed all-time winner, Michelle Pfeiffer, and a look at the stars who have dazzled their way onto more than one of our Most Beautiful People lists.

6-Timers
Michelle Pfeiffer

5-Timers
Tom Cruise
Mel Gibson
John F. Kennedy Jr.

4-Timers
Halle Berry
Julia Roberts

3-Timers
Antonio Banderas
Kevin Costner
Nicole Kidman
Demi Moore
Brad Pitt
Claudia Schiffer
Denzel Washington

2-Timers
Tyra Banks
Juliette Binoche
Toni Braxton
Pierce Brosnan
Sandra Bullock
George Clooney
Cindy Crawford
Daniel Day-Lewis
Princess Diana
Leonardo DiCaprio
Emme
Whitney Houston
Helen Hunt
Matt Lauer
Jared Leto
Jennifer Lopez
Paul Newman
Gwyneth Paltrow
Paulina Porizkova
Jason Priestley
Rebecca Romijn-Stamos
Isabella Rossellini
Winona Ryder
Jaclyn Smith
Hunter Tylo
Meredith Vieira
Katarina Witt

1999'S PICKS
Ben Affleck
Jennifer Aniston
Christina Applegate
Burt Bacharach
Evan Bayh
Jessica Biel
Cate Blanchett
David Boreanaz
Benjamin Bratt
Tom Brokaw
Josh Brolin
Sandra Bullock
Andrea Casiraghi
Daljit Dhaliwal
Taye Diggs
Jenna Elfman
Emme
Joseph Fiennes
Toland Grinnell
Emmylou Harris
Lauryn Hill
Kate Hudson
Jonathan Jackson
Stephan Jenkins
Derek Jeter
Melina Kanakaredes
Nicole Kidman
Queen Latifah
Lucy Liu
Howie Long
Jennifer Lopez
Ricky Martin
Matthew McConaughey
Michael Michele
Monica
Carlos Moya
Aimee Mullins
Gwyneth Paltrow
Matthew Perry
Michelle Pfeiffer
Freddie Prinze Jr.
Rebecca Romijn-Stamos
Gena Rowlands
Keri Russell
Rick Schroder
Jaclyn Smith
Britney Spears
Jon Stewart
Meredith Viera
Alek Wek

Cathleen Webb—The New Hampshire housewife says she faked a rape that sent a man to prison for years, and suddenly finds herself an unlikely celebrity.

Madonna—She's a big girl now—rich, famous, and married to actor Sean Penn—but once upon a time, the reigning queen of all things pop was just another wannabe.

Rupert Murdoch—The empire-building publisher of the *New York Post* and freshly minted American citizen takes on television, Hollywood, and morality.

Dwight Gooden—Vulnerable only to kryptonite, baseball's best pitcher is quiet but deadly, playing a game he hasn't learned how to lose.

Don Johnson—Every woman wants his body, every man wants his clothes—that's why he's America's Friday night vice.

Princess Diana—No matter where she is she embodies dreams and always looks just like a princess.

Mel Fisher—In a season of shipwreck salvagings, Captain Audacious ends a 17-year search for buried treasure, pulling 34 tons of Spanish silver from the Key West waters.

Michael J. Fox—The comedy star of the year's No. 1 movie, *Back to the Future*, and the No. 2 TV show, *Family Ties*, puts on the dog as the boy king of Hollywood.

Mengele's Bones—Discovery of the moldering remains of the Nazis' infamous "Angel of Death" ends the most intense manhunt of the century.

Whoopi Goldberg—She's been on welfare and on Broadway; now she's on-screen in *The Color Purple.*

Rock Hudson—His name stood for Hollywood's golden age of wholesome heroics and lighthearted romance—until he becames the most famous person to die of AIDS.

The Springsteens—The storybook year of Beauty and the Boss ends on a harmonious note with Bruce and Julianne Phillips at ease at last in New Jersey.

Gracie Mansion—A hip gallery owner brings world fame to the brassy, flashy, sometimes trashy art that grows in Manhattan's revitalized East Village.

1986

Sarah, Duchess of York—Breaking out of the royal mold, a commoner marries her prince and wins a nation's heart without losing her independent personality.

Ivan Boesky—It isn't insight but inside tips that make this risk arbitrageur the demon of Wall Street.

Dr. Seuss—*You're Only Old Once!* made us hoot, made us cheer / Seuss wrote it for oldsters, it came out this year.

Bette Midler—No longer the wacked-out Divine Miss M, she becomes a mother and mainstream box-office draw in two hugely successful Disney films.

David Letterman—The *Late Night* host's askew humor finally finds a home in the heartland.

Pat Robertson—A television preacher bids to move from God's House to the White House.

Daniel Ortega—The 41-year-old president of Nicaragua wears baseball caps, wields his own AK-47, and bedevils the Reagan state department.

Raymond Hunthausen—Seen by the Vatican as the shepherd who strayed, Seattle's progressive archbishop believes he's keeping the faith.

Bob Hoskins—A pudgy, pint-size dynamo known as the Cockney Cagney shapes up as the actor of the year with appearances in *Sweet Liberty* and *Mona Lisa.*

Oliver North—After a series of bombshell disclosures, the question remains—was the President's marine a hero or a loose cannon?

Terry Waite—An envoy from the Church of England inspires international trust and obtains freedom for hostages in Beirut.

Paul Hogan—An Aussie smoothy makes *Crocodile Dundee* America's favorite easy-watching movie.

Howard the Duck—George Lucas's feathered friend turns out to be a turkey, as *Howard the Duck* loses $35 million.

Greg LeMond—Becoming the first American to win the Tour de France is no easy feat for the 25-year-old cyclist, who has to battle a mentor's betrayal.

Run–D.M.C.—Rap's Kings of (Hollis) Queens persuade skeptical rock fans to "Walk This Way."

Debi Thomas—The U.S. women's figure-skating champion finds the time to study microbiology at Stanford.

Helga—A Pennsylvania housekeeper bewitches the art world, as it is revealed that she posed for hundreds of previously unknown Andrew Wyeth paintings.

Vanna White—The latest in the line of Lite Celebrities, the letter-turning bombshell of *Wheel of Fortune* rakes in endorsements, writes a book, and leaves some wondering why she's famous at all.

Beth Henley—A Mississippi playwright goes Hollywood with a trio of quirky comedies: *True Stories, Nobody's Fool,* and *Crimes of the Heart.*

Jerome P. Horwitz—AZT, the anticancer drug he developed 22 years ago, is now our best hope in the battle against AIDS.

David Byrne—Letting down his avant-garde, the Talking

Head celebrates a wondrous, wacky America in his movie *True Stories.*

William Rehnquist—In all matters large and small, the new chief justice of the Supreme Court goes his own way.

Tom Cruise—A fave rave of the teen scene grows up to be the box-office *Top Gun* of 1986.

Max Headroom—With electrons for blood, computers for brains, and an ego as big as all TV, this nonhuman talk show host is Chairman of the Tube.

Whitney Houston—Singer Cissy Houston's shy daughter emerges as pop's prettiest commercial monster.

1987

Ronald Reagan—Entering his eighth year in office, the president remains vigorous and completes his term with a Hollywood finish.

Mikhail Gorbachev—The Russian leader who put a human face on communism takes the West by storm and ushers in an age of optimism.

Baby Jessica McClure—Up and running after her fall down a Midland, Texas, well and her televised rescue, she gets on with a normal toddler's life.

Gary Hart—Undaunted by negative press on his personal life, the Colorado senator re-enters the 1988 presidential race.

Oliver North—An all-American marine charms his way through the Iran-Contra hearings. Will he ever pay for his involvement in the arms-for-hostages scandal?

Michael Douglas—Playing a lech in *Fatal Attraction* and a slimy corporate raider in *Wall Street,* Kirk's son steps into the spotlight.

Patient Zero—Randy Shilts's book *And the Band Played On* identifies French Canadian Gaetan Dugas as a major transmitter of the AIDS virus. Forty of the 248 homosexuals diagnosed with the disease in 1982 had either had sexual relations with the flight steward or with someone else who had.

Donald Trump—Emerging as an icon for the '80s, this real estate mogul is pushing his way around in the media and in the marketplace.

Cher—Sonny's onetime partner, who says she "refuses to accept other people's limitations," soars as her roles in *The Witches of Eastwick* and *Moonstruck* bring her power, happiness, and a wider audience.

Christian Lacroix—A new designer's whimsical approach to his trade revolutionizes the high-fashion world and caters to the most chic of the stars.

Oprah Winfrey—The leading voice among talk show hosts is using television to fight apartheid as well as racism at home.

Vincent Van Gogh—Despite bouts with depression so severe they drove him to suicide, Vincent Van Gogh is emerging as the most marketable Postimpressionist of the twentieth century.

Magic Johnson—This talented point guard is leading the Los Angeles Lakers to the top of the NBA—and smiling all the way.

Church Lady—*Saturday Night Live*'s most biting holy roller flourishes in a year of sex scandals, church scams, and other *special* sins.

Princess Diana—Hints of discord follow the princess into her sixth year of marriage, as she and Charles spend more and more time apart and she begins to test the limits of acceptable royal behavior.

Donna Fawn Hahn—Rice, Hall, and Jessica, the women who fell with Gary Hart, Ollie North, and Jim Bakker, are actually all the same person—the three faces of Eve.

Bono—Struggling with sainthood, this rock musician spray-paints a work of art in San Francisco and tries to chip away at his heroic status.

Brigitte Nielsen—Newly divorced from Sylvester Stallone, she remains notorious for her leggy sexuality and questionable motives in love.

Tracey Ullman—Host of her own show on Fox, this British comedian astonishes and delights her audience, always hoping to avoid the bland.

Jerry Garcia—Despite more than just a touch of gray, the middle-aged hippie priest is still getting by—and is singing to a new generation of Deadheads.

Glenn Close—A 40-year-old actress battles her earth-mother image and becomes a screen siren with fatal attraction.

Garrison Keillor—The creator of National Public Radio's *A Prairie Home Companion* is happy with life in the aftermath of his show.

William Casey—Dying before he is able to testify in the Iran-Contra hearings, Ronald Reagan's CIA director admitted using any means necessary to defend the free world as he saw it.

Dennis Quaid—His sure-footed sex appeal and engaging grin ignite the screen in *The Big Easy*

Tammy Faye Bakker—Hurt by a drug addiction and her husband's alliance with Jessica Hahn, America's most unusual makeup consumer stuns *Nightline* audiences and makes herself a national joke.

1988

George Bush—The president–elect is a gentleman of the old school and a family man who is not above a bare-knuckled brawl when it comes to politics.

Jodie Foster—No longer haunted by would-be Reagan assassin John Hinckley, she makes an acclaimed comeback as a rape victim who fights back in *The Accused.*

Roseanne Barr—Looking at her, it's difficult to distinguish art from life—Roseanne plays the larger-than-life housewife both on and off the small screen.

Athina Roussel—Now only three, she will inherit over $1 billion when she turns 18—but money won't buy the love she lost with the death of her mother, Christina Onassis.

The Cyberpunk—The nerds rise again, as "misfit" hackers wreak havoc on America's information networks.

Florence Griffith Joyner—She may have won four medals as a sprinter at the Seoul Olympics, but she's still got two feet firmly on the ground.

Lisa Marie Presley—The King's daughter lives down a princess image by marrying a sober fellow and settling down.

Benazir Bhutto—A Radcliffe-and-Oxford-educated feminist becomes prime minister of Pakistan and discovers the challenges posed in being the first woman to lead an Islamic nation.

Liz Taylor—In another roller-coaster year, Liz writes an upbeat autobiography, raises millions to fight AIDS, and descends again into a drug addiction so severe that a staffer at the Betty Ford Center calls her the "female version of Elvis."

Michelle Pfeiffer—*Married to the Mob, Tequila Sunrise,* and *Dangerous Liaisons* prove that this actress is more than just a pretty face.

Jesse Jackson—He may not have clinched the nomination, but Jesse Jackson's presidential campaign shows that he is a political force to be reckoned with.

Phantom of the Opera—Rising from his lonely catacomb, this anguished spirit of the night beguiles us once again with a vision of the tragic depths of love.

Merv Griffin—At 63, the former talk show host becomes a billionaire and takes over ownership of Trump's Resorts International, beating Donald at his own game.

Anne Tyler—With her new novel *Breathing Lessons* and a film adaptation of her 1985 bestseller, *The Accidental Tourist,* a reclusive novelist is faced by an adoring public.

Orel Hershiser—Squeaky clean or tough and mean? Off the diamond he may be an angel, but this World Series MVP is uncompromising when he pitches.

Shi Peipu—Posing as a woman throughout his 20-year relationship with French diplomat Bernard Boursicot, a onetime singer with the Peking opera inspires David Hwang's Tony Award–winning play, *M. Butterfly.*

Kevin Costner—*Bull Durham*'s down-to-earth romantic lead sends hearts aflutter and critics abuzz.

Tracy Chapman—A serious black folk musician sings about a revolution and becomes one of the most successful recording artists of the year.

David Hockney—Twenty-Five years after making the move from England to sunny California, artist David Hockney and his bright canvases are the talk of the art scene.

Jessica Rabbit—The hottest woman on celluloid isn't a woman at all, according to fans of this sultry 'toon.

Stephen Hawking—Plagued by Lou Gehrig's disease, a Cambridge University mathematics professor works to unwind the mysteries of the universe—and writes a bestselling book.

Tom Hanks—A familiar face hits the *Big* time with his portrayal of a 13-year-old trapped in a 35-year-old's body.

Fergie—The Duchess of York's first year with the Windsors is not the fairy tale it had been cut out to be.

Mike Tyson—The heavyweight champion's most formidable opponent proves to be his beautiful wife, Robin Givens.

Sage Volkman—Thanks to a strong will and the miracles of modern surgery, this six-year-old burn survivor gets back her smile.

1989

George and Barbara Bush—After a successful meeting with Gorbachev abroad, George turns his gaze to domestic matters while Barbara helps Millie write her book.

Jack Nicholson—As *Batman*'s Joker, he romps in a role that fits him as closely as his white grease paint.

Arsenio Hall—This hippest night-owl of them all hops to the top of the talk-show totem pole.

Julio Berumen—The San Francisco Bay Area earthquake's pluckiest survivor takes his first steps with a new leg.

Princess Anne—Once Britain's least-liked royal, she becomes an object of desire.

Mikhail Gorbachev—He shrugs when the Eastern Bloc

cracks and proves he's serious about *perestroika*.

Salman Rushdie—For publishing the controversial *The Satanic Verses* he now lives with the threat he'll perish.

John Goodman—The TV Barr-tender and newly minted movie star is an extra-large hit in any medium

Gaia—The Greek earth goddess lends her name to James Lovelock's daring theory that the planet itself is alive.

Manuel Noriega—The Panamanian dictator gives American leaders fits, but he may be nearing his last hurrah.

Michael Milken—A junk bond entrepreneur makes $1.1 billion financing corporate takeovers—but his indictment brings an era to an end.

Paula Abdul—No longer just Janet Jackson's footwork coach, she steps out as a song-and-dance sensation.

Deborah Gore Dean—As the HUD scandal unravels, it's clear that she saw government as a game show and helped her friends win valuable prizes.

Robert Fulghum—His unlikely bestseller, *All I Really Need To Know I Learned in Kindergarten*, goes to the head of the class.

Madonna—In another typical year, she irks some Christians, splits from Sean, dallies with Warren, and gets canned by Pepsi.

Spike Lee—The director raises a ruckus—and important questions—with his film *Do The Right Thing*.

Ellen Barkin—She's tough, vulnerable, smart, very sexy, and doesn't quite add up; which may be why she's so riveting on-screen.

Billy Crystal—Learning that an orgasm can be faked, he becomes a genuine sex symbol in *When Harry Met Sally....*

Pete Rose—Charlie Hustle battles bad press, baseball commissioner A. Bartlett Giamatti, and his own demons.

Pablo Escobar—A Colombian drug lord markets death by the kilo while evading an outraged citizenry.

Michelle Pfeiffer—In *The Fabulous Baker Boys* she adds a dash of hot pepper to a delicious dish.

Elizabeth Morgan—Jailed for shielding her daughter from alleged sexual abuse, she is freed at last.

Robert Mapplethorpe—The photographer rattles the art world and Jesse Helms with a shocking retrospective.

Captain Al Haynes—In crash-landing a crippled DC-10 in Sioux City, Iowa, he saves lives with grit and cool.

Donna Karan—Her DKNY collection secures the designer's position as high fashion's newest mogul.

1990

George Bush—His place in history insecure, he faces a sea of troubles—and his most daunting crisis lies before him in the treacherous Middle East.

Sinead O'Connor—Her haunting rebel voice is heard in an age of flashing legs and lip sync.

Julia Roberts—After becoming the first hit female star of the '90s in *Pretty Woman*, she's sitting pretty.

Ken Burns—The producer of the 11-hour epic *The Civil War* makes a big bang in an unlikely place—public television.

THE SEXIEST MAN ALIVE

PEOPLE has honored someone with this title beginning in 1985. Here is a look at the magazine's hunks of the year. Discerning readers will recall the drought of 1994, when no one made the honor roll.

1985
Mel Gibson

1986
Mark Harmon

1987
Harry Hamlin

1988
John F. Kennedy Jr.

1989
Sean Connery

1990
Tom Cruise

1991
Patrick Swayze

1992
Nick Nolte

1993
Richard Gere and
Cindy Crawford
(The Sexiest Couple Alive)

1994
No winner

1995
Brad Pitt

1996
Denzel Washington

1997
George Clooney

1998
Harrison Ford

Patrick Swayze—More mesomorphic than ectoplasmic in *Ghost*, he's every woman's dream of a heavenly body

Neil Bush—His questionable involvement with a Denver S&L

puts a First Family face on the $500-billion S&L scandal.

Delta Burke—She has unkind words for her *Designing Women* producers; the next thing she loses may not be pounds.

Saddam Hussein—His invasion of Kuwait—bloody politics as usual for him—brings the world to the brink of war.

Michael Ovitz—The man everyone in Hollywood would like to know spins gold out of tinsel.

Nancy Cruzan—Finally off life support after eight years in a coma, she dramatizes the need for living wills.

Colin Powell—America's top man in uniform raises the world's shield in the desert against Saddam Hussein.

Fidel Castro—Cuba's leader stands alone and defiant after watching the lights go out all over the Communist world.

Effi Barry—She's a model of wifely decorum as husband Marion, Washington's mayor, goes up in a puff of smoke.

Dr. Anthony Fauci—He's used to taking the heat: he's America's point man in the fight against AIDS.

M.C. Hammer—He brings showbiz flash and footwork to rap—and cashes in with the year's hottest LP.

Bart Simpson—TV's intemperate urchin suits his audience to a T(shirt)—while authority figures have a cow.

Nancy Ziegenmeyer—A housewife and rape victim goes public to fight a once-unmentionable crime.

Nelson Mandela—He steps from the dim recesses of a South African jail into the harsh reality of freedom.

Francis Ford Coppola—The acclaimed director stages the movies' most ambitious mob

scene with his sequel *The Godfather, Part III*.

Keenan Ivory Wayans—His *In Living Color* brings howls of laughter and out-Foxes the network establishment.

Claudia Schiffer—No guesswork about this supermodel's genes—they come from Germany, via Bardot.

William Styron—His *Darkness Visible*, an account of his bleak depression, helps fellow sufferers see the light.

Laura Palmer—Wasn't washed up when she was washed up—she's the Girl Most Likely To Pique on *Twin Peaks*.

Bo Jackson—He can hit, run, rattle, and roll—and score on Madison Avenue.

Princess Caroline—Eight years after her mother's death Monaco's First Lady is coping once more with tragedy in the year of her husband's violent death.

1991

George and Barbara Bush—The First Couple's first concerns are war, peace, and their kids.

Jodie Foster—As an actor she's known as BLT (bossy little thing) because she isn't silent as a lamb, but the first-time director commands respect on the set with *Little Man Tate* .

Magic Johnson—He copes with testing HIV-positive by mounting a full-court press against AIDS.

Julia Roberts—With a busted engagement and a box-office bust that's no sleeper, she ends the year flying off to Never-Never Land.

Luke Perry—This hunk steals not only the *Beverly Hills 90210* spotlight but also the hearts of girls in all zip codes.

Anita Hill—Her testimony doesn't stop Clarence Thomas,

but it starts a national debate on sexual harassment.

Garth Brooks—His country album *Ropin' the Wind* crosses over to lasso the attention of all America.

Princess Diana—Surviving digs at her marriage and her AIDS activism, she turns a very regal 30.

William Kennedy Smith—He beats a charge of rape, but his famous family may never be the same again.

Terry Anderson—Unbowed after nearly seven years as a Beirut hostage, he emerges eager to catch up.

Boris Yeltsin—By elbowing aside both Gorby and the Kremlin hard-liners, he becomes Russia's new voice.

Kenneth Branagh—Taking a break from the Bard, he goes Hollywood with the hit noir thriller *Dead Again*.

Anjelica Huston—Recovered from the loss of a father and a lover, she emerges as Morticia, the *Addams*'s coolest ghoul.

Jeffrey Dahmer—His confession could not explain why his grisly serial killings went so long undetected.

Elizabeth Taylor—She must be the world's most incurable romantic; will altar trip No. 8 be her last?

Robert Bly—He says there's a bit of "hairy primate" in us all, and *Iron John*'s (mostly male) readers go ape.

John Singleton—His *Boyz N the Hood* opens middle-class eyes to inner-city life—not bad for a 23-year-old.

Naomi Campbell—With her drop-dead looks and her diva's temperament, she reigns over high-fashion runways.

Axl Rose—Lowering the sonic boom onstage and off befits the rock monster who is Guns N' Roses' lead pistol.

The 4,600-Year-Old Man— Freed from an Alpine deep freeze, he becomes the modern world's unlikeliest souvenir.

Mariah Carey—She becomes pop's queen by sharing her musical *Emotions*, not by truth-or-baring her life.

Derek Humphry—His best-selling suicide manual, *Final Exit*, ignites a passionate public debate about the right to die.

Pee-Wee Herman—Loses his image at an X-rated theater— but not his public, nor the support of Hollywood.

Norman Schwarzkopf—A hero after the Gulf, he now faces the challenges of a post-army career.

Jimmy Connors—Written off as a tennis has-been, he defiantly returns to the present tense at the U.S. Open.

1992

Bill Clinton—The president-elect and his family recoup from a rough campaign and prepare to leave Little Rock behind for Washington.

Hillary Clinton—Barbara's successor is a savvy lawyer who loves her country and her husband and is determined to make a difference.

Cindy Crawford—She shows the brains behind the beauty, becoming a video celebrity.

Ross Perot—Trying to crash the two major parties, he goes from can-do to quitter and back.

Denzel Washington—As a mesmerizing *Malcolm X* he catapults to superstardom.

Princess Diana—She dumps her hubby but gets to keep the kids, the perks, and the palace.

Woody Allen—His breakup

with Mia Farrow is like *Annie Hall Goes Ballistic.*

Larry King—*Larry King Live* is the whistle-stop that White House contenders have to visit this year.

Barney—The purple dino fossilizes the Ninja Turtles and gives kid-vid a Jurassic spark.

Billy Ray Cyrus—All pecs and no talent, said critics, but he's raising Nashville's pulse.

Terry McMillan—She can breathe easy now that her novel *Waiting To Exhale* is a surprise smash.

Gregory K.—He changes his name and sets legal precedents by divorcing his mother.

Desiree Washington—She scores a knockout in court over heavyweight champ Mike Tyson.

Diane English—The producer makes *Murphy Brown* a single mom and herself a lightning rod.

Madonna—She bares her body, blankets the media, and leaves fans asking, "What next?"

George Smoot—He finds the missing ripples that confirm the universe began with a Big Bang.

Katie Couric—With political know-how and a chipper personality, she boosts the *Today* show.

Fabio—Once a fantasy figure on romance-novel covers, he actually moves and speaks.

Arthur Ashe—He brings eloquence, guts, and grace to his instructive fight against AIDS.

Dana Carvey—Whether he's doing Bush, Perot, or *Wayne*'s Garth, he's always hilariously on target.

Bernadine Healy—The first woman to head the National Institutes of Health is brash and brainy, and gives women's health research a shot in the arm.

Carol Moseley Braun—The first black woman to be a U.S.

senator defies naysayers to win a place in the history books.

Henri Matisse—Sybarite and family man, this glorious painter has crowds standing in line to see his work.

Whoopi Goldberg—The actor is suddenly a Hollywood force more prolific than some studios.

Sharon Stone—She shows a *Basic Instinct* for sensuality and stardom—and doesn't sit like a lady.

1993

Bill Clinton—The president faces tough issues and a skeptical nation.

Hilary Rodham Clinton—She reflects on family life and the value of prayer while heading the committee on health care reform.

Princess Diana—She may be out of power in the palace, but she still has a place in Britons' hearts.

Michael Jackson—The pop star can moonwalk but he can't hide from career-threatening allegations of child abuse.

Yasir Arafat—With a handshake seen around the world, the PLO leader makes peace with his sworn enemy.

Oprah Winfrey—This talk show host becomes the world's highest-paid entertainer, sheds 60 pounds, and stays single.

Andrew Wiles—A shy Princeton prof you've never heard of awes the great minds of math.

David Letterman—Once an after-hour prankster, now he's the leader of the late-night pack.

Janet Reno—She wows Washington with her guts and candor, though you can't please everyone.

Susan Powter—Her hot *Stop The Insanity!* suggests anger might be the best weight-loss prescription.

Howard Stern—Radio's raffish raconteur exposes his *Private Parts,* and everybody wants a peek.

Baby Jessica—She focuses our eyes and hearts on the tangled arguments over parental rights.

Lyle Lovett—Country's wry specialist in heartache and rue wins the hand of winsome Julia Roberts.

Ol' Man River—The Mississippi inspires words of awe and rage, from days gone by to last summer's rampaging floods.

Jerry Seinfeld—He's got TV's most buzzed-about sitcom, a hot book—and an 18-year-old girlfriend.

Katherine Ann Power—In facing her bloody past she prompts a rethinking of '60s ideals.

Eddie Vedder—His hellbound vocals make Pearl Jam jell. Now he's got just one problem—he's a star.

Vincent Foster—His suicide brings sadness and self-examination to Clinton's inner circle.

Sheik Omar Abdel Rahman—A blind cleric is accused of inciting his U.S. followers to bomb and kill.

Michael Jordan—His surprise retirement shows that even the highest fliers need to be well grounded.

Rush Limbaugh—He bashes liberals for fun, profit, and the devotion of a fanatic following on air and in print.

Shannen Doherty—Unlike *Beverly Hills 90210*'s Brenda, the feisty actress runs amok in several zip codes.

Tommy Lee Jones—He's not the man you want on your tail, but you sure want to see him on the big screen.

Lorena Bobbitt—She provokes the national imagination with an act few could view with detachment.

Tom Hanks—Seen this year in three diverse and challenging roles, this star doesn't get caught up in the glitz of Hollywood.

1994

Bill Clinton—Foiled by failed politics and gloating Republicans, the president strives to restore voter confidence.

Tim Allen—Good things come in threes for the still-climbing star; with a hit film, book, and sitcom, he has the last ho-ho-ho.

O.J. Simpson—Once an All-American, he finds his greatest fame as the murder suspect of the decade.

The Pope—Despite failing health he delivers his message to millions in a book that lands at No. 1.

Princess Diana—She tries to resume private life amid allegations of adultery and instability.

Gerry Adams—The Sinn Fein leader calls for his Irish countrymen to lay down their arms.

Shannon Faulkner—The 19-year-old "Lady Bulldog" fights tenaciously to become the Citadel's first female cadet.

Michael Fay—In Singapore, the American teen is charged with vandalism and sentenced to a caning that sets off a worldwide debate: Is it spanking or torture?

Whitney Houston—Pop's top songstress takes her show on the road but walks a rocky path at home.

Ricki Lake—Less than 3.6 rating points from Oprah, she trounces her competition, walks down the aisle, and lands in jail for an antifur protest.

Vinton Cerf—The hearing-impaired Father of the Internet is working toward a universal network—his brainchild has doubled every year for the past six.

Michael Jordan—Basketball's king tries the summer game, gracing baseball during the labor strife that threatened to steal the season.

Heather Locklear—When not luring living rooms to join sizzling *Melrose Place*, she's planning her real life marriage to Bon Jovi's Richie Sambora.

Jim Carrey—He may look *Dumb and Dumber*, but that comic *Mask* shows off rare slapstick style.

Tonya Harding—The feisty figure skating champion slides into scandal and ices her dream.

Jeffrey Katzenberg—The Disney exec ditches Mickey and Pluto for Spielberg and Geffen.

Nadja Auermann—Forget the waif: This year's supermodel is a German import who gives fashion a shot of '30s glamour.

Aldrich Ames—For nine years before his arrest, this rogue CIA agent brazenly betrayed his country.

Christine Todd Whitman—New Jersey's new governor becomes a darling of G.O.P. moderates and moves up in line for the 1996 ticket.

James Redfield—His philosophical thriller, *The Celestine Prophecy*, breathes new life into New Age.

Andre Agassi—With Brooke in his court and a win at the U.S. Open, tennis's reformed bad boy serves notice he's back to stay.

Liz Phair—Alternative rock's hottest star looks perky and sings dirty, communicating that wholesome girls have prurient thoughts.

Power Rangers—Six multicultural teenage superheroes battle evil (and the once invincible Barney), but adults worry they are models of violence.

John Travolta—From disco prancing to ponytailed *Pulp Fiction*, he proves to be Hollywood's most durable comeback kid.

Newt Gingrich—The new Speaker of the House uses tough talk to tame Democrats.

1995

Bill Clinton—Taking on Bosnia and the budget, the rejuvenated President sees approval ratings soar.

Princess Diana—With a stunning confession to the BBC, she opens a bid to become "queen of people's hearts."

Christopher Reeve—Injured but not defeated, he finds a new role as a moving inspirational spokesperson.

Elizabeth Hurley—Actress, model, and Hugh Grant's better half, this Brit puts her career in high gear and her beau on a leash.

Colin Powell—The once and possibly future presidential candidate decides to stay high and dry above the fray.

Nicole Kidman—*To Die For* gives birth to a star and puts an end to the "Mrs. Cruise" label.

O. J. Simpson—After the verdict, the unsettling image of a fallen idol remains.

Marcia Clark—A beleaguered working mother loses the O. J. trial but wins in the court of public opinion.

Susan Smith—Convicted of drowning her sons, she's sentenced to a life of punishing memory.

Jay Leno—With a new set and a gentle bite, Mr. Nice Guy becomes late night's top dog.

C. Delores Tucker—Alarmed by what gangsta rap was doing to children, she declares war on media giant Time-Warner—and wins.

Jane Austen—Her novel Brit wit makes her hot in Hollywood—178 years after death.

Shania Twain—A Canadian honky-tonker sings her hard-luck heart out and watches her fortunes change in Nashville.

Brad Pitt—*Seven* proves this star's appeal to be more than skin-deep.

Babe—The sty's no limit to a charming porker who wants to be a real pig star.

Louis Farrakhan—Taking a step from hate toward healing, a demagogue tests the mainstream.

Ted Turner—The titan cheers his champion Braves and hitches his wagon to Time Warner.

Hootie & The Blowfish—What's in a name? For this fun-loving frat band, the sweet sound of success.

The Unabomber—America's most mysterious serial killer issues another bomb, more threats and a "manifesto."

Jennifer Aniston—Gen X's Mary Tyler Moore makes *Friends* and influences hairstyles.

JFK Jr.—With his own magazine, *George*, a political prince gets focused.

Monica Seles—Healed and whole, a leading lady of tennis returns to center court.

R. L. Stine—Churning out two dozen bestsellers a year, he gives young readers *Goosebumps*.

Selena—Not silenced by death, the Latina Madonna takes *Tejano* mainstream.

Cal Ripken Jr.—The Oriole restores the glory to baseball by playing 2,131 consecutive games.

1996

Rosie O'Donnell—The Queen of Nice cleans up the talk show.

Ted Kaczynski—A Harvard-educated hermit is charged as the Unabomber.

Carolyn Bessette Kennedy—She weds JFK Jr. and become's America's most watched woman.

Dennis Rodman—Nude, lewd, and tattooed, he cross-dressed for success, but is he all Bull?

Diana—Out of the Palace and into the world, she tried to find her separate peace.

George Clooney—The new Batman wages a real-life war against stalkerazzi.

Richard Jewell—Cleared as a bombing suspect, he struggles to restore his name

Binta-Jua—The world goes ape over a gorilla with a humanitarian streak.

Jenny McCarthy—MTV's rising star looks pretty and acts anything but!

Christopher Reeve—Undeterred by his paralysis, he works tirelessly for the disabled.

Kathie Lee Gifford—At first she cried...then pushed to put an end to sweatshops.

Dilbert—The office drudge conceived by cartoonist Scott Adams gets the last laugh.

Gwyneth Paltrow—For this hot actress, Brad Pitt is just the icing on the cake.

Marian Wright Edelman—Fighting for children's rights, she loses a White House ally.

Tom Cruise—Mission Accomplished: two blockbusters and three rescues.

Alanis Morissette—The pied piper of teen angst sets a music industry record.

Shannon Lucid—A working mom logs 188 trailblazing days in space.

Brooke Shields—With an unlikely turn to comedy, she's Hollywood's comeback kid.

Conan O'Brien—After a

stumbling start, he's the big man of the wee small hours.

Carolyn McCarthy—A victim of tragedy wins a seat in Congress.

Madonna—The people behind her latest reinvention are named Lourdes and Evita.

Tiger Woods—No longer a sport just for geezers, golf gets a Gen-X superstar.

Goldie Hawn—With two acclaimed movies at 51, her career is golden.

Chelsea Clinton—The First Daughter gracefully takes the stage.

Bob Dole—He loses his presidential bid but makes 'em laugh on Letterman.

1997

Princess Diana—Her sudden death becomes the year's defining event.

Bill Cosby—TV's model father copes with the slaying of his only son and the extortion trial of his would-be daughter.

Ellen DeGeneres—Out and about, she's reshaping TV's take on sexual identity.

Leonardo DiCaprio—In *Titanic,* he sinks—and swims toward big-star status.

Kathie Lee Gifford—Chipper no more, she adds cheating husband to her list of public travails.

Rudolph W. Giuliani—The mayor cleans up New York City —but not his antagonistic act.

Elton John—Mourning friends, he finds new inspiration.

Sheryl Swoopes—A basketball star controls the dribble at home and on the hardwood.

Beck—An ambitious iconoclast brings a fresh voice to pop music.

Andrew Cunanan—A killing binge ending with the murder of

Gianni Versace makes a chilling stranger an all-too-familiar face.

Michael Moore—Big Tobacco's worst headache wins billions in Medicaid costs.

Lucy Lawless—As Xena, she clears the path for powerful female role models.

Tommy Hilfiger—His bright, relaxed styles prove their cross-cultural appeal.

Frank McCourt—In childhood misery, a writer finds wisdom— and poetry.

Brenda Hoster—A retired sergeant major blows the whistle on sexual harassment in the army.

John F. Kennedy Jr.—Successful and settled, he comes into his own.

Bobbi McCaughey—Defying the odds and the critics, she makes history with healthy septuplets.

Madeleine Albright—America's top-ranking woman uses magnetism—and muscle—to foster diplomacy.

Drew Carey—TV's average Joe finds his audience—and bares a long-held secret.

Bill McCartney—A onetime coach exhorts men to tackle their familial and spiritual duties.

Jewel—Folk music gets a '90s poster girl.

Joseph Hartzler—Without grandstanding, this U.S. attorney wins a swift guilty verdict against Oklahoma bomber Timothy McVeigh.

Julia Roberts—Rediscovering her roots in romantic comedy, she's once more sitting pretty.

Dolly—Poor little lamb with no daddy and no mommy, she's all a clone.

Bill Clinton—The president faces an empty nest at home and a full docket of White House controversies.

1998

Mark McGwire—With 70 glorious home runs, he brought our field of dreams to life again.

Cameron Diaz—As the sweet center of a giddily vulgar comedy, she was really *Something.*

Kenneth Starr—He turned up the heat on the president so high, his own reputation got scorched.

Lauryn Hill—Canny and hardly *Miseducated,* she took hip hop to new heights with a dazzling solo doubt.

John Glenn—His triumphant return to space put the country in orbit as well.

Katie Couric—Rocked by the death of her husband, Jay, she carried on with courage and strength.

Chris Rock—His edgy comic candor made him a major player.

Edward Fugger—His quest to help you choose your baby's sex bore fruit.

Geri Halliwell—On her own, she emerged as a surprisingly admirable post–Spice Woman.

The WWII Soldier—Brought to vivid life on the big screen, won the gratitude of a new generation.

James Brolin—He stole Barbra's heart with an easy confidence, but he'll never be Mr. Streisand.

Camryn Manheim—She conquered large-size bias to triumph as a fully rounded Emmy-winning star.

Judy Blume—The queen of preteen fiction hit home with grown-up fans.

David Kaczynski—A concerned brother reached out to the Unabomber's victims.

Michael J. Fox—Sharing his private battle with Parkinson's disease, he offered a lesson in courage.

Oprah Winfrey—Though her Midas touch seemed to falter, she brought a *Beloved* project to completion.

Alan Greenspan—The mighty Fed chief held the world's markets steady.

Leonardo DiCaprio—Amid *Titanic* fanfare, he took a puzzling break.

Matt Drudge—This wired Walter Winchell spread gossip that all too often became news.

Calista Flockhart—Catapulted to fame as Ally McBeal, she faced scrutiny of body and role.

Adam Sandler—He perfected his sophomoric humor to become head of the Hollywood class.

Joan Kroc—Blessed with billions from burgers, she quietly

shared the wealth.

Emeril Legasse—The Food Network's star chef became hotter than haute.

Hillary Rodham Clinton—In a difficult year, she embraced dignity.

The American People—Whether voting, viewing, or investing, we defied expectations.

CYBERSPACE'S MOST WANTED

Search sites help Web crawlers find pages devoted to their favorite stars and shows. Here's who and what surfers sought out most often at Lycos (www.lycos.com) from March through July of 1999.

FEMALE CELEBRITIES

1. Britney Spears
2. Anna Kournikova
3. Pamela Anderson Lee
4. Jennifer Lopez
5. Jenna Jameson
6. Sable
7. Heather Graham
8. Shania Twain
9. Salma Hayek
10. Jennifer Love Hewitt

MALE CELEBRITIES

1. Ricky Martin
2. Justin Timberlake
3. Nick Carter
4. Howard Stern
5. Will Smith
6. Brad Pitt
7. Marilyn Manson
8. Stephen King
9. Tupac Shakur
10. Adam Sandler

BANDS

1. Backstreet Boys
2. N'Sync
3. Limp Bizkit
4. Metallica
5. Pearl Jam
5. The Beatles
7. Blink 182
8. Pink Floyd
9. Dave Matthews Band
10. Dru Hill

FICTIONAL CHARACTERS

1. Austin Powers
2. The Simpsons
3. Barbie
4. Winnie the Pooh
5. Lara Croft
6. Xena: Warrior Princess
7. Teletubbies
8. Darth Maul
9. Barney

CYBERWORLD: 20 ESSENTIAL BOOKMARKS

Some Web sites are good for a one-time giggle, and some will have you going back again and again. PEOPLE staff writer Samantha Miller selects some of the best—the useful, the dishy, and the downright indispensable.

1. Yahoo! (www.yahoo.com)
Yahoo! breaks down the Web like a card catalog, sorting through sites by subject. It's the perfect starting point for any Web expedition—or you can stay on the site for the news stories, stock tickers, and other extras.

2. Excite (www.excite.com)
Pepsi to Yahoo!'s Coke. Each of these two top search sites has its diehard proponents, but we say: just pick out which color scheme you like better, because the content is pretty much the same.

3. Deja.com (www.deja.com)
The easiest way to browse the thousands of Usenet newsgroups, the Internet's freewheeling forums on every conceivable topic.

4. The Internet Movie Database (us.imdb.com)
Everything you ever wanted to know about nearly every movie ever made. Cast, crew, reviews, release dates, and more—all linked so you can play your own version of Six Degrees of Kevin Bacon.

5. The Weather Channel (www.weather.com)
A stormy paradise for weather junkies, minus the Muzak. And handy for anyone without a window office.

6. Quote.com (www.quote.com)
This and other stock sites give you the most current market prices you can get for free.

7. ESPN SportsZone (espn.sportszone.com)
Whether your pleasure is baseball or roller hockey, this site dishes out more up-to-the-minute stats and scores than you can shake a stick (bat, racquet, javelin…) at.

8. Tripod (www.tripod.com)
Aimed at those headed from college to the real world, this friendly site's tips, forums, and news you can use are applicable to browsers of all ages—and its offer of free home pages has made it one of the biggest communities in cyberspace.

9. Infospace (www.infospace.com)
National yellow pages, white pages, e-mail address directories, and more—all the better to help you track down that old buddy or lost love.

10. FAQs
(www.cis.ohiostate.edu/hypertext/faq/usenet/top.html)
One of many sites archiving Usenet newsgroups' Frequently Asked Questions lists—one of the great inventions of geek culture.

THE MOST BEAUTIFUL PEOPLE ON THE WEB

Every year, PEOPLE's print editors name the 50 Most Beautiful People in the World. PEOPLE Online (America Online Keyword: People), meanwhile, asks Net surfers to nominate their own favorites. Here are the lookers who received the most e-mail votes in 1999.

1. Ricky Martin
2. Michelle Pfeiffer
3. Britney Spears
4. Jennifer Lopez
5. Jennifer Aniston
6. Freddie Prinze Jr.
7. Gwyneth Paltrow
8. Rebecca Romijn-Stamos
9. Keri Russell
10. David Boreanaz

11. Liszt (www.liszt.com)

A directory of the tens of thousands of e-mail discussion groups for devotees of everything from Japanese anime to Zoroastrianism. Net vets know private mailing lists are the best way to carry on an intelligent conversation.

12. The Obscure Store and Reading Room (www.obscurestore.com)

One guy's daily roundup of wacky and/or provocative tidbits from the nation's newspapers. If a blind golfer scores a hole in one—or a crook in drag holds up a bank—this site is sure to have a link.

13. Salon (www.salon.com)

Probably the most prestigious Webzine, with lots of arts, politics, and media coverage by marquee-name writers and those newly making big bylines for themselves.

14. The Drudge Report (www.drudgereport.com)

See ground zero of the Monica Lewinsky mess—the snappy, salacious site of one-man gossip machine Matt Drudge.

15. Ain't It Cool News (www.aint-it-cool-news.com)

Proprietor Harry Knowles commands an army of moles who attend advance movie screenings, providing early dish and perturbing Hollywood execs.

16. The Onion (www.theonion.com)

A humor magazine that's actually funny. Long a Net pleasure, it made the big time in '99 with its bestselling book, *Our Dumb Century*.

17. The Food Network (www.foodtv.com)

Watch the cable channel's goofy cooks, then head here to download the recipes free. Just the convenience to get couch potatoes into the kitchen.

18. MapQuest (www.mapquest.com)

Another great thing about the Net: enter any two places in the United States and get free personalized point-to-point driving instructions.

19. Microsoft Expedia (expedia.msn.com)

If you're picky about your travel plans—and who isn't?—it pays to book your own plane tickets. Here and on other sites (but hey, Bill Gates really needs the money) you can shop from a full range of flights and pick your own seat assignment.

20. Amazon.com (www.amazon.com)

You don't have to spend, spend, spend at this ever-expanding shopping site (although it's sooo easy...). Browsing its well-written and artfully designed book, music, and video info—plus reviews from users around the world—is free.

MOST POPULAR WEB SITES

Ranking the popularity of Web sites is far from an exact science. One method follows the approach of TV's Nielsen ratings—it keeps tabs on a sample of selected surfers and sees where they're clicking. For this May 1999 survey, Internet measurement company Media Metrix tracked more than 50,000 computer users and came up with the following most-visited list.

TOP NEWS AND ENTERTAINMENT SITES

1. ZDNet, Ziff-Davis computer magazines (www.zdnet.com)
2. MSNBC (www.msnbc.com)
3. Pathfinder, Time Inc. magazines (www.pathfinder.com)
4. About.com, online guides (www.about.com)
5. The Weather Channel (www.weather.com)
6. CNN Interactive (www.cnn.com)
7. Disney.com (www.disney.com)
8. Sony Online (www.sony.com)
9. ESPN SportsZone (espn.sportszone.com)
10. Warner Bros. Online (www.wb.com)
11. Digital City, city guides (www.digitalcity.com)
12. iVillage.com, news and info for women (www.ivillage.com)
13. Go2Net, financial and other info (www.go2net.com)
14. ABC News (abc.go.com)
15. Broadcast.com, audio and video programs (www.broadcast.com)
16. CNET, computer news (www.cnet.com)
17. CBS Sportsline (www.sportsline.com)
18. Star Wars, movie home page (www.starwars.com)
19. USA Today (www.usatoday.com)
20. The Globe, online community (www.theglobe.com)

TOP SHOPPING SITES

1. America Online Shopping
2. Blue Mountain Arts, greeting cards (www.bluemountainarts.com)
3. Amazon.com, books, music, auctions, etc. (www.amazon.com)
4. eBay, auctions (www.ebay.com)
5. CNET, computer software (www.cnet.com)

TOP TRAVEL AND TOURISM SITES

1. America Online Travel
2. Microsoft Sidewalk, city guides (www.sidewalk.com)
3. Microsoft Expedia, travel info and ticket bookings (expedia.msn.com)
4. Travelocity, travel info and ticket bookings (www.travelocity.com)
5. Preview Travel, travel info and tickets (www.previewtravel.com)

TOP SEARCH SITES

1. Yahoo! (www.yahoo.com)
3. Excite (www.excite.com)
2. Go (www.go.com)
4. Lycos (www.lycos.com)
5. AltaVista (altavista.digital.com)

THE PEOPLE 500

Previous editions of the *Almanac* have assembled essential dossiers and fascinating facts on an imaginary guest list of the 400 most compelling, fastest-rising, and indisputably established stars and starmakers, for a fantasy party to put Mrs. Astor's original 400 to shame. To welcome the millennium and accommodate the infinitely expanding galaxy of pop culture stars, we've made room at the Ball for another 100 hotly contested seats. Join us for the richest feast of star stats ever, and welcome our newest guests.

A HEARTY WELCOME (OR WELCOME BACK)

Marc Anthony
Fiona Apple
Christina Applegate
Rowan Atkinson
Steve Austin
Burt Bacharach
Gil Bellows
Roberto Benigni
Cate Blanchett
Billy Blanks
Andrea Bocelli
Helena Bonham Carter
Benjamin Bratt
Steve Buscemi
Cher
Shawn Colvin
Patricia Cornwell
Elvis Costello
Jeff Daniels
Judi Dench
Brian Dennehy
Portia De Rossi
Taye Diggs
Shannen Doherty
Robert Downey Jr.
Matt Drudge
Carmen Electra
Rupert Everett
Joseph Fiennes
Vivica A. Fox
James Gandolfini
Andy Garcia
Goldberg

Jeff Gordon
Geri Halliwell
Thomas Harris
Salma Hayek
Faith Hill
Katie Holmes
D. L. Hughley
Sammo Hung
Enrique Iglesias
Natalie Imbruglia
Wyclef Jean
Angelina Jolie
James Earl Jones
Mike Judge
Melinda Kanakaredes
Heidi Klum
Jane Krakowski
Ralph Lauren
Denis Leary
Emeril Legasse
Jennifer Jason Leigh
Rush Limbaugh
Laura Linney
Lucy Liu
Jennifer Lopez
Sophia Loren
Rob Lowe
Peter MacNicol
William H. Macy
Camryn Manheim
Marilyn Manson
Ricky Martin
Master P
Stella McCartney
Mark McGwire

Natalie Merchant
Debra Messing
Alyssa Milano
Jay Mohr
Monica
Leslie Nielsen
Nick Nolte
Suze Orman
Ozzy Osbourne
Robin Wright Penn
Bernadette Peters
Ryan Phillippe
Joaquin Phoenix
Natalie Portman
Freddie Prinze Jr.
Al Roker
Ray Romano
Rebecca Romijn-
  Stamos
Diana Ross
Keri Russell
Jeri Ryan
Laura Schlessinger
Rick Schroder
Judith Sheindlin
Kevin Sorbo
Sammy Sosa
Britney Spears
R. L. Stine
Charlize Theron
Courtney Thorne-Smith
Vince Vaughn
Cassandra Wilson
Reese Witherspoon
Catherine Zeta-Jones

BEN AFFLECK

Birthplace: Berkeley, CA
Birthdate: 8/15/72
Occupation: Actor, screenwriter
Education: Attended University of Vermont and Occidental College
Debut: (Film) *Mystic Pizza*, 1988
Signature: *Good Will Hunting*, 1997
Facts: Became friends with Matt Damon in elementary school. By high school, the pair held "business meeting lunches" in the cafeteria to plot their future acting careers.

Wrote *Good Will Hunting* with Damon out of frustration when they weren't getting many acting jobs. Eventually sold the script to Miramax for $800,000.
Famous Relative: Casey Affleck, actor, brother
Major Award: Oscar, Best Original Screenplay, *Good Will Hunting*, 1997
Quote: "To watch updates of your relationships on CNN is bizarre in a way I cannot explain. You think, isn't there something happening in Bosnia, by God?"

JASON ALEXANDER

Real Name: Jay Scott Greenspan
Birthplace: Newark, NJ
Birthdate: 9/23/59
Occupation: Actor
Education: Boston University
Debut: (Film) *The Burning*, 1981; (TV) *Senior Trip!*, 1981
Signature: *Seinfeld*
Facts: *Seinfeld* creator Larry David modeled the George character after himself.

Is an accomplished dancer and operatic tenor.
Marriage: Daena E. Title, 1979
Child: Gabriel, 1992; Noah, 1996
Major Awards: Tony, Best Actor, *Jerome Robbins' Broadway*, 1989; Grammy, Best Cast Show Album, *Jerome Robbins' Broadway* (with others), 1989
Quote: "I started losing my hair when I was a wee kid of 16."

TIM ALLEN

Real Name: Tim Allen Dick
Birthplace: Denver, CO
Birthdate: 6/13/53
Occupation: Comedian, actor
Education: Western Michigan University
Debut: (TV) *Showtime Comedy Club All-Stars II*
Signature: *Home Improvement*
Facts: Has nine brothers and sisters.

Appeared in Mr. Goodwrench commercials.

Provided the voice for Buzz Lightyear in *Toy Story*, 1995.

Paid $2 million for 26 acres of Michigan campground with the intention of keeping it in its natural, undeveloped state.
Infamy: He served 28 months in jail in 1978 for attempting to sell cocaine.

Pled guilty to impaired driving in 1997. When stopped by police, Allen failed four sobriety tests, including counting backward and reciting the alphabet.
Original Job: Creative director for an advertising agency
Marriage: Laura Deibel, 1978
Child: Kady, 1990

WOODY ALLEN

Real Name: Allen Stewart Konigsberg; legal name Heywood Allen
Birthplace: Brooklyn, NY
Birthdate: 12/1/35
Occupation: Actor, director, writer
Education: New York University, City College of New York
Debut: (Film) *What's New Pussycat?*, 1965
Signature: *Annie Hall*, 1977
Facts: Played clarinet every Monday night at Michael's Pub in Manhattan. Missed the Academy Awards ceremony for *Annie Hall* because it was on a Monday night. Now plays at the Café Carlyle.

Among his many neuroses: won't take showers if the drain is in the middle.

Was suspended from New York University for inattention to his work.

His daughter is named after jazz great Sidney Bechet.
Infamy: After details became known of his affair with Soon-Yi, Mia Farrow's oldest adopted daughter, Farrow accused him of sexual abuse of her younger children. In 1993, he was denied custody but retained visitation rights of their adopted children, Dylan (since renamed Malone) and Moses, and biological son Satchel (since renamed Seamus).

After adopting a daughter with wife Soon-Yi, Farrow commented: "I don't know how the courts permitted this, especially in light of a judge not allowing Mr. Allen to see his own children."
Original Job: During high school, he supplied comic snippets to newspaper columnists Walter Winchell and Earl Wilson; he later became a hired gag-writer on a retainer of $25 a week.
Marriages: Harlene Rosen (divorced), Louise Lasser (divorced); Soon-Yi Previn, 1997
Children: Moses,1978 (adopted); Malone, 1985 (originally Dylan, changed to Eliza, changed again; adopted); Seamus, 1987 (formerly Satchel); (with Mia Farrow). Bechet Dumaine, 1998 (adopted)
Major Awards: Oscar, Best Director, *Annie Hall*, 1977; Oscar, Best Original Screenplay, *Annie Hall*, 1977; Oscar, Best Original Screenplay, *Hannah and Her Sisters*, 1986
Quote: "I've never had an audience in any medium."

TORI AMOS

Real Name: Myra Ellen Amos
Birthdate: 8/22/63
Occupation: Singer, songwriter
Education: High school
Debut: (Album) *Y Kant Tori Read?*, 1988
Signature: "Crucify," 1992
Facts: She started playing the piano

at age three. At age 5 she won a scholarship to study piano in a conservatory in Baltimore but was kicked out by age 11 for refusing to practice.

Father was an evangelical preacher, a fact that figures heavily into her sex-laden lyrics in songs like "Leather" and "God."

Original Job: Piano player in Los Angeles lounges
Marriage: Mark Hawley, 1998
Quote: "I have vivid memories of being a prostitute in another life."

GILLIAN ANDERSON

Birthplace: Chicago, IL
Birthdate: 8/9/68
Occupation: Actor
Education: DePaul University
Debut: (Stage) *Absent Friends*, 1991
Signature: *The X-Files*
Facts: Lived in London during her childhood.

As a teenager smitten by British punk rock, she spiked her hair, pierced her nose, put a safety pin through her cheek, and dated a rock musician almost a decade her senior.

To hide her pregnancy, Anderson wore bulky trench coats and took three episodes off during an alleged alien abduction.

Believes in UFOs, ESP, and other paranormal phenomena.

Thousands of male fans have formed an online Gillian Anderson Testosterone Brigade.

Marriage: Clyde Klotz, 1994 (separated, 1996); Rodney Rowland (relationship)
Child: Piper, 1994
Major Award: Emmy, Best Actress in a Drama Series, *The X-Files*, 1997

JULIE ANDREWS

Birthplace: Walton-on-Thames, England
Birthdate: 10/1/35
Occupation: Actor, singer
Education: High school

Debut: (Stage) *Starlight Roof*, 1947; (Film) *Mary Poppins*, 1964
Signature: *Mary Poppins*
Facts: By age 8, had a fully formed adult throat and a four-octave voice.

The 1965 film *The Sound of Music*, in which she played Maria Von Trapp, was the highest-grossing film of its day.

She and husband Edwards adopted two Vietnamese girls during the war.

Under married name Julie Edwards, wrote two children's books in the 1970s, *Mandy* and *The Last of the Really Great Whangdoodles*.

Before starring in *Victor/Victoria*, was last on Broadway 33 years ago.

Rejected her 1996 Tony award nomination for best actress for *Victor/Victoria* because the show was snubbed in all other categories.

After surgery to remove noncancerous throat nodules threatened her singing voice, she appeared in the 1999 Tony Awards telecast in a duet with Carol Burnett and was in fine tune.

Infamy: Tried to shed *Mary Poppins* image by baring her breasts in 1981's *S.O.B.*
Original Job: Toured from age 12 with mother and alcoholic stepfather in a vaudeville act.
Marriages: Tony Walton, 1959 (divorced, 1968); Blake Edwards, 1969
Children: Emma, 1962 (with Tony Walton). Jennifer (stepdaughter); Geoffrey (stepson); Amy Leigh, 1974 (adopted); Joanna Lynne, 1975 (adopted).
Major Award: Oscar, Best Actress, *Mary Poppins*, 1964

MAYA ANGELOU

Real Name: Margueritte Annie Johnson
Birthplace: St. Louis, MO
Birthdate: 4/4/28
Occupation: Writer, actor, singer, dancer
Education: California Labor School

Debut: (Film) *Calypso Heatwave*, 1957
Signature: *I Know Why the Caged Bird Sings*, 1979
Facts: Nicknamed "Maya" by her brother, who called her "My" or "Mine."

At age 7, she was raped by her mother's boyfriend. Several days after her testimony at the trial, her assailant was found dead—killed by her uncles. She blamed herself for the death and did not speak for the next five years.

Tried to join the army in the late 1940s, but was turned down after a security check revealed that the California Labor School was listed as subversive.

Has received over 30 honorary degrees.

Read the inaugural poem at President Clinton's inauguration ceremony.

Infamy: In the late 1950s, she worked as a madam, managing two prostitutes in San Diego. Her guilty conscience caused her to quit after only a short stint.
Original job: The first black—and the first female—streetcar conductor in San Francisco at age 16.
Marriages: Tosh Angelou (divorced, c.1952); Vusumze Make (divorced); Paul Du Feu, 1973 (divorced, 1981)
Child: Guy Johnson, 1945
Major Award: Grammy, Best Spoken Word Recording, *On the Pulse of Morning*, 1993

JENNIFER ANISTON

Birthplace: Sherman Oaks, CA
Birthdate: 2/11/69
Occupation: Actor
Education: High School of Performing Arts
Debut: (TV movie) *Camp Cucamonga*, 1990
Signature: *Friends*
Facts: Actor Telly Savalas was her godfather.

Like her *Friends* character, Aniston

worked as a waitress after graduating from school.

The rail-thin Aniston actually used to be fat. When she realized that was keeping her from landing acting parts, she went on the Nutri/System diet and lost 30 pounds.

Because of her often-emulated shag, she was dubbed America's First Hairdo by *Rolling Stone* magazine.

Infamy: Caused a stir in 1996 when she posed nude in *Rolling Stone*.
Relationship: Brad Pitt
Famous Relative: John Aniston, actor, father

MARC ANTHONY

Real Name: Antonio Marco Muniz
Birthplace: East Harlem, New York City
Birthdate: 9/16/69
Occupation: Salsa singer
Education: High school
Debut: (Album) *When the Night Is Over,* 1991; (Film) *Hackers,* 1995; (Broadway) *Capeman,* 1998
Signature: *Contra la Corriente (Against the Flood),* 1997
Facts: Was discovered at age 12 by commercial producer David Harris.

First exposed to salsa music in his family's kitchen, where his father would play with a salsa band.

Changed his name not only because his listeners were primarily English-speaking but also because there was a known Mexican singer with the same name.

His first solo salsa album, *Otra nota,* which included "El ultimo beso," a song written by his father, went gold five months after its release in 1992.

Rejecting the typical flashy salsa dress, he often wears a pair of jeans, a T-shirt, and a baseball cap on stage.

During his performances, he always pays a tribute to the Puerto Rican flag.

Original Job: Backup singer for TV commercials

Child: Arianna, 1994
Famous Relative: Felipe Muniz, Puerto Rican jibaro guitarist, father
Quote: "I liked salsa, but I sort of saw it as guys with open collars and gold chains. I looked at my friends and I didn't know anybody like that."

FIONA APPLE

Real Name: Fiona Apple McAfee Maggart
Birthplace: New York, NY
Birthdate: 9/13/77
Occupation: Singer-songwriter
Education: High school
Debut: (Album) *Tidal,* 1996
Signature: "Criminal," 1997
Facts: Named after a character in *Brigadoon.*

A rape by a stranger at age 12 precipitated years of therapy and inspired the lyrics to her song "Sullen Girl."

After her parents divorced, she lived with her mother and sister in New York City. Leaving school to join her father in Los Angeles, she finished her high school requirements through a correspondence course.

Lack of a driver's education course has kept her from earning her diploma. She still doesn't have a driver's license.

Regarded as a loner in high school and was nicknamed "Dog" by classmates.

Began taking piano lessons when she was about 8 years old and debuted an original composition at her first recital.

At age 18, she produced a demo tape for a publicist and was instantly signed by a manager.

Follows a vegetarian diet and her typical preperformance meal is split pea soup.

Infamy: Used profanity at the 1997 *MTV Video Music Awards* show.
Famous Relative: Brandon Maggart, actor, father; Diana McAfee, singer, dancer, mother
Major Awards: Grammy, Best Rock

Vocal—Female, "Criminal," 1997
Quote: "If I'm going to end up a role model, then I'd rather not end up being the kind of role model that pretends to be perfect and pretends that she always has the right thing to say."

CHRISTINA APPLEGATE

Birthplace: Los Angeles, CA
Birthdate: 11/25/71
Occupation: Actor
Debut: (TV) *Days of Our Lives,* 1971; (Film) *Jaws of Satan,* 1979
Signature: *Married...With Children*
Facts: When she was 3 months old, she appeared in her mother's arms on *Days of Our Lives.*

During her period of "image-experimentation," she appeared on a poster wearing battered cut-offs and a black leather vest with nothing underneath. A falcon is sitting on one arm and a snake is wrapped around the other.

Bought her first house when she was 11 years old, using her investment money.

Her mother, poor and at one time on food stamps, took her along on casting calls.

She has 3 tatoos.

Relationship: Jonathan Schaech, actor (1998)
Famous Relative: Nancy Priddy, actor, mother
Quote: "As a kid, I was pretty wild. Now I think I'm boring."

GIORGIO ARMANI

Birthplace: Piacenza, Italy
Birthdate: 7/11/34
Occupation: Fashion designer
Facts: Entered medical school but after two years decided to join the military.

Designed uniforms for the Italian Air Force (1980).
Original Job: Medical assistant for Italian military, window dresser in a Milan department store
Major Awards: Neiman-Marcus

Award, Distinguished Service in the Field of Fashion, 1979; Cutty Sark Award, Outstanding International Designer, 1981

THE ARTIST FORMERLY KNOWN AS PRINCE

Real Name: Prince Rogers Nelson
Birthplace: Minneapolis, MN
Birthdate: 6/7/58
Occupation: Singer, songwriter, actor
Education: High school dropout
Debut: (Album) *For You,* 1978
Signature: *Purple Rain,* 1984
Facts: Named after the Prince Roger Trio, a jazz group led by his father.

Can play over two dozen instruments.

Now known as a symbol, or referred to as "The Artist Formerly Known as Prince," sometimes abbreviated to "TAFKAP."

After annulling his marriage, he said he believes marriage contracts "guarantee the possibility of divorce," though he did remain with his Mayte.

Marriage: Mayte Garcia, 1996 (annulled, 1999)
Child: name unreported (deceased)
Major Awards: Grammy, Best Rock Performance—Duo or Group, *Purple Rain* (with The Revolution), 1984; Grammy, Best Rhythm and Blues Song, "I Feel for You," 1984; Grammy, Best Soundtrack Album, *Purple Rain* (with The Revolution, John L. Nelson, Lisa & Wendy), 1984; Oscar, Best Original Song Score, *Purple Rain,* 1984; Grammy, Best R&B Duo or Group, "Kiss" (with The Revolution), 1986

ROWAN ATKINSON

Birthplace: Newcastle-upon-Tyne, England
Birthdate: 1/6/55
Occupation: Actor, comedian, writer
Education: Newcastle University, Oxford University
Debut: (Stage) *Beyond a Joke,* 1978; (TV) BBC series *Not the Nine O'Clock*

News, 1979; (Film) *Bean: The Ultimate Disaster Movie,* 1997
Signature: Mr. Bean
Facts: Earned a B.S. in electrical engineering but was rejected for a job at the BBC. Later earned a masters degree in computer engineering.

His middle name is Sebastian.

In elementary school, his fellow students referred to him as "Moon Man," "Doopie," and "Zoonie."

He drives go-carts, collects classic sports cars, and has written for automobile magazines.

His one-man Broadway show closed after only 14 performances.

He met his wife on the set of *The Black Adder*; she was a make-up artist at the time.

In 1994, he won raves for his well-known comical cameo as the misspeaking vicar in *Four Weddings and a Funeral.*

He is very protective of his private life and reveals very little about his family in interviews.
Original Job: Actor
Marriage: Sunetra Sastry, 1990
Children: Two children
Quote: "I am essentially a rather quiet, dull person who just happens to be a performer."

STEVE AUSTIN

Real Name: Steven Williams
Birthplace: Edna, TX
Birthdate: 12/18/65
Occupation: Wrestler
Education: Attended University of North Texas
Facts: Dropped out of school in 1987, a few credits short of a degree in physical education.

Began wrestling in 1989 for $20 per day.

Known as "Stone Cold" Steve Austin, he once shouted in a fight against Bible-quoting Jake "The Snake" Roberts, "Talk about your psalms, talk about John 3:16; Austin 3:16 says I just whipped your [butt.]!" Since then, he sells some 1

million self-designed T-shirts each month, with his Austin 3:16 logo.

Before he married Jeannie Clark, she was his valet, Lady Blossom.

His stats are listed at 6'2", 252 pounds.

He wrestles 180 shows a year.

Suffered a spinal injury in 1997 after wrestler Owen Hart landed on his head in a "tombstone piledriver," which left him unsure of his future with the WWF.
Original Job: Loaded trucks at a freight terminal
Marriage: Jeannie Clark (separated)
Children: Jade, 1981 (stepdaughter); Stephanie, 1992; Cassidy, 1996
Quote: "A lot of people relate to me. Look, I dumped my boss on his head. I think that everybody would like to do that."

DAN AYKROYD

Birthplace: Ottawa, Canada
Birthdate: 7/1/52
Occupation: Actor, writer
Education: Carleton University
Debut: (TV) *Saturday Night Live,* 1975; (Film) *1941,* 1979
Signature: *Ghostbusters,* 1984
Facts: His grandfather was a Mountie.

Was expelled for delinquency from St. Pious X Preparatory Seminary.

Had a cameo role in *Indiana Jones and the Temple of Doom,* 1984.

A police buff, he rides an Ontario Provincial Police motorcycle, collects police badges, sometimes rides shotgun with detectives in squad cars, and owns, in partnership with several Toronto police officers, a Toronto bar called Crooks.

He is very interested in the supernatural and has an extensive collection of books on the subject. He admits, "I've never seen a full apparition, but I once saw what could be termed ectoplasmic light, and that scared the hell out of me."

Co-founder of the House of Blues restaurant/music club chain.

Original Job: Stand-up comedian
Marriages: Maureen Lewis (divorced), Donna Dixon, 1983
Children: Oscar; Mark; Lloyd; (with Maureen Lewis). Danielle Alexandra, 1989; Belle Kingston, 1993; Stella Irene Augustus, 1998
Major Award: Emmy, Best Writing in a Comedy, Variety, or Music Series, *Saturday Night Live,* 1977

BURT BACHARACH

Birthplace: Kansas City, MO
Birthdate: 5/12/28
Occupation: Songwriter, composer, producer, arranger
Education: Attended Mannes College of Music, New York City
Debut: (First No. 1 hit) "The Story of My Life," 1957; (First film as composer of theme song) *The Sad Sack,* 1957
Signature: "I'll Never Fall in Love Again," 1960
Facts: He toured army bases as a concert pianist from 1950 to 1952.

Following army service, he was accompanist for Polly Bergen, Georgia Gibbs, the Ames Brothers, Imogene Coca, Joel Grey, and Paula Stewart.

Once he's left the recording studio, he does not want to hear the record again.

Unwillingly studied piano during childhood to please his mother.

As a child, he attempted to grow taller and fulfill his dream of becoming a football player by eating jars of peanut butter.

In 1957, he met lyricist Hal David and began years of collaboration— some 150 songs—and No. I hits, including "Magic Moments" (Perry Como, 1958).

Bacharach and David teamed with Dionne Warwick in 1962, and they had 39 chart records in 10 years, eight of which made it to the Top 10.

He cowrote with Carole Bayer Sager the Grammy-winning song "That's What Friends Are For," which became the popular anthem for the struggle against AIDS.

By the mid-1990s, his music enjoyed a revival, and five of his songs were used in the 1997 film *My Best Friend's Wedding.*

Bacharach now enjoys breeding and racing thoroughbred race horses.

Original Jobs: Pianist
Marriages: Paula Stewart (divorced); Angie Dickinson, 1965 (divorced, 1981); Carole Bayer Sager, 1981 (divorced, c. 1991); Jane Hanson, 1991
Children: Lea Nikki, 1966 (with Dickinson). Cristopher Elton, c. 1986 (adopted); Oliver, c. 1993; Raleigh, c. 1996 (with Sager)
Famous Relative: Bert Bacharach, men's fashion columnist and author, father
Major Awards: Grammy Award, Best Instrumental Arrangement, "Alfie," 1967; Academy Award, Best Original Music Score, *Butch Cassidy and the Sundance Kid,* 1969; Academy Award, Best Original Song, "Raindrops Keep Fallin' on My Head," *Butch Cassidy and the Sundance Kid*; 1969; Grammy Award, Best Original Score Written for Motion Picture, *Butch Cassidy and the Sundance Kid,* 1969; Grammy Award, Best Score from an Original Cast Album, *Promises, Promises,* 1969; Emmy Award, Outstanding Single Program, Variety or Musical, *Singer Presents Burt Bacharach,* 1970/71; Academy Award, Best Song, "Best That You Can Do," theme from *Arthur,* 1984; Grammy Award, Song of the Year, "That's What Friends Are For," 1986; Grammy Award, Pop Collaboration With Vocals, "I Still Have That Other Girl" (with Elvis Costello), 1999
Quote: "With technology today, you can make perfect garage music, but when you peel it back, maybe what's missing is melody."

KEVIN BACON

Birthplace: Philadelphia, PA
Birthdate: 7/8/58
Occupation: Actor
Education: Manning St. Actor's Theatre, Circle in the Square Theater School
Debut: (Film) *National Lampoon's Animal House,* 1978
Signature: *Footloose,* 1984
Facts: Nervous about Bacon's sex appeal, Paramount's Dawn Steel took his photo around the studio when casting *Footloose* asking everyone, "Is this guy f--kable?" (Obviously he was; he got the teen idol part in the 1984 film.)

For *Murder in the First,* went on a 600 calorie-a-day diet, shaved his head, and wore uncomfortable contacts that completely covered his eyes. When filming the "dungeon" scenes, he put crickets in his hair (to simulate lice) and got welts from being hit with a leather blackjack.

In 1994, formed band the Bacon Brothers with Emmy-winning composer, older brother Michael.
Marriage: Kyra Sedgwick, 1988
Children: Travis, 1989; Sosie Ruth,1992
Famous Relatives: Michael Bacon, composer, brother

ERYKAH BADU

Real Name: Erica Wright
Birthplace: Dallas, TX
Birthdate: 2/26/71
Occupation: Singer, songwriter
Education: Attended Grambling State University
Debut: (Album) *Baduizm,* 1997
Signature: *Baduizm*
Facts: As a teen, wanted to change her "slave name"; when her mother objected, respelled her first name, with the *y* symbolizing "origin" and the *kah,* ancient Egyptian for "pure inner light." Later changed her surname, choosing a riff she favored.

Is influenced by "mathematics," a type of numerology that equates numbers with personal growth and self-knowledge.

Formed the group Erykah Free with cousin Robert "Free" Bradford, but she alone was signed by a label. To symbolize his presence, she began lighting a candle at her concerts.

Gave birth to son, Seven (named because that number cannot be divided by anything but itself), in a planned home birth.
Original Jobs: Teacher, waiter
Relationship: Andre "Dre" Benjamin
Child: Seven Sirius, 1997
Major Awards: Grammy, Best R&B Album, *Baduizm,* 1997; Grammy, Best Female R&B Vocal Performance, "On and On," 1997

ALEC BALDWIN

Real Name: Alexander Rae Baldwin III
Birthplace: Massapequa, NY
Birthdate: 4/3/58
Occupation: Actor
Education: New York University, Lee Strasberg Theatre Institute
Debut: (TV) *The Doctors,* 1963
Signature: *The Hunt for Red October,* 1990
Facts: He is not naturally tall, dark, and handsome—he dyes his fair hair black.

Originally wanted to be a lawyer.
Was engaged to Janine Turner (*Northern Exposure*); she had the wedding dress ready and the invitations were sent out when they broke up.
Infamy: Was taken to court for assaulting a paparazzo, who had staked out the actor's house for a photo of his newborn; Baldwin's acquittal was applauded weeks later by the audience at the Oscars.
Original Job: Waiter and doorman at Studio 54
Marriage: Kim Basinger, 1993
Child: Ireland Eliesse, 1995
Famous Relatives: Daniel Baldwin, actor, brother; William Baldwin, actor, brother; Stephen Baldwin, actor, brother

ANTONIO BANDERAS

Birthplace: Málaga, Spain
Birthdate: 8/10/60
Occupation: Actor
Education: School of Dramatic Art, Málaga, Spain
Debut: (Stage) *Los Tarantos,* 1981; (Film) *Labyrinth of Passion,* 1982
Signature: *The Mask of Zorro,* 1998
Facts: Modeled for Ralph Lauren and Gucci.

Would love to play the Hunchback of Notre Dame, but thinks he won't be able to because of his good looks.

Studied fencing with the U.S. National Olympic Team.
Original Job: Model, waiter
Marriages: Ana Leza (divorced), Melanie Griffith, 1996
Child: Estela del Carmen, 1996
Quote: "I thought to myself, 'Oh my God. How disgusting.' Then I went to the first rehearsal and it was...so easy. I didn't lose my fingers, my ear didn't fall down. Nothing happens if you're sure of who you are." (On his first kiss in a role as a homosexual, in the 1988 Almodóvar movie *Law of Desire.*)

TYRA BANKS

Birthplace: Inglewood, CA
Birthdate: 12/4/73
Occupation: Model, actor
Education: High school
Debut: (TV) *Fresh Prince of Bel Air,* 1994; (Film) *Higher Learning,* 1995
Facts: The August before she was to enroll in college, she was asked by a French modeling agent to work at the couture shows in Paris. Within a week of that first stroll, "Miss Tyra" (as the fashion cognoscenti call her) had accumulated 25 more bookings.

Became the second-ever black model (Lana Ogilvie was the first) under contract with Cover Girl Cosmetics.

Director John Singleton saw her on the cover of *Essence* and felt she'd be perfect for a part in his *Higher Learning.* He arranged for an audition,

and during the drawn-out casting process they fell in love for a spell.
Relationship: Craig Taylor

DREW BARRYMORE

Birthplace: Los Angeles, CA
Birthdate: 2/22/75
Occupation: Actor
Education: High school dropout
Debut: (Film) *Altered States,* 1980
Signature: *The Wedding Singer,* 1998
Facts: Starred in a TV commercial for Gainsburgers when she was 11 months old.

After drug rehabilitation, she starred in *Fifteen and Getting Straight* (1989), a TV movie about drug abuse, and wrote her own autobiography, *Little Lost Girl,* at age 14 to clear the air. Credits musician David Crosby for helping her get over drugs.
Infamy: Began drinking at age 9 and started taking drugs at 10.

In 1992, posed nude for *Interview* magazine.

In 1995, posed nude for *Playboy.*

While on the *Late Show with David Letterman* in 1995, pulled down her trousers to display tattoos on her behind, then pulled up her shirt and flashed her breasts at Letterman.

She has six tattoos.
Marriage: Jeremy Thomas (divorced, 1994); Jeremy Davies (relationship)
Famous Relatives: John Barrymore Jr., actor and director, father; Ethel Barrymore, actor, great-aunt; Lionel Barrymore, actor, great-uncle; John Barrymore Sr., actor, grandfather
Quote: "I was born 10 years old."

KIM BASINGER

Birthplace: Athens, GA
Birthdate: 12/8/53
Occupation: Actor
Education: University of Georgia
Debut: (Film) *Hard Country,* 1981
Signature: *9 1/2 Weeks,* 1986
Facts: Filed for bankruptcy in May 1993 after an $8.1 million verdict

was rendered against her in favor of Main Line Pictures, after she dropped out of the movie *Boxing Helena*. Had to limit her monthly living expenses to $10,000 under bankruptcy plan. An appeals court later reversed the verdict, setting the stage for another trial.

Developed agoraphobia while a model. Threw her modeling portfolio off the Brooklyn Bridge.

Was involved with The Artist Formerly Known as Prince before marrying Alec Baldwin.
Infamy: In 1983, she appeared in an eight-page *Playboy* spread.

Bought Braselton, a town in Georgia, for $20 million in 1989, with plans to develop it into a tourist attraction. Dumped her interest in the town after she declared bankruptcy, leaving residents angry and fearful for their futures.
Original Job: Breck shampoo model, then a Ford model; pursued a singing career under the nom-de-chant Chelsea
Marriages: Ron Britton (divorced), Alec Baldwin, 1993
Child: Ireland Eliesse, 1995
Major Award: Oscar, Best Actress, *L.A. Confidential,* 1997
Quote: On *L.A. Confidential:* "It's great to be in a movie where people come up to me and say something besides, 'Uh, what were you thinking?' "

ANGELA BASSETT

Birthplace: New York, NY
Birthdate: 8/16/58
Occupation: Actor
Education: Yale University
Debut: (Film) *F/X,* 1986
Signature: *What's Love Got to Do With It,* 1993
Facts: Helped integrate her high school, where she was on the honor roll and the cheerleading squad. Went to college on a scholarship.
Original Job: Hair stylist, photo researcher at *U.S. News and World Report*
Marriage: Courtney B. Vance, 1997

KATHY BATES

Real Name: Kathleen Doyle Bates
Birthplace: Memphis, TN
Birthdate: 6/28/48
Occupation: Actor
Education: Southern Methodist University
Debut: (Film) *Taking Off,* 1971; (Stage) *Casserole,* 1975; (TV) *The Love Boat,* 1977
Signature: *Misery,* 1990
Facts: She lost the screen roles of characters she originated on the stage (Frankie in *Frankie and Johnny in the Claire de Lune* and Lenny McGrath in *Crimes of the Heart*) to Michelle Pfeiffer and Diane Keaton.

Terrence McNally created the character Frankie (in *Frankie and Johnny in the Claire de Lune*) with her in mind.
Original Job: Singing waitress in the Catskills, cashier in the gift shop of Museum of Modern Art in New York
Marriage: Tony Campisi (divorced, 1997)
Major Award: Oscar, Best Actress, *Misery,* 1990

WARREN BEATTY

Real Name: Henry Warren Beaty
Birthplace: Richmond, VA
Birthdate: 3/30/37
Occupation: Actor, producer, director, screenwriter
Education: Northwestern University
Debut: (Film) *Splendor in the Grass,* 1961
Signature: *Shampoo,* 1975
Facts: Rejected football scholarships to go to drama school.

Is famed for his reluctance to do interviews and his tendency to pause for a minute or more before giving a yes or no answer.

The longtime womanizer broke the hearts of many famous actresses, including Natalie Wood, Leslie Caron, and Joan Collins. (Collins even had a wedding dress hanging in a wardrobe for almost a year.)

A behind-the-scenes political player and auteur of *Bulworth,* made

noises about seeking the 2000 Democratic presidential nomination.
Original Job: Bricklayer, dishwasher, construction worker, piano player
Marriage: Annette Bening, 1992
Children: Kathlyn, 1992; Benjamin, 1994; Isabel, 1997
Famous Relative: Shirley MacLaine, actor, sister
Major Award: Oscar, Best Director, *Reds,* 1981.
Quote: "For me, the highest level of sexual excitement is in a monogamous relationship."

BECK

Real Name: Beck Hansen
Birthplace: Los Angeles, CA
Birthdate: 7/8/70
Occupation: Singer, songwriter
Education: High school dropout
Debut: (Album) *Mellow Gold,* 1994
Signature: *Odelay,* 1996
Facts: In 1993, making just four dollars an hour, lived in a rat-infested shed behind a house.

Mellow Gold, which includes "Loser," was recorded for $500, mostly at his friend's house.

Hung out in New York's East Village in the late '80s, where the "anti-folk scene" convinced him that there are no restrictions on subject matter for songs.

Mom was once a regular at Andy Warhol's Factory.
Original Jobs: Painting signs, moving refrigerators, taking ID photos at New York's YMCA, clerking in a video store
Relationship: Leigh Limon
Famous Relatives: Bibbe Hansen, guitarist, mother; Al Hansen, artist, grandfather
Major Awards: Grammy, Best Rock Vocal—Male, "Where It's At," 1996; Grammy, Best Alternative Album, *Odelay,* 1996

GIL BELLOWS

Birthplace: Vancouver, British Columbia, Canada
Birthdate: 6/28/67
Occupation: Actor
Education: American Academy of Dramatic Arts
Debut: (Film) *The First Season* (Canadian), 1987; (TV) *Law & Order,* 1991; (Stage) *True West*
Signature: *Ally McBeal*
Facts: First appeared in several low-budget films, one-act plays, and Off-Broadway shows. In 1995, he enjoyed his first lead in the TV movie *The Silver Strand.*

Proposed to his wife on Valentine's Day.

Landed a 10-minute role in 1994's *Shawshank Redemption,* playing the pivotal part of the thief who provided information about the murder of Tim Robbins's wife.

Co-founded a small theater group called Seraphim.

His first child was born in his home; a mirror fell and shattered as the baby let out her first screams.
Original Job: Hotel doorman
Marriage: Rya Kihlstedt, actress, 1994
Child: Ava Emmanuelle, 1999

ROBERTO BENIGNI

Birthplace: Arrezzo, Tuscany, Italy
Birthdate: 10/27/52
Occupation: Actor, comedian, screenwriter, director, producer
Education: Accounting school, Prado, Italy
Debut: (U.S. Film) *Down by Law,* 1986
Signature: *Life Is Beautiful,* 1998
Facts: Originally planning to become a priest, he attended a seminary in Florence, Italy, but left when the building was damaged by a flood.

The idea for *Life Is Beautiful* came from Benigni's father, who was imprisoned in Bergen-Belsen concentration camp for two years before being liberated in 1945. His father always added humor in the telling of his story.

When he was a child, his family spent three weeks sleeping in a friend's stable.

He was discovered at age 16 by the director of an experimental theater group while delivering an improvised, satirical, political speech in a Tuscan town square.

At 19 he began acting with a theater group in Rome while doing stand-up comedy.

In 1983, *You Disturb Me* launched his career as an actor-writer-director. It was also his first of many collaborations with Nicoletta Braschi, whom he later married.

A passionate Dantista as a youth, he could recite *The Divine Comedy* by heart.

The number Benigni wears on his concentration camp uniform in *Life Is Beautiful* is the same number that his role model, Charlie Chaplin, wore in *The Great Dictator.*
Infamy: In 1980, he mocked Pope John Paul II on Italian TV, and, facing obscenity charges, was fined and given a one-year suspended sentence. Years later, he exuberantly kissed Pope John Paul II instead of his papal ring during an audience and private screening of *Life Is Beautiful.*
Original Jobs: Musician, clown, magician's assistant
Marriage: Nicoletta Braschi, actor, 1991
Major Awards: Oscars, Best Actor and Best Foreign Film, *Life Is Beautiful,* 1998
Quote: "I am so full of joy. Every organ in my body is moving in a very bad way."

ANNETTE BENING

Birthplace: Topeka, KS
Birthdate: 5/29/58
Occupation: Actor
Education: Mesa College, San Francisco State University, American Conservatory Theater, San Francisco
Debut: (Stage) *Coastal Disturbances,* 1986; (Film) *The Great Outdoors,* 1988
Signature: *The Grifters,* 1990
Fact: Originally cast as Catwoman in *Batman Returns,* she got pregnant and lost the role to Michelle Pfeiffer.
Original Job: Cook on a charter boat for a year, to pay for college
Marriages: Steve White (divorced), Warren Beatty, 1992
Children: Kathlyn, 1992; Benjamin, 1994; Isabel, 1997

TONY BENNETT

Real Name: Anthony Dominick Benedetto
Birthplace: Astoria, NY
Birthdate: 8/3/26
Occupation: Singer
Education: Manhattan's School of Industrial Art
Debut: (Album) *The Boulevard of Broken Dreams,* 1950
Signature: "I Left My Heart in San Francisco," 1962
Facts: Marched with Martin Luther King Jr. in Selma in 1965 at the urging of Harry Belafonte.

Used the name Joe Bari until Bob Hope introduced him as Tony Bennett in 1949.

Served two years as an infantryman in Europe during World War II.

An avid painter, his works have been exhibited in galleries around the country.

Had released 98 albums as of 1999.
Original Job: Singing waiter
Marriages: Patricia Beech, 1952 (divorced, 1971); Sandra Grant, 1971 (divorced, 1984)
Children: D'andrea (Danny), 1954; Daegal, 1955 (with Patricia Beech). Joanna, 1970; Antonia, 1974
Major Awards: Grammy, Best Pop Vocal—Male, "I Left My Heart in San Francisco," 1962; Grammy, Record of the Year, "I Left My Heart in San Francisco," 1962; Grammy, Album of the

Year, *MTV Unplugged*, 1994; Grammy, Best Traditional Pop Vocal Performance, *MTV Unplugged*, 1994; Grammy, Best Traditional Pop Vocal Performance, *Tony Bennett on Holiday*, 1997

CANDICE BERGEN

Birthplace: Beverly Hills, CA
Birthdate: 5/9/46
Occupation: Actor, photojournalist
Education: University of Pennsylvania
Debut: (Film) *The Group*, 1966
Signature: *Murphy Brown*
Facts: Her father's puppet, Charlie McCarthy, had a bigger bedroom and more clothes than she did as a child.

As a photojournalist, was published in *Life* and *Playboy*.

Wrote a play, *The Freezer*, which is included in *Best Short Plays of 1968*.
Original Job: Model
Marriage: Louis Malle, 1981 (deceased); Marshall Rose (relationship)
Child: Chloe, 1985
Famous Relative: Edgar Bergen, ventriloquist, father
Major Awards: Emmy, Best Actress in a Comedy Series, *Murphy Brown*, 1989, 1990, 1992, 1993, 1995

HALLE BERRY

Birthplace: Cleveland, OH
Birthdate: 8/14/66
Occupation: Actor
Education: Cuyahoga Community College
Debut: (TV) *Living Dolls*, 1989
Signature: *Boomerang*, 1992
Facts: Elected prom queen her senior year in high school, she was accused of stuffing the ballot box. Was forced to share the title with a "white, blond, blue-eyed, all-American girl."

Raised by her white mother after her black father left when she was four years old.

Lost 80 percent of the hearing in her left ear from an injury sustained from a physically abusive lover. (She rarely wears her hearing aid.)

Learned she was a diabetic when she collapsed in a coma while filming the TV series *Living Dolls*.

She was first runner-up in the 1986 Miss USA pageant.

Played a crackhead in Spike Lee's *Jungle Fever* (1991) and did not bathe for days to prepare for the role.
Infamy: Sued by a Chicago dentist (and former boyfriend) who claims she never repaid the $80,000 she borrowed from him. Refused to settle and, spending $50,000 defending herself, won in court.
Original Job: Model
Marriage: David Justice (divorced, 1996)

JULIETTE BINOCHE

Birthplace: Paris, France
Birthdate: 3/9/64
Occupation: Actor
Education: Attended Paris's National Conservatory of Dramatic Arts
Debut: (Film) *La Vie de famille*, 1984
Signature: *The English Patient*, 1996
Facts: A big star in France, she is known simply as "la Binoche."

Was replaced in the title role of *Lucie Aubrac* while filming was already underway; Binoche felt some of her lines were out of character and wanted to rewrite them.

Her lucrative Lancôme deal requires only 10 working days a year.

Her parents divorced when she was four; grew up shuttling between each parent and a Catholic boarding school.
Relationship: Olivier Martinez
Child: Raphael, 1993 (with Andre Halle)
Major Awards: Cesar (France's Oscar), Best Actress, *Blue*, 1994; Oscar, Best Supporting Actress, *The English Patient*, 1996

CATE BLANCHETT

Birthplace: Melbourne, Australia
Birthdate: 5/14/69
Occupation: Actor
Education: Attended Melbourne University
Debut: (TV) *Police Rescue*, 1994; (Film) *Paradise Road*, 1997; (Stage) *Plenty*, 1999
Signature: *Elizabeth*, 1998
Facts: Her father died of a heart attack when she was 10 years old.

Dropped out of college after two years to attend drama school in Sydney.

After leaving England due to an improper visa, she found a job as an extra in a boxing movie filmed in Egypt.

She bites her nails.

Director Shekhar Kapur decided that he wanted Cate for the lead role in *Elizabeth* based on the trailer for 1997's *Oscar and Lucinda*.
Marriage: Andrew Upton, 1997
Quote: "Growing up in Australia, I always bemoaned the fact that I wasn't a bronzed surfer chick."

BILLY BLANKS

Birthplace: Erie, Pennsylvania
Birthdate: 9/1/55
Occupation: Fitness expert, actor
Debut: (Film) *Bloodfist*, 1989
Signature: Tae-Bo fitness program
Facts: Grew up with 14 brothers and sisters.

Inspired by Bruce Lee as Kato on TV's *The Green Hornet*, he took karate lessons and ultimately became an international karate champion.

Has trained Paula Abdul, Brooke Shields, Shaquille O'Neal, Ashley Judd, and Carmen Electra, among others.

Has been diagnosed with dyslexia.

He developed Tae-Bo, which combines aerobics, jazz, dance, karate, and boxing, to introduce women to martial arts.

Tae-Bo is an acronym that stands for *T*otal *A*wareness, *E*xcellence, *B*ody *O*bedience.

449

Billy Blanks World Training Center in Sherman Oaks, Calif., is the only place where the patented and copy-righted Tae-Bo is taught.

Was paid $1.5 million for his book.

By early 1999, his workout video had grossed $75 million.

Original Jobs: Garbage man
Marriage: Gayle Godfrey
Children: Shellie (stepdaughter); Billy Jr., 1976
Quote: "If you want to sweat, go sit in a whirlpool. I want you to get some power, I want you to feel like you can overcome anything."

MARY J. BLIGE

Birthplace: Bronx, NY
Birthdate: 1/11/71
Occupation: Singer, songwriter
Education: High school dropout
Debut: (Album) *What's the 411?*, 1992
Signature: "I'm Goin' Down"
Facts: Her father left the family when she was 4, leaving her mother to raise Blige and three siblings in a Yonkers, N.Y., housing project.

While hanging out with buddies at a suburban New York mall, made a karaoke-style recording of an Anita Baker song. That tape found its way to Uptown Records' CEO, who signed her to his label.

This Queen of Hip-Hop Soul has been dubbed the Aretha Franklin of Generation X.

Infamy: Developed a reputation for having an "attitude problem" after being sullen, withdrawn, and even nasty during interviews.

Sued for $1 million by her ex-managers for breach of contract, who claimed Blige was a "selfish artist" who forgot the people who worked to make her a success.

Relationship: Jodeci lead singer K-Ci (engaged)
Major Award: Grammy, Best Rap Performance by a Duo or Group, "I'll Be There for You/You're All I Need to Get By" 1995

ANDREA BOCELLI

Birthplace: Lajatico, Italy
Birthdate: 9/22/58
Occupation: Opera singer
Education: University of Pisa
Debut: (U.S.) Kennedy Center, Spring Gala, 1998
Signature: "Con te partiro," ("Time to Say Goodbye") 1995
Facts: Took piano, saxophone, and flute lessons in his youth.

Born with visually debilitating glaucoma, he was left fully blind by a brain hemorrhage at age 12 after hitting his head playing soccer.

His parents own a farm with a small vineyard from which his father still produces Chianti Bocelli.

Obtained law degree while singing professionally in piano bars; he then studied opera.

Big break came in 1992 when he recorded "Miserere" with Italian rock star Zucchero Fornaciari.

In December 1997, PBS aired an *In the Spotlight* special of "Andrea Bocelli: Romanza in Concert." He reached a huge pop audience with this concert of opera renditions in Pisa.

Loves horseback riding and skiing.

With over 20 million albums sold worldwide by early 1999, he ranks as one of the bestselling classical recording artists of all time.

Original Job: Lawyer, piano bar entertainer
Marriage: Enrica Cenzatti, 1992
Children: Amos, Matteo, 1997
Quote: "I don't feel I'm really credible enough yet as an opera singer. I still have to suffer a little while longer."

STEVEN BOCHCO

Birthplace: New York, NY
Birthdate: 12/16/43
Occupation: Producer, screenwriter
Education: Carnegie Institute of Technology
Debut: (TV) *A Fade to Black,* 1967
Signature: *NYPD Blue*
Facts: *Hill Street Blues* won 26 Emmys.

His father, Rudolph Bochco, was a child prodigy violinist who later played with orchestras in Broadway shows and with leading artists at Carnegie Hall.

Wrote material for *Ironside* and was the story editor for *Columbo*.

Turned down the presidency of CBS Entertainment in 1987.

Original Job: Assistant to the head of the story department at Universal Studios
Marriage: Barbara Bosson (divorced, 1998); Dayna Flanagan (relationship)
Children: Melissa, 1970; Jesse, 1975 (with Barbara Bosson)
Famous Relative: Alan Rachins, actor, brother-in-law
Major Awards: Emmy, Outstanding Drama Series, *Hill Street Blues,* 1981, 1982, 1983, 1984; Emmy, Outstanding Drama Series, *L.A. Law,* 1987, 1989, 1990, 1991

MICHAEL BOLTON

Real Name: Michael Bolotin
Birthplace: New Haven, CT
Birthdate: 2/26/53
Occupation: Singer, songwriter
Education: High school dropout
Debut: (EP) *Blackjack* (with Black-jack), 1979; (Album) *Michael Bolton* (solo), 1983
Facts: Wrote ballads and love songs for other artists, including Laura Branigan, Cher, The Pointer Sisters, and Barbra Streisand.

After the breakup of his band, Blackjack, he began recording solo in 1983.

In the mid '80s, he was a regular opening act for metal acts such as Ozzy Osbourne and Krokus.

A research library in the New York Medical College was dedicated to him in 1993 for his work as honorary chairman of This Close for Cancer Research.

Infamy: After a two-week trial in 1994, a jury ruled that Bolton's "Love Is a Wonderful Thing" is remarkably similar to the Isley Brothers song "Love Is a Wonderful Thing."

Marriage: Maureen McGuire, 1975 (divorced, 1991); Ashley Judd (relationship)

Children: Isa, 1975; Holly, 1977; Taryn, 1979; (with Maureen McGuire).

Major Awards: Grammy, Best Pop Vocal—Male, "How Am I Supposed to Live Without You," 1989; Grammy, Best Pop Vocal—Male, "When a Man Loves a Woman," 1991

HELENA BONHAM CARTER

Birthplace: London, England
Birthdate: 5/26/66
Occupation: Actor
Education: Attended Westminster School
Debut: (TV) *A Pattern of Roses,* 1982; (Film) *Lady Jane,* 1985
Facts: Lived with her parents until she was 30, helping care for her paralyzed father.

As a child, she wanted to be a spy because she loved *Charlie's Angels.*

At age 13, she entered a national writing contest and used the money that she won to pay for her entry into the actors' directory *Spotlight.*

Has made four films based on E. M. Forster novels (*A Room with a View; Maurice; Where Angels Fear to Tread; Howard's End*).

Famous Relatives: Herbert Henry Asquith, Britain's prime minister, 1908–1916, great-grandfather; Anthony "Puffin" Asquith, director,

screenwriter, great-uncle; Lady Violet Bonham Carter, a.k.a. Baroness Asquith, grandmother
Quote: "Period movies are my destiny. I should get a few ribs taken out, because I'll be in a corset for the rest of my life."

JON BON JOVI

Real Name: John Bongiovi
Birthplace: Sayreville, NJ
Birthdate: 3/2/62
Occupation: Singer, songwriter
Education: High school
Debut: (Album) *Bon Jovi,* 1984
Signature: Bon Jovi
Facts: Polygram executives gave the band a contract with the following conditions: John Bongiovi would become Jon Bon Jovi and only he would be given a contract. The other four members of the band would become Jon Bon Jovi's employees.

His first solo album, *Blaze of Glory* (1990), was "written for and inspired by" the film *Young Guns II,* in which he had a cameo role.

Title of Bon Jovi's album, *7800° Fahrenheit,* refers to the temperature of an exploding volcano.

Infamy: Had a legal dispute with cousin Tony Bongiovi, who owned the Record Plant, a New York City recording studio, over the extent to which Tony had aided his cousin's career. In 1984, Tony brought a lawsuit against Bon Jovi, the outcome of which gave him a producer's credit, a fee, royalties from Bon Jovi's first album, a cash award, and a one percent royalty from the group's next two albums.
Original Job: Floor sweeper at the Record Plant
Marriage: Dorothea Hurley, 1989
Children: Stephanie Rose, 1993; Jesse James Louis, 1995

BONO

Real Name: Paul Hewson
Birthplace: Dublin, Ireland
Birthdate: 5/10/60
Occupation: Singer, songwriter
Education: High school
Debut: (EP) *U2:3* (with U2), 1979
Signature: U2
Facts: Got his nickname from a billboard advertising Bono Vox, a hearing aid retailer.

In November 1987, U2 opened for themselves at the L.A. Coliseum as the country-rock group The Dalton Brothers.
Infamy: Was the first winner in Grammy history to say "f--k"during its live telecast (1994).
Marriage: Ali Hewson, 1982
Children: Jordan, 1989; Eve, c.1993; Elijah Bob, 1999
Major Awards: Grammy, Album of the Year, *The Joshua Tree,* 1987; Grammy, Best Rock Performance—Duo or Group, *The Joshua Tree,* 1987; Grammy, Best Video—Long Form, *Where the Streets Have No Name,* 1988; Grammy, Best Rock Performance—Duo or Group, "Desire," 1988; Grammy, Best Rock Performance—Duo or Group, *Achtung Baby,* 1992; Grammy, Best Alternative Performance, *Zooropa,* 1993

KENNETH BRANAGH

Birthplace: Belfast, Northern Ireland
Birthdate: 12/10/60
Occupation: Actor, director
Education: Royal Academy of Dramatic Arts
Debut: (Stage) *Another Country,* 1982
Signature: *Henry V,* 1989
Facts: Grew up in poverty in the shadow of a tobacco factory in Belfast.

Co-founded England's Renaissance Theater Company.

To prepare for *Henry V,* Branagh received an audience with Prince Charles to gain insight on being heir to the throne.
Marriage: Emma Thompson (divorced, 1996)

MARLON BRANDO

Birthplace: Omaha, NE
Birthdate: 4/3/24
Occupation: Actor
Education: Expelled from Shattuck Military Academy, attended New School for Social Research
Debut: (Stage) *I Remember Mama,* 1944; (Film) *The Men,* 1950
Signature: *The Godfather,* 1972
Fact: Exiled himself to his private island, Tetiaroa, near Tahiti, which he bought after filming *Mutiny on the Bounty* there in 1960.

Wrote an autobiography, *Brando: Songs My Mother Taught Me* (1994) to raise money for son Christian's legal fees, but the book was panned for omitting his many wives and lovers, the latter including Shelley Winters and Rita Moreno.
Infamy: Son Christian killed daughter Cheyenne's boyfriend and served time for manslaughter (1990). Distraught, Cheyenne took her own life in 1995.
Original Job: Tile fitter, elevator operator
Marriages: Anna Kashfi, 1957 (divorced, 1959); Movita Castenada, 1960 (annulled); Tarita Teripia, 1966 (divorced)
Children: Christian Devi, 1958 (with Anna Kashfi). Sergio, 1960 (a.k.a. Miko; with Movita Castenada). Teihotu Teripaia, 1963. Maya Gabriella Cui, 1963 (with Marie Cui). Tarita Cheyenne, 1970 (deceased, 1995), (with Tarita Teriipaia). Rebecca, 1966; Pietra Barrett, 1970 (adopted; birth father as James Clavell). Ninna Priscilla, 1989 (with Cristina Ruiz).
Major Awards: Oscar, Best Actor, *On the Waterfront,* 1955, Oscar, Best Actor, *The Godfather,* 1972; Emmy, Best Supporting Actor in a Limited Series, *Roots,* 1979

BRANDY

Real Name: Brandy Norwood
Birthplace: McComb, MS
Birthdate: 2/11/79
Occupation: Singer, actor
Education: Pepperdine University
Debut: (Album) *Brandy,* 1994
Signature: "The Boy is Mine," 1998
Facts: From ages 12 to 14, sang backup for the R&B group Immature.

Brandy's famous braids are styled every three weeks, with fake hair extensions added for thickness, in an eight-hour process.

Before starring in UPN's *Moesha,* played the daughter in the short-lived 1993 TV comedy, *Thea.*

Her dad was choir director at their church, so as a child Brandy was always showcased as a featured singer.

Wasn't allowed to date until she was 16, but her mother/manager did provide her with a $500/week allowance.

Enjoys jelly-and-fried-egg sandwiches.
Infamy: Sued by a management and production company for $5 million for allegedly breaking an oral contract to represent her.
Relationship: Wanya Morris
Famous Relative: Ray-J, actor, singer, brother
Major Award: Grammy, R&B Performance—Duo or Group with vocal, "The Boy Is Mine" (with Monica), 1998.

BENJAMIN BRATT

Birthplace: San Francisco, CA
Birthdate: 12/16/63
Occupation: Actor
Education: University of California, Santa Barbara
Debut: (Stage) Utah Shakespeare Festival, 1987; (TV) *Knightwatch,* 1988; (Film) *Bright Angel,* 1990
Signature: *Law & Order*
Facts: He is of Peruvian and German-English lineage.

At age 5, he participated in a takeover of Alcatraz Island with his Peruvian mother and Native American activists. He has remained active on behalf of Native Americans.

Was nicknamed "Scarecrow" in high school for being too thin.

Graduated with honors from college but left the masters program at American Conservatory Theater to begin his career.
Relationship: Julia Roberts
Famous Relative: George Bratt, Broadway actor, grandfather

TONI BRAXTON

Birthplace: Severn, MD
Birthdate: 10/7/66
Occupation: Singer
Education: Bowie State University
Signature: "Breathe Again," 1994
Fact: Learned to sing in a church choir. Her three sisters sing backup vocals on her albums. She and her sisters were only allowed to listen to gospel music, but she would "sneak

into empty rooms to watch *Soul Train*."

Declared bankruptcy in 1998. Some observers saw the move as a tactic to dissolve her recording contract, from which she had sought legal release on grounds of a low royalty rate.

Relationship: Curtis Martin
Major Awards: Grammy, Best New Artist, 1993; Grammy, Best R&B Vocal—Female, "Another Sad Love Song," 1993; Grammy, Best R&B Vocal—Female, "Breathe Again," 1994; Grammy, Best Pop Vocal—Female, "Un-break My Heart," 1996; Grammy, Best R&B Vocal—Female, "You're Makin' Me High," 1996

JEFF BRIDGES

Birthplace: Los Angeles, CA
Birthdate: 12/4/49
Occupation: Actor
Education: High school, Herbert Berghof Studio
Debut: (Film) *The Company She Keeps*, 1950; (TV) *Sea Hunt*, 1957
Signature: *The Fabulous Baker Boys*, 1989
Facts: Joined the Coast Guard Reserves in 1968 to avoid the draft.

At age 16, he wrote a song included on the soundtrack of the 1969 film *John and Mary*, which starred Dustin Hoffman and Mia Farrow, and sold two compositions to Quincy Jones. To date, he has written over 200 songs.

Has exhibited his paintings and photographs in art galleries.
Infamy: In high school, developed a dependency on marijuana. He joined DAWN (Developing Adolescents Without Narcotics) and kicked the habit.
Marriage: Susan Gaston, 1977
Children: Isabelle, 1982; Jessica, 1984; Hayley, 1988
Famous Relatives: Lloyd Bridges, actor, father; Beau Bridges, actor, brother

CHRISTIE BRINKLEY

Birthplace: Malibu, CA
Birthdate: 2/2/54
Occupation: Supermodel
Education: UCLA
Debut: (Film) *National Lampoon's Vacation*, 1983
Signature: Cover Girl Cosmetics model
Facts: An avid Francophile, Brinkley transferred from her local high school to the Lycée Français in Los Angeles. She later dropped out of college and worked at odd jobs selling ice cream, clothes, and plants to earn money for a ticket to Paris.

Designed the cover for Billy Joel's *River of Dreams* album.

Married Taubman atop a ski mountain, a symbolic acknowledgment of the helicopter crash they both survived while heli-skiing in 1994.
Original Job: Painter
Marriages: Jean Francois Allaux (divorced); Billy Joel (divorced); Rick Taubman (divorced); Peter Cook, 1996
Children: Alexa Ray, 1985 (with Billy Joel). Jack Paris, 1995 (with Ricky Taubman). Sailor Lee, 1998
Famous Relative: David Brinkley, scriptwriter, producer, father

MATTHEW BRODERICK

Birthplace: New York, NY
Birthdate: 3/21/62
Occupation: Actor
Debut: (Stage) *Torch Song Trilogy*, 1982; (Film) *Max Dugan Returns*, 1983
Signature: *Ferris Bueller's Day Off*, 1986
Fact: Was heavily influenced by father James Broderick, who played the father in the TV series *Family* and died of cancer in 1982.
Infamy: While on vacation in Northern Ireland in 1987 with his then-girlfriend, actress Jennifer Grey, Broderick suffered a broken leg when the car he was driving collided with another automobile, killing its two occupants. Broderick was acquitted of one count of manslaughter and reckless driving.
Marriage: Sarah Jessica Parker, 1997
Famous Relative: James Broderick, character actor, father
Major Awards: Tony, Best Featured Actor (Dramatic), *Brighton Beach Memoirs*, 1983; Tony, Best Actor (Musical), *How To Succeed in Business Without Really Trying*, 1995

TOM BROKAW

Birthplace: Yankton, SD
Birthdate: 2/6/40
Occupation: Anchor, correspondent, managing editor
Education: University of South Dakota
Debut: (TV) KTIV, Sioux City, IA, 1960
Signature: *NBC Nightly News*
Facts: Served as president of high school student body. Also met future wife who became Miss South Dakota in high school.

Began with NBC as their White House correspondent in 1973.

Was the only network anchor present at the collapse of the Berlin Wall in 1989.
Marriage: Meredith, 1962
Children: Jennifer, 1966; Andrea, 1968; Sarah, 1970
Major Awards: 6 News and Documentary Emmys: 4 as anchor, 1 as interviewer, 1 as managing editor

GARTH BROOKS

Real Name: Troyal Garth Brooks
Birthplace: Tulsa, OK
Birthdate: 2/7/62
Occupation: Singer, songwriter
Education: Oklahoma State University
Debut: (Album) *Garth Brooks*, 1989
Signature: *Ropin' the Wind*, 1991
Facts: In 1990 at age 28, Garth became the youngest member of Nashville's Grand Ole Opry.

Brooks met his future wife while

working as a bouncer. (He threw her out for fighting.)

In 1991, *Ropin' the Wind* became the first country album ever to reach No. 1 on the *Billboard* pop chart.

The video for "The Thunder Rolls," about a cheating husband shot by his battered wife after coming home drunk, was banned by Country Music Television and The Nashville Network. Thousands of shelters for battered women in America used the video in group counseling sessions.

Brooks' half sister is his bassist, his brother handles the books, and a college roommate is one of his guitarists.

Refused the Artist of the Year title from the American Music Awards in 1996, later explaining "I just couldn't accept it, just out of the love of the fellow musicians. I think we're all one."

Took time off from music to try and play professional baseball. He joined the San Diego Padres for spring training but did not make the team. Playing left field, Brooks went 1 for 22 at the plate.

Original Job: Bouncer in a nightclub
Marriage: Sandy Mahl, 1986
Children: Taylor Mayne Pearl, 1992; August Anna, 1994; Allie Colleen, 1996
Famous Relative: Colleen Carroll, singer, mother
Major Awards: Grammy, Best Country Vocal—Male, *Ropin' the Wind,* 1991; Grammy, Best Country Vocal—Collaboration, "In Another's Eyes" (with Trisha Yearwood), 1997

JAMES L. BROOKS

Birthplace: North Bergen, NJ
Birthdate: 5/9/40
Occupation: Producer, director, actor, screenwriter
Education: New York University
Debut: (TV) *Room 222,* 1969; (Film) *Starting Over,* 1979
Signature: *The Mary Tyler Moore Show*

Facts: Founded Gracie Films, which produces *The Simpsons,* in 1984.

With fellow writer Allan Burns, created *The Mary Tyler Moore Show* in 1970.
Original Job: Copyboy for CBS News
Marriages: Marianne Catherine Morrissey (divorced), Holly Beth Holmberg, 1978
Children: Amy Lorraine, 1971 (with Morrissey); Chloe, c. 1984; Cooper, c. 1986; Joseph, c. 1993 (with Holmberg)
Major Awards: Emmy, Best Writing in a Comedy Series, *The Mary Tyler Moore Show,* 1971, 1977; Emmy, Best Comedy Series, *The Mary Tyler Moore Show,* 1975, 1976, 1977; Emmy, Best Comedy Series, *Taxi,* 1979, 1980, 1981; Oscar, Best Director, *Terms of Endearment,* 1983; Oscar, Best Adapted Screenplay, *Terms of Endearment,* 1983; Emmy, Outstanding Variety, Music, or Comedy Program, *The Tracey Ullman Show,* 1989; Emmy, Outstanding Animated Program, *The Simpsons,* 1990, 1991

MEL BROOKS

Real Name: Melvin Kaminsky
Birthplace: Brooklyn, NY
Birthdate: 6/28/26
Occupation: Actor, writer, director, producer
Education: Boston College
Debut: (Stage) *Broadway Revue,* 1949; (TV) *Your Show of Shows,* 1950
Signature: *Blazing Saddles,* 1974
Facts: Fought in Battle of the Bulge during World War II.

Co-creator of the TV series *Get Smart.*
Original Job: Drummer
Marriages: Florence Baum, 1950 (divorced); Anne Bancroft, 1964
Children: Stephanie; 1951; Nicholas, 1952; Edward, 1953; (with Florence Baum). Maximillian, 1972
Major Awards: Emmy, Best Writing in a Variety or Music Program, *Howard Morris Special,* 1967; Oscar,

Best Original Screenplay, *The Producers,* 1968; Emmy, Best Guest Actor in a Comedy Series, *Mad About You,* 1997; Grammy, Best Comedy Album, *The 2000 Year Old Man In The Year 2000* (with Carl Reiner), 1998

PIERCE BROSNAN

Birthplace: Navan, County Meath, Ireland
Birthdate: 5/16/52
Occupation: Actor
Debut: (Stage) *Wait Until Dark,* 1976; (Film) *The Mirror Crack'd,* 1980; (TV) *Remington Steele,* 1982
Signature: *Tomorrow Never Dies,* 1997
Facts: Wife, Cassandra (best known for playing Countess Lisl in *For Your Eyes Only,* 1981), introduced Brosnan to Albert Broccoli, producer of the 007 series. Brosnan almost replaced Roger Moore as James Bond, but couldn't get out of his contract with NBC's *Remington Steele.*

In 1995, he finally played Bond in *Goldeneye,* and is credited with helping to revive the then-ailing series.

Ran away with the circus as a fire eater in his teens.
Original Job: Commercial artist
Marriages: Cassandra Harris, 1977 (deceased, 1991); Keely Shaye-Smith (relationship).
Children: Charlotte, 1971 (stepdaughter); Christopher, 1972 (stepson); Sean William, 1984; (with Cassandra Harris). Dylan Thomas, 1997

KOBE BRYANT

Birthplace: Philadelphia, PA
Birthdate: 8/23/78
Occupation: Basketball player
Education: High school
Debut: (N.B.A.) Los Angeles Lakers, 1996
Facts: Was named for the Kobe steak house in suburban Philadelphia.

His family moved to Italy for eight years when he was six; there his father played pro ball.

In high school, shattered all of Wilt Chamberlain's Pennsylvania school scoring records by more than 500 points.

Took *Moesha*'s Brandy to his prom.

Has written "spiritual rap" with the rap group Cheizaw. His hip-hop name is "Kobe One Kenobe the Eighth."

Famous Relative: Joe "Jelly Bean" Bryant, basketball player, father

JIMMY BUFFETT

Birthplace: Pascagoula, MS
Birthdate: 12/25/46
Occupation: Singer, songwriter
Education: University of Southern Mississippi
Debut: (Album) *Down to Earth*, 1970
Signature: "Margaritaville"
Facts: Has chaired Florida's Save the Manatee Club since its inception in 1981. In 1992, sued the parent Florida Audubon Society for independent control of the club, arguing that the society was "too cozy" with many of the businesses he felt were polluters.

Wrote a children's book, *The Jolly Man*, with his eight-year-old daughter in 1987. Also wrote two novels, including *Tales from Margaritaville* (1989) and a bestselling memoir, *A Pirate Looks at Fifty*. Received a $3-million advance for a collection of tropical short stories.

In 1991, four Cuban exiles seeking political asylum swam to Buffett's Florida house. He handed them over to the authorities after offering them refreshments.

Also owns the Margaritaville Cafe franchise.

Original Job: Reviewer for *Billboard* magazine and freelance writer for *Inside Sports* and *Outside* magazines
Marriage: Jane Slagsvol, 1977
Children: Savannah Jane, 1979; Sarah, 1992; Cameron Marley (adopted).

SANDRA BULLOCK

Birthplace: Arlington, VA
Birthdate: 7/26/64
Occupation: Actor
Education: East Carolina University, Neighborhood Playhouse with Sanford Meisner
Debut: (Film) *Fire on the Amazon*, 1990
Signature: *Speed*, 1994
Facts: Her mother was a European opera singer, so as a child Bullock shuttled between Austria, Germany, and the U.S.

Was a cheerleader in high school.

Played lead actress in the short-lived TV series *Working Girl*.

Her role in *While You Were Sleeping* was originally offered to Demi Moore, whose salary demands were out of reach.
Original Job: Waitress
Famous Relative: Helga Bullock, mother, opera singer

ED BURNS

Birthplace: Valley Stream, NY
Birthdate: 1/29/68
Occupation: Director, actor, writer
Education: Attended Hunter College
Debut: (Film) *The Brothers McMullen*, 1995
Signature: *The Brothers McMullen*
Facts: His first seven screenplays were rejected by agents and producers.

The Brothers McMullen was shot in eight months for around $20,000 (primarily a loan from dad), with Burns's parents' home the principal set.

Won the Catholic Daughters of America Poetry Award in sixth grade for a poem "about Jesus and a tree."
Original Job: Production assistant, *Entertainment Tonight*
Relationship: Heather Graham
Quote: "I try not to read reviews unless they're absolutely glowing. I don't read mixed or negative at all, because life's too short."

STEVE BUSCEMI

Birthplace: Brooklyn, NY
Birthdate: 12/13/57
Occupation: Actor, director
Education: Attended Nassau Community College and Lee Strasberg Institute
Debut: (Film) *The Way It Is, or Eurydice in the Avenues*, 1984; (TV) *Miami Vice*, 1988
Signature: *Fargo*, 1996
Facts: Was hit by a bus when he was a child and received a settlement that he later used to finance acting lessons.

His wife, a performance artist-choreographer-filmmaker, has cast him in several of her performances.

Directed and starred in *Trees Lounge* in 1996, a film based on what his life on Long Island would have been like if he'd never moved to Manhattan to pursue acting. Also directed TV commercials for Nike, and a 1998 episode of *Homicide*. Will direct a series of episodes of HBO's *Oz* for the 1999–2000 season.
Infamy: When he was 16, he was arrested for trespassing in a Burger King parking lot.

He used to squeeze through the back window of a bar to steal crates of beer for his friends.
Original Jobs: Ice cream truck driver, comedian, firefighter
Marriage: Jo Andres
Child: Lucian, 1991
Famous Relatives: Michael Buscemi, actor, brother
Quote: "I guess I sometimes get frustrated about having played too many seedy, ratty guys. But, I'm working."

NICOLAS CAGE

Real Name: Nicholas Coppola
Birthplace: Long Beach, CA
Birthdate: 1/7/64
Occupation: Actor
Education: High school dropout
Debut: (TV) *The Best of Times*, 1980; (Film) *Valley Girl*, 1983
Signature: *Con Air*, 1997

Facts: Was expelled from elementary school.

Changed his last name to have an identity independent of his famous uncle. He assumed the name Cage in admiration of the avant-garde composer John Cage and comic-book character Luke Cage.

His method-acting techniques have involved having wisdom teeth removed without Novocaine for his role as a wounded war veteran in *Birdy*, slashing his arm with a knife in *Racing with the Moon*, and consuming a live cockroach for *Vampire's Kiss*.

Eight years before marrying Patricia Arquette, Cage proposed to her by volunteering to go on "a quest" for her. When he came up with a few of her chosen items—including J. D. Salinger's signature and a (spray-painted) black orchid—Arquette called off the deal.

Infamy: In 1999 was criticized by friend Sean Penn, who said Cage "is no longer an actor . . . now he's more like a . . . performer." Nick Nolte and Stephen Baldwin added their own complaints about Cage's recent oeuvre.

Marriage: Patricia Arquette, 1995

Child: Weston, 1990 (by ex-girlfriend Kristina Fulton)

Famous Relatives: Francis Ford Coppola, director, uncle; Talia Shire, actor, aunt

Major Award: Oscar, Best Actor, *Leaving Las Vegas*, 1995.

Quote: "I've seen a lot of actors get high on their own importance with the Academy Award, and they snob themselves right out of the industry."

JAMES CAMERON

Birthplace: Kapuskasing, Ontario
Birthdate: 8/16/54
Occupation: Director, producer, screenwriter, editor
Education: Attended California State University
Debut: (Film) *Piranha II: The Spawning*, 1981

Signature: *Titanic*, 1997
Facts: After seeing *Star Wars*, the physics-majoring college dropout knew what he wanted for his career. Following frequent trips to the USC library, he acquired camera equipment, built a dolly track in his living room, and began making a film.

When the Italian producers who hired him to direct his first film prepared the final cut without him, he flew to Rome, broke into the editing room, and secretly recut the film himself.

Co-founded his own special effects company, Digital Domain.

Went so far over budget for *Terminator 2* that distributor Carolco had to file for bankruptcy. When he again vastly exceeded his budget for *Titanic*, he voluntarily relinquished all pay except for screenwriting. After it became the biggest box-office grosser of all time, studio executives reinstated his original contract terms.

Infamy: A perfectionist, is known to be verbally abusive to his crew during filming, which frequently runs months behind schedule and tens of millions over budget.

Original Jobs: Machinist, truck driver, school-bus driver

Marriages: first wife (divorced); Gale Anne Hurd (divorced); Kathryn Bigelow (divorced); Linda Hamilton, 1981 (filed for divorce, 1999); Suzy Amis (relationship)

Child: Dalton Abbott, 1989 (stepson); Josephine Archer, 1993 (with Linda Hamilton).

Major Award: Oscar, Best Director, *Titanic*, 1997

NAOMI CAMPBELL

Birthplace: London, England
Birthdate: 5/22/70
Occupation: Supermodel
Education: London School of Performing Arts
Debut: (Magazine) *British Elle*, 1985
Facts: In an effort to extend her talents beyond her modeling career,

she wrote a novel, *Swan*, starred in the movie *Miami Rhapsody*, and recorded an album for Epic Records.

Has been romantically involved with Mike Tyson, Robert De Niro, and U2's Adam Clayton.

Opened Fashion Cafe in 1995 in New York City with fellow supermodels Elle MacPherson and Claudia Schiffer.

Infamy: Staged an impromptu stripping episode during lesbian night at a Manhattan bar.

Relationship: Muhammad Al Habtoor

NEVE CAMPBELL

Birthplace: Guelph, Ontario
Birthdate: 10/3/73
Occupation: Actor
Education: National Ballet School of Canada
Debut: (Stage) Toronto production, *Phantom of the Opera*, 1988; (TV) *Catwalk*, 1992
Signature: *Party of Five*
Facts: Beat out 300 other actors for her *Po5* role.

At age 9, joined the prestigious National Ballet of Canada. Is also trained in jazz, modern, flamenco, and hip-hop.

Drama may be in her blood: her mother once owned a dinner theater and her father was a high school drama teacher. They divorced when she was a toddler.

Her first name is her mother's Dutch maiden name and means "snow."

Auditioned for *Baywatch*. The casting director turned her down, in part, because "she is pale."

Original Job: Ballerina, model
Marriage: Jeff Colt, 1995 (divorced, 1997); Matthew Lillard (relationship)
Famous Relative: Christian, actor, brother

DREW CAREY

Birthplace: Cleveland, OH
Birthdate: 5/23/58
Occupation: Actor, comedian, writer
Education: Attended Kent State University
Debut: (TV) *Star Search,* 1987
Signature: *The Drew Carey Show*
Facts: Served in the marines for six years.

Got into comedy when a DJ friend paid him to write some comedy material; Carey decided to try out the jokes himself on stage.

Battled depression for years, stemming from his grief over his father's death from a brain tumor when Drew was 8. Attempted suicide on several occasions.
Original Job: Waiter at Las Vegas Denny's

MARIAH CAREY

Birthplace: New York, NY
Birthdate: 3/27/69
Occupation: Singer
Education: High school
Debut: (Album) *Mariah Carey,* 1990
Signature: "Vision of Love," 1990
Facts: Her vocal range spans five octaves.

Her wedding cost half a million dollars. She watched tapes of the 1981 wedding of Charles and Diana in preparation.
Infamy: Sued by her stepfather in 1992 for failing to share profits from her 1990 album.
Original Job: Waitress, hat checker, restaurant hostess
Marriage: Tommy Mottola, 1993 (divorced, 1998); Luis Miguel (relationship)
Major Awards: Grammy, Best Pop Vocal—Female, "Vision of Love," 1990; Grammy, Best New Artist, 1990

MARY CHAPIN CARPENTER

Birthplace: Princeton, NJ
Birthdate: 2/21/58
Occupation: Singer, songwriter, guitarist
Education: Brown University
Debut: (Album) *Hometown Girl,* 1988
Signature: "He Thinks He'll Keep Her"
Facts: Father, Chapin Carpenter, was a high-level *Life* magazine executive, so she spent her youth in Princeton, Tokyo, and Washington, DC.

Goes by the name Chapin, not Mary.

After college, considered music something to do for extra cash until she found her real career. Only after landing a nine-to-five job did she realize how much music meant to her, and began to focus on it.

Wrote Wynonna Judd's hit "Girls with Guitars" and co-wrote Cyndi Lauper's "Sally's Pigeon."
Infamy: Became an alcoholic after performing for years in bars.
Major Awards: Grammy, Best Country Vocal—Female, "Down at the Twist and Shout," 1991; Grammy, Best Country Vocal—Female, "I Feel Lucky," 1992; Grammy, Best Country Vocal—Female, "Passionate Kisses," 1993; Grammy, Best Country Vocal—Female, "Shut Up and Kiss Me," 1994; Grammy, Best Country Album, *Stones in the Road,* 1994

JIM CARREY

Birthplace: Jacksons Point, Canada
Birthdate: 1/17/62
Occupation: Actor
Debut: (TV) *The Duck Factory,* 1984; (Film) *Finders Keepers,* 1984
Signature: *Ace Ventura: Pet Detective,* 1994
Fact: When his accountant father was laid off, he quit high school to make money doing janitorial work.

His $20 million paycheck for *The Cable Guy* was the highest salary yet paid to a comedian.

A coalition of fire prevention groups demanded that his Fire Marshall Bill sketches on *In Living Color* be taken off the air because of the negative effect they were having on children.
Marriages: Melissa Womer, 1987 (divorced, 1993); Lauren Holly, 1996 (divorced, 1997); Renee Zellweger (relationship)
Child: Jane, 1987 (with Melissa Womer).

JOHNNY CARSON

Birthplace: Corning, IA
Birthdate: 10/23/25
Occupation: Talk show host
Education: University of Nebraska
Debut: (TV) *Carson's Cellar,* 1951
Signature: *The Tonight Show*
Facts: Declined role to play lead in the series that became *The Dick Van Dyke Show.*

As a 12-year-old, performed at local parties as "The Great Carsoni."

His son Richard was killed when his car plunged off a road.

Third wife Joanna Holland received $20 million in cash and property in a 1983 divorce settlement.

Served with the U.S. Naval Reserve during World War II.

Suffered a heart attack and underwent quadruple-bypass surgery in 1999.
Original Job: Radio announcer, ventriloquist, magician
Marriages: Jody Wolcott, 1949 (divorced, 1963); Joanne Copeland, 1963 (divorced, 1972); Joanna Holland, 1972 (divorced, 1983); Alexis Maas, 1987
Children: Christopher, 1950; Richard, 1952 (deceased, 1991); Cory, 1953; (with Jody Wolcott).
Major Awards: Elected to the Emmy Hall of Fame in 1987; Kennedy Center honoree, 1993

JOHNNY CASH

Real Name: J. R. Cash
Birthplace: Kingsland, AR
Birthdate: 2/26/32
Occupation: Singer, songwriter

Debut: (Song) "Hey Porter," 1955
Signature: "I Walk The Line," 1955
Facts: Cash is one-fourth Cherokee Indian.

He cannot read music.

Created 75 cuts for his 1994 album, produced by Rick Rubin (of Beastie Boys fame), which included songs written for him by Red Hot Chili Pepper Flea and Glenn Danzig.

Known as "the Man in Black," which is the title of his 1975 autobiography. Cash adopted this persona while working in a trio that only wore matching black outfits.

Wrote a novel, *Man in White,* in 1986.

He chose John as a first name when the military wouldn't accept initials.

Has Parkinson's disease.
Infamy: Cash was addicted to Dexadrine in the '60s.
Original Job: Door-to-door appliance salesman, factory worker
Marriages: Vivian Liberto, 1954 (divorced, 1967); June Carter, 1968
Children: Rosanne, 1955; Kathleen, 1956; Cindy, 1958; Tara, 1961; (with Vivian Liberto). John Carter, 1970; Rebecca Carlene (stepdaughter); Rozanna Lea (stepdaughter).
Major Awards: Grammy, Best Country Performance—Duo or Group, "Jackson" (with June Carter), 1967; Grammy, Best Country Vocal—Male, "Folsom Prison Blues," 1968; Grammy, Best Country Vocal—Male, "A Boy Named Sue," 1969; Grammy, Best Country Performance—Duo or Group, "If I Were a Carpenter" (with June Carter), 1970; elected to Country Music Hall of Fame, 1980; Grammy, Best Spoken Word Recording, *Interviews from the Class of '55* (with others), 1986; Grammy, Legend Award, 1991; elected to the Rock and Roll Hall of Fame, 1992; Grammy, Best Contemporary Folk Album, *American Recordings*, 1994; Grammy, Best Country Album, *Unchained*, 1997

ROSANNE CASH

Birthplace: Memphis, TN
Birthdate: 5/24/55
Occupation: Singer, songwriter
Education: State Community College; Vanderbilt University and Lee Strasberg Theatre Institute
Debut: (Song) "Blue Moon with Heartache," 1979
Signature: "I Don't Know Why You Don't Want Me," 1985
Fact: Never intended to become a musician. Her original ambition was to become a serious fiction writer.
Infamy: In 1982, entered a drug rehabilitation program for a cocaine dependency she had developed in 1979.
Original Job: Worked in wardrobe department during her father's tour. One day the tour managers asked her to come on stage and sing harmony.
Marriage: Rodney J. Crowell, 1979 (divorced, 1992); John Leventhal
Children: Caitlin Rivers, c.1980; Chelsea Jane, 1982; Carrie Kathleen, 1988 (with Rodney J. Crowell). Jakob William, 1999
Famous Relatives: Johnny Cash, country singer, father; June Carter Cash, country singer, stepmother; Carlene Carter, country singer, stepsister
Major Award: Grammy, Best Country Vocal—Female, "I Don't Know Why You Don't Want Me," 1985

JACKIE CHAN

Real Name: Chan Kwong-Sang
Birthplace: Hong Kong
Birthdate: 4/7/54
Occupation: Actor, writer, producer, director
Education: Chinese Opera Research Institute
Debut: *Big and Little Wong Tin Bar*, 1962; American debut, *The Big Brawl*, 1980
Signature: *Rumble in the Bronx*, 1995
Facts: Considered the biggest non-Hollywood movie star in the world; has been in more than 40 Asian action comedies. His fan club once topped 10,000 mostly young-girl members, one of whom killed herself when she read Chan was involved with someone.

His first attempts to break into Hollywood in the early '80s led to movie flops.

Nearly died making a 1986 film, when, leaping from a castle to a tree, he fell nearly 40 feet and broke his skull. He's also broken his jaw, shoulder, fingers and nose three times making movies.

To perfect his comic approach, studied old Hollywood Buster Keaton movies.

Impoverished parents left him at the Chinese Opera Institute at age 7 when they moved to Australia. During this militaristic-type training, he was beaten nearly every day.
Original Job: Stuntman
Marriage: Lin Feng-Chiao, 1983 (separated)
Child: Chan Cho-Ming, 1982
Quote: "I have a few rules that I tell my manager: No sex scenes! No make love! The kids who like me don't need to see it. It would gross them out."

CHER

Real Name: Cherilyn Sarkisian La Piere
Birthplace: El Centro, CA
Birthdate: 5/20/46
Occupation: Actor, singer
Education: High school dropout

Debut: (Film) *Wild on the Beach,* 1965; (TV) *The Sonny and Cher Comedy Hour,* 1971; (Stage) *Come Back to the Five and Dime, Jimmy Dean, Jimmy Dean,* 1981
Signature: "I Got You Babe," 1965
Facts: Abandoned by father when she was a few months old and placed in a home until her mother, who is part Cherokee, could save money to support her, she was eventually adopted by her mother's fifth husband, Gilbert La Piere.

Quit school as a teenager, ran away from home, and landed in L.A.

In 1964 began performing with Sonny Bono as Caesar & Cleo. The following year they changed their names to Sonny and Cher.

At one point, sold hair products by infomercial, was the spokesperson for the sweetener Equal, and started her own mail-order home decor business.

Has been linked to many famous men, including David Geffen, Mark Hudson, Gene Simmons, Val Kilmer, and Richie Sambora.

Nine days after her marriage to Gregg Allman, she filed for divorce.

Nominated for Best Supporting Actress Oscar for her role in 1983's *Silkwood,* she formed Isis, her own film production company, two years later and soon found herself in acclaimed roles in *Mask* (1985) and *Moonstruck* (1987).

Her daughter, Chastity Bono, a lesbian activist, was outed in 1990 by a tabloid and later wrote a book, *Family Outing.*

Enjoyed yet another comeback with her 1999 hit single "Believe."

Is seeking a share of Sonny's estate, claiming he owed her back alimony payments.
Original Job: Background vocalist for the Crystals and Ronettes
Marriage: Sonny Bono, 1964 (divorced,1975); Gregg Allman, 1975 (divorced,1977)
Children: Chastity, 1969 (with Bono); Elijah Blue, 1976 (with Allman)
Major Awards: Oscar, Best Actress,

Moonstruck, 1987
Quote: "I still feel pretty kick-ass. I'm pretty vital. I have my truck and my motorcycle."

DEEPAK CHOPRA

Birthplace: India
Birthdate: April 1947
Occupation: Author
Education: All-India Institute of Medicine
Signature: *Ageless Body, Timeless Mind*
Facts: Was a mainstream endocrinologist and chief of staff at New England Memorial Hospital before embracing alternative healing methods.

Dr. Chopra practices a form of Ayurvedic medicine called Maharishi Ayur-Veda, named after the Indian spiritual leader who taught transcendental meditation to the Beatles. The system is based on a 5,000-year-old Indian holistic health system involving herbal remedies, massage, yoga, and transcendental meditation. (Ayur-Veda is derived from the Sanskrit roots for "life" and "knowledge.")
Marriage: Rita, c. 1970
Children: Gautama, Mallika

TOM CLANCY

Birthplace: Baltimore, MD
Birthdate: 4/12/47
Occupation: Author
Debut: (Book) *The Hunt for Red October,* 1984
Facts: First short story was rejected by *Analog* science fiction magazine. Had just one article (on the MX missile system) to his credit when *Hunt for Red October* was published.

In the U.S. Army Reserve Officers' Training Corps, his poor eyesight kept him from serving in the Vietnam War.

Part-owner of the Baltimore Orioles, he also led the effort to bring an NFL expansion team to Baltimore for the 1994 season. He

was successful, and is now part-owner of the Baltimore Ravens.

Clear and Present Danger was the bestselling book of the '80s.
Original Job: Insurance agent
Marriage: Wanda Thomas (divorced, 1999); Alexandra Llewellyn, 1999
Children: Michelle, 1973; Christine, 1974; Tom, c.1983; Kathleen, 1985
Quote: "What do I care if someone reads my books a hundred years from now? I will be dead. And it's kind of hard to make money when you're dead."

ERIC CLAPTON

Real Name: Eric Clapp
Birthplace: Ripley, England
Birthdate: 3/30/45
Occupation: Singer, guitarist, songwriter
Education: Kingston Art School
Debut: (Album) *The Yardbirds,* 1963
Signature: "Layla," 1992
Facts: At the Ealing Club in London, occasionally substituted for lead singer Mick Jagger in Blues, Inc.

Earned the nickname "Slowhand" because his powerful playing regularly broke his guitar strings, which he then changed onstage to the accompaniment of a slow handclap from listeners.

The song "Layla" was reportedly inspired by an affair that Clapton had at the time with George Harrison's wife Patti, and was dedicated "to the wife of my best friend."

Tragedy struck in 1991, when his 4-year-old son died in a fall from Clapton's ex-girlfriend's apartment. The song "Tears in Heaven" is a tribute to him.

Was among 1,080 Britons recognized on Queen Elizabeth's honors list at the end of 1994.

In 1999, sold 100 of his guitars at auction for over $5 million, to benefit Crossroads Center, a clinic he founded in Antigua to treat drug and alcohol abuse.
Infamy: After release of *Layla and Other Assorted Love Songs* (1970),

dropped out of sight for two-and-a-half years because of a heroin addiction. He was brought out of seclusion by Pete Townshend of The Who. A bout with alcoholism followed. Now, he says he hasn't touched a drink since 1987.
Original Job: Construction worker
Marriage: Patricia Anne Boyd-Harrison (divorced, 1988)
Child: Conor (deceased)
Major Awards: Grammy, Album of the Year, *The Concert for Bangladesh* (with George Harrison and Friends), 1972; Grammy, Best Rock Vocal—Male, "Bad Love," 1990; Grammy, Album of the Year, *Unplugged*, 1992; Grammy, Best Rock Vocal—Male, "Layla," 1992; Grammy, Record of the Year, Song of the Year, and Best Pop Vocal—Male, "Tears in Heaven," 1992; Grammy, Best Traditional Blues Album, *From the Cradle*, 1994; Grammy, Record of the Year, "Change the World," 1996; Grammy, Best Pop Vocal—Male, "Change the World," 1996; Grammy, Best Pop Vocal—Male, "My Father's Eyes," 1998.

GEORGE CLOONEY

Birthplace: Lexington, KY
Birthdate: 5/6/61
Occupation: Actor
Education: Northern Kentucky University
Debut: (TV) *E/R*, 1984
Signature: *ER*
Facts: Got his Hollywood break playing a medical intern on the short-lived CBS comedy series *E/R*, set in a Chicago hospital emergency room. On NBC's *ER*, also set in a Chicago hospital emergency room, he graduated to full-fledged doctor.

Appeared as Roseanne's boss and Jackie's boyfriend during the first season of *Roseanne*.

Is reportedly being paid $2 million an episode to guest star on *ER* in the 1999–2000 season.
Original Jobs: Sold insurance door to door; cut tobacco

Marriage: Talia Balsam, 1989 (divorced, 1992)
Famous Relatives: Rosemary Clooney, singer, aunt; Nick Clooney, TV host, father; Miguel Ferrer, actor, cousin

GLENN CLOSE

Birthplace: Greenwich, CT
Birthdate: 3/19/47
Occupation: Actor
Education: The College of William and Mary
Debut: (Stage) *Love for Love*, 1974; (TV) *Too Far To Go*, 1979; (Film) *The World According to Garp*, 1982
Signature: *Fatal Attraction*, 1987
Facts: When she was 13, her father opened a clinic in the Belgian Congo (now Zaire) and ran it for 16 years. During most of that time, the Close children lived alternately in Africa and at boarding schools in Switzerland.

Her voice was dubbed over that of Andie MacDowell in the her starring role in *Greystroke: The Legend of Tarzan, Lord of the Apes*. Fifteen years later, Close's voice was used in Disney's animated *Tarzan* (1999).

Chosen by Andrew Lloyd Webber to replace Patti LuPone in *Sunset Boulevard*, 1994.
Infamy: When she went on a two-week vacation from *Sunset Boulevard* in 1995, the production company released erroneous box-office figures implying that Close's absence had no effect on ticket sales. Close sent a scathing letter of complaint to composer-producer Andrew Lloyd Webber, which was obtained and published in the media.
Original Job: Toured Europe and the U.S. as a member of Up With People
Marriages: Cabot Wade, 1969 (divorced, 1971); James Marlas, 1984 (divorced, 1987); Steve Beers (engaged, 1995)
Child: Annie Maude Starke, 1988 (from relationship with John Starke)
Major Awards: Tony, Best Actress (Dramatic), *The Real Thing*, 1984; Tony, Best Actress (Dramatic), *Death

and the Maiden, 1992; Tony, Best Actress (Musical), *Sunset Boulevard*, 1995; Emmy, Best Actress in a Miniseries or Special, *Serving in Silence: The Margarethe Cammermeyer Story*, 1995

PAULA COLE

Birthplace: Manchester, CT
Birthdate: 4/5/68
Occupation: Singer, songwriter
Education: Berklee College of Music
Debut: (Album) *Harbinger*, 1994
Signature: "Where Have All the Cowboys Gone?" 1996
Facts: In high school, was a self-proclaimed "goody two-shoes," holding posts as three-time class president and junior prom queen.

Had a nervous breakdown and contemplated suicide while in college. Wrote "Bethlehem" during that period.

This Fire's seven Grammy nominations included one for best producer, the first ever for a woman.
Relationship: Seyi Sonuga
Major Award: Grammy, Best New Artist, 1997

SHAWN COLVIN

Birthplace: Vermillion, SD
Birthdate: 1/10/56
Occupation: Singer, songwriter, guitarist
Education: Southern Illinois University
Debut: Shawn Colvin Band, 1976
Signature: "Sunny Came Home," 1997
Facts: At a young age, she sang in the church choir, learned guitar, and designed album covers.

Played folk and rock during her college years, and later played small clubs in California and with the country rock group Dixie Diesels in Texas.

Had to quit in 1978 to let her throat heal after years of singing hard rock with the Shawn Colvin Band.

Sang back-up on Suzanne Vega's 1987 hit "Luka," which led to a tour and signing with Vega's manager.
Marriage: Simon Tassano (divorced, 1995); Mario Erwin, 1997
Child: Caledonia Jean-Marie, 1998
Major Awards: Grammy, Best Contemporary Folk Recording, *Steady On,* 1991; Grammies, Song of the Year and Record of the Year, "Sunny Came Home," 1998
Quote: "I think at best my voice sounds honest."

SEAN "PUFFY" COMBS

Birthplace: New York, NY
Birthdate: 11/4/69
Occupation: Rap singer, producer, executive
Education: Attended Howard University
Debut: (Album) *No Way Out,* 1997
Signature: Puff Daddy
Facts: His father died when Combs was 3; until age 14, he believed it was in a car accident, but later discovered it likely resulted from involvement in illegal street activities.

While in college in Washington, D.C., would ride a four-hour train to New York on weekends to intern at Uptown Records. Was named VP there at age 21. Became CEO of Bad Boy Entertainment at age 24.

Got the nickname "Puffy" as a child because he would huff and puff when angry.

His clothes label, Sean John, is monikered after his first and middle names.
Infamy: Nine people died during a stampede at a hip-hop celebrity basketball game Combs organized in 1991; he was later cleared of criminal charges but settled private lawsuits with the families after a report revealed he had delegated most of the arrangements to inexperienced assistants.

In 1996, was found guilty of criminal mischief after threatening a *New York Post* photographer.

Was arrested in April 1999 on charges that he and his bodyguards beat up Interscope Records executive Steve Stoute. He plead guilty to a reduced violation, and was sentenced to a day of "anger management." A civil suit settlement is being negotiated.
Children: Justin Dior, 1993 (with ex-girlfriend Tanieka Misa Hylton); Christopher Casey, 1998 (with Kim Porter)
Major Awards: Grammy, Best Rap Album, *No Way Out,* 1997; Grammy, Best Rap Performance By Duo Or Group, "I'll Be Missing You," 1997

SEAN CONNERY

Real Name: Thomas Connery
Birthplace: Edinburgh, Scotland
Birthdate: 8/25/30
Occupation: Actor
Debut: (Stage) *South Pacific,* 1951
Signature: James Bond
Facts: Connery grew up in a poor, industrial district of Scotland. At age 7, he took a job delivering milk before school, and by age 13 he quit school.

Served in the British Navy from 1947 to 1950. Was discharged due to ulcers.

In 1950, represented Scotland in London's Mr. Universe competition.

Was denied for knighthood in 1998.

New Woman voted him sexiest man of the century.
Original Job: Lifeguard, milkman, bricklayer, plasterer, coffin polisher, and usher
Marriages: Diane Cilento, 1962 (divorced, 1973); Micheline Roquebrune, 1975
Child: Jason Joseph, 1963 (with Diane Cilento)
Major Awards: Oscar, Best Supporting Actor, *The Untouchables,* 1987; Tony, Best Play, *Art* (coproducer), 1997

HARRY CONNICK JR.

Birthplace: New Orleans, LA
Birthdate: 9/11/67
Occupation: Singer
Education: Loyola University, Hunter College, Manhattan School of Music
Debut: (Album) *Harry Connick, Jr.,* 1987
Signature: "It Had To Be You"
Facts: Performed annually at the New Orleans Jazz & Heritage Festival from the time he was 8.

He also recorded two albums of Dixieland music on little-known labels—the first when he was nine and the second when he was 10.

Learned jazz music from Ellis Marsalis, the patriarch of the Marsalis family at the New Orleans Center for the Creative Arts.
Infamy: Arrested for having a gun in his luggage at New York's JFK airport.
Marriage: Jill Goodacre, 1994
Children: Georgia Tatom, 1996; Sara Kate, 1997
Major Awards: Grammy, Best Jazz Vocal—Male, *When Harry Met Sally,* 1989; Grammy, Best Jazz Vocal—Male, "We Are in Love," 1990

DAVID COPPERFIELD

Real Name: David Kotkin
Birthplace: Metuchen, NJ
Birthdate: 9/16/56
Occupation: Magician
Education: Fordham University
Debut: (TV) *The Magic of ABC,* 1977
Facts: In his act, has levitated a Ferrari, walked through the Great Wall of China, and made the Statue of Liberty disappear. He has also extricated himself from a safe in a building about to be demolished by explosives and a steel box on a raft heading for Niagara Falls.

By age 12, had performed at local birthday parties for a fee of five dollars, under the name "Davino, the Boy Magician."

In 1982 developed Project Magic, a program designed to help people with physical and mental disabilities by teaching them magic.

Was engaged to Claudia Schiffer, but they never married.

FRANCIS FORD COPPOLA

Birthplace: Detroit, MI
Birthdate: 4/7/39
Occupation: Director and writer
Education: Hofstra University, UCLA Film School
Debut: (Film) *Dementia 13,* 1963
Signature: *The Godfather,* 1972
Facts: First dreamed of becoming a filmmaker at age 10, while bedridden with polio. He put on shows for himself using puppets, a tape recorder, a film projector, and a television set.

Coppola's interest in producing a film about the automaker Preston Tucker—*Tucker: The Man and His Dream* (1988)—began when his father invested and lost $5,000 in the automaker's company.

Directed Michael Jackson in the 15-minute Epcot Center feature *Captain EO.*

First son, Gian Carlo, was killed in a boating accident in 1986.

Owns a vineyard in California's Napa Valley. Also owns a restaurant in San Francisco and property in Belize; he hopes to make that country the hub for a huge telecommunications center.

Successfully sued Warner Bros. for thwarting his attempts to develop "dream project," a new version of *Pinocchio,* at another studio; Coppola was awarded $80 million.
Original Job: Worked for famous B-movie producer/director Roger Corman as dialogue director, sound man, and associate producer
Marriage: Eleanor Neil, 1962
Children: Gian Carlo, 1963 (deceased, 1986); Roman, 1965; Sofia, 1971
Famous Relatives: Talia Shire, actor, sister; Nicholas Cage, actor, nephew

Major Awards: Oscar, Best Original Screenplay, *Patton* (with Edmund H. North), 1970; Oscar, Best Adapted Screenplay, *The Godfather* (with Mario Puzo), 1972; Oscar, Best Director, *The Godfather Part II,* 1974; Oscar, Best Adapted Screenplay, *The Godfather Part II* (with Mario Puzo), 1974

PATRICIA CORNWELL

Real Name: Patricia Daniels
Birthplace: Miami, FL
Birthdate: 6/9/56
Occupation: Author
Education: Davidson College
Signature: Kay Scarpetta, hero of her medical examiner–crime series
Facts: After her father had abandoned her and her siblings, her mother sought help from neighbors—evangelist Billy Graham and his wife, Ruth—who placed the children with Christian missionaries.

Her first book was an authorized biography of Ruth Graham, which strained their friendship for several years because of a "misunderstanding."

As a teenager, Cornwell was hospitalized for anorexia.

She married her English professor, 16 years her senior, after college.

Was a cartoonist for her college newspaper.

She travels with at least two bodyguards and hires armed, off-duty police officers for book signings.

She owns a .357 Colt Python, a .380 Walther semi-automatic, and a .38 Smith & Wesson.

Has a history of impulse buying and once spent $27,000 on a furniture shopping spree.

Was rescued by a jaws of life tool after her Mercedes crashed into a stalled van and flipped over three times.

She was known to behave erratically and suffered manic depression, which went undiagnosed for several years. In 1993, she

checked into a clinic for recovering alcoholics.

Thoroughly researches technical details for her novels. Has attended approximately 600 autopsies for these purposes.

Gave $1.5 million to help the state of Virginia create an institute to train forensic scientists and pathologists.
Infamy: In 1992, had a lesbian affair with a married F.B.I. agent whose husband, also with the F.B.I., tried to ambush and kill his estranged wife.
Original Jobs: Police reporter for the *Charlotte Observer;* computer analyst in Richmond, Virginia, morgue
Marriage: Charles Cornwell (divorced, 1990)
Famous Relatives: Descendant of Harriet Beecher Stowe, author
Major Award: Mystery Writers of America, for *Post Mortem,* 1990
Quote: "I have this very cagey way of worming myself in; I'm an infection. You try to pacify me, and before you know it, you can't get me out of your system."

BILL COSBY

Birthplace: Philadelphia, PA
Birthdate: 7/12/37
Occupation: Actor, comedian, producer, author
Education: Temple University; Doctor of Education, University of Massachusetts at Amherst
Debut: (TV) *I Spy,* 1965; (Film) *Hickey and Boggs,* 1971
Signature: *The Cosby Show*
Facts: Grew up in a housing project in Philadelphia.

A gifted athlete, he was noticed by a scout for the Green Bay Packers.

Has played the drums since he was 11. A jazz aficionado, is president of the Rhythm and Blues Hall of Fame.
Infamy: In 1997, Cosby admitted having an adulterous "rendezvous" with Shawn Thompson in the early 1970s. The one-night stand came to

light when Thompson's daughter, Autumn Jackson, threatened to tell the media that Cosby was her father unless he gave her $40 million. Jackson, whose education was financed by the entertainer, was convicted of extortion and sentenced to 26 months in jail, though a federal appeals court subsequently overturned the conviction. Unlike Cosby, Jackson reportedly never submitted DNA samples, thereby precluding a conclusive paternity test.

Original Job: Shined shoes, delivered groceries

Marriage: Camille Hanks

Children: Erika Ranee, 1965; Erinn Charlene, 1966; Ennis William, 1969 (deceased); Ensa Camille, 1973; Evin Harrah, 1976

Major Awards: Grammy, Best Comedy Recording, *I Started Out as a Child,* 1964; Grammy, Best Comedy Recording, *Why Is There Air,* 1965; Grammy, Best Comedy Recording, *Wonderfulness,* 1966; Grammy, Best Comedy Recording, *Revenge,* 1967; Emmy, Best Actor in a Drama Series, *I Spy,* 1966, 1967, 1968; Grammy, Best Comedy Recording, *To Russell, My Brother, Whom I Slept With,* 1968; Grammy, Best Comedy Recording, *Bill Cosby,* 1969; Emmy, *Bill Cosby Special,* 1969; Grammy, Best Recording for Children, *Bill Cosby Talks to Kids About Drugs,* 1971; Grammy, Best Recording for Children, *The Electric Company* (with Lee Chamberlin and Rita Moreno), 1972; NAACP Image Award, 1976; Emmy, *The New Fat Albert Show,* 1981; Emmy, Best Comedy Series, *The Cosby Show,* 1985; Grammy, Best Comedy Recording, *Those of You with or without Children, You'll Understand,* 1986; elected to the Emmy Hall of Fame, 1991

ELVIS COSTELLO

Real Name: Declan Patrick McManus

Birthplace: London, England

Birthdate: 8/25/54

Occupation: Singer, songwriter

Education: High school dropout

Debut: (Album) *My Aim Is True,* 1977

Signature: "Alison"

Facts: "Costello" is his mother's maiden name.

Began playing guitar at age 15 after testing out the violin, among other instruments.

Strongly influenced by American songwriters John Prine and Lowell George.

Got his first contract with CBS Records by performing on the sidewalk in front of the hotel where the label's sales conference was in progress. Was arrested for disturbing the peace but achieved his purpose.

From 1977 to 1986, he performed with the Attractions, including a tour in the U.S. and a spot on *Saturday Night Live.* He was asked on the show to perform "Less Than Zero" after the Sex Pistols cancelled. Instead, he played "Radio, Radio," a song that comments on media manipulation. Many thought the appearance would end his career.

His album *King of America* identifies him by his real name, adding on the imaginary second middle name "Aloysius."

Composed "She," the Charles Aznavour ballad from *Notting Hill.*

Infamy: In a drunken argument in 1979, used racial epithets in referring to Ray Charles and James Brown. American disc jockeys took his records off their playlists, and he received numerous death threats.

Original Job: Computer programmer at Elizabeth Arden's factory in England

Marriage: Mary, 1974 (divorced, c.1985); Caitlin O'Riordan, 1986

Child: Matthew, c.1973 (with Mary)

Famous Relatives: Ross McManus, jazz singer with Joe Loss Band, father

Major Awards: Grammy Pop Collaboration with Vocals (with Burt Bacharach) "I Still Have That Other Girl," 1998

Quote: "I'm not interested in

courting people. If people don't like me, there's no way I'm going to be nice to them so they do like me. All I want is for the records to be heard. I'm not out there saying, 'Love me, love me.'"

KEVIN COSTNER

Birthplace: Lynwood, CA

Birthdate: 1/18/55

Occupation: Actor, director, producer

Education: California State University at Fullerton

Debut: (Film) *Sizzle Beach,* 1979

Signature: *The Untouchables,* 1987

Facts: At 18, built a canoe and paddled down the same rivers that Lewis and Clark had navigated on their way to the Pacific.

As a teenager, he sang in the church choir.

Turned down the leading role in *War Games* (played by Matthew Broderick) to play Alex, the character who commits suicide, in *The Big Chill.* Only two weeks before the film's release, Alex's part was cut. But director Lawrence Kasdan promised Costner that he would write a part for him in another film, and tailored the role of Jake in *Silverado* (1985) for Costner.

Infamy: In February 1995, Costner and his brother Dan began building an entertainment complex in the Black Hills of South Dakota, on land that the Lakota Indians consider sacred and have been trying to recover since 1887. Costner had been made an honorary Lakota in 1990 after working with them on *Dances with Wolves.*

Original Job: Worked in marketing, stage-managed Raleigh Studios in L.A.

Marriage: Cindy Silva (divorced, 1995)

Children: Annie, c.1984; Lily, c.1986; Joe, c.1988; (with Cindy Silva). Liam, 1996 (with Bridget Rooney).

Major Awards: Oscar, Best Director, *Dances with Wolves,* 1990; Oscar,

Best Picture, *Dances with Wolves* (produced with Jim Wilson), 1990.

KATIE COURIC

Birthplace: Arlington, VA
Birthdate: 1/7/57
Occupation: Broadcast journalist
Education: University of Virginia
Signature: *Today*
Fact: Was a cheerleader in high school.

After hearing Couric read a report on the air, the president of CNN banned the young assignment editor from further television appearances, complaining about her high-pitched, squeaky voice. Keeping her spirits, Couric began working with a voice coach.

Original Job: Desk assistant at ABC News in Washington, DC
Marriage: Jay Monahan, 1989 (deceased, 1998)
Children: Elinor Tully, 1991; Caroline, 1996
Quote: "Bob Costas is short and cute, but I've never heard him being called 'perky.' "
Major Awards: Daytime Emmy Outstanding Special Class Program, *Macy's Thanksgiving Day Parade*, 1996, 1997, 1998 (shared awards)

COURTENEY COX

Birthplace: Birmingham, AL
Birthdate: 6/15/64
Occupation: Actor
Education: Mt. Vernon College (Washington, DC)
Debut: (TV) *Misfits of Science*, 1985; (Film) *Down Twisted*, 1987
Signature: *Friends*
Facts: Discovered in 1984 Brian De Palma video "Dancing in the Dark" with Bruce Springsteen.

Played Michael J. Fox's girlfriend on *Family Ties* and Jim Carrey's love interest in *Ace Ventura: Pet Detective*.
Original Job: Model
Marriage: David Arquette, 1999

CINDY CRAWFORD

Birthplace: De Kalb, IL
Birthdate: 2/20/66
Occupation: Supermodel
Education: Northwestern University
Debut: (Film) *Fair Game*, 1995
Facts: Crawford was the valedictorian of her high school class, and received a full scholarship to study chemical engineering in college. There, a professor accused Crawford of cheating after she received a perfect score on a calculus midterm exam.

Supports P-FLAG (Parents and Friends of Lesbians and Gays) and leukemia research (her brother died of the disease at age 3).
Infamy: Posed for the cover of *Vanity Fair* shaving lesbian singer k.d. lang, prompting a renewal of international rumors she and then-husband Richard Gere were each homosexual and maintained the marriage for appearances only. In May 1994, the couple took out a $30,000 ad in the *Times* of London denying the rumors.
Original Job: Spent summers during high school detasseling corn in fields
Marriages: Richard Gere (divorced, 1994); Rande Gerber, 1998
Child: Presley Walker Gerber, 1999

MICHAEL CRICHTON

Real Name: John Michael Crichton
Birthplace: Chicago, IL
Birthdate: 10/23/42
Occupation: Writer, director, producer
Education: Harvard, Harvard Medical School
Debut: (Book) *Odds On* (under the pseudonym John Lange), 1966; (Film) *Westworld*, 1973
Signature: *Jurassic Park*
Facts: Published a travel article in *The New York Times* when he was 14.

Developed FilmTrak, a computer program for film production, and is creator of the computer game Amazon.

As a college student, turned in a paper written by George Orwell to test whether or not a professor was grading him fairly. The professor, who had been giving Crichton C-plusses, gave the Orwell paper in Crichton's name a B-minus.
Infamy: In 1974 was fired as screenwriter of the film adaptation of *The Terminal Man* when his screenplay deviated too much from the book.
Original Job: Anthropology professor
Marriages: Joan Radam, 1965 (divorced, 1970); Kathy St. Johns, 1978 (divorced, 1980); Suzanne Childs (divorced); Anne–Marie Martin, 1987
Child: Taylor, 1989

SHERYL CROW

Birthplace: Kennett, MO
Birthdate: 2/11/62
Occupation: Singer, songwriter
Education: University of Missouri
Debut: (Album) *Tuesday Night Music Club*, 1994
Signature: "All I Wanna Do," 1994
Facts: Her mother and father played piano and trumpet, respectively, with a big band on weekends. Their four children were encouraged to learn music and often practiced on the four pianos in the house simultaneously.

Sang backup for Michael Jackson's 18-month *Bad* tour and, later, for Don Henley.

Went through a severe depression in the late '80s and didn't get out of bed for six months.

Played at Woodstock '94.
Major Awards: Grammy, Record of the Year, "All I Wanna Do," 1994; Grammy, Best New Artist, 1994; Grammy, Best Pop Vocal—Female, "All I Wanna Do," 1994; Grammy, Bet Rock Vocal—Female, "If It Makes You Happy," 1996; Grammy, Best Rock Album, *The Globe Sessions*, 1998.

TOM CRUISE

Real Name: Thomas Cruise Mapother IV
Birthplace: Syracuse, NY
Birthdate: 7/3/62
Occupation: Actor
Education: High school dropout
Debut: (Film) *Endless Love*, 1981
Signature: *Jerry Maguire*, 1996
Facts: Dyslexia put him in remedial reading courses in school, but Cruise proved himself in sports.

At age 14, enrolled in a seminary to become a priest. Dropped out after one year.

Took up acting after losing his place on a high school wrestling team due to a knee injury.

Member of the Church of Scientology.

Developed an ulcer while filming *Eyes Wide Shut*.

Has saved three lives, rescuing people in Santa Monica, London, and off the island of Capri.
Infamy: Author Anne Rice publicly criticized David Geffen for casting Cruise in *Interview with a Vampire* in 1994. After Rice saw the film she admitted Geffen had been right.

Won $580,000 in libel damages in 1998 from Britain's *Express on Sunday* for a story that claimed Cruise and his wife might be closet gays in a sham marriage.

Sued the *Star* in 1999 for claiming that sex experts had to coach Cruise and his wife in the art of lovemaking for *Eyes Wide Shut*.
Original Job: Busboy
Marriages: Mimi Rogers (divorced), Nicole Kidman, 1990
Children: Isabella Jane, 1993; Connor Antony, 1995; (both adopted).
Quote: "I'm not the Stanislavski kind of actor. I just want to communicate with the people in the scene."

BILLY CRYSTAL

Birthplace: New York, NY
Birthdate: 3/14/48
Occupation: Comedian, actor
Education: Marshall University; Nassau Community College; New York University
Debut: (TV) *Soap*, 1977; (Film) *Rabbit Test*, 1978
Signature: *When Harry Met Sally...*, 1989
Facts: Went to college on a baseball scholarship and hosted a campus-radio talk show.

First theater job as a house manager for *You're a Good Man Charlie Brown*, 1968.

Studied directing under Martin Scorsese at New York University.
Infamy: Walked off the set of his first *Saturday Night Live* appearance after his seven-minute monologue was cut from the show.
Original Job: Substitute teacher, writer
Marriage: Janice Goldfinger, 1970
Children: Jennifer, 1973; Lindsay, 1977
Famous Relative: Milt Gabler, founded Commodore Records and later headed Decca Records, uncle
Major Awards: Emmy, Best Writing in a Variety or Music Program, *Midnight Train to Moscow*, 1990; Emmy, Best Individual Performance in a Variety or Music Program, *The 63rd Annual Oscars,* 1991, *The 70th Annual Academy Awards, 1998*; Emmy, Best Writing in a Variety or Music Program, *The 63rd Annual Oscars,* 1991; Emmy, Best Writing in a Variety or Music Program, *The 64th Annual Oscars,* 1992
Quote: "My father used to bring home jazz musicians at Passover. We had swinging seders."

JAMIE LEE CURTIS

Birthplace: Los Angeles, CA
Birthdate: 11/22/58
Occupation: Actor
Education: Choate; University of the Pacific
Debut: (TV) *Operation Petticoat*, 1977; (Film) *Halloween*, 1978
Signature: *A Fish Called Wanda*, 1988
Facts: Very athletic, Curtis was trained as a dancer and appeared on *Circus of the Stars* as an acrobat.

Curtis became interested in her husband Christopher Guest when she saw his picture in *Rolling Stone*. She gave him her home number through an agent.

When her husband inherited his grandfather's English peerage title, Curtis earned the right to be addressed as "Lady Haden-Guest."

She has authored several best-selling children's books, including *When I Was Little: A 4-Year-Old's Memoir of Her Youth* and *Today I Feel Silly and Other Moods That Make My Day.*
Infamy: Admitted to using cocaine, even with her father, although not abusing it. She quit completely in 1983.
Marriage: Christopher Guest, 1983
Children: Annie, 1986; Thomas Haden, 1996 (adopted)
Famous Relatives: Tony Curtis, actor, father; Janet Leigh, actor, mother

JOHN CUSACK

Birthplace: Evanston, IL
Birthdate: 6/28/66
Occupation: Actor, writer, producer
Education: Attended New York University
Debut: (Film) *Class*, 1983
Signature: *Grosse Pointe Blank*, 1997
Facts: Grew up in a tightknit Irish Catholic family, always putting on neighborhood plays. Four of the five kids appear in *Grosse Pointe Blank*, which Cusack wrote and produced.

His parents were active in the anti-war and social protest movements; today he chooses most roles with an eye towards their social statements. During the Gulf War, he even wrote an op-ed for the *Chicago Sun-Times* protesting "police brutality" during an anti-war rally outside a rap concert.

At 20, started his own Chicago

theater group, New Crime Productions.
Famous Relative: Joan Cusack, actor, sister
Quote: "I was a teen star. That's disgusting enough."

MATT DAMON

Birthplace: Cambridge, MA
Birthdate: 10/8/70
Occupation: Actor, screenwriter
Education: Attended Harvard University
Debut: (Film) *School Ties*, 1992
Signature: *Good Will Hunting*, 1997
Facts: As a teenager, occasionally break-danced for money in Harvard Square.

Left Harvard two semesters shy of an English degree.

Good Will Hunting, co-written with Ben Affleck, grew out of a scene Damon wrote for a Harvard playwriting class.

Lost 40 pounds in three months to play heroin addict in *Courage Under Fire*, creating an anorexia-like medical condition that injured his adrenal glands, requiring months of medication.
Relationship: Winona Ryder
Major Award: Oscar, Best Original Screenplay, *Good Will Hunting*, 1997

CLAIRE DANES

Birthplace: New York, NY
Birthdate: 4/12/79
Occupation: Actor
Education: Attending Yale University
Debut: (TV) *Law & Order*, 1992; (Film) *Little Women*, 1995
Signature: *My So-Called Life*
Facts: Winona Ryder was so taken with Danes's portrayal of Angela Chase on *My So-Called Life* that she called her director on *Little Women* to suggest Danes for the part of Beth.

First auditioned for *My So-Called Life* when she was 13, but it took two more years for the show to get a firm commitment from ABC.
Relationship: Ben Lee, musician

JEFF DANIELS

Real Name: Jeffrey Daniels
Birthplace: Athens, GA
Birthdate: 2/19/55
Occupation: Actor
Education: Attended Central Michigan University
Debut: (Stage) *Fifth of July*, 1980; (TV) *A Rumor of War*, 1980; (Film) *Ragtime*, 1981
Signature: *Dumb and Dumber*, 1995
Facts: Starred in McDonald's commercials as a child.

He married his high school sweetheart on Friday the 13th because he used to wear the number 13 on his baseball uniform.

He won an Obie in 1982 for his one-man show, *Johnny Got His Gun*.

Worked four summers in his dad's lumber company in Chelsea, Michigan, and eventually moved there with his family. In 1990, he founded and financed Purple Rose Theater Company in Chelsea, where several of his original plays have been produced.

Learned how to moonwalk for the high school reunion scene in *Something Wild*.

During *The Fifth of July*, he shared a stage kiss, in successive productions, with William Hurt and Christopher Reeve.

His most prized possessions are an autographed Al Kaline–Norm Cash baseball and a 1968 Kaline trading card.
Marriage: Kathleen Traedo, 1979
Children: Benjamin, 1984; Lucas, 1987; Nellie, 1990
Quote: "Sometimes you have to do things that will put the kids through college, in an industry that will spit you out tomorrow and forget your name."

TED DANSON

Real Name: Edward Bridge Danson III
Birthplace: San Diego, CA
Birthdate: 12/29/47
Occupation: Actor

Education: Stanford University, Carnegie-Mellon University
Debut: (TV) *Somerset*, 1975; (Film) *The Onion Field*, 1979
Signature: *Cheers*
Facts: Father was the director of a local Native American museum.

In 1981, was the Aramis man on TV ads for cologne and men's toiletry products.

While at Stanford, followed a good-looking waitress to an audition "just to be near her" and ended up winning a part.

Tap dances.
Infamy: Appeared at then-companion Whoopi Goldberg's 1993 Friars Club roast in blackface.
Marriages: Randall Lee Gosch (divorced), Casey Coates (divorced), Mary Steenburgen, 1995
Children: Kate, 1979 (with Casey Coates). Alexis, 1985
Major Awards: Emmy, Best Actor in a Comedy Series, *Cheers*, 1990, 1993; Golden Globe, Best Actor in a Comedy Series, *Cheers*, 1990, 1991

GEENA DAVIS

Real Name: Virginia Davis
Birthplace: Wareham, MA
Birthdate: 1/21/56
Occupation: Actor
Education: Boston University
Debut: (Film) *Tootsie*, 1982; (TV) *Buffalo Bill*, 1983
Signature: *Thelma & Louise*, 1991
Facts: Six-foot Davis, two inches taller than the cutoff established by professional modeling agencies, worked as a waitress to pay her bills. Finally she lied about her height and was accepted by the Zoli agency.

While working as a saleswoman at Anne Taylor, Davis got a job as a human mannequin in the store window.

Tried to qualify for the U.S. women's Olympic archery team in 1999.
Marriages: Richard Emmolo (divorced); Jeff Goldblum (divorced); Renny Harlin, 1993 (divorced, 1997).
Major Award: Oscar, Best

Supporting Actress, *The Accidental Tourist,* 1988

DANIEL DAY-LEWIS

Birthplace: London, England
Birthdate: 4/29/57
Occupation: Actor
Education: Old Vic Theatre School
Debut: (Film) *Sunday, Bloody Sunday,* 1971
Signature: *My Left Foot,* 1989
Fact: At 16, accidentally overdosed on migraine medicine and suffered from two weeks of hallucinations. Because of this, he was mistakenly diagnosed as a heroin addict and placed in a mental hospital. To escape, he had to put on his "greatest performance of sanity."
Original Job: Loaded trucks
Marriage: Rebecca Miller, 1996
Child: Gabriel Kane, 1995 (with Isabelle Adjani). son, 1998
Famous Relatives: C. Day-Lewis, former poet laureate of Britain, father; Sir Michael Balcon, producer, grandfather; Jane Balcon, actress, mother
Major Award: Oscar, Best Actor, *My Left Foot,* 1989

ELLEN DEGENERES

Birthplace: New Orleans, LA
Birthdate: 1/26/58
Occupation: Actor, comedian
Signature: *Ellen*
Facts: Considered becoming a professional golfer.

In the 1980s the Showtime cable network, looking to name someone Funniest Person in America, found DeGeneres at a comedy club in New Orleans. She was given the title, and toured the country in a Winnebago with a big nose above the front bumper. It earned her the scorn of other comics, who thought she received the title undeservedly.

Was the first female comic ever to be invited to sit on Carson's couch in her first appearance on *The Tonight Show.*

Ellen's title character became the first uncloseted TV lead when she declared herself a lesbian; weeks before the "coming out" episode aired, DeGeneres herself did the same.
Original Job: Vacuum cleaner saleswoman, waitress
Relationship: Anne Heche
Major Awards: Emmy, Best Writing in a Comedy Series, *Ellen,* 1997

JUDI DENCH

Real Name: Judith Olivia Dench
Birthplace: York, England
Birthdate: 12/9/34
Occupation: Actor, director
Education: Central School of Speech and Drama, London
Debut: (London stage) *Hamlet,* 1957; (Broadway) *Henry V,* 1958; (Film) *The Third Secret,* 1964
Signature: *Shakespeare in Love,* 1998
Facts: A much heralded actress, a member of the Old Vic Theatre Company since 1957 and the Royal Shakespeare Company since 1969, she has received numerous awards in England for her performances.

When she was young, she attended the Mount School and became a Quaker, a decision that she stands by to this day.

She has portrayed a wide range of characters, from Shakespeare's Ophelia and Lady Macbeth to historic queens Victoria and Elizabeth I to M, James Bond's boss in *GoldenEye* and *Tomorrow Never Dies.*

In 1980, she was awarded an Order of the British Empire and in 1987, named a Dame Commander of the British Empire.

Was the original choice to play Grizabella in *Cats.*

Was on screen for only eight minutes in *Shakespeare in Love,* for which she won an Academy Award.

She, along with Audrey Hepburn, is one of only a few actresses who have won an Oscar and a Tony in the same year.

Marriage: Michael Williams, actor, 1971
Child: Finty, a.k.a. Tara Cressida Frances, actor, 1972
Famous Relatives: Jeffrey Dench, actor, brother
Major Awards: Academy Award, Best Supporting Actress, *Shakespeare In Love,* 1999; Tony Award, Best Actress in a Play, *Amy's View,* 1999
Quote: "If anyone called me Judith they'd get a black eye. Judi, Judi, I like best."

ROBERT DE NIRO

Birthplace: New York, NY
Birthdate: 8/17/43
Occupation: Actor
Education: Attended the High School of Music and Art and dropped out, studied at the Dramatic Workshop, the Luther James Studio, the Stella Adler Studio, and the Actor's Studio
Debut: (Film) *Greetings,* 1969
Signature: *Taxi Driver,* 1976
Facts: Although commonly regarded as Italian-American, De Niro is more Irish in ancestry.

First acting experience was playing the Cowardly Lion in a Public School 41 production of *The Wizard of Oz.*

Co-owns Rubicon, a San Francisco restaurant, with Francis Ford Coppola.

The pop group Bananarama recorded a song (1984) called "Robert De Niro's Waiting." They originally wanted to use Al Pacino's name, but Pacino refused to let them.

De Niro grew up in New York City's Little Italy, just a few blocks away from his future friend, Martin Scorsese.

Three years after their breakup, De Niro was sperm donor for his ex-girlfriend Toukie Smith; a surrogate mother delivered her twin boys, Aaron and Julian

Was questioned by French police for nine hours regarding an international prostitution ring. Charging that the detectives' only reason for interrogating him was to heighten their profile, De Niro won a defamation case against the paper that printed the investigators' leak, returned his Legion of Honor medal, and vowed never to return to France.

Marriages: Diahnne Abbott (divorced, 1988), Grace Hightower, 1997 (separated, 1999)

Children: Drena, 1967; Raphael, c.1976 (with Diahnne Abbott). Aaron, 1995; Julian, 1995; (with Toukie Smith). Elliot, 1998

Major Awards: Oscar, Best Supporting Actor, *The Godfather Part II*, 1974; Oscar, Best Actor, *Raging Bull*, 1980.

BRIAN DENNEHY

Birthplace: Bridgeport, CT
Birthdate: 7/9/38
Occupation: Actor
Education: Columbia University; attended Yale University, graduate program
Debut: (Stage) *Streamers*, 1976; (Film) *Semi-Tough*, 1977; (TV) *It Happened at Lakewood Manor*, 1977
Signature: *Death of a Salesman*, 1999
Facts: Was in the Marines for over five years and served eight months in Vietnam before returning home because of shrapnel wounds and a concussion.

He made his TV screenwriting-directing debut in 1994, with *Jack Reed: A Search for Justice*.

Attended college on football scholarship and, although he loved the theater, never auditioned because he was a member of the team.

Admits to being a "functional alcoholic" in the beginning of his career.

Owns a cottage on the coast of Ireland.

Collects art and enjoys sailing.
Infamy: Arrested for drunk driving while with actor Steve Guttenberg.
Original Jobs: Meat truck driver, bartender, salesman
Marriage: Judy (divorced); Jennifer Arnott, 1988

Children: Elizabeth, 1960; Kathleen, 1962; Deirdre, 1964 (with Judy). Cormack, 1993 (adopted; with Arnott); Sarah, 1995 (adopted, biological sister of Cormack; with Arnott).
Famous Relatives: Edward Dennehy Jr., acting teacher, theater director, brother
Major Award: Tony, Actor, *Death of a Salesman*, 1999
Quote: "People always ask me if my size has helped or hurt me in this business. It's pretty much an even split."

JOHNNY DEPP

Birthplace: Owensboro, KY
Birthdate: 6/9/63
Occupation: Actor
Education: High school dropout
Debut: (Film) *Nightmare on Elm Street*, 1984
Signature: *21 Jump Street*
Facts: Dropped out of school at age 16 and joined a series of garage bands, one of which (The Kids) opened for Iggy Pop. Moved to L.A., where his ex-wife introduced him to actor Nicolas Cage, who spawned Depp's career.

Once owned a painting of a clown by executed serial killer John Wayne Gacy; now Depp has a pathological fear of clowns.

Tattoos: "Betty Sue" and "Wino Forever" (formerly "Winona Forever").

Co-owns the Viper Room, the '30s-style nightclub in L.A., outside of which River Phoenix died (1994).

Member of the band P, with ex-Sex Pistol Steve Jones and Red Hot Chili Pepper Flea.
Infamy: Charged with trashing a $1,200/night hotel room in New York City in September 1994. He agreed to pay the $9,767.12 in damages.
Original Job: Rock guitarist, sold pens over the phone
Marriages: Lori Anne Allison (divorced); Sherilyn Fenn (engaged, never married); Jennifer Grey (engaged, never married); Winona

Ryder (engaged, never married); Vanessa Paradis (relationship)
Child: Lily-Rose Melody, 1999
Quote: "I've built a career at being a failure. I'm always shocked when I get a job."

PORTIA DE ROSSI

Real Name: Amanda Rogers
Birthplace: Melbourne, Australia
Birthdate: 1/31/73
Occupation: Actor
Education: Attended Melbourne University
Debut: (Film) *Sirens*, 1994
Signature: *Ally McBeal*
Facts: Began modeling at 11 and took professional name at 14.

Attended college as law major but dropped out to pursue career. She still holds on to *Black's Law Dictionary* for reference.

Modeled and appeared in TV commercials in Melbourne to pay tuition when a local film producer suggested she audition for *Sirens*.

Nicknamed "Portia de Froggy" after an episode of *Ally McBeal* where she had several scenes involving frogs.
Original Job: Model
Quote: "I think playing a lawyer alleviates some of my guilt at not becoming one."

DANNY DEVITO

Birthplace: Neptune, NJ
Birthdate: 11/17/44
Occupation: Actor, director, producer
Education: American Academy of Dramatic Arts
Debut: (Stage) *The Man with a Flower in His Mouth*, 1969
Signature: *Taxi*
Facts: After high school he worked in his sister's hair salon and was known as "Mr. Danny."

Got his part in *One Flew Over the Cuckoo's Nest* (1975) through producer Michael Douglas, whom DeVito had met in summer stock a

few years before. Kirk Douglas had directed DeVito in *Scalawag* in 1973.
Original Job: Hairdresser, theatrical makeup artist, valet
Marriage: Rhea Perlman, 1982
Children: Lucy Chet, 1983; Gracie Fan, 1985; Jake Daniel Sebastian, 1987
Major Award: Emmy, Best Supporting Actor in a Comedy Series, *Taxi,* 1981

CAMERON DIAZ

Birthplace: San Diego, CA
Birthdate: 8/30/72
Occupation: Actor, model
Education: High school
Debut: (Film) *The Mask,* 1994
Signature: *There's Something About Mary,* 1998
Facts: The 5' 9" beauty signed with the Elite Modeling Agency at age 16; as a teen, made up to $2,000 a day.

Was a cheerleader in high school.

Says she "nearly killed herself" with her excessive drinking as she traveled the world as a successful —and fun-loving—model.

Nicknamed "Skeletor" as a child for being so skinny.

Competed in the Long Beach celebrity Grand Prix.

Since her only acting experience was in a school play, she originally auditioned for the smaller part of a reporter in *The Mask;* she was called back 12 times before snaring the lead.

Her looks spring from a combination of her dad's Cuban ethnicity and her mother's heritage of German, English, and American Indian. First name means "crooked stream" in Gaelic.

Her favorite authors are Charles Bukowski and Raymond Carver.
Relationship: Jared Leto
Quote: " 'Model turned actress' is a silly phrase. People just assume you don't have the capacity to think."

LEONARDO DICAPRIO

Birthdate: 11/11/74
Occupation: Actor
Debut: (TV) *Romper Room;* (Film) *Poison Ivy,* 1992
Signature: *Titanic,* 1997
Facts: Rejected by a talent agent when he was 10 years old for having a bad haircut.

First memory is of wearing red-and-yellow tap shoes and being lifted onto a stage by his father to entertain people waiting for a concert.

First acting experience was in a Matchbox car commercial.

Successfully sued *Playgirl* to block publication of unauthorized nude photos.
Relationship: Kirsten Zang
Famous Relative: Adam Farrar, actor, stepbrother
Quote: "I hate when I see myself [with] those other cute faces. I feel I'm just part of a meat factory."

TAYE DIGGS

Birthplace: Essex County, NJ
Birthdate: 1/2/71
Occupation: Actor
Education: Syracuse University
Debut: (Stage) *Carousel,* 1994; (TV) *New York Undercover,* 1996; (Film) *How Stella Got Her Groove Back,* 1998
Signature: *How Stella Got Her Groove Back,* 1998
Facts: Spent nine months singing and dancing in the *Caribbean Revue* at Tokyo's Disneyland.

Landed feature role in Broadway's *Rent* and continued TV spots in *Guiding Light.*

Upon learning he landed the *Stella* role, he ran naked through the aisles of *Rent's* theater.

Costarred in the 1999 films *Go* and *The Wood.*
Relationship: Idina Menzel, singer
Quote: "If you could have seen me in high school, you would laugh. I loved sports and I loved women, but I was always a little too small and geeky."

CELINE DION

Birthplace: Charlemagne, Canada
Birthdate: 3/30/68
Occupation: Singer
Education: High school dropout
Signature: "My Heart Will Go On," 1997
Fact: Celine had nine best-selling French albums behind her before she recorded *Unison* in 1990.

She has over 500 pairs of shoes, with not letup in sight.

Announced she would retire after her 1999 tour, in part to focus on having children.
Infamy: In 1990, refused to accept a Quebec music award as anglophone artist of the year, declaring she was "proud to be Quebecoise." The anglophone press criticized her harshly for exploiting the incident for its publicity value.
Marriage: Rene Angélil, 1994
Major Awards: Grammy, Best Pop Performance—Duo or Group, "Beauty and the Beast" (with Peabo Bryson), 1992; Grammy, Best Song Written Specifically for a Movie, "Beauty and the Beast" (with Peabo Bryson), 1992; Grammy, Record of the Year, "My Heart Will Go On," 1998; Grammy, Best Pop Vocal—Female, "My Heart Will Go On," 1998.

SHANNEN DOHERTY

Birthplace: Memphis, TN
Birthdate: 4/12/71
Occupation: Actor
Education: High school
Debut: (Film) *Night Shift,* 1982; (TV) *Father Murphy,* 1982
Signature: *Beverly Hills, 90210*
Facts: Before her role on *90210,* she starred in *Little House on the Prairie* with Melissa Gilbert and *Our House* with Wilfred Brimley.

Gained attention as a teen lead in *90210* for her temperamental behavior.

Subject of *I Hate Brenda* newsletter.

Reteamed with Aaron Spelling for *Charmed* in 1998.

Led the Pledge of Allegiance at the Republican National Convention in 1992.

Was asked to audition for *The Class of Beverly Hills* (a.k.a. *Beverly Hills, 90210*) based on her performance in *Heathers*.

She has three dogs.

Met ex-husband, Ashley Hamilton, only two weeks before they were married.

At her backyard wedding, Doherty wore a silk bathrobe and went barefoot.

Infamy: Highly volatile, she engaged in a bar fight with an aspiring actress and several public brawls with boyfriends.

Cited for thousands of dollars in unpaid rent.

Admits to abusing drugs and alcohol.

Marriage: Dean Factor (engaged, 1990; never married); Chris Foufas (engaged, 1991; never married); Ashley Hamilton (divorced, 1994); Rob Weiss (engaged, never married).

Quote: "Don't judge me for who I am, because everybody makes mistakes."

MICHAEL DOUGLAS

Birthplace: New Brunswick, NJ
Birthdate: 9/25/44
Occupation: Actor, producer, director
Education: University of California, Santa Barbara
Debut: (TV) *The Experiment*, 1969; (Film) *Hail, Hero!*, 1969
Signature: *Fatal Attraction*, 1987
Facts: His film company produced *One Flew over the Cuckoo's Nest* (1975) and *The China Syndrome* (1979), in which he starred.

Directed two episodes of TV show *The Streets of San Francisco*, in which he costarred.

Flunked out of college during his freshman year.

Is a UN Ambassador of Peace.
Marriage: Diandra Luker, 1977

(separated, 1995); Catherine Zeta-Jones (relationship)
Child: Cameron, 1978 (with Diandra Luker)
Famous Relatives: Kirk Douglas, actor, father; Diana Dill, actress, mother; Eric Douglas, comedian, half brother
Major Awards: Oscar, Best Actor, *Wall Street*, 1987

ROMA DOWNEY

Birthplace: Derry, Northern Ireland
Birthdate: 5/6/60
Occupation: Actor
Education: London Drama Studio
Debut: (Stage) *The Circle*, 1989; (TV) *A Woman Named Jackie*, 1991
Signature: *Touched by an Angel*
Facts: An Irish Catholic, was raised in war-torn Northern Ireland, where she sometimes heard gunshots in the night.

Her mother collapsed from a heart attack in front of her when she was 10. Her father died from a heart attack 11 years later.

Turned down for a grant to attend drama school; her tuition was paid by a local theater director and two other teachers who believed in her talent.

Angel costar Della Reese, a minister, officiated at her Salt Lake City wedding, then entertained guests with a jazzy, romantic set.
Marriage: One prior marriage; David Anspaugh, 1995 (divorced, 1998).
Child: Reilly Marie, 1996

ROBERT DOWNEY JR.

Birthplace: New York, NY
Birthdate: 4/4/65
Occupation: Actor
Education: High school dropout
Debut: (Film) *Pound*, 1970; (TV) *Mussolini: The Untold Story*, 1985
Signature: *Chaplin*, 1992
Facts: His middle name is John.

At age 5, he played a puppy in his father's film *Pound*.

Was the live-in companion of

Sarah Jessica Parker for seven years.

In 1985, he took a turn as a regular cast member on *Saturday Night Live*.

To play the part of Charlie Chaplin, Downey learned to pantomime, speak two British dialects, and play left-handed tennis.

An avid musician, Downey plays the piano and sings opera. He composed the closing theme song for *Two Girls and a Guy* as well as recording a version of "Smile" for *Chaplin*.
Infamy: In 1987, he began therapy at a substance rehabilitation center.

Arrested in 1996 on charges of driving while under the influence, carrying a concealed weapon, and drug possession.

Arrested a month later for criminal trespass and leaving a court-ordered rehab, he spent time in a drug clinic and, in 1997, was sentenced to time served and three years' probation.

Arrested again in June 1999 for admitting that he was still doing drugs, he was sentenced to 3 years in prison for violating his probation. With credit for time spent in county jail and treatment centers, he'll probably serve about a year.
Marriage: Deborah Falconer (separated, 1996)
Child: Indio, 1993
Famous Relatives: Robert Downey, actor, director, screenwriter, father; Elsie Downey, actor, singer, mother; Laura Downey, screenwriter, step-mother
Quote: "Stopping isn't hard. Not starting again is."

FRAN DRESCHER

Birthplace: Queens, NY
Birthdate: 9/30/57
Occupation: Actor
Education: Queens College
Debut: (Film) *Saturday Night Fever*, 1977

Signature: *The Nanny*
Facts: Her husband (since 1979) is a writer and executive producer of *The Nanny*.

Her five-line part in *Saturday Night Fever* included memorably asking John Travolta, "Are you as good in bed as you are on the dance floor?"

Before pursuing acting, went to beauty school to have a profession to fall back on. Uses that knowledge to do her own "AstroTurf of hairdos—nothing can hurt it": first mousse, then gel, then voluminize.

Studied with a vocal coach to lose her accent, but gave that up when she stopped getting acting work.

During the writer's strike in the late '80s, started a gourmet crouton business, a product that recently grossed seven figures annually.
Marriage: Peter Marc Jacobson, 1978 (separated, 1997); Michael Angelo (relationship).

MINNIE DRIVER

Real Name: Amelia Driver
Birthplace: Barbados
Birthdate: 1/31/70
Occupation: Actor
Education: England's Webber-Douglas Academy of Dramatic Art
Debut: (Film) *Circle of Friends*, 1995
Signature: *Good Will Hunting*, 1997
Facts: Grew up in the Caribbean until age 9, when she was sent to an English boarding school.

Gained over 20 pounds for *Circle of Friends*, then shed every ounce to play a thin Bond woman in *Goldeneye*.

Stands 5'10".
Original Jobs: Jazz singer, guitarist
Relationship: Josh Brolin

MATT DRUDGE

Birthplace: Tacoma Park, MD
Birthdate: 10/27/66
Occupation: Cybercolumnist, television commentator
Education: High school

Signature: *Drudge Report*
Facts: He reportedly graduated 325th of 350 in his high school class.

When he was younger, he watched television talk shows, listened to talk radio, and sat in his bedroom with a microphone and tape recorder, narrating his own show.

He works out of his Hollywood apartment.

After moving to L.A., he managed a CBS Studio Center gift shop, and in 1995 began his Internet column with tidbits garnered from trashcans.

In 1997, he posted items about Kathleen Willey, the former Clinton campaign worker who would later allege unwanted sexual advances from the Oval Office, and the following year he reported that *Newsweek* held back on a story about intimacies between Clinton and Monica Lewinsky.
Infamy: In 1997, his unsubstantiated report accusing White House aide Sidney Blumenthal of wife-beating was retracted, but because Drudge would not divulge his sources, he was slapped with a $30 million defamation suit, which remains unresolved.
Original Job: Night shift manager at 7-Eleven.
Quote: "I know it's unethical as hell, but it's fun."

DAVID DUCHOVNY

Birthplace: New York, NY
Birthdate: 8/7/60
Occupation: Actor
Education: Princeton; master's degree from Yale
Debut: (Film) *Working Girl*, 1988
Signature: *The X-Files*
Facts: As a six-year-old, Duchovny wanted to be a bathtub.

Duchovny was working on his Ph.D. dissertation, "Magic and Technology in Contemporary Fiction," when he got his first acting job in a Lowenbrau beer commercial.

Played Denise the transvestite detective on *Twin Peaks*, 1990–91.

America Online has two separate folders devoted to messages about him; as one fan explained, "the drool is too heavy to be confined to one."
Infamy: In 1999, filed suit against 20th Century Fox, alleging that the studio has cheated him out of millions of dollars in profits from his TV series.
Original Jobs: Teaching assistant at Yale, bartender
Marriage: Téa Leoni, 1997
Child: Madelaine West, 1999
Quote: "I assumed there was no way it (*The X Files*) would last. It wasn't that interesting and I thought it was silly. Obviously I was wrong."

BOB DYLAN

Real Name: Robert Zimmerman
Birthplace: Duluth, MN
Birthdate: 5/24/41
Occupation: Singer, songwriter
Education: University of Minnesota
Debut: (Album) *Bob Dylan*, 1961
Signature: "Blowin' in the Wind," 1963
Facts: Took stage name from Dylan Thomas.

His backup band, The Hawks, later evolved into The Band.

Motorcycle crash in July 1966 led to a brief retirement.

Became a born-again Christian in 1979.
Infamy: Sued by Ruth Tryangiel in 1994. She claims she was his lover on and off for 19 years, and that she cowrote much of his music and helped manage his career. The lawsuit asks for $5 million plus damages and palimony.
Original Job: Performed with a Texas carnival
Marriage: Sarah Lowndes (divorced, 1977)
Children: Jesse, 1966; Maria, 1961 (stepdaughter, adopted); Samuel, 1968; Anna, 1967; Jakob, 1969
Major Awards: Grammy, Album of the Year, *The Concert for*

Bangladesh (with George Harrison and Friends), 1972; Grammy, Best Rock Vocal—Male, "Gotta Serve Somebody," 1979; Grammy, Lifetime Achievement Award, 1991; Grammy, Best Traditional Folk Album, *World Gone Wrong*, 1994; Grammy, Album of the Year, *Time Out of Mind*, 1997; Grammy, Best Rock Vocal—Male, "Cold Irons Bound," 1997; Grammy, Best Contemporary Folk Album, *Time Out of Mind*, 1997

JAKOB DYLAN

Birthplace: New York, NY
Birthdate: 12/9/69
Occupation: Singer, songwriter
Education: Attended Parsons School of Design
Debut: (Album) *The Wallflowers*, 1992
Signature: The Wallflowers
Facts: The youngest of five children, is rumored to be the inspiration for his father's classic "Forever Young." As a child, often went on the road with dad.

Lived with his mother, Sarah Lowndes, after parents' bitter 1977 divorce. In an incident during custody suit, Sarah tried to take Dylan and his siblings out of school, chasing them down the halls and even assaulting an uncooperative teacher.

Had a D average in high school. Began career wearing anonymous knit caps for seven years, playing L.A.'s clubs and delis without identifying himself as Dylan's son.

Having grown up the protected child of a famous celebrity, Dylan says privacy and security are crucial to his own family as well: he won't even reveal his son's first name.

Debut album bombed at only 40,000 copies, causing Virgin Records to drop him; took more than a year to find a new label.
Marriage: Paige
Child: Son
Famous Relative: Bob Dylan, singer, songwriter, father
Major Awards: Grammy, Best Rock

Vocal—Duo or Group, "One Headlight" (with the Wallflowers), 1997; Grammy, Best Rock Song, "One Headlight," 1997

CLINT EASTWOOD

Birthplace: San Francisco, CA
Birthdate: 5/31/30
Occupation: Actor, director
Education: Los Angeles City College
Debut: (Film) *Revenge of the Creature*, 1955
Signature: *Dirty Harry*, 1972
Facts: He was drafted in 1951 but en route to Korea his plane crashed. He swam miles to shore and was made swimming instructor at a boot camp, where he met actors Martin Milner and David Janssen, who sparked his acting career.

Elected mayor of Carmel, CA, in 1986; reelected in 1988.

Jazz musician and self-taught piano player, he plays three songs in the movie *In the Line of Fire*. Also composed two Cajun-inspired instrumentals for *A Perfect World*.

Has own beer "Pale Rider Ale," named for his 1985 Western *Pale Rider*.

Reportedly had a son and a daughter with Jacelyn Reeves. Names were not released.

Is a part-owner of the famed golf courses at Pebble Beach.
Infamy: Slapped with palimony suit by former lover Sondra Locke.
Original Job: Lumberjack, forest-fire fighter, steelworker
Marriages: Maggie Johnson (divorced); Dina Ruiz, 1996
Children: Kimber, 1964 (with Roxanne Tunis). Kyle, 1968; Alison, 1972; (with Maggie Johnson). Francesca, 1993 (with Frances Fisher). Morgan, 1996
Major Awards: Oscar, Best Picture, *Unforgiven*, 1992, Academy of Motion Pictures Arts and Sciences, Irving G. Thalberg Memorial Award, 1995

ROGER EBERT

Birthplace: Urbana, IL
Birthdate: 6/18/42
Occupation: Film critic, writer
Education: University of Illinois; University of Cape Town, South Africa; University of Chicago
Debut: Film critic for the *Chicago Sun-Times*, 1967
Signature: Siskel & Ebert
Facts: While at the University of Illinois, was editor of the *Daily Illini* and president of the U.S. Student Press Association, 1963–64.

Wrote the screenplay for *Beyond the Valley of the Dolls*, 1970. Also wrote a novel, *Behind the Phantom's Mask*, which was released in 1993.

Is a member of the Studebaker Drivers' Club.
Marriage: Chaz Hammel-Smith, 1993
Major Award: Pulitzer Prize for Distinguished Criticism, 1975

KENNETH "BABYFACE" EDMONDS

Birthplace: Indianapolis, IN
Birthdate: 4/10/58
Occupation: Singer, songwriter, producer
Debut: (Album) *Lovers*, 1989
Facts: While in ninth grade, phoned concert promoters pretending to be his teacher, asking if musicians would grant his gifted young charge—actually himself—an interview. Through this ruse, chatted with Stevie Wonder, the Jackson 5, and Earth, Wind and Fire.

Given his moniker in the early '80s by funk guitarist Bootsy Collins because of his youthful looks.

Has written or produced hits for Mariah Carey, Whitney Houston, Bobby Brown, TLC, Boyz II Men, and Toni Braxton.

Produced the movie *Soul Food* with his wife; they both cameo as film executives in *Hav Plenty*.
Marriages: Denise (divorced); Tracey McQuarn, 1992

Major Awards: Grammy, Best R&B Song, "End of the Road" (with L.A. Reid and Daryl Simmons), 1992; Grammy, Producer of the Year (with L.A. Reid), 1992; Grammy, Album of the Year (producer), *The Bodyguard*, 1993; Grammy, Best R&B Song, "I'll Make Love to You," 1994; Grammy, Best R&B Vocal—Male, "When Can I See You," 1994; Grammy, Producer of the Year, 1995; Grammy, Record of the Year, "Change the World," 1996; Best R&B Song, "Exhale (Shoop Shoop)," 1996; Grammy, Producer of the Year, 1996; Grammy, Producer of the Year, 1997

ANTHONY EDWARDS

Birthplace: Santa Barbara, CA
Birthdate: 7/19/62
Occupation: Actor
Education: University of Southern California
Debut: (IV) *The Killing of Randy Webster*, 1981; (Film) *Heart Like a Wheel*, 1982
Signature: *ER*
Facts: His classmates at USC included Forest Whitaker and Ally Sheedy.

Played a burnt-out surfer in 1982's *Fast Times at Ridgemont High*, and one of the two head nerds in 1984's *Revenge of the Nerds*.

Somewhat bored with acting, he was planning to direct a low-budget children's feature, *Charlie's Ghost Story*, when he was called for *ER*. Originally turned down the *ER* role when production dates for the two projects initially overlapped.
Original Job: Actor in commercials for McDonald's and Country Time Lemonade
Marriage: Jeanine Lobell, 1995
Child: Bailey, 1994; Esme, 1997

CARMEN ELECTRA

Real Name: Tara Leigh Patrick
Birthplace: Cincinnati, OH
Birthdate: 4/20/72

Occupation: Actor, model, singer, dancer
Education: High school
Debut: (Album) *Carmen Electra*, 1992; (TV) *Baywatch Nights*, 1994
Signature: *Baywatch*
Facts: As a protégé of The Artist Formerly Known As Prince, she changed her name and flopped with her debut album. She later scored with *Playboy*, replaced Jenny McCarthy in 1997 as cohost of *Singled Out,* then played a *Baywatch* lifeguard when Pamela Anderson left the hit show, and is now a regular on *Hyperion Bay*.

She's the youngest of five children.

She lost her mother and her sister within a week of each other.

Wore Capri pants, a black Mark Wong Nark shirt, and black high-heel platform shoes to her wedding.

After marrying her in Las Vegas, Dennis Rodman sought an annulment of their marriage, issuing a statement that claimed he was drunk at the time. They remained married for months thereafter, though. Even after Rodman filed for divorce, the two were still linked.
Infamy: Posed nude for *Playboy* in 1996 and appeared in the video *Playboy Cheerleaders*
Original Job: Model
Marriage: Dennis Rodman,1998 (filed for divorce, 1999)
Quote: "I love being in front of an audience. It's so stimulating. You get that adrenaline rush in your body and there's nothing like it in the world. I also love to barbecue."

JENNA ELFMAN

Real name: Jenna Butala
Birthplace: Los Angeles, CA
Birthdate: 9/30/71
Occupation: Actor, dancer
Education: Attended Cal State University and Beverly Hills Playhouse
Debut: (Film) *Grosse Pointe Blank*, 1997
Signature: *Dharma & Greg*

Facts: Became a member of the Church of Scientology in 1991.

Trained in classical dance from age 5, she considered joining Seattle's Pacific Northwest Ballet.

Was a chorus line tap dancer at the 1991 Academy Awards and a "Legs Girl" in ZZ Top's 1994 World Tour.
Marriage: Bodhi Elfman, 1994
Famous Relative: Danny Elfman, composer, rocker, uncle-in-law

NORA EPHRON

Birthplace: New York, NY
Birthdate: 5/19/41
Occupation: Screenwriter, director
Education: Wellesley College
Debut: (Book) *Wallflower at the Orgy*, 1970; (TV) *Perfect Gentleman*, 1978
Signature: *Sleepless in Seattle*, 1993
Facts: She was the subject of the play *Take Her, She's Mine*, written by her parents.

Her book *Heartburn* was adapted into a 1986 movie starring Jack Nicholson and Meryl Streep. Wrote screenplays for *Silkwood* and *When Harry Met Sally...*
Marriages: Dan Greenburg, 1967 (divorced); Carl Bernstein, 1976 (divorced, 1979); Nicholas Pileggi, 1987
Children: Jacob, 1978; Max, 1979; (with Carl Bernstein).
Famous Relatives: Henry Ephron, screenwriter, father; Phoebe Ephron, screenwriter, mother; Delia Ephron, writer, sister
Quote: "No matter how cynical I get, I just can't keep up."

MELISSA ETHERIDGE

Birthplace: Leavenworth, KS
Birthdate: 5/29/61
Occupation: Singer, songwriter, guitarist
Education: Berklee College of Music
Debut: *Melissa Etheridge,* 1988
Facts: Played in women's bars

around L.A. for six years beginning in 1982.

Came out by leaping onstage at one of Bill Clinton's presidential inaugural bashes, kissing cult figure Elvira, and proclaiming herself a proud lifelong lesbian.
Relationship: Julie Cypher
Child: Bailey Jean, 1997; Beckett, 1998
Major Awards: Grammy, Best Rock Vocal—Female, "Ain't It Heavy," 1992; Grammy, Best Rock Vocal—Female, "Come to My Window," 1994
Quote: "I like to bring the sexual energy out by seducing the audience, and, when it's there, building on it. I would like to say that, maybe, going to a concert of mine is like foreplay."

RUPERT EVERETT

Birthplace: Norfolk, England
Birthdate: 5/29/59
Occupation: Actor
Education: High school dropout
Debut: (Film) *A Shocking Accident,* 1982; (TV) *Princess Daisy,* 1983; (American stage) *The Vortex,* 1991
Signature: *My Best Friend's Wedding,* 1997
Facts: As a child, he was very thin with huge buck teeth.

Was expelled for insubordination from Central School of Speech and Drama.

At his all-male, Catholic boarding schools, he was often cast in female roles in plays.

While a struggling actor, he supported himself as a male prostitute. Everett publicly disclosed his homosexuality in 1989.

Scenes from *My Best Friend's Wedding* were reshot to give him more screen time after focus groups praised his performance.

In 1991, he published his first novel, *Hello Darling, Are You Working?*
Original Job: Model
Quote: "I don't think anyone's particularly shocked by anything any more. Are they? We are all such old sluts now."

MIA FARROW

Birthplace: Los Angeles, CA
Birthdate: 2/9/45
Occupation: Actor
Education: Marymount in Los Angeles and Cygnet House in London
Debut: (Stage) *The Importance of Being Earnest,* 1963
Signature: *Rosemary's Baby,* 1968
Facts: Mother—biological or adoptive—of 15 kids.

Was on first cover of PEOPLE, March 4, 1974.
Infamy: Was awarded custody of the two children she and Woody Allen adopted, as well as their biological son, after a highly publicized case involving allegations of molestation by Allen.
Marriages: Frank Sinatra, 1966 (divorced, 1968); André Previn 1970 (divorced, 1977).
Children: Matthew, 1970; Sascha, 1970; Soon-Yi, 1970 (adopted); Lark, 1973 (adopted); Fletcher, 1974; Daisy, 1974 (adopted); (with André Previn).

Moses, 1978 (adopted); Tam, c.1981 (adopted by Mia alone); Malone, 1985 (originally Dylan, changed to Eliza, changed again; adopted); Seamus (formerly Satchel), 1987; (with Woody Allen).

Thaddeus, c.1989 (adopted); Frankie-Minh, c.1991 (adopted); Isaiah Justus, 1992 (adopted); Kaeli-Shea, 1994 (adopted); Gabriel Wilk (adopted); (by Mia alone)
Famous Relatives: Maureen O'Sullivan, actor, mother; John Farrow, director, father

SALLY FIELD

Birthplace: Pasadena, CA
Birthdate: 11/6/46
Occupation: Actor
Education: Columbia Pictures Workshop, Actor's Studio
Debut: (TV) *Gidget,* 1965
Signature: *The Flying Nun*
Facts: Was a cheerleader in high school.

Won the lead role in *Gidget* from among 150 other finalists.

Though entertaining, *The Flying Nun* discouraged people from thinking of her as a serious actress; the producers of the movie *True Grit* refused even to give her an audition. She was paid $4,000 a week for the television show.

According to PEOPLE's Pop Profiles for 3 consecutive years, Field was among the top three female celebrities most appreciated by the public.
Marriages: Steve Craig (divorced); Alan Greisman (divorced, 1994)
Children: Peter, 1969; Elijah, 1972; (with Steve Craig). Samuel, 1987
Famous Relatives: Mary Field Mahoney, actor, mother; Jock Mahoney, actor, stepfather
Major Awards: Emmy, *Sybil,* 1977; Oscar, Best Actress, *Norma Rae,* 1979; Oscar, Best Actress, *Places in the Heart,* 1984

JOSEPH FIENNES

Birthplace: Wiltshire, England
Birthdate: 5/27/70
Occupation: Actor
Education: Guildhall School of Music and Drama
Debut: (Stage) *A Month in the Country,* 1994; (TV) *The Vacillations of Poppy Carew,* 1995; (Film) *Stealing Beauty,* 1996
Signature: *Shakespeare in Love,* 1998
Facts: His middle name is Alberic.

He has a fraternal twin.

He began his career on stage with

Helen Mirren and the Royal Shakespeare Company.
Original Job: Dresser, National Theatre
Famous Relatives: Ralph Fiennes, actor, brother; Martha Fiennes, director, sister; Magnus Hubert Fiennes, musician, brother; Sophie Victoria Fiennes, producer, sister; Jennifer Lash, mother, novelist (deceased)

RALPH FIENNES

Birthplace: Suffolk, England
Birthdate: 12/22/62
Education: London's Royal Academy of Dramatic Art
Debut: (Film) *Wuthering Heights*, 1992
Signature: *Schindler's List*, 1993
Facts: Fiennes gained 28 pounds to play Amon Goeth in *Schindler's List*, 1993. He was chosen for the role after director Steven Spielberg saw Fiennes's performance in the British TV movie *A Dangerous Man: Lawrence After Arabia.*
His name is pronounced "Rafe."
Marriage: Alex Kingston (divorced, 1997); Francesca Annis (relationship)
Famous Relative: Joseph, actor, brother; Martha Fiennes, director, sister; Magnus Hubert Fiennes, musician, brother; Sophie Victoria Fiennes, producer, sister; Jennifer Lash, mother, novelist (deceased)
Major Award: Tony, Best Actor (Dramatic), *Hamlet*, 1995

LAURENCE FISHBURNE

Birthplace: Augusta, GA
Birthdate: 7/30/61
Occupation: Actor
Education: Lincoln Square Academy
Debut: (Stage) *Section D*, 1975; (Film) *Cornbread, Earl and Me*, 1975
Signature: *Boyz N the Hood*, 1991
Facts: Appeared regularly on soap opera *One Life to Live* for four years starting when he was 9.
At 14, went with his mother to the

Philippines for what was supposed to be a three-month shoot for *Apocalypse Now;* the shoot lasted 18 months.
A theater buff, he wrote, directed, and starred in a play, *Riff Raff*, in 1994.
Marriage: Hanja Moss, 1985 (divorced, c.1993)
Children: Langston, 1987; Montana, 1991
Major Awards: Tony, Featured Actor (Dramatic), *Two Trains Running*, 1992; Emmy, Best Guest Actor in a Drama, *Tribeca*, 1993

CARRIE FISHER

Birthplace: Burbank, CA
Birthdate: 10/21/56
Occupation: Actor, novelist, screenwriter
Education: Dropped out of Beverly Hills High School, attended Sarah Lawrence College and Central School of Speech and Drama, London
Debut: (Stage) *Irene*, 1972
Signature: *Star Wars*, 1977
Facts: Sang in her mother's Las Vegas nightclub act.
Her first public appearance was in a *Life* magazine photograph with her mother shortly after her father had run off to marry Elizabeth Taylor.
Infamy: Was a user of LSD and Percodan; almost overdosed, 1985.
Marriage: Paul Simon, 1983 (divorced, 1984)
Child: Billie Catherine Lourd, 1992
Famous Relatives: Debbie Reynolds, actress, mother; Eddie Fisher, singer, father
Quote: "You find me a kid that thinks he got enough affection and attention as a child and I'll show you Dan Quayle."

CALISTA FLOCKHART

Birthplace: Freeport, IL
Birthdate: 11/11/64
Occupation: Actor
Education: Rutgers University
Debut: (TV) *Darrow*, 1991
Signature: *Ally McBeal*

Facts: Named after her great-grandmother, "Calista" means "most beautiful" in Greek.
Was a cheerleader in high school.
Has performed in several lead roles on Broadway.
In 1992, she joined Malaparte, a small Manhattan theater group headed by Ethan Hawke.
Turned down an audition for *Ally McBeal* because she was busy with theater and reluctant to do TV. The producers were persistent and she eventually agreed, flying to L.A. between the Sunday-matinee and Monday-evening performances. She was hired on the spot.
Infamy: After a local TV station aired an unconfirmed report that she was anorexic, a flurry of rumors led her to publicly declare, "Am I anorexic?...No."
Quote: "I live vicariously through my rumors."

BRIDGET FONDA

Birthplace: Los Angeles, CA
Birthdate: 1/27/64
Occupation: Actor
Education: New York University, studied at the Lee Strasberg Institute and with Harold Guskin
Debut: (Film) *Aria*, 1987; (TV) *21 Jump Street*, 1989
Signature: *Singles*, 1992
Facts: Named after Bridget Hayward, a woman her father had loved who had committed suicide.
Her movie debut was in *Aria*, in which she stripped naked, had sex, then committed suicide during her eight minutes on screen with no dialogue.
Dated Eric Stoltz for eight years.
Famous Relatives: Peter Fonda, actor, father; Susan Brewer, actor, mother; Henry Fonda, actor, grandfather; Jane Fonda, actor, aunt

JANE FONDA

Birthplace: New York, NY
Birthdate: 12/21/37
Occupation: Actor, political activist, fitness instructor
Education: Vassar College, studied method acting in Lee Strasberg's Actors Studio
Debut: (Film) *Tall Story,* 1960
Signature: *Barbarella,* 1968
Facts: Mother committed suicide in a sanitarium in 1953.

Jane Fonda's Workout is the best-selling nondramatic video in history.

Spent much of the '70s speaking for the Black Panthers and against the Vietnam War and was almost arrested for treason, earning her the nickname "Hanoi Jane."

Reportedly has an adopted daughter whom she refuses to speak about.
Marriages: Roger Vadim, 1965 (divorced, 1973); Tom Hayden, 1973 (divorced, 1990); Ted Turner, 1991
Children: Vanessa, 1968 (with Vadim); Troy Garrity, 1973 (with Hayden)
Famous Relatives: Henry Fonda, actor, father; Peter Fonda, actor, brother; Bridget Fonda, actor, niece
Major Awards: Oscar, Best Actress, *Klute,* 1971; Oscar, Best Actress, *Coming Home,* 1978; Emmy, Lead Actress in a Limited Series or Special, *The Dollmaker,* 1983
Quote: "A director wanted me to break my jaw and reset it. The head of the studio [wanted me] to wear falsies. No wonder I had low self-esteem."

HARRISON FORD

Birthplace: Chicago, IL
Birthdate: 7/13/42
Occupation: Actor, director
Education: Ripon College
Debut: (Film) *Dead Heat on a Merry-Go-Round,* 1966
Signature: Indiana Jones
Fact: Scar beneath his lower lip is the result of a motorcycle accident.

Ford had his ear pierced at age 54, explaining that he had always wanted one; he was accompanied by already-pierced old friends Jimmy Buffett and Ed Bradley.

Recently purchased a helicopter to compliment the three planes he already owns.
Original Job: Carpenter
Marriages: Mary Marquardt (divorced), Melissa Mathison, 1983
Children: Benjamin, 1966; Willard, 1969; (with Mary Marquardt). Malcolm, 1987; Georgia, 1990
Quote: "I'm like old shoes. I've never been hip. I think the reason I'm still here is that I was never enough in fashion that I had to be replaced by something new."

JODIE FOSTER

Real Name: Alicia Christian Foster
Birthplace: Los Angeles, CA
Birthdate: 11/19/62
Occupation: Actor, director
Education: Yale University
Debut: (TV) *Mayberry RFD,* 1969; (Film) *Napoleon and Samantha,* 1972
Signature: *The Silence of the Lambs,* 1991
Facts: Started at 3 years old as the bare-bottomed Coppertone child in the then ubiquitous advertisement. She got the job when, too young to wait in the car, she was noticed at her brother's casting call. By age 8, she had appeared in over 40 commercials.

At 13, played a hooker in *Taxi Driver.* Because she was so young, the film's producers hired her sister Constance to double for her in a nude scene. Before she got the role, she had to pass psychological tests. "I spent four hours with a shrink to prove I was normal enough to play a hooker. Does that make sense?"

As valedictorian in high school, she gave her graduation speech in French.

Object of would-be presidential assassin John Hinckley's obsession.

Has not identified the father of her child.

Child: Charles, 1998
Famous Relative: Buddy Foster, actor, brother
Major Awards: Oscar, Best Actress, *The Accused,* 1988; Oscar, Best Actress, *The Silence of the Lambs,* 1991

MATTHEW FOX

Birthplace: Crowheart, WY
Birthdate: 7/14/66
Occupation: Actor
Education: Columbia University
Debut: (TV) *Freshman Dorm,* 1992
Signature: *Party of Five*
Facts: Grew up on a 120-acre Wyoming ranch, attending a one-room schoolhouse until the fourth grade.

Pondered becoming a farmer like his father, but dad suggested he go east for college. During a year of prep at Massachusetts' Deerfield Academy, snooty classmates voted him "Most Likely to Appear on *Hee-Haw.*"

Played football at college, where he was wide receiver and an economics major.
Original Job: Model
Marriage: Margherita Ronchi, 1992
Child: Kyle Allison, 1997

MICHAEL J. FOX

Birthplace: Edmonton, Canada
Birthdate: 6/9/61
Occupation: Actor
Education: High school dropout
Debut: (TV) *Palmerstown, U.S.A,* 1980; (Film) *Midnight Madness,* 1980
Signature: *Family Ties*
Facts: When he got the audition for *Family Ties,* he was $35,000 in debt, living on macaroni and cheese, and had been forced to sell off a sectional couch piece by piece to raise money.

Eric Stoltz was first cast in *Back to the Future,* but when he proved to be "too intense for the comedy," Fox got the role. For seven weeks he played Alex on *Family Ties* by day, then transformed himself into Marty McFly for the film.

Heavy smoker, but asks not to be

photographed smoking to avoid becoming a negative role model for his younger fans.

Announced in 1998 that he suffers from Parkinson's Disease. First diagnosed seven years prior, he underwent brain surgery to alleviate his tremors.

Purchased two of Eric Clapton's guitars at auction for $79,300.
Marriage: Tracy Pollan, 1988
Children: Sam Michael, 1989; Aquinnah Kathleen, 1995; Schuyler Frances, 1995
Major Awards: Emmy, Best Actor in a Comedy Series, *Family Ties,* 1985, 1986, 1987, 1988

VIVICA A. FOX

Birthplace: Indianapolis, IN
Birthdate: 7/30/64
Occupation: Actor
Education: High school
Debut: (TV) *Days of Our Lives*; (Film) *Born on the Fourth of July,* 1989
Signature: *Independence Day,* 1996
Facts: She was a cheerleader in high school.

Her nickname for her husband is "Big Daddy."

Her middle name is Agnetta.

She has two cats named Tiger and Snookie.

She got her first big break in 1988 when a producer saw her in a restaurant and recommended an agent.

Appeared in *Days of Our Lives*; *Family Matters*; *Matlock*; *Beverly Hills, 90210*; *The Fresh Prince of Bel-Air*; and *The Young and the Restless* before being tapped to play Will Smith's girlfriend in *Independence Day.*

She and Christopher Harvest arrived at their wedding in a horse-drawn carriage. She wore a diamond tiara and was presented with a thousand red roses from her husband.
Original Job: Model, waitress
Marriage: Christopher Harvest (a.k.a. SixxNine),1998

ARETHA FRANKLIN

Birthplace: Memphis, TN
Birthdate: 3/25/42
Occupation: Singer
Education: High school dropout
Debut: (Song) "Rock-A-Bye Your Baby with a Dixie Melody," 1961
Signature: "Respect," 1967
Facts: Started out as a gospel singer in her father's Baptist church in Detroit in the '50s. Her father was minister of the New Bethel Baptist Church, one of the largest pastorates in the U.S., until 1979, when he went into a coma after being shot in his home by a burglar.
Infamy: Was sued for breach of contract in 1984 when she was unable to open in the Broadway musical *Sing, Mahalia, Sing,* mainly because of her fear of flying.
Marriages: Ted White (divorced), Glynn Turman, 1978 (divorced, 1984).
Children: Edward, 1957; Clarence, c.1958;(father undisclosed). Theodore Jr., 1963 (with Ted White). Kecalf, 1970 (with Ken Cunningham).
Major Awards: Grammy, Best Rhythm and Blues Song, "Respect," 1967; Grammy, Best R&B Vocal—Female, "Respect," 1967; Grammy, Best R&B Vocal—Female, "Chain of Fools," 1968; Grammy, Best R&B Vocal—Female, "Share Your Love with Me," 1969; Grammy, Best R&B Vocal—Female, "Don't Play That Song," 1970; Grammy, Best R&B Vocal—Female, "Bridge over Troubled Water,"1971; Grammy, Best R&B Vocal—Female,*Young, Gifted, & Black,* 1972; Grammy, Best R&B Vocal—Female, "Master of Eyes," 1973; Grammy, Best R&B Vocal—Female, "Ain't Nothing Like the Real Thing," 1974; Grammy, Best R&B Vocal—Female, "Hold On I'm Comin'," 1981; Grammy, Best R&B Vocal—Female, "Freeway of Love," 1985; Grammy, Best R&B Vocal—Female, *Aretha,* 1987; Grammy, Best R&B Duo or Group, "I Knew You Were Waiting (For Me)" (with George Michael), 1987; Grammy Legend

Award, 1991; inducted into the Rock and Roll Hall of Fame, 1987; NARAS Lifetime Achievement Award, 1994

DENNIS FRANZ

Birthplace: Chicago, IL
Birthdate: 10/28/44
Occupation: Actor
Debut: (TV) *The Chicago Story,* 1981
Signature: *NYPD Blue*
Facts: Claims he was the "worst postman in the history of the post office" before becoming an actor. "I used to start my route at daybreak, and I would finish long after dark. I'd stop for donuts, I'd play with animals, I'd go home with my bag of mail and just lay around the house a bit."

Served 11 months in Vietnam with an elite Airborne division.
Marriage: Joanie Zeck, 1995
Children: Tricia, 1974 (step-daughter); Krista, 1976 (stepdaughter)
Major Awards: Emmy, Best Actor in a Drama Series, *NYPD Blue,* 1994, 1996, 1997, 1999

BRENDAN FRASER

Birthplace: Indianapolis, IN
Birthdate: 12/3/68
Occupation: Actor
Education: Cornish College of the Arts
Debut: (Film) *Dogfight,* 1991
Signature: *The Mummy,* 1999
Facts: His Canadian-tourism-exec father had the family moving every three years. As a child, lived in Cincinnati, Detroit, Ottawa, Holland and Toronto, among others.

Stands 6'3".

Underwent six months of intensive weight training and a strict high-protein, low carb diet to beef up for his *George of the Jungle* role.
Marriage: Afton Smith, 1998

MORGAN FREEMAN

Birthplace: Memphis, TN
Birthdate: 6/1/37
Occupation: Actor, director
Education: Attended Los Angeles City College
Debut: (Stage, Broadway) *Hello, Dolly,* 1967; (Film) *Brubaker,* 1980
Signature: *Driving Miss Daisy,* 1989
Facts: Got his show business start as a dancer at the 1964 New York World's Fair. He had studied ballet, tap, and jazz.

Played Easy Reader for five years in the 1970s on the PBS series *Electric Company.*

Moved from New York City, where he lived for 25 years, to a Mississippi farm. Is raising one of his nine grandchildren there.
Marriage: Jeanette Adair Bradshaw (divorced), Myrna Colley-Lee, 1984
Children: Alphonse; Saifoulaye; Deena (adopted); Morgana

JAMES GANDOLFINI

Birthplace: Westwood, NY
Birthdate: 9/18/61
Occupation: Actor
Education: Rutgers University
Debut: (Broadway) *A Streetcar Named Desire,* 1992; (Film) *A Stranger Among Us,* 1992; (TV) *The Sopranos,* 1999
Signature: *The Sopranos*
Facts: Began as a theater actor before Hollywood found him.

He plays the trumpet and saxophone.

Got a late start as an actor when a friend took him to his first acting class in the late 1980s.

Having never been in therapy, he struggles with the therapy scenes of his character, Tony Soprano.
Original Jobs: Bouncer, night club manager, truck driver
Quote: "Human frailty and confusion are what interest me. The more sensitive the character and the more he's in touch with things, the more confusion there is."

ANDY GARCIA

Real Name: Andres Arturo Garcia-Menendez
Birthplace: Havana, Cuba
Birthdate: 4/12/56
Occupation: Actor, director, songwriter
Education: Florida International University
Debut: (TV) *Hill Street Blues,* 1981; (Film) *Blue Skies Again,* 1983
Signature: *The Godfather Part III,* 1990
Facts: His family moved to Florida from Cuba after the Bay of Pigs invasion. He was 5 years old at the time and claims to have vivid memories of the event.

He was athletic as a child, until he was sidelined by a case of mononucleosis and began to take an interest in performing.

After college, he went to L.A. and waited tables while working improv and the Comedy Store.

In 1993, he produced and directed a documentary about Cuban mambo artist Cachao, called *Cachao: Like His Rhythm, There Is No Other.*

He wrote and performed several songs for 1995's *Steal Little, Steal Big.* His daughter Dominik made an appearance in this film.

He proposed to his wife on the first night he met her. They were married seven years later.

He produced, helped score, and starred in 1999's *Just the Ticket.*

Owns 25 conga drums, collects hats, and wears a beret in the winter.

Wore his father's pearl tie-pin, his most personal keepsake from Cuba, in *When a Man Loves a Woman.*
Original Job: Waiter
Marriage: Maria (Marvi) Victoria Lorido, 1982
Children: Dominik, 1984; Daniella, 1988; Alessandra, 1991
Quote: "First and foremost, I am a father—who just happens to act."

JANEANE GAROFALO

Birthplace: New Jersey
Birthdate: 9/28/64
Occupation: Actor, comedian
Education: Providence College
Debut: (TV) *The Ben Stiller Show,* 1992; (Film) *Reality Bites,* 1994
Signature: *The Truth About Cats and Dogs,* 1996
Fact: Has "Think" tatooed on her arm.
Original Job: Bike messenger, receptionist
Marriage: Rob Cohn (divorced); Craig Bierko (relationship)
Quote: "I really am not full of self-loathing. People think that because the name of my company is I Hate Myself Productions."

BILL GATES

Birthplace: Seattle, WA
Birthdate: 10/28/55
Occupation: Computer software entrepreneur-executive
Education: Harvard University
Signature: Microsoft Windows
Facts: After learning how to crash an operating system while a high school student, did it to the Control Data Corporation. Their reprimand caused him to abandon computers for a year.

Formed a company to sell a computerized traffic counting system to cities, which made $20,000 its first year. Business fell off when customers learned Gates was only 14.

Became the youngest billionaire ever at age 31.

As head of fast-growing Microsoft, took a total of six vacation days in the company's first six years.

Owns the Bettmann Archive, one of the world's greatest collections of documentary images.

His $30 million "smart house" in Lake Washington features a 20-vehicle garage; dining space for 100; and music, artwork, lighting, and TV shows that follow individuals from room to room.

Infamy: Accused by competitors of using clout from operating systems software to quash software competitors.

Marriage: Melinda French, 1994

Child: Jennifer Katharine, 1996; Rory John, 1999

SARAH MICHELLE GELLAR

Birthplace: New York, NY
Birthdate: 4/14/77
Occupation: Actor, model
Education: Professional Children's High School
Debut: (TV movie) *Invasion of Privacy*, 1983
Signature: *Buffy the Vampire Slayer*
Facts: At age 4, she chided McDonald's for their skimpy patties in a Burger King ad, for which BK was sued for libel. Gellar appeared in court, though the case was soon settled. Has appeared in more than 100 commercials.

Has five holes in each earlobe and one for a navel ring. Tattooed the Chinese character for integrity on her lower back.

Possesses a brown belt in tae kwon do, and was a competitive figure skater as a child.

Major Award: Emmy, Outstanding Younger Actress, *All My Children*, 1994

Quote: "It's really hard to be a vampire slayer if you're scared of cemeteries." (which she is)

RICHARD GERE

Birthplace: Philadelphia, PA
Birthdate: 8/31/49
Occupation: Actor
Education: University of Massachusetts
Debut: (Film) *Report to the Commissioner*, 1975
Signature: *Pretty Woman*, 1990
Facts: Won a gymnastics scholarship to the University of Massachusetts.

In 1973, first studied the "middle way" of Siddhartha Gotama Buddha as preached by a Japanese sect. In 1982, switched faith to the Tibetan school of Buddhism. In 1986, became a student of the exiled Dalai Lama.

First three big film roles (*Days of Heaven*, 1978, *American Gigolo*, 1980, and *An Officer and a Gentleman*, 1982) were roles turned down by John Travolta.

His photographs of Tibetans were published in the book *Pilgrims*.

Infamy: Took out a $30,000 ad with then-wife Cindy Crawford in the *Times* of London in May 1994 denying rumors of their homosexuality.

Original Job: Rock musician

Marriage: Cindy Crawford (divorced, 1994); Carey Lowell (relationship)

Quote: "I think most actors go into acting because there's a lot of self-loathing and confusion."

MEL GIBSON

Birthplace: Peekskill, NY
Birthdate: 1/3/56
Occupation: Actor, director
Education: University of New South Wales
Debut: (Film) *Summer City*, 1977
Signature: *Lethal Weapon*, 1987
Facts: Father moved the family from New York to Australia in the '60s so his sons wouldn't be drafted.

The night before his audition for *Mad Max*, he got into a barroom fight in which his face was badly beaten, an accident that won him the role.

Took up acting only because his sister submitted an application to the National Institute of Dramatic Art behind his back.

For *Lethal Weapon 4*, was dragged on a freeway at 35 mph.

Marriage: Robyn Moore, 1980

Children: Hannah, c.1980; Edward, 1982; Christian, 1982; Will, 1984; Louis, 1987; Milo, 1989; son, 1999 (name unreleased).

Famous Relative: Eva Mylott, opera singer, grandmother

Major Awards: Oscars for Best Director and Best Picture, *Braveheart*, 1995

KATHIE LEE GIFFORD

Real Name: Kathie Epstein
Birthplace: Paris, France
Birthdate: 8/16/53
Occupation: Talk show host, singer
Education: Oral Roberts University
Debut: (TV) *$100,000 Name That Tune*, 1976
Signature: *Live with Regis and Kathie Lee*
Facts: Despite having a Jewish father, became a born-again Christian at age 11.

Organized a folk singing group while at Oral Roberts University.

Was a cheerleader in high school. Named her dog Regis.

Infamy: A human rights crusader accused Gifford's Honduran-manufactured clothing line of using exploitative child labor.

Original Job: Gospel singer

Marriages: Paul Johnson (divorced); Frank Gifford, 1986

Children: Cody Newton, 1990; Cassidy Erin, 1993

Quote: "I am irreverent, I am opinionated, but I'm not perky."

VINCE GILL

Birthplace: Norman, OK
Birthdate: 4/12/57
Occupation: Singer, songwriter, guitarist
Education: High school
Debut: (Song) "Turn Me Loose," 1984

Signature: "When I Call Your Name," 1990

Facts: After high school, contemplated a career as a pro golfer, but dropped that idea when offered a spot in a top progressive bluegrass group, Bluegrass Alliance.

Joined the band Sundance to play with its great fiddler, Bryon Berline; later joined The Cherry Bombs to be with singer-songwriter Rodney Crowell.

Lead singer for Pure Prairie League in the late '70s.

In the 1980s, worked in Nashville as a studio session vocalist and musician with such stars as Bonnie Raitt, Rosanne Cash, and Patty Loveless.

Dubbed "The Benefit King," he sponsors his own pro-celebrity golf tournament and annual celebrity basketball game and concert.

Marriage: Janis Oliver, 1980 (filed for divorce, 1997)

Child: Jennifer, 1982

Major Awards: Grammy, Best Country Vocal—Male, "When I Call Your Name," 1990; Grammy, Best Country Vocal Collaboration (with Steve Wariner and Ricky Skaggs), "Restless," 1991; Grammy, Best Country Song, "I Still Believe in You" (with John Barlow Jarvis), 1992; Grammy, Best Country Vocal—Male, "I Still Believe in You," 1992; Grammy, Best Country Instrumental "Red Wing" (with Asleep at the Wheel), 1993; Grammy, Best Country Vocal—Male, "When Love Finds You," 1994; Grammy, Best Country Vocal—Male, "Go Rest High on That Mountain," 1995; Grammy, Best Country Song, "Go Rest High on That Mountain," 1995; Grammy, Best Country Vocal—Male, "Worlds Apart," 1996; Grammy, Best Country Vocal—Male, "Pretty Little Adriana," 1997; Grammy, Best Country Vocal—Male, "If You Ever Have Forever In Mind," 1998; Grammy, Best Country Instrumental Performance, "A Soldier's Joy" (with Randy Scruggs), 1998.

SAVION GLOVER

Birthplace: Newark, NJ
Birthdate: 11/19/73
Occupation: Dancer, choreographer
Education: Newark Arts High School
Debut: (Stage) *The Tap Dance Kid*, 1984; (Film) *Tap*, 1989
Signature: *Bring In 'Da Noise, Bring in 'Da Funk*, 1996
Facts: At age 7, played drums in a band.

Made choreography debut at age 16 at New York's Apollo Theater.

Began a featured run on *Sesame Street* in 1990 as a character also named Savion.

His name is his mother's variation on the word "savior."

Infamy: Arrested in late 1995 for driving under the influence of marijuana and criminal possession of bags of marijuana, hidden in his socks. Pled guilty to the reduced charge of disorderly conduct.

Famous Relatives: Yvette Glover, actress and singer, mother

Major Award: Tony, Best Choreography, *Bring In 'Da Noise, Bring in 'Da Funk*, 1996

GOLDBERG

Real Name: Bill Goldberg
Birthplace: Tulsa, OK
Birthdate: 12/27/66
Occupation: Wrestler
Education: University of Georgia
Debut: (Film) *Universal Soldier, the Sequel*, 1999
Facts: Attended World Championship Wrestling Power Plant training school.

On scholarship at University of Georgia, he majored in psychology and was an all-conference nose tackle before going into pro football.

An eleventh round draft pick in 1990 for the Los Angeles Rams, he was cut after pulling a hamstring muscle and spent three seasons as a defensive lineman for the Atlanta Falcons. He finally opted for wrestling after an abdominal injury.

He dips snuff.

He weighs in at some 285 pounds.

He enjoys fishing and collects vintage muscle cars.

His signature finishing move is the "Jackhammer," in which he drives his opponent headfirst into the mat.

His girlfriend of six years is a former "Diamond Doll," who used to escort wrestler Diamond Dallas Page to and from the ring.

Original Job: Bouncer
Relationship: Lisa Shekter
Famous Relatives: Ethel Goldberg, concert violinist with Oklahoma City Philharmonic, mother
Quote: "I never aspired to wrestle. But here I am, wearing my underwear on national television in front of millions of people."

WHOOPI GOLDBERG

Real Name: Caryn Johnson
Birthplace: New York, NY
Birthdate: 11/13/49
Occupation: Actor, comedian
Education: School for the Performing Arts, New York
Debut: (Film) *The Color Purple*, 1985
Signature: *Ghost*, 1990
Facts: Kicked a heroin addiction in the '70s.

Began performing at age 8 with the Helena Rubenstein Children's Theater and later enrolled in the Hudson Guild children's arts program.

Co-owns the West Hollywood restaurant Eclipse with Steven Seagal and Joe Pesci.

She hates to fly and travels on a customized bus.

Infamy: Was roasted by black-faced companion Ted Danson at a Friars Club event, 1993.

Original Job: Bricklayer, hairdresser, bank teller, and makeup artist for a funeral parlor

Marriages: One prior marriage, David Claessen (divorced), Lyle Trachtenberg (divorced, 1995); Frank Langella (relationship)

Child: Alexandrea Martin, 1974
Major Awards: Grammy, Best Comedy Recording, *Whoopi Goldberg*, 1985; Oscar, Best Supporting Actress, *Ghost*, 1990

JEFF GOLDBLUM

Birthplace: Pittsburgh, PA
Birthdate: 10/22/52
Occupation: Actor
Education: Trained at Sanford Meisner's Neighborhood Playhouse
Debut: (Stage) *Two Gentlemen of Verona*, 1971; (Film) *Death Wish*, 1974
Signature: *The Big Chill*, 1983
Facts: Brother Rick died at 23 from a rare virus picked up on a North African trip.

Starred as a stockbroker-turned-P.I. with Ben Vereen in the TV series *Tenspeed and Brownshoe*, 1980.
Marriages: Patricia Gaul (divorced), Geena Davis (divorced)

CUBA GOODING JR.

Birthplace: Bronx, NY
Birthdate: 1/2/68
Occupation: Actor
Education: High school dropout
Debut: (Film) *Coming to America*, 1988
Signature: *Jerry Maguire*, 1996
Facts: His first professional job was at age 16, breakdancing with Lionel Richie at the 1984 Olympic Games.

Big money came to his family when Cuba was a child, after his father's band (The Main Ingredient) hit it big with "Everybody Plays the Fool," but dad split two years later (they have since reunited), leaving mom and the kids on welfare.

Became a born-again Christian at age 13.
Original Jobs: Construction worker, busboy
Marriage: Sara Kapfer, 1994
Children: Spencer, 1994; Mason, 1996
Famous Relative: Cuba Gooding, singer, father

Quote: "The first time I saw myself naked in a school locker room, I was like, 'Wow.' After that, everything had to be trimmed, oiled, and together."
Major Awards: Oscar, Best Supporting Actor, *Jerry Maguire*, 1996

JOHN GOODMAN

Birthplace: Afton, MO
Birthdate: 6/20/52
Occupation: Actor
Education: Southwest Missouri State University
Debut: (Film) *Eddie Macon's Run*, 1983
Signature: *Roseanne*
Facts: Made a living doing dinner and children's theater before Broadway debut in 1979 in *Loose Ends*.

Acted in college with Kathleen Turner and Tess Harper.

Appeared in commercials for Coors beer, Crest toothpaste, and 7UP.
Original Job: Bouncer
Marriage: Anna Beth Hartzog, 1989
Child: Molly, 1990
Major Award: Golden Globe, Best Actor in a Comedy Series, *Roseanne*, 1993

JEFF GORDON

Birthplace: Vallejo, CA
Birthdate: 8/4/71
Occupation: Race car driver
Education: High school
Facts: Began racing at age five when his stepfather bought him a race car. By age eight he was a national champion. By age 11, he won 25 of 25 races in the go-cart division.

After donning his racing suit, he always puts right glove on first. In 1993 Gordon, the first rookie in 30 years to win Daytona's 125-mile qualifying race, went on to become Rookie of the Year in the Winston Cup Series, and the first driver to win rookie honors in NASCAR's two

top divisions.

Polite, slim, and slight, Gordon loses some eight pounds during a race. After races, his eye sockets ache.
Major Awards: Three-time NASCAR Winston Cup winner
Marriage: Brooke

HEATHER GRAHAM

Birthplace: Milwaukee, WI
Birthdate: 1/29/70
Occupation: Actor, model
Education: Attended UCLA
Debut: (Film) *License to Drive*, 1988
Signature: *Boogie Nights*, 1997
Facts: Raised in a religious Catholic household; her parents once encouraged her to become a nun.

Had a six-month romance with actor James Woods, who was twice her age at the time.

Regularly practices Transcendental Meditation.
Original Job: Usher at Hollywood Bowl
Relationship: Edward Burns
Famous Relative: Aimee Graham, actor, sister
Quote: "I love telling dirty jokes. Sex is funny."

KELSEY GRAMMER

Birthplace: St. Thomas, Virgin Islands
Birthdate: 2/21/55
Occupation: Actor
Education: Juilliard School
Debut: (TV) *Another World*, 1983
Signature: *Frasier*
Facts: Father and sister were murdered; his two half brothers died in a scuba accident.

His unborn child died when his ex-wife attempted suicide.

Was nominated five times before finally winning an Emmy in 1994.
Infamy: Arrested for driving under the influence of drugs in 1987; failed to show up for two arraignments for a cocaine arrest in 1988;

sentenced to community service and 30 days in prison in 1990.

In 1995, faced allegations of sexual assault by a 17-year-old, who claimed they had had sex when she was 15. The New Jersey grand jury declined to charge him.

In 1996, crashed his Viper and wound up in the Betty Ford Clinic.
Original Job: Theatrical painter
Marriages: Doreen Alderman (divorced), Leigh-Anne Csuhany (divorced), Camille Donatucci, 1997
Children: Spencer,1985 (with Doreen Alderman). Greer, 1992 (with Barrie Buckner)
Major Awards: Emmy, Best Actor in a Comedy, *Frasier*, 1994, 1995, 1998

HUGH GRANT

Birthplace: London, England
Birthdate: 9/9/60
Occupation: Actor
Education: New College, Oxford University
Debut: (Film) *Privileged*, 1982
Signature: *Four Weddings and a Funeral*, 1994
Facts: Grant opted not to do a nude scene with Andie MacDowell in *Four Weddings and a Funeral* when a makeup artist asked if he wanted definition painted on his body.

While at Oxford, formed a revue group, The Jockeys of Norfolk.

Grant is very popular in Japan, and there are two books on him published there, *Hugh Grant Vol. 1* and *Hugh Grant Vol. 2*.
Infamy: Arrested in June 1995 in Hollywood for picking up a prostitute. Was sentenced to two years' probation, fined $1,180 (which included court costs), and ordered to complete an AIDS education program.
Relationship: Elizabeth Hurley
Quote: "So many dogs have their day. I'm having mine now—and though I'd love it to go on and on, I suspect I'll be back doing BBC radio drama next spring."

MELANIE GRIFFITH

Birthplace: New York, NY
Birthdate: 8/9/57
Occupation: Actor
Education: Pierce College
Debut: (Film) *Night Moves*, 1975
Signature: *Working Girl*, 1988
Facts: Alfred Hitchcock, who was in love with Griffith's mother, gave Melanie a tiny wooden coffin containing a wax replica of her mother, outfitted in the same clothes she had worn in *The Birds,* on her sixth birthday.

At 14, left home to move in with Don Johnson, who was then 22. She married him at 18 and was divorced a year later. In 1988, on her way to the Hazelden Clinic for rehab, she called Don from the plane and renewed their love.

Was clawed in the face by a lioness in the filming of *Roar* (1981).
Infamy: Was addicted to drugs and alcohol in the late '70s and early '80s, and studio executives refused to speak with her. In 1980, she was hit by a car while crossing Sunset Boulevard. She suffered a broken leg and arm, but her doctor said that if she hadn't been so drunk she probably would have been killed.
Original Job: Model
Marriages: Don Johnson (divorced), Steven Bauer (divorced), Don Johnson (divorced), Antonio Banderas, 1996
Children: Alexander, 1985 (with Steven Bauer). Dakota, 1989 (with Don Johnson). Stella del Carmen, 1996
Famous Relatives: Tippi Hedren, actor, mother; Tracy Griffith, actor, half-sister
Quote: "I'm done with stupid movies—I want to be taken seriously again."

JOHN GRISHAM

Birthplace: Arkansas
Birthdate: 2/8/55
Occupation: Author
Education: Mississippi State, University of Mississippi Law School

Debut: (Book) *A Time To Kill,* 1989
Signature: *The Firm*
Facts: Little League baseball coach.

Wife edits his books as he writes them.

Was inspired to write *A Time To Kill* by testimony he heard at the De Soto County courthouse from a 10-year-old girl who was testifying against a man who had raped her and left her for dead.

Served as a Democrat in the Mississippi State Legislature for seven years (1983–90).

Shaves only once a week, before church on Sunday.

In 1989 formed Bongo Comics Group.

A 16th cousin of Bill Clinton.
Original Job: Attorney
Marriage: Renee Jones, 1981
Children: Ty, c.1983; Shea, c.1986

CHARLES GRODIN

Real Name: Charles Grodinsky
Birthplace: Pittsburgh, PA
Birthdate: 4/21/35
Occupation: Actor, writer
Education: University of Miami, Pittsburgh Playhouse School, studied with Lee Strasberg and Uta Hagen
Debut: (Stage) *Tchin-Tchin,* 1962
Signature: *Midnight Run,* 1988
Facts: Grodin was almost cast in the lead role in *The Graduate* but lost it due to an argument with the producers over salary.

Only leases white or gray Cadillac DeVille sedans because he doesn't like to attract attention.

Took his "self-parodying loutishness," as one reviewer called it, to his own cable TV talk show in 1995, to entertaining results.
Marriages: Julia (divorced), Elissa, 1985
Children: Marion, 1960 (with Julia). Nicky, c.1987
Quote: On a *Tonight Show* appearance, Grodin told Johnny Carson, "It's hard for me to answer a question from someone who really

doesn't care about the answer."
Carson banned Grodin from the
show.

MATT GROENING

Birthplace: Portland, OR
Birthdate: 2/15/54
Occupation: Cartoonist
Education: Evergreen College
Debut: (Comic Strip) *Life in Hell* (in
the *Los Angeles Reader*), April 1980
Signature: *The Simpsons*
Facts: Elected student-body presi-
dent in high school. Once elected,
tried to rewrite the student govern-
ment constitution to switch absolute
power to himself.

In Los Angeles, ghostwrote the
autobiography of an elderly film
director who also employed him as a
chauffeur, and worked as a land-
scaper for a sewage treatment
plant.

The members of the Simpson
family bear the same names as
members of Groening's family
(although Bart is an anagram for
brat).

Groening's home in Venice, CA, is
near a canal so he can canoe easily.
Original Job: Writer, rock critic
Marriage: Deborah Caplin, 1986
(separated, 1999)
Children: Homer, 1989; Abraham,
1991
Major Award: Emmy, Outstanding
Animated Program, *The Simpsons*,
1990, 1991

GENE HACKMAN

Birthplace: San Bernardino, CA
Birthdate: 1/30/30
Occupation: Actor
Education: Pasadena Playhouse,
University of Illinois, School of Radio
Technique in NY
Debut: (Stage) *Any Wednesday*, 1964
Signature: *The French Connection*,
1971
Facts: Did his own driving in the
car-chase scenes in *The French
Connection*.

At the Pasadena Playhouse, he
and classmate Dustin Hoffman were
voted the two least likely to succeed.
Original Job: Doorman, truck driver,
shoe salesman, soda jerk, furniture
mover
Marriages: Faye Maltese (divorced),
Betsy Arakawa, 1991
Children: Christopher, 1960;Eliza-
beth, 1962; Leslie, 1966; (with Faye
Maltese)
Major Awards: Oscar, Best Actor, *The
French Connection*, 1971; Oscar,
Best Supporting Actor, *Unforgiven*,
1992

GERI HALLIWELL

Real Name: Geraldine Estelle Halli-
well
Birthplace: Watford, England
Birthdate: 8/6/72
Education: College graduate, UK
Debut: (Album) *Spice*, 1997; (Solo
album) *Schizophonic*, 1999
Signature: Ginger Spice
Facts: After leaving the Spice Girls,
auctioned her performance clothing,
earning $246,000 for charity.

Had a benign lump in her breast
when she was 18, which inspired in
part her current role as a Goodwill
Ambassador of the United Nations
Population Fund, promoting population control and reproductive health
care.

At Prince Charles's 50th birthday
party, she sang in a manner reminiscent of Marilyn Monroe's famous
serenade of John F. Kennedy.

Lived with friend George Michael
and his boyfriend for 3 months after
leaving the Spice Girls.

Was a game-show host on Turkish
television.
Infamy: Was first photographed
nude by Sebastian Amengual when
she was 17, and subsequently posed
nude for numerous other photographers. She also appeared nude in
Playboy.
Quote: "I haven't had a boyfriend for
five years. I am more creative when I
don't have sex."

TOM HANKS

Birthplace: Concord, CA
Birthdate: 7/9/56
Occupation: Actor
Education: Chabot College, Cali-
fornia State University–Sacramento
Debut: (Film) *He Knows You're Alone*,
1980
Signature: *Forrest Gump*, 1994
Facts: Attended at least five
different elementary schools.

In high school, became a born-
again Christian for a couple of
years. Converted to Greek Orthodox
after marrying Wilson.

After a one-shot guest spot on
Happy Days, producer Ron Howard
asked him to read for a secondary
part in *Splash*, but he got the lead
instead.

Played Michael J. Fox's alcoholic
uncle on the sitcom *Family Ties*.

Doesn't like to talk on the phone,
is a bit of a hermit at times.

Collects 1940s typewriters.
Marriages: Samantha Lewes
(divorced), Rita Wilson, 1988
Children: Colin, 1977; Elizabeth,
1982; (with Samantha Lewes).
Chester, 1990; Truman Theodore,
1995
Major Awards: Oscar, Best Actor,
Philadelphia, 1993; Oscar, Best
Actor, *Forrest Gump*, 1994

WOODY HARRELSON

Real Name: Woodrow Tracy
Harrelson
Birthplace: Midland, TX
Birthdate: 7/23/61
Occupation: Actor
Education: Hanover College
Debut: (Film) *Wildcats*, 1986
Signature: *Cheers*
Facts: A hyperactive child, some-
times prone to violence, he was
placed in a school for problem
students. "Violence was almost an
aphrodisiac for me." Took Ritalin.

His absent father was convicted of
murdering a federal judge and

sentenced to life in prison when Woody was a freshman in college.

Sang and composed for a 10-piece "blues-a-billy" band, Manly Moondog and the Three Kool Kats.

Dated Brooke Shields, Carol Kane, Glenn Close, and Moon Unit Zappa. **Infamy:** Admits to having been a sex addict.

Arrested for marijuana possession when he planted four hemp seeds in July 1996 to challenge a state law making it illegal to grow industrial hemp.

Arrested November 1996 for climbing the Golden Gate Bridge. Harrelson was intending to hang banners calling for federal protection for 60,000 acres of redwood trees in Northern California. He was charged with trespassing, being a public nuisance, and failing to obey a peace officer. Agreed to pay a $1,000 fine and spend 25 hours teaching children about the environment.
Original Job: Claims he had over 17 different jobs in one year, including waiting tables and short-order cooking, and was fired from almost all of them
Marriages: Nancy Simon (divorced), Laura Louie, 1998
Children: Deni Montana, 1993; Zoe, 1996
Major Award: Emmy, Best Supporting Actor in a Comedy Series, *Cheers,* 1989

ED HARRIS

Birthplace: Tenafly, NJ
Birthdate: 11/28/50
Occupation: Actor
Education: California Institute of the Arts
Debut: (Film) *Coma,* 1978
Signature: *Apollo 13,* 1995
Facts: Twelve years before *Apollo 13,* appeared in the space film *The Right Stuff.*

His highly lauded *Apollo* scene where he reacts to the astronauts'

splashing down was perfected in a single take.

Played more than 20 film roles in 17 years.
Marriage: Amy Madigan, 1983
Child: Lily, 1993

THOMAS HARRIS

Birthplace: Jackson, TN
Birthdate: 9/22/40
Occupation: Author
Education: Baylor University
Debut: (Novel) *Black Sunday,* 1973
Signature: *Silence of the Lambs,* 1988
Facts: As a seemingly shy crime reporter for the *Waco Herald Tribune* after college, he tooled off to assignments on his motorcycle. One such story involved a Mexican child-prostitution racket, which some consider the beginning of his interest in the darker side.

While working at the Associated Press in New York, he and two colleagues came up with a premise for a thriller about terrorists, which soon became *Black Sunday.*

A reclusive perfectionist, he meticulously researches his material.

He refuses to lecture, promote his books, or grant interviews. (He stopped giving interviews in the early '80s after he was asked if you had to be a homicidal psycho to write about serial killers.)
Original Job: Newspaper copy boy
Marriage: One previous marriage (divorced); Pace Barnes (relationship)
Child: Anne, c. 1962
Quote: "I think really everything that I know is in my books."

MELISSA JOAN HART

Birthplace: Sayville, NY
Birthdate: 4/18/76
Occupation: Actor
Education: Attended New York University

Debut: (TV) *The Lucie Arnaz Show,* 1984
Signature: *Sabrina, the Teenage Witch*
Facts: By age five, had already appeared in 22 commercials. In the next few years she would star in more than a hundred.

She was so young at the time of her 1984 performance on *Saturday Night Live* that she couldn't stay up for the entire show.

Her mom developed *Sabrina,* and became its executive producer.
Famous Relatives: Emily, actor, sister; Alexandra Hart-Gilliams, actor, sister
Quote: "If your butt looks good, your outfit looks good."

DAVID HASSELHOFF

Birthplace: Baltimore, MD
Birthdate: 7/17/52
Occupation: Actor
Education: California Institute of the Arts
Debut: (TV) *The Young and the Restless,* 1975
Signature: *Knight Rider,* 1991
Facts: Hasselhoff is a successful recording star in Europe, and has toured Germany and Austria. He performed a concert in front of 500,000 people at the Berlin Wall.

Baywatch was the first American show to appear in mainland China. It is the most watched show on the planet, seen by almost a billion people every day.
Marriages: Catherine Hickland (divorced), Pamela Bach, 1989
Children: Taylor Ann, 1990; Hayley Amber, 1992

ETHAN HAWKE

Birthplace: Austin, TX
Birthdate: 11/6/70
Occupation: Actor, director, writer
Education: New York University, studied acting at the McCarter Theatre in Princeton, the British

Theatre Association, and Carnegie-Mellon University
Debut: (Film) *Explorers*, 1985; (Stage) *The Seagull*, 1992
Signature: *Dead Poets Society*, 1989
Facts: Was seen out drinking and dancing with the married Julia Roberts in April 1994. He claims they were just discussing a possible movie project.

Starred in *Explorers* when he was 14 with River Phoenix.

His own singing was featured in the *Reality Bites* soundtrack.

Dropped out of Carnegie Mellon after two months to act in *Dead Poets Society*.

Co-founded the New York theater company Malaparte.

Raised eyebrows when *The Hottest State*, his first published novel, attracted advance payments much higher than other novice authors'.
Marriage: Uma Thurman, 1998
Child: Maya Ray Thurman-Hawke, 1998

GOLDIE HAWN

Birthplace: Takoma Park, MD
Birthdate: 11/21/45
Occupation: Actor
Education: American University
Debut: (Film) *The One and Only Genuine Family Band*, 1968
Signature: *Private Benjamin*, 1980
Facts: Discovered while dancing in the chorus of an Andy Griffith TV special in 1967. Became a regular on *Laugh-In*.

Father performed as a musician at the White House.
Original Job: Go-go dancer
Marriages: Gus Trikonis (divorced, 1976); Bill Hudson, (divorced, 1982); Kurt Russell (relationship)
Children: Oliver Rutledge, 1976; Kate Garry, 1979; (with Bill Hudson). Wyatt, 1986
Major Award: Oscar, Best Supporting Actress, *Cactus Flower*, 1969

SALMA HAYEK

Birthplace: Coastzacoalcos, Veracruz, Mexico
Birthdate: 9/2/66
Occupation: Actor
Education: Attended National University of Mexico and Stella Adler Conservatory
Debut: (TV) *Nurses,* 1992; (TV movie) *Roadracers,* 1994; (Film) *Mi vida loca ("My Crazy Life"),* 1993
Signature: *Desperado,* 1995
Facts: Attained stardom on Mexican TV, then moved to L.A. in 1991 to study English and acting.

She is of Lebanese descent.

When she was a child, her grandmother frequently shaved Salma's head and clipped her eyebrows, believing that it would add body to her dark, thick hair.

She finished high school in two years, but her mother was afraid of "college boys" and made her live in Houston until the age of 17.

Discovered by director Robert Rodriguez on a Spanish-language cable-access talk show while he was channel surfing.
Infamy: Expelled from a boarding school in Louisiana for setting alarm clocks back three hours.
Relationship: Edward Atterton
Famous Relatives: Diana Hayek, opera singer, mother
Quote: "When I was a little girl, they told me I couldn't wear tiaras to school. Now I get to wear whatever I want!"

ANNE HECHE

Birthplace: Aurora, OH
Birthdate: 5/25/69
Occupation: Actor
Education: High school
Debut: (TV) *Another World,* 1988; (Film) *The Adventures of Huck Finn,* 1993
Signature: *Volcano,* 1969
Facts: Her father was a Baptist church choir director who was secretly gay; Heche found out at age 12 when he was dying of AIDS.

The same year her father died, her brother was killed in a car accident. To help support her family while in junior high school, Heche sang in a local dinner theater.

Was asked to be in a soap opera by a Procter & Gamble talent scout who happened to see her in a high school play.

Dated Steve Martin, costar of her film *A Simple Twist of Fate* for two years until she broke it off.
Infamy: Shortly after her relationship with Ellen DeGeneres was announced, the pair was criticized for nuzzling and hugging during the annual White House Correspondents' Dinner.
Relationship: Ellen DeGeneres
Quote: "I put a very high premium on honesty. If you don't accept your own sexuality, it will kill you."
Major Awards: Emmy, Outstanding Younger Actress, *Another World,* 1990

KATHARINE HEPBURN

Birthplace: Hartford, CT
Birthdate: 5/12/07
Occupation: Actor
Education: Bryn Mawr College
Debut: (Stage) *The Czarina,* 1928; (Film) *A Bill of Divorcement,* 1932
Signature: *The African Queen,* 1951
Facts: In her strict New England home, where her father was a surgeon and her mother a militant suffragette, Hepburn and her

siblings took cold showers every morning.

Since she was considered too much of a tomboy, she was educated by home tutors.

Decided to take up acting once she realized there was little opportunity for a woman to become a doctor.

According to a 1995 biography, she settled for Tracy after her true love, Catholic director John Ford, couldn't get a divorce from his wife.
Original Job: Sold balloons
Marriages: Ludlow Ogden Smith (divorced, 1934), Spencer Tracy (relationship, deceased)
Major Awards: Oscar, Best Actress, *Morning Glory,* 1933; Oscar, Best Actress, *Guess Who's Coming to Dinner,* 1967; Oscar, Best Actress, *The Lion in Winter,* 1968; Emmy, Best Actress in a Drama Special, *Love Among the Ruins,* 1975; Oscar, Best Actress, *On Golden Pond,* 1981; Kennedy Center Honor for Lifetime Achievement, 1990
Quote: "I am revered rather like an old building."

JENNIFER LOVE HEWITT

Birthplace: Waco, TX
Birthdate: 2/21/79
Occupation: Actor, dancer, singer
Education: High school
Debut: (Film) *Sister Act 2,* 1993
Signature: *Party of Five*
Facts: Made her acting debut at age 6 in a pig barn at a Texas livestock show.

Her debut CD, *Love Songs,* was released in Japan, but not the U.S., when she was 13.

The "starstruck" star has a large celebrity autograph collection.

She sung "How Do I Deal" on the soundtrack for *I Still Know What You Did Last Summer.*

TOMMY HILFIGER

Birthplace: Elmira, NY
Birthdate: 3/24/51
Occupation: Designer
Education: High school
Debut: (Clothes line) Tommy Hilfiger, 1985
Facts: As a child, struggled with dyslexia and, consequently, was a poor student.

Opened his first store, People's Place, selling bell bottoms and other trendy clothes, at age 18. After expanding to several cities, the chain went bankrupt.

Sales of his clothes went up $90 million in 1994, the year Snoop Dogg wore his oversized jersey on *Saturday Night Live.*

Bought a blimp in 1998.
Marriage: Susie, 1980
Children: Alexandra, c.1985; Richard; Elizabeth; Kathleen Anne, 1995
Major Award: Council of Fashion Designers of America, Menswear Designer of the Year, 1995

FAITH HILL

Real Name: Audrey Faith Hill
Birthplace: Jackson, MI
Birthdate: 9/21/67
Occupation: Country singer
Education: High school
Debut: (Album) *Take Me As I Am,* 1994
Signature: *This Kiss,* 1998
Facts: Adopted and raised in Star, Mississippi, she sang in church and formed her first country band by age 16, performing first at a Tobacco Spit competition and eventually at rodeos and country fairs.

Her break came when a talent scout heard her sing harmony with Gary Burr at the Bluebird Cafe.

After some 150 performances in 1994, she endured vocal surgery, followed by three weeks of complete silence.

At the last minute, she was asked to join Tina Turner, Elton John, Cher,

and Whitney Houston for the *VH1 Divas Live* concert event.

Husband Tim McGraw proposed to her in his trailer during 1996's "Spontaneous Combustion" tour. She responded by scrawling "I'm going to be your wife" on the mirror while he was performing on stage.
Marriage: Dan Hill (divorced); Scott Hendricks (engaged, 1995; never married); Tim McGraw, 1996
Children: Gracie Katherine, 1997; Maggie Elizabeth, 1998
Quotes: "I'm not even sure I know what a diva is. But I'm very glad I was there."

LAURYN HILL

Birthplace: South Orange, NJ
Birthdate: 5/25/75
Occupation: Singer
Education: Attended Columbia University
Debut: (Album) *Blunted on Reality,* 1993
Signature: *The Miseducation of Lauryn Hill,* 1998
Facts: Originally called Tranzlator Crew, the group changed their name to The Fugees when a long-forgotten 1980s new-wave act called Translator objected.

The Fugees sprang from the trio's feeling of being refugees from mainstream culture and even hip-hop, and from their sense that they found refuge in the music they made.

Hill met fellow group member Pras Michel when the two attended the same high school. Wyclef Jean, who soon joined forces with them, is Michel's cousin.

Her five-Grammy haul for *The Miseducation of Lauryn Hill* tied her with Carole King for most trophies by a female artist in a single year.

Her fiancé is an ex-college football star and the son of the late Bob Marley.

Relationship: Rohan Marley (engaged)
Children: Zion David, 1997; Selah Louise, 1998
Major Award: Grammy, Best R&B Group with Vocal, "Killing Me Softly," 1996; Grammy, Album of the Year, *The Miseducation of Lauryn Hill,* 1998; Grammy, Best New Artist, 1998; Grammy, Best R&B Song, "Doo Wop (That Thing)," 1998; Grammy, Best R&B Vocal—Female, "Doo Wop (That Thing)," 1998; Grammy, Best R&B Album, *The Miseducation of Lauryn Hill,* 1998.

DUSTIN HOFFMAN

Birthplace: Los Angeles, CA
Birthdate: 8/8/37
Occupation: Actor
Education: Los Angeles Conservatory of Music, Santa Monica City College; studied at the Pasadena Playhouse and the Actor's Studio
Debut: (Stage) *Yes Is for a Very Young Man,* 1960; (Film) *Tiger Makes Out,* 1967
Signature: *The Graduate,* 1967
Facts: Played Tiny Tim in junior high school.

Slept on Gene Hackman's kitchen floor while looking for work.

Achieved Ratso's distinctive walk in *Midnight Cowboy* by putting pebbles in his shoe.

When taking the screen test for *The Graduate,* Hoffman said, "I don't think I'm right for the role. He's a kind of Anglo-Saxon, tall, slender, good-looking chap. I'm short and Jewish." During the screen test he forgot his lines and was nervous and clumsy.

Hoffman originally wanted to be a concert pianist. Also studied to be a doctor.

Los Angeles magazine paid Hoffman $1.5 million for running a computer–altered image of him in an evening dress and high heels. The judge said the magazine violated Hoffman's publicity rights.

Original Job: Washing dishes, checking coats, waiting tables, cleaning a dance studio, selling toys at Macy's, attendant in a psychiatric institution
Marriages: Anne Byrne (divorced); Lisa Gottsegen, 1980
Children: Karina, 1966; Jenna, 1970; (with Anne Byrne). Jacob, 1981; Rebecca, 1983; Max, 1984; Alexandra, 1987
Major Awards: Oscar, Best Actor, *Kramer vs. Kramer,* 1979; Oscar, Best Actor, *Rain Man,* 1988; Emmy, Best Actor in a Made-for-TV Movie, *Death of a Salesman,* 1986

LAUREN HOLLY

Birthplace: Geneva, NY
Birthdate: 10/28/63
Occupation: Actor
Education: Sarah Lawrence College
Debut: (Film) *Band of the Hand,* 1986
Signature: *Picket Fences* (TV series)
Facts: Personal tragedy struck in 1992 when her parents ended their 30-year marriage and, a short time later, her 14-year-old brother died in a house fire.

Her very public 1994 divorce from Anthony Quinn's struggling actor son, Danny, had him claiming that her careless spending squandered their fortune and her accusing him of having affairs and refusing to work.

Roomed with Robin Givens in college.

Marriages: Danny Quinn (divorced), Jim Carrey (divorced, 1997)

KATIE HOLMES

Real Name: Kate Noelle Holmes
Birthplace: Toledo, OH
Birthdate: 12/18/78
Occupation: Actor
Education: High school
Debut: (Film) *The Ice Storm,* 1997; (TV) *Dawson's Creek,* 1998
Signature: *Dawson's Creek*
Facts: Was cast as Joey Potter on *Dawson's Creek* based on a videotape that she made in her basement.

She grew up in a strict Catholic household as the youngest of five children.

The Ice Storm was the first movie she ever auditioned for.

Her mother sent her to modeling school at age 10 to expose her to the field and to teach her how to be graceful. At 16 she attended a modeling convention in New York City, but she never pursued the career.

Earned a 4.0 average in high school and graduated in 1997, deferring enrollment twice at Columbia University.

Quote: "It isn't my fault that I come from a really normal, dream family."

ANTHONY HOPKINS

Birthplace: Port Talbot, South Wales
Birthdate: 12/31/37
Occupation: Actor
Education: Welsh College of Music and Drama, Royal Academy of Dramatic Art, London

Debut: (Stage) *Julius Caesar*, 1964; (Film) *The Lion in Winter*, 1968
Signature: *The Silence of the Lambs*, 1991
Facts: Debuted as conductor with the New Symphony Orchestra at Royal Albert Hall, 1982.

Was knighted in 1993.

Understudied for Laurence Olivier in *Dance Of Death*, 1966.

Wrote the music for his 1996 film *August*.
Infamy: Had a long bout with alcohol addiction.
Original Job: Steelworker
Marriages: Petronella Barker, 1967 (divorced, 1972); Jennifer Ann Lynton, 1973
Child: Abigail, 1968 (with Petronella Barker)
Major Awards: Emmy, Best Actor in a Drama or Comedy Special, *The Lindbergh Kidnapping Case*, 1976; Emmy, Best Actor in a Miniseries, *The Bunker*, 1981; Oscar, Best Actor, *The Silence of the Lambs*, 1991
Quote: "I don't like slow movies. I don't like *Masterpiece Theater*."

WHITNEY HOUSTON

Birthplace: Newark, NJ
Birthdate: 8/9/63
Occupation: Singer
Education: High school
Debut: (Album) *Whitney Houston*, 1985
Signature: "The Greatest Love of All," 1987
Facts: Got her start at age 8 singing in the New Hope Baptist Junior Choir.

Sang backup for Chaka Khan, Lou Rawls, and Dionne Warwick.

As a model, appeared on the cover of *Seventeen*.

Was an actress in her early days, appearing on *Silver Spoons* and *Gimme a Break*.
Original Job: Model
Marriage: Bobby Brown, 1992
Child: Bobbi Kristina, 1993
Famous Relatives: Cissy Houston, singer, mother; Thelma Houston, singer, aunt; Dionne Warwick, singer, cousin
Major Awards: Emmy, Best Individual Performance in a Variety or Music Program, *The 28th Annual Grammy Awards*, 1986; Grammy, Best Pop Vocal—Female, "Saving All My Love for You," 1985; Grammy, Best Pop Vocal—Female, "I Wanna Dance with Somebody," 1987; Grammy, Best Pop Vocal—Female, "I Will Always Love You," 1993; Grammy, Record of the Year, "I Will Always Love You," 1993; Grammy, Album of the Year, *The Bodyguard Soundtrack*, 1993

RON HOWARD

Birthplace: Duncan, OK
Birthdate: 3/1/54
Occupation: Actor, director, producer
Education: University of Southern California
Debut: (Film) *Frontier Woman*, 1956; (TV) *Playhouse 90, 1959*
Signature: *Cocoon*, 1985
Facts: Starred on *The Andy Griffith Show* as Opie when just 6 years old.

The long-running hit *Happy Days* actually struggled in the ratings when it focused mostly on the misadventures of Howard's teenage character; it took off a year later when Henry Winkler's Fonzie became the star.

First directing effort, 1977's *Grand Theft Auto*, was shot in 20 days for $602,000; grossed $15 million.

True to his All-American persona, married his high school sweetheart.
Marriage: Cheryl Alley, 1975
Children: Bryce, 1980; Jocelyn, 1985; Paige, 1985; Reed, 1987
Famous Relatives: Rance Howard, actor, father; Jean Howard, actor, mother; Clint Howard, actor, brother

D. L. HUGHLEY

Real Name: Darryl Lynn Hughley
Birthplace: Los Angeles, CA
Birthdate: 3/6/63
Occupation: Comedian
Education: High school
Debut: (TV) *Def Comedy Jam*
Signature: *The Hughleys*
Facts: Urged by his barber to enter a stand-up comedy contest, then booked on the so-called "Chitlin Circuit." Big break came after 10 years and a million frequent-flyer miles as a stand-up comic.

Expelled from high school in tenth grade for fighting, he later completed his GED.

Sitcom *The Hughleys* is based on his personal experiences living in a white neighborhood.
Infamy: One-time member of the notorious L.A. gang the Bloods, he turned his life around after his cousin, a member of rival gang the Crips, was murdered.
Original Job: Telemarketer for *Los Angeles Times*
Marriage: LaDonna, 1986
Children: Ryan, 1987; Kyle, 1989; Tyler, 1991
Quote: "I don't sing, I don't dance, I don't do impressions. I'm just a guy who gets up there and talks trash."

SAMMO HUNG

Real Name: Samo Hung Kam-Bo
Birthplace: Hong Kong
Birthdate: 1/7/52
Occupation: Actor, director,

producer, fight choreographer

Education: Chinese Opera Research Institute

Debut: (Film) *Education of Love,* 1961; (Directorial) *The Iron-Fisted Monk,* 1978; (TV) *Martial Law,* 1998

Signature: *Martial Law*

Facts: Inspired to be an actor, he studied at the Beijing Opera School, combining physical conditioning with dramatic study, and became star member of the Seven Little Fortunes children's troupe, performing in local nightclubs.

Instructed younger classmates, including Jackie Chan, in Opera-style martial arts, earning him the nickname of "Big Brother."

He's completely colorblind.

His wife, who also acts as his dialogue coach, is a former Miss Hong Kong.

His trademark scar, that runs from the side of his nose to the top of his lip, is the result of being slashed with a cracked soda bottle at age 16.

With some 140 films to his credit in Hong Kong, he is best known in America for his fight with Bruce Lee at the beginning of 1973's *Enter the Dragon.*

Marriages: Jo Yuen Ok, 1973 (divorced,1994); Joyce Mina Godenzi, 1995

Children: Timmy, c. 1974; Jimmy, c. 1975; Sammy, c. 1979; Stephanie, c. 1983; (with Jo Yuen Ok)

Quote: "A sprained ankle to me is like a paper cut to you."

HELEN HUNT

Birthplace: Los Angeles, CA
Birthdate: 6/15/63
Occupation: Actor
Education: UCLA
Debut: (TV) *The Mary Tyler Moore Show,* 1970; (Film) *Rollercoaster,* 1977
Signature: *Mad About You*
Facts: Hunt studied acting, got an agent, and got a part in the TV movie *Pioneer Woman* by age 9.

Began a two-year romance with

actor Matthew Broderick while working on *Project X* (1986).

Played Murray Slaughter's daughter on *The Mary Tyler Moore Show.*

Autograph Collector named her as 1999's Worst Signer. If she does give you an autograph, complains the publication, it's "just an H with a sloppy line after it."

Marriage: Hank Azaria, 1999
Famous Relatives: Gordon Hunt, director, father; Peter Hunt, director, uncle
Major Awards: Emmy, Best Actress in a Comedy Series, *Mad About You,* 1996, 1997, 1998, 1999; Oscar, Best Actress, *As Good As It Gets,* 1997

HOLLY HUNTER

Birthplace: Conyers, GA
Birthdate: 3/20/58
Occupation: Actor
Education: Carnegie Mellon University
Debut: (Film) *The Burning,* 1981; (Stage) *Crimes of the Heart,* 1981
Signature: *Broadcast News*
Facts: Director Jane Campion was originally looking for a tall, statuesque Sigourney Weaver type for the lead in *The Piano.*

Youngest of seven children, grew up on a cattle and hay farm in Georgia, where she drove a tractor.

Appeared in pilot for television series *Fame* (1982).

Marriage: Janusz Kaminski, 1995
Major Awards: Emmy, Best Actress in a Miniseries, *Roe vs. Wade,* 1989; Emmy, Best Actress in a Miniseries, *The Positively True Adventures of the Alleged Texas Cheerleader-Murdering Mom,* 1993; Oscar, Best Actress, *The Piano,* 1993

ELIZABETH HURLEY

Birthplace: Hampshire, England
Birthdate: 6/10/65
Occupation: Actor, model
Education: London Studio Centre
Debut: (Stage) *The Man Most Likely*

To..., (Film) *Rowing in the Wind,* 1986
Signature: *Austin Powers: International Man of Mystery,* 1997
Facts: Long recognized only as actor Hugh Grant's girlfriend. In 1995 when she accompanied Grant on a guest appearance on *The Joan Rivers Show,* Rivers asked, "And who are you?" The two have dated since 1987.

At the opening of Grant's movie *Four Weddings and a Funeral,* she wore a Versace dress held together by 24 safety pins.

Replaced Paulina Porizkova as the face of Estée Lauder cosmetics. Defied conventional stardom by beginning as an actor and becoming a supermodel at age 29.

Characterizes herself as an army brat; her father was a major.

Notorious in her early 20s for her punk-rock phase. She pierced her nose, spiked and painted her hair pink and frequented punk rock bars.

Needlepoint is one of her favorite pastimes.

Was a candidate for the position of ambassador for the United Nations High Commissioner for Refugees.

Won a libel suit against a London paper that claimed she could be "hired" for private functions. Money she has been awarded from such suits has funded an island preserve for abandoned or abused chimpanzees.

Infamy: Was expelled from the London Studio Centre after leaving school and going to a Greek Island.
Relationship: Hugh Grant
Quote: "I've always wanted to be a spy, and frankly I'm a little surprised that British intelligence has never approached me."

ICE CUBE

Real Name: O'Shea Jackson
Birthplace: Los Angeles, CA
Birthdate: 6/15/69
Occupation: Rap artist, actor

Education: Phoenix Institute of Technology
Debut: (Album) *Boyz N the Hood* (with N.W.A.), 1986; (Album) *Amerikkka's Most Wanted* (solo), 1990
Signature: *Boyz N the Hood,* 1991
Facts: Former lyricist of the rap group N.W.A. His 1991 album, *Death Certificate,* stirred controversy because it contained racist attacks on Koreans and called for the murder of a Jewish man.
  Began writing rap lyrics at age 14.
Marriage: Kim
Child: Darrell, 1986 (stepson); O'Shea Jackson Jr., 1991; Kareema, 1994
Quote: "Rap is the network newscast black people never had."

ENRIQUE IGLESIAS

Birthplace: Madrid, Spain
Birthdate: 5/8/75
Occupation: Singer
Education: Attended University of Miami
Debut: (Album) *Enrique Iglesias,* 1995; (Single) "Si Tu Te Vas," 1995
Facts: After parents divorced in 1979 and his grandfather had been kidnapped in Spain, he went to Miami to live with his father, Julio, not only to learn English but also for safety.
  Began singing and writing music at 15 with a couple of older musicians in a Morales basement studio. He kept these meetings secret from his family.
  He hates to have his picture taken.
  When he first began performing, he was known only as Enrique because he wanted to succeed (or fail) on his own. Walked out of a New York radio interview because he was introduced as Julio's son, and, for the same reason, turned down a spot on Oprah's scheduled show about sons of famous fathers.
  Dubbed Sexiest Man by *PEOPLE en Español.*

He loves to windsurf.
Major Awards: Grammy, Best Latin Pop Performer, 1997
Famous Relatives: Julio Iglesias, singer, father; Julio Jose, actor, model, brother; Chabelli, Spanish television personality, sister
Quote: "I say stuff in my music that I would never dare say face-to-face; I'd be too embarrassed."

NATALIE IMBRUGLIA

Birthplace: Campsie, Sydney, Australia
Birthdate: 2/4/75
Occupation: Singer, actor
Education: High school dropout
Debut: (TV, Australia) *Neighbours,* 1992; (Album) *Left of the Middle,* 1998
Signature: "Torn," 1998
Facts: Started dance lessons at age 2 and attended six days a week.
  At 14 she turned down the offer of an Australian entrepreneur for a solo recording act.
  She left parochial high school at 16, did some commercials, attended a performing arts college in Sydney, and landed a role in *Neighbours,* an Australian teen-oriented soap.
  "Torn" was originally recorded by Ednaswap, an L.A. punk band, though it received no airplay.

DON IMUS

Real Name: John Donald Imus Jr.
Birthplace: Riverside, CA
Birthdate: 7/23/40
Occupation: Radio talk-show host
Education: High school dropout
Debut: KUTY, Palmdale, CA, 1968
Signature: "Imus in the Morning"
Facts: Fired from an early window dressing job for staging striptease shows with mannequins to amuse passersby.
  Once called a fast-food restaurant while on the air and ordered 1,200 specially-prepared hamburgers to go, an incident that contributed to

an FCC ruling that DJs must identify themselves when phoning listeners.
  Wrote the novel *God's Other Son,* based on his lecherous evangelist radio character. Originally published in 1981, it was reissued in 1994 and hit the bestseller list for 13 weeks.
Infamy: Caused a stir among media members when his jokes insulted Bill and Hillary Clinton during a televised correspondents' dinner.
  Had a severe alcohol and cocaine abuse problem, for which he was fired from his New York station in 1977. Finally kicked the habit in 1987, after a nine-day drinking binge scared him into a treatment center.
Original Job: Department store window dresser
Marriage: Harriet (divorced, 1979); Deirdre Coleman, 1994
Children: Nadine, 1960 (stepdaughter); Antoinette, 1962 (stepdaughter); Elizabeth, 1966; Ashleigh, 1967; (with Harriet). Fredric Wyatt, 1998
Major Award: Inducted into the Broadcast Hall of Fame, 1996

JEREMY IRONS

Birthplace: Isle of Wight, England
Birthdate: 9/19/48
Occupation: Actor
Education: Bristol Old Vic Theatre School
Debut: (Stage) *Godspell,* 1972
Signature: *The French Lieutenant's Woman,* 1982
Facts: At school, excelled at rugby, the fiddle, and clarinet and headed the cadet corps.
  Made his mark with the BBC series *Brideshead Revisited,* 1981.
  Played a dual role as twin brothers in *Dead Ringers,* a 1988 movie he considers his best work.
Original Job: Housecleaner, gardener, assistant stage manager, busker (singing and playing guitar outside movie theaters)
Marriage: Sinéad Moira Cusack, 1978

Children: Samuel James, 1978; Maximilian Paul, 1985
Major Awards: Tony, Best Actor (Dramatic), *The Real Thing*, 1984; Oscar, Best Actor, *Reversal of Fortune*, 1990

ALAN JACKSON

Birthplace: Newnan, GA
Birthdate: 10/17/58
Occupation: Singer, songwriter
Education: South Georgia College
Debut: (Album) *Here in the Real World*, 1989
Signature: "Neon Rainbow"
Facts: In 1985, his wife got Jackson his big break. A flight attendant, she cornered Glen Campbell in the Atlanta airport and asked him to listen to her husband's tape.

Started wearing his trademark white Stetson to hide scars above his left eyebrow (a result of a childhood accident with a coffee table).
Original Job: Forklift operator, car salesman, home builder
Marriage: Denise, 1979
Children: Mattie, 1990; Alexandra, 1993; Dani Grace, 1997

JANET JACKSON

Birthplace: Gary, IN
Birthdate: 5/16/66
Occupation: Singer, actor
Debut: (TV) *Good Times*, 1977
Signature: *Control*, 1986
Facts: With 1986 song "When I Think of You," she and brother Michael became the first siblings in the rock era to have No. 1 songs as soloists.

Paula Abdul was Janet's choreographer before starting her own career.

Played Charlene DuPrey on the TV series *Diff'rent Strokes*.
Marriages: James DeBarge, 1984 (annulled, 1985); Johnny Gill (relationship)
Famous Relatives: Michael, singer, brother; La Toya, singer, sister; Tito, singer, brother; Randy, singer, brother; Marlon, singer, brother;

Jermaine, singer, brother; Jackie, singer, brother
Major Awards: Grammy, Best Music Video—Long Form, *Rhythm Nation 1814*, 1989; Grammy, Best R&B Song, "That's the Way Love Goes," 1993; Grammy, Best Short Form Music Video, "Got 'Till It's Gone," 1997
Quote: "It was always my dream for no one to know I was a Jackson."

MICHAEL JACKSON

Birthplace: Gary, IN
Birthdate: 8/29/58
Occupation: Singer, songwriter, actor
Debut: (Stage) Mr. Lucky's, Gary, IN (with Jackson 5), 1966
Signature: *Thriller*, 1983
Facts: Built amusement park on property and maintains a menagerie of animals including Bubbles the Chimp.

Gave Elizabeth Taylor away at her marriage to Larry Fortensky in 1991.

Surgery includes four nose jobs, two nose adjustments, and cleft put in his chin. J. Randy Taraborrelli's unauthorized biography claims that Michael had the surgery to avoid resembling his abusive father as much as possible.

Bought the Best Picture statuette awarded by the Academy for *Gone with the Wind* at auction for $1.54 million.
Infamy: Settled out of court a civil lawsuit alleging child molestation. The boy then refused to testify in a criminal proceeding, so prosecutors declined to press charges.

Accused of including anti-Semitic lyrcs in his song "They Don't Care About Us" on *HIStory;* to stem the controversy, the offending lines were altered on later pressings.

In 1999, an Italian judge ruled that he plagiarized the work of songwriter Al Bano when composing the 1991 song, "Will You Be There." Jackson is appealing.
Famous Relatives: Janet, singer, sister; LaToya, singer, sister; Tito, singer, brother; Randy, singer, brother; Marlon, singer, brother; Jermaine, singer, brother; Jackie, singer, brother

Marriage: Lisa Marie Presley (divorced); Debbie Rowe, 1997
Children: Prince Michael Jr, 1997; Paris Michael Katherine, 1998
Major Awards: Grammy, Best R&B Vocal—Male, "Don't Stop Till You Get Enough," 1979; Grammy, Album of the Year, *Thriller*, 1983; Grammy, Best Pop Vocal—Male, *Thriller*, 1983; Grammy, Best R&B Song, "Billie Jean," 1983; Grammy, Best R&B Vocal—Male, "Billie Jean," 1983; Grammy, Best Recording for Children, *E.T., the Extra-Terrestrial*, 1983; Grammy, Record of the Year, "Beat It," 1984; Grammy, Best Pop Vocal—Male, "Beat It," 1984; Grammy, Song of the Year, "We Are the World" (with Lionel Richie), 1985; Grammy, Best Music Video, Short Form, *Leave Me Alone*, 1989; Grammy, Legend Award, 1993; Grammy, Best Music Video, "Scream," 1995

SAMUEL L. JACKSON

Birthplace: Chattanooga, TN
Birthdate: 12/21/48
Occupation: Actor
Education: Morehouse College
Debut: (Film) *Ragtime*, 1981
Signature: *Pulp Fiction*, 1994
Facts: Angry at Morehouse College's lack of African-American studies and its control by a white governing body, he participated in a protest involving locking up the school's board of trustees, and was expelled in 1969. He later returned to graduate.

In 1991's *Jungle Fever*, Jackson's performance as crackhead Gator won him the first-ever supporting actor award given by the Cannes Film Festival.

Was Bill Cosby's stand-in for three years on *The Cosby Show*.
Infamy: Had a problem with drugs and alcohol for several years. Ironically, his first role after taking a vow of sobriety was as the crack addict Gator.
Original Job: Security guard
Marriage: LaTanya Richardson, 1980
Child: Zoe, 1982

MICK JAGGER

Birthplace: Dartford, England
Birthdate: 7/26/43
Occupation: Singer, songwriter
Education: London School of Economics
Debut: (Song) "Come On" (cover of Chuck Berry original), 1963
Signature: The Rolling Stones
Facts: Went to elementary school with guitarist Keith Richards but lost touch with him until they met again on a London train in 1960.

Sang backup on Carly Simon's 1973 hit, "You're So Vain."

Co-owned the Philadelphia Furies, a soccer team, with Peter Frampton, Rick Wakeman, and Paul Simon.

In agreeing to an annullment, Hall capitulated to Jagger's claim that their 1990 Hindu wedding on Bali was invalid due to incomplete paperwork. She received a reported settlement of $15 million and ownership of their $8 million, 26-room London mansion.

Denied fathering son Lucas until a blood test proved paternity.
Marriages: Bianca Perez Morena de Macias (divorced); Jerry Hall, 1990 (annulled, 1999)
Children: Karis, 1970 (with Marsha Hunt). Jade, 1971 (with Bianca Jagger). Elizabeth Scarlett, 1984; James Leroy Augustine, 1985; Georgia May Ayeesha, 1992; Gabriel Luke Beauregard, 1997 (with Jerry Hall). Lucas, 1999 (with Luciana Morad)
Major Awards: Grammy, Best Album Package, *Tattoo You* (with the Rolling Stones), 1981; Grammy, NARAS Lifetime Achievement Award, 1986; inducted into the Rock and Roll Hall of Fame (with the Rolling Stones), 1989; Grammy, Best Rock Album, *Voodoo Lounge* (with the Rolling Stones), 1994
Quote: "It's a good way of making a living. I think we'll just keep right on doing it."

WYCLEF JEAN

Real Name: Nelust Wyclef Jean
Birthplace: Port-au-Prince, Haiti
Birthdate: 10/17/69
Education: High school
Occupation: Rap artist, guitarist
Debut: (Album) *Blunted on Reality*, 1993; (Solo Album) *The Carnival*, 1997
Signature: The Fugees
Facts: At age nine, he came to the U.S. with his family, as his Baptist preacher father fled the reign of "Baby Doc" Duvalier.

His mother bought him an acoustic guitar to keep him off the streets. He mastered it—along with the organ, drums, and bass.

Learned English by listening to rap music.

His devout parents would not allow him to listen to any music that was not religious.

Bandmate Prakazrel "Pras" Michel is his cousin; Lauryn Hill he knew from high school.

Originally called Tranzlator Crew, the group changed their name to The Fugees when a long-forgotten 1980s new-wave act called Translator objected.

The Fugees sprang from the trio's feeling of being refugees from mainstream culture and even hip-hop, and from their sense that they found refuge in the music they made.

At one performance, he played the guitar with his teeth, then put on a hockey mask (like Jason from *Friday the 13th*) to thrill the crowd.

Sang at the memorial service for John F. Kennedy Jr. in 1999.
Major Awards: Grammy Award, R&B Vocal by a Duo or Group, "Killing Me Softly with His Song," 1997; Grammy Award, Best Rap Album, 1997
Quote: "My father would whup my ass for playing rap."

PETER JENNINGS

Birthplace: Toronto, Canada
Birthdate: 7/29/38
Occupation: Anchor, senior editor
Education: Carleton University and Rider College
Debut: At age nine, hosted *Peter's People,* a CBC radio show for children, 1947
Signature: *ABC's World News Tonight*
Facts: At 26, was the youngest network anchor ever. ABC removed him after three years. Took over as permanent anchor in 1983.
Original Job: Bank teller and late-night radio host
Marriages: First marriage (divorced); Valerie Godsoe (divorced); Kati Marton (divorced); Kayce Freed, 1997
Children: Elizabeth, 1979; Christopher, c.1982; (with Kati Marton).
Famous Relative: Charles Jennings, vice president of programming at CBC, father

JEWEL

Real Name: Jewel Kilcher
Birthplace: Payson, UT
Birthdate: 5/23/74
Occupation: Singer, songwriter
Education: Interlochen Arts Academy High School
Debut: (Album) *Pieces of You,* 1995; (TV) *The Wizard of Oz in Concert*
Signature: *Pieces of You*
Facts: Was raised by her father in a log cabin on an 800-acre farm near Homer, Alaska, with no running water, an outhouse for a bathroom, and only a coal stove for heat.

Before they divorced, her parents, Atz and Nedra Kilcher, recorded two LPs as a folk duo.

Jewel has been a crackerjack yodeler since she was a small child; experts told her parents it was supposed to be impossible for someone so young to yodel, since the vocal cords aren't well developed.

As a teenager, she spelled her name, "Juel."

When she began singing at coffeehouses, she and her mom lived in adjacent vans, surviving on fruit from nearby orchards and free happy-hour fare from bars.

Ex-boyfriend Sean Penn directed the video for "You Were Meant for Me"; Jewel had it refilmed after their breakup.

Still suffers from a past kidney infection that hospitals refused to treat due to Jewel's then-low income.

Infamy: Is being sued by former manager, Inga Vainshtein, for $10 million. The suit includes charges that Jewel's mother and current manager, Nedra Carroll, consulted channeler Jackie Snyder on business decisions. Snyder, a friend of Jewel's, died of cancer in 1998.

Original Job: Restaurant worker
Relationship: Christopher Douglas
Quote: "I'm just this cute blonde folk singer who should be patted on the head. My motto is, 'Candy bars for everybody.'"

BILLY JOEL

Birthplace: Bronx, NY
Birthdate: 5/9/49
Occupation: Singer, songwriter, piano player
Education: High school
Debut: (Song) "You Got Me Hummin'" (cover of Sam and Dave original, with The Hassles), 1965
Signature: "Piano Man," 1973
Facts: Had a suicidal period when he was in his early 20s; after taking pills and swallowing furniture polish, he spent three weeks in Meadowbrook Hospital.

As a Long Island teenager, was a local welterweight boxing champion.

Wrote "New York State of Mind" within 20 minutes of returning home from California in 1975.

Original Job: Rock critic for *Changes* magazine
Marriages: Elizabeth Weber (divorced); Christie Brinkley (divorced, 1994); Carolyn Beegan (relationship)

Child: Alexa Ray, 1985
Major Awards: Grammy, Record of the Year, "Just the Way You Are," 1978; Grammy, Song of the Year, "Just the Way You Are," 1978; Grammy, Album of the Year, *Billy Joel,* 1979; Grammy, Best Pop Vocal—Male, *52nd Street,* 1979; Grammy, Best Rock Vocal—Male, *Glass Houses,* 1980; Grammy, Best Recording for Children, *In Harmony 2* (with others), 1982; Grammy, Legend Award, 1991; inducted into Rock and Roll Hall of Fame, 1999

ELTON JOHN

Real Name: Reginald Kenneth Dwight
Birthplace: Pinner, England
Birthdate: 3/25/47
Occupation: Singer, songwriter, piano player
Education: Royal Academy of Music, London
Debut: (Album) *Come Back Baby* (with Bluesology), 1965
Signature: "Candle in the Wind"
Facts: Took his name from first names of Bluesology members Elton Deal and John Baldry.

Wrote "Philadelphia Freedom" in 1975 for Billie Jean King.

Is godfather to Sean Lennon.

Attended London's Royal Academy of Music but quit three weeks before final exams.

Has donated more than $5.5 million—profits from his singles—to his nonprofit care and education foundation.

"Candle in the Wind" is the best-selling single of all time, having sold over 35 million copies.

Had a pacemaker installed in 1999.

Infamy: In 1994, *Star* magazine alleged that he was in a romantic relationship with an Atlanta man. He denied being involved with the man and sued the magazine over the article.

Original Job: Worked at Mills Music Publishers

Marriage: Renate Blauer (divorced, 1988)
Major Awards: Grammy, Best Pop Performance—Duo or Group, "That's What Friends Are For" (with Dionne & Friends), 1986; Grammy, Best Pop Vocal Performance—Male, "Can You Feel the Love Tonight," 1994; inducted into the Rock and Roll Hall of Fame, 1994; Oscar, Best Original Song, "Can You Feel the Love Tonight," 1994; Grammy, Best Pop Vocal—Male, "Candle in the Wind 1997," 1997

DON JOHNSON

Birthplace: Flat Creek, MO
Birthdate: 12/15/49
Occupation: Actor
Education: University of Kansas, studied at the American Conservatory Theater in San Francisco
Debut: (Stage) *Fortunes and Men's Eyes,* 1969; (Film) *The Magic Garden of Stanley Sweetheart,* 1970
Signature: *Miami Vice*
Facts: At age 12, seduced his babysitter. At 16, moved out of his dad's place and moved in with a 26-year-old cocktail waitress. At the University of Kansas, became romantically involved with a drama professor.

Infamy: When he was 12, was caught stealing a car and sent to a juvenile detention home.

Admits to having been addicted to alcohol and cocaine. Says he was sober for ten years, but was treated again for a drinking problem in 1994.

Original Job: Worked in a meat-packing plant
Marriages: a first and second marriage; Melanie Griffith (divorced, remarried, divorced); Kelley Phleger, 1999
Children: Jesse, 1982 (with Patti D'Arbanville). Dakota, 1989 (with Melanie Griffith).

MAGIC JOHNSON

Real Name: Earvin Johnson
Birthplace: Lansing, MI
Birthdate: 8/14/59
Occupation: Basketball player (retired)
Education: Michigan State University
Facts: On November 7, 1991, announced that he was retiring from basketball after being diagnosed HIV positive. Was diagnosed only months after marrying longtime friend Earleatha "Cookie" Kelly, who was in the early stages of pregnancy. Neither Cookie nor the child have tested positive for the disease.

After his diagnosis, became one of the world's major fundraisers and spokesmen for AIDS.

Given his nickname in high school by a local sportswriter after a game in which he scored 36 points and had 18 rebounds.

Hosted short-lived late-night talk show in 1998.

Now a leading businessman, he has helped launch movie theaters in urban locations in Los Angeles and other cities; owns Starbucks and TGIFriday's franchises, has a music management agency with such clients as Boys II Men and Mase, and a music label with MCA Records.
Infamy: In 1992, admitted he caught the AIDS virus from "messing around with too many women."
Marriage: Earleatha "Cookie" Kelly, 1991
Children: Andre, 1982; Earvin III, 1992; Elisa, 1995 (adopted)
Major Awards/Titles: MVP, National Collegiate Athletic Association Final Four playoff tournament, 1979; MVP, NBA Finals, 1980, 1982, 1987; 3 Time NBA Regular Season MVP; 9 Time All-NBA First Team; 11 Time NBA All-Star; Olympic Gold Medal 1992; Grammy, Best Spoken Word Album, *What You Can Do To Avoid AIDS* (with Robert O'Keefe), 1992

ANGELINA JOLIE

Real Name: Angelina Jolie Voight
Birthplace: Los Angeles, CA
Birthdate: 6/4/75
Occupation: Actor
Education: Attended New York University
Debut: (Film) *Lookin' to Get Out,* 1982. (Stage) *Room Service*
Signature: *Gia,* 1998
Facts: Collects daggers, reads about Vlad the Impaler, and has the Japanese word for death tatooed on her shoulder.

Six years after film debut, began studying acting at age 11.

Originally wanted to be a funeral director.

Dropped last name to develop individual identity.

Appeared in numerous music videos, including some by Meat Loaf, The Lemonheads, and the Rolling Stones.

First lead in a theatrical release was *Hackers,* which costarred her future husband, Jonny Lee Miller.

For her wedding, she wore black rubber pants and a white shirt with Miller's name written in blood across the back.

Nominated for an Emmy for her roles in *George Wallace* and *Gia.*

She never goes anywhere without Blistex lip balm.
Original Job: Model
Marriage: Jonny Lee Miller (separated, 1999); Timothy Hutton (relationship)
Famous Relatives: Jon Voight, actor, father; Marcheline Bertrand, actor, mother; James Haven Voight, director, brother
Quote: "I love to put on lotion. Sometimes I'll watch TV and go into a lotion trance for an hour."

JAMES EARL JONES

Birthplace: Arkabutla, MS
Birthdate: 1/17/31
Occupation: Actor
Education: Attended University of Michigan
Debut: (Broadway) *The Egghead,* 1957 (understudy); (Film) *Dr. Strangelove,* 1964; (TV) *As the World Turns,* 1966
Facts: Raised by his maternal grandparents after his father left home before he was born and his mother left when he was very young.

He developed a serious stutter at age six, which necessitated communication through written notes in school.

Was drawn to acting after seeing a magazine photo of his father appearing in a Broadway play.

One of his favorite roles was in 1989's *Field of Dreams.*

He was one of the first black regulars on a daytime drama.
Original Job: Floor waxer, janitor
Marriages: Julienne Marie Hendricks (divorced); Cecilia Hart, 1982
Child: Flynn Earl Jones, 1983
Famous Relatives: Robert Earl Jones, prizefighter (known as "Battling Bill Stovall") and actor, father
Major Awards: Tony Award, Outstanding Actor in a Play, *The Great White Hope,* 1969; Grammy Award, Best Spoken Word Recording, *Great American Documents,* 1976 (with Orson Welles, Helen Hayes, and Henry Fonda); Tony Award, Best Actor in a Play, *Fences,* 1987; Emmy Award, *Gabriel's Fire,* 1990; Emmy Award, Outstanding Supporting Actor in a Miniseries or Special, *Heatwave,* 1990.
Quote: "I was a stutterer, a stammerer, totally impaired vocally, and I still am. I worked on it all my life and I still do. From the beginning of high school through the end of college, my extracurricular activity was using my voice."

QUINCY JONES

Birthplace: Chicago, IL
Birthdate: 3/14/33
Occupation: Composer, producer
Education: Seattle University; Berklee College of Music, Boston Conservatory

Debut: Trumpeter, arranger, for Lionel Hampton Orchestra, 1950
Signature: Produced *Off the Wall, Thriller,* and *Bad*
Facts: Established his own label, Qwest, in 1981 and founded *Vibe* magazine.

Scored the TV series *Roots* in 1977.

Has worked with many prominent pop and jazz artists, including Ray Charles, Miles Davis, Ella Fitzgerald, Dizzy Gillespie, Ice-T, Chaka Khan, and Sarah Vaughan.

Middle name is Delight.
Marriages: Jeri Caldwell (divorced); Ulla Anderson (divorced); Peggy Lipton (divorced, 1989); Donya Fiorentino (relationship)
Children: Jolie, Martina-Lisa, Quincy III, Kidada, Rashida, Kenya
Major Award: Grammy, Album of the Year, *Back on the Block,* 1991; Oscar, Jean Hersholt Humanitarian Award, 1995

TOMMY LEE JONES

Birthplace: San Saba, TX
Birthdate: 9/15/46
Occupation: Actor
Education: Harvard University
Debut: (Stage) *A Patriot for Me,* 1969; (TV) *One Life To Live,* 1969; (Film) *Love Story,* 1970
Signature: *The Fugitive,* 1993
Facts: Roomed with Vice President Al Gore while attending Harvard.

Is a champion polo player.

Raises Black Angus cattle on his ranch in San Antonio.
Original Job: Worked in oil fields
Marriages: Katherine Lardner (divorced); Kimberlea Gayle Cloughley (divorced, 1995); Dawn Laurel (relationship)
Children: Austin, c. 1992; Victoria, c. 1991 (with Cloughley)
Major Awards: Emmy, Best Actor in a Miniseries, *The Executioner's Song,* 1983; Oscar, Best Supporting Actor, *The Fugitive,* 1993

Quote: "I like to cook. I'm really interested in killing things and eating them."

MICHAEL JORDAN

Birthplace: Brooklyn, NY
Birthdate: 2/17/63
Occupation: Basketball player
Education: University of North Carolina
Signature: Ability to fly.
Facts: He was cut from the varsity basketball team in high school.

Though he said, "This is my dream," after hitting his first homer playing professional baseball in the minor leagues, he soon left baseball to return to basketball.

In his first game back as a Bull against archrival Knicks in 1995, some fans paid scalpers more than $1,000 a ticket. They were not disappointed; he scored 55 points.
Marriage: Juanita Vanoy, 1989
Children: Jeffrey Michael, 1988; Marcus James, 1990; Jasmine Mickael, 1992
Major Awards/Titles: NCAA College Player of the Year 1984; MVP NBA Finals, 1991, 1992, 1993, 1996, 1998; four-time NBA Regular Season MVP; eight-time All NBA First Team; ten-time NBA All-Star; eight-time Winner of NBA Scoring Title; Gold Medal at 1984 and 1992 Olympics.

ASHLEY JUDD

Birthplace: Los Angeles, CA
Birthdate: 4/19/68
Occupation: Actor
Education: University of Kentucky
Debut: (Film) *Ruby in Paradise,* 1993
Signature: *Kiss the Girls,* 1997
Facts: Grew up dirt poor in various Kentucky homes lacking electricity, running water or a telephone. Was shuttled around to 12 different schools while Naomi and Wynonna tried to make it in the music business.

Graduated Phi Beta Kappa from college.

Suffered a severe depression in 1996 that lasted for several months.

Famous Relatives: Naomi Judd, singer, mother; Wynonna, singer, sister

MIKE JUDGE

Birthplace: Guayaqyuil, Ecuador
Birthdate: 10/17/62
Occupation: Animator, voice actor
Education: University of California at San Diego
Debut: (Film short) *Office Space* 1991; (TV) *Beavis and Butt-head,* 1993; (Film) *Beavis and Butt-head Do America,* 1996
Signature: *Beavis and Butt-head*
Facts: Grew up in Albuquerque, New Mexico, with his father, an archaeology professor, and his school librarian mother.

Was employee of the month at Whataburger, a fast-food emporium, in June 1979. He drew on his early experiences in such jobs to form Beavis and Butt-head.

While studying physics in college, he took a year off to play bass. After receiving his degree and suffering tedium of two engineering jobs, he moved to Texas to briefly try his hand as a blues musician.

After its 1993 debut, *Beavis and Butt-head* was blamed for several destructive acts committed by young people. MTV eventually responded by moving the program to a later time slot and requesting that Judge tone down references to pyromania and animal cruelty.

He taught himself animation, drawing on books from the library and using an old Bolex 16mm movie camera with his own system of track reading.
Original Job: Electrical engineer, professional musician
Marriage: Francesca Morocco, 1989
Children: Julia, 1991; daughter, 1994
Quote: "Sometimes the truth comes out if you let yourself be simple-minded."

MELINA KANAKAREDES

Birthplace: Akron, OH
Birthdate: 4/23/67
Occupation: Actor
Education: Attended Ohio State University, Point Park College
Debut: (Film) *Bleeding Hearts*, 1994; (TV) *One Life to Live*, 1989
Signature: *Providence*
Facts: Growing up, she spent many hours in her family's candy store.

First performed at age 8 in a local community theater and was a runner-up in the Miss Ohio beauty pageant.

Had a recurring role as Jimmy Smits's reporter girlfriend on *NYPD Blue* before landing *Providence*.

Known for researching her projects, she visited a coroner's office for *Leaving L.A.* and plastic surgeons for *Providence*.

Her extended family is so large that she and her husband invited 550 guests to their wedding.

She was cast for *Providence* without an audition and the other members of the cast were chosen on the basis of their chemistry with her.

She never leaves home without her Braun electric toothbrush.

Met her husband at Ohio State in Sigma Epsilon Phi, a group that tried to get Greek-American kids to socialize with the hope that they will eventually marry.
Original Jobs: Singer, dancer, model, waitress on World Yacht
Marriage: Peter Constantinides, 1992
Quote: "My sanity is my family. Actually, my sanity and my insanity is my family. I'm Greek, and togetherness is a big part of our culture."

DONNA KARAN

Real Name: Donna Faske
Birthplace: Forest Hills, NY
Birthdate: 10/2/48
Occupation: Fashion designer
Education: Parsons School of Design
Signature: DKNY clothes

Facts: While in college, worked for designers Chuck Howard and Liz Claiborne.

After serving a long apprenticeship with the Anne Klein collection, at age 26 was given full creative control by the principal owner of the firm after Anne Klein died of cancer in 1974.

Close personal friend to many stars including Barbra Streisand.
Original Job: Sales clerk at a Long Island dress shop
Marriages: Mark Karan (divorced), Stephen Weiss, 1983
Child: Cory, 1955 (stepson); Lisa, 1957 (stepdaughter); Gabrielle, 1974 (with Mark Karan)
Major Awards: Coty Award, 1977, 1981; named to Coty Hall of Fame, 1984

HARVEY KEITEL

Birthplace: Brooklyn, NY
Birthdate: 5/13/39
Occupation: Actor, producer
Education: Studied with Lee Strasberg at the Actor's Studio and Stella Adler
Debut: (Film) *Who's That Knocking at My Door?*, 1968
Signature: *The Piano*
Facts: Joined the U.S. Marine Corps at age 16 and served in Lebanon.

Answered a newspaper ad placed by Martin Scorsese, then an NYU student director, seeking actors for his first film in 1965, which started their professional relationship.

Was cast as the lead in *Apocalypse Now*, but had a falling out with director Francis Ford Coppola and was fired on location in the Philippines. He was replaced by Martin Sheen.

As a child, Keitel had a severe stutter.

Unusual among Hollywood actors for his willingness to show frontal nudity in his films *(The Piano, Bad Lieutenant)*.
Infamy: Was asked to leave the Alexander Hamilton Vocational School in Brooklyn because of truancy.

His ex-wife filed for Chapter 11 protection in 1999, and claimed that her protracted custody battle (she was awarded sole custody in 1996, now being challenged) with Keitel was the cause after paying nearly $2 million in legal fees.
Original Job: Shoe salesman
Marriage: Lorraine Bracco (divorced, 1992)
Child: Stella, 1986

DAVID E. KELLEY

Birthplace: Waterville, ME
Birthdate: 4/4/56
Occupation: Producer, scriptwriter
Education: Princeton University, Boston University Law School
Debut: (TV writing) *L.A. Law*, 1986
Signature: *Ally McBeal*
Facts: While working at a law firm, wrote a screenplay about young lawyers which an agent sent to Steven Bochco. Soon hired for the then-fledgling *L.A. Law*, he took a leave from his firm rather than resign.

Simultaneously wrote every episode of *Chicago Hope* and *Picket Fences* in 1994 and *Ally McBeal* and *The Practice* several years later.
Original Job: Attorney
Marriage: Michelle Pfeiffer, 1993
Children: Claudia Rose, 1993 (adopted); John Henry, 1994
Major Awards: Emmy, Outstanding Drama Series, *L.A. Law*, 1989; Emmy, Outstanding Drama Series, *L.A. Law*, 1990; Emmy, Outstanding Writing in a Drama Series, *L.A. Law*, 1990; Emmy, Outstanding Drama Series, *L.A. Law*, 1991; Emmy, Outstanding Writing in a Drama Series, *L.A. Law*, 1991; Emmy, Outstanding Drama Series, *Picket Fences*, 1993; Emmy, Outstanding Drama Series, *Picket Fences*, 1994; Emmy, Outstanding Drama Series, *The Practice*, 1998, 1999; Emmy, Outstanding Comedy Series, *Ally McBeal*, 1999

NICOLE KIDMAN

Birthplace: Hawaii
Birthdate: 6/20/67
Occupation: Actor
Education: St. Martin's Youth Theatre, Melbourne, Australia
Debut: (Film) *Bush Christmas,* 1983
Signature: *To Die For,* 1995
Facts: Became an overnight star in Australia with her performance in the miniseries *Vietnam,* 1988.

Joined the Church of Scientology, of which husband Cruise is a devoted member.

Her husband calls her "Nic."
Infamy: Won $580,000 in libel damages in 1998 from Britain's *Express on Sunday* for a story that claimed Kidman and her husband might be closet gays in a sham marriage.

Appeared nude on stage (for approximately 14 seconds) in a limited-run Broadway production of David Hare's *The Blue Room* in 1999.

Sued the *Star* in 1999 for claiming that sex experts had to coach Kidman and her husband in the art of lovemaking for *Eyes Wide Shut.*
Marriage: Tom Cruise, 1990
Children: Isabella Jane, 1993; Connor Antony, 1995; (both adopted)

CRAIG KILBORN

Birthplace: Hastings, MN
Birthdate: 8/24/62
Occupation: Comedian, sports announcer
Education: Montana State University
Debut: (TV) Salinas, CA's KCBA-TV

sports anchor, 1987
Signature: *The Daily Show*
Facts: After college, was offered a spot on a professional basketball team in Luxembourg. Turned down the $600/month job to try his luck in Hollywood.

Stands 6'4".

Daily Show's "5 Questions" was inspired by a failed pickup line he once used in a Manhattan bar.
Infamy: Long-running feud with *Daily Show* female head writer resulted in his one-week suspension after he called her and other female staffers a derogatory name in *Esquire* magazine and suggested that she would perform a sex act on him if requested.

In 1999, admitted to having an 11-year-old son after a tabloid prepared to break the story.
Original Job: Traffic school instructor
Child: son

VAL KILMER

Birthplace: Los Angeles, CA
Birthdate: 12/31/59
Occupation: Actor
Education: Hollywood Professional School, Juilliard
Debut: (Stage) *Slab Boys,* 1983; (TV) *One Too Many,* 1985; (Film) *Top Secret!,* 1984
Signature: *The Doors,* 1991
Facts: Grew up in Chatsworth, CA, across the road from the Roy Rogers ranch. Was the middle child of three boys.

His younger brother, Wesley, drowned right before he left for Juilliard.

At 17, was the youngest person ever accepted to Juilliard's drama school. Cowrote a play with Juilliard classmates, *How It All Began;* starred in an off-Broadway production at the New York Shakespeare Festival.

Met Joanne Whalley on the set of *Willow* in 1988. Pursued her persistently until she finally agreed to marry him.

Provided much of the vocals for the film *The Doors.*

Lives in a cabin in Tesuque, NM. Is part Cherokee and spends his leisure time exploring the Southwest.
Infamy: On the set of *The Island of Dr. Moreau,* Kilmer burned a cameraman's face with a cigarette.
Marriage: Joanne Whalley (divorced, 1995)
Children: Mercedes, 1991; Jack, 1995
Famous Relatives: Joyce Kilmer, poet, second cousin twice removed
Quote: "I don't make any pretense about being normal. I'm not."

LARRY KING

Real Name: Lawrence Harvey Zeiger
Birthplace: Brooklyn, NY
Birthdate: 11/19/33
Occupation: Talk show host
Facts: In February of 1992, Ross Perot announced his bid for the presidency on *Larry King Live.*

Father died of a heart attack when he was 10, and he grew up on public assistance.

As a teenager, ran away to get married. Had the ceremony annulled shortly thereafter.

Graduated from high school just one point above passing.
Infamy: In December of 1971, he was arrested for stealing money a financier had given him for the New Orleans D.A.'s investigation into the death of John F. Kennedy. King had used the money to pay taxes after he had blown his own money on Cadillacs, expensive restaurants, and gambling debts. The charge was eventually dropped.
Original Job: Janitor at a local AM radio station in Florida
Marriages: Frada Miller, c.1953 (annulled); Alene Akins, c.1961 (divorced, remarried, divorced, 1963); Mickey Sutphin, 1964 (divorced, 1968); Sharon Leporte, 1976 (divorced, 1983); Julie Alexander, 1989 (divorced, 1992);

Rama Fox (engaged, 1992; never married); Deanna Lund (engaged, 1995; never married); Shawn Southwick, 1997
Children: Andy (adopted); Chaia, 1967; (with Alene Akins). Larry Jr., 1961 (mother unknown). Kelly (with Mickey Sutphin). Chance Armstrong, 1999
Major Award: 1 News and Documentary Emmy, as interviewer

STEPHEN KING

Birthplace: Portland, ME
Birthdate: 9/21/47
Occupation: Author
Education: University of Maine
Debut: (Book) *Carrie,* 1974
Signature: *The Shining*
Facts: Family was deserted by father, who went out for a pack of cigarettes and never returned.

Wrote first short story at age 7.

Had his first story published in a comic book fan magazine, *Comics Review,* in 1965.

Was working as a high school English teacher at Hampden Academy, in Maine, when his first book was published.

Used the pseudonym Richard Bachman for five novels, including *The Running Man* (made into an Arnold Schwarzenegger film, 1987).

His tales have been turned into seven TV movies and 26 feature films.

Rob Reiner's production company Castle Rock is named after the fictional Maine town in which many King tales are set.

Was seriously injured by an out-of-control motorist in 1999 while walking alongside the road in Maine.
Original Job: Laborer in an industrial laundry
Marriage: Tabitha Spruce, 1971
Children: Naomi, 1970; Joe, 1972; Owen, 1977

GREG KINNEAR

Birthplace: Logansport, IN
Birthdate: 6/17/63
Occupation: Actor
Education: University of Arizona
Debut: (TV) *Movietime,* 1987; (Film) *Sabrina,* 1995
Signature: *As Good As It Gets,* 1997
Facts: Lived in Beirut, Lebanon, with family and then evacuated to Athens, Greece, when the Lebanese civil war broke out.

Worked on the advertising campaigns for such films as *Space Sluts in the Slammer, The Imp,* and the *Ghoulies* series.

Hosted syndicated action game show, *College Mad House.*
Marriage: Helen Labdon, 1999

CALVIN KLEIN

Real Name: Richard Klein
Birthplace: New York, NY
Birthdate: 11/19/42
Occupation: Fashion designer
Education: Fashion Institute of Technology
Facts: Rescued his daughter from kidnappers in 1978.

As a boy in the Bronx, grew up around the corner from Ralph Lifshitz (now Ralph Lauren).

Former junk bond czar Michael Milken issued $80 million in high-interest Klein bonds in the '80s.
Infamy: Was addicted to valium and alcohol in the '80s, and attended a Minnesota rehabilitation center for 31 days in 1988.
Marriages: Jayne Centre, 1964 (divorced, 1974); Kelly Rector, 1986 (separated, 1996)
Child: Marci, 1966 (with Jayne Centre)
Major Awards: Coty Award, 1973, 1974, 1975; elected to American Fashion Critics Circle Hall of Fame, 1975; Council of Fashion Designers of America Award, 1994
Quote: "Anything I've ever wanted to do, I've done. Anyone I've wanted to be with, I've had."

HEIDI KLUM

Birthplace: Germany
Birthdate: 1973
Occupation: Model
Facts: She was the 1998 *Sports Illustrated* swimsuit-issue cover girl. Has been nicknamed "The Body." She's 5'9".

Her husband proposed to her atop the Empire State Building.
Marriage: Ric Pipino, 1997
Quotes: "On the runway you always wish your body was a little tighter, and you worry that if you walk too fast things start to jiggle."

TED KOPPEL

Birthplace: Lancashire, England
Birthdate: 2/8/40
Occupation: Broadcast journalist
Education: Syracuse University, Stanford University
Debut: (Radio) WMCA radio
Signature: *Nightline*
Facts: Author, *Adlai Stevenson: In the National Interest.*

When he joined ABC in 1963, he was the youngest news reporter ever to join a network.

Emigrated to the U.S. from England in 1953.
Marriage: Grace Anne Dorney, 1963
Children: Andrea, 1963; Deidre, 1965; Andrew, 1970; Tara, 1971
Major Award: Elected to the Emmy Hall of Fame, 1991

JANE KRAKOWSKI

Birthplace: Parsippany, NJ
Birthdate: 9/11/68
Occupation: Actor, singer, dancer
Education: Professional Children's School
Debut: (Film) *National Lampoon's Vacation,* 1983; (TV) *Search for Tomorrow,* 1984; (Stage) *Starlight Express,* 1987
Facts: Twice nominated for a Daytime Emmy for her role in *Search for Tomorrow,* which she landed at age 14.

Made her broadway debut in *Starlight Express* at the age of 18. She was one of only four cast members to stay for its two-year run.

Earned a Tony nomination for her role in *Grand Hotel* in 1990.

She has recorded music by Sondheim, Burt Bacharach, and Paul Simon, and recently signed a contract for a new solo album.

Original Job: Performing at industrial fashion shows
Relationship: Charles Hart

LISA KUDROW

Birthplace: Encino, CA
Birthdate: 7/30/63
Occupation: Actor
Education: Vassar College
Debut: (TV) *Cheers*, 1982
Signature: *Friends*
Facts: Earned her B.S. in sociobiology, intent on being a doctor like her father, a renowned headache expert. Decided to become a comic actor when she saw Jon Lovitz, her brother's childhood friend, make it on *Saturday Night Live*.

Her movie debut in 1990's *Impulse* ended up completely cut from the film. Later, she was hired but soon fired as Roz on the pilot for *Frasier*.

Grew up with a pool table in her house and is something of a pool shark, able to perform many difficult trick shots.

Marriage: Michel Stern, 1995
Child: Julian Murray, 1998
Major Award: Emmy, Best Supporting Actress in a Comedy Series, *Friends*, 1998

RICKI LAKE

Birthplace: New York, NY
Birthdate: 9/21/68
Occupation: Actor, talk show host
Education: Ithaca College
Debut: (Film) *Hairspray*, 1988
Signature: *The Ricki Lake Show*
Facts: This once-dumpy star of John Waters' cult films like *Cry Baby* lost 125 pounds over a three-year period.

Plays the flute, piccolo, clarinet, and piano.

Infamy: Arrested in 1994 for criminal mischief for her part in a People for the Ethical Treatment of Animals attack on the offices of designer Karl Lagerfeld.

Original Job: Cabaret singer, appeared off-Broadway in 1983
Marriage: Rob Sussman, 1994
Child: Milo Sebastian, 1997

NATHAN LANE

Real Name: Joseph Lane
Birthplace: Jersey City, NJ
Birthdate: 2/3/56
Occupation: Actor
Education: High school
Debut: (Stage) *A Midsummer Night's Dream*, 1978; (Film) *Ironweed*, 1987
Signature: *The Birdcage*, 1996
Facts: Took the name Nathan at age 22 after playing Nathan Detroit in a *Guys and Dolls* dinner-theater show, since there was another Joe Lane in Actors' Equity.

His truckdriver father drank himself to death when Lane was 11. Lane, too, had a drinking problem for two decades, one he kicked only a few years ago.

Playwright Terrence McNally wrote several plays specifically for him.

Played the voice of Timon, the wisecracking meerkat in *The Lion King*.

Original Job: Police bail interviewer
Major Award: Tony, Best Actor (Musical), *A Funny Thing Happened on the Way to the Forum*, 1996

K.D. LANG

Real Name: Katherine Dawn Lang
Birthplace: Consort, Canada
Birthdate: 11/2/61
Occupation: Singer, songwriter
Education: Attended college in Red Deer, Alberta, Canada
Debut: (Album) *A Truly Western Experience*, 1984
Signature: "Constant Craving," 1992

Facts: Acted in the movie *Salmonberries,* 1991.

Recorded a duet with Roy Orbison on a remake of his song "Crying" in 1988, shortly before he died.

Infamy: Her recordings have been boycotted in the conservative areas of the South and cattle ranching areas of central Canada because she is a lesbian and an animal rights activist.

Original Job: Performance artist
Relationship: Leisha Hailey
Major Awards: Grammy, Best Country Vocal—Collaboration, "Crying" (with Roy Orbison), 1988; Grammy, Best Country Vocaynl—Female, "Absolute Torch and Twang," 1989; Grammy, Best Pop Vocal—Female, "Constant Craving," 1992
Quote: "I have a little bit of penis envy. They're ridiculous, but they're cool."

JESSICA LANGE

Birthplace: Cloquet, MN
Birthdate: 4/20/49
Occupation: Actor
Education: University of Minnesota
Debut: (Film) *King Kong*, 1976
Signature: *Frances*, 1982
Facts: Raised in a depression-prone family with an alcoholic father who moved the family repeatedly, Lange adopted a full-blown, travel-and-party lifestyle as a young adult.

Had a relationship (and a child) with Mikhail Baryshnikov.

The 1994 film *Blue Sky*, for which she won a best actress Academy Award (after four previous nominations), languished in a bank vault after it was made in 1991 because its studio, Orion Pictures, had declared bankruptcy.

Original Job: Dancer, model
Marriages: Paco Grande (divorced, 1982); Sam Shepard (relationship)
Children: Alexandra,1981 (with Mikhail Baryshnikov). Hannah Jane, 1985; Samuel Walker, 1987
Major Awards: Oscar, Best

Supporting Actress, *Tootsie*, 1982; Oscar, Best Actress, *Blue Sky*, 1994
Quote: "I did bail on the glamor thing early. And now I look back and think oh, hell, I should have done it for another five or 10 years…I'm tired of thinking I have to rip my heart out for every character."

ANGELA LANSBURY

Birthplace: London, England
Birthdate: 10/16/25
Occupation: Actor
Education: Webber-Douglas School of Singing and Dramatic Art, Feagin School of Drama and Radio
Debut: (Film) *Gaslight*, 1944
Signature: *Murder, She Wrote*
Facts: Immigrated with her family to the U.S. when the Germans began to bomb London in World War II.

In 1943, went to MGM to audition for *The Picture of Dorian Gray* and was told the studio was looking for someone to play the role of the maid in *Gaslight*. She auditioned and got it.

In the seven years she was under contract to MGM, she appeared in 70 films.
Original Job: Ticket-taker in the theater in which her mother worked, clerk in department store
Marriages: Richard Cromwell (divorced); Peter Pullen Shaw, 1949
Children: David, 1944 (stepson); Anthony Peter, 1952; Deidre Angela, 1953
Famous Relatives: Moyna McGill, actor, mother; David Lansbury, actor, nephew
Major Awards: Tony, Best Actress (Musical), *Mame*, 1966; Tony, Best Actress (Musical), *Dear World*, 1969; Tony, Best Actress (Musical), *Gypsy*, 1975; Tony, Best Actress (Musical), *Sweeney Todd*, 1979

ERIQ LASALLE

Birthplace: Hartford, CT
Birthdate: 7/23/62
Occupation: Actor, director
Education: New York University; attended Julliard
Debut: (Film) *Coming to America*, 1988
Signature: *ER*
Facts: Was once a competitor in martial arts.

After four years of unsuccessfully shopping a screenplay he wrote and wanted to direct, he borrowed $140,000 and some equipment and filmed a short version of the work himself.

Along with the four other original, continuing *ER* cast members, received a $1 million bonus in 1998 from Warner Bros. Television.
Marriage: Angela Johnson

MATT LAUER

Birthplace: New York, NY
Birthdate: 12/30/57
Occupation: Newscaster, producer
Education: Ohio University
Debut: (TV) WOWK-TV, Huntington, WV, 1980
Signature: *Today*
Facts: Quit college for a TV job four credits shy of graduation in 1979; finally got the degree 18 years later by writing a paper on his work experience.

Hosted *9 Broadcast Plaza*, a low-budget tabloid talk show, for two years, but was fired when he refused to do live commercials during the program. Months later, desperate for a job, he applied for a tree-trimming position in upstate New York. When the phone rang, however, it was NBC, asking him to host a local news show.

Appeared 150 times as guest-host of *Today* before landing the permanent slot.

Has an impressive 8 handicap in golf.
Marriage: Nancy Alspaugh (divorced); Annette Roque

RALPH LAUREN

Real Name: Ralph Lifshitz
Birthplace: Bronx, NY
Birthdate: 10/14/39
Occupation: Designer
Education: Attended City College of New York
Facts: Growing up in the Moshulu Park area of New York, Lauren lived two blocks from Calvin Klein.

As a youth, he was drawn to movies and the novels of F. Scott Fitzgerald.

While attending high school in the Bronx, he worked part-time as a department store stockboy and spent most of his earnings on clothes.

After a stint in the army, he was hired as a designer by Beau Brummell Ties. His unusual, wider products sold well, and within a year he formed his own company—Polo—with a loan of $50,000.

He is the only American designer who manufactures and licenses his own designs.

Met his wife when he went to get his eyes tested—she was the optician's receptionist.
Original Job: Salesman
Marriage: Ricky Low Beer, 1964
Children: Andrew, 1969; David, 1971; Dylan, 1974
Quotes: "Being comfortable is more important than being slinky."

LUCY LAWLESS

Birthplace: Mount Albert, Auckland, New Zealand
Birthdate: 3/28/68
Occupation: Actor
Education: Attended Auckland University
Debut: (TV) *Funny Business*, 1988
Signature: *Xena: Warrior Princess*
Facts: Got the part of Xena when the original actor became ill and the producers needed someone to fill in quickly. They turned to Lawless, who had been cast in bit parts in the show.

Stands at 5' 11".

Original Jobs: Picking grapes along Germany's Rhine River, working a gold mine in Australia.
Marriages: Garth Lawless (divorced); Rob Tapert, 1998
Child: Daisy, 1988 (with Garth Lawless)

MARTIN LAWRENCE

Birthplace: Frankfurt, Germany
Birthdate: 4/16/65
Occupation: Actor
Education: High school
Debut: (TV) *What's Happening Now,* 1985; (Film) *Do the Right Thing,* 1989
Signature: *Martin*
Facts: He was a *Star Search* winner, a street performer in Washington Square Park, and a stand-up comedian at the Improv's open-mike night.

Worked at Sears in Queens with Salt-N-Pepa and Kid 'N Play.
Infamy: After a 1994 appearance on *Saturday Night Live* in which he told women to "put a Tic-Tac in your ass" to remain clean, Lawrence was banned from all NBC productions.

Yelled at passersby and brandished a pistol in the middle of a busy L.A. intersection. Tried to board a plane while carrying a Baretta.

In 1997, former *Martin* costar Tisha Campbell filed a suit claiming that he groped and kissed her, among other things, in front of the cast and crew.
Original Job: Gas station attendant, store clerk
Marriage: Patricia Southall, 1995 (divorced, 1996)
Child: Jasmine Page, 1996

DENIS LEARY

Birthplace: Worcester, MA
Birthdate: 8/18/57
Occupation: Actor
Education: Emerson College
Debut: (Off-Broadway) *No Cure for Cancer,* 1991; (Film) *Strictly Business,* 1992

Signature: *Dennis Leary: Lock 'n' Load,* 1997
Facts: Co-founded Comedy Workshop in Boston before moving to New York City in 1990, where he formed Apostle Productions.

Made Fiona Apple cry with a joke about her MTV Awards speech in his HBO special *Lock 'n' Load.*

Known as a "bad boy of comedy" for his aggressive smoking and politically incorrect jokes.

To make extra money while teaching drama, he drove a delivery truck and worked in a sulfuric-acid plant.

During a weekend trip to London with his wife, their first son was born prematurely and they were forced to live there for five months.
Original Job: Acting teacher
Marriage: Ann Lembeck, c. 1990
Children: Jack, c. 1990; Devin, c. 1992
Quote: "I have a lot of anger about the loss of the way things used to be. Like how you can't get coffee-flavored coffee anymore because everything is frappuccino or mochaccino."

MATT LEBLANC

Birthplace: Newton, MA
Birthdate: 7/25/67
Occupation: Actor
Education: Wentworth Institute of Technology
Debut: (TV) *TV 101,* 1988
Signature: *Friends*
Facts: First big breaks were in TV commercials, including an award-winning Heinz spot that ran four years.

Actually of mixed heritage—Italian, French, English, Irish, and Dutch—though usually cast as Italian.

After receiving his first motorcycle at age 8, began entering amateur competitions with hopes of racing professionally, a dream his mother quickly quashed.

A passion for landscape photog-

raphy has taken him all over the world.

Before *Friends,* starred in three TV flops; interest in him soon cooled, and he sold his truck and motorcycle and moved to a smaller apartment to stay afloat financially.
Marriage: Melissa McKnight (engaged, 1999)

PAMELA ANDERSON LEE

Birthplace: Comox, Canada
Birthdate: 7/1/67
Occupation: Actor
Education: High school
Debut: (TV) *Home Improvement,* 1991; (Film) *Barb Wire,* 1995
Signature: *V.I.P*
Facts: Got her first commercial job after her image was projected on a giant scoreboard screen at a Canadian football game in 1989.

Says her mother encouraged her to pose for her several *Playboy* covers, telling her it was a compliment (8 in all—a record).

Writes fairy tales and poetry and regularly keeps a dream diary.

Married Mötley Crüe drummer Tommy Lee in Cancun, Mexico, in 1995 wearing a tiny white bikini. (Lee wore white Bermuda shorts.)

Lost a court request to halt distribution of a homemade video showing her and then-husband Tommy Lee having sex; the two claim the tape was stolen from their home.

Filed for divorce from Lee on grounds of spousal abuse. He spent 3 months in jail for kicking her and was put on probation. In 1999, Lee asked that a restraining order against Lee be lifted.

In 1999, had her silicone breast implants removed, going from a size 34 D to a 34 C. (Surgery revealed that the implants had been leaking.)
Original Job: Beer company spokesmodel
Marriage: Tommy Lee
Child: Brandon Thomas, 1996; Dylan Jagger, 1997
Quote: "Tommy has been fixed."

Actually, he has been neutered or spayed. What do you call it?"

SPIKE LEE

Real Name: Shelton Lee
Birthplace: Atlanta, GA
Birthdate: 3/20/57
Occupation: Filmmaker, director
Education: Morehouse College, New York University
Debut: (Film) *She's Gotta Have It,* 1986
Signature: *Do the Right Thing,* 1989
Facts: Known as an unofficial New York Knick, sitting courtside and shouting out to players on both teams. During the 1994 Eastern Conference Championships, some fans felt that his harassment of an Indiana Pacer caused the player to score the most points in the game and defeat the Knicks.

Taught at Harvard as a visiting professor in 1992.

A film he made at NYU, *Joe's Barbershop: We Cut Heads,* was the first student work ever selected for Lincoln Center's "New Directors, New Films" showcase and won a student award from the Academy of Motion Pictures Arts and Sciences.
Infamy: Accused by the Anti-Defamation League of B'Nai Brith of fostering anti-Semitism through his films, most notably via his portrayal of two Jewish nightclub owners in *Mo' Better Blues.*
Original Job: Advertising copywriter
Marriage: Tonya Linette Lewis, 1993
Children: Satchel Lewis, 1994; Jackson Lewis, 1997

EMERIL LEGASSE

Birthplace: Fall River, MA
Birthdate: 10/15/59
Occupation: Chef, television show host
Education: Johnson and Wales University
Debut: (TV) *Essence of Emeril,* 1993
Signature: "Whoo!" "Bam!" "Pow!"
Facts: Interest in cooking began when he was growing up with his French-Canadian father and Portuguese mother.

Had taught himself how to play trombone, trumpet, flute, and drums, played in a Portuguese band, but turned down a scholarship to the New England Conservatory of Music to pursue culinary arts.

Raises hogs to produce farm-fresh andouille sausage, bacon, and ham, and is a firm believer in organically grown produce.
Original Job: Dishwasher in a Portuguese bakery
Marriages: Elizabeth (divorced, c. 1982); Tari Hohn (divorced, 1996)
Children: Jessica, c. 1980; Jillian, c. 1982 (with Elizabeth)
Quote: "I've been a big Spam fan for a long time."

JENNIFER JASON LEIGH

Real Name: Jennifer Leigh Morrow
Birthplace: Los Angeles, CA
Birthdate: 2/5/62
Occupation: Actor
Education: High school dropout
Debut: (TV) *The Young Runaways,* 1978; (Film) *Eyes of a Stranger,* 1980; (Off Broadway) *Sunshine,* 1989
Signature: *Single White Female,* 1992
Facts: Dropped out of high school six weeks before graduation to act in her debut film.

Since another Jennifer Leigh was already registered with the Screen Actors Guild, she added Jason in honor of family friend Jason Robards.

For her role in 1981 as an anorexic teen in TV's *The Best Little Girl in the World,* she dropped her weight to 86 pounds.

Her father was killed in a helicopter accident on the set of *Twilight Zone: The Movie.*

She is very shy and dreads parties. As a result, she spends her free time reading or going to movies.
Famous Relatives: Barbara (Freedman) Turner, TV scriptwriter, mother; Vic Morrow, actor, father; Mina Badie, actor, half-sister
Quote: "I like the idea of being able to play anything from waif to prostitute."

JACK LEMMON

Birthplace: Boston, MA
Birthdate: 2/8/25
Occupation: Actor
Education: Harvard University
Debut: (Film) *It Should Happen to You,* 1954
Signature: *Odd Couple,* 1968
Facts: Underwent three ear surgeries as a boy, forcing him to miss a year of school.

Son of a top donut executive, he went to the elite Phillips Academy in Andover. (He was a cheerleade there.)

At Harvard, was president of the Hasty Pudding Club.

Has made more than 60 films in almost 50 years.

Was handed the 1997 TV drama Golden Globe award by actor Ving Rhames who believed Lemmon deserved it even though he won.

Odd Couple II marked the tenth movie with pal Walter Matthau.

Infamy: Had a longtime problem with alcohol abuse, eventually sobering up through AA.

Marriages: Cynthia Stone, 1950 (divorced); Felicia Farr, 1962

Children: Christopher, 1954 (with Cynthia Stone). Courtney, 1966

Major Awards: Oscar, Best Supporting Actor, *Mister Roberts*, 1955; Oscar, Best Actor, *Save the Tiger*, 1973

JAY LENO

Real Name: James Leno
Birthplace: New Rochelle, NY
Birthdate: 4/28/50
Occupation: Talk show host, comedian
Education: Emerson College
Debut: (TV) *The Marilyn McCoo & Billy Davis Jr. Show,* 1977; (Film) *Silver Bears,* 1978
Signature: *The Tonight Show*
Facts: Collects antique cars and motorcycles.

Made his first appearance on *The Tonight Show* in 1977.

While in grade school, Leno executed such pranks as flushing tennis balls down the toilet and hiding a dog in his locker. His fifth grade teacher wrote on his report card, "If Jay spent as much time studying as he does trying to be a comedian, he'd be a big star."

Was made a contributing editor at *Popular Mechanics* magazine in 1999. He pens the "Jay Leno's Garage" column.

Original Job: Rolls-Royce mechanic, deliveryman
Marriage: Mavis Nicholson, 1980

TÉA LEONI

Birthplace: New York, NY
Birthdate: 2/25/66
Occupation: Actor
Education: Sarah Lawrence College

Debut: (TV) *Santa Barbara,* 1984; (Film) *Swirch,* 1994
Signature: *Deep Impact,* 1998
Facts: A sufferer of stage fright, was so nervous shooting the pilot for *The Naked Truth* she threw up five times.

Got into acting when, on a dare, entered a mass audition for the remake of *Charlie's Angels* and was chosen, although the show never aired.

Caused a stir when *The Naked Truth* producer Chris Thompson left his wife and children to date her.

Original Job: Teaching Japanese men how to interact with American women
Marriage: One prior marriage; David Duchovny, 1997
Child: Madelaine West, 1999

DAVID LETTERMAN

Birthplace: Indianapolis, IN
Birthdate: 4/12/47
Occupation: Talk show host
Education: Ball State University
Debut: (TV) *The Starland Vocal Band Show,* 1977
Signature: *Late Show with David Letterman*
Facts: While working as a weather announcer at a local TV station, he congratulated a tropical storm on being upgraded to a hurricane.

Was the announcer for the late-night movie program *Freeze Dried Movies.* On the program, he blew up a model of the television station at which he was working.

Margaret Ray stalked him at his New Canaan, Conn., home. She was caught at or in his home eight times from 1988 to 1993.

Original Job: TV announcer, weatherman
Marriage: Michelle Cook (divorced, 1977); Regina Lasko (relationship)
Major Awards: Emmy, Best Host of a Daytime Variety Series, *The David Letterman Show,* 1981; Emmy, Writing in a Variety or Music Show,

Late Night with David Letterman, 1984, 1985, 1986, 1987

RUSH LIMBAUGH

Birthplace: Cape Girardeau, MO
Birthdate: 1/12/51
Occupation: Political commentator, radio and TV broadcaster, author
Education: Elkins Institute of Radio and Technology; attended Southeastern Missouri State University
Facts: After dropping out of college, he left home in 1971 in pursuit of a big-time radio career. Fired from various stations, he left radio seven years later and worked in the public relations office of the Kansas City Royals baseball team.

He targets radical-liberals, environmentalists, do-gooders, and anyone further left than he.

More than 300 "Rush rooms" have opened in restaurants nationwide for the purpose of broadcasting Rush Limbaugh's programs to patrons.

Met his wife, Marta, via electronic mail on CompuServe Information Service. They were married by Supreme Court Justice Clarence Thomas.

He named his radio web *The Excellence in Broadcasting Network,* which began with 56 AM stations and 250,000 listeners. Within three years, his broadcast had an estimated 2 million listeners at any given moment

Infamy: His recurring AIDS Update enraged activists. He ultimately apologized, withdrew the segment, and donated $10,000 to the Pediatric AIDS Foundation.

In February 1994, the Florida Citrus Commission advertised orange juice on Limbaugh's show. The ads generated 7,500 calls to the commission protesting their choice of such a controversial figure to promote their product. The National Organization for Women, as well as various gay and lesbian groups, urged people to boycott Florida orange juice. Meanwhile, about 30 Rush supporters bought out the entire supply of orange juice at an Orlando, Florida, store in counter-protest.

Original job: Apprentice at KGMO radio station

Marriages: Roxie Maxine McNeely (divorced); Michelle Sixta (divorced); Marta Fitzgerald

Famous Relatives: Rush Limbaugh Sr., President Eisenhower's ambassador to India, grandfather; Stephen Limbaugh, federal judge appointed by Ronald Reagan, uncle.

Quotes: "My first real interest in radio can be traced to a dislike for school."

LAURA LINNEY

Birthplace: New York, NY
Birthdate: 2/5/64
Occupation: Actor
Education: Attended Northwestern University, Brown University, Juilliard School
Debut: (Stage) *Six Degrees of Separation*, 1990; (Film) *Lorenzo's Oil*, 1992; (TV) *Class of '61*, 1993
Signature: *The Truman Show*, 1998
Facts: First recognized in 1994 for her portrayal of Mary Ann Singleton in *Armistead Maupin's Tales of the City*.

Her middle name is Legett.

During her years at Juilliard, she suffered from severe stage fright.

She is afraid to fly.

In elementary school she tried to con her teachers into letting her act out book reports instead of writing them.

Based on her performance in *Primal Fear*, she was handpicked by Clint Eastwood to star in 1997's *Absolute Power*.

Original Job: Backstage hand in New England theaters
Marriage: David Adkins, 1995
Famous Relative: Romulus Linney, playwright
Quote: "I have the Cindy Brady complex. You know that episode of

The Brady Bunch where Cindy goes catatonic when she appears on a TV show? That was me."

TARA LIPINSKI

Birthplace: Sewell, NJ
Birthdate: 6/10/82
Occupation: Ice skater
Debut: (TV) *The Young and the Restless*, 1999
Facts: At age 11, she and her mother left Texas so she could train year-round with prestigious coaches.

Practiced only two weeks before landing her signature triple-loop combination—the first ice skater ever to do so.

Stood 4'10" and weighed 82 pounds when she won her Olympic medal.

At age 14, she was the youngest-ever winner of the U.S. Figure Skating Championship.

Major Award: Olympics, Gold medal, women's figure skating, 1998

JOHN LITHGOW

Birthplace: Rochester, NY
Birthdate: 10/19/45
Occupation: Actor
Education: Harvard University, London Academy of Music and Dramatic Arts
Debut: (Film) *Dealing: or The Berkeley-to-Boston Forty-Brick Lost-Bag Blues*, 1972; (TV) *Mom, the Wolfman and Me*, 1980
Signature: *3rd Rock from the Sun*
Facts: His father ran the Antioch Shakespeare Festival, and John had small parts in the plays from early childhood.

Stars in a children's videotape, *John Lithgow's Kid-Size Concert*.

Some years ago he read the book *Forrest Gump* and wanted to acquire the movie rights so he could play the lead, but he didn't get around to it.

Known as a serious dramatic actor, but actually did more than 40 comedies on stage.

Son Ian appears in *3rd Rock* as Professor Solomon's slowest student.
Marriage: Jean Taynton, 1966 (divorced); Mary Yeager, 1981
Children: Ian, 1972 (with Jean Taynton). Phoebe, 1982; Nathan, c.1984
Major Awards: Tony, Best Supporting Actor (Dramatic), *The Changing Room*, 1973; Emmy, Outstanding Guest Performance in a Drama Series, *Amazing Stories*, 1986; Emmy, Best Actor in a Comedy Series, *3rd Rock from the Sun*, 1996, 1997, 1999
Quote: "God bless television."

LUCY LIU

Birthplace: New York, NY
Birthdate: 12/2/67
Occupation: Actor
Education: Attended New York University; University of Michigan
Debut: (TV) *Beverly Hills, 90210*, 1991; (Film) *Jerry Maguire*, 1996
Signature: *Ally McBeal*
Facts: Her middle name is Alexis.

While earning her B.A. in Chinese language and culture, Liu became serious about acting when she played the lead in a campus production of *Alice in Wonderland*.

Her mixed-media photo collages have been exhibited frequently in New York and Los Angeles. After her show at SoHo's Cast Iron Gallery, she was awarded a grant in 1994 to study in China.

She was originally signed on to *Ally McBeal* for only six episodes but her popularity among audiences won her a recurring role.

She practices martial arts.

She treats her long hair with olive oil and lavender.

Nickname among friends is "Curious George."

Original Job: Artist, caterer, aerobics instructor

Quote: "I wanted to be Barbie and I was as opposite to Barbie as you could get."

HEATHER LOCKLEAR

Birthplace: Los Angeles, CA
Birthdate: 9/25/61
Occupation: Actor
Education: UCLA
Debut: (TV) *Dynasty,* 1981
Signature: *Melrose Place*
Facts: Served over six years as the spokesperson for the Health and Tennis Corporation of America.

Played officer Stacy Sheridan on the crime drama series *T.J. Hooker* with William Shatner, 1982–87.

When she joined the cast of *Melrose Place*, the series's audience jumped 50 percent.

Marriage: Tommy Lee (divorced), Richie Sambora, 1994
Child: Ava Elizabeth, 1997

JENNIFER LOPEZ

Birthplace: Bronx, NY
Birthdate: 7/24/70
Occupation: Actor, singer
Debut: (TV) *In Living Color,* 1990;

(Film) *Mi Familia ("My Family"),* 1995; (Album) *On the 6,* 1999
Signature: *Selena,* 1997; "If You Had My Love," 1999
Facts: The daughter of Puerto Rican parents, she danced for music videos and on stage, and then was selected to be a Fly Girl for TV's *In Living Color.*

Her role as Selena was protested by some Latinos because she is of Puerto Rican rather than Mexican descent.

She is the highest paid Latina actress in history.

When she was younger she wanted to be a hairstylist.

On the 6 is named for the subway line that she took to Manhattan when she was growing up.
Original Job: Dancer
Marriage: Ojani Noa (divorced, 1998)
Quote: "Some guys like skinny girls, but they're missing out. When a dress is on a woman, it shouldn't look like it's on a coat hanger."

SOPHIA LOREN

Real Name: Sophia Villani Scicolone
Birthplace: Rome, Italy
Birthdate: 9/20/34
Education: Catholic parochial school, Teachers' Institute
Occupation: Actor
Debut: (Film) *Variety Lights,* 1950; (TV) *The World of Sophia Loren,* 1962
Signature: *Two Women,* 1961
Facts: Although her parents never married, her father, Ricardo Scicolone, granted her the legal right to use his last name.

Growing up poor with her sister and mother in Pozzuoli, a small industrial town near Naples, Italy, she attended a Catholic school, where she has said she was plain, thin, and nicknamed *"Stecchetto"* ("the stick") or *"Stuzzicadenti"* ("toothpick").

At age 12, she enrolled in the Teachers' Institute, where she studied teaching for three years.

Met producer and future husband Carlo Ponti during a beauty contest where he was a judge and she was a contestent. She was 15 years old.

She and her mother worked as extras in *Quo Vadis,* earning a total income of $33.

Sophia began modeling for Italian magazines and in 1952 was given the name Sophia Loren by a director.

She did her famous striptease in 1963 in the film *Yesterday, Today and Tomorrow,* which she reprised in 1994's *Ready to Wear* at age 59.

Suffered two miscarriages and two difficult pregnancies.

Her marriage to Ponti was annulled due to charges by the Italian government that Ponti was a bigamist, claiming that his divorce from a previous wife was invalid. They were married again in 1966.

She is the only actress to have won an Oscar for a foreign-language film.

Infamy: Spent 17 days in jail in 1982 for underpaying her taxes in Italy.
Original Job: Model
Marriage: Carlo, 1957 (annulled in 1962; remarried, 1966)
Children: Carlo Ponti Jr., 1968; Eduardo, 1972
Major Awards: Academy Award, Best Actress, *Two Women,* 1961; Honorary Academy Award, as "one of the genuine treasures of world cinema," 1990
Quotes: "I am not a sexy pot."

JULIA LOUIS-DREYFUS

Birthplace: New York, NY
Birthdate: 1/13/61
Occupation: Actor
Education: Northwestern University
Debut: (TV) *Saturday Night Live,* 1982; (Film) *Hannah and Her Sisters,* 1986
Signature: *Seinfeld*
Facts: Parents were divorced when she was only 1 year old.

Met husband in college and

worked with him on *Saturday Night Live*.

Her role in *Seinfeld* was not in the original mix created by Jerry Seinfeld and Larry David, but was imposed by the network, which felt a female perspective was needed.
Original Job: Member of the Second City comedy troupe
Marriage: Brad Hall, 1987
Child: Henry, 1992; Charles, 1997
Major Award: Emmy, Best Supporting Actress, *Seinfeld,* 1996

COURTNEY LOVE

Real Name: Courtney Menely
Birthplace: San Francisco, CA
Birthdate: 7/9/64
Occupation: Singer, songwriter
Education: High school dropout
Debut: (Album) *Pretty on the Inside,* 1991
Signature: Hole
Facts: Ran away to Europe at 15; her grandfather's death left her a millionaire.

Mother was the psychologist who examined Katherine Anne Power ('60s radical and fugitive who recently confessed to being an accessory to bank robbery).

Appeared in the film *Straight to Hell,* 1987.

Before founding Hole, Love was lead vocalist for the rock band Faith No More in the early '80s "for about a week" (before they found Chuck Mosely). She also played with Kat Bjelland of the Minneapolis all-girl band Babes in Toyland and future L7 member Jennifer Finch in Sugar Baby Doll.

Named daughter after the '30s actress Frances Farmer, who is the subject of Nirvana song "Frances Farmer Will Have Her Revenge on Seattle."
Infamy: In her early teens, was sent to a juvenile detention center after stealing a Kiss T-shirt from a department store.

A *Vanity Fair* article described Love as shooting heroin while pregnant. Though she denied the charge, child-welfare authorities temporarily removed the baby after she was born.

Arrested in 1995 for verbally abusing a flight attendant aboard an Australian flight. She was not convicted, but ordered to remain on good behavior for one month.
Original Job: Danced in strip joints in L.A. and Alaska
Marriage: Kurt Cobain, 1992 (deceased)
Child: Frances Bean, 1992
Famous Relatives: Linda Carroll, psychologist, mother; Hank Harrison, author, father
Quote: "Once you've cleared a million bucks, excuse me, you're not a punk anymore"

LYLE LOVETT

Birthplace: Klein, TX
Birthdate: 11/1/57
Occupation: Singer, songwriter
Education: Texas A&M
Debut: (Album) *Lyle Lovett,* 1986
Facts: Played guitar in coffee shops while in college.

Lives in a clapboard house built by his grandparents.

Is afraid of cows.
Marriage: Julia Roberts, 1993 (divorced, 1995)
Major Awards: Grammy, *Lyle Lovett and His Large Band,* 1989; Grammy, Best Pop Vocal Collaboration, "Funny How Time Slips Away" (with Al Green), 1994; Grammy, Best Country Group Performance with Vocal, "Blues for Dixie" (with Asleep at the Wheel), 1994

ROB LOWE

Birthplace: Charlottesville, VA
Birthdate: 3/17/64
Occupation: Actor
Education: High school
Debut: (TV) *A New Kind of Family,* 1978 (Broadway) *A Little Hotel on the Side,* 1992; (Film) *The Outsiders,* 1983

Signature: *St. Elmo's Fire,* 1985
Facts: His middle name is Helper.

While in high school, he appeared in Super 8 movies made by class-mates Sean Penn and Charlie Sheen.

He is deaf in his right ear.

As the "crown prince" of the Brat Pack, he was romantically linked to Melissa Gilbert, Chynna Phillips, and Princess Stephanie of Monaco.

Wears a gold cross and a gold medallion around his neck with the Serenity Prayer used in 12-step recovery programs, both given to him by his wife.
Infamy: After being caught on videotape with two young women, one of whom was only 16, while attending 1988's Democratic National Convention in Atlanta, he avoided prosecution by agreeing to perform 20 hours of community service.

During the 1989 Academy Awards, in a disastrously bad number, he crooned "Proud Mary" with a Snow White impostor. The Academy apologized to the Walt Disney Company for the potential trademark infringe-ment.
Original Job: Actor in TV commercials
Marriage: Sheryl Berkoff, 1991
Children: Matthew Edward, 1993; John Owen, 1995
Famous Relative: Chad Lowe, actor, brother
Quote: "I drank too much. I had no sense of what should be private and what should be public. And I was very unfocused and not even aware of how the onrush of really being a *man*—as opposed to a young man—was scaring me."

GEORGE LUCAS

Birthplace: Modesto, CA
Birthdate: 5/14/44
Occupation: Director, producer, screenwriter
Education: University of Southern California

Debut: (Film) *THX-1138,* 1971
Signature: *Star Wars,* 1977
Facts: Has sold more than $3 billion in licensed *Star Wars* merchandise, money Lucas got to keep because licensing rights were thrown into his contract in exchange for his having given up an extra director's fee (he forfeited the higher fee to ensure that 20th Century Fox would bankroll his sequel).

His empire includes the Industrial Light & Magic special effects firm, LucasArts interactive media, and a group selling his advanced THX theater sound system.

Still writes scripts in longhand, using the same three-ring binder he used in college.

As an 18-year-old, nearly killed himself while joyriding on a country road when his Fiat hit a car, flipped over, and crashed into a tree. He survived only because his seat belt broke and threw him from the car before impact.

Has received permission from the government to develop 23 acres of land at the former Presidio Army base in San Francisco for his Letterman Digital Arts Center, which will house part of Lucas's film and technology empire.
Marriage: Marcia Griffin (divorced, 1983)
Children: Amanda, 1981; Katie, 1988; Jett, 1993; (all adopted).
Major Awards: Academy of Motion Pictures Arts and Sciences, Irving Thalberg Award, 1992

SUSAN LUCCI

Birthplace: Scarsdale, NY
Birthdate: 12/23/46
Education: Marymount College
Debut: (TV) *All My Children,* 1969
Signature: *All My Children*
Facts: Was nominated 19 times for the best actress in a daytime series, and finally won in 1999.

Was a cheerleader in high school.

Made the semifinals in New York State Miss Universe pageant, 1968.

Dropped out of the competition to finish her college exams.

As Erica Kane, Lucci has impersonated a nun, been kidnapped, rescued a lover from prison using a helicopter, and stared down a grizzly bear.

Daughter Liza appears on the new daytime drama, *Passions.*
Original Job: "Color girl" for CBS, sitting for cameras as a new lighting system for color TV was being developed
Marriage: Helmut Huber, 1969
Children: Liza Victoria, actor, 1975; Andreas Martin, 1980
Major Award: Emmy, Best Actress in a Daytime Drama Series, *All My Children,* 1998–99

LORETTA LYNN

Real Name: Loretta Webb
Birthplace: Butcher Hollow, KY
Birthdate: 4/14/35
Occupation: Singer, songwriter
Debut: (Single) "Honky Tonk Girl," 1960
Signature: "Coal Miner's Daughter"
Facts: First woman to earn a certified gold country album.

While her kids were still young, her husband gave her a guitar to accompany the singing she did around the house. She taught herself to play.

Her first No. 1 single, "Don't Come Home A-Drinkin' (With Lovin' on Your Mind)" was banned from several stations. Many of her songs have been banned, including "Rated X" and "The Pill."

Married when she was 13. "By the time I was 17, I had four kids, and I had never been anywhere." She was a grandmother at 31, one year after her twins (her last children) were born.
Marriage: Oliver Vanetta Lynn Jr., 1948 (deceased, 1996)
Children: Betty Sue Lynn Markworth, c.1948; Jack Benny, 1949 (deceased, 1984); Ernest Ray, 1953; Clara

Marie Lynn Lyell, 1954; Peggy, 1964; Patsy, 1964
Famous Relative: Crystal Gayle, singer, sister
Major Awards: Grammy, Best Country Performance—Duo or Group, "After the Fire Is Gone" (with Conway Twitty), 1971; Grammy, Best Recording for Children, *Sesame Country* (with others), 1981; inducted into the Country Music Hall of Fame, 1988

ANDIE MACDOWELL

Real Name: Rosalie Anderson MacDowell
Birthplace: Gaffney, SC
Birthdate: 4/21/58
Occupation: Actor
Education: Attended Winthrop College
Debut: (Film) *Greystoke: The Legend of Tarzan, Lord of the Apes,* 1984
Signature: *Sex, Lies and Videotape,* 1989
Facts: After *Greystoke* was filmed, MacDowell's part was overdubbed with a British accent provided by Glenn Close.

Played Jimi Hendrix's "Angel" at her wedding.
Original Job: McDonald's, Elite model
Marriage: Paul Qualley, 1986 (separated, 1999)
Children: Justin, 1986; Rainey, 1989; Sarah Margaret, 1994

SHIRLEY MACLAINE

Real Name: Shirley MacLean Beaty
Birthplace: Richmond, VA
Birthdate: 4/24/34
Occupation: Actor, author
Education: Washington School of Ballet
Debut: (Stage) *Oklahoma!,* 1950
Signature: *Terms of Endearment,* 1983
Facts: Starred in her own TV series, *Shirley's World* (1971–72).

Was performing with the Washington School of Ballet by the time she was 12, but soon grew too tall to be a ballerina.

Following a showbiz cliché, she got the lead in the 1954 Broadway show *The Pajama Game* when the lead hurt her ankle.

As a young girl, often had to come with fists blazing to the aid of her bookish and picked-on younger brother.

Infamy: Ridiculed for her oft-expressed beliefs in reincarnation, detailed in her best-selling books *Out on a Limb* and *Dancing in the Light.* Satirized herself in the "Pavilion of Former Lives" in the film *Defending Your Life* (1991).

Had an open marriage with husband Parker, but was stunned to learn from a channeler (later confirmed by a private eye) that he had transferred millions of dollars to his girlfriend's account.

Wrote a tell-all book in 1995, detailing how Debra Winger mooned her and broke wind, and describing Frank Sinatra as "a perpetual kid" and "someone who muscled others." Sinatra's response to the book: "It's amazing what a broad will do for a buck."

Original Job: Dancer
Marriage: Steve Parker (divorced, 1983); Andrew Peacock (relationship)
Child: Stephanie Sachiko, 1956
Famous Relative: Warren Beatty, actor, brother
Major Awards: Emmy, Outstanding Comedy-Variety or Musical Special, *Shirley MacLaine: If They Could See Me Now*, 1974; Emmy, Outstanding Comedy-Variety or Musical Special, *Gypsy in My Soul*, 1976; Emmy, Outstanding Writing of Variety or Music Program, *Shirley MacLaine... Every Little Movement*, 1980; Oscar, Best Actress, *Terms of Endearment*, 1983

PETER MACNICOL

Birthplace: Texas
Birthdate: 4/10/58
Education: Attended University of Minnesota
Occupation: Actor

Debut: (Film) *Dragonslayer*, 1981; (Stage) *Crimes of the Heart*
Signature: *Ally McBeal*
Facts: Originally planned a career in paleontology.

After his first movie experience, he left New York and traveled around Europe and the United States without telling anyone where he was going. When he finally called his agent, he found out that he had an audition for *Sophie's Choice*.
Marriage: Marsue Cumming

ELLE MACPHERSON

Real Name: Eleanor Gow
Birthplace: Sydney, Australia
Birthdate: 3/29/64
Occupation: Supermodel, actor
Debut: *Sports Illustrated* swimsuit model, (Film) *Sirens*, 1994
Facts: Appeared in every issue of *Elle* magazine from 1982 to 1988.

Launched a designer lingerie line in Australia and New Zealand in 1991.

Opened Fashion Cafe in New York City in 1995 with supermodels Claudia Schiffer and Naomi Campbell.

Named the world's wealthiest model by *Business Age* in 1998.
Marriage: Gilles Bensimon (divorced, 1989); Arpad Busson (relationship)
Children: Arpad Flynn, 1998

WILLIAM H. MACY

Birthplace: Miami, FL
Birthdate: 3/13/50
Occupation: Actor, stage director, screenwriter
Education: Goddard College
Debut: (Broadway) *Our Town*, 1988; (TV) *The Awakening Land*, 1978; (Film) *House of Games*, 1987
Signature: *Fargo*, 1996
Facts: Initially planning on a career in veterinary medicine, he transferred from Bethany College to major in theater at Goddard, where he studied under David Mamet.

Moved to Chicago with Mamet and Steven Schacter and founded the St.

Nicholas Theater, where he appeared in 1975 in its first production, *American Buffalo,* and landed small roles in TV.

Is actively involved with Boy Scout Troop 184 in L.A.

His middle name is Hall.

During the 1980s, he performed in more than 50 Broadway and Off-Broadway productions. He and Mamet founded the Atlantic Theatre Company in New York in 1983.
Original Jobs: Musician, acting teacher
Marriage: Felicity Huffman, actor, 1997
Quote: "I'm sort of an odd duck. I look really odd sometimes, then other times I look okay. I tend to get cast for who I am, which is a white guy who can talk a good game."

MADONNA

Real Name: Madonna Louise Veronica Ciccone
Birthplace: Bay City, MI
Birthdate: 8/16/58
Occupation: Singer
Education: University of Michigan
Debut: Dancer, Alvin Ailey Dance Company, 1979
Signature: "Material Girl"
Facts: Was a cheerleader in high school.

She starred in an exploitation film called *A Certain Sacrifice* in 1980.

Early in her career, posed nude for a New York photographer. Those photos later appeared in *Playboy.*

She appears in a nightclub scene from the 1983 movie *Vision Quest,* singing "Crazy for You" in the background.

Her hobby is making scrapbooks.

Has been drinking "kabbalah water," blessed by a rabbi versed in the Jewish mystical tradition, to help with her insomnia.
Infamy: In 1994, swore 14 times while on *The Late Show with David Letterman,* to get revenge for his many jokes at her expense. She also

handed Letterman a pair of her panties and told him to smell them.

Her video for "Justify My Love" (1990) was banned from MTV.

Her book *Sex* (1992) was originally banned in Japan, where it is against the law to show pubic hair. Officials eventually relented since the book was being distributed anyway.

Original Job: Model, worked in a doughnut shop

Marriage: Sean Penn (divorced, 1988)

Child: Lourdes Maria Ciccone Leon, 1996

Major Award: Grammy, Best Music Video—Long Form, *Madonna—Blonde Ambition World Tour Live,* 1991; Grammy, Best Dance Recording, "Ray of Light," 1998; Grammy, Best Shortform Music Video, "Ray of Light," 1998; Grammy, Best Pop Album, *Ray of Light,* 1998.

BILL MAHER

Birthplace: New York, NY
Birthdate: 1/20/56
Occupation: Comedian, talk show host
Education: Cornell University
Debut: *The Tonight Show,* 1982
Signature: *Politically Incorrect*
Facts: Says the most politically incorrect thing he ever did was to say "f--k" in front of the president.

Originally did stand-up on the New York club circuit with other up-and-coming comics, including Jerry Seinfeld and Paul Reiser.

Wrote *True Story: A Comedy Novel.*

JOHN MALKOVICH

Birthplace: Christopher, IL
Birthdate: 12/9/53
Occupation: Actor
Education: Eastern Illinois University, Illinois State University
Debut: (Stage) *True West,* 1982
Signature: *Dangerous Liaisons,* 1988

Facts: Played football and tuba in high school.

Took up acting in college when he fell for a female drama student.

Co-founded the Steppenwolf Theatre in Chicago, in 1976.

Original Job: Enrolled in Eastern Illinois University with plans of becoming an environmentalist

Marriages: Glenne Headly, 1982 (divorced, c.1988); Nicoletta Peyran (relationship)

Children: Amandine, 1990; Lowey, 1992

Major Award: Emmy, Best Supporting Actor in a Made-for-TV Movie, *Death of a Salesman,* 1986

DAVID MAMET

Birthplace: Chicago, IL
Birthdate: 11/30/47
Occupation: Writer, director
Education: Goddard College, studied at the Neighborhood Playhouse in New York
Debut: (Stage) *The Duck Variations,* 1972
Signature: *Glengarry Glen Ross,* 1984
Facts: Has written several books and children's plays, including *Revenge of the Space Pandas, or Binky Rudich and the Two-Speed Clock.*

Has worked as a busboy, driven a cab, worked at *Oui* magazine, and waited tables. Was an assistant office manager for a real estate company and taught drama at Yale, New York University, and the University of Chicago.

Wrote the screenplays for *The Postman Always Rings Twice* (1981), *The Verdict* (1982), and *The Untouchables* (1987).

Published his first novel, *The Village,* in 1994.

Still writes on a '70s manual typewriter and uses a pencil.

Co-founded the Atlantic Theater Company as a summer workshop in Vermont for his NYU students.

Original Job: Worked backstage at the Hull House Theatre in Chicago
Marriages: Lindsay Crouse, 1977 (divorced); Rebecca Pidgeon, 1991
Children: Willa, 1982; Zosia, 1988; (with Lindsay Crouse). Clara, 1994; Noah, 1999
Major Award: Pulitzer Prize, *Glengarry Glen Ross,* 1984

CAMRYN MANHEIM

Real Name: Debra Manheim
Birthplace: Caldwell, NJ
Birthdate: 3/8/61
Occupation: Actor
Education: Cabrillo Junior College; University of California at Santa Cruz; New York University (MFA)
Debut: (Stage) *Hydriotaphia,* 1987; (Film) *The Bonfire of the Vanities,* 1990; (TV) *Law & Order,* 1991
Signature: *The Practice*
Facts: While at NYU she took crystal methedrine to lose weight, became addicted, and accidentally overdosed.

Between sporadic acting gigs in New York, she was a sign language interpreter for the deaf in theaters and hospitals.

The success in 1993 of her one-woman Off-Broadway show, *Wake Up, I'm Fat!,* caught the eye of David E. Kelley, who cast her in the series pilot of *The Practice.*

Has 12 piercings in her right ear, a tattoo of Pegasus above her ankle, and drives a motorcycle.

Accepting her Emmy Award in

1998, she held it up and said, "This is for all the fat girls!"

Influenced by her activist parents, she was once arrested for marching in a pro-choice demonstartion.

Original Job: Sign language interpreter, improvisation teacher

Major Awards: Emmy Award, Outstanding Supporting Actress in Drama Series, *The Practice,* 1998

Quote: "I'm a five-foot-ten Amazon who isn't afraid to be naked or to kiss men or to be sexual anymore."

MARILYN MANSON

Real Name: Brian Hugh Warner
Birthplace: Canton, OH
Birthdate: 1/5/69
Occupation: Singer, band leader
Education: High school
Debut: (Album) *Portrait of an American Family,* 1994
Facts: An only child, he was sent to a private conservative Christian school for the best possible education, but he resented the restrictions and the warnings about evil rock music. He eventually caused sufficient trouble to be expelled and finished his last two years in a public school.

He formed his band in 1990 and created his alter ego based on Marilyn Monroe and Charles Manson, considering them the most popular personalities of the 1960s.

For his music and stage show, he drew from pornography, horror films, and Satanism because they were the forbidden items of youth.

The title of his album *Antichrist Superstar* is a twist on Andrew Lloyd Webber's *Jesus Christ Superstar.*

He proposed to Rose on Valentine's Eve with an antique diamond ring.

After candlelight vigils and bomb threats at some venues, Manson had a hard time getting booked in certain cities.

Infamy: His group was banned in Salt Lake City after he ripped apart a Mormon Bible on stage.

He sold T-shirts imprinted "Kill God...Kill Your Mom and Dad...Kill Yourself."

During a 1998 rampage in Poughkeepsie, NY, he trashed and burned his dressing room and destroyed four hotel rooms.

Relationship: Rose McGowan (engaged)

Quotes: "To the people who are afraid of things like me, the answer is to raise your kids to be more intelligent."

JULIANNA MARGULIES

Birthplace: Spring Valley, NY
Birthdate: 6/8/66
Occupation: Actor
Education: Sarah Lawrence College
Debut: (Film) *Out for Justice,* 1991
Signature: *ER*
Facts: Her father was the ad executive who wrote the Alka Seltzer "Plop, plop, fizz, fizz" jingle.

Her parents divorced early, and her mother, a former dancer with the American Ballet Theatre, moved her to Paris and then London.

A perfectionist in high school, once threw a 50-page, illustrated research report into the mud because it got an A-minus.

While waiting for an acting break, waitressed at some of New York's trendiest restaurants.

Relationship: Ron Eldard
Major Award: Emmy, Best Supporting Actress (Drama), *ER,* 1995

WYNTON MARSALIS

Birthplace: New Orleans, LA
Birthdate: 10/18/61
Occupation: Trumpeter
Education: Attended Juilliard on a full scholarship
Debut: (Band) Art Blakey's Jazz Messengers, 1980
Facts: His first trumpet was a hand-me-down from bandleader Al Hirt.

Played with New Orleans Philharmonic at age 14.

Released his first classical album, *Trumpet Concertos,* in 1983. Was first artist ever to receive—or be nominated for—awards in both jazz and classical categories in a single year.

Children: Wynton, 1990; Simeon, 1992; Jasper Armstrong, 1996
Famous Relatives: Ellis Marsalis, musician, father; Branford Marsalis, musician, brother
Major Awards: Grammy, Best Jazz Performance—Soloist, "Think of One," 1983; Grammy, Best Jazz Performance—Soloist, "Hot House Flowers," 1984; Grammy, Best Jazz Performance—Soloist, "Black Codes from the Underground," 1985; Grammy, Best Jazz Performance—Group, "Black Codes from the Underground," 1985; Grammy, Best Jazz Performance—Group, "J Mood," 1986; Grammy, Best Jazz Performance—Group, *Marsalis Standard Time Volume I,* 1987; Pulitzer Prize, *Blood on the Fields,* 1997

PENNY MARSHALL

Real Name: Carole Penny Marshall
Birthplace: New York, NY
Birthdate: 10/15/43
Occupation: Actor, director
Education: University of New Mexico
Debut: (TV) *The Danny Thomas Hour,* 1967
Signature: *Laverne and Shirley*
Facts: Even though the family was Congregationalist, Marshall's mother was convinced that Jewish men make the best husbands, so she sent Penny to a Jewish summer camp each year.

Lost the part of Gloria on TV's *All in the Family* to Sally Struthers.

Was first woman director to have a film take in more than $100 million at the box office (*Big*).

Original Job: Dance instructor, secretary
Marriages: Michael Henry (divorced); Rob Reiner, 1971 (divorced, 1979)
Child: Tracy Lee, 1964
Famous Relatives: Garry Marshall, director, producer, brother; Tony Maschiarelli, producer, father

RICKY MARTIN

Real Name: Enrique José Martin Morales
Birthplace: San Juan, PR
Birthdate: 12/24/71
Occupation: Singer
Education: High school
Debut: (Solo Album) *Ricky Martin,* 1988; (Solo English-Language Album, *Ricky Martin,* 1999); (TV) *Getting By,* 1993; (Broadway) *Les Misérables,* 1996
Signature: "Livin' La Vida Loca"
Facts: At age six, he began appearing in local television commercials.

When he first tried out the singing group Menudo, he was considered too short. By 1984, he joined as its youngest member, and took "mandatory retirement" before turning 18.

In 1985, legally changed his name from Enrique to Ricky

Played a singing bartender in the soap *General Hospital* in 1993 and by 1994, he had a regular role.

Considers himself a "spiritual" person, is a student of yoga and Buddhism, and shaved his head in India in December, 1998.

Sang the Spanish-language version of the theme to Disney's *Hercules.*

Ricky Martin (1999) has sold over 5 million copies in the U.S. and is the best-selling album ever by a Latin artist.
Major Awards: Grammy, Best Latin Pop Performance, *Vuelve,* 1999
Quote: "I have no butt. Everybody tells me that. It's tiny...not even rock climbing helps."

STEVE MARTIN

Birthplace: Waco, TX
Birthdate: 8/14/45
Occupation: Actor, writer
Education: Long Beach State College, UCLA
Debut: (TV) *The Smothers Brothers Comedy Hour,* 1967
Signature: "A wild and crazy guy"

Facts: Lived behind Disneyland and got his start there performing magic tricks and playing the banjo.

Was a cheerleader in high school.

Is a dedicated art collector.

Dated Anne Heche for two years before she broke it off.

Has published sophisticated satirical pieces in *The New Yorker* and the book *Pure Drivel.*
Original Job: Sold guidebooks at Disneyland
Marriage: Victoria Tennant (divorced, 1993)
Major Awards: Emmy, Best Writing in a Comedy, Variety, or Music Program, *The Smothers Brothers Comedy Hour,* 1969; Grammy, Best Comedy Recording, *Let's Get Small,* 1977; Grammy, Best Comedy Recording, *A Wild and Crazy Guy,* 1978

MASTER P

Real Name: Percy Miller
Birthplace: New Orleans, LA
Birthdate: 2/9/69
Occupation: Rapper, actor, movie producer, record and film company executive
Education: Junior college
Debut: (Album) *The Ghetto's Tryin' to Kill Me,* 1994
Signature: *No Limits*
Facts: The eldest of five children, he grew up in a housing project in an area with a high crime rate and a reputation for violence.

Attended University of Houston on a basketball scholarship but left when he was sidelined with a leg injury.

Moved to Richmond, Virginia, and opened a small record store, No Limits, which has become a very successful independent record company and has made him a multi-millionaire.

He sold his debut album out of the trunk of his car in Oakland and New Orleans. It became an underground hit, selling 200,000 copies without radio play.

His film, *I'm 'Bout It,* which he produced, directed, and acted in, was a fictionalized version of his brother's murder.

He tried out for the Continental Basketball Association's team in 1998 and signed on as a free agent, earning $1,000 per week with a $15 per day allowance. Several months later, he tried out for the Charlotte Hornets, an NBA team, but did not make the cut.

In 1997 he started No Limit Sports Management, a company that represented young NBA players, including Ron Mercer (Boston Celtics) and Derek Anderson (Cleveland Cavaliers).

In 1998 *Forbes* ranked him tenth of highest paid entertainers.
Original Job: Record store owner
Marriage: Sonya Miller
Children: Four children
Quote: "What I learned in the ghetto is that everybody wants more for their money. You gotta be able to give your customers more for their money, 'cause that's how you're going to keep them coming back to you."

WALTER MATTHAU

Real Name: Walter Matuschanskavasky
Birthplace: New York, NY
Birthdate: 10/1/20
Occupation: Actor
Education: Attended Columbia University
Debut: (Film) *The Kentuckian,* 1955
Signature: *Odd Couple,* 1968
Facts: Grew up in poverty on Manhattan's Lower East Side.

Started acting at age 11 when he played bit parts (and sold sodas) at a Yiddish theater.

Neil Simon created the role of Oscar Madison specifically for him; he first played it on Broadway opposite Art Carney.
Infamy: Illegal gambling with bookies was a longtime passion.
Marriage: Grace Johnson (divorced); Carol Marcus, 1959
Children: David, 1953; Jenny, 1956;

(with Grace Johnson); Charles, 1962
Major Awards: Tony, Best Dramatic
Actor, *A Shot in the Dark*, 1962; Tony,
Best Actor in a Play, *Odd Couple*,
1965; Oscar, Best Supporting Actor,
Fortune Cookie, 1966

PAUL MCCARTNEY

Real Name: James Paul McCartney
Birthplace: Liverpool, England
Birthdate: 6/18/42
Occupation: Singer, songwriter,
bassist
Education: High school
Debut: Formed the Quarry Men,
Moondogs, and the Silver Beatles
with John Lennon and George
Harrison, 1956–1962
Signature: The Beatles
Facts: When he wanted to use
"Yesterday" in his 1984 film *Give My
Regards to Broad Street,* he had to
apply to the publishers for its use;
he no longer owned the copyright of
the most recorded song in history
(over 2,500 cover versions exist).

Was the first Beatle to quit in
1970, releasing his solo album
McCartney almost simultaneously
with the band's release of *Let It Be.*

His version of "Mary Had a Little
Lamb" hit No. 9 on the British
charts in June 1972.

In the Paul McCartney Kindergarten in Krakow, Poland, children
are taught English through McCartney's songs.

Was knighted by Queen Elizabeth
in 1996.
Infamy: Admitted to taking LSD and
was arrested numerous times with
Linda for possession of marijuana
and for growing it at their Scotland
farmhouse. Because of this, his
application for a U.S. passport was
refused many times.
Marriage: Linda Eastman, 1969
(deceased)
Children: Heather, 1962 (stepdaughter); Mary, 1969; Stella, 1971;
James, 1977
Major Awards: Grammy, Best New
Artist (with The Beatles), 1964;

Grammy, Best Pop Vocal—Duo or
Group, *A Hard Day's Night* (with The
Beatles), 1964; Grammy, Song of the
Year, "Michelle" (with John Lennon),
1966; Grammy, Best Rock Vocal,
"Eleanor Rigby," 1966; Grammy,
Album of the Year, *Sgt. Pepper's
Lonely Hearts Club Band* (with The
Beatles), 1967; Grammy, Best Score,
Let It Be (with The Beatles), 1970;
Grammy, Best Pop Performance—
Duo or Group, *Band on the Run* (with
Wings), 1974; Grammy, Hall of Fame
Winner, *Sgt. Pepper's Lonely Hearts
Club Band* (with The Beatles), 1992;
Oscar, Best Score, *Let It Be* (with The
Beatles), 1970; inducted into the
Rock and Roll Hall of Fame (with The
Beatles), 1988; NARAS Lifetime
Achievement Award, 1990; Grammy,
Best Pop Vocal, Duo or Group with
Vocal, "Free as a Bird" (with the
Beatles), 1996; inducted into Rock
and Roll Hall of Fame, 1999.

STELLA MCCARTNEY

Birthplace: England
Birthdate: 9/13/71
Occupation: Fashion designer
Education: Central St. Martin's
College of Art and Design
Facts: At 15 she worked at Patou,
the French couture house, but left
because she was opposed to the use
of fur in fashion.

Apprenticed with a Savile Row
tailor, enabling her to sew as well as
to design.

Her graduation fashion show for
St. Martin's featured a song by her
father, and her clothes were modeled
by friends Kate Moss, Yasmin Le Bon,
and Naomi Campbell.

A brief stint running her own
company failed, and she was hired
by Chloe. Now head designer, she
has revitalized the house's line.

Like her parents, she is an active
member of PETA, and narrated a
video about animal curelty at fur
ranches.

Her father advised her, "Nobody is
Beatle-proof."

Famous Relatives: Linda Eastman
McCartney, photographer/musician,
mother, deceased 1998; Paul
McCartney, ex-Beatle, father
Quote: "Of course my name opens
doors. But they can close just as
quickly if I don't deliver."

MATTHEW MCCONAUGHEY

Birthplace: Uvalde, TX
Birthdate: 11/4/69
Occupation: Actor
Education: University of Texas
Debut: (Film) *Dazed and Confused,*
1993
Signature: *A Time To Kill*, 1996
Facts: Endlessly rereads the motiva-
tional book, *The Greatest Salesman
in the World.* Used its techniques to
sell his talents to get acting parts.

Was cast in *Kill* after executives
vetoed Kevin Costner, Keanu Reeves,
Val Kilmer and others in a year-long
search. Received just $200,000 to
play the part.
Quote: "There are certain nights you
and your image just aren't in the
same bed."

DYLAN MCDERMOTT

Birthplace: Waterbury, CT
Birthdate: 10/26/61
Occupation: Actor
Education: Fordham University; also
trained under Sanford Meisner at
the Neighborhood Playhouse
Debut: (Theater) *Biloxi Blues,* 1985;
(Film) *Hamburger Hill,* 1987
Signature: *The Practice*
Facts: Moved to Greenwich Village
as a teen to live with his father. His
playwright-stepmother soon wrote a
part for him.

Engagement to Julia Roberts was
broken off by her after she fell for
Kiefer Sutherland on a movie set.
Original job: Busboy
Marriage: Shiva Afshar, 1995
Child: Colette, 1996
Famous Relative: Eve Ensler, play-
wright, stepmother

FRANCES MCDORMAND

Birthplace: Illinois
Birthdate: 6/23/57
Occupation: Actor
Education: Bethany College, Yale Drama School
Debut: (Film) *Blood Simple,* 1984
Signature: *Fargo,* 1996
Facts: Born to a Disciples of Christ preacher. The family moved repeatedly throughout the Midwest when she was a child.

Met Holly Hunter when the two studied at Yale. After graduation, Hunter told her she had auditioned for "two weird guys" (the Coen brothers) and that McDormand should too. After repeated failed attempts to get an audition, McDormand finally succeeded. *Blood Simple* not only launched her (and Hunter's) career, it introduced her to future husband Joel.

Was nominated in 1988 for Oscar's best supporting actress (for *Mississippi Burning*), the same year she was also nominated for a Tony for *A Streetcar Named Desire.*
Marriage: Joel Coen, 1994
Child: Pedro, c.1994 (adopted)
Famous Relative: Ethan Coen, writer, director, producer, brother-in-law
Major Award: Oscar, Best Actress, *Fargo,* 1996

REBA MCENTIRE

Birthplace: Chockie, OK
Birthdate: 3/28/55
Occupation: Singer, songwriter
Education: Southeastern State University
Debut: (Song) "I Don't Want To Be a One-Night Stand," 1976
Signature: "Is There Life Out There?"
Facts: As a teenager, performed with her siblings in the Singing McEntires. Their first single was a tribute to her grandfather, rodeo rider John McEntire.

Appeared in the 1990 movie *Tremors,* as well as other film and TV roles.

Her longtime tour manager and seven of her band members died in a plane crash in 1991.
Original Job: Cattle rancher, rodeo barrel racer
Marriages: Charlie Battles (divorced), Narvel Blackstock, 1989
Child: Shelby, 1990 (with Blackstock)
Major Awards: Grammy, Best Country Vocal—Female, "Whoever's in New England," 1986; Grammy, Best Country Female Vocalist, 1987; Grammy, Best Country Vocal—Collaboration, "Does He Love You" (with Linda Davis), 1993

TIM MCGRAW

Birthplace: Jacksonville, FL
Birthdate: 5/11/66
Occupation: Singer
Education: Attended Northeast Louisiana University
Debut: (Album) *Tim McGraw,* 1993
Signature: *Not a Moment Too Soon*
Facts: Mom Betty was an 18-year-old dancer when she and then bachelor Tug consummated their summer romance while Tug was in baseball camp. Tim learned who his father was only when he found his birth certificate at age 11. Tim met Tug but had little contact until high school, when Tug agreed to help pay for his son's college education.

Started his own management company, Breakfast Table Management, to launch other groups.

The lyrics to his "Indian Outlaw" outraged some Native American groups, who had it banned from radio stations in several states.
Marriage: Faith Hill, 1996
Child: Gracie Katherine, 1997; Maggie Elizabeth, 1998
Famous Relative: Tug McGraw, baseball player, father

EWAN MCGREGOR

Birthplace: Crieff, Scotland
Birthdate: 3/31/71
Occupation: Actor

Education: Attended London's Guildhall School of Music and Drama
Debut: (Film) *Being Human,* 1993
Signature: *Star Wars: Episode 1—The Phantom Menace,* 1999
Facts: Inspired by his uncle, knew he wanted to be in theater at age 9. Left home at 16 to work backstage at Scotland's Perth Repertory Theatre.

Lost nearly 30 pounds and shaved his head for his role in *Trainspotting.* Debated trying to shoot heroin but decided that it would be disrespectful to the recovering addicts acting as technical advisors to the film.
Marriage: Eve Maurakis, 1995
Child: Clara Mathilde, 1996
Famous Relative: Dennis Lawson, actor, uncle

MARK MCGWIRE

Birthplace: Pomona, CA
Birthdate: 10/1/63
Occupation: Baseball player
Education: University of Southern California
Debut: (Major League Baseball) Oakland Athletics, 1986
Signature: Record-setting home-run hitter
Facts: Began playing Little League baseball at 8. Hit a home run in his first at-bat, against a 12-year-old pitcher.

Has 4 brothers, all of whom are over 6 feet tall and weigh more than 200 pounds.

His ex-wife was a bat girl at USC.

Brother Dan played quarterback for the Seattle Seahawks and the Miami Dolphins.

Was drafted by the Montreal Expos out of high school, but when they offered a signing bonus of only $8,500, he opted for college, where he intended to be a pitcher.

Was rookie of the year in 1987, hitting 49 home runs, the most ever for a rookie.

In 1998 smashed Roger Maris's legendary record of 61 home runs in a season, finishing with a total of 70.

His biceps are 20 inches wide.

Hit 500 home runs sooner in his career than any other slugger.

Loves classical music and watching the Learning Channel.

His on-again, off-again girlfriend runs the Mark McGwire Foundation.

Very close to his son, who fills in as a St. Louis Cardinal's batboy and is contractually guaranteed a seat on the team plane with his father.

Infamy: Has admitted to taking androstenedione pills. Though legal and allowed in baseball, this testosterone-producing substance is banned by the NFL and IOC. Also took creatine, a muscle-building substance.

Marriage: Kathy Williamson (divorced, 1988); Ali Dickson (relationship)

Child: Matthew, 1987

SARAH MCLACHLAN

Birthplace: Halifax, Nova Scotia, Canada

Birthdate: 1/28/68

Occupation: Singer, songwriter, concert promoter

Education: Attended Nova Scotia College of Art and Design

Debut: (Album) *Touch,* 1988

Signature: Lilith Fair

Facts: She and two brothers were adopted; at age 19, met her birth mother by coincidence.

Offered a chance to record demo tapes for a Vancouver independent label while in high school, but her parents refused to let her.

Was harassed for years by an obsessive fan, with his letters inspiring the song "Possession." Recognizing his words, he sued, but committed suicide before the matter was resolved.

Named the Lilith concert after Adam's first wife in Jewish mythology, a woman tossed out of Eden for being too independent and forced to make it alone.

Marriage: Ashwin Sood, 1997

Major Awards: Grammy, Best

Female Pop Vocal Performance, "Building a Mystery," 1997; Grammy, Best Pop Instrumental Performance, "Last Dance," 1997

Quote: "Don't think I don't count the horseshoes on my ass daily."

NATALIE MERCHANT

Birthplace: Jamestown, NY

Birthdate: 10/26/63

Occupation: Singer

Education: High school dropout

Debut: (Album, with 10,000 Maniacs) *Human Conflict No. 5*; (Solo album) *Tigerlily,* 1995

Signature: "Carnival"

Facts: After her mother remarried, the family moved to a commune: "I fell in love with those people."

At 16 she dropped out of high school, took college courses, and worked three jobs, including one at a whole foods bakery.

Frequently in the audience for 10,000 Maniacs' performances, she was suddenly invited up to sing, and at 17 joined the group as lead singer. Quit the group in 1992 to go solo.

Dated R.E.M.'s Michael Stipe on and off for three years.

Quote: "People need to change within first, with their hearts before their minds. Now, instead of wanting to change people, I just want to move them."

DEBRA MESSING

Birthplace: Brooklyn, NY

Birthdate: 8/15/68

Occupation: Actor

Education: Brandeis University, New York University (MFA)

Debut: (Off-Broadway) *Four Dogs and a Bone*; (TV) *NYPD Blue,* 1994; (Film) *A Walk in the Clouds,* 1995

Signature: *Will & Grace*

Facts: Graduated summa cum laude from college.

She won her own series, *Ned and Stacey,* after four episodes of *NYPD Blue.*

Appeared twice on *Seinfeld* as Jerry's unavailable crush.

Relationship: Daniel Zelman (engaged, 1998)

BETTE MIDLER

Birthplace: Honolulu, HI

Birthdate: 12/1/45

Occupation: Singer, comedian, actor, producer

Education: Attended University of Hawaii

Debut: (Album) *The Divine Miss M,* 1972; (Film) *Hawaii,* 1966

Signature: "Wind Beneath My Wings," 1989

Facts: Named after Bette Davis, which her mother mistakenly thought was pronounced "Bet."

Spent her first 21 years in Hawaii, then worked carefully to cultivate a New Yorker image.

Was married in a Las Vegas chapel by an Elvis impersonator.

Wrote a best-selling children's book, *The Saga of Baby Divine.*

Infamy: Became a gay icon in the 1970s by singing in New York's bath houses, often with then-unknown Barry Manilow as her pianist.

Original Jobs: Pineapple cannery worker, radio station secretary, go-go dancer

Marriage: Martin Von Haselburg, 1984

Child: Sophie, 1986

Major Awards: Grammy, Best New Artist, 1973; Grammy, Best Contemporary/Pop Female Solo Vocal, *The Rose,* 1980; Grammy, Best Children's Recording, *In Harmony, A Sesame Street Record,* 1980; Grammy, Record of the Year, "Wind Beneath My Wings,"1989; Grammy, Song of the Year, "Wind Beneath My Wings," 1989; Grammy, Song of the Year, "From a Distance," 1990; Emmy, Best Individual Performance—Variety or Music Show, *The Tonight Show Starring Johnny Carson,* 1992; Emmy, Outstanding Special — Comedy, Variety, or Music, *Ol' Red Hair Is Back,* 1978; Emmy,

Best Individual Performance—Variety or Music Show, *Diva Las Vegas*, 1997; Tony, special award, 1974

ALYSSA MILANO

Birthplace: Brooklyn, NY
Birthdate: 12/19/72
Occupation: Actor
Education: High school dropout
Debut: (Stage) *Annie*, 1980; (Film) *Old Enough*, 1982; (TV) *Who's the Boss*, 1984
Signature: *Who's the Boss*
Facts: Began acting at age eight, as Molly in a national touring company production of *Annie*.

Made an exercise video, *Teen Steam*, and released three albums in Japan.

Says she is "obsessed with religious art" and has an impressive collection of Madonnas, cruicifixes, statues, and rosaries. Also collects Barbie and Madame Alexander dolls.

Her tatoos include an angel, a sacred heart, a garland of flowers, a fairy kneeling in grass, and rosary beads.
Infamy: Successfully sued multiple parties to get images of herself, including both real and fake nude photos, removed from the Internet, and contributed the settlements toward funding Web site www.safe-searching.com, which she developed with her mother to direct surfers to celebrity sites.
Marriage: Scott Wolf (engaged; never married); Cinjun Tate, singer and guitarist for rock band Remy Zero, 1999
Quote: "Every part I play, I change my hair."

JAY MOHR

Real Name: Jon Ferguson Mohr
Birthplace: Verona, NJ
Birthdate: 8/23/71
Occupation: Actor, comedian
Education: High school
Debut: (TV) MTV's *Lip Service*, 1991; (Film) *For Better or Worse*, 1995

Signature: *Jerry Maguire* (1996)
Facts: After graduating from high school in 1988, Mohr spent two years racking up 10 national comedy shows.

In 1993 he began a two-year stint on *Saturday Night Live*, known for his impersonations of Tony Bennett and Christopher Walken. Though well known for his time on the show, he complains about "All that waiting around for a glimmer of stage time, just getting angry every week…It was just an oppressive, horrible, horrible place to be. I went to work feeling nauseous."

The inside of his left arm is tatooed with "Will 12-27," in honor of his cousin who was killed by a drunk driver in 1995, two days after Christmas.
Wife: Nicole Chamberlain, model, actor, 1998
Quote: "Hey, I'm no nancy boy. I've got my bitchin' truck and my rottweiler. I'm a dude…But I still admit to my girlfriend when I'm wrong."

MONICA

Real Name: Monica Arnold
Birthplace: College Park, GA
Birthdate: 12/24/80
Occupation: Singer
Education: High school
Debut: (Single) "Don't Take It Personal," 1995; (Album) *Miss Thang*, 1995; (TV) *Living Single*
Signature: "The Boy Is Mine" (1998)
Facts: Began to sing publicly in church at age 2, and at 12 was discovered at a talent show.

At age 14 with her debut single became the youngest artist to top the Billboard charts. Her 1998 album, *The Boy Is Mine*, produced three consecutive No. 1 singles.

Had a 4.0 average at Atlanta County Day School.

Rapper Queen Latifah is her manager.
Major Award: Grammy, R&B Performance—Duo or Group with vocal,

"The Boy Is Mine" (with Brandy), 1998

DEMI MOORE

Real Name: Demetria Guynes
Birthplace: Roswell, NM
Birthdate: 11/11/62
Occupation: Actor
Education: Left high school to model in Europe, studied with Zina Provendie
Debut: (Film) *Choices*, 1981; (TV) *General Hospital*, 1981
Signature: *Ghost*, 1990
Facts: Was cross-eyed as a child and had an operation to correct it, wearing a patch over one eye.

Decided to become an actor in high school when she lived in the same building as Nastassja Kinski.

In order to play coke addict Jules in the 1985 movie *St. Elmo's Fire*, she had to sign a contract stipulating that she would stop her own alcohol and drug abuse, an agreement that caused her to turn her life around.

Was engaged to Emilio Estevez.

She and Bruce Willis were married by singer Little Richard.
Infamy: Posed nude and pregnant on the cover of *Vanity Fair*.
Original Job: Model
Marriages: Freddy Moore (divorced), Bruce Willis, 1987 (separated, 1998); Oliver Whitcomb (relationship)
Children: Rumer Glenn, 1988; Scout Larue, 1991; Tallulah Belle, 1994

ALANIS MORISSETTE

Birthplace: Ottawa, Canada
Birthdate: 6/1/74
Occupation: Singer, songwriter
Education: High school
Debut: (Album) *Alanis*, 1991
Signature: "You Oughta Know," 1995
Facts: At age 10, appeared as a sweet little girl on Nickelodeon's *You Can't Do That on Television*. At 17, was a Queen of Disco, dubbed the Canadian Debbie Gibson.

During her dance pop days, toured with Vanilla Ice.

Has a twin brother, Wade.

Claimed it took 15 to 45 minutes to write most of the songs on *Jagged Little Pill*.

Major Awards: Grammy, Album of the Year, *Jagged Little Pill*, 1995; Grammy, Best Rock Album, *Jagged Little Pill*, 1995; Grammy, Best Female Rock Vocalist, "You Oughta Know," 1995; Grammy, Best Rock Song, "You Oughta Know," 1995; Grammy, Best Long Form Music Video, *Jagged Little Pill Live*, 1997; Grammy, Best Rock Song, "Uninvited," 1998

TONI MORRISON

Real Name: Chloe Anthony Wofford
Birthplace: Lorain, OH
Birthdate: 2/18/31
Occupation: Author
Education: Howard University, Cornell University
Debut: (Book) *The Bluest Eye*, 1969
Signature: *Beloved*
Facts: Has served as an editor at Random House, helping to publish the works of other black Americans like Toni Cade Bambara, Angela Davis, and Muhammad Ali.

Has taught at Harvard, Yale, and Princeton.

Original Job: Textbook editor
Marriage: Harold Morrison, 1958 (divorced, 1964)
Children: Harold Ford, 1961; Slade Kevin, 1965
Major Awards: National Book Critics Circle Award, *Song of Solomon*, 1977; Pulitzer Prize, *Beloved*, 1988; Nobel Prize for Literature, 1993
Quote: "Although we women are coming into our own, we still love you men for what you are, just to let you know."

VAN MORRISON

Real Name: George Ivan Morrison
Birthplace: Belfast, Northern Ireland.
Birthdate: 8/31/45
Occupation: Singer, songwriter
Education: High school dropout
Debut: (Song) "Don't Start Crying" (with Them), 1964
Signature: "Brown Eyed Girl"
Facts: Was lead singer of Them from 1964 to 1967 and has worked solo ever since.

In 1965, wrote "Gloria," which achieved moderate success but didn't hit the U.S. top ten until it was covered by The Shadows of Knight in 1966.

Marriage: Janet Planet, 1968 (divorced, 1973)
Child: Shana, 1970
Major Award: Grammy, Best Pop Vocal Collaboration (with Sinead O'Connor and the Chieftains), "Have I Told You Lately That I Love You," 1995

EDDIE MURPHY

Birthplace: Hempstead, NY
Birthdate: 4/3/61
Occupation: Actor
Education: Nassau Community College
Debut: (TV) *Saturday Night Live*, 1980
Signature: *Beverly Hills Cop*, 1984
Facts: Father was a policeman who died when Eddie was 5.

Was voted most popular at Roosevelt Jr.-Sr. High School in Roosevelt, NY.

Created and produced the TV series *The Royal Family*, which was cut short upon the sudden death of the star Redd Foxx.

Co-created the controversial animated comedy *The PJ's* (complaints, from Spike Lee among others, arose about its racial depictions, though TV reviewers found it hilarious)and provides the voice of lead character Thurgood Stubbs

Co-owns the L.A. restaurant Georgia with Denzel Washington.
Infamy: In May 1997, police tracking a transvestite prostitute pulled Murphy's Toyota over at 4:45 a.m.; police arrested the prostitute and immediately released Murphy, who explained he was only giving the streetwalker a lift. In the aftermath Murphy sued the *National Enquirer* for publishing interviews with transvestite prostitutes claiming to have had sex with Murphy; the suit was eventually dropped.
Original Job: Shoe store clerk
Marriage: Nicole Mitchell, 1992
Children: Ashlee, 1987; Bria, 1989; (with Nicolle Rader). Eddie Jr., c.1989; (with Paulette McNeeley). Christian Edward, 1990 (with Tamara Hood). Miles Mitchell, 1992; Shayne Audra, 1994
Major Award: Grammy, Best Comedy Recording, *Eddie Murphy— Comedian*, 1983
Quote: "You get born only once in this business, but you can die over and over again. Then you make comebacks."

BILL MURRAY

Birthplace: Wilmette, IL
Birthdate: 9/21/50
Occupation: Actor, writer
Education: Loyola Academy, Regis College, Second City Workshop in Chicago
Debut: (TV) *Saturday Night Live*, 1977
Signature: *Ghostbusters*, 1984
Facts: Was a pre-med student at St. Regis College.

Provided the voice of Johnny Storm, the Human Torch, on Marvel Comics' radio show, *The Fantastic Four*. This is where he was heard by the producers of *Saturday Night Live*.

Bill's son, Homer Banks, is named after legendary Chicago Cub Ernie Banks.

In 1981, performed the song "The Best Thing (Love Song)" for John Waters' *Polyester*.
Original Job: Pizza maker

Marriage: Margaret Kelly (divorced, 1996)
Children: Homer, 1982; Luke, 1985
Famous Relative: Brian Doyle-Murray, actor, brother
Major Award: Emmy, Best Writing in a Comedy Series, *Saturday Night Live,* 1977

MIKE MYERS

Birthplace: Scarborough, Canada
Birthdate: 5/25/63
Occupation: Actor, writer
Education: High school
Debut: (TV) *Mullarkey & Myers,* 1984; (Film) *Elvis Stories,* 1989
Signature: Austin Powers
Facts: When he was a child, Myers's comedy-loving father would wake his three sons at night to watch *Monty Python.*

First appeared in TV commercials when he was 4, and at 8 he did a commercial with Gilda Radner. Also appeared as a kid on Canadian TV programs such as the dance show, *Boogie Junior.*

Modeled his *Saturday Night Live* character Linda "Coffee Talk" Richman on his mother-in-law.

Wrote the script for the original *Austin Powers* in three weeks.

Started a retro-mod band, Ming Tea.

Hobbies are watching old war footage and painting toy soldiers.
Marriage: Robin Ruzan, 1993
Major Awards: Emmy, Outstanding Writing in a Comedy Series, *Saturday Night Live,* 1989

LIAM NEESON

Birthplace: Ballymena, Northern Ireland
Birthdate: 6/7/52
Occupation: Actor
Debut: (Stage) *In the Risen,* 1976; (Film) *Excalibur,* 1981
Signature: *Schindler's List,* 1993
Facts: At age 9, joined a boxing team run by a priest. Nose was broken during an early match, and had it set on site by his manager. Quit boxing at age 17.

First starring role was the disfigured hero of the film *Darkman,* 1990.
Original Job: Forklift operator, architect's assistant, amateur boxer
Marriage: Natasha Richardson, 1994
Children: Micheál, 1995; Daniel Jack N., 1996
Quote: "You have these people in therapy 25 years because, what, their moms didn't cuddle them? I'm sorry. Get a f---in' life."

WILLIE NELSON

Birthplace: Abbott, TX
Birthdate: 4/30/33
Occupation: Singer, songwriter, guitarist, actor
Education: Baylor University
Debut: (Album) *...And Then I Wrote,* 1962; (Film) *The Electric Horseman,* 1979
Signature: "Mamas, Don't Let Your Babies Grow Up To Be Cowboys," 1978
Facts: Nelson taught at Baptist Sunday school until officials objected to him playing in seedy bars.

Sold his first song, "Family Bible," for $50 to feed his family; it became a huge hit, performed by more than 70 country artists.

Organized Farm Aid concerts to help midwestern farmers stricken by drought and threatened with foreclosure.

Began writing songs at age 7.
Infamy: In 1991, after a seven-year dispute with the IRS over $16.7 million in back taxes, the government seized most of Nelson's possessions (country club, recording studio, 44-acre ranch, 20 other properties in four states, instruments, recordings, and memorabilia).

Arrested in 1994 for possession of marijuana. Charges were later dismissed.
Original Job: Janitor, door-to-door salesman (Bibles, encyclopedias, vacuum cleaners, sewing machines), hosted country music shows on Texas radio stations
Marriages: Martha Matthews, 1952 (divorced, 1962); Shirley Collie, 1963 (divorced, 1971); Connie Koepke (divorced, 1989); Annie D'Angelo, 1991
Children: Lana, 1953; Susie, 1957; Billy, 1958 (deceased, 1991); (with Martha Matthews). Paula Carlene, 1969; Amy, 1973; (with Connie Koepke). Lukas Autry, 1988; Jacob Micah, 1990
Major Awards: Grammy, Best Country Vocal—Male, "Blue Eyes Cryin' in the Rain," 1975; Grammy, Best Country Vocal—Male, "Georgia on My Mind," 1978; Grammy, Best Country Performance—Duo or Group, "Mamas Don't Let Your Babies Grow Up To Be Cowboys" (with Waylon Jennings), 1978; Grammy, Best Country Song, "On the Road Again," 1980; Grammy, Best Country Vocal—Male, "Always on My Mind," 1982; Grammy, Best Country Song, "Always on My Mind," 1982; Grammy, Legend Award, 1990; inducted into the Country Music Hall of Fame in 1993

PAUL NEWMAN

Birthplace: Cleveland, OH
Birthdate: 1/26/25
Occupation: Actor, director, producer
Education: Kenyon College, Yale School of Drama, Actors Studio
Debut: (Film) *The Silver Chalice,* 1954

Signature: *The Hustler*, 1961
Facts: Briefly attended Ohio University and was allegedly asked to leave for crashing a beer keg into the president's car.

The Newman's Own food company he founded in 1987 with writer friend A.E. Hochner has donated more than $90 million to charity.

Has worked on more than nine movies with actor wife Joanne Woodward.

A die-hard, marching liberal, he invested in the leftist opinion-making magazine, *The Nation*.

Is a professional race car driver.
Marriages: Jacqueline Witte (divorced), Joanne Woodward, 1958
Children: Scott, 1950 (deceased); Susan, 1953; Stephanie, 1955; (with Jacqueline Witte). Elinor "Nell" Teresa, 1959; Melissa Steward, 1961; Claire Olivia, 1965
Major Awards: Oscar, Jean Hersholt Humanitarian Award, 1993; Oscar, Lifetime Achievement, 1985; Oscar, Best Actor, *The Color of Money*, 1986;

WAYNE NEWTON

Birthplace: Norfolk, VA
Birthdate: 4/3/42
Occupation: Entertainer
Education: High school dropout
Debut: (TV) *Jackie Gleason and His American Scene Magazine*, 1962; (Film) *80 Steps to Jonah*, 1969
Signature: "Danke Schoen"
Facts: Protégé of Jackie Gleason.

Partly Native American.

Earns $250,000 a week for his Las Vegas performances.
Infamy: In 1992, declared bankruptcy, listing debts of more than $20 million.

In 1994 his creditors again went to court, charging that, despite millions in current earnings, he continued spending lavishly on himself (including a reported $75,000 repairing his home pond for his pet penguins) and made little effort to pay what he owed them.
Marriages: Elaine Okamura

(divorced, 1985); Kathleen McCrone, 1994
Child: Erin, 1976 (with Elaine Okamura)

JACK NICHOLSON

Birthplace: Neptune, NJ
Birthdate: 4/22/37
Occupation: Actor, director, producer, screenwriter
Education: Studied with the Players Ring acting group
Debut: (Stage) *Tea and Sympathy*, 1957; (Film) *Cry-Baby Killer*, 1958
Signature: *One Flew Over the Cuckoo's Nest*, 1975
Facts: Recorded *The Elephant's Child*, a children's record, with Bobby McFerrin (1987).

Abandoned by his father in childhood, he was raised believing his grandmother was his mother and his real mother was his older sister. The truth was revealed to him years later when a *Time* magazine researcher uncovered the truth while preparing a story on the star.

Has been nominated 11 times for the Academy Award.
Infamy: Known for being a ladies' man, Nicholson had a 17-year relationship with actress Anjelica Huston that ended in 1990 when Nicholson revealed that actor Rebecca Broussard, his daughter's best friend, was carrying his child.

During a later two-year falling out period with Broussard, he dated a 20-year-old and allegedly fathered her baby girl.

Allegedly used a golf club to strike the windshield of a '69 Mercedes that had cut him off in traffic in 1994. The driver's civil suit was settled out of court.

Admitted the paternity of Caleb Goddard, an adult New York City producer and writer. The public acknowledgment arose out of a messy civil battle between Nicholson and Goddard's mother, actress Susan Anspach.

Original Job: Office boy in MGM's cartoon department
Marriage: Sandra Knight, 1961 (divorced, 1966); Lara Flynn Boyle (relationship)
Children: Jennifer Norfleet, c.1964 (with Sandra Knight). Caleb Goddard, 1970 (with Susan Anspach). Lorraine, 1990; Raymond, 1992 (with Rebecca Broussard)
Major Awards: Oscar, Best Actor, *One Flew over the Cuckoo's Nest*, 1975; Oscar, Best Supporting Actor, *Terms of Endearment*, 1983; Grammy, Best Recording for Children, *The Elephant's Child*, 1987; Oscar, Best Actor, *As Good As It Gets*, 1997
Quote: "More good times—that's my motto."

LESLIE NIELSEN

Real Name: Leslie Nielsen
Birthplace: Regina, Saskatchewan
Birthdate: 2/11/26
Occupation: Actor
Education: Lorne Greene's Academy of Radio Arts, Toronto
Debut: (TV) *Studio One's Battleship Bismarck*, 1950; (Film) *The Vagabond King*, 1956
Signature: *The Naked Gun*
Facts: Spent his childhood 100 miles from the Arctic Circle.

Father was a Royal Canadian Mountie.

A prolific actor, he appeared on countless television programs—over 45 live dramas in 1950 alone, and over 1,500 shows to date—including everything from *Playhouse 90, Wagon Train, Dr. Kildare*, and *Bonanza* to *M*A*S*H* and *The Love Boat*.

Comedic career was launched with *Airplane!*

Author of *The Naked Truth* (1993) and *Bad Golf My Way*, 1996.
Original Job: Royal Canadian Air Force; D.J. and radio announcer
Marriages: Monica Boyer, singer (1950; divorced 1955); Alisand "Sandy" Ullman (1958; divorced, 1974); Brooks Nielsen (divorced, 1982); Barbaree Earl (relationship,

since 1981)
Children: Thea, 1961; Maura, 1963 (with Ullman)
Famous Relative: Jean Hersholt, character actor, uncle.
Quote: "At this stage of my life, I don't give a damn. If they want to type me, let 'em. I just want to maintain whatever celebrity status I have, so they'll keep inviting me to golf tournaments."

NICK NOLTE

Real Name: Nicholas King Nolte
Birthplace: Omaha, NE
Birthdate: 2/8/41
Occupation: Actor, producer
Debut: (TV) *The Framing of Billy the Kid*, 1973; (Film) *Return to Macon County*, 1975
Signature: *Prince of Tides*, 1991
Facts: Did runway and print modeling and appeared on Clairol box for many years.

Was 35 before gaining attention for his role in *Rich Man, Poor Man.*

Known to show up in public wearing pajama bottoms.

Has openly admitted lying to the press to create a persona. He has lied about his educational background, claiming that he won football scholarships to several different universities, and once told a reporter, as a lark, that his ex-wife had been a high-wire circus performer.
Infamy: Convicted in 1962 for selling fake draft cards.

Was sued for palimony by longtime companion Karen Louise Eklund; suit was settled out of court.
Original Jobs: Model, ironworker
Marriages: Sheila Page (divorced 1971); Sharon Haddad (divorced 1983); Rebecca Linger (divorced 1991); Vicki Lewis (relationship)
Children: Brawley King, 1986 (with Linger)
Quote: "Early on I decided that I was going to lie to the press. The best approach to talking about my personal life was to lie."

EDWARD NORTON

Birthplace: Columbia, MD
Birthdate: 8/18/69
Occupation: Actor
Education: Yale University
Debut: (Film) *Primal Fear*, 1996
Signature: *Primal Fear*
Facts: When Leonardo DiCaprio dropped out of *Primal Fear,* Paramount launched an international search of 2,100 actors with no success. Costar Richard Gere was ready to walk from the project until Norton read for the part.

Grandfather James Rouse designed Boston's Faneuil Hall and New York's South Street Seaport. Father Ed Sr., a lawyer, was a federal prosecutor under Jimmy Carter.

Studied astronomy and Japanese (he's fluent) in college before getting a degree in history.
Original Job: Proofreader, waiter, low-income housing worker
Famous Relative: James Rouse, architect, grandfather

CONAN O'BRIEN

Birthplace: Brookline, MA
Birthdate: 4/18/63
Occupation: Talk show host
Education: Harvard University
Debut: (TV) *Not Necessarily the News,* 1985
Signature: *NBC's Late Night with Conan O'Brien*
Facts: Has written for *Saturday Night Live* and *The Simpsons.*

While at Harvard, served as president of *The Harvard Lampoon* for two years, the first person to do so since Robert Benchley in 1912.

First TV producing credit was *Lookwell* (1991), a sitcom pilot starring Adam West as a former TV detective who becomes a real cop.

Once dated Lisa Kudrow, who he met while performing with the Groundlings.
Relationship: Lynn Kaplan
Major Award: Emmy, Best Writing in a

Variety or Music Program, *Saturday Night Live,* 1989
Quote: "The nightmare is that you spend the rest of your life being funny at parties and people say, 'Why didn't you do *that* when you were on television?' "

CHRIS O'DONNELL

Birthplace: Chicago, IL
Birthdate: 6/26/70
Occupation: Actor
Education: Boston College, UCLA
Debut: (TV) *Jack and Mike,* 1986; (Film) *Men Don't Leave,* 1990
Signature: *Scent of a Woman,* 1992
Facts: Youngest of seven children (four sisters and two brothers), grew up in Winnetka, IL.

Began modeling and appearing in commercials in 1983, at age 13. Appeared in a McDonald's commercial opposite Michael Jordan.

Was 17 when he auditioned for *Men Don't Leave.* His mother had to promise him a new car to get him to try out. He is still waiting for that car.

Originally cast as Barbra Streisand's son in *Prince of Tides,* but she decided to have her real-life son play the role instead.

Took time off from pursuing a degree in marketing from Boston College in order to work with Al Pacino on *Scent of a Woman.*
Marriage: Caroline Fentress, 1997
Child: Lily Anne, 1999

ROSIE O'DONNELL

Birthplace: Commack, NY
Birthdate: 3/21/62
Occupation: Actor, comedian
Education: Dickinson College and Boston University
Debut: (TV) *Gimme a Break,* 1986; (Film) *A League of Their Own,* 1992; (Stage) *Grease,* 1994
Signature: *The Rosie O'Donnell Show*
Facts: Won the *Star Search* comedy competition five times.

Fascinated with the blue-collar mundane, she began extensively collecting McDonald's Happy Meal figurines.

Against her agent's advice, she auditioned for—and won—the role of Betty Rizzo in the Broadway revival of *Grease* in 1994. She had no theater experience and says she'd never sung in public before.

In a 1999 interview with Tom Selleck, who once filmed a commercial for the NRA, she began a heated debate about gun control. Selleck finally declared, "I didn't come on your show to have a debate, I came on your show to plug a movie."

Children: Parker Jaren, 1995; Chelsea Belle, 1997; (both adopted).

Major Awards: Emmy, Best Host—Talk or Service Show, *The Rosie O'Donnell Show*, 1995–96; Emmy, Best Host—Talk or Service Show, *The Rosie O'Donnell Show*, 1996–97; Emmy, Best Host—Talk or Service Show, *The Rosie O'Donnell Show*, 1997–98; 1998–99

ASHLEY OLSEN

Birthdate: 6/13/86
Occupation: Actor
Debut: (TV) *Full House*, 1987
Facts: Two minutes older than fraternal twin sister Mary-Kate and has a freckle under her nose.

Their mother says, "When they need someone to be more active or emotional, they let Ashley do it."

How is she different from her twin? "My voice is deeper."

Famous Relative: Jamie Olsen, former dancer with the Los Angeles Ballet, mother

MARY-KATE OLSEN

Birthdate: 6/13/86
Occupation: Actor
Debut: (TV) *Full House*, 1987
Facts: Wants to be a candymaker or a cowgirl when she grows up.

Both twins earned income not only from the show but also through sale of the talking Michelle doll.

"Mary-Kate is more serious, so she

gets the serious lines to do," says her mother.

Famous Relative: Jamie Olsen, former dancer with the Los Angeles Ballet, mother

SHAQUILLE O'NEAL

Birthplace: Newark, NJ
Birthdate: 3/6/72
Occupation: Basketball player
Education: Louisiana State University
Facts: His rap album, *Shaq Diesel*, sold more than one million copies. Got his rap start by singing on "What's Up Doc," a song put out in 1993 by his favorite rap group, FU-Schnickens.

He stands seven feet one inch, weighs 303 pounds, and wears size 21 triple-E shoes.

His first name translates, ironically, to "little one."

Spent most of his adolescence in Germany, where his stepfather was an army sergeant.

Major Awards: NBA Rookie of the Year, 1993; 4 Time NBA All-Star; Winner of NBA Scoring Title 1995; Gold Medal at 1996 Olympics
Relationship: Arnetta (engaged)
Children: Taheara, 1996

SUZE ORMAN

Real Name: Suzie Orman
Birthdate: 6/5/51
Occupation: Author, financial guru
Education: University of Illinois at Urbana-Champaign
Signature: *Nine Steps to Financial Freedom* (1997)
Facts: As a child, her parents lost their boardinghouse in a liability suit, and 10 years later her father's deli burned down. He suffered third-degree burns on his arms after he ran inside to save the cash register. She claims that incident taught her that money is "more important than life."

During college, she roomed with John Belushi and his wife, Judy. "I told Judy he'd never amount to any-

thing. Shows you what I know about picking husbands."

Her degree is in social work.

After college, she waitressed at the Buttercup Bakery in Berkeley, Califonia, for seven years before talking her way into a stockbroker's job at Merrill Lynch. One of the first female brokers in northern California, she sought out unusual clients, like truck drivers and waitresses, and consulted a crystal on investment decisions.

In 1987 opened her own investment/financial advisory firm, which failed in six months because of an employee dispute over commissions, which was finally settled in court.

Receives up to $20,000 for lecture appearances. Is the most successful personality ever on PBS pledge drives.

She lives alone in the same one-bedroom, one-story home she bought 23 years ago, and drives a 1987 BMW.

Quote: "I don't care that I don't look like a hotshot and my English isn't always proper. People can relate to that. I've helped people realize their dreams."

OZZY OSBOURNE

Real Name: John Michael Osbourne
Birthplace: Birmingham, England
Birthdate: 12/3/48
Occupation: Singer
Debut: (Album) *Black Sabbath*, 1969; (Solo album) *Blizzard of Oz*, 1980
Signature: Godfather of heavy metal
Facts: Was the vocalist with Black Sabbath until he was kicked out of the band in 1979.

The original band members reunited in 1997 for a series of concerts in Birmingham and to record an album.

Gave a facelift to his favorite bulldog Baldrick, whose face wrinkles produced sores.

Collects art, particularly Victorian nudes.

A member of the Church of England, he kneels to pray backstage before performances.

Has 15 tattoos.

Infamy: He spent years on various drugs, was often in a clinic to kick his addictions. Doctors determined he has a chemical imbalance resulting from years of alcohol and drugs, and he has been drug- and alcohol-free since 1991.

In 1982 he bit off the head of a live bat, thinking it was made of rubber, but when it bit him back and lashed his face with its wings, he rushed for a rabies shot.

Bit the head off a white dove in front of American businessmen.

Shot his ex-wife's 17 cats.

Was arrested in San Antonio for urinating on the Alamo (he was drunk and wearing a dress).

In 1989 he was charged with attempted manslaughter after allegedly trying to strangle his wife, Sharon, but she later dropped the charges.

In the mid-'80s, he was taken to court by parents who accused him of recording subliminal messages urging teens to commit suicide.

Original Jobs: Car-horn assembly-line worker; slaughterhouse worker
Marriage: Thelma (divorced 1981); Sharon Arden, 1982
Children: Elliott, c. 1966; Jessica, c. 1972; Louis, c. 1975 (with Thelma; Elliott was her son from a previous relationship but took Osbourne's name). Aimee, 1983; Kelly, c. 1984; Jack, c. 1985.
Major Award: Grammy, Best Heavy Metal Performance, "I Don't Want to Change the World," 1994
Quote: "I used to be an alcoholic drug addict, now I'm a workaholic. I've gotta keep moving all the time."

AL PACINO

Real Name: Alfredo James Pacino
Birthplace: New York, NY
Birthdate: 4/25/40
Occupation: Actor
Education: High School of the Performing Arts, Actor's Studio

Debut: (Stage) *The Peace Creeps*, 1966; (Film) *Me, Natalie*, 1969
Signature: *The Godfather*, 1972
Fact: Has been involved with actresses Jill Clayburgh, Marthe Keller, and Diane Keaton.
Original Job: Mail deliverer at *Commentary* magazine, messenger, movie theater usher, building superintendent
Relationship: Beverly D'Angelo
Child: Julie Marie, 1989 (with Jan Tarrant)
Major Awards: Tony, Best Supporting Actor (Dramatic), *Does a Tiger Wear a Necktie?*, 1969; Tony, Best Actor (Dramatic), *The Basic Training of Pavlo Hummel*, 1977; Oscar, Best Actor, *Scent of a Woman*, 1992

SE RI PAK

Birthplace: Taejon, South Korea
Birthdate: 9/28/77
Occupation: Golfer
Education: Student at David Leadbetter Golf Academy
Facts: Was avid track athlete before turning to golf at age 14.

Her father, who admits to being a thug in his past, occasionally left her alone in a dark cemetery to develop her courage.

At 20, was the youngest winner of a major women's golf tournament in 30 years.
Major Awards: Winner, U.S. Women's Open, 1998; Winner, McDonald's LPGA Championship, 1998

GWYNETH PALTROW

Birthplace: Los Angeles, CA
Birthdate: 9/27/72
Occupation: Actor
Education: University of California, Santa Barbara
Debut: (Film) *Shout*, 1991
Signature: *Shakespeare in Love*, 1998
Facts: Nude pictures of her and former beau Brad Pitt that were taken with a telephoto lens while the couple vacationed in privacy in St.

Bart's were circulated on the Internet and published in the tabloids. Pitt filed suit against the photographer. The couple split in 1997 after more than two years together.

Says a major goal for her life is to have babies.
Relationship: Lee Eastman
Famous Relatives: Blythe Danner, actor, mother; Bruce Paltrow, producer, father; Jake Paltrow, actor, director, brother; Hillary Danner, actor, cousin
Major Award: Academy Award, Best Actress, *Shakespeare In Love*, 1998
Quote: "I'm so sick of myself, my boring voice and my stupid sound bites."

SARAH JESSICA PARKER

Birthplace: Nelsonville, OH
Birthdate: 3/25/65
Occupation: Actor
Education: American Ballet Theater, Professional Children's School in New York
Debut: (TV) *The Little Match Girl*, 1973; (Stage) *The Innocents*, 1976
Signature: *Sex in the City*
Facts: Sang in Metropolitan Opera productions of *Hansel and Gretel*, *Cavalleria Rusticana*, *Pagliacci*, and *Parade*.

Starred as nerdy Patty Green on the CBS TV sitcom *Square Pegs*, 1982–83.

Played Annie in the Broadway musical, 1979–80.

Lived with Robert Downey Jr. for seven years.

Wears a size two.
Original Job: Dancer with Cincinnati Ballet and the American Ballet Theatre
Marriage: Matthew Broderick, 1997

DOLLY PARTON

Birthplace: Sevierville, TN
Birthdate: 1/19/46
Occupation: Singer, songwriter
Education: High school

Debut: (Song) "Puppy Love," 1956
Signature: "9 to 5," 1981
Facts: Met her husband in the Wishy Washy laundromat.

Has her own theme park, Dollywood, located in Gatlinburg at the edge of the Smoky Mountains. In her hometown of Sevierville, Tennessee, there is a statue of her on the Sevier County Courthouse lawn.
Marriage: Carl Dean, 1966
Major Awards: Grammy, Best Country Vocal—Female, *Here You Come Again*, 1978; Grammy, Best Country Vocal—Female, "9 to 5," 1981; Grammy, Best Country Performance—Duo or Group, *Trio* (with Linda Rondstadt and Emmylou Harris), 1987
Quote: "Left to my own, I'd rather look like trash. I love tacky clothes. My look came from a very serious honest place, and that was a country girl's idea of what glamour was."

JANE PAULEY

Real Name: Margaret Jane Pauley
Birthplace: Indianapolis, IN
Birthdate: 10/31/50
Occupation: Broadcast journalist
Education: Indiana University
Debut: (TV) WISH-TV, Indiana, 1972
Signature: *Dateline NBC*
Facts: Succeeded Barbara Walters on the *Today* show two weeks shy of her 26th birthday in 1976; left 13 years later in a controversy over Deborah Norville's role that generated enormous sympathy for Pauley.

Limits her children's TV viewing to one hour a day.
Marriage: Garry Trudeau, 1980
Children: Richard Ross,1983; Rachel Grandison, 1983; Thomas Moore, 1986
Major Awards: 3 News and Documentary Emmys: 2 as correspondent, 1 as writer

LUCIANO PAVAROTTI

Birthplace: Modena, Italy
Birthdate: 10/12/35
Occupation: Singer

Education: Istituto Magistrale Carlo Sigonio
Debut: (Stage) *La Bohème*, 1961
Facts: Established Opera Company of Philadelphia/ Luciano Pavarotti Vocal Company, 1980.

Makes at least $100,000 per concert. His fortune is estimated to be between $25 and $50 million.

Dreads the anticipation of singing more than singing itself. "The 10 minutes before the performance you wouldn't wish on your worst enemies."

Half a billion people saw the televised "Three Tenors" concert (with Placido Domingo and José Carreras) in 1990.

In 1990, the only musicians who sold more recordings than Pavarotti were Madonna and Elton John.
Infamy: He was sued by the BBC when it found out that a 1992 Pavarotti concert it had bought for broadcast had really been lip-synched.

An ongoing affair with his 26-year old secretary, Nicoletta Mantovani, led to his separation.
Original Job: Elementary school teacher, salesman
Marriage: Adua Veroni (separated, 1996); Nicoletta Mantovani (relationship)
Children: Lorenza, Cristina, Giuliana
Major Awards: Grammy, Best Classical Vocal Performance, *Luciano Pavarotti—Hits from London Center*, 1978; Grammy, Best Classical Vocal Performance, *O Sole Mio (Favorite Neapolitan Songs)*, 1979; Grammy, Best Classical Vocal Performance, *Live from Lincoln Center—Sutherland—Horne—Pavarotti* (with Joan Sutherland and Marilyn Horne), 1981; Grammy, Best Classical Vocal Performance, *Luciano Pavarotti in Concert*, 1988; Grammy, Best Classical Vocal Performance, *Carreras, Domingo, Pavarotti in Concert* (with José Carreras and Placido Domingo), 1990

BILL PAXTON

Birthplace: Ft. Worth, TX
Birthdate: 5/17/55
Occupation: Actor
Education: New York University
Debut: (Film) *Mortuary*, 1981
Signature: *Twister*, 1996
Facts: Spent much of his career making B-grade movies like *Pass the Ammo* and *Brain Dead*.

For his *Mortuary* character's wardrobe, Paxton bought secondhand sweaters, from which he caught scabies.

Directed *Fishheads*, a cult music video that aired on MTV in the early 1980s.

Has had several long bouts of depression that sometimes took months to shake.

Wife is 10 years younger than he is. They met when he followed her onto a bus.
Original Job: Set dresser
Marriages: First wife (divorced), Louise Newbury, 1985
Children: James, 1994; Lydia, 1997

ROBIN WRIGHT PENN

Real Name: Robin Wright
Birthplace: Dallas, TX
Birthdate: 4/8/66
Occupation: Actor
Education: High school
Debut: (TV) *The Yellow Rose*, 1984; (Film) *Hollywood Vice Squad*, 1986
Signature: *Forrest Gump*, 1994
Facts: Began modeling after a talent scout spotted her roller-skating.

She was waiting tables in Hawaii when she found out that she had won the role of Kelly on NBC soap opera *Santa Barbara*; received two daytime Emmy nominations for her work on the show.

Met future husband, Sean Penn, at a coffee shop where he bummed a cigarette off of her. He was married to Madonna at the time.

Paired with Sean in 1990's *State of Grace*, directed by him in 1995 in

The Crossing Guard, then costarred with him again in *She's So Lovely,* 1997.

Was the victim of a carjacking in front of her home in 1996.

On Oscar night, 1996, she needed emergency gall bladder surgery and Sean skipped the ceremony to be with her.

Son, Hopper Jack, is named after Dennis Hopper and Jack Nicholson.

Original Job: Model
Marriage: Dane Witherspoon (divorced); Sean Penn, 1996
Children: Dylan Frances, 1991; Hopper Jack, 1993
Quote: "I don't want my daughter to think she should go to the front of the line just because her daddy is Sean Penn. I want us to wait like everybody else."

SEAN PENN

Birthplace: Burbank, CA
Birthdate: 8/17/60
Occupation: Actor, director, writer
Education: High school
Debut: (Film) *Taps,* 1981
Signature: *Dead Man Walking,* 1995
Facts: His lavish house burned to the ground in the 1993 Malibu brushfires. Rather than rebuilding, he put a 27 1/ foot trailer on the land and moved in there.

Wears a tattoo saying "NOLA deliver me!," a reference to a frightening night spent in New Orleans (the NOLA) after drinking a glass of water spiked with seven hits of acid.

While growing up, his director father was blacklisted as a Communist, and had trouble getting work for years.

Infamy: Punched several photographers attempting to take his picture, and allegedly fired a gun at a hovering helicopter covering his first wedding. Spent 34 days in jail in 1987 for smacking a film extra while on probation for hitting someone who tried to kiss then wife Madonna.

Was so volatile during his marriage to Madonna she called a

SWAT team to help her retrieve her possessions. Now says he "was drunk all the time" during their marriage.

Marriages: Elizabeth McGovern (engaged, never married); Madonna, 1985 (divorced,1989); Robin Wright, 1996
Children: Dylan Frances, 1991; Hopper Jack, 1993
Famous Relatives: Leo Penn, director, father; Eileen Ryan, actor, mother; Christopher Penn, actor, brother
Quote: "I'm not an alcoholic. I'm just a big drinker, and there's a difference."

MATTHEW PERRY

Birthplace: Williamstown, MA
Birthdate: 8/19/69
Occupation: Actor, writer
Education: High school
Debut: (Film) *A Night in the Life of Jimmy Reardon,* 1988
Signature: *Friends*
Facts: His father is best known for Old Spice commercials.

Moved to his mother's native Ottawa after his parents split when he was a year old. His journalist mother became press aide to Canadian Prime Minister Pierre Trudeau.

An avid tennis player, at 13 was ranked the No. 2 junior player in Ottawa.

Frustrated by the lack of good parts, he and a friend wrote a sitcom about six twentysomethings, which interested NBC. When the network ultimately decided to go with a similar sitcom, *Friends,* Perry decided since he couldn't beat 'em, he'd join 'em.

Infamy: Checked into rehab to overcome addiction to prescription painkillers.
Famous Relative: John Bennett Perry, actor, father

JOE PESCI

Birthplace: Newark, NJ
Birthdate: 2/9/43
Occupation: Actor
Education: High school dropout
Debut: (Radio) *Star Kids,* 1947; (Film) *Hey, Let's Twist!,* 1961
Signature: *My Cousin Vinny,* 1992
Facts: Played guitar for Joey Dee and The Starliters.

At age 5 appeared in Broadway musicals and Eddie Dowling plays. At age 10 became a regular on TV's *Star Time Kids* doing impersonations and singing.

Was managing a restaurant in the Bronx when called by Robert De Niro and Martin Scorsese to play Jake LaMotta's brother in *Raging Bull,* 1978.

He appears in some of his films under the psuedonym Joe Ritchie.
Original Job: Has worked as a nightclub singer, stand-up comedian, barber, postal worker, delivery boy, produce manager, answering service worker, and restaurant manager
Marriages: Two prior marriages; Martha Haro, 1988 (divorced, 1991).
Child: Tiffany, 1966
Major Award: Oscar, Best Supporting Actor, *GoodFellas,* 1990

BERNADETTE PETERS

Real Name: Bernadette Lazzara
Birthplace: Ozone Park, Queens, NY
Birthdate: 2/28/48
Occupation: Actress, comedian, singer, dancer
Education: Quintano's School for Young Professionals, New York City
Debut: (TV) *Juvenile Jury,* 1951; (Stage) *Most Happy Fella,* 1959; (Broadway) *Johnny No Trump,* 1967; (Film) *Ace Eli and Rodger of the Skies,* 1973

Signature: *Sunday in the Park with George*
Facts: At age 3 appeared on a TV game show; two years later, won $800 on *Name That Tune.*

At 9, joined Actors' Equity, and when she was 10, she changed her name (after her father's first name); by 15 she was in a national tour of *Gypsy.*

Her Broadway debut closed after one performance.

First attained success in *Dames at Sea,* a 1967 Off-Broadway spoof.

In 1999, after a five-year absence from the theater, she returned to the stage to star in a remake of the 1946 Irving Berlin classic *Annie Get Your Gun.*

Marriage: Michael Wittenberg, 1997
Major Awards: Tony Award, *Song and Dance,* 1985
Quotes: "I've done it all—everything but circus acrobatics."

TOM PETTY

Birthplace: Gainesville, FL
Birthdate: 10/20/50
Occupation: Singer, songwriter, guitarist
Education: High school dropout
Debut: *Tom Petty and the Heartbreakers,* 1977
Signature: "Free Fallin' "
Facts: Toured for two years as Bob Dylan's backing band.

Recorded two albums with The Traveling Wilburys, comprised of George Harrison, Bob Dylan, Roy Orbison, Jeff Lynne, and Petty.
Marriage: Jane (divorced, 1996)
Children: Adria, Anna Kim

MICHELLE PFEIFFER

Birthplace: Santa Ana, CA
Birthdate: 4/29/58
Occupation: Actor
Education: Golden West College and Whitley College for Court Reporting
Debut: (TV) *Delta House,* 1979; (Film) *The Hollywood Knights,* 1980
Signature: *The Fabulous Baker Boys,* 1989
Facts: Had one line on TV show *Fantasy Island.*

Got her first break by winning the Miss Orange County Beauty Pageant.

In 1993, she decided to be a single mother and adopted a baby girl, who was given the last name Kelley after Pfeiffer married.

Had the leading role in *Grease 2,* 1982.
Original Job: Supermarket cashier, court reporter, model
Marriages: Peter Horton (divorced); David E. Kelley, 1993
Children: Claudia Rose, 1993 (adopted); John Henry, 1994
Famous Relatives: DeDee Pfeiffer, actor, sister

REGIS PHILBIN

Birthplace: New York, NY
Birthdate: 8/25/31
Occupation: Talk show host
Education: University of Notre Dame
Debut: (TV) KOGO news anchor, San Diego, 1960
Signature: *Live With Regis and Kathie Lee*
Facts: Named after Regis High, a Manhattan Catholic boys' school and his father's alma mater.

Son Dan was born with two malformed legs, which were later amputated.

Between 1970 and 1990, hosted nearly a dozen talk and game shows and went through a series of co-hosts before clicking with Kathie Lee.

In 1999, hosted the top-rated quiz show, *Who Wants to Be a Millionaire?*
Marriages: Kay Faylan, 1955 (divorced,1968); Joy Senese, 1970
Children: Amy, 1958; Dan, 1965; (with Kay Faylan). Joanna, 1973; Jennifer, 1974
Quote: "I've worked with Kathie Lee for 15 years. That builds stamina and endurance. A lesser man would be in his grave by now."

RYAN PHILLIPPE

Birthplace: Iowa
Birthdate: 9/10/74
Occupation: Actor
Education: High school
Debut: (TV) *One Life to Live,* 1992;

(Film) *Crimson Tide,* 1995
Signature: *54,* 1998
Facts: Was getting a haircut when a stranger approached him and suggested that he consider an acting career. The man gave him the name of an agent whom Phillippe met and signed with shortly afterward. He had no acting experience at the time.

Played first openly gay male on daytime TV in *One Life to Live.*
Marriage: Reese Witherspoon, 1999
Child: daughter, 1999

JOAQUIN PHOENIX

Real Name: Joaquin Rafael Bottom
Birthplace: Puerto Rico
Birthdate: 10/28/74
Occupation: Actor
Education: Dropped out of ninth grade; home-schooled
Signature: *To Die For* (1995)
Debut: (TV musical) *Seven Brides for Seven Brothers,* (with brother River) 1982; (Film) *Space Camp,* 1986
Facts: The son of missionaries for the Children of God, he traveled throughout Puerto Rico, Mexico, South America, Venezuela, and, returning to the U.S., lived in Florida. When siblings Rainbow and River won talent contests, the family moved to Los Angeles.

Changed his name to Leaf around age 6 or 7; changed it back to Joaquin as a teenager.

Has been a strict vegan since he was 3. (He turned down a part as a bullfighter.)

Drives a yellow '72 Pontiac LeMans.

Was in a relationship with Liv Tyler.
Infamy: Made the 911 call as his brother River suffered a drug overdose on Sunset Strip.
Original Job: Model
Famous Relatives: River Phoenix, a.k.a. River Jude Bottom, who died of a drug overdose in 1993, actor, brother; Rain Joan of Arc Phoenix, a.k.a. Rainbow Phoenix, actor, sister; Liberty Butterfly Phonex, former

actor, sister; Summer Joy Phoenix, actor, sister

Quote: "The reason why I keep making movies—which is the reason why I keep doing interviews—is because I hate the last thing that I did. I'm always trying to rectify my wrongs."

DAVID HYDE PIERCE

Birthplace: Saratoga Springs, NY
Birthdate: 4/3/59
Occupation: Actor
Education: Yale University
Debut: (Stage) *Beyond Therapy,* 1982; (Film) *The Terminator,* 1984; (TV) *Powers That Be,* 1991
Signature: *Frasier*
Facts: Realized he had a strong resemblance to his TV brother Frasier (Kelsey Grammer) after being mistaken for Grammer many times before he even accepted the role. In the original storyline for *Frasier,* Pierce's character (Niles) didn't exist but was added after producers, who saw Pierce in *The Powers That Be,* noticed the resemblance.
Original Job: Clothing salesman, church organist
Major Award: Emmy, Best Supporting Actor in a Comedy Series, *Frasier,* 1995, 1998, 1999

BRAD PITT

Real Name: William Bradley Pitt
Birthplace: Shawnee, OK
Birthdate: 12/18/63
Occupation: Actor
Education: University of Missouri at Columbia, studied acting with Roy London
Debut: (TV) *Dallas;* (Film) *Cutting Class,* 1989
Signature: *Legends of the Fall,* 1994
Facts: Got his big break when he was seen in a sexy Levi's TV ad in 1989. Was cast as the hitchhiker in the 1991 movie *Thelma and Louise* only after William Baldwin turned down the role, choosing to star in *Backdraft* instead.

Dated Robin Givens for six months when they both acted in the TV series *Head of the Class.* Also lived with Juliette Lewis for several years; was engaged to Gwyneth Paltrow.

While at college, posed shirtless for a campus fundraising calendar.

His earliest movie work was filmed in Yugoslavia and lost during its civil war; eight years later, in 1996, the producer finally found all the scattered footage.

Infamy: Aspiring actress Athena Marie Rolando, 19, broke into his home in 1999. A three-year restraining order bars any communication with Pitt and requires that she stay at least 100 yards away from him.
Relationship: Jennifer Aniston
Original Job: Chauffeur for Strip-O-Gram women, dressed up as the El Pollo Loco restaurant chicken
Quote: "Being a sex symbol all the time hampers my work."

NATALIE PORTMAN

Real Name: Unreleased; real family name has been kept from the press
Birthplace: Jerusalem, Israel
Birthdate: 6/9/81
Occupation: Actor, model
Education: High school
Debut: (Film) *The Professional,* 1994; (Broadway) *The Diary of Anne Frank,* 1997
Signature: *Star Wars: Episode I— The Phantom Menace* (1999)
Facts: After spending her first four years in Israel, she and her parents moved to the U.S., eventually settling on Long Island.

Was discovered by a Revlon scout in a pizza parlor in 1991.

Her first professional acting job was as an understudy in the Off-Broadway show *Ruthless.*

Turned down the title role in the *Lolita* remake, heeding her father's advice to do on screen only what she had experienced in real life.

A high school honor student, she is fluent in Hebrew and has studied

French and Japanese.

Calls acting her "extra-curricular activity."

Role models include the late AIDS activist Elisabeth Glaser and the late prime minister of Israel Yitzhak Rabin. Favorite actor is Ben Kingsley.

Her last name has been kept from the press to protect the privacy of her and her family.

Is committed to play Queen Amidala in Episodes II and III of *Star Wars.*
Relationship: Lukas Haas, actor
Quote: "I'm going to college. I don't care if it ruins my career. I'd rather be smart than a movie star."

PARKER POSEY

Birthplace: Baltimore, MD
Birthdate: 11/8/68
Occupation: Actor
Education: Attended North Carolina School for the Arts and State University of New York, Purchase
Debut: (Film) *Dazed and Confused,* 1993
Signature: *House of Yes*
Facts: Was named after the super-model Suzy Parker.

Roomed with *ER*'s Sherry Stringfield while at SUNY. Left school three weeks short of graduation to appear on *As the World Turns.*

Appeared in more than 20 films, the vast majority independents, in a five-year period.

Has a twin brother.

LISA MARIE PRESLEY

Birthplace: Memphis,TN
Birthdate: 2/1/68
Facts: Daughter of Elvis and Priscilla Presley

Inherited an estate of upwards of $150 million from her father.

When Lisa Marie once said she had never seen snow, Elvis flew her to Utah. She also received a tiny mink coat from her father and $100 bills from the Tooth Fairy.

Is a devoted follower of the Church of Scientology.

Marriages: Danny Keough (divorced); Michael Jackson (divorced, 1996); John Oszajza, musician, relationship

Children: Danielle, 1989; Benjamin, 1992

FREDDIE PRINZE JR.

Birthplace: Los Angeles, CA
Birthdate: 3/8/76
Occupation: Actor
Education: High school
Debut: (TV) *Family Matters*, 1994; (Film) *To Gillian on Her 37th Birthday*, 1996
Signature: *She's All That* (1999)
Facts: His father committed suicide when Freddie was 10 months old (his father nicknamed him "Pie").

His mother is of English, Irish, and Native American descent.

Relationship: Kimberly McCullough, actor (1996)

Famous Relative: Freddie Prinze, comedian, actor (*Chico and the Man*), father; high on prescription drugs and despondent over divorce from his wife, he committed suicide in 1977.

Quote: "I know one day I'm going to be the best father in the world. Me not having a father makes me want to be a great one. I have so much love I wanted to give him, and I'll be damned if I don't give it to a child of mine."

DENNIS QUAID

Birthplace: Houston, TX
Birthdate: 4/9/54
Occupation: Actor
Education: University of Houston
Debut: (Film) *September 30, 1955*, 1978
Signature: *The Big Easy*, (1987)
Fact: Wrote songs for three of his films: *The Night the Lights Went Out in Georgia* in 1981, *Tough Enough* in 1983, and *The Big Easy* in 1987.

Shed 47 pounds over a three-month period before playing the scrawny Doc Holliday in 1994's *Wyatt Earp*.

Infamy: Admitted to having a cocaine addiction, a problem he overcame with help from then girlfriend Meg Ryan.

Marriages: Pamela Jayne Soles (divorced), Meg Ryan, 1991
Child: Jack Henry, 1992
Famous Relative: Randy Quaid, actor, brother

QUEEN LATIFAH

Real Name: Dana Owens
Birthplace: East Orange, NJ
Birthdate: 3/18/70
Occupation: Rap artist, actor
Education: High school
Debut: (Album) *All Hail the Queen*, 1989; (TV) *The Fresh Prince of Bel-Air*, 1991; (Film) *Jungle Fever*, 1991
Facts: Was a power forward on two state championship basketball teams in high school.

Trained in karate and use of firearms by her policeman father.

CEO of Flavor Unit, a management and production company whose clients have included Naughty by Nature and FU-Schnickens.

Brother Lance Owens Jr. died at age 24 in a motorcycle accident in 1992; "Winky's Theme" on the album *Black Reign* was dedicated to him.

Starred in sitcom *Living Single*.

Infamy: Charged in a municipal misdemeanor complaint in 1995 after 240 illegally copied tapes were found in a video store she had sold in 1994.

Arrested by California Highway Patrolman in west L.A. and cited for speeding, driving under the influence, carrying a concealed firearm, carrying a loaded firearm, and possession of marijuana.

Original Job: Worked at Burger King, cashier at the Wiz
Major Award: Grammy, Best Rap Solo Performance, "U.N.I.T.Y.", 1994

BONNIE RAITT

Birthplace: Burbank, CA
Birthdate: 11/8/49
Occupation: Singer, songwriter
Education: Radcliffe College
Debut: (Album) *Bonnie Raitt*, 1971
Signature: "Something To Talk About," 1991
Facts: Grew up in a Quaker family in L.A.

Got her first guitar for Christmas when she was eight.

Founded the annual Rhythm & Blues Awards, to provide money to deserving R&B stars who may have been cheated in the early days by managers and/or record labels.

Infamy: Was an avid drinker until giving up all alcohol and drugs a decade ago.

Marriage: Michael O'Keefe, 1991
Child: One son
Famous Relative: John Raitt, actor, father

Major Awards: Grammies, Album of the Year, Best Rock Vocal—Female, and Best Pop Vocal—Female, "Nick of Time," 1989; Grammy, Best Pop Vocal—Female, "Something To Talk About," 1991; Grammy, Best Rock Vocal—Female, "Luck of the Draw," 1991; Grammy, Best Rock Duo with Vocal, "Good Man, Good Woman" (with Delbert McClinton), 1991; Grammy, Best Pop Album, *Longing in Their Hearts*, 1994

DAN RATHER

Birthplace: Wharton, TX
Birthdate: 10/31/31
Occupation: Anchor, correspondent, editor
Education: Sam Houston State College
Debut: (TV) KHOU-TV, Houston, 1960
Signature: *CBS Evening News with Dan Rather*
Facts: Succeeded Walter Cronkite in anchoring the evening news upon Cronkite's retirement in 1981.

In his 1994 book, *The Camera Never Blinks Twice*, he devotes less than a page to his former co-anchor Connie Chung.

Was attacked on the street by two men who called him "Kenneth" and repeatedly demanded "What's the frequency?" R.E.M. used the cryptic phrase as a song title and later performed the tune with Rather on *Late Show with David Letterman.*
Infamy: Angry over a delay in the start of the news, he walked off the set, leaving IV screens blank for six minutes. He also had a stormy pre-election interview with then vice-president George Bush in 1988.
Marriage: Jean Goebel, 1958
Children: Robin, 1958; Danjack, 1960
Major Awards: 28 News and Documentary Emmys: 19 as correspondent, 9 as anchor

ROBERT REDFORD

Real Name: Charles Robert Redford Jr.
Birthplace: Santa Monica, CA
Birthdate: 8/18/36
Occupation: Actor, director, producer
Education: University of Colorado, Pratt Institute of Design, the American Academy of Dramatic Arts
Debut: (Stage) *Tall Story,* 1959; (Film) *War Hunt,* 1962
Signature: *Butch Cassidy and the Sundance Kid,* 1969
Facts: In 1959, his first child died of Sudden Infant Death Syndrome.

Went to college on a baseball scholarship but lost it due to alcohol abuse. Left school in 1957 to go to Europe; lived in Paris and Florence as a painter.

Was burned in effigy in 1976 for opposing a $3.5 billion power plant.

Founded the nonprofit Sundance Institute in Park City, UT, which sponsors an annual film festival and provides support for independent film production.
Infamy: As a teenager, Redford stole and resold hubcaps.
Original Job: Carpenter, shop assistant, oil field worker
Marriage: Lola Van Wagenen (divorced, 1985); Sibylle Szaggars (relationship)
Children: Shauna, 1960; James, 1962; Amy, 1970
Major Awards: Oscar, Best Director, *Ordinary People,* 1980; Cecil B. DeMille Lifetime Achievement Award, 1994

CHRISTOPHER REEVE

Birthplace: New York, NY
Birthdate: 9/25/52
Occupation: Actor
Education: Cornell University, Juilliard graduate program
Debut: (Film) *Gray Lady Down,* 1977
Signature: *Superman,* 1978
Facts: While studying at Juilliard under John Houseman, shared an apartment with then-unknown Robin Williams.

Turned down a lucrative offer to do cigarette commericals in Japan in 1990.

Says the accident that fractured his first and second vertebrae happened on an easy jump, when his Thoroughbred Eastern Express suddenly halted and his hands became entangled in the bridle so he couldn't break his fall.

Completely paralyzed, though with some sensation in his left leg, he gets around by motorized wheelchair, which he directs by puffing air through a tube.
Marriage: Dana Morosini, 1992

Children: Matthew, 1979; Alexandra, 1983; (with Gae Exton). Will, 1992
Major Award: Grammy, Best Spoken Word Album, *Still Me,* 1998

KEANU REEVES

Birthplace: Beirut, Lebanon
Birthdate: 9/2/64
Occupation: Actor
Education: High school dropout; studied with Jasper Deeter
Debut: (Film) *Youngblood,* 1986
Signature: *Speed,* 1994
Facts: His father is Chinese-Hawaiian and his mother is English.

Hasn't seen his father, who is currently serving a ten-year prison term in Hawaii for cocaine possession, since he was 13.

His first name means "cool breeze over the mountains" in Hawaiian.

Had traveled around the world by the time he was 2 years old.

Was the MVP on his high school hockey team in Toronto. A skilled goalie, Reeves earned the name "The Wall."

Turned down the Al Pacino/Robert De Niro film *Heat* to play Hamlet on stage in Winnipeg, Canada. The February 1995 sold-out run was critically acclaimed.

He plays bass in the band Dogstar. His mother was a costume designer for rock stars.
Relationship: Jennifer Syme

PAUL REISER

Birthplace: New York, NY
Birthdate: 3/30/56
Occupation: Actor, comedian
Education: SUNY-Binghamton
Debut: (Film) *Diner,* 1982
Signature: *Mad About You*
Facts: Has appeared in several hit films, including *Beverly Hills Cop* (1984), *Aliens* (1986), and *Beverly Hills Cop II* (1987).

Dubbed by reporters as part of the Four Funniest Men in the World Club, which includes Jerry Seinfeld, Larry Miller, and Mark Schiff. The members

527

meet every New Year's Day for lunch (once they even met in London when Reiser was there filming *Aliens*).
Original Job: Health food distributor
Marriage: Paula, 1988
Child: Ezra Samuel, 1995

GLORIA REUBEN

Birthplace: Toronto, Canada
Birthdate: 6/9/65
Occupation: Actor
Education: Attended Canadian Royal Conservatory
Debut: (TV) *The Round Table*, 1988
Signature: *ER*
Facts: Her father, who died when she was 11, was a white Jamaican while her mother is a black Jamaican.

Studied ballet and jazz dancing at a prestigious music college, and plays classical piano.
Original Job: Model
Famous Relative: Denis Simpson, brother, actor

BURT REYNOLDS

Birthplace: Waycross, GA
Birthdate: 2/11/36
Occupation: Actor, director
Education: Attended Florida State University, Palm Beach Junior College and Hyde Park Playhouse
Debut: (Stage) *Mister Roberts*, 1956; (Film) *Angel Baby*, 1961
Signature: *Smokey and the Bandit*, 1977
Facts: Was signed to play football with the Baltimore Colts, but a car accident derailed that career and led him to acting.

Has dated Dinah Shore (19 years his senior), Chris Evert, and Sally Field.

Is part Cherokee, part Italian.
Infamy: Appeared nude in *Cosmopolitan* magazine centerfold in 1972.

Untrue rumors circulated in the late 1980s that Reynolds had AIDS; he was actually suffering from a joint disorder.

Ugly divorce from Loni Anderson cost him fans and product endorsement contracts, partly contributing to a 1996 bankruptcy filing.
Original Jobs: Bouncer, dishwasher, stuntman
Marriages: Judy Carne (divorced); Loni Anderson (divorced, 1993); Pam Seals (engaged)
Child: Quentin, c.1988 (adopted)
Major Award: Emmy, Best Actor in a Comedy Series, *Evening Shade*, 1991

TRENT REZNOR

Birthplace: Mercer, PA
Birthdate: 5/17/65
Occupation: Singer, keyboardist
Education: Allegheny College
Debut: (Album) *Pretty Hate Machine*, 1989
Signature: Nine Inch Nails
Facts: Reznor makes all Nine Inch Nails albums himself, using a band only for live shows.

In 1990, misplaced video footage of a half-naked Reznor being thrown from a building landed in the hands of the FBI, who thought it was an actual murder. They led an investigation and found Reznor, alive and well and on tour. The publicity helped put Nine Inch Nails in the spotlight.

Mixed the soundtrack LP for Oliver Stone's film *Natural Born Killers* in 1994.

Lived for a year in the Benedict Canyon, CA, house where Sharon Tate and others were murdered by Charles Manson followers.

In what he says was possibly an unconscious attempt to identify with Woodstock '94 fans, he tripped his guitar player on the way to the stage, who fell flat in the mud and started the whole band in a mud match. They performed covered in the stuff.
Original Job: Odd jobs—including cleaning toilets—at a recording studio

Major Awards: Grammy, Best Metal Performance, "Wish," 1992

CHRISTINA RICCI

Birthplace: Santa Monica, CA
Birthdate: 2/12/80
Occupation: Actor
Education: Professional Children's School
Debut: (Film) *Mermaids*, 1990
Signature: *The Opposite of Sex*, 1998
Facts: While starring in her second-grade pageant, she caught the eye of a local movie critic in the audience, who told her parents to get her an agent.

Was a schoolmate of Macaulay Culkin.

Fellow teen actress Natalie Portman was initially approached for the role in *The Ice Storm*, but her parents decided it was too sexual.
Quote: "Basically, I'm like a whore. I'll give people whatever they want so they'll like me."

ANNE RICE

Real Name: Howard Allen O'Brien
Birthdate: 10/4/41
Occupation: Writer
Education: North Texas State University, San Francisco State College
Debut: (Book) *Interview with a Vampire*, 1976
Facts: Is the author of a series of pornographic novels under the name A. N. Roquelaure (which means "cloak").

Is afraid of the dark.

Was originally named after her father and mother's maiden name; changed name to Anne by the time she was in first grade.

In 1972 her six-year-old daughter died of leukemia.
Original Job: Waitress, cook, insurance claims adjuster
Marriage: Stan Rice, 1961
Children: Michelle, 1966 (deceased, 1972); Christopher, 1978

MICHAEL RICHARDS

Birthplace: Culver City, CA
Birthdate: 7/24/49
Occupation: Actor
Education: Los Angeles Valley College, California Insitute of the Arts
Debut: (TV) *Fridays,* 1980
Signature: *Seinfeld*
Facts: Has appeared in guest spots on *Hill Street Blues* and *Miami Vice.*

Starred with Weird Al Yankovic in the film *UHF,* 1989.

He was drafted at the height of the Vietnam War in 1970: "When the drill sergeant yelled at me on the first day, I tried to explain the duffel bag was too heavy."
Original Job: Postal worker, schoolbus driver
Marriages: Cathleen (divorced, 1993); Ann Talman (relationship)
Child: Sophia, 1975
Major Award: Emmy, Best Supporting Actor in a Comedy Series, *Seinfeld,* 1992, 1993, 1997

NATASHA RICHARDSON

Birthplace: London, England
Birthdate: 5/11/63
Occupation: Actor
Education: Central School for Speech and Drama
Debut: (Stage) *On the Razzle,* 1983
Signature: *The Handmaid's Tale,* 1990
Facts: At age 4, appeared as a bridesmaid of Vanessa Redgrave in *The Charge of the Light Brigade.*

Was named after the heroine in Tolstoy's *War and Peace.*
Marriages: Robert Fox (divorced); Liam Neeson, 1994
Children: Micheál, 1995; Daniel Jack N., 1996
Famous Relatives: Vanessa Redgrave, actor, mother; Tony Richardson, director, father; Joely Richardson, actor, sister; Lynn Redgrave, actor, aunt
Quote: "I've spent half my life trying to get away from being Vanessa

Redgrave's daughter, and now I've got to get away from being Liam Neeson's wife."
Major Award: Tony, Best Actress (Musical), *Cabaret,* 1998

LEANN RIMES

Birthplace: Flowood, MS
Birthdate: 8/28/82
Occupation: Singer
Debut: (Album) *Blue,* 1996
Signature: *Blue*
Facts: Was singing songs like "Jesus Loves Me"—on pitch—at 18 months. Appeared on *Star Search* at age 8 and signed a major record deal at 11.

"Blue" was actually written for Patsy Cline in 1963 but was never recorded because she died that year. When songwriter Bill Mack heard Rimes sing the "Star-Spangled Banner" at a Texas Rangers game he was so impressed he sent her the tune.
Major Awards: Grammy, Best New Artist, 1996; Grammy, Best Country Vocal—Female, "Blue," 1996

GERALDO RIVERA

Birthplace: New York, NY
Birthdate: 7/4/43
Occupation: Broadcast journalist, talk show host
Education: University of Arizona; J.D., Brooklyn School of Law; Columbia Journalism School post-graduate
Debut: (TV) *Eyewitness News,* WABC-TV, New York, 1968
Signature: *Geraldo!*
Facts: In the late '60s was involved with a Latino activist group, the Young Lords. Appeared so many times on the evening news the station eventually hired him as a temporary reporter—a good way to satisfy federal minority hiring quotas.

Was fired from ABC-TV in 1985 when the network tired of his sensationalist style and arrogance. At the time, was making $800,000 a year.

In the late '80s, promised a junior

high school class he would pay for their college education. Five years later paid $180,000 for nine of the graduates' schooling.

In 1993, opened the Broadcast Boxing Club fitness center in New York.
Infamy: Arrested several times at demonstrations, as well as at a TV filming of a rally, when he got into a scuffle with a Ku Klux Klansman.

Accused of leading talk shows into the gutter. Once even had his nose broken during a brawl on his show.
Original Job: Attorney
Marriage: Linda Coblentz, c.1965 (divorced); Edith Bucket Vonnegut, 1971 (divorced); Sherryl Raymond, 1976 (divorced, 1984); C. C. Dyer, 1987 (separated, 1999)
Children: Gabriel Miguel, 1979 (with Sherryl Raymond); Cruz, 1987 (born after a brief liaison); Isabella Holmes, 1992; Simone Cruickshank, 1994 (with Dyer)
Major Awards: 3 national and 4 local Emmy Awards

JOAN RIVERS

Real Name: Joan Alexandra Molinsky
Birthplace: Brooklyn, NY
Birthdate: 6/8/33
Occupation: Talk show host
Education: Connecticut College for Women, Barnard College
Debut: (TV) *The Tonight Show,* 1965
Facts: Wrote for *Candid Camera* and *The Ed Sullivan Show.*
Original Job: Publicist at Lord & Taylor, fashion coordinator for Bond Clothing Stores, temporary office secretary, syndicated columnist
Marriage: Edgar Rosenberg, 1965 (deceased); Orin Lehman (relationship)
Child: Melissa, 1968
Major Award: Emmy, Best Host of a Talk Show, *The Joan Rivers Show,* 1990

TIM ROBBINS

Birthplace: West Covina, CA
Birthdate: 10/16/58
Occupation: Writer, director, actor
Education: New York University, SUNY-Plattsburgh, and UCLA
Debut: (Film) *No Small Affair*, 1984
Signature: *The Player*, 1992
Facts: Was kicked off the hockey team in high school for fighting.

Founded Los Angeles theater group Actors' Gang.

Has been an outspoken political activist and peace advocate.
Original Job: Factory worker
Relationship: Susan Sarandon
Children: Jack Henry, 1989; Miles, 1992

JULIA ROBERTS

Birthplace: Smyrna, GA
Birthdate: 10/28/67
Occupation: Actor
Education: High school
Debut: (TV) *Crime Story*, 1986
Signature: *Pretty Woman*, 1990
Facts: Originally wanted to be a veterinarian.

Her middle name is Fiona.

In 1986, she played opposite her brother (actor Eric Roberts) in the film *Blood Red*.

Was set to marry Kiefer Sutherland in 1991, but canceled the wedding at the last minute with virtually no explanation. And she had taken up with Sutherland after breaking off an engagement to Dylan McDermott.

Has also been linked to Liam Neeson, Jason Patric, Daniel Day-Lewis, Ethan Hawke, and Matthew Perry.
Original Job: Worked in a shoe store and an ice cream shop
Marriage: Lyle Lovett, 1993 (divorced, 1995); Benjamin Bratt (relationship)
Famous Relatives: Eric Roberts, actor, brother; Lisa Roberts, actor, sister
Quote: "I used to think I was weird. Now I think I'm just interesting."

CHRIS ROCK

Birthplace: Brooklyn, NY
Birthdate: 2/7/65
Occupation: Actor, comedian
Education: High school dropout (later got his GED)
Debut: (Film) *Beverly Hills Cop II*, 1987; (TV) *Saturday Night Live*, 1990
Signature: *The Chris Rock Show*
Facts: Grew up in Brooklyn's Bedford-Stuyvesant but was bused to an all-white grade school in Bensonhurst, where he was often the victim of racial violence and discrimination.

Discovered by Eddie Murphy at age 18 during open-mike night at a New York comedy club.

Created the voice of the Little Penny puppet on the Penny Hardaway Nike ads.
Marriage: Malaak Compton
Major Awards: Emmy, Best Writing in a Variety or Music Program, *Chris Rock: Bring the Pain*, 1997; Grammy, Best Spoken Comedy Album, *Roll With the New*, 1997; Emmy, Best Writing in a Variety or Music Program, *The Chris Rock Show*, 1999
Quote: "Cool is comedy's biggest enemy."

AL ROKER

Birthplace: Queens, NY
Birthdate: 8/20/54
Occupation: TV host, weatherman
Education: SUNY, Oswego
Debut: (TV) WTVH in Syracuse, NY, 1974
Signature: *Today*
Facts: While a sophomore in college, Roker worked as a weatherman for a Syracuse station and found his calling. After graduation, he was a weathercaster in Washington, D.C., (where he befriended Willard Scott), then Cleveland, where he was a pioneer in the use of computer graphics for weather forcasts.

Has hosted *Remember This?*, a college quiz show (MSNBC) and *The Al Roker Show*. His production company produced *Savage Skies* (PBS), a weather documentary series, and *Going Places* (PBS), a series on time- and cost-efficient vacations.

Received the American Meteorological Society's Seal of Approval, awarded to fewer than 2 percent of TV weather reporters.

Won Cleveland's "International Rib Burn-Off" cooking contest twice.

Has served on the board of Outward Bound.

For his website, roker.com, he creates "Rokertoon of the Day" cartoons.

His wife used to think he was "kind of annoying, overly chatty."

His descendants were slaves on a plantation on the Caribbean island of Exuma, which he has visited. Relatives still live on the island.
Marriages: Alice (divorced); ; Deborah Ann Roberts, NY correspondent for ABC's *20/20*, 1995
Children: Courtney Roker, c. 1988 (with Alice); Leila Ruth, 1998
Major Awards: Daytime Emmys, Outstanding Special Class Program, *Macy's Thanksgiving Day Parade*, 1996, 1997, 1998 (shared awards)
Quote: "I really wanted to write comedy or direct. But my college professors told me that I had the perfect face for radio."

RAY ROMANO

Birthplace: Queens, NY
Birthdate: 12/21/57
Occupation: Actor, comedian
Education: High school
Debut: (TV, stand-up) *The Tonight Show Starring Johnny Carson,* 1991; (TV) *Dr. Katz: Professional Therapist,* cartoon voice, 1995
Signature: *Everybody Loves Raymond*
Facts: While working a variety of jobs, he appeared at clubs as a stand-up comic.

Lived in the basement of his parents' home in Forest Hills, New York, until he was 29.

Was replaced by Joe Rogan after two days of rehearsal on *NewsRadio.*

David Letterman's production company developed the sitcom *Everybody Loves Raymond.*

Published his autobiography, *Everything and a Kite,* in 1998.
Original Job: Gas station attendant, futon delivery man
Marriage: Anna Scarpulla, 1987
Children: Alexandra, 1990; twins Matthew and Gregory, 1993; Joseph, 1998

REBECCA ROMIJN-STAMOS

Birthdate: 11/6/72
Occupation: Model, actor
Education: University of California, Santa Cruz
Debut: (TV) *House of Style*
Signature: *Sports Illustrated* swimsuit issue cover

Facts: Was nicknamed "Jolly Blonde Giant" in high school.

Likes craft projects, including building an elaborate dollhouse.
Marriage: John Stamos, actor, 1998
Quote: "Fashion is intimidating, and I'm intimidated by most designers I meet. It's a scary thing, and I think other women are intimidated too."

ROSEANNE

Birthplace: Salt Lake City, UT
Birthdate: 11/3/52
Occupation: Actor
Education: High school dropout
Debut: (TV) *Funny,* 1983; (Film) *She-Devil,* 1989
Signature: *Roseanne*
Facts: Dropped out of high school to hitchhike cross country, landing in a Colorado artists' colony at age 18.

Had cosmetic surgery and weight reduction in 1993. Breasts were reduced from 40DD to 38C.

Had a tattoo on her upper right thigh that read: "Property of Tom Arnold." When the pair split, she tattooed over it with a flying fairy and flowers.

Claims she was physically and sexually abused as a child. Suppressed memory of the abuse until an adult.

Gave up first baby girl, Brandi, for adoption at age 18.

Born to Jewish parents but raised as a Mormon in Salt Lake City. Her dad sold crucifixes door to door.

In 1999, four of her children developed an animated autobiographical comedy pilot: "The kids live off her money and have to do what she says," described ringleader Jenny.
Infamy: Grabbed her crotch, spat, and screeched while singing the national anthem at a San Diego baseball game in 1990.
Original Job: Window dresser, cocktail waitress
Marriages: Bill Pentland, 1974 (divorced, 1990); Tom Arnold (divorced); Ben Thomas, 1995 (separated, 1998)

Children: Brandi Brown, 1971. Jessica, 1975; Jennifer, 1976; Jake, c.1978; (with Bill Pentland). Buck, 1995
Major Award: Emmy, Best Actress in a Comedy Series, *Roseanne,* 1993

DIANA ROSS

Real Name: Diane Ernestine Ross
Birthplace: Detroit, MI
Birthdate: 3/26/44
Occupation: Singer, actor
Education: High school
Debut: *The Primettes,* 1959; (TV) *Tarzan,* 1968; (Film) *Lady Sings the Blues,* 1972
Signature: *Ain't No Mountain High Enough,* 1970
Facts: Sung with the Primettes as a teenager until the group was reformed as the Supremes in 1961 and signed on with Motown. Six years later the group, then called Diana Ross and the Supremes, became the most successful black recording artists of their time. Nominated for an Oscar for her first feature film role in 1972's *Lady Sings the Blues,* she went on to appear in 1978's *The Wiz,* which proved unsuccessful and ended her movie career.

She often insists that subordinates address her as "Miss Ross."

Received rave reviews in 1994 for her role as a paranoid schizophrenic in the TV movie *Out of Darkness.*

In the late 1970s, she turned down the role that would become Whitney Houston's in *The Bodyguard.*
Infamy: Kept secret the fact that Motown mogul Berry Gordy fathered her first child.
Original Job: fashion designer, cafeteria busgirl
Marriage: Robert Ellis Silberstein (divorced, 1976); Arne Naess (divorced, 1999)
Children: Rhonda Suzanne, 1971 (with Berry Gordy). Tracee Joy, 1972; Chudney Lane, 1975 (with Silberstein). Ross Arne, 1987; Evan, 1988 (with Naess).

531

Major Awards: Grammy, Best Vocal (Contemporary) Performance by a Female, "Ain't No Mountain High Enough," 1970; Special Tony for *An Evening with Diana Ross,* 1977
Quote: "I never thought this little Detroit girl would ever go to Nepal, climb the Himalayas, or be in the bush country in Africa".

GAVIN ROSSDALE

Birthplace: London, England
Birthdate: 10/30/67
Occupation: Singer, songwriter, guitarist
Education: High school
Debut: (Album) *Sixteen Stone,* 1994
Signature: Bush
Facts: His parents divorced when he was eleven. He lived with his physician father in the well-heeled North London Kilburn district, attending the posh Westminster high school. After graduating, became a regular party animal at London's clubs.

As a teen, played semi-pro soccer in London and even tried out for a top pro team, Chelsea.

His former band, the pop-oriented Midnight, had a record deal in the mid-1980s but produced no hits.

Originally signed by Disney's Hollywood Records, but exec Frank G. Wells, a major fan, was killed in a helicopter crash just as *Sixteen Stone* was completed. Other execs deemed the album unacceptable, so it went into limbo until being rescued by Interscope.
Original Job: Music video production assistant
Relationship: Gwen Stefani

KERI RUSSELL

Birthplace: Fountain Valley, CA
Birthdate: 3/23/76
Occupation: Actor
Education: High school
Debut: (TV) Disney Channel's *All New Mickey Mouse Club,* 1991; (Film) *Honey, I Blew Up the Kid,* 1992
Signature: *Felicity*
Facts: A successful audition in Denver led to her three-year stint as a Mouseketeer, launching her career and her long romance with Tony Lucca, with whom she also costarred in TV's 1996 *Malibu Shores.*

Her middle name is Lynn.

At age 17 she set off on her own to L.A. and got a role right away on Dudley Moore's sitcom *Daddy's Girl.*

Producers originally thought she was too pretty for the role of Felicity—even though she dressed down for the audition to make herself look plain.

Her favorite things are massages, fresh flowers, live music, and trips to Ireland and Big Sur.
Original Job: Model
Relationship: Tony Lucca
Quote: "You gotta be low maintenance."

KURT RUSSELL

Birthplace: Springfield, MA
Birthdate: 3/17/51
Occupation: Actor, screenwriter, producer
Education: High school

Debut: (Film) *The Absent-Minded Professor,* 1960
Signature: *Stargate,* 1994
Facts: At 12, starred in his own Western series, *The Travels of Jaimie McPheeters,* featuring Charles Bronson and the very young Osmond brothers.

Left acting in 1971 to play minor league baseball. Returned to acting two years later after tearing a shoulder muscle.

His actor father played the sheriff for 14 years on *Bonanza.*
Marriages: Season Hubley, 1979 (divorced, 1983); Goldie Hawn (relationship)
Children: Boston, 1980 (with Season Hubley). Wyatt, 1986
Famous Relatives: Bing Russell, actor, father

RENE RUSSO

Birthplace: Burbank, CA
Birthdate: 2/17/54
Occupation: Actor
Education: High school dropout
Debut: (Film) *Major League,* 1989
Signature: *Lethal Weapon 3,* 1992
Facts: Considered herself unattractive as a teen because she wore a body cast to correct a curved spine from ages 10 to 14. Shy and uninterested in school (where high school classmates included Ron Howard), she dropped out in 10th grade and worked in an eyeglass factory.

Was discovered by a modeling agent in the parking lot following a Rolling Stones concert. A few weeks later, she was in New York shooting a Revlon ad with Richard Avedon.

At age 30, depressed by being too old to model, she discovered Christian theology, which she spent the next three years studying. Religion gave her the confidence to try an acting career.

Met her future husband on the set of *Freejack,* a film for which she had originally turned down an acting role and for which Gilroy had originally rejected the job of script rewriting.

Original Job: Supermodel
Marriage: Danny Gilroy (divorced)
Child: Rose, 1993
Quote: (on her nude scenes in *The Thomas Crown Affair*): "It never really dawned on me that, gee, I'm 45 and I'm taking off my clothes."

JERI RYAN

Real Name: Jeri Lynn Zimmerman
Birthplace: Munich, Germany
Birthdate: 2/22/68
Occupation: Actor
Education: Northwestern University
Debut: (TV movie) *Nightmare in Columbia County,* 1991
Signature: Seven of Nine in *Star Trek: Voyager*
Facts: From 1993 to 1997, she appeared in episodes of *Who's the Boss*; *Murder, She Wrote*; *Diagnosis Murder*; *Melrose Place*; and the short-lived *Dark Skies*.

Was a National Merit Scholar.

Her original *Voyager* suit was so tight that she passed out four times and required oxygen on the set.
Marriage: Jack Ryan (John Clemens Ryan), 1991 (separated, 1998)
Child: Alex Ryan, c. 1994
Quote: "I don't mind being called a babe. It's better than being called a dog."

MEG RYAN

Real Name: Margaret Hyra
Birthplace: Fairfield, CT
Birthdate: 11/19/61
Occupation: Actor
Education: New York University
Debut: (Film) *Rich and Famous,* 1981; (TV) *As the World Turns, 1983*
Signature: *When Harry Met Sally...,* 1989
Fact: Became high school homecoming queen when the original queen was suspended.

Her strained relationship with her mother became tabloid-show fodder when her stepfather wrote an article about the pair's discord in a

magazine in 1992. Ryan subsequently ended all contact with them.

Met husband Quaid on the set of the comedy film, *Innerspace,* in 1987. A year later, they professionally reunited for the unsuccessful film *D.O.A.*
Marriage: Dennis Quaid, 1991
Child: Jack Henry, 1992
Quote: "I have remained consistently and nauseatingly adorable. In fact, I have been known to cause diabetes."

WINONA RYDER

Real Name: Winona Laura Horowitz
Birthplace: Winona, MN
Birthdate: 10/29/71
Occupation: Actor
Education: High school
Debut: (Film) *Lucas,* 1986
Signature: *Beetlejuice,* 1988
Facts: Her childhood home in Elk, CA, had no electricity.

In junior high school, was attacked and beaten by fellow students during her first week at a new school, apparently because they mistook her for a boy.

Has read *The Catcher in the Rye* countless times, and travels with a copy.

Dated Christian Slater and David Pirner; was engaged to Johnny Depp.

Timothy Leary, the famous psychologist and countercultural philosopher, was her godfather.
Relationship: Matt Damon

ADAM SANDLER

Birthplace: Brooklyn, NY
Birthdate: 9/9/66
Occupation: Comedian, actor
Education: New York University
Debut: (TV) *The Cosby Show,* 1987; (Film) *Shakes the Clown,* 1992
Signature: *Big Daddy,* 1999
Facts: Became a writer for *Saturday Night Live* in 1990, but his sketches were often too eccentric for others to make their own. He soon became a

"featured player" doing those skits and, after the success of his Opera Man, became a regular cast member.

As a developing comic, was so taken by Rodney Dangerfield he memorized many of Dangerfield's routines.
Original Job: Stand-up comedian
Relationship: Margaret Ruden (engaged, never married); Jackie Titone
Quote: "If you don't get the best grades, don't fret—I didn't do too well in school and I'm a multimillionaire."

SUSAN SARANDON

Real Name: Susan Abigail Tomaling
Birthplace: New York, NY
Birthdate: 10/4/46
Occupation: Actor
Education: Catholic University of America
Debut: (Film) *Joe,* 1970
Signature: *Thelma & Louise,* 1991
Facts: Her background is Welsh-Italian. Was one of nine children, and attended Catholic school.

Is 12 years older than beau Tim Robbins.

An activist for numerous political, cultural, and health causes, she digressed during her 1991 Academy Awards presentation to speak for a half-minute on behalf of Haitian refugees with AIDS.

Starred in cult classic *The Rocky Horror Picture Show.*

She and Robbins keep all their awards in the "famous bathroom."
Original Job: While in college, worked in the drama department, modeled, and cleaned apartments.
Marriages: Chris Sarandon, 1967 (divorced, 1979); Tim Robbins (relationship)
Children: Eva Maria Livia, 1985 (with Franco Amurri). Jack Henry, 1989; Miles, 1992 (with Tim Robbins)
Major Awards: Oscar, Best Actress, *Dead Man Walking,* 1995

DIANE SAWYER

Birthplace: Glasgow, KY
Birthdate: 12/22/45
Occupation: Broadcast journalist
Education: Wellesley College
Debut: (TV) WLKY-TV, Louisville, 1967
Signature: *Primetime Live*
Facts: Was national Junior Miss, largely on the strength of her interview and essays.

As a weathercaster in Louisville, KY, she spruced up forecasts with quotes from her favorite poems.

Served as staff assistant to former President Nixon and helped him research his memoirs.
Marriage: Mike Nichols, 1988
Major Awards: 10 News and Documentary Emmys: 9 as correspondent, 1 as anchor

CLAUDIA SCHIFFER

Birthplace: Dusseldorf, Germany
Birthdate: 8/25/70
Occupation: Supermodel
Education: High school
Facts: Tripped during her runway modeling debut in 1990.

Earns as much as $50,000 a day.

Opened Fashion Cafe in New York City in 1995 with fellow supermodels Elle MacPherson and Naomi Campbell.

Was engaged to David Copperfield, but they never married.

LAURA SCHLESSINGER

Birthdate: 1947
Occupation: Radio talk show host
Education: SUNY, Stony Brook; Columbia University, Ph.D. in physiology; University of Southern California, post-doctoral certificate in marriage and family therapy
Debut: (Radio) *The Dr. Laura Schlessinger Show,* 1990
Signature: "Dr. Laura"
Facts: Had a tubal ligation at age 30, which she later had reversed.

Has been estranged from her

mother since before the birth of her son.

Converted to Judaism in 1994.

Her house burned almost entirely in an electrical fire in 1992.

Has a black belt in Karate.

Her radio call-in show now has an audience of some 20 million listeners on 450 U.S. stations and 30 Canadian stations, and is even heard in South Africa.

In addition to her adult best-sellers, recently began writing children's picture books, her first entitled *Why Do You Love Me?*

Owns a Harley and a rose-colored Mercedes-Benz.

Her radio show was sold in 1997 for $71.5 million, 40 percent more than an earlier deal for Rush Limbaugh's show.

It's estimated that 60,000 people call into to her show every day.
Infamy: In 1998 tried unsuccessfully to have a court keep a dozen nude photos of her, taken by a former lover decades earlier, from being posted on the Internet.
Marriages: First husband (divorced, 1978); Lewis Bishop, 1984
Child: Deryk Schlessinger, 1986
Quotes: "I do not see it as my mission to make anybody feel better. I want them to get better."

RICK SCHRODER

Birthplace: Staten Island, NY
Birthdate: 4/13/70
Occupation: Actor
Education: Mesa State College
Debut: (Film) *The Champ,* 1979; (TV) *Silver Spoons,* 1982
Signature: *Silver Spoons*
Facts: "Ricky" began making TV commercials as a toddler, appearing in some 60 by age 7.

Following his youthful sitcom run, he landed his first starring role in the TV movie *Something So Right* in 1982. He later won a key role in the miniseries *Lonesome Dove* and its sequel.

Owns 800 head of cattle, quarter

horses, 2,000 deer, and 3 trout lakes on his 45,000-acre Colorado ranch.

He takes time out of his days to indulge in yoga and receives weekly massages.

He wishes he were taller.
Original Job: Model
Marriage: Andrea Bernard, 1992
Children: Holden, 1992; Luke, 1993; Cambrie, 1996
Major Awards: Golden Globe Award, New Star of the Year, *The Champ,* 1979
Quote: "I guess I've come to terms with myself and what I look like. These are the cards I was dealt, so I play 'em the best I know how."

ARNOLD SCHWARZENEGGER

Birthplace: Graz, Austria
Birthdate: 7/30/47
Occupation: Actor, director, body-builder
Education: University of Wisconsin
Debut: (Film) *Hercules in New York,* 1969
Signature: *The Terminator,* 1984
Facts: After coming to the U.S. in the '60s, founded a bricklaying business, Pumping Bricks, to finance his body-building career.

Won the Austrian Junior Olympic weightlifting championship as well as Junior Mr. Europe and several curling titles.

In 1974, acted in *Happy Anniversary and Goodbye,* an unsold CBS sitcom pilot starring Lucille Ball and Art Carney.

Has killed over 275 people on screen.
Infamy: Named in a 1995 paternity suit by a Texas woman who claims he fathered her daughter 12 years earlier.
Original Job: Managed a Munich health club
Marriage: Maria Owings Shriver, 1986
Children: Katherine Eunice, 1989; Christina Maria Aurelia, 1991; Patrick, 1993; Christopher, 1997
Quote: "Everything I have ever done

in my life has always stayed. I've just added to it...But I will not change. Because when you are successful and you change, you are an idiot."

DAVID SCHWIMMER

Birthplace: Queens, NY
Birthdate: 11/2/66
Occupation: Actor
Education: Northwestern University
Debut: (TV movie) *A Deadly Silence*, 1989; (Film) *Crossing the Bridge*, 1992
Signature: *Friends*
Facts: His mother is the attorney who handled Roseanne's first divorce. Since his father is also an attorney, he flirted with becoming one before settling on acting.

Appeared in the 1994 Henry Winkler flop, *Monty.*

Started Chicago's Lookingglass Theater Company in 1988 with seven other Northwestern graduates.
Relationship: Mili Avital

MARTIN SCORSESE

Birthplace: New York, NY
Birthdate: 11/17/42
Occupation: Director
Education: New York University
Debut: (Film) *Boxcar Bertha*, 1972
Signature: *Taxi Driver*, 1976
Facts: Collaborated on the production of Michael Jackson's *Bad* video in 1987.

Was originally enrolled as an English major before switching to film.
Original Job: Faculty assistant and instructor in film department at NYU
Marriages: Larraine Marie Brennan, 1965 (divorced); Julia Cameron, 1975 (divorced); Isabella Rosellini, 1979 (divorced, 1983); Barbara DeFina, 1985 (divorced); Helen Morris, 1999
Children: Catherine Terese, 1965 (with Larraine Marie Brennan).

Domenica Elizabeth, 1976 (with Julia Cameron).
Major Award: Cannes Film Festival, Palme d'Or, *Taxi Driver*, 1976

STEVEN SEAGAL

Birthplace: Lansing, MI
Birthdate: 4/10/52
Occupation: Actor, producer
Education: Orange Coast College
Debut: (Film) *Above the Law*, 1988
Signature: *Hard To Kill*, 1990
Facts: Founder, Aikido Ten Shin Dojo, Los Angeles.

First non-Asian to successfully open a martial arts academy in Japan.

In 1968, moved to Japan, where he taught English and wrote articles for Japanese magazines and newspapers.

Organized security for the departure of the Shah's family from Iran.

Commands the title of Shihan (Master of Masters).

The high lama of the Nyingma school of Buddhism ceremonially recognized Seagal as a *tulku*—a reincarnated holy man.
Infamy: Was sued by a film assistant for sexual harassment. Paid money to settle out of court in 1990.

Was married to both his first and second wives simultaneously.

Scriptwriter Lars Hansson claimed in 1994 that Seagal threatened him with death after he refused to sell him film rights to a CIA hit-man story.

In 1995, was accused by ex-girlfriend Cheryl Shuman of harassing her. A judge threw out her lawsuit, calling it unintelligible.
Original Job: Martial arts instructor, bodyguard
Marriages: Miyako Fujitani (divorced); Adrienne LaRussa (annulled); Kelly LeBrock, 1994; Arissa Wolf (relationship)
Children: Justice (a.k.a. Kentaro), 1975; Ayako, c.1980; (with Miyako Fujitani). Anna-lisa, c.1987; Dominick San Rocco, 1990; Arissa,

1993; (with Kelly LeBrock). Savannah, 1996
Quote: "I just care about bringing joy into this world in my little way."

SEAL

Real Name: Sealhenry Samuel
Birthplace: Paddington, England
Birthdate: 2/19/63
Occupation: Singer, songwriter
Education: High school dropout
Debut: (Album) *Seal*, 1991
Signature: "Kiss from a Rose," 1995
Facts: His name comes from his Brazilian father's custom of having the grandparents select the name (they chose Seal) coupled with his parents' fascination with British royalty (they wanted Henry).

As an infant, lived with a white foster family until his Nigerian mother reclaimed him. When she became ill several years later, went to his father's, whom he says beat him mercilessly.

Plays a six-string guitar upside down; left-handed, learned on guitars borrowed from studios and they were all right-handed.

The scars on his face are remnants of lupus contracted at age 23.
Major Awards: Grammy, Record of the Year, "Kiss from a Rose," 1995; Grammy, Song of the Year, "Kiss from a Rose," 1995; Grammy, Best Male Pop Vocal Performance, "Kiss from a Rose," 1995

JERRY SEINFELD

Birthplace: Brooklyn, NY
Birthdate: 4/29/54
Occupation: Actor, comedian
Education: Queens College
Debut: (Stand-up) Catch a Rising Star, Manhattan, 1976
Signature: *Seinfeld*
Facts: At his first stage appearance, he was so nervous he forgot his routine and only mumbled the words "The beach. Driving. Shopping. Parents," and walked off.

Owns several dozen pairs of

sneakers, including a custom pair of "Air Seinfelds."

Has practiced yoga for 20 years and is a strict vegetarian.

Infamy: Created a stir when he began dating 18-year-old Shoshanna Lonstein in 1993. They broke up in 1997.

His relationship with newlywed Jessica Sklar, 27, broke up her marriage

Original Job: Sought the worst jobs possible, including selling light bulbs over the phone and costume jewelry on the streets of New York, to force himself to succeed at comedy

Major Award: Emmy, Best Comedy Series, *Seinfeld,* 1993

Quote: "I'm hardly interested in my own life. I don't know how you could be interested."

JANE SEYMOUR

Real Name: Joyce Frankenberg
Birthplace: Hillingdon, England
Birthdate: 2/15/51
Occupation: Actor
Education: Arts Educational School, London
Debut: (Film) *Oh, What a Lovely War,* 1968
Signature: *Dr. Quinn, Medicine Woman*
Facts: Danced with the London Festival Ballet at 13.

Named Honorary Citizen of Illinois by Governor Thompson in 1977.

Original Job: Ballet dancer
Marriages: Michael Attenborough (divorced); Geoffrey Planer (divorced); David Flynn (divorced); James Keach, 1993
Children: Kalen; 1977 (stepson, with James Keach). Jennifer, 1980; Katie, 1982; Sean, 1985 (with David Flynn). John, 1995; Kristopher, 1995
Major Awards: Emmy, Best Supporting Actress in a Miniseries, *Onassis,* 1988

GARRY SHANDLING

Birthplace: Chicago, IL
Birthdate: 11/29/49
Occupation: Actor, writer, comedian
Education: University of Arizona
Debut: (TV) *Sanford & Son,* 1976
Signature: *The Larry Sanders Show*
Fact: Wrote for *Sanford & Son, Welcome Back, Kotter,* and *Three's Company.*

Named *The Tonight Show*'s permanent guest host in 1986 and was widely expected to be Johnny Carson's successor, but decided he didn't enjoy it enough so he left.

Infamy: A former co-star sued Shandling for sexual harassment; she claimed her firing from *Sanders* was tied to the break-up of their relationship.

In 1998, Shandling sued his 18-year friend and manager, Brad Grey, for $100 million, claiming that Grey didn't protect his interests and built a management/production empire on Shandling's talents. Grey counter-sued for $10 million, alleging breach of contract and fiduciary duty. They settled their respective suits in 1999 by exchanging "certain interests in various television properties."

Major Award: Emmy, Writing for a Comedy Series, *The Larry Sanders Show,* 1998

Quote: "It's really to the point now, when I envision myself walking down the aisle with a woman in white, it's a nurse."

WILLIAM SHATNER

Birthplace: Montreal, Canada
Birthdate: 3/22/31
Occupation: Actor, author, producer, director
Education: McGill University
Debut: (TV) *Goodyear TV Playhouse,* 1956
Signature: *Star Trek*
Facts: Has written a series of books, beginning with *TekWar,* which were turned into movies in which he stars.

Most celebrated pre-*Trek* experience was as a guest on one of the most famous *Twilight Zone* episodes, "Nightmare at 20,000 Feet," in 1963.

One of his leisure activities is breeding horses.

Became CEO of a special effects company, CORE Digital Pictures, in 1995.

Original Job: Novelist
Marriages: Gloria Rand (divorced); Marcy Lafferty, 1973 (divorced, 1996); Nerine Kidd, 1997 (deceased)
Children: Leslie, 1958; Lisabeth, 1961; Melanie, 1964; (with Gloria Rand).

JUDITH SHEINDLIN

Real Name: Judy Blum
Birthplace: Brooklyn, NY
Birthdate: 10/21/42
Occupation: TV judge
Education: American University, New York Law School
Signature: *Judge Judy*
Facts: Married while in law school and the only woman in the graduating class of 1965, she practiced law for a few years before staying home to care for her young children.

Returned to work in 1972 as a prosecutor in New York's family court, then served as family court judge in New York for 24 years.

Following publication of her 1996 book, *Don't Pee on My Leg and Tell Me It's Raining,* she began her successful courtroom TV show.

Original Job: Lawyer
Marriage: Ronald Levy, 1964 (divorced, 1976); Jerry Sheindlin, 1978
Children: Adam (with Levy); Jamie Hartwright (with Sheindlin)
Quote: "You do the right thing, the right thing usually happens to you. But you can be sure if you do the wrong thing, it's going to bite you in the [posterior]."

BROOKE SHIELDS

Birthplace: New York, NY
Birthdate: 5/31/65
Occupation: Actor
Education: Princeton University
Debut: (Film) *Alice, Sweet Alice*, 1978
Signature: *Suddenly Susan*
Facts: Began her career as an Ivory Snow baby when she was 11 months old. Appeared on more than 30 magazine covers at age 16.

Says now that her overbearing ex-manager stage-mother, Teri, was an alcoholic. Shields was conceived out of wedlock and her father was around only for the first few months of her life.

Has previously been linked romantically to Liam Neeson, Prince Albert of Monaco, George Michael, Michael Bolton, and Michael Jackson.

Her divorce papers cited "incompatible tastes [and] temperament."
Infamy: As the 12-year-old star of *Pretty Baby*, played a prostitute in various states of undress.
Original Job: Model
Marriage: André Agassi, 1997 (separated, 1999); Chris Henchy (relationship)
Quote: "Every time I go to the doctor I say, 'Can I still make a baby?... How much time do I have? What am I going to have to do, find a sire?'"

ELISABETH SHUE

Birthplace: Wilmington, DE
Birthdate: 10/6/63
Occupation: Actor

Education: Wellesley College, Harvard University
Debut: (Film) *The Karate Kid*, 1984
Signature: *Leaving Las Vegas*, 1995
Facts: Admits to drinking heavily and going to class stoned while in high school.

Encouraged her baby brother Andrew to join her in acting.

Older brother Will died in an accident at age 27.
Marriage: Davis Guggenheim, 1994
Child: Miles William, 1997
Famous Relatives: Andrew Shue, actor, brother

ALICIA SILVERSTONE

Birthplace: San Francisco, CA
Birthdate: 10/4/76
Occupation: Actor
Education: High school equivalency
Debut: (Film) *The Crush*, 1993
Signature: *Clueless*, 1995
Facts: Filed for emancipation from her parents at 15 so she could work in films as an adult.

Was a cheerleader in high school.

Won MTV's Villain of the Year award in 1993 for her performance as the lovestruck psychopath in *The Crush*.
Quote: "People who say I'm sexy don't really understand what sexy means. I'm always dirty and always in sweats. That's the real me."

NEIL SIMON

Real Name: Marvin Neil Simon
Birthplace: Bronx, NY
Birthdate: 7/4/27
Occupation: Playwright, screenwriter, producer
Education: New York University
Debut: (Stage) *Adventures of Marco Polo: A Musical Fantasy*, 1959; (Film) *After the Fox*, 1966
Signature: *The Odd Couple*, 1965
Facts: Flew in the U.S. Air Force, 1945–46.

Met his third wife in 1985 when she was handing out perfume

samples at the Beverly Hills Neiman Marcus store.

Owns Eugene O'Neill Theatre in New York.

Has written nearly 30 Broadway shows.
Original Job: Mail room clerk
Marriages: Joan Baim (deceased), Marsha Mason (divorced), Diane Lander (divorced, remarried, divorced, 1998); Elaine Joyce, 1999
Children: Ellen, 1957; Nancy, 1963; (with Joan Biam). Bryn, c.1984 (stepdaughter)
Major Awards: Tony, Best Author (Dramatic), *The Odd Couple*, 1965; Tony, Special Award, 1975, Tony, Best Play, *Biloxi Blues*, 1985; Tony, Best Play, *Lost in Yonkers*, 1991; Pulitzer Prize, Best Play, *Lost in Yonkers*, 1991

PAUL SIMON

Birthplace: Newark, NJ
Birthdate: 10/13/41
Occupation: Singer, songwriter
Education: Queens College, Brooklyn Law School
Debut: (Song) "Hey Schoolgirl" (with Art Garfunkel, under the name Tom and Jerry), 1957
Signature: *Graceland*, 1986
Facts: In sixth grade, he played the White Rabbit to Garfunkel's Cheshire Cat in *Alice in Wonderland*.

Co-owned the Philadelphia Furies, a soccer team, with Mick Jagger, Peter Frampton, and Rick Wakeman.

Composed music and cowrote book for *The Capeman*, a Broadway show that played briefly in 1998.
Marriages: Peggy Harper (divorced), Carrie Fisher (divorced), Edie Brickell, 1992
Children: Harper, 1992; Adrian Edward, 1993; Lulu, 1995
Famous Relative: Louis Simon, bassist, father
Major Awards: Grammy, Record of the Year, "Mrs. Robinson" (with Simon & Garfunkel), 1968; Grammy, Best Pop Performance—Duo or Group, "Mrs. Robinson" (with Simon

& Garfunkel), 1968; Grammy, Best Soundtrack Album, *The Graduate* (with Dave Grusin), 1968; Grammy, Record of the Year, "Bridge over Troubled Water" (with Simon & Garfunkel), 1970; Grammy, Album of the Year, *Bridge over Troubled Water* (with Simon & Garfunkel), 1970; Grammy, Song of the Year, "Bridge over Troubled Water," 1970; Grammy, Best Rock/Contemporary Song, "Bridge over Troubled Water," 1970; Grammy, Album of the Year, *Still Crazy After All These Years,* 1975; Grammy, Best Pop Vocal—Male, "Still Crazy After All These Years," 1975; Grammy, Album of the Year, *Graceland,* 1986; Emmy, Best Writing in a Comedy, Variety, or Music Special, *The Paul Simon Special,* 1978; inducted into the Rock and Roll Hall of Fame (with Art Garfunkel), 1990

SINBAD

Real Name: David Adkins
Birthplace: Benton Harbor, MI
Birthdate: 11/10/56
Occupation: Actor, comedian
Education: University of Denver
Debut: (TV) *Comedy Tonight,* 1985; (Film) *That's Adequate,* 1989
Signature: *A Different World*
Facts: Finalist in the comedy competition on *Star Search* in 1984.
  Original dream was to play pro basketball.
Infamy: While in the Air Force, impersonated officers and went AWOL.
Marriage: Meredith Adkins (divorced, 1992)
Children: Paige, c.1986; Royce, c.1989

CHRISTIAN SLATER

Real Name: Christian Hawkins
Birthplace: New York, NY
Birthdate: 8/18/69
Occupation: Actor
Education: Dalton School, Professional Children's School

Debut: (TV) *One Life To Live,* 1976; (Film) *The Legend of Billie Jean,* 1985
Signature: *Heathers,* 1989
Facts: Began his career in the stage revival of *The Music Man,* at the age of 9.
  Dated Winona Ryder, Christy Turlington, and Samantha Mathis.
  Was born on the final day of Woodstock.
Infamy: Arrested twice for drunk driving, served ten days in jail in 1990.
  Arrested in 1994 for attempting to carry a 9mm pistol through an airport metal detector. He was ordered to spend three days working with homeless children on a plea-bargained misdemeanor charge in 1995.
  Was sued in 1995 for palimony seeking $100,000 plus property worth $2 million by ex-fiancée Nina Peterson Huang, who claims she had an agreement with Slater to put her career on hold during their five years of living together. Four months after they got engaged, Huang left the volatile actor and broke off the relationship.
  Was arrested in 1997 for assault and battery for acts which encompassed stomach-biting; later admitted to being on alcohol, heroin, and cocaine at the time. He served 59 days in jail and 90 days of community service.
Relationship: Ryan Haddon (engaged)
Child: Jaden Christopher, 1999
Famous Relatives: Mary Jo Slater, casting director, mother; Michael Gainsborough, stage and soap actor, father

JADA PINKETT SMITH

Birthplace: Baltimore, MD
Birthdate: 9/18/71
Occupation: Actor
Education: Attended North Carolina School for the Arts
Debut: (TV) *A Different World,* 1991; (Film) *Menace II Society,* 1993

Signature: *The Nutty Professor*
Facts: Her parents divorced around the time of her birth. She was raised in a rough Baltimore neighborhood by her mother and grandmother.
  In addition to acting, has directed rap music videos, performed poetry readings, appeared at inner-city schools as a motivational speaker, and started a mail-order clothing line of T-shirts and dresses bearing feminist slogans.
  Five feet tall and just 100 pounds, she often buys her clothes from stores' children's departments.
Infamy: Reportedly gave $100,000 bail to rapper/actor friend Tupac Shakur to gain his release from jail while awaiting an appeal on a sexual abuse conviction.
Marriage: Will Smith, 1997
Child: Jaden Christopher Syre, 1998

WILL SMITH

Birthplace: Philadelphia, PA
Birthdate: 9/25/68
Occupation: Actor, rap artist
Education: High school
Debut: Rapper as part of DJ Jazzy Jeff & The Fresh Prince
Signature: *Men In Black,* 1997
Facts: Turned down a scholarship to MIT to pursue music.
  By 1989 had made and lost his first million dollars, the latter due to excessive spending.
  Earned his nickname, the Prince, from a teacher in Overbrook High School because of his regal attitude and ability to talk his way out of difficult situations.
Original Job: Rap artist
Marriage: Sheree Zampino (divorced); Jada Pinkett, 1997
Children: Willard C. "Trey" III, 1992 (with Sheree Zampino). Jaden Christopher Syre, 1998
Major Awards: Grammy, Best Rap Performance—Solo, "Parents Just Don't Understand" (with D.J. Jazzy Jeff & The Fresh Prince), 1988; Grammy, Best Rap Performance—Duo or Group, "Summertime" (with D.J. Jazzy

Jeff & The Fresh Prince), 1991; Grammy, Best Rap Performance—Solo, "Men in Black," 1997; Grammy, Best Rap Performance—Solo, "Gettin' Jiggy Wit It," 1998

Quote: "I have no idea what my limits are. I believe that if I set my mind to it, within the next 15 years, I would be the President of the United States."

WESLEY SNIPES

Birthplace: Orlando, FL
Birthdate: 7/31/62
Occupation: Actor
Education: New York City's High School of the Performing Arts, SUNY-Purchase
Debut: (Film) *Wildcats,* 1985
Signature: *New Jack City,* 1991
Facts: Has studied martial arts, including the African/Brazilian version Capoeira, since his youth.

Was "in the Girl Scouts when I was 9 or 10"—in a helper capacity. "I sold cookies like anybody else, so I could get to go on the field trip."

Appeared in commercials for Levi's 501 Jeans and Coca-Cola Classic.

Snipes came to director Spike Lee's attention when he played a young punk who threatens Michael Jackson in the Martin Scorsese–directed video *Bad,* 1987.

Infamy: Arrested in 1994 for reckless driving for speeding at up to 120 mph on his motorcycle in Florida, leading state troopers on a 30-mile chase. Sentenced to eighty hours of community service, six months' probation, and $7,000 in fines and court costs.

Original Jobs: Street and puppet theater in his troupe, Struttin' Street Stuff, telephone installer, parking attendant
Marriages: One marriage (divorced), Donna Wong (relationship)
Child: Jelani Asar, 1988
Quote: "What I may be lacking in terms of my physical beauty, I make up for in personality and experience."

SNOOP DOGG

Real Name: Cordozar "Calvin" Broadus
Birthplace: Long Beach, CA
Birthdate: 10/20/71
Occupation: Rap artist
Education: High school
Debut: (Album) *Doggystyle,* 1993
Facts: Nickname "Snoop" was given to him by his mother; "Doggy Dogg" came from a cousin who used to call himself Tate Doggy Dog. In 1999 he shortened his moniker, dropping the "Doggy."

Says his musical heroes are Al Green, Curtis Mayfield, and L. J. Reynolds of the Dramatics.

He's 6'4".

Infamy: One month after graduating from Long Beach Polytechnic High School, was arrested and incarcerated on a drug charge.

Dogg went on trial for the murder of L.A. gang member Phil Woldemariam; Snoop was driving the Jeep from which his bodyguard fired two fatal gunshots. The two were found not guilty of murder; the jury deadlocked on manslaughter charges and a mistrial was declared.

In 1994, was arrested in Lake Charles, La., when deputies attempting to deliver civil court papers smelled marijuana outside his hotel room. Charged with possession of marijuana and drug paraphernalia.

Original Job: Sold candy, delivered newspapers, bagged groceries
Marriage: Shanté Taylor, 1997
Child: Cordé, c. 1994; Cordell, 1997

TOM SNYDER

Birthplace: Milwaukee, WI
Birthdate: 5/12/36
Occupation: Talk show host
Education: Marquette University
Debut: (Radio) WRIT-AM, Milwaukee; (TV) KNBC-TV News, Los Angeles, 1970
Signature: *Late Late Show with Tom Snyder*
Facts: David Letterman, whose company produces Snyder's new late-night talk show, *Late Late Show with Tom Snyder,* is the one who took over Snyder's time slot when NBC dropped *Tomorrow* in 1982.
Marriage: One marriage (divorced)
Child: Anne Marie, 1964
Major Award: Emmy, Best Host, *Tomorrow,* 1974

STEPHEN SONDHEIM

Birthplace: New York, NY
Birthdate: 3/22/30
Occupation: Composer, lyricist
Education: Williams College
Debut: (Stage) *Girls of Summer,* 1956
Signature: *West Side Story*
Facts: In May 1992, turned down the NEA's Medal of Arts Award, claiming the agency is "a symbol of censorship and repression rather than encouragement and support."

When Sondheim left home at age 15, he was taken in by Oscar Hammerstein II (lyricist of *Oklahoma!*), who taught him how to structure songs.

Original Job: Wrote for *Topper* TV series, 1953, crossword puzzle writer
Major Awards: Grammy, Best Cast Show Album, *Company,* 1970; Tony, Best Score, *Company,* 1971; Tony, Best Score; *Follies,* 1972; Tony, Best Score, *A Little Night Music,* 1973; Grammy, Best Cast Show Album, *A Little Night Music,* 1973; Grammy, Song of the Year, "Send in the Clowns," 1975; Tony, Best Score, *Sweeney Todd,* 1979; Grammy, Best Cast Show Album, *Sweeney Todd,* 1979; Grammy, Best Cast Show Album, *Sunday in the Park with George,* 1984; Pulitzer Prize, Best Play, *Sunday in the Park with George,* 1985; Grammy, Best Cast Show Album, *West Side Story,* 1985; Grammy, Best Cast Show Album *Follies in Concert,* 1986; Tony, Best Score, *Into the Woods,* 1988; Grammy, Best Cast Show Album, *Into the Woods,* 1988; Oscar, Best Song, "Sooner or Later (I Always Get My Man)," 1990; Tony, Best Score, *Passion,* 1994

Quote: "I like neurotic people. I like troubled people. Not that I don't like squared away people, but I prefer neurotic people…Songs can't develop uncomplicated characters or unconflicted people. You can't just tell the sunny side and have a story with any richness to it."

KEVIN SORBO

Real Name: Kevin Sorbo
Birthplace: Bound, MN
Birthdate: 9/24/58
Occupation: Actor
Education: Attended University of Minnesota
Debut: (TV) *Murder, She Wrote,* 1993; (Film) *Kull, the Conqueror*
Signature: *Hercules*
Facts: Sorbo, who aspired to act from age 11, joined a theater group in Dallas after dropping out of college.

During the 1980s he filmed numerous TV commercials, including Diet Coke, Budweiser, BMW, and Lexus, before heading for Hollywood in 1987.

Lost the role of Superman in *Lois and Clark: The New Adventures of Superman* after seven auditions.
Original Job: Model
Marriage: Sam Jenkins, actor, 1998
Quotes: "I've paid my dues. It's not like I was an accountant and all of a sudden I said, 'Hey, I want a series.'"

MIRA SORVINO

Birthplace: Tenafly, NJ
Birthdate: 9/28/67
Occupation: Actor
Education: Harvard University
Debut: (Film) *Amongst Friends,* 1993
Signature: *Mighty Aphrodite,* 1995
Facts: The East Asian Studies major speaks fluent Chinese Mandarin.

Discouraged from acting by her father, took up ballet and performed in a professional production of *The Nutcracker* at age 12.

In addition to playing the female in *Amongst Friends*, was casting director and third assistant director.
Original Job: Script reader
Relationship: Olivier Martinez
Famous Relative: Paul Sorvino, actor, father
Major Award: Oscar, Best Supporting Actress, *Mighty Aphrodite,* 1995

SAMMY SOSA

Birthplace: San Pedro de Macoris, Dominican Republic
Birthdate: 11/10/68
Occupation: Baseball player
Debut: (Major League Baseball) Texas Rangers, 1989
Signature: record-breaking home-run hitter
Facts: As a child, after his father died when he was 7, Sosa sold oranges, shined shoes, and worked as a janitor to help support his family.

His first "baseball glove" was made out of a milk carton.

Signed with the Philadelphia Phillies when he was 15, but the contract was voided because he was too young. Signed the following year with the Texas Rangers, and gave the $3,500 bonus to his mother after buying himself a bicycle.

In 1993, was the first Chicago Cubs players to have 30 home runs and 30 stolen bases in a season.

His hometown was also produced major leaguers George Bell, Pedro Guererro, and Tony Fernandez.

Wears number 21 on his jersey in honor of Roberto Clemente.

In 1998 smashed Roger Maris's legendary record of 61 home runs in a season, hitting 66, but lost the record to Mark McGwire, who hit 70.
Marriage: Sonia
Children: Keysha; Kenia; Sammy; Michael
Major Award: National League Most Valuable Player, 1998
Quote: "My life is kind of like a miracle."

KEVIN SPACEY

Birthplace: South Orange, NJ
Birthdate: 7/26/59
Occupation: Actor
Education: Los Angeles Valley College, Juilliard
Debut: (Film) *Heartburn,* 1986
Signature: *Seven,* 1995
Facts: Kicked out of a military academy as a kid for hitting a classmate with a tire.

Worked in New York theater in classic Shakespeare, Chekhov, and O'Neill roles before coming to Hollywood.
Major Awards: Tony, Best Featured Actor (Dramatic), *Lost in Yonkers,* 1991; Oscar, Best Supporting Actor, *The Usual Suspects,* 1995

DAVID SPADE

Birthplace: Birmingham, MI
Birthdate: 7/22/64
Occupation: Comedian, actor
Education: Attended Arizona State University
Debut: (Film) *Police Academy 4,* 1987
Signature: *Just Shoot Me*
Facts: His father abandoned the family when he was 5.

In his debut year on *Saturday Night Live* he appeared on camera just three times.
Infamy: Many criticized his decision not to attend friend Chris Farley's funeral.
Original Job: Skateboard shop employee
Famous Relative: Kate Spade, handbag designer, sister-in-law

BRITNEY SPEARS

Birthplace: Kentwood, LA
Birthdate: 12/2/81
Occupation: Singer
Education: home-schooled
Debut: Album *[Hit Me]...Baby One More Time,* 1998; (Song) "[Hit Me]...Baby One More Time," 1998

Signature: "[Hit Me]...Baby One More Time"
Facts: Was turned away from *The Mickey Mouse Club* at age 9 as too young, but admitted 2 years later, joining such future stars as 'N Sync's JC Chasez and Justin Timberlake and Felicity's Keri Russell.

In 1991, was in the off-Broadway show *Ruthless*.

Was a *Star Search* champion in 1992.

Had arthroscopic surgery on her left knee in 1999 to remove cartilage damaged while rehearsing for a video.

Misses eating crawfish when she is on tour.

Favorite authors include Danielle Steel and Jackie Collins.

Her hometown has a population of approximately 2,500.
Quote: "I have really strong morals, and just because I look sexy on the cover of *Rolling Stone* doesn't mean that I'm a naughty girl."

AARON SPELLING

Birthplace: Dallas, TX
Birthdate: 4/22/23
Occupation: Producer, writer
Education: The Sorbonne, Southern Methodist University
Signature: *Beverly Hills 90210*
Facts: Served in U.S. Army Air Force, 1942–45; awarded the Bronze Star and Purple Heart with Oak Leaf Cluster.

In 1969, founded Thomas-Spelling Productions with actor Danny Thomas.

Has produced network hit series such as *The Mod Squad, Starsky and Hutch, S.W.A.T., Charlie's Angels, Family, Dynasty, Beverly Hills 90210,* and *Melrose Place.*
Original Job: Actor
Marriage: Carole Gene Marer, 1968
Children: Victoria "Tori" Davey, 1973; Randall Gene, 1976
Famous Relative: Tori Spelling, actor, daughter
Major Awards: Emmy, Outstanding

Drama/Comedy Special, *Day One,* 1989; Emmy, Outstanding Made-for-TV Movie, *And the Band Played On,* 1993
Quote: "I just got tired of the critics saying that I was the master of schlock. It didn't bother me until my kids began growing up and reading it. Well, I'm proud of those entertainment shows they call schlock."

STEVEN SPIELBERG

Birthplace: Cincinnati, OH
Birthdate: 12/18/46
Occupation: Director, producer
Education: California State College at Long Beach
Debut: (TV) *Night Gallery,* 1969
Signature: *E.T., the Extra-Terrestrial,* 1982
Facts: Made the film *Firelight* at age 16, about the reflecting telescope he made himself, and his father hired a Phoenix, AZ, movie house to show it.

Became a TV director at Universal Pictures at age 20 after finding an empty office and pretending he belonged there.

Was not accepted by the University of Southern California's film department.

Co-owns the Las Vegas restaurant Dive! with Jeffrey Katzenberg.

A 22-minute film he made in college, *Amblin',* brought him the attention of Sidney Sheinberg, at the time head of Universal Television. It also provided the name for his production company.

Directed the first episode of *Columbo,* as well as installments of *Marcus Welby, M.D.*
Marriages: Amy Irving (divorced), Kate Capshaw, 1991
Children: Jessica, 1976 (stepdaughter); Max, 1985; (with Amy Irving). Theo, 1988 (adopted); Sasha, 1990; Sawyer, 1992; Mikaela George, 1996 (adopted); Destry Allyn, 1996
Famous Relative: Anne Spielberg, screenwriter, sister
Major Awards: Academy of Motion

Picture Arts and Sciences, Irving G. Thalberg Award, 1986; Oscar, Best Director, *Schindler's List,* 1993; American Film Institute Lifetime Achievement Award, 1995; Oscar, Best Director, *Saving Private Ryan,* 1998

JERRY SPRINGER

Birthplace: London, England
Birthdate: 2/13/44
Occupation: Talk-show host
Education: Tulane University, Northwestern Law School
Signature: *The Jerry Springer Show*
Facts: His family emigrated from London when he was 5.

Elected mayor of Cincinnati at age 33; later ran for governor of Ohio but lost.

Was a serious news anchor and commentator before hosting his talk show.

His daughter was born without nasal passages and is legally blind and deaf in one ear.
Infamy: Early in his career while vice mayor of Cincinnati, police found his check to a whorehouse and he resigned in disgrace.

A Chicago TV station's offer that he do commentaries for the news prompted the resignation of two esteemed anchors.

Several ex-guests accused his show of staging dialogue, situations, and those notorious fights—charges Springer denied.
Original Job: Presidential campaign worker for Robert Kennedy
Marriage: Micki Velton, 1973 (divorced 1994)
Child: Katie, 1976
Major Awards: Seven local Emmys for nightly news commentaries

BRUCE SPRINGSTEEN

Birthplace: Freehold, NJ
Birthdate: 9/23/49
Occupation: Singer, songwriter
Education: Ocean City Community College

Debut: (Album) *Greetings from Asbury Park,* 1973
Signature: *Born in the USA*
Facts: E Street Band, formed in 1973, was named after the road in Belmar, NJ, where keyboardist David Sancious's mother lives.

After a 1976 Memphis concert, was caught climbing over the wall to Graceland.

Gave the song "Because the Night" to Patti Smith's producer, who was working in the adjacent recording studio.

In 1986, he rejected a $12-million offer from Lee Iococca to use "Born in the U.S.A." for Chrysler commercials.
Marriages: Julianne Phillips (divorced); Patti Scialfa, 1991
Children: Evan, 1990; Jessica, 1991; Sam, 1994
Major Awards: Grammy, Best Recording for Children, *In Harmony 2* (with others), 1982; Grammy, Best Rock Vocal, "Dancing in the Dark," 1984; Grammy, Best Rock Vocal, "Tunnel of Love," 1987; Oscar, Best Song, "Streets of Philadelphia," 1993; Grammy, Song of the Year, "Streets of Philadelphia," 1994; Grammy, Best Rock Vocal—Male, "Streets of Philadelphia," 1994; Grammy, Best Rock Song, "Streets of Philadelphia," 1994; Grammy, Best Song Written for a Motion Picture, "Streets of Philadelphia," 1994; Grammy, Best Contemporary Folk Recording, *The Ghost of Tom Joad,* 1996; inducted into Rock and Roll Hall of Fame, 1999

SYLVESTER STALLONE

Birthplace: Hell's Kitchen, New York
Birthdate: 7/6/46
Occupation: Actor, writer, director
Education: American School of Switzerland, University of Miami
Debut: (Film) *Bananas,* 1971
Signature: *Rocky,* 1976
Facts: When he was born, the forceps severed a nerve in his face and partially paralyzed his lip, chin, and half of his tongue.

Had rickets as a child.

In high school he played football, fenced, and threw discus.

His paintings have been featured in galleries.

In *Bananas* (1971), played a goon who was thrown off a subway by Woody Allen.

As a boy was kicked out of fourteen schools in eleven years.

In 1971 appeared in a soft-core porn film, *A Party at Kitty & Stud's.*

Finally completed his degree at the University of Miami nearly 30 years after he dropped out.
Infamy: In March 1994, dumped longtime girlfriend Jennifer Flavin via letter sent FedEx. They have since reconciled.

Romanced Janice Dickinson, until DNA tests revealed that her newborn daughter wasn't his. She claimed to be pregnant by him again, then miscarried.
Original Job: Usher, fish salesman, zoo attendant, bookstore detective, teacher at American School of Switzerland.
Marriages: Sasha Czack (divorced), Brigitte Nielsen (divorced), Jennifer Flavin, 1997
Children: Sage, 1976; Seargeoh, 1979; (with Sasha Czack). Sophia Rose, 1996; Sistine Rose, 1998
Famous Relative: Frank Stallone, musician, brother; Jacqueline Stallone, astrologer, mother

DANIELLE STEEL

Real Name: Danielle Schuelein-Steel
Birthplace: New York, NY
Birthdate: 8/14/47
Occupation: Writer
Education: Lycée Français, Parsons School of Design, New York University
Debut: (Book) *Going Home,* 1973
Facts: Wrote over 30 best-selling novels in 20 years, including *The Ring* (1980), *Secrets* (1985), and *Daddy* (1989).

Vowed to wear only black until the one-year anniversary of her son's death.
Infamy: Two of her ex-husbands were convicts; she married one while he was still in prison, the other when she was eight months pregnant with his child.
Original Job: Vice president of public relations and new business for Supergirls, Ltd., a PR and ad agency
Marriages: Claude-Eric Lazard (divorced), Danny Zugelder (divorced), Bill Toth (divorced), John Traina (divorced); Tom Perkins, 1998 (separated, 1999)
Children: Beatrix, 1968 (with Claude-Eric Lazard). Nicholas, 1978 (deceased, 1997); (with Bill Toth). Samantha, 1982; Victoria, 1983; Vanessa, 1984; Max, 1986; Zara, 1987 (with John Traina).

GWEN STEFANI

Birthplace: Anaheim, CA
Birthdate: 10/3/69
Occupation: Singer, songwriter
Education: Attended California State—Fullerton
Debut: (Album) *No Doubt,* 1992
Signature: No Doubt
Facts: Older brother Eric recruited her in 1986 to sing in the band he formed with his Dairy Queen coworker John Spence, their flamboyant front man who the following year fatally shot himself in a local park. Gwen was eventually encouraged to step out front so the group could continue.

The bouncy group gave away kazoos at the album-release party for their first record. Released at the height of grunge's popularity, the album bombed.

Started wearing the stick-on *pottu* dots, the jewel-like Hindi forehead decoration, when she dated fellow band member Tony Kanal, whose parents are Indian. Many of the songs on *Tragic Kingdom* reflect her distress about their breakup after seven years.
Relationship: Gavin Rossdale

HOWARD STERN

Birthplace: New York, NY
Birthdate: 1/12/54
Occupation: Radio DJ
Education: Boston University
Signature: *The Howard Stern Show*
Facts: 1994 Libertarian gubernatorial candidate in New York but dropped out of race before the elections.

Once fired for referring to station management as "scumbags" on the air during a salary dispute.

Practices transcendental meditation each morning in the limo ride to work.
Infamy: After angry listeners provided the FCC with transcripts of Stern's show about masturbating to thoughts of Aunt Jemima and having rough sex with actress Michelle Pfeiffer, the commission fined Infinity Broadcasting, which owns WNBC-New York, $600,000.

Stern made fun of singer Selena Quintanilla Perez after her murder in April 1995, playing her music with sounds of gunfire in the background and parodying her mourners. The League of United Latin American Citizens said it intended to drive Stern's program off the air. Stern later apologized for his conduct.

Refusing to apologize for calling French-speakers "scumbags," Stern reasoned, "I can't imagine anybody would take what I say seriously."

In 1999, he signed a deal to produce his own animated cartoon series about people in motor homes searching for family values in post–apocalyptic America.
Marriage: Alison Berns, 1978
Children: Emily, Debra, Ashley Jade, 1993

JON STEWART

Real Name: Jon Stuart Liebowitz
Birthplace: Lawrence, NJ
Birthdate: 11/28/62
Occupation: Comedian, actor
Education: College of William and Mary
Debut: (TV) *Short Attention Span Theater*, 1991
Signature: *The Daily Show, with Jon Stewart*
Facts: Got the idea to do stand-up at age 24, when using puppets to teach schoolkids about disabled people—a gig that honed his prop-wielding skills. Went on the road doing stand-up for the next six years.

His parents divorced when he was 9, and his relationship with his dad became increasingly strained over the years as Stewart gleefully aired the family's dirty laundry in his club acts.
Original Job: Bartender, bike mechanic, porter in a bakery, research lab assistant
Quote: "As long as I can remember, I wanted to sleep late, stay up late, and do nothing in between."

MARTHA STEWART

Birthplace: Nutley, NJ
Birthdate: 8/3/41
Occupation: Entertainment and lifestyle consultant
Education: Barnard College
Debut: (Book) *Entertaining*, 1981
Signature: *Martha Stewart Living*
Facts: Has published more than a dozen books on entertaining.

Discovered her love for decorating, gardening, and cooking when she and her husband bought a Connecticut farmhouse and fixed it up themselves in 1971. Over the years, she added a barn-turned-party-room, a greenhouse, pool, vegetable gardens, orchards, an English border garden, and beehives, turkeys, chickens, and cats.

Sleeps four hours a night with the lights on so when she wakes up she can get right to work.

Has filed an extortion, coercion, and defamation suit against a land-scaper who claims she and her car pinned him against a security box.
Original Job: Model, stockbroker, take-out gourmet food store owner
Marriage: Andy Stewart (divorced, 1990)
Child: Alexis, 1965

PATRICK STEWART

Birthplace: Mirfield, England
Birthdate: 7/13/40
Occupation: Actor, writer
Education: Bristol Old Vic Theatre School
Debut: (Stage) *Treasure Island*, 1959
Signature: *Star Trek: The Next Generation*
Facts: Was so sure that he was going to be fired from the initial season of *Star Trek: The Next Generation* that he didn't unpack his bags for six weeks.
Original Job: Journalist
Marriage: Sheila Falconer, 1966 (divorced, 1990); Wendy Neuss (engaged, 1997)
Children: Daniel Freedom, 1968; Sophie Alexandra, 1973
Quote: "I was brought up in a very poor and very violent household. I spent much of my childhood being afraid."

BEN STILLER

Birthplace: New York, NY
Birthdate: 11/30/65
Occupation: Actor, director
Education: UCLA
Debut: (Film) *Empire of the Sun*, 1987
Signature: *Reality Bites*, 1994
Facts: At age 10, began making Super-8 movies about getting revenge on bullies in his neighborhood.

Learned swimming from the Pips, Gladys Knight's backup vocalists.

His short film parody of *The Color of Money* landed him a job at *Saturday Night Live* and his own show on MTV.

Was once engaged to Jeanne Triplehorn.
Famous Relatives: Jerry Stiller, comedian, father; Anne Meara,

comedian, mother; Amy Stiller, actor, sister
Major Award: Emmy, Best Writing in Variety or Music Program, *The Ben Stiller Show* (with others), 1992

R. L. STINE

Real Name: Robert Lawrence Stine
Birthplace: Columbus, OH
Birthdate: 10/8/43
Occupation: Writer
Education: Ohio State University, New York University
Signature: The Goosebumps series
Facts: Noted author of the Goosebumps and Fear Street series of books for children among others, he has sold over 170 million books.

Before hitting it big, wrote everything from coloring books to bubble gum cards.

Types only with his left index finger.

In 1997 he published his autobiography, *It Came from Ohio.*

Has written under the pseudonyms Eric Affabee, Zachary Blue, Jovial Bob Stine.
Original Jobs: Social studies teacher; magazine editor
Marriage: Jane Waldhorn, 1969
Children: Matthew, 1980
Quote: "I've been called a literary training bra for Stephen King."

STING

Real Name: Gordon Matthew Sumner
Birthplace: Newcastle upon Tyne, England
Birthdate: 10/2/51
Occupation: Singer, songwriter, actor
Education: Warwick University
Debut: (Song) "Fall Out" (with The Police), 1977
Signature: The Police
Facts: Rejected the villain role in James Bond film *A View to a Kill.*

He gained his nickname by wearing a black-and-yellow striped shirt, like a bee.

Received a seaman's card and worked as a bass player with The Ronnie Pierson Trio on Princess Cruise Lines at age 17.

Claimed in a 1993 *Rolling Stone* interview that by practicing meditation, he can make love for more than five hours at a time.
Original Job: Teacher, construction worker, clerk for Inland Revenue
Marriages: Frances Eleanor Tomelty (divorced); Trudie Styler, 1996
Children: Joseph, 1977; Katherine "Kate," 1982 (with Tomelty); Michael "Mickey," 1984; Jake, 1985; Eliot Pauline "Coco," 1990; Giacomo Luke, 1995 (with Styler)
Major Awards: Grammy, Best Rock Performance—Duo or Group, "Don't Stand So Close to Me" (with The Police), 1981; Grammy, Song of the Year, "Every Breath You Take," 1983; Grammy, Best Pop Performance—Duo or Group, "Every Breath You Take" (with The Police), 1983; Grammy, Best Pop Vocal—Male, "Bring On the Night," 1987; Grammy, Best Rock Song/Vocal Performance, "Soul Cages," 1991; Grammy, Best Pop Vocal—Male, "If I Ever Lose My Faith in You," 1993; Grammy, Best Music Video—Long Form, *Ten Summoner's Tales,* 1993

MICHAEL STIPE

Birthplace: Decatur, GA
Birthdate: 1/4/60
Occupation: Singer, songwriter
Education: Southern Illinois University, University of Georgia
Debut: *Chronic Town* (with R.E.M.), 1982
Signature: R.E.M.
Facts: In the early years of R.E.M., traveled to 49 states by the time he was 24.

Planned to record with friend Kurt Cobain. Cobain had tickets to come to Stipe's in Atlanta but called to cancel, and committed suicide soon after.
Infamy: Was rumored to have AIDS because, he says, he is thin, has bad

skin, and is sexually ambiguous. He denies being HIV-positive.
Major Awards: Grammy, Best Alternative Performance, *Out of Time,* 1991; Grammy, Best Pop Vocal—Group, "Losing My Religion," 1991

OLIVER STONE

Birthplace: New York, NY
Birthdate: 9/15/46
Occupation: Director, writer, producer
Education: Yale University, New York University film school
Debut: (Film) *Seizure,* 1974
Signature: *Platoon,* 1986
Facts: Served in the U.S. Merchant Marine, 1966; in the Army in Vietnam, 1967–68. Awarded Bronze Star and Purple Heart with Oak Leaf Cluster.

Made acting debut as a bum in *The Hand* (1981), which he wrote and directed.
Infamy: At least 10 real killings were linked to his ode to violence, *Natural Born Killers,* with one 14-year-old decapitator even telling friends he wanted to be famous like the killers in the movie.

Was arrested in 1999 for allegedly driving under the influence and possession of hashish. Plead no contest on the DUI count and guilty to possession, and was ordered to enter drug and alchohol treatment programs.
Original Job: Taxi driver in New York City, teacher at Free Pacific Institute in South Vietnam
Marriages: Majwa Sarkis (divorced); Elizabeth Burkit Cox (divorced, 1993)
Children: Sean, 1984; Michael, 1991; (with Elizabeth Cox Stone). Tara, 1995 (with Chong Son Chong).
Major Awards: Oscar, Best Adapted Screenplay, *Midnight Express,* 1978; Oscar, Best Director, *Platoon,* 1986; Oscar, Best Director, *Born on the Fourth of July,* 1991

SHARON STONE

Birthplace: Meadville, PA
Birthdate: 3/10/58
Occupation: Actor
Education: Edinboro State University
Debut: (Film) *Stardust Memories,* 1981
Signature: *Basic Instinct,* 1992
Facts: She has an I.Q. of 154.

Between 1977 and 1980, became one of the top 10 models at the Ford Agency.

Infamy: Posed nude for *Playboy* just days after finishing *Total Recall,* 1990.
Original Job: Model
Marriages: Michael Greenburg (divorced), Phil Bronstein, 1998
Famous Relative: Michael Stone, actor, brother
Quote: "If I was just intelligent, I'd be OK. But I am fiercely intelligent, which most people find threatening... I have a strong point of view based on my experience. It may or may not be the correct one, but it is an informed one, and I'm willing to fight for it. If I were a petite, brunette, ethnic lawyer then my behavior would be totally acceptable. But we Barbie dolls are not supposed to behave the way I do."

GEORGE STRAIT

Birthplace: Pearsall, TX
Birthdate: 5/18/52
Occupation: Singer, songwriter
Education: Southwest Texas State
Debut: (Album) *Let's Get Down To It,* 1976
Signature: "Carrying Your Love With Me"
Facts: Grew up on a Texas ranch his family owned for decades.

Before joining the army, eloped with his high school sweetheart.

Frustrated by his lack of success, gave up singing in 1979 and went back to his agriculture roots. Returned soon after to give it one more try.

Original Job: Cattle-pen employee

Marriage: Norma
Children: Jenifer (deceased), George Jr.

MERYL STREEP

Real Name: Mary Louise Streep
Birthplace: Summit, NJ
Birthdate: 6/22/49
Occupation: Actor
Education: Vassar College; MFA, Yale University
Debut: (Stage) *Trelawny of the Wells,* NY Shakespeare Festival, 1975; (Film) *Julia,* 1977
Signature: *Sophie's Choice,* 1982
Facts: When she was 12, began studying with vocal coach Estelle Liebling, who had also taught diva Beverly Sills.

In high school, was a cheerleader and homecoming queen.

Formed a child support group with Annette Bening, Carrie Fisher, and Tracey Ullman, in which they watch each other's children.

When New York theater giant Joseph Papp—who ran New York's Public Theater and Shakespeare in the Park—knew he was dying, he asked Streep to succeed him; she turned him down so she could devote more time to her family.

Original Job: Waitress
Marriage: Don Gummer, 1978
Children: Henry, 1979; Mary Willa, 1983; Grace Jane, 1986; Louisa Jacobson, 1991
Major Awards: Emmy, Best Actress in a Miniseries, *Holocaust,* 1978; Oscar, Best Supporting Actress, *Kramer vs. Kramer,* 1979; Oscar, Best Actress, *Sophie's Choice,* 1982

BARBRA STREISAND

Real Name: Barbara Streisand
Birthplace: Brooklyn, NY
Birthdate: 4/24/42
Occupation: Singer, actor, director
Education: Yeshiva University
Debut: (Stage) *Another Evening with Harry Stoones,* 1961; (Film) *Funny Girl,* 1968

Signature: "The Way We Were"
Facts: Her father died when she was 15 months old.

She graduated from high school two years early.

Although she had never sung before an audience before, she won a talent contest in a Greenwich Village bar and won a singing job at another bar.

Her Academy Award for *Funny Girl* (1968) was shared with Katharine Hepburn for *A Lion in Winter;* it's only tie for the Best Actress Oscar to date.

Reportedly has a pet name from her husband: "Beezer."

Behind Elvis Presley, she's only the second artist to claim 40 gold albums. Her *Christmas Album* is the only vocal holiday album to sell over 5 million copies.

Original Job: Theater usher, switchboard operator, waitress
Marriages: Elliot Gould (divorced); James Brolin, 1998
Child: Jason Emanuel, 1966 (with Elliot Gould)
Famous Relative: Roslyn Kind, singer, sister
Major Awards: Grammy, Best Female Pop Vocalist 1963–65; Emmy, Outstanding Program Achievements in Entertainment, *My Name Is Barbra,* 1965; Oscar, Best Actress, *Funny Girl,* 1968; Tony, Special Award, 1970; Oscar, Best Song, "Evergreen" (with Paul Williams), 1976; Grammy, Best Songwriter (with Paul Williams), 1977; Grammy, Best Female Pop Vocalist, 1977, 1986; Grammy, Legend Award, 1992; Emmy, Best Individual Performance in a Variety or Music Program, *Barbra Streisand: The Concert,* 1995

QUENTIN TARANTINO

Birthplace: Knoxville, TN
Birthdate: 3/27/63
Occupation: Director, writer, actor
Education: High school dropout
Debut: (Film) *Reservoir Dogs,* 1992 (writer, director, and actor)

Signature: *Pulp Fiction*, 1994
Facts: Studied movies while working at an L.A. video store for four years. Got the idea for *Reservoir Dogs* when he saw that no one had made a heist movie in a long time.

Once played an Elvis impersonator on *The Golden Girls*.

Is said to have an I.Q. of 160.

Had already tried his hand at screenwriting as a teenager, penning *Captain Peachfuzz and the Anchovy Bandit*.
Infamy: Once went to jail for failing to pay his parking tickets.

Physically attacked *Natural Born Killers* producer Don Murphy in an L.A. restaurant; recounted the episode on Keenan Ivory Wayans's talk show as a "bitch-slap." Got into another bar brawl in the spring of 1998.
Original Job: Video sales clerk
Major Awards: Cannes Film Festival, Palme d'Or, *Pulp Fiction*, 1994; Oscar, Best Original Screenplay, *Pulp Fiction*, 1994
Quotes: "People ask me if I went to film school. And I tell them, 'No, I went to films.' "

ELIZABETH TAYLOR

Birthplace: London, England
Birthdate: 2/27/32
Occupation: Actor
Education: Byron House, Hawthorne School, Metro-Goldwyn-Mayer School
Debut: (Film) *There's One Born Every Minute*, 1942
Signature: *Cleopatra*
Facts: Almost died from pnuemonia and had an emergency tracheotomy in 1961.

When she was three years old she danced before Queen Elizabeth and Princess Margaret.

After friend Rock Hudson died from AIDS, became the founding chair of the American Foundation for AIDS Research (AMFAR) in 1985.

She met construction worker Larry Fortensky, whom she married in 1992, at the Betty Ford Clinic.

Infamy: Checked herself into the Betty Ford Clinic to overcome alcohol dependency, 1983. Returned in 1988 to overcome painkiller dependency.
Marriages: Nicholas Conrad Hilton Jr. (divorced); Michael Wilding (divorced); Mike Todd (deceased); Eddie Fisher (divorced); Richard Burton (divorced, remarried, divorced); John Warner (divorced); Larry Fortensky (divorced, 1996)
Children: Michael, 1953; Christopher, 1955; (with Michael Wilding). Liza, 1957 (with Mike Todd). Maria Carson, c.1961 (adopted with Richard Burton).
Major Awards: Oscar, Best Actress, *Butterfield 8*, 1960; Oscar, Best Actress, *Who's Afraid of Virginia Woolf*, 1966; Oscar, Jean Hersholt Humanitarian Award, 1992; American Film Institute Lifetime Achievement Award, 1993
Quote: "I've been known to swim in my emeralds."

JOHN TESH

Birthplace: Garden City, NY
Birthdate: 7/9/52
Occupation: Television host, composer, pianist
Education: Attended Juilliard during high school, North Carolina State University
Signature: *Entertainment Tonight*
Facts: Anchored local TV news in Durham, N.C.; Orlando; Nashville; and New York before signing with CBS Sports and, in 1986, *Entertainment Tonight*.

An incurable romantic, he proposed to Selleca by reserving an entire Monterey restaurant; hiring a string quartet to serenade her with a song he had written, "Concetta"; and arranging for a fireworks display outside the window.

He and Selleca, who pledged to avoid premarital sex during their year-long courtship, starred in a late-night infomercial for a series of videos about relationships.

Composed songs for sporting

events he was covering for CBS, including the Tour de France and the Pan-American Games, both of which won Emmys.

His own recording label, GTS Records, has sold more than two million of his CDs. His *Romantic Christmas,* with Selleca, went gold, selling more than 500,000 copies.

Whenever Tesh performs a concert, the event's promoters are contractually bound to provide at least one World Wrestling Foundation action figure for his dressing room.

In 1998 he graced 12 million Kellogg's Complete Oat Bran Flakes cereal boxes (his late parents both suffered from heart-related ailments).
Original Job: TV reporter
Marriages: Julie Wright (divorced); Connie Selleca, 1992
Child: Prima, 1994
Major Awards: Emmy, Best Musical Composition for a Sports Program, Pan-American Games, 1983; Emmy, Best Musical Score, Tour de France, 1987

CHARLIZE THERON

Birthplace: Benoni, South Africa
Birthdate: 8/7/75
Occupation: Actor, model
Debut: (Film) *Two Days in the Valley,* 1996
Facts: Had a pet goat as a child.

Afrikaans was her first language. She mastered English by watching television.

Her father was French, her mother German.

At 16 entered a modeling contest on a whim and won. After a brief modeling stint, she studied with the Joffrey Ballet until a knee injury halted her career.

By 1994 she settled in Los Angeles and caught the attention of a personal manager when she caused a fuss because a bank would not cash her check.

She and her mother have matching fish tattoos.

Original Job: Model
Relationships: Stephan Jenkins, musician with Third Eye Blind, 1998
Quotes: "A nice pair of pumps, a skirt that goes to your knees, that Vargas-red-lipstick glamour—to me, that's what a girl is."

JONATHAN TAYLOR THOMAS

Real Name: Jonathan Weiss
Birthplace: Bethlehem, PA
Birthdate: 9/8/81
Occupation: Actor
Debut: (TV) *The Bradys,* 1990
Signature: *Home Improvement*
Facts: Was the voice of Simba in *The Lion King,* as well as several other characters in kids' cartoons.

Got straight A's when attending public school during breaks in filming.

Has received nearly 50,000 pieces of fan mail a month.
Original Job: Model
Quote: "On occasion, I've taken the test that's been in the teen magazines about me and I've failed. Isn't that scary?"

KRISTIN SCOTT THOMAS

Birthplace: Redruth, Cornwall, England
Birthdate: 5/24/60
Occupation: Actor
Education: Attended London's Central School of Speech and Drama and Paris's Ecole Nationale des Arts et Techniques de Theatre
Debut: (Film) *Under the Cherry Moon,* 1986
Signature: *The English Patient,* 1996
Facts: Her father, a naval pilot, was killed in a flying accident when she was 5. Some years later her stepfather, another naval pilot, was killed in a nearly identical crash.

At 16, enrolled in a convent school with aspirations to be a nun.

Was married in Dorset, a beautiful part of England made famous by novelist Thomas Hardy. Two days of ceremonies included one civil and one before a rabbi and a priest (she's Catholic).
Marriage: Francois Oliviennes
Children: Hannah, c.1989; Joseph, 1991
Famous Relative: Serena Scott Thomas, model, actor, sister

EMMA THOMPSON

Birthplace: London, England
Birthdate: 4/15/59
Occupation: Actor
Education: Cambridge University
Debut: (Film) *Henry V,* 1989
Signature: *Howards End,* 1992
Facts: Wrote screenplay adaptation of *Sense and Sensibility* by Jane Austen, whose novels she began reading at age 9.

When first met her ex-husband, Kenneth Branagh, she "thought he had strange hair."

Lives on the street on which she was raised, opposite her mother and down the street from her younger sister, Sophie.
Marriage: Kenneth Branagh (divorced, 1996); Greg Wise (relationship)
Famous Relatives: Eric Thompson, producer, father; Phyllida Law, actor, mother; Sophie Thompson, actor, sister
Major Award: Oscar, Best Actress, *Howards End,* 1992; Oscar, Best Adapted Screenplay, *Sense and Sensibility,* 1995

COURTNEY THORNE-SMITH

Birthplace: San Francisco, CA
Birthdate: 11/8/67
Occupation: Actor
Education: High school
Debut: (Film) *Lucas,* 1986; (TV) *Fast Time,* 1986
Signature: *Melrose Place*
Facts: Her hyphenated name is a combination of her mother's maiden name, Thorne, and her father's name, Smith.

Drew attention with her recurring role in *L.A. Law* in 1990.

Used to date actor Andrew Shue.
Relationship: Andrew Conrad, engaged 1998

BILLY BOB THORNTON

Birthplace: Alpine, AR
Birthdate: 8/4/55
Occupation: Actor, screenwriter, director
Education: Attended Henderson State University
Debut: (Film) *Hunter's Blood,* 1986
Signature: *Sling Blade,* 1996
Facts: Grew up in a rural area with coal-oil lamps and an outhouse, where supper was whatever grandpa happened to shoot.

Mother Virginia was a psychic, who once predicted that Thornton would work with Burt Reynolds, which he did on *Evening Shade* in 1990.

Broke for years in L.A., he ate nothing but potatoes during a particularly bleak period in 1984, which resulted in nearly fatal heart failure.

Sling Blade's character Karl came to Thornton in 1985 while in a B-movie trailer awaiting his four-line part. The character later appeared in his 1994 short film *Some Folks Call It a Sling Blade,* a forerunner to the feature.

Terrified of flying, he got distributor Miramax to drive him to the New York Film Festival from L.A. in a limousine.
Original Job: Drummer (one of his bands, Tres Hombres, once opened for Hank Williams Jr.), singer, screen-door factory worker, pizza maker
Marriage: Melissa Lee Gatlin, 1978 (divorced, 1980); Toni Lawrence, 1986 (divorced, 1988); Cynda Williams (divorced, 1992); Pietra Dawn Cherniak, 1993 (divorced, 1997); Laura Dern (relationship)
Children: Amanda, 1979 (with Melissa Lee Gatlin). William

Langston, 1993; Harry James, 1994; (with Pietra Dawn Cherniak).
Major Award: Oscar, Best Adapted Screenplay, *Sling Blade*, 1996
Quote: "I prefer eating with plastic—I can't use real silver. Swear to God. I think some big old mad king used to use it or something."

UMA THURMAN

Birthplace: Boston, MA
Birthdate: 4/29/70
Occupation: Actor
Education: Professional Children's School
Debut: (Film) *Kiss Daddy Good Night,* 1987
Signature: *Pulp Fiction,* 1994
Facts: Her father, Robert, a professor of Asian religion, named her Uma after a Hindu goddess.

Her Swedish mother, a psychotherapist, was once married to Timothy Leary.

The nearly six-foot actress quit school and headed for New York at age 16. Modeling jobs and movies quickly followed.
Original Job: Model, dishwasher
Marriage: Gary Oldman (divorced); Ethan Hawke, 1998
Child: Maya Ray Thurman-Hawke, 1998

JOHN TRAVOLTA

Birthplace: Englewood, NJ
Birthdate: 2/18/54
Occupation: Actor
Education: High school dropout
Debut: (Stage) *Who Will Save the Plow,* 1966; (Film) *The Devil's Rain,* 1975; (TV) *Welcome Back, Kotter,* 1975
Signature: *Saturday Night Fever,* 1977
Facts: Holds the record for the most *Rolling Stone* covers for an actor: four.

An avid flyer since the age of 16, he turned down the lead in *An Officer and a Gentleman,* a part reportedly

written for him, because the shooting conflicted with his attendance of American Airlines' month-long jet pilot training school. In 1995, a plane he owns and was piloting lost electrical power over Washington, DC, and had a mid-air near-miss with a commercial jetliner.

His first love, actor Diana Hyland, was 18 years older than the then 22-year-old Travolta. Nine months into the romance she died of cancer—in Travolta's arms.

Languished for nearly a decade in forgettable and/or unpopular films until *Pulp Fiction* restored him to Hollywood's A-list. He earned just $140,000 for his part in the film, far less than the millions-per-picture he once commanded and now receives again.

Has been a member of the Church of Scientology for more than 20 years.
Marriage: Kelly Preston, 1991
Child: Jett, 1992
Famous Relatives: Ellen Travolta, actor, sister; Joey Travolta, actor, brother

CHRIS TUCKER

Birthplace: Atlanta, GA
Birthdate: 8/31/71
Occupation: Comedian, actor
Education: High school
Debut: (Film) *House Party 3,* 1994
Signature: *Fifth Element*
Facts: Is the youngest of six children.

Was voted Most Humorous in his high school, dubbed a Little Eddie Murphy.

Personally rewrote or improvised most of his trademark quick dialogue in *Money Talks.*

TANYA TUCKER

Birthplace: Seminole, TX
Birthdate: 10/10/58
Occupation: Singer
Education: High school dropout
Debut: (Album) *Delta Dawn,* 1972
Signature: "Delta Dawn"
Facts: Her family moved to Las

Vegas when she was 12, on the theory that it was a good city to launch a new entertainer. Within two years she had a hit in "Delta Dawn," a $1.5 million record deal, and a cover story in *Rolling Stone.*

High-profile romances included Merle Haggard, Don Johnson, the late Andy Gibb, and Glen Campbell.

Has released more than 30 country albums.

A reported $700,000 advance and the prodding of friends convinced her to write the tell-all, *Nickel Dreams.*
Infamy: Began drinking in her late teens and quickly developed a reputation as a wild party girl. The cocaine, alcohol, and violence that was integral to her 1980 relationship with Glen Campbell became a national symbol of celebrity excess (the pair split in 1981, and Tucker continued her drinking and drugging until entering the Betty Ford clinic in 1988).

In 1997, with a TV crew in attendance to film a *Dateline* profile segment, Tucker flashed her breasts to a roomful of Nashville music-industry partygoers.
Relationship: Jerry Laseter (engaged)
Children: Presley Tanita, 1989; Beau Grayson, 1991 (both with Ben Reed)

CHRISTY TURLINGTON

Birthplace: Walnut Creek, CA
Birthdate: 1/2/69
Occupation: Supermodel
Education: New York University
Facts: Her face was used on mannequins at the Metropolitan Museum of Art's costume galleries.

Dated screenwriter Roger Wilson for seven years; they had a Buddhist service together, though they were never officially married. Also dated Jason Patric.

Plans to attend graduate school—possibly in a writing program.

TED TURNER

Real Name: Robert Edward Turner III
Birthplace: Cincinnati, OH
Birthdate: 11/19/38
Occupation: Media executive, owner of Atlanta Braves and Hawks
Education: Brown University
Debut: In 1970, bought failing Atlanta TV station, which he turned into WTBS
Signature: CNN
Facts: Won the America's Cup in his yacht, *Courageous,* in 1977.

Interested in owning a major TV network, he made a failed bid for CBS in 1985, and launched negotiations with NBC in 1994 that ultimately broke down.

Owns four bison ranches out west, making him America's largest private bison rancher.
Infamy: Was "asked to leave" Brown University in 1967 for having a girl in his room after hours; was later awarded an honorary degree.
Original Job: Selling space on billboards in family business
Marriages: Judy Nye (divorced), Janie Shirley Smith (divorced), Jane Fonda, 1991
Children: Laura Seydel, 1961; Robert Edward IV, 1963; (with Judy Nye). Rhett, 1965; Beau, 1968; Sara Jean "Jennie," 1969; (with Janie Shirley Smith).
Major Award: Elected to the Emmy Hall of Fame, 1991

TINA TURNER

Real Name: Anna Mae Bullock
Birthplace: Nutbush, TN
Birthdate: 11/26/39
Occupation: Singer, actor
Debut: (Song) "Fool in Love," 1960
Signature: "What's Love Go to Do with It?" 1984
Facts: "River Deep, Mountain High" (1966) was No. 1 in Britain and earned The Ike and Tina Turner Revue the chance to open for The Rolling Stones in 1969.

Became a Buddhist in the early '80s.

Endured years of physical abuse and extramarital affairs by then husband Ike.
Marriage: Ike Turner, 1956 (divorced, 1978); Erwin Bach (relationship)
Children: Raymond Craig Hill, 1958 (with Raymond Hill); Ronald Renelle "Ronnie," 1960 (with Ike Turner)
Major Awards: Grammy, Best R&B Duo or Group, "Proud Mary" (with Ike Turner), 1972; Grammy, Record of the Year and Best Pop Vocal—Female, "What's Love Got to Do with It?," 1984; Grammy, Best Rock Vocal of the Year, "Better Be Good to Me," 1985; Grammy, Best Rock Vocal of the Year, "One of the Living," 1986; Grammy, Best Rock Vocal of the Year, "Back Where You Started," 1986; Grammy, Best Rock Vocal of the Year, *Tina Live in Europe,* 1988; inducted into Rock and Roll Hall of Fame, 1991

SHANIA TWAIN

Real name: Eileen Regina Twain
Birthplace: Windsor, Ontario
Birthdate: 8/28/65
Occupation: Singer, songwriter
Education: High school
Debut: (Album) *Shania Twain,* 1993
Signature: *The Woman in Me,* 1995
Facts: Grew up so poor her Canadian family often went without heat.

Says she's of Ojibwa Indian ancestry, but was actually adopted by her Indian stepfather. Shania means "I'm on my way" in Ojibwa dialect.

Raised her three younger siblings after her parents died in an auto accident when she was 21.
Original job: secretary
Marriage: Robert "Mutt" Lange, 1993
Major Awards: Grammy, Best Country Album, *The Woman in Me,* 1995; Best Country Song, "You're Still The One" (with Robert John "Mutt" Lange), 1998; Grammy, Best

Country Vocal—Female, "You're Still The One," 1998

LIV TYLER

Birthplace: New York, NY
Birthdate: 7/1/77
Occupation: Actor
Education: High school
Debut: (Film) *Silent Fall,* 1994
Signature: *Armageddon,* 1998
Facts: First came to the world's attention as the girl wearing a silver bra in the Aerosmith's 1994 video "Crazy," which also starred Alicia Silverstone.

As a child, believed her father was rocker Todd Rundgren, who was married to her mother, '70s Playboy Playmate Bebe Buell. But at an Aerosmith concert at age 11, she realized she greatly resembled Steven Tyler.

Likes to shop with her father: "We both wear the same size, and we'll just try on clothes for hours."

Was in a relationship with Joaquin Phoenix.
Original Job: Model
Famous Relative: Steve Tyler, Aerosmith lead singer, father
Quote: "It's important to surround yourself with beautiful friends and family who will say, 'You are a dork today.'"

STEVEN TYLER

Real Name: Steven Tallarico
Birthplace: Boston, MA
Birthdate: 3/26/48
Education: High school dropout
Debut: (Album) *Aerosmith,* 1973
Signature: Aerosmith
Facts: Met future Aerosmith members Joe Perry and Tom Hamilton at Lake Sunapee, NH, where their families had vacation houses.

Seriously injured in a motorcycle accident in 1981, capping a long period of discord and debauchery among band members. "I lay there in the hospital crying and flipping out, knowing some other group was going to step into our space. Through the stupor of my medication, I pictured a spotlight. We walked out of it."

When the band reformed in 1984, they got a contract with Geffen but had to audition first.

Aerosmith co-owns the West Hollywood restaurant House of Blues with Dan Aykroyd and Jim Belushi.
Infamy: Alcohol and drug use including heroin addiction.

Sued his ex-wife in 1999 in an attempt to get her to return photographs taken of him in the nude after reading that she intended to publish them.
Marriages: Cyrinda Fox (divorced); Kathleen Tallarico (divorced, 1987); Theresa Barrick
Children: Liv, 1977 (with Bebe Buell). Mia, 1978 (with Cyrinda Fox). Chelsea, 1988; Taj, 1992.
Major Awards: Grammy, Best Rock Performance by a Duo or Group with Vocal, "Janie's Got a Gun," 1990; Grammy, Best Rock Performance by a Duo or Group with Vocal, "Crazy," 1994; Grammy, Best Rock Performance by a Duo or Group with Vocal, "Pink," 1998
Quote: On what is left for his band to accomplish: "I'm looking to be the lounge act on the space shuttle so I can sing 'Walk This Way' on the ceiling."

JOHN UPDIKE

Birthplace: Shillington, PA
Birthdate: 3/18/32
Occupation: Writer
Education: Harvard College, Oxford University
Debut: (Book) *The Carpentered Hen and Other Tame Creatures,* 1958
Signature: *Rabbit, Run*
Facts: Collected Walt Disney comic books.
Marriages: Mary Entwhistle Pennington, 1953 (divorced, 1974); Martha R. Bernhard, 1977
Children: Elizabeth, c. 1955; David, c. 1957; Michael, c. 1959; Miranda,

c. 1960; (with Pennington). Three stepchildren
Major Awards: Pulitzer Prize, *Rabbit Is Rich,* 1982, *Rabbit at Rest,* 1991; American Book Award, *Rabbit Is Rich,* 1982

USHER

Real Name: Usher Raymond IV
Birthplace: Chattanooga, TN
Birthdate: 10/14/78
Occupation: Singer, songwriter, actor
Education: High school
Debut: (Album) *Usher,* 1994
Signature: *My Way*
Facts: Appeared on *Star Search* at age 13 and won as best teen vocalist. Was signed by a record label while still in high school.

When he travels, decoys dressed like the singer head for packs of screaming fans so he can quietly escape.

Does up to 1,000 stomach crunches a day.
Quote: "I'm a ladies' man. But it really shocks me how attached women are to their emotions, whereas a man thinks more in terms of realities."

VINCE VAUGHN

Birthplace: Buffalo Grove, IL
Birthdate: 3/28/70
Occupation: Actor
Education: High school
Debut: (TV) *China Beach,* 1989; (Film) *Rudy,* 1993
Signature: *Swingers*
Facts: First film role was a sex-education short, in which he played a guy trying to persuade his girlfriend to have sex with him.

Met *Swingers* writer and star Jon Favreau while filming *Rudy.* Favreau based the script on his late-night adventures in L.A. with Vaughn.

His father is named Vernon, and both of his sisters and all three family dogs have names beginning with "V."

Stands 6' 5".
Relationship: Jody Lauren Adams, actor
Quote: "I made an independent movie thinking I'll have chicks crawling all over me. Instead, I got guys who emulate me because they—wrongly—think I'm some kind of real swinger."

JAMES VAN DER BEEK

Birthplace: Cheshire, CT
Birthdate: 3/8/77
Occupation: Actor
Education: Attended Drew University
Debut: (Film) *Angus,* 1995
Signature: *Dawson's Creek*
Facts: Was identified as dyslexic in kindergarden and learned to read in a special class. Later became an honors student.

In eighth grade, he was sidelined from football with a concussion and discovered acting in community theater.

Depressed after reading about successful up-and-comers when he was unemployed, he went backpacking in Europe for six weeks. Upon returning, was offered a movie, play, and *Dawson's Creek.*

LUTHER VANDROSS

Birthplace: New York, NY
Birthdate: 4/20/51
Occupation: Singer, songwriter
Education: Attended Western Michigan University
Debut: (Song) "Everybody Rejoice (A Brand New Day)" from *The Wiz,* 1978
Signature: "Here and Now," 1990
Facts: Started playing the piano at age 3.

Sister was a member of the '50s group The Crests.

His first group, Listen My Brother, formed while he was a high school student, played at the Apollo and appeared on the first episode of *Sesame Street.*

He fights a continuous battle with

his weight; he has seesawed between189 and 340 pounds.

His middle name is Ronzoni, the only food his mother could keep down during a diffcult pregnancy.

At one point, supported himself singing jingles for Pepsi-Cola, Juicy Fruit gum, and the U.S. Army.
Original Job: S&H Green Stamp defective-merchandise clerk
Major Awards: Grammy, Best R&B Vocal—Male, "Here and Now," 1990; Grammy, Best R&B Song, "Power of Love/Love Power," 1991; Grammy, Best R&B Vocal—Male, *Power of Love,* 1991; Grammy, Best R&B Vocal—Male, "Your Secret Love," 1996

MARK WAHLBERG

Birthplace: Dorchester, MA
Birthdate: 6/5/71
Occupation: Actor, model, rap artist
Education: High school dropout
Debut: (Album) *Music for the People,* 1991; (Film) *Renaissance Man,* 1994
Signature: *Boogie Nights,* 1997
Facts: Left school at 14 to hustle on the street.

An original member with older brother in New Kids on the Block, he dropped out after six months.

Debut album under nom de rap.

Marky Mark was produced by his brother with his brother's money.

Has a third nipple, which was airbrushed out of Calvin Klein underwear ads.

Wore a 13-inch prosthetic penis and lost 30 pounds for his role in *Boogie Nights.*
Infamy: Convicted at age 16 for his involvement in the beating of two Vietnamese men during a robbery. Served 45 days in jail.

Was arrested on two occasions for yelling racial epithets at black schoolchildren. Gays and Asian-Americans also accused him of bias.

His public misconduct included a catfight with Madonna and an alleged assault on a security guard.
Famous Relative: Donnie Wahlberg,

singer (original New Kids on the Block member), brother

BARBARA WALTERS

Birthplace: Boston, MA
Birthdate: 9/25/31
Occupation: Broadcast journalist
Education: Sarah Lawrence College
Debut: (TV) *The Today Show,* 1974
Signature: *20/20*
Facts: In 1957, Don Hewitt, now executive producer of *60 Minutes,* told Walters: "You're marvelous, but stay out of television."

Walters was the only woman reporter in the press group that accompanied President Nixon on his historic trip to China in 1972.
Original Job: Intent on becoming a teacher, went for her master's in education while working as a secretary
Marriages: Robert Henry Katz (annulled); Lee Guber (divorced); Merv Adelson (divorced, 1992); Sen. John Warner (relationship)
Child: Jacqueline Dena, 1968
Major Awards: Emmy, Best Host on a Talk Show, *Today,* 1975; Emmy, Best Interviewer, *The Barbara Walters Show,* 1982; 4 News and Documentary Emmys as correspondent; elected to the Television Hall of Fame, 1990

VERA WANG

Birthplace: New York, NY
Birthdate: 6/27/49
Occupation: Designer
Education: Sarah Lawrence College
Signature: Mariah Carey's wedding dress
Facts: Her parents emigrated from China and built a multimillion-dollar oil and pharmaceutical company in the U.S.

Competed in figure skating at the U.S. national championship in 1968.

Began designing bridal gowns after she saw a niche when she couldn't find anything mature and

elegant for her own nuptials. Has designed wedding-wear for Sharon Stone, Holly Hunter, Uma Thurman and Chynna Phillips.
Original Job: *Vogue* fashion editor
Marriage: Arthur Becker, 1989
Children: Cecilia, 1990; Josephine, 1993; (both adopted).

DENZEL WASHINGTON

Birthplace: Mt. Vernon, NY
Birthdate: 12/28/54
Occupation: Actor
Education: Fordham University, studied acting at the American Conservatory Theatre, San Francisco
Debut: (Film) *Carbon Copy,* 1981
Signature: *Malcolm X,* 1992
Facts: Played Malcolm X in *When The Chickens Come Home To Roost* on Broadway, as well as in the 1992 Spike Lee movie.

In college, played football and basketball and wrote poetry before deciding to try acting.
Original Job: Drama instructor
Marriage: Pauletta Pearson, 1983
Children: John David, 1984; Katia, 1987; Malcolm, 1991; Olivia, 1991
Major Award: Oscar, Best Supporting Actor, *Glory,* 1989

WENDY WASSERSTEIN

Birthplace: Brooklyn, NY
Birthdate: 10/18/50
Occupation: Playwright
Education: Mount Holyoke College, City College of New York, Yale University School of Drama
Debut: (Stage) *Any Woman Can't,* 1973
Signature: *The Heidi Chronicles*
Facts: Almost enrolled in business school rather than pursuing drama.

Brother sent her a note prior to a premiere: "Can't come to play tonight. Am buying Nabisco."
Famous Relative: Bruce Wasserstein, investment banking star, brother
Major Awards: Pulitzer Prize, *The*

Heidi Chronicles, 1988; Tony, Best Play, *The Heidi Chronicles,* 1989

DAMON WAYANS

Birthplace: New York, NY
Birthdate: 9/4/60
Occupation: Comedian, actor, writer, director
Education: High school
Debut: (Film) *Beverly Hills Cop,* 1984; (TV) *Saturday Night Live,* 1985
Signature: *In Living Color*
Facts: Grew up poor as one of 11 children.

Began career performing stand-up in clubs.
Marriage: Lisa
Children: Damon Jr., 1983; Michael, 1985; Cara Mia, c. 1987; Kyla, c. 1990
Famous Relatives: Keenan Ivory Wayans, actor/producer/writer/director, brother; Kim Wayans, actor, sister; Marlon Wayans, actor, brother; Shawn Wayans, actor, brother

SIGOURNEY WEAVER

Real Name: Susan Weaver
Birthplace: New York, NY
Birthdate: 10/8/49
Occupation: Actor
Education: Stanford University; Yale University (MFA)
Debut: (Stage) *The Constant Wife* (with Ingrid Bergman), 1974
Signature: *Alien*
Facts: Took her name from a character in *The Great Gatsby.*

As a senior at Stanford, she dressed as an elf and lived in a treehouse with her boyfriend.

Accepted at Yale Drama School as "Mr." Sigourney Weaver.
Marriage: Jim Simpson, 1984
Child: Charlotte, 1990
Famous Relatives: Sylvester "Pat" Weaver, president of NBC, father; Elizabeth Inglis, actor, mother

VERONICA WEBB

Birthplace: Detroit, MI
Birthdate: 2/25/65
Occupation: Model, writer, actor
Education: Attended New School for Social Research
Signature: *Veronica Webb Sight*
Facts: Was a cashier in a SoHo boutique when spotted by a makeup artist for the Click modeling agency. Fearing he was a fraud, she resisted calling him back until she was fired from her job.

While a top model for Chanel and Revlon, wrote articles for *Esquire, Details,* and other magazines.

Broke the color barrier in modeling when she became a multimillion-dollar Revlon model.
Original Job: Cashier

ANDREW LLOYD WEBBER

Birthplace: London, England
Birthdate: 3/22/48
Occupation: Composer, producer
Education: Magdelen College of Oxford University, Royal Academy of Music, Oxford, Guildhall School of Music, Royal College of Music
Debut: (Stage) *Joseph and the Amazing Technicolor Dreamcoat,* 1968
Signature: *The Phantom of the Opera*
Fact: In 1969, was commissioned by RCA to write an opera based on a single, "Jesus Christ Superstar."
Infamy: After firing Faye Dunaway from the play *Sunset Boulevard* in 1994 because, he said, she couldn't sing, Webber wrote a confidential letter of apology that he then allowed the *London Standard* to print in its entirety. Dunaway, claiming she could indeed sing, sued, and settled for a reported $1.5 million.
Marriages: Sarah Jane Tudor Hugill (divorced), Sarah Brightman (divorced), Madeleine Astrid Gurdon, 1991

Children: Nicholas; Imogen; Alastair, 1992; Richard, 1993; Billy, 1994; Isabella Aurora, 1996
Famous Relative: William Webber, London College of Music director, father
Major Awards: Grammy, Best Cast Show Album, *Evita* (with Tim Rice), 1980; Grammy, Best Cast Show Album, *Cats,* 1983; Grammy, Legend Award, 1990; New York Drama Critics Award, *Evita,* 1980; Tony, Best Score, *Evita* (music; Tim Rice, lyrics), 1980; Tony, Best Score, *Cats* (music; T. S. Eliot, lyrics), 1983; Tony, Best Musical, *The Phantom of the Opera,* 1988; Academy Award, Best Song, "You Must Love Me," (music; Tim Rice, lyrics), 1996

ROBIN WILLIAMS

Birthplace: Chicago, IL
Birthdate: 7/21/51
Occupation: Actor
Education: Claremont Men's College, College of Marin, Juilliard
Debut: (TV) *Laugh-In,* 1977
Signature: *Mork and Mindy*
Facts: Grew up on a 30-room estate in Bloomfield Hills, MI.

Spent most of childhood playing with his 2,000 toy soldiers.

Second wife was a former nanny of Robin's children and his personal assistant. She served as a producer for *Mrs. Doubtfire,* 1994.
Infamy: Sued for $6.2 million in 1986 by former companion Michelle Tish Carter, who claimed that he gave her herpes during their two-year relationship. Williams countersued for extortion. The suits were settled out of court for an undisclosed amount.

Shared cocaine with John Belushi only a few hours before Belushi's death.
Original Job: Street mime
Marriages: Valeri Velardi (divorced, 1978); Marsha Garces, 1989
Children: Zachary, 1983 (with Valeri Velardi). Zelda, 1989; Cody Alan, 1991

Major Awards: Grammy, Best Comedy Recording, *Reality...What a Concept,* 1979; Emmy, Best Individual Performance in a Variety or Music Program, *A Carol Burnett Special,* 1987; Grammy, Best Comedy Recording, *A Night at the Met,* 1987; Emmy, Best Individual Performance in a Variety or Music Program, *ABC Presents a Royal Gala,* 1988; Grammy, Best Comedy Recording, *Good Morning, Vietnam,* 1988; Grammy, Best Recording for Children, *Pecos Bill,* 1988; Oscar, Best Supporting Actor, *Good Will Hunting,* 1997

VANESSA WILLIAMS

Birthplace: New York, NY
Birthdate: 3/18/63
Occupation: Singer, actor
Education: Syracuse University
Debut: (Album) *The Right Stuff,* 1988; (Film) *The Pick-Up Artist,* 1987
Signature: *Kiss of the Spider Woman*
Facts: Was the first black Miss America. Got hate mail from white-supremacist groups and also from blacks claiming she was too white.

Her debut album sold more than 500,000 copies.
Infamy: Forced to resign as Miss America in 1984, after *Penthouse* printed nude photos of her in leather bondage gear with another woman that had been taken several years earlier.
Marriage: Ramon Hervey, 1988 (divorced, 1996); Rick Fox, professional basketball player, 1999
Children: Melanie, 1987; Jillian, 1989; Devin, 1993
Quote: "Me in a hotel room on location with a whole pie is not a pretty thing."

KEVIN WILLIAMSON

Birthplace: Bern, NC
Birthdate: 3/14/65
Occupation: Screenwriter, director, executive producer

Education: Attended East Carolina State University
Debut: (Filmwriting) *Scream,* 1996
Signature: *Dawson's Creek*
Facts: In high school, an English teacher told him he had little talent and shouldn't consider a writing career.

The real Dawson's Creek is located a few miles from his childhood home and was a favored hangout.

Like Dawson, Williamson has memorized many lines from *Jaws.*
Original Jobs: Actor, music-video director's assistant, dog-walker

BRUCE WILLIS

Real Name: Walter Bruce Willis
Birthplace: Idar-Oberstein, Germany
Birthdate: 3/19/55
Occupation: Actor
Education: Montclair State College
Debut: (Stage) *Heaven and Earth,* 1977
Signature: *Die Hard,* 1988
Facts: Was student council president in high school.

The stammer he'd had since childhood disappeared whenever he performed.

Willis and Demi Moore were married by singer Little Richard.

Has his own band, Bruno.

He and his family live in once sleepy Hailey, Idaho, in the Rockies. Attempting to revitalize the town, Willis bought nearly every building on Main Street.
Infamy: During his senior year in high school, was expelled after a racial disturbance and was only permitted to graduate because his father hired an attorney to get him reinstated.
Original Job: Du Pont plant worker, bartender, commercial actor for Levi's 501 jeans
Marriage: Demi Moore, 1987 (separated, 1998); Maria Bravo, model (relationship)
Children: Rumer Glenn, 1988; Scout Larue, 1991; Tallulah Belle, 1994

Major Award: Emmy, Best Actor in a Drama Series, *Moonlighting,* 1987
Quote: "Being famous, it's like alcohol—whatever you are, it's just a little more of that. If you're an ---hole, you're more of an ---hole; if you're a nice guy, you're more of a nice guy."

AUGUST WILSON

Real Name: Frederick August Kittel
Birthplace: Pittsburgh, PA
Birthdate: 4/27/45
Education: High school dropout
Occupation: Playwright
Debut: (Play) *Ma Rainey's Black Bottom,* 1981
Signature: *The Piano Lesson,* 1990
Fact: Founded the black activist theater company Black Horizon on the Hill in the 1960s.
Marriages: One prior marriage, Judy Oliver (divorced), Constanza Romero, 1994
Child: Sakina Ansari, 1970
Major Awards: Tony, Best Play, *Fences,* 1987; Pulitzer Prize, Best Play, *Fences,* 1987; Pulitzer Prize, Best Play, *The Piano Lesson,* 1990

CASSANDRA WILSON

Birthplace: Jackson, Mississippi
Birthdate: 12/4/55
Occupation: Jazz singer, composer
Education: attended Millsaps College; Jackson State University
Debut: (Album) *Point of View,* 1985
Signature: *New Moon Daughter,* 1995
Facts: Widely considered one of the top jazz singers of the 1990s, she studied classical piano for six years, then learned acoustic guitar. By age 15, she had written some 20 songs.

After moving to New York, joined forces with the Brooklyn-based M-Base movement (stands for macro-basic array of structured extemporizations), which tried to create music inspired from jazz and the contemporary urban scene.

Was selected by Wynaton Marsalis

for the lead vocal role in his jazz oratorio *Blood on the Fields,* which won the 1997 Pulitzer Prize for Music.
Original Job: Television station public-affairs assistant
Marriage: Bruce Lincoln (divorced); Isaach de Bankole, actor (engaged)
Child: Jeris, 1990
Major Award: Grammy, Best Jazz Vocal Recording, *New Moon Daughter,* 1995
Quote: "People don't see things in streams, they don't see what tends to connect us all together. That's what I see. That's what I try to get to."

OPRAH WINFREY

Birthplace: Kosciusko, MS
Birthdate: 1/29/54
Occupation: Talk show host
Education: Tennesee State University
Debut: (Radio Reporter) WVOL, Nashville, 1971–72
Signature: *The Oprah Winfrey Show*
Facts: Delivered Easter sermon to congregation when she was 2 years old.

Once approached Aretha Franklin as she was stepping out of a limo and convinced Franklin that she had been abandoned. Aretha gave her $100, which Oprah used to stay in a hotel.

After being sexually abused at age 9 by an older cousin and later by a family friend, she ran away from home at age 13.

She bore a child when she was 14, though the baby died as an infant.

As a college sophomore, was the first African-American news co-anchor on a local TV station.

In college, won the title of Miss Tennessee and competed in the Miss Black America contest.

She left college in 1975, just a few credits shy of her degree. She finally received a B.S. in communications and theater in 1987, at age 33.

Formed Oxygen Media with Marcy Carsey and Geraldine Laybourne. She says she'll give up her talk show in 2002 and focus on the female-oriented channel.

Along with her steady boyfriend, taught a course entitled Dynamics of Leadership to 110 graduate students at Northwestern University in 1999.
Original Job: News reporter, WVOL radio, WTVF television, Nashville, TN
Relationship: Stedman Graham (engaged)
Major Awards: Emmy, Best Host of a Talk Show, *The Oprah Winfrey Show,* 1986, 1990, 1991, 1992, 1993, 1994, 1997

KATE WINSLET

Birthplace: Reading, England
Birthdate: 10/5/75
Occupation: Actor
Education: High school
Debut: (Film) *Heavenly Creatures,* 1994
Signature: *Titanic,* 1997
Facts: Her grandparents ran a local repertory theater, where uncle Robert Bridges and father Roger Winslet both worked as actors.

Appeared in a breakfast cereal commercial frolicking with a "honey monster" creature at age 11. By age 17, starred in her first feature film.

Weighing 180 pounds in high school, she had the unhappy nickname Blubber. Went on Weight Watchers to drop 50 pounds.
Original Job: Delicatessen worker
Marriage: Jim Threapleton, 1998

REESE WITHERSPOON

Real Name: Laura Jean Reese Witherspoon
Birthplace: New Orleans, LA
Birthdate: 3/22/76
Occupation: Actor
Education: Attended Stanford University
Debut: (Film) *The Man in the Moon,* 1991; (TV) *Wildflower,* 1991
Signature: *Election,* 1999
Facts: She began acting and modeling at age 7.

Won a 10-state talent search and,

at age 15 debuted in *The Man in the Moon.* By 23 she had appeared in 10 films.

Met future husband, Ryan Phillippe, at her twenty-first birthday party before they became an on-screen couple in 1999's *Cruel Intentions.*
Original Job: Model
Marriage: Ryan Phillippe, 1999
Child: daughter, 1999
Quote: "Thank God none of my movies have made any money. God forbid they should ever make any money."

SCOTT WOLF

Birthplace: Boston, MA
Birthdate: 6/4/68
Occupation: Actor
Education: George Washington University
Debut: (TV) *Evening Shade,* 1990
Signature: *Party of Five*
Facts: Majored in finance in college.

Played doubles tennis with Tony the Tiger in a long-running early 1990s Frosted Flakes commercial.

Proposed to actress Alyssa Milano by hiding a 1940s-vintage diamond engagement ring in a pumpkin, getting down on one knee to pop the question, then carving the gourd with a big heart. The pair subsequently broke off their engagement. For a time after, Wolf dated fellow *Po5* costar Paula Devicq.

ELIJAH WOOD

Birthplace: Cedar Rapids, IA
Birthdate: 1/28/81
Occupation: Actor
Debut: (Film) *Back to the Future II*, 1989
Signature: *The War*, 1994
Facts: His first acting role was when he was seven, playing the pint-sized executive in Paula Abdul's "Forever Your Girl" video.

Has appeared in more than 15 national commercials.

Gets more than 700 fan letters every week from adoring teenage girls.

Favorite actors include Tim Roth and Gary Oldman.
Original Job: Model, commercial actor

JAMES WOODS

Birthplace: Vernal, UT
Birthdate: 4/18/47
Occupation: Actor
Education: Massachusetts Institute of Technology
Debut: (Film) *The Visitors*, 1972
Signature: *Ghosts of Mississippi*
Facts: Majored in political science in college. His mother was also interested in politics and was once asked to run for lieutenant governor of Rhode Island, though she declined.

Modeled his voice as Hades for Disney's *Hercules* after an oily William Morris agent he knows.

Left the set of John Savage's *Salvador* in the middle of shooting in a rural Mexican area after an argument with Savage. Walked for five kilometers until Savage finally got in a helicopter and apologized from overhead.
Infamy: He and then fiancé Sarah Owen were allegedly the objects of harassment in the late 1980s by actress Sean Young, with whom Woods supposedly had an affair. Hate mail and gifts of mutilated dolls arrived, though nothing was

ever proven. After Owen split with Woods following their four-month marriage, she accused him in the tabloids of spousal abuse. Woods countered by saying that Owen had been the one staging the earlier harassment.
Marriage: Kathryn Greko, 1980 (divorced, 1983); Sarah Owen, 1989 (divorced, 1990); Missy Crider (engaged)
Major Awards: Emmy, Best Actor in a Miniseries, *The Promise*, 1986; Emmy, Best Actor in a Special, *My Name Is Bill W*, 1988

TIGER WOODS

Real Name: Eldrick Woods
Birthplace: Cypress, CA
Birthdate: 12/30/75
Occupation: Golfer
Education: Attended Stanford University
Facts: Was introduced to golf by his athletic father at nine months; by age 2 had outputt Bob Hope on *The Mike Douglas Show*, by 6 had hit his first hole-in-one, and by 8 had broken 80.

Began listening to subliminal tapes at age 6, featuring such messages as "I believe in me," and "My will moves mountains."

A gifted athlete, is also a switch-hitter in baseball, plays shooting guard in basketball, runs 400-meter track, and has played wide receiver in football.

His ethnicity includes parts African-American, Thai, Chinese, and Indian. On applications requesting ethnic identity, he has described himself as Asian.

The nickname Tiger comes from father Earl's Green Beret army past; it was the moniker of a South Vietnamese officer who saved Earl's life on several occasions.
Major Awards: U.S. Golf Association National Junior Amateur Champion, 1991-1993; U.S. Amateur Golf Champion, 1994-1996; Masters

Tournament winner, 1997; PGA Championship winner, 1999

NOAH WYLE

Birthplace: Los Angeles, CA
Birthdate: 6/4/71
Occupation: Actor
Education: High school
Debut: (TV) *Blind Faith*, 1990
Signature: *ER*
Facts: Is a Civil War buff.

Was given George Clooney's 1960 Oldsmobile Dynamic 88, with the hope that his so-called makeoutmobile would be as lucky for him as it had been for Clooney.

Plays billiards like a pool shark at the Hollywood Athletic Club and at his pool table at home.
Relationship: Tracy Warbin (engaged)

WYNONNA

Real Name: Christina Claire Ciminella
Birthplace: Ashland, KY
Birthdate: 5/3/64
Occupation: Singer
Education: High school
Debut: (Song) "Had a Dream" (with The Judds), 1984
Signature: *Wynonna*
Facts: Drives a 1957 Chevy and a turquoise Harley-Davidson.

Had asthma as a child.

Adopted her name after the town of Wynona, OK, mentioned in the song "Route 66."

The Judds got their first recording contract when mother Naomi, a nurse, gave a tape to patient Diana Maher, daughter of record producer Brent Maher.
Marriage: Arch Kelley III, 1996 (divorced, 1999)
Children: Elijah, 1995; Pauline Grace, 1996
Famous Relatives: Naomi Judd, country singer, mother; Ashley Judd, actor, sister
Major Awards: Best Country Performance by a Group or Duo, "Mama He's

Crazy," 1984; "Why Not Me," 1985; "Grandpa (Tell Me 'Bout the Good Old Days)," 1986; "Give a Little Love," 1988; "Love Can Build a Bridge," 1991; Grammy, Best Country Song, "Love Can Build a Bridge," 1991

YANNI

Real Name: Yanni Chrysomallis
Birthplace: Kalamata, Greece
Birthdate: 11/4/54
Occupation: Musician, pianist
Education: University of Minnesota
Debut: (Album) *Optimystique*, 1986
Facts: Former member of the Greek National Swimming Team.

Toured with the cult rock band Chameleon.

His music has been used on broadcasts of numerous sporting events, including the Tour de France, the Olympic Games, and the World Series.

Spent nine years as Linda Evans's signficant other.

RENEE ZELLWEGER

Birthplace: Katy, TX
Birthdate: 4/25/69
Occupation: Actor
Education: University of Texas
Debut: (Film) *The Texas Chainsaw Massacre 2*, 1986
Signature: *Jerry Maguire*, 1996

Facts: Her Texas hometown was so small it had neither a movie theater nor cable television.

Signed up for her first drama class in college simply because she needed the credit to complete her English degree. Fell in love with acting and declared herself a professional actor upon graduation.

Though practically every well-known actress under age 35 auditioned during a four-month hunt for the *Jerry Maguire* part, the relatively obscure Zellweger impressed Tom Cruise and writer Cameron Crowe with her freshness and offbeat quality—and the fact that she wasn't intimidated by her sizzling co-star.
Original Job: Bartender assistant
Relationship: Jim Carrey

CATHERINE ZETA-JONES

Birthplace: Swansea, Wales
Birthdate: 9/25/69
Occupation: Actor
Signature: *The Mask of Zorro*, 1998
Debut: (Film) *Sheherazade/Les 1001 Nuits*, 1990; (TV) *The Young Indiana Jones Chronicles*, 1992
Facts: As an infant, she contracted a virus which caused difficulty breathing, and has a tracheotomy scar.

As a child, she appeared on the

stage in various British musicals, starting with Annie.

Was a major television star in the U.K. in the early '90s for her role in *The Darling Buds of May*. Moved to Hollywood to avoid the British press.

Zeta, her grandmother's Christian name, was added to distinguish herself from another Catherine Jones in Actors Equity.

Reportedly turned down producer and former studio chief Jon Peters' marriage proposal in 1996 because "I want to be known as an actress rather than a Hollywood wife."
Relationship: Angus Macfadyen, actor (engaged, never married); Michael Douglas
Quote: "I think I came out of the womb loving makeup."

THE REGISTER OF THOUSANDS

Here's a celebrity database covering the multitudes of shakers and shapers, the near-great and notorious, those who grace the screen and the tube, the page and the stage—a resource to discover the real names, birthdates, birthplaces, occupations, and claims to fame of a large slice of pop culture. Those who are coy about their birthdates or are too new on the scene to be sufficiently well documented have been passed over for this year's list—but stay tuned.

AAMES, WILLIE (Willie Upton). Los Angeles, CA, 7/15/60. Actor. *Eight Is Enough.*

ABBOTT, JIM. Flint, MI, 9/19/67. One-handed baseball pitcher.

ABDUL, PAULA. Los Angeles, CA, 6/19/62. Singer, dancer, choreographer, divorced from Emilio Estevez. "Straight Up."

ABRAHAM, F. MURRAY. Pittsburgh, PA, 10/24/39. Actor. *Amadeus.*

ABRAHAMS, JIM. Milwaukee, WI, 5/10/44. Producer, writer, director. *Airplane!; The Naked Gun.*

ABRAHAMS, MICK. Luton, England, 4/7/43. Guitarist. Jethro Tull.

AD-ROCK, KING (Adam Horovitz). New York, NY, 10/31/66. Rap artist. The Beastie Boys.

ADAMS, BROOKE. New York, NY, 2/8/49. Actor. *Invasion of the Body Snatchers.*

ADAMS, BRYAN. Kingston, Canada, 11/5/59. Singer, songwriter. "(Everything I Do) I Do It for You."

ADAMS, DON. New York, NY, 4/19/26. Actor. Maxwell Smart on *Get Smart.*

ADAMS, DOUGLAS. Cambridge, England, 3/11/52. Novelist. *The Hitchhiker's Guide to the Galaxy.*

ADAMS, EDIE (Elizabeth Edith Enke). Kingston, PA, 4/16/29. Actor. *The Ernie Kovacs Show.*

ADAMS, MAUD (Maud Wikstrom). Lulea, Sweden, 2/12/45. Actor. *Octopussy.*

ADAMS, VICTORIA. 4/7/74. Singer. Posh Spice of the Spice Girls.

ADAMSON, STUART (William Adamson). Manchester, England, 4/11/58. Guitarist, singer. Big Country.

ADJANI, ISABELLE. Paris, France, 6/27/55. Actor. *Camille Claudel.*

AGAR, JOHN. Chicago, IL, 1/31/21. Actor, formerly married to Shirley Temple. *The Sands of Iwo Jima.*

AGASSI, ANDRÉ Las Vegas, NV, 4/29/70. Tennis Player.

AGNEW, PETE. Scotland, 9/14/46. Bassist, singer. Nazareth.

AGUTTER, JENNY. Taunton, England, 12/20/52. Actor. *Logan's Run.*

AIELLO, DANNY. New York, NY, 6/20/33. Actor, writer. *Moonstruck.*

AIKMAN, TROY KENNETH. Cerritos, CA, 11/21/66. Football player. Quarterback for the Dallas Cowboys.

AIMEE, ANOUK (Françoise Soyra Dreyfus). Paris, France, 4/27/32. Actor. *A Man and a Woman.*

AKERS, KAREN. New York, NY, 10/13/45. Cabaret singer.

ALBERT, EDDIE (Eddie Albert Heimberger). Rock Island, IL, 4/22/08. Actor, father of Edward. Oliver Wendell Douglas on *Green Acres.*

ALBERT, EDWARD. Los Angeles, CA, 2/20/51. Actor, son of Eddie. *Midway.*

ALBERT, MARV. 6/12/41. Sportscaster.

ALBRECHT, BERNIE (Bernard Dicken). Salford, England, 1/4/56. Guitarist. Joy Division; New Order.

ALDA, ALAN (Alphonso D'Abruzzo). New York, NY, 1/28/36. Actor, writer, director, son of Robert Alda. Benjamin Franklin "Hawkeye" Pierce on *M*A*S*H.*

ALDRIN, BUZZ (Edwin Eugene Aldrin Jr.). Montclair, NJ, 1/20/30. Astronaut, businessman.

ALEXANDER, GARY. Chattanooga, TN, 9/25/43. Singer, guitarist. The Association.

ALEXANDER, JANE (Jane Quigley). Boston, MA, 10/28/39. Actor. *All the President's Men.* Head of the National Endowment for the Arts.

ALI, MUHAMMAD (Cassius Clay). Louisville, KY, 1/17/42. Boxing great.

ALLEN, DEBBIE. Houston, TX, 1/16/50. Choreographer, actor, sister of Phylicia Rashad. *Fame.*

ALLEN, DUANE. Taylortown, TX, 4/29/43. Singer. The Oak Ridge Boys.

ALLEN, JOAN. Rochelle, IL, 8/20/56. Actor. *Face/Off.*

ALLEN, KAREN. Carrollton, IL, 10/5/51. Actor. *Raiders of the Lost Ark.*

ALLEN, NANCY. New York, NY, 6/24/50. Actor. *Robocop.*

ALLEN, PAPA DEE (Thomas Allen). Wilmington, DE, 7/18/31. Keyboardist, singer. War.

ALLEN, RICK. Sheffield, England, 11/1/63. One-armed drummer. Def Leppard.

ALLEN, ROD (Rod Bainbridge). Leicester, England, 3/31/44. Bassist, singer. The Fortunes.

ALLEN, STEVE. New York, NY, 12/26/21. Writer, performer, variety show host, husband of Jayne Meadows. *The Steve Allen Show.*

ALLEN, VERDEN. Hereford, England, 5/26/44. Keyboardist. Mott The Hoople.

ALLEY, KIRSTIE. Wichita, KS, 1/12/51. Actor. Formerly married to Parker Stevenson. Rebecca Howe on *Cheers.*

ALLISON, JERRY. Hillsboro, TX, 8/31/39. Drummer. Buddy Holly & The Crickets.

ALLMAN, GREGG. Nashville, TN, 12/8/47. Keyboardist, guitarist, singer, formerly married to Cher. The Allman Brothers Band.

ALLSUP, MIKE. Modesto, CA, 3/8/47. Guitarist. Three Dog Night.

ALLYSON, JUNE (Ella Geisman). Westchester, NY, 10/7/17. Actor. *The Dupont Show Starring June Allyson; Lassie.*

ALMOND, MARC (Peter Almond). Southport, England, 7/9/59. Singer. Soft Cell.

ALONSO, MARIA CONCHITA. Cuba, 6/29/56. Actor. *The Running Man.*

ALPERT, HERB. Los Angeles, CA, 3/31/35. Trumpeter, band leader, cofounder of A&M Records. The Tijuana Brass.

ALSTON, BARBARA. Brooklyn, NY, 1945. Singer. The Crystals.

ALSTON, SHIRLEY (Shirley Owens). Passaic, NJ, 6/10/41. Singer. The Shirelles.

ALT, CAROL. Queens, NY, 8/18/60. Supermodel.

ALTMAN, ROBERT. Kansas City, MO, 2/20/25. Director, writer, producer. *The Player.*

ALVARADO, TRINI. New York, NY, 1/10/67. Actor. *Rich Kids.*

AMIS, SUZY. Oklahoma City, OK, 1/5/61. Actor. *Blown Away.*

AMOS, JOHN. Newark, NJ, 12/27/41. Actor. James Evans on *Good Times.*

AMOS, WALLY JR. Tallahassee, FL, 7/1/36. Business executive. Famous Amos chocolate chip cookies.

ANDERSON, ALFA. 9/7/46. Singer. Chic.

ANDERSON, HARRY. Newport, RI, 10/14/52. Actor. Judge Harry Stone on *Night Court.*

ANDERSON, IAN. Edinburgh, Scotland, 8/10/47. Singer, flautist. Jethro Tull.

ANDERSON, JON. Lancashire, England, 10/25/44. Singer, drummer. Yes.

ANDERSON, KEVIN. Illinois, 1/13/60. Actor. *Sleeping with the Enemy.*

ANDERSON, LAURIE. Chicago, IL, 6/5/47. Singer, performance artist.

ANDERSON, LONI. St. Paul, MN, 8/5/45. Actor. Receptionist Jennifer Marlowe on *WKRP in Cincinnati.*

ANDERSON, MELISSA SUE. Berkeley, CA, 9/26/62. Actor. Mary Ingalls Kendall on *Little House on the Prairie.*

ANDERSON, MELODY. Edmonton, Canada, 1/3/55. Actor. Dale Arden in *Flash Gordon.*

ANDERSON, RICHARD. Long Branch, NJ, 8/8/26. Actor. Oscar Goldman on *The Six Million Dollar Man* and *The Bionic Woman.*

ANDERSON, RICHARD DEAN. Minneapolis, MN, 1/23/50. Actor. *MacGyver.*

ANDERSON, RICK. St. Paul, MN, 8/1/47. Bassist. The Tubes.

ANDERSON, TERRY. 10/27/47. Journalist, former hostage.

ANDERSSON, BENNY (Goran Andersson). Stockholm, Sweden, 12/16/46. Keyboards, singer. Abba.

ANDERSSON, BIBI. Stockholm, Sweden, 11/11/35. Actor. *The Seventh Seal.*

ANDES, MARK. Philadelphia, PA, 2/19/48. Bassist. Spirit.

ANDRESS, URSULA. Berne, Switzerland, 3/19/36. Actor. *Dr. No.*

ANDRETTI, MARIO. Montana Trieste, Italy, 2/28/40. Auto racer.

ANDREW, PRINCE. London, England, 2/19/60. British royalty, son of Queen Elizabeth II.

ANDREWS, ANTHONY. London, England, 1/12/48. Actor. *Brideshead Revisited.*

ANDREWS, BARRY. London, England, 9/12/56. Keyboardist. XTC.

ANKA, PAUL. Ottawa, Canada, 7/30/41. Singer, songwriter. "Diana."

ANN-MARGRET (Ann-Margret Olsson). Valsjobyn, Sweden, 4/28/41. Actor, singer. *Viva Las Vegas.*

ANNAUD, JEAN-JACQUES. Draveil, France, 10/1/43.

Writer, director. *Quest for Fire; The Lover.*

ANNE, PRINCESS. London, England, 8/15/50. British royalty, daughter of Queen Elizabeth II.

ANSPACH, SUSAN. New York, NY, 11/23/42. Actor. *Five Easy Pieces.*

ANT, ADAM (Stewart Goddard). London, England, 11/3/54. Singer. Adam & The Ants.

ANTHONY, MICHAEL. Chicago, IL, 6/20/55. Bassist. Van Halen.

ANTON, SUSAN. Oak Glen, CA, 10/12/50. Actor, singer. *Goldengirl.*

ANWAR, GABRIELLE. Laleham, England, 2/4/70. Actor. Tangoed with Al Pacino in *Scent of a Woman.*

APPICE, CARMINE. New York, NY, 12/15/46. Drummer. Vanilla Fudge.

AQUINO, CORAZON. Tarlac, Philippines, 1/25/33. Political leader. Former president of the Philippines.

ARAFAT, YASIR. Cairo, Egypt, 8/24/29. Political leader. Head of the PLO.

ARCHER, ANNE. Los Angeles, CA, 8/25/47. Actor. Wife of Michael Douglas in *Fatal Attraction.*

ARENHOLZ, STEPHEN. The Bronx, NY, 4/29/69. Actor.

ARGENT, ROD. St. Albans, England, 6/14/45. Keyboardist. The Zombies.

ARKIN, ALAN. New York, NY, 3/26/34. Actor, director, writer, folk singer, member of Second City, father of Adam Arkin (*Chicago Hope*). *The In-Laws.*

ARMATRADING, JOAN. Basseterre, West Indies, 12/9/50. Singer, songwriter. "Me, Myself, I."

ARMSTRONG, BESS. Baltimore, MD, 12/11/53. Actor. Julia Peters on *On Our Own.*

ARMSTRONG, BILLIE JOE. Rodeo, CA, 2/17/72, Singer, songwriter, guitarist, Green Day.

ARMSTRONG, NEIL. Wapakoneta, OH, 8/5/30. Astronaut.

ARNAZ, DESI JR. Los Angeles, CA, 1/19/53. Actor, singer, son of Lucille Ball and Desi Arnaz. *Here's Lucy.*

ARNAZ, LUCIE. Los Angeles, CA, 7/17/51. Actor, daughter of Lucille Ball and Desi Arnaz, married to Laurence Luckinbill. *Here's Lucy.*

ARNESS, JAMES (James Aurness). Minneapolis, MN, 5/26/23. Actor, brother of Peter Graves. *Gunsmoke.*

ARNOLD, TOM Ottumwa, IA, 3/6/59. Actor, ex-husband of Roseanne. *Roseanne, True Lies.*

ARQUETTE, PATRICIA. New York, NY, 4/8/68. Actor, granddaughter of Cliff Arquette, sister of Rosanna, David and Alexis. *True Romance.*

ARQUETTE, ROSANNA. New York, NY, 8/10/59. Actor, granddaughter of Cliff Arquette, sister of Patricia, and inspiration for Toto song "Rosanna." *Desperately Seeking Susan.*

ARTHUR, BEATRICE (Bernice Frankel). New York, NY, 5/13/26. Actor. *Maude.*

ASH, DANIEL. 7/31/57. Guitarist, singer. Bauhaus; Love and Rockets.

ASHER, PETER. London, England, 6/22/44. Singer. Peter and Gordon.

ASHFORD, NICKOLAS. Fairfield, SC, 5/4/42. Singer. Ashford and Simpson.

ASHFORD, ROSALIND. Detroit, MI, 9/2/43. Singer. Martha & The Vandellas.

ASHLEY, ELIZABETH (Elizabeth Ann Cole). Ocala, FL, 8/30/39. Actor. *Evening Shade.*

ASNER, EDWARD. Kansas City, KS, 11/15/29. Actor. *Lou Grant.*

ASSANTE, ARMAND. New York, NY, 10/4/49. Actor. *The Doctors.*

ASTBURY, IAN. Heswall, England, 5/14/62. Singer. The Cult.

ASTIN, JOHN. Baltimore, MD, 3/30/30. Actor, formerly married to Patty Duke, father of Sean Astin. Gomez Addams on *The Addams Family.*

ASTIN, SEAN. Santa Monica, CA, 2/25/71. Actor, son of John Astin and Patty Duke. *Encino Man.*

ASTLEY, RICK. Warrington, England, 2/6/66. Singer, songwriter. "Never Gonna Give You Up."

ASTON, JAY. London, England, 5/4/61. Singer. Bucks Fizz.

ASTON, JOHN. England, 11/30/57. Guitarist. Psychedelic Furs.

ATKINS, CHET. Luttrell, TN, 6/20/24. Virtuoso guitarist.

ATKINS, CHRISTOPHER. Rye, NY, 2/21/61. Actor. *The Blue Lagoon.*

ATKINSON, PAUL. Cuffley, England, 3/19/46. Guitarist. The Zombies.

ATTENBOROUGH, RICHARD. Cambridge, England, 8/29/23. Actor, producer, director. *Gandhi.*

ATWOOD, MARGARET. Ottawa, Canada, 11/18/39. Author, poet. *The Handmaid's Tale.*

AUBERJONOIS, RENE. New York, NY, 6/1/40. Actor. Security Chief Odo on *Deep Space Nine.*

AUERMANN, NADJA. Berlin, Germany, 1971, Supermodel.

AUTRY, ALAN. Shreveport, LA, 7/31/52. Actor. Bubba Skinner on *In the Heat of the Night.*

AVALON, FRANKIE (Francis Thomas Avallone). Philadelphia, PA, 9/18/40. Singer, actor. *Beach Blanket Bingo.*

AVORY, MICK. London, England, 2/15/44. Drummer. The Kinks.

AXTON, HOYT. Duncan, OK, 3/25/38. Singer, songwriter, actor. *Gremlins.*

AZARIA, HANK. 4/25/64. Actor. *The Simpsons.*

AZNAVOUR, CHARLES (Shahnour Varenagh Aznourian). Paris, France, 5/22/24. Singer, songwriter, actor. *Shoot the Piano Player.*

BACALL, LAUREN (Betty Perske). New York, NY, 9/16/24. Actor, widow of Humphrey Bogart, formerly married to Jason Robards. *Key Largo.*

BACH, BARBARA. Queens, NY, 8/27/47. Actor, married to Ringo Starr. *The Spy Who Loved Me.*

BACHMAN, RANDY. Winnipeg, Canada, 9/27/43. Guitarist, singer. Bachman-Turner Overdrive; The Guess Who.

BACHMAN, ROBBIE. Winnipeg, Canada, 2/18/53. Drummer. Bachman-Turner Overdrive.

BADANJEK, JOHN. 1948. Drummer. Mitch Ryder & The Detroit Wheels.

BAEZ, JOAN. Staten Island, NY, 1/9/41. Folk singer and songwriter, peace and civil rights activist.

BAILEY, PHILIP. Denver, CO, 5/8/51. Singer, conga player, percussionist. Earth, Wind & Fire.

BAILEY, TOM. Halifax, England, 6/18/57. Singer, keyboardist. Thompson Twins.

BAIN, BARBARA. Chicago, IL, 9/13/31. Actor. *Mission: Impossible.*

BAIO, SCOTT. Brooklyn, NY, 9/22/61. Actor. Charles "Chachi" Arcola on *Happy Days.*

BAIUL, OKSANA. 11/16/77. Figure skater. Olympic Gold Medalist.

BAKER, ANITA. Detroit, MI, 12/20/57. R&B singer.

BAKER, CARROLL. Johnstown, PA, 5/28/31. Actor. *Kindergarten Cop.*

BAKER, CHERYL (Rita Crudgington). London, England, 3/8/54. Singer. Bucks Fizz.

BAKER, GINGER (Peter Baker). Lewisham, England, 8/19/40. Drummer. Cream; Blind Faith.

BAKER, JOE DON. Groesbeck, TX, 2/12/36. Actor. *Walking Tall.*

BAKER, KATHY. Midland, TX, 6/8/50. Actor. *Picket Fences.*

BAKER, MICKEY (McHouston Baker). Louisville, KY, 10/15/25. Singer. Mickey & Sylvia.

BAKKER, JIM. Muskegon, MI, 1/2/40. TV evangelist, participant in the PTL scandal.

BAKSHI, RALPH. Haifa, Palestine, 10/29/38. Animator, writer, director. *Fritz the Cat.*

BAKULA, SCOTT. St. Louis, MO, 10/9/55. Actor. *Quantum Leap.*

BALABAN, BOB. Chicago, IL, 8/16/45. Actor. *Midnight Cowboy, Little Man Tate.*

BALDWIN, ADAM. Chicago, IL, 2/27/62. Actor. *My Bodyguard.*

BALDWIN, DANIEL. Massapequa, NY, 10/5/60. Actor. *Homicide.*

BALDWIN, STEPHEN. Massapequa, NY, 5/12/66. Actor. *Threesome.*

BALDWIN, WILLIAM. Massapequa, NY, 2/21/63. Actor, married to Chynna Phillips. *Backdraft.*

BALIN, MARTY (Martyn Jerel Buchwald). Cincinnati, OH, 1/30/43. Singer. Jefferson Airplane/Starship.

BALL, DAVID. Blackpool, England, 5/3/59. Keyboardist. Soft Cell.

BALL, ROGER. Dundee, Scotland, 6/4/44. Alto and baritone saxophonist. Average White Band.

BALLARD, HANK. Detroit, MI, 11/18/36. Singer/songwriter. "Work with Me Annie."

BALLARD, KAYE (Catherine Gloria Balotta). Cleveland, OH, 11/20/26. Actor, singer.

BALSLEY, PHILIP. 8/8/39. Singer. Kingsmen; Statler Brothers.

BAMBAATAA, AFRIKA. The Bronx, NY, 1958. Rap/hip-hop DJ.

BAN BREATHNACH, SARAH. 5/5/47. Author. *Simple Abundance.*

BANALI, FRANKIE. 11/14/55. Musician. Quiet Riot.

BANANA (Lowell Levinger). Cambridge, MA, 1946. Keyboardist, guitarist. The Youngbloods.

BANCROFT, ANNE (Anna Maria Italiano). The Bronx, NY, 9/17/31. Actor. Mrs. Robinson in *The Graduate.*

BANKS, TONY. East Heathly, England, 3/27/51. Keyboardist. Genesis.

BARANSKI, CHRISTINE Buffalo, NY, 5/2/52. Actor. *Cybill.*

BARBATA, JOHN. 4/1/45. Drummer. The Turtles; Jefferson Starship.

BARBEAU, ADRIENNE. Sacramento, CA, 6/11/45. Actor. Carol on *Maude.*

BARBIERI, RICHARD. 11/30/57. Keyboardist. Japan.

BARDOT, BRIGITTE (Camille Javal). Paris, France, 9/28/34. Sex goddess. *And God Created Woman.*

BARGERON, DAVE. Massachusetts, 9/6/42. Trombonist. Blood, Sweat and Tears.

BARKER, BOB. Darrington, WA, 12/12/23. Game show host. *The Price Is Right.*

BARKER, CLIVE. Liverpool, England, 10/5/52. Author. *The Inhuman Condition.*

BARKIN, ELLEN. The Bronx, NY, 4/16/54. Actor. Separated from Gabriel Byrne. *Sea of Love.*

BARNES, LEO. 10/5/55. Musician. Hothouse Flowers.

BARRE, MARTIN. 11/17/46. Guitarist. Jethro Iull.

BARRERE, PAUL. Burbank, CA, 7/3/48. Lead guitarist. Little Feat.

BARRETT, ASTON. Kingston, Jamaica, 11/22/46. Bassist. Bob Marley & The Wailers.

BARRETT, MARCIA. St. Catherine's, Jamaica, 10/14/48. Singer. Boney M.

BARRETT, RONA. New York, NY, 10/8/36. News correspondent, columnist.

BARRETT, SYD (Roger Barrett). Cambridge, England, 1/6/46. Singer, guitarist. Pink Floyd.

BARRY, DAVE. 7/3/47. Columnist, author. *Dave's World.*

BARRY, MARION. Itta Bena, MS, 3/6/36. Mayor of Washington, served six-month prison term for cocaine possession.

BARRYMORE, JOHN DREW. Beverly Hills, CA, 6/4/32. Actor, father of Drew Barrymore.

BARSON, MIKE. England, 5/21/58. Keyboardist. Madness.

BARTEL, PAUL. New York, NY, 8/6/38. Director, writer, actor. *Eating Raoul.*

BARTHOL, BRUCE. Berkeley, CA, 1947. Bassist. Country Joe & The Fish.

BARYSHNIKOV, MIKHAIL. Riga, Latvia, 1/28/48. Dancer, actor. *White Nights.*

BATEMAN, JASON. Rye, NY, 1/14/69. Actor, brother of Justine. David on *The Hogan Family.*

BATEMAN, JUSTINE. Rye, NY, 2/19/66. Actor, sister of Jason. Mallory Keaton on *Family Ties.*

BATES, ALAN. Allestree, England, 2/17/34. Actor. *An Unmarried Woman.*

BATTLE, KATHLEEN. Portsmouth, OH, 8/13/48. Opera singer.

BAUER, JOE. Memphis, TN, 9/26/41. Drummer. The Youngbloods.

BAUER, STEVEN (Steven Echevarria). Havana, Cuba, 12/2/56. Actor, formerly married to Melanie Griffith. *Wiseguy.*

BAUMGARTNER, STEVE. Philadelphia, PA, 10/28/67. Writer. *Permanent Vacation.*

BAXTER, JEFF "SKUNK." Washington, DC, 12/13/48. Lead Guitarist. Steely Dan; The Doobie Brothers.

BAXTER, KEITH. Monmouthshire, Wales, 4/29/33. Actor.

BAXTER, MEREDITH. Los Angeles, CA, 6/21/47. Actor, formerly married to David Birney. Elyse Keaton on *Family Ties.*

BAY, WILLOW. 12/28/63. Model, television journalist.

BEACHAM, STEPHANIE. Hertfordshire, England, 2/28/47. Actor. Sable Scott Colby on *The Colbys.*

BEAKY (John Dymond). Salisbury, England, 7/10/44. Guitarist. Dave Dee, Dozy, Beaky, Mick and Tich.

BEALS, JENNIFER. Chicago, IL, 12/19/63. Actor. *Flashdance.*

BEARD, FRANK. Dallas, TX, 12/10/49. Drummer. ZZ Top.

BEASLEY, ALLYCE. Brooklyn, NY, 7/6/54. Actor. Agnes Dipesto on *Moonlighting.*

BEATRICE, PRINCESS. London, England, 8/8/88. British royalty, daughter of Prince Andrew and the Duchess of York.

BEATTY, NED. Lexington, KY, 7/6/37. Actor. *Deliverance.*

BECK, JEFF. Wallington, England, 6/24/44. Guitarist. The Yardbirds; The Jeff Beck Group; The Jan Hammer Group.

BECK, JOHN. Chicago, IL, 1/28/43. Actor. Mark Graison on *Dallas.*

BECK, MICHAEL. Memphis, TN, 2/4/49. Actor. *The Warriors.*

BECKER, BORIS. Liemen, Germany, 11/22/67. Tennis player.

BECKER, WALTER. New York, NY, 2/20/50. Bassist. Steely Dan.

BECKLEY, GERRY. Texas, 9/12/52. Singer, guitarist. America.

BEDELIA, BONNIE. New York, NY, 3/25/48. Actor. *Presumed Innocent.*

BEDFORD, MARK. London, England, 8/24/61. Bassist. Madness.

BEEFHEART, CAPTAIN (Don Van Vliet). Glendale, CA, 1/15/41. Singer, high school friend of Frank Zappa. Captain Beefheart & The Magic Band.

BEERS, GARY. 6/22/57. Bassist, singer. INXS

BEGLEY, ED JR. Los Angeles, CA, 9/16/49. Actor. Dr. Victor Ehrlich on *St. Elsewhere.*

BEL GEDDES, BARBARA New York, NY, 10/31/22. Actor. *Dallas.*

BELAFONTE, HARRY. New York, NY, 3/1/27. Actor, singer, father of Shari. "The Banana Boat Song."

BELAFONTE, SHARI. New York, NY, 9/22/54. Actor, daughter of Harry. *Hotel.*

BELL, ANDY. Peterborough, England, 4/25/64. Singer. Erasure.

BELL, RICKY. Boston, MA, 9/18/67. Singer. New Edition.

BELL, ROBERT. Youngstown, OH, 10/8/50. Bassist. Kool & The Gang.

BELL, RONALD. Youngstown, OH, 11/1/51. Saxophonist. Kool & The Gang.

BELLADONNA, JOEY. Oswego, NY. Singer. Anthrax.

BELLAMY, GEORGE. Sunderland, England, 10/8/41. Guitarist. The Tornados.

BELLAMY, TONY. Los Angeles, CA, 9/12/40. Singer, guitarist. Redbone.

BELLO, FRANK. 7/9/65. Bassist. Anthrax.

BELMONDO, JEAN-PAUL. Paris, France, 4/9/33. Actor. *Breathless.*

BELUSHI, JIM. Chicago, IL, 6/15/54. Actor, brother of late John Belushi. *K-9.*

BENATAR, PAT (Pat Andrzejewski). Brooklyn, NY, 1/10/53. Singer. "Heartbreaker."

BENBEN, BRIAN. Newburgh, NY. Actor. Dream On. Married to Madeline Stowe.

BENEDICT, DIRK (Dirk Niewoehner). Helena, MT, 3/1/45. Actor. Lt. Templeton Peck on *The A-Team.*

BENJAMIN, RICHARD. New York, NY, 5/22/38. Actor, director. *Love at First Bite; Goodbye, Columbus.*

BENNETT, BRIAN. London, England, 2/9/40. Drummer. The Shadows.

BENNETT, ESTELLE. New York, NY, 7/22/44. Singer. The Ronettes.

BENNETT, PATRICIA. New York, NY, 4/7/47. Singer. The Chiffons.

BENSON, GEORGE. Pittsburgh, PA, 3/22/43. Singer, guitarist. "Give Me the Night."

BENSON, RENALDO. Detroit, MI, 1947. Singer. The Four Tops.

BENSON, ROBBY (Robby Segal). Dallas, TX, 1/21/56. Actor, writer, director. *Ice Castles.*

BERENDT, JOHN. 12/5/39. Author. *Midnight in the Garden of Good and Evil.*

BERENGER, TOM. Chicago, IL, 5/31/49. Actor. *Platoon.*

BERENSON, MARISA. New York, NY, 2/15/47. Actor. *Barry Lyndon.*

BERGEN, POLLY (Nellie Paulina Burgin). Knoxville, TN, 7/14/30. Singer, actor. *The Winds of War.*

BERGER, ALAN. 11/8/49. Bassist. Southside Johnny & The Asbury Jukes.

BERGMAN, INGMAR. Uppsala, Sweden, 7/14/18. Writer, director. *The Silence.*

BERKLEY, ELIZABETH. 7/28/72. Actor. *Showgirls.*

BERKOWITZ, DAVID. New York, NY, 6/1/53. Serial killer. Son of Sam.

BERLE, MILTON (Milton Berlinger). New York, NY, 7/12/08. Actor. *The Milton Berle Show.*

BERNHARD, SANDRA. Flint, MI, 6/6/55. Actor, singer. *Roseanne.*

BERNSEN, CORBIN. Los Angeles, CA, 9/7/54. Actor, married to Amanda Pays. Arnie Becker on *L.A. Law.*

BERRI, CLAUDE (Claude Langmann). Paris, France,

7/1/34. Actor, director, producer of films.

BERRY, BILL. Hibbing, MN, 7/31/58. Drummer. R.E.M.

BERRY, CHUCK. San Jose, CA, 10/18/26. Rock and Roll legend, singer and guitarist. "Johnny B. Goode."

BERRY, JAN. Los Angeles, CA, 4/3/41. Singer. Jan & Dean.

BERTINELLI, VALERIE. Wilmington, DE, 4/23/60. Actor, married to Eddie Van Halen. Barbara Cooper Royer on *One Day at a Time.*

BETTS, DICKEY. West Palm Beach, FL, 12/12/43. Guitarist, singer. The Allman Brothers Band.

BIALIK, MAYIM. San Diego, CA, 12/12/75. Actor. *Blossom.*

BIEHN, MICHAEL. Anniston, AL, 7/31/56. Actor. *The Terminator.*

BIG FIGURE, THE (John Martin). 1947. Drummer. Dr. Feelgood.

BILLINGSLEY, BARBARA. Los Angeles, CA, 12/22/22. Actor. June Cleaver on *Leave It to Beaver.*

BILLINGSLEY, PETER. New York, NY, 1972. Child actor. *A Christmas Story.*

BILLINGSLEY, RAY. Wake Forest, NC, 7/25/57. Cartoonist. *Curtis.*

BIRD, LARRY. West Baden, IN, 12/7/56. Basketball great. Boston Celtics.

BIRNEY, DAVID. Washington, DC, 4/23/39. Actor, formerly married to Meredith Baxter. *St. Elsewhere.*

BIRRELL, PETE. Manchester, England, 5/9/41. Bassist. Freddie & The Dreamers.

BIRTLES, BEEB (Gerard Birtlekamp). Amsterdam, Netherlands, 11/28/48. Guitarist. The Little River Band.

BISHOP, JOEY (Joseph Gottlieb). The Bronx, NY, 2/3/18. Actor. *The Joey Bishop Show.*

BISSET, JACQUELINE. Waybridge, England, 9/13/44. Actor. *The Deep.*

BISSET, JOSIE. Seattle, WA, 10/5/70. Actor. *Melrose Place.*

BIVINS, MICHAEL. 8/10/68. Singer. New Edition, Bell Biv DeVoe.

BLACK, CILLA (Cilla White). Liverpool, England, 5/27/43. Singer, TV personality.

BLACK, JET (Brian Duffy). England, 8/26/58. Drummer. The Stranglers.

BLACK, KAREN (Karen Ziegler). Park Ridge, IL, 7/1/42. Actor. *Easy Rider.*

BLACK, LISA HARTMAN. 6/1/56. Actor, married to Clint Black. *Knot's Landing.*

BLACKMON, LARRY. New York, 5/29/56. Singer, drummer. Cameo.

BLACKMORE, RITCHIE. Weston-Super-Mare, England, 4/14/45. Guitarist. Deep Purple; Rainbow.

BLADD, STEPHEN JO. Boston, MA, 7/13/42. Drummer, singer. The J. Geils Band.

BLADES, RUBEN. Panama City, Panama, 7/16/48. Actor, singer. *The Milagro Beanfield War.*

BLAIR, BONNIE. Cornwall, NY, 3/18/64. Speed skater.

BLAIR, LINDA. Westport, CT, 1/22/59. Actor. *The Exorcist.*

BLAKE, ROBERT (Michael Gubitosi). Nutley, NJ, 9/18/33. Actor. *Baretta.*

BLAKELY, SUSAN. Frankfurt, Germany, 9/7/50. Actor. *Rich Man, Poor Man.*

BLAKLEY, ALAN. Bromley, England, 4/1/42. Guitarist. Brian Poole & The Tremeloes.

BLAND, BOBBY. Rosemark, TN, 1/27/30. Singer.

BLASS, BILL. Ft. Wayne, IN, 6/22/22. Fashion designer.

BLEDSOE, TEMPESTT. Chicago, IL, 8/1/73. Actor. Vanessa Huxtable on *The Cosby Show.*

BLEETH, YASMINE. 6/14/68. Actor. *Baywatch.*

BLOOM, CLAIRE. London, England, 2/15/31. Actor. *Richard III.*

BLOOM, ERIC. Long Island, NY, 12/1/44. Lead guitarist, keyboardist. Blue Oyster Cult.

BLOW, KURTIS (Kurtis Walker). New York, NY, 8/9/59. DJ, rapper. "The Breaks."

BLUECHEL, TED JR. San Pedro, CA, 12/2/42. Singer, drummer. The Association.

BLUME, JUDY. Elizabeth, NJ, 2/12/38. Novelist. *Are You There God? It's Me Margaret.*

BLUNSTONE, COLIN. Hatfield, England, 6/24/45. Singer. The Zombies.

BOBBY G. (Bobby Gubby). London, England, 8/23/53. Singer. Bucks Fizz.

BOGERT, TIM. Richfield, NJ, 8/27/44. Bassist. Vanilla Fudge.

BOGLE, BOB. Portland, OR, 1/16/37. Guitarist, bassist. The Ventures.

BOGOSIAN, ERIC. Woburn, MA, 4/24/53. Actor, writer. *Talk Radio.*

BOLDER, TREVOR. 6/9/50. Bassist. Spiders from Mars; Uriah Heep.

BOLOGNA, JOSEPH. Brooklyn, NY, 12/30/34. Actor. *Chapter Two.*

BONADUCE, DANNY. 8/13/59. Actor, radio personality. Danny on *The Partridge Family.*

BOND, RONNIE (Ronnie Bullis). Andover, England, 5/4/43. Drummer. The Troggs.

BONDS, GARY (Gary Anderson). Jacksonville, FL, 6/6/39. Singer.

BONET, LISA. San Francisco, CA, 11/16/67. Actor, formerly married to Lenny Kravitz. Denise Huxtable on *The Cosby Show.*

BONNER, FRANK. Little Rock, AR, 2/28/42. Actor. Herb Tarlek on *WKRP in Cincinnati.*

BONO, CHASTITY. Los Angeles, CA, 3/4/69. Daughter of Sonny and Cher.

BONSALL, BRIAN. 12/3/82. Child actor. *Family Ties.*

BONSALL, JOE. Philadelphia, PA, 5/18/48. Singer. The Oak Ridge Boys.

BOONE, PAT. Jacksonville, FL, 6/1/34. Singer, actor. *The Pat Boone Show.*

BOONE, STEVE. North Carolina, 9/23/43. Bassist, singer. The Lovin' Spoonful.

BOOTHE, POWERS. Snyder, TX, 6/1/49. Actor. *Guyana Tragedy: The Story of Jim Jones.*

BORGNINE, ERNEST (Ernest Borgnino). Hamden, CT, 1/24/17. Actor. *McHale's Navy.*

BOSSON, BARBARA. Charleroi, PA, 11/1/39. Actor, married to producer Steven Bochco. Fay Furillo on *Hill Street Blues.*

BOSTWICK, BARRY. San Mateo, CA, 2/24/45. Actor. *The Rocky Horror Picture Show.*

BOTTOMS, JOSEPH. Santa Barbara, CA, 4/22/54. Actor. *The Black Hole.*

BOTTOMS, SAM. Santa Barbara, CA, 10/17/55. Actor. *Apocalypse Now.*

BOTTOMS, TIMOTHY. Santa Barbara, CA, 8/30/51. Actor. *Johnny Got His Gun.*

BOTTUM, RODDY. Los Angeles, CA, 7/1/63. Keyboardist. Faith No More.

BOUCHARD, JOE. Long Island, NY, 11/9/48. Bassist, singer. Blue Öyster Cult.

BOWE, RIDDICK. New York, NY, 8/10/67. Boxer, former heavyweight champion of the world.

BOWERS, TONY. 10/31/56. Bassist. Simply Red.

BOWIE, DAVID (David Jones). Brixton, England, 1/8/47. Singer, actor, married to Iman. *Ziggy Stardust and the Spiders from Mars.*

BOX, MICK. London, England, 6/8/47. Guitarist, songwriter. Uriah Heep.

BOXLEITNER, BRUCE. Elgin, IL, 5/12/50. Actor, married to Melissa Gilbert. *Scarecrow and Mrs. King.*

BOY GEORGE (George O'Dowd). Eltham, England, 6/14/61. Singer. Culture Club.

BOYLE, LARA FLYNN. Davenport, IA, 3/24/70. Actor. *Twin Peaks.*

BOYLE, PETER. Philadelphia, PA, 10/18/33. Actor. *Young Frankenstein.*

BRACCO, LORRAINE. Brooklyn, NY, 10/2/54. Actor. *GoodFellas.*

BRADBURY, RAY. Waukegan, IL, 8/22/20. Novelist. *The Martian Chronicles.*

BRAGG, BILLY (Steven Bragg). Barking, England, 12/20/57. Punk/R&B singer, songwriter.

BRAID, LES (William Braid). Liverpool, England, 9/15/41. Bassist. The Swinging Blue Jeans.

BRAMLETT, BONNIE. Acton, IL, 11/8/44. Singer. Delaney & Bonnie.

BRAMLETT, DELANEY. Pontotoc County, MS, 7/1/39. Guitarist, singer. Delaney & Bonnie.

BRANDAUER, KLAUS MARIA. Altaussee, Austria, 6/22/44. Actor. *Out of Africa.*

BRATTON, CREED. Sacramento, CA, 2/8/43. Guitarist. The Grass Roots.

BRAUNN, ERIK. Boston, MA, 8/11/50. Guitarist, singer. Iron Butterfly.

BREATHED, BERKE. Encino, CA, 6/21/57. Cartoonist. *Bloom County.*

BRENNAN, EILEEN. Los Angeles, CA, 9/3/34. Actor. *Private Benjamin.*

BRENNEMAN, AMY. New London, CT, 6/22/64. Actor. *NYPD Blue.*

BRENNER, DAVID. Philadelphia, PA, 2/4/45. Stand-up comedian. *Nightlife.*

BREWER, DONALD. Flint, MI, 9/3/48. Drummer. Grand Funk Railroad.

BRICKELL, EDIE. Oak Cliff, TX, 1966. Singer, songwriter, married to Paul Simon. Edie Brickell and New Bohemians.

BRIDGES, BEAU (Lloyd Vernet Bridges III). Los Angeles, CA, 12/9/41. Actor, director, brother of Jeff. *The Fabulous Baker Boys.*

BRIDGES, TODD. San Francisco, CA, 5/27/65. Actor. Willis Jackson on *Diff'rent Strokes.*

BRIGATI, EDDIE. Garfield, NJ, 10/22/46. Singer, percussionist. The (Young) Rascals.

BRIGGS, DAVID. Melbourne, Australia, 1/26/51. Guitarist. The Little River Band.

BRILEY, ALEX. 4/12/56. Singer. The Village People.

BRIMLEY, WILFORD. Salt Lake City, UT, 9/27/34. Actor. *Cocoon.*

BRINKLEY, DAVID. Wilmington, NC, 7/10/20. Pioneer news journalist and anchor. *This Week with David Brinkley.*

BRIQUETTE, PETE (Patrick Cusack). Ireland, 7/2/54. Bassist, singer. The Boomtown Rats.

BRITTANY, MORGAN (Suzanne Cupito). Los Angeles, CA, 12/5/51. Actor. Katherine Wentworth on *Dallas.*

BRITTON, CHRIS. Watford, England, 6/21/45. Guitarist. The Troggs.

BROLIN, JAMES (James Bruderlin). Los Angeles, CA, 7/18/40. Actor, father of Josh.

Dr. Steven Kiley on *Marcus Welby, M.D.*

BRONSON, CHARLES (Charles Buchinsky). Ehrenfield, PA, 11/3/21. Actor, widower of Jill Ireland. *Death Wish.*

BROOKER, GARY. Southend, England, 5/29/45. Singer, keyboardist. Procol Harum.

BROOKS, ALBERT (Albert Einstein). Los Angeles, CA, 7/22/47. Actor, writer, director. *Defending Your Life.*

BROOKS, LALA. Brooklyn, NY, 1946. Singer. The Crystals.

BROTHERS, JOYCE (Joyce Bauer). New York, NY, 10/20/27. Psychologist.

BROWN, BLAIR. Washington, DC, 1948. Actor. *The Days and Nights of Molly Dodd.*

BROWN, BOBBY. Boston, MA, 2/5/69. Singer, dancer. "My Perogative."

BROWN, BRYAN. Panania, Australia, 6/23/47. Actor, married to Rachel Ward. *FX.*

BROWN, DAVID. Houston, TX, 2/15/47. Bassist. Santana.

BROWN, ERROL. Kingston, Jamaica, 11/12/48. Singer. Hot Chocolate.

BROWN, GEORG STANFORD. Havana, Cuba, 6/24/43. Actor. *Colossus: The Forbin Project.*

BROWN, GEORGE. Jersey City, NJ, 1/5/49. Drummer. Kool and The Gang.

BROWN, HAROLD. Long Beach, CA, 3/17/46. Drummer. War.

BROWN, IAN. Sale, England, 2/20/63. Singer. Stone Roses.

BROWN, JAMES. Augusta, GA, 5/3/33. The Godfather of Soul.

BROWN, JIM. St. Simons Island, GA, 2/17/36. Football player, actor. *The Dirty Dozen.*

BROWN, JIMMY. Birmingham, England, 11/20/57. Drummer. UB40.

BROWN, MELANIE. 5/29/75. Singer. Scary Spice of the Spice Girls.

BROWN, MICHAEL (Michael Lookofsky). New York, NY, 4/25/49. Keyboardist. The Left Banke.

BROWNE, JACKSON. Heidelberg, Germany, 10/9/48. Singer, songwriter.

BRUCE, JACK. Glasgow, Scotland, 5/14/43. Singer, bassist. Cream.

BRUCE, MICHAEL. 3/16/48. Guitarist, keyboardist. Alice Cooper.

BRUFORD, BILL. London, England, 5/17/48. Drummer. Yes.

BRYAN, DAVID (David Rashbaum). New Jersey, 2/7/62. Keyboardist. Bon Jovi.

BRYON, DENNIS. Cardiff, Wales, 4/14/49. Drummer. Amen Corner.

BRYSON, PEABO. (Robert Peabo Bryson), Greenville, SC, 4/13/51, Singer.

BRZEZICKI, MARK. Slough, England, 6/21/57. Drummer. Big Country.

BUCHANAN, PAUL. Scotland. Singer, synthesizer player. Blue Nile.

BUCHHOLZ, FRANCIS. 2/19/50. Guitarist. Scorpions.

BUCK, PETER. Athens, GA, 12/6/56. Guitarist. R.E.M.

BUCK, ROBERT. Guitarist. 10,000 Maniacs.

BUCKINGHAM, LINDSEY. Palo Alto, CA, 10/3/47. Guitarist, singer. Fleetwood Mac.

BUCKLER, RICK (Paul Buckler). 12/6/56. Drummer, singer. The Jam.

BUCKLEY, BETTY. Big Spring, TX, 7/3/47. Actor. *Eight Is Enough.*

BUJOLD, GENEVIEVE. Montreal, Canada, 7/1/42. Actor. *Dead Ringers.*

BUNKER, CLIVE. Blackpool, England, 12/12/46. Drummer. Jethro Tull.

BUNNELL, DEWEY. Yorkshire, England, 1/19/51. Singer, guitarist. America.

BUNTON, EMMA. 1/21/76. Singer. Baby Spice of the Spice Girls.

BURCHILL, CHARLIE. Glasgow, Scotland, 11/27/59. Guitarist. Simple Minds.

BURDEN, IAN. 12/24/57. Synthesizer player. Human League.

BURDON, ERIC. Walker-on-Tyne, England, 5/11/41. Singer, songwriter. The Animals; War.

BURGHOFF, GARY. Bristol, CT, 5/24/43. Actor. Radar O'Reilly on *M*A*S*H.*

BURKE, DELTA. Orlando, FL, 7/30/56. Actor, married to Gerald McRaney. *Designing Women.*

BURKE, SOLOMON. Philadelphia, PA, 1936. Country-gospel-R&B singer, songwriter.

BURNEL, JEAN-JACQUES. London, England, 2/21/52. Bassist. The Stranglers.

BURNETT, CAROL. San Antonio, TX, 4/26/33. Actor. *The Carol Burnett Show.*

BURNS, BOB. Drummer. Lynyrd Skynyrd.

BURR, CLIVE. 3/8/57. Drummer. Iron Maiden.

BURRELL, BOZ (Raymond Burrell). Lincoln, England, 1946. Bassist. Bad Company.

BURROWS, DARREN E. Winfield, KS, 9/12/66. Actor. Ed Chigliak on *Northern Exposure.*

BURSTYN, ELLEN (Edna Rae Gillooly). Detroit, MI, 12/7/32. Actor. *Alice Doesn't Live Here Anymore.*

BURT, HEINZ. Hargin, Germany, 7/24/42. Bassist. The Tornados.

BURTON, LEVAR. Landstuhl, Germany, 2/16/57. Actor. Geordi LaForge on *Star Trek: The Next Generation.*

BURTON, TIM. 8/25/58. Director. *Edward Scissorhands.*

BURTON, TREVOR. Aston, England, 3/9/44. Lead guitarist. The Move.

BUSEY, GARY. Goose Creek, TX, 6/29/44. Actor. *The Buddy Holly Story.*

BUSFIELD, TIMOTHY. Lansing, MI, 6/12/57, Actor, *thirtysomething.*

BUSH, BARBARA. Rye, NY, 6/8/25. Former First Lady, married to George Bush.

BUSH, GEORGE. Milton, MA, 6/12/24. Political leader, husband of Barbara. Forty-first president of the U.S.

BUSH, KATE. Bexleyheath, England, 7/30/58. Singer, songwriter.

BUSHY, RONALD. Washington, DC, 9/23/45. Drummer. Iron Butterfly.

BUTKUS, DICK. Chicago, IL, 12/9/42. Football player, actor. *My Two Dads.*

BUTLER, GEEZER (Terry Butler). Birmingham, England, 7/17/49. Bassist. Black Sabbath.

BUTLER, JERRY. Sunflower, MS, 12/8/39. Singer. The Impressions.

BUTLER, BRETT Montgomery, AL, 1/30/58. Actor, comedian. *Grace Under Fire.*

BUTLER, JOE. Glen Cove, NY, 9/16/43. Drummer, singer. The Lovin' Spoonful.

BUTLER, RICHARD. Surrey, England, 6/5/56. Singer, lyricist. Psychedelic Furs.

BUTLER, TONY. Ealing, England, 2/13/57. Bassist. Big Country.

BUTTAFUOCO, JOEY. Massapequa, NY. 3/11/56. Mechanic. Had affair with Amy Fisher.

BUXTON, GLEN. Akron, OH, 11/10/47. Guitarist. Alice Cooper.

BUZZI, RUTH. Westerly, RI, 7/24/36. Actor. *Laugh-In.*

BYRNE, DAVID. Dumbarton, Scotland, 5/14/52, Singer, songwriter, director, Talking Heads.

BYRNE, GABRIEL. Dublin, Ireland, 12/5/50. Actor. Separated from Ellen Barkin. *Miller's Crossing.*

BYRON, DAVID. Essex, England, 1/29/47. Singer. Uriah Heep.

CAAN, JAMES. The Bronx, NY, 3/26/40. Actor. *The Godfather.*

CADDY, ALAN. London, England, 2/2/40. Guitarist. The Tornados; Johnny Kidd & The Pirates.

CAESAR, SID. Yonkers, NY, 9/8/22. Performer. *Your Show of Shows.*

CAFFEY, CHARLOTTE. Santa Monica, CA, 10/21/53. Singer. The Go-Gos.

CAIN, DEAN Mt. Clemens, MI, 7/31/66. Actor. *Lois & Clark: The New Adventures of Superman.*

CAIN, JONATHAN. Chicago, IL, 2/26/50. Keyboardist. Journey.

CAINE, MICHAEL (Maurice Joseph Micklewhite). London, England, 3/14/33. Actor. *Hannah and Her Sisters.*

CALABRO, THOMAS. 2/3/59. Actor. Michael Mancini on *Melrose Place.*

CALE, JOHN. Garnant, Wales, 3/9/42. Bassist, keyboardist, violist, singer. The Velvet Underground.

CALIFORNIA, RANDY (Randy Wolfe). Los Angeles, CA,

2/20/51. Guitarist, singer. Spirit.

CALLOW, SIMON. London, England, 6/15/49. Actor. *A Room with a View.*

CALVERT, BERNIE. Burnley, England, 9/16/43. Bassist. The Hollies.

CAMERON, KIRK. Panorama City, CA, 10/12/70. Actor, brother of Candace. Mike Seaver on *Growing Pains.*

CAMILLETTI, ROB. 8/1/64. Singer. Milli Vanilli.

CAMP, COLLEEN. San Francisco, CA, 1953. Actor. Kristin Shepard on *Dallas.*

CAMPBELL, ALI (Alastair Campbell). Birmingham, England, 2/15/59. Lead singer, guitarist. UB40.

CAMPBELL, BILL. Chicago, IL, 1960. Actor. *The Rocketeer.*

CAMPBELL, BRUCE. Royal Oak, MI, 6/22/58. Actor, producer, screenwriter. *The Adventures of Briscoe County Jr.*

CAMPBELL, GLEN. Delight, AR, 4/22/36. Actor, singer. *The Glen Campbell Goodtime Hour.*

CAMPBELL, MIKE. Panama City, FL, 2/1/54. Guitarist. Tom Petty & The Heartbreakers.

CAMPBELL, ROBIN. Birmingham, England, 12/25/54. Lead guitarist, singer. UB40.

CAMPBELL, TISHA. Oklahoma City, OK, 10/13/70. Actor. *Martin.*

CAMPION, JANE. Wellington, New Zealand, 4/30/54. Director, screenwriter, daughter of Richard and Edith. *The Piano.*

CANN, WARREN. Victoria, Canada, 5/20/52. Drummer. Ultravox.

CANNON, DYAN (Samille Diane Friesen). Tacoma, WA, 1/4/39. Actor. *Bob & Carol & Ted & Alice.*

CAPALDI, JIM. Evesham, England, 8/24/44. Drummer, singer. Traffic.

CAPRIATI, JENNIFER. Long Island, NY, 3/29/76. Tennis player

CAPSHAW, KATE (Kathleen Sue Nail). Ft. Worth, TX, 11/3/53. Actor, married to Steven Spielberg. *Indiana Jones and the Temple of Doom.*

CARA, IRENE. New York, NY, 3/18/59. Actor, singer. *Fame.*

CARDIN, PIERRE. Venice, Italy, 7/7/22. Fashion designer.

CARDINALE, CLAUDIA. Tunis, Tunisia, 4/15/39. Actor. *The Pink Panther.*

CAREY, TONY. 10/16/53. Keyboardist. Rainbow.

CARLIN, GEORGE. New York, NY, 5/12/37. Actor. "Seven Dirty Words."

CARLISLE, BELINDA. Hollywood, CA, 8/17/58. Singer, songwriter.

CARLOS, BUN (Brad Carlson). Rockford, IL, 6/12/51. Drummer. Cheap Trick.

CARMEN, ERIC. Cleveland, OH, 8/11/49. Singer. The Raspberries.

CARNE, JUDY (Joyce Botterill). Northampton, England, 3/27/39. Actor. *Laugh-In.*

CARNEY, ART. Mt. Vernon, NY, 11/4/18. Actor and comedian. Ed Norton on *The Honeymooners.*

CAROLINE, PRINCESS. Monte Carlo, Monaco, 1/23/57. Daughter of Princess Grace of Monaco.

CARON, LESLIE. Paris, France, 7/1/31. Actor. *Lili.*

CARPENTER, JOHN. Carthage, NY, 1/16/48. Director, writer. *Halloween.*

CARPENTER, RICHARD. New Haven, CT, 10/15/46. Keyboardist, singer. The Carpenters.

CARR, DAVID. Leyton, England, 8/4/43. Keyboardist. The Fortunes.

CARRACK, PAUL. Sheffield, England, 4/21/51. Singer, songwriter. Squeeze; Ace; Mike and the Mechanics.

CARRADINE, DAVID. Hollywood, CA, 12/8/36. Actor, son of John Carradine, brother of Keith and Robert. *Kung Fu.*

CARRADINE, KEITH. San Mateo, CA, 8/8/49. Actor, son of John, brother of David and Robert, father of Martha Plimpton. *The Will Rogers Follies.*

CARRADINE, ROBERT. Hollywood, CA, 3/24/54. Actor, son of John, brother of David and Keith. *Revenge of the Nerds.*

CARRERA, BARBARA. Managua, Nicaragua,

12/31/47. Model, actor. *Dallas.*

CARROLL, DIAHANN (Carol Diahann Johnson). New York, NY, 7/17/35. Actor, singer, married to Vic Damone. *I Know Why the Caged Bird Sings.*

CARRY, JULIUS. Actor. Mitchell Baldwin on *Murphy Brown.*

CARTER, DIXIE. McLemoresville, TN, 5/25/39. Actor. Julia Sugarbaker on *Designing Women.*

CARTER, JIMMY. Plains, GA, 10/1/24. Political leader. Thirty-ninth president of the U.S.

CARTER, LYNDA. Phoenix, AZ, 7/24/51. Actor. *Wonder Woman.*

CARTER, NELL. Birmingham, AL, 9/13/48. Actor, singer. *Gimme a Break.*

CARTERIS, GABRIELLE. 1/2/61. Actor. Andrea Zuckerman on *Beverly Hills 90210.*

CARTWRIGHT, VERONICA. Bristol, England, 1950. Actor. *Alien.*

CARVEY, DANA. Missoula, MT, 4/2/55. Actor. *Saturday Night Live, Wayne's World.*

CARUSO, DAVID. Queens, NY, 1/17/56, Actor, *NYPD Blue.*

CASADY, JACK. Washington, DC, 4/13/44. Bass guitarist. Jefferson Airplane/Starship.

CASEY, HARRY WAYNE (Harold Casey). Hialeah, FL, 1/31/51. Singer, keyboardist. KC & The Sunshine Band.

CASS, PEGGY (Mary Margaret Cass). Boston, MA, 5/21/24. Actor. Panelist on *To Tell the Truth.*

CASSIDY, DAVID. New York, NY, 4/12/50. Actor, half brother of Shaun, son of Jack, step-son of Shirley Jones. Keith in *The Partridge Family.*

CASSIDY, ED. Chicago, IL, 5/4/31. Drummer. Spirit.

CASSIDY, JOANNA. Camden, NJ, 8/2/44. Actor. Jo Jo White on *Buffalo Bill.*

CASTRO, FIDEL (Fidel Ruz). Mayari, Cuba, 8/13/26. Political leader. President of Cuba.

CATES, PHOEBE. New York, NY, 7/16/63. Actor, married to Kevin Kline. *Fast Times at Ridgemont High.*

CATHERALL, JOANNE. Sheffield, England, 9/18/62. Singer. Human League.

CATTINI, CLEM. 8/28/39. Drummer. Johnny Kidd & The Pirates; Tornados.

CATTRALL, KIM. Liverpool, England, 8/21/56. Actor. *The Bonfire of the Vanities.*

CAVALIERE, FELIX. Pelham, NY, 11/29/44. Singer, keyboardist. The (Young) Rascals.

CAVETT, DICK. Gibbon, NE, 11/19/36. Actor, talk show host. *The Dick Cavett Show.*

CEASE, JEFF. Nashville, TN, 6/24/67. Guitarist. The Black Crowes.

CETERA, PETER. Chicago, IL, 9/13/44. Singer, songwriter. Chicago.

CHABERT, LACEY. 9/30/82. Actor. *Party of Five.*

CHADWICK, LES (John Chadwick). Liverpool, England, 5/11/43. Bassist. Gerry & The Pacemakers.

CHAMBERLAIN, RICHARD (George Chamberlain). Los Angeles, CA, 3/31/34. Actor. *Dr. Kildare.*

CHAMBERLAIN, WILT. West Philadelphia, PA, 8/21/36. Basketball great.

CHAMBERS, GEORGE. Flora, MS, 9/26/31. Bassist, singer. The Chambers Brothers.

CHAMBERS, JOE. Scott County, MS, 8/24/42. Guitarist, singer. The Chambers Brothers.

CHAMBERS, LESTER. Flora, MS, 4/13/40. Harmonicist, singer. The Chambers Brothers.

CHAMBERS, MARTIN. Hereford, England, 9/4/51. Drummer. The Pretenders.

CHAMBERS, TERRY. England, 7/18/55. Drummer. XTC.

CHAMBERS, WILLIE. Flora, MS, 3/3/38. Guitarist, singer. The Chambers Brothers.

CHANDLER, GENE (Gene Dixon). Chicago, IL, 7/6/37. Singer, songwriter.

CHANNING, CAROL. Seattle, WA, 1/31/21. Actor. *Hello, Dolly!*

CHANNING, STOCKARD (Susan Williams Antonia Stockard). New York, NY, 2/13/44. Actor. *Grease.*

CHAO, ROSALIND. Los Angeles, CA. Actor. Soon-Lee on *M*A*S*H.*

CHAPLIN, GERALDINE. Santa Monica, CA, 7/31/44. Actor. *Dr. Zhivago.*

CHAPMAN, ROGER. Leicester, England, 4/8/44. Singer. Family.

CHAPMAN, TRACY. Cleveland, OH, 3/30/64. Folk singer, songwriter.

CHAQUICO, CRAIG. 9/26/54. Singer, guitarist. Jefferson Starship.

CHARISSE, CYD (Tula Ellice Finklea). Amarillo, TX, 3/8/22. Actor. *Brigadoon.*

CHARLES, RAY (Ray Robinson). Albany, GA, 9/23/30. Singer, songwriter. "Georgia on My Mind."

CHARLTON, MANUEL. 7/25/41. Guitarist, singer, songwriter. Nazareth.

CHARO. Murcia, Spain, 1/15/41. Actor, singer. *The Love Boat.*

CHASE, CHEVY (Cornelius Crane Chase) New York, NY, 10/8/43, Actor, *National Lampoon's Vacation* movies.

CHECKER, CHUBBY (Ernest Evans). Spring Gulley, SC, 10/3/41. Singer, songwriter. Popularized the Twist and Limbo.

CHERRY, NENEH. Stockholm, Sweden, 3/10/64. Rap/pop singer, songwriter.

CHILD, JULIA. Pasadena, CA, 8/15/12. TV chef, author. *Mastering the Art of French Cooking.*

CHILES, LOIS. Alice, TX, 4/15/47. Model, actor. *The Way We Were.*

CHILTON, ALEX. Memphis, TN, 12/28/50. Guitarist, singer. The Box Tops; Big Star.

CHISHOLM, MELANIE. 1/12/74. Singer. Sporty Spice of the Spice Girls.

CHONG, RAE DAWN. Vancouver, Canada, 1962. Actor, daughter of Thomas Chong. *The Color Purple.*

CHONG, THOMAS. Edmonton, Canada, 5/24/38. Singer, actor, writer, director, former partner of Cheech Marin, father of Rae Dawn Chong. *Up in Smoke.*

CHRISTIAN, GARRY. Merseyside, England, 2/27/55. Singer. The Christians.

CHRISTIAN, ROGER. 2/13/50. Singer. The Christians.

CHRISTIAN, RUSSELL. 6/8/56. Singer. The Christians.

CHRISTIE, JULIE. Chukua, India, 4/14/41. Actor. *Dr. Zhivago.*

CHRISTIE, LOU (Lugee Sacco). Glenwillard, PA, 2/19/43. Singer, songwriter. "Lightnin' Strikes."

CHRISTO (Christo Javacheff). Gabrovo, Bulgaria, 6/13/35. Artist. The Umbrellas.

CHRISTOPHER, WILLIAM. Evanston, IL, 10/20/32. Actor. Father Francis Mulcahy on *M*A*S*H.*

CHUCK D. (Charles Ridenhour). 1960. Rap artist. Public Enemy.

CHUNG, CONNIE (Constance Yu-Hwa Chung) Washington, DC, 8/20/46, TV journalist, CBS.

CHURCHILL, CHICK. Mold, Wales, 1/2/49. Keyboardist. Ten Years After.

CIPOLLINA, JOHN. Berkeley, CA, 8/24/43. Guitarist. Quicksilver Messenger Service.

CLAIBORNE, LIZ (Elisabeth Claiborne). Brussels, Belgium, 3/31/29. Fashion designer.

CLARK, ALAN. Durham, NC, 3/5/52. Keyboardist. Dire Straits.

CLARK, DAVE. Tottenham, England, 12/15/42. Drummer. The Dave Clark Five.

CLARK, DICK. Mt. Vernon, NY, 11/30/29. Producer, music/game show host. *American Bandstand.*

CLARK, GRAEME. Glasgow, Scotland, 4/15/66. Bassist. Wet Wet Wet.

CLARK, NEIL. 7/3/55. Guitarist. Lloyd Cole & The Commotions.

CLARK, PETULA. Surrey, England, 11/15/32. Actor, singer. *Downtown.*

CLARK, ROY. Meherrin, VA, 4/15/33. Country singer, songwriter. *Hee Haw.*

CLARK, STEVE. Hillsborough, England, 4/23/60. Guitarist. Def Leppard.

CLARKE, ALLAN (Harold Clarke). Salford, England, 4/5/42. Singer. The Hollies.

CLARKE, EDDIE. 10/5/50. Guitarist. Motörhead.

CLARKE, MICHAEL (Michael Dick). New York, NY, 6/3/44. Drummer. The Byrds.

CLARKE, VINCE. Basildon, England, 7/3/61. Keyboardist. Erasure.

CLAY, ANDREW DICE. Brooklyn, NY, 1958. Actor. *The Adventures of Ford Fairlaine.*

CLAYBURGH, JILL. New York, NY, 4/30/44. Actor. *An Unmarried Woman.*

CLAYTON, ADAM. Ireland, 3/13/60. Bassist. U2.

CLAYTON-THOMAS, DAVID (David Thomsett). Surrey, England, 9/13/41. Lead singer. Blood, Sweat & Tears.

CLEESE, JOHN. Weston-Super-Mare, England, 10/27/39. Actor. *Monty Python's Flying Circus.*

CLIFF, JIMMY (Jimmy Chambers). Somerton, Jamaica, 1949. Reggae singer, songwriter.

CLIFFORD, DOUG. Palo Alto, CA, 4/24/45. Drummer. Creedence Clearwater Revival.

CLINTON, BILL. Hope, AK, 8/19/46. Husband of Hillary Rodham, father of Chelsea. 42nd President of the United States.

CLINTON, CHELSEA. Arkansas, 2/27/80. Daughter of Bill and Hillary.

CLINTON, GEORGE. Kannapolis, NC, 7/22/41. Funk pioneer, singer. Parliament; Funkadelic.

CLINTON, HILLARY RODHAM. Park Ridge, IL, 10/26/47. Wife of Bill, mother of Chelsea. First Lady.

CLOONEY, NICK. 1/13/35. Actor, father of George Clooney. American Movie Classics.

CLOONEY, ROSEMARY. Maysville, KY, 5/23/28. Actor, singer, aunt of George Clooney.

CLYDE, JEREMY. England, 3/22/44. Singer, guitarist. Chad & Jeremy.

COBURN, JAMES. Laurel, NE, 8/31/28. Actor. *The Magnificent Seven.*

COCA, IMOGENE. Philadelphia, PA, 11/18/08. Actor. *Your Show of Shows.*

COCHRANE, TOM. 5/14/53. Singer, guitarist. Red Rider.

COCKER, JOE (John Cocker). Sheffield, England, 5/20/44. Singer.

COEN, ETHAN. St. Louis Park, MN, 1958. Director, writer. Brother of Joel. *Raising Arizona.*

COEN, JOEL. St. Louis Park, MN, 1955. Director, writer. Brother of Ethan. *Fargo.*

COGHLAN, JOHN. Dulwich, England, 9/19/46. Drummer. Status Quo.

COHEN, DAVID. Brooklyn, NY, 1942. Keyboardist. Country Joe & The Fish.

COHEN, LEONARD. Montreal, Canada, 9/21/34. Singer, songwriter, poet.

COLE, BRIAN. Tacoma, WA, 9/8/42. Singer, bassist. The Association.

COLE, LLOYD. Derbyshire, England, 1/31/61. Singer, guitarist. Lloyd Cole & The Commotions.

COLE, NATALIE (Stephanie Natalie Maria Cole). Los Angeles, CA, 2/6/50. Singer. *Unforgettable.*

COLEMAN, DABNEY. Austin, TX, 1/3/32. Actor. *Buffalo Bill.*

COLEMAN, GARY. Zion, IL, 2/8/68. Actor. Arnold Jackson on *Diff'rent Strokes.*

COLEY, DORIS. Passaic, NJ, 8/2/41. Singer. The Shirelles.

COLLA, JOHNNY. California, 7/2/52. Saxophonist, guitarist. Huey Lewis & The News.

COLLEN, PHIL. London, England, 12/8/57. Guitarist. Def Leppard.

COLLINS, ALLEN. Jacksonville, FL, 7/19/52. Guitarist. Lynyrd Skynyrd.

COLLINS, GARY. Boston, MA, 4/30/38. Actor, talk show host. *Home.*

COLLINS, JACKIE. 10/4/39. Author. *Lucky.*

COLLINS, JOAN. London, England, 5/23/33. Actor. Alexis Carrington Colby on *Dynasty.*

COLLINS, JUDY. Seattle, WA, 5/1/39. Folk/rock guitarist, singer, songwriter. "Send in the Clowns."

COLLINS, PHIL. Chiswick, England, 1/30/51. Singer, drummer. Genesis.

COLLINS, STEPHEN. Des Moines, IA, 10/1/47. Actor. *Tales of the Gold Monkey.*

COLOMBY, BOBBY. New York, NY, 12/20/44. Drummer, singer. Blood, Sweat & Tears.

COLT, JOHNNY. Cherry Point, NC, 5/1/66. Bassist. The Black Crowes.

COLUMBUS, CHRIS. Spangler, PA, 9/10/58. Director. *Home Alone.*

CONAWAY, JEFF. New York, NY, 10/5/50. Actor. Bobby Wheeler on *Taxi.*

CONNELLY, JENNIFER. New York, NY, 12/12/70. Actor. *The Rocketeer.*

CONNOLLY, BRIAN. Hamilton, Scotland, 10/5/49. Singer. Sweet.

CONNORS, JIMMY. Belleville, IL, 9/2/52. Tennis player.

CONNORS, MIKE (Krekor Ohanian). Fresno, CA, 8/15/25. Actor. *Mannix.*

CONROY, KEVIN. Westport, CT, 11/30/55. Actor. Voice of Batman in *Batman: The Animated Series.*

CONROY, PAT. 10/26/45. Author. *Prince of Tides.*

CONSTANTINE, MICHAEL (Constantine Joanides). Reading, PA, 5/22/27. Actor. *Room 222.*

CONTI, TOM. Paisley, Scotland, 11/22/41. Actor. *Reuben Reuben.*

CONWAY, KEVIN. New York, NY, 5/29/42. Actor. *Slaughterhouse Five.*

CONWAY, TIM (Thomas Daniel Conway). Willoughby, OH, 12/15/33. Actor. *The Carol Burnett Show.*

COODER, RY (Ryland Cooder). Los Angeles, CA, 3/15/47. Folk blues guitarist, composer.

COOK, JEFF. Fort Payne, AL, 8/27/49. Singer, fiddler, guitarist, keyboardist. Alabama.

COOK, NORMAN (Quentin Cook). Sussex, England, 7/31/63. Singer. The Housemartins.

COOK, PAUL. London, England, 7/20/56. Drummer. The Sex Pistols.

COOK, STU. Oakland, CA, 4/25/45. Bassist. Creedence Clearwater Revival.

COOLIO Los Angeles,CA, 8/1/63. Rap Artist. "Gangsta's Paradise."

COONCE, RICKY. Los Angeles, CA, 8/1/47. Drummer. The Grass Roots.

COOPER, ALICE (Vincent Furnier). Detroit, MI, 2/4/48. Singer, songwriter. Alice Cooper.

COOPER, JACKIE (John Cooper Jr.). Los Angeles, CA, 9/15/22. Actor, director. *Superman*.

COPE, JULIAN. Bargoed, Wales, 10/21/57. Singer, bassist. The Teardrop Explodes.

COPELAND, STEWART. Alexandria, Egypt, 7/16/52. Drummer, singer. The Police.

CORBIN, BARRY. Dawson County, TX, 10/16/40. Actor. Maurice Minnifield on *Northern Exposure*.

CORGAN, BILLY. Chicago, IL, 3/17/67. Singer, songwriter, guitarist. Smashing Pumpkins.

CORLEY, PAT. Dallas, TX, 6/1/30. Actor. Phil the bartender on *Murphy Brown*.

CORNELL, CHRIS. Seattle, WA, 7/20/64. Singer, songwriter, drummer. Soundgarden.

CORNICK, GLENN. Barrow-in-Furness, England, 4/24/47. Bassist. Jethro Tull.

CORNISH, GENE. Ottowa, Canada, 5/14/45. Guitarist. The (Young) Rascals.

CORNWELL, HUGH. London, England, 8/28/49. Singer, guitarist. The Stranglers.

CORT, BUD (Walter Edward Cox). New Rochelle, NY, 3/29/48. Actor. *Harold and Maude*.

COSTELL, DAVID. Pittsburgh, PA, 3/15/44. Bassist. Gary Lewis and the Playboys.

COULIER, DAVID. Detroit, MI. Actor. Joey Gladstone on *Full House*.

COVERDALE, DAVID. Saltburn-by-the-Sea, England, 9/22/49. Singer. Whitesnake.

COWSILL, BARRY. Newport, RI, 9/14/54. Bassist, singer. The Cowsills.

COWSILL, BILL. Newport, RI, 1/9/48. Guitarist, singer. The Cowsills.

COWSILL, BOB. Newport, RI, 8/26/49. Guitarist, singer. The Cowsills.

COWSILL, JOHN. Newport, RI, 3/2/56. Drummer. The Cowsills.

COWSILL, PAUL. Newport, RI, 11/11/52. Keyboardist, singer. The Cowsills.

COWSILL, SUE. Newport, RI, 5/20/60. Singer. The Cowsills.

COX, ANDY. Birmingham, England, 1/25/60. Guitarist. Fine Young Cannibals.

COX, RONNY. Cloudcroft, NM, 8/23/38. Actor. *Beverly Hills Cop*.

COYOTE, PETER (Peter Cohon). New York, NY, 1942. Actor. *Jagged Edge*.

CRAIG, MIKEY. Hammersmith, England, 2/15/60. Bassist. Culture Club.

CRAVEN, WES. Cleveland, OH, 8/2/39. Director, novelist. *A Nightmare on Elm Street*.

CRAWFORD, JOHN. 1/17/60. Bassist, singer. Berlin.

CRAWFORD, MICHAEL (Michael Dumble-Smith). Salisbury, England, 1/19/42. Actor, singer. *The Phantom of the Opera*.

CRAWFORD, RANDY (Veronica Crawford). Macon, GA, 2/18/52. Rock-R&B singer, songwriter.

CRAY, ROBERT. Columbus, GA, 8/1/53. Contemporary blues singer, songwriter. "Smoking Gun."

CREGAN, JIM. 3/9/46. Guitarist. Steve Harley & Cockney Rebel.

CREME, LOL. Manchester, England, 9/19/47. Singer, guitarist. 10cc; Godley & Creme.

CRENNA, RICHARD. Los Angeles, CA, 11/30/27. Actor. *Rambo: First Blood Part II*.

CREWSDON, ROY. Manchester, England, 5/29/41. Guitarist. Freddie & The Dreamers.

CRISS, PETER (Peter Crisscoula). Brooklyn, NY, 12/27/47. Drummer, singer. Kiss.

CROFTS, DASH. Cisco, TX, 8/14/40. Singer, guitarist, mandolinist. Seals & Crofts.

CRONIN, KEVIN. Evanston, IL, 10/6/51. Singer. REO Speedwagon.

CRONKITE, WALTER. St. Joseph, MO, 11/4/16. News journalist and anchor. *CBS Evening News*.

CRONYN, HUME. London, Canada, 7/18/11. Actor, writer, director, widower of Jessica Tandy. *The Postman Always Rings Twice*.

CROPPER, STEVE. Willow Springs, MO, 10/21/41.

Guitarist. Booker T. & The MG's.

CROSBY, CATHY LEE. Los Angeles, CA, 12/2/49. Actor. *That's Incredible!*

CROSBY, DAVID (David Van Cortland). Los Angeles, CA, 8/14/41. Singer, guitarist. The Byrds; Crosby, Stills, Nash & Young.

CROSBY, DENISE. Hollywood, CA, 1958. Actor, granddaughter of Bing Crosby. *Star Trek: The Next Generation*.

CROSBY, HARRY. Los Angeles, CA, 8/8/58. Actor, singer.

CROSS, BEN. London, England, 12/16/48. Actor. *Chariots of Fire*.

CROSS, CHRIS (Chris St. John). London, England, 7/14/52. Bassist, synthesizer player. Ultravox.

CROSS, CHRISTOPHER (Christopher Geppert). San Antonio, TX, 5/3/51. Guitarist, singer, songwriter. "Ride Like the Wind."

CROUSE, LINDSAY. New York, NY, 5/12/48. Actor. *The Verdict*.

CRYER, JON. New York, NY, 4/16/65. Actor. *Pretty in Pink*.

CULKIN, MACAULAY. New York, NY, 8/26/80. Actor. *Home Alone, My Girl*.

CULLIMORE, STAN. Hull, England, 4/6/62. Bassist. The Housemartins.

CULLUM, JOHN. Knoxville, TN, 3/2/30. Actor. Holling Vincoeur on *Northern Exposure*.

CULP, ROBERT. Oakland, CA, 8/16/30. Actor. *I Spy*.

CUMMINGS, BURTON. Winnipeg, Canada, 12/31/47. Singer, keyboardist. The Guess Who.

CUMMINGS, GEORGE. Meridian, MS, 7/28/38. Lead guitarist. Dr. Hook.

CUNNINGHAM, BILL. Memphis, TN, 1/23/50. Bassist, pianist. The Box Tops; Big Star.

CUNNINGHAM, TOM. Glasgow, Scotland, 6/22/65. Drummer. Wet Wet Wet.

CUOMO, MARIO. Queens, NY, 6/15/32. Political leader. Former Governor of New York.

CURRIE, ALANNAH. Auckland, New Zealand, 9/20/59. Singer, saxophonist, percussionist. Thompson Twins.

CURRIE, BILLY. Huddersfield, England, 4/1/52. Synthesizer player, keyboardist. Ultravox.

CURRIE, CHERIE. Los Angeles, CA, 1960. Singer, married to Robert Hays. The Runaways.

CURRY, TIM. Cheshire, England, 4/19/46. Actor. *The Rocky Horror Picture Show*.

CURTIN, JANE. Cambridge, MA, 9/6/47. Actor. *Kate & Allie*.

CURTIS, CHRIS (Chris Crummy). Oldham, England, 8/26/41. Singer, drummer. The Searchers.

CURTIS, SONNY. Meadow, TX, 5/9/37. Guitarist. Buddy Holly & The Crickets.

CURTIS, TONY (Bernard Schwartz). New York, NY, 6/3/25. Actor, father of Jamie Lee Curtis, formerly married to Janet Leigh. *Some Like It Hot*.

CUSACK, JOAN. Evanston, IL, 10/11/62. Actor. *Working Girl*.

CUSACK, SINEAD. Ireland, 2/18/48. Actor, married to Jeremy Irons, daughter of Cyril Cusack.

CYRUS, BILLY RAY. Flatwoods, NY, 8/25/61. Singer, son of politician Ronald Ray Cyrus. "Achy-Breaky Heart."

D'ABO, OLIVIA. 1/22/69. Actor. *The Wonder Years*.

D'ALEO, ANGELO. The Bronx, NY, 2/3/41. Singer. Dion & The Belmonts.

D'ANGELO, BEVERLY. Columbus, OH, 11/15/51. Actor. *Hair*.

D'ARBANVILLE, PATTI. 5/25/51. Actress

D'ARBY, TERENCE TRENT. New York, NY, 3/15/62. R&B singer, songwriter. "Wishing Well."

D'ONOFRIO, VINCENT. 6/30/59. Actor. *The Newton Boys*.

DAFOE, WILLEM. Appleton, WI, 7/22/55. Actor. *Mississippi Burning*.

DALE, GLEN (Richard Garforth). Deal, England, 4/2/43. Guitarist, singer. The Fortunes.

DALEY, ROSIE. South Seaville, NJ, 1961. Chef. *In the Kitchen with Rosie*.

DALLIN, SARAH. Bristol, England, 12/17/61. Singer. Bananarama.

DALTON, TIMOTHY. Colwyn Bay, Wales, 3/21/44. Actor.

James Bond in *The Living Daylights.*

DALTREY, ROGER. London, England, 3/1/44. Lead singer. The Who.

DALY, GARY. Merseyside, England, 5/5/62. Singer. China Crisis.

DALY, TIMOTHY. New York, NY, 3/1/56. Actor. *Wings.*

DALY, TYNE (Ellen Tyne Daly). Madison, WI, 2/21/46. Actor. *Cagney & Lacey.*

DAMMERS, JERRY (Jerry Dankin). 5/22/54. Keyboardist. The Specials.

DAMONE, VIC (Vito Farinola). Brooklyn, NY, 6/12/28. Singer, married to Diahann Caroll. *The Vic Damone Show.*

DANCE, CHARLES. Worcestershire, England, 10/10/46. Actor. *The Jewel in the Crown.*

DANDO, EVAN. 3/4/67. Musician. The Lemonheads.

DANELLI, DINO. New York, NY, 7/23/45. Drummer. The (Young) Rascals.

DANGERFIELD, RODNEY (Jacob Cohen). Babylon, NY, 11/22/21. Actor. *Back to School.*

DANIEL, JEFFREY. Los Angeles, CA, 8/24/55. Singer. Shalamar.

DANIELS, WILLIAM. Brooklyn, NY, 3/31/27. Actor. *St. Elsewhere.*

DANKO, RICK. Simcoe, Canada, 12/9/43. Bassist, singer. The Band.

DANNER, BLYTHE. Philadelphia, PA, 2/3/43. Actor. *The Prince of Tides.*

DANTE, MICHAEL (Ralph Vitti). Stamford, CT, 1935. Actor. Crazy Horse in *Custer.*

DANZA, TONY. Brooklyn, NY, 4/21/51. Actor. Tony Micelli on *Who's the Boss?*

DAVIDOVICH, LOLITA. Ontario, Canada, 7/15/61. Actor. *Blaze.*

DAVIDSON, JAYE. Riverside, CA, 1967. Actor. *The Crying Game.*

DAVIDSON, JOHN. Pittsburgh, PA, 12/13/41. Game show host. *Hollywood Squares.*

DAVIDSON, LENNY. Enfield, England, 5/30/44. Guitarist. The Dave Clark Five.

DAVIES, DAVE. Muswell Hill, England, 2/3/47. Singer, guitarist. The Kinks.

DAVIES, IVA. Australia, 5/22/55. Guitarist, singer. Icehouse.

DAVIES, RAY. Muswell Hill, England, 6/21/44. Singer, guitarist. The Kinks.

DAVIES, RICHARD. England, 7/22/44. Singer, keyboardist. Supertramp.

DAVIS, BILLY JR. St. Louis, MO, 6/26/38. Singer. The 5th Dimension.

DAVIS, CLIFTON. Chicago, IL, 10/4/45. Actor, singer, composer. *Never Can Say Goodbye.*

DAVIS, JIM. Marion, IN, 7/28/45. Cartoonist. *Garfield.*

DAVIS, MAC (Morris Mac Davis). Lubbock, TX, 1/21/42. Singer, songwriter, actor. *The Mac Davis Show.*

DAVIS, MARTHA. Berkeley, CA, 1/15/51. Singer. The Motels.

DAVIS, OSSIE. Cogdell, GA, 12/18/17. Actor, writer. *Evening Shade.*

DAVIS, PAUL. Manchester, England, 3/7/66. Keyboardist. Happy Mondays.

DAVIS, ROB. Carshalton, England, 10/1/47. Lead guitarist, singer. Mud.

DAVIS, SPENCER. Swansea, Wales, 7/17/42. Guitarist. The Spencer Davis Group.

DAVIS, WILLIE. 1940. Drummer. Joey Dee and the Starliters.

DAWBER, PAM. 10/18/50. Actor. Married to Mark Harmon. *Mork and Mindy.*

DAY, DORIS (Doris von Kappelhoff). Cincinnati, OH, 4/3/24. Actor, performer. *The Doris Day Show.*

DAY, MARK. Manchester, England, 12/29/61. Guitarist. Happy Mondays.

DE BURGH, CHRIS (Chris Davidson). Argentina, 10/15/48. Singer, songwriter. "Lady in Red."

DE HAVILLAND, OLIVIA. Tokyo, Japan, 7/1/16. Actor. *Gone with the Wind.*

DE LAURENTIS, DINO. Torre Annunziata, Italy, 8/8/19. Producer. *King Kong; Conan the Barbarian.*

DEACON, JOHN. Leicester, England, 8/19/51. Bassist. Queen.

DEAN, JIMMY. Plainview, TX, 8/10/28. Performer. *The Jimmy Dean Show.*

DEBARGE, EL (Eldra DeBarge). Grand Rapids, MI, 6/4/61. Singer, keyboardist, record producer.

DEE, DAVE (Dave Harman). Salisbury, England, 12/17/43. Lead singer, tambourinist. Dave Dee, Dozy, Beaky, Mick and Tich.

DEE, JOEY (Joey DiNicola). Passaic, NJ, 6/11/40. Singer. Joey Dee and the Starliters.

DEE, KIKI. Bradford, England, 3/6/47. Pop singer.

DEE, RUBY. Cleveland, OH, 10/27/24. Actor. *Do the Right Thing.*

DEE, SANDRA (Alexandra Zuck). Bayonne, NJ, 4/23/42. Actor. *Gidget.*

DEFOREST, CALVERT. Brooklyn, NY, 1923. Actor, Larry "Bud" Melman.

DEKKER, DESMOND (Desmond Dacris). Kingston, Jamaica, 7/16/42. Reggae singer, songwriter.

DELANEY, KIM. 11/29/61. Actress. *NYPD Blue.*

DELANY, DANA. New York, NY, 3/11/56. Actor. *China Beach.*

DELON, ALAIN. Sceaux, France, 11/8/35. Actor. *Le Samourai.*

DELP, BRAD. Boston, MA, 6/12/51. Guitarist, singer. Boston.

DELUISE, DOM. Brooklyn, NY, 8/1/33. Actor. *The Dom DeLuise Show.*

DELUISE, PETER. Hollywood, CA, 1967. Actor. Doug Penhall on *21 Jump Street.*

DEMME, JONATHAN. Rockville Centre, MD, 2/22/44. Director, producer, writer. *The Silence of the Lambs.*

DEMORNAY, REBECCA. Santa Rosa, CA, 8/29/59. Actor. *The Hand That Rocks the Cradle.*

DEMPSEY, PATRICK. Lewiston, ME, 1/13/66. Actor. *Loverboy.*

DENEUVE, CATHERINE (Catherine Dorleac). Paris, France, 10/22/43. Actor. *Belle de Jour.*

DENSMORE, JOHN. Los Angeles, CA, 12/1/44. Drummer. The Doors.

DENVER, BOB. New Rochelle, NY, 1/9/35. Actor. Gilligan on *Gilligan's Island.*

DEPARDIEU, GERARD. Chateauroux, France, 12/27/48. Actor. *Green Card.*

DEREK, BO (Mary Cathleen Collins). Long Beach, CA, 11/20/56. Actor, married to John Derek. *10.*

DERN, BRUCE. Chicago, IL, 6/4/36. Actor, father of Laura. *Coming Home.*

DERN, LAURA. Los Angeles, CA, 2/10/67. Actor, daughter of Bruce Dern and Diane Ladd, engaged to Jeff Goldblum. *Jurassic Park.*

DERRINGER, RICK (Richard Zehringer). Fort Recovery, OH, 8/5/47. Singer, songwriter, producer. The McCoys.

DESTRI, JIMMY. 4/13/54. Keyboardist. Blondie.

DEVANE, WILLIAM. Albany, NY, 9/5/39. Actor. Greg Sumner in *Knots Landing.*

DEVITO, TOMMY. Montclair, NJ, 6/19/36. Singer, guitarist. The Four Seasons.

DEVOE, RONALD. 11/17/67. Singer. New Edition; Bell Biv DeVoe.

DEY, SUSAN. Pekin, IL, 12/10/52. Actor. *L.A. Law.*

DEYOUNG, CLIFF. Inglewood, CA, 2/12/45. Actor. *The Hunger.*

DEYOUNG, DENNIS. Chicago, IL, 2/18/47. Singer, keyboardist. Styx.

DIAMOND, NEIL (Noah Kaminsky). New York, NY, 1/24/41. Singer, songwriter. *The Jazz Singer.*

DIAMONDE, DICK (Dingeman Van Der Sluys). Hilversum, Holland, 12/28/47. Bassist. The Easybeats.

DICKEN (Jeff Pain). 4/4/50. Singer. Mr. Big.

DICKERSON, B. B. (Morris Dickerson). Torrance, CA, 8/3/49. Bassist, singer. War.

DICKINSON, ANGIE (Angie Brown). Kulm, ND, 9/30/32. Actor. *Police Woman.*

DICKINSON, BRUCE (Paul Dickinson). Worksop, England, 8/7/58. Singer. Iron Maiden.

DIDDLEY, BO (Otha Bates). McComb, MS, 12/30/28. Legendary blues guitarist, singer, songwriter.

DIFFORD, CHRIS. London, England, 11/4/54. Singer, guitarist. Squeeze.

DILLER, PHYLLIS (Phyllis Driver). Lima, OH, 7/17/17. Actor. *The Phyllis Diller Show.*

DILLON, KEVIN. Mamaroneck, NY, 8/19/65. Actor. *The Doors.*

DILLON, MATT. New Rochelle, NY, 2/18/64. Actor. *The Outsiders.*

DIMAGGIO, JOE. Martinez, CA, 11/25/14. Baseball great. New York Yankees. Once married to Marilyn Monroe.

DIMUCCI, DION. The Bronx, NY, 7/18/39. Lead singer. Dion & The Belmonts.

DIO, RONNIE JAMES. Cortland, NY, 7/10/48. Singer. Rainbow; Black Sabbath.

DITKA, MIKE. Carnegie, PA, 10/18/39. NFL football player, coach.

DIXON, DONNA. Alexandria, VA, 7/20/57. Actor, married to Dan Aykroyd. *Bosom Buddies.*

DOBSON, KEVIN. New York, NY, 3/18/43. Actor. *Knots Landing.*

DOHERTY, DENNY. Halifax, Canada, 11/29/41. Singer. The Mamas and the Papas.

DOLENZ, MICKEY (George Dolenz). Los Angeles, CA, 3/8/45. Singer, drummer. The Monkees.

DOMINO, FATS (Antoine Domino). New Orleans, LA, 2/26/28. Legendary singer, songwriter.

DONAHUE, PHIL. Cleveland, OH, 12/21/35. Talk show host.

DONAHUE, TROY (Merle Johnson). New York, NY, 1/27/36. Actor. *Hawaiian Eye.*

DONALDSON, SAM. El Paso, TX, 3/11/34. News reporter and anchor. *Prime Time Live.*

DONEGAN, LAWRENCE. 7/13/61. Bassist. Lloyd Cole & The Commotions.

DONEGAN, LONNIE (Anthony Donegan). Glasgow, Scotland, 4/29/31. Folk/blues guitarist, banjoist, and singer.

DONOVAN (Donovan Leitch). Glasgow, Scotland, 2/10/46. Folk/psychedelic singer, songwriter, father of Ione Skye and Donovan Leitch. "Mellow Yellow."

DONOVAN, JASON. Malvern, Australia, 6/1/68. Singer, actor.

DORMAN, LEE. St. Louis, MO, 9/19/45. Bassist. Iron Butterfly.

DOUGHTY, NEAL. Evanston, IL, 7/29/46. Keyboardist. REO Speedwagon.

DOUGLAS, BUSTER (James Douglas). Columbus, OH, 4/7/60. Boxer. Defeated Mike Tyson.

DOUGLAS, DONNA (Dorothy Bourgeois). Baywood, LA, 9/26/35. Actor. Elly May Clampett on *The Beverly Hillbillies.*

DOUGLAS, KIRK (Issur Danielovitch). Amsterdam, NY, 12/9/16. Actor, producer, father of Michael. *Spartacus.*

DOW, TONY. Hollywood, CA, 4/13/45. Actor. Wally Cleaver on *Leave It to Beaver.*

DOWN, LESLEY-ANN. London, England, 3/17/54. Actor. *Dallas.*

DOWNEY, BRIAN. Dublin, Ireland, 1/27/51. Drummer. Thin Lizzy.

DOWNEY, MORTON JR. 12/9/33. Controversial talk show host, actor.

DOWNS, HUGH. Akron, OH, 2/14/21. Host, actor, commentator. *20/20.*

DOZY (Trevor Davies). Enford, England, 11/27/44. Bassist. Dave Dee, Dozy, Beaky, Mick and Tich.

DRAGON, DARYL. Los Angeles, CA, 8/27/42. Keyboardist. The Captain & Tennille.

DR. DRE. Compton, CA, 1965. Rap artist, record producer. *The Chronic.*

DREJA, CHRIS. Surbiton, England, 11/11/44. Guitarist. The Yardbirds.

DREYFUSS, RICHARD. Brooklyn, NY, 10/29/47. Actor. *Close Encounters of the Third Kind.*

DRYDEN, SPENCER. New York, NY, 4/7/38. Drummer. Jefferson Airplane/Starship.

DUBROW, KEVIN. 10/29/55. Lead singer. Quiet Riot.

DUDIKOFF, MICHAEL. Redondo Beach, CA, 10/8/54. Actor. *American Ninja.*

DUFFY, BILLY. 5/12/61. Lead guitarist. The Cult.

DUFFY, JULIA. Minneapolis, MN, 6/27/51. Actor. *Newhart.*

DUFFY, KAREN. 5/23/61. TV personality. MTV.

DUFFY, PATRICK. Townsend, MT, 3/17/49. Actor. Bobby Ewing on *Dallas.*

DUKAKIS, OLYMPIA. Lowell, MA, 6/20/31. Actor. *Moonstruck.*

DUKE, DAVID. Tulsa, OK, 1951. White supremacist, politician.

DUKE, PATTY (Anna Marie Duke). New York, NY, 12/14/46. Actor, formerly married to John Astin, mother of Sean Astin. *The Patty Duke Show.*

DUKES, DAVID. San Francisco, CA, 6/6/45. Actor. *Sisters.*

DULLEA, KEIR. Cleveland, OH, 5/30/36. Actor. *2001: A Space Odyssey.*

DUNAWAY, DENNIS. Cottage Grove, OR, 12/9/48. Bassist. Alice Cooper.

DUNAWAY, FAYE. Bascom, Fl, 1/14/41. Actor. *Mommie Dearest.*

DUNCAN, GARY (Gary Grubb). San Diego, CA, 9/4/46. Guitarist. Quicksilver Messenger Service.

DUNCAN, SANDY. Henderson, TX, 2/20/46. Actor. *Funny Face.*

DUNN, DONALD. Memphis, TN, 11/24/41. Bassist. Booker T. & The MG's.

DUNN, LARRY. Colorado, 6/19/53. Keyboardist. Earth, Wind & Fire.

DUNNE, GRIFFIN. New York, NY, 6/8/55. Actor, director, son of Dominick. *After Hours.*

DUNST, KIRSTEN. 4/30/82. Actor. *Interview With A Vampire.*

DURBIN, DEANNA (Edna Durbin). Winnipeg, Canada, 12/4/21. Actor. *One Hundred Men and a Girl.*

DURNING, CHARLES. Highland Falls, NY, 2/28/23. Actor. *Evening Shade.*

DURY, IAN. Upminster, England, 5/12/42. Singer. Ian Dury & The Blockheads.

DUTTON, CHARLES. Baltimore, MD, 1/30/51. Actor. *Roc.*

DUVALL, ROBERT. San Diego, CA, 1/5/31. Actor. *Tender Mercies.*

DUVALL, SHELLEY. Houston, TX, 7/7/49. Actor, producer. *The Shining.*

DYSART, RICHARD. Brighton, MA, 3/30/29. Actor. Leland McKenzie on *L.A. Law.*

EARLE, STEVE. Fort Monroe, VA, 1/17/55. Country/rock singer, songwriter. Guitar Town.

EASTON, ELLIOT (Elliot Shapiro). Brooklyn, NY, 12/18/53. Guitarist. The Cars.

EASTON, SHEENA (Sheena Orr). Bellshill, Scotland, 4/27/59. Rock/R&B singer.

EBSEN, BUDDY (Christian Ebsen Jr.). Belleville, IL,

4/2/08. Actor. Jed Clampell on *The Beverly Hillbillies.*

ECHOLS, JOHN. Memphis, TN, 1945. Lead guitarist. Love.

EDDY, DUANE. Corning, NY, 4/26/38. Legendary rock guitarist.

EDEN, BARBARA (Barbara Huffman). Tucson, AZ, 8/23/34. Actor. Jeannie in *I Dream of Jeannie.*

EDGE, GRAEME. Rochester, England, 3/30/42. Drummer. The Moody Blues.

EDGE, THE (David Evans). Wales, 8/8/61. Guitarist. U2.

EDMONTON, JERRY. Canada, 10/24/46. Drummer. Steppenwolf.

EDWARD, PRINCE. London, England, 3/10/64. British royalty, son of Queen Elizabeth II.

EDWARDS, BERNARD. Greenville, NC, 10/31/52. Bassist. Chic.

EDWARDS, BLAKE (William Blake McEdwards). Tulsa, OK, 7/26/22. Writer, director. The *Pink Panther* series. Married to Julie Andrews.

EDWARDS, NOKIE. Washington, DC, 5/9/39. Lead guitarist. The Ventures.

EGGAR, SAMANTHA. London, England, 3/5/39. Actor. *The Collector.*

EIKENBERRY, JILL. New Haven, CT, 1/21/47. Actor. Ann Kelsey on *L.A. Law.*

EKBERG, ANITA. Malmo, Sweden, 9/29/31. Actor. *La Dolce Vita.*

EKLAND, BRITT. Stockholm, Sweden, 10/6/42. Actor. *After the Fox.*

ELIZONDO, HECTOR. New York, NY, 12/22/36. Actor. *Freebie and the Bean.*

ELLERBEE, LINDA. Bryan, TX, 8/15/44. News commentator. *Our World.*

ELLIOTT, BOBBY. Burnley, England, 12/8/42. Drummer. The Hollies.

ELLIOTT, CHRIS. New York, NY, 1960. Comedy writer, actor. *Get a Life.*

ELLIOTT, DENNIS. London, England, 8/18/50. Drummer. Foreigner.

ELLIOTT, JOE. Sheffield, England, 8/1/59. Singer. Def Leppard.

ELLIOTT, SAM. Sacramento, CA, 8/9/44. Actor. *Tombstone.*

ELLIS, RALPH. Liverpool, England, 3/8/42. Guitarist, singer. The Swinging Blue Jeans.

ELMORE, GREG. San Diego, CA, 9/4/46. Drummer. Quicksilver Messenger Service.

ELSWIT, RIK. New York, NY, 7/6/45. Guitarist, singer. Dr. Hook.

ELVIRA (Cassandra Peterson). Manhattan, KS, 9/17/51. Horror film hostess.

ELWES, CARY. Liverpool, England, 10/26/62. Actor. *The Princess Bride.*

EMERSON, KEITH. Todmorden, England, 11/1/44. Keyboardist. Emerson, Lake & Palmer.

ENGEL, SCOTT (Noel Engel). Hamilton, OH, 1/9/44. Singer. The Walker Brothers.

ENGLUND, ROBERT. Hollywood, CA, 6/6/49. Actor. Freddie Krueger in *Nightmare on Elm Street* series.

ENNIS, RAY. Liverpool, England, 5/26/42. Lead guitarist, singer. The Swinging Blue Jeans.

ENO, BRIAN. Woodbridge, England, 5/15/48. Synthesizer player, producer. Cofounder of Roxy Music.

ENTNER, WARREN. Boston, MA, 7/7/44. Singer, guitarist. The Grass Roots.

ENTWISTLE, JOHN. Chiswick, England, 10/9/44. Bassist. The Who.

ENYA (Eithne Ni Bhraona). Gweedore, Ireland, 1962. Singer, composer.

ERRICO, GREG. San Francisco, CA, 9/1/46. Drummer. Sly & The Family Stone.

ERVING, JULIUS. Roosevelt, NY, 2/22/50. Basketball great. Philadelphia 76ers.

ESIASON, BOOMER (Norman Julius Esiason Jr.). West Islip, NY, 4/17/61. NFL football player.

ESPOSITO, GIANCARLO. Copenhagen, Denmark, 4/26/61. Actor. *Do the Right Thing.*

ESSEX, DAVID (David Cook). Plaistow, England, 7/23/47. Drummer, singer, songwriter, actor. *Stardust.*

ESTEFAN, GLORIA (Gloria Fajardo). Havana, Cuba,

9/1/57. Latin pop singer. The Miami Sound Machine.

ESTEVEZ, EMILIO. New York, NY, 5/12/62. Actor, writer, divorced from Paula Abdul, son of Martin Sheen. *Repo Man.*

ESTRADA, ERIK. New York, NY, 3/16/49. Actor. Frank "Ponch" Poncherello on *CHiPS.*

EUGENIE, PRINCESS. London, England, 3/23/90. British royalty, daughter of Prince Andrew and the Duchess of York.

EVANGELISTA, LINDA. Canada, 5/10/65. Supermodel.

EVANS, DALE (Francis Smith). Uvalde, TX, 10/31/12. Actor. *The Yellow Rose of Texas.*

EVANS, LINDA (Linda Evanstad). Hartford, CT, 11/18/42. Actor. *Dynasty.*

EVANS, MARK. Melbourne, Australia, 3/2/56. Bassist. AC/DC.

EVANS, MIKE (Michael Jonas Evans). Salisbury, NC, 11/3/49. Actor. Lionel on *The Jeffersons.*

EVERETT, CHAD (Raymond Lee Cramton). South Bend, IN, 6/11/36. Actor. *Medical Center.*

EVERLY, DON (Isaac Everly). Brownie, KY, 2/1/37. Singer, guitarist. The Everly Brothers.

EVERLY, PHIL. Chicago, IL, 1/19/39. Singer, guitarist. The Everly Brothers.

EVERT, CHRIS. Ft. Lauderdale, FL, 12/21/54. Tennis player.

EVIGAN, GREG. South Amboy, NJ, 10/14/53. Actor. *B.J. and the Bear.*

FABARES, SHELLEY (Michelle Marie Fabares). Santa Monica, CA, 1/19/44. Actor, married to Mike Farrell, niece of Nanette Fabray. Christine Armstrong on *Coach.*

FABIAN (Fabian Forte). Philadelphia, PA, 2/6/43. Singer, actor. *American Bandstand.*

FABIO (Fabio Lanzoni). Milan, Italy, 3/15/61. Model.

FABRAY, NANETTE (Ruby Nanette Fabares). San Diego, CA, 10/27/20. Actor, aunt of Shelley Fabares. *One Day at a Time.*

FAGEN, DONALD. Passaic, NJ, 1/10/48. Singer, keyboardist. Steely Dan.

FAHEY, SIOBHAN. 9/10/60. Singer. Bananarama.

FAIRBANKS, DOUGLAS JR. New York, NY, 12/9/09. Actor. *Gunga Din.*

FAIRCHILD, MORGAN (Patsy McClenny). Dallas, TX, 2/3/50. Actor. *Falcon Crest.*

FAIRWEATHER-LOW, ANDY. Ystrad Mynach, Wales, 8/8/50. Singer, guitarist. Amen Corner.

FAITH, ADAM (Terence Nelhams). Acton, England, 6/23/40. Singer, actor, financial adviser.

FAITHFULL, MARIANNE. Hampstead, England, 12/29/46. Folk/rock singer.

FAKIR, ABDUL. Detroit, MI, 12/26/35. Singer. The Four Tops.

FALANA, LOLA (Loletha Elaine Falana). Philadelphia, PA, 9/11/43. Singer.

FALCONER, EARL. Birmingham, England, 1/23/59. Bassist. UB40.

FALK, PETER. New York, NY, 9/16/27. Actor. *Columbo.*

FALTSKOG, AGNETHA. Jonkoping, Sweden, 4/5/50. Singer. Abba.

FAMBROUGH, HENRY. 5/10/38. Singer. The (Detroit) Spinners.

FAME, GEORGIE (Clive Powell). Leigh, England, 9/26/43. Singer, keyboardist. Georgie Fame & The Blue Flames.

FARENTINO, JAMES. Brooklyn, NY, 2/24/38. Actor. *Dynasty.*

FARINA, DENNIS. Chicago, IL, 2/29/44. Actor. *Crime Story.*

FARNER, MARK. Flint, MI, 9/29/48. Singer, guitarist. Grand Funk Railroad.

FARR, JAMIE (Jameel Joseph Farah). Toledo, OH, 7/1/34. Actor. Maxwell Klinger on *M*A*S*H.*

FARRAKHAN, LOUIS (Louis Eugene Walcott). New York, NY, 5/11/33. Controversial Muslim minister.

FARRELL, BOBBY. Aruba, West Indies, 10/6/49. Singer. Boney M.

FARRELL, MIKE. St. Paul, MN, 2/6/39. Actor, writer, director, married to Shelley Fabares. B. J. Hunnicutt on *M*A*S*H.*

FARRIS, STEVE. 5/1/57. Guitarist. Mr. Mister.

FARRISS, ANDREW. Perth, Australia, 3/27/59. Keyboardist. INXS.

FARRISS, JON. Perth, Australia, 8/10/61. Drummer, singer. INXS.

FAULKNER, ERIC. Edinburgh, Scotland, 10/21/55. Guitarist. The Bay City Rollers.

FAWCETT, FARRAH. Corpus Christi, TX, 2/2/47. Actor. Jill Munroe on *Charlie's Angels.*

FELDMAN, COREY. Reseda, CA, 7/16/71. Actor. *Stand By Me.*

FELDON, BARBARA (Barbara Hall). Pittsburgh, PA, 3/12/41. Actor. Agent 99 on *Get Smart.*

FELDSHUH, TOVAH. New York, NY, 12/27/53. Actor. *The Idolmaker.*

FELICIANO, JOSE. Lares, Puerto Rico, 9/10/45. Singer, guitarist. *Chico and the Man.*

FENN, SHERILYN. Detroit, MI, 2/1/65. Actor. *Twin Peaks.*

FERGUSON, JAY (John Ferguson). Burbank, CA, 5/10/47. Singer. Spirit.

FERGUSON, LARRY. Nassau, Bahamas, 4/14/48. Keyboardist. Hot Chocolate.

FERGUSON, SARAH. London, England, 10/15/59. Duchess of York. Formerly married to Prince Andrew.

FERRARO, GERALDINE. Newburgh, NY, 8/26/35. Politician, first woman vice-presidential candidate.

FERRER, MEL (Melchor Gaston Ferrer). Elberon, NJ, 8/25/12. Producer, director, actor, formerly married to Audrey Hepburn. *Falcon Crest.*

FERRER, MIGUEL. Santa Monica, CA, 2/7/54. Actor, son of Jose Ferrer and Rosemary Clooney. *Twin Peaks.*

FERRIGNO, LOU. Brooklyn, NY, 11/9/52. Actor, bodybuilder. *The Incredible Hulk.*

FERRIS, BARBARA. London, England, 10/3/40. Actor. *The Strauss Family.*

FERRY, BRYAN. Durham, England, 9/26/45. Singer, songwriter. Roxy Music.

FIEGER, DOUG. Detroit, MI, 8/20/52. Singer, guitarist. The Knack.

FIELDER, JIM. Denton, TX, 10/4/47. Bassist. Blood, Sweat & Tears.

FIELDS, KIM. Los Angeles, CA, 5/12/69. Actor. Dorothy

"Tootie" Ramsey on *The Facts of Life.*

FIERSTEIN, HARVEY. Brooklyn, NY, 6/6/54. Actor, writer. *Mrs. Doubtfire.*

FILIPOVIC, ZLATA. Sarajevo, Bosnia-Herzegovina, 12/3/81. Author. *Zlata's Diary.*

FINCH, RICHARD. Indianapolis, IN, 1/25/54. Bassist. KC & The Sunshine Band.

FINER, JEM. Ireland. Banjoist. The Pogues.

FINGERS, JOHNNIE (Johnnie Moylett). Ireland, 9/10/56. Keyboardist, singer. The Boomtown Rats.

FINN, TIM (Te Awamutu). New Zealand, 6/25/52. Singer, keyboardist. Split Enz.

FINNEY, ALBERT. Salford, England, 5/9/36. Actor. *Shoot the Moon.*

FIORENTINO, LINDA (Clorinda Fiorentino). Philadelphia, PA, 3/9/58. Actor. *The Last Seduction.*

FIRTH, COLIN. Grayshott, England, 9/10/60. Actor. *Another Country.*

FISH (Derek Dick). Dalkeith, Scotland, 4/25/58. Singer. Marillion.

FISHER, AMY. New York, NY, 1974. The "Long Island Lolita."

FISHER, EDDIE. Philadelphia, PA, 8/10/28. Singer, formerly married to Debbie Reynolds, Elizabeth Taylor, and Connie Stevens, father of Carrie Fisher. *The Eddie Fisher Show.*

FISHER, JOELY. 10/29/67. Actor, daughter of Eddie Fisher. *Ellen.*

FISHER, MATTHEW. Croydon, England, 3/7/46. Keyboardist. Procol Harum.

FISHER, ROGER. Seattle, WA, 2/14/50. Guitarist. Heart.

FITZGERALD, GERALDINE. Dublin, Ireland, 11/24/14. Actor. *Wuthering Heights.*

FLACK, ROBERTA. Black Mountain, NC, 2/10/40. Pop singer. "The First Time Ever I Saw Your Face."

FLATLEY, MICHAEL. 7/16/58. Dancer. *Lord of the Dance.*

FLEA (Michael Balzary). Melbourne, Australia. Singer, bassist. The Red Hot Chili Peppers.

FLEETWOOD, MICK. London, England, 6/24/42. Drummer. Fleetwood Mac.

FLEMING, PEGGY. San Jose, CA, 7/27/48. Ice skater. Olympic gold medalist.

FLETCHER, ANDY. Basildon, England, 7/8/60. Keyboardist. Depeche Mode.

FLETCHER, LOUISE. Birmingham, AL, 7/22/34. Actor. *One Flew over the Cuckoo's Nest.*

FLOYD, EDDIE. Montgomery, AL, 6/25/35. R&B singer, songwriter.

FOGELBERG, DAN. Peoria, IL, 8/13/51. Guitarist, singer, songwriter.

FOGERTY, JOHN. Berkeley, CA, 5/28/45. Singer, guitarist. Creedence Clearwater Revival.

FOLLOWS, MEGAN. Toronto, Canada, 3/14/68. Actor. *Anne of Green Gables.*

FONDA, PETER. New York, NY, 2/23/40. Actor, son of Henry Fonda, brother of Jane, father of Bridget. *Easy Rider.*

FONTAINE, JOAN (Joan de Havilland). Tokyo, Japan, 10/22/17. Actor, sister of Olivia de Havilland. *Suspicion.*

FONTANA, WAYNE (Glyn Ellis). Manchester, England, 10/28/40. Singer. Wayne Fontana & The Mindbenders.

FORD, FAITH. Alexandria, LA, 9/14/64. Actor. Corky Sherwood Forrest on *Murphy Brown.*

FORD, FRANKIE (Frankie Guzzo). Gretna, LA, 8/4/40. Singer.

FORD, LITA. London, England, 9/23/59. Lead guitarist. The Runaways.

FOREMAN, CHRIS. England, 8/8/58. Guitarist. Madness.

FOREMAN, GEORGE. Marshall, TX, 1/10/49. Boxer, actor. *George.*

FORSSI, KEN. Cleveland, OH, 1943. Bassist. Love.

FORSTER, ROBERT. Rochester, NY, 7/13/41. Actor. *Banyon.*

FORSYTHE, JOHN (John Freund). Penns Grove, NJ, 1/29/18. Actor. Blake Carrington on *Dynasty.*

FORTUNE, JIMMY. Newport News, VA, 3/1/55. Musician. Statler Brothers.

FORTUNE, NICK (Nick Fortuna). Chicago, IL, 5/1/46. Bassist. The Buckinghams.

FOSTER, MEG. Reading, PA, 5/14/48. Actor. *Cagney and Lacey.*

FOX, JACKIE. California, 1960. Bassist. The Runaways.

FOX, JAMES. London, England, 5/19/39. Actor. *The Loneliness of the Long Distance Runner.*

FOX, SAMANTHA. England, 4/15/66. Singer. "Naughty Girls (Need Love Too)."

FOX, TERRY (Terrance Stanley Fox). Winnipeg, Canada, 7/28/58. Track athlete, fund-raiser.

FOXTON, BRUCE. Woking, Surrey England, 9/1/55. Guitarist. The Jam.

FOXWORTH, ROBERT. Houston, TX, 11/1/41. Actor. Chase Gioberti on *Falcon Crest.*

FOXWORTHY, JEFF Hapeville, GA, 9/6/58. Comedian, actor. "You Might Be a Redneck If…"

FRAKES, JONATHAN. Bethlehem, PA, 8/19/52. Actor. Commander William Riker on *Star Trek: The Next Generation.*

FRAME, RODDY. East Kilbride, Scotland, 1/29/64. Singer, guitarist. Aztec Camera.

FRAMPTON, PETER KENNETH. Beckenham, England, 4/22/50. Guitarist, singer, songwriter.

FRANCIOSA, ANTHONY (Anthony Papaleo). New York, NY, 10/25/28. Actor. *The Long Hot Summer.*

FRANCIS, ANNE. Ossining, NY, 9/16/30. Actor, former child model.

FRANCIS, BILL. Mobile, AL, 1/16/42. Keyboardist, singer. Dr. Hook.

FRANCIS, CONNIE (Concetta Franconero). Newark, NJ, 12/12/38. Singer. "Where the Boys Are."

FRANCIS, GENIE. 5/26/62. Actor. *General Hospital.*

FRANKEN, AL. 5/21/51. Actor, author. *Rush Limbaugh's a Big Fat Idiot.*

FRANKLIN, BONNIE. 1/6/44. Actor. *One Day At A Time.*

FRANTZ, CHRIS (Charlton Frantz). Fort Campbell, KY, 5/8/51. Drummer. Talking Heads.

FRASER, ANDY. London, England, 8/7/52. Bassist. Free.

FRAZIER, JOE. Beaufort, SC, 1/17/44. Boxer, former heavyweight champ.

FREDRIKSSON, MARIE. Sweden, 5/30/58. Singer. Roxette.

FREEMAN, BOBBY. San Francisco, CA, 6/13/40. Singer, songwriter.

FREEMAN, MORGAN. Memphis, TN, 6/1/37. Actor. *Driving Miss Daisy.*

FREHLEY, ACE (Paul Frehley). The Bronx, NY, 4/22/51. Guitarist, singer. Kiss.

FREIBERG, DAVID. Boston, MA, 8/24/38. Bassist. Quicksilver Messenger Service.

FREWER, MATT. Washington, DC, 1/4/58. Actor. *Max Headroom.*

FREY, GLENN. Detroit, MI, 11/6/48. Singer, songwriter. The Eagles.

FRICKER, BRENDA. Dublin, Ireland, 2/17/45. Actor. *My Left Foot.*

FRIPP, ROBERT. Wimborne Minster, England, 1946. Guitarist. King Crimson.

FROST, CRAIG. Flint, MI, 4/20/48. Keyboardist. Grand Funk Railroad.

FRY, MARTIN. Manchester, England, 3/9/58. Singer. ABC.

FUNICELLO, ANNETTE. Utica, NY, 10/22/42. Actor, Mouseketeer. *Beach Blanket Bingo.*

FURAY, RICHIE. Yellow Springs, OH, 5/9/44. Singer, guitarist. Buffalo Springfield; Poco.

FURUHOLMEN, MAGS. Oslo, Norway, 11/1/62. Keyboardist, singer. a-ha.

G, KENNY. 6/5/56. Musician. *Breathless.*

GABLE, JOHN CLARK. Los Angeles, CA, 3/20/61. Actor. Son of Clark Gable.

GABOR, ZSA ZSA (Sari Gabor). Budapest, Hungary, 2/6/17. Actor. *Moulin Rouge.*

GABRIEL, PETER. Cobham, England, 2/13/50. Singer, songwriter. Genesis.

GAHAN, DAVE. Epping, England, 5/9/62. Singer. Depeche Mode.

GAIL, MAXWELL. Derfoil, MI, 4/5/43. Actor. Sergeant

Stanley Wojohowicz on *Barney Miller.*

GALLAGHER, PETER. Armonk, NY, 8/19/55. Actor. *sex, lies and videotape.*

GARDNER, CARL. Tyler, TX, 4/29/27. Lead singer. The Coasters.

GARFAT, JANCE. California, 3/3/44. Bassist, singer. Dr. Hook.

GARFUNKEL, ART. New York, NY, 11/5/41. Singer, actor, former partner of Paul Simon. *Carnal Knowledge.*

GARLAND, BEVERLY. Santa Cruz, CA, 10/17/26. Actor. *My Three Sons.*

GARNER, JAMES (James Baumgarner). Norma, OK, 4/7/28. Actor, producer. *The Rockford Files.*

GARR, TERI. Lakewood, OH, 12/11/44. Actor. *Tootsie.*

GARRETT, BETTY. St. Joseph, MO, 5/23/19. Actor. *All in the Family.*

GARRITY, FREDDIE. Manchester, England, 11/14/40. Singer. Freddie & The Dreamers.

GARTH, JENNIE. Champaign, IL, 4/3/72. Actor. Kelly Taylor on *Beverly Hills 90210.*

GARTSIDE, GREEN (Green Strohmeyer-Gartside). Cardiff, Wales, 6/22/56. Singer. Scritti Politti.

GARY, BRUCE. Burbank, CA, 4/7/52. Drummer. The Knack.

GATES, DAVID. Tulsa, OK, 12/11/40. Keyboardist, singer. Bread.

GATLIN, RUDY. 8/20/52. Singer. The Gatlin Brothers.

GATLIN, STEVE. 4/4/51. Singer. The Gatlin Brothers.

GAUDIO, BOB. The Bronx, NY, 11/17/42. Singer, organist. The Four Seasons.

GAYLE, CRYSTAL (Brenda Webb). Paintsville, KY, 1/9/51. Country singer.

GAYLORD, MITCH. Van Nuys, CA, 1961. Gymnast.

GAYNOR, MITZI (Francesca Marlene Von Gerber). Chicago, IL, 9/4/31. Actor. *Anything Goes.*

GAZZARA, BEN (Biago Gazzara). New York, NY, 8/28/30. Actor. *Inchon.*

GEARY, ANTHONY. Coalville, UT, 5/29/47. Actor. Luke Spencer on *General Hospital.*

GEARY, CYNTHIA. Jackson, MS, 3/21/66. Actor. *Northern Exposure.*

GEFFEN, DAVID Brooklyn, NY, 2/21/43. Procucer, executive. Geffen Records, Dreamworks SKG.

GEILS, J. (Jerome Geils). New York, NY, 2/20/46. Guitarist. The J. Geils Band.

GELDOF, BOB. Dublin, Ireland, 10/5/54. Singer. The Boomtown Rats.

GERARD, GIL. Little Rock, AR, 1/23/43. Actor. *Buck Rogers in the 25th Century.*

GERARDO. Ecuador, 1965. Rap artist. "Rico Suave."

GERTZ, JAMI. Chicago, IL, 10/28/65. Actor. *Less Than Zero; Twister.*

GESSLE, PER. 1/12/59. Guitarist, singer. Roxette.

GETTY, BALTHAZAR. 1/22/75. Actor, grandson of J. Paul Getty. *Where the Day Takes You.*

GETTY, ESTELLE. New York, NY, 7/25/23. Actor. Sophia Petrillo on *The Golden Girls.*

GHOSTLEY, ALICE. Eve, MO, 8/14/26. Actor. *Bewitched.*

GIAMMARESE, CARL. Chicago, IL, 8/21/47. Guitarist. The Buckinghams.

GIANNINI, GIANCARLO. Spezia, Italy, 8/1/42. Actor. *Seven Beauties.*

GIBB, BARRY. Isle of Man, England, 9/1/46. Singer, guitarist. The Bee Gees.

GIBB, CYNTHIA. Bennington, VT, 12/14/63. Actor. *Madman of the People.*

GIBB, MAURICE. Manchester, England, 12/22/49. Singer, bassist. The Bee Gees.

GIBB, ROBIN. Manchester, England, 12/22/49. Singer. The Bee Gees.

GIBBINS, MIKE. Swansea, Wales, 3/12/49. Drummer. Badfinger.

GIBBONS, BILLY. Houston, TX, 12/16/49. Guitarist, singer. ZZ Top.

GIBBONS, LEEZA. 3/26/57. TV personality. *Entertainment Tonight.*

GIBBS, MARLA (Margaret Bradley). Chicago, IL, 6/14/31. Actor. Florence Johnston on *The Jeffersons.*

GIBSON, DEBORAH. Long Island, NY, 8/31/70. Singer, songwriter, actor. "Foolish Beat."

GIBSON, HENRY. Germantown, PA, 9/21/35. Actor. Poet from *Laugh-In.*

GIFFORD, FRANK. Santa Monica, CA, 8/16/30. Football player turned sports commentator, married to Kathie Lee Gifford. *Monday Night Football.*

GIFT, ROLAND. Birmingham, England, 5/28/62. Singer. Fine Young Cannibals.

GIGUERE, RUSS. Portsmouth, NH, 10/18/43. Singer, guitarist. The Association.

GILBERT, GILLIAN. Manchester, England, 1/27/61. Keyboardist. New Order.

GILBERT, MELISSA. Los Angeles, CA, 5/8/64. Actor, daughter of Robert and Barbara Crane. *Little House on the Prairie.*

GILBERT, SARA (Rebecca Sara MacMahon). Santa Monica, CA, 1/29/75. Actor, sister of Melissa and Jonathan Gilbert. Darlene Conner on *Roseanne.*

GILES, MIKE. Bournemouth, England, 1942. Drummer. King Crimson.

GILL, PETER. Liverpool, England, 3/8/64. Drummer. Frankie Goes to Hollywood.

GILLAN, IAN. Hounslow, England, 8/19/45. Singer. Deep Purple.

GILLIAM, TERRY. Minneapolis, MN, 11/22/40. Writer, director, actor. *Monty Python and the Holy Grail.*

GILMORE, JIMMIE DALE. Tulia, TX, 1945. Country singer. "Dallas."

GILMOUR, DAVID. Cambridge, England, 3/6/44. Singer, guitarist. Pink Floyd.

GINTY, ROBERT. New York, NY, 11/14/48. Actor. *Baa Baa Black Sheep.*

GILPIN, PERI. 5/27/61. Actor. *Frasier.*

GIVENS, ROBIN. New York, NY, 11/27/64. Actor, formerly married to Mike Tyson. *Head of the Class.*

GLASER, PAUL MICHAEL. Cambridge, MA, 3/25/43. Actor, director. Det. Dave Starsky on *Starsky and Hutch.*

GLASS, RON. Evansville, IN, 7/10/45. Actor. *Barney Miller.*

GLEASON, JOANNA. Winnipeg, Canada, 6/2/50. Actor, daughter of Monty Hall. *Into the Woods.*

GLENN, SCOTT. Pittsburgh, PA, 1/26/42. Actor. *Urban Cowboy.*

GLESS, SHARON. Los Angeles, CA, 5/31/43. Actor. Chris Cagney on *Cagney and Lacey.*

GLITTER, GARY (Paul Gadd). Banbury, England, 5/8/40. Singer, songwriter.

GLOVER, CRISPIN. New York, NY, 9/20/64. Actor. George McFly in *Back to the Future.*

GLOVER, DANNY. San Francisco, CA, 7/22/47. Actor. *Lethal Weapon.*

GLOVER, JOHN. Kingston, NY, 8/7/44. Actor. *Shamus.*

GLOVER, ROGER. Brecon, Wales, 11/30/45. Bassist. Deep Purple.

GOBLE, GRAHAM. Adelaide, Australia, 5/15/47. Guitarist. Little River Band.

GODLEY, KEVIN. Manchester, England, 10/7/45. Singer, drummer. 10cc; Godley & Creme.

GOLD, TRACEY. New York, NY, 5/16/69. Actor. *Growing Pains.*

GOLDEN, WILLIAM LEE. Brewton, AL, 1/12/39. Singer. The Oak Ridge Boys.

GOLDING, LYNVAL. Coventry, England, 7/24/51. Guitarist. The Specials.

GOLDTHWAIT, BOBCAT. Syracuse, NY, 5/26/62. Actor. *Police Academy* series.

GOLDWYN, TONY. Los Angeles, CA, 5/20/60. Actor. *Ghost.*

GOLINO, VALERIA. Naples, Italy, 10/22/66. Actor. *Rain Man.*

GOODALL, JANE. London, England, 4/3/34. Author, anthropologist. *In the Shadow of Man.*

GOODEN, SAM. Chattanooga, TN, 9/2/39. Singer. The Impressions.

GORBACHEV, MIKHAIL. Privolnoye, Russia, 3/2/31. Former leader of the USSR.

GORE, ALBERT JR. Washington, DC, 3/31/48. Vice president of the United States.

GORE, LESLEY. New York, NY, 5/2/46. Singer. "It's My Party."

GORE, MARTIN. Basildon, England, 7/23/61. Keyboardist. Depeche Mode.

GORHAM, SCOTT. Santa Monica, CA, 3/17/51. Guitarist. Thin Lizzy.

GORMAN, STEVE. Hopkinsville, KY, 8/17/65. Drummer. The Black Crowes.

GORME, EYDIE. New York, NY, 8/16/32. Singer. Steve and Eydie.

GORRIE, ALAN. Perth, Scotland, 7/19/46. Singer, bassist. Average White Band.

GORSHIN, FRANK. Pittsburgh, PA, 4/5/33. Actor. The Riddler on *Batman*.

GOSSETT, LOUIS JR. Brooklyn, NY, 5/27/37. Actor. *An Officer and a Gentleman*.

GOTTI, JOHN. New York, NY, 10/27/41. Reputed mob leader.

GOUDREAU, BARRY. Boston, MA, 11/29/51. Guitarist. Boston.

GOULD, BILLY. Los Angeles, CA, 4/24/63. Bassist. Faith No More.

GOULD, BOON. 3/14/55. Guitarist. Level 42.

GOULD, ELLIOTT (Elliott Goldstein). Brooklyn, NY, 8/29/38. Actor. Formerly married to Barbra Streisand. *Bob & Carol & Ted & Alice*.

GOULD, PHIL. 2/28/57. Drummer. Level 42.

GOULDMAN, GRAHAM. Manchester, England, 5/10/45. Singer, guitarist. 10cc.

GOULET, ROBERT (Stanley Applebaum). Lawrence, MA, 11/26/33. Singer, actor. *Blue Light*.

GRAF, STEFFI. Bruhl, Germany, 6/14/69. Tennis player, youngest woman to win French Open.

GRAHAM, BILLY. Charlotte, NC, 11/7/18. Evangelist. *Billy Graham Crusades*.

GRAHAM, LARRY. Beaumont, TX, 8/14/46. Bass guitarist. Sly & The Family Stone.

GRAMM, LOU. Rochester, NY, 5/2/50. Singer. Foreigner.

GRANDMASTER FLASH (Joseph Saddler). New York, NY, 1958. Rap artist. Grandmaster Flash; Melle Mel & The Furious Five.

GRANDY, FRED. Sioux City, IA, 6/29/48. Actor, politician. Burl "Gopher" Smith on *The Love Boat*.

GRANGER, FARLEY. San Jose, CA, 7/1/25. Actor. *Strangers on a Train*.

GRANT, AMY. Augusta, GA, 11/25/60. Singer. *Age to Age*.

GRANT, EDDY (Edmond Grant). Plaisance, Guyana, 3/5/48. Reggae singer, songwriter.

GRANT, LEE (Lyova Rosenthal). New York, NY, 10/31/27. Actor, mother of Dinah Manoff. *Peyton Place*.

GRANTHAM, GEORGE. Cordell, OK, 11/20/47. Drummer, singer. Poco.

GRATZER, ALAN. Syracuse, NY, 11/9/48. Drummer. REO Speedwagon.

GRAVES, PETER (Peter Aurness). Minneapolis, MN, 3/18/26. Actor, brother of James Arness. Jim Phelps on *Mission: Impossible*.

GRAY, EDDIE. 2/27/48. Guitarist. Tommy James & The Shondells.

GRAY, LES. Carshalton, England, 4/9/46. Singer. Mud.

GRAY, LINDA. Santa Monica, CA, 9/12/40. Actor. *Dallas*.

GRAY, SPALDING. Barrington, RI, 6/5/41. Actor, writer, performance artist. *The Killing Fields*.

GREBB, MARTY. Chicago, IL, 9/2/46. Keyboardist. The Buckinghams.

GREEN, AL (Al Greene). Forrest City, AR, 4/13/46. R&B singer, songwriter.

GREEN, BRIAN AUSTIN. 7/15/73. Actor. *Beverly Hills 90210*.

GREEN, KARL. Salford, England, 7/31/47. Bassist. Herman's Hermits.

GREENAWAY, PETER. Newport, Wales, 4/5/42. Director, writer. *The Cook, the Thief, His Wife and Her Lover*.

GREENFIELD, DAVE. Keyboardist. The Stranglers.

GREENSPOON, JIMMY. Los Angeles, CA, 2/7/48. Organist. Three Dog Night.

GREENWOOD, ALAN. New York, NY, 10/20/51. Keyboardist. Foreigner.

GREGG, BRIAN. Bassist. Johnny Kidd & The Pirates.

GREGORY, GLENN. Sheffield, England, 5/16/58. Singer. Heaven 17.

GRETZKY, WAYNE. Brantford, Canada, 1/26/61. Hockey player.

GREY, JENNIFER. New York, NY, 3/26/60. Actor, daughter of Joel. *Dirty Dancing*.

GREY, JOEL (Joel Katz). Cleveland, OH, 4/11/32. Musical comedy performer, father of Jennifer. *Cabaret*.

GRIER, DAVID ALAN. Detroit, MI, 6/30/55. Actor. *In Living Color*.

GRIER, PAM. 5/26/49. Actor. *Jackie Brown*.

GRIER, ROSEY (Roosevelt Grier). Cuthbert, GA, 7/14/32. Football player, actor.

GRIFFEY, KEN JR. 11/21/69. Baseball player.

GRIFFITH, ANDY. Mt. Airy, NC, 6/1/26. Actor, writer, producer. *The Andy Griffith Show*.

GRIFFITH, NANCI. Austin, TX, 7/6/53. Singer, songwriter. "From a Distance."

GRILL, ROB. Los Angeles, CA, 11/30/44. Bassist, singer. The Grass Roots.

GROSS, MARY. Chicago, IL, 3/25/53. Actor, sister of Michael. *Saturday Night Live*.

GROSS, MICHAEL. Chicago, IL, 6/21/47. Actor, brother of Mary. Steven Keaton on *Family Ties*.

GRUNDY, HUGH. Winchester, England, 3/6/45. Drummer. The Zombies.

GUCCIONE, BOB. New York, NY, 12/17/30. Publisher, founder of *Penthouse*.

GUEST, CHRISTOPHER. New York, NY, 2/5/48. Actor, writer, married to Jamie Lee Curtis. *This Is Spinal Tap*.

GUEST, LANCE. Saratoga, CA, 7/21/60. Actor. *Knots Landing*.

GUEST, WILLIAM. Atlanta, GA, 6/2/41. Singer. Gladys Knight & The Pips.

GUILLAUME, ROBERT (Robert Williams). St. Louis, MO, 11/30/27. Actor. Benson DuBois on *Soap*.

GUINNESS, ALEC. London, England, 4/2/14. Actor. *The Bridge on the River Kwai*.

GUISEWITE, CATHY. 9/5/50. Cartoonist. *Cathy*.

GULAGER, CLU. Holdenville, OK, 11/16/28. Actor. *The Last Picture Show*.

GUMBEL, BRYANT. New Orleans, LA, 9/29/48. News show host and sportscaster. *Today*.

GUSTAFSON, KARIN. Miami, FL, 6/23/59. Actor. *Taps*.

GUSTAFSON, STEVEN. Bassist. 10,000 Maniacs.

GUTHRIE, ARLO. New York, NY, 7/10/47. Folk singer, songwriter. "Alice's Restaurant."

GUTTENBERG, STEVE. Brooklyn, NY, 8/24/58. Actor. *Three Men and a Baby*.

GUY, BILLY. Attasca, TX, 6/20/36. Baritone. The Coasters.

GUY, BUDDY (George Guy). Lettsworth, LA, 7/30/36. Blues guitarist.

GUY, JASMINE. Boston, MA, 3/10/62. Actor. Whitley Gilbert on *A Different World*.

HAAS, LUKAS. West Hollywood, CA, 4/16/76. Actor. *Witness*.

HACK, SHELLEY. Greenwich, CT, 7/6/52. Actor. *Charlie's Angels*.

HACKETT, BUDDY (Leonard Hacker). Brooklyn, NY, 8/31/24. Actor. *It's a Mad Mad Mad Mad World; The Love Bug*.

HADLEY, TONY. Islington, England, 6/2/59. Singer. Spandau Ballet.

HAGAR, SAMMY. Montcrcy, CA, 10/13/47. Singer, guitarist. Van Halen.

HAGERTY, JULIE. Cincinnati, OH, 6/15/55. Actor. *Airplane!*

HAGMAN, LARRY (Larry Hageman). Fort Worth, TX, 9/21/31. Actor, son of Mary Martin. J. R. Ewing on *Dallas*.

HAHN, JESSICA. Massapequa, NY, 7/7/59. *Playboy* model, involved in PTL/Jim Bakker scandal.

HAID, CHARLES. San Francisco, CA, 6/2/43. Actor, director, producer. Andrew Renko on *Hill Street Blues*.

HAIM, COREY. Toronto, Canada, 12/23/71. Actor. *The Lost Boys*.

HALE, BARBARA. DeKalb, IL, 4/18/22. Actor, mother of William Katt. Della Street on *Perry Mason*.

HALFORD, ROB. Birmingham, England, 8/25/51. Singer. Judas Priest.

HALL, ANTHONY MICHAEL. Boston, MA, 4/14/68. Actor. *Sixteen Candles*.

HALL, ARSENIO. Cleveland, OH, 2/12/56. Actor. *The Arsenio Hall Show*.

HALL, BRIDGET. Dallas, TX, 12/14/77. Supermodel.

HALL, BRUCE. Champaign, IL, 5/3/53. Bassist. REO Speedwagon.

HALL, DARYL (Daryl Hohl). Pottstown, PA, 10/11/46. Singer, guitarist. Hall & Oates.

HALL, DEIDRE. 10/31/47. Actor. Marlena Evans on *Days of Our Lives*.

HALL, FAWN. Annandale, VA, 9/4/59. Secretary for Oliver North. Iran-Contra scandal.

HALL, JERRY. 7/2/56. Model, married to Mick Jagger.

HALL, MONTY. Winnipeg, Canada, 8/25/21. TV personality. *Let's Make a Deal*.

HALL, TERRY. Coventry, England, 3/19/59. Singer. The Specials.

HAM, GREG. Australia, 9/27/53. Saxophonist, keyboardist, flautist. Men at Work.

HAM, PETE. Swansea, Wales, 4/27/47. Guitarist, pianist, singer. Badfinger.

HAMEL, VERONICA. Philadelphia, PA, 11/20/43. Actor. Joyce Davenport on *Hill Street Blues*.

HAMILL, DOROTHY. Chicago, IL, 7/26/56. Ice skater. Olympic gold medalist.

HAMILL, MARK. Oakland, CA, 9/25/51. Actor. Luke Skywalker in *Star Wars* trilogy.

HAMILTON, GEORGE. Memphis, TN, 8/12/39. Actor. *Love at First Bite*.

HAMILTON, LINDA. Salisbury, MD, 9/26/56. Actor. Sarah Connor in *The Terminator*. Separated from James Cameron.

HAMILTON, SCOTT. Haverford, PA, 8/28/58. Ice skater.

HAMILTON, TOM. Colorado Springs, CO, 12/31/51. Bassist. Aerosmith.

HAMLIN, HARRY. Pasadena, CA, 10/30/51. Actor. *L.A. Law*.

HAMLISCH, MARVIN. New York, NY, 6/2/44. Composer. *The Way We Were; The Sting*.

HAMMER, MC. (Stanley Kirk Burrell). Oakland, CA, 3/30/62. Rap artist, dancer. *Please Hammer Don't Hurt 'Em*.

HAMMETT, KIRK. 11/18/62. Guitarist. Metallica.

HAMPSHIRE, SUSAN. London, England, 5/12/41. Actor. *The Forsythe Saga*.

HANCOCK, HERBIE. Chicago, IL, 4/12/40. Jazz pianist, composer. "Rockit."

HANNAH, DARYL. Chicago, IL, 12/3/60. Actor. *Splash*.

HANSON, ISAAC. 11/17/80. Singer. "MMMbop."

HANSON, TAYLOR. 3/14/83. Singer. "MMMbop."

HANSON, ZAC. 10/22/85. Singer. "MMMbop."

HARDING, TONYA. Portland, OR, 11/12/70. Figure skater. Pled guilty to hindering prosecution in Nancy Kerrigan attack.

HARDISON, KADEEM. Brooklyn, NY, 7/24/66. Actor. Dwayne Wayne on *A Different World*.

HAREWOOD, DORIAN. Dayton, OH, 8/6/50. Actor. *Roots—The Next Generation*.

HARKET, MORTEN. Konigsberg, Norway, 9/14/59. Lead singer. a-ha.

HARLEY, STEVE (Steve Nice). London, England, 2/27/51. Singer. Steve Harley & Cockney Rebel.

HARLIN, RENNY. 3/15/58. Director, formerly married to Geena Davis.

HARMON, MARK. Los Angeles, CA, 9/2/51. Actor. *Chicago Hope*. Married to Pam Dawber.

HARPER, JESSICA. Chicago, IL, 10/10/49. Actor.

HARPER, TESS (Tessie Jean Washam). Mammoth Spring, AR, 8/15/50. Actor. *Crimes of the Heart*.

HARPER, VALERIE. Suffern, NY, 8/22/39. Actor. Rhoda Morgenstern on *The Mary Tyler Moore Show*.

HARRINGTON, PAT. New York, NY, 8/13/29. Actor. Dwayne Schneider on *One Day at a Time*.

HARRIS, BARBARA (Sandra Markowitz). Evanston, IL, 7/25/35. Actor. *Family Plot*.

HARRIS, JULIE. Grosse Point, MI, 12/2/25. Actor. *Knots Landing*.

HARRIS, EMMYLOU. 4/2/47. Singer.

HARRIS, MEL (Mary Ellen Harris). Bethlehem, PA, 7/12/56. Actor. Hope Murdoch Steadman on *thirtysomething*.

HARRIS, RICHARD. Limerick, Ireland, 10/1/33. Actor. *A Man Called Horse*.

HARRISON, BILLY. Belfast, Ireland, 10/14/42. Lead guitarist. Them.

HARRISON, GEORGE. Liverpool, England, 2/25/43. Singer, lead guitarist. The Beatles.

HARRISON, GREGORY. Catalina Island, CA, 5/31/50. Actor. *Trapper John, MD*.

HARRISON, JENILEE. Northridge, CA, 6/12/59. Actor. Jamie Ewing Barnes on *Dallas*.

HARRISON, JERRY. Milwaukee, WI, 2/21/49. Keyboardist. Talking Heads.

HARRISON, NOEL. London, England, 1/29/34. Singer, actor. *The Girl from U.N.C.L.E.*

HARRY, DEBORAH. Miami, FL, 7/1/45. Singer. Blondie.

HART, MARY. Sioux Falls, SD, 11/8/51. TV hostess. *Entertainment Tonight*.

HART, MICKY (Michael Hart). New York, NY, 9/11/44. Drummer, songwriter. Grateful Dead.

HARTLEY, MARIETTE. New York, NY, 6/21/40. Actor. *Peyton Place*.

HARTMAN, DAVID. Pawtucket, RI, 5/19/35. Actor, talk show host. *Good Morning America*.

HARTMAN, JOHN. Falls Church, VA, 3/18/50. Drummer. The Doobie Brothers.

HASSAN, NORMAN. Birmingham, England, 11/26/57. Percussionist. UB40.

HATCHER, TERI. 12/8/64. Actor. *Lois and Clark: The New Adventures of Superman*.

HATFIELD, BOBBY. Beaver Dam, WI, 8/10/40. Singer. The Righteous Brothers.

HATTON, BILLY. Liverpool, England, 6/9/41. Bassist. The Fourmost.

HAUER, RUTGER. Breukelen, Netherlands, 1/23/44. Actor. *Blade Runner*.

HAVENS, RICHIE. Brooklyn, NY, 1/21/41. Folk/blues guitarist, singer, songwriter.

HAWKING, STEPHEN. Oxford, England, 1/8/42. Theoretical physicist, author of *A Brief History of Time*.

HAY, COLIN. Scotland, 6/29/53. Singer. Men at Work.

HAY, ROY. Southend, England, 8/12/61. Guitarist, keyboardist. Culture Club.

HAYDOCK, ERIC. Stockport, England, 2/3/42. Bassist. The Hollies.

HAYES, CHRIS. California, 11/24/57. Lead guitarist. Huey Lewis & The News.

HAYES, ISAAC. Covington, TN, 8/20/42. R&B/rock saxophonist, keyboardist, singer, songwriter, radio personality, actor. *South Park*.

HAYS, ROBERT. Bethesda, MD, 7/24/47. Actor, married to Cherie Currie. *Airplane!*

HAYWARD, JUSTIN. Wiltshire, England, 10/14/46. Singer, songwriter. The Moody Blues.

HEADLY, GLENNE. New London, CT, 3/13/55. Actor, formerly married to John Malkovich. *Dirty Rotten Scoundrels*.

HEADON, NICKY. Bromley, England, 5/30/55. Drummer. The Clash.

HEALEY, JEFF. Toronto, Canada, 1966. Singer, songwriter, guitarist.

HEARD, JOHN. Washington, DC, 3/7/46. Actor. Father in *Home Alone*.

HEATON, PAUL. Birkenhead, England, 5/9/62. Singer, guitarist. The Housemartins.

HEDREN, TIPPI (Natalie Kay Hedren). New Ulm, MN, 1/19/35. Actor. Mother of Melanie Griffith. *The Birds*.

HEFNER, HUGH. Chicago, IL, 4/9/26. Publisher, founder of *Playboy*.

HELL, RICHARD (Richard Myers). Lexington, KY, 10/2/49. Bassist. Television.

HELLER, JOSEPH. New York, NY, 5/1/23. Author, dramatist. *Catch-22*.

HELLIWELL, JOHN. England, 2/15/45. Saxophonist. Supertramp.

HELM, LEVON. Marvell, AR, 5/26/42. Drummer, singer. The Band.

HELMSLEY, LEONA. New York, NY, 7/4/20. Hotel executive. Convicted of tax evasion.

HEMINGWAY, MARIEL. Ketchum, ID, 11/22/61. Actor, granddaughter of Ernest Hemingway, sister of Margaux. *Manhattan*.

HEMSLEY, SHERMAN. Philadelphia, PA, 2/1/38.

Actor. George on *The Jeffersons*.

HENDERSON, ALAN. Belfast, Ireland, 11/26/44. Bassist. Them.

HENDERSON, BILLY. Detroit, MI, 8/9/39. Singer. The (Detroit) Spinners.

HENDERSON, FLORENCE. Dale, IN, 2/14/34. Actor. Carol Brady on *The Brady Bunch*.

HENLEY, DON. Linden, TX, 7/22/47. Singer, songwriter, drummer, guitarist. The Eagles.

HENNER, MARILU. Chicago, IL, 4/6/52. Actor. Elaine Nardo on *Taxi*.

HENNING, DOUG. Fort Gary, Canada, 5/3/47. Magician. *The Magic Show*.

HENRIKSEN, LANCE. New York, NY, 5/5/40. Actor. *Aliens*.

HENRY, BUCK (Buck Zuckerman). New York, NY, 12/9/30. Actor, writer. *Get Smart; That Was the Week That Was*.

HENRY, CLARENCE. Algiers, LA, 3/19/37. Singer. "Ain't Got No Home."

HENRY, JUSTIN. Rye, NY, 5/25/71. Actor. *Kramer vs. Kramer*.

HENRY, PRINCE. London, England, 8/15/84. British royalty, son of Prince Charles and Princess Diana.

HENSLEY, KEN. England, 8/24/45. Keyboardist, guitarist, singer, percussionist. Uriah Heep.

HENSLEY, PAMELA. Los Angeles, CA, 10/3/50. Actor. C. J. Parsons on *Matt Houston*.

HENSTRIDGE, NATASHA. 8/15/74. Actor. *Species*.

HERMAN, PEE-WEE (Paul Reubens). Peekskill, NY, 8/27/52. Children's performer. *Pee-Wee's Playhouse*.

HERRMANN, EDWARD. Washington, DC, 7/21/43. Actor. *The Paper Chase*.

HERSHEY, BARBARA (Barbara Herzstein). Hollywood, CA, 2/5/48. Actor. *Hannah and Her Sisters*.

HERVEY, JASON. Los Angeles, CA, 4/6/72. Actor. Wayne Arnold on *The Wonder Years*.

HESSEMAN, HOWARD. Salem, OR, 2/27/40. Actor. Dr. Johnny Fever on *WKRP in Cincinnati*.

HESTON, CHARLTON (Charles Carter). Evanston, IL, 10/4/24.

Actor. *The Ten Commandments*.

HETFIELD, JAMES. 8/3/63. Singer, guitarist. Metallica.

HEWETT, HOWARD. Akron, OH, 10/1/55. Singer. Shalamar.

HEYWARD, NICK. Kent, England, 5/20/61. Guitarist, singer. Haircut 100.

HICKS, CATHERINE. New York, NY, 8/6/51. Actor. *Peggy Sue Got Married*.

HICKS, TONY. Nelson, England, 12/16/43. Guitarist. The Hollies.

HILL, ANITA. Tulsa, OK, 7/30/56. Lawyer, law professor. Accused Supreme Court nominee Clarence Thomas of sexual harrassment.

HILL, ARTHUR. Saskatchewan, Canada, 8/1/22. Actor. *Owen Marshall, Counsellor at Law*.

HILL, DAVE. Fleet Castle, England, 4/4/52. Guitarist. Slade.

HILL, DUSTY. Dallas, TX, 5/19/49. Bassist, singer. ZZ Top.

HILL, STEVEN. Seattle, WA, 2/24/22. Actor. *Law and Order*.

HILLERMAN, JOHN. Denison, TX, 12/20/32. Actor. Jonathan Quayle Higgins III on *Magnum P.I.*

HILLERMAN, TONY. Sacred Heart, OK, 5/27/25. Novelist.

HILLMAN, CHRIS. Los Angeles, CA, 12/4/42. Singer, bassist. The Byrds.

HINES, GREGORY. New York, NY, 2/14/46. Actor, dancer. *The Cotton Club*.

HINGLE, PAT (Martin Patterson Hingle). Denver, CO, 7/19/23. Actor. *Gunsmoke*.

HINSLEY, HARVEY. Northampton, England, 1/19/48. Guitarist. Hot Chocolate.

HIRSCH, GARY "CHICKEN." England, 1940. Drummer. Country Joe & The Fish.

HIRSCH, JUDD. New York, NY, 3/15/35. Actor. Alex Rieger on *Taxi*.

HITCHCOCK, RUSSELL. Melbourne, Australia, 6/15/49. Singer. Air Supply.

HO, DON. Kakaako, HI, 8/13/30. Singer. "Tiny Bubbles."

HOBBS, RANDY. 3/22/48. Bassist. The McCoys.

HODGE, PATRICIA. Lincolnshire, England, 9/29/46. Actor. *The Elephant Man*.

HODGSON, ROGER. Portsmouth, England, 3/21/50. Guitarist. Supertramp.

HODO, DAVID. 7/7/50. Singer. The Village People.

HOFFS, SUSANNA. Newport Beach, CA, 1/17/57. Guitarist, singer. The Bangles.

HOGAN, HULK (Terry Gene Bollea). Augusta, GA, 8/11/53. Wrestler, former World Federation heavyweight champion.

HOGAN, PAUL. Lightning Ridge, Australia, 10/8/39. Actor. *Crocodile Dundee*.

HOLBROOK, HAL. Cleveland, OH, 2/17/25. Actor. *All the President's Men*.

HOLDER, NODDY (Neville Holder). Walsall, England, 6/15/50. Guitarist, singer. Slade.

HOLLAND, JOOLS (Julian Holland). 1/24/58. Keyboardist. Squeeze.

HOLLIMAN, EARL. Delhi, LA, 9/11/28. Actor. *Police Woman*.

HOLLIS, MARK. Tottenham, England, 1955. Singer, guitarist, keyboardist. Talk Talk.

HOLM, CELESTE. New York, NY, 4/29/19. Actor. *All About Eve*.

HOLMES, LARRY. Cuthbert, GA, 11/3/49. Boxer. Former heavyweight champ.

HOOK, PETER. Salford, England, 2/13/56. Bassist. Joy Division; New Order.

HOOKER, JOHN LEE. Clarksdale, MS, 8/22/17. Legendary blues guitarist, singer, songwriter.

HOOKS, JAN. Decatur, GA, 4/23/57. Actor. Carlene Frazier Dobber on *Designing Women*.

HOPE, BOB (Leslie Hope). Eltham, England, 5/29/03. Actor, performer for overseas troops. *The Road* movies with Bing Crosby.

HOPE, DAVE. Kansas, 10/7/49. Bassist. Kansas.

HOPKIN, MARY. Pontardawe, Wales, 5/3/50. Singer, discovered by the Beatles. "Those Were the Days."

HOPKINS, TELMA. Louisville, KY, 10/28/48. Singer, actor, former member of Tony

Orlando & Dawn. *Family Matters*.

HOPPER, DENNIS. Dodge City, KS, 5/17/36. Actor, director. *Easy Rider*.

HOPPER, SEAN. California, 3/31/53. Keyboardist. Huey Lewis & The News.

HOPWOOD, KEITH. Manchester, England, 10/26/46. Guitarist. Herman's Hermits.

HORNE, LENA. Brooklyn, NY, 6/30/17. Singer, actor.

HORNSBY, BRUCE. Williamsburg, VA, 11/23/54. Singer, keyboardist, accordionist. Bruce Hornsby & The Range.

HOSKINS, BOB. Bury St. Edmunds, England, 10/26/42. Actor. *Who Framed Roger Rabbit*.

HOWARD, ALAN. Dagenham, England, 10/17/41. Bassist. Brian Poole & The Tremeloes.

HOWARD, ARLISS. Independence, MO, 1955. Actor. *Full Metal Jacket*.

HOWARD, KEN. El Centro, CA, 3/28/44. Actor. *The White Shadow*.

HOWE, STEVE. London, England, 4/8/47. Guitarist, singer. Yes; Asia.

HUCKNALL, MICK "RED." Manchester, England, 6/8/60. Singer. Simply Red.

HUDLIN, REGINALD. Centerville, IL, 12/15/61. Director, writer, producer, brother of Warrington. *House Party*.

HUDLIN, WARRINGTON. East St. Louis, IL, 1952. Producer, director, brother of Reginald. *House Party*.

HUDSON, GARTH. London, Canada, 8/2/37. Organist. The Band.

HUGG, MIKE. Andover, England, 8/11/42. Drummer. Manfred Mann.

HUGHES, GLENN. 7/18/50. Singer. The Village People.

HULCE, TOM. White Water, WI, 12/6/53. Actor. *Amadeus*.

HUMPERDINCK, ENGELBERT (Arnold Dorsey). Madras, India, 5/2/36. Pop singer. *The Engelbert Humperdinck Show*.

HUMPHREYS, PAUL. London, England, 2/27/60. Keyboardist. Orchestral Manoeuvres in the Dark (OMD).

HUNT, BILL. 5/23/47. Keyboardist. Electric Light Orchestra (ELO).

HUNT, LINDA. Morristown, NJ, 4/2/45. Actor. *The Year of Living Dangerously.*

HUNTER, IAN. Shrewsbury, England, 6/3/46. Singer, guitarist. Mott The Hoople.

HUNTER, TAB (Arthur Gelien). New York, NY, 7/11/31. Actor. *Damn Yankees.*

HUPPERT, ISABELLE. Paris, France, 3/16/55. Actor. *Entre Nous.*

HURT, JOHN. Shirebrook, England, 1/22/40. Actor. *The Elephant Man.*

HURT, MARY BETH (Mary Beth Supinger). Marshalltown, IA, 9/26/48. Actor, formerly married to William Hurt. *The World According to Garp.*

HURT, WILLIAM. Washington, DC, 3/20/50. Actor, formerly married to Mary Beth Hurt. *Children of a Lesser God.*

HUSSEIN, SADDAM. Tikrit, Iraq, 4/28/37. Leader of Iraq.

HUSSEY, WAYNE. Bristol, England, 5/26/59. Guitarist, singer. The Mission.

HUSTON, ANJELICA. Santa Monica, CA, 7/8/51. Actor, daughter of John Huston. *Prizzi's Honor.*

HUTTER, RALF. Krefeld, Germany, 1946. Keyboardist, drummer, singer. Kraftwerk.

HUTTON, DANNY. Buncrana, Ireland, 9/10/42. Singer. Three Dog Night.

HUTTON, LAUREN (Mary Hutton). Charleston, SC, 11/17/43. Actor, model. *American Gigolo.*

HUTTON, TIMOTHY. Malibu, CA, 8/16/60. Actor, director. *Ordinary People.*

HUXLEY, RICK. Dartford, England, 8/5/42. Guitarist. The Dave Clark Five.

HYNDE, CHRISSIE. Akron, OH, 9/7/51. Singer, divorced from Jim Kerr. The Pretenders.

IACOCCA, LEE (Lido Anthony Iacocca). Allentown, PA, 10/15/24. Auto executive, author. *Iacocca.*

IAN, JANIS (Janis Fink). New York, NY, 4/7/51. Folk/rock singer, songwriter.

ICE-T Newark, NJ, 2/16/58. Rap artist, actor. *New Jack City, Breakin'.*

IDLE, ERIC. Durham, England, 3/29/43. Actor. *Monty Python's Flying Circus.*

IDOL, BILLY (Billy Broad). Stanmore, England, 11/30/55. Singer, songwriter.

IGLESIAS, JULIO. Madrid, Spain, 9/23/43. Pop singer, songwriter.

ILLSLEY, JOHN. Leicester, England, 6/24/49. Bassist. Dire Straits.

IMAN. Mogadishu, Somalia, 7/25/55. Model, married to David Bowie.

INGELS, MARTY. Brooklyn, NY, 3/9/36. Actor, agent, married to Shirley Jones. *The Pruitts of Southampton.*

INGLE, DOUG. Omaha, NE, 9/9/46. Singer, keyboardist. Iron Butterfly.

INGRAM, JAMES. Akron, OH, 2/16/56. R&B singer, songwriter.

INNES, NEIL. Essex, England, 12/9/44. Singer, keyboardist. The Bonzo Dog Doo-Dah Band.

INNIS, ROY. Saint Croix, Virgin Islands, 6/6/34. Civil rights leader.

IOMMI, TONY. Birmingham, England, 2/19/48. Guitarist. Black Sabbath.

IRELAND, KATHY. Santa Barbara, CA, 3/20/63. Model, sister of Mary and Cynthia. *Sports Illustrated* swimsuit cover girl.

IRELAND, PATRICIA. Oak Park, IL, 10/19/45. Political activist. President of NOW.

IRVING, AMY. Palo Alto, CA, 9/10/53. Actor. *Yentl.*

IRVING, JOHN. Exeter, NH, 3/2/42. Author. *The World According to Garp.*

IRWIN, BILL. Santa Monica, CA, 4/11/50. Actor. *Eight Men Out.*

ISAAK, CHRIS. Stockton, CA, 6/26/56. Singer, songwriter, actor. "Wicked Game."

ISLEY, O'KELLY. Cincinnati, OH, 12/25/37. Singer. The Isley Brothers.

ISLEY, RONALD. Cincinnati, OH, 5/21/41. Lead singer. The Isley Brothers.

ISLEY, RUDOLPH. Cincinnati, OH, 4/1/39. Singer. The Isley Brothers.

IVEY, JUDITH. El Paso, TX, 9/4/51. Actor. *Designing Women.*

IVORY, JAMES. Berkeley, CA, 6/7/28. Director, producer. *Howards End.*

JABS, MATTHIAS. 10/25/56. Guitarist. Scorpions.

JACKEE (Jackee Harry). Winston-Salem, NC, 8/14/56. Actor. *227.*

JACKSON, BO. Bessemer, AL, 11/30/62. Pro football, baseball player.

JACKSON, EDDIE. 1/29/61. Bassist, singer. Queensryche.

JACKSON, FREDDIE. New York, NY, 10/2/56. R&B singer, songwriter.

JACKSON, GLENDA. Birkenhead, England, 5/9/36. Actor. *Women in Love.*

JACKSON, JACKIE (Sigmund Jackson). Gary, IN, 5/4/51. Singer, brother of Michael and Janet Jackson. The Jacksons.

JACKSON, JERMAINE. Gary, IN, 12/11/54. Singer, brother of Michael and Janet. The Jacksons.

JACKSON, JESSE. Greenville, SC, 10/8/41. Civil rights leader, politician. Founded the Rainbow Coalition.

JACKSON, JOE. Burton-on-Trent, England, 8/11/55. Singer, songwriter.

JACKSON, KATE. Birmingham, AL, 10/29/48. Actor. Sabrina Duncan on *Charlie's Angels.*

JACKSON, LATOYA. 5/29/56. Sister of Michael and Janet.

JACKSON, MARLON. Gary, IN, 3/12/57. Singer, brother of Michael and Janet. The Jacksons.

JACKSON, PERVIS. 5/17/38. Singer. The (Detroit) Spinners.

JACKSON, TITO (Toriano Jackson). Gary, IN, 10/15/53. Singer, brother of Michael and Janet. The Jacksons.

JACKSON, TONY. Liverpool, England, 7/16/40. Singer, bassist. The Searchers.

JACKSON, VICTORIA. Miami, FL, 8/2/59. Actor. *Saturday Night Live.*

JACOBI, DEREK. London, England, 10/22/38. Actor. *The Day of the Jackal.*

JACOBI, LOU. Toronto, Canada, 12/28/13. Actor. *Irma La Douce.*

JAGGER, BIANCA. Managua, Nicaragua, 5/2/45. Socialite, actor. Divorced from Mick Jagger.

JAM MASTER JAY (Jason Mizell). New York, NY, 1965. DJ. Run-D.M.C.

JAMES, CLIFTON. Portland, OR, 5/29/25. Actor. *Cool Hand Luke.*

JAMES, ETTA. Los Angeles, CA, 1/25/38. Singer. Bridged R&B and rock.

JAMES, RICK (James Johnson). Buffalo, NY, 2/1/48. Funk singer, songwriter. "Super Freak."

JAMES, TOMMY (Tommy Jackson). Dayton, OH, 4/29/47. Singer. Tommy James & The Shondells.

JANIS, CONRAD. New York, NY, 2/11/28. Actor, musician. Frederick McConnell on *Mork and Mindy.*

JARDINE, AL. Lima, OH, 9/3/42. Guitarist, singer. The Beach Boys.

JARREAU, AL. Milwaukee, WI, 3/12/40. Jazz singer, sang theme song to *Moonlighting.*

JAZZIE B. (Beresford Romeo). London, England, 1/26/63. Rap artist. Soul II Soul.

JEFFRIES, LIONEL. London, England, 6/10/26. Actor, director. *The Water Babies.*

JENNER, BRUCE. Mount Kisco, NY, 10/28/49. Track athlete, sportscaster. Olympic gold medalist.

JENNINGS, WAYLON. Littlefield, TX, 6/15/37. Country singer, songwriter. *The Dukes of Hazzard* theme song.

JETER, MICHAEL. Lawrenceburg, TN, 8/26/52. Actor. *Evening Shade.*

JETT, JOAN. Philadelphia, PA, 9/22/58. Singer, guitarist. "I Love Rock 'n' Roll."

JILLIAN, ANNE (Anne Nauseda). Cambridge, MA, 1/29/51. Actor. *It's a Living.*

JOHANSEN, DAVID. Staten Island, NY, 1/9/50. Actor, singer, a.k.a. Buster Poindexter. *Scrooged.*

JOHN, DR. (Malcolm Rebennack). New Orleans, LA, 11/21/41. Rock/cajun/ blues singer, songwriter. "Right Place Wrong Time."

JOHN PAUL II, POPE. Wadowice, Poland, 5/18/20. First non-Italian pope since the Renaissance.

JOHNS, GLYNIS. Durban, South Africa, 10/5/23. Actor. *Glynis.*

JOHNSON, ARTE. Benton Harbor, MI, 1/20/29. Actor. *Laugh-In.*

JOHNSON, BEVERLY. Buffalo, NY, 10/13/52. Model, actor.

JOHNSON, HOLLY (William Johnson). Khartoum, Sudan, 2/19/60. Singer. Frankie Goes to Hollywood.

JOHNSON, HOWIE. Washington, DC, 1938. Drummer. The Ventures.

JOHNSON, LADY BIRD. Karnack, TX, 12/22/12. Former First Lady, wife of Lyndon.

JOHNSON, MATT. 8/15/61. Singer, guitarist. The The.

JOHNSON, VAN. Newport, RI, 8/25/16. Actor. *The Caine Mutiny.*

JOHNSON, WILKO (John Wilkinson). 1947. Guitarist. Dr. Feelgood.

JON, JOHN. 2/26/61. Musician. Bronski Beat.

JONES, ALAN. Swansea, Wales, 2/6/47. Baritone saxophonist. Amen Corner.

JONES, BOOKER T. Memphis, TN, 12/11/44. Keyboardist. Booker T. & The MG's.

JONES, DAVY. Manchester, England, 12/30/45. Singer, actor. The Monkees.

JONES, DEAN. Decatur, AL, 1/25/31. Actor. *The Shaggy D.A.*

JONES, GRACE. Spanishtown, Jamaica, 5/19/52. Singer, actor. *A View to a Kill.*

JONES, GRAHAM. North Yorkshire, England, 7/8/61. Guitarist. Haircut 100.

JONES, HOWARD. Southampton, England, 2/23/55. Singer, songwriter.

JONES, JEFFREY. Buffalo, NY, 9/28/47. Actor. Principal Ed Rooney in *Ferris Bueller's Day Off.*

JONES, JENNIFER (Phyllis Isley). Tulsa, OK, 3/2/19. Actor. *The Song of Bernadette.*

JONES, JOHN PAUL (John Paul Baldwin). Sidcup, England, 1/31/46. Bassist. Led Zeppelin.

JONES, KENNY. London, England, 9/16/48. Drummer. The Small Faces.

JONES, MICK. Brixton, England, 6/26/55. Guitarist, singer. The Clash; Big Audio Dynamite.

JONES, MICK. London, England, 12/27/44. Guitarist. Foreigner.

JONES, NEIL. Llanbradach, Wales, 3/25/49. Guitarist. Amen Corner.

JONES, PAUL (Paul Pond). Portsmouth, England, 2/24/42. Singer, harmonicist. Manfred Mann.

JONES, RANDY. 9/13/52. Singer. The Village People.

JONES, RAY. Oldham, England, 10/22/39. Bassist. Billy J. Kramer & The Dakotas.

JONES, RICKIE LEE. Chicago, IL, 11/8/54. Rock/jazz singer, songwriter.

JONES, SAM J. Chicago, IL, 8/12/54. Actor. *Flash Gordon.*

JONES, SHIRLEY. Smithton, PA, 3/31/34. Actor, married to Marty Ingels. *The Partridge Family.*

JONES, STAR. 3/24/62. TV host. *The View.*

JONES, STEVE. London, England, 9/3/55. Guitarist. The Sex Pistols.

JONES, TERRY. Colwyn Bay, Wales, 2/1/42. Actor, director, writer. *Monty Python's Life of Brian.*

JONES, TOM (Tom Woodward). Pontypridd, Wales, 6/7/40. Pop singer.

JORDAN, LONNIE (Leroy Jordan). San Diego, CA, 11/21/48. Keyboardist, singer. War.

JOURARD, JEFF. 1955. Guitarist. The Motels.

JOURDAN, LOUIS (Louis Gendre). Marseilles, France, 6/19/19. Actor. *Gigi.*

JOVOVICH, MILLA. 12/17/75. Actor. *The Fifth Element.*

JOYCE, MIKE. Manchester, England, 6/1/63. Drummer. The Smiths.

JOYNER-KERSEE, JACKIE. St. Louis, IL, 3/3/62. Track athlete. Olympic gold medalist.

JUDD, NAOMI (Diana Judd). Ashland, KY, 1/11/46. Country singer, mother of Wynonna and Ashley. The Judds.

JUMP, GORDON. Dayton, OH, 4/1/32. Actor. Arthur Carlson on *WKRP in Cincinnati.*

JUSTMAN, SETH. Washington, DC, 1/27/51. Keyboardist, singer. The J. Geils Band.

KAHN, MADELINE. Boston, MA, 9/29/42. Actor. *Blazing Saddles.*

KALE, JIM. 8/11/43. Bassist. The Guess Who.

KANE, BIG DADDY. New York, NY, 9/10/68. Rap artist, songwriter. "Long Live the Kane."

KANE, CAROL. Cleveland, OH, 6/18/52. Actor. Simka Graves on *Taxi.*

KANTNER, PAUL. San Francisco, CA, 3/12/42. Guitarist. Jefferson Airplane; Starship.

KAPRISKY, VALERIE. Paris, France, 1963. Actor. *Breathless.*

KARPOV, ANATOLY. Zlatoust, Russia, 5/23/51. Chess player. International grandmaster, world champion.

KARRAS, ALEX. Gary, IN, 7/15/35. Former football player, actor. *Webster.*

KASPAROV, GARRY. Baku, Russia, 4/13/63. Chess player. International grandmaster, world champion.

KATH, TERRY. Chicago, IL, 1/31/46. Guitarist. Chicago.

KATT, WILLIAM. Los Angeles, CA, 2/16/55. Actor, son of Barbara Hale. *The Greatest American Hero.*

KATZ, STEVE. New York, NY, 5/9/45. Guitarist, harmonicist, singer. Blood, Sweat & Tears.

KATZENBERG, JEFFREY. New York, NY, 12/21/50. Studio executive.

KAUKONEN, JORMA. Washington, DC, 12/23/40. Guitarist. Jefferson Airplane; Hot Tuna.

KAVNER, JULIE. Los Angeles, CA, 9/7/50. Actor. Voice of Marge Simpson on *The Simpsons; Rhoda.*

KAY, JOHN (Joachim Krauledat). Tilsit, Germany, 4/12/44. Guitarist, singer. Steppenwolf.

KAYLAN, HOWARD (Howard Kaplan). New York, NY, 6/22/47. Singer, saxophonist. The Turtles.

KAZURINSKY, TIM. Johnstown, PA, 3/3/50. Actor. *Saturday Night Live.*

KEACH, STACY (William Keach Jr.). Savannah, GA, 6/2/41.
Actor. *Mickey Spillane's Mike Hammer.*

KEANE, BIL. Philadelphia, PA, 10/5/22. Cartoonist. *The Family Circus.*

KEATON, DIANE (Diane Hall). Los Angeles, CA, 1/5/46. Actor. *Annie Hall.*

KEATON, MICHAEL (Michael Douglas). Coraopolis, PA, 9/9/51. Actor. *Batman.*

KEEBLE, JON. London, England, 7/6/59. Drummer. Spandau Ballet.

KEEL, HOWARD (Harold Leek). Gillespie, IL, 4/13/17. Actor. Clayton Farlow on *Dallas.*

KEENAN, BRIAN. New York, NY, 1/28/44. Drummer. The Chambers Brothers; Manfred Mann.

KEESHAN, BOB (Robert James Keeshan). Lynbrook, NY, 6/27/27. TV personality, author. *Captain Kangaroo.*

KEFFORD, ACE (Christopher Kefford). Mosely, England, 12/10/46. Bassist. The Move.

KEILLOR, GARRISON. 8/7/42. Author, radio personality. *Lake Wobegon Days.*

KEITH, DAVID LEMUEL. Knoxville, TN, 5/8/54. Actor. *An Officer and a Gentleman.*

KELLER, MARTHE. Basel, Switzerland, 1/28/45. Actor. *Marathon Man.*

KELLERMAN, SALLY. Long Beach, CA, 6/2/37. Actor. Hot Lips in the movie *M*A*S*H.*

KELLEY, DEFOREST. Atlanta, GA, 1/20/20. Actor. Dr. Leonard "Bones" McCoy on *Star Trek.*

KELLEY, KITTY. Spokane, WA, 4/4/42. Unauthorized biographer.

KELLING, GRAEME. Paisley, Scotland, 4/4/57. Guitarist. Deacon Blue.

KELLY, MARK. Dublin, Ireland, 4/9/61. Keyboardist. Marillion.

KELLY, MOIRA. 1968. Actor. *The Cutting Edge.*

KEMP, GARY. Islington, England, 10/16/60. Guitarist, brother of Martin. Spandau Ballet.

KEMP, MARTIN. London, England, 10/10/61. Bassist, brother of Gary. Spandau Ballet.

KENDRICKS, EDDIE. Birmingham, AL, 12/17/39. Singer. The Temptations.

KENNEDY, GEORGE. New York, NY, 2/18/25. Actor. *Cool Hand Luke*.

KENNEDY, TED. Brookline, MA, 2/22/32. Politician, brother of John and Robert.

KENNIBREW, DEE DEE (Dolores Henry). Brooklyn, NY, 1945. Singer. The Crystals.

KENNY G (Kenneth Gorelick). Seattle, WA, 6/5/56. Jazz saxophone player.

KENSIT, PATSY. London, England, 3/4/68. Actor, formerly married to Jim Kerr; married to Liam Gallagher. *Lethal Weapon 2*.

KERNS, JOANNA (Joanna De Varona). San Francisco, CA, 2/12/53. Actor. Maggie Seaver on *Growing Pains*.

KERR, DEBORAH. Helensburg, Scotland, 9/30/21. Actor. *The King and I*.

KERR, JIM. Glasgow, Scotland, 7/9/59. Singer. Simple Minds.

KERRIGAN, NANCY. Stoneham, MA, 10/13/69. Figure skater. Olympic silver medalist, victim of knee attack.

KHAN, CHAKA (Yvette Marie Stevens). Great Lakes, IL, 3/23/53. Singer. Rufus.

KIDD, JOHNNY (Frederick Heath). London, England, 12/23/39. Singer. Johnny Kidd & The Pirates.

KIDDER, MARGOT. Yellow Knife, Canada, 10/17/48. Actor. Lois Lane in *Superman*.

KIEDIS, ANTHONY. Grand Rapids, MI, 11/1/62. Singer. Red Hot Chili Peppers.

KIEL, RICHARD. Detroit, MI, 9/13/39. Actor. Jaws in *The Spy Who Loved Me*.

KILPATRICK, JAMES JR. Oklahoma City, OK, 11/1/20. Journalist. *60 Minutes*.

KIMBALL, BOBBY (Bobby Toteaux). Vinton, LA, 3/29/47. Lead singer. Toto.

KING, ALAN (Irwin Kniberg). Brooklyn, NY, 12/26/27. Producer, comedian. *The Andersen Tapes*.

KING, B. B. (Riley King). Itta Bena, MS, 9/16/25. Legendary blues guitarist, singer, songwriter.

KING, BEN E. (Ben E. Nelson). Henderson, NC, 9/23/38. Singer. The Drifters.

KING, BILLIE JEAN. Long Beach, CA, 11/22/43. Tennis player.

KING, CAROLE (Carole Klein). Brooklyn, NY, 2/9/42. Singer, songwriter.

KING, CORETTA SCOTT. Marion, AL, 4/29/27. Author, lecturer, widow of Martin Luther King Jr.

KING, DON. Cleveland, OH, 8/20/31. Boxing promoter.

KING, MARK. Isle of Wight, England, 10/20/58. Singer, bassist. Level 42.

KING, PERRY. Alliance, OH, 4/30/48. Actor. Cody Allen on *Riptide*.

KING, WILLIAM. Alabama, 1/30/49. Trumpeter, keyboardist. The Commodores.

KINGSLEY, BEN (Krishna Bhanji). Snaiton, England, 12/31/43. Actor. *Gandhi*.

KINSKI, NASTASSJA (Nastassja Nakszynski). Berlin, Germany, 1/24/61. Actor, daughter of Klaus Kinski. *Cat People*.

KIRBY, BRUNO (Bruce Kirby Jr.). New York, NY, 4/28/49. Actor. *City Slickers*.

KIRKE, SIMON. Wales, 7/28/49. Drummer. Bad Company; Free.

KIRKLAND, SALLY. New York, NY, 10/31/41. Actor. *Anna*.

KIRKMAN, TERRY. Salina, KS, 12/12/41. Singer, keyboardist. The Association.

KIRKPATRICK, JEANE. Duncan, OK, 11/19/26. Diplomat. Former U.S. representative to the U.N.

KISSINGER, HENRY. Fuerth, Germany, 5/27/23. Richard Nixon's secretary of state.

KITT, EARTHA. North, SC, 1/17/27. Actor, singer. *The Mark of the Hawk*.

KLEIN, DANNY. New York, NY, 5/13/46. Bassist. The J. Geils Band.

KLEIN, ROBERT. New York, NY, 2/8/42. Actor. *Comedy Tonight*.

KLEMPERER, WERNER. Cologne, Germany, 3/22/20. Actor. Colonel Wilhelm Klink on *Hogan's Heroes*.

KLINE, KEVIN. St. Louis, MO, 10/24/47. Actor, married to Phoebe Cates. *The Big Chill*.

KLUGMAN, JACK. Philadelphia, PA, 4/27/22. Actor. Oscar Madison on *The Odd Couple*.

KNIGHT, GLADYS. Atlanta, GA, 5/28/44. Singer. Gladys Knight & The Pips.

KNIGHT, JONATHAN. Boston, MA, 11/29/69. Singer. New Kids on the Block.

KNIGHT, JORDAN. Boston, MA, 5/17/71. Singer. New Kids on the Block.

KNIGHT, MERALD. Atlanta, GA, 9/4/42. Singer. Gladys Knight & The Pips.

KNIGHT, MICHAEL E. Princeton, NJ, 5/7/59. Actor. Tad Martin on *All My Children*.

KNIGHT, SHIRLEY. Goessell, KS, 7/5/36. Actor. *The Dark at the Top of the Stairs*.

KNIGHT, SUGE. 4/19/65. Musician.

KNIGHTS, DAVE. Islington, England, 6/28/45. Bassist. Procol Harum.

KNOPFLER, DAVID. Glasgow, Scotland, 12/27/52. Guitarist. Dire Straits.

KNOPFLER, MARK. Glasgow, Scotland, 8/12/49. Singer, guitarist. Dire Straits.

KNOTTS, DON. Morgantown, WV, 7/21/24. Actor. Barney Fife on *The Andy Griffith Show*.

KNOWLES, PATRIC (Reginald Lawrence Knowles). Horsforth, England, 11/11/11. Actor. *How Green Was My Valley*.

KNUDSEN, KEITH. Ames, IA, 10/18/52. Drummer, singer. The Doobie Brothers.

KOCH, ED. New York, NY, 12/12/24. Former mayor of New York.

KOENIG, WALTER. Chicago, IL, 9/14/36. Actor, writer, director, producer. Pavel Chekov on *Star Trek*.

KOOL ROCK (Damon Wimbley). 11/4/66. Rap artist. Fat Boys.

KOPELL, BERNIE. New York, NY, 6/21/33. Actor. Dr. Adam Bricker on *The Love Boat*.

KORMAN, HARVEY. Chicago, IL, 2/15/27. Actor. *The Carol Burnett Show*.

KOSSOFF, PAUL. London, England, 9/14/50. Guitarist. Free.

KOTTO, YAPHET. New York, NY, 11/15/39. Actor. *Live and Let Die*.

KRABBE, JEROEN. Amsterdam, The Netherlands, 12/5/44. Actor. *The Fugitive*.

KRAMER, BILLY J. (Billy J. Ashton). Bootle, England,

8/19/43. Singer. Billy J. Kramer & The Dakotas.

KRAMER, JOEY. New York, NY, 6/21/50. Drummer. Aerosmith.

KRANTZ, JUDITH. New York, NY, 1/9/28. Novelist. *Scruples*.

KRAVITZ, LENNY. New York, NY, 5/26/64. Singer, songwriter, formerly married to Lisa Bonet. "Are You Gonna Go My Way?"

KREUTZMANN, BILL JR. Palo Alto, CA, 5/7/46. Drummer. Grateful Dead.

KRIEGER, ROBBIE. Los Angeles, CA, 1/8/46. Guitarist. The Doors.

KRIGE, ALICE. Upington, South Africa, 6/28/55. Actor. *Chariots of Fire*.

KRISTOFFERSON, KRIS. Brownsville, TX, 6/22/36. Singer, songwriter, actor. *Amerika*.

KUHLKE, NORMAN. Liverpool, England, 6/17/42. Drummer. The Swinging Blue Jeans.

KURTZ, SWOOSIE. Omaha, NE, 9/6/44. Actor. *Sisters*.

KWAN, NANCY. Hong Kong, 5/19/39. Actor. *The World of Suzie Wong*.

LABELLE, PATTI (Patricia Holt). Philadelphia, PA, 10/4/44. Pop/soul singer.

LADD, CHERYL (Cheryl Stoppelmoor). Huron, SD, 7/12/51. Actor. Kris Munroe on *Charlie's Angels*.

LADD, DIANE (Diane Ladner). Meridian, MS, 11/29/39. Actor, mother of Laura Dern. *Alice Doesn't Live Here Anymore*.

LAGASSE, EMERIL. 10/15/59. Chef, author, TV personality.

LAGERFELD, KARL. Hamburg, Germany, 9/10/38. Fashion designer. Chanel.

LAHTI, CHRISTINE. Birmingham, MI, 4/4/50. Actor. *Swing Shift*.

LAINE, DENNY (Brian Hines). Jersey, England, 10/29/44. Singer, guitarist. The Moody Blues.

LAKE, GREG. Bournemouth, England, 11/10/48. Bassist, singer. Emerson, Lake & Palmer; King Crimson.

LAMARR, HEDY (Hedwig Kiesler). Vienna, Austria, 11/9/13. Actor. *Ecstasy*.

LAMAS, LORENZO. Los Angeles, CA, 1/20/58. Actor. Lance Cumson on *Falcon Crest*.

LAMBERT, CHRISTOPHER. New York, NY, 3/29/57. Actor. *Greystoke: The Legend of Tarzan, Lord of the Apes.*

LAMM, ROBERT. New York, NY, 10/13/44. Singer, keyboardist. Chicago.

LANCASTER, ALAN. London, England, 2/7/49. Bassist. Status Quo.

LANDAU, MARTIN. Brooklyn, NY, 6/20/28. Actor. *Mission: Impossible.*

LANDERS, AUDREY. Philadelphia, PA, 7/18/59. Actor. Afton Cooper on *Dallas.*

LANDESBERG, STEVE. The Bronx, NY, 11/3/45. Actor. Detective Arthur Dietrich on *Barney Miller.*

LANDIS, JOHN. Chicago, IL, 8/3/50. Director. *Twilight Zone—The Movie.*

LANE, ABBE. Brooklyn, NY, 12/14/34. Actor, formerly married to Xavier Cugat. *Xavier Cugat Show.*

LANE, CHARLES. New York, NY, 12/5/53. Director. *Sidewalk Stories.*

LANE, DIANE. New York, NY, 1/22/65. Actor. *Rumble Fish.*

LANG, BOB. Manchester, England, 1/10/46. Bassist. Wayne Fontana & The Mindbenders.

LANGE, HOPE. Redding Ridge, CT, 11/28/31. Actor. *The Ghost and Mrs. Muir.*

LANGE, TED. Oakland, CA, 1/5/47. Actor. Isaac Washington on *The Love Boat.*

LANGELLA, FRANK. Bayonne, NJ, 1/1/38. Actor. *Dracula.*

LANIER, ALLEN. 6/25/46. Guitarist, keyboardist. Blue Öyster Cult.

LANSING, ROBERT (Robert Brown). San Diego, CA, 6/5/29. Actor. *The Man Who Never Was.*

LAPREAD, RONALD. Alabama, 9/4/50. Bassist, trumpeter. The Commodores.

LARDIE, MICHAEL. 9/8/58. Musician. Great White.

LARROQUETTE, JOHN. New Orleans, LA, 11/25/47. Actor. *Night Court.*

LARUE, FLORENCE. Pennsylvania, 2/4/44. Singer. The 5th Dimension.

LASSER, LOUISE. New York, NY, 4/11/39. Actor, formerly married to Woody Allen. *Bananas.*

LAUDER, ESTEE. New York, NY, 7/1/08. Fashion designer.

LAUPER, CYNDI. New York, NY, 6/22/53. Singer, actor, professional wrestling promoter. *She's So Unusual.*

LAURIE, PIPER (Rosetta Jacobs). Detroit, MI, 1/22/32. Actor. Mother in *Carrie.*

LAVERN, ROGER (Roger Jackson). Kidderminster, England, 11/11/38. Keyboardist. The Tornados.

LAVIN, LINDA. Portland, ME, 10/15/37. Actor, singer. *Alice.*

LAWRENCE, CAROL (Carol Laraia). Melrose Park, IL, 9/5/34. Actor, singer. *West Side Story.*

LAWRENCE, JOEY. Montgomery, PA, 4/20/76. Actor, singer. *Blossom.*

LAWRENCE, VICKI. Inglewood, CA, 3/26/49. Actor. *Mama's Family.*

LAWSON, LEIGH. Atherston, England, 7/21/45. Actor. *Tess.*

LAWTON, JOHN. 6/11/46. Singer. Uriah Heep.

LEA, JIMMY. Melbourne Arms, England, 6/14/52. Bassist, keyboardist, violinist. Slade.

LEACH, ROBIN. London, England, 8/29/41. TV host. *Lifestyles of the Rich and Famous.*

LEACHMAN, CLORIS. Des Moines, IA, 4/30/26. Actor. Phyllis Lyndstrom on *The Mary Tyler Moore Show.*

LEADON, BERNIE. Minneapolis, MN, 7/19/47. Guitarist, singer. The Eagles.

LEAR, NORMAN. New Haven, CT, 7/27/22. Producer, director, formerly married to Frances. *All in the Family.*

LEARNED, MICHAEL. Washington, DC, 4/9/39. Actor. Olivia on *The Waltons.*

LEBON, SIMON. Bushey, England, 10/27/58. Lead singer. Duran Duran.

LEBROCK, KELLY. 3/22/60. Actor, married to Steven Seagal. *Weird Science.*

LEE, ALVIN. Nottingham, England, 12/19/44. Guitarist, singer. Ten Years After.

LEE, ARTHUR. Memphis, TN, 1945. Guitarist, singer. Love.

LEE, BARBARA. New York, NY, 5/16/47. Singer. The Chiffons.

LEE, BEVERLY. Passaic, NJ, 8/3/41. Singer. The Shirelles.

LEE, BRENDA (Brenda Tarpley). Lithonia, GA, 12/11/44. Singer.

LEE, GEDDY. Willowdale, Canada, 7/29/53. Singer, bassist. Rush.

LEE, JASON SCOTT. Los Angeles, CA, 1966. Actor. *Dragon: The Bruce Lee Story.*

LEE, JOHNNY. Texas City, TX, 7/3/46. Singer. "Lookin' for Love."

LEE, MICHELE (Michele Dusiak). Los Angeles, CA, 6/24/42. Actor. Karen Fairgate MacKenzie on *Knots Landing.*

LEE, PEGGY (Norma Delores Egstrom). Jamestown, ND, 5/26/20. Actor, singer. *The Jazz Singer.*

LEE, RIC. Cannock, England, 10/20/45. Drummer. Ten Years After.

LEE, STAN. New York, NY, 12/28/22. Artist, writer, Marvel Comics legend.

LEE, TOMMY (Tommy Bass). Athens, Greece, 10/3/62. Drummer, married to Pamela Anderson Lee, formerly married to Heather Locklear. Mötley Crüe.

LEEDS, GARY. Glendale, CA, 9/3/44. Drummer. The Walker Brothers.

LEESE, HOWARD. Los Angeles, CA, 6/13/51. Keyboardist, guitarist. Heart.

LEEVES, JANE. East Grinstead, England, 4/18/61. Actor. Daphne Moon on *Frasier.*

LEEWAY, JOE. London, England, 1957. Percussionist. Thompson Twins.

LEGUIZAMO, JOHN. Bogota, Columbia, 7/22/60. Actor. *Carlito's Way.*

LEIBMAN, RON. New York, NY, 10/11/37. Actor. *Kaz.*

LEIFER, CAROL. 7/27/56. Comic. *Alright Already.*

LEIGH, JANET (Jeannette Helen Morrison). Merced, CA, 7/6/27. Actor, mother of Jamie Lee Curtis. *Psycho.*

LEIGHTON, LAURA (Laura Miller). Iowa City, IA, 7/24/68. Actor. *Melrose Place.*

LEITCH, DONOVAN. 8/16/67. Actor, son of folk singer Donovan, brother of Ione Skye.

LEMAT, PAUL. Rahway, NJ, 9/22/52. Actor. *American Graffiti.*

LEMIEUX, MARIO. Montreal, Canada, 10/5/65. NHL hockey player. Pittsburgh Penguins.

LEMMON, CHRIS. Los Angeles, CA, 1/22/54. Actor, son of Jack Lemmon. *Swing Shift.*

LEMMY (Ian Kilmister). Stoke-on-Trent, England, 12/24/45. Bassist, singer. Motorhead.

LEMON, MEADOWLARK. Wilmington, NC, 4/25/32. Basketball player. Harlem Globetrotters.

LENNON, JULIAN (John Charles Julian Lennon). Liverpool, England, 4/8/63. Singer, songwriter, son of John Lennon. Half brother of Sean.

LENNON, SEAN. 10/9/75. Musician. Son of John Lennon and Yoko Ono. Half brother of Julian Lennon.

LENNOX, ANNIE. Aberdeen, Scotland, 12/25/54. Singer, songwriter. Eurythmics.

LEONARD, ROBERT SEAN. Westwood, NJ, 2/28/69. Actor. *Dead Poets Society.*

LEONARD, SUGAR RAY. Wilmington, NC, 5/17/56. Boxer.

LERNER, MICHAEL. Brooklyn, NY, 6/22/41. Actor. *Barton Fink.*

LESH, PHIL (Phil Chapman). Berkeley, CA, 3/15/40. Bassist. Grateful Dead.

LESTER, ROBERT "SQUIRREL." 1/13/30. Singer. The Chi-Lites.

LEVERT, EDDIE. Canton, OH, 6/16/42. Singer. The O'Jays.

LEVIN, DRAKE. Guitarist. Paul Revere & The Raiders.

LEVY, EUGENE. Hamilton, Canada, 12/17/46. Actor, writer. *SCTV.*

LEWINSKY, MONICA. 7/23/73. Former White House intern, had "inappropriate" relationship with Bill Clinton.

LEWIS, AL (Alexander Meister). New York, NY, 4/30/10. Actor. *The Munsters.*

LEWIS, CARL (Carl Frederick Carlton). Birmingham, AL, 7/1/61. Track athlete. Olympic gold medalist.

LEWIS, EMMANUEL. New York, NY, 3/9/71. Actor. Webster Long on *Webster.*

LEWIS, GARY (Gary Levitch). New York, NY, 7/31/46. Singer, drummer, son of Jerry Lewis. Gary Lewis & The Playboys.

LEWIS, HUEY (Hugh Cregg III). New York, NY, 7/5/50. Singer. Huey Lewis & The News.

LEWIS, JERRY (Joseph Levitch). Newark, NJ, 3/16/26. Actor, father of Gary Lewis. *The Nutty Professor.*

LEWIS, JERRY LEE. Ferriday, LA, 9/29/35. Legendary rock keyboardist, singer, songwriter.

LEWIS, JULIETTE. San Fernando Valley, CA, 6/21/73. Actor. *Cape Fear.*

LEWIS, PETER. Los Angeles, CA, 7/15/45. Guitarist, singer. Moby Grape.

LEWIS, RICHARD. 6/29/47. Comic. *Anything But Love.*

LIDDY, G. GORDON. New York, NY, 11/30/30. Watergate participant, talk show host. *The G. Gordon Liddy Show.*

LIFESON, ALEX. Fernie, Canada, 8/27/53. Guitarist. Rush.

LIGHT, JUDITH. Trenton, NJ, 2/9/49. Actor. Angela on *Who's the Boss?*

LIGHTFOOT, GORDON. Orillia, Canada, 11/17/38. Folk guitarist, singer, songwriter.

LINCOLN, ABBEY (Anna Marie Woolridge). Chicago, IL, 8/6/30. Singer, actor. *For Love of Ivy.*

LINDEN, HAL (Hal Lipschitz). The Bronx, NY, 3/20/31. Actor. *Barney Miller.*

LINDES, HAL. Monterey, CA, 6/30/53. Guitarist. Dire Straits.

LINDSAY, MARK. Eugene, OR, 3/9/42. Singer, saxophonist. Paul Revere & The Raiders.

LINDUP, MIKE. 3/17/59. Keyboardist, singer. Level 42.

LINKLETTER, ART. Moose Jaw, Canada, 7/17/12. TV personality. *People Are Funny.*

LINN-BAKER, MARK. St. Louis, MO, 6/17/54. Actor. Cousin Larry Appleton on *Perfect Strangers.*

LINVILLE, LARRY. Ojai, CA, 9/29/39. Actor. Frank Burns on *M*A*S*H.*

LIOTTA, RAY. Newark, NJ, 12/18/54. Actor. *GoodFellas.*

LIPNICKI, JONATHAN. 10/22/90. Actor. *Jerry Maguire.*

LITTLE EVA (Eva Narcissus Boyd). Bellhaven, NC, 6/29/45. Singer. "The Loco-Motion."

LITTLE RICHARD (Richard Penniman). Macon, GA, 12/5/32. Legendary singer, songwriter.

LIVGREN, KERRY. Kansas, 9/18/49. Guitarist. Kansas.

L.L. COOL J (James Todd Smith). New York, NY, 1/14/68. Rap artist.

LLOYD, CHRISTOPHER. Stamford, CT, 10/22/38. Actor. "Reverend Jim" Ignatowski on *Taxi.*

LLOYD, EMILY. London, England, 9/29/70. Actor. *Wish You Were Here.*

LOCKE, JOHN. Los Angeles, CA, 9/25/43. Keyboardist. Spirit.

LOCKE, SONDRA. Shelbyville, TN, 5/28/47. Actor. *The Gauntlet.*

LOCKHART, JUNE. New York, NY, 6/25/25. Actor. *Lost in Space.*

LOCKWOOD, GARY. Van Nuys, CA, 2/21/37. Actor. *2001: A Space Odyssey.*

LOCORRIERE, DENNIS. Union City, NJ, 6/13/49. Lead singer. Dr. Hook.

LODGE, JOHN. Birmingham, England, 7/20/45. Bassist. The Moody Blues.

LOEB, LISA. 3/11/68. Singer. "Stay."

LOFGREN, NILS. Chicago, IL, 6/21/51. Guitarist, keyboardist, singer, songwriter.

LOGGIA, ROBERT. Staten Island, NY, 1/3/30. Actor. *Mancuso, FBI.*

LOGGINS, KENNY. Everett, WA, 1/7/48. Singer, songwriter.

LOLLOBRIGIDA, GINA. Subiaco, Italy, 7/4/27. Actor. *Circus.*

LOM, HERBERT. Prague, Czechoslovakia, 1/9/17. Actor. *Spartacus.*

LONG, SHELLEY. Ft. Wayne, IN, 8/23/49. Actor. Diane Chambers on *Cheers.*

LONGMUIR, ALAN. Edinburgh, Scotland, 6/20/53. Bassist. The Bay City Rollers.

LONGMUIR, DEREK. Edinburgh, Scotland, 3/19/55. Drummer. The Bay City Rollers.

LORD, JON. Leicester, England, 6/9/41. Keyboardist. Deep Purple.

LORDS, TRACI (Norma Kuzma). Steubenville, OH,

5/7/68. Actor, former porn star. *Melrose Place.*

LOUGANIS, GREG. El Cajon, CA, 1/29/60. Diver. Olympic gold medalist.

LOUGHNANE, LEE. Chicago, IL, 10/21/46. Trumpeter. Chicago.

LOUISE, TINA (Tina Blacker). New York, NY, 2/11/34. Actor. Ginger Grant on *Gilligan's Island.*

LOVE, MIKE. Baldwin Hills, CA, 3/15/41. Singer. The Beach Boys.

LOVELADY, DAVE. Liverpool, England, 10/16/42. Drummer. The Fourmost.

LOVELESS, PATTY. Belcher Holler, KY, 1/4/57 Singer.

LOVITZ, JON. Tarzana, CA, 7/21/57. Actor. *Saturday Night Live.*

LOWE, CHAD. Dayton, OH, 1/15/68. Actor, brother of Rob Lowe. *Life Goes On.*

LOWE, CHRIS. Blackpool, England, 10/4/59. Keyboardist. Pet Shop Boys.

LUCIA, PETER. 2/2/47. Drummer. Tommy James & The Shondells.

LUCKINBILL, LAURENCE. Fort Smith, AR, 11/21/34. Actor, married to Lucie Arnaz. *The Boys in the Band.*

LUDLUM, ROBERT. New York, NY, 5/25/27. Novelist, actor, producer. *The Gemini Contenders.*

LUFT, LORNA. Los Angeles, CA, 11/21/52. Actor, half-sister of Liza Minnelli, daughter of Judy Garland. *Where the Boys Are.*

LUKATHER, STEVE. Los Angeles, CA, 10/21/57. Lead guitarist. Toto.

LULU (Marie Lawrie). Glasgow, Scotland, 11/3/48. Singer, actor. *To Sir with Love.*

LUNDEN, JOAN. Fair Oaks, CA, 9/19/50. Host. *Good Morning America.*

LUNDGREN, DOLPH. Stockholm, Sweden, 11/3/59. Actor. *Rocky IV.*

LUPONE, PATTI. Northport, NY, 4/21/49. Actor. *Life Goes On.*

LUPUS, PETER. Indianapolis, IN, 6/17/37. Actor. Willie Armitage on *Mission: Impossible.*

LWIN, ANNABELLA (Myant Aye). Rangoon, Burma, 10/31/65. Singer. Bow Wow Wow.

LYDON, JOHN. London, England, 1/31/56. Singer, a.k.a. Johnny Rotten. The Sex Pistols; Public Image Ltd.

LYNCH, STAN. Gainesville, FL, 5/21/55. Drummer. Tom Petty & The Heartbreakers.

LYNGSTAD, FRIDA (Anni-Frid Lyngstad). Narvik, Sweden, 11/15/45. Singer. Abba.

LYNNE, JEFF. Birmingham, England, 12/30/47. Singer, guitarist. Electric Light Orchestra (ELO).

LYNOTT, PHIL. Dublin, Ireland, 8/20/51. Singer, bassist. Thin Lizzy.

LYONS, LEO. Standbridge, England, 11/30/43. Bassist. Ten Years After.

LYTE, MC. New York, NY, 1971. Rap artist.

MA, YO-YO. Paris, France, 10/7/55. Cello virtuoso.

MACARTHUR, JAMES. Los Angeles, CA, 12/8/37. Actor, son of Helen Hayes. Danny Williams on *Hawaii Five-O.*

MACCHIO, RALPH. Long Island, NY, 11/4/62. Actor. *The Karate Kid.*

MACCORKINDALE, SIMON. Cambridge, England, 2/12/52. Actor. *Falcon Crest.*

MACDONALD, EDDIE. St. Asaph, Wales, 11/1/59. Bassist. The Alarm.

MACDONALD, ROBIN. Nairn, Scotland, 7/18/43. Guitarist. Billy J. Kramer & The Dakotas.

MACGOWAN, SHANE. Kent, England, 12/25/57. Guitarist, singer. The Pogues.

MACGRAW, ALI. Pound Ridge, NY, 4/1/38. Actor. *Love Story.*

MACKAY, ANDY. London, England, 7/23/46. Saxophonist, woodwindist. Roxy Music.

MACKAY, DUNCAN. 7/26/50. Keyboardist. Steve Harley & Cockney Rebel.

MACLACHLAN, KYLE. Yakima, WA, 2/22/59. Actor. *Twin Peaks.*

MACLEAN, BRYAN. Los Angeles, CA, 1947. Guitarist, singer. Love.

MACLEOD, GAVIN. Mt. Kisco, NY, 2/28/31. Actor. Captain Stubing of *The Love Boat.*

MACNAUGHTON, ROBERT. New York, NY, 12/19/66. Actor. *E.T., the Extra-Terrestrial.*

MACNEE, PATRICK. London, England, 2/6/22. Actor. *The Avengers.*

MACNEIL, ROBERT. Montreal, Canada, 1/19/31. Broadcast journalist. *MacNeil/Lehrer Report.*

MACNELLY, JEFF. New York, NY, 9/17/47. Cartoonist. *Shoe.*

MACNICOL, PETER. Dallas, TX, 4/10/54. Actor. *Sophie's Choice.*

MADDEN, JOHN. Austin, MN, 4/10/36. Sportscaster, football analyst.

MADIGAN, AMY. Chicago, IL, 9/11/51. Actor. *Places in the Heart.*

MADSEN, MICHAEL. Chicago, IL, 1959. Actor, brother of Virginia. *Reservoir Dogs.*

MADSEN, VIRGINIA. Winnetka, IL, 9/11/61. Actor, sister of Michael. *Electric Dreams.*

MAGNUSON, ANN. Charleston, WV, 1/4/56. Actor. Catherine Hughes on *Anything but Love.*

MAGUIRE, LES. Wallasey, England, 12/27/41. Keyboardist, saxophonist. Gerry & The Pacemakers.

MAHONEY, JOHN. Manchester, England, 6/20/40. Actor. Father of Dr. Crane on *Cheers* and *Frasier.*

MAJORS, LEE (Harvey Lee Yeary II). Wyandotte, MI, 4/23/39. Actor, formerly married to Farrah Fawcett. *The Six Million Dollar Man.*

MAKEPEACE, CHRIS. Montreal, Canada, 4/22/64. Actor. *My Bodyguard.*

MAKO (Makoto Iwamatsu). Kobe, Japan, 12/10/33. Actor. *The Sand Pebbles.*

MALDEN, KARL (Mladen Sekulovich). Gary, IN, 3/22/12. Actor, American Express spokesperson. *The Streets of San Francisco.*

MALONE, DOROTHY. Chicago, IL, 1/30/25. Actor. *Written on the Wind.*

MALTIN, LEONARD. New York, NY, 12/18/50. Film critic. *Entertainment Tonight.*

MANDEL, HOWIE. Toronto, Canada, 11/29/55. Actor. Dr. Wayne Fiscus on *St. Elsewhere.*

MANDELA, NELSON. Umtata, South Africa, 7/18/18. President of South Africa.

MANDELA, WINNIE. Transkei, South Africa, 9/26/34.

Political activist, formerly married to Nelson Mandela.

MANDRELL, BARBARA. Houston, TX, 12/25/48. Country singer. Barbara Mandrell & The Mandrell Sisters.

MANETTI, LARRY. Chicago, IL, 7/23/47. Actor. Rick on *Magnum, P. I.*

MANILOW, BARRY (Barry Alan Pincus). Brooklyn, NY, 6/17/43. Singer, songwriter. *I Write the Songs.*

MANN, MANFRED (Michael Lubowitz). Johannesburg, South Africa, 10/21/40. Keyboardist. Manfred Mann.

MANN, TERRENCE. Kentucky, 1945. Actor. *Les Misérables.*

MANOFF, DINAH. New York, NY, 1/25/56. Actor, daughter of Lee Grant. Carol Weston on *Empty Nest.*

MANSON, CHARLES. Cincinnati, OH, 11/12/34. Murderer, cult leader.

MANTEGNA, JOE. Chicago, IL, 11/13/47. Actor. *The Godfather, Part III.*

MANZANERA, PHIL. London, England, 1/31/51. Guitarist. Roxy Music.

MANZAREK, RAY. Chicago, IL, 2/12/39. Keyboardist. The Doors.

MARCEAU, MARCEL. Strasbourg, France, 3/22/23. Actor, pantomimist. *Bip.*

MARCHAND, NANCY. Buffalo, NY, 6/19/28. Actor. *Lou Grant.*

MARCOS, IMELDA. Talcoban, the Philippines, 7/2/31. Wife of late Ferdinand Marcos.

MARCOVICCI, ANDREA. New York, NY, 11/18/48. Actor, singer. *Trapper John, MD.*

MARGO, MITCH. Brooklyn, NY, 5/25/47. Tenor singer. The Tokens.

MARGO, PHIL. Brooklyn, NY, 4/1/42. Bass singer. The Tokens.

MARIN, CHEECH (Richard Marin). Los Angeles, CA, 7/13/46. Actor, writer, former partner of Tommy Chong. *Up in Smoke.*

MARINARO, ED. New York, NY, 3/31/50. Actor, football player. *Hill Street Blues.*

MARK, MARKY (Mark Wahlberg). Dorchester, MA, 6/5/71. Rap artist, Calvin Klein underwear model, brother of Donny Wahlberg.

MARLEY, ZIGGY (David Marley). Jamaica, 10/17/68. Singer, songwriter, son of Bob Marley. Ziggy Marley & The Melody Makers.

MARR, JOHNNY. Manchester, England, 10/31/63. Guitarist. The Smiths.

MARRIOTT, STEVE. Bow, England, 1/30/47. Singer, guitarist. The Small Faces.

MARS, MICK (Bob Deal). Terre Haute, IN, 4/4/55. Guitarist. Mötley Crüe.

MARSALIS, BRANFORD. Breaux Bridge, LA, 8/26/60. Jazz musician, bandleader, saxophonist. Brother of Wynton Marsalis. Former musical director of *The Tonight Show.*

MARSDEN, FREDDIE. Liverpool, England, 10/23/40. Drummer. Gerry & The Pacemakers.

MARSDEN, GERRY. Liverpool, England, 9/24/42. Singer, lead guitarist. Gerry & The Pacemakers.

MARSH, IAN. Sheffield, England, 11/11/56. Keyboardist. The Human League; Heaven 17.

MARSHALL, PETER (Pierre La Cock). Huntington, WV, 3/30/30. TV personality. Host of *The Hollywood Squares.*

MARTELL, VINCE. New York, NY, 11/11/45. Guitarist. Vanilla Fudge.

MARTIN, ANDREA. Portland, ME, 1/15/47. Writer, actor. *SCTV.*

MARTIN, DEWEY. Chesterville, Canada, 9/30/42. Singer, drummer. Buffalo Springfield.

MARTIN, DICK. Battle Creek, MI, 1/30/22. Actor. Cohost of *Laugh-In.*

MARTIN, JIM. Oakland, CA, 7/21/61. Guitarist. Faith No More.

MARTIN, PAMELA SUE. Westport, CT, 1/15/53. Actor. *Dynasty.*

MARTINDALE, WINK (Winston Conrad Martindale). Bells, TN, 12/4/34. TV personality. Host of *Tic Tac Dough* and *Debt.*

MARTINI, JERRY. Colorado, 10/1/43. Saxophonist. Sly & The Family Stone.

MARVIN, HANK (Brian Rankin). Newcastle, England, 10/28/41. Lead guitarist. The Shadows.

MARX, RICHARD. Chicago, IL, 9/16/63. Singer, songwriter.

MASON, DAVE. Worcester, England, 5/10/47. Singer, guitarist. Traffic.

MASON, JACKIE. Sheboygan, WI, 6/9/34. Actor. *Chicken Soup.*

MASON, MARSHA. St. Louis, MO, 4/3/42. Actor. *The Goodbye Girl.*

MASON, NICK. Birmingham, England, 1/27/45. Drummer. Pink Floyd.

MASSI, NICK (Nick Macioci). Newark, NJ, 9/19/35. Singer, bassist. The Four Seasons.

MASTELOTTO, PAT. 9/10/55. Drummer. Mr. Mister.

MASTERSON, MARY STUART. Los Angeles, CA, 6/28/66. Actor, daughter of Peter. *Fried Green Tomatoes.*

MASTERSON, PETER. Houston, TX, 6/1/34. Actor, writer, director, father of Mary Stuart. *The Exorcist.*

MASTRANGELO, CARLO. The Bronx, NY, 10/5/39. Bass singer. Dion & The Belmonts.

MASTRANTONIO, MARY ELIZABETH. Oak Park, IL, 11/17/58. Actor. *The Color of Money.*

MASUR, RICHARD. New York, NY, 11/20/48. Actor, Screen Actors Guild president. *One Day at a Time.*

MATHERS, JERRY. Sioux City, IA, 6/2/48. Actor. Theodore "Beaver" Cleaver on *Leave It to Beaver.*

MATHESON, TIM. Glendale, CA, 12/31/47. Actor. *National Lampoon's Animal House.*

MATHEWS, DENISE (formerly Vanity). Niagara, Canada, 1/3/63. Former singer and actor (a.k.a. D.D. Winters), now Christian Evangelist, bible student, married to L.A. Raiders defensive end Anthony Smith. *The Last Dragon.*

MATHIS, JOHNNY. San Francisco, CA, 9/30/35. Pop singer.

MATLOCK, GLENN. 8/27/56. Bassist. The Sex Pistols.

MATTHEWS, IAN (Ian McDonald). Lincolnshire, England, 6/16/45. Singer, guitarist. Matthew's Southern Comfort.

MAUS, JOHN. New York, NY, 11/12/43. Singer. The Walker Brothers.

MAXFIELD, MIKE. Manchester, England, 2/23/44. Lead guitarist. Billy J. Kramer & The Dakotas.

MAY, BRIAN. Twickenham, England, 7/19/47. Guitarist. Queen.

MAY, ELAINE (Elaine Berlin). Philadelphia, PA, 4/21/32. Actor, director, writer. *Ishtar.*

MAY, PHIL. Dartford, England, 11/9/44. Singer. The Pretty Things.

MAYALL, JOHN. Macclesfield, England, 11/29/33. Singer, keyboardist, harmonicist. The Bluesbreakers.

MAYFIELD, CURTIS. Chicago, IL, 6/3/42. Singer, songwriter, record producer, paralyzed in an accident during a concert. "Superfly."

MAYS, WILLIE. Fairfield, AL, 5/6/31. Baseball player. San Francisco Giants.

MAZAR, DEBI. Queens, NY, 1964. Actor. *Civil Wars; L.A. Law.*

MAZURSKY, PAUL. Brooklyn, NY, 4/25/30. Producer, director, writer, actor. *Down and Out in Beverly Hills.*

M.C. ERIC. 8/19/70. Rap artist. Technotronic.

MCA (Adam Yauch). Brooklyn, NY, 8/15/67. Rap artist. The Beastie Boys.

MCBRIDE, MARTINA. Sharon, KS, 7/29/66. Singer.

MCCALLUM, DAVID. Glasgow, Scotland, 9/19/33. Actor. *The Great Escape.*

MCCARTHY, ANDREW. Westfield, NJ, 11/29/62. Actor. *Less Than Zero.*

MCCARTHY, JENNY Chicago, IL, 11/1/72. *Singled Out.*

MCCARTHY, KEVIN. Seattle, WA, 2/15/14. Actor. *Invasion of the Body Snatchers.*

MCCARTY, JIM. Liverpool, England, 7/25/44. Drummer. The Yardbirds; Mitch Ryder & The Detroit Wheels.

MCCAULEY, JACKIE. Coleraine, Ireland, 12/14/46. Keyboardist. Them.

MCCAULEY, PATRICK. Northern Ireland, 3/17/44. Drummer. Them.

MCCLANAHAN, RUE. Healdton, OK, 2/21/34. Actor. Blanche Devereaux on *The Golden Girls.*

MCCLARY, THOMAS. 10/6/50. Lead guitarist. The Commodores.

MCCLINTON, DELBERT. Lubbock, TX, 11/4/40. Singer, songwriter.

MCCLURG, EDIE. Kansas City, MO, 7/23/50. Actor. *The Hogan Family.*

MCCLUSKEY, ANDY. Wirral, England, 6/24/59. Singer. Orchestral Manoeuvres in the Dark (OMD).

MCCOO, MARILYN. Jersey City, NJ, 9/30/43. Singer, cohost of *Solid Gold.* The 5th Dimension.

MCCREADY, MIKE. 4/5/66. Guitarist. Pearl Jam.

MCCULLOCH, IAN. Liverpool, England, 5/5/59. Singer. Echo & The Bunnymen.

MCDANIELS, DARRYL D. New York, NY, 1964. Rap artist. Run-D.M.C.

MCDONALD, COUNTRY JOE. El Monte, CA, 1/1/42. Guitarist, singer. Country Joe & The Fish.

MCDONALD, IAN. London, England, 6/25/46. Saxophonist. King Crimson.

MCDONALD, MICHAEL. St. Louis, MO, 12/2/52. Singer, songwriter, keyboardist. The Doobie Brothers.

MCDONALD, PAT. 8/6/52. Musician. Timbuk 3.

MCDONNELL, MARY. Ithaca, NY, 1952. Actor. *Dances with Wolves.*

MCDOWELL, MALCOLM. Leeds, England, 6/19/43. Actor. *A Clockwork Orange.*

MCENROE, JOHN JR. Wiesbaden, Germany, 2/16/59. Tennis player. Formerly married to Tatum O'Neal, relationship with Patty Smyth.

MCFADDEN, CYNTHIA. 5/27/56. Television journalist.

MCFERRIN, BOBBY. New York, NY, 3/11/50. Singer. "Don't Worry, Be Happy."

MCGAVIN, DARREN. Spokane, WA, 5/7/22. Actor. *The Night Stalker.*

MCGEOCH, JOHN. Guitarist. Siouxsie & The Banshees.

MCGILLIS, KELLY. Newport Beach, CA, 7/9/57. Actor. *Witness.*

MCGOVERN, ELIZABETH. Evanston, IL, 7/18/61. Actor. *Ragtime.*

MCGOVERN, MAUREEN. Youngstown, OH, 7/27/49. Singer, actor. "The Morning After."

MCGUINN, ROGER "JIM" (James Joseph McGuinn). Chicago, IL, 7/13/42. Singer, guitarist. The Byrds.

MCGUINNESS, TOM. Wimbledon, England, 12/2/41. Bassist. Manfred Mann.

MCINTOSH, LORRAINE. Glasgow, Scotland, 5/13/64. Singer. Deacon Blue.

MCINTYRE, FRITZ. 9/2/58. Keyboardist. Simply Red.

MCINTYRE, JOE. Needham, MA, 12/31/73. Singer. New Kids on the Block.

MCINTYRE, ONNIE. Lennox Town, Scotland, 9/25/45. Guitarist. Average White Band.

MCJOHN, GOLDY. 5/2/45. Organist. Steppenwolf.

MCKAGAN, DUFF ROSE (Michael McKagan). Seattle, WA. Bassist. Guns N' Roses.

MCKEAN, MICHAEL. New York, NY, 10/17/47. Actor, writer. Lenny Kosnowski on *Laverne & Shirley.*

MCKELLAR, DANICA. 1/3/75. La Jolla, CA. Actor. Winnie Cooper on *The Wonder Years.*

MCKELLEN, IAN. Burnley, England, 5/25/39. Shakespearian actor.

MCKEON, NANCY. Westbury, NY, 4/4/66. Actor. Jo Polniaczek on *The Facts of Life.*

MCKEOWN, LESLIE. Edinburgh, Scotland, 11/12/55. Singer. The Bay City Rollers.

MCKUEN, ROD. Oakland, CA, 4/29/33. Poet. *Laugh-In.*

MCLAGAN, IAN. England, 5/12/46. Keyboardist. The Faces.

MCLEAN, DON. New Rochelle, NY, 10/2/45. Singer, songwriter.

MCLEMORE, LAMONTE. St. Louis, MO, 9/17/39. Singer. The 5th Dimension.

MCMAHON, ED. Detroit, MI, 3/6/23. Announcer and host. *The Tonight Show; Star Search.*

MCNALLY, JOHN. Liverpool, England, 8/30/41. Singer, guitarist. The Searchers.

MCNEIL, MICK. Scotland, 7/20/58. Keyboardist. Simple Minds.

MCNICHOL, KRISTY. Los Angeles, CA, 9/11/62. Actor. Barbara Weston on *Empty Nest.*

MCPHERSON, GRAHAM. Hastings, England, 1/13/61. Singer. Madness.

MCVIE, CHRISTINE (Christine Perfect). Birmingham, England, 7/12/44. Keyboardist, singer. Fleetwood Mac.

MCVIE, JOHN. London, England, 11/26/45. Bassist. Fleetwood Mac.

MEADOWS, JAYNE (Jayne Cotter). Wu Chang, China, 9/27/24. Actor, quiz show regular, married to Steve Allen, sister of Audrey.

MEANEY, COLM. Dublin, Ireland, 1953. Actor. Miles O'Brien on *Star Trek: The Next Generation.*

MEARA, ANNE. Brooklyn, NY, 9/20/29. Actor, partner/married to Jerry Stiller, mother of Ben Stiller. *The Out-of-Towners.*

MEAT LOAF (Marvin Lee Aday). Dallas, TX, 9/27/51. Singer. *Bat out of Hell.*

MEDLEY, BILL. Santa Ana, CA, 9/19/40. Singer. The Righteous Brothers.

MEDRESS, HANK. Brooklyn, NY, 11/19/38. Tenor singer. The Tokens.

MEHTA, ZUBIN. Bombay, India, 4/29/36. Conductor.

MEINE, KLAUS. 5/25/48. Singer. Scorpions.

MEISNER, RANDY. Scottsbluff, NE, 3/8/47. Bassist, singer. The Eagles; Poco.

MELLENCAMP, JOHN. Seymour, IN, 10/7/51. Guitarist, singer, songwriter.

MENDOZA, MARK. Long Island, NY, 6/13/54. Bassist. Twisted Sister.

MENKEN, ALAN. New Rochelle, NY, 1949. Composer. *Beauty and the Beast.*

MERCHANT, JIMMY. New York, NY, 2/10/40. Singer. Frankie Lymon & The Teenagers.

MESSINA, JIM. Maywood, CA, 12/5/47. Guitarist, singer. Poco.

MESSNER, TAMMY FAYE. International Falls, MN, 3/7/42. Former wife of PTL founder Jim Bakker.

METCALF, LAURIE. Edwardsville, IL, 6/16/55. Actor. Jackie Conner Harris on *Roseanne.*

METHENY, PAT. Lee's Summit, MO, 8/12/54. Jazz guitarist. "Offramp."

MEYERS, ARI. San Juan, Puerto Rico, 4/6/69. Actor. Emma McArdle on *Kate & Allie.*

MEYERS, AUGIE. San Antonio, TX, 5/31/40. Keyboardist. Texas Tornados.

MIALL, TERRY LEE. England, 11/8/58. Drummer. Adam & The Ants.

MICHAEL, GEORGE (Georgios Kyriacou Panayiotou). London, England, 6/25/63. Singer, songwriter. Wham!

MICHAELS, LORNE Toronto, Canada, 11/17/44. Producer, writer. *Saturday Night Live.*

MICK (Michael Wilson). Amesbury, England, 3/4/44. Drummer. Dave Dee, Dozy, Beaky, Mick and Tich.

MIDORI. Osaka, Japan, 10/25/71. Violinist.

MIKE D. (Mike Diamond). New York, NY, 11/20/65. Rap artist. The Beastie Boys.

MILANO, FRED. The Bronx, NY, 8/26/40. Tenor singer. Dion & The Belmonts.

MILES, SARAH. Ingatestone, England, 12/31/41. Actor. *Ryan's Daughter.*

MILES, SYLVIA. New York, NY, 9/9/34. Actor. *Midnight Cowboy.*

MILES, VERA (Vera Ralston). Boise City, OK, 8/23/30. Actor. *Psycho.*

MILKEN, MICHAEL. Van Nuys, CA, 1946. Financier. Convicted of securities violations.

MILLER, ANN (Lucille Ann Collier). Chireno, TX, 4/12/23. Actor. *On the Town.*

MILLER, CHARLES. Olathe, KS, 6/2/39. Saxophonist, clarinetist. War.

MILLER, DENNIS. Pittsburgh, PA, 11/3/53. TV personality. *Saturday Night Live.*

MILLER, JERRY. Tacoma, WA, 7/10/43. Guitarist. Moby Grape.

MILLER, PENELOPE ANN. Santa Monica, CA, 1/13/64. Actor. *Carlito's Way.*

MILLER, STEVE. Milwaukee, WI, 10/5/43. Singer, guitarist. The Steve Miller Band.

MILLS, HAYLEY. London, England, 4/18/46. Actor, daughter of John Mills, sister of Juliet Mills. *The Parent Trap.*

MILLS, JOHN. Suffolk, England, 2/22/08. Actor, father of Hayley and Juliet Mills. *Ryan's Daughter.*

MILLS, JULIET. London, England, 11/21/41. Actor, daughter of John Mills, sister of Hayley Mills. *Nanny and the Professor.*

MILLS, MIKE. 12/17/58. Bassist. R.E.M.

MILLS, STEPHANIE. New York, NY, 3/22/57. Actor, singer. *The Wiz.*

MILLWARD, MIKE. Bromborough, England, 5/9/42. Guitarist, singer. The Fourmost.

MIMIEUX, YVETTE. Los Angeles, CA, 1/8/42. Actor. *The Black Hole.*

MINNELLI, LIZA. Los Angeles, CA, 3/12/46. Singer, actor, daughter of Vincente Minnelli and Judy Garland, half-sister of Lorna Luft. *Cabaret; The Sterile Cuckoo.*

MINOGUE, KYLIE. Melbourne, Australia, 5/28/68. Actor, singer.

MIOU-MIOU (Sylvette Hery). Paris, France, 2/22/50. Actor. *Going Places.*

MIRABELLA, GRACE. Maplewood, NJ, 6/10/29. Fashion editor, publishing executive. *Mirabella.*

MIRREN, HELEN. 7/26/45. Actor. *Prime Suspect.*

MITCHELL, JONI (Roberta Anderson). Fort McLeod, Canada, 11/7/43. Folk singer, songwriter.

MITCHELL, LIZ. Clarendon, Jamaica, 7/12/52. Singer. Boney M.

MITCHELL, MITCH (John Mitchell). Middlesex, England, 7/9/46. Drummer. The Jimi Hendrix Experience.

MITCHELL, NEIL. Helensborough, Scotland, 6/8/67. Keyboardist. Wet Wet Wet.

MITCHUM, JAMES. Los Angeles, CA, 5/8/41. Actor, son of Robert. *Thunder Road.*

MODINE, MATTHEW. Loma Linda, CA, 3/22/59. Actor. *Vision Quest.*

MOFFAT, DONALD. Plymouth, England, 12/26/30. Actor. *Clear and Present Danger.*

MOL, GRETCHEN. 11/8/72. Actor.

MOLL, RICHARD. Pasadena, CA, 1/13/43. Actor, stands 6' 8". Bailiff Nostradamus "Bull" Shannon on *Night Court.*

MOLLAND, JOEY. Liverpool, England, 6/21/48. Guitarist, keyboardist, singer. Badfinger.

MONARCH, MICHAEL. Los Angeles, CA, 7/5/50. Guitarist. Steppenwolf.

MONDALE, WALTER "FRITZ." Ceylon, MN, 1/5/28. Politician, former Vice President of the United States, former presidential candidate. Father of Eleanor.

MONEY, EDDIE (Eddie Mahoney). Brooklyn, NY, 3/21/49. Singer.

MONTALBAN, RICARDO. Mexico City, Mexico, 11/25/20. Actor. *Fantasy Island.*

MONTANA, JOE. New Eagle, PA, 6/11/56. Football great.

MONTGOMERY, GEORGE (George Letz). Brady, MT, 8/29/16. Actor. *The Texas Rangers.*

MONTGOMERY, JOHN MICHAEL. Lexington, KY, 1/20/65. Country singer.

MOODY, MICKY. 8/30/50. Guitarist. Whitesnake.

MOONEY, KEVIN. England, 5/5/62. Bassist. Adam & The Ants.

MOORE, DUDLEY. Dagenham, England, 4/19/35. Actor. *Arthur.*

MOORE, JULIANNE. 12/3/60. Actor. *Boogie Nights.*

MOORE, MARY TYLER. Brooklyn, NY, 12/29/36. Actor. *The Mary Tyler Moore Show.*

MOORE, MELBA (Beatrice Hill). New York, NY, 10/29/45. R&B singer, actor. *Purlie.*

MOORE, ROGER. London, England, 10/14/27. Actor, replaced Sean Connery as James Bond. *Live and Let Die.*

MOORE, SAM. Miami, FL, 10/12/35. Singer. Sam & Dave.

MORAN, ERIN. Burbank, CA, 10/18/61. Actor. Joanie Cunningham on *Happy Days.*

MORANIS, RICK. Toronto, Canada, 4/18/54. Actor, writer. *Honey, I Shrunk the Kids.*

MOREAU, JEANNE. Paris, France, 1/23/28. Actor. *Jules et Jim.*

MORENO, RITA (Rosita Dolores Alverio). Humacao, PR, 12/11/31. Actor. *West Side Story.*

MORGAN, LORRIE (Loretta Lynn Morgan). Nashville, TN, 6/27/59. Singer.

MORIARTY, CATHY. The Bronx, NY, 11/29/60. Actor. *Raging Bull.*

MORIARTY, MICHAEL. Detroit, MI, 4/5/41. Actor. *Law and Order.*

MORITA, NORIYUKI "PAT." Isleton, CA, 6/28/32. Actor. *The Karate Kid.*

MORRIS, STEPHEN. Macclesfield, England, 10/28/57. Drummer. New Order.

MORRISSEY (Stephen Morrissey). Manchester, England, 5/22/59. Singer. The Smiths.

MORROW, ROB. New Rochelle, NY, 9/21/62. Actor. *Northern Exposure.*

MORSE, DAVID. Hamilton, MA, 10/11/53. Actor. *St. Elsewhere.*

MORTON, JOE. New York, NY, 10/18/47. Actor. *Terminator 2: Judgment Day.*

MORVAN, FABRICE. Guadeloupe, 5/14/66. "Singer." Milli Vanilli.

MOSLEY, BOB. Paradise Valley, CA, 12/4/42. Bassist. Moby Grape.

MOSS, JON. Wandsworth, England, 9/11/57. Drummer. Culture Club.

MOSS, KATE. London, England, 1/16/74. Supermodel.

MOST, DONNY. New York, NY, 8/8/53. Actor. Ralph Malph on *Happy Days.*

MOSTEL, JOSH. New York, NY, 12/21/46. Actor. *City Slickers.*

MOULDING, COLIN. Swindon, England, 8/17/55. Bassist. singer. XTC.

MOUNT, DAVE. Carshalton, England, 3/3/47. Drummer, singer. Mud.

MOYERS, BILL. Hugo, OK, 6/5/34. Journalist, commentator. *Bill Moyers' Journal*.

MOYET, ALISON (Genevieve Moyet). Basildon, England, 6/18/61. Singer. Yazoo.

MUDD, ROGER. Washington, DC, 2/9/28. Broadcast journalist, newscaster.

MULDAUR, DIANA. New York, NY, 8/19/38. Actor. *L.A. Law; Star Trek: The Next Generation*.

MULGREW, KATE. Dubuque, IA, 4/29/55. Actor. Capt. Kathryn Janeway on *Star Trek: Voyager*.

MULHERN, MATT. Philadelphia, PA, 7/21/60. Actor. 2nd Lt. Gene Holowachuk on *Major Dad*.

MULL, MARTIN. Chicago, IL, 8/18/43. Actor. *Mary Hartman, Mary Hartman*.

MULLEN, LARRY JR. Dublin, Ireland, 10/31/61. Drummer. U2.

MULLIGAN, RICHARD. New York, NY, 11/13/32. Actor. Dr. Harry Weston on *Empty Nest*.

MUMY, BILLY. El Centro, CA, 2/1/54. Actor. *Lost in Space*.

MURPHY, MICHAEL. Los Angeles, CA, 5/5/38. Actor. *Manhattan*.

MURPHY, PETER. 7/11/57. Singer. Bauhaus.

MURRAY, DAVE. London, England, 12/23/58. Lead guitarist. Iron Maiden.

MUSIC, LORENZO. Brooklyn, NY, 5/2/37. Actor, writer. Carlton the Doorman on *Rhoda*.

NABORS, JIM. Sylacauga, GA, 6/12/32. Actor. Gomer Pyle on *The Andy Griffith Show*.

NADER, RALPH. Winsted, CT, 2/27/34. Political activist, author. *Unsafe at Any Speed*.

NAMATH, JOE. Beaver Falls, PA, 5/31/43. Football great, endorser.

NASH, BRIAN. Liverpool, England, 5/20/63. Guitarist. Frankie Goes to Hollywood.

NASH, GRAHAM. Blackpool, England, 2/2/42. Guitarist. The Hollies; Crosby, Stills, Nash & Young.

NAUGHTON, DAVID. West Hartford, CT, 2/13/51. Actor, brother of James. *An American Werewolf in London*.

NAUGHTON, JAMES. Middletown, CT, 7/6/45. Actor,

brother of David. *The Good Mother*.

NAVRATILOVA, MARTINA. Prague, Czechoslovakia, 10/18/56. Tennis player.

NEAL, PATRICIA. Packard, KY, 1/20/26. Actor. *Hud*.

NEGRON, CHUCK. The Bronx, NY, 6/8/42. Singer. Three Dog Night.

NEIL, VINCE (Vince Wharton). Hollywood, CA, 2/8/61. Singer. Mötley Crüe.

NEILL, SAM. Ireland, 9/14/47. Actor. *Jurassic Park*.

NELLIGAN, KATE. London, Canada, 3/16/51. Actor. *The Prince of Tides*.

NELSON, CRAIG T. Spokane, WA, 4/4/46. Actor, writer. Hayden Fox on *Coach*.

NELSON, DAVID. New York, NY, 10/24/36. Actor, son of Ozzie and Harriet, brother of Ricky. David Nelson on *The Adventures of Ozzie and Harriet*.

NELSON, JUDD. Portland, ME, 11/28/59. Actor. *The Breakfast Club*.

NELSON, SANDY. Santa Monica, CA, 12/1/38. Rock/jazz drummer.

NELSON, TRACY. Santa Monica, CA, 10/25/63. Actor, daughter of Rick Nelson. *Father Dowling Mysteries*.

NEMES, LES. Surrey, England, 12/5/60. Bassist. Haircut 100.

NESMITH, MIKE (Robert Nesmith). Houston, TX, 12/30/42. Singer, guitarist, actor. The Monkees.

NEVILLE, AARON New Orleans, LA, 1/24/41. Singer. The Neville Brothers.

NEVILLE, ART. New Orleans, LA, 12/17/37. Singer, keyboardist. The Neville Brothers.

NEVILLE, CHARLES. New Orleans, LA, 12/28/38. Saxophonist. The Neville Brothers.

NEVILLE, CYRIL. 1/10/48. Singer, percussionist. The Neville Brothers.

NEWHART, BOB (George Newhart). Chicago, IL, 9/5/29. Actor, comedian. *The Bob Newhart Show*.

NEWLEY, ANTHONY. Hackney, England, 9/24/31. Actor, composer. "The Candy Man."

NEWMAN, RANDY. Los Angeles, CA, 11/28/43. Singer, songwriter.

NEWTON, JUICE. Lakehurst, NJ, 2/18/52. Country singer. "Angel of the Morning."

NEWTON-JOHN, OLIVIA. Cambridge, England, 9/26/48. Singer, actor. *Grease*.

NGUYEN, DUSTIN. Saigon, Vietnam, 1962. Actor. *21 Jump Street*.

NICHOL, AL. Winston-Salem, NC, 3/31/46. Guitarist, keyboardist, singer. The Turtles.

NICKS, STEVIE. Phoenix, AZ, 5/26/48. Singer. Fleetwood Mac.

NIELSEN, LESLIE Regina, Canada, 2/11/26. Actor, writer. *The Naked Gun*.

NIELSEN, RICK. Rockford, IL, 12/22/46. Singer, guitarist. Cheap Trick.

NIELSON, BRIGITTE. Denmark, 7/15/63. Actor, formerly married to Sylvester Stallone. *Red Sonja*.

NIMOY, LEONARD. Boston, MA, 3/26/31. Actor, director. Mr. Spock on *Star Trek*.

NOIRET, PHILIPPE. Lille, France, 10/1/31. Actor. *Cinema Paradiso*.

NOLAN, MIKE. Dublin, Ireland, 12/7/54. Singer. Bucks Fizz.

NOONAN, PEGGY. New York, NY, 9/7/50. Author, presidential speechwriter. Responsible for phrase "a kinder, gentler nation."

NOONE, PETER. Manchester, England, 11/5/47. Singer. Herman's Hermits.

NORRIS, CHUCK (Carlos Ray). Ryan, OK, 3/10/40. Karate champion, actor. *Good Guys Wear Black*.

NORTH, OLIVER. San Antonio, TX, 10/7/43. Presidential aide, senatorial candidate. Iran-Contra.

NORTON, KEN. Jacksonville, IL, 8/9/45. Boxer, actor. *The Gong Show*.

NOURI, MICHAEL. Washington, DC, 12/9/45. Actor. *Flashdance*.

NOVAK, KIM (Marilyn Novak). Chicago, IL, 2/13/33. Actor. *Vertigo*.

NOVELLO, DON. Ashtabula, OH, 1/1/43. Actor. Father Guido Sarducci.

NUGENT, TED. Detroit, MI, 12/13/48. Hard rock guitarist, actor.

NUMAN, GARY (Gary Webb). Hammersmith, England, 3/8/58. Singer. "Cars."

O'CONNOR, CARROLL. New York, NY, 8/2/24. Actor. Archie Bunker on *All in the Family*.

O'CONNOR, DONALD. Chicago, IL, 8/28/25. Actor. *Singin' in the Rain*.

O'CONNOR, SANDRA DAY. El Paso, TX, 3/26/30. Supreme Court Justice.

O'CONNOR, SINEAD. Dublin, Ireland, 12/8/66. Singer.

O'HARA, BRIAN. Liverpool, England, 3/12/42. Guitarist, singer. The Fourmost.

O'HARA, CATHERINE. Toronto, Canada, 3/4/54. Actor. Mother in *Home Alone*.

O'HARA, MAUREEN (Maureen FitzSimons). Dublin, Ireland, 8/17/21. Actor. *How Green Was My Valley*.

O'NEAL, ALEXANDER. 11/14/53. Singer, songwriter.

O'NEAL, RYAN (Patrick Ryan O'Neal). Los Angeles, CA, 4/20/41. Actor, father of Tatum O'Neal. *Love Story*.

O'NEAL, TATUM. Los Angeles, CA, 11/5/63. Actor, daughter of Ryan, formerly married to John McEnroe. *Paper Moon*.

O'NEILL, ED. Youngstown, OH, 4/12/46. Actor. Al Bundy on *Married ... with Children*.

O'NEILL, JENNIFER. Rio de Janeiro, Brazil, 2/20/48. Actor, former model. *Summer of '42*.

O'NEILL, JOHN. 8/26/57. Guitarist. The Undertones.

O'SHEA, MILO. Dublin, Ireland, 6/2/26. Actor. *The Verdict*.

O'SULLIVAN, GILBERT (Raymond O'Sullivan). Waterford, Ireland, 12/1/46. Singer, songwriter.

O'SULLIVAN, MAUREEN. Byle, Ireland, 5/17/11. Actor, mother of Mia Farrow. *Hannah and Her Sisters*.

O'TOOLE, ANNETTE (Annette Toole). Houston, TX, 4/1/53. Actor. *Superman III*.

O'TOOLE, MARK. Liverpool, England, 1/6/64. Bassist. Frankie Goes to Hollywood.

O'TOOLE, PETER. Connemara, Ireland, 8/2/32. Actor. *Lawrence of Arabia*.

OAKEY, PHILIP. Sheffield, England, 10/2/55. Singer. The Human League.

OAKLEY, BERRY. Chicago, IL, 4/4/48. Bassist. The Allman Brothers Band.

OATES, JOHN. New York, NY, 4/7/48. Singer, guitarist. Hall & Oates.

OCASEK, RIC (Ric Otcasek). Baltimore, MD, 3/23/49. Singer, guitarist, married to Paulina Porizkova. The Cars.

OCEAN, BILLY (Leslie Charles). Fyzabad, Trinidad, 7/21/50. Rock/R&B singer, songwriter.

OLDFIELD, MIKE. Reading, England, 5/15/53. Bassist, composer. "Tubular Bells."

OLDMAN, GARY. New Cross, England, 3/21/58. Actor, formerly married to Uma Thurman. *Bram Stoker's Dracula.*

OLIN, KEN. Chicago, IL, 7/30/54. Actor, director. Michael Steadman on *thirtysomething.*

OLIN, LENA. Stockholm, Sweden, 3/22/55. Actor. *Havana.*

OLMOS, EDWARD JAMES. East Los Angeles, CA, 2/24/47. Actor. Martin Castillo on *Miami Vice.*

ONO, YOKO. 2/18/33. Singer, wife of John Lennon, mother of Julian Lennon and Sean Lennon.

ONTKEAN, MICHAEL. Vancouver, Canada, 1/24/46. Actor. *Twin Peaks.*

OPPENHEIMER, ALAN. New York, NY, 4/23/30. Actor. Gene Kinsella on *Murphy Brown.*

ORANGE, WALTER. Florida, 12/10/47. Singer, drummer. The Commodores.

ORBACH, JERRY. The Bronx, NY, 10/20/35. Actor. *Law and Order.*

ORLANDO, TONY (Michael Cassivitis). New York, NY, 4/3/44. Singer. Tony Orlando & Dawn.

ORMOND, JULIA. Epsom, England, 1/4/65. Actor. *Legends of the Fall.*

ORR, BENJAMIN (Benjamin Orzechowski). Cleveland, OH, 8/9/55. Singer, bass guitarist. The Cars.

ORZABAL, ROLAND (Roland Orzabal de la Quintana). Portsmouth, England,

8/22/61. Guitarist, keyboardist. Tears for Fears.

OSBORNE, JEFFREY. Providence, RI, 3/9/48. Singer, songwriter, drummer. L.T.D.

OSBOURNE, OZZY (John Michael Osbourne). Anston, England, 12/3/48. Singer. Black Sabbath.

OSGOOD, CHARLES. New York, NY, 1/8/33. Broadcast journalist, author.

OSKAR, LEE (Oskar Hansen). Copenhagen, Denmark, 3/24/46. Harmonicist. War.

OSMOND, ALAN. Ogden, UT, 6/22/49. Singer, member of the Osmond family. The Osmonds.

OSMOND, DONNY. Ogden, UT, 12/9/57. Singer, member of the Osmond family. *The Donny & Marie Show.*

OSMOND, JAY. Ogden, UT, 3/2/55. Singer, member of the Osmond family. The Osmonds.

OSMOND, MARIE (Olive Marie Osmond). Ogden, UT, 10/13/59. Singer, member of the Osmond family. *The Donny & Marie Show.*

OSMOND, MERRILL. Ogden, UT, 4/30/53. Singer, member of the Osmond family. The Osmonds.

OSMOND, WAYNE. Ogden, UT, 8/28/51. Singer, member of the Osmond family. The Osmonds.

OTIS, CARRE. 9/28/68. Model, actor, married to Mickey Rourke.

OTIS, JOHNNY (John Veliotes). Vallejo, CA, 12/28/21. R&B drummer, pianist, and songwriter.

OWEN, RANDY. Fort Payne, AL, 12/13/49. Singer, guitarist. Alabama.

OWENS, SHIRLEY. Passaic, NJ, 6/10/41. Lead singer. The Shirelles.

OVITZ, MICHAEL. Encino, CA, 12/14/46. Studio executive.

OXENBERG, CATHERINE. New York, NY, 9/21/61. Actor. Amanda Carrington on *Dynasty.*

OZ, FRANK. Hereford, England, 5/25/44. Puppeteer, film director. *The Muppet Show.*

PACULA, JOANNA. Tamaszow Lubelski, Poland, 1/2/57. Actor. *Gorky Park.*

PAGE, JIMMY. Heston, England, 1/9/44. Guitarist. Led Zeppelin.

PAICE, IAN. Nottingham, England, 6/29/48. Drummer. Deep Purple.

PAICH, DAVID. Los Angeles, CA, 6/25/54. Keyboardist, singer. Toto.

PALANCE, JACK (Walter Palanuik). Lattimer, PA, 2/18/20. Actor. *City Slickers.*

PALIN, MICHAEL. Sheffield, England, 5/5/43. Actor, writer. *Monty Python's Flying Circus.*

PALMER, BETSY. East Chicago, IN, 11/1/26. Actor, panelist on *I've Got a Secret.*

PALMER, CARL. Birmingham, England, 3/20/51. Drummer. Emerson, Lake & Palmer; Asia.

PALMER, JOHN. 5/25/43. Keyboardist. Family.

PALMER, ROBERT (Alan Palmer). Batley, England, 1/19/49. Singer, songwriter. "Addicted to Love."

PALMINTERI, CHAZZ (Chalogero Lorenzo Palminteri). Bronx, NY, 5/15/51. Actor, playwright, screenwriter. *A Bronx Tale.*

PANKOW, JAMES. Chicago, IL, 8/20/47. Trombonist. Chicago.

PANOZZO, CHUCK. Chicago, IL, 9/20/47. Bassist. Styx.

PAQUIN, ANNA. Wellington, New Zealand, 7/24/82. Actor. *The Piano.*

PARAZAIDER, WALTER. Chicago, IL, 3/14/45. Saxophonist. Chicago.

PARE, MICHAEL. Brooklyn, NY, 10/9/59. Actor. *Eddie and the Cruisers.*

PARFITT, RICK (Richard Harrison). Redhill, England, 10/25/43. Guitarist, singer. Status Quo.

PARILLAUD, ANNE. France, 1961. Actor. *La Femme Nikita.*

PARKER, FESS. Fort Worth, TX, 8/16/24. Actor. *Daniel Boone.*

PARKER, GRAHAM. Deepcut, England, 11/18/50. Singer. Graham Parker & The Rumour.

PARKER, JAMESON. Baltimore, MD, 11/18/47. Actor. *Simon and Simon.*

PARKER, MARY-LOUISE. Ft. Jackson, SC, 8/2/64. Actor. *Fried Green Tomatoes.*

PARKER, RAY JR. Detroit, MI, 5/1/54. Singer, songwriter. "Ghostbusters."

PARKER, TREY. 10/19/69. Actor, cartoonist. *South Park.*

PARSONS, ESTELLE. Lynn, MA, 11/20/27. Actor. *Roseanne.*

PARTRIDGE, ANDY. Malta, 11/11/53. Guitarist, singer. XTC.

PASTORELLI, ROBERT. 6/21/54. Actor. *Murphy Brown.*

PATERSON, GERRY. Winnepeg, Canada, 5/26/45. Drummer. The Guess Who.

PATINKIN, MANDY (Mandel Patinkin). Chicago, IL, 11/30/52. Actor. *Yentl.*

PATRIC, JASON (Jason Patrick Miller). Queens, NY, 6/17/66. Actor. *Rush.*

PATRICK, ROBERT. Marietta, GA, 1959. Actor. Evil T-1000 in *Terminator 2: Judgment Day.*

PATTEN, EDWARD. Atlanta, GA, 8/2/39. Singer. Gladys Knight & The Pips.

PATTERSON, LORNA. Whittier, CA, 6/1/57. Actor. *Private Benjamin.*

PATTERSON, MELODY. Los Angeles, CA, 1947. Actor. Wrangler Jane on *F Troop.*

PATTINSON, LES. Ormskirk, England, 4/18/58. Bassist. Echo & The Bunnymen.

PATTON, MIKE. Eureka, CA, 1/27/68. Lead singer. Faith No More.

PATTON, WILL. Charleston, SC, 6/14/54. Actor. *No Way Out.*

PAYCHECK, JOHNNY (Donald Eugene Lytle). Greenfield, OH, 5/31/41. Singer. "Take This Job and Shove It."

PAYNE, BILL. Waco, TX, 3/12/49. Keyboardist. Little Feat.

PAYS, AMANDA. Berkshire, England, 6/6/59. Actor, married to Corbin Bernsen. *The Flash.*

PAYTON, DENIS. Walthamstow, England, 8/11/43. Saxophonist. The Dave Clark Five.

PAYTON, WALTER. Columbia, MS, 6/25/54. Football player.

PEARSON, DELROY. Romford, England, 4/11/70. Singer. Five Star.

PEARSON, DENIECE. Romford, England, 6/13/68. Lead singer. Five Star.

PEARSON, DORIS. Romford, England, 6/8/66. Singer. Five Star.

PEARSON, LORRAINE. Romford, England, 8/10/67. Singer. Five Star.

PEARSON, STEDMAN. Romford, England, 6/29/64. Singer. Five Star.

PEART, NEIL. Hamilton, Canada, 9/12/52. Drummer. Rush.

PECK, GREGORY (Eldred Peck). La Jolla, CA, 4/5/16. Actor, producer. *To Kill a Mockingbird.*

PEEK, DAN. Panama City, FL, 11/1/50. Singer, guitarist. America.

PELE, PEROLA NEGRA (Edson Arantes do Nascimento). Tres Coracoes, Brazil, 10/23/40. Soccer legend.

PELLOW, MARTI (Mark McLoughlin). Clydebank, Scotland, 3/23/66. Singer. Wet Wet Wet.

PENA, ELIZABETH. Elizabeth, NJ, 9/23/61. Actor. *La Bamba.*

PENDER, MIKE (Michael Prendergast). Liverpool, England, 3/3/42. Singer, lead guitarist. The Searchers.

PENDERGRASS, TEDDY. Philadelphia, PA, 3/26/50. R&B singer, songwriter, drummer.

PENDLETON, AUSTIN. Warren, OH, 3/27/40. Actor. *What's Up Doc?*

PENDLETON, BRIAN. Wolverhampton, England, 4/13/44. Guitarist. The Pretty Things.

PENGILLY, KIRK. 7/4/58. Guitarist, saxophonist, singer. INXS.

PENNY, JOE. London, England, 9/14/56. Actor. Jake Styles on *Jake and the Fatman.*

PEPA (Sanda Denton). Queens, NY, 9/9/64. Rap artist. Salt-N-Pepa.

PEREZ, ROSIE. Brooklyn, NY, 9/4/66. Actor, choreographer. *Do the Right Thing.*

PERKINS, ELIZABETH. Queens, NY, 11/18/61. Actor. *Big.*

PERLMAN, RHEA. Brooklyn, NY, 3/31/48. Actor, married to Danny DeVito. Carla Tortelli LeBec on *Cheers.*

PERLMAN, RON. New York, NY, 4/13/50. Actor. The Beast in *Beauty and the Beast.*

PEROT, HENRY ROSS. Texarkana, TX, 6/27/30. Self-made billionaire businessman, former presidential candidate.

PERRINE, VALERIE. Galveston, TX, 9/3/43. Actor. *Lenny.*

PERRY, JOE. Boston, MA, 9/10/50. Guitarist. Aerosmith.

PERRY, LUKE (Perry Coy III). Fredericktown, OH, 10/11/66. Actor. *Beverly Hills 90210.*

PERRY, STEVE. Hanford, CA, 1/22/53. Singer. Journey.

PERRY, WILLIAM "THE REFRIGERATOR." Aiken, SC, 12/16/62. Very large football player. Chicago Bears.

PESCOW, DONNA. Brooklyn, NY, 3/24/54. Actor. *Saturday Night Fever.*

PETERS, BROCK. New York, NY, 7/2/27. Actor, singer. *To Kill a Mockingbird.*

PETERS, MIKE. Prestatyn, Wales, 2/25/59. Guitarist, singer. The Alarm.

PETERSEN, WILLIAM. Chicago, IL, 1953. Actor. *To Live and Die in L.A.*

PETERSON, DEBBI. Los Angeles, CA, 8/22/61. Drummer, singer. The Bangles.

PETERSON, SYLVIA. New York, NY, 9/30/46. Singer. The Chiffons.

PETERSON, VICKI. Los Angeles, CA, 1/11/58. Guitarist, singer. The Bangles.

PETERSSON, TOM. Rockford, IL, 5/9/50. Singer, bassist. Cheap Trick.

PETTY, LORI. Chattanooga, TN. Actor. *A League of Their Own.*

PFEIFFER, DEDEE. 1/1/64. Actor, sister of Michelle Pfeiffer. *Cybill.*

PFISTERER, ALBAN. Switzerland, 1947. Drummer, keyboardist. Love.

PHANTOM, SLIM JIM (Jim McDonnell). 3/20/61. Drummer. The Stray Cats.

PHAIR, LIZ. New Haven, CT, 4/17/67. Singer, songwriter. *Exile in Guyville.*

PHILIP, PRINCE (Philip Mountbatten). Corfu, Greece, 6/10/21. Husband of Queen Elizabeth II, Duke of Edinburgh.

PHILLIPS, CHYNNA. Los Angeles, CA, 1/12/68. Singer, half-sister of Mackenzie, daughter of John and Michelle, married to Billy Baldwin. Wilson Phillips.

PHILLIPS, JOHN. Parris Island, SC, 8/30/35. Singer, formerly married to Michelle, father of Mackenzie and Chynna. The Mamas & the Papas.

PHILLIPS, LOU DIAMOND (Lou Upchurch). Philippines, 2/17/62. Actor. *La Bamba.*

PHILLIPS, MACKENZIE (Laura Mackenzie Phillips). Alexandria, VA, 11/10/59. Actor, daughter of John Phillips, half-sister of Chynna. Julie Cooper Horvath on *One Day at a Time.*

PHILLIPS, MICHELLE (Holly Gilliam). Santa Ana, CA, 6/4/44. Actor, formerly married to John, mother of Chynna. Anne Matheson on *Knots Landing.*

PHILTHY ANIMAL (Philip Taylor). Chesterfield, England, 9/21/54. Drummer. Motorhead.

PICKETT, WILSON. Prattville, AL, 3/18/41. Singer, songwriter. "In the Midnight Hour."

PIERSON, KATE. Weehawken, NJ, 4/27/48. Organist, singer. The B-52's.

PINCHOT, BRONSON. New York, NY, 5/20/59. Actor. Balki Bartokomous on *Perfect Strangers.*

PINDER, MIKE. Birmingham, England, 12/12/42. Keyboardist. The Moody Blues.

PINKNEY, BILL. Sumter, NC, 8/15/25. Bassist. The Drifters.

PIRNER, DAVE. Green Bay, WI, 4/16/64. Singer, songwriter, guitarist. Soul Asylum.

PIRRONI, MARCO. England, 4/27/59. Guitarist. Adam & The Ants.

PISCOPO, JOE. Passaic, NJ, 6/17/51. Actor. *Saturday Night Live.*

PITNEY, GENE. Hartford, CT, 2/17/41. Singer, songwriter.

PLACE, MARY KAY. Tulsa, OK, 9/23/47. Actor. *The Big Chill.*

PLANT, ROBERT. Bromwich, England, 8/20/48. Singer. Led Zeppelin.

PLATT, OLIVER. 1/12/60. Actor. *Flatliners.*

PLESHETTE, JOHN. New York, NY, 7/27/42. Actor. Richard Avery on *Knots Landing.*

PLESHETTE, SUZANNE. New York, NY, 1/31/37. Actor. Emily Hartley on *The Bob Newhart Show.*

PLOWRIGHT, JOAN. Brigg, England, 10/28/29. Actor, widow of Laurence Olivier. *Enchanted April.*

PLUMB, EVE. Burbank, CA, 4/29/58. Actor. Jan Brady on *The Brady Bunch.*

PLUMMER, AMANDA. New York, NY, 3/23/57. Actor, daughter of Christopher Plummer. *The Fisher King.*

PLUMMER, CHRISTOPHER. Toronto, Canada, 12/13/27. Actor, father of Amanda Plummer. Baron von Trapp in *The Sound of Music.*

POINTER, ANITA. East Oakland, CA, 1/23/48. Singer. Pointer Sisters.

POINTER, BONNIE. East Oakland, CA, 6/11/51. Singer. Pointer Sisters.

POINTER, JUNE. East Oakland, CA, 11/30/54. Singer. Pointer Sisters.

POINTER, RUTH. East Oakland, CA, 3/19/46. Singer. Pointer Sisters.

POITIER, SIDNEY. Miami, FL, 2/20/27. Actor. *Guess Who's Coming to Dinner.*

POLANSKI, ROMAN. Paris, France, 8/18/33. Director, writer. *Rosemary's Baby.*

POLLAK, KEVIN. 10/30/57. Actor.

POLLACK, SYDNEY. South Bend, Indiana, 7/1/34. Director, producer, actor. *The Way We Were.*

POLLAN, TRACY. New York, NY, 6/22/60. Actor, married to Michael J. Fox. *Family Ties.*

POOLE, BRIAN. Barking, England, 11/2/41. Singer. Brian Poole & The Tremeloes.

POP, IGGY (James Osterburg). Ann Arbor, MI, 4/21/47. Singer, songwriter.

POPCORN, FAITH. New York, NY, 5/11/43. Trend analyst, consultant.

PORCARO, STEVE. Los Angeles, CA, 9/2/57. Keyboardist, singer. Toto.

PORTZ, CHUCK. Santa Monica, CA, 3/28/45. Bassist. The Turtles.

POST, MARKIE. Palo Alto, CA, 11/4/50. Actor. Christine Sullivan on *Night Court.*

POTTER, CAROL. Tenafly, NJ, 5/21/48. Actor. *Beverly Hills 90210.*

POTTS, ANNIE. Nashville, TN, 10/28/52. Actor. Mary Jo Shively on *Designing Women*.

POUNDSTONE, PAULA. Alabama, 12/29/60. Comedian, actor.

POVICH, MAURY. Washington, DC, 1/17/39. Talk show host, married to Connie Chung. *A Current Affair*.

POWELL, BILLY. Florida, 6/3/52. Keyboardist. Lynyrd Skynyrd.

POWELL, COLIN. New York, NY, 4/5/37. Military leader.

POWELL, DON. 9/10/50. Drummer. Slade.

POWERS, STEPHANIE (Stefania Federkiewicz). Hollywood, CA, 11/12/42. Actor. Jennifer on *Hart to Hart*.

POWTER, SUSAN. Sydney, Australia, 1957. Weight-loss expert. *Stop the Insanity!*

PRENTISS, PAULA (Paula Ragusa). San Antonio, TX, 3/4/38. Actor. *What's New Pussycat?*

PRESLEY, PRISCILLA. Brooklyn, NY, 5/24/45. Actor, producer, married and divorced Elvis Presley.

PRESLEY, REG (Reginald Ball). Andover, England, 6/12/43. Singer. The Troggs.

PRESTON, KELLY. Honolulu, HI, 10/13/62. Actor, married to John Travolta. *52 Pick-Up*.

PRICE, ALAN. Fairfield, Durham, 4/19/41. Keyboardist. The Animals.

PRICE, LLOYD. Kenner, LA, 5/9/33. Singer, songwriter.

PRICE, RICK. 6/10/44. Bassist. Wizzard.

PRIDE, CHARLEY. Sledge, MS, 3/18/38. Country singer, songwriter.

PRIEST, STEVE. London, England, 2/23/50. Bassist. Sweet.

PRIESTLEY, JASON. Vancouver, Canada, 8/28/69. Actor. Brandon Walsh on *Beverly Hills 90210*.

PRIESTMAN, HENRY. 7/21/58. Singer. The Christians.

PRIME, JAMES. Kilmarnock, Scotland, 11/3/60. Keyboardist. Deacon Blue.

PRINCE MARK D. 2/19/60. Rap artist. Fat Boys.

PRINCIPAL, VICTORIA. Fukuoka, Japan, 1/3/50. Actor. Pam Ewing on *Dallas*.

PRITCHARD, BARRY. Birmingham, England, 4/3/44. Guitarist, singer. The Fortunes.

PROBY, P. J. (James Smith). Houston, TX, 11/6/38. Singer, actor.

PRYCE, JONATHAN. North Wales, 6/1/47. Actor. *Miss Saigon*.

PRYOR, NICHOLAS. Baltimore, MD, 1/28/35. Actor. *Risky Business*.

PRYOR, RICHARD. Peoria, IL, 12/1/40. Actor. *Stir Crazy*.

PUERTA, JOE. 7/2/51. Bassist, singer. Bruce Hornsby & The Range.

PULLMAN, BILL. Hornell, NY, 12/17/53. Actor. *While You Were Sleeping*.

PURCELL, SARAH. Richmond, IN, 10/8/48. TV personality. Cohost on *Real People*.

QADDAFI, MUAMMAR. Sirta, Libya, 1942. Political leader. Libyan head of state.

QUAID, RANDY. Houston, TX, 10/1/50. Actor, brother of Dennis. *The Last Picture Show*.

QUAIFE, PETE. Tavistock, England, 12/31/43. Bassist. The Kinks.

QUATRO, SUZI (Suzi Quatrocchio). Detroit, MI, 6/3/50. Singer, songwriter, actor.

QUAYLE, DAN. Indianapolis, IN, 2/4/47. Vice president under George Bush.

QUAYLE, MARILYN. Indianapolis, IN, 7/29/49. Lawyer, author, married to Dan. *Embrace the Serpent*.

QUEEN LATIFAH. 3/18/70. Singer, actor. *Living Single*.

QUINLAN, KATHLEEN. Mill Valley, CA, 11/19/54. Actor. *Apollo 13*.

QUINN, AIDAN. Chicago, IL, 3/8/59. Actor. *The Playboys*. Married to Elizabeth Bracco.

QUINN, ANTHONY. Chihuahua, Mexico, 4/21/15. Actor. *Zorba the Greek*.

QUINN, DEREK. Manchester, England, 5/24/42. Lead guitarist. Freddie & The Dreamers.

QUIVERS, ROBIN. 8/8/52. Radio personality, author. *The Howard Stern Show*.

RAFFERTY, GERRY. Paisley, Scotland, 4/16/47. Singer, songwriter. "Baker Street."

RAFFI. Cairo, Egypt, 7/8/48. Singer, songwriter, children's performer. *Everything Grows*.

RAFFIN, DEBORAH. Los Angeles, CA, 3/13/53. Actor. *Once Is Not Enough*.

RALPH, SHERYL LEE. Waterbury, CT, 12/30/56. Actor. *The Distinguished Gentleman*.

RALPHS, MICK. Hereford, England, 3/31/44. Guitarist. Mott The Hoople; Bad Company.

RAMIS, HAROLD. Chicago, IL, 11/21/44. Writer, director, actor. Egon Spengler in *Ghostbusters*.

RAMONE, DEE DEE (Douglas Colvin). Fort Lee, VA, 9/18/52. Bassist. The Ramones.

RAMONE, JOEY (Jeffrey Hyman). Forest Hills, NY, 5/19/52. Singer. The Ramones.

RAMONE, JOHNNY (John Cummings). Long Island, NY, 10/8/48. Guitarist. The Ramones.

RAMONE, TOMMY (Thomas Erdelyi). Budapest, Hungary, 1/29/49. Drummer. The Ramones.

RAMOS, LARRY JR. (Hilario Ramos Jr.). Kauai, HI, 4/19/42. Singer, guitarist. The Association.

RAMPLING, CHARLOTTE. Surmer, England, 2/5/46. Actor. *The Verdict*.

RAMSEY, AL. New Jersey, 7/27/43. Guitarist. Gary Lewis & The Playboys.

RANDALL, TONY (Leonard Rosenberg). Tulsa, OK, 2/26/20. Actor. Felix Unger on *The Odd Couple*.

RAPHAEL, SALLY JESSY. Easton, PA, 2/25/43. talk show hostess. *Sally Jessy Raphäel*.

RAPP, DANNY. Philadelphia, PA, 5/10/41. Lead singer. Danny & The Juniors.

RAREBELL, HERMAN. 11/18/49. Drummer. Scorpions.

RASCHE, DAVID. St. Louis, MO, 8/7/44. Actor. *Sledge Hammer*.

RASHAD, AHMAD. Portland, OR, 11/19/49. Football player, sportscaster, husband of Phylicia.

RASHAD, PHYLICIA. Houston, TX, 6/19/48. Actor, sister of Debbie Allen, wife of Ahmad. Clair Huxtable on *The Cosby Show*.

RATZENBERGER, JOHN. Bridgeport, CT, 4/6/47. Actor. Cliff Claven on *Cheers*.

RAWLS, LOU. Chicago, IL, 12/1/36. R&B singer. "Lady Love."

RAY, JAMES EARL. Alton, IL, 3/10/28. Assassin. Killed Martin Luther King Jr.

REA, CHRIS. Middlesbrough, England, 3/4/51. Singer, songwriter, guitarist.

REAGAN, NANCY. New York, NY, 7/6/21. Former First Lady, married to president Ronald Reagan.

REAGAN, RONALD. Tampico, IL, 2/6/11. Politician, actor, father of Ron Jr., husband of Nancy. Fortieth U.S. president. *Bedtime for Bonzo*.

REAGAN, RONALD JR. Los Angeles, CA, 5/20/58. Performer, son of former president Ronald Reagan.

REASON, REX. Berlin, Germany, 11/30/28. Actor. *This Island Earth*.

RECORD, EUGENE. 12/23/40. Lead singer. The Chi-Lites.

REDDING, NOEL. Folkestone, England, 12/25/45. Bassist. The Jimi Hendrix Experience.

REDDY, HELEN. Melbourne, Australia, 10/25/41. Pop singer. *The Helen Reddy Show*.

REDGRAVE, CORIN. London, England, 6/16/39. Actor, brother of Lynn and Vanessa. *A Man for All Seasons*.

REDGRAVE, LYNN. London, England, 3/8/43. Actor, sister of Corin and Vanessa. *House Calls*.

REDGRAVE, VANESSA. London, England, 1/30/37. Actor, sister of Corin and Lynn. *Playing for Time*.

REED, LOU (Louis Firbank). Long Island, NY, 3/2/43. Singer, songwriter. The Velvet Underground.

REED, PAMELA. Tacoma, WA, 4/2/53. Actor. *The Right Stuff*.

REEMS, HARRY (Herbert Streicher). The Bronx, NY, 8/27/47. Actor. *Deep Throat*.

REESE, DELLA. 7/6/32. Actor. *Touched By An Angel*.

REEVES, MARTHA. Alabama, 7/18/41. Lead singer. Martha & The Vandellas.

REEVES, STEVE. Glasgow, MT, 1/21/26. Actor. *Hercules*.

REGALBUTO, JOE. Brooklyn, NY. Actor. Frank Fontana on *Murphy Brown*.

REID, DON. Staunton, VA, 6/5/45. Musician, brother of Harold. Statler Brothers.

REID, HAROLD. Staunton, VA, 8/21/39. Musician, brother of Don. Statler Brothers.

REID, JIM. East Kilbride, Scotland, 1961. Guitarist, singer. The Jesus & Mary Chain.

REID, TIM. Norfolk, VA, 12/19/44. Actor, producer. Gordon "Venus Flytrap" Sims on *WKRP in Cincinnati*.

REID, WILLIAM. East Kilbride, Scotland, 1958. Guitarist, singer. The Jesus & Mary Chain.

REINER, CARL. New York, NY, 3/20/22. Actor, writer, and director. *The Dick Van Dyke Show*.

REINER, ROB. New York, NY, 3/6/45. Actor, writer, producer, director, son of Carl, formerly married to Penny Marshall. Mike Stivic on *All in the Family*.

REINHOLD, JUDGE (Edward Ernest Reinhold Jr.). Wilmington, DE, 5/21/57. Actor. Rosewood in *Beverly Hills Cop*.

REINKING, ANN. Seattle, WA, 11/10/49. Actor, dancer. *Annie*.

REITMAN, IVAN. Komarno, Czechoslovakia, 10/26/46. Director, producer. *Ghostbusters*.

REVERE, PAUL. Harvard, NE, 1/7/38. Keyboardist. Paul Revere & The Raiders.

REYNOLDS, DEBBIE (Mary Frances Reynolds). El Paso, TX, 4/1/32. Actor, formerly married to Eddie Fisher, mother of Carrie Fisher. *Singin' in the Rain*.

RHAMES, VING. 5/12/59. Actor. *Only in America: The Don King Story*.

RHODES, NICK (Nicholas Bates). Mosely, England, 6/8/62. Keyboardist. Duran Duran.

RIBEIRO, ALFONSO. New York, NY, 9/21/71. Actor, dancer. *Fresh Prince of Bel Air*.

RICH, ADAM. New York, NY, 10/12/68. Actor. Nicholas Bradford on *Eight Is Enough*.

RICHARD, CLIFF (Harry Webb). Lucknow, India, 10/14/40. Singer, drummer. The Shadows.

RICHARDS, KEITH. Dartford, England, 12/18/43. Guitarist. The Rolling Stones.

RICHARDSON, MIRANDA. Lancashire, England, 3/3/58. Actor. *The Crying Game*.

RICHARDSON, SUSAN. Coatesville, PA, 3/11/52. Actor. Susan Bradford on *Eight Is Enough*.

RICHIE, LIONEL. Tuskegee, AL, 6/20/49. Singer, songwriter. The Commodores.

RICHRATH, GARY. Peoria, IL, 10/18/49. Guitarist. REO Speedwagon.

RICKLES, DON. New York, NY, 5/8/26. Actor. *The Don Rickles Show*.

RICKMAN, ALAN. Hammersmith, England, 1946. Actor. *Die Hard*.

RIDGELEY, ANDREW. Windlesham, England, 1/26/63. Guitarist. Wham!

RIEGERT, PETER. New York, NY, 4/11/47. Actor. *Crossing Delancey*.

RIGBY, CATHY. Long Beach, CA, 12/12/52. Gymnast, actor.

RIGG, DIANA. Doncaster, England, 7/20/38. Actor. Emma Peel on *The Avengers*.

RIGGS, BOBBY. Los Angeles, CA, 2/25/18. Tennis player, defeated by Billie Jean King.

RILEY, PAT. Rome, NY, 3/20/45. Basketball coach. Former New York Knicks coach.

RINGWALD, MOLLY. Sacramento, CA, 2/18/68. Actor. *Sixteen Candles*.

RITTER, JOHN. Burbank, CA, 9/17/48. Actor, producer. Jack Tripper on *Three's Company*.

RIVERA, CHITA. Washington, DC, 1/23/33. Singer.

RIVERS, JOHNNY (John Ramistella). New York, NY, 11/7/42. Soul/rock singer, songwriter.

RIZZUTO, PHIL. New York, NY, 9/25/18. Baseball great, sports announcer.

ROBARDS, JASON. Chicago, IL, 7/26/22. Actor, formerly married to Lauren Bacall. *Inherit the Wind*.

ROBERTS, ERIC. Biloxi, MS, 4/18/56. Actor, brother of Julia. *The Pope of Greenwich Village*.

ROBERTS, ORAL. Ada, OK, 1/24/18. Evangelist. Oral Roberts University.

ROBERTS, TANYA (Tanya Leigh). The Bronx, NY, 10/15/55. Actor. *Charlie's Angels*.

ROBERTS, TONY. New York, NY, 10/22/39. Actor. *Play It Again, Sam*.

ROBERTS, XAVIER. Cleveland, GA, 10/31/55. Businessman. Creator of Cabbage Patch Kids.

ROBERTSON, BRIAN. Glasgow, Scotland, 9/12/56. Guitarist. Thin Lizzy.

ROBERTSON, CLIFF. La Jolla, CA, 9/9/23. Actor. *Charly*.

ROBERTSON, PAT (Marion Gordon Robertson). Lexington, VA, 3/22/30. Evangelist, TV personality. Founder of Christian Broadcasting Network.

ROBERTSON, ROBBIE (Jaime Robertson). Toronto, Canada, 7/5/44. Guitarist, singer. The Band.

ROBINSON, CHRIS. Atlanta, GA, 12/20/66. Singer. The Black Crowes.

ROBINSON, CYNTHIA. Sacramento, CA, 1/12/46. Trumpeter. Sly & The Family Stone.

ROBINSON, JAY. New York, NY, 4/14/30. Actor. *The Robe*.

ROBINSON, RICH. Atlanta, GA, 5/24/69. Guitarist. The Black Crowes.

ROBINSON, SMOKEY (William Robinson). Detroit, MI, 2/19/40. Motown singer, songwriter. Smokey Robinson & The Miracles.

ROCKER, LEE (Leon Drucher). 1961. Double bassist. The Stray Cats.

ROCKWELL (Kenneth Gordy). Detroit, MI, 3/15/64. Singer, son of Berry Gordy. "Somebody's Watching Me."

RODGERS, NILE. New York, NY, 9/19/52. Guitarist. Chic.

RODGERS, PAUL. Middlesbrough, England, 12/17/49. Singer. Free; Bad Company.

RODMAN, DENNIS Trenton, NJ, 5/13/61. Basketball player. Married to Carmen Electra.

ROE, TOMMY. Atlanta, GA, 5/9/42. Singer, songwriter.

ROGERS, KENNY. Houston, TX, 8/21/38. Country singer, actor. "The Gambler."

ROGERS, MIMI. Coral Gables, FL, 1/27/55. Actor. Formerly married to Tom Cruise. *Someone To Watch Over Me*.

ROGERS, FRED. Latrobe, PA, 3/20/28. Children's host, producer. *Mr. Rogers' Neighborhood*.

ROGERS, ROY (Leonard Slye). Cincinnati, OH, 11/5/12. TV cowboy, singer. *Happy Trails with Roy and Dale*.

ROGERS, WAYNE. Birmingham, AL, 4/7/33. Actor. Trapper John on *M*A*S*H*.

ROGERS, WILL JR. New York, NY, 10/20/12. Actor, lecturer. *The Story of Will Rogers*.

ROLLE, ESTHER. Pompano Beach, FL, 11/8/22. Actor. *Driving Miss Daisy*.

RONSTADT, LINDA. Tucson, AZ, 7/15/46. Singer, actor. *The Pirates of Penzance*.

ROONEY, ANDY. Albany, NY, 1/14/19. News commentator. *60 Minutes*.

ROONEY, MICKEY (Joe Yule Jr.). Brooklyn, NY, 9/23/20. Actor. *National Velvet*.

ROSE, AXL (William Bailey). Lafayette, IN, 1962. Singer. Guns N' Roses.

ROSE, PETE. Cincinnati, OH, 4/14/41. Baseball player and manager. Cincinnati Reds.

ROSS, KATHARINE. Hollywood, CA, 1/29/43. Actor. *The Graduate*.

ROSS, MARION. Albert Lea, MN, 10/25/28. Actor. Marion Cunningham on *Happy Days*.

ROSS, RICKY. Dundee, Scotland, 12/22/57. Singer. Deacon Blue.

ROSSELLINI, ISABELLA. Rome, Italy, 6/18/52. Actor, formerly married to Martin Scorsese. *Blue Velvet*.

ROSSI, FRANCIS. Forest Hill, England, 4/29/49. Guitarist, singer. Status Quo.

ROSSINGTON, GARY. Jacksonville, FL, 12/4/51. Guitarist. Lynyrd Skynyrd.

ROTH, DAVID LEE. Bloomington, IN, 10/10/54. Singer. Van Halen.

ROTH, TIM. London, England, 1961. Actor. *Reservoir Dogs*.

ROTHERY, STEVE. Brampton, England, 11/25/59. Guitarist. Marillion.

ROTHWELL, RIC. Stockport, England, 3/11/44. Drummer. Wayne Fontana & The Mindbenders.

ROUNDTREE, RICHARD. New Rochelle, NY, 9/7/42. Actor. *Shaft.*

ROURKE, MICKEY. Schenectady, NY, 9/16/56. Actor, married to Carre Otis. *9 1/2 Weeks.*

ROWLAND, KEVIN. Wolverhampton, England, 8/17/53. Singer, guitarist. Dexy's Midnight Runners.

ROWLANDS, GENA. Cambria, WI, 6/19/30. Actor. *Gloria.*

RUCKER, DARIUS Charleston, SC, 5/13/66. Singer, songwriter, guitarist. Hootie & The Blowfish.

RUDD, PHILIP. Australia, 5/19/46. Drummer. AC/DC.

RUDNER, RITA. Miami, FL, 9/11/55. Actor, comedian.

RUEHL, MERCEDES. Queens, NY, 2/28/52. Actor. *Lost in Yonkers.*

RUFFIN, DAVID. Meridian, MS, 1/18/41. Singer. The Temptations.

RUNDGREN, TODD. Philadelphia, PA, 6/22/48. Singer, songwriter.

RUSH, GEOFFREY Toowoomba, Australia, 7/6/51. Actor. *Shine.*

RUSHDIE, SALMAN. Bombay, India, 6/19/47. Author. *The Satanic Verses.*

RUSSELL, GRAHAM. Nottingham, England, 6/1/50. Singer. Air Supply.

RUSSELL, JACK. 12/5/60. Singer. Great White.

RUSSELL, JANE. Bemidji, MN, 6/21/21. Actor, pinup girl. *The Outlaw.*

RUSSELL, LEON (Hank Wilson). Lawton, OK, 4/2/41. Country/blues singer, songwriter.

RUSSELL, NIPSEY. Atlanta, GA, 10/13/24. Actor. *Car 54, Where Are You?*

RUSSELL, THERESA (Theresa Paup). San Diego, CA, 3/20/57. Actor. *Black Widow.*

RUTHERFORD, MIKE. Guildford, England, 10/2/50. Guitarist. Genesis; Mike & The Mechanics.

RUTHERFORD, PAUL. Liverpool, England, 12/8/59. Singer. Frankie Goes to Hollywood.

RUTTAN, SUSAN. Oregon City, OR, 9/16/48. Actor. Roxanne on *L.A. Law.*

RYAN, TOM. Anderson, IN, 6/6/26. Cartoonist. *Tumbleweeds.*

RYDER, MITCH (William Levise Jr.). Detroit, MI, 2/26/45. Singer. Mitch Ryder & The Detroit Wheels.

RYDER, PAUL. Manchester, England, 4/24/64. Bassist. Happy Mondays.

RYDER, SHAUN. Little Hulton, England, 8/23/62. Singer. Happy Mondays.

SABATINI, GABRIELA. Buenos Aires, Argentina, 5/16/70. Tennis player.

SADE (Helen Folasade Adu). Ibadan, Nigeria, 1/16/59. Singer.

SAGAL, KATEY. Los Angeles, CA, 1/19/54. Actor. Peg on *Married ... with Children.*

SAGET, BOB. Philadelphia, PA, 5/17/56. Actor. *Full House.*

SAHM, DOUG. San Antonio, TX, 11/6/41. Singer, guitarist. Sir Douglas Quintet.

SAINT, EVA MARIE. Newark, NJ, 7/4/24. Actor. *On the Waterfront.*

SAINT JAMES, SUSAN (Susan Miller). Los Angeles, CA, 8/14/46. Actor. Kate on *Kate & Allie.*

SAJAK, PAT. Chicago, IL, 10/26/46. Game show host. *Wheel of Fortune.*

SALAZAR, ALBERTO. Havana, Cuba, 8/7/58. Track athlete, won New York City Marathon.

SALES, SOUPY (Milton Supman). Franklinton, NC, 1/8/26. TV personality. *The Soupy Sales Show.*

SALINGER, J. D. (Jerome David Salinger). New York, NY, 1/1/19. Author. *The Catcher in the Rye.*

SALT (Cheryl James). Brooklyn, NY, 3/8/64. Rap artist. Salt-N-Pepa.

SALT, JENNIFER. Los Angeles, CA, 9/4/44. Actor. *Midnight Cowboy.*

SAMBORA, RICHIE. 7/11/59. Guitarist, married to Heather Locklear. Bon Jovi.

SAMMS, EMMA. London, England, 8/28/60. Actor.

Fallon Carrington Colby on *Dynasty* and *The Colbys.*

SAMPRAS, PETE. Washington, DC, 8/12/71. Tennis player.

SAMWELL-SMITH, PAUL. Richmond, England, 5/8/43. Bassist. The Yardbirds.

SAN GIACOMO, LAURA. Denville, NJ, 11/14/61. Actor. *sex, lies and videotape.*

SANDERS, RICHARD. Harrisburg, PA, 8/23/40. Actor. Les Nessman on *WKRP in Cincinnati.*

SANDS, JULIAN. Yorkshire, England, 1/15/58. Actor. *A Room with a View.*

SANDY, GARY. Dayton, OH, 11/3/46. Actor. Andy Travis on *WKRP in Cincinnati.*

SANFORD, ISABEL. New York, NY, 8/29/17. Actor. Louise on *The Jeffersons.*

SANTANA, CARLOS. Autlan de Navarro, Mexico, 7/20/47. Guitarist, singer. Santana.

SANTIAGO, HERMAN. New York, NY 2/18/41. Singer. Frankie Lymon & The Teenagers.

SARANDON, CHRIS. Beckley, WV, 7/24/42. Actor, former husband of Susan. Leon in *Dog Day Afternoon.*

SASSOON, VIDAL. London, England, 1/17/28. Hairstylist.

SAVAGE, FRED. Highland Park, IL, 7/9/76. Actor, brother of Ben. Kevin Arnold on *The Wonder Years.*

SAVAGE, JOHN (John Youngs). Long Island, NY, 8/25/49. Actor. *The Deer Hunter.*

SAVAGE, RICK. Sheffield, England, 12/2/60. Bassist. Def Leppard.

SAVANT, DOUG. 6/21/64. Actor. *Melrose Place.*

SAWYER, RAY. Chickasaw, AL, 2/1/37. Lead singer. Dr. Hook.

SAYER, LEO (Gerard Sayer). Shoreham-by-Sea, England, 5/21/48. Singer, songwriter. "You Make Me Feel Like Dancing."

SAYLES, JOHN. 9/28/50. Director.

SCABIES, RAT (Chris Miller). Kingston-upon-Thames, England, 7/30/57. Drummer. The Damned.

SCACCHI, GRETA. Milan, Italy, 2/18/60. Actor. *Presumed Innocent.*

SCAGGS, BOZ (William Scaggs). Ohio, 6/8/44.

Guitarist, singer, songwriter. "Lowdown."

SCALIA, JACK. Brooklyn, NY, 11/10/51. Actor. *Wolf.*

SCARPELLI, GLENN. Staten Island, NY, 7/6/68. Actor. Alex Handris on *One Day at a Time.*

SCAVULLO, FRANCESCO. 1/16/29. Photographer.

SCHACHER, MEL. Flint, MI, 4/3/51. Bassist. Grand Funk Railroad.

SCHEIDER, ROY. Orange, NJ, 11/10/32. Actor. Chief Brody in *Jaws.*

SCHELL, MAXIMILIAN. Vienna, Austria, 12/8/30. Actor. *Judgment at Nuremberg.*

SCHENKER, RUDOLPH. 8/31/48. Guitarist. Scorpions.

SCHERMIE, JOE. Madison, WI, 2/12/45. Bassist. Three Dog Night.

SCHNEIDER, FRED. Newark, GA, 7/1/51. Keyboardist, singer. The B-52's.

SCHNEIDER, MARIA. Paris, France, 3/27/52. Actor. *Last Tango in Paris.*

SCHNEIDER-ESLEBEN, FLORIAN. Dusseldorf, Germany, 1947. Keyboardist, drummer, singer, woodwindist. Kraftwerk.

SCHOLZ, TOM. Toledo, OH, 3/10/47. Guitarist, keyboardist. Boston.

SCHON, NEAL. San Mateo, CA, 2/27/54. Guitarist. Journey.

SCHORR, DANIEL. New York, NY, 8/31/16. Broadcast journalist. NPR.

SCHULTZ, DWIGHT. Baltimore, MD, 11/24/47. Actor. H. M. "Howling Mad" Murdock on *The A-Team.*

SCHULZ, CHARLES. Minneapolis, MN, 11/26/22. Cartoonist. *Peanuts.*

SCHWARZKOPF, NORMAN. Trenton, NJ, 8/22/34. Retired army general, Gulf War hero.

SCHYGULLA, HANNA. Katlowitz, Germany, 12/25/43. Actor. *Dead Again.*

SCIORRA, ANNABELLA. New York, NY, 3/24/64. Actor. *The Hand That Rocks the Cradle.*

SCOLARI, PETER. New Rochelle, NY, 9/12/54. Actor. *Bosom Buddies.*

SCOTT, ANDY. Wrexham, Wales, 6/30/51. Guitarist. Sweet.

SCOTT, BON (Ronald Scott). Kirriemuir, Scotland, 7/9/46. Singer. AC/DC.

SCOTT, GORDON (Gordon Werschkul). Portland, OR, 8/3/27. Actor. *Tarzan's Hidden Jungle.*

SCOTT, HOWARD. San Pedro, CA, 3/15/46. Guitarist, singer. War.

SCOTT, MIKE. Edinburgh, Scotland, 12/14/58. Singer, guitarist. The Waterboys.

SCOTT, RIDLEY. South Shields, England, 11/30/37. Director, brother of director Tony. *Thelma and Louise.*

SCOTT, WILLARD. Alexandria, VA, 3/7/34. Weatherman. *Today.*

SEAL, ELIZABETH. Genoa, Italy, 8/28/33. Actor. *Irma La Douce.*

SEALE, BOBBY. Dallas, TX, 10/20/36. Political activist, author. Cofounder of the Black Panthers.

SEALS, JIM. Sidney, TX, 10/17/41. Singer, guitarist, saxophonist, violinist. Seals & Crofts.

SEAVER, TOM. Fresno, CA, 11/17/44. Baseball pitcher.

SEBASTIAN, JOHN. New York, NY, 3/17/44. Singer, guitarist, harmonicist, autoharpist. "The Lovin' Spoonful."

SEDAKA, NEIL. Brooklyn, NY, 3/13/39. Pop singer, songwriter. "Laughter in the Rain."

SEDGWICK, KYRA. New York, NY, 8/19/65. Actor, married to Kevin Bacon. *Phenomenon.*

SEEGER, PETE. New York, NY, 5/3/19. Folk singer, songwriter, guitarist, social activist. Founded The Weavers.

SEGAL, ERICH. 6/16/37. Author. *Love Story.*

SEGAL, GEORGE. New York, NY, 2/13/34. Actor. *Look Who's Talking.*

SEGER, BOB. Dearborn, MI, 5/6/45. Singer, songwriter. The Silver Bullet Band.

SELLECCA, CONNIE (Concetta Sellecchia). The Bronx, NY, 5/25/55. Actor, married to John Tesh. *Hotel.*

SELLECK, TOM. Detroit, MI, 1/29/45. Actor. *Magnum, P.I.*

SENDAK, MAURICE. New York, NY, 1/10/28. Author,

illustrator. *Where the Wild Things Are.*

SENSIBLE, CAPTAIN (Ray Burns). England, 4/23/55. Bassist. The Damned.

SERAPHINE, DANNY. Chicago, IL, 8/28/48. Drummer. Chicago.

SERGEANT, WILL. Liverpool, England, 4/12/58. Guitarist. Echo & The Bunnymen.

SETZER, BRIAN. 4/10/60. Guitarist, singer. The Stray Cats.

SEVERIN, STEVE. 9/25/55. Bassist. Siouxsie & The Banshees.

SEYMOUR, STEPHANIE. San Diego, CA, 7/23/68. Supermodel.

SHAFFER, PAUL. Toronto, Canada, 11/28/49. Musician, bandleader. *Late Show with David Letterman.*

SHALIT, GENE. New York, NY, 1932. Critic. *Today.*

SHAPIRO, HELEN. Bethnal Green, England, 9/28/46. Singer, actor, cabaret performer.

SHARIF, OMAR (Michel Shalhoub). Alexandria, Egypt, 4/10/32. Actor. *Dr. Zhivago.*

SHARKEY, FEARGAL. Londonderry, Northern Ireland, 8/13/58. Singer. The Undertones.

SHARP, DAVE. Salford, England, 1/28/59. Guitarist. The Alarm.

SHARPTON, AL. Brooklyn, NY, 1954. Politician, activist, clergyman.

SHAVER, HELEN. St. Thomas, Canada, 2/24/51. Actor. *The Amityville Horror.*

SHAW, SANDIE (Sandra Goodrich). Dagenham, England, 2/26/47. Pop singer.

SHAW, TOMMY. Montgomery, AL, 9/11/52. Lead guitarist. Styx.

SHAWN, WALLACE. New York, NY, 11/12/43. Playwright, actor. *My Dinner with Andre.*

SHEA, JOHN. North Conway, NH, 4/14/49. Actor. *Lois & Clark.*

SHEARER, HARRY. Los Angeles, CA, 12/23/43. Actor. *This Is Spinal Tap.*

SHEEDY, ALLY. New York, NY, 6/13/62. Actor. *WarGames.*

SHEEHAN, FRAN. Boston, MA, 3/26/49. Bassist. Boston.

SHEEN, CHARLIE. Los Angeles, CA, 9/3/65. Actor. *Platoon.*

SHEEN, MARTIN (Ramon Estevez). Dayton, OH, 8/3/40. Actor, father of Charlie Sheen and Emilio Estevez. *Apocalypse Now.*

SHEILA E. (Sheila Escovedo). Oakland, CA, 12/12/57. Drummer, singer.

SHELDON, SIDNEY. Chicago, IL, 2/11/17. Novelist, producer. *The Other Side of Midnight.*

SHELLEY, CAROLE. London, England, 8/16/39. Actor. *The Elephant Man.*

SHELLEY, PETE (Peter McNeish). Lancashire, England, 4/17/55. Guitarist, singer. The Buzzcocks.

SHEPARD, SAM (Sam Rogers). Ft. Sheridan, IL, 11/5/43. Playwright, actor. *True West; The Right Stuff.*

SHEPHERD, CYBILL. Memphis, TN, 2/18/50. Actor. *Cybill.*

SHERIDAN, JIM. Dublin, Ireland, 1949. Director, writer. *My Left Foot.*

SHERIDAN, NICOLLETTE. Worthington, England, 11/21/63. Actor, model. *The Sure Thing.*

SHIRE, TALIA (Talia Rose Coppola). Lake Success, NY, 4/25/45. Actor, sister of Francis Ford Coppola. *Rocky I–V.*

SHORE, PAULY. 2/1/68. Actor. "The Weez."

SHORROCK, GLENN. Rochester, England, 6/30/44. Singer. The Little River Band.

SHORT, MARTIN. Toronto, Canada, 3/26/50. Actor. Ed Grimley on *Saturday Night Live.*

SHOW, GRANT. Detroit, MI, 2/27/62. Actor. *Melrose Place.*

SHOWALTER, MAX (Casey Adams). Caldwell, KS, 6/2/17. Actor. First Ward Cleaver in the *Leave It to Beaver* pilot, "It's a Small World."

SHRIVER, MARIA. Chicago, IL, 11/6/55. Broadcast journalist, married to Arnold Schwarzenegger. *First Person with Maria Shriver.*

SHUE, ANDREW. South Orange, NJ, 2/20/67. Actor, brother of Elizabeth Shue. *Melrose Place.*

SIEGEL, JAY. Brooklyn, NY, 10/20/39. Baritone singer. The Tokens.

SIKKING, JAMES B. Los Angeles, CA, 3/5/34. Actor. Lt. Howard Hunter on *Hill Street Blues.*

SILLS, BEVERLY. New York, NY, 5/25/29. Opera singer.

SILVER, RON. New York, NY, 7/2/46. Actor, director. *Reversal of Fortune.*

SILVERMAN, JONATHAN. Los Angeles, CA, 8/5/66. Actor. *The Single Guy.*

SIMMONS, GENE (Chaim Witz). Haifa, Israel, 8/25/49. Long-tongued bassist, singer. Kiss.

SIMMONS, JEAN. London, England, 1/31/29. Actor. *The Thorn Birds.*

SIMMONS, JOSEPH. Queens, NY, 1964. Rap artist. Run-D.M.C.

SIMMONS, PATRICK. Aberdeen, WA, 1/23/50. Guitarist, singer. The Doobie Brothers.

SIMMONS, RICHARD. New Orleans, LA, 7/12/48. Health guru. *Sweatin' to the Oldies.*

SIMON, CARLY. New York, NY, 6/25/45. Singer, songwriter, childrens' book author.

SIMONE, NINA. Tryon, NC, 2/21/33. Singer. Soundtrack for *The Crying Game.*

SIMONON, PAUL. Brixton, England, 12/15/55. Bassist. The Clash.

SIMPSON, O.J. San Francisco, CA, 7/9/47. Football player, actor, indicted for murder of ex-wife, guilty in a civil trial but not the criminal one.

SINGER, LORI. Corpus Christi, TX, 5/6/62. Actor. *Fame.*

SINGLETON, JOHN. Los Angeles, CA, 1/6/68. Director, writer. *Boyz N the Hood.*

SINGLETON, STEPHEN. Sheffield, England, 4/17/59. Saxophonist. ABC.

SIOUX, SIOUXSIE (Susan Dallon). Chiselhurst, England, 5/27/57. Singer. Siouxsie & The Banshees.

SIXX, NIKKI (Frank Ferrano). Seattle, WA, 12/11/58. Bassist. Mötley Crüe.

SKERRITT, TOM. Detroit, MI, 8/25/33. Actor. *Picket Fences.*

SKYE, IONE (Ione Leitch). London, England, 9/4/71. Actor, daughter of folk singer

Donovan, sister of Donovan Leitch. *Say Anything.*

SLASH (Saul Hudson). Stoke-on-Trent, England, 1965. Guitarist. Guns N' Roses.

SLATER, HELEN. New York, NY, 12/15/65. Actor. *Supergirl.*

SLATER, RODNEY. Lincolnshire, England, 11/8/44. Saxophonist, trumpeter. The Bonzo Dog Doo-Dah Band.

SLEDGE, DEBBIE. Philadelphia, PA, 7/9/54. Singer. Sister Sledge.

SLEDGE, JONI. Philadelphia, PA, 9/13/56. Singer. Sister Sledge.

SLEDGE, KATHY. Philadelphia, PA, 1/6/59. Singer. Sister Sledge.

SLEDGE, KIM. Philadelphia, PA, 8/21/57. Singer. Sister Sledge.

SLEDGE, PERCY. Leighton, AL, 11/25/41. Singer. "When a Man Loves a Woman."

SLICK, GRACE (Grace Wing). Chicago, IL, 10/30/39. Singer. Jefferson Airplane/Starship.

SLIWA, CURTIS. New York, NY, 3/26/54. Founder of the Guardian Angels.

SMIRNOFF, YAKOV (Yakov Pokhis). Odessa, Russia, 1/24/51. Actor. *What a Country!*

SMITH, ADRIAN. Huckney, England, 2/27/57. Guitarist. Iron Maiden.

SMITH, BOBBIE. 4/10/36. Singer. The (Detroit) Spinners.

SMITH, CHARLES MARTIN. Los Angeles, CA, 10/30/53. Actor. *American Graffiti.*

SMITH, CLAYDES (Charles Smith). Jersey City, NJ, 9/6/48. Guitarist. Kool & The Gang.

SMITH, CURT. Bath, England, 6/24/61. Singer, bassist. Tears for Fears.

SMITH, JACLYN. Houston, TX, 10/26/45. Actor. Kelly Garrett on *Charlie's Angels.*

SMITH, JEFF. Seattle, WA, 1/22/39. TV personality, chef, author. *The Frugal Gourmet.*

SMITH, JEROME. Miami, FL, 6/18/53. Guitarist. KC & The Sunshine Band.

SMITH, LARRY. Oxford, England, 1/18/44. Drummer. The Bonzo Dog Doo-Dah Band.

SMITH, LIZ. Fort Worth, TX, 2/2/23. Gossip columnist.

SMITH, MAGGIE. Ilford, England, 12/28/34. Actor. *Sister Act.*

SMITH, MIKE. Neath, Wales, 11/4/47. Tenor saxophonist. Amen Corner.

SMITH, MIKE. Edmonton, England, 12/12/43. Singer, keyboardist. The Dave Clark Five.

SMITH, PATTI. Chicago, IL, 12/30/46. Singer, songwriter.

SMITH, PHIL. 5/1/59. Saxophonist. Haircut 100.

SMITH, ROBERT. Crawley, England, 4/21/59. Guitarist, singer. The Cure.

SMITS, JIMMY. New York, NY, 7/9/55. Actor. Victor Sifuentes on *L.A. Law.*

SMOTHERS, DICK. New York, NY, 11/20/38. Actor, singer, brother of Tom. *The Smothers Brothers Comedy Hour.*

SMOTHERS, TOM. New York, NY, 2/2/37. Actor, singer, brother of Dick. *The Smothers Brothers Comedy Hour.*

SMYTH, PATTY. New York, NY, 6/26/57. Singer, relationship with John McEnroe. "The Warrior."

SNEED, FLOYD. Calgary, Canada, 11/22/43. Drummer. Three Dog Night.

SNODGRESS, CARRIE. Chicago, IL, 10/27/46. Actor. *Diary of a Mad Housewife.*

SOMERS, SUZANNE (Suzanne Mahoney). San Bruno, CA, 10/16/46. Actor. *Three's Company.*

SOMERVILLE, JIMMY. Glasgow, Scotland, 6/22/61. Dance/rock singer, keyboardist.

SOMMER, ELKE (Elke Schletz). Berlin, Germany, 11/5/40. Actor. *A Shot in the Dark.*

SORVINO, PAUL. New York, NY, 4/13/39. Actor, father of Mira. *GoodFellas.*

SOTHERN, ANN (Harriet Lake). Valley City, ND, 1/22/09. Actor. *The Ann Sothern Show.*

SOUL, DAVID (David Solberg). Chicago, IL, 8/28/43. Actor. Kevin "Hutch" Hutchinson on *Starsky and Hutch.*

SOUTH, JOE. Atlanta, GA, 2/28/40. Rock/country guitarist, singer, songwriter.

SOUTHSIDE JOHNNY (Johnny Lyon). Neptune Park, NJ, 12/4/48. Singer. Southside Johnny & The Asbury Jukes.

SPACEK, SISSY (Mary Elizabeth Spacek). Quitman, TX, 12/25/49. Actor. *Coal Miner's Daughter.*

SPADER, JAMES. Boston, MA, 2/7/60. Actor. *sex, lies, and videotape.*

SPANO, JOE. San Francisco, CA, 7/7/46. Actor. Henry Goldblume on *Hill Street Blues.*

SPANO, VINCENT. New York, NY, 10/18/62. Actor. *Rumble Fish.*

SPEAR, ROGER. London, England, 6/29/43. Saxophonist, kazooist. The Bonzo Dog Doo-Dah Band.

SPECTOR, PHIL. New York, NY, 12/26/39. Music producer. Wall of sound.

SPECTOR, RONNIE (Veronica Bennett). New York, NY, 8/10/43. Lead singer. The Ronettes.

SPELLING, TORI. Los Angeles, CA, 5/16/73. Actor, daughter of Aaron Spelling. Donna on *Beverly Hills, 90210.*

SPENCE, ALEXANDER. Windsor, Canada, 4/18/46. Guitarist, lead singer. Moby Grape.

SPENCER, JEREMY. West Hartlepoole, England, 7/4/48. Guitarist. Fleetwood Mac.

SPILLANE, MICKEY (Frank Morrison). New York, NY, 3/9/18. Author. Mike Hammer detective stories.

SPINKS, LEON. St. Louis, MO, 7/11/53. Boxer, former heavyweight champion, brother of Michael.

SPINKS, MICHAEL. St. Louis, MO, 7/29/56. Boxer. Olympic gold medalist, brother of Leon.

SPOONER, BILL. Phoenix, AZ, 4/16/49. Guitarist. The Tubes.

SPRINGFIELD, DUSTY (Mary O'Brien). Hampstead, England, 4/16/39. Folk/pop singer.

SPRINGFIELD, RICK (Richard Spring Thorpe). Sydney, Australia, 8/23/49. Singer, actor. *General Hospital.*

SQUIER, BILLY. Wellesley, MA, 5/12/50. Singer. "Everybody Wants You."

SQUIRE, CHRIS. London, England, 3/4/48. Bassist. Yes.

SQUIRE, JOHN. Sale, England, 11/24/62. Lead guitarist. The Stone Roses.

ST. JOHN, JILL (Jill Oppenheim). Los Angeles, CA, 8/19/40. Actor, married to Robert Wagner. *Diamonds Are Forever.*

STACK, ROBERT. Los Angeles, CA, 1/13/19. Actor. Eliot Ness on *The Untouchables.*

STAFFORD, JIM. Eloise, FL, 1/16/44. Singer, songwriter. "Spiders and Snakes."

STAMOS, JOHN. Cypress, CA, 8/19/63. Actor. *Full House.*

STAMP, TERENCE. London, England, 7/23/38. Actor. *Superman II.*

STANLEY, PAUL (Paul Eisen). Queens, NY, 1/20/50. Guitarist, singer. Kiss.

STANSFIELD, LISA. Rochdale, England, 4/11/66. Singer, songwriter. "All Around the World."

STANTON, HARRY DEAN. West Irvine, KY, 7/14/26. Actor. *Paris, Texas.*

STAPLES, NEVILLE. 4/11/56. Singer, percussionist. The Specials.

STAPLES, PETE. Andover, England, 5/3/44. Bassist. The Troggs.

STAPLETON, JEAN (Jeanne Murray). New York, NY, 1/19/23. Actor. Edith Bunker on *All in the Family.*

STAPLETON, MAUREEN. Troy, NY, 6/21/25. Actor. *Airport.*

STARR, RINGO (Richard Starkey). Liverpool, England, 7/7/40. Drummer, singer, actor, married to Barbara Bach. The Beatles.

STAUBACH, ROGER. Cincinnati, OH, 2/5/42. NFL football player. Dallas Cowboys.

STAX, JOHN (John Fullegar). London, England, 4/6/44. Bassist. The Pretty Things.

STEEL, JOHN. Gateshead, England, 2/4/41. Drummer. The Animals.

STEELE, DAVID. Birmingham, England, 9/8/60. Keyboardist, bassist. Fine Young Cannibals.

STEELE, MICHAEL. 6/2/54. Bassist, singer. The Bangles; The Runaways.

STEELE, TOMMY (Thomas Hicks). Bermondsey, England, 12/17/36. Guitarist, singer, actor.

STEENBURGEN, MARY. Newport, AR, 2/8/53. Actor,

married to Ted Danson. *Parenthood.*

STEIGER, ROD. Westhampton, NY, 4/14/25. Actor. *In the Heat of the Night.*

STEIN, CHRIS. Brooklyn, NY, 1/5/50. Guitarist. Blondie.

STEIN, MARK. Bayonne, NJ, 3/11/47. Singer, organist. Vanilla Fudge.

STEINBERG, DAVID. Winnipeg, Canada, 8/9/42. Actor, director. *Paternity.*

STEINEM, GLORIA. Toledo, OH, 3/25/34. Women's rights activist.

STERBAN, RICHARD. Camden, NJ, 4/24/43. Singer, bassist. The Oak Ridge Boys.

STERN, DANIEL. Bethesda, MD, 8/28/57. Actor, narrator of *The Wonder Years. City Slickers.*

STERN, ISAAC. Kreminiecz, Russia, 7/21/20. Violinist.

STERNHAGEN, FRANCES. Washington, DC, 1/13/30. Actor. *Driving Miss Daisy.*

STEVENS, ANDREW. Memphis, TN, 6/10/55. Actor, son of Stella. *Dallas.*

STEVENS, CAT (Steven Georgiou). Soho, England, 7/21/47. Folk singer, songwriter—left recording upon conversion to Islam.

STEVENS, CONNIE (Concetta Ann Ingolia). Brooklyn, NY, 8/8/38. Actor. *Hawaiian Eye.*

STEVENS, FISHER. Chicago, IL, 11/27/63. Actor. *Short Circuit.*

STEVENS, RAY (Ray Ragsdale). Clarksdale, GA, 1/24/39. Singer. *Andy Williams Presents Ray Stevens.*

STEVENS, SHAKIN' (Michael Barratt). Ely, Wales, 3/4/48. Singer, actor.

STEVENS, STELLA (Estelle Eggleston). Hot Coffee, MS, 10/1/36. Actor, mother of Andrew. *Santa Barbara.*

STEVENSON, DON. Seattle, WA, 10/15/42. Drummer. Moby Grape.

STEVENSON, PARKER. Philadelphia, PA, 6/4/52. Actor. Formerly married to Kirstie Alley. *Falcon Crest.*

STEWART, AL. Glasgow, Scotland, 9/5/45. Guitarist, singer, songwriter.

STEWART, DAVE. Sunderland, England, 9/9/52. Keyboardist, guitarist. Eurythmics.

STEWART, ERIC. Manchester, England, 1/20/45. Singer, guitarist. 10cc.

STEWART, MARTHA (Martha Haworth). Bardwell, KY, 10/7/22. Actor. *Holocaust.*

STEWART, ROD. Highgate, England, 1/10/45. Singer, songwriter.

STIERS, DAVID OGDEN. Peoria, IL, 10/31/42. Actor. Dr. Charles Emerson Winchester on *M*A*S*H.*

STILES, RAY. Carshalton, England, 11/20/46. Bassist, singer. Mud.

STILLER, JERRY. New York, NY, 6/8/27. Actor, partner/married to Anne Meara, father of Ben. *Seinfeld.*

STILLS, STEPHEN. Dallas, TX, 1/3/45. Singer, guitarist. Buffalo Springfield; Crosby, Stills, Nash & Young.

STOCKDALE, JAMES. Abington, IL, 12/23/23. Vietnam POW, running mate of presidential candidate Ross Perot.

STOCKWELL, DEAN. Hollywood, CA, 3/5/36. Actor. Al Calavicci on *Quantum Leap.*

STOCKWELL, JOHN (John Samuels). Galveston, TX, 3/25/61. Actor. *My Science Project.*

STOLTZ, ERIC. American Samoa, 9/30/61. Actor. *Mask.*

STONE, DEE WALLACE (Deanna Bowers). Kansas City, MO, 12/14/48. Actor. Mother in *E.T., the Extra-Terrestrial.*

STONE, FREDDIE. Dallas, TX, 6/5/46. Guitarist. Sly & The Family Stone.

STONE, MATT. 5/26/71. Actor, cartoonist. *South Park.*

STONE, ROSIE. Vallejo, CA, 3/21/45. Singer, keyboardist. Sly & The Family Stone.

STONE, SLY (Sylvester Stewart). Dallas, TX, 3/15/44. Singer, keyboardist, guitarist. Sly & The Family Stone.

STORCH, LARRY. New York, NY, 1/8/23. Actor. *F Troop.*

STORM, GALE (Josephine Cottle). Bloomington, TX, 4/5/22. Actor. *My Little Margie.*

STOWE, MADELEINE. Los Angeles, CA, 8/18/58. Actor. *The Last of the Mohicans.*

STRASSMAN, MARCIA. New York, NY, 4/28/48. Actor. Julie Kotter on *Welcome Back Kotter.*

STRATHAIRN, DAVID. San Francisco, CA, 1949. Actor. *Matewan.*

STRATTON, DENNIS. London, England, 11/9/54. Guitarist. Iron Maiden.

STRAUSS, PETER. Croton-on-Hudson, NY, 2/20/47. Actor. *The Jericho Mile.*

STRINGFIELD, SHERRY. Colorado Springs, CO, 6/24/67. Actor. *ER.*

STRICKLAND, KEITH. Athens, GA, 10/26/53. Drummer. The B-52's.

STRITCH, ELAINE. Detroit, MI, 2/2/25. Actor. *September.*

STRUMMER, JOE (John Mellors). Ankara, Turkey, 8/21/52. Singer, guitarist. The Clash.

STRUTHERS, SALLY. Portland, OR, 7/28/47. Actor. Gloria Bunker Stivic on *All in the Family.*

STRYKERT, RON. Australia, 8/18/57. Guitarist. Men at Work.

STUART, CHAD. England, 12/10/43. Singer, guitarist. Chad & Jeremy.

STUART, HAMISH. Glasgow, Scotland, 10/8/49. Singer, guitarist. Average White Band.

STUBBS, LEVI (Levi Stubbles). Detroit, MI, 6/6/36. Lead singer. The Four Tops.

SUCH, ALEC. 11/14/56. Bassist. Bon Jovi.

SULLIVAN, SUSAN. New York, NY, 11/18/44. Actor. Maggie Gioberti Channing on *Falcon Crest.*

SULLIVAN, TOM. Boston, MA, 3/27/47. Singer, actor, composer. "If You Could See What I Hear."

SUMMER, DONNA (LaDonna Gaines). Boston, MA, 12/31/48. Disco/pop singer. "Love To Love You Baby."

SUMMERS, ANDY (Andrew Somers). Poulton le Fylde, France, 12/31/42. Guitarist, singer. The Police.

SUMNER, BARNEY (Bernard Dicken). Salford, England, 1/4/56. Guitarist, singer. New Order.

SUTHERLAND, DONALD. St. John, Canada, 7/17/35. Actor,

father of Kiefer. *Ordinary People.*

SUTHERLAND, KIEFER. Los Angeles, CA, 12/21/66. Actor, son of Donald. *Flatliners.*

SUZMAN, JANET. Johannesburg, South Africa, 2/9/39. Actor. *Nicholas and Alexandra.*

SVENSON, BO. Goreborg, Sweden, 2/13/41. Actor. *Walking Tall.*

SWAGGART, JIMMY. Ferriday, LA, 3/15/35. Evangelist.

SWAIN, DOMINIQUE. 8/12/80. Actor. *Lolita.*

SWANN, LYNN. Alcoa, TN, 3/7/52. NFL football player.

SWAYZE, PATRICK. Houston, TX, 8/18/52. Actor, dancer. *Dirty Dancing.*

SWEENEY, D. B. (Daniel Bernard Sweeney). Shoreham, NY, 11/14/61. Actor. *The Cutting Edge.*

SWEET, DERRELL. 5/16/47. Drummer, percussionist, singer. Nazareth.

SWEET, MATTHEW. Lincoln, NE, 10/6/64. Singer, songwriter, guitarist. "Girlfriend."

SWENSON, INGA. Omaha, NE, 12/29/32. Actor. Gretchen Kraus on *Benson.*

SWIT, LORETTA. Passaic, NJ, 11/4/37. Actor. Margaret "Hot Lips" Houlihan on *M*A*S*H.*

SYLVIAN, DAVID (David Batt). Lewisham, England, 2/23/58. Singer, guitarist. Japan.

T, MR. (Lawrence Tero). Chicago, IL, 5/21/52. Actor and wrestler. Bosco "B.A." Baracus on *The A-Team.*

TAJ MAHAL. New York, NY, 5/17/42. Singer, songwriter, composer. "Sounder."

TAKEI, GEORGE. Los Angeles, CA, 4/20/39. Mr. Sulu on *Star Trek.*

TALBOT, MICK. London, England, 9/11/58. Keyboardist. The Style Council.

TALLEY, GARY. Memphis, TN, 8/17/47. Guitarist. The Box Tops/Big Star.

TALLEY, NEDRA. New York, NY, 1/27/46. Singer. The Ronettes.

TAMBLYN, RUSS. Los Angeles, CA, 12/30/34. Actor. *West Side Story.*

TAMBOR, JEFFREY. San Francisco, CA, 7/8/44. Actor. *The Larry Sanders Show.*

TANDY, RICHARD. Birmingham, England, 3/26/48. Bassist. Electric Light Orchestra (ELO).

TARKENTON, FRAN. Richmond, VA, 2/3/40. Football player, sportscaster. *Monday Night Football.*

TAUPIN, BERNIE. Sleaford, England, 5/22/50. Lyricist. Wrote for Elton John.

TAYLOR, ANDY. Tynemouth, England, 2/16/61. Guitarist. Duran Duran.

TAYLOR, CLIVE. Cardiff, Wales, 4/27/49. Bassist. Amen Corner.

TAYLOR, DICK. Dartford, England, 1/28/43. Lead guitarist. The Pretty Things.

TAYLOR, JAMES. South Carolina, 8/16/53. Lead singer. Kool & The Gang.

TAYLOR, JAMES. Boston, MA, 3/12/48. Folk-oriented singer, songwriter.

TAYLOR, JOHN. Birmingham, England, 6/20/60. Bassist. Duran Duran.

TAYLOR, LARRY. Brooklyn, NY, 6/26/42. Bassist. Canned Heat.

TAYLOR, LILI. Chicago, IL, 1967. Actor. *Mystic Pizza.*

TAYLOR, ROD. Sydney, Australia, 1/11/30. Actor. *The Time Machine.*

TAYLOR, ROGER. King's Lynn, England, 7/26/49. Drummer. Queen.

TENCH, BENMONT. Gainesville, FL, 9/7/54. Keyboardist. Tom Petty & The Heartbreakers.

TENNANT, NEIL. Gosforth, England, 7/10/54. Singer. Pet Shop Boys.

TENNANT, VICTORIA. London, England, 9/30/50. Actor, formerly married to Steve Martin. *L.A. Story.*

TENNILLE, TONI. Montgomery, AL, 5/8/43. Singer. The Captain & Tennille.

TERRANOVA, JOE. 1/30/41. Baritone. Danny & The Juniors.

THICKE, ALAN. Ontario, Canada, 3/1/47. Actor. *Growing Pains.*

THISTLETHWAITE, ANTHONY. Leicester, England, 8/31/55. Saxophonist. The Waterboys.

THOMAS, B. J. (Billy Joe Thomas). Hugo, OK, 8/7/42.

Pop singer. "Raindrops Keep Fallin' on My Head."

THOMAS, BETTY. Saint Louis, MO, 7/27/47. Actor, director. Lucy Bates on *Hill Street Blues.*

THOMAS, DAVE. Saint Catharines, Canada, 6/20/49. Actor. Doug MacKenzie on *SCTV.*

THOMAS, HENRY. San Antonio, TX, 9/8/72. Actor. Elliot in *E.T., the Extra-Terrestrial.*

THOMAS, JAY. New Orleans, LA, 7/12/48. Actor, radio personality. *Murphy Brown.*

THOMAS, MARLO (Margaret Thomas). Detroit, MI, 11/21/37. Actor, married to Phil Donahue, daughter of Danny Thomas. *That Girl.*

THOMAS, MARY. Brooklyn, NY, 1946. Singer. The Crystals.

THOMAS, PHILIP MICHAEL. Columbus, OH, 5/26/49. Actor. Ricardo Tubbs on *Miami Vice.*

THOMAS, RAY. Stourport-on-Severn, England, 12/29/42. Flautist, harmonicist, singer. The Moody Blues.

THOMAS, RICHARD. New York, NY, 6/13/51. Actor. John Boy on *The Waltons.*

THOMPKINS, RUSSELL JR. Philadelphia, PA, 3/21/51. Lead singer. The Stylistics.

THOMPSON, LEA. Rochester, MN, 5/31/61. Actor. *Caroline in the City.*

THOMPSON, PAUL. Jarrow, England, 5/13/51. Drummer. Roxy Music.

THOMPSON, SADA. Des Moines, IA, 9/27/29. Actor. *Family.*

THOMSON, DOUGIE. Glasgow, Scotland, 3/24/51. Bassist. Supertramp.

THORN, TRACEY. Hartfordshire, England, 9/26/62. Singer. Everything but the Girl.

THORNTON, BLAIR. Vancouver, Canada, 7/23/50. Guitarist. Bachman-Turner Overdrive.

THOROGOOD, GEORGE. Wilmington, DE, 1951. Singer, guitarist. George Thorogood and the Delaware Destroyers.

TICH (Ian Amey). Salisbury, England, 5/15/44. Lead guitarist. Dave Dee, Dozy, Beaky, Mick and Tich.

TIEGS, CHERYL. Alhambra, CA, 9/25/47. Model, author. *The Way to Natural Beauty.*

TIFFANY (Tiffany Renee Darwish). Norwalk, CA, 10/2/71. Singer.

TILBROOK, GLENN. London, England, 8/31/57. Singer, lead guitarist. Squeeze.

TILLIS, MEL. Pahokee, FL, 8/8/32. Singer, songwriter, father of Pam Tillis.

TILLIS, PAM. Plant City, FL, 7/24/57. Singer, daughter of Mel Tillis.

TILLY, MEG. Texada, Canada, 2/14/60. Actor, sister of Jennifer. *The Big Chill.*

TILTON, CHARLENE. San Diego, CA, 12/1/58. Actor. Lucy Ewing Cooper on *Dallas.*

TIPTON, GLENN. Birmingham, England, 10/25/48. Guitarist. Judas Priest.

TOLHURST, LOL (Laurence Tolhurst). 2/3/59. Keyboardist. The Cure.

TOLKAN, JAMES. Calumet, MI, 6/20/31. Actor. Principal in *Back to the Future.*

TOMEI, MARISA. Brooklyn, NY, 12/4/64. Actor. *My Cousin Vinny.*

TOMLIN, LILY (Mary Jean Tomlin). Detroit, MI, 9/1/39. Actor. *Rowan & Martin's Laugh-In.*

TONE-LOC. Los Angeles, CA, 3/3/66. Rap artist. "Wild Thing."

TOPHAM, ANTHONY "TOP." England, 1947. Guitarist. The Yardbirds.

TORK, PETER (Peter Halsten Thorkelson). Washington, DC, 2/13/44. Keyboardist, bassist, actor. The Monkees.

TORN, RIP. (Elmore Rual Torn Jr). Temple, TX, 2/6/31. Actor. *Blind Ambition.*

TORRENCE, DEAN. Los Angeles, CA, 3/10/40. Singer. Jan & Dean.

TOWNSEND, ROBERT. Chicago, IL, 2/6/57. Actor. *Hollywood Shuffle.*

TOWNSHEND, PETE. Chiswick, England, 5/19/45. Guitarist. The Who.

TOWNSON, RON. St. Louis, MO, 1/20/33. Singer. The 5th Dimension.

TRAVANTI, DANIEL J. Kenosha, WI, 3/7/40. Actor. Captain Frank Furillo on *Hill Street Blues.*

TRAVERS, BILL. Newcastle-upon-Tyne, England, 1/3/22.

Actor, producer, director. *Born Free.*

TRAVERS, BRIAN. Birmingham, England, 2/7/59. Saxophonist. UB40.

TRAVIS, NANCY. 9/21/61. Singer.

TRAVIS, RANDY (Randy Traywick). Marshville, NC, 5/4/59. Country singer, songwriter.

TREBEK, ALEX. Sudbury, Canada, 7/22/40. Game show host. *Jeopardy!*

TRESVANT, RALPH. Boston, MA, 5/16/68. Singer. New Edition.

TREVOR, CLAIRE (Claire Wemlinger). New York, NY, 3/8/10. Actor. *Key Largo.*

TREWAVAS, PETER. Middlesborough, England, 1/15/59. Keyboardist. Marillion.

TRIPPLEHORN, JEANNE. Tulsa, Oklahoma, 1963. Actor. *The Firm.*

TRITT, TRAVIS. Marietta, GA, 2/9/63. Country singer, songwriter.

TROWER, ROBIN. Southend, England, 3/9/45. Guitarist. Procol Harum.

TRUDEAU, GARRY (Garretson Beckman Trudeau). New York, NY, 1948. Cartoonist, married to Jane Pauley. *Doonesbury.*

TRUGOY THE DOVE (David Jolicoeur). 9/21/68. Musician. De La Soul.

TRUMP, DONALD. New York, NY, 6/14/46. Real estate developer, author. Married to Marla Maples, formerly married to Ivana Winkelmayr Trump.

TRUMP, MARLA MAPLES. 10/27/63. Actor. Married to Donald Trump. *The Will Rogers Follies.*

TUCKER, JIM. Los Angeles, CA, 10/17/46. Guitarist. The Turtles.

TUCKER, MICHAEL. Baltimore, MD, 2/6/45. Actor, married to Jill Eikenberry. *L.A. Law.*

TUCKER, MICK. Harlesden, England, 7/17/49. Drummer. Sweet.

TUFANO, DENNIS. Chicago, IL, 9/11/46. Guitarist, lead singer. The Buckinghams.

TUNE, TOMMY. Wichita Falls, TX, 2/28/39. Actor, director, choreographer, dancer.

TURBO B. (Durron Maurice Butler). Pittsburgh, PA, 4/30/67. Rap artist. Snap.

TURNER, C. F. Winnipeg, Canada, 10/16/43. Bassist, singer. Bachman-Turner Overdrive.

TURNER, IKE. Clarksdale, MS, 11/5/31. Singer, songwriter, formerly married to Tina Turner. Ike & Tina Turner.

TURNER, JANINE (Janine Gauntt). Lincoln, NE, 12/6/63. Actor. *Northern Exposure.*

TURNER, KATHLEEN Springfield, MO, 6/19/54. Actor. *Romancing the Stone.*

TURNER, LONNIE. Berkeley, CA, 2/24/47. Bassist, singer. The Steve Miller Band.

TUROW, SCOTT. Chicago, IL, 4/12/49. Author. *The Burden of Proof.*

TURTURRO, JOHN. Brooklyn, NY, 2/28/57. Actor. *Barton Fink.*

TWIGGY (Lesley Hornby). London, England, 9/19/49. Model, actor. *The Boy Friend.*

TWIST, NIGEL. Manchester, England, 7/18/58. Drummer. The Alarm.

TYLER, BONNIE (Gaynor Hopkins). Swansea, Wales, 6/8/53. Singer. "Total Eclipse of the Heart."

TYLER, RICHARD. Sunshine, Australia, 1948. Designer.

TYSON, CICELY. New York, NY, 12/19/24. Actor. *The Autobiography of Miss Jane Pittman.*

TYSON, MIKE New York, NY, 6/30/66. Boxer, convicted of rape.

UECKER, BOB. Milwaukee, WI, 1/26/35. Actor. *Mr. Belvedere.*

UGGAMS, LESLIE. New York, NY, 5/25/43. Singer, actor. Kizzy in *Roots.*

ULLMAN, TRACEY. Hackbridge, England, 12/30/59. Actor. *The Tracey Ullman Show.*

ULLMANN, LIV. Tokyo, Japan, 12/16/39. Actor. *Persona.*

ULVAEUS, BJORN. Gothenburg, Sweden, 4/25/45. Guitarist, singer. Abba.

UNDERWOOD, BLAIR. Tacoma, WA, 8/25/64. Actor. *L.A. Law.*

URICH, ROBERT. Toronto, Canada, 12/19/46. Actor. *Spenser: For Hire.*

VACCARO, BRENDA. Brooklyn, NY, 11/18/39. Actor. *Midnight Cowboy.*

VADIM, ROGER (Roger Vadim Plemiannikov). Paris, France, 1/26/28. Movie director, formerly married to Jane Fonda.

VALE, JERRY. New York, NY, 7/8/32. Pop singer. "Innamorata."

VALE, MIKE. 7/17/49. Bassist. Tommy James & The Shondells.

VALENTINE, HILTON. North Shields, England, 5/21/43. Guitarist. The Animals.

VALENTINE, SCOTT. Saratoga Springs, NY, 6/3/58. Actor. Nick Moore on *Family Ties.*

VALLI, FRANKIE (Frank Castelluccio). Newark, NJ, 5/3/37. Lead singer. The Four Seasons.

VALLONE, RAF (Raffaele Vallone). Tropea, Italy, 2/17/18. Actor. *Obsession.*

VALORY, ROSS. San Francisco, CA, 2/2/49. Bassist. Journey.

VAN ARK, JOAN. New York, NY, 6/16/43. Actor. Val Ewing Knots Landing.

VAN DAMME, JEAN-CLAUDE Brussels, Belgium, 10/18/60. Actor, martial arts expert. *Kickboxer.*

VAN DEVERE, TRISH (Patricia Dressel). Englewood Cliffs, NJ, 3/9/45. Actor, married to George C. Scott. *The Day of the Dolphin.*

VAN DOREN, MAMIE (Joan Lucile Olander). Rowena, SD, 2/6/31. Actor. *Ain't Misbehavin'.*

VAN DYKE, DICK. West Plains, MO, 12/13/25. Actor and performer, brother of Jerry. *The Dick Van Dyke Show.*

VAN DYKE, JERRY. Danville, IL, 7/27/31. Actor, brother of Dick. *Coach.*

VAN HALEN, ALEX. Nijmegen, Holland, 5/8/55. Drummer. Van Halen.

VAN HALEN, EDDIE Nijmegen, Holland, 1/26/55. Singer, guitarist. Van Halen.

VAN PATTEN, DICK. New York, NY, 12/9/28. Actor. *Eight Is Enough.*

VAN PEEBLES, MARIO. New York, NY, 1/15/57. Actor, director, writer, son of Melvin. *Posse.*

VAN PEEBLES, MELVIN. Chicago, IL, 8/21/32. Actor, writer, composer, father of

Mario. *Sweet Sweetback's Badasssss Song.*

VAN ZANDT, DONNIE. Florida, 6/11/52. Singer, guitarist. .38 Special.

VAN ZANDT, STEVIE. Boston, MA, 11/22/50. Bassist. E Street Band.

VANDA, HARRY (Harry Vandenberg). The Hague, The Netherlands, 3/22/47. Guitarist. The Easybeats.

VANDERBILT, GLORIA. New York, NY, 2/20/24. Fashion designer. Gloria Vanderbilt Jeans.

VANIAN, DAVE (David Letts). 10/12/56. Singer. The Damned.

VANNELLI, GINO. Montreal, Canada, 6/16/52. Singer, songwriter. "Living Inside Myself."

VARNEY, JIM. Lexington, KY, 6/15/49. Actor. *Ernest Goes to Camp.*

VAUGHN, ROBERT. New York, NY, 11/22/32. Actor. *The Man from U.N.C.L.E.*

VEDDER, EDDIE Chicago, IL, 12/23/64. Pearl Jam.

VEE, BOBBY (Robert Velline). Fargo, ND, 4/30/43. Singer, songwriter.

VEGA, SUZANNE. New York, NY, 8/12/59. Folk-oriented guitarist, singer, songwriter. "Luka."

VELEZ, EDDIE (Edwin Velez). New York, NY, 6/4/58. Actor. *Extremities.*

VELJOHNSON, REGINALD. Queens, NY, 8/16/52. Actor. *Family Matters.*

VENDELA (Vendela Kirsebom). Sweden, 1/12/67. Supermodel.

VERDON, GWEN. Culver City, CA, 1/13/25. Actor, dancer, choreographer. *The Cotton Club.*

VEREEN, BEN. Miami, FL, 10/10/46. Actor, performer. Chicken George Moore on *Roots.*

VERLAINE, TOM (Thomas Miller). Mt. Morris, NJ, 12/13/49. Singer, lead guitarist. Television.

VERUSCHKA. 1943. Model, actor. *Blow Up.*

VESTINE, HENRY. Washington, DC, 12/25/44. Guitarist. Canned Heat.

VICKERS, MIKE. Southampton, England, 4/18/41. Guitarist. Manfred Mann.

VIDAL, GORE (Eugene Luther Vidal). West Point, NY, 10/3/25. Author, dramatist. *Lincoln: A Novel.*

VINCENT, JAN-MICHAEL. Denver, CO, 7/15/45. Actor. *The Mechanic.*

VINTON, BOBBY. Canonsburg, PA, 4/16/35. Singer, songwriter.

VIRTUE, MICKEY. Birmingham, England, 1/19/57. Keyboardist. UB40.

VOIGHT, JON. Yonkers, NY, 12/29/38. Actor. *Midnight Cowboy.*

VOLMAN, MARK. Los Angeles, CA, 4/19/47. Singer, saxophonist. The Turtles.

VON BULOW, CLAUS. Copenhagen, Denmark, 8/11/26. Businessman. Subject of the motion picture *Reversal of Fortune.*

VON SYDOW, MAX. Lund, Sweden, 7/10/29. Actor. *The Greatest Story Ever Told.*

VONNEGUT, KURT JR. Indianapolis, IN, 11/11/22. Author. *Slaughterhouse Five.*

WAAKTAAR, PAUL. Oslo, Norway, 9/6/61. Guitarist, singer. a-ha.

WAGGONER, LYLE. Kansas City, KS, 4/13/35. Actor. *Wonder Woman.*

WAGNER, JACK. Washington, MO, 10/3/59. Actor, singer. Frisco Jones on *General Hospital.*

WAGNER, LINDSAY. Los Angeles, CA, 6/22/49. Actor. *The Bionic Woman.*

WAGNER, ROBERT. Detroit, MI, 2/10/30. Actor, widower of Natalie Wood, married to Jill St. John. Jonathan Hart on *Hart to Hart.*

WAHL, KEN. Chicago, IL, 2/14/57. Actor. Vinnie Terranova on *Wiseguy.*

WAHLBERG, DONNIE. Dorchester, MA, 8/17/69. Singer, brother of Mark. New Kids on the Block.

WAILER, BUNNY (Neville O'Riley Livingston). Kingston, Jamaica, 4/10/47. Singer, percussionist. Bob Marley & The Wailers.

WAITE, JOHN. Lancaster, England, 7/4/54. Singer, songwriter.

WAITS, TOM. Pomona, CA, 12/7/49. Singer, actor, composer. *Short Cuts*.

WALKEN, CHRISTOPHER. Astoria, NY, 3/31/43. Actor. *The Deer Hunter*.

WALKER, ALICE. Eatonton, GA, 2/9/44. Author. *The Color Purple*.

WALKER, CLINT. Hartford, IL, 5/30/27. Actor. *Cheyenne*.

WALKER, DAVID. Montgomeryville, AL, 5/12/43. Keyboardist. Gary Lewis & The Playboys.

WALKER, JIMMIE. New York, NY, 6/25/48. Actor. J. J. Evans on *Good Times*.

WALKER, JUNIOR (Autry DeWalt II). Blytheville, AR, 1942. Saxophonist, singer. Junior Walker & The All-Stars.

WALKER, MORT. El Dorado, KS, 9/3/23. Cartoonist. *Beetle Bailey*.

WALLACE, MIKE (Myron Leon Wallace). Brookline, MA, 5/9/18. News reporter and interviewer, anchor. *60 Minutes*.

WALLACH, ELI. Brooklyn, NY, 12/7/15. Actor. *The Good, the Bad and the Ugly*.

WALLER, GORDON. Braemar, Scotland, 6/4/45. Singer. Peter and Gordon.

WALLER, ROBERT JAMES. Rockford, IA, 8/1/39. Author. *The Bridges of Madison County*.

WALLINGER, KARL. Prestatyn, Wales, 10/19/57. Keyboardist, guitarist. World Party.

WALSH, JOE. Cleveland, OH, 11/20/47. Guitarist, singer. The Eagles; The James Gang.

WALSH, M. EMMET. Ogdensburg, NY, 3/22/35. Actor. *Blood Simple*.

WALSTON, RAY. New Orleans, LA, 11/2/14. Actor. Uncle Martin on *My Favorite Martian*.

WALTER, JESSICA. Brooklyn, NY, 1/31/41. Actor. *Play Misty for Me*.

WALTER, TRACEY. Jersey City, NJ. Actor. Bob the Goon in *Batman*.

WARD, BILL. Birmingham, England, 5/5/48. Drummer. Black Sabbath.

WARD, BURT. Los Angeles, CA, 7/6/46. Actor. *Batman*.

WARD, FRED. San Diego, CA, 12/30/42. Actor. *Henry and June*.

WARD, RACHEL. London, England, 1957. Actor. *Against All Odds*.

WARD, SELA. Meridian, MS, 7/11/56. Actor. *Sisters*.

WARDEN, JACK (Jack Warden Lebzelter). Newark, NJ, 9/18/20. Actor. Harry Fox on *Crazy Like a Fox*.

WARE, MARTYN. Sheffield, England, 5/19/56. Synthesizer player. The Human League; Heaven 17.

WARFIELD, MARSHA. Chicago, IL, 3/5/55. Actor. Roz Russell on *Night Court*.

WARNER, DAVID. Manchester, England, 7/29/41. Actor. *The Omen*.

WARNER, JULIE. New York, NY, 1965. Actor. *Doc Hollywood*.

WARNER, MALCOLM-JAMAL. Jersey City, NJ, 8/18/70. Actor. Theo Huxtable on *The Cosby Show*.

WARNES, JENNIFER. Orange County, CA, 1947. Pop singer.

WARREN, LESLEY ANN. New York, NY, 8/16/46. Actor. *Mission: Impossible*.

WARRICK, RUTH. St. Joseph, MO, 6/29/15. Actor. Phoebe Wallingford on *All My Children*.

WARWICK, CLINT (Clinton Eccles). Birmingham, England, 6/25/40. Bassist. The Moody Blues.

WARWICK, DIONNE (Marie Warrick). East Orange, NJ, 12/12/40. Gospel/pop singer.

WATERS, JOHN. Baltimore, MD, 4/22/46. Director, writer, actor. *Hairspray; Pink Flamingos; Serial Mom*.

WATERS, ROGER. Great Bookham, England, 9/9/44. Singer, bassist. Pink Floyd.

WATERSTON, SAM. Cambridge, MA, 11/15/40. Actor. *The Killing Fields*.

WATLEY, JODY. Chicago, IL, 1/30/59. Singer. Shalamar.

WATSON, BRUCE. Ontario, Canada, 3/11/61. Guitarist. Big Country.

WATT, BEN. 12/6/62. Guitarist, keyboardist, singer. Everything but the Girl.

WATTS, CHARLIE. Islington, England, 6/2/41. Drummer. The Rolling Stones.

WATTS, OVEREND (Peter Watts). Birmingham, England, 5/13/49. Bassist. Mott The Hoople.

WAXMAN, AL. Toronto, Canada, 3/2/34. Actor. Bert Samuels on *Cagney and Lacey*.

WAYANS, KEENEN IVORY. New York, NY, 6/8/58. Actor, director, writer. *In Living Color*.

WAYBILL, FEE (John Waldo). Omaha, NE, 9/17/50. Singer. The Tubes.

WAYNE, CARL. Mosely, England, 8/18/44. Singer. The Move.

WAYNE, PATRICK. Los Angeles, CA, 7/15/39. Actor, son of John. *McClintock!*

WEATHERS, CARL. New Orleans, LA, 1/14/48. Actor. Apollo Creed in *Rocky*.

WEAVER, BLUE (Derek Weaver). Cardiff, Wales, 3/3/49. Organist. Amen Corner.

WEAVER, DENNIS. Joplin, MO, 6/4/24. Actor. *McCloud*.

WEAVER, FRITZ. Pittsburgh, PA, 1/19/26. Actor. *Marathon Man*.

WEBB, PAUL. 1/16/62. Bassist. Talk Talk.

WEIDER, JOHN. England, 4/21/47. Bassist. Family.

WEIR, BOB. San Francisco, CA, 10/6/47. Guitarist. Grateful Dead.

WEITZ, BRUCE. Norwalk, CT, 5/27/43. Actor. Mick Belker on *Hill Street Blues*.

WELCH, BRUCE (Bruce Cripps). Bognor Regis, England, 11/2/41. Guitarist. The Shadows.

WELCH, RAQUEL (Raquel Tejada). Chicago, IL, 9/5/40. Actor. *One Million Years B.C.*

WELD, TUESDAY (Susan Weld). New York, NY, 8/27/43. Actor. *Looking for Mr. Goodbar*.

WELLER, PAUL. 5/25/58. Singer, bassist. The Jam.

WELLER, PAUL. Woking, England, 5/25/58. Singer, guitarist. The Style Council.

WELLER, PETER. Stevens Point, WI, 6/24/47. Actor. *Robocop*.

WELLS, CORY. Buffalo, NY, 2/5/42. Singer. Three Dog Night.

WELLS, KITTY (Muriel Deason). Nashville, TN, 8/30/19. Country singer.

WELNICK, VINCE. Phoenix, AZ, 2/21/51. Keyboardist. The Tubes.

WENDT, GEORGE. Chicago, IL, 10/17/48. Actor. Norm Peterson on *Cheers*.

WEST, ADAM (William Anderson). Walla Walla, WA, 9/19/28. Actor. *Batman*.

WEST, JOHN. Uhrichsville, OH, 7/31/39. Guitarist. Gary Lewis & The Playboys.

WEST, RICK. Dagenham, England, 5/7/43. Lead guitarist. Brian Poole & The Tremeloes.

WESTHEIMER, RUTH (Karola Ruth Siegel). Frankfurt, Germany, 6/4/28. Sex therapist. *Ask Dr. Ruth*.

WETTON, JOHN. Derbyshire, England, 7/12/49. Lead singer, bassist. Asia.

WEYMOUTH, TINA. Coronado, CA, 11/22/50. Bassist. Talking Heads.

WHALEY, FRANK. Syracuse, NY, 1963. Actor. *The Doors*.

WHALLEY, JOANNE. Manchester, England, 8/25/64. Actor, formerly married to Val Kilmer. *Willow*.

WHELCHEL, LISA. Fort Worth, TX, 5/29/63. Actor. Blair Warner on *The Facts of Life*.

WHITAKER, FOREST. Longview, TX, 7/15/61. Actor, director. *The Crying Game*.

WHITAKER, JOHNNY. Van Nuys, CA, 12/13/59. Actor. Jody on *Family Affair*.

WHITE, BARRY. Galveston, TX, 9/12/44. R&B singer, songwriter.

WHITE, BETTY. Oak Park, IL, 1/17/22. Actor. Rose Nylund on *The Golden Girls*.

WHITE, CHRIS. Barnet, England, 3/7/43. Bassist. The Zombies.

WHITE, DAVE (David Tricker). Philadelphia, PA, 9/1/40. Singer. Danny & The Juniors.

WHITE, JALEEL. Los Angeles, CA, 11/27/76. Actor. Steve Urkel on *Family Matters*.

WHITE, MARK. Sheffield, England, 4/1/61. Guitarist. ABC.

WHITE, MAURICE. Memphis, TN, 12/19/41. Singer, drummer, kalimba player. Earth, Wind & Fire.

WHITE, VANNA (Vanna Rosich). North Myrtle Beach, SC, 2/18/57. Letter turner extraordinaire. *Wheel of Fortune.*

WHITE, VERDINE. Illinois, 7/25/51. Singer, bassist. Earth, Wind & Fire.

WHITELAW, BILLIE. Coventry, England, 6/6/32. Actor. *Charlie Bubbles.*

WHITFORD, BRAD. Winchester, MA, 2/23/52. Guitarist. Aerosmith.

WHITMORE, JAMES. White Plains, NY, 10/1/21. Actor. *Will Rogers, USA.*

WHITNEY, CHARLIE. Leicester, England, 6/4/44. Guitarist. Family.

WIEST, DIANNE. Kansas City, MO, 3/28/46. Actor. *Hannah and Her Sisters.*

WILCOX, LARRY. San Diego, CA, 8/8/47. Actor. Officer Jon Baker on *CHiPS.*

WILDE, KIM (Kim Smith). London, England, 11/18/60. Singer, songwriter.

WILDER, ALAN. 6/1/59. Singer, synthesizer player. Depeche Mode.

WILDER, GENE (Jerome Silberman). Milwaukee, WI, 6/11/33. Actor, director, writer, widower of Gilda Radner. *Young Frankenstein.*

WILLIAM, PRINCE. London, England, 6/21/82. British royalty, son of Prince Charles and Princess Diana.

WILLIAMS, ANDY. Wall Lake, IA, 12/3/27. Pop singer. "Where Do I Begin?"

WILLIAMS, BARRY. Santa Monica, CA, 9/30/54. Actor. Greg on *The Brady Bunch.*

WILLIAMS, BILLY DEE. New York, NY, 4/6/37. Actor. *Lady Sings the Blues.*

WILLIAMS, CINDY. Van Nuys, CA, 8/22/47. Actor. Shirley Feeney on *Laverne & Shirley.*

WILLIAMS, CLARENCE III. New York, NY, 8/21/39. Actor. Lincoln Hayes on *The Mod Squad.*

WILLIAMS, CLIFF. Rumford, England, 12/14/29. Bass guitarist. AC/DC.

WILLIAMS, DENIECE (Deniece Chandler). Gary, IN, 6/3/51. Gospel/pop singer.

WILLIAMS, ESTHER. Los Angeles, CA, 8/8/21. Actor,

swimmer, widow of Fernando Lamas. *Bathing Beauty.*

WILLIAMS, HANK JR (Randall Hank). Shreveport, LA, 5/26/49. Country singer, songwriter. "Texas Women."

WILLIAMS, JOBETH. Houston, TX, 12/6/48. Actor. *The Big Chill.*

WILLIAMS, JOHN TOWNER. Queens, NY, 2/8/32. Composer, conductor. *Jaws; Star Wars.*

WILLIAMS, MAISIE. Montserrat, West Indies, 3/25/51. Singer. Boney M.

WILLIAMS, MILAN. Mississippi, 3/28/48. Keyboardist, trombonist, guitarist, drummer. The Commodores.

WILLIAMS, MONTEL. Baltimore, MD, 7/3/56. Talk show host. *The Montel Williams Show.*

WILLIAMS, OTIS (Otis Miles). Texarkana, TX, 10/30/49. Singer. The Temptations.

WILLIAMS, PAUL. Birmingham, AL, 7/2/39. Singer. The Temptations.

WILLIAMS, TREAT (Richard Williams). Rowayton, CT, 12/1/51. Actor. *Prince of the City.*

WILLIAMS, WALTER. 8/25/42. Singer. The O'Jays.

WILLIAMS, WENDY O. (Wendy Orlean Williams). Rochester, NY, 1946. Entertainer, singer.

WILLIAMSON, NICOL. Hamilton, Scotland, 9/14/38. Actor. *Excalibur.*

WILLIG, GEORGE. New York, NY, 6/11/49. Actor, stuntman. Climbed World Trade Center.

WILSON, AL "BLIND OWL." Boston, MA, 7/4/43. Guitarist, singer, harmonicist. Canned Heat.

WILSON, ANN. San Diego, CA, 6/19/51. Lead singer. Heart.

WILSON, BARRY J. London, England, 3/18/47. Drummer. Procol Harum.

WILSON, BRIAN. Inglewood, CA, 6/20/42. Bassist, keyboardist, singer, father of Wendy and Carnie. The Beach Boys.

WILSON, CARNIE. Los Angeles, CA, 4/29/68. Singer, daughter of Brian, sister of Wendy. Wilson Phillips.

WILSON, CINDY. Athens, GA, 2/28/57. Guitarist, singer. The B-52's.

WILSON, DEMOND. Valdosta, GA, 10/13/46. Actor. *Sanford and Son.*

WILSON, DON. Tacoma, WA, 2/10/37. Guitarist. The Ventures.

WILSON, JOYCE. Detroit, MI, 12/14/46. Singer. Tony Orlando & Dawn.

WILSON, MARY. Greenville, MS, 3/6/44. Singer. The Supremes.

WILSON, NANCY. Chillicothe, OH, 2/20/37. R&B singer.

WILSON, NANCY. San Francisco, CA, 3/16/54. Guitarist, singer. Heart.

WILSON, TOM. Grant Town, WV, 8/1/31. Cartoonist. *Ziggy.*

WILSON, TONY. Trinidad, 10/8/47. Bassist, singer. Hot Chocolate.

WILSON, WENDY. Los Angeles, CA, 10/16/69. Singer, sister of Carnie, daughter of Brian. Wilson Phillips.

WINCHELL, PAUL. New York, NY, 12/21/22. Ventriloquist, actor. *The Paul Winchell-Jerry Mahoney Show.*

WINDOM, WILLIAM. New York, NY, 9/28/23. Actor. *Murder She Wrote.*

WINFIELD, DAVE. Saint Paul, MN, 10/3/51. Baseball player.

WINFIELD, PAUL. Los Angeles, CA, 5/22/41. Actor. *Sounder.*

WINGER, DEBRA (Mary Debra Winger). Cleveland, OH, 5/16/55. Actor. *Terms of Endearment.*

WINKLER, HENRY. New York, NY, 10/30/45. Actor, producer, director. Arthur "The Fonz" Fonzarelli on *Happy Days.*

WINNINGHAM, MARE. Phoenix, AZ, 5/6/59. Actor. *St. Elmo's Fire.*

WINSTON, JIMMY (James Langwith). London, England, 4/20/45. Organist. The Small Faces.

WINTER, EDGAR. Beaumont, TX, 12/28/46. Blues/rock keyboardist, brother of Johnny.

WINTER, JOHNNY. Beaumont, TX, 2/23/44. Blues/rock guitarist, brother of Edgar.

WINTERS, JONATHAN. Dayton, OH, 11/11/25. Actor. *The Jonathan Winters Show.*

WINTERS, SHELLEY (Shirley Schrift). St. Louis, MO,

8/18/20. Actor. *The Poseidon Adventure.*

WINWOOD, MUFF (Mervyn Winwood). Birmingham, England, 6/14/43. Singer, songwriter, bassist. The Spencer Davis Group.

WINWOOD, STEVE. Birmingham, England, 5/12/48. Singer, songwriter. The Spencer Davis Group; Traffic; Blind Faith.

WITHERS, BILL. Slab Fork, WV, 7/4/38. Pop singer, songwriter, guitarist.

WITHERS, JANE. Atlanta, GA, 4/12/26. Actor. Josephine the Plumber on TV commercials.

WOLF, PETER (Peter Blankfield). New York, NY, 3/7/46. Singer. The J. Geils Band.

WOLTERS, JOHN. 4/28/45. Drummer, singer. Dr. Hook.

WOMACK, BOBBY. Cleveland, OH, 3/4/44. Gospel/R&B singer, songwriter, guitarist.

WONDER, STEVIE (Steveland Morris). Saginaw, MI, 5/13/50. Singer, songwriter, formerly married to Syreeta Wright.

WONG, B. D. San Francisco, CA, 10/24/62. Actor. *M. Butterfly.*

WOOD, DANNY. Boston, MA, 5/14/71. Singer. New Kids on the Block.

WOOD, RON. London, England, 6/1/47. Guitarist. The Rolling Stones.

WOOD, ROY (Ulysses Adrian Wood). Birmingham, England, 11/8/46. Singer, guitarist, cellist. Electric Light Orchestra (ELO); Wizzard; The Move.

WOOD, STUART. Edinburgh, Scotland, 2/25/57. Guitarist. The Bay City Rollers.

WOODARD, ALFRE. Tulsa, OK, 11/8/53. Actor. *Cross Creek.*

WOODWARD, EDWARD. Croydon, England, 6/1/30. Actor. *The Equalizer.*

WOODWARD, JOANNE. Thomasville, GA, 2/27/30. Actor, married to Paul Newman. *The Three Faces of Eve.*

WOODWARD, KEREN. Bristol, England, 4/2/61. Singer. Bananarama.

WORLEY, JO ANNE. Lowell, IN, 9/6/39. Actor, singer. *Laugh-In.*

WRAY, FAY. Alberta, Canada, 9/10/07. Actor. *King Kong.*

WRIGHT, ADRIAN. Sheffield, England, 6/30/56. Projector operator for on-stage slides and films. The Human League.

WRIGHT, LITTLE STEVIE. Leeds, England, 12/20/48. Singer. The Easybeats.

WRIGHT, MAX. Detroit, MI, 8/2/43. Actor. Willie Tanner on *ALF*.

WRIGHT, PAT. Brooklyn, NY, 1945. Singer. The Crystals.

WRIGHT, RICK. London, England, 7/28/45. Keyboardist. Pink Floyd.

WRIGHT, STEVEN. Burlington, MA, 12/6/55. Comedian.

WRIGHT, SYREETA. Pittsburgh, PA, 1946. Singer, songwriter, formerly married to Stevie Wonder.

WUHL, ROBERT. Union City, NJ, 10/9/51. Actor, writer. *Bull Durham*.

WYATT, JANE. Campgaw, NJ, 8/13/12. Actor. *Father Knows Best*.

WYMAN, BILL (William Perks). London, England, 10/24/36. Bassist. The Rolling Stones.

WYMAN, JANE (Sarah Jane Fulks). St. Joseph, MO, 1/4/14. Actor, formerly married to Ronald Reagan. Angela Channing on *Falcon Crest*.

YAMAGUCHI, KRISTI. Hayward, CA, 7/12/71. Skater, Olympic gold medalist.

YANKOVIC, WEIRD AL (Alfred Matthew Yankovic). Los Angeles, CA, 10/23/59. Singer, spoof artist. "Like a Surgeon."

YANOVSKY, ZAL. Toronto, Canada, 12/19/44. Guitarist, singer. The Lovin' Spoonful.

YARROW, PETER. New York, NY, 5/31/38. Composer, author, singer. Peter, Paul and Mary.

YEARWOOD, TRISHA. Monticello, GA, 9/19/64. Singer.

YELTSIN, BORIS. Burka, Russia, 2/1/31. Russian political leader.

YESTER, JIM. Birmingham, AL, 11/24/39. Singer, guitarist. The Association.

YOAKAM, DWIGHT. Pikesville, KY, 10/23/56. Country singer. "Honky Tonk Man."

YORK, MICHAEL. Fulmer, England, 3/27/42. Actor. *Logan's Run*.

YORK, PETE. Redcar, England, 8/15/42. Drummer. The Spencer Davis Group.

YOUNG, ANGUS. Glasgow, Scotland, 3/31/59. Guitarist. AC/DC.

YOUNG, GEORGE. Glasgow, Scotland, 11/6/47. Guitarist. The Easybeats.

YOUNG, JAMES. Chicago, IL, 11/14/48. Guitarist. Styx.

YOUNG, JESSE COLIN (Perry Miller). New York, NY, 11/11/41. Guitarist, bassist, singer. The Youngbloods.

YOUNG, LORETTA (Gretchen Young). Salt Lake City, UT, 1/6/13. Actor. *The Farmer's Daughter*.

YOUNG, MALCOLM. Glasgow, Scotland, 1/6/53. Guitarist. AC/DC.

YOUNG, NEIL. Toronto, Canada, 11/12/45. Singer, songwriter, guitarist. Buffalo Springfield; Crosby, Stills, Nash & Young.

YOUNG, PAUL. Luton, England, 1/17/56. Singer, songwriter.

YOUNG, RUSTY. Long Beach, CA, 2/23/46. Pedal steel guitarist. Poco.

YOUNG, SEAN. Louisville, KY, 11/20/59. Actor. *No Way Out*.

YOUNG MC (Marvin Young). London, England, 1968. Rap artist.

ZADORA, PIA. New York, NY, 5/4/56. Actor. *Naked Gun 33 1/3*.

ZAHN, PAULA. Naperville, IL, 2/24/56. Broadcast journalist. *CBS This Morning*.

ZAL, ROXANA. Los Angeles, CA, 11/8/69. Actor. *Something About Amelia*.

ZANDER, ROBIN. Rockford, IL, 1/23/53. Singer, guitarist. Cheap Trick.

ZAPPA, DWEEZIL. Los Angeles, CA, 9/5/69. Guitarist, son of Frank, brother of Moon Unit.

ZAPPA, MOON UNIT. Hollywood, CA, 9/28/67. Singer, daughter of Frank, sister of Dweezil. "Valley Girl."

ZEMECKIS, ROBERT Chicago, IL, 5/14/51. Director, producer, screenwriter. *Forrest Gump*.

ZEVON, WARREN. Chicago, IL, 1/24/47. Singer, songwriter. "Werewolves of London."

ZIERING, IAN. 3/30/64. Actor. *Beverly Hills 90210*.

ZIMBALIST, STEPHANIE. Encino, CA, 10/8/56. Actor, daughter of Efrem. Laura Holt on *Remington Steele*.

ZMED, ADRIAN. Chicago, IL, 3/4/54. Actor. Vince Romano on *T. J. Hooker*.

ZUNIGA, DAPHNE. Berkeley, CA, 10/28/62. Actor. *Melrose Place*.

HAPPY BIRTHDAY! THE GREATS' NATAL DATES

JANUARY 1
Frank Langella
Don Novello
Dedee Pfeiffer
J.D. Salinger

JANUARY 2
Jim Bakker
Gabrielle Carteris
Chick Churchill
Taye Diggs
Cuba Gooding Jr.
Joanna Pacula

JANUARY 3
Melody Anderson
Dabney Coleman
Mel Gibson
Robert Loggia
Danica McKellar
Victoria Principal
Stephen Stills
Bill Travers

JANUARY 4
Bernie Albrecht
Dyan Cannon
Matt Frewer
Ann Magnuson
Julia Ormond
Michael Stipe
Barney Sumner
Jane Wyman

JANUARY 5
Suzy Amis
George Brown
Robert Duvall
Diane Keaton
Ted Lange
Marilyn Manson
Walter Mondale
Chris Stein

JANUARY 6
Rowan Atkinson
Syd Barrett
Bonnie Franklin
Mark O'Toole
John Singleton
Kathy Sledge
Loretta Young
Malcolm Young

JANUARY 7
Nicolas Cage
Katie Couric
Sammo Hung
Kenny Loggins
Paul Revere

JANUARY 8
David Bowie
Stephen Hawking
Robbie Krieger
Yvette Mimieux
Charles Osgood
Soupy Sales
Larry Storch

JANUARY 9
Joan Baez
Bill Cowsill
Bob Denver
Scott Engel
Crystal Gayle
David Johansen
Judith Krantz
Herbert Lom
Jimmy Page

JANUARY 10
Trini Alvarado
Pat Benatar
Shawn Colvin
Donald Fagen
George Foreman
Bob Lang
Cyril Neville
Maurice Sendak
Rod Stewart

JANUARY 11
Mary J. Blige
Naomi Judd
Vicki Peterson
Rod Taylor

JANUARY 12
Kirstie Alley
Anthony Andrews
Melanie Chisholm
Per Gessle
William Lee
  Golden
Rush Limbaugh
Oliver Platt
Chynna Phillips
Cynthia Robinson
Vendela

JANUARY 13
Kevin Anderson
Nick Clooney
Patrick Dempsey
Robert "Squirrel"
  Lester
Julia Louis-
  Dreyfus
Graham
  McPherson

Penelope Ann
  Miller
Richard Moll
Robert Stack
Frances
  Sternhagen
Gwen Verdon

JANUARY 14
Jason Bateman
Faye Dunaway
L.L. Cool J
Andy Rooney
Carl Weathers

JANUARY 15
Captain Beefheart
Charo
Martha Davis
Chad Lowe
Andrea Martin
Pamela Sue
  Martin
Julian Sands
Peter Trewavas
Mario Van Peebles

JANUARY 16
Debbie Allen
Bob Bogle
John Carpenter
Bill Francis
Kate Moss
Sade
Laura
  Schlessinger
Jim Stafford
Paul Webb

JANUARY 17
Muhammad Ali
Jim Carrey
David Caruso
John Crawford
Steve Earle
Joe Frazier
Susanna Hoffs
James Earl Jones
Eartha Kitt
Maury Povich
Vidal Sassoon
Betty White
Paul Young

JANUARY 18
Kevin Costner
David Ruffin
Larry Smith

JANUARY 19
Desi Arnaz Jr.
Dewey Bunnell

Michael Crawford
Phil Everly
Shelley Fabares
Tippi Hedren
Harvey Hinsley
Robert MacNeil
Robert Palmer
Dolly Parton
Katey Sagal
Jean Stapleton
Mickey Virtue
Fritz Weaver

JANUARY 20
Buzz Aldrin
Arte Johnson
Lorenzo Lamas
David Lynch
Bill Maher
John Michael
  Montgomery
Patricia Neal
Paul Stanley
Eric Stewart
Ron Townson

JANUARY 21
Robby Benson
Emma Bunton
Geena Davis
Mac Davis
Jill Eikenberry
Richie Havens
Steve Reeves

JANUARY 22
Linda Blair
Olivia D'Abo
Balthazar Getty
John Hurt
Diane Lane
Piper Laurie
Chris Lemmon
Steve Perry
Jeff Smith
Ann Sothern

JANUARY 23
Richard Dean
  Anderson
Princess Caroline
Bill Cunningham
Earl Falconer
Gil Gerard
Rutger Hauer
Jeanne Moreau
Anita Pointer
Chita Rivera
Patrick Simmons
Robin Zande

JANUARY 24
Ernest Borgnine
Neil Diamond
Jools Holland
Nastassja Kinski
Michael Ontkean
Oral Roberts
Yakov Smirnoff
Ray Stevens
Warren Zevon

JANUARY 25
Corazon Aquino
Andy Cox
Richard Finch
Etta James
Dean Jones
Dinah Manoff

JANUARY 26
Jazzie B
David Briggs
Ellen DeGeneres
Scott Glenn
Wayne Gretsky
Paul Newman
Andrew Ridgeley
Bob Uecker
Roger Vadim
Eddie Van Halen

JANUARY 27
Bobby Bland
Troy Donahue
Brian Downey
Bridget Fonda
Gillian Gilbert
Seth Justman
Nick Mason
Mike Patton
Mimi Rogers
Nedra Talley

JANUARY 28
Alan Alda
Mikhail
  Baryshnikov
John Beck
Brian Keenan
Marthe Keller
Sarah McLachlan
Nicholas Pryor
Dave Sharp
Dick Taylor
Elijah Wood

JANUARY 29
David Byron
Ed Burns
John Forsythe
Roddy Frame

Sara Gilbert
Heather Graham
Noel Harrison
Eddie Jackson
Anne Jillian
Greg Louganis
Tommy Ramone
Katharine Ross
Tom Selleck
Oprah Winfrey

JANUARY 30
Marty Balin
Phil Collins
Charles Dutton
Gene Hackman
William King
Dorothy Malone
Steve Marriott
Dick Martin
Vanessa Redgrave
Joe Terranova
Jody Watley

JANUARY 31
John Agar
Harry Wayne
  Casey
Carol Channing
Lloyd Cole
Portia De Rossi
Minnie Driver
John Paul Jones
Terry Kath
John Lydon
Phil Manzanera
Suzanne Pleshette
Jean Simmons

FEBRUARY 1
Mike Campbell
Don Everly
Dennis Farina
Sherilynn Fenn
Sherman Hemsley
Rick James
Terry Jones
Billy Mumy
Lisa Marie
  Presley-Jackson
Ray Sawyer
Pauly Shore
Boris Yeltsin

FEBRUARY 2
Christie Brinkley
Garth Brooks
Alan Caddy
Farrah Fawcett
Gale Gordon
Peter Lucia
Graham Nash

Liz Smith
Tom Smothers
Elaine Stritch
Ross Valory

FEBRUARY 3
Joey Bishop
Thomas Calabro
Angelo D'Aleo
Blythe Danner
Dave Davies
Morgan Fairchild
Eric Haydock
Nathan Lane
Fran Tarkenton
Lol Tolhurst

FEBRUARY 4
Gabrielle Anwar
Michael Beck
Clint Black
David Brenner
Alice Cooper
Natalie Imbruglia
Florence LaRue
Dan Quayle
John Steel

FEBRUARY 5
Bobby Brown
Christopher Guest
Barbara Hershey
Jennifer Jason
  Leigh
Laura Linney
Charlotte
  Rampling
Roger Staubach
Cory Wells

FEBRUARY 6
Rick Astley
Tom Brokaw
Natalie Cole
Fabian
Mike Farrell
Zsa Zsa Gabor
Alan Jones
Patrick Macnee
Ronald Reagan
Rip Torn
Robert Townsend
Michael Tucker
Mamie Van Doren

FEBRUARY 7
David Bryan
Miguel Ferrer
Jimmy Greenspoon
Alan Lancaster
Chris Rock
James Spader
Brian Travers

FEBRUARY 8
Brooke Adams
Brian Bennett

Creed Bratton
Gary Coleman
John Grisham
Robert Klein
Ted Koppel
Vince Neil
Nick Nolte
Mary Steenburgen
John Williams

FEBRUARY 9
Mia Farrow
Carole King
Judith Light
Master P
Roger Mudd
Joe Pesci
Janet Suzman
Travis Tritt
Alice Walker

FEBRUARY 10
Laura Dern
Donovan
Roberta Flack
Jimmy Merchant
Mark Spitz
Robert Wagner
Don Wilson

FEBRUARY 11
Jennifer Aniston
Brandy
Sheryl Crow
Conrad Janis
Tina Louise
Leslie Nielsen
Burt Reynolds
Sidney Sheldon

FEBRUARY 12
Maud Adams
Joe Don Baker
Judy Blume
Cliff DeYoung
Arsenio Hall
Joanna Kerns
Simon
  MacCorkindale
Ray Manzarek
Christina Ricci
Joe Schermie

FEBRUARY 13
Tony Butler
Stockard
  Channing
Roger Christian
Peter Gabriel
Peter Hook
David Naughton
Kim Novak
George Segal
Jerry Springer
Bo Svenson
Peter Tork

FEBRUARY 14
Hugh Downs
Roger Fisher
Florence
  Henderson
Gregory Hines
Meg Tilly
Paul Tsongas
Ken Wahl

FEBRUARY 15
Mick Avory
Marisa Berenson
Claire Bloom
David Brown
Ali Campbell
Mikey Craig
Matt Groening
John Helliwell
Harvey Korman
Kevin McCarthy
Jane Seymour

FEBRUARY 16
LeVar Burton
James Ingram
William Katt
John McEnroe Jr.
Andy Taylor

FEBRUARY 17
Billie Joe
  Armstrong
Alan Bates
Jim Brown
Brenda Fricker
Hal Holbrook
Michael Jordan
Lou Diamond
  Phillips
Gene Pitney
Rene Russo
Raf Vallone

FEBRUARY 18
Robbie Bachman
Randy Crawford
Sinead Cusack
Dennis DeYoung
Matt Dillon
George Kennedy
Toni Morrison
Juice Newton
Yoko Ono
Jack Palance
Molly Ringwald
Herman Santiago
Greta Scacchi
Cybill Shepherd
John Travolta
Vanna White

FEBRUARY 19
Mark Andes
Justine Bateman
Francis Buchholz

Lou Christie
Jeff Daniels
Tony Iommi
Holly Johnson
Smokey Robinson
Seal

FEBRUARY 20
Edward Albert
Robert Altman
Charles Barkley
Walter Becker
Ian Brown
Randy California
Cindy Crawford
Sandy Duncan
J. Geils
Kelsey Grammer
Jennifer O'Neill
Sidney Poitier
Andrew Shue
Peter Strauss
Gloria Vanderbilt
Nancy Wilson

FEBRUARY 21
Christopher Atkins
William Baldwin
Jean-Jacques
  Burnel
Mary Chapin
  Carpenter
Tyne Daly
David Geffen
Kelsey Grammer
Jerry Harrison
Jennifer Love
  Hewitt
Gary Lockwood
Rue McClanahan
Nina Simone
Vince Welnick

FEBRUARY 22
Drew Barrymore
Jonathan Demme
Julius Erving
Ted Kennedy
Kyle MacLachlan
John Mills
Miou-Miou

FEBRUARY 23
Peter Fonda
Howard Jones
Mike Maxfield
Steve Priest
David Sylvian
Brad Whitford
Johnny Winter
Rusty Young

FEBRUARY 24
Barry Bostwick
James Farentino
Steven Hill
Paul Jones

Edward James
  Olmos
Helen Shaver
Lonnie Turner
Paula Zahn

FEBRUARY 25
Sean Astin
George Harrison
Téa Leoni
Mike Peters
Sally Jessy
  Raphael
Bobby Riggs
Veronica Webb
Stuart Wood

FEBRUARY 26
Erykah Badu
Michael Bolton
Jonathan Cain
Johnny Cash
Fats Domino
John Jon
Tony Randall
Mitch Ryder
Sandie Shaw

FEBRUARY 27
Adam Baldwin
Garry Christian
Chelsea Clinton
Eddie Gray
Steve Harley
Howard Hesseman
Paul Humphreys
Ralph Nader
Neal Schon
Grant Show
Adrian Smith
Elizabeth Taylor
Joanne Woodward

FEBRUARY 28
Mario Andretti
Stephanie
  Beacham
Frank Bonner
Charles Durning
Phil Gould
Robert Sean
  Leonard
Gavin MacLeod
Bernadette Peters
Mercedes Ruehl
Bubba Smith
Joe South
Tommy Tune
John Turturro
Cindy Wilson

MARCH 1
Harry Belafonte
Dirk Benedict
Roger Daltrey
Timothy Daly
Jimmy Fortune

Ron Howard
Alan Thicke

MARCH 2
Jon Bon Jovi
John Cowsill
John Cullum
Mark Evans
Mikhail Gorbachev
John Irving
Jennifer Jones
Jay Osmond
Lou Reed
Al Waxman

MARCH 3
Willie Chambers
Jance Garfat
Jackie Joyner-
  Kersee
Tim Kazurinsky
Dave Mount
Mike Pender
Miranda
  Richardson
Tone-Loc
Blue Weaver

MARCH 4
Chastity Bono
Evan Dando
Patsy Kensit
Catherine O'Hara
Paula Prentiss
Chris Rea
Chris Squire
Shakin' Stevens
Bobby Womack
Adrian Zmed

MARCH 5
Alan Clark
Samantha Eggar
Eddy Grant
James B. Sikking
Dean Stockwell
Marsha Warfield

MARCH 6
Tom Arnold
Marion Barry
Kiki Dee
David Gilmour
Hugh Grundy
D.L. Hughley
Ed McMahon
Shaquille O'Neal
Rob Reiner
Mary Wilson

MARCH 7
Tammy Faye
  Messner
Paul Davis
Matthew Fisher
John Heard
Willard Scott

Lynn Swann
Daniel J. Travanti
Chris White
Peter Wolf

MARCH 8

Mike Allsup
Cheryl Baker
Clive Burr
Cyd Charisse
Mickey Dolenz
Ralph Ellis
Peter Gill
Camryn Manheim
Randy Meisner
Gary Numan
Aidan Quinn
Lynn Redgrave
Claire Trevor
James Van Der
  Beek

MARCH 9

Juliette Binoche
Trevor Burton
John Cale
Jim Cregan
Linda Fiorentino
Martin Fry
Marty Ingels
Emmanuel Lewis
Mark Lindsey
Jeffrey Osborne
Mickey Spillane
Robin Trower
Trish Van Devere

MARCH 10

Neneh Cherry
Prince Edward
Jasmine Guy
Chuck Norris
James Earl Ray
Tom Scholz
Sharon Stone
Dean Torrence

MARCH 11

Douglas Adams
Sam Donaldson
Lisa Loeb
Bobby McFerrin
Susan Richardson
Ric Rothwell
Mark Stein
Bruce Watson

MARCH 12

Barbara Feldon
Mike Gibbins
Marlon Jackson
Al Jarreau
Paul Kantner
Liza Minnelli
Brian O'Hara
Bill Payne

James Taylor

MARCH 13

Adam Clayton
Dana Delany
Glenne Headly
William H. Macy
Deborah Raffin
Neil Sedaka

MARCH 14

Michael Caine
Billy Crystal
Megan Follows
Boon Gould
Taylor Hanson
Quincy Jones
Walter Parazaider
Kevin Williamson

MARCH 15

Ry Cooder
David Costell
Terence Trent
  D'Arby
Fabio
Renny Harlin
Judd Hirsch
Phil Lesh
Mike Love
Bret Michaels
Rockwell
Howard Scott
Sly Stone
Jimmy Lee
  Swaggart

MARCH 16

Michael Bruce
Erik Estrada
Isabelle Huppert
Jerry Lewis
Kate Nelligan
Nancy Wilson

MARCH 17

Harold Brown
Lesley-Anne Down
Patrick Duffy
Scott Gorham
Mike Lindup
Rob Lowe
Patrick McCauley
Kurt Russell
John Sebastian

MARCH 18

Bonnie Blair
Irene Cara
Kevin Dobson
Peter Graves
John Hartman
Wilson Pickett
Charley Pride
Queen Latifah
John Updike

Vanessa Williams
Barry J. Wilson

MARCH 19

Ursula Andress
Paul Atkinson
Glenn Close
Terry Hall
Clarence Henry
Derek Longmuir
Ruth Pointer
Bruce Willis

MARCH 20

John Clark Gable
Holly Hunter
William Hurt
Kathy Ireland
Spike Lee
Hal Linden
Carl Palmer
Slim Jim Phantom
Carl Reiner
Mr. Rogers
Theresa Russell

MARCH 21

Matthew Broderick
Timothy Dalton
Cynthia Geary
Roger Hodgson
Eddie Money
Rosie O'Donnell
Gary Oldman
Rosie Stone
Russell
  Thompkins Jr.

MARCH 22

George Benson
Jeremy Clyde
Randy Hobbs
Werner Klemperer
Kelly LeBrock
Andrew
  Lloyd Webber
Karl Malden
Marcel Marceau
Stephanie Mills
Matthew Modine
Lena Olin
Pat Robertson
William Shatner
Harry Vanda
M. Emmet Walsh
Reese
  Witherspoon

MARCH 23

Princess Eugenie
Chaka Khan
Ric Ocasek
Marti Pellow
Amanda Plummer
Keri Russell

MARCH 24

Lara Flynn Boyle
Robert Carradine
Tommy Hilfiger
Star Jones
Lee Oskar
Donna Pescow
Annabella Sciorra
Dougie Thomson

MARCH 25

Hoyt Axton
Bonnie Bedelia
Aretha Franklin
Paul Michael
  Glaser
Mary Gross
Jeff Healey
Elton John
Neil Jones
Sarah Jessica
  Parker
Gloria Steinem
John Stockwell
Maisie Williams

MARCH 26

Alan Arkin
James Caan
Leeza Gibbons
Jennifer Grey
Vicki Lawrence
Leonard Nimoy
Teddy Pendergrass
Diana Ross
Fran Sheehan
Martin Short
Curtis Sliwa
Richard Tandy
Steven Tyler

MARCH 27

Tony Banks
Mariah Carey
Judy Carne
Andrew Farriss
Austin Pendleton
Maria Schneider
Tom Sullivan
Quentin Tarantino
Michael York

MARCH 28

Dirk Bogarde
Ken Howard
Lucy Lawless
Reba McEntire
Chuck Portz
Salt
Dianne Wiest
Milan Williams

MARCH 29

Jennifer Capriati
Bud Cort
Eric Idle

Bobby Kimball
Christopher
  Lambert
Elle Macpherson

MARCH 30

John Astin
Warren Beatty
Tracy Chapman
Eric Clapton
Richard Dysart
Graeme Edge
Hammer
Peter Marshall
Paul Reiser
Ian Ziering

MARCH 31

Rod Allen
Herb Alpert
Richard
  Chamberlain
Liz Claiborne
William Daniels
Albert Gore
Sean Hopper
Shirley Jones
Ewen McGregor
Ed Marinaro
Al Nichol
Rhea Perlman
Mick Ralphs
Christopher
  Walken
Angus Young

APRIL 1

John Barbata
Alan Blakley
Billy Currie
Rudolph Isley
Gordon Jump
Ali MacGraw
Phil Margo
Annette O'Toole
Debbie Reynolds
Mark White

APRIL 2

Dana Carvey
Glen Dale
Buddy Ebsen
Alec Guinness
Emmylou Harris
Linda Hunt
Pamela Reed
Leon Russell
Keren Woodward

APRIL 3

Alec Baldwin
Jan Berry
Marlon Brando
Doris Day
Jennie Garth
Jane Goodall

Marsha Mason
Eddie Murphy
Wayne Newton
Tony Orlando
Barry Pritchard
Mel Schacher

APRIL 4

Maya Angelou
Robert Downey Jr.
Steve Gatlin
Dave Hill
David E. Kelley
Kitty Kelley
Graeme Kelling
Christine Lahti
Mick Mars
Nancy McKeon
Craig T. Nelson
Berry Oakley

APRIL 5

Allan Clarke
Paula Cole
Agnetha Faltskog
Maxwell Gail
Frank Gorshin
Peter Greenaway
Mike McCready
Michael Moriarty
Gregory Peck
Colin Powell
Gale Storm

APRIL 6

Stan Cullimore
Marilu Henner
Jason Hervey
Ari Meyers
John Ratzenberger
John Stax
Billy Dee Williams

APRIL 7

Mick Abrahams
Patricia Bennett
Jackie Chan
Francis Ford
  Coppola
Buster Douglas
Spencer Dryden
James Garner
Bruce Gary
Janis Ian
Elaine Miles
John Oates
Wayne Rogers

APRIL 8

Patricia Arquette
Roger Chapman
Steve Howe
Julian Lennon
Robin Wright Penn

APRIL 9
Jean-Paul Belmondo
Les Gray
Hugh Hefner
Mark Kelly
Michael Learned
Dennis Quaid

APRIL 10
Kenneth "Babyface" Edmonds
Peter MacNicol
John Madden
Steven Seagal
Brian Setzer
Omar Sharif
Bobbie Smith
Bunny Wailer

APRIL 11
Stuart Adamson
Joel Grey
Bill Irwin
Louise Lasser
Delroy Pearson
Peter Riegert
Richie Sambora
Lisa Stansfield
Neville Staples

APRIL 12
Alex Briley
David Cassidy
Tom Clancy
Claire Danes
Shannen Doherty
Andy Garcia
Vince Gill
Herbie Hancock
John Kay
David Letterman
Ann Miller
Ed O'Neill
Will Sergeant
Scott Turow
Jane Withers

APRIL 13
Peabo Bryson
Jack Casady
Lester Chambers
Jimmy Destri
Tony Dow
Al Green
Garry Kasparov
Howard Keel
Brian Pendleton
Ron Perlman
Rick Schroder
Paul Sorvino
Lyle Waggoner

APRIL 14
Ritchie Blackmore

Dennis Bryon
Julie Christie
Larry Ferguson
Sarah Michelle Gellar
Anthony Michael Hall
Suge Knight
Buddy Knox
Jay Robinson
Pete Rose
John Shea
Rod Steiger

APRIL 15
Claudia Cardinale
Lois Chiles
Graeme Clark
Roy Clark
Samantha Fox
Emma Thompson

APRIL 16
Edie Adams
Ellen Barkin
Jon Cryer
Lukas Haas
Gerry Rafferty
Bill Spooner
Dusty Springfield
Bobby Vinton

APRIL 17
Boomer Esiason
Liz Phair
Pete Shelley
Stephen Singleton

APRIL 18
Barbara Hale
Melissa Joan Hart
Jane Leeves
Hayley Mills
Rick Moranis
Conan O'Brien
Les Pattinson
Eric Roberts
Alexander Spence
Mike Vickers
James Woods

APRIL 19
Don Adams
Tim Curry
Ashley Judd
Dudley Moore
Alan Price
Larry Ramos Jr.
Mark Volman

APRIL 20
Carmen Electra
Craig Frost
Jessica Lange
Joey Lawrence
Ryan O'Neal

George Takei
Luther Vandross
Jimmy Winston

APRIL 21
Paul Carrack
Tony Danza
Queen Elizabeth II
Charles Grodin
Patti LuPone
Andie MacDowell
Elaine May
Iggy Pop
Anthony Quinn
Robert Smith
John Weider

APRIL 22
Eddie Albert
Joseph Bottoms
Glen Campbell
Peter Kenneth Frampton
Ace Frehley
Chris Makepeace
Jack Nicholson
Aaron Spelling
John Waters

APRIL 23
Valerie Bertinelli
David Birney
Steve Clark
Sandra Dee
Jan Hooks
Melinda Kanakaredes
Lee Majors
Alan Oppenheimer
Captain Sensible

APRIL 24
Eric Bogosian
Doug Clifford
Glenn Cornick
Billy Gould
Shirley MacLaine
Paul Ryder
Richard Sterban
Barbra Streisand

APRIL 25
Hank Azaria
Andy Bell
Michael Brown
Stu Cook
Meadowlark Lemon
Paul Mazursky
Al Pacino
Talia Shire
Bjorn Ulvaeus
Renee Zellweger

APRIL 26
Carol Burnett
Duane Eddy

Giancarlo Esposito

APRIL 27
Anouk Aimee
Sheena Easton
Pete Ham
Jack Klugman
Kate Pierson
Marco Pirroni
Clive Taylor

APRIL 28
Ann-Margret
Saddam Hussein
Bruno Kirby
Jay Leno
Marcia Strassman
John Wolters

APRIL 29
Andre Agassi
Duane Allen
Stephen Arenholz
Keith Baxter
Daniel Day-Lewis
Lonnie Donegan
Carl Gardner
Celeste Holm
Tommy James
Coretta Scott King
Rod McKuen
Zubin Mehta
Kate Mulgrew
Michelle Pfeiffer
Eve Plumb
Francis Rossi
Jerry Seinfeld
Uma Thurman
Carnie Wilson

APRIL 30
Turbo B
Jill Clayburgh
Gary Collins
Kirsten Dunst
Perry King
Cloris Leachman
Al Lewis
Willie Nelson
Merrill Osmond
Bobby Vee

MAY 1
Judy Collins
Johnny Colt
Steve Farris
Nick Fortune
Joseph Heller
Tim McGraw
Ray Parker Jr.
Phil Smith

MAY 2
Christine Baranski
Lesley Gore
Lou Gramm

Engelbert Humperdinck
Bianca Jagger
Goldy McJohn
Lorenzo Music

MAY 3
David Ball
James Brown
Christopher Cross
Bruce Hall
Doug Henning
Mary Hopkin
Pete Seeger
Pete Staples
Frankie Valli
Wynonna

MAY 4
Nickolas Ashford
Jay Aston
Ronnie Bond
Ed Cassidy
Jackie Jackson
Randy Travis
Pia Zadora

MAY 5
Sarah Ban Breathnach
Gary Daly
Lance Henriksen
Ian McCulloch
Kevin Mooney
Cathy Moriarty
Michael Murphy
Michael Palin
Bill Ward

MAY 6
George Clooney
Roma Downey
Willie Mays
Bob Seger
Lori Singer
Mare Winningham

MAY 7
Michael Knight
Bill Kreutzmann Jr.
Traci Lords
Darren McGavin
Rick West

MAY 8
Philip Bailey
Rick Derringer
Chris Frantz
Melissa Gilbert
Gary Glitter
Enrique Iglesias
David Lemuel Keith
James Mitchum
Don Rickles

Paul Samwell-Smith
Toni Tennille
Alex Van Halen

MAY 9
Candice Bergen
Pete Birrell
James L. Brooks
Sonny Curtis
Nokie Edwards
Albert Finney
Richie Furay
Dave Gahan
Paul Heaton
Glenda Jackson
Billy Joel
Steve Katz
Mike Millward
Tom Petersson
Dave Prater
Lloyd Price
Tommy Roe
Mike Wallace

MAY 10
Jim Abrahams
Bono
Linda Evangelista
Henry Fambrough
Jay Ferguson
Graham Gouldman
Dave Mason
Danny Rapp

MAY 11
Eric Burdon
Les Chadwick
Louis Farrakhan
Faith Popcorn
Natasha Richardson

MAY 12
Burt Bacharach
Stephen Baldwin
Bruce Boxleitner
George Carlin
Lindsay Crouse
Billy Duffy
Ian Dury
Emilio Estevez
Kim Fields
Susan Hampshire
Katharine Hepburn
Ian McLagan
Ving Rhames
Tom Snyder
Billy Squier
David Walker
Steve Winwood

MAY 13
Beatrice Arthur

Harvey Keitel
Danny Klein
Lorraine McIntosh
Dennis Rodman
Darius Rucker
Paul Thompson
Overend Watts
Stevie Wonder

MAY 14
Ian Astbury
Cate Blanchett
Jack Bruce
David Byrne
Tom Cochrane
Gene Cornish
Meg Foster
George Lucas
Fabrice Morvan
Danny Wood
Robert Zemeckis

MAY 15
Brian Eno
Graham Goble
Mike Oldfield

MAY 16
Pierce Brosnan
Tracey Gold
Glenn Gregory
Janet Jackson
Barbara Lee
Gabriela Sabatini
Derrell Sweet
Debra Winger
Ralph Tresvant

MAY 17
Bill Bruford
Dennis Hopper
Pervis Jackson
Jordan Knight
Sugar Ray
  Leonard
Maureen
  O'Sullivan
Bill Paxton
Trent Reznor
Bob Saget
Taj Mahal

MAY 18
Joe Bonsall
Pope John Paul II
George Strait

MAY 19
Nora Ephron
James Fox
David Hartman
Dusty Hill
Grace Jones
Nancy Kwan
Joey Ramone
Philip Rudd

Pete Townshend
Martyn Ware

MAY 20
Warren Cann
Cher
Joe Cocker
Sue Cowsill
Tony Goldwyn
Nick Heyward
Brian Nash
Bronson Pinchot
Ronald Reagan Jr.

MAY 21
Mike Barson
Peggy Cass
Al Franken
Ronald Isley
Stan Lynch
Carol Potter
Judge Reinhold
Leo Sayer
Mr. T
Hilton Valentine

MAY 22
Charles Aznavour
Richard Benjamin
Naomi Campbell
Michael
  Constantine
Jerry Dammers
Iva Davies
Morrissey
Bernie Taupin
Paul Winfield

MAY 23
Drew Carey
Rosemary Clooney
Joan Collins
Betty Garrett
Bill Hunt
Jewel
Anatoly Karpov

MAY 24
Gary Burghoff
Roseanne Cash
Thomas Chong
Bob Dylan
Priscilla Presley
Derek Quinn
Rich Robinson
Kristin Scott
  Thomas

MAY 25
Dixie Carter
Patti D'Arbanville
Anne Heche
Justin Henry
Lauryn Hill
Robert Ludlum
Mitch Margo

Ian McKellen
Klaus Meine
Mike Myers
Frank Oz
John Palmer
Connie Sellecca
Beverly Sills
Leslie Uggams
Paul Weller

MAY 26
Verden Allen
James Arness
Helena Bonham-
  Carter
Ray Ennis
Genie Francis
Bobcat Goldthwait
Pam Grier
Levon Helm
Wayne Hussey
Lenny Kravitz
Peggy Lee
Stevie Nicks
Gerry Paterson
Matt Stone
Philip Michael
  Thomas
Hank Williams Jr.

MAY 27
Cilla Black
Todd Bridges
Joseph Fiennes
Peri Gilpin
Louis Gossett Jr.
Tony Hillerman
Henry Kissinger
Cynthia McFadden
Siouxsie Sioux
Bruce Weitz

MAY 28
Carroll Baker
John Fogerty
Roland Gift
Gladys Knight
Sondra Locke
Kylie Minogue

MAY 29
Annette Bening
Larry Blackmon
Gary Brooker
Melanie Brown
Kevin Conway
Roy Crewsdon
Melissa Etheridge
Rupert Everett
Anthony Geary
Bob Hope
Clifton James
Lisa Whelchel

MAY 30
Lenny Davidson

Keir Dullea
Marie Fredriksson
Nicky Headon
Ted McGinley
Clint Walker

MAY 31
Tom Berenger
Clint Eastwood
Sharon Gless
Gregory Harrison
Augie Meyers
Joe Namath
Johnny Paycheck
Brooke Shields
Lea Thompson
Peter Yarrow

JUNE 1
Rene Auberjonois
David Berkowitz
Lisa Hartman
  Black
Pat Boone
Powers Boothe
Pat Corley
Jason Donovan
Morgan Freeman
Andy Griffith
Mike Joyce
Peter Masterson
Alanis Morissette
Lorna Patterson
Jonathan Pryce
Graham Russell
Alan Wilder
Ron Wood
Edward Woodward

JUNE 2
Joanna Gleason
William Guest
Tony Hadley
Charles Haid
Marvin Hamlisch
Stacy Keach
Sally Kellerman
Jerry Mathers
Charles Miller
Milo O'Shea
Max Showalter
Michael Steele
Charlie Watts

JUNE 3
Michael Clarke
Tony Curtis
Ian Hunter
Curtis Mayfield
Billy Powell
Suzi Quatro
Scott Valentine
Deniece Williams

JUNE 4
Roger Ball

John Drew
  Barrymore
El DeBarge
Bruce Dern
Angelina Jolie
Michelle Phillips
Parker Stevenson
Eddie Velez
Gordon Waller
Dennis Weaver
Ruth Westheimer
Charlie Whitney
Scott Wolf
Noah Wyle

JUNE 5
Laurie Anderson
Richard Butler
Spalding Gray
Kenny G
Robert Lansing
Marky Mark
Bill Moyers
Don Reid
Freddie Stone
Mark Wahlberg

JUNE 6
Sandra Bernhard
Gary Bonds
David Dukes
Robert Englund
Harvey Fierstein
Roy Innis
Amanda Pays
Tom Ryan
Levi Stubbs
Billie Whitelaw

JUNE 7
The Artist Formerly
  Known as Prince
James Ivory
Tom Jones
Liam Neeson

JUNE 8
Kathy Baker
Mick Box
Barbara Bush
Russell Christian
Griffin Dunne
Mick "Red"
  Hucknall
Julianna
  Margulies
Neil Mitchell
Chuck Negron
Doris Pearson
Nick Rhodes
Joan Rivers
Boz Scaggs
Jerry Stiller
Bonnie Tyler
Keenen Ivory
  Wayans

JUNE 9
Trevor Bolder
Patricia Cornwell
Johnny Depp
Michael J. Fox
Billy Hatton
Jon Lord
Jackie Mason
Natalie Portman

JUNE 10
Shirley Alston
Human Beatbox
Lionel Jeffries
Tara Lipinski
Grace Mirabella
Shirley Owens
Prince Philip
Rick Price
Andrew Stevens

JUNE 11
Adrienne Barbeau
Joey Dee
Chad Everett
John Lawton
Joe Montana
Bonnie Pointer
Donnie Van Zandt
Gene Wilder
George Willig

JUNE 12
Marv Albert
Timothy Busfield
George Bush
Bun Carlos
Vic Damone
Brad Delp
Jenilee Harrison
Jim Nabors
Reg Presley

JUNE 13
Tim Allen
Christo
Bobby Freeman
Howard Leese
Dennis Locorriere
Mark Mendoza
Deniece Pearson
Ally Sheedy
Richard Thomas

JUNE 14
Rod Argent
Jasmine Bleeth
Boy George
Marla Gibbs
Steffi Graf
Jimmy Lea
Will Patton
Donald Trump
Muff Winwood

JUNE 15
Jim Belushi
Simon Callow
Courteney Cox
Mario Cuomo
Julie Hagerty
Russell Hitchcock
Noddy Holder
Helen Hunt
Waylon Jennings
Jim Varney

JUNE 16
Eddie Levert
Ian Matthews
Laurie Metcalf
Corin Redgrave
Erich Segal
Joan Van Ark
Gino Vannelli

JUNE 17
Greg Kinnear
Norman Kuhlke
Mark Linn-Baker
Peter Lupus
Barry Manilow
Jason Patric
Joe Piscopo

JUNE 18
Tom Bailey
Roger Ebert
Carol Kane
Paul McCartney
Alison Moyet
Isabella Rossellini
Jerome Smith

JUNE 19
Paula Abdul
Tommy DeVito
Larry Dunn
Louis Jourdan
Nancy Marchand
Malcolm McDowell
Phylicia Rashad
Gena Rowlands
Salman Rushdie
Kathleen Turner
Ann Wilson

JUNE 20
Danny Aiello
Michael Anthony
Chet Atkins
Olympia Dukakis
John Goodman
Billy Guy
Martin Landau
Alan Longmuir
John Mahoney
Lionel Richie
John Taylor
Dave Thomas
James Tolkan

Brian Wilson

JUNE 21
Meredith Baxter
Berke Breathed
Chris Britton
Mark Brzezicki
Ray Davies
Michael Gross
Mariette Hartley
Bernie Kopell
Joey Kramer
Juliette Lewis
Nils Lofgren
Joey Molland
Robert Pastorelli
Jane Russell
Doug Savant
Maureen
   Stapleton
Prince William

JUNE 22
Peter Asher
Gary Beers
Bill Blass
Klaus Maria
   Brandauer
Amy Brenneman
Bruce Campbell
Tom Cunningham
Green Gartside
Howard Kaylan
Kris Kristofferson
Cyndi Lauper
Michael Lerner
Alan Osmond
Tracy Pollan
Todd Rundgren
Jimmy Somerville
Meryl Streep
Lindsay Wagner

JUNE 23
Bryan Brown
Adam Faith
Karin Gustafson
Frances
   McDormand

JUNE 24
Nancy Allen
Jeff Beck
Colin Blunstone
Georg Stanford
   Brown
Jeff Cease
Mick Fleetwood
John Illsley
Michele Lee
Andy McCluskey
Curt Smith
Sherry Stringfield
Peter Weller

JUNE 25
Tim Finn
Eddie Floyd
Allen Lanier
June Lockhart
Ian McDonald
George Michael
David Paich
Walter Payton
Carly Simon
Pearly Sweets
Jimmie Walker
Clint Warwick

JUNE 26
Billy Davis Jr.
Chris Isaak
Mick Jones
Chris O'Donnell
Larry Taylor

JUNE 27
Isabelle Adjani
Julia Duffy
Bob Keeshan
Lorrie Morgan
Henry Ross Perot
Vera Wang

JUNE 28
Kathy Bates
Gil Bellows
Mel Brooks
John Cusack
Dave Knights
Alice Krige
Mary Stuart
   Masterson
Noriyuki "Pat"
   Morita

JUNE 29
Maria Conchita
   Alonso
Gary Busey
Fred Grandy
Colin Hay
Richard Lewis
Little Eva
Ian Paice
Stedman Pearson
Roger Spear
Ruth Warrick

JUNE 30
Vincent D'Onofrio
David Alan Grier
Lena Horne
Hal Lindes
Andy Scott
Glenn Shorrock
Mike Tyson
Adrian Wright

JULY 1
Wally Amos Jr.

Pamela Anderson
Dan Aykroyd
Claude Berri
Karen Black
Roddy Bottum
Delaney Bramlett
Genevieve Bujold
Leslie Caron
Olivia De
   Havilland
Princess Diana
Jamie Farr
Farley Granger
Deborah Harry
Estee Lauder
Carl Lewis
Alanis Morissette
Sydney Pollack
Fred Schneider
John Tesh
Liv Tyler

JULY 2
Pete Briquette
Johnny Colla
Jerry Hall
Imelda Marcos
Brock Peters
Joe Puerta
Ron Silver
Paul Williams

JULY 3
Paul Barrere
Dave Barry
Betty Buckley
Neil Clark
Vince Clarke
Tom Cruise
Johnny Lee
Montel Williams

JULY 4
Leona Helmsley
Gina Lollobrigida
Kirk Pengilly
Geraldo Rivera
Eva Marie Saint
Neil Simon
Jeremy Spencer
John Waite
Al "Blind Owl"
   Wilson
Bill Withers

JULY 5
Shirley Knight
Huey Lewis
Michael Monarch
Robbie Robertson

JULY 6
Allyce Beasley
Ned Beatty
Gene Chandler
Rik Elswit

Nanci Griffith
Shelley Hack
Bill Haley
Jon Keeble
Janet Leigh
James Naughton
Nancy Reagan
Della Reese
Geoffrey Rush
Glenn Scarpelli
Sylvester Stallone
Burt Ward

JULY 7
Pierre Cardin
Shelley Duvall
Warren Entner
Jessica Hahn
David Hodo
Joe Spano
Ringo Starr

JULY 8
Kevin Bacon
Beck
Andy Fletcher
Anjelica Huston
Graham Jones
Raffi
Jeffrey Tambor
Jerry Valy

JULY 9
Marc Almond
Frank Bello
Brian Dennehy
Tom Hanks
Jim Kerr
Kelly McGillis
Mitch Mitchell
Fred Savage
Bon Scott
O.J. Simpson
Debbie Sledge
Jimmy Smits
John Tesh

JULY 10
David Brinkley
Ronnie James Dio
Ron Glass
Arlo Guthrie
Jerry Miller
Neil Tennant
Max Von Sydow

JULY 11
Giorgio Armani
Tab Hunter
Peter Murphy
Leon Spinks
Sela Ward

JULY 12
Milton Berle
Bill Cosby

Mel Harris
Cheryl Ladd
Christine McVie
Liz Mitchell
Richard Simmons
Jay Thomas
John Wetton
Kristi Yamaguchi

JULY 13
Stephen Jo Bladd
Lawrence
   Donegan
Harrison Ford
Robert Forster
Cheech Marin
Roger "Jim"
   McGuinn
Patrick Stewart
Spud Webb

JULY 14
Polly Bergen
Ingmar Bergman
Chris Cross
Matthew Fox
Rosey Grier
Harry Dean
   Stanton

JULY 15
Willie Aames
Brian Austin
   Green
Alex Karras
Peter Lewis
Brigitte Nielsen
Linda Ronstadt
Jan-Michael
   Vincent
Patrick Wayne
Forest Whitaker

JULY 16
Ruben Blades
Phoebe Cates
Stewart Copeland
Desmond Dekker
Corey Feldman
Michael Flatley
Tony Jackson

JULY 17
Lucie Arnaz
Geezer Butler
Diahann Carroll
Spencer Davis
Phyllis Diller
David Hasselhoff
Art Linkletter
Donald Sutherland
Mick Tucker
Mike Vale

JULY 18
Papa Dee Allen

James Brolin
Terry Chambers
Hume Cronyn
Dion DiMucci
Glenn Hughes
Audrey Landers
Robin MacDonald
Nelson Mandela
Elizabeth
  McGovern
Martha Reeves
Nigel Twist

JULY 19
Allen Collins
Alan Gorrie
Anthony Edwards
Pat Hingle
Bernie Leadon
Brian May

JULY 20
Paul Cook
Chris Cornell
Donna Dixon
John Lodge
Mike McNeil
Diana Rigg
Carlos Santana

JULY 21
Lance Guest
Edward Herrmann
Don Knotts
Leigh Lawson
Jon Lovitz
Jim Martin
Matt Mulhern
Billy Ocean
Henry Priestman
Isaac Stern
Cat Stevens
Robin Williams

JULY 22
Estelle Bennett
Albert Brooks
George Clinton
Willem Dafoe
Richard Davies
Louise Fletcher
Danny Glover
Don Henley
John Leguizamo
David Spade
Alex Trebek

JULY 23
Dino Danelli
David Essex
Martin Gore
Woody Harrelson
Eriq LaSalle
Andy Mackay
Don Imus
Larry Manetti

Edie McClurg
Stephanie
  Seymour
Terence Stamp
Blair Thornton

JULY 24
Heinz Burt
Ruth Buzzi
Lynda Carter
Lynval Golding
Kadeem Hardison
Robert Hays
Laura Leighton
Jennifer Lopez
Anna Paquin
Michael Richards
Chris Sarandon

JULY 25
Ray Billingsley
Manuel Charlton
Estelle Getty
Barbara Harris
Iman
Matt LeBlanc
Jim McCarty
Verdine White

JULY 26
Sandra Bullock
Blake Edwards
Dorothy Hamill
Mick Jagger
Duncan Mackay
Jason Robards
Kevin Spacey
Roger Taylor

JULY 27
Peggy Fleming
Norman Lear
Carol Leifer
Maureen
  McGovern
Helen Mirren
John Pleshette
Al Ramsey
Betty Thomas
Jerry Van Dyke

JULY 28
Elizabeth Berkley
George Cummings
Jim Davis
Terry Fox
Simon Kirke
Sally Struthers
Rick Wright

JULY 29
Neal Doughty
Peter Jennings
Geddy Lee
Martina McBride
Marilyn Quayle

Michael Spinks
David Warner

JULY 30
Paul Anka
Delta Burke
Kate Bush
Larry Fishburne
Vivica A. Fox
Buddy Guy
Anita Hill
Lisa Kudrow
Ken Olin
Rat Scabies
Arnold Schwarz-
  enegger

JULY 31
Daniel Ash
Alan Autry
Bill Berry
Michael Biehn
Dean Cain
Geraldine Chaplin
Norman Cook
Karl Green
Gary Lewis
Wesley Snipes
John West

AUGUST 1
Rick Anderson
Tempestt Bledsoe
Rob Camilletti
Coolio
Ricky Coonce
Robert Cray
Dom DeLuise
Joe Elliott
Giancarlo Giannini
Arthur Hill
Robert James
  Waller
Tom Wilson

AUGUST 2
Joanna Cassidy
Doris Coley
Wes Craven
Garth Hudson
Victoria Jackson
Carroll O'Connor
Peter O'Toole
Mary-Louise
  Parker
Edward Patten
Max Wright

AUGUST 3
Tony Bennett
B.B. Dickerson
James Hetfield
John Landis
Beverly Lee
Gordon Scott
Martin Sheen

Martha Stewart

AUGUST 4
David Carr
Frankie Ford
Jeff Gordon
Billy Bob Thornton

AUGUST 5
Loni Anderson
Neil Armstrong
Rick Derringer
Rick Huxley
Jonathan
  Silverman

AUGUST 6
Paul Bartel
Geri Halliwell
Dorian Harewood
Catherine Hicks
Abbey Lincoln
Pat McDonald

AUGUST 7
Bruce Dickinson
Andy Fraser
John Glover
Garrison Keillor
David Rasche
Alberto Salazar
B. J. Thomas

AUGUST 8
Richard Anderson
Philip Balsley
Princess Beatrice
Keith Carradine
Harry Crosby
Dino De Laurentiis
The Edge
Andy Fairweather-
  Low
Chris Foreman
Dustin Hoffman
Donny Most
Robin Quivers
Connie Stevens
Mel Tillis
Larry Dee Wilcox
Esther Williams

AUGUST 9
Gillian Anderson
Kurtis Blow
Sam Elliott
Melanie Griffith
Billy Henderson
Whitney Houston
Ken Norton
Benjamin Orr
David Steinberg

AUGUST 10
Ian Anderson
Rosanna Arquette

Antonio Banderas
Veronica Bennett
Michael Bivins
Riddick Bowe
Jimmy Dean
Jon Farriss
Eddie Fisher
Bobby Hatfield
Lorraine Pearson

AUGUST 11
Erik Braunn
Eric Carmen
Hulk Hogan
Mike Hugg
Joe Jackson
Jim Kale
Denis Payton
Claus Von Bulow

AUGUST 12
George Hamilton
Roy Hay
Sam J. Jones
Mark Knopfler
Pat Metheny
Pete Sampras
Dominique Swain
Suzanne Vega
Jane Wyatt

AUGUST 13
Kathleen Battle
Danny Bonaduce
Fidel Castro
Dan Fogelberg
Pat Harrington
Don Ho
Feargal Sharkey

AUGUST 14
Halle Berry
Dash Crofts
David Crosby
Alice Ghostley
Larry Graham
Jackee
Magic Johnson
Steve Martin
Susan Saint
  James
Danielle Steel

AUGUST 15
Princess Anne
Ben Affleck
Julia Child
Mike Connors
Linda Ellerbee
Tess Harper
Natasha
  Henstridge
Matt Johnson
MCA
Debra Messing
Bill Pinkney

Rose-Marie
Pete York

AUGUST 16
Bob Balaban
Angela Bassett
James Cameron
Robert Culp
Frank Gifford
Kathie Lee Gifford
Eydie Gorme
Timothy Hutton
Madonna
Fess Parker
Carole Shelley
James Taylor
Reginald
  Veljohnson
Lesley Ann Warren

AUGUST 17
Belinda Carlisle
Robert De Niro
Steve Gorman
Colin Moulding
Maureen O'Hara
Sean Penn
Kevin Rowland
Gary Talley
Donnie Wahlberg

AUGUST 18
Carol Alt
Dennis Elliott
Dennis Leary
Martin Mull
Edward Norton
Roman Polanski
Robert Redford
Christian Slater
Madeleine Stowe
Ron Strykert
Patrick Swayze
Malcolm-Jamal
  Warner
Carl Wayne
Shelley Winters

AUGUST 19
Ginger Baker
Bill Clinton
John Deacon
Kevin Dillon
Jonathan Frakes
Peter Gallagher
Ian Gillan
Billy J. Kramer
M.C. Eric
Diana Muldaur
Matthew Perry
Jill St. John
John Stamos

AUGUST 20
Joan Allen
Connie Chung

Doug Fieger
Rudy Gatlin
Isaac Hayes
Don King
Phil Lynott
James Pankow
Robert Plant
Al Roker

AUGUST 21

Kim Cattrall
Wilt Chamberlain
Carl Giammarese
Kenny Rogers
Kim Sledge
Joe Strummer
Melvin Van
 Peebles
Clarence
 Williams III

AUGUST 22

Ray Bradbury
Valerie Harper
John Lee Hooker
Roland Orzabal
Debbi Peterson
Norman
 Schwarzkopf
Cindy Williams

AUGUST 23

Kobe Bryant
Ronny Cox
Barbara Eden
Bobby G.
Shelley Long
Vera Miles
Shaun Ryder
Richard Sanders
Rick Springfield

AUGUST 24

Yasir Arafat
Mark Bedford
Jim Capaldi
Joe Chambers
John Cipollina
Jeffrey Daniel
David Freiberg
Steve Guttenberg
Ken Hensley
Craig Kilborn
Marlee Matlin
Claudia Schiffer

AUGUST 25

Anne Archer
Sean Connery
Elvis Costello
Billy Ray Cyrus
Mel Ferrer
Rob Halford
Monty Hall
Van Johnson
Regis Philbin

John Savage
Gene Simmons
Tom Skerritt
Blair Underwood
Joanne Whalley
Walter Williams

AUGUST 26

Jet Black
Bob Cowsill
Macaulay Culkin
Chris Curtis
Geraldine Ferraro
Michael Jeter
Branford Marsalis
Fred Milano
John O'Neill

AUGUST 27

Barbara Bach
Tim Bogert
Jeff Cook
Daryl Dragon
Pee-Wee Herman
Alex Lifeson
Glenn Matlock
Harry Reems
Tuesday Weld

AUGUST 28

Clem Cattini
Hugh Cornwell
Ben Gazzara
Scott Hamilton
Donald O'Connor
Wayne Osmond
Jason Priestley
LeAnn Rimes
Emma Samms
Elizabeth Seal
Danny Seraphine
David Soul
Daniel Stern

AUGUST 29

Richard
 Attenborough
Tim Burton
Rebecca
 DeMornay
Elliott Gould
Michael Jackson
Robin Leach
George
 Montgomery
Isabel Sanford

AUGUST 30

Elizabeth Ashley
Timothy Bottoms
Cameron Diaz
John McNally
Micky Moody
John Phillips
Kitty Wells

AUGUST 31

Jerry Allison
James Coburn
Richard Gere
Debbie Gibson
Buddy Hackett
Van Morrison
Harold Reid
Rudolph Schenker
Daniel Schorr
Anthony
 Thistlethwaite
Glenn Tilbrook
Chris Tucker

SEPTEMBER 1

Billy Blanks
Greg Errico
Gloria Estefan
Bruce Foxton
Barry Gibb
Lily Tomlin
Dave White

SEPTEMBER 2

Rosalind Ashford
Jimmy Connors
Sam Gooden
Marty Grebb
Mark Harmon
Salma Hayek
Fritz McIntyre
Steve Porcaro
Keanu Reeves

SEPTEMBER 3

Eileen Brennan
Donald Brewer
Al Jardine
Steve Jones
Gary Leeds
Valerie Perrine
Charlie Sheen
Mort Walker

SEPTEMBER 4

Martin Chambers
Gary Duncan
Greg Elmore
Mitzi Gaynor
Fawn Hall
Judith Ivey
Merald Knight
Ronald LaPread
Rosie Perez
Jennifer Salt
Ione Skye
Damon Wayans

SEPTEMBER 5

William Devane
Cathy Guisewhite
Carol Lawrence
Bob Newhart
Al Stewart
Raquel Welch

Dweezil Zappa

SEPTEMBER 6

Dave Bargeron
Jane Curtin
Jeff Foxworthy
Swoosie Kurtz
Claydes Smith
Paul Waaktaar
Jo Anne Worley

SEPTEMBER 7

Alfa Anderson
Corbin Bernsen
Susan Blakely
Chrissie Hynde
Julie Kavner
Peggy Noonan
Richard Roundtree
Benmont Tench

SEPTEMBER 8

Sid Caesar
Brian Cole
Michael Lardie
David Steele
Henry Thomas
Jonathan Taylor
 Thomas

SEPTEMBER 9

Doug Ingle
Michael Keaton
Sylvia Miles
Cliff Robertson
Adam Sandler
Dave Stewart
Roger Waters

SEPTEMBER 10

Chris Columbus
Siobhan Fahey
Jose Feliciano
Johnnie Fingers
Colin Firth
Danny Hutton
Amy Irving
Big Daddy Kane
Pat Mastelotto
Joe Perry
Ryan Phillippe
Don Powell
Fay Wray

SEPTEMBER 11

Harry Connick Jr.
Lola Falana
Mickey Hart
Earl Holliman
Jane Krakowski
Amy Madigan
Virginia Madsen
Kristy McNichol
Jon Moss
Tommy Shaw
Mick Talbot

Dennis Tufano

SEPTEMBER 12

Barry Andrews
Gerry Beckley
Tony Bellamy
Darren E. Burrows
Linda Gray
Neil Peart
Brian Robertson
Peter Scolari
Barry White

SEPTEMBER 13

Fiona Apple
Barbara Bain
Jacqueline Bisset
Nell Carter
Peter Cetera
David Clayton-
 Thomas
Randy Jones
Richard Kiel
Joni Sledge

SEPTEMBER 14

Pete Agnew
Barry Cowsill
Faith Ford
Morten Harket
Walter Koenig
Paul Kossoff
Sam Neill
Joe Penny
Nicol Williamson

SEPTEMBER 15

Les Braid
Jackie Cooper
Prince Henry
Tommy Lee Jones
Oliver Stone

SEPTEMBER 16

Marc Antony
Lauren Bacall
Ed Begley Jr.
Joe Butler
Bernie Calvert
David Copperfield
Peter Falk
Anne Francis
Kenny Jones
B.B. King
Richard Marx
Mickey Rourke
Susan Ruttan

SEPTEMBER 17

Anne Bancroft
Elvira
Jeff MacNelly
Lamonte
 McLemore
John Ritter
Fee Waybill

SEPTEMBER 18

Frankie Avalon
Ricky Bell
Robert Blake
Joanne Catherall
James Gandolfini
Kerry Livgren
Dee Dee Ramone
Jada Pinkett
 Smith
Jack Warden

SEPTEMBER 19

Jim Abbott
John Coghlan
Lol Creme
Lee Dorman
Jeremy Irons
Joan Lunden
Nick Massi
David McCallum
Bill Medley
Nile Rodgers
Twiggy
Adam West

SEPTEMBER 20

Alannah Currie
Crispin Glover
Sophia Loren
Anne Meara
Chuck Panozzo

SEPTEMBER 21

Leonard Cohen
Henry Gibson
Larry Hagman
Faith Hill
Stephen King
Ricki Lake
Rob Morrow
Bill Murray
Catherine
 Oxenberg
Philthy Animal
Alfonso Ribeiro
Nancy Travis
Trugoy the Dove

SEPTEMBER 22

Scott Baio
Shari Belafonte
Andrea Bocelli
David Coverdale
Thomas Harris
Joan Jett
Paul LeMat

SEPTEMBER 23

Jason Alexander
Steve Boone
Ronald Bushy
Ray Charles
Lita Ford
Julio Iglesias
Ben E. King

Elizabeth Pena
Mary Kay Place
Mickey Rooney
Bruce Springsteen

SEPTEMBER 24
Gerry Marsden
Anthony Newley
Kevin Sorbo

SEPTEMBER 25
Gary Alexander
Michael Douglas
Mark Hamill
John Locke
Heather Locklear
Onnie McIntyre
Christopher Reeve
Phil Rizzuto
Steve Severin
Will Smith
Cheryl Tiegs
Barbara Walters

SEPTEMBER 26
Melissa Sue
 Anderson
Joe Bauer
George Chambers
Craig Chaquico
Donna Douglas
Georgie Fame
Bryan Ferry
Linda Hamilton
Mary Beth Hurt
Winnie Mandela
Olivia Newton-
 John
Tracey Thorn

SEPTEMBER 27
Randy Bachman
Wilford Brimley
Greg Ham
Jayne Meadows
Gwyneth Paltrow
Meat Loaf
Sada Thompson

SEPTEMBER 28
Brigitte Bardot
Jeffrey Jones
Carre Otis
Se Ri Pak
John Sayles
Helen Shapiro
Mira Sorvino
William Windom
Moon Unit Zappa

SEPTEMBER 29
Anita Ekberg
Mark Farner
Bryant Gumbel
Patricia Hodge
Madeline Kahn

Jerry Lee Lewis
Larry Linville
Emily Lloyd

SEPTEMBER 30
Angie Dickinson
Lacey Chabert
Fran Drescher
Jenna Elfman
Deborah Kerr
Dewey Martin
Johnny Mathis
Marilyn McCoo
Sylvia Peterson
Victoria Tennant
Barry Williams

OCTOBER 1
Julie Andrews
Jean-Jacques
 Annaud
Jimmy Carter
Stephen Collins
Rob Davis
Richard Harris
Howard Hewett
Jerry Martini
Walter Matthau
Mark McGwire
Philippe Noiret
Randy Quaid
Stella Stevens
James Whitmore

OCTOBER 2
Lorraine Bracco
Richard Hell
Freddie Jackson
Donna Karan
Don McLean
Philip Oakey
Mike Rutherford
Sting
Tiffany

OCTOBER 3
Lindsey
 Buckingham
Neve Campbell
Chubby Checker
Barbara Ferris
Pamela Hensley
Tommy Lee
Gwen Stefani
Gore Vidal
Jack Wagner
Dave Winfield

OCTOBER 4
Armand Assante
Jackie Collins
Clifton Davis
Jim Fielder
Charlton Heston
Patti LaBelle
Chris Lowe

Anne Rice
Susan Sarandon
Alicia Silverstone

OCTOBER 5
Karen Allen
Daniel Baldwin
Clive Barker
Leo Barnes
Josie Bissett
Eddie Clarke
Jeff Conaway
Brian Connolly
Bob Geldof
Glynis Johns
Bil Keane
Mario Lemieux
Carlo Mastrangelo
Steve Miller
Kate Winslet

OCTOBER 6
Kevin Cronin
Britt Ekland
Bobby Farrell
Thomas McClary
Elizabeth Shue
Matthew Sweet
Bob Weir

OCTOBER 7
June Allyson
Toni Braxton
Kevin Godley
Dave Hope
Yo-Yo Ma
John Mellencamp
Oliver North

OCTOBER 8
Rona Barrett
Robert Bell
George Bellamy
Chevy Chase
Matt Damon
Michael Dudikoff
Paul Hogan
Jesse Jackson
Sarah Purcell
Johnny Ramone
R.L. Stine
Hamish Stuart
Sigourney Weaver
Tony Wilson
Stephanie
 Zimbalist

OCTOBER 9
Scott Bakula
Jackson Browne
John Entwistle
Sean Lennon
Michael Pare
Robert Wuhl

OCTOBER 10
Charles Dance
Jessica Harper
Martin Kemp
Alan Rachins
David Lee Roth
Tanya Tucker
Ben Vereen

OCTOBER 11
Joan Cusack
Daryl Hall
Ron Leibman
David Morse
Luke Perry
Grant Shaud

OCTOBER 12
Susan Anton
Kirk Cameron
Sam Moore
Luciano Pavarotti
Adam Rich
Dave Vanian

OCTOBER 13
Karen Akers
Tisha Campbell
Sammy Hagar
Beverly Johnson
Nancy Kerrigan
Robert Lamm
Marie Osmond
Kelly Preston
Nipsey Russell
Demond Wilson

OCTOBER 14
Harry Anderson
Marcia Barrett
Greg Evigan
Billy Harrison
Justin Hayward
Ralph Lauren
Roger Moore
Cliff Richard
Usher

OCTOBER 15
Mickey Baker
Richard Carpenter
Chris De Burgh
Sarah Ferguson
Lee Iacocca
Tito Jackson
Emeril Lagasse
Linda Lavin
Penny Marshall
Tanya Roberts
Don Stevenson

OCTOBER 16
Tony Carey
Barry Corbin
Gary Kemp
Angela Lansbury

Dave Lovelady
Tim Robbins
Suzanne Somers
C.F. Turner
Wendy Wilson

OCTOBER 17
Sam Bottoms
Beverly Garland
Alan Howard
Wyclef Jean
Mike Judge
Margot Kidder
Ziggy Marley
Michael McKean
Howard Rollins Jr.
Jim Seals
Jim Tucker
George Wendt

OCTOBER 18
Chuck Berry
Peter Boyle
Pam Dawber
Mike Ditka
Russ Giguere
Keith Knudsen
Melina Mercouri
Erin Moran
Joe Morton
Martina
 Navratilova
Gary Richrath
Vincent Spano

OCTOBER 19
Richard Dreyfuss
Patricia Ireland
John Lithgow
Trey Parker
Karl Wallinger

OCTOBER 20
Joyce Brothers
William
 Christopher
Snoop Dogg
Alan Greenwood
Mark King
Ric Lee
Jerry Orbach
Tom Petty
Will Rogers Jr.
Bobby Seale
Jay Siegel

OCTOBER 21
Charlotte Caffey
Julian Cops
Steve Cropper
Eric Faulkner
Lee Loughnane
Steve Lukather
Manfred Mann
Judith Sheindlin

OCTOBER 22
Eddie Brigati
Catherine
 Deneuve
Joan Fontaine
Annette Funicello
Jeff Goldblum
Valeria Golino
Zac Hanson
Derek Jacobi
Ray Jones
Christopher Lloyd
Jonathan Lipnicki
Tony Roberts

OCTOBER 23
Johnny Carson
Michael Crichton
Freddie Marsden
Perola Negra Pele
Weird Al Yankovic
Dwight Yoakam

OCTOBER 24
F. Murray Abraham
Jerry Edmonton
Kevin Kline
David Nelson
B.D. Wong
Bill Wyman

OCTOBER 25
Jon Anderson
Anthony Franciosa
Matthias Jabs
Midori
Tracy Nelson
Rick Parfitt
Helen Reddy
Marion Ross
Glenn Tipton

OCTOBER 26
Hillary Rodham
 Clinton
Pat Conroy
Cary Elwes
Keith Hopwood
Bob Hoskins
Dylan McDermott
Ivan Reitman
Pat Sajak
Jaclyn Smith
Keith Strickland

OCTOBER 27
Terry Anderson
Roberto Benigni
John Cleese
Ruby Dee
Matt Drudge
Nanette Fabray
John Gotti
Simon LeBon
Marla Maples
Carrie Snodgress

OCTOBER 28

Jane Alexander
Steve
  Baumgartner
Wayne Fontana
Dennis Franz
Bill Gates
Jami Gertz
Lauren Holly
Telma Hopkins
Bruce Jenner
Hank Marvin
Stephen Morris
Joan Plowright
Annie Potts
Julia Roberts
Daphne Zuniga

OCTOBER 29

Ralph Bakshi
Kevin Dubrow
Joely Fisher
Kate Jackson
Denny Laine
Melba Moore
Winona Ryder

OCTOBER 30

Harry Hamlin
Kevin Pollak
Gavin Rossdale
Grace Slick
Charles Martin
  Smith
Otis Williams
Henry Winkler

OCTOBER 31

King Ad-Rock
Barbara
  Bel Geddes
Tony Bowers
Bernard Edwards
Dale Evans
Lee Grant
Deidre Hall
Sally Kirkland
Annabella Lwin
Johnny Marr
Larry Mullen Jr.
Jane Pauley
Dan Rather
Xavier Roberts
David Ogden
  Stiers
Chris Tucker

NOVEMBER 1

Rick Allen
Ronald Bell
Barbara Bosson
Keith Emerson
Robert Foxworth
Mags Furuholmen
James Kilpatrick
  Jr.

Lyle Lovett
Eddie MacDonald
Jenny McCarthy
Betsy Palmer
Dan Peek

NOVEMBER 2

k.d. lang
Brian Poole
David Schwimmer
Ray Walston
Bruce Welch
Alfre Woodard

NOVEMBER 3

Adam Ant
Roseanne Arnold
Charles Bronson
Kate Capshaw
Mike Evans
Larry Holmes
Steve Landesberg
Lulu
Dolph Lundgren
Dennis Miller
James Prime
Gary Sandy

NOVEMBER 4

Art Carney
Sean "Puffy"
  Combs
Walter Cronkite
Chris Difford
Ralph Macchio
Delbert McClinton
Matthew
  McConaughey
Markie Post
Kool Rock
Mike Smith
Loretta Swit

NOVEMBER 5

Bryan Adams
Art Garfunkel
Peter Noone
Tatum O'Neal
Roy Rogers
Sam Shepard
Paul Simon
Elke Sommer
Ike Turner

NOVEMBER 6

Sally Field
Glenn Frey
Ethan Hawke
P.J. Proby
Rebecca Romijn
Doug Sahm
Maria Shriver
George Young

NOVEMBER 7

Billy Graham

Joni Mitchell
Johnny Rivers

NOVEMBER 8

Alan Berger
Bonnie Bramlett
Alain Delon
Mary Hart
Rickie Lee Jones
Terry Lee Miall
Gretchen Mol
Parker Posey
Bonnie Raitt
Esther Rolle
Rodney Slater
Courtney Thorne-
  Smith
Roy Wood
Roxana Zal

NOVEMBER 9

Joe Bouchard
Lou Ferrigno
Alan Gratzer
Hedy Lamarr
Phil May
Pepa
Dennis Stratton

NOVEMBER 10

Glen Buxton
Greg Lake
MacKenzie Phillips
Ann Reinking
Jack Scalia
Roy Scheider
Sammy Sosa

NOVEMBER 11

Bibi Andersson
Paul Cowsill
Chris Dreja
Calista Flockhart
Patric Knowles
Roger Lavern
Ian Marsh
Vince Martell
Demi Moore
Andy Partridge
Kurt Vonnegut Jr.
Jonathan Winters
Jesse Colin Young

NOVEMBER 12

Errol Brown
Tonya Harding
Charles Manson
John Maus
Leslie McKeown
Stephanie Powers
Wallace Shawn
Neil Young

NOVEMBER 13

Whoopi Goldberg

Joe Mantegna
Richard Mulligan

NOVEMBER 14

Frankie Banali
Prince Charles
Freddie Garrity
Robert Ginty
Alexander O'Neal
Laura San
  Giacomo
Alec Such
D. B. Sweeney
Yanni
James Young

NOVEMBER 15

Edward Asner
Petula Clark
Beverly D'Angelo
Yaphet Kotto
Frida Lyngstad
Sam Waterston

NOVEMBER 16

Oksana Baiul
Lisa Bonet
Dwight Gooden
Clu Gulager

NOVEMBER 17

Martin Barre
Danny DeVito
Ronald DeVoe
Bob Gaudio
Isaac Hanson
Lauren Hutton
Gordon Lightfoot
Mary Elizabeth
  Mastrantonio
Lorne Michaels
Martin Scorsese
Tom Seaver

NOVEMBER 18

Margaret Atwood
Hank Ballard
Imogene Coca
Linda Evans
Kirk Hammett
Andrea Marcovicci
Graham Parker
Jameson Parker
Elizabeth Perkins
Herman Rarebell
Susan Sullivan
Brenda Vaccaro
Kim Wilde

NOVEMBER 19

Dick Cavett
Jodie Foster
Savion Glover
Larry King
Jeane Kirkpatrick
Calvin Klein

Hank Medress
Kathleen Quinlan
Ahmad Rashad
Meg Ryan
Ted Turner

NOVEMBER 20

Kaye Ballard
Jimmy Brown
Mike D
Bo Derek
George Grantham
Veronica Hamel
Richard Masur
Estelle Parsons
Dick Smothers
Ray Stiles
Joe Walsh
Sean Young

NOVEMBER 21

Ken Griffey Jr.
Goldie Hawn
Dr. John
Lonnie Jordan
Laurence
  Luckinbill
Lorna Luft
Juliet Mills
Harold Ramis
Nicollette
  Sheridan
Marlo Thomas

NOVEMBER 22

Aston Barrett
Boris Becker
Tom Conti
Jamie Lee Curtis
Rodney
  Dangerfield
Terry Gilliam
Mariel Hemingway
Billie Jean King
Floyd Sneed
Stevie "Little
  Steven" Van
  Zandt
Robert Vaughn
Tina Weymouth

NOVEMBER 23

Susan Anspach
Bruce Hornsby

NOVEMBER 24

Donald Dunn
Geraldine
  Fitzgerald
Chris Hayes
Dwight Schultz
John Squire
Jim Yester

NOVEMBER 25

Christina
  Applegate
Joe DiMaggio
Amy Grant
John Larroquette
Ricardo
  Montalban
Steve Rothery
Percy Sledge

NOVEMBER 26

Cyril Cusack
Robert Goulet
Norman Hassan
Alan Henderson
John McVie
Charles Schulz
Tina Turner

NOVEMBER 27

Charlie Burchill
Dozy
Robin Givens
Fisher Stevens
Jaleel White

NOVEMBER 28

Beeb Birtles
Ed Harris
Hope Lange
Judd Nelson
Randy Newman
Jon Stewart

NOVEMBER 29

Felix Cavaliere
Kim Delaney
Denny Doherty
Barry Goudreau
Jonathan Knight
Diane Ladd
Howie Mandel
John Mayall
Andrew McCarthy
Garry Shandling

NOVEMBER 30

John Aston
Richard Barbieri
Dick Clark
Kevin Conroy
Richard Crenna
Roger Glover
Rob Grill
Robert Guillaume
Billy Idol
Bo Jackson
G. Gordon Liddy
Leo Lyons
Mandy Patinkin
June Pointer
Rex Reason
Ridley Scott
Ben Stiller

DECEMBER 1
Woody Allen
Eric Bloom
John Densmore
Bette Midler
Sandy Nelson
Gilbert O'Sullivan
Richard Pryor
Lou Rawls
Charlene Tilton
Treat Williams

DECEMBER 2
Steven Bauer
Ted Bluechel Jr.
Cathy Lee Crosby
Julie Harris
Lucy Liu
Michael McDonald
Tom McGuinness
Rick Savage
Howard Stern

DECEMBER 3
Brian Bonsall
Brendan Fraser
Julianne Moore
Ozzy Osbourne
Andy Williams

DECEMBER 4
Tyra Banks
Jeff Bridges
Deanna Durbin
Chris Hillman
Wink Martindale
Bob Mosley
Gary Rossington
Southside Johnny
Marisa Tomei

DECEMBER 5
John Berendt
Morgan Brittany
Gabriel Byrne
Jeroen Krabbe
Charles Lane
Little Richard
Jim Messina
Les Nemes
Jack Russell

DECEMBER 6
Peter Buck
Rick Buckler
Tom Hulce
Janine Turner
Ben Watt

JoBeth Williams
Steven Wright

DECEMBER 7
Larry Bird
Ellen Burstyn
Mike Nolan
Tom Waits
Eli Wallach

DECEMBER 8
Gregg Allman
Kim Basinger
Jerry Butler
David Carradine
Phil Collen
Bobby Elliott
Teri Hatcher
James MacArthur
Sinead O'Connor
Paul Rutherford
Maximilian Schell

DECEMBER 9
Joan Armatrading
Beau Bridges
Dick Butkus
Rick Danko
Judi Dench
Kirk Douglas
Morton Downey Jr.
Dennis Dunaway
Douglas
 Fairbanks Jr.
Buck Henry
Neil Innes
John Malkovich
Michael Nouri
Donny Osmond
Dick Van Patten

DECEMBER 10
Frank Beard
Kenneth Branagh
Susan Dey
Ace Kefford
Mako
Walter Orange
Chad Stuart

DECEMBER 11
Bess Armstrong
Teri Garr
David Gates
Jermaine Jackson
Booker T. Jones
Brenda Lee
Rita Moreno
Nikki Sixx

DECEMBER 12
Bob Barker
Dickey Betts
Mayim Bialik
Clive Bunker
Jennifer Connelly
Sheila E.
Connie Francis
Terry Kirkman
Ed Koch
Rush Limbaugh
Mike Pinder
Cathy Rigby
Mike Smith
Dionne Warwick

DECEMBER 13
Jeff "Skunk"
 Baxter
Steve Buscemi
John Davidson
Ted Nugent
Randy Owen
Christopher
 Plummer
Dick Van Dyke
Tom Verlaine
Johnny Whitaker

DECEMBER 14
Patty Duke
Cynthia Gibb
Bridget Hall
Abbe Lane
Jackie McCauley
Mike Scott
Dee Wallace Stone
Cliff Williams
Joyce Wilson

DECEMBER 15
Carmine Appice
Dave Clark
Tim Conway
Reginald Hudlin
Don Johnson
Paul Simonon
Helen Slater

DECEMBER 16
Benny Andersson
Benjamin Bratt
Steven Bochco
Ben Cross
Billy Gibbons
Tony Hicks
William Perry
Liv Ullmann

DECEMBER 17
Sarah Dallin
Dave Dee
Bob Guccione
Milla Jovovich
Eddie Kendricks
Eugene Levy
Mike Mills
Art Neville
Bill Pullman
Paul Rodgers
Tommy Steele

DECEMBER 18
Steve Austin
Ossie Davis
Elliot Easton
Katie Holmes
Ray Liotta
Leonard Maltin
Brad Pitt
Keith Richards
Steven Spielberg

DECEMBER 19
Jennifer Beals
Alvin Lee
Robert
 MacNaughton
Alyssa Milano
Tim Reid
Cicely Tyson
Robert Urich
Maurice White
Zal Yanovsky

DECEMBER 20
Jenny Agutter
Anita Baker
Billy Bragg
Bobby Colomby
John Hillerman
Chris Robinson
Little Stevie
 Wright

DECEMBER 21
Phil Donahue
Chris Evert
Jane Fonda
Samuel L. Jackson
Jeffrey Katzenberg
Josh Mostel
Ray Romano
Kiefer Sutherland
Kurt Waldheim
Paul Winchell

DECEMBER 22
Barbara
 Billingsley
Hector Elizondo
Maurice Gibb
Robin Gibb
Lady Bird Johnson
Rick Nielsen
Ricky Ross
Diane Sawyer

DECEMBER 23
Corey Haim
Jorma Kaukonen
Johnny Kidd
Susan Lucci
Dave Murray
Eugene Record
Ruth Roman
Harry Shearer
James Stockdale
Eddie Vedder

DECEMBER 24
Ian Burden
Lemmy

DECEMBER 25
Jimmy Buffett
Robin Campbell
O'Kelly Isley
Annie Lennox
Shane MacGowan
Barbara Mandrell
Noel Redding
Hanna Schygulla
Sissy Spacek
Henry Vestine

DECEMBER 26
Steve Allen
Abdul Fakir
Alan KingDonald
 Moffat
Phil Spector

DECEMBER 27
John Amos
Goldberg
Peter Criss
Gerard Depardieu
Tovah Feldshuh
Mick Jones
David Knopfler
Les Maguire

DECEMBER 28
Willow Bay
Alex Chilton

Dick Diamonde
Lou Jacobi
Stan Lee
Charles Neville
Johnny Otis
Maggie Smith
Denzel
 Washington
Edgar Winter

DECEMBER 29
Ted Danson
Mark Day
Marianne Faithfull
Mary Tyler Moore
Paula Poundstone
Inga Swenson
Ray Thomas
Jon Voight

DECEMBER 30
Joseph Bologna
Bo Diddley
Davy Jones
Matt Lauer
Jeff Lynne
Mike Nesmith
Sheryl Lee Ralph
Russ Tamblyn
Tracey Ullman
Fred Ward
Tiger Woods

DECEMBER 31
Barbara Carrera
Rosalind Cash
Burton Cummings
Tom Hamilton
Anthony Hopkins
Val Kilmer
Ben Kingsley
Tim Matheson
Joe McIntyre
Sarah Miles
Pete Quaife
Patti Smith
Donna Summer
Andy Summers

2000'S WATERSHED BIRTHDAYS

The following folks will have reason to celebrate (or toast themselves) a little harder this year as they reach birthday milestones.

TURNING 90
Al Lewis
Claire Trevor

TURNING 80
Ray Bradbury
David Brinkley
Nanette Fabray
Leona Helmsley
Pope John Paul II
James Kilpatrick
 Jr.
Werner Klemperer
Peggy Lee
Walter Matthau
Ricardo
 Montalban
Jack Palance
Tony Randall
Mickey Rooney
Isaac Stern
Jack Warden
Shelley Winters

TURNING 75
Robert Altman
Mickey Baker
Barbara Bush
Johnny Carson
Mike Connors
Tony Curtis
Farley Granger
Julie Harris
Tony Hillerman
Hal Holbrook
Clifton James
George Kennedy
B.B. King
Angela Lansbury
Jack Lemmon
John Lockhart
Dorothy Malone
Paul Newman
Donald O'Connor
Bill Pinkney
Maureen
 Stapleton
Rod Steiger
Elaine Stritch
Dick Van Dyke
Gwen Verdon
Gore Vidal
Jonathan Winters

TURNING 70
Buzz Aldrin
Neil Armstrong
John Astin
Polly Bergen
Bobby Bland
Ray Charles
Sean Connery
Pat Corley
John Cullum
Robert Culp
Clint Eastwood
Anne Francis
Ben Gazzara
Frank Gifford
Bob Guccione
Gene Hackman
Buck Henry
Don Ho
G. Gordon Liddy
Abbey Lincoln
Robert Loggia
Peter Marshall
Paul Mazursky
Vera Miles
Donald Moffat
Sandra Day
 O'Connor
Alan Oppenheimer
Henry Ross Perot
Pat Robertson
Jay Robinson
Gena Rowlands
Maximillian Schell
Stephen Sondheim
Frances
 Stenhagen
Rod Taylor
Robert Wagner
Edward Woodward
Joanne Woodward

TURNING 65
Woody Allen
Herb Alpert
Bibi Anderson
Julie Andrews
Diahann Carroll
Christo
Nick Clooney
Alain Delon
Bob Denver
Phil Donohue
Donna Douglas
Abdul Fakir
Geraldine Ferraro
Eddie Floyd

Henry Gibson
Charles Grodin
Barbara Harris
David Hartman
Tippi Hedren
Judd Hirsh
Alex Karras
Jerry Lee Lewis
Loretta Lynn
Nick Massi
Johnny Mathis
Dudley Moore
Sam Moore
Jerry Orbach
Luciano Pavarotti
John Phillips
Nicholas Pryor
Donald Sutherland
Jimmy Swaggart
Bob Uecker
Bobby Vinton
Lyle Waggoner
M. Emmet Walsh

TURNING 60
Mario Andretti
Rene Auberjonois
Tony Bellamy
Brian Bennett
Tom Brokaw
James L. Brooks
James Caan
Alan Caddy
Lester Chambers
George Clinton
Barry Corbin
Dash Crofts
Joey Dee
Adam Faith
Barbara Ferris
Roberta Flack
Peter Fonda
Wayne Fontana
Frankie Ford
Bobby Freeman
Freddie Garrity
David Gates
Terry Gilliam
Gary Glitter
Linda Gray
Charles Grodin
Herbie Hancock
Bobby Hatfield
Mariette Hartley
Lance Henrikson
Howard Hesseman
John Hurt

Tony Jackson
Tom Jones
Don Imus
Al Jarreau
Jorma Kaukonen
Ted Koppel
Phil Lesh
Loretta Lynn
John Mahoney
Manfred Mann
Freddie Marsden
Delbert McClinton
Bill Medley
Jimmy Merchant
Augie Meyers
Fred Milano
Nick Nolte
Chuck Norris
Al Pacino
Perola Negra Pele
Austin Pendleton
Richard Pryor
Eugene Record
Cliff Richard
Richard Sanders
Martin Sheen
Elke Sommer
Joe South
Jill St. John
Ringo Starr
Patrick Stewart
Fran Tarkenton
Dean Torrence
Daniel J. Travanti
Alex Trebek
Jessica Walter
Clint Warwick
Dionne Warwick
Sam Waterston
Raquel Welch
Dave White

TURNING 50
Debbie Allen
Nancy Allen
Richard Dean
 Anderson
Princess Anne
Susan Anton
Joan Armatrading
Kathy Baker
Walter Becker
Robert Bell
Susan Blakely
Trevor Bolder
Bruce Boxleitner
Erik Braunn

Francis Buchholz
Gabriel Byrne
Jonathan Cain
David Cassidy
Alex Chilton
Roger Christian
Eddie Clarke
Natalie Cole
Jeff Conaway
Bud Cort
Bill Cunningham
Pam Dawber
Dicken
Julia Duffy
Dennis Elliot
Julius Erving
Morgan Fairchild
Andy
 Fairweather-Low
Agnetha Faltskog
Roger Fisher
Peter Kenneth
 Frampton
Peter Gabriel
Joanna Gleason
Lou Gramm
Cathy Guisewite
Dorian Harewood
Tess Harper
Ed Harris
Gregory Harrison
Mary Hart
John Hartman
Pamela Hensley
Roger Hodgson
David Hodo
Hoddy Holder
Mary Hopkin
Glenn Hughes
William Hurt
Bill Irwin
David Johansen
Jeffrey Katzenberg
Tim Kazurinsky
Paul Kossoff
Joey Kramer
Christine Lahti
John Landis
Ronald Lapread
Jay Leno
Huey Lewis
Joan Lunden
Duncan Mackay
William H. Macy
Leonard Maltin
Ed Marinaro
Thomas McClary

Edie McClurg
Bobby McFerrin
Miou-Miou
Michael Monarch
Mickey Moody
Bill Murray
Peggy Noonan
Billy Ocean
Graham Parker
Jane Pauley
Dan Peek
Teddy Pendergrass
Ron Perlman
Joe Perry
Tom Peterson
Tom Petty
Markie Post
Don Powell
Steve Priest
Victoria Principal
Randy Quaid
Suzi Quatro
Graham Russell
Mike Rutherford
John Sayles
Cybill Shepherd
Martin Short
Patrick Simmons
Billy Squier
Paul Stanley
Chris Stein
Bernie Taupin
Victoria Tenant
Blair Thornton
Stevie Van Zandt
Wendy
 Wasserstein
Fay Waybill
Tina Weymouth
Stevie Wonder

TURNING 40
Willie Aames
Carol Act
Kevin Anderson
Prince Andrew
Daniel Baldwin
Antonio Banderas
Valerie Bertinelli
Bono
Kenneth Branagh
Steve Clark
Adam Clayton
Sue Cowsill
Andy Cox
Mickey Craig
John Crawford

Buster Douglas
Roma Downey
David Duchovny
Prince Edward
Siobhan Fahey
Colin Firth
Andy Fletcher
Hugh Grant
Tony Goldwyn
Amy Grant
Jennifer Grey
Lance Guest
Mick "Red"
  Hucknall
Paul Humphreys
Daryl Hannah
Les Hemes

Timothy Hutton
Holly Johnson
Gary Kemp
Kelly Lebrock
John Leguizamo
Greg Louganis
Branford Marsalis
Julianne Moore
Cathy Moriarty
Matt Muchern
Sean Penn
Oliver Platt
Tracy Pollan
Paula Poundstone
James Prime
Mark D. Prince
Jack Russell

Emma Samms
Rick Savage
Gretta Scacchi
Brian Setzer
James Spader
Danielle Steele
Michael Stipe
John Taylor
Kristin Scott
  Thomas
Meg Tilly
Jean Claude Van
  Damme
Damon Wayans
Kim Wilde

TURNING 30

Andre Agassi
Gabrielle Anwar
Beck
Josie Bisset
Lara Flynn Boyle
Kirk Cameron
Naomi Campbell
Jennifer Connelly
Matt Damon
Minnie Driver
Deborah Gibson
Heather Graham
Tonya Harding
Ethan Hawke
Queen Latifah

Emily Lloyd
Eric M.C.
Chris O'Donnell
Delroy Pearson
Gabriela Sabatini
Claudia Schiffer
Uma Thurman
Malcolm—Jamal
  Warner

TURNING 21

Lance Bass
Brandy
Claire Danes
Jennifer Love
  Hewitt
Kate Hudson

TURNING 20

Chelsea Clinton
Macaulay Culkin
Isaac Hanson
Monica
Christina Ricci
Dominique Swain